Association for
Computing Machinery

Advancing Computing as a Science & Profession

25th Anniversary
International Conference on Supercomputing
1987-2011

ICS 25th Anniversary Volume

Sponsored by:

ACM SIGARCH

Edited by:

Utpal Banerjee

Association for
Computing Machinery

Advancing Computing as a Science & Profession

The Association for Computing Machinery
2 Penn Plaza, Suite 701
New York, New York 10121-0701

Notice to Past Authors of ACM-Published Articles
ACM intends to create a complete electronic archive of all articles and/or other material previously published by ACM. If you have written a work that has been previously published by ACM in any journal or conference proceedings prior to 1978, or any SIG Newsletter at any time, and you do NOT want this work to appear in the ACM Digital Library, please inform permissions@acm.org, stating the title of the work, the author(s), and where and when published.

ISBN: 978-1-4503-3581-2

Additional copies may be ordered prepaid from:

ACM Order Department
PO Box 30777
New York, NY 10087-0777, USA

Phone: 1-800-342-6626 (USA and Canada)
+1-212-626-0500 (Global)
Fax: +1-212-944-1318
E-mail: acmhelp@acm.org
Hours of Operation: 8:30 am – 4:30 pm ET

Printed in the USA

Foreword

The International Conference on Supercomputing (ICS) was born in 1987 in Athens, Greece. Some of us have been associated with this conference since its very beginning, and we take great joy and pride in seeing it become successful and now pass the quarter century mark. A decision was made to celebrate the silver jubilee by publishing a 25th Anniversary Volume consisting of some of the most important papers presented at the conference over the years, together with the authors' retrospectives. The ideal would have been to pick one paper from each of the 25 years that had the greatest impact, and making sure that no more than one paper was from the same author or set of authors. I am happy to report that we did not follow these rules too rigidly and did not rely blindly on citation counts of papers. The distinguished committee that made the final decisions was a group of former ICS program committee chairs: Eduard Ayguade, Kyle Gallivan, Avi Mendelson, Alex Nicolau, Constantine Polychronopoulos, Mateo Valero, Alex Veidenbaum, Harry Wijshoff and myself.

The committee selected 35 papers after extensive discussion. These papers and their authors' retrospectives appear in this volume. Several selected papers are included without a retrospective; their authors chose not to write one or had a very tough work schedule and could not do it in time. Only 32 of the selected papers are reprinted in this volume however, because ACM does not hold the copyright to papers from ICS'87.

I would like to thank each committee member for the time and effort he put in to review and discuss a very large set of papers. Sometimes it was a difficult process since for each good paper there were many close competitors. I would also like to thank ACM SIGARCH for supporting ICS for over 25 years and for giving the green light to this project.

It is with deep sorrow I remember here the passing of Ken Kennedy, Theodore Papatheodorou and Stamatis Vassiliadis, all friends and past chairs, who made tremendous contributions to ICS. They were taken from us far too soon.

Utpal Banerjee
Volume Editor

Table of Contents

NOTE: That the authors of the retrospectives included in this Special 25th Anniversary Volume may differ from the authorhip of the original paper (which start on third page of this table of contents).

Original ICS Papers

Author Retrospective for PTRAN's Analysis and Optimization Techniques

Ron K. Cytron
Computer Science and Engineering
Washington University Box 1045
One Brookings Drive
St Louis, MO 63130
cytron@cs.wustl.edu

Jeanne Ferrante
Computer Science and Engineering
UC, San Diego
9500 Gilman Drive
La Jolla CA, 92093-0404
jferrante@ucsd.edu

ABSTRACT
The PTRAN (Parallel Translator) system at IBM had as its goal the analysis and optimization of sequential programs for parallel architectures. In this paper, we give our perspective on what has changed since PTRAN, and what is still relevant.

http://dl.acm.org/citation.cfm?id=73950.73962

Categories and Subject Descriptors
D.3.3 [**Programming Languages**]: Compilers; Transformation systems.

Keywords
Automatic parallelization; program analysis; interprocedural analysis; control dependence; data dependence; program dependence graph; program restructuring; program optimization.

1. INTRODUCTION
The PTRAN system project was initiated in 1984 at IBM's T.J. Watson Center to investigate automatic parallelization of scientific programs, particularly those written in FORTRAN. Led by Fran Allen, it became one of the top research groups in this area. [1] highlights overall advances in PTRAN.

Further PTRAN advances in code restructuring and scheduling for parallel machines are detailed in [1,2]. The PTRAN technologies formed the basis for several high performance parallel products, including the Parallel Fortran compiler at IBM.

2. CHANGES IN THE ARCHITECTURAL LANDSCAPE
There has been a major change in the diversity and degree of parallelism available in present day architectures. In 1987, multiprocessor and vector supercomputers were the main targets; today, parallelism is present from the chip level with multiple cores, to the Cloud, and with much greater diversity, for example, GPU's. Even uniprocessors can be considered to be parallel due to out-of-order execution, and multiple execution units with long pipelines. Another architectural trend is that data movement and the associated latencies have become increasingly more important; computation has become cheap, but communication relatively more expensive. These changes have made optimizing data movement (rather than parallelism) the key goal.

ICS 25th Anniversary Volume. 2014.
ACM 978-1-4503-2840-1/14/06.
http://dx.doi.org/10.1145/2591635.2591638

3. WHAT IS STILL RELEVANT
Although automatic parallelization of arbitrary sequential programs is no longer a sought-after goal, the many levels of parallelism prevalent in today's architectures make PTRAN's analysis and transformations relevant to this day to enable small-scale parallelism (i.e. loop level and below). Research continues in the area of automatic parallelization, but such efforts are usually focused on specialized application domains [16], specialized hardware [24], or languages that make the discovery of such paralleism more straightforward [11]. Many of these efforts use structures that appeared in our paper. For example, trace-based optimization [12] relies on data persistently associated with programs.

Ideas from the PTRAN system have found their way into research and industrial compilers (LLVM, gcc, Intel) that are crucial for the success of today's architectures. We summarize below the concepts and structures from the PTRAN system that are most prevalent today in program translation and transformation tools.

3.1 Intermediate Representations
Compilers often use multiple intermediate representations of the program beyond the usual control flow graph in order to most efficiently analyze and transform the code. Several new representations were used in the PTRAN system, and we give historical background as well as a current perspective on each.

3.1.1 Program Dependence Graph (PDG)
The PDG is a program representation which removes unnecessary constraints on program order while compactly representing the essential control and data constraints, thereby exposing potential parallelism. Earlier work of Ottenstein [20] had developed a data flow graph intermediate representation allowing direct links of program regions connected by data flow. Subsequently, [8] extended this work to include a single graphical representation for both control and data flow for structured, reducible programs. The PDG [9,10] representation further extends these advantages to unstructured programs by supplying an efficient algorithm to construct control dependence for all programs. Many traditional optimizations were shown to operate more efficiently on the PDG.

The PDG in some version is used to this day in diverse settings, and is included in many compiler textbooks. It was cited in Allen's Turing award citation as "the primary structuring method used by most parallelizing compilers"[13]. Besides the other obvious applications to program slicing, debugging, and testing, it has been used widely, from register allocation [19] to generate abstract interpreters [18] to gene splicing algorithms [14]. As noted in [23], the PDG's use has been primarly as the basis for academic research rather than industry, but the growing prevalence of parallelism may make it more more relevant today than in the past decade. It has recently been used in the context of CUDA and GPU's [17].

3.1.2 Static Single Assignment Form (SSA)

SSA form, like the PDG, also leads to more efficient and powerful transformations in compilers. SSA was intiated by the search for a more powerful and efficient algorithm for constant propagation by Wegman and Zadeck [25,26]. Several of the PTRAN co-authors were proceeding in a similar direction [5], participated in the subsequent development of SSA [6,7], and it was implemented in PTRAN. The two representations are also related algorithmically. A critical requirement for the adoption of SSA was an algorithm for its efficient construction, and the earlier work on control dependence [10] supplied this necessary step. SSA is used in many compilers, including GCC and others [23].

3.2 Analysis

Restructuring sequential code with loops requires understanding the iteration space and dependences in a program. The techniques developed in the PTRAN system had their roots in the work of David Kuck's group at the University of Illinois. These efforts found success using *approximate* techniques: relationships found to be independent were truly so, but some relationships evaded analysis. PTRAN's hierarchical approach to dependence testing [3] continues to be used where direction vectors are of interest. Exact techniques trace their roots to the work of Paul Feautrier's group (then at Ecole des Mines), but such methods were not used in PTRAN because they were more expensive computationally and they were generally no more successful than the approximate techniques when applied to arbitrary sequential programs.

The bane of such analysis as applied to popular programming languages (then Fortran, today Java or C++) has been the extent to which alias relationships between references are clear or murky. Cognescenti developers could write code so that compilers could discover concurrency, or use languages in which such concurrency is easily discovered. Unforunately, as we lament below, the application of even the most sophisticated analysis to code in the wild had limited success.

However, there is continued interest today in exact techniques. For example, Sanjay Rajopadhye and colleagues have published widely on the polyhedral model and its analysis [21]. For code where indexing and alias relationships are clear, this form of analysis has found success. An application could be transformed to concurrent execution, but more relevant today are the ways in which this analysis leads to program restructuring that better suits a storage hierarchy, as discussed next.

3.3 Transformations

As noted in the original paper, the aim of PTRAN analysis was program transformations on multiprocessors, particularly for parallelism. However, as we stated earlier, optimizing data movement rather than finding parallelism has become key. While tiling and other loop transformations were already well known, PTRAN's use of tiling and other loop transformations may still be relevant today. For example, [4] introduced the notion of hierarchical tiling for multiple levels of memory hierarchy and parallelism. As noted in [15], the use of multilevel tiling is approaching that of a design pattern. (See, for example, [27]).

Thanks in part to the gaming industry, high speed graphics processing units (GPUs) are available for general use. These units are essentially today's vector processors, and program transformations are available in compilers that target these processors [17,24]. The proper staging of data into and out of these processors is crucial for their performance. Many of the loop transformations present in PTRAN and similar systems can be applied here with success.

4. EPITAPH FOR AUTOMATIC PARALLELIZATION

As a practical technique in the supercomputer setting of 25 years past, the goal of automatic parallelization did not succeed. Much more can be gained by thoughtful algorithmic and memory-conscious design prior to writing programs. However, the analysis and transformations developed, and their corresponding intermediate representations, may be increasingly relevant at different levels of modern architectures. Parellelizing compilers such as Intel's C++ and Fortran compilers are still in place, and new ones are still being developed (for example [22]), and are often combined with other runtime and user-driven tools.

5. WHEREABOUTS OF CO-AUTHORS

Fran Allen is IBM Fellow Emeritus and recipient of the 2006 Turing Award, in part for her work on PTRAN [13]. Ron Cytron is currently professor of computer science and engineering at Washington University. Michael Burke and Philippe Charles are both on the computer science research staff at Rice University. Jeanne Ferrante is professor of computer science at UC San Diego.

6. ACKNOWLEDGMENTS

Our thanks to everyone who was part of IBM's PTRAN team, and especially to Fran Allen for her leadership.

7. REFERENCES

[1] Allen, F. E. Burke, M., Charles, P., Cytron, R., Ferrante, J., Hsieh, W., and Shields, D. 1988. An Overview of the PTRAN Analysis System for Multiprocessing, In *Proceedings of the International Conference on Supercomputing,* 1987. Also published in *Journal of Parallel and Distributed Computing,* 5, 1988.

[2] Allen, F.E., Compiling for Parallelism: An Overview, In *Proceedings of the IBM Institute Europe*, North Holland Press, 1986.

[3] Burke, M. and Cytron, R. Interprocedural Dependence Analysis and Parallelization (with retrospective). In *20 Years of PLDI (1979-1999): A Selection,* 2004.

[4] Carter, L., Ferrante, J. and Hummel, S.J.. 1995. Hierarchical tiling for improved superscalar performance. In *Proceedings of the 9th International Symposium on Parallel Processing* (IPPS '95), 239-245.

[5] Cytron, R. and Ferrante, J. 1987. What's in a name? In *Proceedings of the International Conference on Parallel Processing* (Aug. 1987), 19-27.

[6] Cytron, R., Ferrante, J., Rosen, B. K., Wegman, M. N.and Zadeck, F. K. 1989. An efficient method of computing static single assignment form. In *Proceedings of the 16th ACM SIGPLAN-SIGACT symposium on Principles of programming languages* Association for Computing Machinery, 25-35. DOI=10.1145/75277.75280 http://doi.acm.org/10.1145/75277.75280

[7] Cytron, R., Ferrante, J., Rosen, B. K., Wegman, M. N.and Zadeck, F. K. 1991. Efficiently computing static single assignment form and the control dependence graph. *ACM Trans. Program. Lang. Syst*. 13, 4 (October 1991), 451-490. DOI=10.1145/115372.115320 http://doi.acm.org/10.1145/115372.115320

[8] Ferrante, J. and Ottenstein, K. J. 1983. A program form based on data dependency in predicate regions. In *Proceedings of the 10th ACM SIGACT-SIGPLAN symposium on Principles of programming languages (POPL '83)*. ACM, New York, NY, 217-236. DOI=10.1145/567067.567089 http://doi.acm.org/10.1145/567067.567089

[9] Ferrante, J., Ottenstein, K.J., and Warren, J. 1984. The program dependence graph and its use in optimization, In *Proceedings of the 6th Colloquium on International Symposium on Programming*, 125-132.

[10] Ferrante, J., Ottenstein, K., and Warren, J. 1987. The program dependence graph and its use in optimization, *ACM Transactions on Programming Languages and Systems*, 9, 3, 319–349.

[11] Martin Hirzel, Robert Soulé, Scott Schneider, Buğra Gedik, and Robert Grimm. 2014. A catalog of stream processing optimizations. *ACM Comput. Surv.* 46, 4, Article 46 (March 2014), 34 pages.

[12] Justin Holewinski, Ragavendar Ramamurthi, Mahesh Ravishankar, Naznin Fauzia, Louis-Noël Pouchet, Atanas Rountev, and P. Sadayappan. 2012. Dynamic trace-based analysis of vectorization potential of applications. *SIGPLAN Not.* 47, 6 (June 2012), 371-382.

[13] http://amturing.acm.org/award_winners/allen_1012327.cfm

[14] Hu, Y. et. al. DiffSplice: the genome-wide detection of differential splicing events with RNA-seq *Nucl. Acids Res.* (2013) 41 (2): e39

[15] Kim, D., Renganarayanan, L., Rostron, D., Rajopadhye, S. and Mills Strout, M. 2007. Multi-level tiling: M for the price of one. In *Proceedings of the Conference on Supercomputing* (SC '07). DOI=10.1145/1362622.1362691 http://doi.acm.org/10.1145/1362622.1362691

[16] Sriram Krishnamoorthy, Muthu Baskaran, Uday Bondhugula, J. Ramanujam, Atanas Rountev, and P Sadayappan. 2007. Effective automatic parallelization of stencil computations. In *Proceedings of the 2007 ACM SIGPLAN conference on Programming language design and implementation* (PLDI '07). ACM, New York, NY, USA, 235-244

[17] Lee, Y. et al. 2013. Convergence and scalarization for data-parallel architectures, In *Proceedings of Code Generation and Optimization (CGO),* Feb. 2013. doi: 10.1109/CGO.2013.6494995

[18] Lim, J. and Reps, T. 2013. TSL: A System for Generating Abstract Interpreters and its Application to Machine-Code Analysis. *ACM Trans. Program. Lang. Syst.* 35, 1, Article 4 (April 2013), 59 pages. DOI=10.1145/2450136.2450139 http://doi.acm.org/10.1145/2450136.2450139

[19] Norris, C. and. Pollock, L.L.. 1998. Experiences with Cooperating Register Allocation and Instruction Scheduling. *Int. J. Parallel Program*. 26, 3 (June 1998), 241-283. DOI=10.1023/A:1018738112639 http://dx.doi.org/10.1023/A:1018738112639

[20] Ottenstein, K. 1978. Data-flow graphs as an intermediate program form. *Ph.D. Dissertation*. Purdue University, West Lafayette, IN, USA. AAI7905807.

[21] Quillere, Fabien, Rajopadhye, Sanjay, and Wilde, Doran. Generation of Efficient Nested Loops from Polyhedra. *International Journal of Parallel Programming* 28, 5 469-498.

[22] Raman, A., Lee, J.W. and August, D.I. 2012. From sequential programming to flexible parallel execution. In *Proceedings of the 2012 international conference on Compilers, architectures and synthesis for embedded systems (CASES '12)*. 37-40. DOI=10.1145/2380403.2380417 http://doi.acm.org/10.1145/2380403.2380417

[23] Stanier, J. and Watson, D. 2013. Intermediate representations in imperative compilers: A survey. *ACM Comput. Surv.* 45, 3, Article 26 (July 2013). DOI=10.1145/2480741.2480743 http://doi.acm.org/10.1145/2480741.2480743

[24] Sven Verdoolaege, Juan Carlos Juega, Albert Cohen, José Ignacio Gómez, Christian Tenllado, and Francky Catthoor. 2013. Polyhedral parallel code generation for CUDA. *ACM Trans. Archit. Code Optim.* 9, 4, Article 54 (January 2013), 23 pages. DOI=10.1145/2400682.2400713 http://doi.acm.org/10.1145/2400682.2400713

[25] Wegman, M.N. and Zadeck, F. K. 1985. Constant propagation with conditional branches. In *Proceedings of the 12th ACM SIGACT-SIGPLAN symposium on Principles of programming languages (POPL '85)*. ACM, New York, NY, USA, 291-299. DOI=10.1145/318593.318659 http://doi.acm.org/10.1145/318593.318659

[26] Wegman, M.N. and Zadeck, F. K. 1991. Constant propagation with conditional branches. *ACM Trans. Program. Lang. Syst.* 13, 2 (April 1991), 181-210. DOI=10.1145/103135.103136 http://doi.acm.org/10.1145/103135.103136

[27] Zhou, X., Giacalone, J., Garzarán, M.J.,. Kuhn, R.H., N, Y., and Padua, D. 2012. Hierarchical overlapped tiling. In *Proceedings of the Tenth International Symposium on Code Generation and Optimization* (CGO '12). 207-218. DOI=10.1145/2259016.2259044 http://doi.acm.org/10.1145/2259016.2259044

Author Retrospective for Code Scheduling and Register Allocation in Large Basic Blocks

James R. Goodman
Emeritus Professor,
Computer Sciences Department
University of Wisconsin-Madison

Wei Chung Hsu
Department of CSIE
National Taiwan University
Taipei, Taiwan, R.O.C.
hsuwc@csie.ntu.edu.tw

In 1987 we were working at the University of Wisconsin-Madison with Jim Smith, JT Hsieh, Koujuch Liou and Andrew Pleszkun on PIPE[4], an unorthodox "decoupled access-execute processor." The driving innovation of PIPE was the separation of instructions dealing with memory through a separate and independent instruction stream racing ahead, initiating load and store instructions in-order, synchronized only with other instructions through architectural queues. The queues eliminated the need for allocating and managing temporary registers.

While the problems of register allocation and instruction scheduling were traditionally treated independently, the genesis of this paper came while developing an optimizing compiler for PIPE, with the insight that in a conventional architecture these two closely related problems have conflicting goals that could be played off against each other to maximize benefit: Code scheduling uses as many temporary registers as possible to achieve a higher level of instruction-level parallelism (ILP), while register allocation minimizes the use of temporary registers so that more data items could be allocated to the available registers. As we gained more experience in optimizing for parallel programs, we came to understand that such conflicting goals were commonplace in the trade-off between parallelism and locality[2].

This work introduced the concept of the DAG-driven register allocation. We defined two terms, width and height of a DAG, in the context of code scheduling. The width of a DAG is the maximal number of mutually independent nodes requiring a destination (i.e. target) register and the height of a DAG is the length of its critical path. The shape of the DAG can be changed due to register allocation. For example, while the width can be reduced by reusing registers, the height could be increased. The purpose of DAG-driven register allocation is to minimize the height while keeping the width smaller than the number of available registers.

Original paper: http://dx.doi.org/10.1145/2591635.2591640

ICS 25th Anniversary Volume. 2014
ACM 978-1-4503-2840-1/14/06.
http://dx.doi.org/10.1145/2591635.2591640.

This work was most obviously relevant in the era of limited registers. By the late 1980s, RISC architectures were popular, and were often equipped with a relatively large register file, so we initially believed this work would have little practical impact, especially since the proceedings were never available in hardcopy after the conference was held. After finishing his PhD and working at Cray Research, however, Wei Hsu applied the techniques on Cray architectures having only 8 A/S registers, yielding significant performance improvements to the Cray CFT77 compilers on both Cray XMP/YMP and Cray 2/3 processors. In addition, the 64 B/T registers in Cray architectures allow low cost spilling, which takes advantage of the integrated scheduling approach proposed in the paper that would trade spilling for reduced pipeline interlocks. Though modern processors generally have many more registers, reducing the conflict between register allocation and code scheduling, these additional registers do not come for free, and the DAG-driven approach allows optimal scheduling with fewer registers. As computer scientists, we would like to produce an optimal algorithm, but if the optimal approach is NP-hard, then we settle for a heuristic guided algorithm. The DAG-driven allocation approach discussed in the paper is based on heuristics, and as such, we have always felt this work to be incomplete.

In the late 1980s, the infrastructure for computer system programming research was primitive. There were no open source compiler frameworks to be leveraged. In the PIPE project, our group had to develop our own compiler (by Honesty Young) and optimizer (by Mark Holiday). Benchmarks were also unrealistic and undemanding. Only an earlier version of the twelve Livermore loops was available. Due to the immature evaluation environments, we were uncertain of the practical value of this work until it was ported to the Cray CFT77 compiler and demonstrated significant performance gain on many important large applications. Today, the LLVM compiler infrastructure [5], and the GCC releases are easy to access in academia and benchmarks like SPEC [1] and ParSec [3] are large and diversified real applications. We are deeply indebted to our many peers who provided more comprehensive and reliable system evaluation infrastructures.

We are grateful especially to the members of the PIPE group at the University of Wisconsin-Madison. In particular, we would like to thank Honesty Young, who developed the early version of the code scheduler for the PIPE architecture. Wei Hsu would like to thank his colleagues at Cray

Research, especially Christopher C. Hsiung and Irene Qualters who encouraged the implementation of this research on a production quality compiler. James Goodman wishes to point out that the order of appearance of authors' names was influenced by advice of senior members of the Computer Sciences Department, who encouraged untenured professors whose names appear early in an alphabetical listing to list all authors in alphabetical order, regardless of their contributions.

1. REFERENCES

[1] http://www.spec.org/benchmarks.html.

[2] J. M. Anderson and M. S. Lam. Global optimizations for parallelism and locality on scalable parallel machines. *SIGPLAN Not.*, 28(6):112–125, June 1993.

[3] C. Bienia, S. Kumar, J. P. Singh, and K. Li. The parsec benchmark suite: Characterization and architectural implications. In *Proceedings of the 17th International Conference on Parallel Architectures and Compilation Techniques*, PACT '08, pages 72–81, New York, NY, USA, 2008. ACM.

[4] J. R. Goodman, J.-t. Hsieh, K. Liou, A. R. Pleszkun, P. B. Schechter, and H. C. Young. Pipe: A vlsi decoupled architecture. *SIGARCH Comput. Archit. News*, 13(3):20–27, June 1985.

[5] C. Lattner and V. Adve. Llvm: A compilation framework for lifelong program analysis & transformation. In *Proceedings of the International Symposium on Code Generation and Optimization: Feedback-directed and Runtime Optimization*, CGO '04, Washington, DC, USA, 2004. IEEE Computer Society.

Author Retrospective for Array Expansion, Array Shrinking, or There and Back Again

Paul Feautrier
Ecole Normale Supérieure de Lyon, Lyon, France
Paul.Feautrier@ens-lyon.fr

In the late 1980's, I was recovering from a long stint as the manager of Paris University computing facility (yes, there were still computing facilities, and PCs were just coming of age) and I was teaching old fashioned automatic parallelization to postgraduate students. I had heard of scalar expansion and privatization, and it was a natural question whether it could be extended to arrays. I first concocted partial solutions – for instance, valid only for the innermost loop – and then decided to try for the general case: converting array accesses to single assignment form. I soon realized that this implied finding the source, or last write before a given read, and that the solution must be a function of the position of the read in the temporal execution of the program. It was obvious that this could not be done for arbitrary complex programs, hence I specified a set of restriction: the polyhedral model. I also introduced the execution order, now known as the "happens-before" relation. Finding the last write then became an integer programming problem with some unfamiliar features: lexicographic order took the place of the economic function, the problem had to be solved exactly, and the coordinates of the read operation were acting as parameters. Hence, I had first to build PIP (a parametric integer programming tool [2]) before solving my problem. PIP was developed on a 80286 PC, using Borland TurboC and LeLisp.

It then took me about two years to have an improved form of the ICS paper published by a journal [3]. Here, the emphasis was more on single assignment conversion and its use for program comprehension. I also formalized a comparison algorithm, which is needed when there are several potential sources. But it was not until [4] that I managed to prove its termination.

Meanwhile, the ICS paper had attracted attention from the other side of the Atlantic. Most important was Bill Pugh's work [6], in which the problem was reformulated in term of affine relations, and solved by Bill's own linear programming tool, Omega. I remember that we exchanged our benchmarks, and found that our results were equivalent. An early example of reproducible research!

It soon became evident that single assignment programs, whose space complexity is equal to their time complexity, could not be run directly. In fact, a progran can run indefinitely, or at least for as long as the MTBF of its target system, while the amount of memory was and still is limited. The aim of array shrinking is to reuse memory when the information it contains is no longer useful, and this may be either the result of sloppy programming or of excessive array expansion. A succession of papers [5, 7, 1] tackled the problem with increasing power and precision.

And that should have been all, but array dataflow analysis reappeared unexpectedly. Many teams, mostly in the USA, were designing parallel programming languages, where deadlock freedom is guaranteed, but determinism is not. Parallel programs have a partial execution order, hence, when searching for the source of a read, one cannot compute a maximum, but only extrema, and a given read may have several sources. This indicates non-determinism. In [8], polyhedral dataflow analysis was applied to the X10 language, using techniques similar to Bill Pugh's. The result was a tool able to detect some non-determinism at compile time.

ICS 25th Anniversary Volume. 2014
ACM 978-1-4503-2840-1/14/06.
http://dx.doi.org/10.1145/2591635.2591641.

1. REFERENCES

[1] A. Darte, R. Schreiber, and G. Villard. Lattice-based memory allocation. *IEEE Transactions on Computers*, 54(10):1242–1257, 2005.

[2] P. Feautrier. Parametric integer programming. *RAIRO Recherche Opérationnelle*, 22:243–268, Sept. 1988.

[3] P. Feautrier. Dataflow analysis of scalar and array references. *Int. J. of Parallel Programming*, 20(1):23–53, Feb. 1991.

[4] P. Feautrier. Array dataflow analysis. In *Compiler Optimizations for Scalable Parallel Systems*, LNCS 1808, pages 173–216. Springer, 2001.

[5] V. Lefebvre and P. Feautrier. Storage management in parallel programs. In *5th Euromicro Workshop on Parallel and Distributed Processing*, pages 181–188, Jan. 1997.

[6] W. Pugh and D. Wonnacott. An evaluation of exact methods for analysis of value-based array data dependences. In *Sixth LCPC*, pages 546–566. Springer-Verlag LNCS 768, Aug. 1993.

[7] F. Quilleré and S. Rajopadhye. Optimizing memory usage in the polyhedral model. *ACM TOPLAS*, 22(5):773–815, 2000.

[8] T. Yuki, P. Feautrier, S. V. Rajopadhye, and V. Saraswat. Array dataflow analysis for polyhedral x10 programs. In *PPOPP*, pages 23–34, 2013.

Author Retrospective for

A *Global* Resource-constrained Parallelization Technique

Kemal Ebcioğlu
Global Supercomputing Corporation
kemal.ebcioglu@global-supercomputing.com

Alexandru Nicolau
University of California, Irvine
nicolau@ics.uci.edu

DOI: http://dx.doi.org/10.1145/318789.318807

Looking back over the last 25 years, we will reflect below on our 1989 paper, "A *global* resource-constrained parallelization technique" published in the Third International Conference on Supercomputing, held in Crete, June 1989.

Automatic parallelization of arbitrary sequential code is a very difficult problem, necessitating multiple innovations by its nature.

A key obstacle to overcome during any effort for automatic parallelization of arbitrary sequential code is the *program serialization point*, which is a barrier point wherein parallel execution effectively comes to a standstill. For example, depending on the parallelization algorithm, program serialization points can occur on conditional branches that are mispredicted, or at inner or outer loop entries and exits, or at operating system calls, or at time consuming memory or I/O accesses which cannot be overlapped with other work. Avoiding serialization points is important: It has been confirmed more than once in limit studies that the further apart serialization points are in the execution trace of a sequential program, the more parallelism can be extracted [Wal91], [The92].

An important technique available at the time of the publication of our 1989 paper for compiler-based parallelization of arbitrary sequential code was Trace Scheduling [Fis79], which scheduled operations on a predicted path through a sequential program, wherein the predicted path was determined by, e.g., software profiling. Serialization points were frequent with trace scheduling: whenever the predicted path (the *trace*) was not followed at run time, programs scheduled by trace scheduling effectively incurred a serialization point penalty, since parallelism was then limited only to the maximum parallelism available within the instruction window starting at the beginning of the trace, and ending at the mispredicted branch.

Our 1989 paper described a core resource-constrained scheduling algorithm, which extended Percolation Scheduling[Nic85] that on its own did not deal with resources and conditional execution.

Our 1989 algorithm was intended for parallelizing arbitrary acyclic sequential code (i.e., program fragments having a control flow graph in the form of a Directed Acyclic Graph (DAG), including both conditional branches and join points).

ICS 25th Anniversary Volume, 2014
ACM 978-1-4503-2840-1/14/06.
http://dx.doi.org/10.1145/2591635.2591642

Our paper's algorithm got rid of any *requirement* for predicting branches, and therefore avoided the associated penalty at branch mispredictions. Note that to solve the all-paths scheduling problem, it was possible use simpler, alternative approaches in 1989, including:

1. Using *select/conditional move* operations (or almost equivalently, *predicated execution*) to execute all operations on all paths in the program, and to finally commit the correct subset of operations on the taken path (*disadvantages:* all paths are forced to take an equal amount of time, even though some paths may inherently be faster, and the computation of operations on untaken paths become wasted computations), or
2. Creating different schedules for each distinct path in the program (where the different schedules share only an initial segment) by converting the DAG program into a tree program, by duplicating code after join points (*disadvantage:* potential high code size increase).

But our paper of 1989 chose neither of these simpler approaches, and instead preserved the join points in the original program, whenever there was no parallelism extraction reason to justify the destruction of join points. The algorithm of 1989 accomplished its goals by:

Speculative execution on *all* paths instead of a single path/trace, therefore avoiding branch misprediction penalties,

while preserving computational resources by:

- Stopping the execution of the remaining operations of a path, as a soon as it is known that that path is not taken, and
- Recognizing common operations on multiple paths, and merging such common operations into a single operation. For example, only a single copy of an $i=i+1$ operation occurring after 10 *if-then-else-endif* statements could exist in the final scheduled VLIW program, as opposed to 2^{10} = 1024 copies.

While this paper's algorithm did not include systematic register renaming to eliminate anti and output dependences (these dependences could be reduced by renaming techniques applied prior to applying the algorithm), it was indeed a first description of a resource constrained all-paths global scheduling technique resilient to branch mispredictions in branch-intensive DAG code. Combined with proper multiway branching and conditional execution hardware, e.g., as in the first IBM Research VLIW machine [Ebc88] and its follow-on designs, the algorithm introduced in this paper could overcome branch misprediction penalties and could also save computational resources as described above. We believe that our 1989 algorithm was therefore one of the essential innovation ingredients on the difficult trajectory toward automatic parallelization of arbitrary sequential code.

Since 1989, many academic and industrial research experiments and at least one major industrial product initiative (The Intel and HP *IA-64®* project [Rie12]) based on the fine-grain parallelism concept within VLIW architectures were carried out, out-of-order execution mechanisms within processors were concomitantly improved, and multi-core processor architectures have flourished, offering additional innovation opportunities for *coarse-grain* parallelism (creation of new parallel synchronized threads), in addition to fine-grain parallelism within each thread, in the context of automatic parallelization of arbitrary sequential code. Automatic parallelization of arbitrary sequential code remains an exciting and active area as of today, and promising research and industry efforts continue [Ebc11], [Ebc12], [Cam12].

References

[Wal91] David W. Wall. 1991. Limits of instruction-level parallelism. SIGARCH Comput. Archit. News 19, 2 (April 1991), 176-188. DOI=10.1145/106975.106991 http://doi.acm.org/10.1145/106975.106991

[The92] Kevin B. Theobald, Guang R. Gao, and Laurie J. Hendren. 1992. On the limits of program parallelism and its smoothability. In Proceedings of the 25th annual international symposium on Microarchitecture (MICRO 25). IEEE Computer Society Press, Los Alamitos, CA, USA, 10-19.

[Fis79] Joseph A. Fisher, 1979. Optimization of horizontal microcode within and beyond basic blocks. An application of processor scheduling with resources. Courant Mathematics and Computing Laboratory. Department of Energy report COO-1077-161. October 1979. http://www.archive.org/stream/optimizationofho00fish

[Nic85] Alexandru Nicolau. 1985. Uniform Parallelism Exploitation in Ordinary Programs. International Conference on Parallel Processing (ICPP): 614-618.

[Ebc88] Kemal Ebcioğlu. Some Design Ideas for a VLIW Architecture for Sequential Natured Software. Parallel Processing (Proc. IFIP WG 10.3 Working Conference on Parallel Processing), M. Cosnard, M.H. Barton, M. Vanneschi (eds.), pp. 3-21, North Holland, 1988. http://global-supercomputing.com/people/kemal.ebcioglu/pdf/Ebcioglu-IFIP88.pdf

[Rie12] Reid J. Riedlinger, Ron Arnold, Larry Biro, William J. Bowhill, Jason Crop, Kevin Duda, Eric S. Fetzer, Olivier Franza, Tom Grutkowski, Casey Little, Charles Morganti, Gary Moyer, Ashley Munch, Mahalingam Nagarajan, Cheolmin Park, Christopher Poirier, Bill Repasky, Edi Roytman, Tejpal Singh, Matthew W. Stefaniw: A 32 nm, 3.1 Billion Transistor, 12 Wide Issue Itanium® Processor for Mission-Critical Servers. J. Solid-State Circuits 47(1): 177-193 (2012).

[Ebc11] Method and system for converting a single-threaded software program into an application-specific supercomputer. Co-inventors: Kemal Ebcioglu, Emre Kultursay, Mahmut Taylan Kandemir. Filed on 11/15/2011 as US non-provisional patent application 13/296,232. http://patentscope.wipo.int/search/en/WO2013074341

[Ebc12] Parallel hardware hypervisor for virtualizing application-specific supercomputers. Co-inventors: Kemal Ebcioglu, Atakan Dogan, Reha Oguz Altug, Mikko Herman Lipasti, Eray Ozkural. Filed on 02/04/2012 as US non-provisional patent application 13/366,318. http://patentscope.wipo.int/search/en/WO2013115928

[Cam12] Simone Campanoni, Timothy Jones, Glenn Holloway, Vijay Janapa Reddi, Gu-Yeon Wei, and David Brooks. "HELIX: automatic parallelization of irregular programs for chip multiprocessing," in Proceedings of the 10th annual IEEE/ACM international symposium on Code generation and optimization (CGO), March 2012.

Author Retrospective

Compiler-Directed Data Prefetching in Multiprocessors with Memory Hierarchies

Eddie Gornish
Nvidia Corporation
2001 Walsh Avenue
Santa Clara, CA 95050
(408) 562-7599
gornish@gmail.com

Elana Granston
Cutting Edge Consulting
cuttingedgeconsulting@outlook.com

Alexander V. Veidenbaum
Dept. of Computer Science
University of California Irvine
Irvine, CA 92697-3435
(949)-824-6188
alexv@ics.uci.edu

ABSTRACT

The ideas of compiler-generated prefetching were first proposed in the late 80's. Two main research directions were pursued, both addressed prefetching for loop-based applications containing arrays with regular access patterns. Our approach assumed a hardware prefetcher controlled by software and prefetching into a separate prefetch buffer and finding the earliest point such a prefetch can possibly be initiated. The other approach proposed to prefetch into a cache using a prefetch instruction. This retrospective examines the decisions made at the time and their applicability in today's high-performance processors.

Original paper: http://dx.doi.org/10.1145/77726.255176

Categories and Subject Descriptors

B.3.2.[**Design Styles**]: Cache Memories, Shared Memory.
D.3.4 [**Processors**]: Compilers, Code Generation.

Keywords: Prefetching; caches; compiler; multi-processor; interconnection network.

1. A HISTORICAL PERSPECTIVE

It is taken for granted today that commercial compilers generate software prefetches and, in general, optimize programs to better use the complex memory hierarchies of modern processors. This was not the case at the time when our paper was written. The use of software to help manage caches was only beginning to be explored, with the focus on parallel programs and multiprocessors. The prevailing view, especially among hardware designers and architects, was that a cache was managed by hardware and was supposed to be invisible to the software. There was already, of course, cache (and TLB) management in a commercial operating systems but it primarily involved page-level invalidation. At the time our paper was written, compiler-managed cache coherence using very simple hardware support for certain types of parallel programs was a new idea [PBG+85, 1][1]. The type of parallel programs considered was akin to OpenMP, i.e. using parallel loop constructs, but OpenMP was not yet defined. Parallel loops were beginning to become available in commercial systems and source to source automatic parallelization [KKLW80, 2] was implemented in research compilers.

Data prefetching for multiprocessors was still a research topic, in both academia and industry. On the architecture side, both prefetching into a prefetch buffer [Lee87, 3] and prefetching into cache [Lee87, 4] were still considered. The latter was a concern as caches were small and cache block fetch could significantly increase the bandwidth requirements for strides > 1 and in the presence of conditionals. Memory latency and bandwidth were major concerns for scalable systems, even though latencies were very low by today's standards. In addition, processors were in-order and had caches allowing only one miss at a time.

Our interest in compiler generating prefetching code was, in part, due to the above-mentioned developments. Another reason was the development of the Cedar multiprocessor [KDLS86, 5] at the Center for Supercomputing Research and Development at the University of Illinois. Cedar implemented a hardware stride prefetcher in each processor. The software loaded prefetch control registers (length, stride, mask) and the prefetch was then initiated by a memory request. Cedar prefetched from shared memory into a 4KB prefetch buffer directly accessible to the processor. The number of outstanding prefetch requests was only limited by the size of the length register.

Compiler generation of prefetch instructions was the subject of a Master's thesis for one of us [Gor89]. We chose to prefetch into a separate prefetch buffer because caches at the time did not allow user control and had other issue mentioned above. We were very concerned about memory latency for multiprocessor scaling and our major goal was to investigate how far in advance a prefetch can be issued. For instance, can it be initiated before a loop nest enclosing a reference? Or even earlier? This was one of the major differences with concurrent work at Rice [Port89], which investigated cache prefetching in vector loops and either in the same or at most one iteration ahead of a reference. In general, our work was equally applicable to cache prefetching if the hardware could support a cache block based prefetch unit.

We were interested in prefetching for sequential loops, whether enclosed by parallel loops or not. In the latter case, we especially wanted to exploit the interleaved memory system and overlap memory requests (today's Memory Level Parallelism or MLP). It was generally assumed that at least a singly-nested sequential loop was enclosed by a parallel loop running across multiple processors.

[1] References starting with a letter are from the original paper.

ICS 25th Anniversary Volume. 2014
ACM 978-1-4503-2840-1/14/06.
http://dx.doi.org/10.1145/2591635.2591644.

On the architecture side, by the time the paper was being written we had developed a clock-cycle accurate memory and network simulator of a Cedar-like system. Thus another goal of the paper was to evaluate the effect of prefetching on the shared memory bandwidth and latency as well as on program speedup. Our results showed that prefetching speedup was lower than our static analysis based model predicted. The main reason was network contention, which increased the memory latency.

Looking back, it is interesting to see that we also evaluated a system without prefetching but allowing overlap of shared memory access and computation. It produced speedups similar to prefetching in most tested programs. This is basically a combination of non-blocking loads and multiple outstanding requests, e.g. MLP. Our simulation model set the prefetch length to 256B, which was experimentally determined to result in lowest contention and latency on this 32 processor system. However, even with this limit we observed a large increase in both latency and arrival rate of requested data due contention. We mentioned but did not investigate at the time issues of prefetch scheduling to alleviate this problem. Dynamic adaptation of prefetch length to reduce contention was not yet considered.

2. DESIGN DECISIONS

Looking back, it is interesting to consider which of our design decision and concerns were justified.

1. We used prefetching into a prefetch buffer rather than a cache, although this was not a critical issue for our compilation approach. We could have easily investigated both approaches, especially if we assumed 1-word cache blocks as in [Port89]. Prefetching directly into the cache was still considered controversial at the time, but clearly is not a concern today.

2. We limited prefetching in two ways:

   A. Only data that would not be overwritten before use was prefetched (this limited what data could be prefetched and how far in advance it could be prefetched). Without this limitation we would need to guarantee that the prefetched data went into a location that was memory coherent. The obvious memory coherent target would be cache; however, as we indicated above, prefetching into the cache was considered controversial at the time. Furthermore, our work assumed that caches were kept coherent by compilers and used weak ordering.

   B. Only data guaranteed to be used was prefetched, so we avoided prefetching any data in a location that was not control-equivalent to the use point. This also limited what data could be prefetched and how far in advance it could be prefetched. A major concern at the time was that unused prefetch data could cause thrashing. While this is true, the concern was blown out of proportion. A well-thought compiler algorithm could get by with only prefetching a small amount of excess data. By the mid 90's many commercial compiler algorithms were not worried about prefetching a few extra cache lines at the end of an array, or prefetching an array that was accessed within a conditional. In the latter case, where several array elements would fit into a cache line, one would need to load elements that would not be accessed, even without prefetching. So, one might as well prefetch them. But again, when we wrote the paper, we were not thinking about caches, cache line size, and how many elements could fit into a cache line. This issue can still be a concern today if one attempts to prefetch in a scalable many-core system.

3. Cache lines in commercial processors were small at the time (16B) and many research papers considered 1-word lines. For these reasons, we tried to focus the paper more on *what* could be prefetched and *how early* it could be prefetched" and stayed away from *where* it could prefetched into and *how* it could be prefetched (e.g. a block prefetch instruction, many little prefetch instructions). Line sizes increased quickly between the writing of this paper and the mid to late 90's allowing for different trade-offs. Digital's Alpha architecture even introduced a 512B prefetch instruction for loading data into an L2 cache. Thus our 256B prefetch length would become a single line prefetch.

4. We assumed a 2-level memory hierarchy and prefetched from memory to the prefetch buffer. Today, processors have 3 or even 4 levels of cache with multiple hardware cache line prefetchers. The caches are large and highly associative, making replacement by prefetched lines less of a concern. Processors are out of order and support a high number of outstanding misses. Latencies are much larger. What and where should the compiler prefetch? Compiler generated prefetch instructions are thus typically treated as hints by the hardware.

5. Finally, our major contribution was determining the earliest point to initiate prefetching. This can lead to too much data being prefetched and should be balanced with the data needs of a program. Today's compilers can achieve almost the same latency hiding effect by moving a cache prefetch instruction as many iterations before data use as necessary.

3. CONCLUSIONS

It is surprising given the vast changes in cache organization and the use of multiple hardware prefetchers that compiler prefetching algorithms are still basically the same as 20+ years ago. They are much better integrated in the compilation process and are not performed at the source level, but are they the best one can do for today's hardware? Overall, similar to the situation we found ourselves in when writing the original paper, it is not clear again what is the best combination of compiler and hardware techniques for prefetching.

4. ACKNOWLEDGMENTS

Our thanks to ACM SIGARCH for publishing this retrospective.

5. REFERENCES

[1] Alexander V. Veidenbaum. A Compiler-Assisted Cache Coherence Solution for Multiprocessors. Intl. Conference on Parallel Processing (ICPP), 1986. pp.1029-1036

[2] Randy Allen, Ken Kennedy. Automatic Translation of Fortran Programs to Vector Form. ACM Trans. Program. Lang. Syst. 9(4), pp. 491-542 (1987).

[3] Norman P. Jouppi. "Improving direct-mapped cache performance by the addition of a small fully-associative cache and prefetch buffers," Intl. Symposium on Computer Architecture (ISCA), 1990. pp.364–373

[4] Todd C. Mowry, Anoop Gupta. Tolerating Latency Through Software-Controlled Prefetching in Shared-Memory

Multiprocessors. J. Parallel Distrib. Comput. 12(2), pp. 87-106 (1991)

[5] David. J Kuck et al. The Cedar System and an Initial Performance Study. Intl. Symposium on Computer Architecture (ISCA), 1993. pp. 213-223

[6] Daniel Lenoski et al. The DASH Prototype: Implementation and Performance. Intl. Symposium on Computer Architecture (ISCA), 1992. pp. 92-103

Author Retrospective for Semantical Interprocedural Parallelization: An Overview of the PIPS Project

François Irigoin
MINES ParisTech
francois.irigoin@mines-paristech.fr

Pierre Jouvelot
MINES ParisTech
pierre.jouvelot@mines-paristech.fr

Rémi Triolet
Simulation Factory
remi.triolet@simulationfactory.net

ABSTRACT

The PIPS project was started in 1988 to investigate the automatic detection of medium- and large-grain parallelism in scientific programs thanks to summarization techniques based on convex array regions. By 1992 the PIPS system had reached its original goals, but it has morphed into a comprehensive, open-source platform still in use today. What were the key scientific and engineering decisions that made this possible in spite of some inevitable shortcomings?

Original paper: http://dx.doi.org/10.1145/109025.109086

Categories and Subject Descriptors:
D.3.4 [Processors]: Compilers, Optimization

Keywords:
Automatic Parallelization; Interprocedural Analysis

1. INTRODUCTION

The goals of the PIPS project were (1) to find automatically medium and large grain *interprocedural* parallelism in Fortran 77 scientific programs and (2) to express it thanks to a *source-to-source* translation process targetting *shared-memory* multiprocessors.

PIPS was based on polyhedral techniques for command abstraction [16], procedure summarization with convex array regions [31] and hence dependence tests, and was to be the first polyhedral compiler.

2. ASSUMPTIONS AND KEY CHOICES

2.1 Six Key Assumptions

The necessary parallelism was to be found in loops dealing with arrays indexed by *affine* expressions only. Unlike data parallelism, task and instruction-level parallelisms were deemed of no use because bounded by the code size and the number of operators.

ICS 25th Anniversary Volume. 2014
ACM 978-1-4503-2840-1/14/06.
http://dx.doi.org/10.1145/2591635.2591645.

Unstructured pieces of code did not require a precise analysis because they do not contain data parallelism.

Recursive functions were not used in scientific code and do not contain data parallelism either. Functional parameters are not common enough to be taken care of either.

Convex array regions are precise enough to find medium-grain parallelism and polyhedral operators are fast enough to analyze whole applications.

PIPS would perform *whole program parallelization.* The source code of all modules is assumed available.

Finally, source-to-source is sufficient to express parallelism and optimizations, while preserving key information for programmers and optimizers.

2.2 Scientific Choices

Because parallelism was to be found in DO loops, PIPS internal representation is not based on a usual control flow graph (CFG). Instead it uses a recursive combination of abstract syntax trees for structured components and CFGs for unstructured ones. This combination was called a hierarchical control flow graph (HCFG).

It was decided to use abstract commands to build abstract stores for interprocedural analysis with only two traversals of the call graph, and, later, to perform convex array region propagation. Abstract commands are also useful to shorten the analysis of nested loops, which are common in scientific codes.

2.3 Design Choices

The design was guided by our knowledge of Parafrase [20] and PTRAN [30] internals, and ended up with a minimal internal representation both for control constructs and for entities. No intrinsics, not even the assignment, are singled out: they all are calls with side effects. Functions, variables, commons... are all entities. Hence, the internal representation [11] is language-independent.

The Newgen [32] data description language was adopted to implement PIPS internal representation. Newgen uses dynamic typing to provide automatically compact data management features, thanks to a layer of macros and functions, including higher-order generic traversal operators.

Multiple implementation languages were available for fast prototyping, CommonLisp, and efficiency, C. Thanks to Newgen, data structures could be shared by the two languages.

A unique symbol table was designed to ease interprocedural analyses.

Persistance was necessary for interprocedural analyses because of the memory size constraint and to allow interactive uses. A make-like system was implemented to ensure the PIPS database consistency and some pass ordering automatically [11]. It also made PIPS modular and evolutive, with an easy declarative way to add new passes [5].

A sparse implementation was chosen for the polyhedral library because few variables are involved in each constraint.

Finally, an interactive window-based interface was added for demonstrations and for pedagogical reasons.

2.4 Future Work of 1991

We anticipated the need for path transformers [18], profitability analyses [36], programming rules, assertions about key parameters and data transformations such as array expansion or privatization [12, 13], as well as improvement in convex array region translation, and feared complexity due to affine transformers.

We assumed that non-convex array regions would be useful in signal processing codes and expected a lack of target machines and parallel languages

3. LOOKING BACKWARD

PIPS later competitors such as Parafrase-2, Polaris, SUIF, SUIF-2 are gone, but PIPS is still with us and has not been rewritten in Java or C++. Why?

3.1 Strong Points

Polyhedral techniques are very flexible [2] and often not too complex [35]. They support loop parallelization, with neither control nor call restrictions [13], and automatic distribution [9, 23].

Interprocedural techniques, which PIPS pioneered, are now key to compilers for heterogeneous targets [14, 1].

A langage-neutral high-level source-to-source internal representation is useful for the user who can recognize her source code, for debugging the compiler since the internal representation can be compiled and executed at any step, and for supporting new input languages.

Automatic consistency is important to manage interprocedural issues and to add new passes. Pass dependencies are managed by PIPS, not by the pass programmer.

The data description language NewGen was useful to update the internal representation without modifying PIPS code. This proved key when adding C to Fortran as a source language.

However, interactivity and multiple implementation languages turned out to be of little use.

3.2 Extensions

To process industrial code, we had to extend the initial Fortran subset to cope with entries, stack allocation, dependent types, while loops and the HPF/OpenMP directives. And then we had to support C99 with pointers and dynamic allocation.

We combined static and dynamic analyses to obtain both safety and efficiency: array overflows, aliasing detection and proper variable initialization [27, 26, 28]. We also had to analyze non-integer variables and non-affine expressions because they control the behaviors of large applications.

To process C, we had to extend and/or to implement usual code analyses and transformations such as use-def chains, points-to analysis, dead-code elimination, control simplification, induction variable substitution, scalarization and loop fusion [5, 1, 22].

We also had to go beyond a simple interprocedural approach and to add procedure cloning, inlining and outlining: procedure boundaries must be moved to fit the target machine [14].

Finally all kinds of parallelism must be detected. Commutative and transitive expression optimization was added to improve ILP [38]. Reduction detection [17], small vector parallelism, SSE or AVX [15], and GPU code generation with data distribution [1, 3] were introduced later. Finally task parallelism must be exploited with multicores [19, 33].

On the implementation side, list-based algorithms were replaced by hash-tables to scale up when large applications are analyzed, modules written in CommonLisp were rewritten in C, and exception management had to be introduced to cope with magnitude overflows in polyhedral operators. A Python embedding, pyps, was introduced to provide the flexibility required with in- and out-lining [14]. The 1.x Par4All initiative [33] also uses Python to increase PIPS robustness and to simplify its use (see `par4all.org`).

4. CONCLUSIONS

PIPS has proved over the years to be a fertile ground for the polyhedral model [21], data transformations [13], communication synthesis [4, 7], compilation for distributed memory machines [9, 23], ILP [37], code maintenance [29, 6], program verification [25], scratchpad management [8], offload compilers [14, 1, 10], and task parallelism [18, 33].

These advances were made possible by PIPS modular and evolutive structure, by its language-neutral internal representation and by new analyzes and a better understanding of their domains [36, 34, 13, 24, 22], but also by many contributors to the PIPS infrastructure, to its classical pass portfolio, to its tutorials and website. And PIPS grew from 50 KLOC in 1991 to about 600 KLOC in 2014.

New challenges are now addressed with PIPS: manycores, heterogeneous systems, complex memory hierarchies, code modelization, tool combinations and parallel languages. On the infrastructure side, we intend to combine robustness for industrial use and openness for research.

5. ACKNOWLEDGMENTS

We owe many thanks to the PIPS contributors, who are too numerous to be all mentioned here, but whose names are listed on its website, `pips4u.org`. Their work was funded by many French and European programs, institutions and companies: ANR, CEA, CNRS, DRET, EDF, ESPRIT, HPC Project/SILKAN, Télécom SudParis and THALES.

We are also thankful to Claude Girault, who helped fund and set up the so-called C3 group, and to the members of this group, especially Corinne Ancourt, Philippe Clauss, Alain Darte, Paul Feautrier, Catherine Montgenet, Guy-René Perrin, Patrice Quinton and Yves Robert.

6. ADDITIONAL REFERENCES

[1] M. Amini. *Source-to-Source Automatic Program Transformations for GPU-like Hardware Accelerators*. PhD thesis, MINES ParisTech, Paris, France, 2012.

[2] M. Amini, C. Ancourt, F. Coelho, F. Irigoin, P. Jouvelot, R. Keryell, P. Villalon, B. Creusillet, and S. Guelton. PIPS Is not (just) Polyhedral Software. In *Intl. Workshop on Polyhedral Compilation Techniques (IMPACT'11)*, Chamonix, France, Apr. 2011.

[3] M. Amini, F. Coelho, F. Irigoin, and R. Keryell. Static Compilation Analysis for Host-Accelerator Communication Optimization. In *LCPC*, pages 237–251, Fort Collins, Colorado., 2011.

[4] C. Ancourt. *Génération automatique de code de transfert pour multiprocesseurs à mémoires locales.* PhD thesis, Université Pierre et Marie Curie (Paris 6), Mar. 1991.

[5] C. Ancourt, F. Coelho, B. Creusillet, and R. Keryell. How to Add a New Phase in PIPS: the Case of Dead Code Elimination. In *Sixth Workshop on Compilers for Parallel Computers (CPC)*, pages 19–30, Aachen, Germany, Dec. 1996.

[6] C. Ancourt and T. V. N. Nguyen. Array resizing for scientific code debugging, maintenance and reuse. In *Proceedings of the 2001 ACM SIGPLAN-SIGSOFT Workshop on Program Analysis for Software Tools and Engineering*, PASTE '01, pages 32–37, New York, NY, USA, 2001. ACM.

[7] C. Ancourt, T. Petrisor, F. Irigoin, and E. Lenormand. Automatic Generation of Communications for Redundant Multi-dimensional Data Parallel Redistributions. In *IEEE International Conference on High Performance Computing and Communications*, pages pp. 800–811, Zhangjiajie, Chine, Nov. 2013.

[8] Y. Bouchebaba. *Optimisation des transferts de données pour le traitement du signal : pavage, fusion et réallocation des tableaux.* PhD thesis, École des mines de Paris, Nov. 2002.

[9] F. Coelho. *Contributions à la compilation du High Performance Fortran.* PhD thesis, École des mines de Paris, Oct. 1996.

[10] F. Coelho and F. Irigoin. API Compilation for Image Hardware Accelerators. *ACM TACO*, 9(4):49:1–49:25, Jan. 2013.

[11] F. Coelho, P. Jouvelot, F. Irigoin, and C. Ancourt. Data and Process Abstraction in PIPS Internal Representation. In *Workshop on Internal Representations (WIR)*, Chamonix, France, Apr. 2011.

[12] B. Creusillet and F. Irigoin. Interprocedural array region analyses. *IJPP*, 24:513–546, Dec. 1996.

[13] B. Creusillet-Apvrille. *Array Region Analyses and Applications.* PhD thesis, École des mines de Paris, Dec. 1996.

[14] S. Guelton. *Building Source-to-Source Compilers for Heterogenous Targets.* PhD thesis, Télécom Bretagne, 2011.

[15] S. Guelton, A. Guinet, and R. Keryell. Building retargetable and efficient compilers for multimedia instruction sets. In *Parallel Architectures and Compilation Techniques*, PACT, Oct. 2011. (poster).

[16] F. Irigoin. Interprocedural analyses for programming environments. In *Environments and Tools for Parallel Scientific Computing*, pages 333–350. Elsevier, Sept. 1993.

[17] P. Jouvelot, B. Dehbonei. A Unified Semantic Approach for the Vectorization and Parallelization of Generalized Reductions. In *Proceedings of the 3rd International Conference on Supercomputing* (ICS '89), pages pp. 186–194, Heraklion, Crete, June 1989.

[18] D. Khaldi. *Automatic Resource-Constrained Static Task Parallelization.* PhD thesis, MINES ParisTech, 2013.

[19] D. Khaldi, P. Jouvelot, C. Ancourt, and F. Irigoin. Task Parallelism and Data Distribution: An Overview of Explicit Parallel Programming Languages. In *LCPC*, pages 174–189, 2012.

[20] D. J. Kuck, R. H. Kuhn, B. Leasure, and M. Wolfe. The structure of an advanced vectorizer for pipelined processors. In *4th International Computer Software and Applications Conference*, Oct. 1980.

[21] A. Leservot. *Analyses interprocédurales du flot des données.* PhD thesis, Université Paris VI, Mar. 1996.

[22] A. Mensi. *Analyse des pointeurs pour le langage C.* PhD thesis, MINES ParisTech, 2013.

[23] D. Millot, A. Muller, C. Parrot, and F. Silber-Chaussumier. STEP: a distributed OpenMP for coarse-grain parallelism tool. In *Proceedings of the 4th International Conference on OpenMP in a New Era of Parallelism*, IWOMP'08, pages 83–99, 2008.

[24] D. Nguyen. *Robust and Generic Abstract Domain for Static Program Analyses: The Polyhedral Case.* PhD thesis, École des mines de Paris, Nov. 2010.

[25] T. V. N. Nguyen. *Efficient and Effective Software Verification for Scientific Applications Using Static Analysis and Code Instrumentation.* PhD thesis, École des mines de Paris, 2002.

[26] T. V. N. Nguyen and F. Irigoin. Alias verification for Fortran code optimization. *Journal of Universal Computer Science*, 9(3):270–297, Mar. 2003.

[27] T. V. N. Nguyen and F. Irigoin. Efficient and effective array bound checking. *ACM Trans. Program. Lang. Syst.*, 27:527–570, May 2005.

[28] T. V. N. Nguyen, F. Irigoin, C. Ancourt, and F. Coelho. Automatic detection of uninitialized variables. In *Proceedings of the 12th International Conference on Compiler Construction*, CC'03, pages 217–231, Berlin, Heidelberg, 2003. Springer-Verlag.

[29] N. W. Preston. New type signatures for legacy Fortran subroutines. In W. G. Griswold and S. Horwitz, editors, *PASTE*, pages 76–85. ACM, 1999.

[30] V. Sarkar. Parallel functional languages and compilers. chapter PTRAN – The IBM Parallel Translation System, pages 309–391. ACM, New York, USA, 1991.

[31] R. Triolet, F. Irigoin, and P. Feautrier. Direct parallelization of call statements. In *SIGPLAN Symp. on Compiler Construction*, pages 176–185, 1986.

[32] R. Triolet and P. Jouvelot. NewGen : A language-independent program generator. Technical Report A-191, CRI, École des mines de Paris, 1989.

[33] N. Ventroux, T. Sassolas, A. Guerre, B. Creusillet, and R. Keryell. SESAM/ Par4All: a tool for joint exploration of MPSoC architectures and dynamic dataflow code generation. RAPIDO'12, pages 9–16, New York, NY, USA, 2012. ACM.

[34] Y.-Q. Yang. *Tests des dépendances et transformations de programme.* PhD thesis, Université Pierre et Marie Curie (Paris 6), Nov. 1993.

[35] Y.-Q. Yang, C. Ancourt, and F. Irigoin. Minimal data dependence abstractions for loop transformations. *IJPP*, 23:359–388, Aug. 1995.

[36] L. Zhou. Complexity estimation in the PIPS parallel programming environment. In *Parallel Processing: CONPAR 92 – VAPP V*, volume 634, pages 845–846. 1992.

[37] J. Zory. *Contributions à l'optimisation de programmes scientifiques.* PhD thesis, École des mines de Paris, Dec. 1999.

[38] J. Zory and F. Coelho. Using algebraic transformations to optimize expression evaluation in scientific codes. In *PACT*, pages 376–384, Oct. 1998.

Author Retrospective for

Optimizing for Parallelism and Data Locality

Kathryn S. McKinley
Microsoft Research
mckinley@microsoft.com

ABSTRACT

Today there is an urgent need for algorithms, programming language systems and tools, and hardware that deliver on the potential of parallelism due to the end of Dennard scaling. This work (from my PhD dissertation, supervised by Ken Kennedy) was one of the early papers to optimize for and experimentally explore the tension between data locality and parallelism on shared memory machines. A key result was that false sharing of cache lines between processors with local caches on separate chips was disastrous to the performance and scaling of applications. This retrospective includes a short personal tour through the history of parallel computing, a discussion of locality and parallelism modeling versus a polyhedral formulation of optimizing dense matrix codes, and how this problem is still relevant to compilers today. I end with a short memorial to my deceased co-author and advisor Ken Kennedy.

Original paper: http://doi.acm.org/10.1145/143369.143427

Categories and Subject Descriptors

D.3.4 [**Programming Languages**]: Processors—*Compilers; Optimization*

Keywords

False Sharing; Loop Transformations; Parallelism; Locality

Parallel Computing: A Personal History

Parallel computing seemed to be entering its heyday in the late 1980s and early 1990s. At Rice in 1989, Ken Kennedy was awarded an NSF Science and Technology Center for the Center for Research on Parallel Computing (CRPC) as the Principal Investigator. The CRPC started with seven sites and eventually included 400 researchers, staff, and graduate students. Their technical expertise spanned parallel algorithms, compilers, runtimes, and hardware. The CRPC vision that Ken, his collaborators, and students shared was to invent parallel algorithms for critical problems in science, coupled with programming language tools, such as compilers, runtime systems, and programming environments, that made them run fast. We were not trying to solve the *dusty-deck* problem of automatically converting sequential algorithms to parallel ones. We understood that parallel and sequential algorithms for the same problem require different solutions. However, tools would do heavy lifting to map application parallelism to hardware parallelism, such that the programmers would not have to reimplement their algorithms for each new parallel architecture. A key aspect of this problem is balancing parallelism, sharing between tasks, and memory usage, which was the topic our paper addressed.

In this same period, a number of established companies and startups, such as Sequent, had introduced parallel machines. The Sequent Symmetry was the machine on which we reported our results. It was not yet clear that the research and development challenges of parallel computing would make it too costly to win in the market place in the short term. By the mid 1990s, this generation of parallel computers together with some of the companies that built them were pulled under by the economic tide and huge success of personal computers with a single processor. Clock scaling was delivering exponential performance improvements. Sequential software was easier to build; the sequential programming interface was stable across generations of hardware and software; and hardware was twice as fast every 18 months. Why invest in parallel computing?

In hindsight, abandoning sustained national funding, much research, and advanced development on parallel computing was a mistake. Today, leakage power and other manufacturing challenges at small feature sizes have ended Dennard scaling and will soon end Moore's Law. Vendors have turned to parallelism as a strategy to continue increasing computer capacity to meet computational demands in science, government, and consumer markets. However, researchers and companies are still struggling to deliver on the potential of parallelism. For example, even though manufacturers can fit 20 to 100 processors on a single chip, many commodity server, client, and mobile chips have 1 to 12 CPUs with 2 to 24 hardware contexts. Building, compiling for, programming, and porting software between parallel systems is still hard.

Parallelism and Data Locality

Part of the reason programming and optimizing parallel machines, even shared memory machines, is hard is due to real sharing and *false sharing* of data between parallel tasks. In a typical shared memory parallel machine, each CPU has some amount of private cache memory and some shared main memory. In the 1990s, the CPUs were on separate chips and today they are on the same chip, but the basic memory hierarchy structure is similar.

Hardware caches exploit the observation that programs often exhibit *temporal locality* – they reuse the same data — and *spatial locality* — they access adjacent data elements — close together in time. For example, a loop that sequentially iterates over a vector of

ICS 25th Anniversary Volume. 2014
ACM 978-1-4503-2840-1/14/06.
http://dx.doi.org/10.1145/2591635.2591646.

integers (allocated as a single vector) exhibits spatial locality with a reuse distance of one iteration. Caches store the most recently used items and cache lines typically contain between 32 B to 256 B of data. The fewer accesses between reuse of data on the same cache line, the more likely the cache will be to still hold the line. Unfortunately, since the architecture only moves and tracks data at a cache line granularity, *false sharing* occurs when two tasks on different CPUs want to write *independent* data that resides on the same cache line at the same time, they cannot. Only one cache can write the line at a time, which requires invalidating and moving the cache line, serializing execution.

Figure 1 in the paper shows the effect of false sharing on 18 processors of a Sequent shared-memory parallel machine executing an addition of three 2D dense matrices and storing the result. For the same amount of work, without false sharing, a speedup of 18 (best) is possible. With false sharing, speedup ranges between 6 and 9 (mem). That figure would have been better labeled "False sharing more than halves speedup."

The remainder of the paper presents an optimization algorithm for dense matrices that seeks (1) to minimize the reuse distance for cache lines for each parallel task, (2) to introduce parallelism at the outermost loop possible, and (3) to eliminate false sharing by strip mining, such that the outer loop is parallel and each parallel iteration never shares a cache line with another parallel iteration.

The algorithm uses data dependence analysis to detect parallelism and temporal reuse [4, 5, 12]. It precisely computes spatial and temporal cache line reuse on inner loops and then generalizes to the entire loop nest. It next determines the loop ordering that maximizes expected cache line reuse, and directly permutes the loops to this order or the closest legal loop order. The next phase introduces parallelism at the coarsest possible granularity (outermost loop) without causing false sharing. It uses a combination of loop permutation and strip mining. A machine specific cost model determines if the parallel loop is of sufficient granularity to deliver speedups. If the parallel loop also provides cache line reuse, the algorithm strip mines the loop based on the line size and number of processors, permuting the iterator loop to the outermost legal position and leaving the *strips* of consecutive iterations with reuse in place to deliver cache locality. This transformation process ensures that none of the outermost parallel loop iterations share cache lines, eliminating false sharing.

Historical Positioning

Our work on optimizing compilers for parallel architectures at Rice was greatly influenced by the research at UIUC, IBM, and Stanford. David Kuck and his PhD students at UIUC introduced the first analyses and optimizations in this area. For example, Uptal Banerjee introduced the first practical dependence tests to detect parallelism [4, 5] and Abu-Sufah introduced the first optimizations for improving data locality [1]. Allen and Kennedy showed how to use dependences to correctly permute loops and introduce parallelism [3], and with Callahan, subsequently showed how to maximize the granularity of parallelism [2].

Irigoin and Triolet introduced the use of a polyhedral model of dependences to increase parallelism [14] and the work of Wolf and Lam extended this theory to introduce parallelism at all possible levels [28]. Wolf and Lam also used this theory to produce all the legal loop permutations and loop skews and then selected the one that maximized cache reuse [27], however they did not consider both locality and parallelism at once.

At the time, the polyhedral and unimodular models were restricted to permuting, reversing, and skewing perfectly nested loops operating on dense matrices. Optimizing one loop in isolation was and is not sufficient for the best performance; data reorganization, loop fusion, and loop distribution add substantial benefits [7, 10, 11, 16, 21, 22, 25]. Our model directly computed the best permutations for locality and parallelism and we showed [7, 16, 20] how to directly derive good loop fusion and distribution choices, which the polyhedral model could not yet perform. Our approach also had the advantage that the resulting code was human readable and suitable for use in an interactive parallelization tool [17]. Several comercial tools implemented our approach, including the DEC Alpha compiler.

Today, the polyhedral approach combines fusion and distribution with other loop optimizations [11, 22, 25] and is in wide use in commercial and research compilers. These techniques use heuristic search based on models, some similar to our model, to specialize code for a variety of parallel architectures.

Loop nest optimization remains an active area of research [11, 22, 25], in part, because each generation of parallel hardware offers new challenges and opportunities. Using the compiler to adapt applications to a parallel machine achieves portability and high performance, substantially reducing developer effort. Loop optimizations are critical to optimization in many modern settings, including GPUs [18], high-level hardware synthesis [8, 19, 24], autotuning [9, 23, 25], and library construction [13, 26].

None of the early work on locality or parallelism considered false sharing and locality and parallelism interactions. Our paper highlighted the problems that false sharing caused, which subsequently other researchers also sought to eliminate. For example, Jeremiassen and Eggers transformed data with padding [15] and Ding and Kennedy performed array regrouping [10] to eliminate false sharing and improve locality. Later my PhD student Emery Berger, others, and I showed how the Hoard memory allocator avoided false sharing to produce more scalable performance, compared to prior C/C++ memory allocators [6]. The Hoard algorithm is now widely used, for example, in Apple's iOS.

Professor Ken Kennedy (1945 - 2007)

Ken loved his research and bringing people together on both a small and large scale. He founded the Rice Computer Science Department in 1985, CRPC, the Los Alamos Computer Science Institute (LACSI), and co-chaired with Bill Joy, the President's Information Technology Advisory Committee (PITAC) from 1997 to 1999. This first PITAC committee initiated the NSF ITR program, which funded the research of 1000s of faculty and graduate students over a 10 year period. In his own research life, he could not bear to cut back on people or research; he would instead raise more money. He felt it was a personal failure if any student who worked with him did not graduate and graduated over 40 PhD students. Together with his students and colleagues, he invented programming language technologies still in use today, such as register allocation, strength reduction, prefetching, loop transformations for scalar, vector, and parallel architectures (this paper is an example), interprocedural analyses, interactive parallel programming tools, FortranD, and telescoping languages.

In the last few years of his life as he struggled with pancreatic cancer, he kept working because he loved his life, his students, and his work. Ken laughed a lot and really loudly, especially at his own jokes. I still miss him.

Acknowledgements I would like to thank again my graduate student colleagues Chau-Wen Tseng, Preston Briggs, Cliff Click, Ervan Darnell, and Nathaniel McIntosh for their contributions to this work. I would also like to thank them as well as David Callahan, Keith Cooper, Mark Hall, Mary Hall, Seema Hiranandani, Marina

Kalem, Amy Pullen, Linda Torczon, and Scotty Strahan (my husband) for making graduate school a wonderful personal and intellectual experience. I thank the anonymous reviewer for improving the first version and Steve Blackburn, Mary Hall, and Todd Mytkowicz for discussions and comments on this version.

References

[1] W. A. Abu-Sufah. *Improving the Performance of Virtual Memory Computers, PhD Dissertation*. PhD thesis, Dept. of Computer Science, University of Illinois at Urbana-Champaign, 1978.

[2] J. R. Allen, D. Callahan, and K. Kennedy. Automatic decomposition of scientific programs for parallel execution. In *ACM Symposium on the Principles of Programming Languages (POPL)*, pages 63–76, Munich, Germany, Jan. 1987.

[3] J. R. Allen and K. Kennedy. Automatic loop interchange. In *ACM Conference on Programming Language Design and Implementation (PLDI)*, pages 75–90, Montreal, Canada, June 1984.

[4] U. K. Banerjee. Data depedence in ordinary programs, Master's Thesis. Technical Report 76-837, Dept. of Computer Science, University of Illinois at Urbana-Champaign, 1976.

[5] U. K. Banerjee. *Depedence Analysis for Supercomputing*. Kluwer Academic Publishers, Norwell, MA, 1988.

[6] E. D. Berger, K. S. McKinley, R. D. Blumofe, and P. R. Wilson. Hoard: A scalable memory allocator for multithreaded applications. In *ACM Conference on Architectural Support for Programming Languages and Operating Systems (ASPLOS)*, pages 117–128, Cambridge, MA, Nov. 2000.

[7] S. Carr, K. S. McKinley, and C. Tseng. Compiler optimizations for improving data locality. In *ACM Conference on Architectural Support for Programming Languages and Operating Systems (ASPLOS)*, pages 252–262, San Jose, CA, Oct. 1994.

[8] J. Cong, P. Zhang, and Y. Zou. Optimizing memory hierarchy allocation with loop transformations for high-level synthesis. In *Annual Design Automation Conference (DAC)*, pages 1233–1238, 2012.

[9] K. Datta, M. Murphy, V. Volkov, S. Williams, J. Carter, L. Oliker, D. Patterson, J. Shalf, and K. Yelick. Stencil computation optimization and auto-tuning on state-of-the-art multicore architectures. In *ACM/IEEE Conference on Supercomputing*, pages 4:1–12, 2008.

[10] C. Ding and K. Kennedy. Inter-array data regrouping. In *Languages and Compilers for Parallel Computing*, pages 149–163, San Diego, CA, Aug. 1999.

[11] S. Girbal, N. Vasilache, C. Bastoul, A. Cohen, D. Parello, M. Sigler, and O. Temam. Semi-automatic composition of loop transformations for deep parallelism and memory hierarchies. *International Journal of Parallel Programming*, 34(3):261–317, June 1995.

[12] G. Goff, K. Kennedy, and C. Tseng. Practical dependence testing. In *ACM Conference on Programming Language Design and Implementation (PLDI)*, pages 15–29, Toronto, Canada, June 1991.

[13] K. Goto and R. van de Geijn. High-performance implementation of the Level-3 BLAS. *ACM Transactions on Mathmatical Software (TOMS)*, 35(1):4:1–14, July 2008.

[14] F. Irigoin and R. Triolet. Supernode partitioning. In *ACM Symposium on the Principles of Programming Languages (POPL)*, pages 319–329, San Diego, CA, Jan. 1988.

[15] T. E. Jeremiassen and S. J. Eggers. Reducing false sharing on shared memory multiprocessors through compile time data transformations. In *ACM Symposium on Principles and Practice of Parallel Programming (PPOPP)*, pages 179–188, Santa Barbara, CA, July 1995.

[16] K. Kennedy and K. S. McKinley. Maximizing loop parallelism and improving data locality via loop fusion and distribution. In *Languages and Compilers for Parallel Computing*, pages 301–321, Portland, OR, Aug. 1993.

[17] K. Kennedy, K. S. McKinley, and C. Tseng. Interactive parallel programming using the ParaScope Editor. *IEEE Transactions on Parallel and Distributed Systems*, 2(3):329–341, July 1991.

[18] M. Khan, G. R. P. Basu, M. Hall, C. Chen, and J. Chame. A script-based autotuning compiler system to generate high-performance CUDA code. *ACM Transactions on Architecture and Code Optimization*, 9(4):31:1–25, 2013.

[19] Q. Liu, G. A. Constantinides, K. Masselos, and P. Y. K. Cheung. Combining data reuse with data-level parallelization for FPGA-targeted hardware compilation: A geometric programming framework. *IEEE Transactions on Computer-Aided Design of Integrated Circuits and Systems*, 28(3):305–315, Mar. 2009.

[20] K. S. McKinley. A compiler optimization algorithm for shared-memory multiprocessors. *IEEE Transactions on Parallel and Distributed Systems*, 9(8):769–787, Aug. 1998.

[21] K. S. McKinley and O. Temam. A quantitative analysis of loop nest locality. In *ACM Conference on Architectural Support for Programming Languages and Operating Systems (ASPLOS)*, pages 94–104, Cambridge, MA, Oct. 1996.

[22] L.-N. Pouchet, U. Bondhugula, C. Bastoul, A. Cohen, J. Ramanujam, P. Sadayappan, and N. Vasilache. Loop transformations: Convexity, pruning and optimization. In *ACM Symposium on the Principles of Programming Languages (POPL)*, pages 549–562, 2011.

[23] M. Puschel, J. Moura, J. R. Johnson, D. Padua, M. M. Veloso, B. W. Singer, J. Xiong, F. Franchetti, A. Gacic, Y. Voronenko, K. Chen, R. W. Johnson, and N. Rizzolo. SPIRAL: Code generation for DSP transforms. *Proceedings of the IEEE*, 93(2):232–275, 2005.

[24] B. So, M. W. Hall, and P. C. Diniz. A compiler approach to fast hardware design space exploration in FPGA-based systems. In *ACM Conference on Programming Language Design and Implementation (PLDI)*, pages 165–176, 2002.

[25] A. Tiwari, C. Chen, J. Chame, M. Hall, and J. K. Hollingsworth. A scalable auto-tuning framework for compiler optimization. In *IEEE International Symposium on Parallel & Distributed Processing (IPDPS)*, pages 1–12, 2009.

[26] R. C. Whaley, A. Petitet, and J. J. Dongarra. Automated empirical optimizations of software and the ATLAS project. *Parallel Computing*, 27(1):3–35, 2001.

[27] M. E. Wolf and M. Lam. A data locality optimizing algorithm. In *ACM SIGPLAN Notices*, pages 30–44, Toronto, Canada, June 1991.

[28] M. E. Wolf and M. Lam. A loop transformation theory and an algorithm to maximize parallelism. *IEEE Transactions on Parallel and Distributed Systems*, 2(4):452–471, Oct. 1991.

Author Retrospective for PYRROS: Static Task Scheduling and Code Generation for Message Passing Multiprocessors

Tao Yang
Department of Computer Science
University of California
Santa Barbara, CA 93106, USA
tyang@cs.ucsb.edu

Apostolos Gerasoulis
Department of Computer Science
Rutgers University
New Brunswick, NJ 08903, USA
gerasoul@cs.rutgers.edu

ABSTRACT

Given a program with annotated task parallelism represented as a directed acyclic graph (DAG), the PYRROS project was focused on fast DAG scheduling, code generation and runtime execution on distributed memory architectures. PYRROS scheduling goes through several processing stages including clustering of tasks, cluster mapping, and task execution ordering. Since the publication of the PYRROS project, there have been new advancements in the area of DAG scheduling algorithms, the use of DAG scheduling for irregular and large-scale computation, and software system development with annotated task parallelism on modern parallel and cloud architectures. This retrospective describes our experience from this project and the follow-up work, and reviews representative papers related to DAG scheduling published in the last decade.

Original paper: http://dx.doi.org/10.1145/143369.143446

Categories and Subject Descriptors

C.1.2 [**Processor Architectures**]: Multiple Data Stream Architectures (Multiprocessors); D.1.3 [**Programming Techniques**]: Parallel Programming; D.4.1 [**Operating Systems**]: Process Management—*Scheduling*

Keywords

DAG, parallel processing, scheduling, task graphs

1. INTRODUCTION

Directed-acyclic task graphs (DAGs) have been widely used for parallelism representation, performance modeling, code generation, and execution optimization of parallel programs. Earlier work in parallelizing compilers and runtime systems [21, 28, 6] adopted DAG-based task parallelism. The contribution of the PYRROS project was to develop fast scheduling algorithms for parallel code generation and resource management in dealing with a large task graph and taking communication cost into consideration. Experience from PYRROS demonstrates that scheduling and code generation systems can be built with low complexity to simplify parallel programming of complex parallel architectures, especially for coarse grain computation with many task components or irregular patterns.

During the last decade, the development in high performance computing infrastructures continues to present a formidable challenge for parallel programming. It is difficult for application users to fully harness the power of multi-core clusters or hybrid platforms with GPU accelerators or other co-processors. DAG-based codes have been suggested as a suitable candidate for exascale applications [1, 14] to exploit modern parallel and distributed architectures. New algorithms and techniques were developed for DAG-based computation execution on emerging architectures. We will give a short survey of those techniques as a retrospective on DAG scheduling in high performance computing.

1.1 The PYRROS system and follow-up work

PYRROS contains a task graph language with an interface to C and Fortran, allowing users to define partitioned programs and data; a scheduling system; a graphic displayer for visualizing task graphs and scheduling results; a code generator that inserts synchronization primitives and performs code optimization for distributed memory machines. PYRROS uses the following multistep approach to fast scheduling: 1) Perform clustering using the Dominant Sequence Algorithm (DSC) [33]. 2) Merge and map the clusters to available physical machines. 3) Order the execution of tasks in each processor using the RCP algorithm [32]. The overall algorithm complexity is $O(e + v\log v)$ for a DAG with v nodes and e edges, and the near-linear complexity allows the system to handle a large task graph efficiently.

The experience learned from the PYRROS system is that an automatic system for scheduling and code generation is useful in many ways. If the scheduling is determined at compile time then the complex parallel architecture can be utilized better. A programmer does not have to get involved in low level programming and synchronization, and the parallel code generated or managed by such a system can provide better portability. The scheduling system can also facilitate performance prediction and comparison of different optimization strategies without actual code execution.

As a follow-up work to leverage DAG-scheduling for unstructured computation [10], we studied the use of PYRROS

ICS 25th Anniversary Volume. 2014
ACM 978-1-4503-2840-1/14/06.
http://dx.doi.org/10.1145/2591635.2591647.

scheduling for irregular code [20] and developed a software system called RAPID based on an inspector/executor approach for runtime parallelization [18, 17, 34]. RAPID provides library functions for specifying irregular data objects and tasks that access these objects, extracts a task dependence graph from data access patterns, and executes tasks efficiently on distributed memory machines. Additional research issues addressed were space/time-efficient DAG scheduling optimization for better data locality and load balancing, the use of advanced hardware features for low-overhead asynchronous communication, efficient task-level synchronization protocols for maintaining data consistency, and runtime memory management for maximizing space reuse. The effectiveness of RAPID was demonstrated in parallelizing irregular problems with static or slowly changing dynamic computation patterns such as sparse matrix solving and the adaptive fast multipole method for n-body simulation. Using RAPID, we developed fast DAG-based parallel code for sparse LU factorization with partial pivoting and set up a new performance record [16, 15].

2. PROGRESS IN DAG-BASED PARALLELIZATION AND SCHEDULING

There has been a large body of active research on DAG-based parallelization and computation scheduling. We summarize a number of representative papers published during the last decade in the following three areas.

Algorithms and compilation support for DAGs. An earlier survey paper on DAG scheduling was by Kwok and Ahmad [24]. Cosnard et al. [11, 12] studied the compact representation and symbolic scheduling of DAGs to avoid the unrolling of dependence structure. Sinnen et al. [29] presented scheduling with task duplication under communication contention. Bozdağ et al. [8] optimized the number of processors required in duplication-based scheduling. Vydyanathan et al. [31] presented DAG scheduling with task duplication in processing a stream of input data. Daoud and Kharma [13] considered the architecture heterogeneity in two-phase task scheduling.

Adve and Sakellariou [2] described parallelizing compiler techniques to automate the task graph constructions for the MPI code generated for a High-Performance-Fortran program. Baskaran et al. [4] discussed compile-time parallelization techniques in the Pluto system to enable dynamic extraction of inter-tile dependences at run-time, and dynamic scheduling of the parallel tiles on multi-core architectures. Bellens et al. [5] presented a programming model called CellSs with annotated functional parallelism. A source-to-source compiler generates the necessary code that builds a runtime task dependency graph and supports a locality-aware task scheduling.

Parallel programming and application experience with DAGs. The DAGuE system developed by Bosilca et al. [7, 14] targets at exascale parallel programming with annotated task parallelism. It uses a concise representation of the DAG to avoid task graph unrolling and reduce the memory usage. The algebraic representation of task dependencies extracts more potential parallelism, while still enabling out-of-order task execution.

Motivated by the need of exascale applications, Meng et al. [25] investigated the portability and scalability of DAG-based computation with the Uintah software on large computing infrastructures. Through their experimental studies, the authors indicate that the adaptive DAG-based approach provides a powerful abstraction for solving challenging multiscale multi-physics engineering problems on the three of the fastest computers appeared in the top 500 list of November 2012. Bueno et al. [9] developed a task graph based programming system called OmpSs that lets a user annotate a sequential application and provides semi-automatic parallelization to simplify programming on GPU clusters.

DAG parallelism on clouds and emerging architectures. Henzinger et. al [22, 23] discussed the DAG scheduling and resource management challenges, and developed a cloud programming and pricing model which considers the tradeoff of execution speed and price on a per-job basis. Tang et al. [30] considered handling of hardware and software failures in task graph scheduling for a grid computing system in which distributed scientific and engineering applications often require multi-institutional collaboration, large-scale resource sharing, and wide-area communication.

Hardware specialization is an important architecture direction to improve microprocessor performance and transistor energy efficiency. One key specialization technique is to map large regions of computation to the hardware with a spatial architecture paradigm. Mercaldi et al. [26] developed a practical DAG scheduling algorithm that generates efficient code schedules for tiled architectures. The scheduler decides where and when an instruction will execute. For example, placing dependent instructions on the same or adjacent tiles reduces producer-to-consumer operand latency. Nowatzkiy et al. [27] studied a scheduling framework usable for various spatial architectures.

One key challenge in high performance quantum computing research is to scale experimental quantum computers from a handful of quantum bits to a large number of quantum bits. Balensiefer et al. [3] presented a set of infrastructural tools that enable the quantitative evaluation of architectures for quantum computers with thousands of quantum bits and billions of time steps. One of its tools is a device scheduler that maps an assembly source into a set of device specific primitive operations for controlling a quantum micro-architecture. The ability to process billions of operations was critical in designing the scheduler. The paper considers a trade-off of optimality for speed and employs a variant of list scheduling [32].

3. CONCLUDING REMARKS

DAG scheduling is an important technique for software tools, compilers, and runtime systems in optimizing the use of parallel computing resource. Our earlier theoretical study on task granularity [19] shows that scheduling needs to take communication overhead into account especially for distributed memory architectures. Fast scheduling heuristic algorithms can attain good performance in solving the resource optimization problem. Those scheduling techniques can be practical with an integration of a software system that aids task graph description or derivation and manages code generation and runtime support for executing DAG computation. Such systems are critical for supporting large-scale scientific and data-intensive applications in the current and future high performance computing platforms.

Acknowledgments. This work was supported in part by NSF IIS-1118106. Any opinions, findings, conclusions or recommendations expressed in this material are those of the authors and do not necessarily reflect the views of the NSF.

4. REFERENCES

[1] D. Brown and P. Messina (Chairs). *Scientific Grand Challenges: Crosscutting Technologies for Computing at the Exascale*. Report from the 2010 Workshop. U.S. Department of Energy, 2010.

[2] Vikram S. Adve and Rizos Sakellariou. Compiler synthesis of task graphs for parallel program performance prediction. In *Proc. of 13th Inter. Workshop on Languages and Compilers for Parallel Computing-Revised Papers*, pages 208–226, 2001.

[3] Steven Balensiefer, Lucas Kregor-Stickles, and Mark Oskin. An evaluation framework and instruction set architecture for ion-trap based quantum micro-architectures. In *Proc. of 32nd Annual Inter. Symposium on Computer Architecture*, pages 186–196, 2005.

[4] Muthu Manikandan Baskaran, Nagavijayalakshmi Vydyanathan, Uday Kumar Reddy Bondhugula, J. Ramanujam, Atanas Rountev, and P. Sadayappan. Compiler-assisted dynamic scheduling for effective parallelization of loop nests on multicore processors. In *Proc. of 14th ACM SIGPLAN Symposium on Principles and Practice of Parallel Programming*, pages 219–228, 2009.

[5] Pieter Bellens, Josep M. Perez, Rosa M. Badia, and Jesus Labarta. Cellss: A programming model for the cell be architecture. In *Proc. of ACM/IEEE Supercomputing'06*.

[6] R. Blumofe, C. Joerg, B. Kuszmaul, C. Leiserson, K. Randall, and Y. Zhou. Cilk: An Efficient Multithreaded Runtime System. In *Proc. of 5th ACM Symposium on Principles and Practice of Parallel Programming*, pages 207–216, 1995.

[7] George Bosilca, Aurelien Bouteiller, Anthony Danalis, Thomas Herault, Pierre Lemarinier, and Jack Dongarra. Dague: A generic distributed dag engine for high performance computing. *Parallel Comput.*, 38(1-2):37–51, January 2012.

[8] Doruk Bozdağ, Füsun Özgüner, and Umit V. Catalyurek. Compaction of schedules and a two-stage approach for duplication-based dag scheduling. *IEEE Trans. Parallel Distrib. Syst.*, 20(6):857–871, June 2009.

[9] Javier Bueno, Judit Planas, Alejandro Duran, Rosa M. Badia, Xavier Martorell, Eduard Ayguade, and Jesus Labarta. Productive programming of gpu clusters with ompss. In *Proc. of 2012 IEEE 26th Inter. Parallel and Distributed Processing Symposium*, pages 557–568, 2012.

[10] F. T. Chong, S. D. Sharma, E. A. Brewer, and J. Saltz. Multiprocessor Runtime Support for Fine-Grained Irregular DAGs. In Rajiv K. Kalia and Priya Vashishta, editors, *Toward Teraflop Computing and New Grand Challenge Applications.*, New York, 1995. Nova Science Publishers.

[11] Michel Cosnard and Emmanuel Jeannot. Compact dag representation and its dynamic scheduling. *J. Parallel Distrib. Comput.*, 58(3):487–514, September 1999.

[12] Michel Cosnard, Emmanuel Jeannot, and Tao Yang. Compact dag representation and its symbolic scheduling. *J. Parallel Distrib. Comput.*, 64(8):921–935, August 2004.

[13] Mohammad I. Daoud and Nawwaf Kharma. A hybrid heuristic-genetic algorithm for task scheduling in heterogeneous processor networks. *J. Parallel Distrib. Comput.*, 71(11):1518–1531, November 2011.

[14] Jack Dongarra. *Achitecture Aware Algorithms and Software for Peta and Exascale.* Presentation at Ken Kennedy Institute of Information Technology, Feb 2014.

[15] C. Fu, X. Jiao, and T. Yang. Efficient Sparse LU Factorization with Partial Pivoting on Distributed Memory Architectures. *IEEE Transactions on Parallel and Distributed Systems*, 9(2):109–125, 1998.

[16] C. Fu and T. Yang. Sparse LU Factorization with Partial Pivoting on Distributed Memory Machines. In *Proc. of ACM/IEEE SuperComputing'96*.

[17] C. Fu and T. Yang. Run-time Compilation for Parallel Sparse Matrix Computations. In *Proc. of ACM Inter. Conf. on Supercomputing*, pages 237–244, 1996.

[18] C. Fu and T. Yang. Space and Time Efficient Execution of Parallel Irregular Computations. In *Proc. of ACM Symposium on Principles & Practice of Parallel Programming*, pages 57–68, 1997.

[19] A. Gerasoulis and T. Yang. On the Granularity and Clustering of Directed Acyclic Task Graphs . *IEEE Trans. on Parallel and Distributed Syst.*, 4(6):686–701, June 1993.

[20] Apostolos Gerasoulis and Jia Jiao. Rescheduling support for mapping dynamic scientific computation onto distributed memory multiprocessors. In *Proc. of Third Inter. Euro-Par Conference on Parallel Processing*, pages 905–912, 1997.

[21] M. Girkar and C. Polychronopoulos. Automatic Extraction of Functinal Parallelism from Ordinary Programs. *IEEE Trans. on Parallel and Distributed Syst.*, 3(2):166–178, 1992.

[22] Thomas A. Henzinger, Anmol V. Singh, Vasu Singh, Thomas Wies, and Damien Zufferey. A marketplace for cloud resources. In *Proc. of Tenth ACM Inter. Conf. on Embedded Software*, pages 1–8, 2010.

[23] Thomas A. Henzinger, Anmol V. Singh, Vasu Singh, Thomas Wies, and Damien Zufferey. Static scheduling in clouds. In *Proc. of 3rd USENIX HotCloud*, 2011.

[24] Yu-Kwong Kwok and Ishfaq Ahmad. Static scheduling algorithms for allocating directed task graphs to multiprocessors. *ACM Comput. Surv.*, 31(4):406–471, 1999.

[25] Qingyu Meng, Alan Humphrey, John Schmidt, and Martin Berzins. Investigating applications portability with the uintah dag-based runtime system on petascale supercomputers. In *Proc. of SC13: Inter. Conf. for High Performance Computing, Networking, Storage and Analysis*, pages 96:1–96:12, 2013.

[26] Martha Mercaldi, Steven Swanson, Andrew Petersen, Andrew Putnam, Andrew Schwerin, Mark Oskin, and Susan J. Eggers. Instruction scheduling for a tiled dataflow architecture. In *Proc. of 12th Inter. Conf. on Architectural Support for Programming Languages and Operating Systems*, pages 141–150, 2006.

[27] Tony Nowatzki, Michael Sartin-Tarm, Lorenzo De Carli, Karthikeyan Sankaralingam, Cristian Estan, and Behnam Robatmili. A general constraint-centric scheduling framework for spatial architectures. In *Proc. of 34th ACM SIGPLAN Conference on Programming Language Design and Implementation*, pages 495–506, 2013.

[28] V. Sarkar. *Partitioning and Scheduling Parallel Programs for Execution on Multiprocessors.* MIT Press, 1989.

[29] Oliver Sinnen, Andrea To, and Manpreet Kaur. Contention-aware scheduling with task duplication. *J. Parallel Distrib. Comput.*, 71(1):77–86, January 2011.

[30] Xiaoyong Tang, Kenli Li, Meikang Qiu, and Edwin H. M. Sha. A hierarchical reliability-driven scheduling algorithm in grid systems. *J. Parallel Distrib. Comput.*, 72(4):525–535, April 2012.

[31] Naga Vydyanathan, Umit Catalyurek, Tahsin Kurc, Ponnuswamy Sadayappan, and Joel Saltz. Optimizing latency and throughput of application workflows on clusters. *Parallel Comput.*, 37(10-11):694–712, 2011.

[32] T. Yang and A. Gerasoulis. List Scheduling With and Without Communication . *Parallel Computing*, 19:1321–1344, 1993.

[33] T. Yang and A. Gerasoulis. DSC: Scheduling Parallel Tasks on An Unbounded Number of Processors. *IEEE Trans. on Parallel and Distributed Syst.*, 5(9):951–967, 1994.

[34] Tao Yang and Cong Fu. Space/time-efficient scheduling and execution of parallel irregular computations. *ACM Trans. Program. Lang. Syst.*, 20(6):1195–1222, November 1998.

Author's Retrospective for: Array Privatization for Parallel Execution of Loops

Zhiyuan Li
Department of Computer Science
Purdue University
250 North University Street
West Lafayette, Indiana, USA
zhiyuanli@purdue.edu

ABSTRACT

Array privatization, as a program transform to increase the opportunity for loop parallelization, was introduced at a time when numerical programs dominated the parallel computing world. Today, with parallel processors becoming ubiquitous, the computer industry faces a new challenge, i.e. how to best utilize hardware parallelism for the next generation of main-stream applications. The author re-examines the technique of array privatization both in its historical context and in view of new developments in recent years.

Original paper:
http://doi.acm.org/10.1145/143369.143426

Categories and Subject Descriptors: D.3.4 [**Programming Languages**]: Processors – *Compilers, run-time environments;* F.3.2 [**Logics And Meanings of Programs**]: Semantics of Programming Languages – *Program Analysis*

Keywords: Program parallelization; loops; memory allocation

1. BACKGROUND

In the fall of 1990, I joined the compiler group of the Center for Supercomputing Research and Development (CSRD) in University of Illinois, Urbana-Champaign (UIUC). Under the leadership of the director, David Kuck, CSRD was designing and building the Cedar multiprocessor cluster [9]. There were groups working on its hardware, the operating system, the compiler, performance analysis tools, numerical libraries and many other issues concerning supercomputing. Many results from the Cedar project were ground-breaking.

The compiler group, led by David Padua, was busy designing and implementing a Fortran dialect called Cedar Fortran [8] that provides syntax for multiple levels of parallelism and data locality. In order to understand how to make it easier to convert existing numerical programs for shared-memory parallel computers, the compiler group also started to hand parallelize a suite of benchmark programs contributed by the PERFECT Club [2]. Continuing UIUC's long tradition of pioneering automatic parallelization techniques, the compiler group wanted to find out what kind of new techniques might be needed to automatically convert the PERFECT benchmark programs into efficient parallel codes.

The initial experience from this hand parallelization effort was presented at International Conference on Parallel Processing in 1991 and a more definitive report was later published in 1993 [6]. These reports identify several new techniques that are instrumental for parallelizing the PERFECT benchmarks, with array privatization being one of the more important.

The basic idea for array privatization is quite simple. If a loop operates on different parts of arrays in different iterations, then these iterations can be executed simultaneously on multiple processors. Often, the intermediate results are stored in arrays that are rewritten from iteration to iteration. Array privatization creates a private copy of such arrays for each processor, such that writes from iterations executing in parallel do not cause conflicts. This transformation is especially important because arrays are the most common data structures in numerical programs to represent physical quantities.

To anyone who is not the author of the original program, determining which arrays can be safely privatized can be a tedious task. One must determine whether the lifetime of an array (or a part of it) may extend across the iterations of the targeted loop. If so, then privatizing that array will cause an incorrect computation result. Moreover, it is necessary to determine whether the values written to a privatized array in the last loop iteration remain live after the parallel loop exits. If so, these values must be copied back to the original shared array to make them accessible to all processors. It is safe to copy the entire array out, but unnecessary copying can incur high overhead. The program scope to be analyzed for array privatization can be extensive, making the analysis both laborious and error-prone. Obviously, there is a strong incentive to automate the analysis.

Prior to the hand parallelization experiment by the CSRD compiler group, the IBM Ptran project team published a framework for automatically converting a sequential program into parallel code using the fork/join shared-memory model [1]. Among the ideas presented within that framework was privatizing scalar variables to remove data dependencies caused by storage conflicts [3].

The idea to duplicate variables in order to increase parallelism dates back to the *scalar expansion* technique for auto-

ICS 25th Anniversary Volume. 2014
ACM 978-1-4503-2840-1/14/06.
http://dx.doi.org/10.1145/2591635.2591648.

matic vectorization [10], which removes data dependencies due to iterative read/write operations on a single scalar by letting such operations be performed on elements of a new array instead. Conceptually, data dependencies caused by storage conflicts can be eliminated completely by fully expanding all variables, including arrays, that are responsible for such conflicts. It is unknown how to automatically perform such conversion in the general case, but under a set of ideal conditions automatic *array expansion* is possible.

In practice, however, it is obvious that excessive variable expansion incurs overheads that are unacceptable. Increasing a single array dimension can increase the storage for that array by an order of magnitude. In 1990's, computers simply did not have enough memory to allow full array expansion. Moreover, storage increases tend to make it difficult to efficiently use faster but smaller memory devices, such as caches, which is perhaps the bigger issue today. The technique of privatization, by making one copy of the variable for each processor, increases loop level parallelism at the minimum storage cost.

Unfortunately, a number of serious challenges stand in the way when one tries to automatically privatize arrays. Some of them are common to all analyses that deal with array references, e.g. how to build a mathematical system that is sufficiently precise to model the analysis problem and yet can be efficiently solved. There is a unique challenge to array privatization, however. Its underlying mathematical system may simultaneously involve all references to the targeted array. This is in contrast to the traditional *data dependence analysis* that answers the question whether array accesses from different iterations interfere with each other. For data dependence analysis, it is sufficient to examine array references one pair at a time, which greatly simplifies both the mathematical system and the information gathering to build the system.

At the highest level, there are two alternative approaches to the construction of the mathematical system for array privatization, which we now discuss.

2. THE TOP-LEVEL DESIGN REEXAMINED

The paper revisited here takes an approach that can be viewed as *write-centric*, and it corresponds to a forward direction in which the mathematical system is built based on program analysis and is solved incrementally. An opposite approach is *read-centric*, corresponding to backward propagation. In a later experiment to actually build a compiler prototype, my student, Junjie Gu, and I took the latter approach [7].

The write-centric approach computes the *cover set* for the array targeted for privatization at every program point in the loop. This is the set of array elements that are known to have been definitely written, no matter what execution path is taken when the specific program point is reached. Naturally, this set must be computed in the forward direction, with every write reference examined for the array elements being written. Note that this set will be parameterized by the execution conditions of the current program point, including the index variables of all nested loops (within the targeted loop) containing the program point.

When analyzing a sequence of program statements, the cover set can be expanded (by union operations) on-the-fly. If a read reference is encountered, its upwardly exposed elements can be determined by subtracting the current cover set from the set of array elements that are read. Different cover sets, however, must be computed for different execution paths until they are intersected.

The read-centric approach propagates, in the backward direction, the set of array elements that may be upwardly exposed to the beginning of any arbitrary iteration of the targeted loop. When a write reference is encountered, the elements written are subtracted from the set being propagated. The difference is propagated further. An obvious potential advantage is that, if most of the time the difference is either empty or in a simple shape, then the cost to propagate the upwardly exposed set is low. In comparison, the write-centric approach must propagate all elements that are written in the targeted loop, which may consume much more storage and time. However, the read-centric approach has a potential down side: if most of the time the set subtraction results in a non-convex set, we will need to decompose the result into several convex sets, because the solvers of the mathematical systems normally require the sets to be convex. Hence, we may end up with propagating a long list of fragmented convex sets. In the experiment mentioned above [7], however, a set representation is devised to allow lazy computation of set differences. A set subtraction is registered but not actually performed until it cannot be postponed any further. The experiment shows that for the PERFECT benchmarks the subtraction operations can often be avoided this way.

3. OTHER DEVELOPMENTS

Numerous efforts have been undertaken by researchers to make array access analyses efficient. Progress has been made on several fronts, some of which are recounted below, as they have direct impact on the quality and efficiency of automatic array privatization.

Set representation.

The set of array elements needs to be represented in a way that allows set operations to be performed efficiently. For array privatization, one can borrow methods originally proposed for interprocedural data dependence analysis. Often, the set of elements accessed by a single array reference forms a *regular array section* and can be denoted by a triplet *(lower bound, upper bound, stride)* [12, 4]. During automatic array privatization, both the cover sets for write references and the sets of upwardly exposed elements can be represented as a list of regular array sections. It is often beneficial to maintain a list of postponed set subtraction operations, as mentioned above, instead of eagerly performing the subtraction and storing the fragmented result as a list of regular array sections.

Solving the underlying mathematical systems.

The problem of determining whether a set of written array elements overlaps a set of upwardly exposed elements can usually be reduced to the problem of determining the feasibility of a set of integer linear inequalities. Such linear inequalities contain loop index variables and possibly other symbols appearing in array subscripts and loop limits. This is an integer programming problem and in general can be very time consuming to solve. Numerous approximation methods have been proposed but are not discussed here. It is worth pointing out that a more comprehensive mathematical model that incorporates execution path conditions may be needed, in practice, for some cases. Today, logical system solvers are mature enough to solve such more complicated systems.

Finding relationship between different symbols.
A more challenging issue than solving a logical system concerns finding sufficient information to build a useful system. In general, the more constraints we can extract from the program the more precise the model is. If two different symbols appear in the system but we know nothing about their relationship, then the system tends to be a poor approximation of the problem and its solution may be useless. For this reason, we ideally want to find a closed-form expression for every symbol such that the expression contains no symbols except for the program input variables. This way, every useful relationship governing the symbols will be represented in the mathematical system. Unfortunately, in practice we are rarely able to obtain such an ideal representation, which means that there will be "unknown symbols" present in the system. We wish to be able to find useful constraints on such symbols via symbolic substitution. The demand-driven substitution method proposed by Tu and Padua synchronizes the substitution steps for two symbols of interest [13]. This method is found to be especially effective for the purpose of automatic array privatization.

Dynamic methods.
For programs that are difficult to analyze at compile time, dynamic privatization methods have been proposed for arrays [11, 5].

Researchers looking into ways to parallelize non-numerical programs have discovered that non-array aggregate variables, such as dynamically allocated irregular data structures, may also be privatized to improve loop level parallelism. Due to the space limit, these new developments are not discussed here.

4. LOOKING FORWARD

Automatic array privatization is motivated mainly by the desire to automatically parallelize programs. Due to the well-known difficulties with parallelizing legacy programs, whether automatic parallelization has a future has constantly been questioned. One has to ask, however, what the effective alternatives are. Based on the difficulties experienced by many when teaching or learning parallel programming, the question seems to be unanswered. It is important to find an effective way to retain the determinism of computational results offered by sequential programming languages and yet, at the same time, to remove the complications that can obscure the inherent parallelism in a computation problem.

5. REFERENCES

[1] F. Allen, M. Burke, P. Charles, R. Cytron, and J. Ferrante. An overview of the PTRAN analysis system for multiprocessing. *The Journal of Parallel and Distributed Computing*, 5(5):617 – 640, October 1988.

[2] M. Berry, D. Chen, P. Koss, D. Kuck, S. Lo, Y. Pang, L. Pointer, R. Roloff, A. Sameh, E. Clementi, S. Chin, D. Schneider, G. Fox, P. Messina, D. Walker, C. Hsiung, J. Schwarzmeier, K. Lue, S. Orszag, F. Seidl, O. Johnson, and R. Goodrum. The PERFECT Club benchmarks: Effective performance evaluation of supercomputers. *International Journal of Supercomputer Applications*, 3:5–40, 1988.

[3] M. Burke, R. Cytron, J. Ferrante, and W. Hsieh. Automatic generation of nested, fork-join parallelism. *Journal of Supercomputing*, 3(2):71 – 88, 1989.

[4] D. Callahan and K. Kennedy. Analysis of interprocedural side effects in a parallel programming environment. *Journal of Parallel and Distributed Computing*, 5(5):517–550, 1988.

[5] F. Dang, H. Yu, and L. Rauchwerger. The R-LRPD test: Speculative parallelization of partially parallel loops. In *Proceedings of the 16th International Symposium on Parallel and Distributed Processing*, IPDPS '02, pages 20–, Washington, DC, USA, 2002. IEEE Computer Society.

[6] R. Eigenmann, J. Hoeflinger, G. Jaxon, Z. Li, and D. A. Padua. Restructuring Fortran programs for Cedar. *Concurrency - Practice and Experience*, 5(7):553–573, 1993. An early version is in *Proceedings of the 1991 International Conference on Parallel Processing*, pages 57–66, 1991.

[7] J. Gu, Z. Li, and G. Lee. Experience with efficient array data flow analysis for array privatization. In *Proceedings of the Sixth ACM SIGPLAN Symposium on Principles and Practice of Parallel Programming*, PPOPP '97, pages 157–167, New York, NY, USA, 1997. ACM.

[8] M. D. Guzzi, J. P. Hoeflinger, D. A. Padua, and D. H. Lawrie. Cedar Fortran and other vector and parallel Fortran dialects. In *Proceedings of the 1988 ACM/IEEE Conference on Supercomputing*, Supercomputing '88, pages 114–121, Los Alamitos, CA, USA, 1988. IEEE Computer Society Press.

[9] D. J. Kuck, E. S. Davidson, D. H. Lawrie, and A. H. Sameh. Parallel supercomputing today and the Cedar approach. *Science*, 231(4741):967 – 974, 1986.

[10] D. J. Kuck, R. H. Kuhn, D. A. Padua, B. Leasure, and M. Wolfe. Dependence graphs and compiler optimizations. In *Proceedings of the 8th ACM SIGPLAN-SIGACT Symposium on Principles of Programming Languages*, POPL '81, pages 207–218, New York, NY, USA, 1981. ACM.

[11] L. Rauchwerger and D. Padua. The privatizing DOALL test: a run-time technique for DOALL loop identification and array privatization. In *Proceedings of the 8th international conference on Supercomputing*, ICS '94, pages 33–43, New York, NY, USA, 1994. ACM.

[12] P. F. Rémi Triolet and F. Irigoin. Direct parallelization of call statements. *Proceedings of the ACM Symposium on Compiler Construction*, 1986.

[13] P. Tu and D. Padua. Gated SSA-based demand-driven symbolic analysis for parallelizing compilers. In *Proceedings of the 9th International Conference on Supercomputing*, ICS '95, pages 414–423, New York, NY, USA, 1995. ACM.

Author Retrospective for Increasing the Instruction Fetch Rate via Multiple Branch Prediction and a Branch Address Cache

Tse-Yu Yeh
Apple Inc.
Cupertino, CA
tyyeh@apple.com

Deborah T. Marr
Intel Corporation
Hillsboro, OR
debbie.marr@intel.com

Yale N. Patt
The University of Texas at Austin
Austin, TX
patt@ece.utexas.edu

Original paper: http://dx.doi.org/10.1145/165939.165956

Categories and Subject Descriptors

C.1.1 [**Computer Systems Organization**]: Processor Architectures—*Single data stream architectures*

Keywords

Branch prediction

"Increasing the Instruction Fetch Rate via Multiple Branch Prediction and a Branch Address Cache" was the first paper to propose a highly accurate hardware mechanism for predicting and fetching multiple non-contiguous basic blocks using leading-edge aggressive branch predictors of the time. Prior to this paper, the methods to increase fetch bandwidth relied on software and compiler mechanisms to increase the size of the basic blocks themselves. The publication of our paper inspired an explosion of research to further improve the accuracy of multiple branch prediction, reduce complexity of fetching multiple basic blocks, or increase the fetch bandwidth in other ways.

Our HPS research group defied conventional wisdom in a 1991 ISCA paper [1] that demonstrated instruction level parallelism (IPC) can be greater than two even for non-scientific workloads. This flew in the face of numerous "proofs" at the time. We showed that there was enough parallelism for an aggressive superscalar out-of-order execution engine to exploit to dramatically improve performance, provided that the penalties caused by incorrect branch predictions, cache misses, and TLB misses could be improved.

Six months later, in our Micro 1991 paper [5], we introduced the Two-level Adaptive Branch Predictor, based on the notion that maintaining two levels of branch history provides far greater accuracy than was possible with simpler branch prediction schemes [4]. Other researchers quickly agreed, and thus a frenzy of branch predictor research began. We followed our first paper with a more comprehensive paper describing alternative implementations of the two-level scheme in ISCA 1992 [6] and Kimming So and his colleagues published their correlation predictor in ASPLOS [3] later that same year. Soon after, Scott McFarling introduced g-share, a variation on the GAs two-level predictor, and hybrid branch prediction [2]. The computer architecture research landscape had changed in favor of aggressive research in branch prediction.

ICS 25th Anniversary Volume. 2014
ACM 978-1-4503-2840-1/14/06.
http://dx.doi.org/10.1145/2591635.2591649.

After we adopted state of the art cache designs and branch prediction schemes for our out-of-order processor research, one bottleneck we faced was predicting only one branch at a time, which meant fetching only to the next branch instruction. Since branches occur approximately every five instructions, this was a serious handicap. Continuing to fetch along the fall-through path brings in more instructions, but a lot more than 50% of branches follow the taken path and it flew counter to the huge performance benefits being realized by the aggressive branch predictor research at the time.

We weren't the only ones thinking about this problem. Compiler teams were working on making basic blocks larger by a variety of techniques, including superpipelining, trace scheduling, and superblocks. However, success was limited to the quality of profiling information and it was already known that dynamic hardware branch predictors were far more accurate and could handle a wider range of behavior. We decided to explore whether it was possible to bring multiple basic blocks into the processor through hardware alone. We came up with a mechanism consisting of essentially three components: (1) a branch predictor that could accurately predict the outcomes of multiple branches each cycle using one of the aggressive and highly accurate predictors of the time, (2) a branch address cache for generating fetch addresses for multiple non-consecutive basic blocks each cycle, and (3) an instruction cache with enough bandwidth to supply a large number of instructions from multiple, non-consecutive basic blocks. The result was an increase in instruction fetch bandwidth of 60% on integer benchmarks at the cost of a complex engine.

The idea was novel and spurred new research – how to greatly increase the fetch bandwidth by bringing in multiple non-contiguous basic blocks with the new highly-accurate branch predictor. Many ideas and papers sprung from this, including trace cache designs and loop buffers. The Intel® Pentium™ 4 Processor was the first commercial processor to include a trace cache.

Microprocessor research has changed direction more than once since 1993. The microprocessor chip containing a single processor gave way to the multi- core chip, where each microprocessor consisted of two, then four, then eight, etc. processors on each silicon die. With the increase in the number of processors on a chip, attention waned from making the individual processor excel in favor of making all processors perform concurrently. The thought was that all the processors could be identical and simple, and maximum benefit would be based on how well concurrent execution was exploited.

Today the research landscape has changed again. In spite of immense research into parallelism, many workloads continue to have significant segments of limited parallelism or serial segments. The notion that processors will be identical and simple has been replaced by the recognition that a collection of heterogeneous processors, each tuned for specific needs, is a better approach. One of those needs is to aggressively handle single-thread performance which requires increasing the fetch rate via better branch predictors and on chip storage structures. The notion of hardware complexity has also changed over time – with far more transistors available, many of the hardware-intense and complex mechanisms of the past are no longer deemed to be complex and in fact are quite feasible. Perhaps we have come full circle!

Tse-Yu Yeh completed his PhD at Michigan in 1993 and has been responsible for many microprocessor designs at a variety of companies including Intel, Broad com, and Apple. He is currently a director at Apple working on chip development. Deborah Marr interrupted her PhD research to take a full time position at Intel, where she was the lead architect for key aspects of Intel's Core/Xeon architecture product lines. She completed her PhD in her spare time from Michigan in 2008. She is currently the Director of the Accelerator Architecture Research Lab at Intel. Yale Patt retired from Michigan in 1999 to become the Ernest Cockrell, Jr. Centennial Chair in Engineering at The University of Texas at Austin. He continues to thrive on directing PhD students in microarchitecture research and teaching both freshmen and graduate students.

1. REFERENCES

[1] M. Butler, T.-Y. Yeh, Y. Patt, M. Alsup, H. Scales, and M. Shebanow. Single instruction stream parallelism is greater than two. In *Proceedings of the 18th Annual International Symposium on Computer Architecture*, pages 276–286, May 1991.

[2] S. McFarling. Combining branch predictors. Technical Report WRL Technical Note TN-36, Digital Equipment Corporation, June 1993.

[3] S.-T. Pan, K. So, and J. T. Rahmeh. Improving the accuracy of dynamic branch prediction using branch correlation. In *Proceedings of the Fifth International Conference on Architectural Support for Programming Languages and Operating Systems*, pages 76–84, September 1992.

[4] J. E. Smith. A study of branch prediction strategies. In *Proceedings of the 8th Annual Symposium on Computer Architecture*, pages 135–148, May 1981.

[5] T.-Y. Yeh and Y. N. Patt. Two-level adaptive training branch prediction. In *Proceedings of the 24th Annual International Symposium on Microarchitecture*, pages 51–61, September 1991.

[6] T.-Y. Yeh and Y. N. Patt. Alternative implementations of two-level adaptive branch prediction. In *Proceedings of the 19th Annual International Symposium on Computer Architecture*, pages 124–134, May 1992.

Author Retrospective for Anatomy of a Message In the Alewife Multiprocessor

John Kubiatowicz
Computer Science Division
University of California, Berkeley
kubitron@cs.berkeley.edu

ABSTRACT

The MIT Alewife project, launched in the Spring of 1988, comprised a dynamic group of researchers who designed and implemented the Alewife multiprocessor [1]. One of the most important and unexpected outcomes of this project was the message-passing interface described in "Anatomy of a Message in the Alewife Multiprocessor," selected for this Retrospective. This interface was essential to the Alewife OS and runtime systems, was important for I/O, and enabled a new and innovative cache-coherence protocol, called LimitLESS [3]. It also enabled direct comparisons between shared memory and message-passing [4].

Original paper: http://dx.doi.org/10.1145/165939.165970

Categories and Subject Descriptors

B.4 [Input/Output and Data Communications]: Interconnections (Subsystems)—*interfaces*; C.2 [Computer-Communication Networks]: Network Architecture and Design—*Packet-switching networks*

Keywords

Parallel computing, message-passing interfaces

1. INTRODUCTION

The MIT Alewife project was an amazing collaboration of students, research staff, and faculty that charted new ground, produced a wide variety of research results, and ultimately built real parallel processing hardware. It spanned the 10-year period from the Spring of 1988 to Spring of 1998—producing almost 30 papers in conferences and journals and 7–10 PhD theses (depending on how you count them). Lead by Anant Agarwal from MIT, the research environment was exciting, occasionally contentious, and always productive. As one of the principle architects of the Alewife hardware, I had the privilege to work directly with many outstanding researchers during the project. Together, we designed the Alewife machine from scratch with a new processor, new cache-coherence protocol, new compiler, novel synchronization support, and a custom operating system.

ICS 25th Anniversary Volume. 2014
ACM 978-1-4503-2840-1/14/06.
http://dx.doi.org/10.1145/2591635.2591650.

Much of the focus behind our papers was aimed at *practical* considerations that ultimately lead to the Alewife machine [1]. This "implementation realism" was one of our strengths as a research team. Whenever one of us would propose a new mechanism or protocol, the others would ask whether or not it was practical. During the course of the project, we constructed at least three different system-level simulators—including one called "the New World Order"—with the express purpose of understanding the complexity and performance of mechanisms under realistic loads.

One of the most important (and unexpected) outcomes of the early phase of the Alewife project was the message-passing interface. The final form of this interface was a collaboration between multiple members of the Alewife team. It rapidly evolved from a novelty to an essential mechanism.

2. THE INTERFACE IS BORN

When I first joined Alewife project in 1989, the team was investigating the design and implementation of limited directory cache-coherence protocols. Anant Agarwal "signed me on" to help design and implement the Alewife machine. At that time, there were some initial thoughts of what mechanisms should be in a good processor (ultimately leading to the April processor paper [2]) as well as a preference for packet-switched, low-dimensional networks over alternatives. The remainder of the details were in the very early stages and quite fungible. Since building a complete machine from scratch was an exciting prospect, I immediately began to flesh out the details.

The genesis for the Alewife message-passing interface was my desire to provide communication support for the operating system and I/O subsystem. In keeping with the fine-grained communication philosophy of Alewife, my initial proposal for the messaging interface included a low-overhead message description process, integrated direct memory access (DMA), and fast interrupt handling. At the time, Technology Square at MIT had a number of competing parallel computer projects, including the J-machine [8], Monsoon [9], and *T [7]. The J-machine, in particular, provided much inspiration to design a low-overhead message-passing interface that was compatible with our standard RISC pipeline[1]. I was quite familiar with the J-machine, since Bill Dally's research group was right next to ours.

As I recall, others in the group were extremely skeptical of my initial proposal. Many, including Daniel Nussbaum

[1]The J-machine included a specialized processor with hardware-support for method dispatch in object-oriented programming models such as Smalltalk.

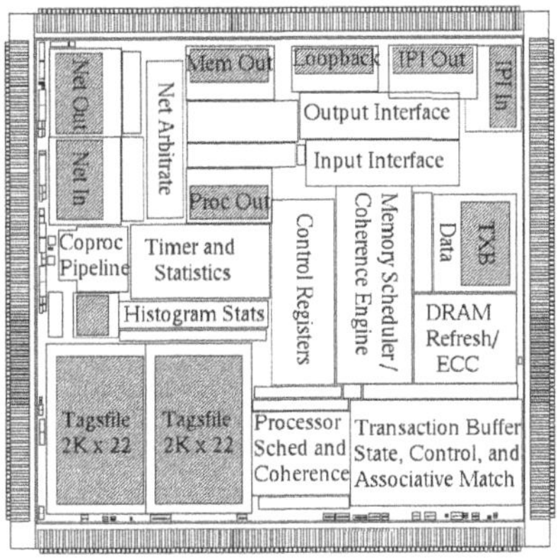

Figure 1: Floorplan for the Alewife CMMU (15mm × 15mm). Shaded regions are standard-cell memories. Remaining blocks are formed from sea-of-gates transistors.

Category	Gate Count	%	Mechanism SM	MP	LT	FG
Processor Requests	11686	12	√		√	√
Full/Empty Decode	2157	2				√
Memory Machine	13351	13	√	√		
DRAM Control	8720	9	√	√		
Transaction Buffer	17399	17	√	√	√	
Tracking Vectors	2108	2	√		√	
Network Interface	11805	12	√	√		
Network Queueing	7363	7	√	√	√	√
CMMU Registers	9308	9	√	√		
Statistics	11958	12				
Miscellaneous	4627	5				

Figure 2: Functional block sizes (in gates) for the Alewife CMMU, as well as contributions to shared memory (SM), message passing (MP), latency tolerance (LT), and fine-grain synchronization (FG). Total chip resources: 100K gates and 120K bits of SRAM.

and David Chaiken, thought it was a distraction from our charter of making distributed shared-memory practical. I persisted, however, and had begun to think about the fact that "message-passing" (packet-switching) networks were going to be underneath any shared-memory implementation for Alewife. Soon, Anant Agarwal and David Chaiken realized that a low-overhead message-passing interface could be used to provide flexibility for the cache coherence protocol—allowing the common-case to be handled in hardware with special cases relegated to software. At that point, both the Alewife network interface and the LimitLESS cache coherence protocol [3] were born.

With the support of the Alewife team, I began designing the message passing mechanism in earnest—adapting it as necessary as others began applying it to their own interests. A flurry of activity followed. Specifically, David Chaiken began designing the LimitLESS coherence protocol; Ben-Hong Lim began designing synchronization mechanisms using messages; David Kranz and Dan Nussbaum began integrating messaging into the compiler and runtime system. Kirk Johnston, Ken Mackenzie, and Donald Yeung provided valuable insights at this time as well.

It is a testimony to our extensive simulation environment (complete with the ability to boot a binary version of our operating system) that we were able to quickly iterate on the design of the messaging interface.

3. A MATURE DESIGN

The "devil is in the details," as they stay. The "Anatomy of a Message" paper, included in this volume, is the result of an intense design process. It represents the (often colliding) combination of many design goals and implementation restrictions. I list a few of them here:

- The inclusion of the *Atomic Send* mechanism was necessary for reasonable integration with operating systems, since it allows the OS to interrupt user-level processes that are sending messages[2].
- The *High-Availability* interrupt mechanism was crucial to permit message-passing and shared memory to exist in the same machine.
- The *Locally-Coherent DMA* mechanism was a logical compromise between programmability and ease of implementation.
- Network overflow support (and corresponding queue topology) was essential, given that Alewife was implemented on top of a network with only a single virtual channel.

The strength of this paper arose, in my opinion, precisely because it was founded in real implementation concerns—without losing the simplicity of mechanism description. At the time that the paper was published, the Alewife communication and memory management unit (CMMU) was already well on its way toward implementation.

Figure 1 shows the final floorplan for the CMMU, illustrating where the message-passing mechanisms were placed. The queues and overall control interfaces (for the "Interprocessor Interrupt" or IPI) can be seen in the upper right corner of this chip. The upper left corner contains the network queuing and hardware interfaces to the network from the coherence protocol mechanisms.

This floorplan came directly from our LSI-Logic layout tool, and represents the final positioning of these components. Figure 2 shows that the message-passing mechanism comprises slightly more than 20% of the chip (it includes some of the CMMU registers), but that it impacts a number of important functions.

As a result of our extensive simulation and testing methodology (which included the ability to run a gate-level simulation of the CMMU in communication with a functional multiprocessor simulator), the first versions of the CMMU and Sparcle processor were substantially functional[3]. In fact, CMMU chips arrived in our lab on May 4th of 1994, and we had a 16-node Alewife machine running by June 17th.

[2]This is an important design flaw, in my opinion, of the J-Machine network interface.

[3]Many thanks to LSI Logic for their help in the design of the Sparcle processor and support with the layout and fabrication of the CMMU.

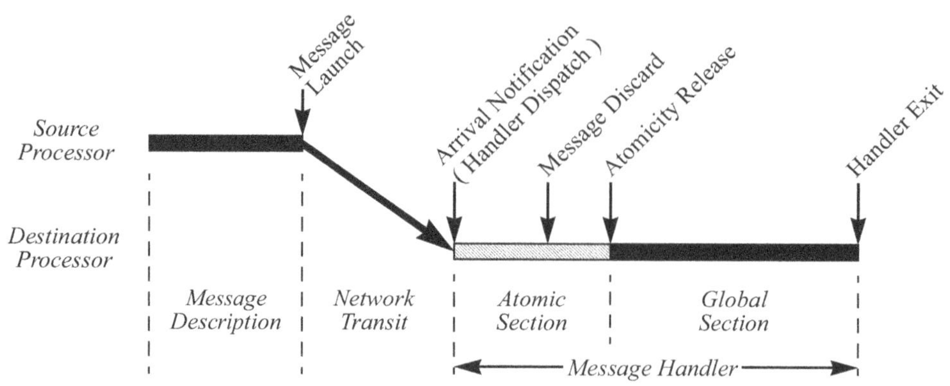

Figure 3: Injection of a User-Direct message and later extraction of this message with a user-level interrupt handler. A crucial aspect of this version of the message send was the *Atomic Section* which was entirely under control of the user-level task receiving messages.

4. EXTENSIONS TO THE SCHEME

The first version of the Alewife message-passing interface had some minor deficiencies with respect to user-level access to the network. Missing from that version was support for user-level control of message interrupts. As a result, Ken Mackenzie and I collaborated with Anant Agarwal and Frans Kaashoek to develop what we called "User-Direct Messaging" [6]. Support for this style of communication appeared in the second iteration of the CMMU.

User-Direct Messaging introduced a novel atomicity mechanism that allows user-level programs to disable message-arrival interrupts as long as they do not "abuse" the privilege; abuses include refusing to consume messages or consuming them too slowly. Figure 3 shows the complete life of a message as embodied in this new interface. Of particular importance to this figure is the *Atomic Section* that is entirely under control of the user.

5. 20 YEARS LATER

I like to think that everyone in the Alewife group eventually came to love the inclusion of a low-overhead message-passing interface into the Alewife universe. It altered our thinking about communication mechanisms significantly, changing the way we constructed essential software services [5] and spurring direct comparisons between message-passing and shared-memory communication styles [4]. The LimitLESS cache coherence protocol [3] immediately garnered attention from a wide audience and subsequently inspired a variety of follow-on work (both inside and outside of MIT) on the benefits of hardware invoked, software-supported cache-coherence protocols.

To this day, I believe that the Alewife message-passing interface is one of the most efficient and practical messaging interfaces ever designed. Its unique features are thanks to a dynamic group of researchers on the 6th floor of MIT's technology square—a group of which I had the distinct privilege to be a member.

6. REFERENCES

[1] Anant Agarwal, Ricardo Bianchini, David Chaiken, Kirk Johnson, David Kranz, John Kubiatowicz, Beng-Hong Lim, Kenneth Mackenzie, and Donald Yeung. The MIT Alewife Machine: Architecture and Performance. In *Proceedings of the 22nd Annual International Symposium on Computer Architecture*, June 1995.

[2] Anant Agarwal, Beng-Hong Lim, and David Kranz. April: A Processor Architecture for Multiprocessing. In *Proceedings of the 17th Annual International Symposium on Computer Architecture*, June 1990.

[3] David Chaiken, John Kubiatowicz, and Anant Agarwal. LimitLESS diectories: A scalable cache coherence scheme. In *Proceedings of the 22nd Annual Conference on Architectural Support for Programming Languages and Operating Systems*, April 1991.

[4] Fredric T. Chong, Rajeev Barua, Fredrik Dahlgren, John Kubiatowicz, and Anant Agarwal. The Sensitivity of Communicaton Mechanisms to Bandwidth and Latency. In *Proceedings of the Fourth Annual Symposium on High-Performance Computer Architecture*, February 1998.

[5] David Kranz, Kirk Johnson, Anant Agarwal, Beng-Hong Lim, and John Kubiatowicz. Integrating Message-Passing and Shared-Memory: Early Experience, May 1993.

[6] Kenneth Mackenzie, John Kubiatowicz, Matthew Frank, Walter Lee, Victor Lee, Anant Agarwal, and M. Frans Kaashoek. Exploiting Two-Case Delivery for Fast Protected Messaging. In *Proceedings of the Fourth Annual Symposium on High-Performance Computer Architecture*, February 1998.

[7] R. S. Nikhil, Greggory Papadopoulos, and David Culler. *T: A Multithreaded Massively Parallel Architecture. In *Proceedings of the 19th Annual International Symposium on Computer Architecture*, May 1992.

[8] Michael Noakes, Deborah Wallach, and William Dally. The J-Machine Multicomputer: An Architectural Evaluation. In *Proceedings of the 20th Annual International Symposium on Computer Architecture*, May 1993.

[9] Gregory Papadopoulos and David Culler. Monsoon: An Explicit Token-Store Archiecture. In *Proceedings of the 17th Annual International Symposium on Computer Architecture*, June 1990.

Author Retrospective

Compilation Techniques for Block-Cyclic Distributions

John Mellor-Crummey
Rice University
johnmc@rice.edu

Seema Hiranandani
Synopsys, Inc.
seemah@synopsys.com

Ajay Sethi
Accel Partners
ajay@accel.com

ABSTRACT

Compilers for data-parallel languages use data distribution specifications to guide code generation for distributed-memory machines. Our 1994 paper described how to generate efficient code for programs that employ block-cyclic data distributions. In subsequent work at Rice University, Darte, Mellor-Crummey, Fowler, and Chavarría-Miranda developed a more general form of block-cyclic partitionings known as generalized multipartitionings. Generalized multipartitionings provide some additional balance properties that make them useful for parallelizing computations that solve recurrences along spatial dimensions. These partitionings were subsequently implemented in Rice University's dHPF compiler for High Performance Fortran. In the years since, the field has changed in many ways; however, variants of block-cyclic data distributions are still used today by modern parallel programming models, algorithms, and compilers.

Original paper: http://dx.doi.org/10.1145/181181.181572

Categories and Subject Descriptors

D.3.4 [**Programming Languages**]: Processors—*code generation, compilers*; D.1.3 [**Software**]: Concurrent Programming—*parallel programming*

General Terms

Data-parallel languages, Compilers, Data distributions

1. INTRODUCTION

Compilers for data-parallel languages, such as High Performance Fortran [8], use data distributions to guide the parallelization of single-threaded programs for distributed memory parallel systems. Data layout directives indicate how to partition an application's data across the processors in a parallel system. By using the *owner computes* rule[1] as a guide, data-parallel compilers partition computation, add data movement, and insert synchronization. Our 1994 paper described a new approach for compiling block-cyclic distributions to load balance dense matrix algorithms on distributed memory systems. Immediate follow-on work to our 1994 paper included papers about communication generation for cyclic(k) distributions [10], a linear-time address generation algorithm for block-cyclic distributions [12], and extensions to this work to handle arbitrary affine subscripts [11]. In this short retrospective, we briefly describe a few related developments in the field that have occurred over the two decades since. In Section 2, we describe generalized multipartitionings [5, 6]—sophisticated variants of a block-cyclic data distribution that have some additional balance properties—that are useful for parallelizing computations that solve recurrences along spatial dimensions. In Section 3, we conclude with a few comments about the use of block-cyclic data distributions today.

2. GENERALIZED MULTIPARTITIONING

While block-cyclic data decompositions are useful for parallelizing and load balancing many matrix computations, they fall short of what is needed to efficiently parallelize programs that perform line-sweeps to solve one-dimensional recurrences along each of the spatial dimensions. Line sweeps are the backbone of numerical methods such as Alternating Direction Implicit (ADI) integration—a technique for solving partial differential equations such as the Navier-Stokes equation [1]. Parallelizing multi-dimensional line-sweep computations is challenging because recurrences along each spatial dimension partially or fully serialize computation along any dimension distributed with conventional block or block-cyclic partitionings.

To support better parallelization of line sweep computations over multi-dimensional arrays, a skewed block-cyclic partitioning of data and computation known as a *multipartitioning* was developed [1, 2, 9, 13]. A multipartitioning partitions an array of two or more dimensions into blocks and assigns each processor a set of blocks so that (1) all processors are active in every step of a line-sweep computation along any array dimension, (2) load-balance is nearly perfect, and (3) only coarse-grain communication is needed. Figure 2 shows a three-dimensional multipartitioning.

A multipartitioning achieves full parallelism and load balance by (1) assigning each processor a balanced number of

[1]With the *owner computes* rule, each processor computes only values for data mapped to it by a data layout.

ICS 25th Anniversary Volume. 2014
ACM 978-1-4503-2840-1/14/06.
http://dx.doi.org/10.1145/2591635.2591651.

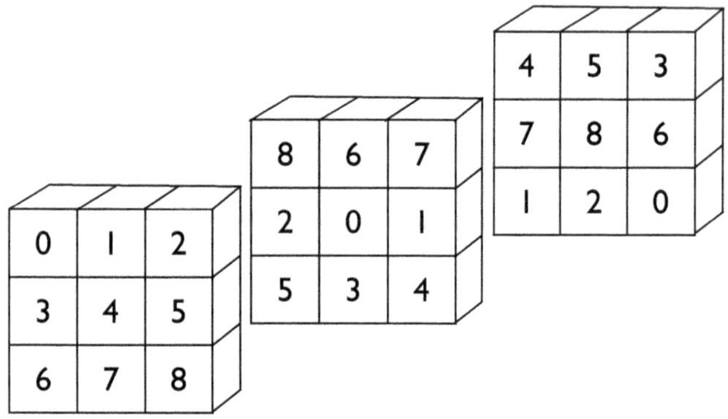

Figure 1: A three-dimensional diagonal multipartitioning on nine processors. The planes along the Z axis are shown separately to show the ownership of each data tile in the volume. The number on each tile represents the processor that owns the tile. Notice that each processor owns exactly one tile in each row, column and plane. As a result, each processor owns exactly one tile in each plane orthogonal to any one of the coordinate axes.

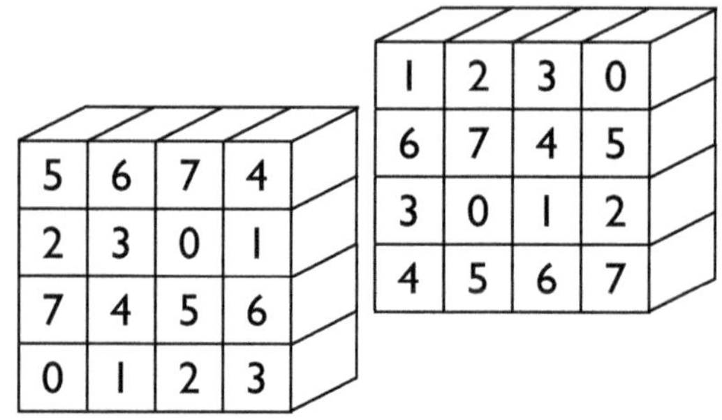

Figure 2: A three-dimensional generalized multipartitioning on eight processors. The planes along the Z axis are shown separately to show the ownership of each data tile in the volume. The number on each tile represents the processor that owns the tile. Notice that each processor owns a balanced number of tiles in each hyperplane perpendicular to any of the coordinate axes. For the xy planes, each processor owns two tiles. For the xz and yz planes, each processor owns one tile. The mapping also satisfies the neighbor property—all neighboring tiles for any processor q in any one direction along a dimension are all owned by some other processor r. The fact that each processor owns more than one tile in some hyperplane makes this a generalized multipartitioning.

tiles in each hyper-rectangular slab defined by a pair of adjacent cuts along a partitioned data dimension and (2) ensuring that for all tiles mapped to a processor, their immediate tile neighbors in any one coordinate direction are all mapped to a single processor. These two properties are known as the *balance* property and the *neighbor* property, respectively. The utility of the balance property is obvious: for a computation solving one dimensional recurrences, all processors will have a balanced number of tiles to work on in every step of the computation. The neighbor property enables a fully-vectorized, directional-shift communication with one message per processor.

As of 2001, multipartitionings described in the literature allowed only one tile per processor per hyperplane of a partitioned array; such multipartitionings are known as *diagonal multipartitionings* [13]. While it is straightforward to compute a diagonal multipartitoning for d-dimensional data arrays by employing p cuts along each dimension, such partitionings cause excessive communication unless $p^{1/(d-1)}$ is integral, where p is the number of processors. For three dimensions, diagonal multipartitionings are only optimal when the number of processors is a perfect square [5]. To support efficient multipartitionings on arbitrary numbers of processors, in 2002, Darte, Mellor-Crummey, Fowler, and Chavarría-Miranda developed an algorithm to compute generalized multipartitionings for d dimensions of a ρ-dimensional array for an arbitrary number of processors, for any d, $2 \leq d \leq \rho$ [5, 6]. Unlike diagonal multipartitionings, generalized multipartitionings allow a processor to own more than one tile per hyperplane of a partitioned array. Figure 2 shows a three-dimensional generalized multipartitioning for eight processors.

The best generalized multipartitioning is the one that has the smallest communication cost. Computing the best generalized multipartitioning of a ρ-dimensional array requires a cost model to select d, the dimensionality of the best partitioning, and $\vec{\gamma}$—the number of cuts along each dimension. For the number of tiles in each hyper-rectangular slab to be divisible by p, $\vec{\gamma}$ must be such that for each dimension i, p divides $\prod_{j \neq i} \gamma_j$. The selection of $\vec{\gamma}$ and the mapping of cuts to data dimensions depends both on the factorization of p and the extent of each data dimension. Unless p is prime, the best generalized multipartitioning for a three dimensional data domain is a three-dimensional multipartitioning; if p is prime, a two-dimensional partitioning yields a superior computation to communication ratio.

In addition to computing the number of cuts along each dimension, a generalized multipartitioning must map each tile to a processor. As for any multipartitioning, the tile-to-processor mapping for a generalized multipartitioning must satisfy the balance and neighbor properties. For a generalized multipartitioning, the balance property means that when the mapping is applied to each tile in any hyper-rectangular slab, it must map an equal number of tiles to each processor. Generalized multipartitionings employ modular mappings to satisfy the balance and neighbor properties. The algorithms for computing generalized multipartitionings are surprisingly simple; a full description of them can be found elsewhere [6].

Compiler and runtime support for generalized multipartitionings is more extensive than that for the block-cyclic partitionings described in our 1994 paper. Support for generalized multipartitionings in Rice University's dHPF compiler includes support for (1) reasoning about communication and computation for tiles of arbitrary dimension with symbolic extents using polyhedral analysis, (2) generating parameterized code so that the selection of which array dimensions will be partitioned can be deferred until execution time when p, the number of processors, is known, and (3) computing tile schedules for loop nests with data dependences so that when each processor performs its computation for a loop nest, it sweeps through its tiles in an order consistent with any data dependences present. The runtime library for dHPF provides routines to (1) factor p, (2) enumerate all elementary partitionings $\vec{\gamma}$ of d, $2 \leq d \leq \rho$, dimensions (elementary partitionings, $\vec{\gamma}$, satisfy the criterion that p divides $\prod_{j \neq i} \gamma_j$ without unnecessary cuts), (3) evaluate the cost of each elementary partitioning using a cost model that assesses the cost of communicating across each partition, and (4) compute the tile to processor mapping for the minimum cost elementary partitioning.

3. BLOCK-CYCLIC MAPPINGS TODAY

While interest in High Performance Fortran has waned over the years, other parallel languages are emerging in its place. Block-cyclic data distributions remain an important feature for these programming models. Today, the Chapel [3] and X10 [4] languages borne of DARPA's High Productivity Computing Systems program both provide a global view of data and support block-cyclic data distributions. XscalableMP [15]—an emerging data-parallel programming model that builds upon ideas from both HPF and Coarray Fortran—also supports block-cyclic data distributions, as does Unified Parallel C [7].

With recent generations of parallel systems, the speed of computation has been increasing much faster than increases in memory and network bandwidth or reductions in memory and network latency. This trend is expected to continue into the future. As a result, there has been a groundswell of interest in communication-avoiding algorithms that minimize the time and energy for a computation by avoiding data movement. Solomonik and Demmel devised a communication-optimal parallel 2.5D matrix multiplication algorithm that employs a skewed cyclic distribution of matrix tiles in combination with a systolic algorithm that rotates tiles after each computation step [14]. Recently, Mellor-Crummey's group has recently been working to adapt HPF compiler technology to reason about communication for such algorithms and generate optimized data movement and synchronization.

4. REFERENCES

[1] J. Bruno and P. Cappello. Implementing the Beam and Warming method on the hypercube. In *Proceedings of 3rd Conference on Hypercube Concurrent Computers and Applications*, pages 1073–1087, Pasadena, CA, Jan. 1988.

[2] J. Bruno and P. Cappello. Implementing the 3D alternating direction method on the hypercube. *Journal of Parallel and Distributed Computing*, 23(3):411–417, Dec. 1994.

[3] B. L. Chamberlain. A brief overview of Chapel. `http://chapel.cray.com/papers/BriefOverviewChapel.pdf`, January 2013.

[4] P. Charles, C. Grothoff, V. Saraswat, C. Donawa, A. Kielstra, K. Ebcioglu, C. von Praun, and V. Sarkar. X10: An object-oriented approach to non-uniform cluster computing. In *Proceedings of the 20th Annual ACM SIGPLAN Conference on Object-oriented Programming, Systems, Languages, and Applications*, OOPSLA '05, pages 519–538, New York, NY, USA, 2005. ACM.

[5] A. Darte, D. Chavarria-Miranda, R. Fowler, and J. Mellor-Crummey. Generalized multipartitioning for multi-dimensional arrays. In *Proceedings of the International Parallel and Distributed Processing Symposium*, April 2002.

[6] A. Darte, J. Mellor-Crummey, R. Fowler, and D. Chavarría-Miranda. Generalized multipartitioning of multi-dimensional arrays for parallelizing line-sweep computations. *J. Parallel Distrib. Comput.*, 63(9):887–911, Sept. 2003.

[7] T. El-Ghazawi, W. Carlson, T. Sterling, and K. Yelick. *UPC: Distributed Shared-Memory Programming*. Wiley-Interscience, 2003.

[8] High Performance Fortran Forum. High Performance Fortran language specification. *Scientific Programming*, 2(1–2):1–170, 1993.

[9] S. L. Johnsson, Y. Saad, and M. H. Schultz. Alternating direction methods on multiprocessors. *SIAM Journal of Scientific and Statistical Computing*, 8(5):686–700, 1987.

[10] K. Kennedy, N. Nedeljkovi?, and A. Sethi. Communication generation for cyclic(k) distributions. In B. Szymanski and B. Sinharoy, editors, *Languages, Compilers and Run-Time Systems for Scalable Computers*, pages 185–197. Springer US, 1996.

[11] K. Kennedy, N. Nedeljkovic, and A. Sethi. Efficient address generation for block-cyclic distributions. In *Proceedings of the 9th International Conference on Supercomputing*, ICS '95, pages 180–184, New York, NY, USA, 1995. ACM.

[12] K. Kennedy, N. Nedeljkovic, and A. Sethi. A linear-time algorithm for computing the memory access sequence in data-parallel programs. In *Proceedings of the Fifth ACM SIGPLAN Symposium on Principles and Practice of Parallel Programming*, PPOPP '95, pages 102–111, New York, NY, USA, 1995. ACM.

[13] N. Naik, V. Naik, and M. Nicoules. Parallelization of a class of implicit finite-difference schemes in computational fluid dynamics. *International Journal of High Speed Computing*, 5(1):1–50, 1993.

[14] E. Solomonik and J. Demmel. Communication-optimal parallel 2.5D matrix multiplication and LU factorization algorithms. In *Proceedings of the 17th International Conference on Parallel Processing - Volume Part II*, Euro-Par'11, pages 90–109, Berlin, Heidelberg, 2011. Springer-Verlag.

[15] XcalableMP Specification Working Group. XcalableMP language specification, version 1.2. `http://www.xcalablemp.org/spec/xmp-spec-1.2.pdf`, November 2013.

Author Retrospective for
The Dual Data Cache

Antonio González
Department of Computer Architecture, UPC
Intel Barcelona Research Center, Intel Labs
antonio@ac.upc.edu

Carlos Aliagas
D. Enginyeria Informàtica I Matemàtiques
Universitat Rovira I Virgili
carles.aliagas@urv.net

ABSTRACT
In this paper we present a retrospective on our paper published in ICS 1995, which to best of our knowledge was the first paper that introduced the concept of a cache memory with multiple subcaches, each tuned for a different type of locality. In this retrospective, we summarize the main ideas of the original paper and outline some of the later work that exploited similar ideas and could have been influenced by our original paper, including two actual industrial microprocessors.

DOI: http://dx.doi.org/10.1145/224538.224622

Categories and Subject Descriptors
B.3.2 [**Memory Structures**]: Design Styles – *Caches memories*

1. INSPIRATION and MOTIVATION
Cache memories had received a lot of attention by the research community prior to our work. There were many research proposals on better prefetching schemes, replacement algorithms, indexing functions, just to name a few. However, we were intrigued by the little use of specialization in cache architectures, as opposed to what was happening in other parts of the microprocessors. There was a trend to include more specialized units for particular program behaviors, but this trend was not seen in caches. For instance, the datapath had different parts for integer, FP and vector instructions; the front-end had hybrid branch predictors to use the most adequate one depending on the type of code. On the other hand, cache memories kept being composed of a monolithic unit with a smart but single policy to deal with all memory references. These observations motivated us to investigate cache architectures that had more than one caching policy, with mechanisms that dynamically choose the most adequate one for each memory reference.

Cache memories are based on exploiting locality but there are different types of locality, so our plan was to investigate whether we could build a cache system that had multiple subcaches, each one specialized for a different type of locality.

2. MAIN CONTRIBUTIONS
Among the different types of locality, the two main categories are spatial and temporal. Some memory references exhibit both, whereas others have only one of them, and some have none. The simplest way to exploit spatial locality is by means of very large cache lines, whereas the most effective way to exploit references with only temporal locality is by means of one-word lines. For memory references without locality, the most effective way to handle them is to bring only the required data (as opposed to a whole cache line) and not store it in the cache, to avoid polluting it. All these were the main goals of the Dual Data Cache [1].

ICS 25th Anniversary Volume, 2014
ACM 978-1-4503-2840-1/14/06.
http://dx.doi.org/10.1145/2591635.2591652

The Dual Data Cache is a novel design with two subcaches, the Temporal Cache and the Spatial Cache. The Temporal Cache has very short lines to better exploit data that only exhibits temporal locality, whereas the Spatial Cache has longer lines to better exploit data with spatial locality and perhaps temporal too.

A key part of the Dual Data Cache is the scheme that decides in which subcache each reference is placed. For this purpose, we proposed a structure called the Locality Prediction Table (LPT), which keeps track at runtime of the behavior of memory instructions and tries to estimate their locality properties. The LPT is based on capturing the stride exhibited by memory instructions. Instructions with strides smaller than the Spatial Cache line size are mapped into the Spatial Cache. Instructions with zero stride (e.g., scalar references) and instructions with strides larger than the Spatial Cache line size that do not interfere with themselves when placed in the Temporal Cache are stored in the Temporal Cache. Other references simply bypass the two subcaches because they have poor locality or they would interfere when placed in cache. Besides, the Spatial Cache uses a very simple next-block prefetching scheme, which is very effective for this type of references.

In the same paper [1] we also propose a Selective Cache, which is a simplified version of the Dual Data Cache, in which there is only one subcache and the LPT that decides which references are cached and which ones are not.

Some previous works related to our paper include:

- Block algorithms [2], [3], [4] deal with large working sets.
- Bypassing [5] deals with pollution due to non-unit strides.
- Victim Cache [6], Skewed-associative Cache [7] and Column-associative Cache [8] deal with interferences (conflict misses).
- Prefetching techniques [9], [10], [11] that are based on dynamically identifying the stride of memory references.

3. IMPACT ON LATER WORKS
To the best of our knowledge, our paper was the first time a data cache with multiple caching strategies tuned to different types of locality was proposed. In the following years, there were multiple proposals that referenced our work and proposed alternative implementations that exploit this concept. In this section, we briefly summarized some of the main proposals in this area. We have classified them into three categories:

- Evolutionary: They normally propose alternative implementations that improve the behavior for some scenarios or combine this concept with others.
- Adapted to other scenarios.
  - Embedded systems.
  - Multicore systems.
- Implementations in commercial processors.
  - Samsung ClamRISC/32.
  - Intel StrongARM SA-1110.

3.1 Evolutionary

3.1.1 *Hardware Oriented Proposals*

A number of papers have studied the spatial/temporal locality characteristics of the memory references in different manners and proposed hardware mechanisms to exploit them.

Moshovos et al. [12] use data dependence information to decide to bypass a memory instruction, to store it in the Transient Value Cache or in the main cache. The TVC has some similarity to the Temporal cache of the Dual Data Cache.

To avoid some conflict misses in the main cache, the Annex cache[13] acts as an entry cache for compulsory misses and when some locality is detected the data is moved to a bigger cache that acts as a conventional cache. It resembles a victim cache but for incoming data as opposed to outgoing.

Johnson et al. focus on integer applications and propose a scheme that decides to do prefetching [14] or bypassing [15] of memory references via hardware monitoring of locality.

Rivers et al. [16] compare several mechanisms to obtain the locality of memory references in the L1 cache. Some uses some bits of the address and others some bits of the PC to access a table to catch the reusability of the memory access. They use this information to place the data in one of the two parts of the cache.

Kumar et al.[17] focus on spatial locality to emulate a large block cache via prefetching of the next predicted block.

Ju et al.[18] claim that it is more beneficial to cache those memory references that are in the critical path of a program instead of the ones that have more reusability.

Juurlink [19] uses a main cache with sub-blocking to emulate blocks of different sizes like those of the dual data cache. This scheme avoids to replicate data when a block has both types of locality.

Qureshi et al.[20] propose a special design for the L2 cache. Like the Dual Data Cache, it consists of two subcaches, a Line-Organized Cache and a Word-Organized Cache. When a line is evicted from the former, the used words of the lines are transferred to the later, and the unused words are discarded.

3.1.2 *Software Oriented Techniques*

These proposals do not require any hardware mechanism to track the behavior of memory references. Instead, this information is derived statically, during compilation, and is passed to the hardware through some ISA feature (e.g. a field in the memory instructions). The hardware uses this information to handle the memory instruction accordingly.

A follow-up work of the same group that proposed the Dual Data Cache [21] shows that a very small full-associative cache can store the data that shows only temporal locality next to the main cache.

Grun et al.[22] propose a software optimization via profiling to best map data in the address space of the application. This can be applied to any cache configuration including Dual Data Cache.

3.1.3 *Survey Papers*

There are a number of papers that survey the main proposals that deal with a cache organization divided in several parts to store different types of memory reference [23] [24] [25].

3.2 Adapted to Other Scenarios

3.2.1 *Embedded Systems*

For embedded systems, most of the works make a special emphasis in energy consumption. At the time when we proposed the Dual Data Cache, mid 90s, energy consumption was not yet a main concern. In our proposal, every memory request has to access both cache modules, then, it has to compute some data and store in a table, and in some cases, has to move or copy data form one subcache to the other. This obviously generates an increase in dynamic energy consumption.

Hsien-hsin et al. [26] propose a three module cache system managed by the type of memory references: stack data go to one module, global data is mapped to another, and the rest go to the main cache, but only one module is accessed for a given memory reference.

Petrov [27] and Kim [28] partition a cache memory in several subcaches and try to use only some of them for power reduction. The former uses static information to decide the partition assigned to each individual load/store instruction. The latter use dynamic information to map memory references to the various cache partitions. This dynamic partitioning can take into account spatial and temporal locality properties among others.

3.2.2 *Multicores*

Cache architectures for multiprocessors have been a hot topic in recent years due to the popularity of multithreaded processors, multicores and network on chips. Some proposals have leveraged the concept of different types of locality to optimize the design.

Sahuquillo et al. [29] study a multiprocessor with a L1 cache organization very similar to the Dual Data Cache, which is composed of two modules, one for temporal locality and another for spatial locality.

Memik et al. [30] investigate the Dual Data Cache in depth and optimize it for a multicore embedded system. They claim that the Dual Data Cache was not optimized for energy consumption, but due to its performance benefits, there is a reduction of the bus activity and the overall energy consumption is reduced.

NUCA caches have been extensively studied for multicore systems. In general, these caches try to move data next to the core for which the data has higher locality.

Kim et al. [31] explain that a D-NUCA is a cache organization that inherently adapts to the data locality. Chishti et al. [32] propose a new NUCA organization that has a flexible placement of blocks to try to keep them near the core that uses them. In both works data with poor locality is placed in farther modules, which has some similarity with our work on selective caching, in which we avoid storing in L1 blocks with poor locality.

3.3 Real implementations

3.3.1 *Samsung*

The CalmRISC [33] uses a "cooperative cache" that resembles the structure of the Dual Data Cache. The TOC (Temporal Cache) is a direct-mapped cache with a block size of 8 bytes and the SOC (Spatial Cache) is a four-way associative cache with a block size of 32 bytes. Both have a capacity of 8Kbytes. They claim that performance increases with respect to a conventional cache while maintaining similar values on energy consumption.

3.3.2 *Intel*

Intel StrongARM SA-1110 [34] uses a design similar to the Dual Data Cache. They use a 'main cache' of 8 Kbytes with a block size of 32 bytes and 32-way associativity and a 'minicache' of 512 bytes with write-back policy, 2-way set-associative and a block size of 32 bytes. The placement is decided by two bits contained in the memory instruction. The C bit indicates to cache or bypass and the B bit decides to store the data in the main cache (Temporal and

Spatial locality) or in the minicache (Spatial locality only). So the placement of the data is decided at compile time. This scheme is similar to a follow up work of our group published in 1997 [21].

4. CONCLUDING REMARKS

This paper has presented a retrospective on our ICS 1995 work on a novel cache architecture with multiple caching strategies to exploit different types of locality. This was the first paper that presented this concept to the best of our knowledge. Afterwards, a large number of papers have appeared which exploit this concept in a different manner and we have reviewed some of them in this retrospective. We have also briefly outlined two implementations in commercial microprocessors that have exploited this idea.

In the era of abundant and transistors that is characterizing our current and future technology, there will be even more opportunities for specialization, and we believe we will see this concept more often applied to all components, including the memory hierarchy.

5. ACKNOWLEDGMENTS

This work is partially supported by the Generalitat of Catalunya under grant 2009SGR-125 and the Spanish Ministry of Economy and Competitiveness under grant TIN 2010-18368.

6. REFERENCES

[1] A. González, C. Aliagas, and M. Valero, "A data cache with multiple caching strategies tuned to different types of locality," in *9th ICS*, 1995, pp. 338–47.

[2] M. Wolfe, "More iteration space tiling," in *3rd ICS*, 1989.

[3] M. D. Lam, E. E. Rothberg, and M. E. Wolf, "The cache performance and optimizations of blocked algorithms," in *ASPLOS-IV*, 1991, pp. 63–74.

[4] S. Carr and K. Kennedy, "Compiler blockability of numerical algorithms," in *6th ICS*, 1992, no. April, pp. 114–24.

[5] S. McFarling, "Cache replacement with dynamic exclusion," *ACM SIGARCH News*, vol. 20, no. 2, pp. 191–200, 1992.

[6] N. P. Jouppi, "Improving direct-mapped cache performance by the addition of a small fully-associative cache and prefetch buffers," *ACM SIGARCH News*, vol. 18, 1990.

[7] A. Seznec, "A case for two-way skewed-associative caches," *ACM SIGARCH News*, vol. 21, no. 2, pp. 169–78, 1993.

[8] A. Agarwal and S. D. Pudar, "Column-associative caches," *ACM SIGARCH News*, vol. 21, no. 2, pp. 179–90, 1993.

[9] J.-L. Baer and T.-F. Chen, "An effective on-chip preloading scheme to reduce data access penalty," *5th ICS*, p. 176, 1991.

[10] J. W. C. Fu, J. H. Patel, and B. L. Janssens, "Stride directed prefetching in scalar processors," *ACM SIGMICRO News*, vol. 23, no. 1–2, pp. 102–10, 1992.

[11] Y. Jégou and O. Temam, "Speculative prefetching," in *7th ICS*, 1993, pp. 57–66.

[12] C. F. Chen, B. Falsafi, and A. Moshovos, "Accurate and Complexity-Effective Spatial Pattern Prediction," in *IEEE 10th HPCA*, 2004, pp. 276–276.

[13] L. John and A. Subramanian, "Design and performance evaluation of a cache assist to implement selective caching," in *ICCD VLSI*, 1997, pp. 510–8.

[14] T. L. Johnson, M. C. Merten, and W. W. Hwu, "Run-time spatial locality detection and optimization," *IEEE/ACM Micro-30*, 1997.

[15] T. Johnson et al., "Run-time cache bypassing," *IEEE Tr. Computers*, vol. 48, no. 12, pp. 1338–54, 1999.

[16] J. A. Rivers et al., "Utilizing reuse information in data cache management," in *12th ICS*, 1998, pp. 449–56.

[17] S. Kumar and C. Wilkerson, "Exploiting spatial locality in data caches using spatial footprints," *ACM SIGARCH News*, vol. 26, no. 3, pp. 357–68, 1998.

[18] R. D. Ju, A. R. Lebeck, and C. Wilkerson, "Locality vs. criticality," *ACM SIGARCH News*, vol. 29, no. 2, 2001.

[19] B. Juurlink, "Unified dual data caches," in *Euromicro DSD*, 2003, pp. 33–40.

[20] M. K. Qureshi, M. A. Suleman, and Y. N. Patt, "Line Distillation: Increasing Cache Capacity by Filtering Unused Words in Cache Lines," *IEEE 13th HPCA*, pp. 250–9, 2007.

[21] F. J. Sanchez, A. Gonzalez, and M. Valero, "Static locality analysis for cache management," in *6th. PACT*, 1997.

[22] P. Grun, N. Dutt, and A. Nicolau, "Access pattern based local memory customization for low power embedded systems," in *DATE*, 2001, pp. 778–84.

[23] J. Sahuquillo and A. Pont, "Splitting the data cache: a survey," *IEEE Concurrency*, vol. 8, no. 3, pp. 30–5, 2000.

[24] J. Sahuquillo, A. Pont, and V. Milutinovic, "The filter data cache: A tour management comparison with related split data cache schemes sensitive to data localities," *HPC*, 2000.

[25] Z. Sustran et al., "A survey of dual data cache systems," in *IEEE ICIT*, 2012, pp. 450–6.

[26] S. L. Hsien-hsin and G. Tyson, "Region-Based Caching: An Energy-Delay Efficient Memory Architecture for Embedded Processors," *Conf. Compilers Archit.*, 2000.

[27] P. Petrov and A. Orailoglu, "Performance and power effectiveness in embedded processors - customizable partitioned caches," *IEEE Tr. CDICS*, vol. 20, no. 11, 2001.

[28] S. Kim et al., "Power-aware partitioned cache architectures," *ISLPED*, pp. 64–7, 2001.

[29] J. Sahuquillo and A. Pont, "The split data cache in multiprocessor systems: an initial hit ratio analysis," in *7th Euromicro PDP*, 1999, pp. 27–34.

[30] G. Memik and W. H. Mangione-Smith, "Increasing power efficiency of multi-core network processors through data filtering," *CASES*, p. 108, 2002.

[31] C. Kim, D. Burger, and S. W. Keckler, "An adaptive, non-uniform cache structure for wire-delay dominated on-chip caches," *ACM SIGARCH News*, vol. 30, no. 5, p. 211, 2002.

[32] Z. Chishti, M. D. Powell, and T. N. Vijaykumar, "Distance associativity for high-performance energy-efficient non-uniform cache architectures," *Digital Avionics Sys-22*, 2003.

[33] K. Lee et al., "The cache memory system for CalmRISC32," in *2nd IEEE AP-ASICs*, 2000, pp. 323–6.

[34] Intel, "Intel StrongARM SA-1110 Microprocessor. Developer's Manual," no. June, 2000.

Author Retrospective for

Optimum Modulo Schedules for Minimum Register Requirements

Alexandre E. Eichenberger
IBM T.J. Watson Research Center
PO Box 218
Yorktown Heights, NY 10514
+1 914 945 1812
alexe@us.ibm.com

Edward S. Davidson
1100 Chestnut Rd.
Ann Arbor, MI 48104
+1 734 973-0751
davidson@umich.edu

Santosh G. Abraham
Advanced Processor Laboratory
Samsung Research America
1732 N. 1st Street
San Jose, CA 95112
+1 408 605-5813
sg.abraham@samsung.com

Original paper: http://dx.doi.org/10.1145/224538.224542

1. Origins

Modulo Scheduling is an approach to scheduling loops where successive iterations of a given loop are initiated at a constant rate using the same instruction schedule for each iteration. This scheduling approach was inspired by work on designing hardware pipelines that maximizes the throughput of a single function pipeline. In this earlier work, the resource pattern of the single pipeline was optimized; namely, when given enough buffers, stages could be delayed, so as to achieve an optimal throughput[1]. This work formalized the resource optimization problem using reservation tables, which had one row per resource and one column per time unit modulo the period of the initiation sequence [1].

As new machines with programmable microcode or assembly operations were coming to market, programmers started to look for efficient approaches to schedule compute-intensive loops. The earliest reports of using techniques akin to the design of throughput-optimized hardware pipelines were reported in the early 80s [2, 3]. Work by Rau and Glaeser [3] described techniques for handling dependences across consecutive loop iterations.

Next came robust modulo-scheduling algorithms, in particular the design of iterative modulo-schedulers [4, 5]. In this work, operations that could not be successfully scheduled in a given cycle could eject conflicting operations that were already scheduled. Ejected operations would then be rescheduled in different time slots, so as to iteratively derive a better schedule. When combined with suitable priority heuristics, such iterative algorithms achieved optimal throughput, as determined by a lower bound, in a large fraction of loops.

A side effect of achieving increasingly high throughput is an increased register pressure, mainly due to the increased instruction-level parallelism. Higher register pressure, in turn, is detrimental to performance when a schedule exceeds the maximum number of registers of the targeted machine, as spill code often adds critical delay and memory operations to an already tightly scheduled loop. As a result, the demand for research on register-sensitive modulo scheduling algorithms became high.

As I transitioned to my Ph.D., Davidson encouraged me to read theses of his former students. Interestingly, Mangione-Smith had included a hint on how one might generalize his results on lowering register-requirements by moving operations between stages of a given modulo schedule for a specific class of dependence graphs [6]. His hint led me to my first publication on finding an optimal stage schedule for arbitrary dependence graphs. In stage scheduling, operations can be moved by multiples of *II* cycles, where *II* is the initiation interval between consecutive loop iterations. While this problem is clearly simpler than the general modulo-scheduling problem, it worked surprisingly well on schedules generated by register-insensitive modulo schedulers.

The next step was to search for optimal modulo schedules with minimum register requirements without being bound to an existing modulo schedule. Work in that area had recently minimized buffer requirements using an integer linear programming formulation [7], and later extended for arbitrary resource usages [8]. That work was minimizing buffers, akin to hardware buffers in the original hardware pipeline work. However, most computers stage values in registers, which are more flexible than buffers as registers can be used to store different values of different variables on a cycle by cycle basis. In retrospect, the main contribution of our ICS paper was to formulate an integer programming model that precisely models the register usages of a modulo schedule. A later extension [9] refined the model to reduce time to solution by almost a factor of ten.

2. Impact

The main result of this paper is the discovery that the modulo-scheduling heuristics of the time were excellent at finding maximum throughput schedules; however, because of their focus on loop performance, the register pressure exhibited by their schedules was far from optimal. Since then heuristics for register-sensitive modulo schedulers [4, 10] have been proposed and are widely used in production compilers (e.g. GCC, LLVM, ...).

While it is generally accepted that integer linear-programming based solutions may be too time-consuming for use within production compilers, I still believe that they can play an important role for tuning heuristics, and for rapidly predicting performance of loop kernels targeting future processing elements with distinct resource and dependence constraints. Unfortunately,

ICS 25th Anniversary Volume, 2014
ACM 978-1-4503-2840-1/14/06.
http://dx.doi.org/10.1145/2591635.2591653

integer-programming solvers have not been widely used in this context. I believe it is not primarily due to their computational complexity, as better formulations [9], smarter solvers, and faster computers have greatly decreased time to solution. Rather, it is mainly due to the lack of easy-to-use optimal scheduling solver packages that can be deployed to engineers not familiar with integer linear-programming solvers. With the advent of more publicly available solvers, one might hope that this situation will change.

3. REFERENCES

[1] J. H. Patel and E. S. Davidson. 1976. Improving the throughput of a pipeline by insertion of delays. In *Proceedings of the 3rd Annual Symposium on Computer Architecture* (ISCA), 159-164.

[2] A. E. Charlesworth. 1981. An Approach to Scientific Array Processing: The Architectural Design of the AP-120B/FPS-164 Family. In *Computer* 14(9), 18-27.

[3] B. R. Rau and C. D. Glaeser. 1981. Some scheduling techniques and an easily schedulable horizontal architecture for high performance scientific computing. In *Proceedings of the Fourteenth Annual Workshop on Microprogramming*, 183-198.

[4] R. A. Huff. 1993. Lifetime-sensitive modulo scheduling. In *Proceedings of the Conference on Programming Language Design and Implementation (PLDI)*, 258-267.

[5] B. R. Rau. 1994. Iterative modulo scheduling: an algorithm for software pipelining loops. In *Proceedings of the 27th Annual International Symposium on Microarchitecture (MICRO)*, 63-74.

[6] W. H. Mangione-Smith, S. G. Abraham, and E. S. Davidson. 1992. Register requirements of pipelined processors. In *Proceedings of the 6th International Conference on Supercomputing (ICS)*, 260-271.

[7] R. Govindrajan, E. R. Altman and G. R. Gao. 1994. Minimizing register requirements under resource-constrained rate-optimal software pipelining. In *Proceedings of the 27th Annual International Symposium on Microarchitecture (MICRO)*, 85-94.

[8] E. R. Altman, R. Govindrajan and G. R. Gao. 1995. Scheduling and mapping: software pipelining in the presence of hazards. In *Proceedings of the Conference on Programming Language Design and Implementation (PLDI)*, 139-150.

[9] A. E. Eichenberger and E. S. Davidson. 1997. Efficient formulation for optimal modulo schedulers. In *Proceedings of the Conference on Programming Language Design and Implementation (PLDI)*, 194-205.

[10] J. Llosa, A. Gonzalez, E. Ayguade, M. Valero. 1996. Swing Modulo Scheduling: A Lifetime-Sensitive Approach. In *Proceedings of the Conference on Parallel Architectures and Compilation Techniques (PACT)*, 80-86.

Author Retrospective for Counting Solutions to Linear and Nonlinear Constraints Through Ehrhart Polynomials: Applications to analyze and transform Scientific Programs

Philippe Clauss
INRIA, ICube Lab., CNRS
University of Strasbourg, France
clauss@unistra.fr

ABSTRACT

Ehrhart polynomials are amazing mathematical objects that I discovered in the early 90's and that have many applications in computer science. This retrospective relates my personal and scientific experience regarding this research work, my meeting with the mathematician Eugène Ehrhart, and addresses some extensions and perspectives of further developments.

Original paper: http://dx.doi.org/10.1145/237578.237617

Categories and Subject Descriptors

D.3.4 [**Programming Languages**]: Processors

Keywords

Ehrhart polynomials; program analysis and optimization; nested loops; polyhedral model; polyhedron; integer points

1. INTRODUCTION

In addition to its scientific significance, the writing of this paper is linked to a personal experience and to the life and oeuvre of the french mathematician Eugène Ehrhart. I had the incommensurable chance of meeting him in the very last years of his life, and this encountering marked me definitely.

A few years after defending my PhD thesis, I was in a step of my career when I was searching for a new impulse. Many readers probably understand what is evoked here. Personally, I was always impressed by mathematics and the intelligence and power of its theorems. Even if computer scientists are often considered as "weak mathematicians", I was always convinced that most answers to scientific issues can be found in mathematics.

After defending my PhD thesis in 1990 and having accomplished my french military service, I targeted a scientific and theoretical goal related to my former PhD work: *what is the exact number of integer points contained in a convex polyhedron, when this polyhedron depends linearly on integer parameters.* While "mathematically speaking", this issue seems straightforward, many computer scientists at that time, including me, proposed solutions that were unsatisfactory. Indeed, this well-defined problem was crucial in computer science, generally because counting is often a way to analyze programs, and more particularly because (nested) loops do play a forefront role in high performance computing. Nested loops were, and are still, an important target in code optimization and parallelization. From the seminal books of Uptal Banerjee [1] and Michael J. Wolfe [15], through the papers of Paul Feautrier and Christian Lengauer [10] introducing the polyhedral model, nested loops are still the topic of many current research papers, some of which referencing the article in question. Later, I noticed that this question was also crucial in many other scientific fields, such as economy, crystallography, probability, etc. Shortly after this publication at ICS, I was contacted by several researchers of these fields who published papers where Ehrhart polynomials are used.

In this retrospective, I will first relate the starting of this research work, my meeting with Eugène Ehrhart and some remarkable points of his career. Then, I will explain the scientific context of this research which is related to the polyhedral model. Some important applications are addressed in Section 4 while extensions and perspectives are addressed in Section 5. Finally, I will conclude in Section 6.

2. EUGÈNE EHRHART (1906-2000)

In 1991, I was recruited as an assistant professor in a business school where students did not have much interest in pure computer science and mathematics, and teaching them word-processor tools was pretty straightforward. Thus, this professional context provided me some time to meditate. This meditation was taking place in the mathematics library of the University of Strasbourg, which is one of the best of this kind in the world, where one can find very old manuscripts of savants such as Euler or Jacobi, some of which are the originals written by these mathematicians themselves!

In 1995, after several weeks spent in the library reading books, articles, going from references to references, I took in my hands a thin manuscript in a really bad shape, writ-

ICS 25th Anniversary Volume. 2014
ACM 978-1-4503-2840-1/14/06.
http://dx.doi.org/10.1145/2591635.2591654.

ten using a typewriter, whose cover was briefly mentioning: "Eugène Ehrhart, Strasbourg". What a revelation when I opened it: polyhedra, counting, polynomials, integer arithmetic, ... a miracle! The solution was there, proposed by someone from my own city in France, and although it solved such a fundamental problem, it looked so underrated and neglected.

I immediately asked the librarian (who was a woman about to complete her professional career and retire): *Do you know someone named Eugène Ehrhart?*. Librarian: *Yes of course! He is still coming regularly at the library.* Me: *What do you mean by "still coming"?*. Librarian: *He is a very old man now, but still very alert!* Me: *If I entrust you a letter, could you forward it to him, please?* The next day, at precisely 8 AM, I received a prominent phone call.

Eugène Ehrhart was an amazing person whose passion for science and mathematics had no limits. During his professional career, he was professor in high-schools (french "lycée"), but always wanted to solve small and often entertaining research problems of mathematics. But in the mid-50's, he started to publish very important results on polygons and integer arithmetic that were mostly issued in reports of the french academy of sciences ("Compte-rendus de l'académie des sciences") [6]. At the end of the 50's, he showed the first version of his *Ehrhart polynomials* which are now part of the universal mathematics culture, and won his first award from the french academy, and later, his second award in 1974. In 1963, he obtained a one-year sabbatical from the french CNRS institute to accomplish his PhD thesis that he defended in 1966, when he was 60 years old! He published a book presenting most of his results related to polyhedra and polynomials in 1977 [7].

Eugène Ehrhart was 89 years old when I met him for the first time at the mathematics library. Although he was still in a very good shape, he was unable to remember all the details of his research work. He still remembered the essential aspects, but I had to understand his reasoning mostly by myself. Next, I extended his solution to an arbitrary number of integer parameters, built an algorithm to compute his wonderful polynomials, and showed many useful applications of his outstanding theory.

At that time, Eugène Ehrhart was concerned by "roulettes of ellipses". His problem was to determine the shape of the curve outlined by a point which is on the circumference of a rolling ellipse. He explained me that things are just like in the desert, with camels (two humps) and dromedaries (one hump). He published his very last paper on this topic in 1995 in the American Mathematical Monthly journal [8].

My meeting with this man has definitely marked my own professional and personal life, Eugène Ehrhart being an example of unconditional and deep devotion to science and its beauty. He disappeared from this world a few days after the defense of my "Habilitation à diriger les recherches" degree. I dedicate him this retrospective and the honour of re-publishing this article in the ICS 25th anniversary volume.

3. THE POLYHEDRAL MODEL

In the field of automatic parallelization and compilation, many research projects focused on loop nests in which scientific codes spend most of the execution time. For loop nests consisting of for-loops whose unique iterators have bounds that are linear functions of the enclosing loop iterators, and where the body statements have as operands only scalar variables or array elements referenced through linear functions of the iterators, Paul Feautrier and Christian Lengauer proposed an advanced mathematical framework called *the polyhedral model* (or *polytope model*, or *polyhedron model*) [10]. In this model, loop nests' iteration domains are represented as polyhedra whose inner integer points are indexed as tuples of iterators values. Thus, analysis and transformation of loop codes translate to a geometrical and arithmetical problem. While general-purpose codes are more difficult to handle, programs amenable to the polyhedral model provide opportunities for very accurate and highly-efficient automatic code optimizations. It is still a research topic generating considerable activity. For instance, I am involved in some recent developments that propose to dynamically optimize loop nests which seem not to be in compliance with the polyhedral model, but which exhibit a "runtime polyhedral behavior" [11].

Thus, it may seem clear that modeling loop nests as polyhedra is equivalent to translating quantitative code analysis to arithmetic analysis of polyhedra. The number of iterations of a loop nest, the number of accessed array elements for memory consumption evaluation, the number of parallel iterations, or the number of cache misses, are typical examples of quantities that might be relevant for automatic optimization and parallelization methods and that can be expressed as Ehrhart polynomials.

Another important point is that scientific loop nests often depend on various size parameters, typically the size of the matrices which are handled. More generally, parametric approaches open the scope to the creation of methods in which determining the value of some parameter translates to optimizing an objective polynomial function. Other possibilities are related to adaptive approaches depending on dynamic parameters that may be unknown before the target loop nest's execution.

All these facts explain the success of this paper which offers an exact and direct solution that is helping many research developments.

4. APPLICATIONS TO ANALYZE AND TRANSFORM...

One interesting application, which is also fundamental in some sense, is the computation of a *ranking polynomial*. A loop nest which is in compliance with the polyhedral model scans iterations in the lexicographic order of the loop iterators. For some purposes, it might be interesting to know the one-dimensional rank of any iteration defined by the tuple of its iterator values. For example, nested loops may be transformed into one unique loop in this manner. It might also be interesting to determine at what iteration rank a given array element is accessed. It then allows to define a new data layout for array elements that are referenced by a loop nest by considering memory as a one-dimensional array, so as to optimize their spatial locality. Thanks to ranking Ehrhart polynomials, array elements may be re-indexed in memory in the same order as they are accessed by the loop nest [4].

Many other applications of Ehrhart polynomials may be found in the literature. Probably one of the most recent and noticeable ones is addressing a currently important topic which is energy saving for computers by software optimization employing data prefetching [12]. Ehrhart polynomials are adopted to guard the amount of prefetching such that the optimization is efficient.

5. EXTENSIONS AND PERSPECTIVES

This 1996 ICS publication resulted in the following months in a software developed by Doran K. Wilde and Vincent Loechner implementing the algorithm which is described in the paper. It was the very first known tool computing Ehrhart polynomials from the definition of a parametrized polyhedron, and was included in the library PolyLib [13]. However, since this algorithm is based on an initial counting of the integer points for small values of the parameters, it is restricted to medium to large domains to be able to count a sufficient number of initial values. In 2007, a more robust method for calculating Ehrhart polynomials [14] was proposed and implemented in the Barvinok library. It extends an existing method, based on Barvinok's decomposition [2].

In 2004, I proposed, together with my former PhD student Irina Tchoupaeva, the use of the Bernstein expansion for symbolic evaluation of the minimum and maximum values of an Ehrhart polynomial over a domain of parameters values, and showed some applications to program analysis [5]. Later, in 2009, this approach was improved to consider polynomials defined over a parametrized polytope. The related paper also shows applications on estimating the memory requirements of programs [3].

Regarding perspectives of further related developments, the inversion of ranking Ehrhart polynomials may provide interesting applications related to code optimization. Since a ranking polynomial is defining a bijection between a polyhedral iteration domain and the interval of integers ranging from one to the total number of integer points of the domain, it may be inverted. This would allow to compute any loop nest using any other loop nest with the same iteration count. A concrete application is, for example, the applicability of the OpenMP `collapse` directive clause to loop nests in which loop bounds are linear functions of the enclosing loop iterators. Some preliminary results are presented in [9].

6. CONCLUSION

My research work on Ehrhart polynomials is accompanied by a wonderful personal and scientific experience. I had the chance of knowing Eugène Ehrhart and, thanks to him, of providing to computer science the solution to many important issues. But the story is far from being finished. I am convinced that many additional researchers in the future will also discover these amazing mathematical objects and use them in their developments. Personally, I am still enthusiastic about imagining some further extensions and applications. Stay in tune with my future publications and those of my students!

7. ACKNOWLEDGMENTS

I would like to thank the organizers of the ICS conference, and specifically the people who had the initiative of this 25th anniversary volume, and who gave me the occasion to relate this wonderful experience.

I would also like to give special thanks to my former PhD student Alexandra Jimborean for her invaluable assistance in preparing this retrospective.

8. REFERENCES

[1] Utpal K. Banerjee. *Loop Transformations for Restructuring Compilers: The Foundations*. Kluwer Academic Publishers, Norwell, MA, USA, 1993.

[2] A.I. Barvinok and J Pommersheim. An algorithmic theory of lattice points in polyhedra. *New Perspectives in Algebraic Combinatorics*, 38:91–147, 1999.

[3] Philippe Clauss, Federico Javier Fernández, Diego Garbervetsky, and Sven Verdoolaege. Symbolic polynomial maximization over convex sets and its application to memory requirement estimation. *IEEE Tr. Very Large Scale Integr. Syst.*, 17:983–996, 2009.

[4] Philippe Clauss and Benoît Meister. Automatic memory layout transformations to optimize spatial locality in parameterized loop nests. *ACM SIGARCH Comp. Arch. News*, 28(1):11–19, March 2000.

[5] Philippe Clauss and Irina Tchoupaeva. A symbolic approach to Bernstein expansion for program analysis and optimization. In Evelyn Duesterwald, editor, *13th International Conference on Compiler Construction, CC 2004*, volume 2985 of *LNCS*, pages 120–133. Springer, April 2004.

[6] Eugène Ehrhart. Propriétés arithmo-géométriques des polygones. *Compte-rendus de l'académie des sciences*, 241:686–689, 1955.

[7] Eugène Ehrhart. *Polynômes arithmétiques et Méthode des Polyèdres en Combinatoire*. Birkhäuser Verlag, Basel und Stuttgart, 1977.

[8] Eugène Ehrhart. On roulettes of ellipses. *The American Mathematical Monthly*, 1995.

[9] Imen Fassi, Philippe Clauss, Matthieu Kuhn, and Yosr Slama. Multifor for Multicore. In Louis-Noël Pouchet Armin Grösslinger, editor, *IMPACT 2013, Third International Workshop on Polyhedral Compilation Techniques*, Berlin, Germany, January 2013. Epubli.

[10] Paul Feautrier and Christian Lengauer. Polyhedron model. In David Padua, editor, *Encyclopedia of Parallel Computing*, pages 1581–1592. Springer US, 2011.

[11] Alexandra Jimborean, Philippe Clauss, Jean-François Dollinger, Vincent Loechner, and Juan Manuel Martinez Caamaño. Dynamic and speculative polyhedral parallelization using compiler-generated skeletons. *Int. J. of Parallel Programming*, 2013.

[12] Alexandra Jimborean, Konstantinos Koukos, Vasileios Spiliopoulos, David Black-Schaffer, and Stefanos Kaxiras. Fix the code. don't tweak the hardware: A new compiler approach to voltage-frequency scaling. In *Proc. of IEEE/ACM Int. Symp. on Code Generation and Optimization*, CGO '14, pages 262–272, 2014.

[13] The PolyLib Polyhedral Library. http://icps.u-strasbg.fr/PolyLib.

[14] Sven Verdoolaege, Rachid Seghir, Kristof Beyls, Vincent Loechner, and Maurice Bruynooghe. Counting Integer Points in Parametric Polytopes using Barvinok's Rational Functions. *Algorithmica*, 48(1):37–66, February 2007.

[15] Michael Joseph Wolfe. *High Performance Compilers for Parallel Computing*. Addison-Wesley Longman Publishing Co., Inc., Boston, MA, USA, 1995.

Author Retrospective

Improving Data Cache Performance by Pre-executing Instructions Under a Cache Miss

Trevor Mudge
University of Michigan
Ann Arbor, MI
tnm@eecs.umich.edu

ABSTRACT

The paper introduces and evaluates a technique, referred to as runahead, that prefetches instructions and data into the L1 caches on cache misses. The results of the experiments reported in the paper show that the CPI of a simple in-order pipeline could be reduced by 30%. The principle advantage of runahead over many other prefetching strategies, is twofold: 1) it prefetches both instructions and date; and 2) it is able to create non-sequential data prefetches.

Original Paper: http://dx.doi.org/10.1145/263580.263597

Categories and Subject Descriptors

C.0 [**Computer Systems Organization**]: General; C.1.1 [**Computer Systems Organization**]: Processor Architectures

Keywords

runahead; speculation; prefetching

1. INTRODUCTION

The work presented in the paper arose from a conversation that Jim Dundas and I had while he was a graduate student at The Univerisity of Michigan in the mid-1990's. We were brainstorming ideas that would improve the performance of a simple in-order pipeline with a minimum of extra logic. The driving factor was that we had been designing and building prototype Gallium Arsenide processors, which suffered from reduced device density compared to silicon [8, 1]. This led us to consider a number of unorthodox architectural ideas, including the topic of this paper: runahead pre-processing. The basic idea behind runahead is to allow a simple, yet very fast, processor pipeline to prefetch and pre-process instructions during cache miss cycles, instead of stalling. The pre-processed instructions are used to generate highly accurate data prefetches. Runahead allowed us to achieve a form of aggressive speculation with a simple in-order pipeline. Important from our point of view, the principal hardware cost is modest, because we make use of the execution pipeline when it would otherwise be idle. The only additional cost is a means of checkpointing the sequential state of the register file and memory hierarchy while instructions are pre-processed. This can be achieved with just a backup register for every register in the register file (simpler than a duplicate register file), because we discard all results that are computed during runahead episodes after the cache miss has been serviced.

ICS 25th Anniversary Volume. 2014
ACM 978-1-4503-2840-1/14/06.
http://dx.doi.org/10.1145/2591635.2591655.

2. BACKGROUND

In the early 1990's our group had been experimenting with Gallium Arsenide (GaAs) as an alternative to silicon. GaAs had the promise of improved performance through increased clock speed because it has a much higher electron mobility than silicon. It also had the promise of lower power—our prototypes ran with a supply voltages of 1-2V when the prevailing silicon supply voltages were 5V (or later in the decade, 3.3V). The drawback with GaAs was that the densities were an order of magnitude less than silicon. This still allowed us to build single chip microprocessors, and, as noted above, we built several MIPS-like cores in the mid-1990's, but those cores had to be relatively simple. This limited the range of architectural alternatives that we could explore to take advantage of this faster technology.

We experimented with a number of ideas that didn't affect gate count too much. We explored much deeper pipelines [7] than used at that time, as well as pipelined cache organizations [6]. The runahead idea also arose from exploring ways to improve performance without substantially increasing gate count. We viewed it as an inexpensive way to retrieve some of the architectural benefits that we had to give up because of logic density limitations. Our early experiments were reported in [3]. Subsequently Jim wrote his Ph.D. [4] thesis on the subject and explored many of the alternatives to the straightforward approach presented in the paper. In particular, he evaluated the idea of removing last level caches and just relying on runahead to maintain performance. The results were mixed and highly dependent on L1 size and benchmarks. He also showed that runahead works well for streaming benchmarks, as might be expected. In the case of STREAM, CPI was reduced by almost 80%. He further examined simpler checkpointing schemes and proposed the idea of a co-processor to perform runahead.

Subsequent work on runahead took a different turn. Rather than viewing it as an inexpensive way to obtain architecture benefits in density constrained designs, runahead was examined in the context of more complex out-or-order machines. Several efforts took this direction. Examples are the work of Mutlu and Patt and their collaborators [5], and the work of Chaudhry and his colleagues at Sun on the ROCK processor [2]. The Sun design used threads to lookahead, coining the term "scout" thread, to describe their lookahead mechanism. The related work section in this paper contains a good overview of related work, if the reader wants to expire more recent developments.

3. REFERENCES

[1] R. Brown, T. Basso, P. Parakh, S. Gold, C. Gauthier, R. Lomax, and T. Mudge. Complementary GaAs technology for a ghz microprocessor. In *Gallium Arsenide Integrated Circuit (GaAs IC) Symposium, 1996. Technical Digest 1996., 18th Annual*, pages 313–316, Nov 1996.

[2] S. Chaudhry, R. Cypher, M. Ekman, M. Karlsson, A. Landin, S. Yip, H. Zeffer, and M. Tremblay. Simultaneous speculative threading: A novel pipeline architecture implemented in Sun's ROCK processor. In *Proceedings of the 36th Annual International Symposium on Computer Architecture*, ISCA '09, pages 484–495, New York, NY, USA, 2009. ACM.

[3] J. Dundas and T. Mudge. Using stall cycles to improve microprocessor performance. Technical Report CSE-TR-301-96, Department of Electrical Engineering and Computer Science, The University of Michigan, Ann Arbor, Michigan, September 1996.

[4] J. D. Dundas. *Using Stall Cycles to Improve Microprocessor Performance.* PhD thesis, The University of Michigan, Ann Arbor, Michigan, 1998.

[5] O. Mutlu, J. Stark, C. Wilkerson, and Y. Patt. Runahead execution: an alternative to very large instruction windows for out-of-order processors. In *High-Performance Computer Architecture, 2003. HPCA-9 2003. Proceedings. The Ninth International Symposium on*, pages 129–140, Feb 2003.

[6] K. Olukotun, T. Mudge, and R. Brown. Performance optimization of pipelined primary cache. In *Proceedings of the 19th Annual International Symposium on Computer Architecture*, ISCA '92, pages 181–190, New York, NY, USA, 1992. ACM.

[7] M. Upton, T. Huff, T. Mudge, and R. Brown. Resource allocation in a high clock rate microprocessor. In *Proceedings of the Sixth International Conference on Architectural Support for Programming Languages and Operating Systems*, ASPLOS VI, pages 98–109, New York, NY, USA, 1994. ACM.

[8] M. Upton, T. Huff, P. Sherhart, P. Barker, R. McVay, T. Stanley, R. Brown, R. Lomax, T. Mudge, and K. Sakallah. A 160 000 transistor GaAs microprocessor. In *Solid-State Circuits Conference, 1993. Digest of Technical Papers. 40th ISSCC., 1993 IEEE International*, pages 92–93, Feb 1993.

Author Retrospective for
Optimizing Matrix Multiply using PHiPAC: a Portable High-Performance ANSI C Coding Methodology

Jeff Bilmes
EE Department
University of Washington, Seattle
bilmes@ee.washington.edu

Krste Asanović
EECS Department
University of California, Berkeley
krste@eecs.berkeley.edu

Chee-Whye Chin
Department of Mathematics
National University of Singapore
cheewhye@math.nus.edu.sg

Jim Demmel
EECS Department
University of California, Berkeley
demmel@cs.berkeley.edu

Original paper: http://dx.doi.org/10.1145/263580.263662

1. INTRODUCTION

PHiPAC was an early attempt to improve software performance by searching in a large design space of possible implementations to find the best one. At the time, in the early 1990s, the most efficient numerical linear algebra libraries were carefully hand tuned for specific microarchitectures and compilers, and were often written in assembly language. This allowed very precise tuning of an algorithm to the specifics of a current platform, and provided great opportunity for high efficiency. The prevailing thought at the time was that such an approach was necessary to produce near-peak performance. On the other hand, this approach was brittle, and required great human effort to try each code variant, and so only a tiny subset of the possible code design points could be explored. Worse, given the combined complexities of the compiler and microarchitecture, it was difficult to predict which code variants would be worth the implementation effort.

PHiPAC circumvented this effort by using code generators that could easily generate a vast assortment of very different points within a design space, and even across very different design spaces altogether. By following a set of carefully crafted coding guidelines, the generated code was reasonably efficient for any point in the design space. To search the design space, PHiPAC took a rather naive but effective approach. Due to the human-designed and deterministic nature of computing systems, one might reasonably think that smart modeling of the microprocessor and compiler would be sufficient to predict, without performing any timing, the optimal point for a given algorithm. But the combination of an optimizing compiler and a dynamically scheduled microarchitecture with multiple levels of cache and prefetching results in a very complex, highly non-linear system. Small changes in the code can cause large changes in performance, thwarting "smart" search algorithms that attempt to build models of the performance surface. PHiPAC instead used massive, diverse, offline, and only loosely informed grid or randomized search, where each point was evaluated by empirically measuring the code running on the machine, which succeeded due to its indifference to the shape of the performance surface.

Of course, a clever human must first create the set of possible design spaces in the first place, as well as efficient search, timing, and code-generation methods, and update everything as technologies change. This is as it should be, with humans operating at higher levels of abstraction where creativity can have broader payoffs.

In retrospect, the idea of using a computer instead of a human to search a combinatorially large design space seems obvious. Techniques analogous to autotuning were of course used previously by many researchers in software and hardware, for example, design-space exploration in CAD. Intelligent search had also already become an integral part of many of the algorithms used to solve problems in artificial intelligence [10]. At the time, however, PHiPAC was received with some skepticism. As we explain below, PHiPAC was able to quickly achieve performance that was on par with some of the best vendor-supplied numerical libraries available at the time. Therefore, the tides quickly turned, and autotuning is now widely used in many fields [5].

2. HISTORY

The PHiPAC project grew out of work in the early 1990s within the Realization Group at the International Computer Science Institute (ICSI), who were using large artificial neural networks (ANN) for speech recognition. The training algorithms for these ANNs were very computationally intensive, but could be formulated using a few dense linear algebra kernels. The ICSI group had built custom DSP multiprocessors (the RAP machine [9]) to accelerate these algorithms, and was building a custom chip, the T0 vector microprocessor [13], to provide higher performance at lower cost.

ICS 25th Anniversary Volume. 2014
ACM 978-1-4503-2840-1/14/06.
http://dx.doi.org/10.1145/2591635.2591656 .

In addition to the custom computing machines, the speech researchers at ICSI regularly used their network of desktop SPARC workstations to run ANN training jobs, with a locally customized version of pmake used to distribute jobs among all the idle machines. Although all the workstations were binary compatible, we noted that six different SPARC microarchitectures were in use around the institute with widely varying floating-point performance. This was also a period of rapid development in RISC workstation architectures, and we wanted to be able to quickly and effectively exploit any new machines as they became available. Although the BLAS library interface was well-established by this time, high-performance library implementations were only available for a few machines and often came at significant additional cost. Freely available portable matrix-vector libraries contained naïve code with low performance. In addition, we wanted to retain a compatible interface to the T0 vector microprocessor, and so we defined our own simple floating-point vector library "fltvec".

The ANN training codes used primarily matrix-vector operations (BLAS2) at this time, and we began handwriting some optimized C matrix-vector routines for fltvec in early 1994. During this process, we figured out most of the portable high-performance C coding rules that eventually appeared in Section 2 of the paper [2], as an explicit goal of the library was to attain good performance across the range of workstations in use at ICSI. The name "PHiPAC" ("fee-pack", following the Greek pronunciation of ϕ) was actually initially coined to refer just to this coding style, though we eventually used it to cover the entire autotuning process.

Later in 1994, the speech group was seeking greater performance and wanted to use faster matrix-matrix operations (BLAS3) on both the workstations and the T0 accelerator. By December 1994, we had completed an initial matrix-multiply routine in C that was parameterized using a very large fixed set of preprocessor macros, and began tuning and evaluating its performance on various machines.

In the spring of 1995, we taught the CS267 "Applications of Parallel Computers" class at Berkeley. In this class, students entered a matrix-multiply contest and had to compare their results with the current version of our matrix-multiply code. We continued to add optimizations and code variants to the matrix-multiply code, but found that the preprocessor macro approach didn't scale due to the combinatorial explosion when combining different options. We decided to change our approach and instead write a program to generate the code variant directly, including only the specific macros that were needed for the given set of blocking parameters. The first version of this new matrix-multiply code generator, which would eventually form the core of the PHiPAC release, was completed around the end of April 1995.

Using the new code generator, we ran timings on many more machines including an SGI MIPS R4000-based Indigo and an IBM RS6000. The IBM RS6000 came with the ESSL BLAS libraries, which were extensively manually tuned and well regarded, and we were pleasantly surprised when we found we could quickly achieve similar performance using our generated code. At this time, we were still manually changing parameters to explore the design space, but realized that it should be possible to automate the search.

In the summer of 1995, Dominic Lam, an undergraduate, joined the project and began work on Perl scripts to automatically search (i.e., generate code and then time instances within) the design space of the generator. We used simple heuristics to limit the design space the autotuner would explore, but within the feasible set we performed a simple exhaustive grid search that could take days to complete. To help us more quickly get a sense of the tuning space, we added a random search strategy, and were surprised at how often this would quickly find a good point, if not the best point, in the space. The summer was spent refining the search strategy, which was complicated by the need to tune for each level of the memory hierarchy, from innermost (register blocking) to outermost (level 2 cache blocking).

Each new machine we tried would usually require some additional optimization or improvements in search strategy to get better performance, though the current version would usually give reasonable performance when first run on a new machine. As an example, in November 1995, Greg Henry started using the PHiPAC generator on the newly introduced Intel Pentium Pro machines, which represented the first x86 machines with performance competitive to the RISC workstations. When run on the Pentium Pro, PHiPAC automatically selected a very different register blocking than for the register-rich RISC workstation floating-point units. Although the initial PHiPAC-generated code was reasonably fast (around 60% of peak), hand-tuned assembly code was running significantly faster (>80% of peak). PHiPAC relies on a optimizing compiler to take care of low-level scheduling, and at the time, the code quality of the available x86 compilers was not as high as that from the RISC workstation vendors. Later modifications to PHiPAC, and better x86 compilers, led to much improved performance on x86 platforms in our later release.

We released the first PHiPAC code in December 1995, and started to receive growing interest in the code and the technique. We also experienced a lot of skepticism from the compiler community, who thought compilers could generate good code for matrix multiply, and library authors, who thought only human-tuned code could attain near-peak performance. Our experiences were that even the most highly regarded commercial compilers failed dismally on matrix multiply code, and that PHiPAC often produced code that matched or beat vendor-supplied hand-tuned libraries. Further, for many machines, high-performance libraries weren't available or were prohibitively expensive to license.

We continued to improve the search strategy and the code generation. The search strategy was made more intelligent to focus on just the runs needed to tune at each level of the memory hierarchy, while the code generator was similarly improved to generate code specialized for each level of the memory hierarchy, the lowest level including special features like explicit software pipelining [3]. Later in 1996, we prepared a submission to the Supercomputing conference, which was rejected partly because a reviewer believed the ESSL numbers against which we were comparing were from the FORTRAN compiler!

We reworked the paper and submitted it to ICS-1997, where thankfully it was accepted [2]. As we worked on the camera-ready version of the paper, we had a particularly satisfying visit to SGI where Ed Rothberg had kindly made available machines containing MIPS R8000 and R10000 processors. Within a single afternoon, we had the autotuner producing matrix-multiply routines that were competitive with the vendor BLAS libraries for these two very different microarchitectures. Given that we had not previously worked with these machines or their compilers, this was strong evidence that the autotuning approach could quickly provide high-performance code for new architectures.

Returning to the original impetus for the project, we used PHiPAC-generated code to improve neural network training, resulting in significant speedups [4]. Due to their excellent performance in many applications such as speech and computer vision, the many layered "deep" variants [8] of neural networks have recently been experiencing a resurgence of interest, making autotuned implementations [4] perhaps even more relevant today.

We released the second and final version of PHiPAC in spring 1998 [3]. By this time, several other efforts had sprung up to produce autotuners, most notably the ATLAS project [1], which was directly inspired by PHiPAC. Independently, but a little later than PHiPAC, a group at MIT started the FFTW effort to produce autotuned FFTs [7].

3. AUTOTUNING TODAY

The field of autotuning, or automated design-space exploration, has grown in many directions over the years. This short retrospective does not permit us to survey the entire field, or even just the hundreds of papers that have cited our early work on PHiPAC. But we can summarize their common motivation: the design space of different ways to implement an algorithm on a particular piece of hardware is so large, and the impact of even small implementation changes on the running time is so difficult to predict, that it is much more productive to automate the process of searching the design space and to use empirical timing results. This still leaves the programmer the challenging problems of defining the design space, and finding an algorithm to search it efficiently, a much better level of abstraction at which to work. Autotuning is now widely used to generate code not just for dense linear algebra [1] but also sparse linear algebra [5], FFTs [6] more general digital signal-processing algorithms [11], and many other examples [12].

The survey paper [5] summarizes a subset of this subsequent work that has been carried on by some of the PHiPAC authors and other more recent contributors, and gives some pointers to other literature. One interesting example is the continued use of the matrix multiply contest as a homework in our CS267 class. Now the students learn about autotuning before the assignment, and are told that autotuning is a possible (but not required!) way to do the assignment. For the class offering discussed in [5], 3-student teams built autotuners in the 2 weeks they had for the assignment, automatically generating and searching over tens of thousands of lines of code. More recently, matrix multiply has been adopted in UC Berkeley's newly reorganized 3rd semester undergraduate programming class CS61C. Again, some of the sophomores choose to build their own autotuners to explore the design space.

Looking at ongoing and future work, the challenges and opportunities are large and growing. Sometimes tuning cannot be done "offline", taking a large amount of time to search the design space and building a library that is called at run-time, but must be done in part at run-time, when the user's input data is available. This is because the best algorithm may strongly depend on the inputs. For example, for sparse-matrix operations, the best algorithm depends on the sparsity pattern of the matrix. Sometimes the tuning space is so large that it is even impractical to tune it exhaustively offline, requiring clever machine learning techniques to search faster. Finally, sometimes the search space includes not just changes to the software, but also changes to the hardware as well [11], e.g. when one is trying to build specialized hardware to solve a problem, making the search space larger still.

To conclude, our work on PHiPAC has been an example of a larger pattern underlying much successful computer science research: the goal of research project $n + 1$ is to automate the successful ideas from research project n.

4. ACKNOWLEDGEMENTS

We would like to thank Dominic Lam for his work on the first release of PHiPAC, and Rich Vuduc for experimenting with PHiPAC after the ICS paper.

5. REFERENCES

[1] ATLAS: Automatically Tuned Linear Algebra Software. math-atlas.sourceforge.net/, 2014.

[2] J. Bilmes, K. Asanović, C. Chin, and J. Demmel. Optimizing matrix multiply using PHiPAC: a Portable, High-Performance, ANSI C coding methodology. In *Proceedings of the International Conference on Supercomputing*, pages 340–347, Vienna, Austria, July 1997. ACM SIGARC.

[3] J. Bilmes, K. Asanović, C.-W. Chin, and J. Demmel. The PHiPAC v1.0 Matrix-Multiply Distribution. Technical Report UCB/CSD-98-1020, Computer Science Division, University of California at Berkeley, 1998. also ICSI technical report TR-98-035.

[4] J. Bilmes, K. Asanović, C. whye Chin, and J. Demmel. Using PHiPAC to speed error back-propagation learning. In *Proceedings of ICASSP*, volume 5, pages 4153–4157, Munich, Germany, April 1997.

[5] J. Demmel, J. Dongarra, A. Fox, S. Williams, V. Volkov, and K. Yelick. Autotuning: Accelerating Time-to-Solution for Computational Science and Engineering. In *SciDAC Review, v. 15*, Winter 2009. available at www.scidacreview.org.

[6] FFTW. www.fftw.org, 2014.

[7] M. Frigo. *Portable High-Performance Programs.* PhD thesis, Massachusetts Institute of Technology, June 1999.

[8] G. E. Hinton, S. Osindero, and Y.-W. Teh. A fast learning algorithm for deep belief nets. *Neural computation*, 18(7):1527–1554, 2006.

[9] N. Morgan, J. Beck, P. Kohn, J. Bilmes, E. Allman, and J. Beer. The Ring Array Processor (RAP): A Multiprocessing Peripheral for Connectionist Applications. *Journal of Parallel and Distributed Computing*, 14:248–259, April 1992.

[10] S. Russell and P. Norvig. *Artificial Intelligence: A Modern Approach.* Prentice Hall, 1995.

[11] Spiral: Software/Hardware Generation for DSP Algorithms. www.spiral.net, 2014.

[12] R. Vuduc, J. W. Demmel, and J. A. Bilmes. Statistical models for empirical search-based performance tuning. *International Journal of High Performance Computing Applications*, 18(1):65–94, 2004.

[13] J. Wawrzynek, K. Asanović, B. Kingsbury, J. Beck, D. Johnson, and N. Morgan. Spert-II: A vector microprocessor system. *IEEE Computer*, 29(3):79–86, March 1996.

Author Retrospective for
Software Trace Cache

Alex Ramirez[1,2], Ayose J. Falcón[3], Oliverio J. Santana[4], Mateo Valero[1,2]
[1] Universitat Politècnica de Catalunya, BarcelonaTech
[2] Barcelona Supercomputing Center
[3] Intel Labs, Barcelona
[4] Universidad de Las Palmas de Gran Canaria
{aramirez@ac.upc.edu}

ABSTRACT
In superscalar processors, capable of issuing and executing multiple instructions per cycle, fetch performance represents an upper bound to the overall processor performance. Unless there is some form of instruction re-use mechanism, you cannot execute instructions faster than you can fetch them.

Instruction Level Parallelism, represented by wide issue out of order superscalar processors, was the trending topic during the end of the 90's and early 2000's. It is indeed the most promising way to continue improving processor performance in a way that does not impact application development, unlike current multicore architectures which require parallelizing the applications (a process that is still far from being automated in the general case). Widening superscalar processor issue was the promise of never-ending improvements to single thread performance, as identified by Yale N. Patt et al. in the 1997 special issue of IEEE Computer about "Billion transistor processors" [1].

However, instruction fetch performance is limited by the control flow of the program. The basic fetch stage implementation can read instructions from a single cache line, starting from the current fetch address and up to the next control flow instruction. That is one basic block per cycle at most.

Given that the typical basic block size in SPEC integer benchmarks is 4-6 instructions, fetch performance was limited to those same 4-6 instructions per cycle, making 8-wide and 16-wide superscalar processors impractical. It became imperative to find mechanisms to fetch more than 8 instructions per cycle, and that meant fetching more than one basic block per cycle.

The Trace Cache [2] [3] [4] quickly established itself as the state of the art in high performance instruction fetch. The trace cache relies on a trace building mechanism that dynamically reorders the control flow of the program, and stores the dynamic instruction sequences in sequential storage, increasing fetch width.

However, it is a complex hardware structure that adds not only another cache memory to the on-chip storage hierarchy, but also requires a branch predictor capable of issuing multiple predictions per cycle to index the contents of the trace cache, and distinguish between multiple dynamic sequences of instructions.

The Software Trace Cache is a compiler transformation, or a post-compilation binary optimization, that extends the seminar work of Pettis and Hansen PLDI'90 to perform the reordering of the dynamic instruction stream into sequential memory locations using profile information from previous executions. The major advantage compared to the trace cache, is that it is a software optimization, and does not require additional hardware to capture the dynamic instruction stream, nor additional memories to store them. Instructions are still captured in the regular instruction cache. The major disadvantage is that it can only capture one of the dynamic instruction sequences to store it sequentially. Any other control flow will result in taken branches, and interruptions of the fetch stream.

Our results show that fetch width using STC was competitive with that obtained with the hardware TC, and was applicable to a wide range of superscalar architectures, because it does not require hardware changes to enable fetching from multiple basic blocks in a single cycle, even if only one branch prediction can be issued. Any front-end architecture built on a BTB that ignores branches as long as they are not taken, will automatically treat such branches as NOP instructions in terms of fetch [5].

This was only the beginning. The impact of this optimization on fetch and superscalar processor architectures went much further than the original ICS paper in 1999

ICS 25th Anniversary Volume. 2014.
ACM 978-1-4503-2840-1/14/06.
http://dx.doi.org/10.1145/2591635.2594508

Categories and Subject Descriptors
D.3.4 [**Programming Languages**]: Processors. Compilers. Code generation. Optimization.

General Terms
Performance, Experimentation.

Keywords
Binary trablslation, ILP. Superscalar processors. Instruction fetch.

1. IMPACT
After the first STC presentation, the first author, Alex Ramirez, was invited for a summer internship in Digital Equipment Corporation's Western Research Lab.((by the time the internship actually happened, DEC and its Research Labs had been acquired by Compaq)) in Palo Alto (CA) in order to implement the STC algorithm in their SPIKE binary optimizer.

This work actually expanded two consecutive summers (1999 and 2000). The first one was required to finalize the implementation, and perform initial simulation studies. The second one allowed finalizing the implementation and performing tests on real workloads and systems.

Using SPIKE we optimized the performance of both a commercial DBMS (Oracle) and the operating system kernel, improving TPC benchmark results on Alpha platforms.

Similar code layout optimizations [6] were implemented in the IBM FDPR binary optimizer, and the STC algorithm is implemented in the Control Flow branch of the GNU gcc compiler [7].

Although 16-wide superscalar processors never happened (so far), we have seen other wide-issue superscalars such as the IBM Power7, and Intel SandyBridge or Haswell, where fetch performance is a potential bottleneck. These architectures have implemented solutions to enable fetching of multiple basic blocks per cycle, from the standard instruction cache, and would greatly benefit from optimizations such as the STC.

Also, fetch performance and fetch scheduling become even more important in simultaneous multithreaded architectures (which also exploit wide-issue superscalar pipelines), such as the IBM Power5 (and its successors), or the AMD Bulldozer. Again, improving the layout of the code could lead to both simpler microarchitectures and better performance.

The hardware trace cache has been actually implemented in the Intel Pentium 4 and Pentium D NetBurst architectures, from Willamette to Presier. However it was widely acknowledged that the main purpose was to store and fetch decoded micro-ops rather than increasing fetch width. As such, it is more closely related to the Decoded Instruction Area [8] or the rePLay framework [9] than to the STC.

2. RELATED AND FOLLOW-UP WORK

There were several papers that derived from this original Software Trace Cache paper. A slightly different version of the code layout algorithm was developed focusing on database workloads, which traverse a very large instruction working set, with lots of subroutine calls and low branch predictability in ICPP'99 [10], with a journal archive version in IJPP'02 [11]. An improved version of the fetch stage microarchitecture avoiding redundancy between software traces in the instruction cache, and dynamic traces in the trace cache was published in HPCA'00 [12].

The final, archive version of the algorithm with new heuristics to totally automate the process, was published in IEEE Transactions on Computers in 2004 [12].

Also, several papers explored in depth analysis of the impact of the STC optimizations in the SPIKE optimizer. A detailed analysis on the instruction cache and fetch performance on Oracle database was published in ISCA'01 [13], showing not only improvements on the instruction cache, but also a mush tighter packaging of useful instructions into cache lines, and a reduction in taken branches that leads to improved fetch width. A detailed analysis on the impact on branch prediction accuracy for various prediction strategies was published in PACT'00 [14], showing that since most branches behave the same way (usually not taken), their interference in the branch prediction tables was constructive, not destructive, achieving the same effect as an Agree prediction strategy.

Finally, based on all these observations, we developed a new fetch stage microarchitecture and a specialized branch predictor that exploit the maximum benefits of these layout optimizations: the instruction stream fetch engine, in MICRO'02 [15].

This fetch architecture for wide superscalar instruction fetch was picked up by the next PhD students in the group, and produced several related papers. A modification of the stream fetch engine for SMT processors was evaluated in HPCA'04 [16], showing relevant impact on the choice of the fetch policy to be used when fetching from a single thread on each cycle. A stream predictor capable of issuing multiple predictions per cycle was shown in ISHP'05 [17]. And a mechanism to store decoded instructions (like the Pentium4 trace cache) in the standard instruction cache was presented in PACT'06 [18] (archive version published in IEEE ToC'09 [19]).

3. DISCUSSION

There have been multiple works, before and after the STC, that have shown the benefits of feedback directed compilation. However, profile feedback is standard practice only in benchmark runs. It has not been adopted by end users in daily usage of computers. This may indicate that we need to change the way we use the compiler and how profile data is generated and stored, to make it easier for users to use them.

At the same time, and for the same reasons, it is very important to develop heuristic analysis techniques that can statically obtain an approximation of the information that would be obtained via profiling, such as the "Branch prediction for free" paper by Ball and Larus in PLDI'93 [20].

Combining profile feedback and heuristics, it is possible to reproduce at compile time many of the complex dynamic mechanisms that we have in out of order execution, leading to significant savings at reduced performance penalties. Even if maximum performance is required, and thus we resort to complex dynamic solutions in hardware, the combination of software and hardware optimizations still leads to improved results.

The combined results of all the STC related research show that code layout optimizations have an impact that goes far beyond a mere reduction in the instruction cache misses.

Even if 16-wide superscalar processors have not been produced yet, there is a significant benefit of wide superscalar instruction fetch in terms of power consumption. As shown by our instruction stream fetch engine, it takes approximately the same effort to fetch 16 instructions in one cycle, than to fetch just 4. That means that we could be fetching instructions only once every 4 cycles, or that we could decouple the clock frequency of the processor front-end from the processor back-end.

All in all, the STC was the seed for a very exciting series of research projects spanning compiler algorithms, superscalar processor microarchitecture, branch prediction, multithreaded processors, and instruction decoding. With the demise of wide issue superscalar processors in favor of multicore processors, interest in this kind of techniques has decreased. However, given the power efficiency difficulties that future processor and multicore architectures are facing, it is likely that techniques originally intended for wide superscalar processors can be revisited focusing on their energy saving potential.

4. ACKNOWLEDGEMENTS

The authors want to thank those industrial partners who expressed interest in the STC-derived technologies (Sun Microsystems, IBM, Intel, Digital Equipment Corporation / Compaq), and specially Luiz Barroso and Kourosh Garachorloo who hosted the first author for two consecutive summers in Compaq's Western Research Lab.

5. REFERENCES

[1] Y. N. Patt y et al., «One Billion Transistors, One Uniprocessor, One Chip,» *IEEE Computer,* pp. 51-58, Sept. 1997.

[2] A. Peleg y U. Weiser, «Dynamic Flow Instruction Cache Memory Organized Around Trace Segments Independent of Virtual Address Line». United States Patente 5,381,533, 1995.

[3] E. Rottenberg, S. Bennett y J. E. Smith, «Trace cache: a low latency approach to high bandwidth instruction fetching,» de *ACM/IEEE international symposium on Microarchitecture (MICRO 29)*, 1996.

[4] D. H. Friendly, S. J. Patel y Y. N. Patt, «Alternative fetch and issue policies for the trace cache fetch mechanism,» de *30th annual ACM/IEEE international symposium on Microarchitecture (MICRO 30)*, 1997.

[5] B. Calder y D. Grunwald, «Reducing branch costs via branch alignment,» de *6th Intl. Conference on Architectural Support for Programming Languages and Operating Systems (ASPLOS)*, 1994.

[6] K. Pettis y R. C. Hansen, «Profile guided code positioning,» de *ACM SIGPLAN Conf. on Programming Language Design and Implementation (PLDI)*, 1990.

[7] «Improving GCC's Infrastructure (Control Flow Graph),» [En línea]. Available: http://www.gnu.org/software/gcc/projects/cfg.html.

[8] O. J. Santana, A. Falcon, A. Ramirez y M. Valero, «Branch predictor guided instruction decoding,» de *15th international conference on Parallel architectures and compilation techniques (PACT '06)*, 2006.

[9] S. J. Patel y S. S. Lumetta, «rePLay: A hardware framework for dynamic optimization,» *IEEE Transactions on Computers,* 2001.

[10] A. Ramirez, J. L. Larriba-Pey, C. Navarro, X. Serrano y M. Valero, «Optimization of Instruction Fetch for Decision Support Workloads,» de *International Conference on Parallel Processing (ICPP)*, 1999.

[11] A. Ramirez, J. L. Larriba-Pey, C. Navarro, M. Valero y J. Torrellas, «Software Trace Cache for Commercial Applications,» *Internatinal Journal of Parallel Programming,* vol. 30, nº 5, pp. 373-395, 2002.

[12] A. Ramirez, J. L. Larriba-Pey y M. Valero, «Trace Cache Redundancy: Red & Blue Traces,» de *Sixth International Symposium on High-Performance Computer Architecture (HPCA)*, 2000.

[13] A. Ramirez, J. L. Larriba-Pey y M. Valero, «Software Trace Cache,» *IEEE Transactions on Computers,* vol. 54, nº 1, pp. 22-35, 2005.

[14] A. Ramirez, L. A. Barroso, K. Gharachorloo, R. Cohn, J. L. Larriba-Pey, G. P. Lowney y M. Valero, «Code layout optimizations for transaction processing workloads,» de *28th Annual International Symposium on Computer Architecture*, 2001.

[15] A. Ramirez, J. L. Larriba-Pey y M. Valero, «The Effect of Code Reordering on Branch Prediction,» de *International Conference on Parallel Architectures and Compilation Techniques*, 2000.

[16] A. Ramirez, O. J. Santana, J. L. Larriba-Pey y M. Valero, «Fetching instruction streams,» de *35th Annual International Symposium on Microarchitecture*, 2002.

[17] A. Falcon, A. Ramirez y M. Valero, «A Low-Complexity, High-Performance Fetch Unit for Simultaneous Multithreading Processors,» de *10th International Conference on High-Performance Computer Architecture*, 2004.

[18] A. Falcon, A. Ramirez y m. Valero, «Tolerating Branch Predictor Latency on SMT,» de *5th International Symposium on High Performance Computing (ISHPC)*, 2005.

[19] O. J. Santana, A. Falcon, A. Ramirez y M. Valero, «Branch predictor guided instruction decoding,» de *15th International Conference on Parallel Architecture and Compilation Techniques*, 2006.

[20] J. S. Oliverio, F. Ayose, R. Alex y V. Mateo, «DIA: A Complexity-Effective Decoding Architecture,» *IEEE Transactions on Computers,* vol. 58, nº 4, pp. 448-462, 2009.

[21] T. Ball y J. R. Larus, «Branch prediction for free,» de *ACM SIGPLAN Conf. on Programming Language Design and Implementation (PLDI'93)*, 1993.

Author Retrospective of Dynamic Application Scheduling Using On-line Analytics – Then and Now

Rich Wolski
Department of Computer Science
University of California, Santa Barbara
Santa Barbara, CA 93106
rich@cs.ucsb.edu

ABSTRACT

This paper attempts, retrospectively, to frame results originally published in the 1998 edition of the ACM International Conference on Supercomputing in the present context. The article entitled *Application Level Scheduling of Gene Sequence Comparison on Metacomputers* described the use of on-line performance prediction to adapt, dynamically, the execution schedule of a gene sequencing code to fluctuating performance conditions in the wide area. This retrospective discusses those results in light of recent technological developments in large-scale, wide area distributed computing.

1. INTRODUCTION

The article entitled *Application Level Scheduling of Gene Sequence Comparison on Metacomputers* authored by Neil Spring and this author appeared in the ACM International Conference on Supercomputing in 1998. Since that time, the ability to use wide-area distributed computing resources as an application platform has improved dramatically. In addition, many of the ideas that we tested with respect to the use of on-line performance measurement and prediction (*i.e.* on-line analytics) to optimize application performance "on-the-fly" are now common practice in one form or another. While it is tempting to try and find a causal relationship between the original work with gene sequencing (and more generally, the AppLeS [3] project, co-led by Dr. Francine Berman, of which it was a part) and the current enthusiasm for distributed computing (in the form of cloud computing), the relationship is most properly viewed as being circuitous. By way of retrospective, this paper makes a modest attempt to "connect the dots" between current trends in large-scale distributed systems and the original work from ICS in 1998.

Then: Metacomputing and The Grid

During the mid 1990s, a number of researchers (including myself and my co-author Neil Spring) who came from a background in high-performance parallel computing began to study the possibility of using resources distributed across the wide area as a platform for high-performance applications. This general field of investigation was originally referred to as *Heterogeneous Computing* (a term due to Dr. Richard Fruend) indicating that applications would need to be able to leverage a mix of processor types. Increasingly, however, it became clear that the language and runtime system would need to be able to control the application's deployment and execution dynamically to account for both performance and reliability variations. Furthermore, the "platform" for application execution had to be programmable to take into account specific application-level requirements. Hence the programmer would now be faced with the problem of writing a program about her program – a metaprogram – subsequently referred to as *Metacomputing.* Metacomputing eventually became *The Grid* with Dr. Ian Foster and Dr. Carl Kesselman's seminal book [6] on the subject as the popular research emphasis shifted toward middleware development and production-quality deployments for scientific applications [5, 7].

It was in this context that we chose to focus on using fast, on-line statistical forecasting techniques to make short-term predictions of research performance and reliability. Using these forecasts, an application scheduler could anticipate future performance capabilities and adjust execution accordingly.

What We Learned

For the genetic sequencing application we investigated in the ICS paper, it was essential that the scheduler combine predictions of resource performance with predictions of application workload when developing a schedule. This approach was controversial for several reasons.

- **Writing the scheduler was a complicated task.** In particular, debugging and tuning a distributed program that ran in an environment which changes from moment to moment was labor intensive and error prone.
- **On-line resource prediction was poorly understood.** Little was known about the efficacy of using streaming, on-line analytics to make real-time decisions about future resource capabilities.
- **Genetic sequencing is a non-uniform workload.** Even when resource performance is stable, the amount of work that the application did at each "step" varied making it necessary to compose a prediction of workload with a resource prediction in order to generate a schedule.

ICS 25th Anniversary Volume. 2014
ACM 978-1-4503-2840-1/14/06.
http://dx.doi.org/10.1145/2591635.2591657.

For these reasons, the conventional approach at the time was to implement some form of work pull or work stealing scheduler. If idle compute nodes simply draw work from a logically centralized queue, the workload appears to balance itself with little need for the added complexities associated with predictive scheduling.

What we learned from the experiment, however, was that it was possible to improve on the performance of simple work pull using on-line analytics. The inspiration stemmed from two observations that, today, are relatively commonplace in large-scale distributed systems.

- **Scale improves statistical accuracy by increasing sample size**. Somewhat counter-intuitively, the larger the system, the greater the opportunity to manage uncertainty by exploiting statistical methods. Simply put, the abundance of data make better inferences possible (although, by no means does more data alone yield better inferences and forecasts).
- **The quantiles matter as much as the moments**. Most statistical methodologies used for scheduling at that time focused on making some inference about the mean performance. Our methodology used an estimate of a large quantile (*e.g.* the upper 0.95 quantile) as a bound on performance to derive performant schedule.

Our approach used a network-facing performance monitoring and forecasting service (The Network Weather Service (NWS) [12, 13]) to gather and forecast resource performance using non-parametric time series techniques. The NWS used an eventually-consistent data model internally to achieve wide-area scale and robustness and it served measurement and forecast data through a well-defined, network-accessible API.

The application scheduler would query the NWS for an instantaneous forecast of the CPU loads and network performance between CPUs associated with a set of machines. It then convolved those forecasts with a statistical prediction of workload to generate an assignment of work to processors.

The research, however, was driven by the two observations about the use of on-line data as a system implementation tool: scale is useful, and statistical techniques need to consider more than distribution summaries. The paper demonstrated that, based on dynamic performance forecasting, it was possible to improve on the performance over the widely-accepted best practice for this type of application in the wide area.

2. THEN AND NOW

Retrospectively, many of the novel ideas explored in the ICS paper from 1998 have become part of common and, in some cases, best practice today when implementing large-scale distributed applications. We cannot claim that our research has led to this circumstance directly. At best, the work should be considered as comprising a combination of some prescience, a little scientific influence, and a great deal of exposition of our of trials and errors. At the same time, some of the questions that the original work did not address definitively remain open and viable as research pursuits.

Now: The Cloud

Large-scale applications are increasingly adopting a model of distributed computation based on the ability to provision and release abstract representations of physical resources dynamically. The abstract resources are implemented using physical resources via some form (or multiple forms) of virtualization. The term "Cloud Computing" refers to the notion that the system deliberately obscures the physical resource topology and characteristics from its users. Thus, in the same way that The Internet implements an abstract communication service without the need to understand physical connectivity, "The Cloud" implements a resource provisioning service without the need to understand physical infrastructure characteristics. Moreover, because the resources are abstract, and users cannot choose a specific resource, it is possible to implement a cloud at very large scale.

Cloud computing was invented by large e-commerce enterprises as a way of implementing scalable, web-service based applications. Since its inception as a general-purpose platform in 2006, however, it has rapidly gained in popularity, so much so, that many industry analyses predict it will become the predominant Information Technology platform within the next 10 years.

Cloud-based Applications

The Cloud is not an evolution of The Grid and/or Metacomputing from a technology perspective since its original motivation was the implementation of large-scale, web-based e-commerce. However, the problems associated with using wide-area distributed resources at scale are fundamental to all three paradigms. Thus several of the concepts originally explored in the ICS paper have proved relevant today.

- **The Use of On-line Analytics** – Cloud applications routinely use on-line performance monitoring and forecasting to "tune" themselves dynamically in response to varying performance and reliability conditions. Streaming video service is, perhaps, the most visible example in which the application attempts to predict bandwidth to the delivery site, and to schedule viewing quality based on these predictions. Indeed, the Netflix OSS (Open Source Software) toolchain [9] (with which Netflix implements its e-commerce platform) uses internal performance forecasting to make wide-area distribution decisions. Similarly, Content Delivery Networks (CDNs) routinely use network monitoring and prediction to control content flows.
- **Resource Scheduling is Application Specific** – Cloud platforms cannot "see" what it is the applications they host intend to do with the resources once they are provisioned. Thus the cloud provides a performance "Service Level Agreement" (SLA) which is expressed as a quantile to the application for the application to use to develop its own schedule. Powerful scripting languages and dashboard services *e.g.* Rightscale [10]) support (and monetize) sophisticated algorithms for building application-specific schedulers based on these SLAs.
- **Quantiles and not Moments** – Like the genetic sequencing application described in the ICS paper, cloud applications consider the resources they use in abstract terms, where the abstraction comes in the form of an SLA. For example, a CPU is simply a service that can deliver a specified computing rate. These SLAs are often expressed in terms of bound rather than expecta-

tions, and the bounds are characterized by a probability. In short, most clouds today quote SLAs as quantiles on a performance or reliability distribution rather than as expectations. As another example, Google's TrueTime [4] time stamp management system is based on quantile and not moment estimation. TrueTime is an attempt to use on-line analytics to implement strongly consistent database transactions in the wide area.

One point of potential confusion with respect to cloud applications concerns their architecture. Cloud applications today are organized as communicating services. Architecturally they are similar to what is described in the SOA (Service Oriented Architecture) web service standards [2] but the APIs are REST [8] based. Thus, the cloud "sees' an application as a collection of asynchronously communicating services (possibly implemented using several separate technologies). The work described in the ICS paper, however, targeted data parallel and/or bulk-synchronous parallel application designs.

3. OPEN QUESTIONS FOR THE FUTURE

This difference in application architecture between Metacomputing/Grid applications and Cloud applications continues to point to questions that plagued us at the time our paper was published in 1998. Writing distributed applications is still a labor-intensive and error-prone task. Writing distributed application schedulers (*i.e.* metaprograms in the 1998 parlance) continues to be even more daunting. From a systems perspective, the platform must now use the same techniques (on-line analytics, eventual consistency, etc.) to implement the resource abstractions as the applications use when provisioning them. These tribulations lead, naturally, to research questions we briefly considered at the time of the ICS paper and quickly decided to leave as future work where some of them continue to remain.

- **Programming Model** – It remains unclear as to what programming model (or models) are best suited to high-performance distributed applications development. The Grid was middleware based. Clouds are REST-based web services. Web-services, high-throughput computing, and some large-scale database applications work well, but data parallel applications have not proved successful (yet). Is there one or more programming language(s) for "The Cloud?" If so, how does that language take into account dynamism? Is virtualization the right way to implement abstract resources for application performance or should it be done at the language level? There are some efforts to understand the "right" level of abstraction for application development but more work is needed.

- **Stability** – It became clear to us that an application scheduler using on-line analytics could make decisions faster, using more data than a human counterpart. One question that remains relevant today is whether a system of applications controlled by such schedulers in which the schedulers were not cooperating will be stable. At present, stability is ensured by restricting the typical application to using a statistically insignificant fraction of the total cloud resource pool (thereby creating a form of statistical isolation). However, as larger application classes move to the cloud, scheduling systems like Google's Omega [11] that support independent application-level schedulers will need to grapple with the problem of performance stability.

- **Policy Effects** – Clouds are governed by policies that, through their influence on SLAs, affect application performance. For the ICS paper, the genetic sequencing application we developed was given "guest" access on all of the resources it used which essentially meant that it could run as a medium or low priority process with no restriction on network usage. Today, cloud policies that control SLAs are far more complex and dynamically changing. Indeed some cloud infrastructures such as AWS [1] include a policy language for users and administrators to specify customized policies. Application schedulers will need to be able to sense policy effects to make the best use of the resources available.

The freshness of these questions as the subjects of research today suggest the value that ICS has provided provided to the research community during its first 25 years. While it would be difficult to tease apart the direct contribution to the current enthusiasm for distributed computing from the general contribution that ICS has made to "what is known" by the system science community, it is clear that the conference has featured work which remains relevant. We are honored to have been included by the ICS community in these contributions, both then and now.

4. REFERENCES

[1] AWS IAM. `http://aws.amazon.com/iam/`.

[2] J. Bean. *SOA and web services interface design: principles, techniques, and standards.* Morgan Kaufmann, 2009.

[3] F. Berman, R. Wolski, S. Figueira, J. Schopf, and G. Shao. Application-level scheduling on distributed heterogeneous networks. In *Supercomputing, 1996. Proceedings of the 1996 ACM/IEEE Conference on*, pages 39–39. IEEE, 1996.

[4] J. C. Corbett, J. Dean, M. Epstein, A. Fikes, C. Frost, J. Furman, S. Ghemawat, A. Gubarev, C. Heiser, P. Hochschild, et al. Spanner: GoogleâĂŹs globally distributed database. *ACM Transactions on Computer Systems (TOCS)*, 31(3):8, 2013.

[5] I. Foster and C. Kesselman. Globus: A metacomputing infrastructure toolkit. *International Journal of Supercomputer Applications*, 1997.

[6] I. Foster and C. Kesselman. The grid: Blueprint for a new computing architecture. 1999.

[7] M. Livny, J. Basney, R. Raman, and T. Tannenbaum. Mechanisms for high throughput computing. *SPEEDUP journal*, 11(1):36–40, 1997.

[8] M. Masse. *REST API design rulebook.* " O'Reilly Media, Inc.", 2011.

[9] Netflix Open Source Software. `http://netflix.github.io/#repo`.

[10] Rightscale Inc. `http://www.rightscale.com`.

[11] M. Schwarzkopf, A. Konwinski, M. Abd-El-Malek, and J. Wilkes. Omega: flexible, scalable schedulers for large compute clusters. In *Proceedings of the 8th ACM European Conference on Computer Systems*, pages 351–364. ACM, 2013.

[12] R. Wolski. Dynamically forecasting network performance to support dynamic scheduling using the network weather service. August 1997.

[13] R. Wolski, N. Spring, and J. Hayes. The network weather service: A distributed resource performance forecasting service for metacomputing. *Future Generation Computer Systems*, 15(5-6):757–768, October 1999.

Author's Retrospective for:

Improving the Performance of Speculatively Parallel Applications on the Hydra CMP

Kunle Olukotun, Lance Hammond, and Mark Willey
Computer Systems Laboratory
Stanford University
Stanford, CA 94305-4070
http://www-hydra.stanford.edu/

ABSTRACT

Our 1999 paper described how to use hardware with thread-level speculation (TLS) support to effectively parallelize a number of serial application benchmarks with minimal programmer intervention required. The ability of TLS hardware to allow programmers to parallelize code almost arbitrarily and then performance tune afterwards, based on feedback supplied by the TLS system, provided significant improvements to programmer productivity and made parallel programming much less error-prone. Since this paper appeared, we investigated other hardware variations that could provide similar benefits in terms of programmer productivity, such as ones based on an extension of transactional memory. Unfortunately, these concepts have not been implemented on any real systems. As a result, there is still an opportunity to implement schemes like the ones that we described in this paper in order to ease parallel programming in future systems dramatically.

Original Paper: http://dx.doi.org/10.1145/305138.305155

Categories and Subject Descriptors

C.1.4. [**Computer Systems Organization**]: Processor architectures — *parallel architectures*. D.1.3. [**Software**]: Programming techniques — *concurrent programming (parallel programming)*.

General Terms

Performance

Keywords

Retrospective, chip multiprocessor (CMP), thread-level speculation (TLS), parallel programming, transactional memory.

ICS 25th Anniversary Volume.
ICS'14, Jun 10-13 2014, Muenchen, Germany
ACM 978-1-4503-2840-1/14/06.
http://dx.doi.org/10.1145/2591635.2591658

1. THE RESEARCH

This paper was nominally about the speculation support that we were designing for inclusion in the Hydra chip multiprocessor, a research design that was under development at the time. There was a strong research push in the 1990's to try and facilitate parallel programming in a more automated way. Many schemes looked at using automatically generated speculative threads. Most of these involved adding additional thread processor units to each processor core and spreading out the speculative threads among them. Because of the tight, register-to-register coupling required between all of these units, they often ended up being similar to the designs for simultaneous multi-threading (SMT [33], or Hyperthreading in Intel parlance [27]) cores that were being described in a variety of papers at about the same time. Sohi, et. al. was one of the first to describe how to use a scheme like this with the Multiscalar papers [3, 4, 5, 18], and a number of other designs quickly followed.

However, we felt that the dependence on such large cores running many threads at once was likely to be untenable in the long run. Building ever-larger cores would add additional complexity, slowing clock rates and making them harder to debug, while performance returns would gradually decrease. Also, when running multiple independent jobs or applications that naturally break up into coarse parallel threads, it did not make sense to hobble performance by making those applications execute all of their independent threads on some humongous and probably slow core, as SMT boosters were advocating. As a result, we favored the design of CMPs, which in turn required a less hardware-intensive scheme for extracting speculative parallelism. The hardware required to support our hardware-software hybrid scheme was more akin to adding a small MMU to each core, instead of the complete core overhauls required by most of the other schemes from that era.

Our support involved adding a special parallel-execution control coprocessor to each core and some extra bits to the cache tags and a few on-chip buses between cores to track data that had been read and written by processors speculatively executing threads of execution out ahead of the "normal" serial execution of any originally serial program. As long as the execution performed by these speculative threads did not conflict with any "older" threads executing in parallel with them, by reading data that the older threads were writing concurrently, one could achieve nearly automatic parallelization of any serial program, in theory. This form of speculation is called "thread-level" speculation (TLS) to clearly delineate it from the instruction-level speculation techniques that are used in most processors to speculate beyond things like predicted branches. Of course, as we had demonstrated in our ASPLOS paper from the previous year, "Data Speculation Support for a Chip Multiprocessor," [7] reality did not always match up to theory, since most serial programs are not written with parallelism in mind. Even programs with blocks of code that were clearly good sources of parallel threads often had minor hazards introduced by the semantics of serial programming practice that foiled our initial, automated system. As a result, we created this follow-up paper to investigate how serial software could be adjusted to make the extraction of parallelism with our scheme more feasible.

There were several optimization schemes examined in this paper. Other than choosing to use a simplified, loop-only speculation control system, all involved manual source adjustments: hand-picking which threads to speculate upon (specifically, choosing which key loops or procedures in the serial code looked like likely sources of parallel threads), moving code around to minimize data dependencies across loop iterations, inserting synchronization points at key dependencies, and adjusting the size of speculative threads by splitting large ones and grouping (i.e. effectively loop unrolling) small ones. These modifications were all performed using a simple methodology:

1. We could start executing our programs by launching them on our system, without any extra tuning, to see how inherently parallel the serial code is when broken up into threads at loops and/or function calls. Usually the code would not speed up, but a few loops (or, occasionally, a procedure) would pop out as good potential targets for performance tuning.

2. The programming environment automatically directed us to the points in our serial code where some additional work would be helpful, based on statistics about where true data dependencies were occurring and how much performance was being lost at each point.

3. We then made a few small and simple modifications, with each one only involving a source change of a line or two, and sometimes just a constant like a loop unrolling factor.

4. Some minor dependencies remained, but we let the speculative hardware handle continue to catch them on the rare occasions when they still occurred.

This methodology is very simple and straightforward. In fact, we were subsequently able to automate much of the process for Java programs with the development of the JRPM system in 2003 [23]. More to the point, this process is much simpler than conventional parallel programming, which requires that one break up a program into parallel threads, each with its own private data, before one can even attempt to execute the program in parallel. The easy experimentation allowed by TLS support is just not possible. Moreover, without the automatic feedback provided by a TLS system to help find all of the communication points, deciding how to divide up a program and its data is often a matter of trial and error. Since one must guarantee that all data is either only used privately by a single thread or that each communication point is fully "protected" by inter-thread synchronization mechanisms, there is usually a lot more "error" than "trial" in this process.

Over the course of the decade after this paper came out, we extended these ideas further with concepts like adapting transactional memory systems to provide TLS-like support. [25] That work took parallel applications, with manually selected threads, and used TLS hardware to eliminate the need for fully privatizing data and marking all synchronization points between cores. This could sometimes improve performance over a conventional parallel system by eliminating synchronization overhead when communication seldom occurs in practice. In other cases, it allowed TLS to scale from just a few cores up to systems with tens of processor cores, for applications with sufficient available parallelism [24]. More critically, though, it made even "conventional" parallel programming much easier by eliminating the error-prone steps of ensuring that all data is either private or fully protected with synchronization primitives. The transactional hardware continued to serialize any occasional conflicting accesses, converting what could have been critical correctness errors in a conventional parallel program into occasional small performance penalties.

2. THE REALITY

Over the past 15 years, our predictions about how processors should be built have largely come true. Core throughput has largely been limited to about 3-6 instructions/cycle and SMT design to about 2 threads/core because of the inherent complexity of building ever-larger cores. Instead, silicon area has been devoted to stamping down more copies of cores, up to the limits of what can be practically cooled within a particular device form factor. For desktop machines, this is currently about 8-16 cores/chip, as this retrospective is written in 2014, while for handheld devices it is about 2-4 cores/chip. Undoubtedly these numbers will continue to scale further as process technology improves.

However, our proposals for thread-level speculation mechanisms have not been implemented in any real systems. As a result, even though more cores are available, those cores are still almost as difficult to program as they were in the 1990s. While we are now blessed with a multitude of cores in virtually every device, there is not always enough parallel work available to utilize them effectively.

Software support for parallel programming has improved somewhat, with standards like MPI [31], pthreads [21], OpenMP [32], and OpenCL [29] becoming well-established, plus platform-specific APIs like Nvidia's CUDA [30] and Apple's Grand Central Dispatch (GCD) [20] to provide more specialized support. However, with these various software APIs it is still the programmer's responsibility to guarantee that all communication between threads is marked explicitly using techniques like messages or synchronization. If one forgets to synchronize any true communication, an error may occur. Even worse, many of these errors can be very intermittent and therefore hard to debug. Also, all of these APIs require some degree of manual load-balancing among the various processors and efforts to keep communication levels between cores manageable. Some improvements, like the use of GPUs as parallel computation coprocessors, have made this task even more difficult by imposing restrictions on the types of threads that can execute on some cores and/or lengthening communication times between some cores.

The closest systems to Hydra's TLS support that we have seen in shipping hardware are the transactional memory mechanisms available in a few chips such as the Intel Haswell [26] and IBM server chips [22, 28], but these are too simple to provide full TLS-on-TM support like the kind proposed in our transactional memory papers. While the current hardware designs are capable of basic transactional memory techniques like lock elision, which converts small lock critical regions to transactional memory regions, they do not support the inter-transaction priority ordering mechanisms needed for TLS and are not really designed to scale up to transaction sizes consisting of hundreds or thousands of instructions per transaction, which is needed for TLS-like support. Hence, the current transactional memory designs only begin to address the range of support that might be possible with hardware-software schemes like we were proposing for use in Hydra 15 years ago.

While all of these improvements are welcome, we still believe that adding true TLS support, probably via an enhanced transactional memory mechanism, would be advantageous because it offers a significantly easier route to parallel code than any of the schemes that have been implemented to date. None of them can compete with the ability of TLS to allow one to divide code up into threads almost arbitrarily and try running them in parallel, just to see what happens, with the hardware guaranteeing that code will still work correctly. This ability to run code in parallel and generate useful feedback about inter-thread dependencies without requiring programmers to find and isolate these dependencies manually beforehand is a key TLS advantage that no existing system has ever been able to emulate. TLS cannot help as much with the process of finding "good" threads in parallel code and load balancing for performance, but these tasks are nowhere near as difficult or error-prone as properly parallelizing the communication within a parallel program.

Even if one ignores the potential savings in programmer time, TLS support would also be useful in shipping products because it allows hardware to seamlessly catch and correct any rare communication events that may remain undetected in a large and complex parallel program and would normally cause an intermittent, hard-to-find bug. What could have been a critical correctness bug that might have required an expensive fix will instead cause a minor performance hiccup or can be handled in a controlled manner using an exception handler.

3. ADDITIONAL REFERENCES

References [1]–[19] are from the original paper's references.

[20] Apple Inc., https://developer.apple.com/library/ios/documentation/Performance/Reference/GCD_libdispatch_Ref/Reference/reference.html.

[21] D. R. Butenhof, Programming with POSIX Threads, Addison-Wesley ISBN 0-201-63392-2.

[22] H. W. Cain, M. M. Michael, B. Frey, C. May, D. Williams, and H. Le, "Robust architectural support for transactional memory in the POWER architecture," in 40th Annual International Symposium on Computer Architecture (ISCA-40), June 2013.

[23] M. K. Chen, K. Olukotun, "The JRPM system for dynamically parallelizing Java programs," in 30th International Symposium on Computer Architecture (ISCA-30), June 2003.

[24] L. Hammond, B. D. Carlstrom, V. Wong, B. Hertzberg, M. Chen, C. Kozyrakis, and K. Olukotun, "Programming with Transactional Coherence and Consistency (TCC)," in 11th ACM Conference on Architectural Support for Programming Languages and Operating Systems (ASPLOS-11), October 2004.

[25] L. Hammond, V. Wong, M. Chen, B. D. Carlstrom, J. D. Davis, B. Hertzberg, M. K. Prabhu, H. Wijaya, C. Kozyrakis, and K. Olukotun, "Transactional Memory Coherence and Consistency," in 31st International Symposium on Computer Architecture (ISCA-31), June 2004.

[26] Intel Corp., "Intel Architecture Instruction Set Extensions Programming Reference (February 2012)," chapter 8, http://software.intel.com/sites/default/files/m/9/2/3/41604.

[27] Intel Corporation, "Intel Hyper-Threading Technology: Technical User's Guide," http://cache-www.intel.com/cd/00/00/01/77/17705_htt_user_guide.pdf.

[28] C. Jacobi, T. Slegel, and D. Greiner, "Transactional Memory Architecture and Implementation for IBM System Z," in 45th Annual International Symposium on Microarchitecture (MICRO-45), 2012.

[29] Khronos.org, https://www.khronos.org/opencl/.

[30] Nvidia Corporation, http://www.nvidia.com/object/cuda_home_new.html.

[31] OpenMPI.org, http://www.open-mpi.org.

[32] OpenMP.org, http://openmp.org/.

[33] D.M. Tullsen, S.J. Eggers, and H.M. Levy, "Simultaneous Multithreading: Maximizing On-Chip Parallelism," in 22nd Annual International Symposium on Computer Architecture (ISCA-22), June 1995.

Author Retrospective for

Characterizing Processor Architectures for Programmable Network Interfaces

Patrick Crowley
Dept. of Computer Science & Engineering
Washington University in St. Louis
St. Louis, MO 63130-4899 USA
pcrowley@wustl.edu

Original paper: http://dx.doi.org/10.1145/335231.335237

Categories and Subject Descriptors

C.1.2 [**Multiple Data Stream Architectures (Multiprocessors)**]
C.2.6 [**Internetworking**]: *Routers*

General Terms

Performance, Design, Experimentation.

1. INTRODUCTION

Our investigation into architectural support for networking tasks began in late 1998, and it began with something of a coincidence. Fiuczynski was an active graduate student participant in the SPIN project at UW [2,3]. He had been writing a SPIN driver for a high-speed network interface card (NIC), and visited Crowley (at the time, a graduate student investigating the relationships between processor & memory architectures and desktop computer applications [4]) one afternoon to discuss the NIC's processor. Had either Fiuczynksi or Crowley been out of the office on that particular day, it is not clear that this collaboration would have emerged.

As it happened, both were in the office that day and the NIC processor was very interesting: a dual-core MIPS-like processor built specifically for the NIC. In ensuing discussions, it became clear that—despite the simplicity of its instruction set and microarchitecture—the NIC processor was as a whole more interesting than the much larger and complex x86 processor of the host system. It was more interesting because, as a dual-core processor, it was different and in no way an incremental improvement upon the deeply pipelined CPUs that dominated computing at the time. (They still dominate PCs and servers, of course, but mobile, graphics and embedded chips represent a huge swath of relevant computing platforms today.) It represented evidence of a combination of commercial and technical justification for designing a new and different processor to handle networking tasks.

ICS 25th Ann. Volume, 2014
ACM 978-1-4503-2840-1/14/06.
http://dx.doi.org/10.1145/2591635.2591659

The question that would drive our work occurred to us almost immediately: if we had the opportunity to design a processor from scratch to support NIC workloads, what processor organization would we choose? As can be seen in the paper, our initial work in answering this question was decomposed into three basic questions.

- What must NICs be capable of doing?
- What are the performance requirements?
- Which processor architectures might meet those requirements?

The effort and activities that went into this investigation are all too familiar to systems graduate students: we developed and extended extensive simulator infrastructure, application-code and an experimental operation system to build the experimental environment needed to pursue these questions. We were fortunate to be a part of research groups that shared their code freely; without that culture of sharing, this project would not have gotten started. An early version of this work appeared as a workshop paper in 1999 [1].

In the end, this effort established two key ideas that remain relevant today. First, packet-level parallelism is abundant in network workloads, and its efficient exploitation is the key to achieving high-bandwidth network processing. Second, real-world networking workloads contain a mix of simple and complex tasks, and the latter will always benefit from more sophisticated and aggressive microarchitecture support.

2. IDEAS, PRODUCTS & IMPACT

The decade following the publication of this paper was a fascinating time for the networking silicon industry. This period saw a flourishing of technologies, startups and large-company initiatives, all aimed at making a substantive impact on the processor-based ecosystem supporting network interface cards and switches & routers.

To be clear, we are not suggesting that our publication caused this innovative time; indeed, we were interested in these problems for many of the same reasons that caused a pair of large industries (microprocessors & networking infrastructure) to become interested in them. It is perhaps just an accident of history that we started publishing our ideas earlier than most others.

The network processor industry has been particularly interesting to follow. Two waves of startup companies managed lucrative acquisitions by large entrenched players. Each of Cisco, IBM, Intel and Motorola made several acquisitions, among others. A wide variety of architectural approaches were used in commercial products, including at least one NP based on simultaneous multithreading; most solutions, however, were multi-core architectures with a variety of hardware accelerators and memory controllers.

While there were many successes—particularly amongst the earliest entrepreneurs and venture capital investors—many of the biggest bets were made in pursuit of the biggest prize of all: to become the primary network processor provider to Cisco. Cisco's dominant position in the switch and router markets made it an attractive and all-important prospect. However, while Cisco was fairly liberal in using third-party network processors in a variety of product lines (and, hence, was generally the biggest customer for **every** NP vendor), Cisco never relinquished the role of producing its own network processors for its top-of-line switch and router products [5].

Intel Corporation made perhaps that largest investment in the development and marketing of network processors for OEMs. Its leading IXP family of NPs, for example, reportedly became a billion-dollar business, resulting in at least two promotions to the rank of Intel Fellow. Ultimately, however, two factors limited the shelf life of the IXP as a core Intel product line. First, most IXPs included an on-chip ARM-based control processor, whose presence continued to be a poor strategic alignment. Second, and likely more influential, was the gradual progress of chip-level integration that saw Intel's server products integrate many NP-like features directly on-chip, comfortably enabling x86-based network processing at 10G line rates.

3. SUBSEQUENT WORK

In addition to commercial activities, considerable subsequent and related work has been published in the research literature. Our initial work focused on the relationship between simple networking tasks and processor organizations. Since the late 90s, both networking tasks and platforms have grown and diversified substantially.

Crowley completed a doctoral dissertation that considered not only processor architectures, but also both memory subsystems, including caches, and architectural support for real-time tasks in order to provide temporal guarantees in multithreaded software systems.

More broadly, a series of Nework Processor Workshops were held in conjunction with the HPCA conference from 2002 through 2004. A corresponding series of books [6,7,8] chronicle the workshop proceedings, and also provide a comprehensive architectural description of commercial network processor products produced in those years. In 2005, the workshop became a full-fledged conference, the ACM/IEEE Symposium on Architectures for Networking and Communications (ANCS), which has been held annually ever since [9].

While processor architectures have been a common topic of research at ANCS, the thrust of "architectural support for networking" and, indeed, many of the investigators and groups involved in that work, have broadened their scope to both lower-level mechanisms (e.g., supporting high-speed networking mechanisms both in software and in hardware accelerators) and higher-level system building projects (e.g., programmable router platforms and distributed platforms for computing and communication). Additionally, enormous new directions have emerged, such as networking support for platform virtualization, network security and monitoring, software-defined radios and software-defined networking.

Uniting all of these topics is the balance between the needs of a networking-related application and the capabilities of a platform to satisfy those needs. Given that both networking tasks and semiconductor technologies continue to evolve and improve, work at this intersection appears poised to remain vibrant and relevant for years to come.

4. ACKNOWLEDGMENTS

This work would not have been possible without the support of two groups. First, the faculty advisors, Jean-Loup Baer and Brian Bershad, were supportive and willing to permit two graduate students to branch out in a new direction. Second, flexible financial support from Intel Corp., NSF and Darpa made it possible to fund this work without a separately funded research agenda.

5. REFERENCES

[1] "Workloads for Programmable Network Interfaces." Patrick Crowley, Marc E. Fiuczynski, Jean-Loup Baer, and Brian N. Bershad. In *Workload Characterization for Computer System Design*, chapter 7. Kluwer Academic Publishers, 2000. Early version appeared in *Proceedings of the 2nd Annual IEEE Workshop on Workload Characterization*, October 1999.

[2] B. N. Bershad, S. Savage, P. Pardyak, E. G. Sirer, M. E. Fiuczynski, D. Becker, C. Chambers, and S. Eggers. 1995. Extensibility safety and performance in the SPIN operating system. *SIGOPS Oper. Syst. Rev.* 29, 5 (December 1995), 267-283.

[3] M.E. Fiuczynski, et al. SPINE: An Operating System for Intelligent Network Adapters. In *Proc. of the Eighth ACM SIGOPS European Workshop*, pp. 7-12. Sintra, Portugal, September 1998.

[4] Dennis C. Lee, Patrick J. Crowley, Jean-Loup Baer, Thomas E. Anderson, and Brian N. Bershad. "Execution characteristics of desktop applications on Windows NT." In *Proc. of the 25th annual International Symposium on Computer Architecture* (ISCA '98) (1998): 27-38.

[5] Cisco Systems. The Cisco QuantumFlow Processor: Cisco's Next Generation Network Processor. 2008.

[6] Mark Franklin, Patrick Crowley, Haldun Hadimioglu, and Peter Onufryk. 2002. Network Processor Design: Issues and Practices, Volume 1. Morgan Kaufmann Publishers Inc., San Francisco, CA, USA.

[7] Mark Franklin, Patrick Crowley, Haldun Hadimioglu, and Peter Onufryk. 2003. Network Processor Design: Issues and Practices, Volume 2. Morgan Kaufmann Publishers Inc., San Francisco, CA, USA.

[8] Mark Franklin, Patrick Crowley, Haldun Hadimioglu, and Peter Onufryk. 2005. Network Processor Design: Issues and Practices, Volume 3. Morgan Kaufmann Publishers Inc., San Francisco, CA, USA.

Author Retrospective for Synthesizing Transformations for Locality Enhancement of Imperfectly-nested Loop Nests*

Keshav Pingali
Department of Computer Science
The University of Texas at Austin
Texas, USA 78712
pingali@cs.utexas.edu

ABSTRACT

This paper describes a technique for transforming imperfectly-nested loops to enhance locality of reference. The key idea is to embed the iteration space of every statement in the loop nest into a special iteration space called the *product space*. The product space is interpreted as a perfectly-nested loop that is transformed to enhance locality and enable tiling; after that, fully permutable loops are tiled, and a new imperfectly-nested loop with better locality than the original one is generated. Experimental results show that this approach is effective in locality enhancement for dense matrix factorization codes and relaxation codes, among others.

Original paper: http://dx.doi.org/10.1023/A:1012293814832

Categories and Subject Descriptors

D.3.4 [**Programming Languages**]: Processors—*Optimization*
General Terms: Algorithms, Languages, Performance
Keywords: restructuring compilers, imperfectly-nested loops, locality enhancement.

1. BACKGROUND

The idea of using loop transformations to enhance locality of reference goes back to the pioneering work of Abu-Sufah, Kuck and Lawrie [1] who showed in 1981 that loop transformations can improve the performance of virtual memory systems. This work demonstrated the utility of loop transformations for locality enhancement, but the transformations were done manually. In the mid-80's, Moldovan and others in the systolic array community explored space-time mappings for mapping loop nests to systolic arrays [7, 13]. Space-time mappings, which can be viewed as composite loop transformations, were represented by integer matrices, and the entries in these integer matrices were obtained by solving Diophantine equations formulated from the dependence distance vectors of the loop nest [7]. Code generation techniques for these transformations were explored by Ancourt and Irigoin [3]. For some reason, this work did not have immediate impact on restructuring compilers, perhaps because the compiler community was busy inventing new dependence tests to improve on the well-known GCD and Banerjee tests that were in vogue at that time.

These ideas were rediscovered and extended in the late 80's and early 90's by the restructuring compiler community, starting with the seminal work of Feautrier [8, 9]. The use of loop transformations to enhance parallelism and locality in perfectly-nested loops was explored by Banerjee [5], Wolf and Lam [18], Li and Pingali [14], and others [4, 16]. Wolf and Lam extended Moldovan's techniques to loop nests for which some dependences are summarized by dependence *directions*, rather than distances. Li and Pingali showed how non-singular integer matrices can be used to simplify the synthesis of loop transformations. Non-singular integer matrices can represent arbitrary compositions of loop permutation, skewing, reversal, and scaling, which are collectively known as *linear loop transformations*.

In most programs however, loop nests are usually *imperfectly-nested* because one or more assignment statements are contained in some but not all of the loops of the loop nest. Cholesky, LU and QR factorizations [10] are imperfectly-nested loop nests. Jacobi iteration for solving pde's approximately using explicit finite difference methods is another example. Figure 1 shows a use of the Jacobi method for solving the two-dimensional heat equation. The outer loop counts time-steps; in each time-step, a smoothing operation (stencil computation) is performed on arrays that represent approximations to the solution to the pde.

It is possible to isolate perfectly-nested loops within imperfectly-nested loops and transform each one separately, but the resulting performance improvements are usually sub-optimal. As an example, consider the Jacobi code fragment in Figure 1. Statements `S1` and `S2` touch the same data in each iteration of the `t` loop; instances of these statements in different iterations of the outer loop touch the same data as well. If the arrays do not fit into cache, this reuse will not be exploited. It is possible to exploit the reuse between statements in a given iteration of the `t` loop if the code is rewritten as in Figure 2. This code can be obtained by peeling the first iterations of the `i1,j1` loops and the last iterations of the `i2` and `j2` loops, and then fusing the remaining `i1` and `i2` loops as well as `j1` and `j2` loops. Furthermore, reuse between different iterations of the `t`-loop can be exploited by skewing the resulting `i` and `j` loops by `2*t` and then tiling all three loops; if the arrays are stored in column major order, interchanging the `i` and `j` loops allows the exploitation of spatial locality as well. These variants are not shown here due to their complexity.

Performing these kinds of transformations automatically requires a theory of loop transformations that models imperfectly-nested loop transformations like loop fusion and fission, and a way of ap-

ICS 25th Anniversary Volume. 2014
ACM 978-1-4503-2840-1/14/06.
http://dx.doi.org/10.1145/2591635.2591660.

```
for t = 1,T
  for i1 = 2,N-1
    for j1 = 2,N-1
S1:   L(i1,j1) = (A(i1,j1+1) + A(i1,j1-1)
                + A(i1+1,j1) + A(i1-1,j1)) / 4
    end
  end
  for i2 = 2,N-1
    for j2 = 2,N-1
S2:   A(i2,j2) = L(i2,j2)
    end
  end
end
```

Figure 1: Jacobi

```
for t = 1,T
  for j1 = 2, N-1
    L(2, j1) = (A(2,j1+1) + A(2,j1-1)
              + A(4,j1) + A(1,j1)) / 4
  end
  for i = 3,N-1
    L(i, 2) = (A(i,3) + A(i,1)
              + A(i+1,2) + A(i-1,2)) / 4
    for j = 3,N-1
      L(i,j) = (A(i,j+1) + A(i,j-1)
                + A(i+1,j1) + A(i-1,j1)) / 4
      A(i-1,j-1) = L(i-1,j-1)
    end
    A(i-1,N-1) = L(i-1,N-1)
  end
  for j2 = 2,N-1
    A(N-1,j2) = L(N-1,j2)
  end
end
```

Figure 2: Fused Jacobi

plying this theory to locality enhancement of imperfectly-nested loops.

As in the case of perfectly-nested loops, the way forward was shown by case studies that investigated how imperfectly-nested loops could be transformed by hand to enhance locality. Carr and Kennedy studied block-matrix factorization codes in the LAPACK library, and showed how the "point" versions of Cholesky factorization can be transformed into the blocked versions using sequences of imperfectly-nested loop transformations [6]. Song and Li did a similar study for Jacobi relaxation [17]. In particular, they showed how the difficult problem of tiling the time loop in Jacobi can be solved by suitable loop transformations.

This was the context in which we performed the research reported in the ICS 1999 paper.

2. OVERVIEW OF SOLUTION

The general approach to locality enhancement of imperfectly-nested loops discussed here builds on the standard approach used for perfectly-nested loops. The strategy is shown in Figure 3. The iteration space of each statement is embedded in a special space called the *product space* using affine embedding functions F_i. These embeddings can be chosen so as to improve reuse in the program, and they generalize transformations like loop fusion and loop fission that have been used in the literature for locality enhancement. Furthermore, the product space itself can be viewed as a perfectly-nested loop nest, so locality enhancement techniques such as height reduction [14] can be applied to the resulting loop nest; when possible, this loop nest is made fully permutable, enabling it to be tiled. Finally, code is generated after projecting out redundant dimensions, using standard techniques from polyhedral algebra; this code generation process may produce imperfectly-nested loop nests if appropriate.

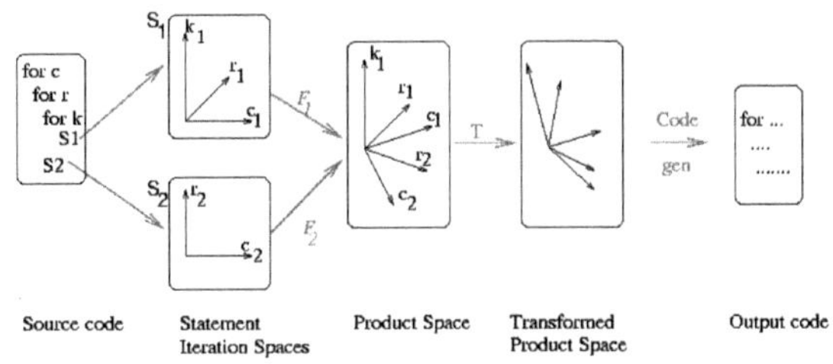

Figure 3: Locality enhancement strategy

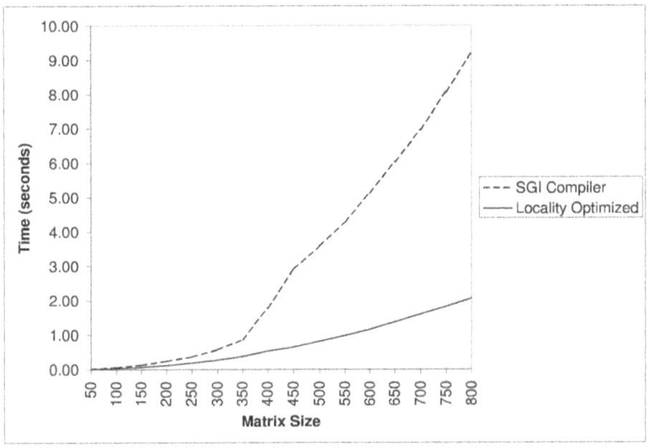

Figure 4: Execution time of Jacobi versions

The effectiveness of our locality enhancement technique is demonstrated for the Jacobi example in Figure 4. It shows the execution times for (i) the code produced by our technique, and (ii) by the SGI compiler, for different grid sizes for a fixed number of time-steps (100). All experiments were run on an SGI Octane workstation based on a R12000 chip running at 300MHz with 32 KB first-level data cache and an unified second-level cache of size 2 MB (both caches are two-way set associative). Our approach is able to tile the time loop, and this results in substantially better performance. To the best of our knowledge, our solution provided the first fully automatic loop transformation technique capable of accomplishing this.

3. CONCLUDING REMARKS

This paper provided one of the first comprehensive solutions to the problem of locality enhancement of imperfectly-nested loops.

Like most loop transformations in the literature, the one presented here relies on knowing dependence information about the loop nest. Pivoting in linear algebra codes introduces a major complication because dependences in such codes cannot be summarized usefully by distance or direction vectors. In 2003, Menon and Pingali showed that a generalized form of symbolic analysis called *fractal symbolic analysis* can solve the problem of restructuring for locality in codes like LU factorization with pivoting [15].

A very different approach to locality enhancement was explored by Kodukula and Pingali in their 1997 work on *data shackling* [11]. Data shackling is a *data-centric* approach to locality enhancement of matrix programs: the matrix is blocked conceptually, and a schedule is chosen for visiting the blocks in some order. All computations that write to a given block are performed when that block is visited. For matrix programs, data shackling offered a data-centric perspective on program transformations that was different from the standard loop-centric view in the literature, but it did not have any special advantages over the standard one. The data-centric point of view came into its own a decade later in 2007 when Kulkarni, Pingali *et al.* showed that it provided the right abstractions for parallelizing irregular applications [12].

4. ACKNOWLEDGEMENTS

Nawaaz Ahmed and Nikolay Mateev are co-authors of the ICS 1999 paper. The work discussed here was part of Ahmed's PhD dissertation at Cornell, which was supervised by Pingali [2]. Mateev was a PhD student in Pingali's group at that time.

References

[1] W. Abu-Sufah, D. Kuck, and D.H.Lawrie. On performance enhancement of paging systems through program analysis and transformations. *IEEE Transactions on Computers*, C-30(5), 1981.

[2] Nawaaz Ahmed. *Locality enhancement of imperfectly-nested loop nests*. PhD thesis, Cornell University, 2000.

[3] C. Ancourt and F. Irigoin. Scanning polyhedra with DO loops. In *Principle and Practice of Parallel Programming*, pages 39–50, April 1991.

[4] E. Ayguadé and Jordi Torres. Partitioning the statement per iteration space using nonsingular matrices. In *1993 ACM International Conference on Supercomputing*, pages 407–415, Tokyo, July 1993.

[5] Uptal Banerjee. A theory of loop permutations. In *Languages and compilers for parallel computing*, pages 54–74, 1989.

[6] Steve Carr and K. Kennedy. Compiler blockability of numerical algorithms. In *Supercomputing*, 1992.

[7] D.I.Moldovan. On the design of algorithms for VLSI systolic arrays. *Proceedings of the IEEE*, 1983.

[8] Paul Feautrier. Some efficient solutions to the affine scheduling problem - part (i): one dimensional time. *International Journal of Parallel Programming*, October 1992.

[9] Paul Feautrier. Some efficient solutions to the affine scheduling problem - part (ii): multi-dimensional time. *International Journal of Parallel Programming*, December 1992.

[10] Gene Golub and Charles Van Loan. *Matrix Computations*. The Johns Hopkins University Press, 1996.

[11] Induprakas Kodukula, Nawaaz Ahmed, and Keshav Pingali. Data-centric multi-level blocking. In *ACM SIGPLAN Conference on Programming Languages Design and Implementation*, PLDI'97, June 1997.

[12] Milind Kulkarni, Keshav Pingali, Bruce Walter, Ganesh Ramanarayanan, Kavita Bala, and L. Paul Chew. Optimistic parallelism requires abstractions. In *ACM SIGPLAN Conference on Programming Language Design and Implementation*, PLDI '07, 2007.

[13] S-Y Kung. *VLSI array processors*. Prentice-Hall, 1988.

[14] W. Li and K. Pingali. Access Normalization: Loop restructuring for NUMA compilers. *ACM Transactions on Computer Systems*, 1993.

[15] Vijay Menon, Keshav Pingali, and Nikolay Mateev. Fractal symbolic analysis. *ACM Trans. Program. Lang. Syst.*, 25(6), November 2003.

[16] J. Ramanujam and P. Sadayappan. Tiling multidimensional iteration spaces for multicomputers. *Journal of Parallel and Distributed Computing*, 16(2):108–120, October 1992.

[17] Yonghong Song and Zhiyuan Li. New tiling techniques to improve cache temporal locality. In *ACM SIGPLAN Conference on Programming Languages Design and Implementation*, PLDI '99, June 1999.

[18] M.E. Wolf and M.S. Lam. A data locality optimizing algorithm. In *ACM SIGPLAN Conference on Programming Languages Design and Implementation*, PLDI '91, June 1991.

Author Retrospective for Adaptive Reduction Parallelization Techniques

Hao Yu
IBM T.J. Watson Research Center
yuh@us.ibm.com

Lawrence Rauchwerger
Parasol Lab, Texas A&M University
rwerger@cse.tamu.edu

ABSTRACT

Modern applications are dynamic and input dependent and algorithm performance is input and environment sensitive. This potential mismatch between algorithmic choice and performance is exacerbated in the case of parallel programs because the penalty for less than optimal locality grows with the size of the machine. Reductions, e.g., *map-reduce* are one of the most important algorithms used in parallel codes are also input sensitive. This led us to develop an adaptive framework that used a statistical method to learn how to select the best algorithm for every execution instance. We applied it to parallel reduction algorithm selection. The importance of better reduction methods as well as adaptive selection methods has only increased since the time this paper was first published.

Original paper: http://dx.doi.org/10.1145/335231.335238

Categories and Subject Descriptors

D.1.3 [**Software**]: Parallel Programming; D.4.8 [**Performance**]: Modeling and Prediction; E.2 [**Data Storage Representation**]: Linked Representations

Keywords

Adaptive Algorithms, Parallel Algorithms, Machine Learning, Reductions, Sorting, Matrix Multiplication

1. ORIGINS OF ADAPTIVE ALGORITHMS

High level algorithm optimization that selects among functionally equivalent versions is today a more pervasive technique than ever before. Due to the complexity of today's computing environments and large and diverse data sets it has become increasingly difficult to tune a single algorithm by finding an optimal setting for its parameters. It has become evident that we can obtain better results (performance) by matching each instance of a problem (input data and machine characteristics) to a specialized algorithms selected from a pre-existing library or from an ad-hoc generated form (e.g., [10]).

In this paper we proposed and implemented one of the first automatic algorithm selection frameworks described in the literature. We used it for matching the best parallel reduction algorithm from our library to the input data of a program on a particular machine. Our system consisted of a library of parallel reduction algorithms, a model (description) of the memory reference characteristic space (based on all possible inputs) and a relative ranking of our library components within this space. The exploration and characterization of the input was done using a factorial experiment on each machine considered. The result was an executable decision tree that could select at run-time the best suited parallel reduction algorithm.

We selected reduction optimization because it was a simple algorithm used in many applications and which consumed a disproportionate amount of execution time. It is a ubiquitous algorithm, perhaps because it implements the principle of superposition. In the parallel processing environment reductions are expensive because they represent a global operation, that generates a lot of communication/synchronization. In our paper we provided several new algorithmic variations to reduction parallelization that were well adapted to the variety of memory reference patterns encountered in various applications. Together with the existing reduction algorithms we put together a fairly comprehensive library of parallel reduction techniques that covered a large input space.

The origins of adaptive algorithm selection can be traced back to John Rice [11] who casted the algorithm selection problem in the framework of approximation theory. Based on practical examples, Rice formulated the algorithm selection problem as a search for a mapping from the elements of a problem space to elements of an algorithm space. Then a performance function mapped (algorithm, problem) tuples to values in a multi-dimensional performance space, in order to optimize some measure of performance, e.g., execution time. The problem space was mapped into a multi-dimensional feature space through a feature extraction function (in itself a complex issue). Rice offered several possible optimization scenarios such as the minimization of execution time of a problem by selecting a per-instance best algorithm. Rice considered offline learning of static single-algorithm selection, both per set and per instance.

Most of the later work in this area can be formulated within this seminal framework. In addition to our own re-

ICS 25th Ann. Volume, Jun 10-13 2014, Muenchen, Germany 2014
ACM 978-1-4503-2840-1/14/06.
http://dx.doi.org/10.1145/2591635.2591661.

search we can in fact note several projects that developed around the same idea and the same time:

The ATLAS [14] library aims to provide automated tuning of BLAS [9], a widely used collection of linear algebra routines. ATLAS made two important contributions to the field. First, it defines a good taxonomy of software adaptation, dividing tuning between parameterized adaptation and source code adaptation. Source code adaptation was further split between multiple implementation (choosing among several implementations) and code generation techniques (i.e., loop unrolling). The viability of the automated library customization approach in ATLAS is demonstrated by its performance which equals or exceeds that of vendor supplied BLAS implementations on a wide variety of platforms.

Similar to our approach, ATLAS uses empirical data gathered at installation to drive customization. Their modeling approach, however, is clearly specialized for the BLAS library. Furthermore, no characteristics of the input data, other than problem size, are employed in the optimization process. Though this may be unimportant for BLAS we found that reductions are sensitive to memory reference characteristics in addition to data structure size.

Brewer [2] built an extensive framework for parallel algorithm selection. Linear system performance models were provided, along with code annotations, by the user, and then a benchmarking phase determined the models' coefficients. The models were then used to estimate the running time of each algorithm, and the algorithm with the shortest predicted execution time was selected. This methodology was shown to be effective for selecting among sorting algorithms and determining data distributions for an equation solver. The use of individual performance models appears to require more effort by the user than our automated approach. Brewer ranks algorithms based on estimated execution time which is more difficult than instance specific relative performance ranking. We have found that our approach yields a sufficiently accurate algorithm selection.

2. LATER WORK

The adaptive algorithm selection ideas presented in our paper have inspired us and other researchers to extend this work [15]. A few years later we applied similar high level adaptive methods to sorting and matrix multiplications algorithms. In [12] we showed how to use a machine learning algorithm to train the adaptive system to select the fastest sorting and matrix multiplication algorithm based on features of the input sequence and the computer system on which it was running. Our work has also influenced other later research such as [7, 5, 13] among others. Currently, almost any software package that is used in a variety of domains with various inputs will use some form of statistical learning technique to adapt to the run-time conditions by tuning parameters or swapping entire algorithms, or even by deriving new ones [10] from high level mathematical specifications. We expect this trend to continue.

Our work has also increased the number of specialized parallel reduction algorithms and influenced (and perhaps motivated) a substantial amount of follow up research. There are tens of citations to our parallel reduction algorithms such as [6, 1, 4, 8, 3].

Today, with the coming of age of parallel processing, the importance of reductions has increased dramatically: Mapreduce is a basic operation in most large scale parallel applications. Thus our paper has aged well. The importance of its topic has only increased with time.

3. REFERENCES

[1] Michael Beynon, *et. al.* Processing large-scale multi-dimensional data in parallel and distributed environments. *Parallel Computing*, 28(5):827–859, May 2002.

[2] Eric A. Brewer. High-level optimization via automated statistical modeling. In *Proc. ACM SIGPLAN Symp. Prin. Prac. Par. Prog.*, pages 80–91, 1995.

[3] Eladio Gutiérrez, Oscar Plata, and Emilio L. Zapata. Data partitioning-based parallel irregular reductions: Research articles. *Concurr. Comput. : Pract. Exper.*, 16(2-3):155–172, Jan. 2004.

[4] Eladio Gutiérrez, Sergio Romero, Luis F. Romero, Oscar Plata, and Emilio L. Zapata. Parallel techniques in irregular codes: Cloth simulation as case of study. *J. Parallel Distrib. Comput.*, 65(4):424–436, April 2005.

[5] Mary W. Hall, Y. Gil, and R.F. Lucas. Self-configuring applications for heterogeneous systems: Program composition and optimization using cognitive techniques. *Proc. of the IEEE*, 96(5):849–862, 2008.

[6] Hwansoo Han and Chau-Wen Tseng. Exploiting locality for irregular scientific codes. *IEEE Trans. Parallel Distrib. Syst.*, 17(7):606–618, July 2006.

[7] Troy A. Johnson and Rudolf Eigenmann. Context-sensitive domain-independent algorithm composition and selection. *SIGPLAN Not.*, 41(6):181–192, June 2006.

[8] Tahsin Kurc, Feng Lee, Gagan Agrawal, Umit Catalyurek, Renato Ferreira, and Joel Saltz. Optimizing reduction computations in a distributed environment. In *Proc. of the 2003 ACM/IEEE Conf. on Supercomputing*, SC '03, New York, NY, 2003.

[9] C. L. Lawson, R. J. Hanson, D. R. Kincaid, and F. T. Krogh. Basic linear algebra subprograms for Fortran usage. *ACM Trans. Math. Softw.*, 5(3):308–323, 1979.

[10] Markus Püschel, *et. al.* Spiral: Code generation for dsp transforms. *Proc. of the IEEE*, 93(2):232–275, 2005. Special issue on 'Program Generation, Optimization, and Adaptation.

[11] J. R. Rice. The algorithm selection problem. *Advances in Computers*, 15:65–118, 1976.

[12] Nathan Thomas, Gabriel Tanase, Olga Tkachyshyn, Jack Perdue, Nancy M. Amato, and Lawrence Rauchwerger. A framework for adaptive algorithm selection in STAPL. In *Proc. ACM SIGPLAN Symp. Prin. Prac. Par. Prog.*, pages 277–288, Chicago, IL, 2005.

[13] Oliver Trachsel and Thomas R. Gross. Variant-based competitive parallel execution of sequential programs. In *Proc. of the 7th ACM Int. Conf. on Computing Frontiers*, pages 197–206, New York, NY, 2010.

[14] R. Clint Whaley, Antoine Petitet, and Jack Dongarra. Automated empirical optimizations of software and the ATLAS project. *Parallel Computing*, 27(1–2):3–35, Jan. 2001.

[15] Hao Yu, Dongmin Zhang, and Lawrence Rauchwerger. An adaptive algorithm selection framework. In *Proc. Intern. Conf. Parallel Architecture and Compilation Techniques*, pages 278–289. IEEE Comp. Soc., 2004.

Author Retrospective

Analytical Cache Models with Applications to Cache Partitioning

G. Edward Suh
Electrical and Computer Engineering
Cornell University
Ithaca, NY
suh@csl.cornell.edu

George Kurian, Srinivas Devadas, Larry Rudolph*
Computer Science and Artificial Intelligence Laboratory
Massachusetts Institute of Technology
Cambridge, MA
{gkurian, devadas, rudolph}@csail.mit.edu

ABSTRACT

This paper presents the author retrospective on the analytical cache modeling work published in the 2001 International Conference on Supercomputing (ICS). We summarize the history of the work, revisit primary observations and lessons that we learned from the modeling effort, and also briefly describe follow-up work to show how the research direction evolved over time.

Original Paper: http://dx.doi.org/10.1145/377792.377797

Categories and Subject Descriptors

B.3.2 [**Design Styles**]: Cache Memories; D.4.1 [**Process Management**]: Scheduling; I.6.5 [**Simulation and Modeling**]: Model Development

Keywords

Cache Partitioning; Process Scheduling; Cache Models

1. HISTORY

The cache modeling work in the 2001 ICS paper was carried out within a larger project named Malleable Caches. While cache design and performance had been extensively researched, the Malleable Caches project was motivated by three observations that were novel at the time: (1) the traditional assumptions on the locality of memory accesses were no longer true for emerging applications such as streaming and real-time applications, (2) the emergence of more spacious caches enabled program blocks to reside longer within the cache, even across scheduling time slices, and (3) caches were increasingly shared amongst multiple processors. The project aimed to improve the efficiency of large caches by dynamically allocating cache resources to run-time workload and sharing behaviors. The analytical model introduced in the ICS paper was a departure from cache optimizations, verified via simulation, that largely focused on static allocation for a single program.

Dynamic partitioning of a shared cache, one thrust of the Malleable Caches project, aimed to more efficiently allocate cache space among multiple tasks. An effective cache partitioning technique requires solving two main challenges: a low-cost, fine-grained mechanism to control cache space for each task, and an algorithm to determine how much cache space that each task needs. For our project, column caching [ ] provided a mechanism to partition caches. However, at the time, there was no work that answered the question of how to determine the best allocation.

The cache modeling work was largely motivated by this need to understand the impact of cache sharing and develop an effective cache allocation policy. The goal of the model was to estimate the overall cache miss-rate (or the number of misses) of a shared cache given individual program characteristics, a cache configuration, and a sharing pattern. The model assumed that a cache is accessed by one program at a time in a time-shared fashion, essentially modeling a single-core system. It was a pleasant surprise to discover that the model can also be used to estimate the performance of shared caches in multicore systems.

The main challenge in characterizing the performance impact of multiple programs sharing a cache is estimating the amount of cache space used by each program without simulating every type of workload combination. One key insight is that the individual isolated program miss-rate curves can be combined to determine the shared cache performance. The miss-rate curve represents the probability of a cache miss as a function of cache size, and enables an estimation of the number of unique cache blocks accessed over a given time period. The number of cache blocks that each program accesses over its time quantum can be combined across context switches to determine the cache footprint of a program at the beginning of its time quantum. Once the initial cache footprint is known, the miss-rate curve can be used to obtain the miss-rate for each program over a time quantum.

2. OBSERVATIONS AND LESSONS

Role of Analytical Modeling.

Analytical methods are rarely used in designing practical systems because it is often extremely difficult, if not impossible, to accurately model complex systems mathematically. As a result, most architectural studies rely on simulations or emulations. This cache modeling effort shows, however,

*Also affiliated with Two Sigma

ICS 25th Anniversary Volume. 2014
ACM 978-1-4503-2840-1/14/06.
http://dx.doi.org/10.1145/2591635.2591662.

that there is a role for analytical studies in system designs. For example, the modeling process forced us to identify first-order effects and tradeoffs in a shared cache, and provided insight and intuition on the range of interference behaviors. The computational efficiency of the analytical model enabled our study of the high-level tradeoffs in a large design space.

It was both interesting and surprising to discover that the individual miss-rate curves were sufficient to accurately capture the performance impact of sharing a cache. The model showed that there were two program properties in the miss-rate curves that largely determine the shared cache performance. One, the number of cache blocks that are accessed over a period largely determines how much cache space is allocated to each program. Traditional cache policies, such as LRU, prioritize recently accessed data. As a result, programs that access a large amount of data quickly are likely to keep more data in the cache compared to the ones with high locality. Two, the cache performance for each program is heavily influenced by how sensitive the program's miss-rate is to the cache size. Some programs may benefit significantly from additional cache space, yet programs such as streaming applications may be largely insensitive to the cache size.

Shared Cache Interference.

While well-known now, our study based on the cache model showed that the performance impact of interference in shared caches could be significant and that the traditional cache management policies could exacerbate the problem.

The study showed that the cache performance of a memory-intensive program with a large cache footprint could be significantly degraded when a cache was simultaneously used by another memory-intensive program. Streaming applications turned out to be particularly damaging because traditional cache policies blindly allocated space to a program with lots of misses even when the program does not benefit from the additional space. In certain cases, we even found that the overall throughput of a multicore system could be improved by leaving some cores idle to reduce the cache interference.

While not as significant as interference from simultaneous sharing, our study also suggested that context switches could have a noticeable impact on cache performance, especially for large shared caches. In a traditional round-robin schedule, the LRU policy evicts cache blocks for old jobs. These blocks may get evicted just before the job is rescheduled leading to lots of cold misses after a context switch.

These observations suggested that cache performance could be significantly improved with more intelligent allocation or scheduling that minimizes harmful cache interference. As an example, for a cache that is shared amongst multiple cores, partitioning can allocate space based on the utility of additional space to each program and limit the pollution from streaming applications. Under time sharing, cold misses can be reduced by keeping a small amount of critical data for each program across context switches.

Limitations.

While the analytical model provided valuable insight, we found that there was still a gap between the model and practical systems. In particular, an accurate prediction for set-associative caches turned out to be difficult because real-world applications often accessed cache sets in a non-uniform manner. In certain cases, this non-uniform access pattern could artificially reduce cache interference among programs because accesses from programs might use different sets. Our attempt to incorporate the non-uniform accesses complicated the cache model with only a limited improvement in its accuracy. In practice, however, we found that the interference that was captured by the fully-associative cache model was often sufficient to make partitioning or scheduling decisions even for set-associative caches.

As another limitation, our cache model targeted multi-programmed workloads and did not consider accesses to common memory locations by multiple threads. As a result, the model could not handle multithreaded programs.

3. OUR FOLLOW-UP WORK

Cache and Memory Monitors [ ].

The cache model showed that miss-rate (or miss) curves contained key program characteristics to understand shared cache performance. To obtain individual program's miss(-rate) curves at run-time for optimizations, we introduced *Recency Hit Counters*. The scheme leverages the LRU stack used for replacement policy decisions. The LRU stack consists of addresses from a sequence of cache or memory accesses such that the distance from the top (i.e., stack distance) represents how recently the address was accessed. A counter, maintained for each LRU stack distance, is incremented when the address in that LRU distance is accessed. Because the stack distance can be used to predict whether an access would be a hit or not given a certain cache/memory size, these counters effectively encode the number of hits as a function of cache size. In essence, the counters represent marginal gains ($g(x)$), which is the number of additional hits for a particular job when the number of allocated memory blocks is increased from $x - 1$ to x.

Thread Scheduling [,].

We studied how thread scheduling could be improved taking memory contention into account in a shared-memory multiprocessor system. The goal was to find the job schedule that minimizes the processor idle time due to either page faults or processors with no jobs scheduled. The study first found that job scheduling has a significant impact on shared memory performance due to interference. We then investigated algorithms to find good schedules. For a small number of jobs, the analytical model could be used to estimate the memory performance of all possible job schedules and determine the best one. For a large number of jobs, a brute-force search based on the model was intractable so a new heuristic method was developed. It first identified the memory needs of jobs by allocating available memory capabilities based on marginal gains. Then, the jobs were grouped together to balance the total memory needs in each time slice.

Cache Partitioning [, ,].

We investigated partitioning of shared last-level caches in the context of both chip multiprocessors (CMP) and simultaneous multithreading (SMT). The recency hit counters were used to obtain marginal gains and cache space was allocated based on the gains. While the high-level approach was simple, a few challenges had to be addressed to make partitioning effective for set-associative caches. First, because the LRU stack was only maintained within a set, the marginal gains were obtained at a coarser granularity, such as one counter for each cache way. Second, partitioning based on cache ways effectively reduced the associativity for each program and increased conflict misses. To address this problem, we introduced a modified LRU policy that replaces a cache block based on the owner and its cache allocation. Finally, cache miss curves were often non-convex and finding the optimal allocation efficiently was difficult. Our solution relied on a heuristic that uses greedy algorithms with multiple starting points.

4. FOLLOW-UP RESEARCH DIRECTIONS

This section provides a brief overview of the research directions that followed our work.

Thread Scheduling.

There has been a large body of work on improving scheduling decisions considering shared cache/memory contention, especially in the context of multi-core processors. For example, Chen et al. [ ] presented a scheduling algorithm that leverages the constructive cache sharing behavior of multithreaded programs. Zhuravlev et al. [ ] proposed to improve scheduling using classification schemes which determine how programs affect each other when competing for shared resources such as caches, memory bus, etc.

Partitioning for Efficiency.

There have been efforts to improve both effectiveness and costs of cache partitioning. Qureshi et al. [ ] proposed utility-based cache partitioning using dynamic set sampling. The sampling enables obtaining a complete isolated miss curve of each application at run-time without maintaining full recency counters for each application. The number of sampled sets is chosen to obtain good accuracy with negligible hardware overhead. The work also uses a lookahead algorithm to avoid local minima when searching for the best allocation.

To avoid losing associativity, partitioning of cache sets instead of ways has also been investigated [ ]. Such schemes, however, require significant redesign of the cache arrays and must do scrubbing, i.e, flush data when resizing partitions. Sanchez et al. proposed Vantage [ ] that allows fine-grained partitioning while maintaining high associativity and strong isolation. Vantage requires cache designs with high associativity and good hash functions (e.g., zcaches).

Partitioning for Commodity Processors.

Researchers have investigated partitioning on commodity processors without custom hardware support. One set of techniques obtained the miss curve (or marginal gains) using existing hardware functions such as performance counters. Tam et al. [ ] proposed to collect the cache references using the Sampled Data Address Register (SDAR) of IBM Power5 processors and build the LRU stack model at regular intervals to estimate the miss curve of an application. West et al. [ ] proposed an analytical model that measures the cache occupancy of an application and combined this with miss rate information from performance counters to estimate the miss curve. Multiple occupancy (/miss-curve) points are obtained by co-scheduling the application with different co-runners or by dynamically throttling its execution rate.

Another set of techniques explored the cache partition space using hill climbing [ ], albeit with non-convex problems. To enforce partitioning policies, these approaches use virtual memory and page coloring to constrain the pages of a process to specific cache sets. Repartitioning requires potentially costly recoloring, involving page mapping updates and copying of physical pages.

Partitioning for Quality of Service.

Researchers have shown that cache partitioning can also be used to improve Quality of Service (QoS). For example, Iyer [ ] designed a QoS framework for shared caches on CMP platforms. The hardware partitions the cache into multiple regions and directs memory references to separate regions to enforce priority. Cook et al. [ ] proposed a partitioning technique that allowed latency-sensitive foreground jobs to run simultaneously with throughput-bound background jobs. The proposal ensures that enough shared cache space is allocated to the foreground job.

5. REFERENCES

[1] S. Chen, P. B. Gibbons, M. Kozuch, V. Liaskovitis, A. Ailamaki, G. E. Blelloch, B. Falsafi, L. Fix, N. Hardavellas, T. C. Mowry, and C. Wilkerson. Scheduling Threads for Constructive Cache Sharing on CMPs. In *Proceedings of the 19th Annual ACM Symposium on Parallel Algorithms and Architectures*, 2007.

[2] D. Chiou, P. Jain, L. Rudolph, and S. Devadas. Application-specific Memory Management for Embedded Systems Using Software-controlled Caches. In *Proceedings of the 37th Annual Design Automation Conference*, 2000.

[3] H. Cook, M. Moreto, S. Bird, K. Dao, D. A. Patterson, and K. Asanovic. A Hardware Evaluation of Cache Partitioning to Improve Utilization and Energy-efficiency While Preserving Responsiveness. In *Proc. of the 40th Annual International Symposium on Computer Architecture*, 2013.

[4] R. Iyer. CQoS: A Framework for Enabling QoS in Shared Caches of CMP Platforms. In *Proceedings of the 18th Annual International Conference on Supercomputing*, 2004.

[5] J. Lin, Q. Lu, X. Ding, Z. Zhang, X. Zhang, and P. Sadayappan. Gaining Insights into Multicore Cache Partitioning: Bridging the Gap between Simulation and Real Systems. In *Proc. of the International Symposium on High Performance Computer Architecture*, 2008.

[6] M. K. Qureshi and Y. N. Patt. Utility-Based Cache Partitioning: A Low-Overhead, High-Performance, Runtime Mechanism to Partition Shared Caches. In *Proceedings of the 39th Annual IEEE/ACM International Symposium on Microarchitecture*, 2006.

[7] D. Sanchez and C. Kozyrakis. Vantage: Scalable and Efficient Fine-grain Cache Partitioning. In *Proc. of the 38th International Symposium on Computer Architecture*, 2011.

[8] G. E. Suh, S. Devadas, and L. Rudolph. A New Memory Monitoring Scheme for Memory-Aware Scheduling and Partitioning. In *Proc. of the 8th International Symposium on High-Performance Computer Architecture*, 2002.

[9] G. E. Suh, L. Rudolph, and S. Devadas. Dynamic Cache Partitioning for Simultaneous Multithreading Systems. In *Proceedings of the IASTED International Conference on Parallel and Distributed Computing and Systems*, 2001.

[10] G. E. Suh, L. Rudolph, and S. Devadas. Effects of Memory Performance on Parallel Job Scheduling. In *Job Scheduling Strategies for Parallel Processing*, Lecture Notes in Computer Science. Springer Berlin Heidelberg, 2001.

[11] G. E. Suh, L. Rudolph, and S. Devadas. Dynamic Partitioning of Shared Cache Memory. *Journal of Supercomputing*, 2004.

[12] D. K. Tam, R. Azimi, L. B. Soares, and M. Stumm. RapidMRC: Approximating L2 Miss Rate Curves on Commodity Systems for Online Optimizations. In *Proc. of the International Conference on Architectural Support for Programming Languages and Operating Systems*, 2009.

[13] K. Varadarajan, S. K. Nandy, V. Sharda, A. Bharadwaj, R. Iyer, S. Makineni, and D. Newell. Molecular Caches: A Caching Structure for Dynamic Creation of Application-specific Heterogeneous Cache Regions. In *Proc. of the 39th Annual International Symposium on Microarchitecture*, 2006.

[14] R. West, P. Zaroo, C. A. Waldspurger, and X. Zhang. Online Cache Modeling for Commodity Multicore Processors. *SIGOPS Oper. Syst. Rev.*, 44(4), 2010.

[15] S. Zhuravlev, S. Blagodurov, and A. Fedorova. Addressing Shared Resource Contention in Multicore Processors via Scheduling. In *Proc. of the International Conference on Architectural Support for Programming Languages and Operating Systems*, 2010.

Author Retrospective for Search and Replication In unstructured Peer-to-peer Networks

Qin Lv
University of Colorado Boulder
qin.lv@colorado.edu

Pei Cao
Google, Inc.
cao@cs.stanford.edu

Edith Cohen
Microsoft Research
edith@cohenwang.com

Kai Li
Princeton University
li@cs.princeton.edu

Scott Shenker
University of California, Berkeley
shenker@icsi.berkeley.edu

ABSTRACT

Does academic research impact popular open-source peer-to-peer systems? Looking back, we find that the simple technique "expanding ring" does find its use in Gnutella and many other contexts.

Original paper:
http://dx.doi.org/10.1145/514191.514206

Categories and Subject Descriptors

C.2.4 [**Distributed Systems**]: Distributed applications

Keywords

unstructured peer-to-peer systems; scalable query algorithms

Our paper, published in 2002, was motivated by the poor scalability of Gnutella software at the time, Gnutella 0.4. Gnutella, released in early 2000, was the first decentralized peer-to-peer file sharing network of its kind. It supported file sharing among its network participants, yet had no central server to be targeted or shut down by authorities. Gnutella 0.4 used a pure flooding query algorithm to facilitate file discovery among its participants. A node looking for a particular file queries every other node until a fixed Time-To-Live (TTL) has been exhausted. The algorithm, though simple, clearly does not scale.

Our paper proposed two new techniques: *expanding ring*, and *k random walkers*. We emphasized the need for *adaptive termination*, that is, instead of using a fixed TTL, each querying node should rein in its lookup requests periodically, and only contact more nodes if it hasn't received enough answers.

How has Gnutella itself evolved since then? In 2002, the Gnutella 0.6 protocol was introduced and made two significant changes to the Gnutella 0.4 protocol. First, nodes are partitioned into two tiers, leaves and ultrapeers, with ultrapeers storing directories of files on leaves and handling all lookup requests. Second, Dynamic Querying, which is a variant of *expanding ring*, is used for initial phase of queries among ultrapeers. Dynamic querying follows the principle of adaptive termination; the lookup is stopped when the querying node received a fixed number of results. Gnutella 0.6 is still in use today with millions of users.

It is both humbling and gratifying to observe how open-source P2P software such as Gnutella and BitTorrent address scalability challenges. On the other hand, it appears that a very simple two-tier technique, where certain nodes are elevated to take on more responsibilities such as ultrapeers or trackers, is enough to solve a lot of the problem. After all, a node with powerful CPUs and good Internet connections can be asked to manage 100 other weaker nodes, giving the system an immediate two orders of magnitude scalability boost, which, many times, is all that is needed! On the other hand, techniques such as expanding ring do find its use in Gnutella. Perhaps this is due to the fact that expanding ring is the simplest algorithm that employs adaptive termination.

Over the years, the two techinques, *expanding ring* and *k random walkers*, have found use in many other dynamic P2P environments such as sensor networks and Vehicular Ad-Hoc NETwork (VANET). Truly unstructured peer-to-peer systems without the use of a two-tier structure do arise in different contexts from time to time, and those techinques remain the simplest solutions for scalable lookups.

ICS 25th Anniversary Volume. 2014
ACM 978-1-4503-2840-1/14/06.
http://dx.doi.org/10.1145/2591635.2591663.

Author Retrospective

Bloom Filtering Cache Misses for Accurate Data Speculation and Prefetching

Jih-Kwon Peir
CISE Department
University of Florida
P.O. Box 116120
Gainesville, FL 32611
(352) 505-1573
peir@cise.ufl.edu

Shih-Chang Kevin Lai
ARM Taiwan Ltd.
7F, No.2, Li-Hsin 6th Road,
Hsinchu,Taiwan, 30078
886-03-5657116
kevin.lai@arm.com

Shih-Lien Liu, Jared Stark, Konrad Lai *
Intel Corporation
2111 NE 25th Ave,
Hillsboro, OR 97124
(503) 712-2750
{shih-lien.l.lu,jared.w.stark}@intel.com

ABSTRACT

In this paper, we provide the authors' retrospective analysis of the paper "Bloom Filtering Cache Misses for Accurate Data Speculative and Prefetching" which was published in the proceedings of 2002 International Conference on Supercomputing.

DOI: http://dx.doi.org/10.1145/514191.514219

Categories and Subject Descriptors

C.1 [**Processor Architectures**]: Processor pipeline, cache access, memory hierarchy, instruction scheduling, single-stream processors.

General Terms: Performance and Design.

Keywords

Bloom filter, cache hit/miss prediction, instruction scheduling, data speculation, prefetching.

BACKGROUND AND MOTIVATION

Cache access involves a tag path to determine cache hit/miss and the location of the data, and a data path to access the data from the hit location. To shorten the access time, these two inherently sequential paths are operated in parallel in modern processors. Early techniques bypass the tag path and use cache index bits to fetch the data from the target set in the data array. They rely on way-prediction methods ranging from simple MRU prediction to more accurate prediction based on matching partial address tags to select the predicted data in the set [1].

* Konrad Lai retired from Intel Corp.

ICS 25th Anniversary Volume, 2014
ACM 978-1-4503-2840-1/14/06.
http://dx.doi.org/10.1145/2591635.2591664

The predicted data is verified after the hit/miss resolution from the tag path. This way-prediction for fast cache data access is the earliest application based on the idea of cache-hit predictions with high accuracy.

Instruction scheduling on pipelined processors plays a critical role in processor performance. To avoid pipeline bubbles, load dependents must be scheduled according to the cache latency of the load before knowing whether the load data is located in the cache. In the case of a cache miss, the load and its dependents must be canceled and rescheduled, which incurs complexity and overhead. To solve this problem, we sought an accurate way to predict cache hit/miss in early pipeline stages. At the time this paper was published, the existing counter-based prediction [2] was inaccurate and the partial-address matching approach [3] was too expensive due to space and access time overhead. For this purpose, we introduced a new approach using the Bloom Filter (BF) technique [4] for identifying cache misses accurately.

A Bloom Filter (BF) is a probabilistic algorithm to quickly test membership in a large set using multiple hash functions into an array of bits [4]. Our goal in this paper was to adopt the fundamentals of a Bloom Filter and modify it for cache hit/miss prediction to accomplish accurate instruction scheduling with low overhead. The theme of a BF for cache hit/miss prediction is when a BF identifies a non-member (cache miss), it is guaranteed. However, when a BF identifies a member (cache hit), it is not guaranteed. Therefore, it is important to design an efficient BF which can identify a majority of cache misses to minimize erroneous scheduling of load dependents.

CHALLENGES

In searching for a BF solution, we faced many challenges, mainly in two aspects; the fitness of the BF fundamentals for cache hit/miss prediction and an efficient integration of the BF into a processor pipeline. We will describe these challenges and our solutions in a retrospective manner.

In the original BF, multiple randomized hashing functions were applied to the key (i.e. block address) of the cached blocks to index a linear array of bits, called the BF array. The hashed bits were turned on when a block was allocated in cache. Therefore, a block was guaranteed not to be located in cache when any hashed bit was off. There were three obstacles to mimic the original BF:

1. In a cache access, the index bits were extracted quickly from the least significant bits in the block address for indexing the tag and the data arrays. Using randomized hashing functions could cause delays in accessing the BF array.
2. Sharing the BF bit array with multiple hashing functions required multiple accesses and could encounter conflicts in accessing the multiple bits and caused further delays.
3. The original BF could not handle the update of the BF array when a block was replaced from the cache since the associated bits in the BF array may have been shared with other cache blocks and could not be turned off.

We handled these issues in the proposed Partition-address BF and Partial-address BF as follows. First, we did not consider randomized hashing functions and stayed with the simple cache indexing mechanism. In the Partition-address BF, we honored the multiple hashing idea. But, instead of hashing to the same BF array, we partitioned the array into equal-size sub-arrays, each of which was indexed by a different portion of the block address. Separated indices and BF arrays allowed parallel accesses and fast BF filtering. However, the accuracy of filtering suffered because of the limited, non-sharing bits in each sub-array. In addition, the challenge of handling the update of the BF array remained as a difficult issue. One expensive solution for an accurate update was to implement a counting BF [5]. In this approach, instead of a single bit, a counter was used in each hashed location in the BF array to count the number of cached blocks hashing to that location. The counter was incremented when a block hashed to the location entered the cache, and was decremented when the block was removed from the cache. We did not consider this solution further due to its space overhead and complexity.

The Partial-address BF handled the BF array update by recognizing the blocks that shared the same bit were allocated in the same cache set as long as the partial-address was wider than the cache index. Hence, the address tags in the target set could be used to determine whether the hashed location in the BF array could be reset when the LRU block was replaced. In this approach, we abandoned the multiple hashing because it complicated the BF array update. Furthermore, the single hashing approach using partial block address had showed high accuracy for filtering cache misses.

We noticed that cache hit/miss prediction based on partial-address matching [3] could also be considered as a form of Bloom filter. It guaranteed a cache miss if the match failed. Again, we did not consider this solution due to its cost and overhead.

The second aspect of the challenges was to integrate the BF for cache misses into the processor pipeline. We needed the block address in order to apply the BF for testing cache membership. However, in a physical cache, the physical block address was not known until after the address was generated and the virtual to physical address translation was performed. In an Alpha 21264-like pipeline design, it was too late for scheduling the load dependent even if the BF could accurately identify a cache miss for the load. The severity of this challenge was largely dependent on the pipeline implementation.

To remedy this difficulty, we decided to use a virtual-address based BF for predicting cache misses to push the prediction one cycle earlier. Once a cache miss was identified using the virtual address, the dependent instructions scheduled in the same cycle to avoid pipeline bubbles were canceled while other independent instructions were unaffected. We had explored other options to push the prediction even earlier in the pipeline. One example we considered was to use the base register ID and displacement of a load so that we could make the cache miss prediction before the memory address was calculated. However, after extensive simulations, we abandoned the idea since the accuracy of prediction was discouraging.

IMPACTS

We introduced the Bloom Filter concept for solving architecture issues. We proposed a Partition-address BF and a Partial-address BF for filtering cache misses. The Partial-address BF described in the paper made a unique observation to handle dynamic update of the BF array for tracking cache membership without using a counting BF. An efficient way of handling updates of the BF array is essential since the cache is updated constantly throughout program execution.

We did a Google Scholar search and found 4349 papers in which the classical Bloom filter paper [4] was cited. Our paper was the first paper to cite the original Bloom filter paper among 53 papers from the five major architecture conferences: ISCA, MICRO, HPCA, ICS and PACT. There are 81 papers which cited our paper. The top 20 most-cited papers among these 81 papers have been cited by 1937 papers. These top 20 highly-cited papers cover a wide-range of architecture-related subjects including transactional memory, processor pipeline design, memory disambiguation and LSQ design, data prefetching, software and memory-related debugging, synchronization and data race detection, cache management and cache coherence, variants of Bloom filter designs, security and denial-of-service, code analysis and optimization, branch prediction, and low-power cache and cache coherence mechanisms.

We also searched the papers published in the five major architecture conferences from 2003 to 2013. We found that there were 42 papers in ISCA, 35 papers in MICRO, 28 papers in HPCA, 10 papers in ICS, and 11 papers in PACT, which either directly or indirectly applied the Bloom filter idea in their paper.

ACKNOWLEDGEMENT

Early discussions of the Bloom filter idea with Windsor Hsu at IBM Research were very helpful. The research funding from NSF, Intel, and IBM for Jih-Kwon Peir are acknowledged. Qi Zeng, Xi Tao helped collecting statistics from Google Scholar and surveying papers in five major architecture conferences.

REFERENCES

[1] J-K. Peir, W. Hsu, and A. Smith, "Functional Implementation Techniques for CPU Cache Memories," *IEEE Trans. on Computers*, Special Issue on Cache Memory, 48(2), pp. 100-110, 1999.

[2] A. Yoaz, M. Erez, R. Ronen, and S. Juordan, "Speculation Techniques for Improving Load Related Instruction Scheduling," *Proc. 26th Int'l Symp. On Computer Architecture*, 1999.

[3] L. Liu, "Cache Design with Partial Address Matching," *Proc. 27th Int'l Symp. On Microarchitecture*, 1994.

[4] B. Bloom, "Space / Time Trade-offs in Hash Coding with Allowable Errors," *Comm. ACM*, 13(7), pp. 422–426, 1970.

[5] L. Fan, P. Cao, J. Almeida, and A. Broder, "Summary Cache: A Scalable Wide-area Web Cache Sharing Protocol," *IEEE/ACM Trans. On Networking*, 8(3), pp. 281-293, 2000.

Author Retrospective

AEGIS: Architecture for Tamper-Evident and Tamper-Resistant Processing

G. Edward Suh*, Christopher Fletcher†, Dwaine Clarke†, Blaise Gassend†, Marten van Dijk‡, Srinivas Devadas†

* Cornell University, ECE – suh@csl.cornell.edu
† Massachusetts Institute of Technology, CSAIL – {declarke, gassend}@alum.mit.edu, {cwfletch, devadas}@mit.edu
‡ University of Connecticut, ECE – vandijk@engr.uconn.edu

ABSTRACT

AEGIS is a single-chip secure processor that can be used to protect the integrity and confidentiality of an application program from both physical and software attacks. We briefly describe the history behind this architecture and its key features, discuss main observations and lessons from the project, and list limitations of AEGIS and how recent research addresses them.

Original paper: http://dx.doi.org/10.1145/782814.782838

Categories and Subject Descriptors

C.1 [**Processor Architectures**]: Miscellaneous; D.4.6 [**Operating Systems**]: Security and Protection

Keywords

Certified execution, software licensing, secure processors

1. HISTORY

The AEGIS project began with the question of what hardware's role in security should be. At the time, security was a relatively new topic to computer architects and there were only a few previous studies in the area of architectural support for security. One notable work from the academic community was XOM [10], which proposed to only trust processor hardware to provide a protected execution environment. XOM needed this level of security to support software copy protection. We found the idea of only trusting a single processor chip to be particularly promising, especially given the trend of remote computation on the Internet such as peer-to-peer or cloud computing and the proliferation of embedded and mobile devices. In this sense, XOM largely inspired the security model and the high-level approach of AEGIS.

We started our work in this direction by developing mechanisms to protect off-chip memory [5], which we believed were essential to enable a "single-chip" secure processor but were missing at the time, including in [10]. This experience and further investigation of potential application scenarios helped us identify key high-level design considerations for AEGIS. First, we found that the cost of protection mechanisms could be substantial and that application scenarios had varying security requirements. Based on these efficiency concerns, we felt that the secure processor should to be able to provide flexible protection that matches each application's needs. Second, to be useful in remote computations, we found that the security of the computation must be verifiable externally in addition to being protected by the processor. Finally, there was a question about how much software needs to be trusted especially because the hardware complexity of completely removing trust in an operating system turned out to be non-trivial.

The AEGIS paper in the 2003 ICS presented the high-level architecture that would enable an application to choose its protection levels and verify its computation externally. The paper also investigated multiple design choices based on the level of trust in system software. In that sense, the main contribution of the paper was to provide a framework for single-chip secure processor designs by identifying key security capabilities, to describe the protections necessary for each type of attack, and to discuss how best to implement those protections. In a subsequent paper, we presented a detailed implementation of one particular design point [13].

AEGIS explicitly identified two protection levels for secure execution environments. First, *tamper-evident computing* is intended to ensure the integrity of a computation. In this environment, any tampering from outside the protected program such as unintended changes to program memory should be detected. Second, *private tamper-resistant computing* requires an additional confidentiality guarantee that an adversary cannot learn about the user's secret data. This distinction means that additional protection overheads are paid only when necessary, depending on application requirements. For example, crowd sourcing applications like SETI@home require integrity, but seldom require confidentiality. On the other hand, users usually expect confidentiality when they outsource computation with their own sensitive data.

The AEGIS paper investigated the tradeoffs based on how much trust is placed on software components, in particular operating system (OS) functions. General-purpose computing systems often rely on OS support to provide the ability to time-share resources (e.g., CPU and memory) and manage multiple users, among other responsibilities. Yet, OS code is often quite complex, which results in vulnerabilities that at-

ICS 25th Anniversary Volume. 2014
ACM 978-1-4503-2840-1/14/06.
http://dx.doi.org/10.1145/782814.782838.

tackers use to break the security of the system. For security, some or all of the OS functions can either be moved to or checked by hardware so the software trusted computing base shrinks. However, more security-related functions in hardware come at the cost of reduced flexibility and increased design complexity. To investigate this tradeoff, AEGIS presented two designs: a version that trusts a small piece of critical OS code, and a version that does not trust any OS code.

AEGIS also described which protection mechanisms are necessary given different attack types. For example, conventional virtual memory and privilege levels are sufficient to protect the memory contents from a pure software attack. On the other hand, to prevent hardware attacks that physically read memory by tapping the main memory bus, encryption is necessary. Similarly, the design that assumes an untrusted OS requires additional protection mechanisms that are not necessary with trusted OS components.

2. OBSERVATIONS AND LESSONS

Hardware Root-of-Trust.

For systems that are physically exposed to potential adversaries, hardware must provide a root of trust that cannot be duplicated or altered. Thus, a system's root keys should be kept secret in hardware. The most fundamental security functions should also be implemented as ROM code or custom hardware to ensure their integrity. For example, today's mobile devices such as smartphones and tablets rely on a secret key inside the processor hardware to authenticate the device and a secure booting mechanism in ROM code to check the integrity of a boot loader.

Single-Chip Trusted Computing Base.

History also suggests that the single-chip approach of minimizing trusted hardware has important benefits in building secure systems in practice. Having multiple chips in the hardware trusted computing base turned out to pose challenges in both securing inter-chip communication channels from physical attacks and coordinating multiple manufacturers. As an example, Intel's TXT technology [2] relies on both an Intel processor and a third-party (external) chip called a TPM [15] to provide hardware-based security functions. TXT+TPM has been successfully attacked by probing or tampering with the processor-TPM bus [12, 16]. While TXT+TPM has been available for several years, the technology has not been widely utilized.

In 2013, Intel announced the next-generation of TXT called Software Guard Extensions (SGX) [9]. SGX works by maintaining one or more enclaves, where each enclave is a memory region that is inaccessible to software running at any non-enclave privilege level. Like TXT, code/data loaded into an enclave is measured and the result/starting state can be signed before it is returned to a user. Interestingly, SGX takes the third-party TPM out of the picture and adopts a single-chip approach, only relying on the main processor. SGX also performs automatic encryption and integrity verification on all data that leaves the processor. AEGIS proposed these techniques to protect against physical attacks.

Similarly, game consoles and mobile devices also integrate their basic security functions into the main processing chip instead of utilizing an auxiliary chip. These decisions are likely to have been taken in order to provide a proper level of security against physical attacks.

Hardware's Role in Reducing the Software TCB.

It is now widely accepted that a complex piece of software cannot be trusted to be secure. For example, a large monolithic OS has been repeatedly shown to have security vulnerabilities. In that sense, hardware support to reduce the software trusted computing base is necessary to build a secure system.

However, exactly how much software should be trusted and how critical security functions should be implemented are open design choices. In the AEGIS project, after investigating two design points with and without trusted software, we implemented the one with a trusted security kernel to get the flexibility of software in executing certain tasks, and the security of hardware for the remaining operations. While the ability to tolerate a completely untrusted OS was attractive, full hardware protection added significant design complexity and could only support a very restrictive protection model. We remark that Intel's SGX also chose to rely on a special piece of system software, which Intel provides, to implement TPM-like functionality.

On one hand, cryptographic primitives are good candidates for hardware implementations because they are relatively static, seldom requiring a patch once implemented correctly, and their efficiency can often benefit significantly from parallelism in hardware. Indeed, AEGIS implemented encryption and hashing functions for memory protection in hardware for performance reasons. Further, a cryptographic operation implemented in hardware is nearly always more resistant to attacks compared to the same operation in software. For example, Intel's hardware AES-NI extensions prevent cache side-channel attacks on AES [8].

On the other hand, for infrequent and control-intensive functions, the added complexity and reduced flexibility of a hardware implementation is often difficult to justify. For example, a context switcher in hardware is likely to be implemented as a sequential state machine and is in a sense equivalent to a fixed microcode routine. Therefore, if the integrity of the software routine can be ensured by, for example, checking the hash at run-time, both hardware and software implementations arguably provide comparable security and performance, and a trusted software implementation will be preferable. In fact, the AEGIS implementation relied on ROM code for infrequent and complex security functions such as entering or exiting a protected execution environment.

In essence, architects need to consider the overall system complexity of both hardware and software combined, in addition to efficiency and security, to make a decision on where to place a security function. For certain cases, we found that the complexity can be reduced by having a trusted component verify the operations of an untrusted one. For example, the AEGIS design with an untrusted OS had a hardware verifier, which is much simpler than the context switcher itself, to check the context switching operation in the OS. However, simply moving one function from software to hardware may not necessarily reduce the overall complexity of the trusted computing base.

3. LIMITATIONS

Untrusted Programs and Side/Covert Channels.

The AEGIS architecture was designed to protect a program from external software and physical attacks, but assumed that the protected program itself is *trusted* and *well-written*. A malicious program, on the other hand, may produce a bogus result or intentionally leak the user's private data. Also, AEGIS did not provide protection against side-channel or covert-channel attacks. As a result, a protected program may still leak confidential information if its observable behaviors, such as memory access patterns [7] or execution time [1], depend on the confidential data.

AEGIS made the above assumptions because it mainly considered application scenarios where a program was written by a trusted party. In fact, these assumptions are fairly common for many secure processor designs. For example, Intel SGX assumes software running inside the enclave is trusted, and requires the user program to wipe register values upon a normal enclave exit if those registers stored confidential data.

However, the assumptions of trusted and well-written programs pose limitations on applicable application scenarios and on the level of security provided by AEGIS. For example, in many cloud computing scenarios today, users do not own or see the program that processes their data (e.g., the algorithms in Google Docs are kept secret by Google). Further, these types of programs are frequently updated. As a result, it is difficult (if not impossible) for users to vet these programs. Second, being "well-written" to prevent unintentional leakage is difficult and/or incurs large overhead. In fact, the only "fool proof" way to quell unintentional leakage channels is to use Fully Homomorphic Encryption [6], which currently has over a billion times overhead when running even simple programs.

To address these issues, a new single-chip secure processor called Ascend is being designed to run *untrusted* programs [3]. The key idea behind Ascend is *program obfuscation*: an adversary should not be able to tell what program or data is running inside Ascend by observing the Ascend chip's external pins. To achieve this security level, Ascend is built with a primitive called Oblivious-RAM (ORAM) that keeps main memory encrypted and additionally shuffles memory to prevent leakage through the program's address pattern [11]. Further, Ascend uses information-theoretic principles to bound leakage over timing channels (e.g., program runtime and ORAM access rate) [4]. On the other hand, Ascend's security comes with a more limited usage model. Currently, Ascend runs programs on bare metal and does not allow sharing resources with other users. Ascend can only run programs whose IO is limited to Ascend's ORAM — such as batch programs and stream computations [17].

Secure User IO.

The AEGIS proposal is also limited in its support for secure IO channels. AEGIS relies on a program itself to secure its communication channels using cryptographic protocols. This approach is relatively easy to apply for network communications where both sides can be authenticated and trusted, but difficult to use for local user interfaces such as displays and keyboards.

In fact, providing secure yet rich user interfaces is a challenge that still needs further investigation [18]. In traditional systems, user interfaces involve multiple components on a system such as a processor, a south bridge, and an IO device. As a result, the processor needs to be able to secure communications among multiple distributed components and also maintain consistent security policies across them. Modern system-on-chip (SoC) designs mitigate this problem by integrating most of the IO components into a single chip. However, even for SoCs, secure user IO requires device drivers to be trusted, adding to the TCB.

Virtualization Support.

AEGIS was designed in the context of traditional systems that run a single operating system. Today, however, virtualization has become a norm especially for cloud computing, allowing a single processor to run multiple operating systems managed by a hypervisor. Recent studies (e.g., [14]) showed that the general secure processor approach in AEGIS can be applied to the virtualization context, protecting a virtual machine (or an application) even from untrusted hypervisors, thereby reducing the trusted computing base.

4. CONCLUSION

In retrospect, the high-level approach in AEGIS that relies only on a single processor chip to protect a program's execution turned out to be a promising direction which continued in more recent systems. The architecture had some limitations and much research still remains to be done to fully realize the promise of single-chip secure processors.

5. REFERENCES

[1] D. J. Bernstein. Cache-Timing Attacks on AES. Technical report, 2005.

[2] David Grawrock. The Intel Safer Computing Initiative: Building Blocks for Trusted Computing, 2006.

[3] C. Fletcher, M. van Dijk, and S. Devadas. Secure Processor Architecture for Encrypted Computation on Untrusted Programs. In *STC; an extended version is located at http://csg.csail.mit.edu/pubs/memos/Memo508/memo508.pdf (Master's thesis)*, 2012.

[4] Fletcher, Christopher and Ren, Ling and Yu, Xiangyao and Van Dijk, Marten and Khan, Omer and Devadas, Srinivas. Suppressing the Oblivious RAM Timing Channel While Making Information Leakage and Program Efficiency Trade-offs. In *HPCA*, 2014.

[5] B. Gassend, G. E. Suh, D. Clarke, M. van Dijk, and S. Devadas. Caches and Merkle Trees for Efficient Memory Integrity Verification. In *HPCA*, 2003.

[6] C. Gentry. Fully Homomorphic Encryption Using Ideal Lattices. In *STOC*, 2009.

[7] O. Goldreich and R. Ostrovsky. Software Protection and Simulation on Oblivious RAMs. In *J. ACM*, 1996.

[8] S. Gueron. Intel Advanced Encryption Standard (AES) New Instructions Set, 2012.

[9] Intel. Software Guard Extensions Programming Reference, 2013.

[10] D. Lie, C. Thekkath, M. Mitchell, P. Lincoln, D. Boneh, J. Mitchell, and M. Horowitz. Architectural Support for Copy and Tamper Resistant Software. In *ASPLOS*, 2000.

[11] Ling Ren and Xiangyao Yu and Christopher Fletcher and Marten van Dijk and Srinivas Devadas. Design Space Exploration and Optimization of Path Oblivious RAM in Secure Processors. In *ISCA*, 2013.

[12] E. Sparks. A Security Assessment of Trusted Platform Modules. Technical Report 597, 2007.

[13] G. E. Suh, C. W. O'Donnell, I. Sachdev, and S. Devadas. Design and Implementation of the AEGIS Single-Chip Secure Processor Using Physical Random Functions. In *ISCA*, 2005.

[14] J. Szefer and R. B. Lee. Architectural Support for Hypervisor-Secure Virtualization. In *ASPLOS*, 2012.

[15] Trusted Computing Group. TCG Specification Architecture Overview Revision 1.2. http://www.trustedcomputinggroup.com/home, 2004.

[16] Winter, Johannes and Dietrich, Kurt. A Hijacker's Guide to the LPC Bus. In *EUROPKI*, 2012.

[17] Yu, Xiangyao and Fletcher, Christopher W and Ren, Ling and van Dijk, Marten and Devadas, Srinivas. Generalized External Interaction with Tamper-Resistant Hardware with Bounded Information Leakage. In *CCSW*, 2013.

[18] Zhou, Zongwei and Gligor, Virgil D. and Newsome, James and McCune, Jonathan M. Building Verifiable Trusted Path on Commodity x86 Computers. In *IEEE S&P*, 2012.

Author Retrospective for Energy Conservation Techniques for Disk Array-based Servers

Eduardo Pinheiro
Google

Ricardo Bianchini
Rutgers University and Microsoft

Abstract. This is a retrospective on our original paper titled "Energy Conservation Techniques for Disk Array-based Servers", which was published in the Proceedings of the International Conference on Supercomputing in 2004.

Original paper: http://dx.doi.org/10.1145/2591635.2591666

Categories and Subject Descriptors

D.4 [**Operating systems**]: Storage management

Keywords

Energy conservation; disk power; disk arrays

Back then... The early 2000s were an exciting time for systems research. At that time, Internet services' datacenters were becoming larger and more sophisticated. In 2001, researchers at Duke University and our own group at Rutgers University published the first papers [4, 16] arguing that energy management would become critical for datacenters. Until then, energy management had only been considered for battery-operated devices, such as laptop computers.

A little later, researchers also started to consider the energy consumption of the storage subsystem in datacenters and supercomputers. This line of research started in 2002 with the MAID (Massive Array of Idle Disks) system [5], which used hard disk drives for large-scale storage, instead of tapes. To cope with the greater energy consumption of disks, MAID proposed that most of them be kept asleep (i.e., off); only a relatively small number of additional "cache disks" would be active at all times. A cache disk miss would then involve the activation of the (sleeping) disk that contained the desired data. Upon reading the data from this disk, the system would store it on any cache disk assuming that more requests for it would arrive. The activated disk would be transitioned back to sleep after a period of idleness.

Another key advance related to our project appeared in the following year. In 2003, researchers at Penn State University and our own group proposed that disks should be able to perform accesses at one of multiple rotation speeds [7, 3]. The idea was to adjust a disk's rotation speed dynamically, according to the amount of load offered to it. Since the spindle motor consumes the largest fraction of a disk's power and reducing rotation speed has a quadratic impact on power consumption [7], this approach can accrue significant energy savings under low and moderate loads.

Our project and PDC. By early 2003, it had become clear to us that neither MAID nor multi-speed disks would produce the highest energy savings in disk array-based servers. MAID involves the energy (and management) overhead of the cache disks and depends heavily on the number of such disks for a good performance/energy tradeoff. Simply using multi-speed disks often limits savings, as the data layout may force all disks to operate at relatively high speeds.

Given these observations and early evidence of a high data popularity skew in certain server workloads [2, 9], we decided to investigate whether segregating popular and unpopular data onto separate disks via migration would enable higher and more robust energy savings [15]. We called this approach Popular Data Concentration (PDC). PDC would not require extra disks and would enable a subset of disks (those storing unpopular data) to be in a low-power state longer.

To avoid performance degradation for popular data, PDC should avoid overloading the popular disks. Thus, we needed to consider the expected access rate of each disk explicitly. We could do this by estimating the future load (in MBytes/second) on each disk to be the sum of the recent load directed to the data to be stored on it. PDC should then only migrate data onto a disk until the expected load on the disk is close to its maximum throughput for the workload. Keeping track of data popularity and offered load efficiently was a challenge, but we could leverage prior work on second-level storage caching algorithms [20].

The final step was to build a PDC-based system that would enable high performance and energy savings, despite the high energy overhead of data migration. We implemented PDC in a system we call Nomad FS. Nomad FS is an energy-aware file server that we implemented at the user level on top of a local UNIX file system. It explicitly caches data blocks in main memory, again at the user level. Although Nomad FS receives requests for 8-KByte file blocks, it migrates entire files according to PDC. To conserve energy in disk arrays composed of conventional (single-speed) disks, Nomad FS spins disks down after a fixed period of idleness. A spun down disk is automatically reactivated on the next access to it. For servers with (autonomous) two-speed disks [3], Nomad FS does not explicitly effect power

ICS 25th Anniversary Volume. 2014
ACM 978-1-4503-2840-1/14/06.
http://dx.doi.org/10.1145/2591635.2591666.

mode transitions. Furthermore, it does not migrate files out of disks that are already running in low speed to reduce the migration overhead.

As commercial two-speed disks were not available and we wanted to explore a large space of parameters quickly, we also built a simulator of Nomad FS. For comparison with PDC, we implemented MAID in a variation of Nomad FS and in simulation. We validated the simulator against our real implementations of PDC and MAID using conventional disks. Our parameter exploration results were positive. In summary, we found that PDC conserves substantial energy during periods of light load on the file server (at a very small response time penalty) with two-speed disks. We also found that PDC can deal more gracefully with high request rates and low file popularity than MAID or two-speed disks without data movement. In addition, PDC achieved consistent energy savings for most of the parameter space. However, the PDC gains degrade substantially for long migration intervals. In comparison, the behavior of MAID is heavily dependent on the number of cache disks used. Furthermore, the energy overhead of these disks is pronounced in several parts of the space. We also found that using two-speed disks without data movement behaves well when disk loads remain light most of the time. For conventional disks, PDC can only conserve energy when the load on the server is low, but those savings come at a high performance overhead for the (typically small) percentage of requests that get delayed by disk spin-ups.

In a 2006 paper [17], we proposed a new energy management technique for redundant large-scale storage systems (called Diverted Accesses) and combined it with PDC, assuming conventional disks.

Impact of PDC. PDC has had an important impact on the community. As of March 2014, our original PDC paper has been cited by 300+ other papers, according to Google Scholar. More importantly, many published systems have clearly been influenced by PDC. For example, Hibernator [21] combines PDC with RAID (Redundant Array of Inexpensive Disks) and multi-speed disks. Hibernator improved on our migration scheme by grouping the disks into "tiers" (all disks in a tier are organized as a RAID and spin at the same speed). Migrations would then only need to happen across tiers. The SEA (Striping Energy-Aware) data placement scheme [19] took a similar approach in combining PDC, RAID, and two-speed disks.

Many papers have combined PDC with solid-state drives (SSDs). For example, Kim *et al.* proposed an extension of PDC, called Pattern-based PDC [12], which migrates frequently read data to a conventional hard disk and frequently written data to an SSD. Deng *et al.* considered combining an SSD, a conventional hard drive, and popularity-based migrations between them in the design of energy-aware disk drives [6]. Lee and Koh took a similar approach for arrays of conventional disks and called their approach PDC-NH [13].

More broadly, PDC has also influenced research in energy-aware distributed systems and even energy-aware main memory systems. GreenHDFS [10] and Lightning [11] are energy-aware distributed file systems that implement popularity-based data migration between "storage zones" comprising groups of servers with conventional disks. For main memory, Huang *et al.* [8] and Wu *et al.* [18], for example, dynamically place data in memory ranks based on popularity. Not surprisingly, we leveraged PDC-style data placement in our own work on energy-aware memory [14].

Finally, Bostoen *et al.* produced an extensive survey of energy management for storage systems [1]. The paper discusses some of the above systems, and also places PDC at their roots.

Looking forward. In recent years, research on techniques tailored to SSDs (often used as caches for disks) and redundant large-scale disk storage (e.g., Diverted Accesses) has become popular. We expect these topics to remain in evidence for the foreseeable future, as SSD costs per bit keep decreasing and cloud storage demand keeps increasing. Despite these more recent topics, interest in PDC is strong as ever: the two years in which the original PDC paper received the most citations have been last year and the year before. With this in mind, we hope that PDC, the concepts that surround it, and the parameter space exploration in our paper will remain relevant for years to come.

Acknowledgements. We would like to thank Vinicio Carrera and Cezary Dubnicki for their help with many aspects of our energy-aware storage work. We are also indebted to the National Science Foundation for its support of our work via grants CCR-0238182 (CAREER award) and EIA-0224428.

1. REFERENCES

[1] T. Bostoen, S. Mullender, and Y. Berbers. Power-Reduction Techniques for Data-Center Storage Systems. *ACM Computing Surveys*, 45(3), 2013.

[2] L. Breslau, P. Cao, L. Fan, G. Phillips, and S. Shenker. Web Caching and Zipf-like Distributions: Evidence and Implications. In *Proceedings of IEEE InfoCom'99*, 1999.

[3] E. V. Carrera, E. Pinheiro, and R. Bianchini. Conserving Disk Energy in Network Servers. In *Proceedings of the 17th International Conference on Supercomputing*, 2003.

[4] J. Chase, D. Anderson, P. Thackar, A. Vahdat, and R. Boyle. Managing Energy and Server Resources in Hosting Centers. In *Proceedings of the 18th Symposium on Operating Systems Principles*, 2001.

[5] D. Colarelli and D. Grunwald. Massive Arrays of Idle Disks For Storage Archives. In *Proceedings of the 15th High Performance Networking and Computing Conference*, 2002.

[6] Y. Deng, F. Wang, and N. Helian. EED: Energy Efficient Disk Drive Architecture. *Information Sciences*, 178(22), 2008.

[7] S. Gurumurthi, A. Sivasubramaniam, M. Kandemir, and H. Franke. DRPM: Dynamic Speed Control for Power Management in Server Class Disks. In *Proceedings of the International Symposium on Computer Architecture*, 2003.

[8] H. Huang, K. G. Shin, C. Lefurgy, and T. Keller. Improving Energy Efficiency by Making DRAM Less Randomly Accessed. In *Proceedings of the 2005 International Symposium on Low Power Electronics and Design*, 2005.

[9] S. Jin and A. Bestavros. GISMO: A Generator of Internet Streaming Media Objects and Workloads. *ACM SIGMETRICS Performance Evaluation Review*, 29(3), 2001.

[10] R. Kaushik and M. Bhandarkar. GreenHDFS: Towards an Energy-Conserving, Storage-Efficient, Hybrid Hadoop Compute Cluster. In *Proceedings of the USENIX Annual Technical Conference*, 2010.

[11] R. Kaushik, L. Cherkasova, R. Campbell, and K. Nahrstedt. Lightning: Self-Adaptive, Energy-Conserving, Multi-Zoned, Commodity Green Cloud Storage System. In *Proceedings of the 19th ACM International Symposium on High Performance Distributed Computing*, 2010.

[12] Y.-J. Kim, K.-T. Kwon, and J. Kim. Energy-efficient File Placement Techniques for Heterogeneous Mobile Storage Systems. In *Proceedings of the 6th ACM/IEEE International Conference on Embedded Software*, 2006.

[13] D. Lee and K. Koh. PDC-NH: Popular Data Concentration on NAND Flash and Hard Disk Drive. In *Proceedings of the 10th IEEE/ACM International Conference on Grid Computing*, 2009.

[14] V. Pandey, W. Jiang, Y. Zhou, and R. Bianchini. DMA-Aware Memory Energy Management. In *Proceedings of the 12th Symposium on High-Performance Computer Architecture*, 2006.

[15] E. Pinheiro and R. Bianchini. Energy Conservation Techniques for Disk Array-Based Servers. In *Proceedings of the 18th International Conference on Supercomputing*, 2004.

[16] E. Pinheiro, R. Bianchini, E. V. Carrera, and T. Heath. Load Balancing and Unbalancing for Power and Performance in Cluster-Based Systems. In *Proceedings of the Workshop on Compilers and Operating Systems for Low Power*, September 2001.

[17] E. Pinheiro, R. Bianchini, and C. Dubnicki. Exploiting Redundancy to Conserve Energy in Storage Systems. In *Proceedings of SIGMETRICS*, 2006.

[18] D. Wu, B. He, X. Tang, J. Xu, and M. Guo. Ramzzz: Rank-aware DRAM Power Management with Dynamic Migrations and Demotions. In *Proceedings of the International Conference on High Performance Computing, Networking, Storage and Analysis*, 2012.

[19] T. Xie. SEA: A Striping-Based Energy-Aware Strategy for Data Placement in RAID-Structured Storage Systems. *IEEE Transactions on Computers*, 57(6), 2008.

[20] Y. Zhou, P. Chen, , and K. Li. The Multi-Queue Replacement Algorithm for Second-Level Buffer Caches. In *Proceedings of the 2001 USENIX Annual Technical Conference*, 2001.

[21] Q. Zhu, Z. Chen, L. Tan, Y. Zhou, K. Keeton, and J. Wilkes. Hibernator: Helping Disk Arrays Sleep Through the Winter. In *Proceedings of the 20th ACM Symposium on Operating Systems Principles*, 2005.

Author Retrospective for A NUCA Substrate for Flexible CMP Cache Sharing

Jaehyuk Huh
KAIST

Changkyu Kim
Google

Hazim Shafi
Samsung

Lixin Zhang
Institute of Computing Technology
Chinese Academy of Sciences

Doug Burger
Microsoft Research

Stephen W. Keckler
NVIDIA and UT-Austin

ABSTRACT

In 2005, as chip multiprocessors started to appear widely, it became possible for the on-chip cores to share the last-level cache. At the time, architects either considered the last-level cache to be divided into per-core private segments, or wholly shared. The shared cache utilized the capacity more efficiency but suffered from high, uniform latencies. This paper proposed a new direction: allowing the caches to be non-uniform, with a varying number of processors sharing each section of the cache. Sharing degree, the number of cores sharing a last-level cache, determines the level of replication in on-chip caches and also affects the capacity and latency for each shared cache. Building on our previous work that introduced non-uniform cache architectures (NUCA), this study explored the design space for shared multi-core caches, focusing on the effect of sharing degree. Our observation of a per-application optimal sharing degree led to a static NUCA design with a reconfigurable sharing degree. This work in multicore NUCA cache architectures has been influential in contemporary systems, including the level-3 cache in the IBM Power 7 and Power 8 processors.

Original paper: http://dx.doi.org/10.1145/1088149.1088154

Categories and Subject Descriptors: C.1.2 [**Processor Architectures**]: Multiple Data Stream Architectures (Multiprocessors); B.3.2 [**Memory Structures**]Design Styles – Shared memory

Keywords: NUCA design, sharing degree, multicore processors

1. BACKGROUND

In the early 2000s, as power limitations hampered single-core performance improvements, the industry shifted *en masse* to chip multiprocessors (CMPs). The on-chip integration of multiple cores and caches expanded the possible space of cache hierarchy designs. Instead of the private, per-core caches used in traditional multi-processors, CMPs enabled shared cache designs. These shared caches reduce cache misses significantly by reducing replication of cache blocks and by resolving capacity imbalances among working sets accessed by multiple cores sharing a cache.

Shared multicore caches, however, also incurred large access latencies. The increased capacity and physical distance from some of the cores led to long hit times, which could reduce or eliminate the benefit of the reduced misses. To mitigate increasing cache latencies, previous work proposed Non-Uniform Cache Architectures (NUCA) which redesigned cache structures to account for variable cache bank access latency [10]. NUCA designs consist of a set of small cache banks connected via an interconnection network to allow hit latency to vary depending on the location of accessed cache blocks. The original NUCA work focused on the last level cache for uniprocessors. The latency problem targeted by the NUCA work is typically worse for shared CMP caches, as the capacity needs to be larger to support multiple working sets.

At that time, the caching efficiency/latency tradeoff was well understood, but the consensus at the time was that caches should either be private or shared by all cores, and that caches would have a uniform access latency. Adding NUCA capabilities brought down the average latencies of large shared caches, making them faster, and thus enabling larger sharing degrees. The study in this paper focused on the tension between cache sharing and latency, using NUCA caches as a way to better balance these two constraints [8].

Other contemporaneous work took a different approach to mitigate the long latencies of large, last-level shared caches. Rather than adjusting the sharing degree, this other approach moved individual cache blocks closer to the requester, either by selectively replicating the blocks, or by migrating them to a closer portion of the cache [4, 13, 2]. This paper's approach instead asked the question of how may cores should share a cache to maximize the caching efficiency, while preserving low cache hit latency. The answer to this question determines how many replications of cache blocks can exist in a processor, how large a shared cache segment should be, and how fast a block access takes in the shared cache.

Our results showed that by adjusting the sharing degree and using a NUCA substrate, a better balance between hit latencies and misses can be struck. We also found that choosing the sharing degree on an application by applica-

ICS 25th Anniversary Volume. 2014
ACM 978-1-4503-2840-1/14/06.
http://dx.doi.org/10.1145/2591635.2591667.

tion basis, or even a cache line by line bases, can improve the CMP performance even further than a single ideal sharing degree. While our paper did not propose a mechanism to identify these ideal sharing degrees for individual applications or individual lines, our conclusion that these were promising approaches have been validated by other researchers' follow-on work.

2. SHARING DEGREE: IDENTIFYING INHERENT TENSIONS

Unlike previous shared cache studies that assumed the entire last-level cache of a CMP is composed of either per-core private caches or a single per-chip shared cache, we generalized the design space into a range of degrees of sharing, including the intermediate points where some cache banks were shared by a subset of the processors. This paper defined the term *sharing degree* to denote the number of cores sharing a given partition of the cache in a CMP design.

The goal of the sharing degree concept was to better balance the tensions inherent in shared cache designs. With a low sharing degree, cache blocks are replicated in more places, reducing caching efficiency and potentially increasing coherence overheads. This additional replication, however, can result in lower latencies, especially when the working sets fit in the local cache partitions and the data are not often written. With a high sharing degree, conversely, the replication is reduced, thus using the cache space more effectively. Also, as more cores share a cache, the chance to share the capacity increases, balancing dynamic shifts in the required capacity among cores. However, the access latencies of shared caches increase with higher sharing degrees.

To empirically identify the tensions caused by the degree of replication, we started from a start-of-the-art cache design for reducing cache hit latencies. Based on NUCA caches, we simulated and evaluated our target processors with several different sharing degrees. Our initial goal was to understand the behaviors of parallel applications with different sharing degrees and hit latencies determined by cache capacity. The performance of each application was evaluated in several different designs with a static sharing degree. The study included three different NUCA designs from static mapping to fully dynamic mapping policies to understand the effect of sharing degree, when dynamic migration within a shared cache is enabled or not.

With static NUCA, a cache block can be located in a fixed position in a shared cache, but in a dynamic NUCA policy, a cache block can be migrated toward a frequently accessing core by block migration mechanism. In single-core NUCA designs, the dynamic NUCA policies exhibited better performance by reducing hit latencies. In our study, we explored both static and dynamic NUCA cache policies to understand their effect on optimal sharing degree.

Our evaluation led to somewhat unexpected results, although the results were (of course) obvious after the tension of sharing degree become understood. We found that each application may respond differently to various sharing degrees. Some applications benefit from reduced cache misses due to higher sharing degrees, while others suffer from increased hit latencies without much benefit from miss reduction. The range of optimal sharing degrees across applications led to the next contribution of this paper: a cache architecture that could flexible support different sharing degrees at different times.

3. FLEXIBLE SHARING DEGREE

Our observation of per-application optimal sharing degree led to a cache design supporting flexible sharing degree. The design borrows its base structure from the single-core NUCA design with an interconnected array of cache banks in a multi-core processor. The NUCA substrate supports a reconfigurable sharing degree, to support a different optimal sharing degree for each application. A key component is a central flexible directory and sharing bits embedded in each cache tag. The central directory provides coherence among different cache partitions, sharing bits in the tags to support coherence among L1 caches within a shared cache domain.

The main contribution of this paper (flexible sharing degree) was a very different result than we set out to demonstrate. Initially, we were trying to provide a single large cache that leveraged D-NUCA techniques to permit the sharing efficiency and use migration to address the latency issue. With this goal in mind, we explored the design space with three NUCA substrates: static NUCA, 1D dynamic NUCA, and 2D dynamic NUCA. We were surprised to find that the performance benefit of the dynamic NUCA organizations over static NUCA was relatively small compared to the benefit of dynamic NUCA in uniprocessor caches. The flexible sharing degree ended up being a more important design factor than dynamic data migration within a shared cache region. If an application has a low optimal sharing degree, cache latencies are already relatively short. If an application has a high optimal sharing degree, there may be highly shared data accessed by many cores. For such highly shared data, dynamic migration of blocks was not very effective as most of the cores attempt to migrate the shared blocks closer to them. We concluded that a static NUCA architecture combined with flexible sharing degree provides an effective design with low complexity. This study showed that the proposed dynamic NUCA designs are not effective, despite their performance potential measured in the earlier paper. The limited gains for multi-cores made them clearly not worth the complexity.

Our paper was limited in that it applied the same sharing degree to all cache lines in an application. However, even within an application, different memory regions may require different optimal sharing degrees. In an extension of this paper, we briefly showed the potential of such sharing degree per cache line or memory region of an application [9]. Although the analysis showed potential performance improvements, we were not able to propose a viable mechanism to support per-line or per-region sharing degree. Hardavellas et al. later proposed to use two sharing degrees, *private and shared*, for different memory regions of the same application [7]. That paper proposed to use the TLB and paging mechanism to separate private and shared pages, and to map them differently to the NUCA substrate.

Another limitation of this study is that it focused primarily on the identification of the sharing degree problem and the NUCA mechanism to change the sharing degree, and did not include a deep study of how to find the optimal sharing degree for each application. A range of techniques that drive profiling, dynamic phase detection and reconfiguration can be applied to this problem.

4. IMPACT

This work has had significant influence on the memory system design for some of industry's contemporary multiprocessor architectures. The L3 cache of the IBM POWER 7 processor is a NUCA design for 8 cores with private L1 and L2 caches [11]. The 32MB eDRAM-based L3 consists of eight L3 regions that are shareable across the cores. In POWER 7, non-uniformity appears at two levels of the L3 organization. First, the access latency to an L3 region depends on the distance between it and the requesting processor core. Second, each L3 region is composed of four banks; access latencies to each bank within a region also varies by the distance to a core. The POWER 7 L3 cache has a mechanism to control sharing degree dynamically. The L3 changes the broadcast scope among L3 regions; if the same copy of a cache block is found in another L3 region in the same broadcast scope, the duplicate copies are merged. By changing the broadcast scope across L3 regions, the L3 can adjust the sharing degree. The subsequent POWER 8 processor extended the NUCA design to a 96MB L3 cache [12]. For twelve 12 cores, the L3 is decomposed into twelve 8MB regions, and each region consists of 8 banks with non-uniform access times even within a region.

In addition the industrial influence, this paper also had significant academic influence. Many follow-on papers have continued to explore the design space of hybrid private and shared cache architectures. Chang and Sohi proposed a hybrid shared cache architecture based on private caches cooperating to hold victim cache blocks from other caches [3]. Such cooperative caching improves caching efficiency of private caches by selectively sharing capacity. Reactive NUCA [7] uses two distinct mapping policies, private and shared, for different memory pages of an applications. It uses private mapping for private memory regions to minimize access latencies, while shared data are mapped differently to avoid replication. Beckmann et al. proposed an adaptive replication mechanism for NUCA-based multi-core caches, which can control per-line sharing degree dynamically [1]. Dybdahl et al. investigated cache partitioning schemes for NUCA-based shared caches [6]. Given that dynamic NUCA showed only marginal improvements for shared CMP caches, Cho et al. investigated a static shared NUCA that used the operating system to optimize the placement of pages by OS-level page mapping [5]. Instead of using complex and expensive hardware-based dynamic migration, the OS page allocation policy places pages in caches close to requesting cores. That paper adapted some of our earlier work that used OS-page placement for on-chip uniprocessor memory for multiprocessor caches [14]. Our earlier paper hypothesized in the conclusions that multicore gains would be higher, but missed the opportunity to apply this technique to caches, which was an inspired leap by Cho et al.

5. REFERENCES

[1] B. M. Beckmann, M. R. Marty, and D. A. Wood. ASR: Adaptive Selective Replication for CMP Caches. In *International Symposium on Microarchitecture (MICRO)*, pages 443–454, December 2007.

[2] B. M. Beckmann and D. A. Wood. Managing wire delay in large chip-multiprocessor caches. In *37th International Symposium on Microarchitecture (MICRO)*, December 2004.

[3] J. Chang and G. S. Sohi. Cooperative Caching for Chip Multiprocessors. In *International Symposium on Computer Architecture (ISCA)*, pages 264–276, June 2006.

[4] Z. Chishti, M. D. Powell, and T. N. Vijaykumar. Optimizing replication, communication, and capacity allocation in cmps. In *Proceedings of the 32nd annual international symposium on Computer Architecture*, 2005.

[5] S. Cho and L. Jin. Managing Distributed, Shared L2 Caches Through OS-Level Page Allocation. In *International Symposium on Microarchitecture (MICRO)*, pages 455–468, December 2006.

[6] H. Dybdahl and P. Stenstrom. An Adaptive Shared/Private NUCA Cache Partitioning Scheme for Chip Multiprocessors. In *International Symposium on High-Performance Computer Architecture (HPCA)*, pages 2–12, February 2008.

[7] N. Hardavellas, M. Ferdman, B. Falsafi, and A. Ailamaki. Reactive NUCA: Near-optimal Block Placement and Replication in Distributed Caches. In *International Symposium on Computer Architecture (ISCA)*, pages 184–195, June 2009.

[8] J. Huh, C. Kim, H. Shafi, L. Zhang, D. Burger, and S. W. Keckler. A NUCA Substrate for Flexible CMP Cache Sharing. In *Proceedings of International Conference on Supercomputing (ICS)*, pages 31–40, June 2005.

[9] J. Huh, C. Kim, H. Shafi, L. Zhang, D. Burger, and S. W. Keckler. A NUCA Aubstrate for Flexible CMP Cache Sharing. *IEEE Transactions on Parallel and Distributed System*, 18(8):1028–1040, August 2007.

[10] C. Kim, D. Burger, and S. W. Keckler. An Adaptive, Non-Uniform Cache Structure for Wire-Delay Dominated On-Chip Caches. In *International Conference on Architectural Support for Programming Languages and Operating Systems (ASPLOS)*, pages 211–222, October 2002.

[11] B. Sinharoy, R. Kalla, W. J. Starke, H. Q. Le, R. Cargnoni, J. A. Van Norstrand, B. J. Ronchetti, J. Stuecheli, J. Leenstra, G. L. Guthrie, D. Q. Nguyen, B. Blaner, C. F. Marino, E. Retter, and P. Williams. IBM POWER7 Multicore Server Processor. *IBM Journal of Research and Development*, 55(3):1:1–1:29, May 2011.

[12] J. Stuecheli. POWER8. *Hot Chips 25: A Symposium of High Performance Chips*, August 2013.

[13] M. Zhang and K. Asanovic. Victim replication: Maximizing capacity while hiding wire delay in tiled chip multiprocessors. In *Proceedings of the 32nd annual international symposium on Computer Architecture*, 2005.

[14] R. Desikan, C.R. Lefurgy, S.W. Keckler, and D. Burger. On-Chip MRAM as a High-Bandwidth, Low-Latency Replacement for DRAM Physical Memories. *Department of Computer Sciences Technical Report TR-02-47*, The University of Texas at Austin, 2002.

Author Retrospective for Design Tradeoffs for Tiled CMP On-Chip Networks

William J. Dally
NVIDIA & Stanford
dally@stanford.edu

James Balfour
Google Inc.
jbalfour@google.com

ABSTRACT

In the eight years that have passed since we published "Design Tradeoffs for Tiled CMP On-Chip Networks," on-chip interconnection networks have become pervasive, as semiconductor scaling has allowed increasing numbers of processor cores and components to be integrated on a chip. The contributions of the paper, in particular the detailed technology models and the use of channel slicing and concentration to improve efficiency, remain as valid today as they were when we began the research that led to the paper. The network-on-chip (NoC) design methodology presented in the paper is widely used today. In this retrospective, we review the more significant contributions of the original paper, and comment on the impact it had on subsequent research.

Original paper: http://dx.doi.org/10.1145/1183401.1183430

Categories and Subject Descriptors

C.1.2 [**Multiple Data Stream Architectures (Multiprocessors)**]: Interconnection architectures; C.2.1 [**Network Architecture And Design**]: Network Topology

Keywords

Network-on-Chip; Energy Modeling; Area Modeling; Network Topology

1. INTRODUCTION

On-chip interconnection networks [4] have become pervasive in the eight years that have passed since we published "Design Tradeoffs for Tiled CMP On-Chip Networks" (DTTN) [2]. The numbers of cores integrated in a modern multi-core processor chip [3] have increased to the point where the choice of network topology critically affects performance. NoCs are also widely used in building system-on-chips (SoCs) [15] where, in addition to providing a high-performance interconnect, they also serve to provide a standard interface to system modules. The contributions of DTTN enable the design of high-performance, cost-efficient NoCs for both multi-core processors and SoCs.

ICS 25th Anniversary Volume. 2014
ACM 978-1-4503-2840-1/14/06.
http://dx.doi.org/10.1145/2591635.2591668.

The DTTN paper made several contributions that in part enabled this widespread use of NoCs, including:

1. Developing a simple, accurate technology model for evaluating the area, energy, and delay of alternative NoC organizations.
2. Comparing alternative tree, torus, and mesh networks considering on-chip layout using the technology model and realistic workloads.
3. Demonstrating that due to quadratic switch cost and non-uniformity in packet sizes, two separate networks can outperform a single, wider network of equal cost.
4. Demonstrating that concentration is a key element of a successful NoC topology by showing that the concentrated mesh (CMesh) topology outperformed the alternative networks by a significant margin.

The contributions of DTTN have stood the modest test of eight years time. The technology model, layout based network comparisons, use of multiple networks, and use of concentration are all still valid today. While the CMesh topology remains superior to the alternatives considered in the paper, the flattened-butterfly topology, introduced [12] in 2007, is an attractive alternative. The two topologies are closely related: the flattened-butterfly is a CMesh with express channels repeated throughout the network interior. Most important, the methodology established by the DTTN paper, performing quantitative comparisons of network alternatives using an accurate technology model and taking layout into account, remains the preferred method to make NoC design choices.

The following sections explore each of the contributions listed above in more detail.

2. ENABLING TECHNOLOGY MODELS

A key contribution of DTTN was developing a simple but accurate technology model for evaluating the area, energy, and delay of alternative NoC designs. This model enables objective comparison of alternative network organizations with much less effort than a detailed logical and physical design of the network would require.

The model developed in DTTN assumes an efficient custom circuit layout rather than a design realized via logic synthesis followed by placement and routing of standard cells. This approach directly reflects industry practice in high-end designs [8] and is also a reasonable estimator of the relative area required by synthesized designs.

The model is particularly useful in enabling sweeps of key network parameters to develop insight into the sensitivity of cost and performance to each variable. Topology, channel latency, channel length, channel width, flow control method, and number of virtual channels can all be varied. As the parameters are varied the model computes the input buffer requirements and then, based on these buffer sizes, computes the area and energy consumed by each element of the network datapath.

Communication is energetically expensive in modern VLSI technology and improves more slowly than logic with technology scaling. Thus, the energy cost of traversing a channel improves more slowly than the energy cost of traversing a router. Consequently, detailed models such as those developed in the paper are required to evaluate the tradeoffs between router and channel energy, particularly when using routing algorithms that increase the average physical distance a packet travels.

3. LAYOUT MATTERS

Semiconductor scaling has enabled very high levels of integration on a chip. The scale of modern chip-multiprocessors and systems-on-chip requires structured approaches to integration and on-chip communication. One consequence is that the replication of components typical in modern designs allows additional engineering effort to be invested in the implementation of critical system components, such as cache memories and processor datapaths. This is particularly true of the highly structured and regular components such as the routers and channels comprising interconnection networks.

One significant aspect of DTTN was the detailed consideration of VLSI design and implementation issues in the development of the area, energy, and delay models. For example, while wires are relatively abundant on chip, allowing wide channels to be constructed, long channels require repeaters that compete with processors and other logic for die area. The parameterized models developed in the DTTN paper captured details such as the the placement of input buffers and switches in routers as well as the allocation of interconnect and die area to repeaters in channels. The network evaluation considered system-level details such as the placement of routers and channels in the chip floor plan and the placement of input buffers and switches inside routers to derive key model parameters for the different networks.

Layout affects a number of network properties that must be modeled accurately in simulations and evaluations. The placement of routers and components comprising channels determines network properties such as channel latency that are critical for accurate simulation. Channel latency contributes directly to credit round-trip delay, which determines the minimum input buffer capacity required to cover the credit round-trip delays and keep the channels fully utilized. It should not be surprising that layout has a significant impact on the channel traversal energy, but the more subtle impact on router traversal energy can be easily missed during evaluation without sufficiently detailed models. And as we found, the tree networks and torus perform poorly compared to the CMesh because VLSI limitations render them less amenable to efficient on-chip implementations.

4. CHANNEL SLICING

DTTN demonstrated that two networks are often better than one, with multiple networks providing better performance and efficiency than a single network. Though we did not explain it as such at the time, the paper demonstrated that channel slicing [5] is an effective technology for improving on-chip network performance and efficiency.

Channel slicing splits a network into multiple parallel networks that operate independently, with communication between the networks limited to the terminal nodes. When the bisection bandwidth is held constant, the reduction in the datapath width that results from channel slicing produces smaller routers, in part because switch area exhibits a quadratic dependence on the datapath width. The reduction in the datapath width can also improve switch bandwidth utilization. However, this form of channel slicing increases packet serialization latency.

Alternatively, the aggregate bisection bandwidth can be increased by replacing a single network with parallel networks whose combined channel width exceeds the original. Because switch traversal latency and energy increase with the datapath width, a second network is a practical way to increase bisection bandwidth without adversely impacting clock cycle times or switch traversal costs. Channel slicing decouples the allocation of resources to different networks, which can improve resource utilization under load.

Systems with multiple parallel on-chip networks are relatively common in commercial on-chip network designs [18], with the independent networks often used instead of virtual-channels to isolate traffic classes. Evaluating the myriad tradeoffs involved in the provisioning of resources between the networks can be complicated, and an effective design space exploration requires detailed models such as those presented in the DTTN paper.

5. CONCENTRATION IS KEY

Concentration combines the traffic of multiple terminal nodes at one router. DTTN showed the importance of concentration as a technology for improving both performance and efficiency. Concentration is typically used to reduce the diameter of a network. Performance improves because concentration affords a reduction in the average number of routers packets traverse. Energy efficiency improves because concentration trades longer channel traversals in exchange for reductions in the number of input buffer and switch traversals.

Much of the performance and efficiency gains of the CMesh network arise from the application of concentration to a conventional Mesh network. Unlike the tree networks evaluated in the paper, where the channel energy dominates, the CMesh networks route most packets on efficient paths that minimize the distance packets travel and the amount of interconnect traversed. However, the results for the synthetic workloads cautioned that concentration can degrade performance on adversarial workloads because of the loss of bisection channels and bandwidth.

Like the CMesh, the flattened-butterfly topology arises from the use of concentration [12]. Flattened-butterfly networks incorporate additional express channels throughout the interior of the network, which increases the bisection channel count and affords additional path diversity, thereby improving the handling of adversarial traffic patterns.

6. CONCLUSION

DTTN developed a methodology for the design and evaluation of NoCs based on simple, accurate technology models.

Combining these models with the techniques of channel slicing and concentration enabled a large number of network alternatives to be quickly evaluated in terms of area, power, and performance. Performing this evaluation in a *layout-conscious* manner gave realistic results that reflected VLSI implementation issues.

In the years since DTTN was published, the methodology it established has been embraced by researchers and used to evolve NoCs in a number of directions. It enabled researchers to understand and explore what were recognized as significant research problems in the design and implementation of on-chip networks, including power and thermal management, topology, and area and energy efficiency [15]. Research flourished as the computer architecture community recognized the important role of on-chip networks as the interconnect of large-scale multiprocessors and systems-on-chips. Subsequent research would reinforce the impact of on-chip networks on the performance of large-scale multiprocessors [17]. Concentration was recognized as an important technology for scaling on-chip interconnect to very large scale multiprocessors [10, 14].

The technology models presented in DTTN were detailed enough to be used in a wide variety of research, ranging from router micro-architecture [11] to scalable on-chip network design [7]. At the same time, the models were simple enough to be used in research exploring the design and evaluation of a range of large-scale chip multi-processors architectures [1, 10]. Subsequent research would use similar methodologies to evaluate novel signaling technologies [13], such as on-chip nanophotonics for channels [9, 16].

In the years to come, we expect the importance of NoCs will continue to increase as the extent of chip-level integration continues to increase. With the end of Dennard scaling [6], energy efficiency becomes even more important, placing a premium on accurate energy models such as those developed in DTTN. Over time, we expect more innovative network topologies to supplant the CMesh and flattened-butterfly. However, we expect such topologies to make use of channel slicing and concentration as demonstrated in DTTN.

7. REFERENCES

[1] A. Bakhoda, J. Kim, and T. M. Aamodt. Throughput effective on-chip networks for manycore accelerators. In *Proceedings of the 43rd Annual IEEE/ACM International Symposium on Microarchitecture*, pages 421–432. IEEE Computer Society, 2010.

[2] J. Balfour and W. J. Dally. Design tradeoffs for tiled CMP on-chip networks. In *Proceedings of the 20th annual international conference on Supercomputing*, pages 187–198. ACM, 2006.

[3] G. Chrysos. Intel Xeon Phi coprocessor (codename Knights Corner). In *Proceedings of the 24th Hot Chips Symposium*, 2012.

[4] W. J. Dally and B. Towles. Route packets, not wires: On-chip interconnection networks. In *Design Automation Conference, 2001. Proceedings*, pages 684–689. IEEE, 2001.

[5] W. J. Dally and B. P. Towles. *Principles and practices of interconnection networks*. Elsevier, 2004.

[6] R. H. Dennard, F. H. Gaensslen, V. L. Rideout, E. Bassous, and A. R. LeBlanc. Design of ion-implanted MOSFET's with very small physical dimensions. *Solid-State Circuits, IEEE Journal of*, 9(5):256–268, 1974.

[7] B. Grot, J. Hestness, S. W. Keckler, and O. Mutlu. Kilo-NoC: a heterogeneous network-on-chip architecture for scalability and service guarantees. *ACM SIGARCH Computer Architecture News*, 39(3):401–412, 2011.

[8] Y. Hoskote, S. Vangal, A. Singh, N. Borkar, and S. Borkar. A 5-GHz mesh interconnect for a teraflops processor. *IEEE Micro*, 27(5):51–61, Sept. 2007.

[9] A. Joshi, C. Batten, Y.-J. Kwon, S. Beamer, I. Shamim, K. Asanovic, and V. Stojanovic. Silicon-photonic clos networks for global on-chip communication. In *Proceedings of the 3rd ACM/IEEE International Symposium on Networks-on-Chip*, pages 124–133. IEEE Computer Society, 2009.

[10] J. H. Kelm, D. R. Johnson, M. R. Johnson, N. C. Crago, W. Tuohy, A. Mahesri, S. S. Lumetta, M. I. Frank, and S. J. Patel. Rigel: An architecture and scalable programming interface for a 1000-core accelerator. In *Proceedings of the 36th Annual International Symposium on Computer Architecture*, pages 140–151. ACM, 2009.

[11] J. Kim. Low-cost router microarchitecture for on-chip networks. In *Proceedings of the 42nd Annual IEEE/ACM International Symposium on Microarchitecture*, pages 255–266. ACM, 2009.

[12] J. Kim, J. Balfour, and W. Dally. Flattened butterfly topology for on-chip networks. In *Proceedings of the 40th Annual IEEE/ACM International Symposium on Microarchitecture*, pages 172–182. IEEE Computer Society, 2007.

[13] J. Kim, K. Choi, and G. Loh. Exploiting new interconnect technologies in on-chip communication. *Emerging and Selected Topics in Circuits and Systems, IEEE Journal on*, 2(2):124–136, 2012.

[14] A. Mahesri, D. Johnson, N. Crago, and S. J. Patel. Tradeoffs in designing accelerator architectures for visual computing. In *Proceedings of the 41st Annual IEEE/ACM International Symposium on Microarchitecture*, pages 164–175. IEEE Computer Society, 2008.

[15] R. Marculescu, U. Y. Ogras, L.-S. Peh, N. E. Jerger, and Y. Hoskote. Outstanding research problems in NoC design: System, microarchitecture, and circuit perspectives. *Transactions on Computer Aided Design, Integrated Circuits and Systems*, 28(1):3–21, Jan. 2009.

[16] Y. Pan, P. Kumar, J. Kim, G. Memik, Y. Zhang, and A. Choudhary. Firefly: Illuminating future network-on-chip with nanophotonics. In *Proceedings of the 36th Annual International Symposium on Computer Architecture*, pages 429–440. ACM, 2009.

[17] D. Sanchez, G. Michelogiannakis, and C. Kozyrakis. An analysis of on-chip interconnection networks for large-scale chip multiprocessors. *ACM Transactions on Architecture and Code Optimization (TACO)*, 7(1):4, 2010.

[18] D. Wentzlaff, P. Griffin, H. Hoffmann, L. Bao, B. Edwards, C. Ramey, M. Mattina, C.-C. Miao, J. F. Brown III, and A. Agarwal. On-chip interconnection architecture of the Tile processor. *IEEE Micro*, 27(5):15–31, Sept. 2007.

Author Retrospective for
Cooperative Cache Partitioning for Chip Multiprocessors

Jichuan Chang
Google, Inc.
jichuan@google.com

Gurindar S. Sohi
University of Wisconsin-Madison
sohi@cs.wisc.edu

ABSTRACT
In this paper, we reflect on our experiences and the lessons learned in designing and evaluating the cooperative cache partitioning technique for chip multiprocessors.

Original paper: http://dx.doi.org/10.1145/1274971.1275005

Categories and Subject Descriptors
B.3.2 [**Memory Structures**]: Design Styles – *Cache Memory.*
C.4 [**Performance of Systems**]: Design Studies.

Keywords
Multicore, last-level cache, cache partitioning, fairness, QoS.

1. BACKGROUND
The 1990s were what have been referred to as the Golden Age of Microarchitecture. There were many innovations in the basic microarchitecture of a uniprocessor, enabled by the increasing number of transistors provided by Moore's Law. Classical uniprocessor organizations were totally transformed as a result of these innovations. At the turn of the decade, chips transitioned from uniprocessors to chip multiprocessors (CMPs). The initial organization (or microarchitecture) of the "multiprocessor portion" of a CMP, i.e., the hardware that was not in the processor cores (e.g., shared caches, interconnect) still resembled a canonical symmetric multiprocessor (SMP). It was clear to the second author that continuing transistor bounty could be used to rethink the microarchitecture of the multiprocessor portion of a CMP. Specifically, since the designers of a CMP had complete control of what hardware it contained and how it would function, they could contemplate and implement techniques that could never be practical if they required interactions between distinct chips over which the designers may not have complete control, as was the case in canonical SMPs. Since caches accounted for a significant portion of this hardware, rethinking the organization and functioning of caches in CMPs was a logical place to start.

Our first foray into different cache operations, albeit in the SMP context, was Coherence Decoupling [1], which targeted the latency of coherence misses. Here we proposed to separate two major operations that are needed for correct cache operation on a coherence miss: obtaining the accessed data, and obtaining the coherence permissions to the data. We observed that data could typically be accessed quicker than all the necessary coherence permissions had been obtained, so a processor could (speculatively) start working with the data while the permissions were still pending, with corrective actions in case the speculative access was incorrect. Encouraged by the promising results over here, we started to contemplate other novel mechanisms for optimizing cache operations.

About the same time, there was a lot of work in the community on optimizing the latency of on-chip caches using novel last-level cache organizations. Although the last-level caches at that time were the L2 caches, the proposed techniques are typically applicable to large on-chip caches (e.g., L3 cache in today's server processors). The NUCA cache work was an early proposal in the direction [2]. Another line of work observed that running parallel programs, or multiple programs, on the shared resources of a CMP introduced new problems due to interference in the shared resources. A significant body of work was already underway in trying to alleviate the negative impact of such interference.

2. DEVELOPING THE IDEAS
The plethora of ongoing work in optimizing L2 cache operation motivated us to try our own proposal for CMP cache organization. We wanted to achieve the latency benefits of private L2 caches, and also the capacity benefits of shared L2 caches. The idea was to use available capacity in another on-chip L2 cache when replacing a cache block from a private L2 cache, rather than evict the block entirely from the chip. We quickly became aware of similar concepts of cooperative caching proposed in file systems research. Further development of the basic ideas led to the "Cooperative Caching for Chip Multiprocessors" paper that appeared in *ISCA 2006*. CMP cooperative caching (CC) enabled fine-grained capacity sharing between private caches to combine the best attributes of both private and shared cache designs.

The observation that led to the work on Cooperative Cache Partitioning (CCP) was actually quite serendipitous. As we experimented with our CC design, we observed some interesting results. In particular, in an experiment with 4 cores running 4 copies of SPEC2000 benchmark `art`, the performance of CC was better than both the private and shared cache baselines. The contemporaneous work on cache partitioning showed that such a result was possible when co-scheduling different benchmarks, due to capacity sharing between applications with different cache footprints. However, it was not clear why this happened when running multiple copies of the same benchmark, which should have the same cache footprint.

Exploring further we observed the interaction of two factors. First, allocating slightly more cache resources to an application

ICS 25th Anniversary Volume, 2014
ACM 978-1-4503-2840-1/14/06.
http://dx.doi.org/10.1145/2591635.2591669

can disproportionately increase its performance while slowing down other co-scheduled applications only slightly. This is because for some applications the miss-rate (and thus performance) vs. capacity curve is non-linear and at certain points additional cache capacity can be very beneficial. This observation was also made by others at about the same time. Serendipitously, benchmark `art` happened to be such an application, and the caches size we were using was the point where `art` exhibited the behavior! Had we been experimenting with another benchmark, or with different cache parameters, we may not have observed the phenomenon. Second, an unintended consequence of CC was that the logically shared cache was being partitioned unequally at a given point in time. However, over time, the different threads each got a chance at an unequal partition, thus leading to overall higher performance, while not compromising fairness.

We were quite excited by these initial observations, since it suggested that CC was also a simple and effective cache partitioning technique, naturally addressing the issues of performance isolation and cache QoS. But as we further studied the related work and ran more experiments, it dawned on us that this was not a simple problem. There were cases where CC was adequate, but there were others where it was not. We needed to find a more systematic approach for leveraging CC for cache partitioning.

We posed two main challenges for ourselves. First, we wanted to develop a technique that would simultaneously achieve better throughput, fairness and QoS. Other proposals had to sacrifice some aspects to optimize others. Second, we felt the need to come up with effective evaluation metrics, since the related work lacked common metrics, measurement standards, baselines and representative co-schedules.

We spent a fair amount of time tuning CC to address the first challenge without much success. One day, Jichuan was discussing the problem with two other students in our research group: Philip Wells and Koushik Chakraborty. They asked: why only spatial partitioning? Wouldn't the time-sharing policies from conventional OS scheduling studies help? This was the spark for introducing temporal techniques to address the problem. The example that we were trying to understand—of 4 copies of `art`—was in a sense already exhibiting this phenomenon, albeit naturally, without explicit control on our part. With the normal CC mechanisms, one `art` thread got an unfairly large partition in one time epoch, and others in a different time epoch. We just needed to come up with a way to deliberately give an unfair share of the L2 cache to a thread in a time epoch, and add a scheme to control these actions so that the overall fairness and QoS would not be compromised.

Using this inspiration, we went back and formulated the basic idea of MTP (multiple time-sharing partitions). Initial experiments quickly revealed that always using MTP wasn't a good idea, since for many cases SSP (single space-sharing partition)—the common root of contemporary work in CMP cache partitioning, including CC— was more effective. Now we needed mechanisms for using MTP when it was likely to be effective and defaulting to SSP otherwise. After a lot of experimentation devoted to understanding behavior in different situations, we fleshed out the detailed algorithm for profiling, determining and enforcing MTPs as well as the policy of when to fall back to the default baseline (CC). This phase of the research was actually the most laborious and took a very large amount of time and effort.

Kyle Nesbit and Jim Smith at University of Wisconsin were also working on partitioning CMP resources at that time. Although we took a different approach, Jichuan enjoyed hearty discussions with them on the selection of baselines and metrics.

3. LOOKING BACK AND AHEAD

Looking back, there were multiple factors that led to the work and ideas reported in the paper. With Cooperative Caching, we started out by considering cache organization techniques that only became viable in a CMP context. Our objective was to optimize memory access latency for a single program, by making effective use of aggregative on-chip cache resources and minimizing off-chip accesses. Quite serendipitously, when experimenting with CC we realized that it was also effective in partitioning the aggregative cache resources for different threads, a problem that was actively being pursued by others using different techniques. And then came the realization that we could also enhance the proposal by adopting time sharing techniques that were proposed to address related problems in different contexts. In summary, the outcome was a mix of a different way of looking at a classical problem, serendipity, and adapting a solution from a different problem area. This is an effective mix that has been the basis of, and is likely to continue to be the basis for, many innovative solutions to problems.

Looking forward, with processing systems becoming more complex with multiple interacting hardware and software components and an increasing number of software threads, hybrid solutions that employ both space- and time-sharing approaches are likely to be more successful than approaches that employ either approach in isolation. This will also require a lot of innovation in algorithms and techniques that can monitor situations dynamically and determine the appropriate mix of techniques to deploy at a given point in time.

4. REFERENCES

1. Jaehyuk Huh, Jichuan Chang, Doug Burger, Gurindar S. Sohi. Coherence decoupling: making use of incoherence. ASPLOS 2004. pp. 97-106.
2. Changkyu Kim, Doug Burger, Stephen W. Keckler. An adaptive, non-uniform cache structure for wire-delay dominated on-chip caches. ASPLOS 2002, pp. 211-222.

Author's Retrospective for: Biomedical Image Analysis on a Cooperative Cluster of GPUs and Multicores

Timothy D. R. Hartley
Intel Corporation
Software and Services Group
Hillsboro, OR
timothy.d.hartley@intel.com

Ümit V. Çatalyürek
Dept. Biomedical Informatics
The Ohio State University
Columbus, OH 43210
umit@bmi.osu.edu

Antonio Ruiz
Computer Architecture Dept.
University of Malaga
Malaga, Spain
aruiz@uma.es

Francisco Igual
Computer Architecture and
Automatic Control Dept.
Univ. Complutense of Madrid
Madrid, Spain
figual@ucm.es

Rafael Mayo
Dept. of Computer Eng. and
Computer Science
University Jaume I
Castellon, Spain
mayo@icc.uji.es

Manuel Ujaldon
Computer Architecture Dept.
University of Malaga
Malaga, Spain
ujaldon@uma.es

Original paper:
http://dx.doi.org/10.1145/1375527.1375533

Categories and Subject Descriptors: C.1[Processor Architectures]: Multiple Data Stream Architectures (Multiprocessors) — *Parallel Processors*; I.3 [Computer Graphics]: Hardware Architecture — *Graphics Processors*; I.4 [Image Processing and Computer Vision]: Applications

General Terms: Algorithms, Languages, Performance

Keywords: GPU, CUDA

1. INTRODUCTION

The last six years has seen Moore's Law continue to produce incredible gains in computational power. Indeed, the November, 2007 list of the top ten fastest supercomputers in the world contained no machines with acceleration of any kind. The same list six years later has four of the ten fastest supercomputers using accelerators, including the top two machines [3] . And the ten greenest supercomputers in November 2013 are using NVIDIA GPUs [1]. This heterogeneity of processing units is present from the top of the computational power spectrum down to the bottom, where GPU hardware coupled with novel CUDA and OpenCL programming paradigms have brought significant performance gains to consumer-grade applications.

Our paper was one of a number of papers riding the wave of greater programming flexibility and computational capability of accelerators in general, and NVIDIA GPUs in particular. This wave has only increased in size, and probably marks the end of the significant computational performance inflection points for general-purpose silicon processors. Advances in networking technology and field-programmability are waiting in the wings for their turn to change the landscape of computing. But for now, we look back at our paper and its peers, and examine their impact.

ICS 25th Anniversary Volume, Jun 10–13 2014, Muenchen, Germany.
ACM 978-1-4503-2840-1/14/06.
http://dx.doi.org/10.1145/2591635.2591670.

2. IMPACT

Our paper sat at the nexus of two exploding fields, biomedical image analysis and supercomputing based on coordinated use of multi-core CPUs and hardware accelerators.

2.1 Biomedical Image Analysis

At the time, whole-slide scanners were new sources of huge amounts of data. Due to the possible benefit to the public through better disease detection, it made sense for researchers to apply effort to increase the quality of the analysis through computational means. Unfortunately, there was a large gap between the researchers versed in creating the biologically supported analysis techniques and those versed in making most efficient use of cutting-edge computational resources. Our paper helped bridge that gap.

Although we used popular methods within image processing, the merit here was to gather a rich and complete set of assorted features, and to implement them efficiently with CUDA, and on a distributed architecture. Therefore, our methods were constructive examples at the time, where simplicity and pedagogy for non-expert programmers was rightly combined.

With progress in imaging systems and algorithms, the computational complexity of image processing has continued its increase. Pratx et al. [16] provide a recent survey about the vast influence of GPU computing in medical image processing. Two fundamental tools within this area are **image registration** (the transformation of two or more images into a common frame of reference) and **image segmentation** (the grouping of voxels with common properties). We have demonstrated the utility of our CUDA kernels in a wide set of applications included within these two subareas [18, 17]. The huge input dataset, usually consisting of a large set of high resolution images (around 100Kx100K) creates a heavy workload which requires parallelization, and where the CUDA paradigm, based on data parallelism, reaches extraordinary speed-up factors.

Signal and image reconstruction are two more areas where our work is useful. For example, Lee et al. [13] discuss the implementation of a wide number of kernels useful in these two areas, and they cite our work as a reference in biomedical imaging. Hartley et al. [9] explore the use of distributed memory cluster computers and GPUs for radar signal analysis applications, particularly backprojection image formation, and also take our implementation as a reference. And finally, Ashtari et al. [4] have implemented novel regularization methods in microwave image reconstruction problems for its application on breast imaging, providing another scenario where our techniques offer great potential.

2.2 Supercomputing with accelerators

At this stage of the GPGPU evolution there were few supercomputers based on GPUs. We used BALE at Ohio Supercomputing Center, which combined many-core GPUs and multi-core CPUs, and we included a detailed performance analysis on platforms belonging to that category. The advent of heterogeneous computing thereafter gave us great visibility as pioneers of this approach [8, 10].

2.2.1 CUDA Programming

The ICS'08 Program included an opening keynote by Mark Harris entitled "Many-core GPU Computing with NVIDIA CUDA" plus a "CUDA Programming" tutorial by Manuel Ujaldon, co-author and presenter of this paper. It was the right forum for showing CUDA optimizations, and we showed novel techniques using shared memory, phantom cells, block geometries, conflicts in memory banks, coalescing and packed datatypes. Most of those optimizations were extensively used thereafter in many disciplines when porting algorithms into CUDA, thus referencing our work. For example, numerical analysis [19], artificial intelligence [7] and signal and image registration [13].

Among all topics covered by our paper, CUDA programming has been the one evolving the fastest. Since its inception at the end of 2006, Google Scholar reports 3636 articles with CUDA in its title. The progress is impressive, as we can see in Table 1. Another relevant data about the popularity reached by CUDA is that more than 800 universities worldwide teach CUDA programing in early 2014. Some of our CUDA kernels, like the color conversion or the histogram of an image, were used in many tutorials worldwide and included in the CUDA SDK provided by NVIDIA, which was downloaded more than two million times during the first six years of use.

Year	2007	2008	2009	2010	2011	2012	2013
Papers	84	231	488	627	720	672	507

Table 1: Number of research papers including CUDA in the title according to Google Scholar [2]

2.2.2 Coordination of multi-core CPUs and GPUs

As we found during our research, one of the hardest problems to address in an infrastructure designed to provide access to GPU-based computing systems is the movement of data. Since GPUs have such high raw computational power, keeping them fed with sufficient input data on which to compute can be a challenge. Thus, contributions [11] were made to automatically deal with the complexities of providing the program a consistent data view, even when dealing with complex data structures.

Another of the vexing problems the literature has continued to battle when dealing with accelerators like GPUs is the fact that certain types of computation are still ill-suited to run on massively parallel processors with high memory latencies. Thus, the technique we used, and which continues to be applied [6, 14, 5] is to match the computation to the correct processor type, leveraging the strengths of each while keeping the overall performance of the system and application in mind.

One of the benefits of the dataflow framework we used in our work is the inherent adaptivity in the platform. The notion of adaptivity continues to be leveraged to great success in the literature [20, 15]. Both of these contributions target peta-scale systems where the overlap of communication and computation is critical. Further, the authors of [20] also make use of another useful feature of dataflow frameworks (which we used in our work), that of software pipelining. Pipelined execution is of critical importance at this scale of computing, to deal with the latencies involved in CPU-GPU communication as well as communication between nodes in the system.

Other notable papers have combined this kind of infrastructure work with additional real-time constraints [12].

3. CONCLUDING REMARKS

The arrival of CUDA in late 2006 reignited data parallelism in scientific computing. In many areas, the number of publications related to the use of GPUs for accelerating computationally demanding kernels has skyrocketed since then, and biomedical image analysis is one of the most successful ones. Our paper, submitted to ICS'08 one year later, was one of the first dealing with a GPU supercomputer composed of multi-core CPUs and many-core GPUs to reach extraordinary speed-ups. Today, GPUs are ubiquitous in the HPC arena, being adopted throughout industry and academia, and nowadays it is usual to find research presented at HPC conferences following a structure and methodology similar to the ones we showed in this early work.

4. REFERENCES

[1] http://green500.org/, Apr. 2014.

[2] http://scholar.google.com/, Apr. 2014.

[3] http://top500.org/, Apr. 2014.

[4] A. Ashtari, S. Noghanian, A. Sabouni, J. Aronsson, G. Thomas, and S. Pistorius. Using a priori information for regularization in breast microwave image reconstruction. *Biomedical Engineering, IEEE Transactions on*, 57(9):2197–2208, 2010.

[5] G. Barlas, A. Hassan, and Y. Al Jundi. An analytical approach to the design of parallel block cipher encryption/decryption: A CPU/GPU case study. In *Parallel, Distributed and Network-Based Processing (PDP), 2011 19th Euromicro International Conference on*, pages 247–251. IEEE, 2011.

[6] P. Benner, P. Ezzatti, E. Quintana-Ortí, and A. Remón. Using hybrid CPU-GPU platforms to accelerate the computation of the matrix sign function. In H.-X. Lin, M. Alexander, M. Forsell, A. KnÃijpfer, R. Prodan, L. Sousa, and A. Streit, editors, *Euro-Par 2009 âĂŞ Parallel Processing Workshops*, volume 6043

of *Lecture Notes in Computer Science*, pages 132–139. Springer Berlin Heidelberg, 2010.

[7] J. M. Cecilia, J. M. García, G. D. Guerrero, M. A. Martínez-del Amor, I. Pérez-Hurtado, and M. J. Pérez-Jiménez. Simulation of p systems with active membranes on cuda. *Briefings in Bioinformatics*, 11(3):313–322, 2010.

[8] A. Cevahir, A. Nukada, and S. Matsuoka. High performance conjugate gradient solver on multi-GPU clusters using hypergraph partitioning. *Computer Science-Research and Development*, 25(1-2):83–91, 2010.

[9] T. D. R. Hartley, A. R. Fasih, C. A. Berdanier, F. Özgüner, and Ü. V. Çatalyürek. Investigating the use of GPU-accelerated nodes for SAR image formation. In *Proc. of the IEEE International Conference on Cluster Computing, Workshop on Parallel Programming on Accelerator Clusters (PPAC)*, 2009.

[10] K. Hawick, A. Leist, and D. Playne. Mixing multi-core CPUs and GPUs for scientific simulation software. *Research Letters in the Information and Mathematical Sciences, Massey University, University of New Zealand*, 2010.

[11] T. B. Jablin, J. A. Jablin, P. Prabhu, F. Liu, and D. I. August. Dynamically managed data for CPU-GPU architectures. In *Proceedings of the Tenth International Symposium on Code Generation and Optimization*, CGO '12, pages 165–174, New York, NY, USA, 2012. ACM.

[12] M. Joselli, M. Zamith, E. Clua, A. Montenegro, A. Conci, R. Leal-Toledo, L. Valente, B. Feijo, M. d'Ornellas, and C. Pozzer. Automatic dynamic task distribution between CPU and GPU for real-time systems. In *Computational Science and Engineering, 2008. CSE '08. 11th IEEE International Conference on*, pages 48–55, July 2008.

[13] S. Lee and S. J. Wright. Implementing algorithms for signal and image reconstruction on graphical processing units. *Optimization Online*, 10, 2008.

[14] Y. Liu, A. Fedorov, R. Kikinis, and N. Chrisochoides. Real-time non-rigid registration of medical images on a cooperative parallel architecture. In *Bioinformatics and Biomedicine, 2009. BIBM'09. IEEE International Conference on*, pages 401–404. IEEE, 2009.

[15] Q. Meng, J. Luitjens, and M. Berzins. Dynamic task scheduling for the uintah framework. In *IEEE Workshop on Many-Task Computing on Grids and Supercomputers (MTAGS)*, pages 1–10, Nov 2010.

[16] G. Pratx and L. Xing. GPU computing in medical physics: A review. *Medical physics*, 38(5):2685–2697, 2011.

[17] A. Ruiz, O. Sertel, M. Ujaldon, Ü. Çatalyürek, J. Saltz, and M. Gürcan. Pathological image analysis using the GPU: Stroma classification for neuroblastoma. In *Proc. of IEEE Int. Conf. on Bioinformatics and Biomedicine*, pages 78–85, 2007.

[18] A. Ruiz, M. Ujaldon, L. Cooper, and K. Huang. Non-rigid registration for large sets of microscopic images on graphics processors. *Journal of Signal Processing Systems*, 55(1-3):229–250, 2009.

[19] S. Tsutsui and N. Fujimoto. Solving quadratic assignment problems by genetic algorithms with GPU computation: a case study. In *Proceedings of the 11th Annual Conference Companion on Genetic and Evolutionary Computation Conference: Late Breaking Papers*, pages 2523–2530. ACM, 2009.

[20] C. Yang, F. Wang, Y. Du, J. Chen, J. Liu, H. Yi, and K. Lu. Adaptive optimization for petascale heterogeneous CPU/GPU computing. In *IEEE International Conference on Cluster Computing (CLUSTER)*, pages 19–28, Sept 2010.

25th Anniversary Volume Editor is proud to include this ICS paper

Strategies for Cache and Local Memory Management by Global Program Transformation

Dennis Gannon; William Jalby; Kyle Gallivan
gallivan@fsu.edu

Link to original article for the readers' convenience:
http://link.springer.com/chapter/10.1007/3-540-18991-2_14
& DOI: DOI: 10.1007/3-540-18991-2_14

25th Anniversary Volume Editor
is proud to include this ICS paper

An Overview of the PTRAN Analysis System for Multiprocessing

Frances E. Allen; Michael G. Burke; Philippe Charles;
Ron Cytron; Jeanne Ferrante
jferrant@eng.ucsd.edu

Link to original article for the readers' convenience:
http://link.springer.com/chapter/10.1007/3-540-18991-2_12
& DOI: 10.1007/3-540-18991-2_12

25th Anniversary Volume Editor
is proud to include this ICS paper

Analysis of Interprocedural Side Effects in a Parallel Programing Environment

David Callahan, Ken Kennedy

DOI of original article for the readers' convenience:
http://link.springer.com/chapter/10.1007/3-540-18991-2_10

Code Scheduling and Register Allocation in Large Basic Blocks

James R. Goodman

Computer Sciences Department
The University of Wisconsin-Madison
Madison, WI 53706

Wei-Chung Hsu[1]

Development Building
Cray Research Inc.
Chippewa Falls, WI 54729

Abstract

We discuss the issues about the interdependency between code scheduling and register allocation. We present two methods as solutions: (1) an integrated code scheduling technique; and (2) a DAG-driven register allocator. The integrated code scheduling method combines two scheduling techniques— one to reduce pipeline delays and the other to minimize register usage— into a single phase. By keeping track of the number of available registers, the scheduler can choose the appropriate scheduling technique to schedule a better code sequence. The DAG-driven register allocator uses a dependency graph to assist in assigning registers; it introduces much less extra dependency than does an ordinary register allocator. For large basic blocks, both approaches were shown to generate more efficient code sequences than conventional techniques in the simulations.

1. Introduction

Pipelining is a common technique used in high-performance computers [Kogg81]. It increases system performance by overlapping instruction execution. Ideally, more pipelined stages (*i.e.* a more finely segmented pipeline) means higher throughput. However, the presence of branch instructions and inter-instruction data dependencies often restricts the effectiveness of a long pipeline. Hardware techniques like out-of-order instruction execution [Toma67, Thor70] have been used occationally to alleviate the data dependency problem. However, they are not used widely because (1) they are expensive; (2) their complexity may slow down the clock rate. On the other hand, code scheduling, a software technique that rearranges the code sequence at compile time to reduce possible run-time delays, has been shown to be effective for improving the performance of pipelined processors [Henn83, Youn85, Gibb86, Weis87].

Code scheduling normally exploits existing parallelism in basic blocks. The code scheduler interleaves several independent instructions so that the latency (both memory latency and function unit latency) can be largely hidden. However, the observed parallelism in typical basic blocks is often limited to a factor of two to three [Tjad70]. This limits the effectiveness of a long pipeline. However, compiler techniques like loop unrolling [Dong79, Weis87] and trace scheduling [Fish81, Elli85] can be used to generate large basic blocks. Large basic blocks are common in scientific applications written for supercomputers, and they provide a better opportunity to exploit parallelism in basic blocks.

While code scheduling is effective in reducing pipeline interlocks and hiding memory latency, it creates a problem for register allocation. Code scheduling increases the time between a write to a register and the reads after the write. Having longer register lifetimes increases the number of simultaneously live registers, interfering with register allocation. Code scheduling may cause the register allocator to spill some registers. This is a major reason why researchers choose postpass code scheduling — code scheduling after the register allocation is done [Henn83, Gibb86] — rather than prepass scheduling. However, since the register allocator may inadvertently introduce dependencies by allocating the same register for unrelated instructions (so called storage-related dependency), postpass code scheduling is more restricted than prepass code scheduling. When basic blocks are small, this restriction makes little difference. But for large basic blocks and long pipelines, it may make a significant difference in performance.

We introduce two approaches to attack the interdependency problem between code scheduling and register allocation. Section 3 describes a code scheduling method which combines two code motion techniques — one to reduce pipeline delays and the other to minimize register usage— into a single phase. By keeping track of the number of available registers, the scheduler can choose a more appropriate scheduling technique. This method also considers spilling as a trade-off with runtime interlocks because for some heavily pipelined processors, spilling may not be more expensive than long interlocks. The other approach is based on a DAG-driven register allocator which uses a Dependency DAG to assist in assigning registers; it introduces much less extra dependency than does an ordinary register allocator. It will be described in section 4.

2. Background

2.1. Code Scheduling Constraints: The Dependency DAG

Code scheduling algorithms generally reorder instructions to improve program execution time [Henn83, Gibb86]. The ordering must preserve the original partial order imposed by operational precedence constraints. DAGs (Directed Acyclic Graphs) are normally used to represent program precedence constraints [Aho86]. A DAG defines legal evaluation orders within a basic block; nodes represent instructions, and edges represent serialization dependencies between instructions. An edge leading from instruction *A* to instruction *B* indicates that *A* must be executed before *B* in the scheduled code sequence. An example code sequence and its dependency DAG are shown in Figure 2.1. This example program will be used repeatedly in this paper.

2.2. The Use of Low Level Intermediate Languages

The use of intermediate languages (IL) simplifies code generation and optimizations. The PL.8 compiler [Ausl82] uses a low

[1] The work described here was done while this author was at University of Wisconsin--Madison.

·el IL with an unlimited number of symbolic registers. In the gister allocation phase, the symbolic registers are mapped into a nited number of physical registers. The IL used in this paper is nilar to the assembly language of a load/store, register-register, ree-address format machine. We will use it to illustrate examples.

```
= a*b
= (c+d)*(a+e)
= f+g
```

urce program

```
Load R1, a
Load R2, b
Mul  R3, R1, R2
Load R4, c
Load R5, d
Add  R6, R4, R5
Load R7, e
Add  R8, R1, R7
Mul  R9, R6, R8
Add  R10, R3, R9
Stor R10, h
```

program

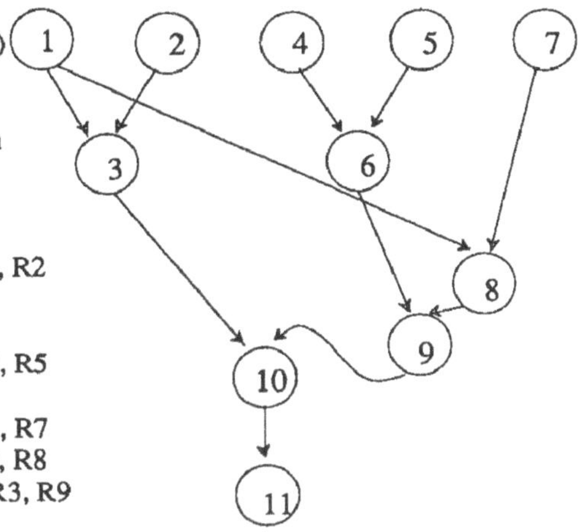

Dependency DAG

Figure 2.1 Example Program and its Dependency DAG

3. Prepass or Postpass?

Code scheduling can be applied to a program in IL either fore the register allocation pass (prepass) or after register allocan (postpass). The advantage of prepass scheduling is that the full rallelism of the program could be exploited. Its drawback is the ssibility of overusing registers which causes excessive register illing. The increased instructions for register spilling will slow wn the computation. Postpass scheduling does not increase illed code, since register allocation has already been done. Hower, the register allocator is likely to assign the same register for related instructions. The reuse of registers introduces new depenncy constraints, making code scheduling more restricted. An ample in Figure 2.2 illustrates the pros and cons of the above two heduling policies. In Figure 2.2, the same program as in Figure 1 is used, PR means pseudo-registers.

In the above example, we assume a stack is used to manage register pool: dead registers are returned to the top of the stack d new registers are allocated from the top of the stack[1]. The DAG Figure 2.1 is used for prepass code scheduling. The original DAG, ich is based on the dependencies of pseudo-registers, preserves aximal parallelism. After the register allocation, the reuse of regiss forces new dependencies. For example, the reuse of register 4 in struction 7 adds a write-after-read (WAR) dependency (or antipendency [Padu86]) from instruction 6 to 7 (Figure 2.3). This wly introduced dependency prevents instruction 7 from overlapg instruction 4 or 5, in postpass scheduling, introducing artificial peline delays. However, the code sequence of prepass code heduling consumes five registers while the code sequence of postss scheduling requires only four. If only four registers are availle, the prepass code needs load and store instructions to spill regiss.

[1]Alternate allocation policies are discussed in section 3.

2.4. Two Conflict Scheduling Techniques

Two code rearranging techniques could be applied during the optimization phases. They are: (1) code scheduling [Henn83, Gibb86, Youn85] to avoid delays in pipelined machines as we have discussed before — we call this technique CSP (Code Scheduling for Pipelined processors) for short, and (2) code reorganization [Davi86] to minimize the number of registers required — we call it

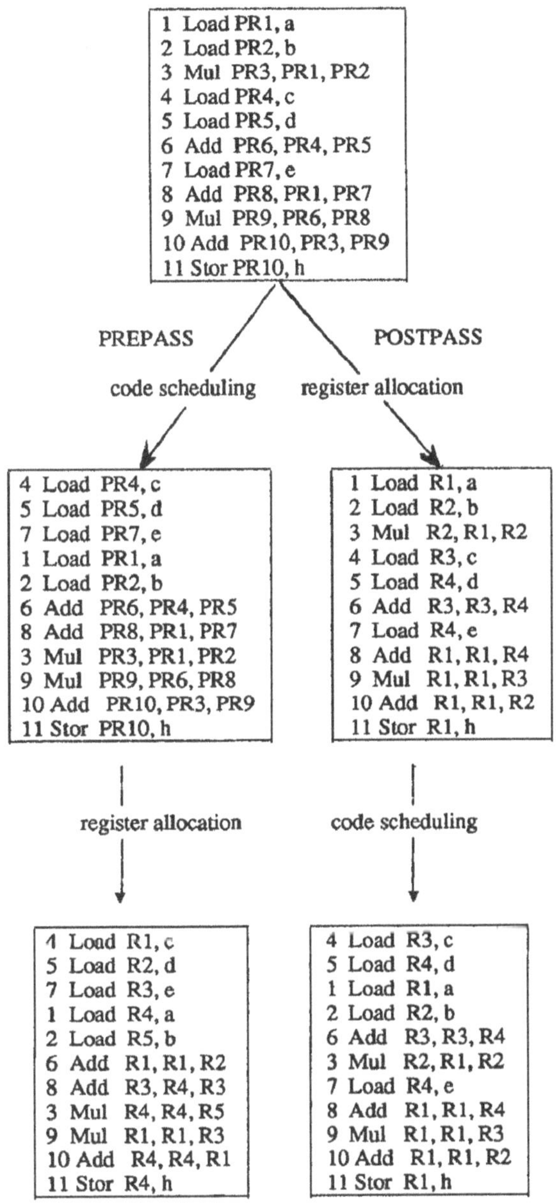

Figure 2.2 Prepass and Postpass Scheduling

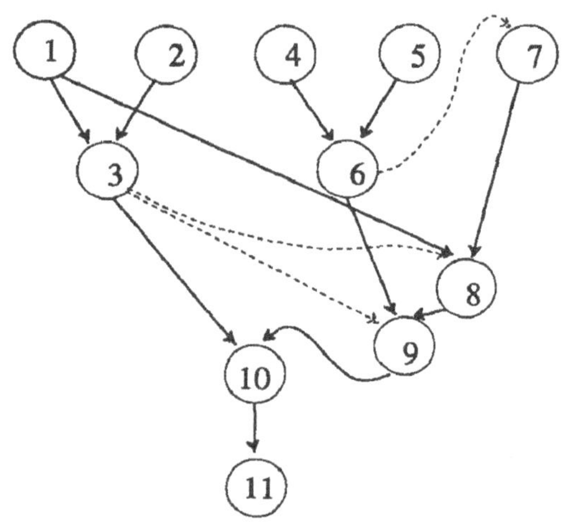

solid lines -- original dependencies.

dashed lines -- dependencies added by register allocation

Figure 2.3 New Dependency Edges Added by Register Allocation

CSR (Code Scheduling to minimize Registers usage) for short. CSP could be applied before and/or after the register allocation phase while it only makes sense to apply CSR before register allocation. The use of CSP has been discussed; we now introduce the use of CSR in the following example.

As in Figure 2.2, a typical register allocation for the IL program requires four registers. The rearranged code sequence using CSR (as in Figure 2.4) needs only three registers.

The rearranging technique that generates the above code sequence has been used in the code generation phase to determine better evaluation orders of expression trees or DAGs. The well-known Sethi-Ullman algorithm [Seth70] generates the optimal evaluation order (using minimal number of registers) of expression trees. Heuristic algorithms are also available for DAGs (with common subexpressions) [Aho77]. Recently, Davidson [Davi86] has separated this optimization technique from the code generation phase and implemented it as an independent code reorganization technique. The key idea of this optimization is to prevent a register from holding a temporary too long. Hence the number of simultaneously live registers could be reduced.

CSP and CSR conflict with each other. CSP tends to increase the lifetime of each pseudo-register while CSR wants to shorten it.

4 Load PR4, c		Load R1, c
5 Load PR5, d		Load R2, d
6 Add PR6, PR4, PR5		Add R1, R1, R2
1 Load PR1, a	after	Load R2, a
7 Load PR7, e	== register ==>	Load R3, e
8 Add PR8, PR1, PR7	allocation	Add R3, R2, R3
9 Mul PR9, PR8, PR6		Mul R1, R3, R1
2 Load PR2, b		Load R3, b
3 Mul PR3, PR1, PR2		Mul R3, R2, R3
10 Add PR10, PR3, PR9		Add R1, R3, R1
11 Stor PR10, h		Stor R1, h

Figure 2.4 CSR Minimizing the Use of Registers

We attempt to integrate CSP and CSR into a single phase so th they will cooperate in generating a better code sequence.

3. Integrated Prepass Scheduling

The major disadvantage of prepass scheduling is that it m overuse registers causing register spilling. We propose to integra CSP and CSR in prepass code scheduling to control register spillir The basic idea is to keep track of the number of available regist during code scheduling. Since each issued instruction may create new live register and terminate the lifetime of some registers, we c keep track of the number of available registers. When there a enough registers, the scheduler uses CSP to reduce pipeline dela When the number of available register is getting low, the schedu switches to CSR to control the use of registers. The followi example explains this approach.

Example

Suppose the input program is the same as in Figure 2.1 a there are four[2] registers available for this program. Our new co scheduler will schedule the program in a sequence like:

4 Load PR4, c
5 Load PR5, d
7 Load PR7, e
1 Load PR1, a

The scheduler must now choose between issuing instruction which activates one register, and instruction 6, which frees one r register. Since the available registers have been used up, CSR tak charge of scheduling, and issues instruction 6. We then return CSP and instruction 2 is issued after instruction 6. The comple reorganized code sequence is as in Figure 3.1.

Notice that this code sequence uses four registers, the sa number as the postpass code sequence used. Compared to the po pass code sequence as in Figure 2.2, however, this code sequen has fewer runtime interlocks.

3.1. Implementation Notes

3.1.1. CSP, CSR and AVLREG

There are two major parts in our approach: CSP and CS The use of CSP in our work is based on the work by You [Youn85]. We also take ideas from others [Gibb86, Henn83] improve the CSP algorithm. Young [Youn85] assumes the targ machine has multiple functional units whose pipelines vary

4 Load PR4, c		Load R1, c
5 Load PR5, d		Load R2, d
7 Load PR7, e		Load R3, e
1 Load PR1, a		Load R4, a
6 Add PR6, PR4, PR5	after	Add R1, R1, R2
2 Load PR2, b	== register ==>	Load R2, b
8 Add PR8, PR1, PR7	allocation	Add R3, R4, R3
3 Mul PR3, PR1, PR2		Mul R4, R4, R2
9 Mul PR9, PR6, PR8		Mul R1, R1, R3
10 Add PR10, PR3, PR9		Add R4, R4, R1
11 Stor PR10, h		Stor R4, h

Figure 3.1 Code Sequence Using Integrated Scheduling

[2] A machine typically has eight or 16 general purpose registers. However, we sume that other registers have already been preallocated to frequently used variab or constants and thus only four are left for this basic block.

length. Instructions complete whenever they leave their particular functional unit pipelines. The estimated execution time of each instruction is used to compute the cumulative cost of each node in the DAG. This cumulative cost identifies which node is on the critical path during instruction scheduling. Instructions are scheduled in a topological sort order of the DAG. Nodes on the current critical path have higher issue priority. In contrast to [Henn83], hardware interlocks are assumed rather than using software to enforce interlocks.

The CSR used in our approach is different from earlier work [Seth70, Aho77], which determines the complete evaluation order of an expression tree or a DAG. In our approach, when CSR is called, the evaluation order of the DAG has been partially determined (some nodes have been issued). The goal of CSR at this point is to find the next instruction which will not increase the number of live registers, or if possible, decrease that number. Our CSR does not decide the total evaluation order. The basic approach of our CSR is to find an instruction that frees more registers than the number of live registers it creates. When no such instructions exist, the scheduler looks for instructions on partially evaluated paths, since once the partially evaluated path is fully evaluated, registers may be freed.

Switching between CSP and CSR is driven by the number of available register, AVLREG. CSP is responsible for code scheduling most of the time. When AVLREG drops below a threshold (say, one) CSR is invoked. After AVLREG is restored to an acceptable value, CSP resumes scheduling. AVLREG is initially determined by the total number of registers minus the number of registers live-on-entry. Global data flow analysis [Aho86] can supply the information of registers live-on-entry. Reference counting is used to determine when pseudo-registers are dead and can be freed. We increase AVLREG when there are freed registers, and decrease AVLREG when instructions create live registers.

Renaming techniques [Padu86] have been used to enforce single assignments — every pseudo-register is written only once statically in a basic block — in order to maintain maximal scheduling flexibility.

3.1.2. Interlock Checking at Scheduling Time

In load/store, register-register architectures, it is easy to resolve all interlocks at the instruction issue stage [Kogg81, Cray82]. The code scheduler can use instruction execution time information to estimate possible runtime interlocks, and schedule instructions to avoid as many interlocks as possible.

3.1.3. Leader Set and Ready Set

A leader of a DAG is a vertex with no predecessors. An instruction can not be issued until it becomes a leader. As instructions are issued, their nodes are removed from the DAG and some successor nodes become new leaders. All leaders are maintained in a *leader set*. Instructions in the leader set lacking interlocks with previously issued instructions are promoted from the leader set to a *ready set*. All the instructions in the ready set are ready to be issued.

3.1.4. Integrated Scheduling Algorithm

(1) Rename pseudo-registers to enforce single assignment.

(2) Input a basic block, create the DAG and calculate the reference count of each pseudo-register.

(3) Compute the cumulative cost of each node in reverse topological sort order.

(4) Issue instructions in topological sort order.

Details of step 4:

```
 4.0 Calculate the leader set.

while (leader set or ready set is not empty) do

 4.1 Move nodes without interlocks from leader set to ready set.
 4.2 if (AVLREG > threshold value) then
        if (ready set is not empty) then
          select one node from ready set with maximum
          cumulative cost.
        else
          select one node from leader set with maximum
          cumulative cost.
        endif
      else {invoke CSR}
        if there are nodes in ready set that can free registers
        then
          select one node which frees the most registers.
          if there are more than one such node then
            select one with maximum cumulative cost.
          endif
        else
          if there are nodes in leader set that can free registers
            then
            select one which frees the most registers.
            if there are more than one such node then
              select one that has the fewest interlocks.
            endif
          else
            find a partially evaluated path, (for example,
                one of its RAW dependency has been lifted)
            select one node from the leaders of this path.
            if there are no such partially evaluated paths then
               select any one node from the ready set
               or from the leader set if the ready set is empty.
            endif
          endif
        endif
      endif

 4.3 Issue the selected instruction
   if the issued instruction creates one live register then
      decrement AVLREG by 1.
   for each pseudo-register referenced in this instruction do
      decrement its reference count by 1
      if the reference count drops to 0 then
         increment AVLREG by 1.
      endif
   end for
   Remove this instruction from the DAG
   Remove all dependencies caused by this instruction
   Reserve the destination register in a reservation table.

 4.4 Insert new leaders into the leader set

end while
```

The input program used in this example is the same one as used in section 2. In addition, we assume the following timing for the relevant functions.

Function	Timing(clock periods)
Load	4
Store	1
Add	2
Multiply	3

We assume that the initial value of AVLREG is 4. The weighted DAG is shown in the Figure 3.2 The code sequences generated by prepass code scheduling, postpass code scheduling, and our algorithm are shown in Figure 3.3. Notice that, since the number of available registers is 4, prepass code scheduling incurs spilling costs.

3.1.5. A Variation on Profitable Register Spilling

In the above algorithm, we have assumed that register spilling is more costly than run-time interlocks. This assumption may not be true for highly pipelined machines.

(1) In highly pipelined machines, a pipeline interlock could be very long compared to the issuance of a couple of spill instructions. Also, for machines that have a back up register file like the B/T registers in Cray-1 and Cray-XMP, spilling is not expensive.

(2) Spill code can often be scheduled to run in otherwise wasted cycles.

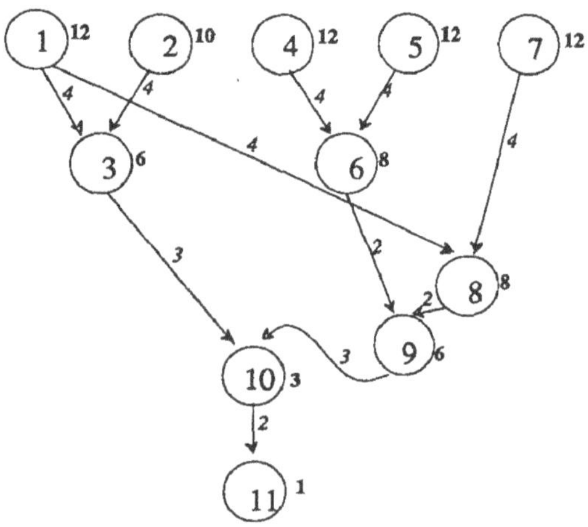

boldface numbers associated with nodes are cumulative costs
italic numbers associated with edges are execution time estimates

Figure 3.2 Weighted DAG Identifying Critical Paths

Prepass	Postpass	Integrated
1 Load R1, a	4 Load R3, c	4 Load R2, c
4 Load R2, c	5 Load R4, d	5 Load R3, d
5 Load R3, d	1 Load R1, a	7 Load R4, e
7 Load R4, e	2 Load R2, b	1 Load R1, a
s Stor R4, templ	6 Add R3, R3, R4	6 Add R2, R2, R3
2 Load R4, b	3 Mul R2, R1, R2	2 Load R3, b
6 Add R2, R2, R3	7 Load R4, e	8 Add R4, R1, R4
s Load R3, templ	8 Add R1, R1, R4	3 Mul R1, R1, R3
8 Add R3, R1, R3	9 Mul R1, R1, R3	9 Mul R2, R2, R4
3 Mul R1, R1, R4	10 Add R1, R1, R2	10 Add R1, R1, R2
9 Mul R2, R2, R3	11 Stor R1, h	11 Stor R1, h
10 Add R1, R1, R2		
11 Stor R1, h		
(22 cycles)	(20 cycles)	(17 cycles)

Figure 3.3 Comparisons of Scheduled Code Sequences

(3) Registers containing loop invariants can be spilled at a low cost.

We have developed a variation of the algorithm to consi profitable register spilling. The variation operates as follows: wh available registers are running out and the next selected instructi has a long interlock with a previously issued instruction, scheduler checks if there is a live pseudo-register which could spilled at a low cost. If there is at least one such register, scheduler will revert to CSP scheduling to favor instructions havi no interlocks and/or are on the critical evaluation path. Because the uncertainties involved in predicting how inserted load instr tions will interfere with subsequent register usage, we have o attempted to guess at a good threshold value for determining wh spilling is worthwhile.

3.2. Simulation Studies and Discussion

3.2.1. Simulations

In this section, we show some experimental results concerni the effectiveness of our new approach. An interpreter and a perf mance simulator have been built to evaluate how fast instructio can be issued for a hypothetical machine. The hypothetical machi architecture has a load/store, register-oriented, three-address instr tion format. It has a single general purpose register file. Its pipelir implementation is shown in the Figure 3.4. The number of gene purpose registers and the degree of pipelining of the machine can varied by changing the parameters in a profile. We assume hypothetical machine has hardware hazard detection and an int lock mechanism.

We use the first twelve Livermore loops [McMa72] for ben mark programs. Loop unrolling [Dong79, Weis87] have been u to obtain large basic blocks. Since unrolled loops may overflow instruction buffer, decreasing performance, we unroll loops u their program size is a little less than some predefined limit. In simulation, this limit is 32 instructions. Although 32 is relativ small compared to the instruction buffer in modern supercomput (CRAY-1 has a buffer size of 256 instruction parcels, CRAY-X has a size of 512), it is large enough to study the interdepende between code scheduling and register allocation. All of the lo are translated into the IL of the hypothetical machine and optimi based on standard optimization techniques [Aho86, Ausl82].

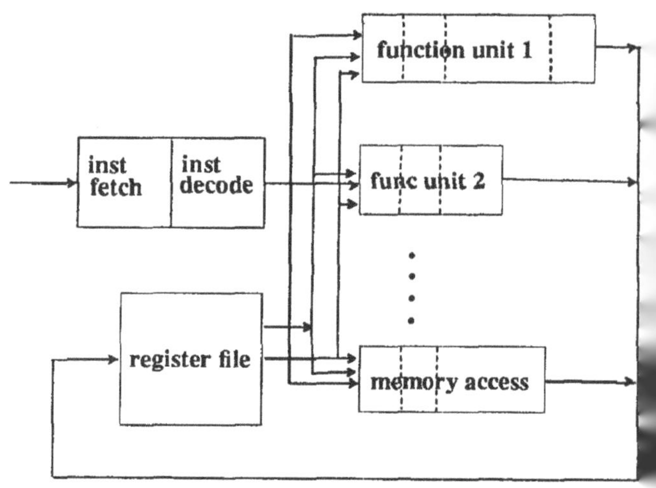

Figure 3.4 Pipelined Implementation of Our Model Architecture

rder to simplify the simulation, all floating point operations have een changed to integer operations.

Different approaches for code scheduling that have been tested n the simulation are:

1) Prepass: IL --> CS --> RA

2) Twopass: IL --> CS --> RA --> CS

code scheduling is performed both before and after register allocation. The second pass scheduling is primarily for the inserted load/stores introduced by register spilling.

3) Postpass: IL --> RA --> CS

4) Postpass with round-robin register allocation (PostRR for short):

The regular register allocation uses a stack to manage register reuse. Some papers [Henn83, Youn85] suggest using round-robin allocation, which cycling through registers, to reduce the inadvertent dependencies introduced by register reuses. Hence we implemented PostRR as a variation of general Postpass. The code scheduling algorithm for approaches (1) through (4) is essentially the CSP part as discussed in previous section.

5) GoodWay0 (GW0): As described in the previous section.

This algorithm does prepass code scheduling with appropriate control of register usages.

6) GoodWay1 (GW1): A variation of GW0.

This version considers spilling a register as an alternative when the next issuing instruction has long interlocks with previously issued instructions.

ll the above approaches used the same register allocator, which ses a replacement-based algorithm [Hsu87].

In Figure 3.5, we present the relative performance of six different approaches. The performance measure is the number of clock ycles needed to issue and execute a program. The number of available registers is varied from 4 to 30. The machine is assumed to be eavily pipelined (HP for short), similar to the CRAY-1 [Cray82]. Ve assume 11 clock periods (CP) for a load, 3 CPs for an integer dd, 6 CPs for an integer multiply, and so on. Figure 3.6 is similar o Figure 3.5 except that the machine has a slower clock rate. In this achine, we assume a load takes 6 CPs, an add takes 2 CPs, an multiply takes 3 CPs, and so on.

Figures 3.5 and 3.7 base on the same machine assumptions, as o Figures 3.6 and 3.8. In Figures 3.7 and 3.8, the measure is the umber of instructions. Since prepass code scheduling often results n register spilling, the sizes of its resulting programs are usually arger than programs of postpass scheduling and our scheduling cheme.

.2.2. Discussion

Using Figures 3.5 through 3.8, we make the following observations.

1) In Figures 3.5 and 3.6, prepass code scheduling usually has better performance than postpass scheduling unless the number of available registers is very low. This is because prepass scheduling has much better flexibility to schedule code, especially when more parallelism exists. However, we should not conclude that prepass scheduling is better than postpass scheduling. In Figures 3.7 and 3.8, the prepass

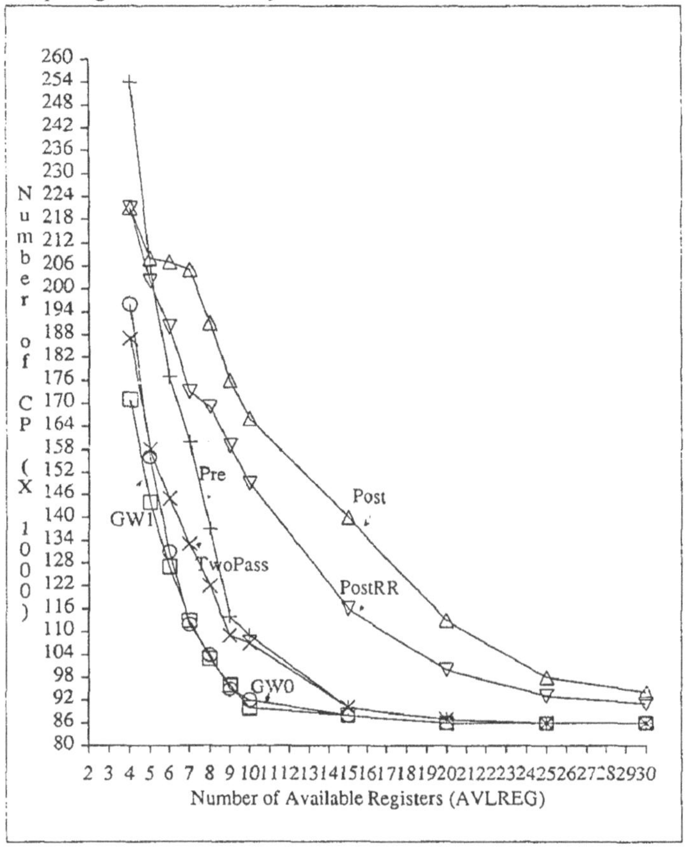

Figure 3.5 Comparisons of Speed (Highly Pipelined Model)

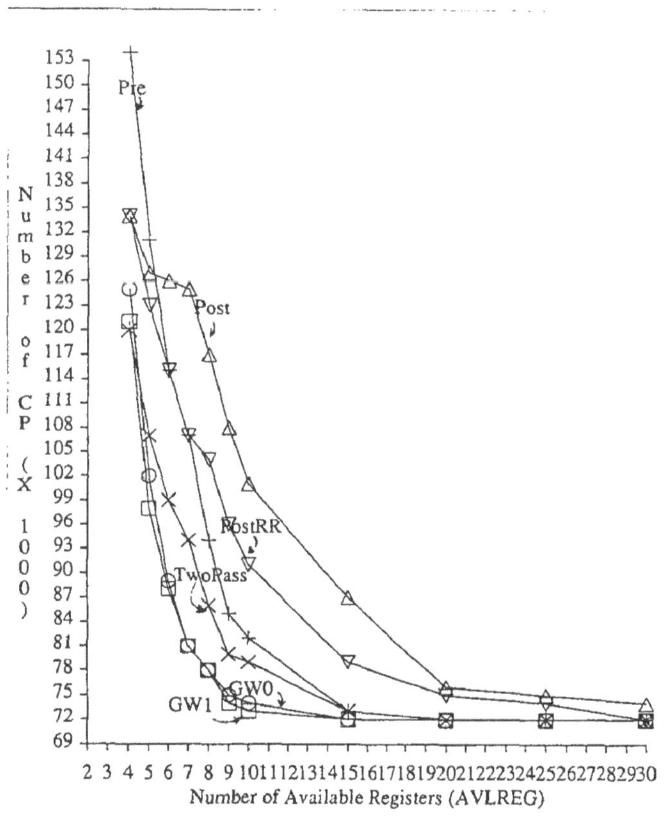

Figure 3.6 Comparisons of Speed (Medium Pipelined Model)

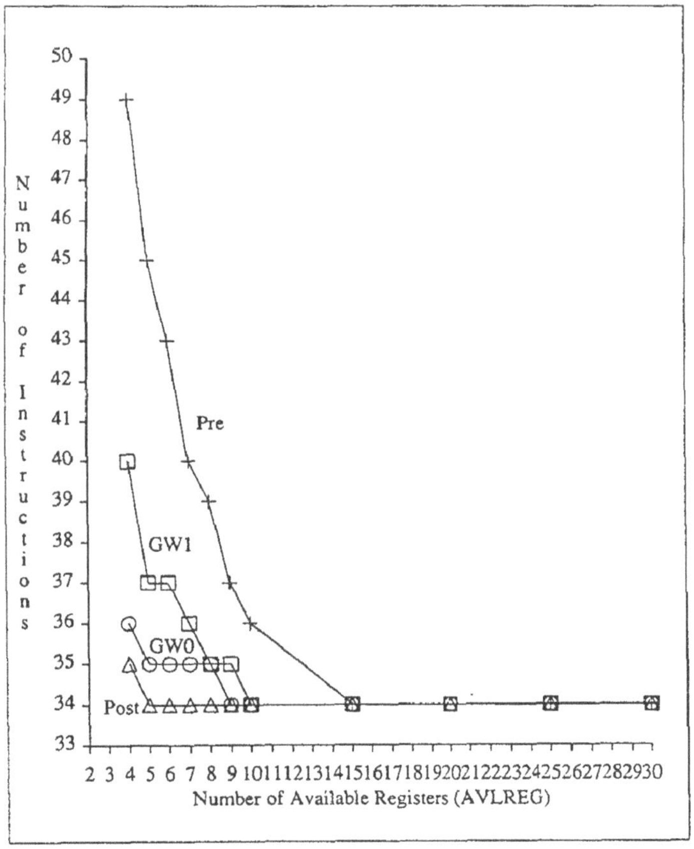

Figure 3.7 Comparisons of Code Size (Highly Pipelined Model)

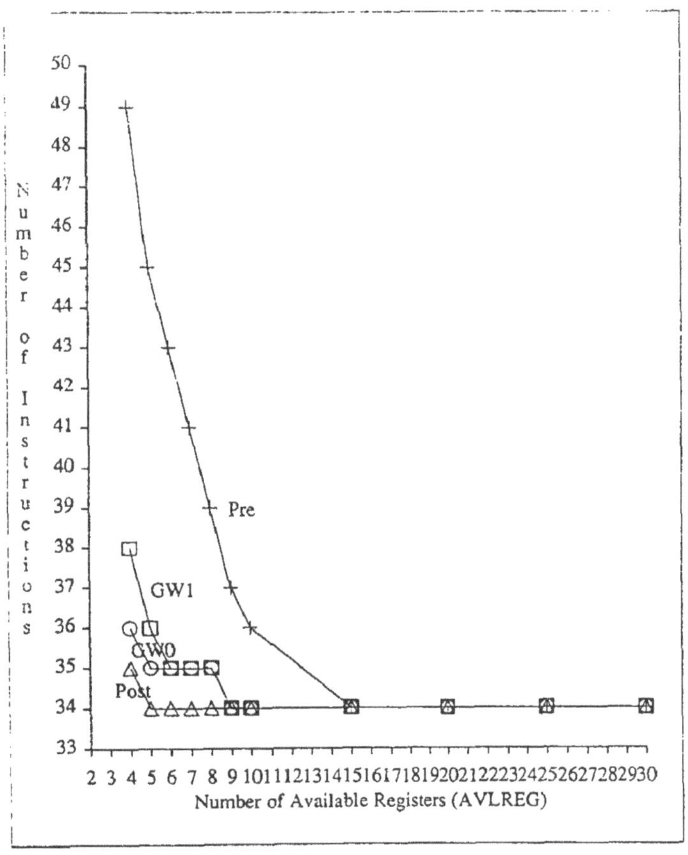

Figure 3.8 Comparisons of Code Size (Medium Pipelined Model)

scheduled programs have significantly larger size than the pr grams of postpass scheduling. Larger programs may execu more slowly, since larger loops are more likely to overflow t instruction buffer, and inserted load/store instructions increa the number of memory fetches and stores. Addition load/stores will slow the computation seriously if memo bandwidth is the performance bottleneck (this is likely in multiprocessor system).

Our approach GW0 outperforms both prepass scheduling a postpass scheduling as shown in Figure 3.5 and 3.6 while t additional load/store instructions of GW0 are only sligh (less than 3%) more than postpass scheduling, as shown Figure 3.7 and 3.8.

(2) In theory, if there are an infinite number of registers, all t different approaches have the same performance. As shown in Figures 3.5 and 3.6, all the curves level off to the sa point when the number of available registers becomes lar However, minimizing the number of registers is critical designing high-performance computers; for register access be fast, the size of the register file should be small [Henn8 Hence, the more important question is how to use limi registers efficiently. As shown in Figures 3.5 and 3.6, curve of our approach levels off more quickly than othe implying that better scheduling can use a (relatively) sm number of registers efficiently.

A register file can be used to hold temporaries and frequen used variables. An efficient algorithm uses fewer registers temporaries, leaving more registers for frequently used co stants and variables. The number of registers is well-defined an architecture. Yet the architecture can have quite differ implementations. A highly pipelined implementation requi more registers for temporaries so that interlocks can reduced. When a highly pipelined implementation is used, approach of using better algorithms to make effective use the register file is more favorable than the approach redesigning the architecture with more registers.

Advances in silicon technologies may make it relatively ea to have a large number of registers on-chip in the near futu However, for GaAs technology, which is much faster than s con technology, the amount of on-chip memory allowed very limited [Milu86]. In a memory hierarchy, the space the top level is always limited, and efficient algorithms necessary to make effective use of the scarce space.

(3) Some compilers designed for pipelined processors use rou robin register allocation, which cycles through the regist available for use. Intuitively, this allocation policy seems avoid the situation of having a long evaluation path due to intensive reuse of certain registers. In Figure 3.6, postp scheduling with round-robin allocation does outperform sta allocation most of the time. It is also true in Figure 3.5 exc when the number of available register is low. Since ev reuse of a register will add a storage-related dependencies the DAG, may combine two parallel evaluation paths into sequential one, without having the detailed information of DAG, no allocation policy will be uniformly superior to oth in balancing the length of merged evaluation paths. One alt native to the current approach is to provide DAG informati to the register allocator. With the DAG information, the reg ter allocator may be able to reuse registers in a way such t the depth of the new DAG can be minimized. Such approach will be described in the next section.

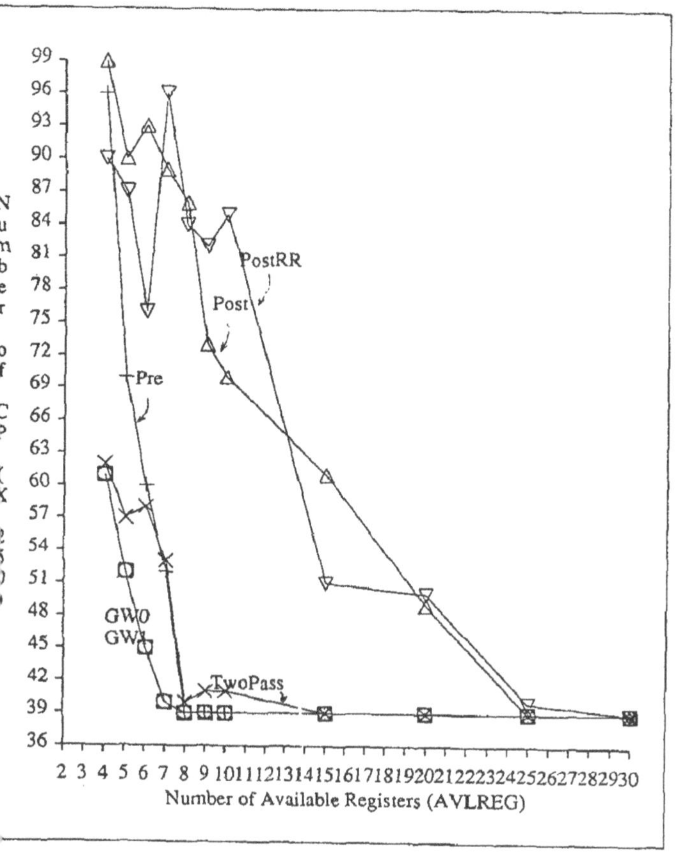

Figure 3.9 Anomalies (from Loop 3)

Some anomalies exist in Twopass and Postpass scheduling :periments. Since they can not be observed from Figure 3.5 and 6 which are figures averaged over all loops, Figure 3.9 is used to esent the curves of a single loop. The following discussions are sed on Figure 3.9.

) The Post curve in Figure 3.9 exhibits a deterioration in performance when the number of registers is increased from five to six. The PostRR curve exhibits a similar anomaly for the transition from six to seven and nine to ten registers. These anomalies result from variations in induced dependencies, as illustrated in Figure 3.10. The DAG on the left hand side has five available registers while the DAG on the right hand side has only four. Round-robin register allocation was used. Notice that after register allocation, the left DAG is more restricted than the right DAG. Because the right tree in the left DAG can not be interleaved with the left tree any more, instructions are forced to be executed in a sequential order.

Figure 3.9 also showed that sometimes Post (stack register allocation) outperforms PostRR (round-robin register allocation) and vise versa. This supports our previous assertion that no allocation policy will be superior to others without detailed DAG information.

Two-pass scheduling is used to improve the performance of prepass scheduling. The second scheduling pass is used to schedule the inserted load/store instructions. In Figures 3.9, the anomaly of the Twopass curve occurs when the number of registers is eight, nine and ten. Not only is the performance poorer than the single pass scheduling but the curve also exhibits a deterioration in performance when the number of registers is increased. When there are enough registers, no inserted load/stores are required for spilling. When there are no inserted load and store instructions, a second pass scheduling is useless. The performance deterioration anomaly is created by the effect of register allocation.

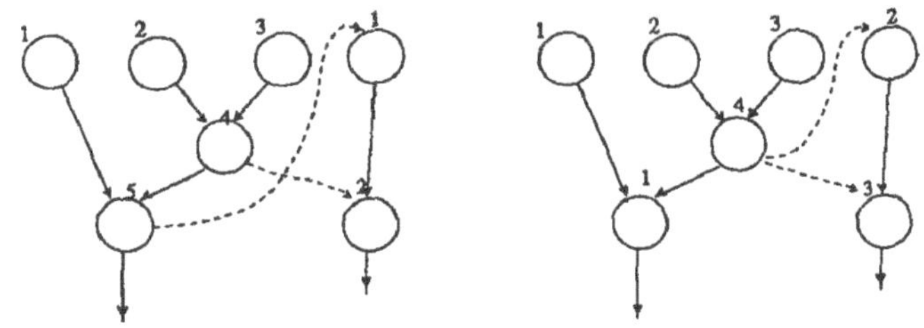

solid lines -- original dependencies.

dashed lines -- dependencies added by register allocation

Figure 3.10 One Explanation of the Anomaly in Postpass Scheduling

4. DAG-Driven Register Allocation

The previous section suggests solving the interdependency problem with an integrated prepass scheduling method. This section discusses an approach which is for the postpass scheduling. We use the dependency DAG to direct register allocation so that very little storage-related dependency are introduced. Two advantages to use postpass scheduling: (1) a postpass scheduler can be applied both to code output from a compiler and to hand-written assembly-language code; (2) unlike prepass scheduling, postpass scheduling will never introduce additional spill code. If minimizing load/stores is the major concern, then postpass scheduling should be favored.

4.1. Balancing DAG Reconstruction

In order to introduce the concept of the DAG-driven register allocation, we define two terms: *width* and *height* of a DAG. The width of a DAG is defined as the maximal number of mutually independent nodes which need a destination register (a store instruction, for example, does not need a destination register), and the *height* of a DAG is the length of its longest path. Since we use the single assignment rule in naming temporaries, the dependency DAG will have a greatest width exposing maximum parallelism. If the number of real registers is larger than the width of the DAG, the shape of the DAG can remain unchanged during register allocation. Otherwise, the register allocator will reduce the width of the DAG to be smaller than or equal to the number of real registers by reusing registers. While the width is reduced, the height is increased since each reuse of registers may merge two evaluation paths into one. The greater the height, the longer the critical path. The longer the critical path, the less efficient the code scheduling. Therefore, our DAG-driven register allocator is trying to minimize the height of the reconstructed DAG. Two strategies to control the growth of the height are: exploiting free WAR dependencies and balancing the growth of the DAG.

4.1.1. Free WAR Dependencies

The reuse of a register creates new dependencies, primarily write-after-read (WAR) dependencies. We have explained that the added WAR dependencies reduce available parallelism and result in less effective code scheduling in section 2. We assumed a pipeline structure in which the operand registers are read at the time an instruction is issued (see Figure 3.4). So long as instructions issue in order (at run time), WAR hazards at register level will never occur. Therefore, the WAR dependency edges are essentially used to enforce the logical order of instructions. We assign WAR dependency a cost of 1, the lowest cost of all dependencies.

Figure 4.1 shows the DAG of the following program segment. Assume there are 5 registers. As the register allocator reads the

1 Load PR1, a
2 Load PR2, b
3 Add PR3, PR1, PR2
4 Load PR4, c
5 Sub PR5, PR4, PR1
6 Addi PR6, PR5, #4
7 Mul PR7, PR5, PR1
.
.

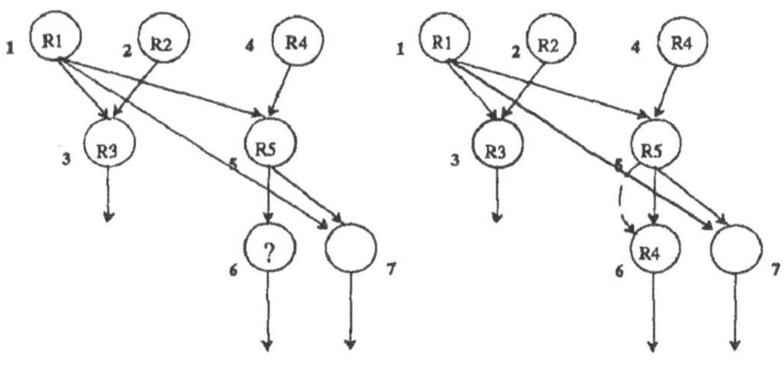

Figure 4.1 Free WAR Dependencies

program, it allocates register R1 through R5 for the destination registers of instruction 1 to instruction 5. At instruction 6, since the available registers have been used up, the register allocator tries to find a dead register to replace. Two registers, register 2 and register 4, are dead before instruction 4. As in Figure 4.1, the reuse of register 4 at instruction 6 introduces a WAR dependency which is represented as a dashed line from instruction node 5 to 4. This dependency is redundant since the logical order of instructions 4, 5 and 6 can be enforced by already existing dependency edges. But if register 2 is allocated rather than register 4 to instruction 6, the added dependency (from node 3 to node 6) is not redundant. Redundant dependencies are *free dependencies*, since they will not increase the height of the DAG.

To minimize the increase in height of the DAG, the register allocator will first select a dead register to replace such that only redundant dependencies are introduced. In other words, the uses of the dead register are on the dependent path of the current instruction. For example, in Figure 4.1, when the register allocator allocates register 4 for instruction 6, the last use of register 4 is instruction 5, which is on the dependent path of instruction 4. Therefore, this allocation introduces no additional dependencies.

4.1.2. Balancing the Growth of the DAG

All register replacements which add new dependencies may increase the height of the DAG. When there are no free dependencies, we allocate registers based on *earliest issue time* and *earliest finish time*. The earliest issue time (EIT for short) of a node is the maximal path cost from the beginning of the DAG to the node. The earliest finish time (EFT for short) of a node is the maximal path cost from the node to the end of the DAG. As the names suggest, the EIT of a node indicates the earliest possible issue time of that instruction from the beginning of the execution of the DAG. The EFT of a node indicates the earliest possible finish time from the issue of that instruction to the end of the execution of the DAG. Figure 4.2 shows the EIT and EFT attributes of each node in a DAG. If the register allocator assigns two independent paths to share a register, then a new WAR dependency connects the two paths into one long path. For example, in Figure 4.1, if the register allocator assigns register 2 to instruction 6, then instruction node 6 is connected with instruction node 3 by a WAR dependency edge. The maximal cost of this new path is apparently $(EIT_3 + EFT_6 + 1)$, where 1 is the cost of the WAR dependency edge.

The key idea in minimizing the height of the DAG is to ba ance the growth of the DAG. The allocator tries not to connect tw nodes such that one has a large EIT and the other has a large EFT. the current instruction has a high EFT, then the allocator woul select a dead register such that all the nodes the current instructio will connect to have a small EIT. But how does the allocator kno if the EFT of the current instruction is relatively large or smal This suggests that the allocator should look at all the unallocate instructions, especially the leader nodes, to determine where th current instruction stands.

Statically computed EIT cannot be used directly in allocatin registers since each register replacement may change the EIT some nodes. The details of implementation can be found elsewhe [Hsu87].

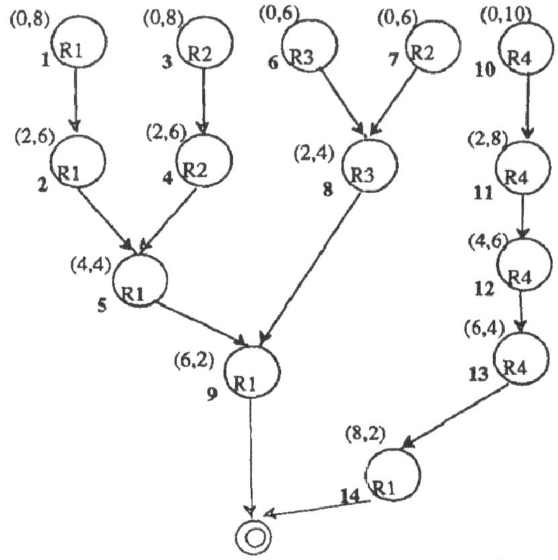

numbers in parenthesis are (EIT, EFT)
assuming each instruction takes 2 clock periods
the double circle is a pseudo node which
indicates the end of the DAG

Figure 4.2 Computations of EIT and EFT

4.1.3. DAG-Driven Allocation Algorithm

(1) Rename pseudo-registers to enforce single assignment

(2) Use CSR to reduce the number of simultaneously live reg ters

(3) Read in the basic block, build the DAG and set up a hash tab of register reference histories

(4) Compute the EFT of each node, set up the adjacency matr representing the dependency relation

(5) Register allocation:

while there are instructions to be allocated **do**

foreach pseudo-register in the instruction, in the order of first operand, second operand, destination **do**

```
ile there are instructions to be allocated do

foreach pseudo-register in the instruction, in the order of
first operand, second operand, destination do

if (pseudo-register Miss) then

   if (Write Miss) then

      if (there are dead registers on the dependent path)
      then
         select one and replace;
         go to 2;
      endif
   endif
   if (there are dead registers) then
      sort them in ascending order on the EIT field,
      count how many remaining leaders have a higher EFT
         than the current instruction into a variable P,
      if (P+1 is greater than the number of dead registers)
      then
         select the dead register with highest EIT to replace;
      else
         select the P+1st dead register to replace;
      endif
   else
      normal replacements;
   endif
endif
dfor

1: update dependent relation incrementally;

2: update EIT of real registers;

dwhile
```

2. The Performance of DAG-driven Register Allocation

Our test results, based on the same test environment described section 3, show DAG-driven register allocation significantly proves the performance of postpass code schedulings (cf. Figures 3 and 4.4). We also compared DAG-driven register allocation to e integrated prepass scheduling. For the highly pipelined model igure 4.3), the integrated prepass scheduling approach that consid-s profitable spilling slightly outperforms the DAG-driven register ocation approach. However, in the medium pipelined model (Fig-e 4.4), DAG-driven allocation approach outperforms all the others. e explain our results as follows: for the highly pipelined model, here an interlock could be relatively expensive, spilling may be ofitable. The integrated prepass scheduling can easily accommo-te profitable spilling, this flexibility creates an opportunity for a tter performance than the DAG-driven allocation approach. The AG-driven allocation approach has the advantage that it does not crease the code size at all. Therefore, it is favored by machines hich discourage code spilling.

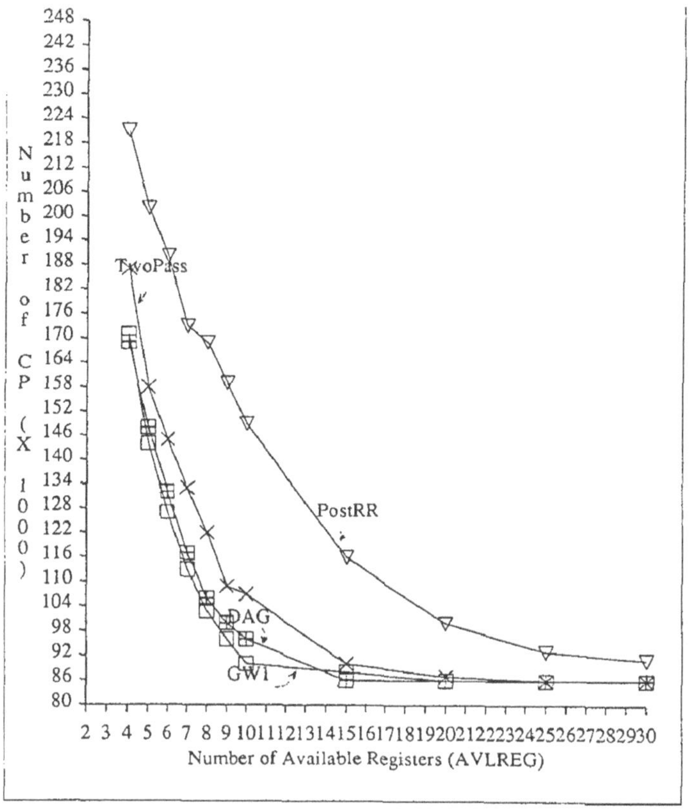

Figure 4.3 Performance of DAG-Driven Allocation (Highly Pipelined)

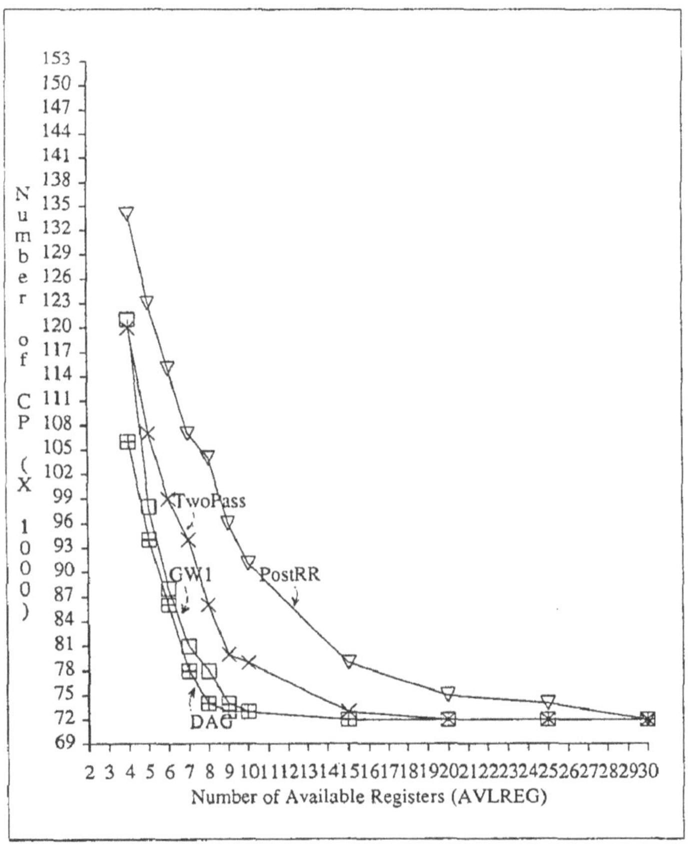

Figure 4.4 Performance of DAG-Driven Allocation (Medium Pipelined)

5. Conclusion

The problems of register allocation and instruction scheduling are often treated independently, although they are closely related. We attempt to look at the two problems at the same time by investigating two approaches: register allocation driven code scheduling and dependence graph driven register allocation. Both the integrated prepass scheduling and the DAG-driven register allocation approaches have been shown to be effective in solving the problem of the interdependency between code scheduling and register allocation.

Conceptually, the DAG-driven register allocation approach is simpler. It attempts to minimize the storage-related dependencies by carefully allocating a limited number of registers available to a basic block. The integrated prepass scheduling is more flexible and more aggresive than the DAG-driven allocation. When long interlocks encounted during code scheduling, our integrated prepass scheduling will force spilling. This is useful in a case where many values in the outer loop are carried through registers, leaving insufficient registers for the inner loop to have a decent scheduling. Our prepass scheduler will force the inner loop to spill (spill code will be moved to the outer loop), creating sufficient registers for code scheduling.

REFERENCES

[Aho77] Aho, A. V., S. C. Johnson, and J. D. Ullman, "Code Generation for expressions with common subexpressions," *JACM*, 24:1, 146-160, 1977

[Aho86] Aho, A. V., J. D. Ullman, and R. Sethi, "Compilers Principles, Techniques, and Tools," Addison-Wesley, Reading, MA, 1986.

[Ausl82] Auslander, M. and M. Hopkins, "An Overview of the PL.8 compiler," *Proceedings of the SIGPLAN '82 Symposium on Compiler Construction*, June, 1982.

[Cray82] Cray Research Inc., *Cray-1 Computer System* S Series Mainframe Reference Manual (HR-0029), 1982.

[Davi86] Davidson, J. W., "A Retargetable Instruction Reorganizer," *Proceedings of the SIGPLAN '86 Symposium on Compiler Construction.* June, 1986

[Dong79] Dongarra, J. J. and A. R. Jinds, "Unrolling Loops in Fortran," *Software Practice and Experience* 9, 3, pp. 219-226, Mar., 1979

[Elli85] Ellis, J. R., "Bulldog: A Compiler for VLIW Architectures," *Ph.D. Thesis*, YaleU/DCS/RR-364, Yale University, Feb., 1985

[Fish81] Fisher, J., "Trace Scheduling: A Technique for Global Microcode Compaction," *IEEE Transactions on Computers*, Vol. C-30, No. 7, July 1981.

[Gibb86] Gibbons P. B., and S. S. Muchnick, "Efficient Instruction Scheduling for a Pipelined Architecture," *Proceedings of the SIGPLAN '86 Symposium on Compiler Construction*, Jun., 1986

[Henn83] Hennessy, J. L., and Thomas Gross, "Postpass Code Optimization of Pipeline Constraints," *ACM Transactions on Programming Languages and Systems* 5, 3, pp. 422-448, July 1983

[Henn84] Hennessy, J. L., "VLSI Processor Architecture," *IEEE Transactions on Computers*, Vol. c-33 No. 12, Dec., 1984.

[Hsu87] Hsu, Wei-Chung, "Register Allocation and Code Schedul ing for Load/Store Architectures" *UW Computer Scienc Technique Report #722*, Oct., 1987

[Kogg81] Kogge, P. M., "The Architecture of Pipelined Compu ers," McGraw-Hill, New York, 1981

[McMa72] McMahon, F. H, "FORTRAN CPU Performanc Analysis", Lawrence Livermore Laboratories, 1972

[Milu86] Milutinovic, Veliko, "GaAs Microprocessor Technology *Computer*, Vol. 19, No. 10, Oct. 1986

[Padu86] Padua, D. and M. J. Wolfe, "Advanced Compiler Optim zations for Supercomputers," *Communication of the AC* Dec. 1986

[Seth70] Sethi, R. and J. D. Ullman, "The Generation of Optim Code for Arithmetic Expressions," *JACM* 17, 6, 1970, p 715-728

[Thor70] Thornton, J. E., "Design of a Computer, The Control Da 6600," Scott, Foresman and Co., Glenview, IL, 1970.

[Tjad70] Tjaden, G. S. and M. J. Flynn, "Detection and Parall Execution of Independent Instructions," *IEEE Transactio on Computers* 19(10):889-895, Oct., 1970

[Toma67] Tomasulo, R. M., "An Efficient Algorithm for Exploiti Multiple Arithmetic Units," *IBM Journal of Research a Development* V 11, pp. 25-33, Jan., 1967.

[Weis87] Weiss, S. and J. E. Smith, "A Study of Scalar Compilati Techniques for Pipelined Supercomputers" *Second Inter tional Conference on Architectural Support for Progra ming* Languages and Operating Systems," Oct., 1987.

[Youn85] Young, H., "Evaluation of a Decoupled Computer Arc tecture and the Design of A Vector Extension," *Compu Sciences Technical Report #603*, July, 1985

ARRAY EXPANSION

Paul FEAUTRIER

M A S I
Université P. et M. Curie
4 place Jussieu
75252 PARIS CEDEX 05
FRANCE

Abstract *A common problem in restructuring programs for vector or parallel execution is the suppression of false dependencies which originate in the reuse of the same memory cell for unrelated values. The method is simple and well understood in the case of scalars. This paper gives the general solution for the case of arrays. The expansion is done in two steps: first, modify all definitions of the offending array in order to obtain the single assignment property. Then, reconstruct the original data flow by adapting all uses of the array. This is done with the help of a new algorithm for solving parametric integer programs. The technique is quite general and may be used for other purposes, including program checking, collecting array predicates, etc...*

1 INTRODUCTION

1.1 Motivation

One of the most striking trends in today's computer architecture is the development of special purpose machines for numerical computations. The idea behind this effort is that by capitalizing on the peculiarities of scientific computing, one may improve on the performance-to-price ratio of general purpose processors.

Scientific computation is characterized by its highly repetitive nature, as found for instance in the use of vectors and arrays with regular adressing patterns. Hence numerical super-computers are parallel or pipelined machines with many processing elements among which the total workload is distributed.

The price to pay for the increased power is a more difficult programming task. When using sequential languages, parallel and vector operations must be translated to lower-level constructions. To make efficient use of a super-computer, one must retrieve these features from the sequential program text or (worse !) from one's sequential thinking.

Many attempts have been made to automate this process by constructing optimizing and restructuring compilers; see [Padu86] for an up-to-date review. Broadly speaking, all such compilers start by detecting dependencies in the source code. Two instructions are dependent if the first one compute a value which is used by the other (Producer-Consumer or data dependency), or if the first one use a variable which is modified by the second (Consumer-Producer or anti-data dependency), or if both modify the same variable (Producer-Producer or output dependency). If two instructions are independent, one may execute them in parallel; in the special case where these instructions are instance of the same program text (as happens in a loop), one may pipeline them.

Most often, the dependence relation is summarized by a dependency graph. There are several algorithms to extract a parallel or vector program from this graph, the most comprehensive being probably the one of [Alle84]. Whatever the algorithm, it is clear that edges in the dependency graph are obstacles to parallelization. Now, any algorithm is susceptible of many different implementations; it is natural to search for programs which, while giving the same ultimate results, have more opportunities for parallel execution, i.e. less edges in their dependency graph.

When looking for such edge cutting transformations, one sees at once that PC edges are inherent to the structure of the algorithm, while the presence of CP and PP edges indicate merely that a memory cell has been reused. If programs where written in single assignment style, there would be no such edges. For instance, if a scalar variable is modified in a loop, this creates a PP edge which precludes parallel execution. Replacing the scalar by an array whose index is the loop counter will cut the PP edge and may (in favorable cases) allow parallel execution. This is the well-known scalar expansion technique [Wolf78]. The aim of this paper is to extend it to the general case, in which one tries to cut a PP edge on an array; hence the name Array Expansion.

1.2 Outline

Paragraph 2 will set the stage for the paper by describing the simple programming language we will work with, and introducing necessary notations and definitions. Paragraph 3 will describe, with the help of an exemple, the two-step expansion process: first, rename or expand arrays definitions as necessary, then restore the correct data flow by rewriting references to the modified arrays. In paragraph 4, we will return to the simpler problem of scalar expansion, and show that classical techniques are particular cases of our general solution. In the conclusion, we will review our results and point to some unsolved problems.

1.3 Related work

1.31 Scalar expansion

Scalar expansion (see [Padu86] or [Wolf78]), is mainly used by vectorizing compilers; the transformation is restricted to innermost loops in which a scalar is assigned to. The situation may be corrected by replacing the scalar by an array whose index is the loop counter.:

```
for i := 1 to n do              for i := 1 to n do
begin                           begin
      ...                             ...
      x := ... ;        =>            xx[i] := ... ;
      ...                             ...
end;                            end;
```

In the loop body, references to x must be replaced by xx[i] if they occur after the defining instruction, and xx[i-1] otherwise. One must also add an initialisation instruction before the loop:

```
xx[0] := x;
```

and restore the contents of x after the loop:

```
x := xx[n];
```

There are various schemes (strip mining, use of vector registers, etc) to limit the amount of memory space which is used up by the new array xx.

A closely related technique is node splitting, in which a subexpression is equated to a temporary, which is then expanded into an array. In this case, neither initialisation nor restoration is necessary.

1.32 Use Def Chains

The computation of use-def chains, (see [Aho85], chapter 11), is a technique which is used in optimizing compilers to summarize the flow of data in a program. Before executing an optimizing transformation (such as code motion or dead code elimination), the information is used to verify that the proposed transformation is valid. To each use (rhs occurence) of a variable x is associated a list of definitions of x which may be the source of the current value of x. Use-def chains are computed by iteratively solving propagation equations.

The theory of use-def chains is both more and less comprehensive than the present one. Its range of applicability is wider, since the source program may contain conditionals and even **goto's**. However, it is a static theory (all executions of an instruction in a loop are lumped as one), and, as such, apply only to scalars (or to arrays considered as a whole). Whether a synthesis is possible will be the subject of future research.

2 NOTATIONS AND CONVENTIONS

We will first describe our source language. We will then discuss the restrictions we superimpose on this language. In some cases, these restrictions may be lifted by more complicated algorithms or by preprocessing. We will then introduce the **sequencing predicate**, as a mean of finding the execution order of instructions instances.

2.1 The source language

The source language may be seen either as a static PASCAL or a rationalized FORTRAN. Data types will be restricted to integers, reals, and n-dimensional arrays of integers and reals. Declarations, which are of interest to the compiler only, will be omited.

2.11 Specifications

The source language will be a one level subset of Pascal. As simple instructions, we will consider only scalar and array assignments. The only control constructions will be the sequence and the `for` loop. We will also use the conditional expression, with the following syntax:

<conditional expression> ::=
`if` <boolean expression> `then` <expression> `else` <expression>

as a mean of expressing the result of index calculations (see e.g. paragraph 3.23). Note the absence of `goto`'s, of conditional instructions, of `while` loops and of procedures.

2.12 Restrictions

The programs we will consider in the sequel must conform to quite stringent restrictions, beside those which are inherent to the above specification.

Some restrictions are enforced merely to simplify the exposition. It is often possible to implement preprocessors to eliminate the offending constructs. Other features (e.g. **while** loops or non-linear indices) prohibit the use of the proposed technique.

The central problem we try to solve here is the following: given an array element, which of several instruction is the source of the value contained therein. Most of the time, the defining instructions will be embedded in loops. The values of indices as a function of the loop counter, and the iteration count of the loop are evidently crucial knowledge for the solution. These informations are easy to obtain for normal **for** loops and for affine indices. While loops, on the other hand, are quite intractable and will be prohibited.

<u>2.111 Normal loops</u>

For the reasons given above, we will only consider **for** loops. Furthermore, in the interest of simplicity, the step will always be 1. It is quite easy to implement a preprocessor to reduce all **for** loops to the above format. It is also possible to eliminate **goto**'s (see for instance [Bake77]), to detect induction variables ([Aho86]) and to detect **while** loops which are **for** loops in disguise.

<u>2.112 Linear indices</u>

All indices will be restricted to affine functions of the loops inductions variables and of other integer variables. Similarly, all loops upper bounds will be affine functions of the surrounding loops induction variables and of other integer variables. These auxilliary variables will be treated as constants throughout this paper. This restriction may sometime be lifted by semantic analysis (see [Cous81] or [Jouv87]).

<u>2.113 The source program is correct!</u>

We will use the fact that in a correct program, array indices are always within the array bounds. Hence, two array references address the same memory location if and only if they are references to the same array and if their indices are equal.

Obviously, it is good programming practice to debug a sequential program before attempting to restructure it for parallel or vector execution. Hence the restriction is not too severe.

2.2 The sequencing predicate

Values in array elements are not produced by instructions, but by instruction executions. Hence we need a notation to designate a specific instance of an instruction.

Our first need is an unambiguous designation of an instruction in a program. Neither the text of the instruction nor its position in the program syntax tree will serve, since there may be several instructions with the same text, and since the program may be modified by a restructuring compiler. Hence we will use a set of arbitrary instruction names, which will be denoted by letters such as r, s, etc... In a practical application, a natural choice for these names may be pointers to records containing the instruction descriptions. In the sequel, we will mostly be interested in simple instructions. However, some discussions will be clearer if all instructions, compound or simple, are named.

In our source language, the only repetitive construct is the **for** loop. Hence, an instruction instance is uniquely defined by the name of the instruction and the values of the surrounding loop induction variables (the iteration vector of [Kuck78]). A pair whose components are an instruction name and an integer list will be called an instruction **coordinate**. To denote an instruction instance, a coordinate must verify two conditions:

- the length of the integer list must be equal to the number of loops surrounding the instruction;

- all integers in the list must be within the corresponding loop limits.

In the following, integer lists will be denoted by **bold** letters. [] will denote the empty list. $\mathbf{a}[i..j]$ will denote the sublist of $\mathbf{a}$ beginning at position i and ending at j, while $\mathbf{a}[i]$ will be an abbreviation for $\mathbf{a}[i..i]$. We will use freely extensions of usual predicates to integer lists and functions whose values are integer lists. For instance,

$$\mathbf{F}(i) \geq 0$$

asserts that function $\mathbf{F}$ return a list whose elements are non negative integers.

To each looping instruction t we may associate a pair of inequalities:

$$lb_t \leq a \leq ub_t ,$$

where a is the loop counter of t. If an instruction s is embedded in a loop nest t_1, t_2, ..., t_N, in that order, then the iteration vector of s, $\mathbf{a}$, must satisfy:

(1) $$\forall p\ (1 \leq p \leq N)\ lb_{tp} \leq \mathbf{a}[p] \leq ub_{tp} .$$

According to 2.113, loop t_p bounds are affine functions of the iteration counters of loops t_j with j<p. (1) may be summarized in matrix form:

(2) $$L_{tp}\,\mathbf{a} + \mathbf{h}_{tp} \geq 0.$$

where L_{tp} is a quasi-triangular matrix.

Obviously, in deciding whether coordinate $(r,\mathbf{a})$ or $(s,\mathbf{b})$ is the source of a given value, we need to know which of $(r,\mathbf{a})$ or $(s,\mathbf{b})$ is executed first. The fact that $(r,\mathbf{a})$ is executed before $(s,\mathbf{b})$ will be expressed by:

$$(r,\mathbf{a}) \prec (s, \mathbf{b})$$

$\prec$, the sequencing predicate, is a strict total order on the set of coordinates. $\prec$ depends on the source program text. In fact, in applications in which we consider several texts (e.g. an initial sequential text and a parallel one), there should be several sequencing predicates, which must be distinguished by subscripting. Our aim is to give a simple expression for $\prec$.

Suppose first that r and s are instructions in the outermost instruction list of the program. $\mathbf{a}$ and $\mathbf{b}$ necessarily are the empty list []. $(r,[]) \prec (s,[])$ iff r precedes s in the program text. Let T_{rs} be a boolean such that T_{rs} is true iff r textually precedes s; in this case:

$$(r,[]) \prec (s,[]) = T_{rs}$$

Note that T_{rr}= **false** and that if $r \neq s$ T_{rs}= not T_{sr}.

Suppose next that r and s are the same instruction. In this case, according to the usual semantics of for loops, $(r,\mathbf{a}) \prec (r,\mathbf{b})$ iff $\mathbf{a}$ is lexicographically smaller than $\mathbf{b}$. Lexicographic ordering will be denoted by the symbol $\ll$.

In the general case, there is an innermost loop t whose body contains both r and s. Let N_{rs} be the depth of this loop. In the body of t, there are two instructions r' and s' such that r is r' or is inside r', and s is s' or is inside s'. Obviously:

$$(r,\mathbf{a}) \prec (s,\mathbf{b}) = (r',\mathbf{a}[1..N_{rs}]) \prec (s', \mathbf{b}[1..N_{rs}])$$

Now, if $\mathbf{a}[1..N_{rs}] \neq \mathbf{b}[1..N_{rs}]$, $(r',\mathbf{a})$ and $(s',\mathbf{b})$ belong to distinct iterations of loop t. In this case, their order is given by a lexical comparison of $\mathbf{a}[1..N_{rs}]$ and $\mathbf{b}[1..N_{rs}]$. Conversely, if $\mathbf{a}[1..N_{rs}] = \mathbf{b}[1..N_{rs}]$, then $(r',\mathbf{a})$ and $(s',\mathbf{b})$ belong to the same iteration of t, and their order is the textual order $T_{r's'} = T_{rs}$. Putting all this together:

(3) $(r,a) \prec (s,b) = a[1..N_{rs}] \ll b[1..N_{rs}]$ or $(a[1..N_{rs}] = b[1..N_{rs}]$ and $T_{rs})$

Knowledge of N_{rs} (a set of integers) and T_{rs} (a set of booleans) is all we need to sequence all instructions in a program. The definition of the $\prec$ predicate may be extended to programs containing parallel constructions. In this case, $\prec$ is no longer a total order. Similarly, in the presence of well structured conditionals, $\prec$ may still be defined. Since instructions in opposite arms of an **if** have no temporal relationship, $\prec$ is a partial order in this case also. Extending the notation to unstructured programs is apparently impossible, especially since there is no longer a uniform method for specifying a particular instruction instance. This is the gist of the classical arguments of Dijkstra against the use of goto's.

In the balance of the paper, we will use the following example:

```
            for k := 0 to m+n do
 {r}            c[k] = 0. ;
            for i := 0 to m do                          {A}
                for j := 0 to n do
 {s}                c[i+j] := c[i+j] + a[i] * b[j];
```

which compute the product of two polynomials a and b of respective degrees m and n. There are two elementary instructions to which we have given the names r and s. A coordinate for r is of the form (r,[x]), where x must satisfy $0 \le x \le m+n$. Similarly, a coordinate for s is (s,[y,z]), where:

(4) $0 \le y \le m$,
$0 \le z \le n$.

It is quite clear that $N_{rs} = 0$ and T_{rs} is true; this is another expression of the obvious fact that all instances of r are executed before any instance of s. On the other hand, $N_{ss} = 2$ and T_{ss} is false; hence:

(5) $(s, [y,z]) \prec (s, [y',z']) = (y < y'$ or $y = y'$ and $z < z')$.

Observe that the elements of the coordinate list act as bound variables. We will feel free to rename them (as we have done in (5)) in order to avoid collisions.

3 THE EXPANSION PROCESS

There is a very strong relation between PP and CP edges. In fact, one may prove that in a correctly written program, if there is a CP dependecy on x from s to t, there exists another instruction r with a PP dependency from r to t.

> In a correct program, each variable must be set before being used. Since s uses (consumes) x, there is another instruction r, which is executed before s and sets x. Now, "before" is transitive; s is executed before t, and s and t are in PP dependency.

From this we deduce that if all PP dependencies on x are deleted, then, as a by-product, CP dependencies will also disappear.

Array expansion is a two step process. First, one selects an array production and rewrites it in such a way that no memory word is written more than once. Next, all uses of the array must be examined to find whether the reference is to the new array or the old; in the first case, new values of the indexing function must be determined.

3.1 Renaming and expanding

Suppose our aim is to cut a PP edge s->t of the dependency graph. In our source language, this implies that s and t are both assignment to the same array or scalar A. To suppress the dependency, we must insure that, in the modified version of the program, s and t assign values to different memory locations. There are two ways of insuring this property. If s and t are different instructions, simply create a new array A' similar to A, and replace in one instruction (say t) the left hand side reference to A by A' (Array Renaming). Obviously, this technique does not work if s and t are the same instruction.

Consider the case of an instruction r with coordinate (r, a):

(6) A[f(a)] := ... ;

There is a PP dependancy on r iff the following system:

$$L_r a + h_r \geq 0 ,$$
$$L_r a' + h_r \geq 0 ,$$
$$f(a) = f(a') ,$$
$$(r,a) \prec (r,a') ,$$

has solutions. Now it is clear that if **f** is the identity function: **f(a) = a**, there is no solution since (r,a) ≺ (r,a) is always false. Hence, to suppress the PP edge, rewrite r as :

A'[**a**] := ...

Clearly, the new array A' has more entries that A, hence the name Array Expansion.

In real cases, the renaming policy may be more complicated. For instance, if the target machine is a pipeline processor, we are interested only in suppressing dependencies in the innermost loop; hence, it is sufficient to expand the lhs of r:

A'[**a**[N_{rr}]] := ...

The study of this and other strategies is left for future research.

In the case of example {A}, there are two PP dependencies, which are due to the fact that both {r} and {s} rewrite several times the same cell of A. It so happens that, by replacing c in {s} by a new two-dimensional array cc, both dependencies are cut. The original program becomes:

```
           for k := 0 to m+n do
{r}                  c[k] = 0. ;
           for i := 0 to m do                            {B}
               for j := 0 to n do
{s}                 cc[i,j] := ? + a[i] * b[j] ;
```

The problem lies in the rewriting of the lhs of {s}.

3.2 Reconstructing the data flow

3.21 Some notations

Suppose that we are given a program conforming to the restrictions of paragraph 2. Let t be an instruction in which an array A is used. Let **b** be the iteration vector of t; the indices of A are affine functions of **b**. In vector form, the reference to A may be written A[**g**(**b**)].

We are interested in finding the origin of the value of A[**g**(**b**)]. Let s_1, s_2, ..., s_n be the instructions wich produce a value for A, a_1, a_2, ..., a_n their iteration vectors. s_i is of the form:

A[$f_i(a_i)$] = ...

3.22 Formal solution

Any instruction s_i may be the source of the value used by t; let us denote by (s_i, $K_i(b)$) a possible source for t. The real source is the latest such instruction; it is (s_i, $K_i(b)$) iff:

(7) $\forall j \neq i, (s_j, K_j(b)) \prec (s_i, K_i(b))$

The correct value of i may depend on **b**. In particular, $K_i(b)$ may be undefined for some value of **b**. We will suppose that an undefined iteration vector (written as Ø) comes earlier than any other coordinate:

(8) $\forall s, t, b : (s,\emptyset) \prec (t,b)$.

The conditions on $K_i(b)$ are:

- Firstly, (s_i, $K_i(b)$) must produce a value for A[**g**(**b**)]:

(9) $f_i(K_i(b)) = g(b)$

- Secondly, (s_i, $K_i(b)$) must be the latest such coordinate:

(10) $f_i(u) = g(b) \Rightarrow u \ll K_i(b)$

- Thirdly, $(s_i, K_i(b))$ must precede (t,b) :

(11) $(s_i, K_i(b)) \prec (t,b)$;

- Lastly, $K_i(b)$ must be a legitimate coordinate:

(12) $L_{si} K_i(b) + h_{si} \geq 0$.

In summary, if «-max denote the lexicographic maximum of a set of integer lists:

(13) $K_i(b) = \text{«-max } \mathcal{Q}_i(b)$

where $\mathcal{Q}_i(b)$ is the set:

(14) $\mathcal{Q}_i(b) = \{ u \mid f_i(u) = g(b); (s_i,u) \prec (t,b), L_{si} u + h_{si} \geq 0\}$

with the convention that the lexical maximum of the empty set is undefined.

One should note the similarity of the above problem with the dependency computation. In fact, there is a dependency between s_i and t precisely when there exists a value of b such that $\mathcal{Q}_i(b)$ is not empty. Hence, the search for K_i may be limited to those instructions s_i such that there actually exists a dependency from s_i to t.

3.23 Evaluation techniques

In this paragraph, we will focus on one particular s_i (i.e. we will dispense with the index i). When the source program conforms to the restrictions of paragraph 2, all terms in formula (14) are linear equalities or inequalities. In fact since indexing functions are affine, the first term is a linear system whose dimension is that of array A. The last term is simply a set of linear inequalities. The second term may be computed with the help of (3). According to the definition of the lexicographic order, it is a disjunction of $N_{st} + 1$ terms. The term at depth p (according to [Allen84] definition of depth) is:

$$u[1..p] = b[1..p] \text{ and } u[p+1] < b[p+1]$$

while the last one is:

$$u[1..N_{st}] = b[1..N_{st}]$$

This term must be omitted if T_{st} is false.

This means that the set $\mathcal{Q}(b)$ splits into $N_{st}+1$ sets $\mathcal{Q}_p(b)$. There is a maximum for each non empty such set; we are interested in the latest one. However, no comparison is necessary since:

$$p < q \Rightarrow \mathcal{Q}_p(b) \ll \mathcal{Q}_q(b).$$

The solution lies in the non empty $\mathcal{Q}_p(b)$ with the highest index p. Now, since all constraints in the definition of $\mathcal{Q}_p(b)$:

(15) $\mathcal{Q}_p(b) = \{u \mid f(u) = g(b); L_s u + h_s \geq 0, u[1..p] = b[1..p], u[p+1] < b[p+1]\}$,

are linear equalities and inequalities, $\mathcal{Q}_p(b)$ is the integer hull of a polyhedron. Finding its lexical maximum is a parametric integer problem, for which the author has devised an efficient algorithm in [Feau88]. The parameters are the components of b and other integer variables (e.g. the variables which occurs in the array bounds). In the sequel, in the interest of legibility, we will not note explicitly these supplementary variables. Note also that the components of b are not arbitrary; they must satisfy various constraints, among which is:

$$L_t b + h_t \geq 0.$$

In [Feau88] terminology, these inequalities form the **context** of the parametric integer problem.

To express the solution, we need the concept of a quasi-linear form. A quasi-linear form is constructed from the parameters and integer constants by the operations of addition, multiplication by an integer, and euclidean division by an integer. The name "quasi-linear" stems from the fact that is is possible to replace the integer quotients by extra parameters; the form is linear in the extended set of parameters, and the quotients may be defined by two supplementary linear constraints.

The solution is then expressed as a multistage conditional expression. The predicates are of the form $f(b) \geq 0$, where f is quasi-linear. The values are quasi-linear forms or the "undefined" sign, Ø. The lexical maximum of $Q_p(b)$ will be noted $k_p(b)$. From the k_p's the construction of K is done by the following algorithm:

Algorithm (K)

-(1) let $p = N_{st}-1$ and $K = k_{N_{st}}$;

-(2) if there are no occurences of Ø in K, stop;

-(3) otherwise, replace all occurences of Ø by k_p;

-(4) if p = 0 stop;

-(5) otherwise decrease p by 1 and go back to step (2)

K may sometime be simplified by detecting non-compatible predicates in the path from the root to a leaf. A set of quasi-linear predicates is non-compatible is the corresponding set of linear inequalities is not feasible. This is easily tested by the methods of [Feau88]. If a non-compatible path is detected, simply delete the leaf and the last test.

We now put together all partial results to obtain the correct expression for A[g(b)]. We first build the following predicates:

(16) $$P_i = \bigwedge_{j>i} (s_j, K_j(b)) \prec (s_i, K_i(b)) ;$$

$$P_n = \text{true} .$$

The conjunction:

$$\text{not } P_1 \wedge \dots \text{not } P_{i-1} \wedge P_i$$

express the fact that s_i is the latest source for A [g(b)].

If instruction s_i has not been modified by the renaming process, let:

(17) $$e_i = A[f_i(K_i(b))] = A[g(b)]$$

by (9).

If instruction s_i has been subjected to Array Expansion, let:

(18) $$e_i = A'[K_i(b)].$$

Lastly, if s_i has been modified by Array Renaming, let:

(19) $$e_i = A'[g(b)]$$

Replace A[g(b)] by:

(20)
$$e = \text{if } P_1 \text{ then } e_1 \text{ else if } P_2 \text{ then } e_2 \dots \text{ else } e_n .$$

In building e, one should take into account as much simplifications as possible. Let us go back, for instance, to example {A} as rewritten into {B}.

There are two possible sources for c in the rhs of s, r and s itself. In the case of r, we must evaluate the function:

$$K_r(i,j) = \prec\text{-max } Q_r(i,j)$$

where:

$$Q_r(i,j) = \{x \mid i + j = x ;(r,[x]) \prec (s,[i,j]);\ 0 \leq x \leq n+m\}$$

in the context $0 \leq i \leq m$, $0 \leq j \leq n$.

In this case, there is no need to use a complicated mathematical programming algorithm. (r,[x]) ◀ (s,[i,j]) is always true as we have already noted. The value x = i+j is the only solution of the first constraint, and it satisfies the second constraint as a consequence of the context. Hence the solution is $K_r(i,j)$ = i+j, always defined.

In the case of s:

$$K_s(i,j) = \text{«-max } Q_s(i,j)$$

$$Q_s(i,j) = \{x,y|\ i+j=x+y;\ 0 \leq x \leq m;\ 0 \leq y \leq n;\ i>x \text{ or } (i=x \text{ and } j>y)\ \}$$

The subset $Q_{s1}(i,j)$ is empty, since the system:

$$i+j = x+y$$
$$i = x$$
$$j \leq y$$

has no solution. Q_{s0} is the set:

$$Q_{s0}(i,j) = \{y,z \mid i+j = y+z;\ 0 \leq y \leq m;\ 0 \leq z \leq n;\ y \leq i\}$$

in the context $0 \leq i \leq m,\ 0 \leq j \leq n$.

In order to apply [Feau88] algorithm, we must first convert all constraints to the form f ≥ 0, and transform the problem to a search for a lexicographic minimum. This is done by the following change of variables:

$$0 \leq y' = m-y \leq n + m$$
$$0 \leq z' = n-z \leq n\ .$$

The problem is cast in the form of a tableau:

```
y' =  y'                      ≥ 0 ,
z' =      z'                  ≥ 0 ,
a  = -y' -z'     -i -j +m +n  ≥ 0 ,
b  =  y' +z'     +i +j -m -n  ≥ 0 ,
c  = -y'               +m     ≥ 0 ,
d  =     -z'              +n  ≥ 0 ,
e  =  y'      -1 +i    -m     ≥ 0 .
```

When the context is taken into account, the algorithm is able to prove that the "parametric term" in row b (i.e. the part of row b which depends only on the parameters), is never positive. Hence b must becomes an independent variable in place of z'. The result is:

```
y' =  y' ,
z' = -y' +b     -i -j +m +n ,
a  =     -b ,
b  =      b ,
c  = -y'              +m ,
d  =  y' -b     +i +j -m ,
e  =  y'     -1 +i    -m .
```

Here again, the context shows that -1 + i -m < 0; y' must be eliminated in favour of e:

```
y' =  e     +1 -i    +m ,
z' = -e +b  -1    -j    +n ,
a  =    -b ,
b  =     b ,
c  = -e     -1 +i ,
d  =  e -b  +1    +j ,
e  =  e .
```

In this case, the context does not determine the sign of n-j-1. We must distinguish two cases. Similarly, i-1 may or may not be positive. If both linear forms are non-negative, all parametric terms are non negative integers, and the solution is found by zeroing the independent variables:

$y' = m - i + 1$, $z' = n - j - 1$,

or

$y = i - 1$,
$z = j + 1$.

(In more complicated cases, the parametric terms may be fractional; one may have to introduce **cuts** to restore integrity, see [Feau88] for details).

Suppose now that i-1 is negative. Inspection of the c row shows that the coefficients of the independent variables are null or negative. Hence bringing the row to a non-negative value is impossible, and the problem has no solution. After one more change of variable, a similar result is obtained in the case n-j-1 < 0. The final result is:

$$\mathbf{k}_0(i,j) = \text{if } (n-j-1 \geq 0) \text{ and } (i-1 \geq 0) \text{ then } \begin{vmatrix} i-1 \\ j+1 \end{vmatrix} \text{ else } \emptyset .$$

Since $\mathbf{k}_1(i,j) = \emptyset$, by algorithm (K), $K_s(i,j) = \mathbf{k}_0(i,j)$. There are only two selection predicates, P_r and P_s = **true**.

$P_r = (r, [i+j]) \lessdot (s, [y,z])$
where $y = \text{if } (n-j-1 \geq 0) \text{ and } (i-1 \geq 0)$ then $i-1$ else $\emptyset$,
and $z = \text{if } (n-j-1 \geq 0) \text{ and } (i-1 \geq 0)$ then $j+1$ else $\emptyset$.

We know that $(r, [x]) \lessdot (s,[y,z])$ is always true unless [y,z] is undefined. Hence:

$P_r = (n-j-1 < 0) \text{ or } (i-1 < 0)$,
$e_r = c\ [i+j]$,
$e_s = cc\ [i-1, j+1]$.

We have simplified the expression of e_s, since it is used only in case $K_s(i,j)$ is defined. Putting all this together, we obtain the final form of s:

```
cc [i,j] = (if (n-j-1 < 0) or (i-1 < 0)
             then c [i+j]
             else cc [i-1, j+1]) + a [i]*b [j];
```

One may further replace c [i+j] by 0, but this is another type of program transformation. Note also that since this expression has no occurence of Ø, we have just proved that the original program is correct in so far as no element of c is used before being defined.

5 SCALAR EXPANSION REVISITED

In the case where the variable which carries the PP dependency is a scalar, the problem is much simpler. In the definition of $Q_i(b)$, (see (14)), the first constraint is void, since a scalar has no indices. We are left with:

(21) $$Q_i(b) = \{ \mathbf{u} \mid (s_i,\mathbf{u}) \lessdot (t,b);\ L_{si}\ \mathbf{u} + \mathbf{h}_{si} \geq 0\},$$

in the context $L_t\ \mathbf{b} + \mathbf{h}_t \geq 0$.

There are $n = N_{sit}$ loops which surround both s_i and t and $N = N_{sisi}$ loops which surround s_i alone.. Hence part of the constraint $L_{si}\ \mathbf{u} + \mathbf{h}_{si} \geq 0$ and part of the context are of the form:

(22) $lb_p \leq \mathbf{u}[p] \leq ub_p$, $1 \leq p \leq n$
(23) $lb_p \leq \mathbf{b}[p] \leq ub_p$, $1 \leq p \leq n$

We will suppose in the sequel that each loop is executed at least once, i.e. that:

(24) $lb_p \leq ub_p$, $1 \leq p \leq n$

It is left to the reader to add the necessary conditional prefixes in case these conditions cannot be proved from the program text.

There are two cases: either T_{sit} is true or not. In the first case, the last term in the sequencing predicate is:

(25) $u[1..N_{sit}] = b[1..n]$,

and we claim that the solution is:

(26) $K_{si}(b) = [b[1..n], ub_{n+1},...,ub_N]$.

This obviously verify (25); (22) is verified as a consequence of (23). Furthermore, there are no other possible values for the n first components of K_{si}, and the next components are as large as possible.

> For readability sake, (26) has been written as if the upper bounds were constants; it is left to the reader to see that if the bounds are affine forms, they may be evaluated from left to right in term of b[1..n].

Suppose now that T_{sit} is false; the sequencing predicate at depth p is:

(27) $u[1..p] = b[1..p]; u[p+1] < b[p+1]$.

A possible solution is:

(28) $K_p(b) = [b\,[1..p], b\,[p+1]-1, ub_{p+2},...,ub_N]$.

This is feasible if and only if $b\,[p+1]-1 \geq lb_{p+1}$, which is not guaranteed by the context. Execution of algorith (K) gives the final solution:

(29) $K_{si}(b)$ = if $b[n] > lb_n$ then

$[b[1..n-1], b[n]-1, ub_{n+1}, ...]$

else if $b[n-1] > lb_{n-1}$ then

$[b[1..n-2], b[n-1]-1, ub_n, ...]$

else ...

else Ø.

From (26) and (29) a complete solution may be developped. In the special case where we are interested only in one loop and one scalar, it is easy to see that application of (26) and (29) is equivalent to the rules of 1.31. But our methods are much more powerful. Take for example the case of the matrix product:

```
         for i := 1 to n do
              for j := 1 to n do
              begin
{r}                   v := 0;
                      for k := 1 to n do
{s}                        v := v + a[i,k] * b[k,j];          {C}
                      c[i,j] := v;
              end;
```

Suppose we decide to promote v to a two dimensional array vv with indices i and j both in {r} and {s}. A straightforward application of (26) and (29), plus some simplifications, gives the following result:

```
         for i := 1 to n do
              for j := 1 to n do
              begin
{r}                   vv[i,j] := 0;                     {D}
                      for k := 1 to n do
{s}                        vv[i,j] := vv[i,j] + a[i,k] * b[k,j];
                      c[i,j] := vv [i,j];
              end;
```

It would be possible to extend the rules in 1.31 to cover such cases, but the result would be very ungainly; application of our technique is probably much simpler.

6 CONCLUSION

We have given a general technique which allows an automatic restructuring compiler to expand or rename an array definition in order to avoid output dependencies. This technique involves solving small parametric integer problems. The algorithm of [Feau88] has been implemented and found to work reliably on examples such as programs {A} and {C}. The method will work under any expansion strategy: one simply has to modify accordingly rules (17) to (19).

The overall complexity of the method depends on several size parameters. On the one hand, the amount of work is proportional to the number of references to be rewritten, i.e. to the number of data dependencies originating in the expanded instruction, t.

On the other hand, at each reference s one must solve N_{ss} Parametric Integer Problems whose size depends on:

- the number of unknowns, n, which is N_{ss};

- the number of parameters, p, which is N_{tt} plus the number of auxilliary parameters (loop limits, etc.);

- the number of constraints, m: there is one equality per dimension of the expanded array, plus $2N_{ss}$ loop limit constraints, plus d+1 sequencing constraints where d is the depth.

In real-life programs, all these values are small integers: for instance, arrays seldom have more than 3 indices. The algorithm proceeds mainly by pivoting steps in the manner of the Gauss-Jordan algorithm, each step having an operation count proportional to (n+p)m. In theory, the step count may be quite large: the simplex is not polynomial. However, it is well known that for most data, the simplex is polynomial with a pivoting count proportional to the number of unknowns. Preliminary experience sustains the conjecture that the Parametric Integer algorithm shares this property.

There are several points which deserve further study. Before real size application is contemplated, systematic techniques for simplifying formulas such as (20) should be devised. Similarly, techniques for avoiding useless computations (e.g., distinguishing between live and dead definitions), would be very useful. It would also be very interesting to lift some of the restrictions we imposed in 2.2 (e.g., to allow conditionals instructions).

There are many degrees of freedom in the choice of rewriting or expansion beyond the simple rules of 3.1. How does one judge a priori the interest of such a transformation? Are there situations in which the data flow reconstruction is simplified? In the case of {C}, this is probably because all use of the offending variable where rewritten in the same way. Is this always possible?

We believe the techniques we have introduced in this paper to be susceptible of many applications beyond array expansion. We have noted that they give a method for testing that no array element is used before being defined. Similarly, the method may be used to build assertions on arrays, in the manner of [Jouve86]. It may even be possible in some cases to solve recurrence equations on array, as for instance to transform:

```
x [0] := 0;
for i := 1 to n do
    x[i] := x[i-1];
```

into

```
for i := 0 to n do
    x[i] := 0;
```

with the attendant increase in parallelism. Finally, let us note that our method would give very interesting information to an optimizing compiler.

REFERENCES

[Aho85] Aho A.V, Sethi R, Ullman J.D
Compilers: Principles, Techniques and Tools
Addison-Wesley, Reading, Mass, 1986

[Alle84] Allen, J.R, Kennedy K.
Automatic Loop Interchange
SIGPLAN Notices, 19, 1984

[Bake77] Baker B.S
An algorithm for structuring programs
JACM 24, 98-120, 1977

[Cous81] Cousot P, Halbwach N.
Automatic Discovery of Linear Restraints among Variables of a Program
ACM POPL, 1978

[Feau88] Feautrier P.
Parametric Integer Programming
to appear in RAIRO Recherche Operationelle, September 1988

[Jouv87] P. Jouvelot
Semantic parallelizatio, a practical exercise in abstract interpretation
ACM-POPL '87, Munich

[Kuck78] Kuck D.J
The structure of computers and computations.
J. Wiley and sons, New York, 1978

[Padu86] Padua D.A, Wolfe M. J
Advanced Compiler optimization for super computers
CACM, 1986

[Wolf78] Wolfe M. J
Techniques for improving the inherent parallelism in programs.
M.S. thesis, Univ of Illinois at Urbana-Champlain, 1978.

A *global* resource-constrained parallelization technique*

Kemal Ebcioglu
IBM Research Division
T.J.Watson Research Center
P.O.Box 218
Yorktown Heights, NY 10598
U.S.A.

Alexandru Nicolau
Dept. of Information and
Computer Science
University of California - Irvine
Irvine, CA 92717
U.S.A.

Abstract

This paper presents a new approach to resource-constrained compiler extraction of fine-grain parallelism, targeted towards VLIW supercomputers, and in particular, the IBM VLIW (Very Large Instruction Word) processor. The algorithms described integrate resource limitations into Percolation Scheduling—a global parallelization technique—to deal with resource constraints, *without* sacrificing the generality and completeness of Percolation Scheduling in the process. This is in sharp contrast with previous approaches which either applied only to conditional-free code, or drastically limited the parallelization process by imposing relatively *local* heuristic resource constraints early in the scheduling process.

1 Introduction

Automatic fine-grain (instruction level) parallelization is critical in exploiting substantially all the parallelism available in a given program, particularly highly irregular forms of parallelism not visible at coarser levels. Since the effect of all levels of parallelism exploitation has a multiplicative effect on overall performance, substantially all parallelism needs to be exploited in order to achieve good performance—an obvious consequence of Amhdal's law.

*This work was supported in part by NSF grant CCR 87-04367, ONR grant N00014-86-K-0215, and IBM.

The importance of fine-grain parallelism exploitation ha already been recognized to some extent, and is reflected i the use of pipelining and/or horizontal microcode in virtu ally all high-performance machines.

Compile-time parallelization (scheduling) of programs a the fine-grain (machine or intermediate code) level is a wa to tap this level of parallelism. The obvious advantage this approach lies in the elimination of runtime schedu ing overheads (by doing the scheduling work at *compil* time), and allows the utilization of sophisticated analys and transformations that would be too expensive to pe form at runtime. Furthermore, this approach can pote tially exploit parallelism that is not readily available coarser levels of granularity, and that is far too tedious be expressed at the user level.

In the last few years, parallelization techniques hav emerged that can effectively *extract* such fine-grain pa allelism from ordinary programs (particularly numeric codes). Unfortunately, while these techniques were able expose parallelism, they did not help specify how the pa allelism was to be exploited on real, resource-constraine machines. While heuristics could be (and in practice hav been) utilized to map the idealized schedules to machine these heuristics either drastically restricted the parallelis extraction capabilities of the system, or did not apply glo ally to the program, potentially weakening effectivenes The approach presented in this paper is the first compil technique, to our knowledge, to allow truly global resourc constrained scheduling. That is, our technique permi speculative execution of operations and conditional jum on multiple paths through the program, while taking in account resource limitations as part of the scheduling pr cess.

1.1 What is Percolation Scheduling?

Percolation Scheduling (PS) is a system of semantic preserving transformations that convert an original *pr gram graph* (control-flow graph) into a more parallel on PS globally rearranges code in an attempt to exploit para lelism. Its core consists of a small set of primitive progra ransformations; the transformations are atomic and thus an be combined with a variety of guidance rules to direct he optimization process. Above this core level, guidance ules and transformations which extend the applicability of the core transformations to exploit coarser parallelism, and/or introduce resource constraints may be applied.

1.1.1 The Core of Percolation Scheduling

The core transformations of PS are defined in terms of adacent nodes in a program graph. Repeatedly applying the ransformations allows operations to "percolate" towards he top of the program graph from the various parts of the code—hence the name Percolation Scheduling. Operations are packed together in nodes as PS is applied to a program graph, thereby yielding more parallel code.

The details of the transformations deal with maintaining the semantic integrity of all affected paths. A complete discussion of percolation scheduling is found elsewhere in he literature [10], [11], [2]. In Section 2.3 of this paper we present the modified algorithms for PS transformations in he context of our resource mapping approach. The transformations presented here are based on a modified version of the PS core transformations that fit the programming model offered by the IBM VLIW machine [6], [7], now being built at the IBM T.J. Watson Research Center.

1.2 Why use PS?

The PS transformations can expose substantial amounts of parallelism even in the presence of multiple, and statically unpredictable, conditional jumps. Furthermore, these transformations are defined independently of any superimposed heuristics, yielding increased flexibility. In [1], it was shown that the core transformations are relatively *complete* with respect to the set of all possible local, dependency-preserving transformations on program trees. Thus, for all practical purposes, no alternate system of transformations based on the same principles (e.g., locality of application, dependency-preservation) can do better at exposing parallelism at this level.

Two additional transformations extend the applicability of the core transformations to arbitrary loops. The first of these meta-transformations allows the exploitation of fine-grain parallelism across multiple nested loops [12], while he second realizes the *full effect* of complete unwinding of loops and fine-grain parallelization, *without* the actual complete unwinding [2]. These transformations work even in the presence of conditional jumps. Together, they combine to overcome the loop-related difficulties encountered by previous fine-grain parallelizing transformations, while synthesizing the desirable parallelism-extraction features of coarser-grain transformations, such as doacross, wavefront, and loop interchange [4], [14], [3].

The resilience of our approach to statically unpredictable conditional jumps and its effectiveness has been confirmed by both our own experimental evidence [2], [11], and by independent work at IBM T.J.Watson research Center [5], [6]. In fact, Percolation Scheduling was found to be so robust in the presence of control-flow unpredictability, that its main target application in the IBM project is in systems, AI, and "casual code" domains, rather than the generally more regular and predictable numerical applications. This is in sharp contrast with previous approaches (e.g., Trace Scheduling (TS) [9]) where the parallelism extraction is either limited to a single path and/or a single rule (heuristic for path selection) which is inseparable from the actual transformation mechanism.

1.3 The IBM VLIW processor

A detailed description of the architecture of the IBM VLIW machine being built at IBM T.J.Watson Research Center is found in [6]. For the purposes of this paper, it is enough to describe the semantics of the execution model of the processor.

The machine can be thought of as executing *program graphs*, one node at a time. Each node in the program graph corresponds to a VLIW *instruction*, and contains a *tree* formed from RISC like *operations* (with control-flow operations forming the tree, and non-control-flow operations (e.g., multiply, load, etc) populating the branches. A precise definition of the structure of the program graph will be given shortly.

The execution of an instruction can be thought of as a three step process. In the first step, all operands for all operations in the instruction are read. In the second step, all conditions are evaluated and a path to the (unique) successor instruction is chosen. This yields the next VLIW instruction to execute. In step three, results of the operations *on the path chosen in step two* are written in their destinations, and control is transferred to the next instruction which is then executed. Note that, as an intentional side-effect of this three-step process, operations in a given instruction can only read the results computed by a previous instruction (since all reads occur before any writes take place). If several operations on the chosen path in the instruction have the same destination, the last operation on the path takes precedence (i.e., gets to set (write) the location). In practice, on the IBM VLIW machine, these three steps are—efficiently—executed as part of the basic machine cycle. Note that all operations in one instruction will have completed before the next instruction is issued. The tree structure of the instructions coupled with the execution mechanism outlined above allows speculative execution of operations and conditional jumps on multiple paths through the program, thus achieving good performance regardless of the branches taken. For a more complete discussion of the advantages and overheads of this approach see [6].

The cycle time of the IBM VLIW machine will vary with the precise technology used; but through the use of RISC-style pipelining techniques with bypass paths, it is comparable with that of state-of-the-art RISC processors implemented in the same technology. Throughout this paper we will assume that there are only single cycle simple operations in the code. Some methods of extending the single cycle model for handling longer, (e.g., floating point) operations are discussed in [6].

The following example illustrates a typical instruction and its execution on the IBM VLIW machine:

```
              L1
               | R2:=R2+2
               | cc1:=R2<R5
              if cc1
            T/     \ F
           /         \ R2:=R5+R5
       if cc2         \
    T /      \ F     L3
     /R3:=0   \
    L2         L3
```

L1 is the label of the instruction. If the *old* values (computed in previously executed instructions) of cc1 and cc2 are initially both true when L1 is executed, then the leftmost path (leading to L2) will be chosen for execution, and the operations R2:=R2+2, cc1:=R2<R5, R3:=0 will be executed (where R2<R5 will use the old value of R2, before it is incremented through R2+2); and the machine will branch to instruction labeled L2. The target instruction L2 will use the new updated values of R2, R3 and cc1; these new values have no effect on either the selection of the path or the calculations of results in the current instruction L1.

The crucial resource limitation in the IBM VLIW machine is the number of *distinct* operations that can be issued in any one cycle, and the number of conditional branches in the instruction. While the approach described in this paper can be applied to other architectures, the "cleanliness" of the resource-constraints imposed by the IBM machine simplifies the task, without making it trivial.

1.3.1 The program graph model

A program-graph consists of *nodes* that contain one or more (connected) *inverted-v*'s. The inverted-v (or iv) is the canonical form of the structures in the program graph. Initially, there is a one-to-one correspondence between nodes and iv's. Latter on, as a result of PS transformations, this correspondence may be destroyed by operations moving from one node to another. The nodes semantically correspond to IBM VLIW machine instructions, being filled through the compaction process.

An iv contains one conditional-jump (the root) and two branches (T/F), each containing zero or more operations. Each iv corresponds to a conditional test in the VLIW machine instruction along with the two (T/F) edges emanating from the test.

For example, the structure of an iv could be represented graphically as:

```
       c
     T/ \F
   o1    o'1
   ...   ...
   o_n   o'm
```

Definitions:
cj-branch(c,T/F) is the set of operations on c's T or F branch. *cj-target(c,T/F)* is the iv pointed to by c's T/F branch.

Since there is a one-to-one correspondence between conditional-jumps and iv's, we will refer to them interchangeably.

To adhere to the execution semantics of the IBM VLIW machine described above, operations that depend on each other are part of separate iv's (and thus separate nodes in the initial program-graph. The program transformations we will later apply, while merging multiple iv's in a single node, will only do so when no dependencies are violated. Furthermore, given the above definition of iv's some operations (notably those constituting targets of *several* jumps) may not be included as part of any existing iv. For completeness, such operations will also form separate iv's (nodes) in the initial program-graph. In these "dummy" iv's, the conditional-jump doesn't read or write any variable (i.e., has no dependencies), and always takes the T branch, while the F branch is grounded (goes to the end-of-program). For example, the code segment bellow

```
a:= b + c      --\      null-test(T)
b:= c + d      --/         T|
                        a:= b + c
                        b:= c + d
CODE SEGMENT           ASSOCIATED IV
```

would be represented by the above iv (the execution semantics of the machine will ensure correct execution of the reads and writes of *b*), while the following code requires two-iv's:

```
                        null-test(T)
                           T|
b:= c + d      --\      b:= c + d
a:= b + c      --/      null-test(T)
                           T|
                        a:= b + c
```

1.4 Previous Approaches to Resource Constrained Scheduling

Since even modest resource limitations make the mapping of programs to machines NP-hard, several heuristic approaches have emerged. The first and probably most widely used, is to use a set of special purpose mapping techniques, and resort to a possibly poor, but always applicable mapping, when none of the special purpose tricks apply. While this approach yields good results in some cases, its average performance is not satisfactory [9].

The second approach is to build the heuristic into the scheduling transformations. While this approach can yield better results, and is much more widely applicable if the heuristic is well chosen, it too will suffer severe drawbacks when the heuristic fails to work well. In addition the intermingling of the scheduling algorithm with the heuristic can be very unyielding to change when the code does not conform to the underlying assumption behind the heuristic, potentially yielding poor performance and rather complex code that is hard to combine with other heuristics.

PS on the other hand, separates the heuristic part of the compiler from the actual transformations. The question is how to introduce resource constraints without violating this separation between transformations and heuristic nd without unduly restricting the transformation process. 'he integration of heuristics designed to manage resources ı the scheduling algorithm tends to limit the global effect f the parallelization algorithm, by forcing it into early deisions as to what should be moved and where. Most of he obvious heuristics used in this context lead to "myopic" ode-generation, due largely to the difficulty of maintainng truly global information from which to chose the best ext step.

The alternate approach, taken by Trace Scheduling and revious PS versions, has been to delay all resource maping till the last possible time. First, idealized schedles that do not take resources into account are generted. These schedules, being only restricted by the ability f the transformations to extract parallelism, can then be apped heuristically onto a given machine. The drawack of this approach is that it is very hard to maintain a lobal view of the code while doing the mapping, particlarly across potential execution paths through the code Vhile this approach often does well, it has the distinct rawback that it may have to undo some of the code moons performed in the unrestricted phase. This is compliated by the fact that some transformations do not have unique inverse, and undoing them may generate different (and potentially worse) code than that of the original rogram. An additional drawback of this approach is that haring of code among several paths becomes particularly roublesome, necessitating extensive changes to the ideal chedule, and potentially degrading performance.

For programs containing no conditional-jumps, or if one ath is truly dominant and can be identified at compileme, List Scheduling [13] will perform very well when maping idealized schedules to resources. In fact, if the evalution function (heuristic) used to prioritize list scheduling ere optimal, the result of list scheduling would be optimal s well.[1] In the presence of conditional jumps, however, the ifficulty to design good evaluation functions, and the difculty in dealing with shared portions of execution paths, ake list scheduling not directly applicable and the quality f scheduling uncertain.

: A New Approach

'he problem with the above approaches is that the heuriscs either control the scheduling too early, and thus interre with the parallelism-extraction, or are superimposed fter the parallelism extraction phase, and may have to ndo much of what was achieved in that phase. In addion, both approaches lack a truly global view of the code eing optimized, and thus have to rely on either local (mypic) or ad-hoc information for their decisions. Both of ese approaches may yield poor code, by interfering with e parallelizing transformations.

Ideally, we would like to apply the full power of the parlelism extraction transformations, while taking resources into account. Furthermore, we would like to keep parallelizing transformations and resource mapping heuristics separate, so that the heuristics can be modified or even drastically changed without affecting the overall compiler design. In other words, given k processors, we would like our algorithm to schedule for execution at each and every instruction in the program the k most important operations available for execution at that point, limited only by the power of the transformations we apply to extract parallelism, and the ability of our heuristics to choose the k most important operations at any given point. Of course, we would also like the heuristics to be based on accurate and global information in making their decision.

2.1 What We Are Proposing

To achieve the goals just mentioned, we need to know, for every machine instruction, what operations can *potentially* be scheduled in it. Then we could use the full power of PS to transform the code, allowing only the most important k operations to move into that instruction, where k is the maximal number of resources available. This framework is analogous to that of classical global optimizations (e.g., constant-folding) with the initial computation of "operations that can be scheduled in instruction k" (*unifiable-ops*) corresponding to data-flow (reaching) information, and the ensuing PS phase corresponding to the optimization itself. In this framework, the heuristics only enter in the choice of the order in which the instructions (and operations within them) are processed.

2.2 The algorithm

The algorithm consists of two phases. First, information on what operations can move, and where, is gathered. Next, the actual scheduling takes place through PS transformations. This, in turn, necessitates a continuous (incremental) updating of the original information, to reflect the changes in the program. The gathering of information in this method, while akin to classical flow-analysis, is less conservative. The information that we compile is the set of *all* operations that may, as a result of PS parallelizing transformations, reach a certain point in the program, even though some of these motions may be mutually exclusive. For example,

```
      (p)  ...
             c
         T/    \F
   (a) a:=1    (b) a:=2
        |            |
      b:=a*c       d:=a-c
```

either operation (a) or (b) may move to point p, (see above) but not both. Thus, the set of operations that can potentially reach point p should initially include both (a) and (b). We will refer to such operations as *mutually blocking*. As PS is actually applied, the information at p should be updated. For example, if operation (a) moves up to p, the set at p should be updated to reflect the fact that (b) cannot reach that point in the code anymore. One

[1] Since the problem is NP-hard, practical evaluation functions annot be, in general, optimal; however, this doesn't preclude e possibility that a good evaluation function will produce opmal code most of the time.

key question is whether this updating can be performed incrementally, since otherwise the approach may be too expensive. We will now describe in detail the algorithms necessary to perform these tasks.

```
MAIN program /* Assumes rooted (single entry)
                program DAG,composed of iv's. */
  compute-unifiable-ops(root);
  schedule-with-resources(node(root));
  /* node(root) = node whose top iv is 'root' */
END MAIN program
```

2.2.1 Computing Unifiable-ops

This section describes the initial computation of *unifiable-ops(n)*, the set of operations that can be *immediately* (i.e., without the need for other operations to move first) moved from *anywhere* in the program up to the top of node n, by PS transformations. In other words, if there exists a sequence of PS transformations involving only the motion of operation o (or copies thereof) from anywhere in the program graph to the top of node n, then o should appear in *unifiable-ops(n)*. This initial computation of *unifiable-ops* is performed on the original (i.e., uncompacted) program-graph, where each iv corresponds to a separate node. For conciseness, we will unambiguously refer to the set such as *unifiable-ops(cj-target(c,dir))* as *unifiable-ops(c,dir)*.

This information will be computed for each node in the program graph, in a process akin to computing data-flow information. For this information to be useful, it should be efficient to compute. Fortunately, since PS by itself is not applied across the backedges of loops (loop pipelining techniques described in [5], [2] can do as well as possible in conjunction with PS on loops), we only need perform one pass on the DAG obtained from the program-graph by removing the back-edges. Thus the time cost of the initial phase is linear in the number of operations in the program.

In the remainder of the paper, we assume we are operating on such a DAG. For simplicity of exposition, we will describe the algorithm in terms of iv's, while the PS transformations are described in terms of nodes. The mapping from iv's to nodes is straight-forward. Since the algorithm performs a single pass over the code, there is no need to actually store the unifiable-ops information at each iv, but rather it can be kept only at the top of each node.

Definitions:

The set of *successors* of a node n ($succs(n)$) is the union of all nodes immediately reachable by paths in n.

The set *reads* of an operation o ($reads(o)$) consists of all the operands of o whose values are (potentially) used by the operation. The set *writes(o)* of an operation o consists of the unique operand of o whose value is (potentially) changed by the operation. In the following, we assume that $reads()$ and $writes()$ apply to sets of operations as well as single operations.

The set of variables *live* at the top of node n (*live-at-top(n)*) consists of all variables which, on some path from n, are read before being written.

A *path* in a node n to a successor node s is the sequence of operations and directions (for conditional branches) by which node s can be reached at execution time from the top of node n. Note that there may be several paths from n to s. We will denote by $paths(n, s)$ the set of paths from the top of node n to node s. A sequence formed by a path in node n_0 (to n_1), followed by a path in n_1 to n_2, etc, will also be called a *path*, the difference between the two being clear from context. The edge emanating from the last iv on a path within a node is called the *tip* of that path.

An operation o is said to *reach* a node n, if there exists a path from o's current node to n along which no data-dependencies that could prevent o from moving exist.

The following definition describes the set of operations that will be prevented (by dependencies) from moving above this iv, assuming they reach as high as this iv.

$$killed\text{-}with\text{-}live\text{-}ops(c,dir) = \{o | (o \in Program) \bigwedge ((\exists o' \neq o \in cj-branch(c, dir)\ s.t.\ o\ dep\ o') \bigvee ((live-vars(c, \overline{dir}) \cap write(o)) \neq \emptyset))\}.$$

where dir is $true$ (T) or $false$ (F), and dep is one of:

- write-before-read (I.e., $o' \in cj-branch(c, dir)$ writes a variable read by o).
- read-before-write (I.e., $o' \in cj-branch(c, dir)$ reads (the old value of) a variable written by o. Note that in this case, both o', o may be in $cj-branch(c, dir)$).

Note that dep should be a true dependency in the sense that the operations should have occurred in such an order as create the dependency; this would not be automatically the case if the sets are implemented as bit vectors, but can easily be enforced by proper numbering so that for all o, o' such that $o\ dep\ o'$, $(\#bit(o') < \#bit(o))$. Also note that write-before-write is not a dependency. The execution model has a well defined mechanism for dealing with multiple writes within a node, and thus there is no reason to disallow them.[2]

The following is the definition of the set of operations not allowed to move above c only because they write a variable being read on (another) branch of c.

$$Killed\text{-}by\text{-}live\text{-}only(c,dir) = \{o | (o \in Program) \bigwedge ((\neg((\exists o' \neq o)(o' \in cj-branch(c, dir) \bigwedge (o\ dep\ o')))) \bigwedge ((live-vars(c, \overline{dir}) \cap write(o)) \neq \emptyset))\}.$$

Note that *killed-with-live-ops(c,dir)* can and should correctly include operations in the *cj-branch(c,dir)* itself. To correctly do this in a bit-vector implementation, operations in the branch must be added *in order* to the set. While this is not automatic, it can be guaranteed by numbering the operations (bits) in DFS order of the program graph.

The Algorithm for compute-unifiable-ops. In the algorithm bellow, "root" stands for the top iv in the dag, not the root node (since this initial pass is computed on the uncompacted graph, there is a one-to-one correspondence between nodes and iv's). Also note that the algorithm assumes the DAG on which it applies has a unique root. This can be trivially enforced, or we can iteratively issue calls for each root, making sure that—for efficiency—common parts of the DAG are not traversed more than once.

[2] In fact, if each write reaches a potential use—on separate paths—then allowing the occurrence of two such writes in the same node may benefit (speed-up) execution; otherwise, dead writes can be removed as part of the PS transformations.

```
PROCEDURE compute-unifiable-ops(root:iv)
  IF  marked(root) = 'visited' THEN  RETURN;
  ELSE FOR s IN successors(root) DO
          compute-unifiable-ops(s)
          ENDFOR
       unifiable-ops(root) :=
                 Set1 U Set2 U Set3 U Set4 U
              [(Set8 U Set6) Intersection
                         (Set7 U Set5)] U Set9;
       marked(root) := 'visited';
       ENDELSE
END compute-unifiable-ops
```

Sets 1-4 are the sets of operations reaching the current iv (sets 1-2) or operations in its branches (sets 3-4) that are unaffected by any dependencies (including live). Sets 5-6 and 7-8 contain operations that are prevented from moving past the current iv *only* by live-dependencies, and thus may be amenable to PS unification. Set9 contains the conditional itself.

Set1 = unifiable-ops(c,T) - killed-with-live-ops(c,T).
Set2 = unifiable-ops(c,F) - killed-with-live-ops(c,F).
Set3 = cj-branch(c,T) - killed-with-live-ops(c,T).[3]
Set4 = cj-branch(c,F) - killed-with-live-ops(c,F).[3]
Set5 = unifiable-ops(c,T) ∩ killed-by-live-only(c,T).
Set6 = unifiable-ops(c,F) ∩ killed-by-live-only(c,F).
Set7 = cj-branch(c,T) ∩ killed-by-live-only(c,T).
Set8 = cj-branch(c,F) ∩ killed-by-live-only(c,F).
Set9 = { c }.

2.2.2 Performing Resource-constrained PS

The scheduling relies on modified PS core transformations, based on [10], [5]. The main procedure *schedule-with-resources* applies to *nodes* in a heuristically-defined order (an optimal solution being NP-hard). The procedure calls an auxiliary routine, migrate, that brings the operation being moved up to, but not into the current node being filled. The filled nodes map directly into instructions for the IBM VLIW machine. The order in which the scheduling occurs is controlled by three routines, *choose-op, choose-branch,* and *choose-node.* Useful heuristics for these routines are discussed in the next section.

The following procedures are expressed in terms of nodes, rather than iv's for convenience of explanation, as the PS transformations conceptually apply to program-graph nodes.

```
PROCEDURE schedule-with-resources (n:node)
WHILE there exist unfilled nodes, n, DO
 choose-node n;
 WHILE (resources not full) DO
   choose-op o in the Union of unifiable-ops(s),
            over all s in successors(n),
            s.t. reads(o) are not set in n;
   IF no operation o was found THEN LEAVE-LOOP;
   ELSE
     choose-branch tp on a path from n to node of o;
         /* tp is an edge out of node n */
      migrate(target-node(tp),o); /* move o to
         (bottom of) node given by target-node(tp) */
      move-op-or-cj(target-node(tp),n,tp,o);
            /* move o into tip of branch tp */
    ENDIF
  ENDWHILE
ENDWHILE
END schedule-with-resources
```

Successors(n) and similar functions on the program-graph are assumed to operate on a DAG of nodes, i.e., should return *nil* when encountering a backedge. Note that *schedule-with-resources* separates the heuristics from the actual parallelizing transformations, and allows nodes, branches and operations to be processed in an arbitrary order (imposed by the choice functions). Of course, there is still an implicit order among the heuristics, nodes being first selected, then paths, and then operations. While this is in fact quite natural, and doesn't impose a great bias, it too could be relaxed.

```
PROCEDURE migrate(n,op)
 /* n is a node, op is in unifiable-ops(n) */
 FOR n' in { s | s in successors(n) s.t. op is in
                    unifiable-ops(s) } DO
     migrate(n',op);
     FOR all branches tp going from n to n' DO
        move-op-or-cj(n',n,tp,op);
        /* move op from n' to tip of tp in n*/
     ENDFOR
 ENDFOR
END migrate
```

2.2.3 Incremental Updating of Unifiable-ops

Fortunately for the practical applicability—of the algorithm, the updating of *unifiable-ops* sets for each node, can be done incrementally and locally on the nodes transformed by *scheduling-with-resources.* There are only two requirements for this process to be correct. First, all predecessors of a node should be scheduled before the node is scheduled. If this condition is not satisfied, unifiable-ops sets for some nodes may contain *more* operations than can actually be moved up to that point (they can never contain less). Second, a slightly more complex splitting scheme is needed to keep paths sharing a common section of the program graph from resulting in incorrect unifiable-ops information in the presence of mutually blocking operations.[4] When an operation that is causing a mutually-blocking conflict moves out of a node[5], the copy node is *always* preserved (even though there may not appear to be multiple paths through the original node). This process then continues along the path on which the operation is being

[3] Assuming killed-with-live-ops contains also ops in cj-branch, as discussed above.

[4] *Splitting* is the duplication of a node that occurs in PS to maintain the semantic correctness on paths through that node that are distinct from the path on which the transformation occurs (see the definition of the PS transformations bellow).

[5] This can be detected on the fly: unifiable-ops(n) will normally lose only the operation being moved out of n; whenever other operations are removed from unifiable-ops(n) as a result of a single move, this identifies all these operations as mutually blocking.

moved, copy nodes always being preserved and threaded into an alternate path. If points where the nodes would normally be split (by regular PS) are encountered, then the split occurs as usual but the copy node is threaded into the alternate, rather than the new, path. If no such points are encountered until the operation's final position, then the alternate path (formed by the copy nodes) is discarded. This different split mechanism would be required to avoid the problem illustrated below.

```
A:[.] B:[.] G:[.]           A:[a:=1;..]  B:[.]  G:[.]
   \    |   /                    |           |      /
    \   |  /                     |           |     /
     C:[...]       --\     C':[...]   C:[a:=1;..]
        |          --/            \    /
     D:[...]                     D:[...]
      /    \                      /    \
E:[a:=1;..]  F:[a:=2;..]      E:[.]   F:[a:=2;..]
     |            |             |          |
 [b:=a+c]      [x:=a-y]     [b:=a+c]   [x:=a-y]
```

Initially, either $a := 1$, or $a := 2$ can move to any of the nodes A, B, , or G, and thus would be part of the *unifiable-ops* sets for these nodes. Moving $a := 1$ from node E to node A, however, leaves a use of a exposed, on paths to B and G, so that $a := 2$ would not be able to move to either B or G. Thus, unless *unifiable-ops* sets are updated for these nodes, they will contain incorrect information. However, since B and G are not touched by the migration of $a := 1$ to A, this would require (in general) an extensive recomputation of *unifiable-ops*, throughout the program graph. The split modification described above, fixes this problem by ensuring that paths get split early enough (in this case at D) so that consistent *unifiable-ops* information is maintained.

Since the PS transformations would check applicability before transforming the program, only efficiency and not correctness could be affected even if unifiable-ops were not updated. Furthermore, even restoring precise unifiable-ops sets in the presence of arbitrary-order scheduling of the nodes may not be prohibitively expensive, since only operations writing the same variables can be mutually blocking, and we only need to propagate unifiable-ops changes (recursively) for such operations into the predecessors of the node(s) being modified.

If the previous conditions are satisfied (i.e., predecessors-first scheduling and modified split mechanism) the simplest method of incrementally updating unifiable-ops sets is to recompute it for any node touched by a PS *move* transformation. Since this recomputation is done locally for the node affected and the changes do not propagate through the program graph, the overall complexity of performing PS is not adversely affected (the cost of moving an operation between two nodes is only increased by a linear factor in the number of operations in the node). Furthermore, since only a fixed number of operations (corresponding to the resources of the machine) are moved to any given node, the overhead due to updating will be bound, in practice, by a constant. The algorithm for performing the updating is given below, together with the move-op-or-cj code.

```
PROCEDURE move-op-or-cj(n',n,tp,op)
   /* also does updating of unifiable-ops */
  IF op is not a conditional-jump THEN
    /* move all syntactic copies of op from
       node n' to the end of path tp of n
       (tp leads to n')  */
    move-op(n', n, tp, op);
    /* PS transformation w/ live info updating */
     IF move was successful THEN
       /*  n'' is a new node created by move-op,
           (a copy of n' with all
           syntactic copies of o deleted */
       update-live-dead(n'');
       update-unifiable-ops(n'');
     ENDIF
  ELSE
    move-cj(n',n,tp,op);
    /* PS transformation w/ live info updating */
    IF move was successful THEN
     /* nT', nF' are partial copies of n',
        for the T/F branch of op */
      update-live-dead(nT');
      update-unifiable-ops(nT');
      update-live-dead(nF');
      update-unifiable-ops(nF');
    ENDIF
  ENDIF
END move-op-or-cj

PROCEDURE update-unifiable-ops(n:node);
 FOR i in (iv's in node n) DO
    /* this restrains compute-unifiable-ops
       from recomputing beyond the current node *
   marked(i) := unvisited;
 compute-unifiable-ops(n);
END update-unifiable-ops;
```

The procedure *compute-unifiable-ops* can be used in *update-unifiable-ops* eventhough it assumes that iv's belong to separate nodes, and thus may appear to conflict with the semantics of nodes containing multiple iv's. For example, if the operations: $a : x := x + 1; b : y := x * 2$ occured in sequence inside a single node, both a, b would use (read) the *old* values of x, while if they occurred in the separate nodes, (in the same order) the value of x computed in a will be used by b. Thus it may appear that the original $compute - unifiable - ops$ routine, with its iv based semantics cannot apply once the $1 : 1$ correspondence between nodes and iv's has been altered by the move transformations described in Section 2.3. This however, is not so. The motion of b (from a successor node) into the same node as a would be disallowed by the PS transformations, precisely because it would change the semantics of the program (the only way in which these two operations would be allowed by PS to occur in the same node is if b preceded a in the original program, preserving the semantics of the original program). Thus, within a single node, the semantics of the original iv's are not changed and $compute - unifiable - ops$ can be safely applied as shown above.

.3 The Actual PS Transformations

he following is an outline of the PS transformations that erform the actual node-level changes, and the incremental pdating of unifiable-ops and live-vars. A formal definition the transformations can be found in [10], [11] and a odified version adapted for the IBM VLIW machine in]. This later version of the PS transformations is given ere; they do not include the modified split as described ove. The modification is easy to perform.

```
ROCEDURE Move-op(o:operation; n:from-node;
                 m:to-node; p:path-for-move);
IF       /* no conflict in m on relevant paths */
    for every o' on path p in m, from m to n,
      intersection(reads(o),writes(o')) = nil
  AND  /* no ops in n read what o writes */
    for every o' in n, o' =/= o,
      intersection(writes(o),reads(o')) = nil
  AND  /* either writes(o) is dead on all paths
           FROM n, or it's killed in n*/
    for every s in succs(n), either
      intersection(live-at-top(s),writes(o))=nil
      OR
      for every path, p', from n to s,
           there exists an operation o' in p',
            s.t. writes(o) = writes(o')
THEN /* move */
  create a copy n' of n;
  delete all occurrences of o in n';/*unification*/
  move o into tip of path p in m;
     /*add o to last cj-branch on m on path p*/
  make m go to n' instead of n (on path p ONLY);
  IF there exists o' s.t. writes(o') = writes(o)
    AND
     o' occurs on a path in m going through
        the newly added o,
  THEN
     delete o' from these paths;
     for all iv's j, occurring on paths encompassing o
                    and the original location of o',
        place o' in cj-branch(j,dir), where dir is
                    the branch not leading to o;
        if o' becomes dead, remove it altogether;
* n is the split copy of itself;
  n' is the transformed version */
  IF n has no predecessors, delete it;
 END /* move */
ND /* move-op */
```

ote that Move-op only moves an operation *into* the node, ut doesn't attempt to push it as high as it can go inside hat node. Such hoisting does not improve speedup if the peration remains inside the node, and could actually hiner motions of other operations. Since not hoisting operaons to the highest point in a node does not hinder their ture motion outside that node, this does not reduce the enerality of move-op in any way.

To move a test *cj* (of the form *if cc*, where *cc* is a condition code register) from n to a node m along path p do:

```
PROCEDURE Move-cj(o:conditional-jump; n:from-node;
                  m:to-node; p:path-for-move);
IF forall operations o' in p
        intersection(writes(o'), reads(o)) = nil
  THEN
    Create copy nT of n, that behaves as if o in n
    always took the true (T) branch, and does not
    contain o (i.e., no syntactic copy of o).
     /* This amounts to unification - merging - of
        multiple copies of conditionals. */
    To do this: Make a copy of n and change its
    label to nT. Change all iv's in nT of the form:
/* o1..ok are either on the T or F branch of iv1 */
           iv1                            iv1
             |o1                           |o1
             |...                          |...
             |ok                           |ok
       o: iv2:if cj         --\            |o'1
         o'1 /T   F\        --/            |
         .../       \                      |o'l
       o'l/          \                   iv3
         iv3        iv4
                      (iv starting at o (iv2) deleted)

    Create a copy nF of n that behaves as if o in n
    always took the F branch,and doesn't contain o.
    Create new iv rooted in o, and place it as the
    last iv on path p in m, and make:
          cj-target(iv(o),T) := nT;
          cj-target(iv(o),F) := nF.
    Fix last iv in m,on path on which move occurs:
             |op1...                     |op1...
             |opi         --\            |opi
             v            --/           o:if cj
        n:node                           /    \
                                   nT:node  nF:node
  /* n has become the 'split copy' of original n;
    (nT and nF are the transformed versions)*/
     If n now has no predecessors remove it.
  ENDIF /* then */
END move-cj;
```

To re-compute live variables of a node n after move-op or move-cj, we can use the following scheme:

```
PROCEDURE update-live-vars(n:node)
 let writes(p:path) be the set of variables
     assigned to along path p.
 let reads(p:path)  be the set of variables
     read along path p.
   livevars(n) := nil;
   FOR each path p from n to {s| s in succs(n)} DO
       livevars(n) :=
         Union(livevars(n),
               Union([livevars(s) - writes(p)],
                     reads(p)));
END update-live-vars;
```

2.4 Choosing Heuristics

One of the advantages of our approach is that the heuristics can be chosen independently of the actual code transformations, and even of the *selection of the candidates* for motions from among which the choices are made (this selection is *not* heuristic).

By reducing the heuristic part of the algorithm as much as possible, and separating it from the rest of the code, we achieve maximum expressiveness, and if a better heuristic is found, or is better suited to an individual user's application context, its incorporation in the system is easy. This is in sharp contrast with previous approaches. The particular heuristics we have chosen to implement are simple, yet appear to be quite powerful:

choose-node: nodes are selected in breadth-first order of the program graph (i.e., shallowest—closest to the root—first). The *depth* of a node is given by the maximum number of nodes on any path from the root to it. A second order heuristic is that nodes with higher probability of execution are scheduled first. Thus from among the successors of a node the most likely to execute is scheduled first.

choose-path: path with the highest probability of execution is chosen first.

choose-op: operation with the highest (probability-of-execution-over-all-copies(op) * number-of-dependents-of-all-copies(op)), should be chosen first (if ops have different latencies, that too should be taken into account instead of just number of dependents, perhaps by adding the lengths of all the dependency chains. This formula may require dynamic updating as the program is compacted for maximum accuracy.

3 Analysis of PS-w-resources

This section outlines a more precise characterization of the behavior of PS with resource constraints, and how it compares with the idealized schedule, as well as with other scheduling techniques, e.g., list-scheduling. While scheduling with resources is NP-hard, we would argue that our approach manages to isolate the NP-hardness from the scheduling, yielding a better resource-constrained schedule, and one that is easier to analyze and make precise claims about. The formal statement and proofs for the following theorems require the development of a tedious and rather long formalism, uninteresting per se. Space considerations prevent us from presenting the proofs in this paper. The interested reader should refer to [8] for more details.

Theorem 0: Live-dead information can be incrementally (locally on the nodes touched by a PS transformation) updated, without loss of correctness or accuracy.

Theorem 1: Updating of unifiable-ops is a necessary and incremental process, when the order of traversal of the nodes and the splitting mechanism in PS are as previously discussed.

Theorem 2: Any operation that can be moved by some sequence of PS transformations (that doesn't involve moving other operations out of the way first) to node n, will appear in unifiable-ops(n).

Theorem 3: *Migrate* can move any operation in Unifiable-ops(n) to node n.

Theorem 4: If the resources available could accommodate the unconstrained PS schedule for a program, then PS-with-resources will generate that schedule. That is, in the presence of enough resources, PS-with-resources places no constraints on the ideal PS schedule.

Theorem 5: Subject to data-dependencies and ordering imposed by the *choice* functions, PS-with-resources is optimal. That is, for each node that can contain k ops, the k most important operations (based on choice (and availability) at the time the node is scheduled) are indeed scheduled in that node.

Theorem 6: For the choice functions we've picked, every path through the code is scheduled as if by list-scheduling subject only to more important paths having preempted certain motions on less important paths.

4 An example of how resource constrained PS works

The following is a simple demonstration of our algorithm. Let us assume that we have an IBM VLIW style machine with a maximum of 2 arithmetic or load/store ops and a maximum of two way branching per instruction. Assume the following is the input sequential code. The initial *unifiable-ops* set of each node is shown above the node. The instructions below are each intended to encode a VLIW tree, we hope that the notation is obvious.

```
/* find the minimum of an array */
/* t:=(ai) means use ai as an address register and
   fetch the word at address ai into register t */
/* unifiable-ops set for node 1: */
   {cc0:=ai<ailim, t:=(ai), ai:=ai+4}
/* node 1: */
   LOOP: cc0:=ai<ailim, goto L2
/* node 2 and associated unifiable-ops set: */
   {~cc0, t:=(ai), ai:=ai+4}
   L2: if ~cc0 (goto EXIT) else (goto L3)
/* node 3 and associated unifiable-ops set: */
   {t:=(ai), ai:=ai+4}     L3: t:=(ai), goto L4
/* node 4 and associated unifiable-ops set: */
   {cc1:=t<min, ai:=ai+4} L4: cc1:=t<min, goto L5
/* node 5 and associated unifiable-ops set: */
   {~cc1, ai:=ai+4}
   L5: if ~cc1 (goto X1) else (goto L6)
/* node 6 and associated unifiable-ops set: */
   {min:=t, ai:=ai+4}     L6: min:=t, goto X1
/* node 7 and associated unifiable-ops set: */
  {ai:=ai+4}              X1: ai:=ai+4, goto LOOP
 EXIT: t is dead here
```

Suppose that the ALU ops and tests that are control dependent on a test (conditional branch) are counted among the "number of dependents" of the test for the purposes of *choose-op*. Scheduling will start, guided by choose-node, with the first node. To fill this node, the candidates in unifiable-ops are considered in the order dictated by choose-op:

```
igible ops to move:
st: t:=(ai): 3 deps,100% prob.
nd: ai:=ai+4:0 dep,100% prob./*no room to move*/
```

d the resulting program will be:

```
{cc0:=ai<ailim, t:=(ai), ai:=ai+4}
OP: cc0:=ai<ailim, t:=(ai), goto L2'
{not cc0, cc1:=t<min, ai:=ai+4}
': if not cc0 (goto exit) else (goto L4)
{cc1:=t<min, ai:=ai+4}
: cc1:=t<min, goto L5
{not cc1, ai:=ai+4}
: if not cc1 (goto X1) else (goto L6)
{min:=t, ai:=ai+4}
: min:=t, goto X1
{ai:=ai+4}
: ai:=ai+4, goto LOOP
```

milarly, the resulting program after L2' is filled will be:

```
igible ops for moving to L2':
1st: cc1:=t<min: 2 deps 100%
2nd: ai:=ai+4   : 0 dep. 100%

..   /* same as before */
{not cc0, cc1:=t<min, ai:=ai+4}
': if not cc0 (goto EXIT)
      else (cc1:=t<min, ai:=ai+4, goto L5')
{not cc1}
': if not cc1 (goto LOOP) else (goto L6')
{min:=t}
': min:=t, goto LOOP
```

he final result, after filling node L5' will be:

```
igible ops for moving to L5':
st: min:=t: 0 dep 20% (guess for probability)

OP:cc0:=ai<ailim, t:=(ai), goto L2'
':if not cc0 (goto exit)
     else (cc1:=t<min, ai:=ai+4, goto L5')
':if not cc1 (goto LOOP) else (min:=t, goto LOOP)
```

hus the execution of the loop was compressed to only cycles/iteration; this is optimal assuming no software pelining or unrolling of the loop.

Conclusions

'e have presented the first modular resource-constrained ne-grain parallelization algorithm to apply uniformly on ultiple paths. This is in contrast to List Scheduling, hich strictly speaking applies only to basic blocks, or race Scheduling which only considers one path at a time. 'ithout additional techniques such as software pipelining nd/or loop unrolling, the technique described in this paer will of course not produce the highest possible parallism, but it can serve as a crucial component of a fineain parallelizing compiler, and is important for this rean. We believe that this work contributes yet another ep on the way to the efficient automatic parallelization ordinary code, *for all applications*.

References

[1] A.Aiken. *Compaction Based Parallelization.* Ph.D.Thesis, Dept.of Comp.Sci., Cornell University, 1988.

[2] A.Aiken and A.Nicolau. *Optimal Loop Parallelization*, Proc. 1988 ACM SIGPLAN Conference on Programming Language Design and Implementation, June 1988.

[3] J.R.Allen and K.Kennedy. *Automatic Loop Interchange.* Proc. Symposium on Compiler Construction, SIGPLAN No.6, 1984.

[4] R.Cytron. *Compile-time Scheduling and Optimization for Asynchronous Machines.* Ph.D. Thesis, CS Dept. Univ of Ill. UC, 1984.

[5] K.Ebcioglu. *A Compilation Technique for Software Pipelining of Loops with Conditional Jumps* Proc.20th Workshop on Microprogramming, December 1987.

[6] K.Ebcioglu. *Some Design Ideas for a VLIW Architecture for Sequential Natured Software* in Parallel Processing (Proc. IFIP WG 10.3 Working Conference on Parallel Processing), M. Cosnard et al. (editors), North Holland, 1988.

[7] K.Ebcioglu. *A Wide Instruction Word Architecture for Fine Grain Parallelism.* Proc. CONPAR-88, Cambridge Press, 1989.

[8] K.Ebcioglu and A.Nicolau. *Resource Constrained Percolation Scheduling.* IBM T.J.Watson Research Center, and U.of Cal. Irvine Dept of ICS Tech.Rep., May 1989.

[9] J.A.Fisher *Trace scheduling: A technique for global microcode compaction.* IEEE Transactions on Computers, Number 7, 1981.

[10] Nicolau.A. *Uniform Parallelism Exploitation in Ordinary Programs.* Proc. International Conf. on Parallel Processing, August 1985.

[11] A.Aiken and A.Nicolau. *A development Environment for Horizontal Microcode.* IEEE Trans. on Software Engineering, May 1988.

[12] A.Nicolau. *Loop Quantization: A Generalized Loop Unwinding Technique.* Journal of Parallel and Distributed Computing, North-Holland, No.5, 1988.

[13] M.Tokoro, E.Tamura, T.Takizuka. *Optimization of Microprograms.* IEEE Transactions on Computers, Number 7, 1981.

[14] M.Wolfe. *Loop Skewing: the Wavefront Method Revisited.* Tech. Rep., CSRD, U.of Ill. Urbana Champaign, April 1987.

The Tera Computer System*

Robert Alverson David Callahan Daniel Cummings Brian Koblenz
Allan Porterfield Burton Smith

Tera Computer Company
Seattle, Washington USA

1 Introduction

The Tera architecture was designed with several major goals in mind. First, it needed to be suitable for very high speed implementations, *i. e.*, admit a short clock period and be scalable to many processors. This goal will be achieved; a maximum configuration of the first implementation of the architecture will have 256 processors, 512 memory units, 256 I/O cache units, 256 I/O processors, and 4096 interconnection network nodes and a clock period less than 3 nanoseconds. The abstract architecture is scalable essentially without limit (although a particular implementation is not, of course). The only requirement is that the number of instruction streams increase more rapidly than the number of physical processors. Although this means that speedup is sublinear in the number of instruction streams, it can still increase linearly with the number of physical processors. The price/performance ratio of the system is unmatched, and puts Tera's high performance within economic reach.

Second, it was important that the architecture be applicable to a wide spectrum of problems. Programs that do not vectorize well, perhaps because of a preponderance of scalar operations or too-frequent conditional branches, will execute efficiently as long as there is sufficient parallelism to keep the processors busy. Virtually any parallelism available in the total computational workload can be turned into speed, from operation level parallelism within program basic blocks to multiuser time- and space-sharing. The architecture even has strong support for implementing non-numeric languages like Lisp and Prolog and highly applicative languages like Sisal and Id.

A third goal was ease of compiler implementation. Although the instruction set does have a few unusual features, these do not seem to pose unduly hard problems for the code generator. There are no register or memory addressing constraints and only three addressing modes. Condition code setting is consistent and orthogonal. Although the richness of the instruction set often allows several ways to do something, the variation in their relative costs as the execution environment changes tends to be small. Because the architecture permits the free exchange of spatial and temporal locality for parallelism, a highly optimizing compiler may work hard improving locality and trade the parallelism thereby saved for more speed. On the other hand, if there is sufficient parallelism the compiler has a relatively easy job.

The Tera architecture is derived from that of Horizon [6, 9, 10]; although they are highly similar multistream MIMD systems, there are many significant differences between the two designs.

2 Interconnection Network

The interconnection network is a three-dimensional mesh of pipelined packet-switching nodes, each of which is linked to some of its neighbors. Each link can transport a packet containing source and destination addresses, an operation, and 64 data bits in both directions simultaneously on every clock tick. Some of the nodes are also linked to *resources*, *i. e.*, processors, data memory units, I/O processors, and I/O cache units. Instead of locating the processors on one side of the network and memories on the other (in what Robert Keller has called a "dancehall" configuration[5]), the resources are distributed more-or-less uniformly throughout the network. This permits data to be placed in memory units near the appropriate processor when that is possible and otherwise generally maximizes the distance between possibly interfering resources.

*This research was supported by the United States Defense Advanced Research Projects Agency under Contract MDA972-89-C-0002. The views and conclusions contained in this document are those of Tera Computer Company and should not be interpreted as representing the official policies, either expressed or implied, of DARPA or the U. S. Government.

The interconnection network of a 256 processor Tera system contains 4096 nodes arranged in a 16x16x16 toroidal mesh; that is, the mesh "wraps around" in all three dimensions. Of the 4096 nodes, 1280 are attached to the resources comprising 256 processors, 512 data memory units, 256 I/O cache units and 256 I/O processors. The 2816 remaining nodes do not have resources attached but still provide message bandwidth. To increase node performance, some of the links are missing. If the three directions are named X, Y, and Z, then X-links and Y-links are missing on alternate Z layers. This reduces the node degree from 6 to 4, or from 7 to 5 counting the resource link.

In spite of its missing links, the bandwidth of the network is very high. Any plane bisecting the network crosses at least 256 links, giving the network a data bisection bandwidth of one 64-bit data word per processor per tick in each direction. This bandwidth is needed to support shared memory addressing in the event all 256 processors are addressing memory on the other side of some bisecting plane simultaneously.

As the Tera architecture scales to larger numbers of processors p, the number of network nodes grows as $p^{3/2}$ rather than the $p\log(p)$ associated with the more commonly used multistage networks. For example, a 1024-processor system would have 32,768 nodes. The reason for the overhead per processor of $p^{1/2}$ instead of $\log(p)$ stems from the fact that the system is speed-of-light limited. One can argue that memory latency is fully masked by parallelism only when the number of messages being routed by the network is at least $p \times l$, where l is the (round-trip) latency. Since messages occupy volume, the network must have volume proportional to $p \times l$; since the speed of light is finite, the volume is also proportional to l^3 and therefore l is proportional to $p^{1/2}$ rather than $\log(p)$.

3 Memory

A full-sized system contains 512 data memory units of 128 megabytes each. Memory is byte-addressable, and is organized in 64-bit words. Four additional *access state* bits, more fully described in section 5, are associated with each word. Data and access state are each equipped with a separate set of single error correcting, double error detecting code bits. Data addresses are randomized in the processors using a scheme similar to that developed for the RP3[8]. The randomization is excellent for avoiding memory bank hotspots and network congestion, but makes it difficult to exploit memory locality using nearby memory units. In the Tera system, the randomization is combined with another notion called *distribution*. The processor data segment map has a distribution factor associated with each segment entry. Consecutive virtual addresses in a segment can be distributed among all 512 data memory units, a single unit, or any power of two in between.

Disk speeds have not kept pace with advances in processor and memory performance in recent years. The only currently reasonable solution to this problem is to lower the level of disks in the memory hierarchy by placing a large semiconductor memory between the disks and data memory. In a fully configured Tera system, the 70 gigabyte per second sustained bandwidth needed between secondary storage and data memory is supplied by 256 I/O cache units comprising a directly addressable memory of 256 gigabytes.

The I/O cache units are functionally identical to data memory. The only difference is that their latency is higher because their memory chips are slower (but denser). The fact that I/O cache has all of the attributes of main memory makes it possible to map I/O buffers directly into the address spaces of the application programs that access them. This is used to avoid copying by remapping segments.

A processor fetches instructions through a special path to a neighboring I/O cache unit. This avoids network traffic and network latency, but requires one copy of a program be made for every processor it is to run on.

4 Processors

Each processor in a Tera computer can execute multiple instruction streams simultaneously. In the current implementation, as few as one or as many as 128 program counters may be active at once. On every tick of the clock, the processor logic selects a stream that is ready to execute and allows it to issue its next instruction. Since instruction interpretation is completely pipelined by the processor and by the network and memories as well, a new instruction from a different stream may be issued in each tick without interfering with its predecessors. When an instruction finishes, the stream to which it belongs thereby becomes ready to execute the next instruction. As long as there are enough instruction streams in the processor so that the average instruction latency is filled with instructions from other streams, the processor is being fully utilized. Thus, it is only necessary to have enough streams to hide the expected latency (perhaps 70 ticks on average); once latency is hidden the processor is running at peak performance and additional streams do not speed the result.

If a stream were not allowed to issue its next instruction until the previous instruction completed then approximately 70 different streams would be required on each processor to hide the expected latency. The lookahead described in section 4.3 allows streams to issue multiple instructions in parallel, thereby reducing the number of streams needed to achieve peak performance.

4.1 Stream State

Each stream has the following state associated with it:

- 1 64-bit Stream Status Word (SSW)
- 32 64-bit General Registers (R0-R31)
- 8 64-bit Target Registers (T0-T7)

Context switching is so rapid that the processor has no time to swap the processor-resident stream state. Instead, it has 128 of everything, *i. e.*, 128 SSW's, 4096 general registers, and 1024 target registers. It is appropriate to compare these registers in both quantity and function to vector registers or words of cache in other architectures. In all three cases, the objective is to improve locality and avoid reloading data.

Program addresses are 32 bits long. Each stream's current program counter is located in the low half of its SSW. The upper half describes various modes (*e. g.* floating point rounding, lookahead disable), the trap disable mask (*e. g.* data alignment, floating overflow), and the four most recently generated condition codes. Most operations have a `_TEST` variant which emits a condition code, and branch operations can examine any subset of the last four condition codes emitted and branch appropriately.

Also associated with each stream are 32 64-bit general registers. Register `R0` is special in that it reads as 0, and output to it is discarded. Otherwise, all general registers are identical.

The target registers are used as branch targets. The format of the target registers is identical to that of the SSW, though most control transfer operations only use the low 32 bits to determine a new PC. Separating the determination of the branch target address from the decision to branch allows the hardware to prefetch instructions at the branch targets, thus avoiding delay when the branch decision is made. Using target registers also makes branch operations smaller, resulting in tighter loops. There are also skip operations, which obviate the need to set targets for short forward branches.

One target register (`T0`) points to the trap handler, which is nominally an unprivileged program. When a trap occurs, the effect is as if a coroutine call to `T0` had been executed. This makes trap handling extremely lightweight and independent of the operating system. Trap handlers can be changed by the user to achieve specific trap capabilities and priorities without loss of efficiency.

4.2 Horizontal Instructions

Processor effectiveness, the utilization of the instruction interpretation resources, has always been constrained by the difficulty of issuing more than one instruction per tick. This difficulty has become known as the Flynn Bottleneck[2]. Vector instructions sidestep this difficulty in part, but are not able to handle frequent conditional branches or heterogeneous scalar operations well. Processors with horizontal instructions, extreme examples of which are sometimes called Very Long Instruction Word (VLIW) architectures, offer a good alternative to vector instructions. In a horizontal instruction, several operations are specified together. Memory operations are usually simple loads and stores, and the others are two- or three-address register-to-register operations. If the overall architecture and organization are capable of achieving one instruction per tick, then every functional unit mentioned in the instruction is well-used. If the instructions are only moderately long, branches can be sufficiently frequent.

Tera instructions are mildly horizontal. They typically specify three operations: a memory reference operation like `UNS_LOADB`(yte), an arithmetic operation like `FLOAT_ADD_MUL`(tiply), and a control operation like `JUMP`. The control operation can also be a second arithmetic operation, `FLOAT_ADD`, or perhaps an `INTEGER_ADD` used in an address computation. Vectorizable loops can be processed at nominal vector rates (one flop per tick) using only horizontal instructions with these three kinds of operations. Matrix-vector multiplication attains nearly two flops per tick via the same technique used for its efficient vectorization.

4.3 Explicit-Dependence Lookahead

If there are enough streams executing on each processor to hide the average latency (about 70 ticks) then the machine is running at peak performance. However, if each stream can execute some of its instructions in parallel (*e. g.* 2 successive loads) then fewer streams and parallel activities are required to achieve peak performance.

The obvious solution to this problem is to introduce instruction lookahead; the only difficulty is controlling it. The traditional register reservation approach requires far too much scoreboard bandwidth in this kind of architecture. Either multi-streaming or horizontal instructions alone would preclude scoreboarding. The traditional alternative, exposing the pipeline, is also impractical because multi-streaming and unpredictable memory operation latency make it impossible to generate code that is both efficient and safe.

The Tera architecture uses a new technique called explicit-dependence lookahead. The idea is quite simple: each instruction contains a three bit lookahead field that explicitly specifies how many instructions from this stream will issue before encountering an instruction that depends on the current one. Since seven is the maximum possible lookahead value, at most eight instructions and twenty-four operations can be concurrently executing from each stream. A stream is ready to issue a new instruction when all instructions with lookahead values referring to the new instruction have completed. Thus, if each stream maintains a lookahead of seven then nine streams are needed to hide 72 ticks of latency.

Lookahead across one or more branch operations is handled by specifying the minimum of all distances involved. The variant branch operations `JUMP_OFTEN` and `JUMP_SELDOM`, for high- and low-probability branches respectively, facilitate optimization by providing a barrier to lookahead along the less likely path. There are also `SKIP_OFTEN` and `SKIP_SELDOM` operations. The overall approach is philosophically similar to exposed-pipeline lookahead except that the quanta are instructions, not ticks.

4.4 Protection Domains

Each processor supports as many as 16 active protection domains that define the program memory, data memory, and number of streams allocated to the computations using that processor. Each executing stream is assigned to a protection domain, but which domain (or which processor, for that matter) is not known to the user program. In this sense, a protection domain is a virtual processor and may be moved from one physical processor to another.

The protection domains share a single 64K data segment map and a 16K program page map. Each protection domain has two pairs of map base and limit registers that describe the region of each map available to it. The upper 2048 data segments and 1024 program pages are not relocated by the map bases, and are used by the operating system. Any active protection domain can use all of either or both maps. The map entries contain the physical address; the levels of privilege needed to read, write, or execute the segment or page; whether the segment or page was read, written, or executed, as appropriate; and the distribution (for the data map).

The number of streams available to a program is regulated by three quantities `slim`, `scur`, and `sres` associated with each protection domain. The current number of streams executing in the protection domain is recorded by `scur`; it is incremented when a stream is created and decremented when a stream quits. A create can only succeed when the incremented `scur` does not exceed `sres`, the number of streams reserved in the protection domain. The operations for reserving streams are unprivileged, and allow several streams to be reserved or released simultaneously. The stream limit `slim` is the operating system limit on the number of streams the protection domain can reserve.

When a stream executes a `CREATE` operation to create a new stream it increments `scur`, generates the initial SSW for the stream using one of its own target registers, copies the trap target `T0` from its own `T0` register, and loads three registers in the new stream from its own general purpose registers. The newly created stream can quickly begin executing useful work in cooperation with its creator as long as significant storage allocation is unnecessary. The `QUIT` operation terminates the stream that executes it, and decrements both `sres` and `scur`. The `QUIT_PRESERVE` operation only decrements `scur`, thereby giving up a stream without surrendering its reservation.

Each protection domain has a *retry limit* that determines how many times a memory reference can fail in testing a location's full/empty bit (see section 5) before it will trap. If a synchronization is not satisfied for a long time, then possibly a heavier weight mechanism that avoids busy waiting should be used to wait for the synchronization. The retry limit should be based on the amount of trap processing overhead, which varies depending on the run-time environment. The trap handler thus can invoke the heavier weight mechanism when appropriate.

4.5 Privilege Levels

The privilege levels apply to each stream independently. There are four levels of privilege: user, supervisor, kernel, and IPL. IPL level operates in absolute addressing mode and is the highest privilege level. User, supervisor, and kernel levels use the program and data maps for address translation, and represent increasing levels of privilege. The data map entries define the minimum levels needed to read and write each segment, and the program map entries define the *exact* level needed to execute from each page. The current privilege level of a stream is stored as part of the privileged stream state and is not available to a user-level stream.

Two hardware operations are provided to allow an executing stream to change its privilege level. The (`LEVEL_ENTER` *lev*) operation sets the current privilege level to the instruction map level if the current level is equal to *lev*. The `LEVEL_ENTER` operation is located at every entry point that can accept a call from a different privilege level. A trap occurs if the current level is not equal to *lev*. The (`LEVEL_RETURN` *lev*) operation is used to return to the original privilege level. A trap occurs if *lev* is greater than the current privilege level.

4.6 Exceptions

Exceptional conditions can occur in two ways. First, an instruction may not be executed due to insufficient privilege, as with a LEVEL_RETURN which attempts to raise the privilege level. This type of exception is quite easy to handle. More commonly, exceptions occur *while* executing instructions. With lookahead, further instructions may already be executing and overwriting registers which would be needed to restart instructions.

Rather than keep shadow copies of registers to support rollback, the Tera architecture defines certain exceptions as a side effect of instruction *completion*. In this model, exceptions are guaranteed to be signaled before they are needed, as indicated by the lookahead field. Thus, if instruction j depends on instruction i, all possible exceptions during the execution of instruction i will be signaled before instruction j begins execution.

To support diagnosis and recovery, certain state must be available to the trap handler. A trap can be caused by any of the three operations in an instruction. For each of the (at most eight) memory operations that trapped, the processor provides the trap handler with the trap reason and enough state to allow the operation to be retried (*e. g.* for demand paged virtual memory).

For arithmetic traps caused by the arithmetic operations no state is automatically provided to the trap handler. The decision to preserve operand values for possible use by the trap handler is made by the compiler. While the lookahead field normally only guards true dependence for registers, operand values may be preserved by limiting lookahead to guard antidependence as well.

5 Tagged Memory

Each memory location in the Tera computer system is equipped with four access state bits in addition to a 64-bit value. These access state bits allow the hardware to implement several useful modifications to the usual semantics of memory reference. The two data trap bits generate application-specific lightweight traps, the forward bit implements invisible indirect addressing, and the full/empty bit is used for lightweight synchronization. The influence of these access state bits can be suppressed by a corresponding set of bits in the pointer value used to access the memory.

The two trap bits in the access state are independent of each other and are available for use by the language implementer. If a trap bit is set in a location and the corresponding trap disable bit in the pointer is clear, a trap will occur. Uses for the trap bits include data breakpoints, demand-driven evaluation, run-time type exception signaling, implementation of "active" memory objects, and even stack limit checking.

The forward bit implements a kind of "invisible indirection". Unlike normal indirection, forwarding is controlled by both the pointer and the location pointed to. If the forward bit is set in the memory location and forwarding is not disabled in the pointer, the value found in the location is to be interpreted as a pointer to the target of the memory reference rather than the target itself. Dereferencing will continue until the pointer either disables forwarding or discovers that the addressed location has its forward bit reset. The primary use of forwarding is for on-the-fly modification of address-location bindings, for example in concurrent storage reclamation involving the copying of live structures from one space to another.

The full/empty bit controls the synchronizing behavior of memory references. Load and store operations can optionally use the full/empty bit in the addressed memory word by setting bits in the access control field. The four values for access control are shown below.

value	LOAD	STORE
0	read regardless	write regardless and set full
1	reserved	reserved
2	wait for full and leave full	wait for full and leave full
3	wait for full and set empty	wait for empty and set full

When access control is 2, loads and stores wait for the memory cell to be full before proceeding. In this context, it is sometimes useful to think of the full state as meaning "available" and the empty state as meaning "unavailable". The reading or writing of any part of an object is conveniently prevented by marking that part of it "unavailable". The access control value of 3 causes loads to be treated as "consume" operations and stores as "produce" operations. A load waits for full and then sets empty as it reads, and a store waits for empty and then sets full as it writes. A forwarded location that is not disabled and that has its full/empty bit set to empty is treated as "unavailable" until it fills again, irrespective of access control.

Additional operations exist to fetch the access state of a given memory location or to set the access state for a given location.

Although the full/empty bit provides a fast way of implementing arbitrary indivisible memory operations, the need for extremely brief mutual exclusion during "integer add to memory" is so important for scheduling applications that this function is done entirely within each memory unit by a single operation, FETCH_ADD. This is the Ultracomputer fetch-and-add operation[3], and differs from it only in that the network hardware does not combine fetch-and-add operations to the same memory location.

6 Arithmetic

The numeric data types directly supported by the Tera architecture include:

- 64 bit twos complement integers
- 64 bit unsigned integers
- 64 bit floating point numbers
- 64 bit complex numbers

Operations on these types include addition, subtraction, multiplication, conversion, and comparison. Reciprocation of unsigned and floating point quantities is provided for using Newton's method.

Other types are supported indirectly, including:

- 8, 16, and 32 bit twos complement integers
- 8, 16, and 32 bit unsigned integers
- arbitrary length unsigned integers
- 32 bit floating point numbers
- 128 bit "doubled precision" numbers

The shorter integers are sign- or zero-extended to 64 bit quantities as they are loaded from memory, and truncated to the appropriate length as they are stored. The fundamental support for arbitrary length integer arithmetic is provided by the operations `INTEGER_ADD_MUL`, `UPPER_ADD_MUL`, and `CARRY_ADD_TEST` that together implement $64 \times n$ bit unsigned multiply-add in approximately $2 \times n^2$ instructions.

The 32 bit floating point numbers are simply the real parts of the 64 bit complex type with imaginary parts set to zero. The 128 bit "doubled precision" type was pointed out to us by Kahan [1, 7, 4]; it represents a real number R as the unevaluated sum of two 64 bit floating point numbers r and ρ, where ρ is insignificant with respect to r and as near as possible to $R-r$. Support for this type is provided by `FLOAT_ADD_LOWER` which (with `FLOAT_ADD`) implements "doubled precision" addition in six instructions, and by `FLOAT_MUL_ADD` which rounds only once and is used to implement "doubled precision" multiplication in five instructions.

References

[1] T. J. Dekker. A floating-point technique for extending the available precision. *Numerische Math.*, 18:224–242, 1971.

[2] M. Flynn. Some computer organizations and their effectiveness. *IEEE Transactions on Computers*, C-21(9):948–960, September 1972.

[3] A. Gottlieb, R. Grishman, C. P. Kruskal, K. P. McAuliffe, L. Rudolph, and M. Snir. The NYU Ultracomputer - designing an MIMD shared memory parallel computer. *IEEE Transactions on Computers*, C-32(2):175–189, 1984.

[4] W. Kahan. Doubled-precision IEEE standard 754 floating-point arithmetic. Unpublished manuscript, February 1987.

[5] R. M. Keller. Rediflow: A proposed architecture for combining reduction & dataflow. In *PAW83: Visuals Used at the 1983 Parallel Architecture Workshop*, University of Colorado, Boulder, 1983.

[6] J. T. Kuehn and B. J. Smith. The Horizon supercomputer system: Architecture and software. In *Proceedings of Supercomputing '88*, Orlando, Florida, November 1988.

[7] S. Linnainmaa. Software for doubled-precision floating-point computations. *ACM Transactions on Mathematical Software*, 7:272–283, 1981.

[8] A. Norton and E. Melton. A class of boolean linear transformations for conflict-free power-of-two stride access. In *Proceedings of the 1987 International Conference on Parallel Processing*, pages 247–254, August 1987.

[9] Frank Pittelli and David Smitley. Analysis of a 3d toriodal network for a sihared memory architecture. In *Proceedings of Supercomputing '88*, Orlando, Florida, November 1988.

[10] M. R. Thistle and B. J. Smith. A processor architecture for Horizon. In *Proceedings of Supercomputing '88*, pages 35–41, Orlando, Florida, November 1988.

Compiler-directed Data Prefetching in Multiprocessors with Memory Hierarchies *

Edward H. Gornish   Elana D. Granston   Alexander V. Veidenbaum

Center for Supercomputing Research and Development
University of Illinois at Urbana-Champaign
Urbana, Illinois, 61801

Abstract

Memory hierarchies are used by multiprocessor systems to reduce large memory access times. It is necessary to automatically manage such a hierarchy, to obtain effective memory utilization. In this paper, we discuss the various issues involved in obtaining an optimal memory management strategy for a memory hierarchy. We present an algorithm for finding the earliest point in a program that a block of data can be prefetched. This determination is based on the control and data dependences in the program. Such a method is an integral part of more general memory management algorithms. We demonstrate our method's potential by using static analysis to estimate the performance improvement afforded by our prefetching strategy and to analyze the reference patterns in a set of Fortran benchmarks. We also study the effectiveness of prefetching in a realistic shared-memory system using an RTL-level simulator and real codes. This differs from previous studies by considering prefetching benefits in the presence of network contention.

1 Introduction

Memory access time has always been a key factor limiting the performance of high-speed computers. For large-scale, shared-memory multiprocessors, memory system performance is even more critical; limited bandwidth in the interconnection between the processors and the memories, coupled with long delays resulting from network and memory conflicts can increase memory access times dramatically [Tur89, GTV90].

Memory hierarchies have traditionally been used to decrease average memory access times. These include registers, caches, additional levels of memory and disks. In addition, a pipelined asynchronous memory access mode has been provided on high-speed machines, such as Cray computers [Cray82], to further decrease the access times. Hierarchical memory systems are used in multiprocessors such as Cedar [KDLS86], the RP3 [PBG+85] and the Ultracomputer [GGK+82]. Unfortunately, no effective techniques currently exist for managing such hierarchical systems. There are many issues involved, and this paper attempts to address some of these issues, focusing on optimization of memory accesses in multiprocessors with multiple levels of memory.

Our target architecture is a large-scale multiprocessor system. The system is assumed to have a memory hierarchy consisting of at least two levels—one private and one shared— in addition to the processors' register sets. Furthermore, the shared-memory subsystem is to be highly interleaved and connected to the processors through multistage interconnection networks (MINs).

To achieve high performance in a hierarchical memory system such as the above, it is necessary to solve the data migration problem. Obviously it would be ideal if we could move all data from global memory to local memory at the beginning of the program and have it remain there throughout the entire program execution. However, this is not possible in the general case as data communication takes place between processors, and data needs to be moved after it is produced. Our goal is, therefore, to move data between the levels of the memory hierarchy in such a way that execution time is minimized.

The best way to move data is by using the asynchronous block transfer mechanism. This pipelining of accesses allows a much higher bandwidth to be obtained from a MIN-based shared-memory subsystem, as compared to individual word transfers [GTV90], and

*This work was supported by NASA Ames Research Center under Grant No. NASA NCC 2-559, the Department of Energy under Grant No. DE-FG02-85ER25001, the National Science Foundation under Grant No. MIP-8410110, Mips, and Cray.

makes it possible to overlap memory accesses and computation. Thus, ideally, we would like to convert each array load or store in a program into a sequence of block moves to utilize the asynchronous block transfer mechanism. This is similar to vector register loads and stores on vector processors such as the Cray-1S. The difference is that we would like to do this transformation for every array access, not just for accesses inside vector loops. Furthermore, we would like to reuse data in both vector and non-vector program segments. Since vector registers are scarce and cannot be used for storing data which will be used in non-vector program segments, we want to be able to keep data in local memory as well. This has the added advantage of allowing data to be fetched in blocks which are larger than the vector register length, provided such a transfer is more efficient. Scheduling these blocks so that the pipelining benefits are not outweighed by the added network contention is a non-trivial task as will be shown later in this study.

Caches can provide a similar functionality, given long cache lines; however, they do not work very well for non-unit strides, and there is no user control of caches. In addition, without hardware prefetching of cache lines, no overlap can occur between a cache miss service and computation.

We note, that if we simply analyze each array reference individually, we might not obtain the optimal data movement strategy. If there is common data used in several loops, then a data move generated from a unified analysis of these loops might be more efficient. In addition, issues such as the effect of one memory access on the access time of another (e.g. contention for the interconnection network) and determining the best way to overlap computation and memory accesses, are important. The organization of the memory hierarchy also plays a role in determining the optimal compilation strategy.

Thus, the following issues determine when data moves can both legally and efficiently take place:

1. control dependences [Wol82]
2. data dependences [Wol82]
3. memory coherence
4. data reuse
5. interference with other data moves
6. overlap between data moves and computation
7. sizes of the different memories in the hierarchy
8. organization of the memory hierarchy.

In this paper, we will concentrate on the problem of data prefetching. We define *prefetching* as the asynchronous block transfers of data from global memory to local memory before the computation using that data. More specifically, we are only concerned with a block of data that can be prefetched at some point before the execution of the innermost loop in which it is used. The complementary problem of data *poststoring* can be treated in a very similar way and will not be discussed in any detail. In order that our approach be more general, we will not discuss items 7 and 8 above, or the effects of an operating system. For now, we concentrate on items 1–4. Items 5 and 6 are discussed in later in the paper.

We take the approach that the compiler should perform the program analysis for data prefetching. Concentrating exclusively on array references, we attempt to determine the earliest point in a program where we can prefetch a block of data. Given our definition of prefetching above, we are only concerned with array references that can be prefetched at some point before the execution of the innermost loop in which they are used. Thus, we determine the largest possible *access window* in the program in which data can be prefetched.

Finding such a window has to be a part of a more general memory management algorithm. In our analysis, we deal with individual array references. By merging the information obtained for different references of the same array, we can produce an overall data movement and placement strategy for the array.

Our analysis is based on the control and data dependences of a program. Control dependence constraints arise because we do not want to access data unless we are sure that the data will be used. Data dependence constraints arise because we do not want to prefetch data that will be modified by another processor before it is used. Ensuring that these constraints are obeyed causes all prefetched data to be read-only between the time it is prefetched and the time it is used; thus, we solve the problem of memory coherence.

A problem can arise if data is prefetched, by a processor, into non-shared memory, and processor reassignment takes place before the prefetched data is used. Then the prefetched data might not be accessible by the correct processor. Therefore, we assume that either the scheduler and data placement algorithm work together to insure that this does not occur or that the prefetch will take place at a later time, within the access window, after the reassignment of processors.

Data reuse—using prefetched data more than once—is a complex issue. Data reuse can be achieved by detecting occasions when multiple global memory references overlap and *combining* the accesses so that each datum is prefetched only once. We use *common subexpression removal* to combine identical references that are in the same basic block. Combining array references where the regions of the array being accessed by each reference are not identical is a significantly more complex problem. So is the task of combining references that are in different basic blocks or in different loop nests. If one of these loops is a parallel loop, the this latter case may be related to the problem of processor reassignment discussed above.

The remainder of this paper is organized as follows. The following section presents work related to our research. In Section 3, we present a method for determining the earliest point in the program at which data can be prefetched. In Section 4, we present static timing estimates of benchmarks to demonstrate the potential of this technique to decrease program run-time. We also analyze these benchmarks to determine the percentage of references which can be prefetched in practice and discuss the reasons why other references can not be prefetched. In Section 5, we present the results of our simulation-based study on the effects of prefetching in a realistic shared-memory system. Finally, in Section 6, we present our conclusions and suggestions for future work.

2 Related Work

Previous studies have used dependence analysis techniques—similar to those presented in this paper—for the purpose of memory management. Some of these studies have dealt specifically with data prefetching, while others have not; however, the techniques involved are related, in either case. Furthermore, the results generated by some of the studies that do not explicitly examine data prefetching can still be applied to data prefetching.

Lee [Lee87] and Marcovitz [Mar88] use a run-time lookahead scheme to prefetch data that has been marked cacheable. A reference is non-cacheable if it is accessed by more than one processor and written to by at least one processor; otherwise it is cacheable. A variable can be cacheable for some parts of a program's execution and non-cacheable for other parts. They divide a program into *epochs*—a parallel loop or the scalar code between parallel loops. A variable can then be cacheable (and therefore prefetchable) in some epochs and non-cacheable (and therefore non-prefetchable) in others. Their method of data dependence analysis finds the same prefetchable data as our method; however, the size of their prefetching window is limited by the size of their hardware prefetch buffer and by epoch boundaries. In our method we are not constrained by epoch boundaries, and local memory is much larger than hardware prefetch buffers. Furthermore, they do not determine their prefetching window at compile time as we do. Rather, the prefetching unit determines at run-time when a particular datum can be prefetched. This requires very complex hardware.

Porterfield [Por89] compares hardware lookahead with the compile-time prefetching technique of fetching vector data one iteration before it is used. He shows that with effective compile-time analysis, software prefetching is often more effective than hardware prefetching because the compiler has knowledge of more than the next few instructions, when determining which data to prefetch. Porterfield's work differs from that presented here because he only deals with prefetching from vector loops and does not attempt to determine the earliest point at which a datum can be fetched. Furthermore, he does not address multiprocessor issues.

Husmann [Hus86], Jackson [Jac85] and Lee [Lee83] discuss dependence analysis to overlap memory fetches, computation and memory stores. That is, they show how the execution of three consecutive iterations, $i, i+1, i+2$, of a parallel loop can be overlapped by storing data from i, executing code of $i+1$ and fetching for $i+2$ at the same time. However, their methods only discuss prefetching data before the execution of the innermost loop using the data, not at the earliest possible point in the program.

In [GJG87] and [Por89], the finite cache problem is addressed. Gannon et al. and Porterfield use data dependence analysis to determine the number of array elements that need to be kept in fast memory to achieve good machine performance. They show how program transformations, such as loop interchanging, can reduce this necessary number of elements. These techniques can also be used to reduce the amount of data that needs to be prefetched.

In [GJG88], Gallivan, Jalby and Gannon discuss issues associated with moving data between global and local memories. They present a method for deciding which data should be moved from global to local memory, and when to move it. This method is based on the number of times the data will be used and whether the data move can be pipelined. In the case where necessary information is unavailable at compile time, they present a method for creating a cost function that can be evaluated at run-time. They acknowledge the problems caused by data and control dependences; however, they do not analyze these constraints in the same detail that we do.

3 Compile Time Prefetching Analysis

3.1 Introduction

To provide maximum flexibility for scheduling and combining memory accesses, we would like to determine the largest possible range in which a memory access can occur. This access window extends from the earliest point at which we can fetch the data for a reference and extends until the reference point itself. In this section, we present a method for finding this earliest point, subject to certain data dependence and control dependence constraints. These constraints are discussed in Section 3.2. We note that while we only discuss intraprocedural prefetching analysis in this section, our method can be the basis for an interprocedural prefetching analysis algorithm.

Example 1 gives an illustration of a prefetch statement.

Example 1

```
prefetch(b(1:n))
do i = 1, n
   a(i) = b(i) + 1
enddo
```

The reference to $b(i)$ uses elements 1 through n. Therefore, we can prefetch these elements before the start of the loop. If these elements are block fetched, then the overall execution time of the program should decrease.

Definition 1 We say that we *pull out* a reference from a loop, if *all* the elements generated by the reference in the loop can be prefetched before the start of the loop. We also say that a prefetch is pulled out from a loop, where we are referring to the prefetch for the reference that was pulled out.

In Example 1, the reference to $b(i)$ is pulled out from the loop.

Calculating the portion of an array which corresponds to a reference depends on:

- the array being referenced
- the reference's subscripts
- the lower bound of the surrounding loop
- the upper bound of the surrounding loop
- the stride of the surrounding loop.

Example 2 shows a prefetch statement that exhibits these points.

Example 2

```
prefetch(b(3:n+2))
do i = 2, n+1
   a(i) = b(i+1) + 1
enddo
```

In Example 3, the reference to $b(i, j)$ lies inside two nested loops.

Example 3

```
prefetch(b(1:n,1:m))
do i = 1, n
   do j = 1, m
      a(i,j) = b(i,j) + 1
   enddo
enddo
```

We can pull out the reference to $b(i, j)$ from both loops, as shown in the example, or we can pull out the reference from only one loop, as shown in Example 4.

Example 4

```
do i = 1, n
   prefetch(b(i,1:m))
   do j = 1, m
      a(i,j) = b(i,j) + 1
   enddo
enddo
```

In the former case, we generate one prefetch of $n * m$ elements. In the latter case, we generate n prefetches of m elements each. The advantage of performing one prefetch, as in Example 3, is that any block fetch startup costs are only accrued once. The disadvantage is that more local memory is required to store this prefetch of $n * m$ elements than is required to store a prefetch of m elements. The opposite is true in Example 4. Less local memory is required to store an individual prefetch; however, startup costs are accrued n times.

In this study, our goal is to determine how far out a reference can be pulled. However, dependence constraints sometimes limit us to only being able to pull out a particular reference from a limited number of loops, or from no loops at all. We now discuss these constraints.

3.2 Prefetch Suppression

In our method of prefetching, we impose certain restrictions in order to ensure both program correctness and that we do not fetch elements that may not be used.

Definition 2 We say that a prefetch is *suppressed* in a given loop if it cannot be pulled out from that loop without the possibility of either:

1. prefetching data that might not be used
2. some of the prefetched data being modified before it is used.

We also can refer to a reference as being suppressed.

Restriction 1 is generally caused by control dependences. Restriction 2 is caused by data dependences.

3.2.1 Control Dependence

We do not pull out a reference whose execution is controlled by a conditional, since we might be prefetching unnecessary data or, worse, non-existent data. Consider Example 5:

Example 5

```
do i = 1, 10
   if i < 5 then
      a(i) = b(i) + 1
   endif
enddo
```

If we were to pull out the reference to $b(i)$ from the loop, there would be two potential problems:

1. We would prefetch elements 1 through 10 of array b, and would, therefore, be prefetching five data that would not be used. This is an important concern, since we would be doing unnecessary work. If we were to prefetch too much data that would not be used, we might offset the gains derived from prefetching. Even worse, we might increase the program's execution time, instead of decreasing it. Jackson [Jac85] also discusses this issue.

2. A more serious problem might exist. If b were declared to contain only elements 1 through 5, we would be prefetching data that did not exist and would encounter an error.

These two problems cause prefetches to be suppressed by control dependences. Therefore, before pulling out a reference from a loop, we want to be sure that the reference's statement is executed every iteration of the loop. Assuming the loop has only one exit and one entrance, this is equivalent to saying that the reference must dominate the last statement of the loop (alternatively post-dominate the first statement of the loop). We therefore perform control flow analysis on a loop by loop basis and only prefetch references that satisfy the previous restriction.

If we want to pull out a reference from multiple loops, then the reference's statement must be executed in each iteration of each loop. In Example 6, the reference to $b(i)$ can be pulled out from the inner loop, but not the outer loop.

Example 6

```
do i = 1, 10
   if i < 5 then
      prefetch(b(i,1:n))
      do j = 1, n
         a(i,j) = b(i,j) + 1
      enddo
   endif
enddo
```

With further analysis, it is sometimes possible to pull out a reference that is modified by a control structure. In the previous example, if we were to analyze the condition $i < 5$, we would realize that we could prefetch $b(1:5, 1:n)$ before the start of the outer loop. Therefore, we could pull the reference out from both loops. If the condition were more complicated or only computable at run-time, we could generate a prefetch statement that was modified by a mode vector, as in Example 7.

Example 7

```
do i = 1, 10
   if i < 5  then
      mask(i) =  true
   endif
enddo
prefetch(b(i,1:n))  where( mask(i) =  true)
do i = 1, 10
   if  mask(i)  then
      do j = 1, n
         a(i,j) = b(i,j) + 1
      enddo
   endif
enddo
```

If a loop is an *exit loop*, that is, its body contains a branch statement whose target is a statement outside of the loop, then, in general, it is difficult to determine if a statement containing a global data reference will be executed every iteration of the loop. More complicated analysis can be used to determine if a reference can be pulled out from an exit loop. This involves splitting out from the rest of the loop those parts of the loop upon which the exit test is dependent [Wol82]. However, since only 4% of the loops we have encountered in our experiments are exit loops, we simply treat all references in exit loops as being suppressed. If a statement branches out from multiple loops, then all the references in those loops are suppressed. In addition, if a statement branches into a loop, the references in that loop are also suppressed.

3.2.2 Data Dependence

Data dependences can cause data to be prefetched unnecessarily or, even worse, cause prefetched data to be invalid when it is used. Example 8 shows why this might happen.

Example 8

```
     do i = 1, n
S1      a(i) = b(i) + 1
S2      c(i) = a(i) + 1
     enddo
```

If we pull out the reference to $a(i)$ in statement 2 from the loop, the prefetched data would be modified before it would be used. Depending on the architecture of a given computer, the program might still execute correctly; however, the prefetch will be useless. For example, we might be prefetching data into a user-controlled global cache. In this case, the values of a assigned by statement 1 would be written into the cache, and the values of a used by statement 2 would be read from the cache. Therefore, while we would not have caused the program to execute incorrectly, we would have hindered its performance.

Now consider Example 9.

Example 9

```
      do i = 1 to n
S1       a(i+2) = b(i) + 1
S2       c(i) = a(i) + 1
      enddo
```

If different iterations of the loop are executed on different processors, then a particular element of a might be written in S_1 by one processor and read in S_2 by a different processor. However, if the values of a in statement 2 come from prefetched data, this data would be invalid. There would be two copies of the data of array a; therefore, the memory would not be coherent. Since we want our method to be generic enough to work under any architecture, we do not prefetch a reference that is suppressed by a data dependence.

When a reference is contained in nested loops, we employ the method of *freezing* loops. Freezing a loop means that we treat the loop as being serial, or, alternatively, only consider one iteration of the loop during dependence analysis. Consider Example 10.

Example 10

```
      prefetch(b(1:n,1:n))
      do i = 1 to n
         prefetch(a(i,1:n))
         do j = 1 to n
S1          a(i+1,j) = b(i,j) + 1
S2          c(i,j) = a(i,j) + 1
         enddo
      enddo
```

In this example, there is a flow dependence, due to a, from S_1 to S_2. This would appear to indicate that the reference to $a(i,j)$ is suppressed in both loops. However, if we freeze the outer loop, then we see that for one iteration of the outer loop, there is no intersection between the elements written by S_1 and read by S_2; hence, there is no dependence. That is, S_1 only references row $i+1$ of a, and S_2 only references row i of a. The reference to $a(i,j)$ can, therefore, be pulled out from the inner loop. When we unfreeze the outer loop, a dependence does exist; therefore, we cannot pull out the reference from the outer loop. We also note that there is no dependence involving the reference to $b(i,j)$; hence, it can be pulled out from both loops.

The general method begins, therefore, by freezing all loops in a nest. Starting from the innermost loop and working our way out, we then successively unfreeze each loop and check for a dependence. If a dependence is detected, we stop. Otherwise, we can pull out the reference from the given loop, and we continue with the next outer loop.

As mentioned at the beginning of this section, a reference's subscripts and loop bounds and strides help to determine the data that is prefetched for a reference. Therefore, a dependence involving one of these items can cause a reference to be suppressed. Example 11 demonstrates this.

Example 11

```
      do i = 1, n
         M = f(a)
         X = f(a)
         prefetch(b(i,1+X:M+X))
         do j = 1, M
            a(i,j) = b(i,j+X)
         enddo
      enddo
```

We can pull out the reference to b from the innermost loop, but there are two reasons why we cannot pull out the reference from both loops. First, we do not know how many elements to prefetch, since the value of M changes with each iteration of the outer loop. Second, we do not know which elements to prefetch, since the value of X is also variant. A similar problem would exist if the stride of the inner loop were a variable whose value was variant within the outer loop.

We note in this section that data dependences can cause a reference to be suppressed since the prefetched data might be modified before it is used. However, a more complex dependence analysis may allow us to determine that only part of a reference might be suppressed. That is, only some of the data would be modified before its use. In this case, we might be able to prefetch the elements that would not be modified before they are used.

3.3 Algorithm

We have implemented an algorithm to execute the method of prefetching, described in Section 3, using PARAFRASE [KKLW80, Wol82]. PARAFRASE is a source-to-source Fortran translator for parallel machines. It automatically detects parallel loops in a program and performs transformations that aid in the detection of parallelism.

In the previous sections, we discussed pulling references out from loops. We note that if our algorithm is successful in pulling out a reference from all enclosing

```
mark all references in exit loops done
freeze all loops
foreach region R that is not an exit loop, in reverse order do
        unfreeze R
        foreach array reference A that is not marked done do

                if A is not executed every iteration of R or
                  a dependence exists, between A and other statements in R, suppressing A then
                        if R is the innermost region surrounding A then
                             mark A unprefetchable
                             mark A done
                        else
                             generate a prefetch for A at A.current_prefetch_location
                             mark A done

                elseif R is the procedure itself or
                       R.outer is an exit loop then
                             generate a prefetch for A at R.start
                             mark A done

                else
                        A.current_prefetch_location = R.start
```

Figure 1: Prefetching Algorithm

loops, it then attempts to pull out the reference from the procedure itself. To facilitate our discussion, we introduce a new term, *regions*. The set of regions in a procedure includes all loops and the actual procedure.

The algorithm works by examining a procedure region by region and incrementally updating the necessary prefetching information for each reference. We examine all regions in an inside-out fashion. That is, we examine the regions in the order they would be encountered when traversing the procedure from the end to the beginning. We refer to this as the *reverse order*. Figure 1 shows our prefetching algorithm.

4 Static Analysis

To determine the potential of prefetching, we tested our algorithm on a set of 35 subroutines. This set is comprised of a subset of EISPACK [SBD+76] subroutines, a subset of LINPACK [DBMS79] subroutines, and REALSET, a collection of benchmark subroutines. The subsets of EISPACK and LINPACK are chosen to be representative of all the algorithms in their respective packages. For example, when the package contains two similar subroutines, one for real numbers and one for complex numbers, we only chose the real number use of the subroutines. We tested our algorithm on a variety of program packages in an attempt to cover a broad range of the application spectrum. We selected a problem size of 1024 for EISPACK and LINPACK. The programs in REALSET have built in sizes which vary between subroutines.

The statistics we generated are divided into three categories:

1. static analysis of execution-time speedup due to prefetching
2. potential for prefetching in subroutines
3. why reference prefetching is suppressed.

The first two categories show how effective the prefetching method is, and the last category shows where its shortcomings come from.

4.1 Speedup Due to Prefetching

In this section we first discuss the various models we use to generate timing statistics. We then present our statistics for speedup due to prefetching.

4.1.1 How Timing Statistics Were Generated

We estimated execution times for programs using two different models:

no-overlap: Data prefetching and computation may not be overlapped.

overlap: Data prefetching and computation may be overlapped.

A more complete description of these two models can be found in [Gor89]. In both models, we assumed that the data for each reference is prefetched at the earliest point in its access window.

4.1.1.1 No-Overlap Model

Static timing analysis for the **no-overlap** model is performed by estimating the number of iterations of all loops and the execution times of all statements in a source-level program. Weights, due to the control structure of the program, are also generated for each statement. If we define n to be the number of statements in a program, nest(s) to be the number of loops surrounding statement s and iterations(s, l) to be the number of iterations of the lth loop surrounding s, then the total execution time of the program is given by:

$$\sum_{s=1}^{n} \left(\prod_{l=1}^{\text{nest}(s)} \text{iterations}(s,l) \right) * \text{execution\_time}(s) * \text{weight}(s)$$

For calculating static timings, we assumed that only one level of parallelism is utilized, and that the outermost parallel loop of a nest is executed in parallel. For a multiprocessed parallel loop, l, the number of iterations is:

$$\left\lceil \frac{\text{serial\_iterations}(l)}{\#\text{processors}} \right\rceil$$

In Section 5, we will relax this restriction and consider an additional level of vector parallelism.

Data access times are calculated as follows; Global memory has a fetch time of GLOB_FETCH_TIME and a store time of GLOB_STORE_TIME. Local memory and registers have access times respectively: LOCAL_TIME and REGISTER_TIME. If n elements are being prefetched from global memory, the first element takes GLOB_FETCH_TIME units to fetch, and the remaining elements take PREF_ELT_TIME units. Thus the entire prefetch takes

$$\text{GLOB\_FETCH\_TIME} + (n-1) * \text{PREF\_ELT\_TIME}$$

Elements are prefetched from global memory into local memory. Thus, an access to data that has been prefetched takes LOCAL_TIME units.

Since register allocation is not the subject of this paper, we assumed an unlimited number of registers, so compiler temporaries and other intermediate values have been allocated to registers whenever possible. Had there been a limited number of registers, some of these values might have been spilled to local memory. Since local memory access is likely to be closer to register access time than to global memory access time, this should not significantly affect the static timings presented in this section.

Name	Value
GLOB_FETCH_TIME	17
GLOB_STORE_TIME	2
LOCAL_TIME	1
OPTIME	2
PREF_ELT_TIME	5
REGISTER_TIME	0

Table 1: Timing Estimation Variables

For simplicity, all arithmetic operations are assumed to take OPTIME units.

Table 1 shows the values we used for the various timing parameters mentioned above. These values are chosen based on MIN-based shared-memory subsystem simulations described in [Tur89] and [GTV90].

4.1.1.2 Overlap Model

In the **overlap** model, our static timing analysis is similar to the **no-overlap** model, except that we assumed that the computation of a loop body begins after the elements for the first iteration have been prefetched. Prefetching and computation is then overlapped, subject to the constraint that execution of the nth iteration cannot begin until prefetching for the nth iteration is finished. If

$$t_f = \text{time for prefetching for one iteration}$$

$$t_l = \text{time for computation for one iteration}$$

then the time to execute a loop is:

$$t_f + (i-1) * \max(t_f, t_l) + t_l$$

where i is the number of iterations of the loop.

4.1.2 Timing Data

Figure 2 shows speedups due to prefetching for the two different timing models we used. These speedups have been averaged over our benchmark suite described in the beginning of this section. The data is shown for varying numbers of processors. As would be expected, the **overlap** model performed better than the **no-overlap** model. The graphs show that prefetching reduced the execution time, regardless of the number of processors. The speedups due to the **overlap** model range from approximately 2.87 to 1.97, and the speedups due to the **no-overlap** model range from approximately 1.78 to 1.47.

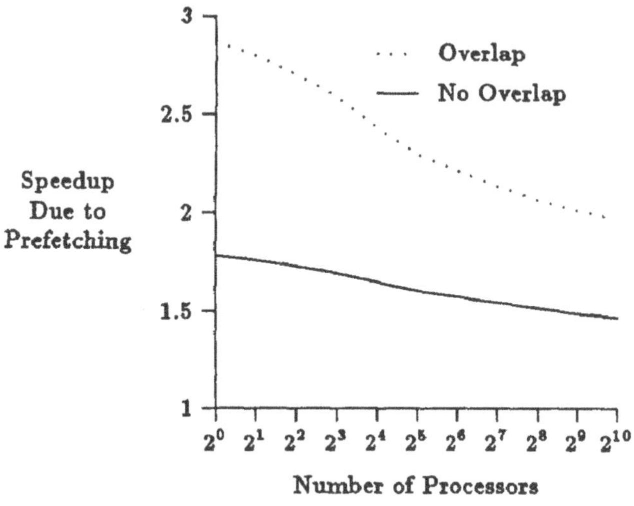

Figure 2: Speedup Due to Prefetching

We note that the theoretical maximum for the **no-overlap** model is:

$$\frac{\text{GLOB\_FETCH\_TIME}}{\text{PREF\_ELT\_TIME}} = 3.4$$

At this theoretical limit, the program execution time is dominated by memory access time of the references that are prefetchable. Therefore, if we do prefetching, these fetches take PREF_ELT_TIME time units. If we do not do prefetching, these fetches take GLOB_FETCH_TIME time units. The theoretical maximum for the **overlap** case is dependent on program structure; hence, it varies from program to program. However, it should be obvious that the theoretical maximum for the **overlap** case will always be greater than or equal to that of the **no-overlap** case.

In both curves in Figure 2, the speedups decrease as the number of processors increases. In Figures 3 and 4, we show the distribution of speedups for our two timing models. These histograms show the number of subroutines that have a speedup falling into a particular category. Similar to Figure 2, the histograms indicate that speedups decrease as the number of processors increases. Example 12 should show why this is so.

Example 12

```
prefetch(b(1:n))
do i = 1, n
   a(i) = b(i) + 1
enddo
```

If we only consider the execution time for accessing the elements of $b(i)$, then the speedup due to prefetching in the serial case is:

$$\frac{n * \text{GLOB\_FETCH\_TIME}}{\text{GLOB\_FETCH\_TIME} + (n-1) * \text{PREF\_ELT\_TIME}} = \frac{\text{serial without prefetching}}{\text{serial with prefetching}}$$

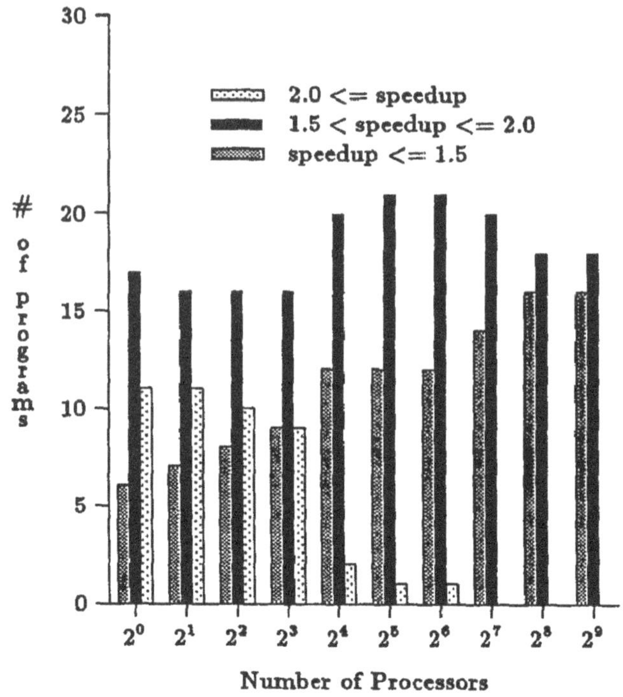

Figure 3: Speedups for the **no-overlap** model

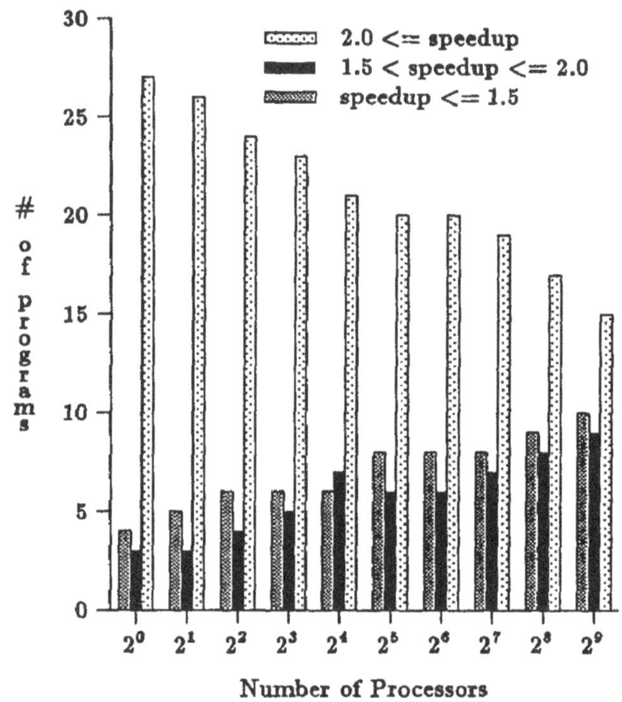

Figure 4: Speedups for the **overlap** model

and the speedup due to prefetching in the parallel case with p processors is:

$$\frac{\left\lceil \frac{n}{p} \right\rceil * \text{GLOB\_FETCH\_TIME}}{\text{GLOB\_FETCH\_TIME} + \left(\left\lceil \frac{n}{p} \right\rceil - 1\right) * \text{PREF\_ELT\_TIME}} = \frac{\text{parallel without prefetching}}{\text{parallel with prefetching}}$$

The GLOB_FETCH_TIME in the denominator becomes more significant as the number of processors increases; therefore, the speedup decreases. Alternatively, the prefetch start-up time becomes more significant as the number of elements to be prefetched decreases. It can be argued, though, that as the number of processors increases, the program size usually increases too, and therefore this is not a problem.

4.2 Potential for Prefetching in Subroutines

In this section, we present results regarding the extent to which references can be pulled out from enclosing loops.

Figure 5 displays the effectiveness of our method in three different categories:

Pulled Out From At Least One Loop: the percentage of references that are prefetchable to any degree,

Pulled Out From All Loops: the percentage of references that can be pulled out from all loops,

Pulled Out From Entire Subroutine: the percentage of references that can be pulled out from the entire subroutine, or, alternatively, out from all regions.

The histogram shows the number of subroutines that have a given percentage range of their references falling into a particular category. Table 2 summarizes these results for each program package and for all the packages combined. Column 2 shows the number of *candidates*—that is, array references inside loops that are not register references. The other data is presented in absolute values and as a percentage of the number of candidates. The values in Figure 5 are also percentages of the number of candidates.

Our method is successful in prefetching 58% of the candidates. This number drops to 22%, due to prefetch suppression, when considering the case of references pulled out from all loops, and to 3%, when considering the case of references pulled out from an entire subroutine.

We now examine the effectiveness of our prefetching method in more depth. Note the loop matrices presented in Table 3. These matrices show the number

EISPACK					
# of loops Pulled Out From	Loop Nest				
	1	2	3	4	Total
0	142	193	40	0	375 (49)
1	69	169	88	3	329 (43)
2	0	15	43	3	61 (8)
3	0	0	3	0	3 (0)
4	0	0	0	0	0 (0)
Total	211 (27)	377 (49)	174 (23)	6 (1)	768 (100)

LINPACK					
# of loops Pulled Out From	Loop Nest				
	1	2	3	4	Total
0	127	36	6	0	169 (49)
1	54	75	10	0	139 (40)
2	0	15	25	0	40 (11)
3	0	0	0	0	0 (0)
4	0	0	0	0	0 (0)
Total	181 (52)	126 (36)	41 (12)	0 (0)	348 (100)

REALSET					
# of loops Pulled Out From	Loop Nest				
	1	2	3	4	Total
0	85	122	46	5	258 (33)
1	104	102	29	11	246 (31)
2	0	113	49	14	176 (22)
3	0	0	106	2	108 (14)
4	0	0	0	0	0 (0)
Total	189 (24)	337 (43)	230 (29)	32 (4)	788 (100)

TOTAL					
# of loops Pulled Out From	Loop Nest				
	1	2	3	4	Total
0	354	351	92	5	802 (42)
1	227	346	127	14	714 (38)
2	0	143	117	17	277 (15)
3	0	0	109	2	111 (6)
4	0	0	0	0	0 (0)
Total	581 (31)	840 (44)	445 (23)	38 (2)	1904 (100)

Table 3: Loop Matrices

Package	Candidates	Prefetchable		All Loops		Subroutine	
EISPACK	768	393	(51%)	86	(11%)	1	(0%)
LINPACK	348	179	(51%)	64	(18%)	5	(1%)
REALSET	788	530	(67%)	275	(35%)	48	(6%)
TOTAL	1904	1102	(58%)	425	(22%)	54	(3%)

Table 2: Prefetching Data Summary

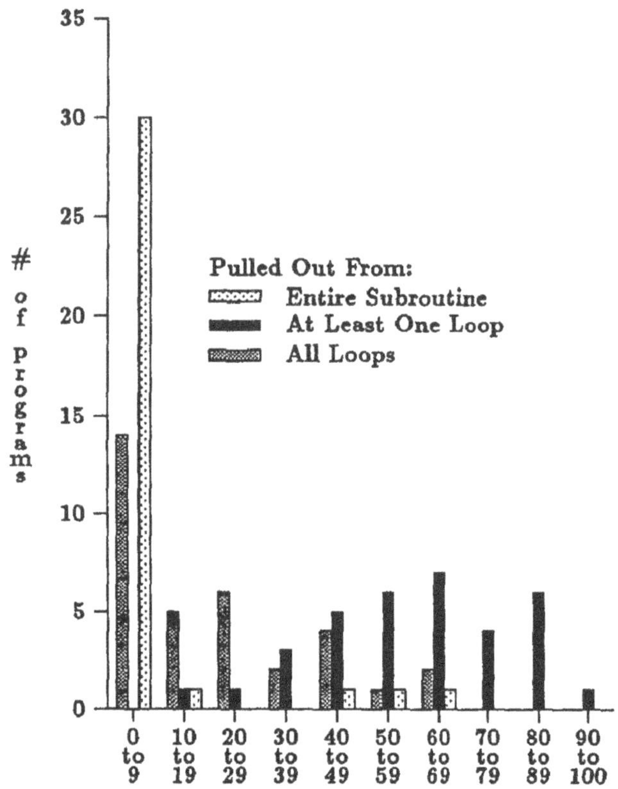

Figure 5: Prefetching Effectiveness

of references, at a particular loop nest level, that are pulled out from a given number of loops. The percentages are based on the number of total candidates. These numbers correlate with those in Table 2. 58% of all references can be pulled out from at least one loop, but only 21% can be pulled out from more than one loop. The matrices also show that we had more success with REALSET than with EISPACK or LINPACK. 49% of the references in both EISPACK and LINPACK are not prefetchable, but this number is only 33% in REALSET. In addition, 8% of the EISPACK references and 11% of the LINPACK references can be pulled out from more than one loop, but this number rises to 36% for REALSET. We further note that the more deeply nested a reference, the more likely it is that it can be pulled out from at least one loop. Of the 581 references that are inside one loop, only 227 (or 39%) can be pulled out from their enclosing loops. However, this number rises to 58%, 79% and 87% for

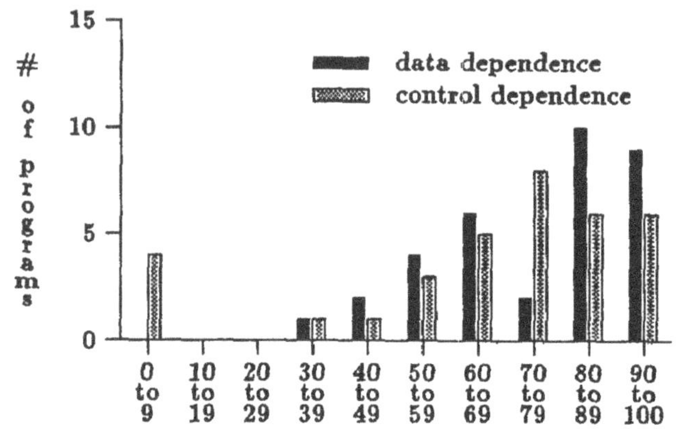

Figure 6: Reasons for Prefetch Suppression

nesting levels of two, three and four, respectively.

4.3 Why Prefetches were Suppressed

In Section 4.2, we discussed the cases where prefetches were completely or partially suppressed. We now present data as to why these prefetches were suppressed, according to the rules discussed in Section 3.2. The data in this section is important as it helps us identify the causes of suppression. This information can then be used to augment our algorithm to overcome some of these limitations (see [Gor89]).

The data presented in Figure 6 and summarized in Table 4 show the effects of control dependence and data dependence suppression. The histograms show the number of subroutines that have a given percentage range of their references suppressed for a particular reason. In this data, we include cases where suppression causes a reference to be non-prefetchable, in addition to cases where suppression causes a reference to only be partially pulled out. Therefore, the only references that do not yield data points for these histograms, are those that can be pulled out from the entire subroutine. From these results, we can see that control dependences and data dependences are equal causes of prefetch suppression and that improvement can only be achieved if both are reduced.

Package	Reason	
	Data Dep.	Cont. Dep.
EISPACK	(73%)	(82%)
LINPACK	(80%)	(72%)
REALSET	(72%)	(61%)
TOTAL	(74%)	(72%)

Table 4: Suppression Data Summary

5 Simulation Results

To explore the actual benefits of prefetching in the presence of network contention, we have simulated the execution of Fortran kernels on a large-scale multiprocessor at the register-transfer level. This section presents the results of this work.

5.1 System Configuration

The system configuration is based on a class of generalized Cedar-like architectures [KDLS86]. The values of some of the parameters have been determined experimentally to provide the best cost/performance ratio as determined by random traffic studies [GTV90]. The remaining parameters are based on Cedar itself. The system is a shared-memory machine with thirty-two processors connected to an equal number of interleaved memory modules via a pair of Omega networks [Law75]. Each processor has an associated prefetch unit with connections to the forward and reverse networks. The prefetch unit can both produce and consume a single word on each clock cycle. Data paths in the network are one word wide. A memory access request for a block of n data words is composed of n messages, where each message consists of an address/control word together with a data word, if required. The machine supports block accesses of up to thirty-two data words and a block of data may have any constant stride.

The switches have a clock rate equal to that of the processors and, barring contention, are capable of transferring a word from any input port into any output port during a single cycle. A contention resolution scheme is employed to ensure fair and bounded waiting. Each switch is equipped with a single-word first-in first-out (FIFO) buffer on each of its output ports. In the forward network, each switch has a two-word input buffer. In the reverse network, thirty-two word input buffers are used, as this has been shown experimentally to be the minimum buffer length necessary to give good performance under heavy loads.

Memory modules are interleaved on consecutive word addresses and have sixty-four and two word FIFO buffers on both their inputs and outputs, respectively. Again, the input buffer length has been determined experimentally. The memory modules require five network cycles to service a request for a single datum. Upon completion of an access, a memory module first places the response message in its output buffer (one word at a time) and then accepts the next message in its input buffer. The entire memory system is pipelined and all components attempt to move a word as soon as possible. Handshaking between components of the memory system causes one component to hold a word in its output buffer when the associated input buffer in the next component is full.

To offload the processing of global memory accesses, the processor sends a request to the prefetch unit to load a block of data into a particular register. The prefetch unit, in turn, issues the memory access request, one word per clock cycle, into the forward network. The messages travel through to the memory modules and back to the prefetch unit, which then notifies the processor that the memory access has completed.

In the **no-overlap** model, as described in Section 4, each instruction must complete before the next can be initiated. In the **overlap** model, the processor continues executing the program after issuing a memory access without waiting for the memory access to complete. A processor may have any number of memory accesses outstanding, so it only needs to wait for a memory access to complete when it needs the data from a pending fetch or when it encounters a processor reassignment instruction.

For simplicity, all scalar operands are assumed to come from registers and each operation is assumed to take one time unit per element.

5.2 Benchmarks

Owing to the added complexity of simulating program execution at the level of detail we have selected, we could not simulate all the the routines used for the static analysis. For this reason we have chosen 6 programs which are characteristic of a range numerical codes. VECSUM calculates a vector sum and TRIDIAG multiplies a tridiagonal matrix and a vector. Both of these are simple, singly-nested loops. The others are more complex. LLL8 is is an example of A.D.I integration, more commonly known as the eighth Lawrence Livermore loop. CFD and EFLUX are subroutines from two dimensional cfd programs. HRDIF1 is a subroutine from a horizontal non-linear diffusion program.

5.3 Prefetching/Scheduling Heuristic

For these experiments, we again assume that outermost parallel loops are distributed amongst processors.

Routine Name	overlap/ no-prefetch	overlap/ prefetch
VECSUM	1.07	1.68
TRIDIAG	1.06	1.08
LLL8	1.07	1.11
CFD	1.08	1.18
EFLUX	1.07	1.13
HRDIF1	1.11	1.18

Table 5: Speedup Relative to **no-overlap/no-prefetch** Case

We use a simple heuristic for scheduling prefetches, which works as follows. Consider a reference to a linearized array a nested in a series of loops such that loop L is the most deeply nested loop whose index i is referenced in the subscript of a. We pull out the reference to a from loop L to a point p immediately preceding L, if the following three conditions are met:

1. The subscript of a is linear in i (the reference has constant stride).
2. p lies in the access window for a.
3. L is not an outermost parallel loop (a is not being pulled across a processor reassignment boundary).

Otherwise, we leave the reference where it is.

Consider the loop nest in Example 13. We pull out the reference to $a(i)$ from both loops and $b(j * j)$ from none.

Example 13

```
prefetch(a(1:n))
do i = 1 to n
   do j = 1 to n
      ... = a(i) + b(j*j)
   enddo
enddo
```

To ensure that prefetches do not exceed the maximum block length, all loops are stripmined [Lov77] into thirty-two word blocks.

5.4 Experimental Results

The PARAFRASE Fortran compiler has been extended to generate pseudo-assembly level output. This output is then used to drive our simulator. Each benchmark routine has been compiled with our prefetching/scheduling heuristic (**prefetch**) and without (**no-prefetch**). We evaluate the performance of each routine under three conditions:

1. **no-overlap/no-prefetch**
2. **overlap/no-prefetch**
3. **overlap/prefetch**.

The **no-overlap/no-prefetch** case is used as a base case. Table 5 shows the speedups of the programs in the other two cases relative to the base case. Table 6 displays the average *request latency* and *message interarrival times* for each routine in all three cases. Request latency is the number of clock cycles which have elapsed between the time the processor initiates a memory access request and the time the first message of that request returns to the prefetch unit. Message interarrival time is the time between the return of successive messages to the prefetch unit.

Approximately a 7% improvement in performance is obtained, without any compiler assistance, by allowing memory accesses to be overlapped with computation and each other. As evidenced by the latencies and interarrival times, the added traffic due to the overlapping of memory accesses does not substantially interfere with the turnaround time for processing a request.

In contrast, the latencies and interarrival times increase dramatically when our simple prefetching/scheduling heuristic is incorporated. While prefetching data affords more opportunity for overlapping a memory access request with both computation and other memory access requests, this technique also leads to added contention. Hence, the run-time of the programs in the **overlap/prefetch** case is reduced by a modest 2% to 61% over the **overlap/no-prefetch** case. Had there been a more direct connection to the memories, we should have been able to realize speedups much closer to the theoretical ones predicted in Section 4. In spite of these problems, however, data is being fetched early enough so that the network delays do not completely offset the prefetching benefits. Overall, the combination of prefetching data early and overlapping requests with computation and other requests reduces the time the processors spend waiting for data to arrive by 32% to 97% over the base case.

As is evidenced by these results, more needs to done to overcome the problem of network contention and more fully realize the potential of data prefetching. In larger codes, loop transformations can sometimes be applied to improve the balance between memory accesses and computation [CCK87], thereby affording more opportunity to overlap memory accesses with computation. However, in simple codes, such as VECSUM, there is relatively little computation with which to overlap memory accesses, so it may not be possible to completely eliminate the time the processor spends waiting on data.

However, it can still be beneficial to overlap memory accesses with each other. If loop unrolling [CCK87] is applied before applying our prefetching/scheduling heuristic, the number of memory accesses which can be pulled out of a loop and overlapped may be increased.

Routine Name	Latency			Interarrival Time		
	no-overlap/ no-pre-fetching	overlap/ no-pre-fetching	overlap/ prefetching	no-overlap/ no-pre-fetching	overlap/ no-pre-fetching	overlap/ prefetching
VECSUM	141	136	1050	5.4	5.3	7.11
TRIDIAG	28	32	223	2.4	2.5	11.2
LLL8	23	50	635	2.2	2.2	7.2
CFD	15	19	627	2.2	2.3	3.7
EFLUX	28	85	448	2.4	2.5	4.9
HRDIF1	22	49	694	2.8	2.3	7.2

Table 6: Request Latencies and Message Interarrival Times

For comparison purposes, the VECSUM code used in these experiments, a loop with a single-statement body, was unrolled four times; TRIDIAG, a loop of several statements, was not. In both cases, all the global memory accesses were prefetchable. Note that VECSUM exhibits the greatest performance improvement from prefetching and TRIDIAG the least.

Longer input buffers on the memories and reverse network would have further improved the performance of memory intensive codes, such as VECSUM. However, since the buffer lengths chosen here suffice for most codes, the cost of these additional buffers is probably not warranted, which is why they have not been used for these experiments.

From other experiments not presented here, we have preliminary indications that with modest hardware support and more sophisticated scheduling strategies, latency and interarrival times can be dramatically reduced, thereby further increasing the attractiveness of compile-time data prefetching. However, this work is beyond the scope of this paper.

6 Conclusions and Future Work

We have presented a method for conservatively determining the earliest point in a program at which data can be prefetched. Control dependences and data dependences are the limiting factors on the range of this access window. Control dependence constraints arise because we do not want to prefetch data unless we are sure that the data will be used. Data dependence constraints arise because we do not want to prefetch data before the execution of a statement that modifies the data. Prefetching in this case would be counterproductive and can cause memory coherence problems.

Given the above constraints, our method is successful in finding opportunities to prefetch 58% of all the candidates in our benchmarks. Barring architectural and operating system considerations, a speedup, of as high as 2.87 from prefetching alone, is predicted. Control dependences and data dependences affect 72% and 74% of all candidates respectively, showing that they are equal causes of prefetch suppression. Only 3% of all candidates can be pulled out from an entire subroutine. This indicates that better intraprocedural results need to be achieved before interprocedural memory management becomes feasible. [Gor89] discusses ways of overcoming prefetch suppression.

We show that in real systems, in the presence of network contention, even a simple algorithm for scheduling prefetches within their access windows can reduce the amount of time a processor spends waiting on global data in Fortran kernels by as much as 32% to 97%. However, the limited bandwidth of the MINs prevents the full potential of prefetching from being realized. However, with hardware support and more sophisticated scheduling of prefetches, even better performance should be obtainable.

We are presently investigating other techniques for further reducing the time a processor must wait for data. These techniques include more sophisticated scheduling algorithms, methods for combining prefetches, and adaptations of the prefetching algorithm to handle poststoring.

Acknowledgements

We would like to thank Stephen Turner for his helpful comments and suggestions.

References

[CCK87] David Callahan, John Cocke, and Ken Kennedy. Estimating interlock and improving balance for pipelined architectures. In *International Conference on Parallel Processing*, pages 295–304, August 1987.

[Cray82] Cray Research Inc. The Cray X-MP series of computers, 1982.

[DBMS79] J. J. Dongarra, J. R. Bunch, C. B. Moler, and G. W. Stewart. *Linpack User's Guide.* Siam Press, Philadelphia, 1979.

[GGK+82] Allan Gottlieb, Ralph Grishman, Clyde P. Kruskal, Kevin P. McAuliffe, Larry Rudolph, and Marc Snir. The NYU Ultracomputer – designing an MIMD shared memory parallel machine. In *Tenth Annual Symposium on Computer Architecture*, 1982.

[GJG87] Dennis Gannon, William Jalby, and Kyle Gallivan. Strategies for cache and local memory management by global program transformation. In *1987 International Conference on Supercomputing*, 1987.

[GJG88] Kyle Gallivan, William Jalby, and Dennis Gannon. On the problem of optimizing data transfers for complex memory systems. In *1988 International Conference on Supercomputing*, July 1988.

[Gor89] Edward H. Gornish. Compile time analysis for data prefetching. Master's thesis, University of Illinois at Urbana-Champaign, December 1989.

[GTV90] Elana D. Granston, Stephen W. Turner, and Alexander V. Veidenbaum. Designing a scalable shared-memory system with support for burst traffic. To be published, 1990.

[Hus86] Harlan Husmann. *Compiler Memory Management and Compound Function Definition for Multiprocessors*. PhD thesis, University of Illinois at Urbana-Champaign, August 1986.

[Jac85] Daniel Thomas Jackson. Data movement in doall loops. Master's thesis, University of Illinois at Urbana-Champaign, May 1985.

[KDLS86] David. J. Kuck, E. S. Davidson, D. H. Lawrie, and A. H. Sameh. Parallel supercomputing today and the Cedar approach. *Science*, 231:967–974, February 1986.

[KKLW80] David J. Kuck, R. H. Kuhn, B. Leasure, and M. Wolfe. The structure of an advanced vectorizer for pipelined processors. In *Fourth International Computer Software and Applications Conference*, October 1980.

[Law75] Duncan H. Lawrie. Access and alignment of data in an array processor. *IEEE Transactions on Computers*, C-24(12):173–183, December 1975.

[Lee83] Kyungsook Yoon Lee. *Interconnection Networks and Compiler Algorithms for Multiprocessors*. PhD thesis, University of Illinois at Urbana-Champaign, 1983.

[Lee87] Roland Lun Lee. *The Effectiveness of Caches and Data Prefetch Buffers in Large-Scale Shared Memory Multiprocessors*. PhD thesis, University of Illinois at Urbana-Champaign, May 1987.

[Lov77] D. B. Loveman. Program improvement by source-to-source transformation. *Journal of the ACM*, 24(1):121–145, January 1977.

[Mar88] David M. Marcovitz. A multiprocessor cache performance metric. Master's thesis, University of Illinois at Urbana-Champaign, October 1988.

[PBG+85] Gregory F. Pfister, W. C. Brantley, D. A. George, S. L. Harvey, W. J. Kleinfeider, K. P. McAuliffe, E. A. Melton, V. A. Norton, and J. Weiss. The IBM Research Parallel Processor Prototype (RP3): Introduction and architecture. In *International Conference on Parallel Processing*, August 1985.

[Por89] Allan K. Porterfield. *Software Methods for Improvement of Cache Cache Performance on Supercomputer Applications*. PhD thesis, Rice University, May 1989.

[SBD+76] B. T. Smith, J. M. Boyle, J. J. Dongarra, B. S. Garbow, Y. Ikebe, V. C. Klema, and C. B. Moler. *Matrix Eigensystem Routines—Eispack Guide*. Springer-Verlag, Heidelberg, 1976.

[Tur89] Stephen Wilson Turner. Shared memory and interconnection network performance for vector multiprocessors. Master's thesis, University of Illinois at Urbana-Champaign, May 1989.

[Wol82] Michael Joseph Wolfe. *Optimizing Compilers for Supercomputers*. PhD thesis, University of Illinois at Urbana-Champaign, October 1982.

Semantical Interprocedural Parallelization: An Overview of the PIPS Project

François Irigoin
Pierre Jouvelot
Rémi Triolet

CRI, Ecole des Mines de Paris, France
{irigoin,jouvelot}@ensmp.fr

Abstract

PIPS is an experimental FORTRAN source-to-source parallelizer that combines the goal of exploring interprocedural and semantical analysis with a requirement for compilation speed. We present in this paper the main features of PIPS, i.e., demand-driven architecture, automatic support for multiple implementation languages, structured control graph, predicates and regions for interprocedural analysis and global nested loop parallelization, with an emphasis on its core data structures and transformation phases. Some preliminary results on the practical impact of our design choices are discussed.

This research is partially funded by DRET, under contract 87-017.

1 Introduction

Detecting the maximum level of parallelism in sequential programs requires a thorough understanding of their behavior. If numerous vectorizing and parallelizing compilers for scientific programs exist in both the academic ([ABCCF88], [KKLW84], [CCHKT88], [SG90], [AS89], [DLTKK90]) and industrial (VAST, FORGE, KAP) worlds, few are able to address the question of parallelism detection on a global basis, i.e. coupled with interprocedural information and comprehensive semantical analysis. The main goal of the PIPS (Parallélisation Interprocédurale de Programmes Scientifiques) project is to address this very issue and explore its effectiveness on real programs written in a real language.

PIPS is a source-to-source parallelizing compiler that transforms Fortran77 programs by replacing parallelizable nests of sequential DO loops with either Fortran90 [A90] vector instructions or DOALL constructs. It is not targeted towards a particular supercomputer, although only shared memory machines have yet been considered.

The principal characteristics of PIPS are:

- Interprocedural parallelization [T84]. It is at the core of PIPS: every step of the parallelizing process is able to cope with interprocedural information. A striking example of this drastic point of view is the parser, which encodes every assignment statement as a function call to a built-in = procedure with two arguments, the right and left hand side expressions. There is no "assign" node in the abstract syntax tree of programs and a user CALL would be encoded in the same way.
- Interprocedural analysis. To be most effective, a parallelizing compiler needs to gather as comprehensive as possible information about the behavior of programs. This is done in PIPS by a set of sophisticated (interprocedural) semantical analysis phases that compute side-effects (SDFI), regions [TIF86] and predicates in the style of [CH78].
- Efficiency. PIPS is fast enough to be used on real life programs. We use benchmarks provided by ONERA, a French research institute in aeronautics, and other more standard suites such as the PERFECT Club or LINPACK.

In the remainder of this paper, we discuss the general architecture of the PIPS parallelizer (Section 2), present the core data structures used within PIPS (Section 3), describe the different semantical analysis phases (Section 4), dependence tests (Section 5) and transformations (Section 6) applied by PIPS, give the current status of the project (Section 7) and conclude (Section 8). Given the breadth of this presentation, no particular section is dedicated to a discussion of the related work; relevant references are provided within each section.

2 PIPS General Design

Since PIPS is mainly a research project, we wanted its architecture to be modular and evolutive enough to adapt to the wide variety of people involved in the project (researchers, students, numerical analysts,...) and to the requirements of interprocedural analysis and interactivity. This dictated a structure in *phases*, all of which manipulate a common intermediate representation of programs that has been carefully designed and whose updates are under top supervision (see figure 1).

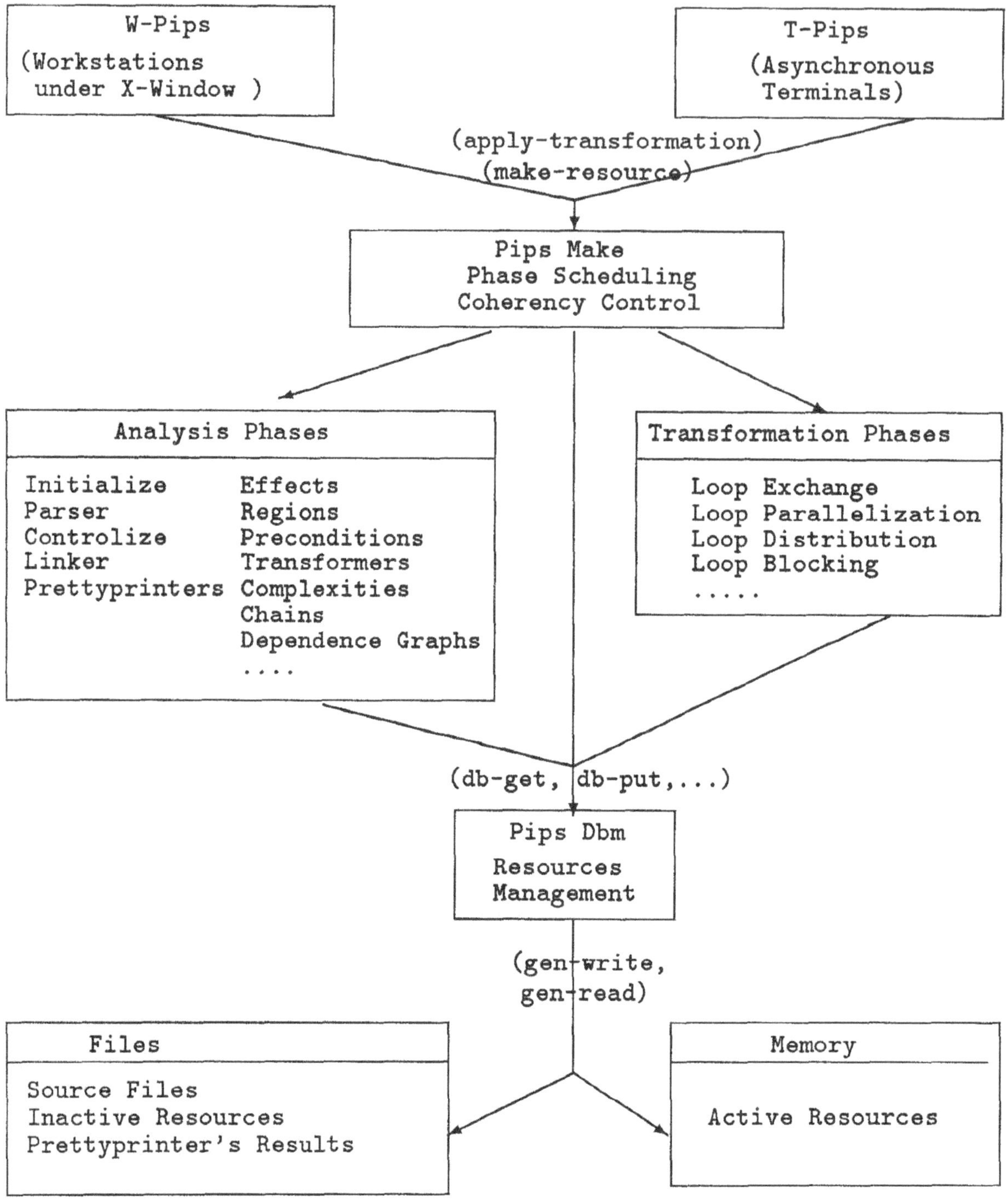

Figure 1: PIPS Structure

This architecture is hardly new. But a major issue is then the determination of the order according to which these different phases of the parallelizing process have to be scheduled to maintain consistency. PIPS adopts a relatively uncommon approach to this problem; the ordering is demand-driven, dynamic and automatically deduced from the declarative specifications of the dependencies between phases, by a program called **pipsmake**. Users are allowed to send requests to **pipsmake**, either to get a particular data structure or to apply a specific function.

Every data structure used, produced or transformed by a phase in PIPS, such as the abstract syntax tree, the control flow graph or the use-def chains, are considered to be *resources* which are under control of a data base manager, called **pipsdbm**. The place where the data actually reside (memory or file) is left to **pipsdbm** which can optimize these transfers according to the current memory space available. Data structures destroyed in memory by side effects performed by a given phase can be retrieved on disk, as well as data structured saved by previous PIPS runs, if they are still consistent.

Called by **pipsmake**, any phase begins by requesting some resources, via the **db_get** function provided by **pipsdbm**, performs some computation and declares the availability of its result via **db_put**. Every data structure is linked to its associated program unit. Currently, the units known by **pipsmake** are the whole `PROGRAM`, a given `MODULE` (i.e. a Fortran77 subroutine or function), the `CALLEES` (i.e., the list of all the modules that are called by a given module) and the `CALLERS` (i.e., the list of all the modules that call the given module). Via the notion of callees and callers, **pipsmake** manages the interprocedurality of PIPS.

Every phase in PIPS, such as the parsing of a source program or the privatization process, denotes a *function*; it may use and/or produce some resources. Every phase that exists in PIPS is declared via production rules; these are stored in a configuration file which is used by **pipsmake** to schedule the execution of each function, according to what the user and each phase (recursively) request. We give below an excerpt of this configuration file:

```
proper_effects  > MODULE.proper_effects
        < PROGRAM.entities
        < MODULE.code
        < CALLEES.summary_effects

cumulated_effects        > MODULE.cumulated_effects
        < PROGRAM.entities
        < MODULE.code
        < MODULE.proper_effects

summary_effects > MODULE.summary_effects
        < PROGRAM.entities
        < MODULE.code
        < MODULE.cumulated_effects
```

Here, for instance, the phase **cumulated_effects** computes the accumulated effects (such as a read on a given variable, called *entity* in PIPS) of all the statements of a `MODULE`. It needs the definition of all the entities of the `PROGRAM` - recall that PIPS is interprocedural -, the code of the module and its proper effects, i.e. the effects of the subroutine calls.

This architecture is demand-driven, since data structures are computed only when needed by some phase, and flexible, since each phase does not have to worry about the others and only requests resources at its outset. This organization permits the interprocedurality to be almost transparent to the programmer of a given phase since he can ignore how resources are computed. Each necessary resource is requested from **pipsdbm** and the appropriate function has previously been automatically activated by **pipsmake**, if the rules are correct. This allows for easy implementations of both top-down and bottom-up algorithms on the call graph of a program. Note however that it relies heavily upon the non-recursivity of Fortran77. It also provides the database structure necessary to combine interprocedural analysis and the speed necessary for interactivity: objects are computed only when they are needed and when they are not already available and up-to-date.

3 Data Structures

PIPS is organized around a core data structure that implements the abstract syntax trees of Fortran77. Since we expected to look at other languages than Fortran77 in the future, we carefully designed our Intermediate Representation (IR) to avoid to stick too closely to Fortran77 idiosyncrasies. Based upon experience, we also knew that numerous constructs in Fortran77 were mere syntactic sugar and could be abstracted as function calls, thus avoiding a huge set of cases that would have to be treated separately, even though they are all of the same. Occam's razor has been applied to its most extreme; there are only three cases of expressions and five cases of statements ! Even so, almost all Fortran77[1] has been embedded inside this IR.

The data structures that implement the IR used in PIPS are defined with the software engineering tool NewGen [JT89], developed by Pierre Jouvelot and Rémi Triolet. NewGen allows the definition of data *domains* in terms of basic ones, like `integer` or `float`, that can be combined to form products, sums, lists or sets. From these definitions, expressed in a simple language, NewGen generates a set of creation, manipulation and destruction functions on objects and values of these domains. We give below, as an example of NewGen compactness and PIPS philosophy, the definition of the expression domain used in PIPS:

```
expression = reference + range + call ;
reference = variable:entity x
            indices:expression* ;
range = lower:expression x
        upper:expression x
        increment:expression ;
call = function:entity x
       arguments:expression* ;
```

Here, we can see that a node for a `call` expression, representing a Fortran77 `FUNCTION` call, includes the `function` entity and the list of `arguments` expressions. As said above, an assignment is encoded in the same way, with a pseudo-intrinsic function = and two arguments denoting the left hand side and the right hand side of the assignment. This is possible since the implicit call mechanism is by reference.

The functions and macros generated by NewGen can be in either C or CommonLISP, the two languages currently

[1] The most significant restrictions are multiple entry points together with assigned and computed gotos, which can, most of the time, be desugared into more standard constructs. The very common BUFFER IN and BUFFER OUT extensions have been added to accept benchmark programs.

supported. These two versions are compatible at the file system level since NewGen automatically generates functions that can read and write data structures on files in a language-independent format. This permits a programming style reminiscent of *persistency*, a feature heavily exploited by pipsdbm.

CommonLISP is used as a prototyping language. For instance, a given exploratory phase can thus be quickly programmed in this highly expressive language before being efficiently recoded in C, once the algorithms have been designed and polished in the Lisp environment. The incremental linker of PIPS was first programmed in CommonLISP and rewritten in C. The implementation of *generalized reduction* detection [JD89] is being carried out in CommonLISP.

4 Semantical Analysis

We discuss in this section the control graph used in PIPS, together with the interprocedural computation of memory effects, regions [T84] and predicates, based on the intraprocedural computation of the same information on the statements of modules.

4.1 Control Graph

Semantical analysis[2] of programs is performed on their Hierarchical Structured Control-flow Graph (HSCG). This data structure is unique to PIPS among parallelizers[3] and its inception can be traced back to the notion of *control effect masking* described in [JG89]. The basic premise is that useful parallelism is only found in structured parts, which are at the same time easier and faster to manipulate and analyze, and very common in scientific programs like the benchmarks we were given. Most analysis algorithms for structured code have a simple recursive description by structural induction on the abstract syntax tree definition of the programming language. The presence of random branches destroys this nice property and imposes the computation of fixed points by iteration on the control graph.

The *controlizer* phase of PIPS, which computes the hierarchical structured control flow graph of a program, tries to keep the influence of branches as local as possible so that if, for instance, a label is only used within and from within a loop body, the loop will appear as a structured construct from the outside; control vagaries are masked. The HSCG is thus a layered data structure where each layer is either a structured construct or a graph-based description of a non-structured piece of code. The algorithms that manipulate HSCGs are successively defined by recursion and fixed point iteration. In particular, note that the presence of local branches in loops does not prevent parallelization, if the data dependences do not create conflicts.

The control graph is defined by the domain `unstructured` whereas structured statements are either basic commands altering the store with side-effects (`call`), sequences (`block`), tests (`test`) or DO loops (`loop`). The NewGen declarations, slightly simplified for the purpose of exposition, look like the following:

```
statement = label:entity x
            number:int x
            comments:string x
            instruction ;

instruction = block:statement* + test + loop +
              call + unstructured ;
test = condition:expression x
       true:statement x
       false:statement ;
loop = index:entity x
       range x
       body:statement x
       label:entity ;

unstructured = control x exit:control ;
control = statement x
          predecessors:control* x
          successors:control* ;
```

All the semantical analysis phases are defined by induction on the `statement` domain.

4.2 Effects

Effects describe the memory operations performed by a given statement. Besides the reference on which the operation is performed and its kind (read or write), PIPS distinguishes between effects that are always performed and the ones that may be performed.

Proper effects are memory references local to a given statement, such as a write on the left-hand side of an assignment or on the index variable of a `DO` loop construct. *Cumulated*[4] effects take into account all effects of a given statement, including those of its substatements (recall that the definition of the PIPS abstract syntax tree is recursive). Contrarily to proper effects, only the variable that is referenced is kept; in particular, in case of array references, index expressions are lost in this aggregation. *Summary* effects abstract the cumulated effects of a module by masking the effects performed on entities local to the module.

The proper effects of a call statement are derived from the cumulated effects of the body of the callee. Proper and cumulated effects are computed by an (automatic) bottom-up scan of the call tree, as can be seen in the following excerpt of the `pipsmake` rules for effects we saw previously:

```
proper_effects > MODULE.proper_effects
        < PROGRAM.entities
        < MODULE.code
        < CALLEES.summary_effects

summary_effects > MODULE.summary_effects
        < PROGRAM.entities
        < MODULE.code
        < MODULE.cumulated_effects

cumulated_effects > MODULE.cumulated_effects
        < PROGRAM.entities
        < MODULE.code
        < MODULE.proper_effects
```

[2] Semantical analysis denotes any kind of abstract interpretation of program and not only type checking or overloading removal as in classical compilers.

[3] High-Level Data Flow Analysis was proposed in [R77] and [S80] for classical compilers. Most academic parallelizers use either a classical low-level control flow graph or a program dependence graph [FOW87] or both. Another approach is to restructure the control flow graph before analysis are performed [TF89].

[4] Cumulated effects are also known as *use-mod* or sdfi information.

To give a better flavor of pipsmake's behavior, suppose no effects are available when the proper effects of some module are requested. Let P be this module and assume it calls Q, a leaf of the call graph. pipsmake will find the program entities and P's code on disk or in memory if parsing and linking have been performed[5] but not Q's summary effects. It will push them as a new goal and try to activate the rule for summary effects. But Q's cumulated effects are not available either, and the new goal becomes Q's proper effects, which can be evaluated because Q has no callees (Q was assumed to be a call graph leaf).

4.3 Predicates

To improve the accuracy of the effect information, to provide more information for dependence testing [TIF86] and to select better program transformations, statements are labelled with *predicates* that express constraints on the integer scalar variables, which are often used in references and loop bounds. This is most useful for array references, for instance to precisely define which subpart of an array is referenced by a memory operation and to refine cumulated effects into *regions* [T84][TIF86]. It is also used to improve dependence testing when inductive variables and triangular loop bounds are involved, and to select one vector loop or one parallel loop among many dependence free loops.

PIPS predicates are abstract commands, mapping a store to a set of stores [S77]. They are relations between the values of integer scalar variables in an initial store and a final store. The relations considered are polyhedra, represented by systems of linear inequalities and equalities and, sometimes, internally by generating systems, as in [CH78], because they provide a sound and general mathematical framework. Constant propagation, as well as inductive variable detection, linear equality detection [K76] or general linear constraints computation [CH78], can be performed in this framework using different operators to deal with PIPS basic control structures: sequences, tests, loops and control graphs (the so-called unstructured). More accurate operators are usually slower and PIPS users can interactively choose which ones are best for their program or module after viewing the results.

Unlike most analysis, we are dealing with abstract commands instead of abstract stores for two reasons. First, variables appearing in references cannot be aggregated to build cumulated and summary effects unless they denote the same value, i.e., they refer to the same store. The module's initial store is a natural candidate to be the unique reference store and, as a result, a relationship between this store and any statement's initial store is needed. Second, dependence tests are performed between *two* statements. Although a relationship between each statement store would be more useful than two stores, each relative to one statement, this would not be realistic because too many predicates would have to be computed. Thus a common reference to the same initial store seems to be a good trade-off between accuracy and complexity.

The drawback for using abstract commands instead of abstract stores is that the polyhedron dimensions are doubled, which is bad news for the exponential algorithms used to deal with polyhedra [CH78]. This was made less of a problem by exploiting the hierarchical structured control graph to compute predicates in an as small as possible environment.

A two-phase algorithm was designed and implemented. The first phase computes abstract commands bottom-up from the call statements to the sequences, tests and loops up to whole modules, and bottom-up from leave procedures to the main module. This is the most CPU intensive part but it benefits from locality. Each procedure is analyzed only once. The second phase is a top down phase. It propagates information about the initial store of the main program downwards to the call statements and to the called procedures, down to the simplest statements of the leaf procedures. Each procedure again is analyzed only once and receives as initial store the convex hull of all stores of its call sites.

It is difficult to compare this analysis with previously published methods either intraprocedural, like [CH78][6], or interprocedural, like [CCKT86], for two reasons. The first one is that many lattices are used, even though some algorithms are lattice independent. The second one is that different sets of operators can be used for a given lattice producing more or less accurate results. To put it in a very simplified way, return functions à la [CCKT86] are computed over a [CH78] lattice in the first phase, while jump functions are computed in the second phase. Example 1 of [CCKT86] could be handled if the assignment in *ralph*:

```
b=a*c/2000;
```

were linear.

4.4 Regions

Regions were defined [T84][TIF86] and implemented a first time in Parafrase [T85] by Rémi Triolet. Since then many different methods have been published and sometimes implemented. They belong to two broad classes [C90]. In the first class, the effects of call statements are somehow aggregated within each procedure using some lattice, at the cost of an accuracy loss and of a dependence test extension, but with the benefit of a reduction in the number of dependence tests to be performed to parallelize the callers [T84][C87][CK88][BK89]. In the second class, these elementary effects are simply gathered, which may benefit accuracy, but have to be tested independently to parallelize each caller, which induces a time penalty [L89] and, sometimes, requires a dependence test modification [BC86].

The region method as described in [T85] et [TIF86] did not look very attractive mainly because the dependence test used was shown to be very slow[7] and because the convex hull algorithm used to aggregate regions is potentially slow too. It was decided to implement it anyway in PIPS because worst-case exponential algorithms are not necessarily exponential on practical cases [TIF86]. This is especially true if restrictive assumptions are made on the region shapes as in [BK89]; once it has been shown that most regions belong to some subset, algorithm complexity should be evaluated on that subset. Experimental results are needed here to usefully compare methods.

[5] If not, pipsmake will activate the parse and link phases whose rules have been omitted here.

[6] In his PhD thesis Halbwachs gave hints about interprocedural extensions and program structure exploitation but no implementation seems to have ever been done.

[7] Slowliness reported in [T85] was also due to the implementation. Rémi Triolet had very little time to finish his work at CSRD.

From a theoretical point of view, regions could (but should they?) be improved by preserving some integer lattice information when possible, instead of giving up by systematically using convexity to reduce the information amount. For instance, convexity reduction in T(2*I) will lose the even parity information of the index expression. This could easily, from a mathematical point of view, be done by characterizing subparts of an array as affine images of polyhedra.

From a practical point of view, region implementation in PIPS is underway and only very simple cases have been handled up to now. Our key benchmarks were also analyzed by hand. Three out of four contain some interprocedural parallelism within DO loop bodies. Since regions would not give better results than array slices, subarray-based detection was quickly implemented as an extension of effect translation, the process that maps the summary effects of the callee to the proper effects of the CALL statement. At each CALL site, the summary effects of the callee are checked and ranges are used to express effects on subarrays, such as columns or set of columns.

5 Dependence Tests

The dependence test algorithm [B88] is a critical part for any parallelizer. Under the usual linear assumptions on loop bounds and array index expressions, integer programming provides an exact test at a very high cost [TF89]. Historically, simpler tests have been developed to speed up dependence testing because the number of tests to perform increases as the square of the number of references in the statements of interest.

Recently people have tried to develop multi-precision tests. Fast tests are used first. If a positive or negative conclusion is obtained, the test is finished. If a *don't know* answer is returned, a more sophisticated test is applied.

Although we know it could be easily improved, we used the Fourier-Motzkin pairwise elimination technique described in [TIF86], with slight variations. First of all, equations can be solved exactly before inequalities are combined and can show dependence or independence very often. Second, the whole dependence system built with the array references and the execution contexts (called *predicates* in PIPS) does not have to be solved for each dependence level [AK87] or for each dependence direction vector [W89].

It is sufficient to project[8] the dependence system on the dependence subspace once and for all, and either to quickly conclude when a constant dependence vector is found or when the equations have no solution, or to add additional constraints to the small system obtained in the dependence space. Its dimension is bounded by the number of enclosing loops[9] and additional constraints are very simple since they are either simple equalities, like $di = 0$, or simple inequalities, like $di > 0$ (i is assumed to be a loop index and di the corresponding dependence direction).

Also, the algorithm complexity seems to adapt to the dependence system intrinsic difficulty although it is very simple to program. Diagonal systems, which do not need *simultaneous testing* [BC86], are solved linearly and constant dependences are detected before inequalities are involved.

[8] Linear programming, as used in [LT85], or integer programming techniques are faster to decide emptiness but do not preserve enough information for projection.

[9] Depending on previous program transformations, inductive variables and the like may have to be taken into consideration, increasing the sub-system size.

Finally, measurements show that dependence testing does not take a noticeable amount of time compared to the whole parallelization process, at least in our implementation.

6 Transformations

A number of transformation phases have been implemented or planned inside the PIPS parallelizer. We will discuss below the following ones : privatization, detection of induction variables and reductions, distribution of loops and loop rescheduling.

6.1 Privatization

Some variables are used as local temporaries inside loop bodies. They are assigned on loop entries and their values on body exit are not used by subsequent iterations. This condition is checked in the *privatization* phase by looking at the use-def chains; all variables that satisfy this condition are flagged as local to the loop. Whenever such a loop is prettyprinted, a **PRIVATE** pragma is inserted into the output and the related dependences are deleted. Privatization increases the potential for parallelism detection, without the memory penalty of scalar expansion [W89].

6.2 Induction Variables and Reductions

Loop invariants, induction variables and reductions such as inner products are special cases of the so-called *generalized reductions*. A prototype implementation of the technique described in [JD89] is being written. It is based on symbolic evaluation of loop bodies and pattern-matching of the resulting symbolic store against a database of known cases.

This phase could be used to replace references to induction variables inside a loop body by appropriate expressions built over loop counters. By eliminating spurious dependences created by these variables, this would improve the potential for parallelism detection. Since inductive variables are also found by the semantic analysis, it will be interesting to compare the two method effectiveness.

The eventual goal is to detect reductions on real variables and to replace sequential loops by parallel reductions or by a proper library call.

6.3 Loop Distribution

The algorithm used in PIPS to generate parallel code is based on the technique described in [AK87]. The dependence graph is structured into strongly connected components, each of which is recursively analyzed with an incremented dependence level. Depending on whether the target architecture has a vector facility or not, it can be interesting to replace parallel loops that have more than one assignment statement in their bodies by a set of single assignment loops. These simple loops can then be replaced by vector instructions by the code generator. This transformation, called *loop distribution*, is provided by PIPS. It is coupled with the prettyprinter which is able to generate instructions with a syntax compatible with Fortran90.

6.4 Nested Loop Parallelization

Even if the initial order in which iterations of a loop nest body are executed prevents the straightforward parallelization of these loops, there may be ways to perform a change of basis in the corresponding iteration space to exhibit some loop parallelism. Based on the dependence directions between loop statements, the *hyperplane* method [L74] is one of the numerous techniques, like loop interchange and loop skewing, that perform a unimodular change of basis and that belong to this class of transformation.

A first prototype of global loop nest parallelization was implemented as an experimental phase in the PTRAN project [I88], using dependence direction vectors [W89]. The unimodular change of basis choice was based on a heuristic and designed for a vector multiprocessor like the IBM 3090 VF. A loop direction with as many as possible contiguous memory accesses was chosen as inner vector loop and another parallel loop was chosen as parallel outer loop to define parallel tasks. Other parallel loops were kept sequential. A more general version, using dependence cones to characterize the loop dependence set, was presented in [IT88b].

A PIPS implementation of this technique is under development. Program transformations are performed automatically, but the choice of the transformation is still left to the user at the time being.

7 Status and Preliminary Results

PIPS has been under development for the last two years and required six man-years of design, programming and testing. It is written in about 50k lines of C, although some prototype phases were written in CommonLISP. A window-based user interface has been added, written on top of the X11 Window System with the XView Toolkit. It runs on Sun 4 and Sparc workstations, under the SunOS operating system.

Parts of our test suite include four medium-sized (from one to three thousand lines of sparsely commented code) numerical programs from ONERA (Office National d'Etudes et de Recherche Aéronautiques), a government-funded agency for aerospace research. They were run on PIPS to assess both its performance and its efficiency.

The performance of the whole system is difficult to assess since it depends on input-output file transfers implicitly performed by `pips_dbm`. Currently, all the data structures are saved on disk, which means that a significant performance penalty is incurred. A more intelligent manager would cache some of them in memory and delay the disk operations to the point where they are required.

A few conclusions can be drawn from our preliminary results. First, interprocedural parallelism detection would benefit from better programming practice :

- Formal arrays should be dimensioned as accurately as possible. Declarations like `A(1)` should be prohibited and declarations like `A(*)` should be avoided as often as possible. Some parameter `N` is usually passed to loop over `A` and should be used to declare `A(N)`.
- Temporary arrays should be avoided. In ONERA benchmarks, many copies could be replaced by better procedure call or index expressions.
- Implicit conditions on key parameters read from disk should be explicitly checked. The program would be safer and semantical analysis could automatically propagate this extra information where it is needed.

Second, new compilation techniques are needed to achieve a reasonably good automatic interprocedural parallelization, while others are not as useful as expected :

- Regions seem to be overprecise to summarize the effects of modules. More attention should be paid to effect translation, from effects on formal parameters to effects on actual ones.
- Interprocedural semantical analysis gathers potentially useful information but, often, a key piece of information is missing.
- Array expansion [F88] or privatization are needed.
- Kill information about arrays would be useful to mask procedure effects on static arrays.
- General cases of array reshaping should be handled.

8 Conclusion

The PIPS project strives to reach three objectives: (1) confirm interprocedural analysis as a useful basis for parallelization, (2) justify the use of sophisticated semantical analysis techniques to improve the effectiveness of parallelism detection and (3) show the practicality of these two approaches with actual programs written in full Fortran77. By using both standard software engineering tools such as Lex and Yacc and the NewGen program generator, developed in-house, these ambitious requirements can be fulfilled with a limited development team of three people.

The PIPS parallelizer is still under development and but preliminary experiments on real programs have been successfully carried out. The effectiveness of parallelism detection cannot be evaluated without hand analysis, almost impossible on real programs, or without another parallelizer. The project evaluation is also hampered by the lack of a target machine; we expect to tune PIPS for Cray-like machines in the near future.

New parallelization techniques are also going to be introduced in or derived from it, such as code partitioning [IT88a] and data movement generation [An90] for shared memory and, eventually, distributed memory supercomputers.

References

[A90] ANSI X3J3/S8.115. Fortran90. June 90

[An90] Ancourt, C. *Génération Automatique de Codes de Transfert pour Multiprocesseurs à Mémoires Locales.* PhD thesis, Université Paris 6, 1991

[ABCCF88] Allen F., Burke M., Charles P., Cytron R., and Ferrante J. An overview of the PTRAN analysis system for multiprocessing. *Journal of Parallel and Distributed Computing* , Vol. 5, No 5, Oct. 1988.

[AK87] Allen, R., and Kennedy K. Automatic translation of FORTRAN programs to vector form. *ACM Transactions on Programming Langages and Systems*, Oct. 87.

[AS89] Appelbe, B., and Smith, K. Start/Pat: A Parallel Programming Toolkit. *IEEE Software*, Jul. 89.

[B88] Banerjee, U. *Dependence Analysis for Supercomputing.* Kluwer Academic Publishers, 1988

[BC86] Burke, M., and Cytron, R. Interprocedural Dependence Analysis and Parallelization. In the *Proceedings of the ACM Symposium on Compiler Construction*, 1986

[BK89] Balasundaram, V., Kennedy, K. A Technique for Summarizing Data Access and its Use in Parallelism Enhancing Transformations. In the *Proceedings of the ACM Symposium on Programming Languages Design and Implementation*, 1989

[C87] Callahan, D. A Global Approach to Detection of Parallelism. PhD Thesis, Rice University, 1987

[C90] Chassany, P. Les méthodes de parallélisation interprocédurale. Tech. Rep. EMP-CAI-I E/129, Ecole des Mines, 1990

[CCHKT88] Callahan, C. D., Cooper, K. D., Hood, R. T., Kennedy, K., and Torczon, L. Parascope: A Parallel Programming Environment. In the *Inter. J. of Supercomputer Applications*, Winter 88.

[CCKT86] Callahan, C. D., Cooper, K. D., Kennedy, K., and Torczon, L. Interprocedural Constant Propagation. In the *Proceedings of the ACM Symposium on Compiler Construction*, 1986

[CH78] Halbwachs, N., and Cousot, P. Automatic Discovery of Linear Restraints Among Variables of a Program. In the *Conference Record of the Tenth ACM Annual Symposium on Principles of Programming Languages*, 1978

[CK88] Callahan, D., and Kennedy, K. Analysis of Interprocedural Side Effects in a Parallel Programming Environment. *Journal of Parallel and Distributed Computing*, v. 5, n. 5, 1988

[DLTKK90] Dehbonei, B., Laurent, C., Tawbi, N., and Kulkarni, R. & S. PMACS: An Environment for Parallel Programming. In the *Proceedings of the International Workshop on Compilers for Parallel Computers*, Paris, Dec. 90.

[F88] Feautrier, P. Array Expansion. In the *Proceedings of the ACM International Conference on Supercomputing*, St-Malo, 1988.

[FOW87] Ferrante, J., Ottenstein, K. J., and Warren, J. D. The Program Dependence Graph and it Use in Optimization. *ACM TOPLAS*, 1987

[I88] Irigoin, F. Loop Reordering with Dependence Direction Vectors. In the *Journées FIRTECH Systèmes et Télématique Architectures Futures: Programmation Parallèle et Intégration VLSI*, Paris, 1988

[IT88a] Irigoin, F., and Triolet, R. Supernode Partitioning. In the *Proceedings of the ACM Symposium on Principles of Programming Languages*, San-Diego, 1988

[IT88b] Irigoin, F., and Triolet, R. Dependence Approximation and Global Parallel Code Generation for Nested Loops. In the *Proceedings of the International Workshop on Parallel and Distributed Algorithms*, Bonas, 1988

[JD89] Jouvelot, P., and Dehbonei, B. A Unified Semantic Approach For The Vectorization And Parallelization Of Generalized Reductions. In the *Proceedings of the ACM International Conf. on Supercomputing*, Crete, 1989

[JG89] Jouvelot, P., and Gifford, D. K. Reasoning about Continuation with Control Effects. In the *Proceedings of the ACM Conference on Programming Languages Design and Implementation*, 1989

[JT89] Jouvelot, P., and Triolet, R. NewGen: A Language Independent Program Generator. Rapport Interne CAII 191, 1989

[K76] Karr, M. Affine Relationships among Variables of a Program. *Acta Informatica*, 1976

[KKLW84] Kuck, D. J., Kuhn, R. H., Leasure, B., and Wolfe, M. J. The Structure of an Advanced Retargetable Vectorizer. In *Supercomputers: Design and Application*, IEEE Comp. Soc. Press, 1984

[L74] Lamport, L. The Parallel Execution of DO Loops. *Communications of the ACM*, 1974

[LT85] Lichnewsky, A., and Thomasset, F. Techniques de base pour l'exploitation automatique du parallélisme dans les programmes. INRIA Report 460, 1985

[L89] Li. Intraprocedural and Interprocedural Data Dependence Analysis for Parallel Computing. CSRD Report 910, 1989

[R77] Rosen, B. K. High-Level Data Flow Analysis. *Communications of the ACM*, 1977

[S77] Stoy, J. E. Denotational Semantics: The Scott-Strachey Approach to Programming Language Theory. MIT Press, 1977

[S80] Sharir, M. Structural Analysis: A New Approach to Flow Analysis in Optimizing Compilers. *Computer Language*, 1980

[SG90] Shei, B., and Gannon, D. SIGMACS: A Programmable Programming Environment. In the *Proceedings of the International Workshop on Programming Languages and Compilers for Parallel Computers*, Irvine, Aug. 90.

[T84] Triolet, R. Contribution à la parallélisation automatique de programmes Fortran comportant des appels de procédure, PhD Thesis, Université Pierre et Marie Curie, 1984

[T85] Triolet, R. Interprocedural Analysis for Program Restructuring with Parafrase. CSRD Report 538, 1985

[TF89] Tawbi, N., and Feautrier, P. Parallélisation automatique de programmes pour ordinateurs multiprocesseurs à mémoire partagée. Tech. Rep. MASI, Université Pierre et Marie Curie, 1989

[TIF86] Triolet, R., Irigoin, F., and Feautrier, P. Direct Parallelization of Call Statements. In the *Proceedings of the ACM Symposium on Compiler Construction*, 1986

[W89] Wolfe, M. J. *Optimizing Supercompilers for Supercomputers*. MIT Press, 1989

Optimizing for Parallelism and Data Locality

Ken Kennedy Kathryn S. McKinley
ken@rice.edu *kats@rice.edu*

Department of Computer Science
Rice University
Houston, TX 77251-1892

Abstract

Previous research has used program transformation to introduce parallelism and to exploit data locality. Unfortunately, these two objectives have usually been considered independently. This work explores the trade-offs between effectively utilizing parallelism and memory hierarchy on shared-memory multiprocessors. We present a simple, but surprisingly accurate, memory model to determine cache line reuse from both multiple accesses to the same memory location and from consecutive memory access. The model is used in memory optimizing and loop parallelization algorithms that effectively exploit data locality and parallelism in concert. We demonstrate the efficacy of this approach with very encouraging experimental results.

1 Introduction

Transformations to exploit parallelism and to improve data locality are two of the most valuable compiler techniques in use today. Independently, each of these optimizations has been shown to result in dramatic improvements. This paper seeks to combine the benefits of both by using a simple memory model to drive optimizations for data locality and parallelism. By unifying the treatment of these optimizations, we are able to place loops with data reuse on inner loops and to introduce parallelism for outer loops. Our strategy produces data locality at the innermost loops, where it is most likely to be exploited by the hardware and places parallelism at the outermost loop, where it is most effective. If these two goals conflict, we present an algorithm that usually reaps the benefits of both.

Optimizing data locality is necessarily both architecture and language dependent. However, the reuse of memory locations and the consecutive access of adjacent memory locations form the foundation of most memory hierarchy optimizations. Reuse of a particular memory reference for arrays can be discovered using *data-dependence* analysis [KKP+81]. However, reuse of consecutive accesses, often called *unit stride* access, is a significant source of reuse that can easily be determined when the storage order of arrays and the cache line size is known. In this paper we introduce a simple model for estimating the cost, in memory references, of executing a given loop nest. The principal advantage of this model over previous models is that it takes into account cache reuse due to consecutive accesses to the same cache line. We show how this model can be used to exploit data locality at multiple levels via loop permutation.

ICS '92-7/92/D.C., USA
© 1992 ACM 0-89791-485-6/92/0007/0323...$1.50

Parallelism is usually most effective when it achieves the highest possible *granularity*, the amount of work per parallel task. Granularity is highest when parallel tasks contain the largest amount of work possible. In this paper, parallelism is introduced via the parallel loop construct for shared-memory multiprocessors. Our algorithm first uses the memory model to find a loop organization that exploits data locality. It then seeks to parallelize the outermost loop or a parallel loop that can be positioned outermost. Given sufficient iterations, it then strip mines the loop into two loops, such that one loop is used to achieve locality and the other is used to introduce parallelism.

1.1 Matrix Multiply Example

As an example of this process, consider the ubiquitous matrix multiply.

```
DO J = 1, N
   DO K = 1, N
      DO I = 1, N
         C(I,J) = C(I,J) + A(I,K) * B(K,J)
```

Assuming arrays are stored such that columns of the arrays are in consecutive memory locations, *i.e. column-major order*, this loop organization exploits data locality in the following manner. The consecutive access on the inner I loop to C(I,J) and A(I,K) provide an opportunity for cache line reuse when the cache line size is greater than 1. There is also a loop-invariant reuse of B(K,J) on the I loop. Additionally, the J and the I loops can be parallel. However, if the number of processors, P, is less than the number of iterations of either loop, it is not profitable to utilize both levels of parallelism at once due to additional scheduling overhead. A better execution time would result by maximizing the granularity of one level of the parallelism and then matching it to the machine. If N = P, selecting J to be executed in parallel preserves data locality and introduces a single level of parallelism with maximum granularity.

```
PARALLEL DO J = 1, N
    DO K = 1, N
        DO I = 1, N
            C(I,J) = C(I,J) + A(I,K) * B(K,J)
```

However, if the number of loop iterations is greater than the number of processors, N > P, it is often useful to combine independent iterations into a single parallel task to achieve granularity that matches the machine. The parallel loop is strip mined by the number of processors where the strip size is SS = ⌈ N/P ⌉. We call the J loop the strip and the JJ loop, which walks between strips, the iterator.

```
PARALLEL DO JJ = 1, N, SS
    DO J = JJ, MIN(JJ + SS - 1, N)
        DO K = 1, N
            DO I = I, N
                C(I,J) = C(I,J) + A(I,K) * B(K,J)
```

The parallel JJ loop carves up the data space nicely, but if each processor's cache is still not large enough to contain all of array A, *tiling* the loop nest further improves performance by providing reuse of A. Tiling combines strip mining and loop interchange to promote reuse across a loop nest [IT88, Wol89a]. For matrix multiply, the loop nest may be tiled by strip mining the K loop by TS and then interchanging it with J.

```
PARALLEL DO JJ = 1, N, SS
    DO KK = 1, N, TS
        DO J = JJ, MIN(JJ + SS - 1, N)
            DO K = KK, MIN(KK + B - 1, N)
                DO I = I, N
                    C(I,J) = C(I,J) + A(I,K) * B(K,J)
```

Here, TS is selected based on the cache size. This organization moves the reuse of A(1:N,KK:KK+TS-1) on the J loop closer together in time, making it more likely to still be in cache.

This optimization approach may be divided into three phases:

1. optimizing to improve data locality,
2. finding and positioning a parallel loop, and
3. performing low-level memory optimizations such as tiling for cache and placing references in registers [LRW91, CCK90].

This paper focuses on the first two phases. We advocate the first two phases be followed by a low-level memory optimizing phase, but do not address it here.

The remainder of this paper is divided into 10 sections. We first present some terms used in this paper to describe data dependence and the machine model. The next section explores and illustrates the effects of parallelism and memory access on performance. The next two sections present a cost model for determining reuse and an algorithm for improving it. Section 6 describes the parallelization strategy. The overall strategy combines the two in Section 7. In Section 8, experimental results are reported. We then overview related work and conclude.

2 Background

2.1 Data Dependence

Dependence analysis is the compile-time analysis of a program's memory accesses. A *data dependence* between two references Ref_1 and Ref_2 indicates that they read or write a common memory location [KKP+81]. True, anti, and output dependences arise when at least one reference is write; the order between Ref_1 and Ref_2 must be preserved to maintain the semantics of the original program. Input dependences arise if both Ref_1 and Ref_2 are reads; they do not restrict program order.

Data dependences may be characterized by their access pattern between loop iterations. The number of loop iterations d separating the source and sink of the dependence is its *dependence distance* [KMC72, Lam74]; it may also be summarized as a *dependence direction* consisting of '<', '=', or '>' [WB87, Wol89b].

Dependence distances and directions are represented as a vector whose elements, displayed left to right, represent the dependence from the outermost to the innermost loop in the nest. By definition all distance and direction vectors are lexicographically positive. We use $\vec{\delta} = (\delta_1, \ldots, \delta_n)$ to represent a distance or direction vector, where δ_i is the dependence distance or direction for the loop at level i.

Dependences may also be characterized as either loop-independent or loop-carried. *Loop-independent* dependences occur on the same iteration of a loop. A dependence between iterations of a loop is called *loop-carried* and prevents the iterations of a loop from being executed in parallel [AK87]. A dependence is carried by the outermost loop for which the element in the direction vector is not an '='.

Data dependence is used to determine the legality of a given loop permutation by checking whether any permuted true, anti, or output dependence vector becomes lexicographically negative [Ban90b, WL90]. Data dependence also characterizes reuse of individual memory locations [CCK90].

2.2 Memory and Language Model

The techniques developed in this paper are intended for shared-memory multiprocessors where each processor has at a local cache and the processors are connected with a common bus. Because we are evaluating reuse, we require some knowledge of the memory hierarchy. However, because our model is very simple, only minimal knowledge of the cache is required; the compiler must know the cache line size (cls). The size, set associativity, and replacement policy of the cache are not important here. In addition, we assume a write-back cache and ignore non-unique write references. If the cache is write-through, these writes should be included.

In addition, we only concern ourselves with memory accesses caused by array references, since they dominate memory access in scientific Fortran codes. We also assume that arrays are stored in *column-major* order,

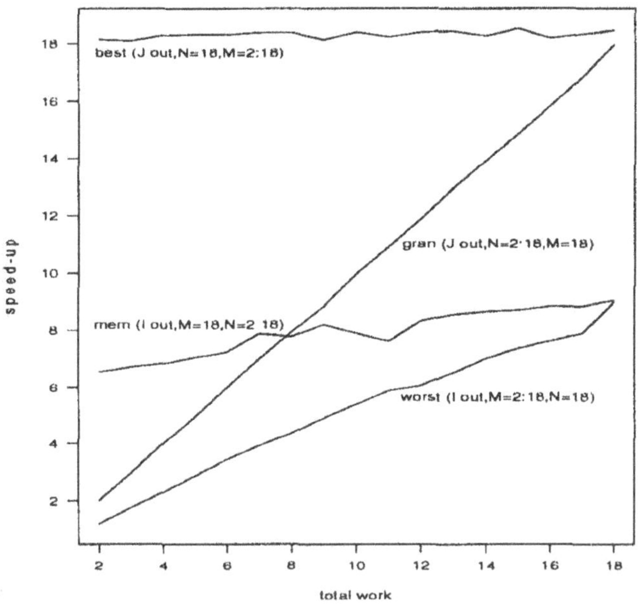

Figure 1: Memory and parallelism tradeoffs

where unit stride accesses in the first array dimension translate into contiguous memory accesses. Our results are also valid for *row-major* arrays such as those found in C with only minor changes.

3 Tradeoffs in Optimization

This section illustrates with an experiment the influence of memory reuse and parallelism granularity on speed-up. As expected, it indicates the best performance is possible only when both are utilized effectively in concert. It also shows that when both cannot be achieved at once, there are situations where favoring one or the other results in the best execution time. Neither always dominates. To illustrate, we phrase the following question.

Given enough computation to make parallelism profitable, what is the effect of reuse and how should it affect the optimization strategy?

Figure 1 presents the results of executing different parallel versions of the following loop nest on 18 processors of a Sequent Symmetry S81 with 20 processors, with increasing amounts of total work.

```
DO J = 1, N
    DO I = 1, M
        DO H = 1, L
            C(I, J) = C(I, J) + A(I, J) + B(I, J)
```

The total amount of work is increased by varying the upper bounds N and M from 2 to the number of processors (P = 18). We consider positioning I or J as the outer parallel loop in the nest. In Figure 1, the *best* version of this loop nest has an outer parallel J loop with 18 iterations (N = 18) and total work is increased by varying M from 2 to 18. Each of the 18 processors accesses distinct columns of each array. This organization exploits cache line reuse on each processor and results in linearly-scalable speed-up.

When the J loop is outermost and the number of parallel iterations of is varied from 2 to 18 along with P and the I loop contains 18 iterations, the total amount of work increases, but the work per processor remains the same. This organization is illustrated by the *gran* line. In this case, the speed-up scales by the number of parallel iterations, but cache line reuse is still facilitated on each processor.

If instead the I loop is made outermost and parallel, then processors must compete for the cache line which contains C(I,J) in order to write it. This competition is called *false sharing*. In addition, multiple processors require cache lines containing A(I,J) and B(I,J), increasing network contention and total memory utilization. When the number of parallel iterations of the I loop as outermost varies from 2 to 18 along with P and the J loop contains 18 iterations, the *worst* line indicates the performance. If the number of parallel iterations of I is held at 18 while the J loop is varied from 2 to 18, the *mem* line results.

Compare the pair of lines *best* and *mem* The factor of two difference is due to the benefit of cache line reuse in *best*, and the limitations of false sharing and increased bus and memory utilization in *mem*. The same comparison holds for the *gran* and *worst* lines. These results indicate that the parallelizing algorithm must recognize reuse and false sharing to be effective.

Now compare the pair of crossing lines *gran* and *mem*. These computations differ only by an interchange. An optimization strategy that only used loop interchange would be forced to pick between the two. To obtain the best performance for this example, the J loop would be outermost when N > 8, otherwise the I loop should be outermost. In addition, this "crossover" point would need to be determined for each computation, a daunting task. Our approach instead combines loop interchange and strip mining in a parallelization strategy that minimizes false sharing and exploits data reuse.

4 Optimizing Data Locality

In this section we describe two sources of data reuse, then we incorporate both in a simple yet realistic cost model. In subsequent sections, this cost model is used to guide optimizations for improving data locality and exploiting parallelism.

4.1 Sources of Data Reuse

We first consider the two major sources of data reuse.

- multiple accesses to the same memory location
- accesses to consecutive memory locations (*i.e.* stride 1 or unit stride access)

Multiple accesses to the same memory location may arise from either a single array reference or multiple array references. These accesses are loop-independent if they occur in the same loop iteration, and are loop-carried if they occur on different loop iterations. Wolf and Lam call this *temporal* reuse [WL91]. The most obvious source of temporal reuse is from loop-invariant references. For instance, consider the reference to A(J) in the following loop nest. It is invariant with respect to the I loop, and is reused by each iteration.

```
DO J = 1,N
    DO I = 1,N
        S = S + A(J) + B(I) + C(J,I)
```

A second source of data reuse is caused by multiple accesses to consecutive memory locations. For instance, each cache line is reused multiple times on the inner I loop for B(I) in the above example. Wolf and Lam call this *spatial* reuse [WL91]. The actual amount of reuse is dependent on the size of B(I) relative to the cache line size and the pattern of intervening references. For the rest of this paper, we assume for simplicity that the cache line size is expressed as a multiple of the number of array elements. For reasonably large computations, references such as C(J,I) do not provide any reuse on the I loop, because the desired cache lines have been flushed by intervening memory accesses.

Previous researchers have studied techniques for improving locality of accesses for registers, cache, and pages [AS79, CCK90, WL91, GJG88]. In this paper we concentrate on improving the locality of accesses for cache; *i.e.* we attempt to increases the locality of access to the same cache line. Empirical results show that improving spatial reuse can be significantly more effective than techniques that consider temporal reuse alone [KMT92]. In addition, consecutive memory access results in reuse at all levels of the memory hierarchy except for registers.

4.2 Simplifying Assumptions

To simplify analysis we make two assumptions. First, our loop cost function assumes that reuse occurs only across iterations of the innermost loop. This assumption decreases precision but greatly simplifies analysis, since it allows the number of cache line accesses to be calculated independent of the permutation of all outer loops. This assumption is accurate if the inner loop contains a sufficiently large number of memory accesses to completely flush the cache after executing all of its iterations. We show later that our optimizations to improve locality can select a desirable permutation of outer loops even with this restriction.

Cache interference refers to the situation where two memory locations are mapped to the same cache line, eliminating an opportunity to exploit reuse for one of the references. Our second assumption is that cache interferences occur rarely for small numbers of inner loop iterations, compared to the total number of distinct cache lines accessed in those iterations. In other words, we expect very few interferences for each cache line being reused, since the cache line is only needed for a small number of consecutive inner loop iterations. Lam *et al.* show that this assumption may not hold if cache lines must remain live for longer periods of time. Considerable interference may take place when loops are tiled to increase reuse across outer loops [LRW91].

Figure 2: Algorithm RefGroup

INPUT:
  $Refs = \{Ref_1 \ldots Ref_n\}$ references
  $\mathcal{DG} = \{\langle Ref_i\ \vec{\delta}\ Ref_j \rangle, \ldots\}$ the dependence graph
  l = candidate innermost loop

OUTPUT:
  $\{RefGroup_1 \ldots RefGroup_m\}$ reference groups for l

ALGORITHM:
  $m = 0$
  while $Refs \neq \emptyset$ **do**
    $m = m + 1$
    $RefGroup_m = \{r\}$, where $r \in Refs$
    $Refs = Refs - \{r\}$
    for each $\langle r\ \vec{\delta}\ r' \rangle$ **or** $\langle r'\ \vec{\delta}\ r \rangle \in \mathcal{DG}$ *s.t.* $r' \in Refs$
      if (δ_l is a constant d) & (δ_l is the only nonzero entry in $\vec{\delta}$)
        $RefGroup_m = RefGroup_m + \{r'\}$
        $Refs = Refs - \{r'\}$
      endif
    endfor
  endwhile

4.3 Loop Cost Function

Given these assumptions, we present a loop cost function *LoopCost* based on our memory model. Its goal is to estimate the total number of cache lines accessed when a candidate loop l is positioned as the innermost loop. The result is used to guide loop permutation to improve data locality. The estimate is computed in two steps. First, references that will access the same cache line in the same or different iterations of the l loop are combined using *RefGroup*. Second, the number of cache lines accessed by all groups is calculated using *LoopCost*.

4.4 RefGroup

The goal of the *RefGroup* algorithm is to partition variable references in the program text into *reference groups* such that all references in a group access the same memory locations, and consequently the same cache line. Wolf and Lam call these groups *equivalence classes* exhibiting *group-temporal* reuse. The partition process is particularly simple here because we only consider reuse for each loop when it is positioned innermost.

Two references are in the same reference group for loop l if they actually access some common memory location (data dependence $\vec{\delta}$ exists between them), and the reuse occurs on l if it is positioned as the innermost loop. The common accesses then occur on either the same iteration of l ($\delta_l = 0$) or across d iterations of l

($\delta_l = d$). More formally we define *RefGroup* as follows.

Definition: Two references Ref_1 and Ref_2 belong to the same *reference group* with respect to loop l if and only if:

1. $\exists\ Ref_1 \vec{\delta} Ref_2$, and
2. $\vec{\delta}$ is a loop-independent dependence, or δ_l, the entry in $\vec{\delta}$ corresponding to loop l, is a constant d (d may be zero) and all other entries are zero.

4.4.1 Jacobi Example

For instance, consider the following Jacobi iteration example.

```
DO I = 2,N-1
   DO J = 2,N-1
      A(J,I) = 0.2* (B(J,I) + B(J-1,I) + B(J,I-1)
               + B(J+1,I) + B(J,I+1))
```

Data dependences connect all references to B. The reference groups for the I loop are:

{A(J,I)}, {B(J,I),B(J,I-1),B(J,I+1)},
{B(J-1,I)}, {B(J+1,I)}.

The reference groups for the J loop are:

{A(J,I)}, {B(J,I),B(J-1,I),B(J+1,I)},
{B(J,I-1)}, {B(J,I+1)}.

Algorithm *RefGroup* is shown in Figure 2. Its efficiency may be improved by pruning all identical array references, since they access the same memory location on each iteration and always fall in the same reference group.

4.5 LoopCost

After the number of reference groups for loop l is computed with *RefGroup*, the algorithm *RefCost* is applied to estimate the total number of cache lines that would accessed by each reference group if l were the innermost loop. Once again, the task is simplified because we only consider reuse between iterations of l.

RefCost works by considering one array reference *Ref* from each reference group; these representative references are classified as loop-invariant, consecutive, or non-consecutive with respect to loop l. Loop-invariant array references have subscripts that do not vary with l; they require only one cache line for all iterations of l.[1] Consecutive array accesses vary with l only in the first subscript dimension. They access a new cache line every cls iterations, resulting in $trip/cls$ cache line accesses, assuming l performs $trip$ iterations. Fewer cache lines are reused for nonunit strides. Non-consecutive array accesses vary with l in some other subscript dimension; they access a different cache line each iteration, yielding a total of $trip$ cache line accesses.

[1] Of course, loop-invariant references should eventually be put in registers by later optimizations [CCK90].

Once *RefCost* is computed, the algorithm *LoopCost* calculates the total number of cache lines accessed by all references when l is the innermost loop. It simply sums *RefCost* for all reference groups, then multiplies the result by the trip counts of all the remaining loops. This calculation will underestimate the number of cache lines accessed on the inner loop, if the distance of the dependences for a particular *RefGroup* set are greater than cls. Also, slight underestimates occurs because the exact alignment of arrays in memory is not known until run-time. *LoopCost* will overestimate the number of cache lines, if there is additional reuse across an outer loop.

LoopCost is expressed more formally in Figure 3 for the following loop nest containing one array reference from each reference group $RefGroup_1 \ldots RefGroup_m$:

$$
\begin{array}{l}
\text{do } i_1 = lb_1, ub_1, s_1 \\
\quad \text{do } i_2 = lb_2, ub_2, s_2 \\
\quad\quad \ldots \\
\quad\quad \text{do } i_n = lb_n, ub_n, s_n \\
\quad\quad\quad Ref_1(f_1(i_1,\ldots,i_n),\ldots,f_j(i_1,\ldots,i_n)) \\
\quad\quad\quad \ldots \\
\quad\quad\quad Ref_m(g_1(i_1,\ldots,i_n),\ldots,g_k(i_1,\ldots,i_n))
\end{array}
$$

Note that *LoopCost* can be used to calculate cache line accesses even for array references with complex subscript expressions. For instance, it determines that A(I+J+N) results in consecutive memory accesses with respect to both the I and J loops.

4.6 Imperfectly Nested Loops

Because of their simplicity, both *RefGroup* and *LoopCost* can also be applied to imperfectly nested loops. Consider the following example, where the first definition of A(J) is imperfectly nested:

```
DO J = 1, 100
   A(J) = 0
   DO I = 1, 100
      A(J) = A(J) + ...
```

RefGroup would place all references to A(J) in the same reference group. When we apply *RefCost* to calculate the number of cache lines accessed by a reference group, we need to select the most deeply nested member of the group. *LoopCost* then multiplies the result by the trip counts of all the loops that actually enclose the reference.

5 Loop Permutation

The previous section presents our cost model for evaluating the data locality of a given loop structure with respect to cache. In this section we show how the simplicity and accuracy of the cost model guides loop permutation to restructure a loop nest for better data locality.

A naive optimization algorithm would simply generate all legal loop permutations and select the permutation that yields the best estimated data locality using *LoopCost*. Unfortunately, generating all possible

Figure 3: Algorithm LoopCost

INPUT:

$\mathcal{L} = \{l_1, \ldots, l_n\}$ a loop nest with headers lb, ub, s

$\mathcal{R} = \{Ref_1, \ldots, Ref_m\}$ representatives from each reference group

$trip_l = (ub_l - lb_l + s_l)/s_l$

cls = the cache line size,

$appear(f)$ = the set of index variables that appears in the subscript expression f

$coeff(i_l, f)$ = the coefficient of the index variable i_l in the subscript f (it may be zero)

OUTPUT:

$LoopCost(l)$ = number of cache lines accessed with l as innermost loop

ALGORITHM:

$$\textbf{LoopCost}(l) = \sum_{k=1}^{m} \left(\textbf{RefCost}(Ref_k(f_1(i_1, \ldots, i_n), \ldots, f_j(i_1, \ldots, i_n))) * \prod_{h \neq l} trip_h \right)$$

$\textbf{RefCost}(Ref_k)$ =

1	**if**	$(i_l \notin appear(f_1)) \wedge \ldots \wedge (i_l \notin appear(f_j))$	**loop invariant**
$trip_l/cls$	**if**	$(i_l \in appear(f_1)) \wedge (\lvert coeff(i_l, f_1)\rvert = 1) \wedge (\lvert s_l \rvert = 1) \wedge$ $(i_l \notin appear(f_2)) \wedge \ldots \wedge (i_l \notin appear(f_j))$	**unit stride**
$trip_l$	**otherwise**		**no reuse**

loop permutations takes time that is exponential in the number of loops and can be very expensive in practice. It becomes increasingly unappealing when transformations such as strip mining introduce even larger search spaces.

Instead of testing all possible permutations, we show how our cost model allows us to design an algorithm to directly compute a preferred loop permutation.

5.1 Memory Order

The locality evaluating function *LoopCost* does not calculate data reuse on outer loops; however, we can still restructure programs to exploit outer loop reuse. The key insight is that if loop l causes more reuse than loop l' when both are considered as innermost loops, l will also promote more reuse than l' when both loops are placed at the same outer loop position.

LoopCost can thus be considered to be a measure of the reuse carried by a loop. This allows us to select a desired permutation of loops called *memory order* that yields the best estimated data locality. We simply rank each loop l using *LoopCost*, ordering the loops from outermost to innermost $(l_1 \ldots l_n)$ such that $LoopCost(l_{i-1}) \geq LoopCost(l_i)$.

5.1.1 Memory Order Algorithm

The algorithm *MemoryOrder* is defined as follows. It computes *LoopCost* for each loop, sorts the loops in order of decreasing cache line accesses (*i.e.* increasing reuse), and returns this loop permutation.

5.1.2 Example

As an example, recall matrix multiply. We compute memory order with $cls = 4$. The reference groups for matrix multiply put the two references to C(I,J) in the same group on all the loops and A(I,K) and B(K,J) are placed in separate groups. *LoopCost* computes the relative reuse on each of the loops as seen below.

	LoopCost as innermost		
references	J	K	I
C(I, J)	$n * n^2$	$1 * n^2$	$1/4n * n^2$
A(I, K)	$1 * n^2$	$n * n^2$	$1/4n * n^2$
B(K, J)	$n * n^2$	$1/4n * n^2$	$1 * n^2$
totals	$2n^3 + n^2$	$5/4n^3 + n^2$	$1/2n^3 + n^2$

The algorithm *MemoryOrder* uses these costs to compute a preferred loop ordering of (J, K, I), from outermost to innermost. The same result is obtained by previous researchers [AK84, WL91].

5.2 Permuting to Achieve Memory Order

We must now decide whether the desired memory order is legal. If it is not, we must select some legal loop permutation close to memory order. To determine whether a loop permutation is legal is straightforward. We permute the entries in the distance or direction vector for every true, anti, and output dependence to reflect the desired loop permutation. The loop permutation is illegal if and only if the first nonzero entry of some vector is negative, indicating that the execution order of a data dependence has been reversed [AK84, Ban90a, Ban90b, WL90].

In many cases, the loop permutation calculated by *MemoryOrder* is legal and we are finished. However, if the desired memory order is prevented by data dependences, we use a simple heuristic for calculating a legal loop permutation near memory order. The algorithm for determining this organization takes $max(D, n^2)$ time in the worst-case where n is the depth of the nest and D is the number of dependences, a definite improvement over considering all legal permutations, which is exponential in n. The algorithm is guaranteed to find a legal permutation with the desired inner loop, if one exists.

5.2.1 Permutation Algorithm

Given a memory ordering $\{i_{\sigma_1}, i_{\sigma_2}, \ldots, i_{\sigma_n}\}$ of the loops $\{i_1, i_2, \ldots, i_n\}$ where i_{σ_1} has the least reuse and i_{σ_n} has the most, we can test if it is a legal permutation directly by performing the equivalent permutation on the elements of the direction vectors. If the result is a legal set of direction vectors, the loops are permuted accordingly.

Otherwise, we attempt to achieve a "nearby" permutation with the algorithm *NearbyPermutation*. The algorithm builds up a legal permutation in $\mathcal{P}$ by first testing to see if the loop i_{σ_1} is legal in the outermost position. If it is legal, it is added to $\mathcal{P}$ and removed from $\mathcal{L}$. If it is not legal, the next loop in $\mathcal{L}$ is tested. Once a loop l is positioned, the process is repeated starting from the beginning of $\mathcal{L} - \{l\}$ until $\mathcal{L}$ is empty. The following theorem holds for the *NearbyPermutation* algorithm.

Theorem: *If there exists a legal permutation where σ_n is the innermost loop, then NearbyPermutation will find a permutation where σ_n is innermost.*

The proof by contradiction of the theorem proceeds as follows. Given an original set of legal direction vectors, each step of the "for" is guaranteed to find a loop which results in a legal direction vector, otherwise the original was not legal [AK84, Ban90a]. In addition, if any loop σ_1 through σ_{n-1} may be legally positioned prior to σ_n it will be.

This characteristic is important because most data reuse occurs on the innermost loop and is due to spatial reuse, so positioning the inner loop correctly will yield the best data locality.

Figure 4: Algorithm NearbyPermutation

INPUT:

$\mathcal{O}$ $= \{i_1, i_2, \ldots, i_n\}$, the original loop ordering
$\mathcal{DV}$ = set of original legal direction vectors for l_n
$\mathcal{L}$ $= \{i_{\sigma_1}, i_{\sigma_2}, \ldots, i_{\sigma_n}\}$, a permutation of $\mathcal{O}$

OUTPUT:

$\mathcal{P}$ a nearby permutation of $\mathcal{O}$

ALGORITHM:

```
P = ∅ ;  k = 0 ;  m = n
while L ≠ ∅
  for j = 1, m
    l = l_j ∈ L
    if direction vectors for {p_1, ..., p_k, l} are legal
      P = {p_1, ..., p_k, l}
      L = L − {l} ;  k = k + 1 ;  m = m − 1
      break for
    endif
  endfor
endwhile
```

6 Parallelism

In the following two subsections, parallelism is evaluated and exploited. We first present a performance estimator that evaluates the potential benefit of parallelism. A parallel code generation strategy then uses performance estimation and the cost model developed in the previous section with other transformations to combine effective parallelism and memory order, making tradeoffs as necessary.

6.1 Performance Estimation

This section uses performance estimation to quantify the effects of parallelism on execution time. Our performance estimator predicts the cost of parallel and sequential performance using a loop model and a *training set* approach.

The goal of our performance estimator is to assist in code generation for both shared and distributed memory multiprocessors [BFKK92, KMM91]. Modeling the target machines at an architectural level would require calculating an analytical model for each supported architecture. Instead our performance estimator uses a training set to characterize each architecture in a machine-independent fashion. A training set is a group of kernel computations that are compiled, executed and timed on each target machine. They measure the cost of operations such as multiplication, branching, intrinsics, and loop overhead. These costs are then made available to the performance estimator via a table of data. Note, the training sets for the performance estimator only measure access times to data in registers or the closest cache.

Of particular interest is the estimation of parallel loops. Given sufficient parallel granularity, using all available processors results in the best execution time. Estimating the cost in this circumstance may be modeled by determining the following.

$c_s =$ cost of starting parallel execution
$c_f =$ cost of forking and synchronizing a parallel process
$P =$ number of processors
$b =$ number of iterations of the parallel loop
$t(B) =$ cost of the loop body

If the loop bounds are unknown, a guess is used that is based on the declared dimension of the arrays accessed in the loop. With these parameters the performance of a parallel loop with sufficient work may be estimated by:

$$c_s + c_f P + \left\lceil \frac{b}{P} \right\rceil t(B) \ .$$

However, if the amount of work is not sufficient, parallel loop execution is more difficult to model. Instead of an equation, a table is used to indicate the appropriate number of processors for the best performance. The model and the table are generated using a training set.

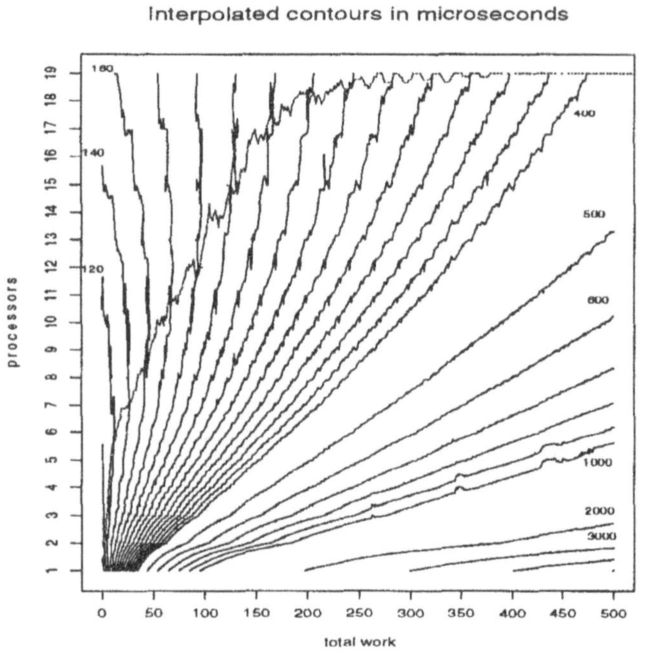

Figure 5: Parallel loop training set

The sample training set for determining parallel loop overhead begins by varying the total amount of work. For each unit of work, the number of processors is varied from 1 to the total available. The number of processors which minimize the execution time of this work is selected. The result of a training run for parallel loops on the Sequent S81 appears in Figure 5.

This particular training run repeatedly performed a single scalar operation that executed for approximately 10 microseconds, which represents one unit of work in Figure 5. Each of the contour lines indicates a particular execution time. The single line cutting across the contour lines represents the minimum execution time for executing a particular work load and the appropriate number of processors. When total work is below 250 a table determines the appropriate number of processors and approximate execution time. Once the total work is over about 250, the parallel loop model is used. The estimator provides a single cost function for evaluating loops that chooses between the techniques based on total work and number of loop iterations.

Estimate(l, *how*) returns $\langle \tau, np \rangle$ where
l is a loop with body B
how indicates whether l may be run in parallel

This function returns a tuple $\langle \tau, np \rangle$ with an estimate τ which is the minimal execution time and the number of processors np necessary to obtain the estimate, based on whether the loop is parallel. Note, if the loop is sequential or it is not profitable to run it in parallel, the sequential running time and $np = 1$ are returned.

6.2 Introducing Parallelism

The key to introducing parallelism is to maintain memory order during parallelization by using strip mining and *loop shifting* (loop shifting moves an inner loop outward across one or more loops). Strip mining performs two functions in parallelization. (1) It preserves cache line reuse in parallel execution. Without strip mining, consecutive iterations may be scheduled on different processors, denying cache line reuse. (2) Because strip mining results in two loops, the parallel iterator loop may be shifted outward to maximize granularity while the sequential strip remains in place providing the data locality introduced using memory order. To illustrate this point, consider the subroutine *dmxpy* from Linpackd written in memory order [DBMS79].

```
DO J = JMIN, N2
    DO I = 1, N1
        Y(I) = Y(I) + X(J) * M(I,J)
```

The J loop is not parallel. The I loop can be parallel. Both contain reuse. A simple parallelization that maximizes granularity would interchange the two loops and make the I loop parallel without strip mining. Unfortunately with this organization, the parallel loop may be scheduled such that consecutive iterations are assigned to different processors causing false sharing of Y and eliminating cache line reuse for consecutive accesses to X and M. In addition, cache lines containing the same array elements would be required at multiple processors, increasing total memory and bus utilization.

We instead strip mine a parallel loop by strip size SS $= \lceil N1/P \rceil$ to provide reuse on the strip and parallelize the resultant iterator. If the parallel loop is outermost, as in matrix multiply, parallelization is complete. If not, we use loop shifting to move the parallel iterator to its outermost legal position, maximizing its granularity. Applying this strategy to *dmxpy*, we begin with the memory ordered loop nest. The I loop is the only parallel loop and it contains reuse. Therefore, it is strip mined. The parallel iterator is not outermost, but it is legally shifted to the outermost position. The compiler shifts the loop, resulting in maximum granularity and data locality as illustrated below.

```
PARALLEL DO I = 1, N1, SS
    DO J = JMIN, N2
        DO II = I, MIN(I + SS - 1, N1)
            Y(II) = Y(II) + X(J) * M(II,J)
```

6.3 Strip Mining Algorithm

If a loop is selected to be performed in parallel, it is strip mined if it contains any reuse. Given sufficient iterations, strip mining exploits data locality and parallelism by using $\lceil N/P \rceil$ as the strip size where N is the number of iterations. Assuming $cls \leq$ P, the iteration space is sufficiently large if P < N. If

$$P < N < cls * P,$$

strip mining by $\lceil N/P \rceil$ is less than the cls and may result in false sharing. However, the granularity of the parallel loop does match P and some reuse will occur. In this case, we still strip mine by $\lceil N/P \rceil$. However, if N < P, strip mining may provide reuse but at the cost of drastically reducing the granularity of parallelism. This

Figure 6: Algorithm Parallelize

INPUT: $\mathcal{L} = \{\sigma_1, \ldots, \sigma_n\}$ a legal permutation

OUTPUT: $\mathcal{T}$ a parallelizing transformation

ALGORITHM:

```
T = ∅
for j = 1, n
  for k = j, n
    if σk legal at position j & parallel
      T = { StripMine(σk),
              shift iterator to j, parallelize it }
      return T
    elseif σk legal at j & σj becomes parallel
      T = {StripMine(σk), shift k iterator to j,
              StripMine(new σj+1),
              parallelize the j+1 iterator }
    endif
  endfor
  if T ≠ ∅ return T
endfor
```

tradeoff is very machine specific. We choose not to strip mine when N < P.

When memory order is computed, the loops are marked to indicate if they contain any reuse. If there is reuse, the strip mining algorithm uses the above equations to select a strip size that maximizes granularity and reuse. If there is no reuse, the strip mining algorithm does not perform strip mining, giving more flexibility to the scheduler.

6.4 Parallelization Algorithm

For memory ordered loop nests that are not parallel on the outermost loop, the *Parallelization* algorithm uses loop shifting to introduce parallelism. It uses loop shifting, rather than a general loop permutation algorithm, in order to minimize the effect of parallelization on data locality. It performs strip mining when the loop contains reuse before shifting for the same reason.

The algorithm for introducing parallelism into memory order appears in Figure 6. It begins by testing whether the outermost loop is parallel. In the first iteration of the "for k" ($j = k = 1$), the first "if" tests if the outermost loop is parallel. Trivially, a shift of loop σ_j to position j is always legal.

If the loop is parallel, it is strip mined and parallelized and the algorithm returns. If the loop is not parallel, a legal shift of an inner loop to position j which is parallel at position j is sought. If a parallel loop is found that can be shifted outermost to j, it is strip mined, parallelized and shifted and the algorithm returns. Otherwise, a shift to position j may cause the next inner loop, *i.e.* the loop originally positioned at j, to be parallel. This situation is determined in the "elseif." Because it is more desirable to parallelize a loop at position j than at $j+1$, all other shifts to position j are considered before this parallelization is returned at the completion of the "for k."

Figure 7: Algorithm Optimizer

INPUT: $\mathcal{L} = \{l_1, \ldots, l_n\}$

OUTPUT: $\mathcal{T}$ an optimization of $\mathcal{L}$

ALGORITHM:

```
O = MemoryOrder(L)
np = Estimate (O, parallel)
if np > 1 (parallelism is profitable)
  T = Parallelize(O)
endif
perform { O, T }
```

In Figure 6 the *Parallelize* algorithm does not detect when strip mining results in a strip size of less than *cls* or strip mining is not performed due to insufficient parallel iterations. As we saw in Section 3 these conditions are unavoidable in some cases and the best possible performance is gained even when they hold. However, we extend *Parallelize* as follows to seek a better parallelization for which neither condition holds.

If *StripMine* returns with a strip size of less than *cls* or does not strip mine due to insufficient parallel iterations, then the number of parallel iterations PI and the size of the strip SS are recorded and the "for k" loop continues instead of returning. If the "for k" finds a parallelization where neither condition holds, it returns. Otherwise, at the completion of the "for k" it selects the parallelization with the largest pair (PI, SS).

7 Optimization Algorithm

The optimization driver for exploiting data reuse and introducing parallelism appears in Figure 7. It combines the component algorithms described in the previous sections and is also $O(n^2)$ time.

It first calls *MemoryOrder* to optimize data locality via loop permutation. It then determines whether the loop contains sufficient computation to pursue parallelism. If it does, the memory ordered loop nest is provided to the algorithm *Parallelize*. If needed, *Parallelize* uses strip mining and loop shifting to introduce loop level parallelism.

The search space in *Parallelize* is constrained to meet our goal of perturbing the memory order as little as possible. If parallelism is not discovered and would be profitable, other optimization strategies that consider all loop permutations, loop skewing [WL90], or loop distribution [McK92] should be explored.

8 Experimental results

We tested the algorithm for optimizing data locality independently and report some of those results here. The overall parallelization strategy was also tested by applying it by hand to several kernels and to the program Erlebacher, provided by Thomas Eidson from ICASE. The results of these experiments are very promising.

8.1 Matrix multiply

We executed all possible loop permutations of matrix multiply for 3 problem sizes, 150×150, 300×300 and 512×512, on a variety of uniprocessors to determine the accuracy of the *MemoryOrder* in predicting the best loop permutations. In Table 1, the permutations are ordered from the most desirable to the least based on the ranking computed by *MemoryOrder*. On all the processors, memory order JKI produced the best results in all but two cases. On all the processors but the Sequent, the entire ranking generally served to accurately predict relative performance. These results illustrate that *LoopCost* is effective in predicting relative reuse on outer loops as well as inner loops.

Table 1: Matrix Multiply (in seconds)

	Loop Permutation					
Processor	JKI	KJI	JIK	IJK	KIJ	IKJ
	150 × 150					
Sequent Weitek	26.0	27.1	31.1	30.7	28.4	26.9
Sun Sparc2	2.33	2.25	3.20	3.16	2.81	2.79
Intel i860	1.16	1.17	1.23	1.18	3.50	3.42
IBM RS6000	0.42	0.46	0.36	0.38	1.08	1.08
	300 × 300					
Sun Sparc2	18.3	17.8	26.1	25.2	24.9	27.1
Intel i860	9.7	10.2	21.7	21.8	59.1	58.9
IBM RS6000	3.37	3.47	12.5	12.5	56.4	56.5
	512 × 512					
Sun Sparc2	91.0	93.6	223	240	277	336
Intel i860	60.2	46.7	143	156	292	292
IBM RS6000	16.7	17.0	183	186	399	399

Interestingly, the disparity in execution times between permutations became greater as the processor speed increased. On the individual processors, execution times varied by significant factors of up to 3.69 on the Sparc2, 6.25 on the i860, and a dramatic 23.89 on the RS6000. These results indicate that data locality *should* be the overwhelming force driving scalar compilers today.

Table 2: Speed-ups for Parallel Matrix Multiply

	speed-up of parallel JKI tiled	
	over sequential JKI	over sequential JKI tiled
	19 processors	
150x150	20.5	18.8
300x300	20.1	18.7
	7 processors	
150x150	7.5	6.8
300x300	7.5	7.0

The speed-ups of a parallel tiled matrix multiply on 7 and 19 processors of a Sequent Symmetry S81 for arrays of size 150×150 and 300×300 are presented in Table 2. We ran a sequential version with the loops in memory order JKI, a sequential tiled version, and the identically tiled parallel version. The parallel version is tiled by 4 and is the same version presented in Section 1.1. Besides tiling, no other low-level memory optimizations were used. The speed-ups were basically linear for both matrix sizes when comparing the two tiled versions.

8.2 Dmxpy

The subroutine *dmxpy* from Linpack was optimized using these algorithms as illustrated in Section 6.2. In scientific programs, there are many instances of this type of doubly-nested loop which iterates over vectors and/or matrices, where only one loop is parallel and it is best ordered at the innermost position. These loops may be an artifact of a vectorizable programming style. They appear frequently in the Perfect benchmarks [CKPK90], the Level 2 BLAS [DCHH88], and the Livermore loops [McM86].

Table 3 illustrates the performance benefits with the organization of *dmxpy* generated by our algorithm on matrices of size 200×200 on 19 processors. For comparison, the performance when the I strip is not returned to its best memory position and a parallel inner I loop were also measured.

Table 3: Dmxpy on 19 processors

	loop organization I loop parallel		
	I J II	I II J	J I
speed-up over sequential JI	16.4	13.8	2.9

8.3 Erlebacher

Erlebacher is a tri-diagonal solver for the calculation of variable derivatives written by Thomas Eidson at ICASE, NASA-Langley. It uses 3 dimensional $64 \times 64 \times 64$ arrays. It contains 1341 lines of Fortran. The *Optimizer* algorithm was performed by hand on the entire program. No low-level memory optimizations were performed. The speed-up from this algorithm on 19 processors was 14.2 for the entire application. The speed-up for the parallel portions of the program was 15.0.

9 Related work

Our work bears the most similarity to research by Wolf and Lam [WL91]. They develop an algorithm that estimates all temporal and spatial reuse for a given loop permutation, including reuse on outer loops. This reuse is represented as a *localized vector space*. Vector spaces representing reuse for individual and multiple references are combined to discover all loops $\mathcal{L}$ carrying some reuse. They then exhaustively evaluate all legal loop permutations where some subset of $\mathcal{L}$ is in the innermost position, and select the one with the best estimated locality.

Wolf and Lam's algorithm for selecting a loop permutation is potentially more precise and powerful than the one presented in this paper. It directly calculates reuse across outer loops and can suggest loop skewing and reversal to achieve reuse; however, how often these transformations are needed is yet to be determined. Skewing in particular is undesirable because it reduces spatial reuse.

Gannon *et al.* also formulate the dependence testing problem to give reuse and volumetric information about array references [GJG88]. This information is then used to tile and interchange the loop nests for cache, after which parallelism is inserted at the outermost possible position. They do not consider how the parallelism affects the volumetric information nor if interchange would improve the granularity of parallelism.

Porterfield presents a formula that approximates the number of cache lines accessed, but is restricted to a cache line size of one and loops with uniform dependences [Por89]. Ferrante *et al.* present a more general formula that approximates the number of cache lines and is applicable across a wider range of loops [FST91]. However, they first compute an estimate for every array reference in a group and then combine them, trying not to do dependence testing. Like Wolf and Lam, they exaustively search for a loop permulation with the lowest estimated cost.

Many algorithms have been proposed in the literature for introducing parallelism into programs. Callahan *et al.* use the metric of minimizing barrier synchronization points via loop distribution, fusion and interchange for introducing parallelism [ACK87, Cal87]. Wolf and Lam [WL90] introduce all possible parallelism via the unimodular transformations: loop interchange, skewing, and reversal. Neither of these techniques try to map the parallelism to a machine, or try take into account data locality, nor is any loop bound information considered. Banerjee also considers introducing parallelism via unimodular transformations, but only for doubly nested loops [Ban90b]. Banerjee does however consider loop bound information.

Because we accept some imprecision, our algorithms are simpler and may be applied to computations that have not been fully characterized in Wolf and Lam's unimodular framework. For instance, we can support imperfectly nested loops, multiple loop nests, and imprecise data dependences. We believe that this approximation is a very reasonable one, especially in view of the fact that we intend to use a scalar cache tiling method as a final step in the code generation process [CCK90]. In addition, the algorithms presented here are $O(n^2)$ time in the worst case, where n is the depth of the loop nest, and are a considerable improvement over work which compares all legal permutations and then picks the best, taking exponential time.

10 Summary and Conclusions

We have addressed the problem of choosing the best loop ordering in a nest of loops for exploiting data locality and for generating parallel code for shared-memory multiprocessors. As our experimental results bear out, the key issue in loop order selection is achieving effective use of the memory hierarchy, especially cache lines. Our approach improves data locality, provides the highest granularity of parallelism, and properly positions loops for low-level memory optimizing transformations. When possible, the benefits of parallelism and data locality are therefore both exploited.

We believe our experimental results provide strong evidence for the effectiveness of this approach. With this method, the programmer is permitted to pay more attention to the correctness of a calculation and less to the explicit loop structure required to achieve high performance.

Acknowledgments

We are especially grateful to Chau-Wen Tseng for his significant contributions to this work. We would like to thank Preston Briggs, Cliff Click, Ervan Darnell, and Nathaniel McIntosh for their many helpful discussions and experiments. We also appreciate the constructive detailed suggestions from one of our reviewers.

This research was supported by the CRPC, the Center for Research on Parallel Computation, a National Science Foundation Science and Technology Center, and by a DARPA/NASA Research Assistantship in Parallel Processing, administered by the Institute for Advanced Computer Studies, University of Maryland. Use of the Sequent Symmetry S81 was provided by the CRPC under NSF Cooperative Agreement # CDA8619893.

References

[ACK87] J. R. Allen, D. Callahan, and K. Kennedy. Automatic decomposition of scientific programs for parallel execution. In *Proceedings of the Fourteenth Annual ACM Symposium on the Principles of Programming Languages*, Munich, Germany, January 1987.

[AK84] J. R. Allen and K. Kennedy. Automatic loop interchange. In *Proceedings of the SIGPLAN '84 Symposium on Compiler Construction*, Montreal, Canada, June 1984.

[AK87] J. R. Allen and K. Kennedy. Automatic translation of Fortran programs to vector form. *ACM Transactions on Programming Languages and Systems*, 9(4):491–542, October 1987.

[AS79] W. Abu-Sufah. *Improving the Performance of Virtual Memory Computers*. PhD thesis, Dept. of Computer Science, University of Illinois at Urbana-Champaign, 1979.

[Ban90a] U. Banerjee. A theory of loop permutations. In D Gelernter, A. Nicolau, and D. Padua, editors, *Languages and Compilers for Parallel Computing*. The MIT Press, 1990.

[Ban90b] U. Banerjee. Unimodular transformations of double loops. In *Proceedings of the Third Workshop on Languages and Compilers for Parallel Computing*, Irvine, CA, August 1990.

[BFKK92] V. Balasundaram, G. Fox, K. Kennedy, and U. Kremer. A static performance estimator in the Fortran D programming system. In J. Saltz and P. Mehrotra, editors, *Languages, Compilers, and Run-Time Environments for Distributed Memory Machines*. North-Holland, Amsterdam, The Netherlands, 1992.

[Cal87] D. Callahan. *A Global Approach to Detection of Parallelism*. PhD thesis, Rice University, March 1987.

[CCK90] D. Callahan, S. Carr, and K. Kennedy. Improving register allocation for subscripted variables. In *Proceedings of the SIGPLAN '90 Conference on Program Language Design and Implementation*, White Plains, NY, June 1990.

[CKPK90] G. Cybenko, L. Kipp, L. Pointer, and D. Kuck. Supercomputer performance evaluation and the Perfect benchmarks. In *Proceedings of the 1990 ACM International Conference on Supercomputing*, Amsterdam, The Netherlands, June 1990.

[DBMS79] J. Dongarra, J. Bunch, C. Moler, and G. Stewart. *LINPACK User's Guide*. SIAM Publications, Philadelphia, PA, 1979.

[DCHH88] J. Dongarra, J. Du Croz, S. Hammarling, and R. Hanson. An extended set of Fortran basic linear algebra subprograms. *ACM Transactions on Mathematical Software*, 14(1):1–17, March 1988.

[FST91] J. Ferrante, V. Sarkar, and W. Thrash. On estimating and enhancing cache effectiveness. In *Proceedings of the Fourth Workshop on Languages and Compilers for Parallel Computing*, Santa Clara, CA, August 1991.

[GJG88] D. Gannon, W. Jalby, and K. Gallivan. Strategies for cache and local memory management by global program transformation. *Journal of Parallel and Distributed Computing*, 5(5):587–616, October 1988.

[IT88] F. Irigoin and R. Triolet. Supernode partitioning. In *Proceedings of the Fifteenth Annual ACM Symposium on the Principles of Programming Languages*, San Diego, CA, January 1988.

[KKP+81] D. Kuck, R. Kuhn, D. Padua, B. Leasure, and M. J. Wolfe. Dependence graphs and compiler optimizations. In *Conference Record of the Eighth Annual ACM Symposium on the Principles of Programming Languages*, Williamsburg, VA, January 1981.

[KMC72] D. Kuck, Y. Muraoka, and S. Chen. On the number of operations simultaneously executable in Fortran-like programs and their resulting speedup. *IEEE Transactions on Computers*, C-21(12):1293–1310, December 1972.

[KMM91] K. Kennedy, N. McIntosh, and K. S. McKinley. Static performance estimation in a parallelizing compiler. Technical Report TR91-174, Dept. of Computer Science, Rice University, December 1991.

[KMT92] K. Kennedy, K. S. McKinley, and C. Tseng. Improving data locality. Technical Report TR92-179, Dept. of Computer Science, Rice University, March 1992.

[Lam74] L. Lamport. The parallel execution of DO loops. *Communications of the ACM*, 17(2):83–93, February 1974.

[LRW91] M. Lam, E. Rothberg, and M. E. Wolf. The cache performance and optimizations of blocked algorithms. In *Proceedings of the Fourth International Conference on Architectural Support for Programming Languages and Operating Systems*, Santa Clara, CA, April 1991.

[McK92] K. S. McKinley. *Automatic and Interactive Parallelization*. PhD thesis, Rice University, April 1992.

[McM86] F. McMahon. The Livermore Fortran Kernels: A computer test of the numerical performance range. Technical Report UCRL-53745, Lawrence Livermore National Laboratory, 1986.

[Por89] A. Porterfield. *Software Methods for Improvement of Cache Performance*. PhD thesis, Rice University, May 1989.

[WB87] M. J. Wolfe and U. Banerjee. Data dependence and its application to parallel processing. *International Journal of Parallel Programming*, 16(2):137–178, April 1987.

[WL90] M. E. Wolf and M. Lam. Maximizing parallelism via loop transformations. In *Proceedings of the Third Workshop on Languages and Compilers for Parallel Computing*, Irvine, CA, August 1990.

[WL91] M. E. Wolf and M. Lam. A data locality optimizing algorithm. In *Proceedings of the SIGPLAN '91 Conference on Program Language Design and Implementation*, Toronto, Canada, June 1991.

[Wol89a] M. J. Wolfe. More iteration space tiling. In *Proceedings of Supercomputing '89*, Reno, NV, November 1989.

[Wol89b] M. J. Wolfe. *Optimizing Supercompilers for Supercomputers*. The MIT Press, Cambridge, MA, 1989.

PYRROS: Static Task Scheduling and Code Generation for Message Passing Multiprocessors

Tao Yang and Apostolos Gerasoulis
Department of Computer Science
Rutgers University
New Brunswick, NJ 08903
Email: tyang or gerasoulis@cs.rutgers.edu

Abstract

We describe a parallel programming tool for scheduling static task graphs and generating the appropriate target code for message passing MIMD architectures. The computational complexity of the system is almost linear to the size of the task graph and preliminary experiments show performance comparable to the "best" hand-written programs.

1 Introduction

In this paper, we consider *static* scheduling and code generation for message passing architectures. There are generally three distinct ways in addressing the programming difficulties for distributed memory architectures.

The first approach considers the problem of automatic parallelization and scheduling from sequential programs. The emphasis has been in the development of compilers or software tools that will assist in programming parallel architectures [2, 16, 18, 19]. Since message passing architectures require coarse grain parallelism to be efficient, one difficulty is the identification of parallelism especially at the procedural level and another is the scheduling and synchronization.

The second approach emphasizes the development of languages with parallel constructs such as KALI [14] and FORTRAN D [13]. Most of those compiler systems have not addressed the scheduling issues.

The third approach uses existing sequential languages, with the addition of communication library functions, to distribute the data and programs, and schedule the execution manually. This approach has been the most successful with respect to utilization of message passing architectures.

As far as we know no automatic parallelization compiler exists that can produce code for message passing machines which is competitive to manually programmed code. This is because of the difficulties in precise dependence analysis and scheduling. However, manually programming is tedious and debugging parallel programs is very hard.

Here, we describe a software system named PYRROS[1] for automatic scheduling and code generation. PYRROS takes as an input parallel program tasks with precedence constraints and produces code for message passing architectures such as nCUBE-2 and INTEL-2.

The paper is organized as follows. Section 2 discusses the macro-dataflow model task graph used to represent parallel computation. Section 3 describes the organization of PYRROS. Section 4 discusses the program and data partitioning for PYRROS along with an example. Section 5 presents a two-step method for scheduling a task graph. Section 6 describes code optimization algorithms for the target code generation. Section 7 presents some preliminary experiments. Section 8 discusses related work.

2 Macro Dataflow Task Graphs

A directed acyclic task graph (DAG) is defined by tuple $G = (V, E, \mathcal{C}, \mathcal{T})$ where V is the set of tasks and $v = |V|$ is the number of tasks, E is the set of communication edges and $e = |E|$ is the number of edges, $\mathcal{C}$ is the set of edge communication costs and $\mathcal{T}$ is the set of task computation costs. The value $c_{i,j} \in \mathcal{C}$ is the communication cost incurred along the edge $e_{i,j} = (n_i, n_j) \in E$, which becomes zero if both tasks n_i and n_j are mapped onto the same processor. The value $\tau_i \in \mathcal{T}$ is the execution time of task $n_i \in V$.

The macro-dataflow model of execution works as follows, e.g. Wu and Gajski [24], Sarkar [22]. The data flow goes through the graph and triggers the execution of tasks. A task receives all data from its predecessors

[1] The name PYRROS comes from PYRRHUS the legendary king of Epirus.

in *parallel*. It then executes without interruption and immediately after completion it sends the data to all successors in *parallel*. We do not allow task *duplication* in separate processors since it results in an increase of the space complexity. This model can overlap communication with computation which is extremely important for message passing architectures.

3 System Organization of PYRROS

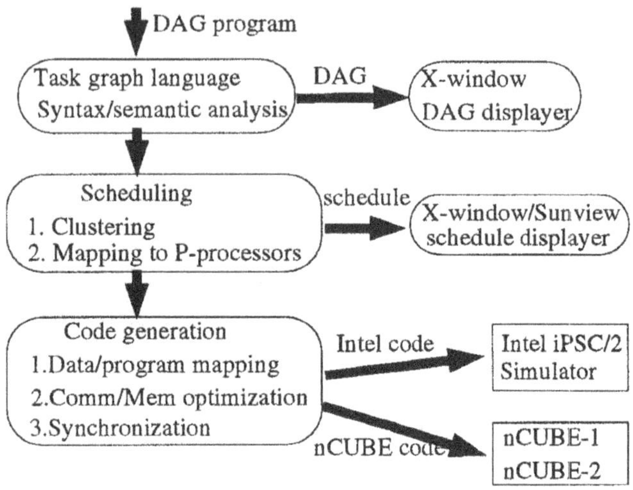

Figure 1: The system organization of PYRROS.

The organization of PYRROS is shown in Figure 1. The current tool has the following components: a task graph language, with an interface to C, allowing users to define partitioned programs and data. A scheduling system for clustering, load balancing and physical mapping, and communication/computation ordering. A graphic displayer for displaying task graphs and scheduling results. A code generator that inserts synchronization primitives and performs code optimization for the INTEL iPSC/2 simulator and the nCUBE-1 and nCUBE-2 hypercube machines.

4 Program and Data Partitioning for PYRROS

Program and data partitionings are given as an input to PYRROS. Let us consider as an example the *kji* form without pivoting of the Gauss-Jordan (GJ) algorithm with interior loop partitioning shown in Figure 2. The task T_k^j defined in Figure 2 uses column k to modify column j of the matrix A. The coarse grain data dependence graph is given in Figure 3. Task T_k^j is a functional task with input data being columns k and j and output data column j. Task T_k^{k+1} is a broadcasting node, sending the same column $k+1$ to all T_{k+1}^j, $j = k+2 : n+1$. The data units are the columns of the matrix on which the tasks operate.

for $k = 1$ **to** n
  for $j = k+1$ **to** $n+1$
    $T_k^j : \{ \quad a_{k,j} = a_{k,j}/a_{k,k}$
      for $i = 1 : n$ **and** $i \neq k$
        $a_{i,j} = a_{i,j} - a_{i,k} * a_{k,j}$
      end$\}$
  end
end

Figure 2: The *kji* form for Gauss-Jordan without pivoting and with interior loop task partitioning.

The communication and computation weights are estimated as follows. We can either symbolically compute the time that it takes to execute and communicate the data for each task or perform an average case estimation, Sarkar [23]. For T_k^j there are about $n\omega$ operations for each task, where ω is the time that it takes for each operation, $a_{i,j} = a_{i,j} - a_{i,k} * a_{k,j}$. For the communication cost we use the linear model $\alpha + n\beta$ time to transfer a vector of size n between two neighbors processors, where α is the start up time and β is the transmission rate. These communication and computation parameters can be found in Dunigan [7]. For example, for the nCUBE-2 hypercube, $\omega = 2.38\mu s$, $\alpha = 160\mu s$ and $\beta = 2.4\mu s$ per word transfer for single precision arithmetic.

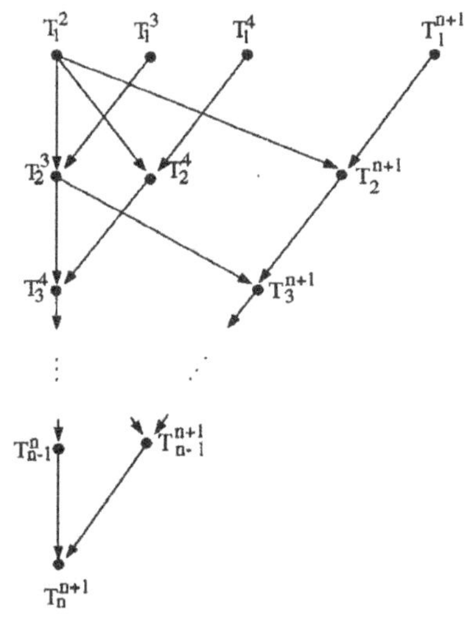

Figure 3: The Gauss-Jordan DAG. The node computation cost is $\tau = n\omega$ and edge communication cost is $c = \alpha + n\beta$.

4.1 Task graph language

The PYRROS system uses a simple language for defining task graphs. The program code in Figure 4 is a description of the GJ DAG shown in Figure 2 and 3. The key words are boldfaced. The semantics of the loop is the same as in Figure 2. The interior loop body contains the data dependence and weight information for a task T_k^j along with the specification of task computation. Task T_k^j has **weight** $n\omega$ and it receives column k and j from T_{k-1}^k and T_{k-1}^j respectively if $k > 1$; otherwise it receives data from the host. The *c_update* is an external C function which defines the task T_k^j. After the *c_update* is executed, then if $k < n$ this task sends column j to T_{k+1}^j and also performs a broadcast to other tasks if $k = j - 1$. When $k = n$, it sends the solution column $k + 1$ to the host.

```
for k=1 to n
  for j = k+1 to n+1
    task T(k,j)
      weight n*w
      receive if(k>1) column[k] T(k-1,k) weight alpha+beta*n
              column[j] T(k-1,j) weight alpha+beta*n
            else
              column[k] host weight alpha+beta*n
              column[j] host weight alpha+beta*n
            endif
      perform c_update(k,j)
      send if (k<n)
            if (k != j-1)
                column[j]      T(k+1,j)      weight alpha+beta*n
            else
              for b = j+1 to n+1
                column[j]      T(k+1,b)      weight alpha+beta*n
              endfor
            endif
          else
            column[k+1] host weight alpha+beta*n
      endif
    endtask
  endfor
endfor
```

Figure 4: PYRROS task specification for the GJ DAG.

PYRROS will read this program and perform lexical and semantics analysis to generate an internal representation of the DAG. Then using the X-window DAG displayer we can verify whether the definition of the task graph is correct.

5 Scheduling in PYRROS

PYRROS uses the two-step method for scheduling:

1. Clustering on an unbounded number of processors of a completely connected architecture.
2. Scheduling the clusters on a fixed number of p processors of the physical architecture.

We have chosen this method for several reasons. First of all it has been shown to be a good approach to scheduling, particularly for coarse grain parallelism, Kim and Browne [15], Sarkar [22], Ortega [17]. Second we can devise low complexity algorithms without affecting performance.

5.1 Clustering

Clustering is defined as a mapping of tasks onto clusters. This is an important part in scheduling, since once tasks are assigned in a cluster they execute in the same processor in the actual architecture. Sarkar [22] was one of the first to recognize the importance of clustering, which he calls internalization pre-pass. A detailed discussion of the clustering problem is in Gerasoulis and Yang [10].

PYRROS uses the Dominant Sequence Algorithm (DSC) to automatically determine the clustering for task graphs. It performs a sequence of clustering refinement steps and at each refinement step, it tries to zero an edge to reduce the parallel time (PT). The parallel time is determined by the longest path in the scheduled graph. We call this path the *Dominant Sequence* (DS).

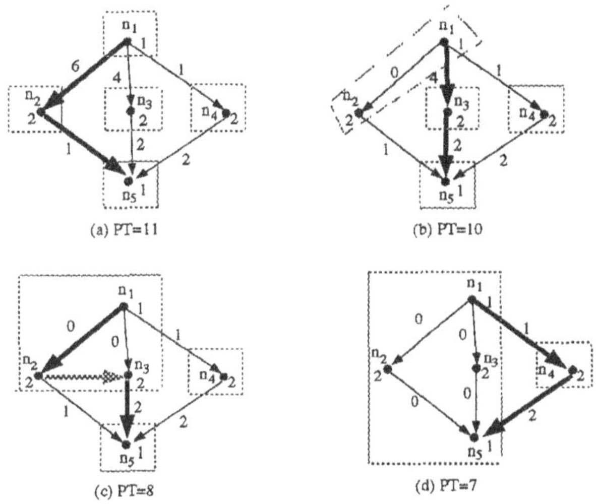

Figure 5: The clustering refinements in DSC.

In Figure 5 (c) three clusters are given, $\{ n_1, n_2, n_3 \}$, $\{ n_4 \}$ and $\{ n_5 \}$. If this clustered graph is scheduled then an execution ordering between the independent tasks n_2 and n_3 must be determined. If we execute n_2 before n_3 then PT is determined by the dominant sequence DS $=< n_1, n_2, n_3, n_5 >$. The DSC algorithm is outlined below:

```
Initially each task is a cluster.
Compute the initial DS. Mark all edges unexamined.
WHILE there is an edge unexamined DO
    Zero an edge in DS if PT does not increase.
    Mark this edge examined.
    Find a new DS.
ENDWHILE
```

For example, Figure 5(a) is the initial clustering. The DS is shown with bold face arrows and PT=11. The first edge in DS is zeroed and PT is reduced to 10, shown Figure 5(b) along with the new DS$=< n_1, n_3, n_5 >$. A zeroing is accepted as long as PT does not increase from the previous step. Thus this zeroing is accepted. Next the edge (n_1, n_3) is zeroed and the new DS=<

$n_1, n_2, n_3, n_5 >$ is shown in Figure 5(c) with PT=8, so this zeroing is also accepted. Since the only unexamined edge in DS is (n_3, n_5) this edge is picked up for zeroing in the next step and the parallel time of the clustering shown in Figure 5(d) is PT=7. In the final step (n_1, n_2) is chosen for zeroing, but this zeroing cannot be accepted since the parallel time increases to PT= 8.

A detailed description of the DSC algorithm is in Yang and Gerasoulis [25]. DSC has been shown to be superior to several other clustering algorithms from the literature in the following sense:

- DSC has an "almost linear" complexity, $O((v + e)\log v))$ time complexity and $O(v + e)$ space complexity. The key idea to keep the complexity low is to find the DS nodes incrementally from one step to the next in $O(\log v)$ time. Most of the algorithms in the literature have complexity higher than $O(v^2)$ which makes them impractical for large task graphs. For the GJ DAG, $v = n^2$ where n is the size of the matrix. Using an $O(v^2)$ algorithm will result in $O(n^4)$ complexity which is higher than the $O(n^3)$ sequential complexity of GJ.

- Experimental results using random graphs and numerical computation DAGs show that DSC outperforms several higher complexity algorithms from the literature [15, 22, 24] in terms of parallel time.

- The general problem of finding the optimum clustering is NP-complete. However there are few classes of task graphs such as join, fork and coarse grain tree for which the optimal solutions are tractable in a polynomial time complexity. DSC is the only general clustering algorithm which finds the optimum for these task graphs. When graph structures become slightly more complicated such as fork/join concatenated graphs and fine grain trees, the time complexity of optimal scheduling jumps to NP-complete, Chretienne [3]. This indicates that DSC has reached a high degree, in terms of parallel time optimality, that a polynomial-time complexity algorithm can attain.

5.2 Scheduling a clustered graph on p processors

Let us assume that the number of clusters is u and the number of available processors is p. We schedule the clusters to p processors in the following three stages:

1. Merge the u clusters into p completely connected virtual processors if $u > p$.
2. Map the p virtual processors into p physical processors.
3. Order the execution of tasks in each processor.

Sarkar [22] has proposed an incremental scheduling method that combines all three stages by performing v iterations. Each iteration of the Sarkar's algorithm selects a task and assigns this task, along with other tasks in the same cluster, to the one of p processors that gives the minimum parallel time increase from the previous iteration. The cost of his algorithm is $O(vp(v + e))$ where $O(v + e)$ comes from the cost in computing the parallel time at each iteration. This complexity is too high for large graphs. Next we describe a low complexity algorithm used in PYRROS.

5.2.1 Cluster merging

PYRROS uses a *work profiling method*, George et. al. [12] for cluster merging. This method is simple, with low complexity and has been shown to work well in practice, e.g. Saad [20], and Ortega [17].

> 1. Compute the arithmetic load LM_j for each cluster.
> 2. Sort the clusters in an increasing order of their loads.
> 3. Use a load balancing algorithm to map u clusters to p virtual processors so that every processor has approximately the same load.

For example, assume there are four clusters as depicted in Figure 6(a) and each task has weight 1. First the clusters are ordered in terms of their loads:

$M_1 = \{T_1^3\}$, $M_2 = \{T_1^4, T_2^4\}$,
$M_3 = \{T_1^5, T_2^5, T_3^5\}$, $M_4 = \{T_1^2, T_2^3, T_3^4, T_4^5\}$.

Then M_1 is merged with M_4, M_2 is merged with M_3 and the arithmetic load is balanced.

5.2.2 Physical mapping

At this stage, we have p virtual processors (or clusters) and p physical processors. Since physical processors are not completely connected, we have to take the processor distance into account. Let $TC_{i,j}$ be the total communication which is the summation of costs of all edges between virtual processor i and j. And Let $CC = \{TC_{i,j} | TC_{i,j} \neq 0\}$ and $m = |CC|$. In general we expect that $m << e$.

The goal of the physical mapping is to determine the physical processor number $P(V_i)$ for each virtual processor V_i that minimizes the following cost function:

$$F(CC) = \sum_{TC_{i,j} \in CC} distance(P(V_i), P(V_j)) \times TC_{i,j}.$$

Figure 6 is a special case of the GJ DAG when $n = 4$. A clustering for this DAG is Figure 6(a) and each cluster corresponds to a virtual processor. Assuming that the edge cost is equal to 3 time units then the total communication between four virtual processors is shown in Figure 6(b).

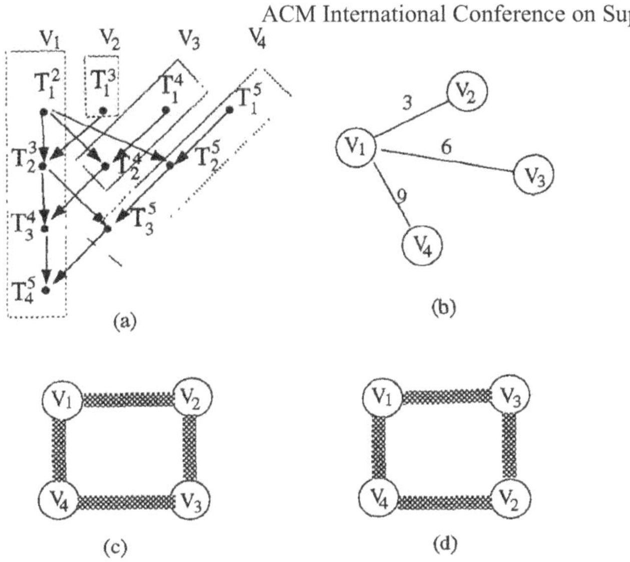

Figure 6: An example of physical mapping. Each nonzero edge cost is 3 time units.

In Figure 6(c) we show one physical mapping to a 4-node hypercube with $F(CC) = 24$ and another mapping is shown in (d) with $F(CC) = 21$.

Determining an optimal physical mapping is very hard. Currently PYRROS uses a heuristic algorithm due to Bokhari [1]. This algorithm starts from an initial assignment, then performs a series of pairwise interchanges so that the $F(CC)$ is reduced monotonically. The complexity is $O(p^3)$.

5.2.3 Task ordering

After the physical mapping has been fixed, the interprocessor communication delay between tasks can be determined. We still need to order the execution of tasks within each processor such that the total parallel time is minimized. Unfortunately, this problem is NP-complete.

PYRROS uses the RCP (ready critical path) algorithm with complexity $O(v \log v + e)$. One major difference between RCP and the classical critical path algorithm is that it maintains a *ready* task list instead of a *free* task list[2]. Our experiments have verified the advantages of the ready list scheduling. A detailed analysis of the task ordering problem is given in Yang and Gerasoulis [26]. The RCP algorithm is outlined below.

[2] A task is free if the predecessors of this task have completed their executions and a task is ready if the data items sent from its predecessors have arrived at the local memory.

1. Adjust the communication edges of the DAG using the information of task processor assignment and processor physical distances.
2. Compute the level priority for each task in the DAG, which is the length of the longest path from it to an exit node, including both computation and nonzero communication costs in that path.
3. Each processor maintains a ready priority list of tasks. The ready task with the highest priority is executed as soon as the processor where this task is assigned becomes available.

Consider an example in Figure 7(a) where six tasks have been assigned to two processors. If the execution ordering is $\{n_4, n_3\}$ on processor 0 and is $\{n_2, n_1, n_5, n_6\}$ on processor 1, then PT is 12 as shown in Figure 7(c). The schedule produced by RCP is shown in Figure 7(b) with PT=7. Task n_4 has level priority 4 and n_3 has level priority 3. At time 1, n_4 and n_3 are both free but not ready on processor 0. At time 2, only n_3 is ready, thus it is scheduled for execution on processor 0. At time 3, n_4 is ready and it is scheduled. If n_4 had been scheduled before n_3 since n_4 was free with higher priority, an idle gap would have been created from time 1 to 3 on processor 0. This is because n_4 could not be executed until time 3.

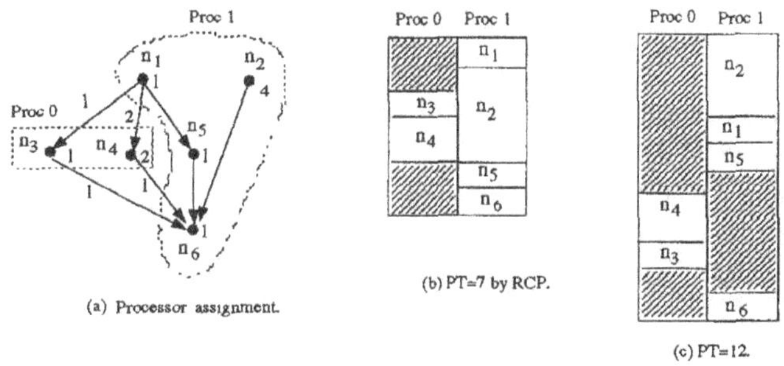

Figure 7: An example of task execution ordering.

6 Code Generation

In order to execute tasks in a target machine, we need to generate the appropriate code based on the previous scheduling result. The complexity of the algorithms described in this section is $O((v + e) \log p)$.

6.1 Machine model

The target machines are MIMD message passing local memory architectures. Each processor has a unique identification and can execute different programs on different data. Data communication and synchronization are implemented by message exchange. The message passing primitives are the following:

- *send(m,i)*
  The message m is sent to processor i. Sending is nonblocking in the sense that this procedure does not have to wait for the receiving processor to get this message.

- *receive(m,i)* and *receive(m)*
  By executing the first procedure a processor will wait until a message from processor i arrives at this processor. It is a blocking receive. For the second "receive" function, a processor will wait until *any* message is received by this processor.

We number processors as $0, 1, 2, \cdots, p-1$. There is a special function *mynode* that returns the processor number where the program resides. There is a special host node, named *host* where the PYRROS host program is executed. The host performs the following functions: (1) allocates the required number of processors, (2) loads node programs, (3) sends the initial data to nodes and (4) collects the final result from nodes.

6.2 Program distribution and data distribution

The scheduling part of PYRROS determines the processor assignment for each task. We define

- $Proc(x)$ – the processor assignment of task x.
- $Tasks(i)$ – the ordered set of tasks executed in processor i.

Using the DAG information, we define the following sets for each task x:

- $InMsg(x)$ – the data items that task x must use to perform a computation. It is expressed by a set of message-to-source pairs:

$$InMsg(x) = \{(t_1, s_1) \cdots (t_k, s_k)\}$$

  where each pair (t_i, s_i) indicates a message t_i sent from processor s_i.

- $Procedure(x)$ – the operational specification of task x.
- $OutMsg(x)$ – the data items produced by x and sent to some successor tasks. It is expressed by a set of message-destination pairs:

$$OutMsg(x) = \{(t_1, s_1) \cdots (t_k, s_k)\}$$

  where each pair (t_i, s_i) indicates a message t_i sent to processor s_i.

We also define

- $fst((t, s)) = t$, the first item of a pair.
- $scnd(t, s)) = s$, the second item of a pair.
- $FirstSet(\{(t_1, s_1), \cdots, (t_k, s_k)\}) = \{t_1, \cdots, t_k\}$, the set composed of the first elements of the message items.

The program distributed to processor i is determined by $Tasks(i)$. The initial data used in processor i is distributed by the host as:

$$InitData(i) = \bigcup_{x \in Tasks(i), m \in InMsg(x)} fst(m) | scnd(m) = host.$$

The data items used in processor i are

$$Data(i) = \bigcup_{x \in Tasks(i), m \in InMsg(x)} fst(m) | scnd(m) \neq i.$$

The final result for processor i to send back to the host is

$$Result(i) = \bigcup_{x \in Tasks(i), m \in OutMsg(x)} fst(m) | scnd(m) = host.$$

Thus the host will collect the following result from the parallel architecture:

$$Result(host) = \bigcup_{0 \le i \le p-1} Result(i).$$

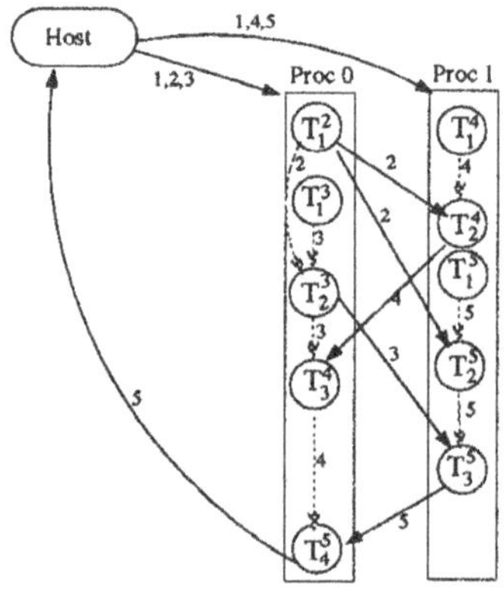

Figure 8: The GJ DAG with $n = 4$ mapped onto 2 processors.

Example: Figure 8 depicts the mapping of GJ DAG of Figure 3 with $n = 4$ onto two processors. Precedence edges are marked with the data items (columns) to be communicated. The dashed arrows within each processor indicate the intra-processor communication. The following table gives examples of $InMsg$ and $OutMsg$ sets:

	$InMsg$	$OutMsg$
T_1^4	$\{(1, host), (4, host)\}$	$\{(4, 1)\}$
T_2^4	$\{(2, 0), (4, 1)\}$	$\{(4, 0)\}$

The following table summarizes the information on data and program distribution for this DAG:

	processor 0	processor 1
$Tasks$	$(T_1^2, T_1^3, T_2^3, T_3^4, T_4^5)$	$(T_1^4, T_2^4, T_1^5, T_2^5, T_3^5)$
$Data$	$\{1, 2, 3, 4, 5\}$	$\{1, 2, 3, 4, 5\}$
$InitData$	$\{1, 2, 3\}$	$\{1, 4, 5\}$
$Result$	$\{5\}$	$\emptyset$

6.3 Program generation

Program generation includes arithmetic computation generation and communication generation. The schedule derived according to the DAG precedence ensures the correctness of the computation ordering. In order to execute each task properly, we need to make sure that each data item referred by this task is available in the local memory of its processor before its execution. After the completion of its computation, each new data item produced by this task should be sent to appropriate processors whose tasks need this data item for further computation.

A naive approach for the program generation for the macro dataflow model is to use the code in Figure 9 for each processor i.

```
FOR each task x in Tasks(i) scanned in the execution
order DO
   FOR each message m in InMsg(x) DO
     IF scnd(m) ≠ i THEN
       allocate some space if necessary and receive this
message.
     ENDIF
   ENDFOR
   Execute procedure(x).
   FOR each message m in OutMsg(x) DO
     IF scnd(m) ≠ i THEN
       send this message to processor scnd(m).
     ENDIF
   ENDFOR
ENDFOR
```

Figure 9: A naive approach to program generation.

There are two problems that we must address to improve the code quality.

- **Communication optimization**

  A task could send the same messages to many tasks in the same processor. Thus we need to eliminate the unnecessary communication operations. Furthermore, one message could be sent to many processors. Using one-to-one message sending repeatedly creates network contention. Thus, a broadcast algorithm is needed that takes advantage of the network topology.

- **Memory utilization improvement**

  Since the size of a local memory is still limited, we need to reuse the memory space. Thus if some data items are no longer used after certain execution point, the space freeing should be performed so that the memory utilization can be improved.

In the next subsection, we discuss how PYRROS addresses the first problem. The memory optimization will not be presented here.

6.4 Communication optimization

6.4.1 Communication procedure selection

The selection of communication procedures depends on the topology of the target machine. Li and Chen [16] have discussed an approach for recognizing some communication patterns such as one-to-all broadcast, uniform-shift, all-to-one-reduce and affine-transform. They have not, however, addressed the optimization and implementation of a specific communication procedure.

Here, we will focus on the selection and optimization of message broadcasting on a *hypercube* architecture. The algorithm for one-to-all spanning tree broadcasting on a hypercube has been developed by Saad and Schultz [21]. This algorithm requires all processors to participate in the message routing, which is not appropriate when many processors do not need this message. Thus, we need a one-to-some multicasting scheme to reduce the number of unnecessary processors involved in message forwarding to alleviate the communication contention.

PYRROS uses a static elimination scheme to reduce the broadcasting range from the entire hypercube to several small subgraphs which sufficiently cover all destinations. The space overhead for storing a subgraph information in a communication packet is $O(1)$. Two types of basic subgraph broadcasting are used:

- *Linear path broadcasting*

  If all nodes belong to a shortest path between the broadcasting node and the farthest receiving node then the message is broadcasted along this linear path. The advantage of this communication is its simplicity. The disadvantage is that there are few instances for which a path covers all destinations.

- *Subcube broadcasting*

  A more complicated broadcasting is to use a spanning tree of a subcube. The advantage is that it can reach scattered nodes in a more efficient manner within a smaller broadcasting scope comparing with the entire hypercube broadcasting. The representation and determination of a subcube will be described below.

PYRROS partitions the destinations into several subsets such that each subset is covered by a path or a subcube. The partitioning method will not be discussed here.

Assume that the source processor is s and the destination processors are $p_1, p_2, \cdots p_k$. One possible linear path for covering these processors can be explored by checking whether a destination p_i is in the path from s to the farthest receiving processor. The nodes in this path can be found by reversing the bits of node binary code numbers from right to left (or from left to right). To determine a subcube where the one-to-some broadcasting is conducted, the following procedure is performed:

> Let
> $$h = EOR(s, p_1, p_2, \cdots, p_k)$$
> where EOR is the bitwise exclusive OR function with $k+1$ arguments, i.e. the i-th bit of h is one if there are different values among the i-th bits of those $k+1$ arguments.
> h is called a ***subcube mask***. The number of non-zero bits in the subcube mask is the subcube dimension.

Example: Figure 10 shows a part of a DAG mapped onto a hypercube of dimension 3. Task n_1 broadcasts a data message to n_2, n_4 and n_5. This communication can be accomplished using subcube broadcasting within the cube composed of processor 000, 001, 011 and 010 where the subcube mask is $h = 011$. The broadcasting from n_2 to n_3, n_6 and n_7 can be implemented as a linear-path communication along processor path 011, 001 and 101.

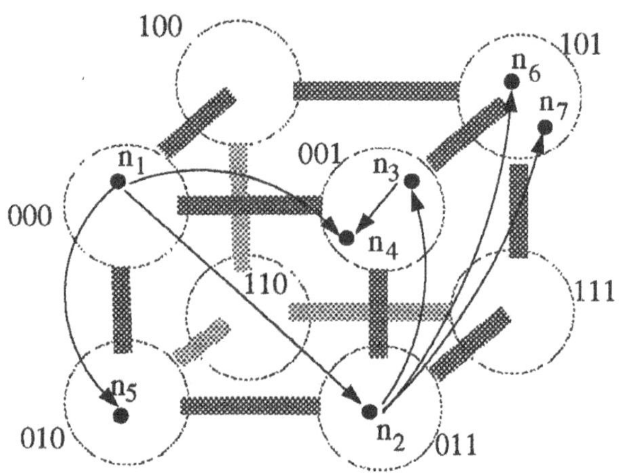

Figure 10: Part of a DAG mapped to a hypercube with 8 nodes.

6.4.2 Redundant communication elimination

The naive approach for generating a program shown in Figure 9 strictly ensures that before the execution of a task, all messages it needs will be received. After the completion of this task, it will send the messages it produces to the tasks that need them. Some redundant communication might be generated by this approach. For instance, in Figure 10 assume that n_2 sends the same message to n_6 and n_7. In the sending site, n_2 only needs to send this message once since n_6 and n_7 are scheduled in the same processor 101. In the receiving site, only one receiving operation is needed to be performed in processor 101. Once a processor receives the same data message, another could get this data item from the local memory. Furthermore, if the redundant receiving is conducted but no message sending corresponds to this receiving, a *deadlock* is created.

Since the communication operation is inserted with respect to each task, it is easy for sending sites to avoid the redundant sending because the produced messages can be sent with respect to the processors that need them instead of tasks. In the receiving site, however, we need to inform the availability of data items in the local memory to the local tasks whose input data items have already been received by a previously executed task.

We will perform a dataflow information computation to determine whether an insertion of receiving operation is necessary before a task execution. Assume that for processor i, the ordered task execution list is $Tasks(i) = (n_1, n_2, \cdots, n_k)$. Define $MsgExist(n_j)$ to be a set of messages that are available in the local memory of processor i before processing task n_j. Then

> $MsgExist(n_1) = \emptyset$
> **FOR** $j = 2$ **TO** k **DO**
> $OutMsg1(n_{j-1}) = FirstSet(OutMsg(n_{j-1})) \odot i.$
> $MsgDef(n_{j-1}) = InMsg(n_{j-1}) \ominus OutMsg1(n_{j-1}) \cup OutMsg1(n_{j-1}).$
> $MsgExist(n_j) = (MsgExist(n_{j-1}) \ominus MsgDef(n_{j-1})) \cup MsgDef(n_{j-1}).$
> **ENDFOR**

where the operator $\ominus$ is defined as:
$X \ominus Y = \{msg \mid msg \in X \wedge fst(msg) \notin FirstSet(Y)\}$
and operator $\odot$ is defined as:
$\{m_1, \cdots, m_k\} \odot s = \{(m_1, s), \cdots, (m_k, s)\}$.

Thus, for each data message in $InMsg(n_j)$, say msg, that message is already in the local memory if $msg \in MsgExist(n_j)$. As a result, a receiving operation can be eliminated.

Example: We show the above dataflow computation for processor 1 in Figure 8:

	$MsgExist$
T_1^4	$\emptyset$
T_2^4	$\{(1, host), (4, 1)\}$
T_1^5	$\{(1, host), (2, 0), (4, 1)\}$
T_2^5	$\{(1, host), (2, 0), (4, 1), (5, 1)\}$
T_3^5	$\{(1, host), (2, 0), (4, 1), (5, 1)\}$

We can eliminate receiving data item 2 from processor 0 for T_2^5 since this item is already in set $MsgExist(T_2^5)$.

6.4.3 Deadlock free communication protocol

Without incorporating the efficient communication procedures, the execution graph is purely acyclic and no deadlock could be caused. But by using specialized communication procedures, each processor not only will execute its tasks but also will be involved in the message routing. As a result, the entire multiprocessor system no longer is executing an acyclic graph. A deadlock could be caused when there is a cycle in message waiting and forwarding.

For example in Figure 10 processor 000 broadcasts a message produced by n_1 to n_4, n_5 and n_2. In order to let n_2 receive this message, processor 001 would have to receive this message from processor 000 and forward this message to processor 011. However, before doing that, processor 001 could be performing the message receiving for n_3 and must wait for the message produced by n_2 at processor 011. This gives rise to a deadlock.

In order to resolve the conflict in message waiting and forwarding, we use an asynchronous communication scheme to allow each processor to receive any arbitrary message that arrives at the message buffer of this processor, to store this message if it is useful and to forward this message if necessary. The routing direction of the message forwarding is recognized according to a communication protocol described below.

For each message, there is a control head indicating the following information: the type of message passing routing, all additional information needed for this routing procedure, the message identification and the message size. The type of message passing could be *one-to-one*, *one-to-all tree broadcasting*, *one-to-some linear path broadcasting*, and *one-to-some subcube broadcasting*. After recognizing that information, a message could be routed accordingly.

For the subcube broadcasting, the following message routing method is then used:

Let *mynode* be the current processor number and m be the received subcube mask.
WHILE $m > 0$ **DO**
Let j be the right most bit of one in the binary code of m.
Forward the message to node $EOR(mynode, 2^{j-1})$ with subcube mask $EOR(m, 2^{j-1})$.
Reset $m = EOR(m, 2^{j-1})$.
ENDWHILE

Example: In Figure 10, task n_1 in processor 000 broadcasts a message in the subcube with mask 011. The routing tree is depicted in Figure 11.

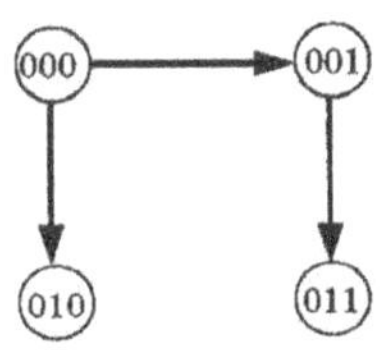

Figure 11: Subcube broadcasting with subcube mask=011.

For linear path broadcasting, the forwarding is terminated if the end point of this linear path is reached otherwise the following routing method is used:

Let s be the starting node in this path, *mynode* be the current node number and j be the leftmost bit of one in the binary code of $EOR(s, mynode)$.
Forward the message to node $EOR(mynode, 2^{j-1})$.

7 Performance Results

We report our experiments on the BLAS-3 GJ algorithm. The LINPACK BLAS-3 based programs are widely used for benchmarking parallel architectures, see Dongarra et. al. [6]. The task graph definition is similar to the one defined for the regular GJ algorithm in Figure 4.

We have also manually written a program that uses natural clustering and wrap mapping along the gray code ring, following the approach by Saad [20]. The sequential time is 1150 seconds for 1000×1000 linear algebraic system on nCUBE-2.

In the following table we compare the performance of automatically-generated code by PYRROS with the hand-written manual program when $n = 1000$. PYRROS first simulates the execution on the host using the nCUBE-2 parameters ($\omega = 2.38\mu s$, $\alpha = 160\mu s$ and $\beta = 2.4\mu s$ per word for single precision arithmetic) and gives a predicted performance. The predicted performance by PYRROS is very close to the real performance in nCUBE-2. Moreover, the performance of the automatically-generated code is comparable with that of our hand-written version. The speedup entry is computed by dividing the sequential time (1150 seconds) by the actual PYRROS code time.

	Pyrros(auto)		Hand	speedup
	predicted	nCUBE		
p=4	299.0	283.4	288.7	4.0
p=8	155.7	150.5	150.4	7.6
p=16	84.5	81.0	81.4	14.1
p=32	50.0	48.7	47.4	24.3
p=64	33.0	31.8	32.8	35.1

8 Related Work

There are several other systems related to PYRROS. PARAFRASE-2 [18] by Polychronopoulos et. al., is a parallelizing compiler system that performs dependence analysis, program partitioning and dynamic scheduling on shared memory machines. SCHEDULER by Dongarra and Sorensen [5] uses centralized dynamic scheduling for the shared memory model of computation. The KALI system by Koelbel and Mehrota [14] addresses parallel code generation and is currently targeted at DOALL parallelism. Kennedy's group [13] is also working on code generation for FORTRAN D on distributed-memory machines. The PARTI system by Saltz's group [4] focuses on irregular dependence graphs determined at run-time and optimizes the performance by precomputing the data accessing pattern. The current FORTRAN D system, KALI and PARTI do not address program scheduling for optimizing the mapping of program and data and the ordering of code execution.

HYPERTOOL by Wu and Gajski [24] uses the same model of computation and produces codes for the hypercube simulator SIMON. TASKGRAPHER by El-Rewini and Lewis [8] schedules task graphs but does not generate codes. The time complexity of the two systems is over $O(v^2)$.

Acknowledgments

Jack Dongarra from University of Tennessee gave us the initial inspiration for PYRROS and Mel Ciment from NSF the initial financial support DMS-8706122 and encouragement to look at parallel computing issues. Partial support has been provided by the Air Force Office of Scientific Research and the Office of Naval research under grant N00014-90-J-4018. We thank Weining Wang for developing the task graph language parser, Milind Deshpande for the X window schedule displayer, and the nCUBE corporation for giving us free time on the nCUBE-2 and also a booth at Supercomputing 91 to demonstrate PYRROS.

References

[1] S.H. Bokhari, *Assignment Problems in Parallel and Distributed Computing*, Kluwer Academic Publisher, 1990.

[2] D. Callahan, K. Kennedy, *Compiling programs for distributed-memory multi-processors,* The Journal of Supercomputing, (2): 151-169, 1988.

[3] Ph. Chretienne, *Task Scheduling over Distributed Memory Machines*, Proc. of the International Workshop on Parallel and Distributed Algorithms, (North Holland, Ed.), 1989.

[4] R. Das, R. Ponnusamy, J. Saltz, and D. Mavriplis, *Distributed Memory Compiler Methods for Irregular Problems: Data Copy Reuse and Runtime Partitioning*, ICASE Report No. 91-73, 1991.

[5] J. J. Dongarra, and D.C. Sorensen, *SCHEDULE: Tools for Developing and Analyzing Parallel Fortran Programs*, in D.B. Gannon, L.H. Jamieson and R.J. Douglass, editors, *The Characteristics of Parallel Algorithms*, pp. 363-394. The MIT Press, Cambridge, Massachusetts, 1987.

[6] J. J. Dongarra, J. Du Croz, I. Duff and S. Hammarling, *A Set of Level 3 Basic Linear Algebra Subprograms*, ACM Trans. on Math. Software, 16(1):1-17, Mar. 1990.

[7] T.H. Dunigan, *Performance of the INTEL iPSC/860 and nCUBE 6400 Hypercube*, ORNL TM-11790, Oak Ridge National Laboratory, Oak Ridge, TN, Nov. 1991.

[8] H.El-Rewini and T.G. Lewis, *Scheduling Parallel Program Tasks onto Arbitrary Target Machines*, J. of parallel and Distributed Computing 9, 138-153(1990).

[9] A. Gerasoulis and T. Yang, *On the Granularity and Clustering of Directed Acyclic Task Graphs*, LCSR-TR-153, Dept. of Computer Science, Rutgers Univ., 1990.

[10] A. Gerasoulis and T. Yang, *A Comparison of Clustering Heuristics for Scheduling DAGs on Multiprocessors*, LCSR-TR-169, Dept. of Computer Science, Rutgers Univ., 1991.

[11] A. Gerasoulis and T. Yang, *Compile-time scheduling and code generation for message-passing architectures*, Report.

[12] A. George, , M.T. Heath, and J. Liu, *Parallel Cholesky Factorization on a Shared Memory Processor*, Lin. Algebra Appl., 77(1986), pp. 165-187.

[13] S. Hiranandani, K. Kennedy and C.W. Tseng, *Compiler Optimizations for Fortran D on MIMD Distributed-Memory Machines*, Supercomputing 91, pp. 86-100.

[14] C. Koelbel and P. Mehrotra, *Compiling global name-space parallel loops for distributed execution*, IEEE Trans. on parallel and Distributed Systems 2(4), 1991.

[15] S.J. Kim and J.C Browne, *A General Approach to Mapping of Parallel Computation upon Multiprocessor Architectures*, Int'l Conf. on Parallel Processing, vol 3, pp. 1-8, 1988.

[16] J. Li and M. Chen, *Compiling Communication-Efficent Programs for Massively Parallel Machines.*, May 1991, accepted in IEEE Trans. on Distributed and Parallel Computing.

[17] J.M. Ortega, *Introduction to Parallel and Vector Solution of Linear Systems*, New York:Plenum, 1988.

[18] C. D. Polychronopoulos, M.B. Girkar, M. R.Haghighat, C.L. Lee, B.P. Leung, and D.A. Schouten, *The Structure of Parafrase-2: an Advanced Parallelizing Compiler for C and Fortran*, in D. Gelernter, A. Nicolau and D. Padua (Eds.), *Languages and Compilers for Parallel Computing*, 1990.

[19] A. Rogers, K. Pingali, *Process Decomposition Through Locality of Reference*, SIGPLAN 1989, pp. 69-80.

[20] Y. Saad, *Gaussian Elimination on Hypercubes*, Parallel Algorithms and Architectures, Cosnard, M. et al. Eds., Elsevier Science Publishers, North-Holland, 1986.

[21] Y. Saad and M. H. Schultz, *Data Communication in Hypercubes*, DCS/RR-428, Research Report, Yale Uiverstiy, 1985.

[22] V. Sarkar, *Partitioning and Scheduling Parallel Programs for Execution on Multiprocessors*, The MIT Press, 1989.

[23] V. Sarkar, *Determining Average Program Execution Times and their Variance*, SIGPLAN 1989, pp. 298-312.

[24] Min-You Wu and D. Gajski, *A Programming Aid for Hypercube Architectures*, The Journal of Supercomputing, vol. 2, pp. 349-372, 1988.

[25] T. Yang and A. Gerasoulis, *A Fast Scheduling Algorithm for DAGs on an Unbounded Number of Processors*, The Proceeding of IEEE Supercomputing 91, pp. 633-642.

[26] T. Yang and A. Gerasoulis, *List Scheduling with and without Communication Delay*, Report.

Array Privatization for Parallel Execution of Loops

Zhiyuan Li*
Department of Computer Science
University of Minnesota
200 Union St. SE, Minneapolis, Minnesota 55455
li@cs.umn.edu

Abstract

In recent experiments, array privatization played a critical role in successful parallelization of several real programs. This paper presents compiler algorithms for the program analysis for this transformation. The paper also addresses issues in the implementation.

1 Introduction

The diversity of parallel architectures makes it difficult to write efficient parallel programs in a machine independent language. For a long time, many researchers have pursued the goal of automatic transformation of sequential programs into parallel machine code. Unfortunately, the result has been unsatisfactory. Many transformation techniques used in existing compilers do not prove to be effective in practice [EB91], mainly because they handle relatively simple cases. On the other hand, recent experiments show significant results by solving more complex cases, using hand-performed new analyses and transformations [EHJ+91], [EHLP91]. A technique called *array privatization*, along with other techniques, improves the performance of all four programs reported in [EHLP91]. Tables 1 and 2 summarize the effect of array privatization on those programs. The fifth column of Table 2 shows the percentage of the sequential execution time (over the whole program) of each loop which is made parallel after array privatization. The percentage indicates the significance of each loop. For every program except OCEAN, no improvement would result without array privatization. We have improved other application programs through array privatization, although we have yet to compile the result data to show the effect. These programs include ADM and SPEC77 in the Perfect program suite [PER89] and WHAMS3D [BT82], a program for structural analysis.

In this paper, we discuss compiler algorithms for automatic *array privatization*. This technique may be viewed as an extension of *scalar privatization* which has been used in parallelizing compilers [ABC+88], [CF87]. We may call both techniques *variable privatization*. If a variable is modified in different iterations of a loop, writing conflicts result when the iterations are executed by multiple processors. Variable privatization removes such conflicts by allocating in each processor a private storage for the offending variable. Parallelism in the program is increased. Data access time may also be reduced, since privatized variables can be allocated to local memories. Of course, the effectiveness of privatization is limited by the memory size.

Table 1. Speedups before and after hand transformations on the Alliant FX/80 (8 vector processors).

Code	Before	After	Array Priv.
MDG	1.1	5.5	Yes
OCEAN	1.42	8.3	Yes
TRACK	0.90	5.1	Yes
TRFD	2.36	13.2	Yes

Table 2. Loops in which arrays are privatized (speedup is over seq. time).

Prog	Loop Label	Routine	Loop Spdup	% of Seq
TRACK	300	nlfilt	5.2	40%
	300	fptrak	6.0	9%
	400	extend	7.0	34%
MDG	1000	interf	6.0	90%
	2000	poteng	5.2	8%
TRFD	100	olda	16.4	69%
	300	olda	12.3	29%
OCEAN	270	ocean	8.0	3%
	480	ocean	6.1	4%
	500	ocean	6.5	3%

Privatization is not always valid. If the value of a

*This work is supported by the Graduate Collage of University of Minnesota.

ICS '92-7/92/D.C., USA
© 1992 ACM 0-89791-485-6/92/0007/0313...$1.50

```
DO j = 1, N
DO i = 3, N
   =  A(i-1)      (r1)
A(i)   =          (w1)
A(i+1) =          (w2)
END DO
END DO
          (a)
```

```
DO j = 1, N
DO i = 3, N
A(i) =            (w1)
   = A(i+1)       (r1)
END DO
END DO
          (b)
```

Figure 1: Examples of SDDs and NSDDs

variable is defined in one iteration and used in another, then the variable cannot be privatized. Privatizable scalars can easily be identified. If any scalar definition reaches the end of the loop body and any use of the same scalar is exposed to the beginning of the loop body, then the definition will certainly reach the use from one iteration to another, which prohibits privatization. However, such a criterion does not apply to array references. In the simple example in Figure 1(a), w_1 and w_2 reach the end of the loop body and r_1 is exposed to the beginning of the loop body. However, r_1 does not read any value generated in previous iterations of the outer loop. Array A, therefore, can be privatized in the outer loop. In contrast, A cannot be privatized in the outer loop in Figure 1(b), because its values are carried from one iteration to another. From the examples, it is clear that new criteria are needed for array privatization.

We organize this paper as follows. In Section 2, we discuss the basic idea and various aspects of array privatization. We also review the related work. In Section 3, we present algorithms to determine array privatizability, which is the key to the technique. In Section 4, we present an algorithm for live array analysis which is used to determine whether *copy-out* is necessary. We summarize in Section 5.

2 Overview and Related Work

Two types of writing conflicts may exist between different iterations of a loop. The first type involves a single definition which overwrites the same array elements in different iterations. The second type involves two different definitions. Privatization is suitable for the first type, while *renaming* is suitable for the second. In Figure 1(a), the writing conflicts between w_1 and w_2 can be removed by renaming, i.e., by letting w_2 write to a new array. This paper covers privatization only.

The problem of privatization may be divided into three issues. The first is the privatizability of an array in a loop. The second is the need to *copy out* the last defined values. The third is the storage allocation for privatized arrays. We describe these issues separately in the following.

2.1 Array privatizability

First, we define the object of privatization.

Definition If a definition of a variable overwrites the same array element(s) in different iterations of a loop L, we call this definition a *self dependent definition* (SDD) in loop L.

In Figure 1(a), both w_1 and w_2 are SDDs in the outer loop, because in every iteration, w_1 writes the same elements, A(3:N), and w_2 writes the same elements, A(4:N+1). However, w_1 and w_2 are not SDDs in the inner loop, because they write different elements in different iterations. Similarly, in Figure 1(b), w_1 is an SDD in the outer loop, but not in the inner loop. SDDs can be recognized by the well-understood analysis of *output dependences* [Ban88].

Definition An SDD w is *privatizable* in loop L *iff* the value generated by w is not used across the iterations of L.

In Figure 1(a), both w_1 and w_2 are privatizable in the outer loop. In Figure 1(b), w_1 is not privatizable. These facts will be explained as our discussion proceeds.

In a DO loop, we can divide the definitions of an array into three categories: the non-self dependent definitions (NSDDs), privatizable definitions, and nonprivatizable definitions. We privatize an array in a DO loop only if the following criteria are both met.

Criterion A The SDDs of the array are all privatizable in the loop.

Criterion B The SDDs do not overlap the NSDDs in the loop. [1]

Breaking the two criteria would make the compiler analysis substantially more complicated. To break Criterion A, the compiler may privatize the privatizable definitions while leave others unchanged. However, the compiler will have to identify which definitions are privatizable and which are not. To break Criterion B, the compiler must be able to handle the situation in which both a privatizable definition and an NSDD may reach an array use. If either of the criteria is broken, the compiler has to analyze array reaching definitions fully and exactly, which is extremely time-consuming. On the other hand, it seems unlikely in practice that a better performance could result by breaking the two criteria. In the experiment reported in [EHLP91], the privatized arrays meet both the above criteria.

To check whether an array A meets Criterion B in a DO loop, we intersect the set of the A elements defined by SDDs and the set of the A elements defined by NSDDs. This is a typical data dependence test problem

[1] They may overlap in an outer loop.

and has been studied extensively [Ban88]. Hence, we need to examine Criterion A only.

Once the privatizable arrays are identified, the compiler can prune the data dependence graph. All *loop carried* dependences whose sources are SDDs can be eliminated. Of course, other transformations such as scalar privatization can also contribute to the graph pruning. Based on the new dependence graph, the compiler decides which loops should be executed in parallel. Variables are privatized in parallel loops only.

2.2 The copy-out issue

If any self dependent definitions (SDDs) in a loop reach the array uses outside the loop, then the last values written by the SDDs must be copied out. When a processor executes a particular iteration, it needs to determine which array elements should be copied out. Figure 2 shows simple examples. In each example, A is privatizable in the outer loop according to Criteria A and B. Copy-out is necessary in (a), but is unnecessary in (b) because the SDDs are *killed* in the following loop by an assignment to A(k). For program TRFD (cf. Table 2), two privatized arrays are copied out from each of the two listed loops. For other programs in Table 2, copy-out is unnecessary either because the privatized arrays are not referenced outside the loops, or because the definitions are killed before reaching any uses.

Definition The *last defining iteration* (LDI) of an array element is the iteration in which the element is last defined in the loop.

IF statements in a loop tend to make it unclear which iteration is the last defining iteration for a particular arary element. In this case, a processor cannot determine independently, i.e. without communicating with others, whether the current iteration is the LDI. We say that, in this case, the LDI is *independently undeterminable.* The LDIs in Figures 2(a) and 2(b) are independently, and easily, determinable. For every A element, the LDI is $i = N$. LDIs of the privatized arrays in program TRFD (cf. Table 2) are also independently, and easily, determinable. In Figure 2(c), however, the LDIs are independently undeterminable. In this case, we do not privatize the array. In our experience so far, the LDIs are independently determinable whenever we need to copy out. However, it is unclear whether this is generally true in practice.

To summarize, we handle the copy-out issue as follows. First, the compiler performs a fast *live array* analysis to see whether the SDDs in a loop reach any outside use. If no SDDs of array A reach any outside use, then no copy-out is necessary for A and we mark A as a *candidate* for privatization. Otherwise, we examine whether the LDIs are independently undeterminable. If they are, we do not privatize A. If they are not, then we mark A as a candidate for privatization. The copy-out code will be described in the next subsection. The algorithms for the live array analysis will be briefly discussed in Section 4. Reference [Li92] discusses algorithms for determining LDIs.

```
DO i = 1, N
DO j = 1, M
A(j)  =
   =  A(j)
END DO
END DO

DO k = 2, M-1
   =  A(k)
END DO
```
(a)

```
DO i = 1, N
DO j = 1, M
   A(j)  =
      =  A(j)
END DO
END DO

DO k = 1, M
A(k)   =
   = A(k)
END DO
```
(b)

```
DO i = 1, N
DO j = 1, N
  IF () THEN
  A(j) =
     = A(j)
  END IF
END DO
END DO
```
(c)

Figure 2: Copy-out and LDIs

2.3 Storage allocation

The storages are allocated as follows. For each parallel loop, the compiler checks to see whether it immediately contains any self dependent definitions (SDDs) of a candidate for privatization. If it does, then in each processor that participates in executing the loop, the compiler allocates a private storage for each of such candidates. This materializes the array privatization. (The storage will be reclaimed as soon as the loop is completed.) Note that sometimes the SDDs in a loop modify a part of an array only. In these cases, it suffices to allocate a private storage just for that part of the array.

In all programs listed in Table 2, the privatized arrays are privatizable at one loop level only. Given a *perfect nest* of loops that have no intervening statements between the loop headers or the loop ends, it always suffices to privatize the array in the innermost loop in which the array is privatizable. However, if a loop nest is imperfect and an array is privatizable in more than one loop, then the array should be privatized in more than one loop. It is clear that a privatizable SDD should write into the private storage allocated to the innermost enclosing loop in which the array is privatized. We call this loop *the home loop* or simply the *home* of the SDD. If the array of an SDD is not privatized in any enclosing loop, then the SDD should write into the storage for the original array. In this case, we say the *home* of the SDD is the whole scope of the original array, say, a subroutine. For an array definition which is not an SDD in any loop, the home is also the scope of the original array. The hierarchy among the homes for the same array can be represented by a tree whose root is the scope of the original array. In the programs in Table 2, all privatized SDDs have one home only Nonetheless, in program SPEC77 in the Perfect code suite [PER89], some SDDs have two homes, one of which being the scope of the original array.

For each array use, the compiler must determine the storage from which it reads. This depends on which array elements are used. The compiler locates the nearest home that satisfies the following: (1) the home contains the array use; and (2) the used element is defined by SDDs in that home. In other words, the used element should not be ***upward exposed*** (defined in Section 3) in the home.

Copy-out, when necessary, is performed as follows. When a processor executes a loop iteration, it checks to see whether the iteration is the last defining iteration of some privatized array elements that must be copied out. The processor writes these elements into the storage allocated to the home, H, at the next upper level. If H is a DO loop and there exist statements outside H which use the copied elements, then the processor which executes the last iteration of H is responsible for copying the elements all the way up to the parent of H. This process continues until all statements that use the copied elements are served. Copy-out in such "relay" style simplifies the analysis of reaching definitions. In our experience so far, e.g. in program TRFD (Table 2), only one step of copy-out is necessary.

We use examples (Figure 3) to show the code before and after array privatization. To make them easy to understand, we present the examples in a self-evident pseudo parallel language. The keyword `DOALL` indicates a parallel loop and the keyword `private` indicates the new name for a privatized array. In example (a), the inner loop is the only home loop. The array use reads most elements generated within the loop. But it also reads an element from outside the loops. Here, we simply copy in that element A(1). In example (b), there are two home loops. An array element is copied from one home to the other.

Implementation of the mechanism described in this subsection is quite straightforward. Therefore, we do not provide algorithms here to formalize the mechanism. Analysis of array privatizability, on the other hand, is essential but not straightforward. Hence, we present its algorithms in Section 3.

2.4 Related work

Literature on data dependence analysis abounds and is well-known. Data dependence analysis, in the commonly understood terms, are concerned about intersection of array regions, which does not support array privatization. Nonetheless, we have shown that the results in data dependence analysis are useful for identification of self dependent definitions and for verification of Criterion B. Our work has been inspired by recent related work. Feautrier studies the technique of *array expansion* [Fea88]. His method expands arrays to higher dimensions to allow a program transformed into a single assignment form. He considers programs which have DO loops, assignment statements and conditional assignment statements. Gross and Steenkiste devise a dataflow analysis on arrays [GS90]. Their algorithm examines whether a definition reaches a use in the same loop iteration and whether it reaches the end of the loop body.

Our work focuses on the information required to determine array privatizability. The essential information is whether an array reference can possibly read a value from previous iterations, suppose the loop is executed in sequential. This information is not provided by either the traditional data dependence analysis or recent related works. To make it more general, we consider arbitrary flow graphs including cases in which a DO loop has multiple exits. Interestingly, in our scheme, if

```
A(1)   =                 A(1)  =
DO i = 1, N              DOALL i = 1, N
DO j = 1, N              DOALL j = 1, N
DO k = 2, N                private A1(1:N)
A(k)   =                 A1(1) = A(1)
   =  A(k-1)             DO k = 2, N
END DO                   A1(k) =
END DO                          = A1(k-1)
END DO                   END DO
                         END DOALL
                         END DOALL
```

(a)

```
DO i = 1, N              DOALL i = 1, N
DO j = 1, N                private A1(1:N)
DO k = 1, N              DOALL j = 1, N
A(k)   =                   private A2(1:N)
   =  A(k)               DO k = 1, N
END DO                   A2(k) =
END DO                          = A2(k)
                         END DO
                         IF(j=N) THEN
                         A1(1) = A2(1)        copy-out
                         END DOALL
DO h = 2, N              DO h = 2, N
A(h)   =                 A1(h) =
   =  A(h-1)                =  A1(h-1)
END DO                   END DO
END DO                   END DOALL
```

(b)

Figure 3: Examples of array privatization

a program's flow graph is reducible, we do not need to propagate information over any cycles.

3 Determination of Array Privatizability

3.1 An assumption on IF conditions

Most data flow analyses are insensitive to the exact content of an IF condition. Unfortunately, for subroutine INTERF of MDG and the main program of OCEAN (cf. Table 2), array privatizability cannot be recognized without considering the exact contents of IF conditions. In the case of MDG, the conditions are in the form of "if (LOC < 1 or LOC+NW-1 > MEMSIZE or NW < 1)", which involves scalars only. In the case of OCEAN, the conditions are in the form of "if (RS(k) > CUT2)", which involves arrays as well. Compiler mechanisms that deal with scalar relations do exist [LT88], [TIF86]. But mechanisms dealing with arrays are yet to be devised. Nonetheless, to separate two different issues, we do not examine the contents of IF conditions in this paper. As a result, we must make the assumption that one branch decision will not affect another.

The above assumption makes our computation of the *upward exposed* array elements (defined below) conservative. It also implies that nonprivatizable definitions exist in loop L if and only if an array element is defined by self dependent definitions (SDDs) in one iteration and is upward exposed in a later iteration, which is a conservative statement.

3.2 Upward exposed array elements

Definition If an array element is always defined before used in iteration i, we say the element is *covered* in iteration i. Otherwise, we say the element is *upward exposed* in iteration i.

In order to determine whether nonprivatizable definitions exist, we introduce the following notations. Consider a nest of DO loops, L_1, L_2, ..., L_n, where L_1 is the outermost, L_2 is nested in L_1, and so on. Suppose the loop index variables are I_1, I_2, ..., I_n, respectively. (Without loss of generality, we assume index steps of 1.) We represent an iteration of L_d, $1 \le d \le n$, by an index vector $\langle i_1, i_2, \ldots, i_d\rangle$ such that $I_1 = i_1$, $I_2 = i_2$, and $I_d = i_d$. For a given array A, let $UE_{\langle i_1,i_2,\ldots,i_d\rangle}$ denote the set of all upward exposed elements in iteration $\langle i_1, i_2, \ldots, i_d\rangle$ and let $D_{\langle i_1,i_2,\ldots,i_d\rangle}$ denote the set of all elements which *may* be written in $\langle i_1, i_2, \ldots, i_d\rangle$ by SDDs. The following formalizes our condition for the existence of nonprivatizable definitions.

Claim 1 *Loop L_d has nonprivatizable definitions of A iff. for some iteration $\langle i_1, i_2, \ldots, i_d\rangle$, the intersection of $UE_{\langle i_1,i_2,\ldots,i_d\rangle}$ and $\bigcup_{l_d \le k \le i_d - 1} D_{\langle i_1,i_2,\ldots,k\rangle}$ is nonempty, where l_d is the lower bound of L_d and $i_d > l_d$.*

Consider the outer loops in Figure 1. In (a), A(2) is the upward exposed element in every iteration, but A(2) is not defined in any iterations, because $D_{\langle j\rangle}$ is A(3:N+1). Therefore, the definitions of A are privatizable in (a). In (b), $D_{\langle j\rangle}$ is A(3:N). A(4:N) are both upward exposed and defined in every iteration. Therefore, w_1 is not privatizable.

The *cover set* defined below is instrumental in computing the set of upward exposed elements. Suppose statement S is nested in L_1, L_2, ..., L_n. Let S_{α} denote the instance of S in iteration $\alpha = \langle i_1, i_2, \ldots, i_n\rangle$ and $S_{\langle i_1,i_2,\ldots,i_d\rangle}$ denote *all* instances of S in iteration $\langle i_1, i_2, \ldots, i_d\rangle$. We may also write $S_{\langle i_1,i_2,\ldots,i_d\rangle}$ as $S_{\alpha|_d}$, where $\alpha|_d$ stands for the first d elements of α.

Definition For array A, the *cover set* of S_{α} *at loop level d* is the set of the A elements that are guaranteed to be defined *within* iteration $\alpha|_d$ before the execution of S_{α}. $C^S_{\alpha}|_d$ denotes this cover set.

Take the examples in Figure 1, where we suppose S is the statement that issues r_1 and α stands for $\langle j, i\rangle$. In (a) and (b), the cover set of S_{α} at loop level 1 is A(3:i). Note that a cover set, like other types of sets in this paper, often has loop index variables as its parameters. If we assign different values to the index variables, we obtain different sets of array elements. Set representation is briefly discussed in [Li92].

Let U^S_{α} denote the array elements used by S_{α}. In iteration $\alpha|_d$, the set of the upward exposed elements used by S_{α} are clearly $U^S_{\alpha} - C^S_{\alpha}|_d$. The set of the upward exposed elements used by all instances of S in iteration $\langle i_1, i_2, \ldots, i_d\rangle$ is the union of $U^S_{\alpha} - C^S_{\alpha}|_d$ over all α such that $\alpha|_d = \langle i_1, i_2, \ldots, i_d\rangle$. Finally, as claimed below, we can determine the set of the upward exposed elements in iteration $\langle i_1, i_2, \ldots, i_d\rangle$.

Claim 2 *$UE_{\langle i_1,i_2,\ldots,i_d\rangle}$ equals to the union of $U^S_{\alpha} - C^S_{\alpha}|_d$ over all α such that $\alpha|_d = \langle i_1, i_2, \ldots, i_d\rangle$ and over all S that make use of array A in loop L_d.*

We illustrate this claim through Figure 1. Let S be the statement which issues r_1 and let α be $\langle j, i\rangle$.

(a) $U^S_{\alpha}|_1$ is A(i-1). $U^S_{\alpha} - C^S_{\alpha}|_1$ is A(i-1) for $i = 3$ and is empty for other i. Hence, $UE_{\langle j\rangle}$ is A(2).

(b) U^S_{α} is A(i+1). $C^S_{\alpha}|_1$ is A(3:i). Hence, $U^S_{\alpha} - C^S_{\alpha}|_1$ is A(i+1). $UE_{\langle j\rangle}$ is $\{$A(i+1) $\mid 3 \le i \le N\}$ = A(4:N+1).

3.3 Computing the cover sets

In this subsection, we discuss how the control flows affect the cover sets. We first consider DO loops that have no exits due to GOTO.

We build the control flow graphs in a hierarchical fashion. Consider again the DO loops $L_1, L_2, \ldots, L_n$. We assume that L_d may contain DO loops in addition to L_{d+1}, $d = 1, 2, \ldots, n-1$. For the loop body of L_d, we construct a *condensed* control flow graph, G_d. Each DO loop, including L_{d+1}, that is immediately nested in L_d is represented by a *condensed* node in G_d. We denote the condensed nodes by $L^{(1)}, L^{(2)}, \ldots, L^{(m)}$. The remaining statements in L_d are grouped into basic blocks in the same way as in the conventional control flow graphs. Each basic block is represented by a regular node in G_d. A condensed node is different from an *interval* [All70], [Coc70] in that only an indexed DO loop may be condensed. A loop of any other type is decomposed into basic blocks and is represented by a number of regular nodes.

It is convenient to index the instances of a basic block, B, or a DO loop, $L^{(i)}$, in L_d. Let $B_{\langle i_1, i_2, \ldots, i_d\rangle}$ denote the instances of basic block B in iteration $\langle i_1, i_2, \ldots, i_d\rangle$. [2] Similarly, let $L^{(i)}_{\langle i_1, i_2, \ldots, i_d\rangle}$ denote the instances of DO loop $L^{(i)}$ in iteration $\langle i_1, i_2, \ldots, i_d\rangle$. In the following, unless we state otherwise, we use the symbol P to denote either a basic block or a DO loop $L^{(i)}$.

Definition For a given array A, the *incoming-cover-set* of $P_{\langle i_1, i_2, \ldots, i_d\rangle}$ in G_d, denoted by $C\_IN^P_{\langle i_1, i_2, \ldots, i_d\rangle}$, is the set of the A elements guaranteed to have been defined in iteration $\langle i_1, i_2, \ldots, i_d\rangle$ before P is entered. The *outgoing-cover-set* of $P_{\langle i_1, i_2, \ldots, i_d\rangle}$ in G_d, denoted by $C\_OUT^P_{\langle i_1, i_2, \ldots, i_d\rangle}$, is the set of the A elements guaranteed to have been defined in iteration $\langle i_1, i_2, \ldots, i_d\rangle$ before the exit of P.

Definition The *must-modify* set of $P_{\langle i_1, i_2, \ldots, i_d\rangle}$, denoted by $M^P_{\langle i_1, i_2, \ldots, i_d\rangle}$, is the set of the A elements defined in $P_{\langle i_1, i_2, \ldots, i_d\rangle}$ no matter what control path is taken within $P_{\langle i_1, i_2, \ldots, i_d\rangle}$. Similarly, $M^S_{\langle i_1, i_2, \ldots, i_d\rangle}$ denotes the set of the A elements defined in $S_{\langle i_1, i_2, \ldots, i_d\rangle}$, an instance of statement S.

We now establish the basic flow equations regarding the sets defined above. First of all, we have

Eq1. $C\_OUT^P_{\langle i_1, i_2, \ldots, i_d\rangle} = C\_IN^P_{\langle i_1, i_2, \ldots, i_d\rangle} \cup M^P_{\langle i_1, i_2, \ldots, i_d\rangle}$.

Eq2. Suppose $P_1, P_2, \ldots, P_p$ are the predecessors of P in G_d. $C\_IN^P_{\langle i_1, i_2, \ldots, i_d\rangle}$ equals $\bigcap_{i=1,p} C\_OUT^{P_i}_{\langle i_1, i_2, \ldots, i_d\rangle}$.

Eq3. $C\_IN^T_{\langle i_1, i_2, \ldots, i_d\rangle} = C\_OUT^T_{\langle i_1, i_2, \ldots, i_d\rangle}$ is empty, where T is the starting node in L_d.

[2] In the presence of **while** or **goto** loops, an instance defined as such may repeat at run time. This, however, does not disturb our discussion.

Now, suppose a basic block B contains s statements which modify A elements. We list these statements by their textual order: $S_0, S_1, \ldots, S_s$. By definitions, we have

Eq4. $M^B_{\langle i_1, i_2, \ldots, i_d\rangle} = \bigcup_{i=1,p} M^{S_i}_{\langle i_1, i_2, \ldots, i_d\rangle}$.

Eq5. For any statement S in B which textually precedes S_0, $C^S_{\langle i_1, i_2, \ldots, i_d\rangle}|_d = C^{S_0}_{\langle i_1, i_2, \ldots, i_d\rangle}|_d = C\_IN^B_{\langle i_1, i_2, \ldots, i_d\rangle}$.

Eq6. For any statement S between S_i and S_{i+1}, $0 \le i \le s-1$, $C^S_{\langle i_1, i_2, \ldots, i_d\rangle}|_d = C^{S_{i+1}}_{\langle i_1, i_2, \ldots, i_d\rangle}|_d = C^{S_i}_{\langle i_1, i_2, \ldots, i_d\rangle}|_d \cup M^{S_i}_{\langle i_1, i_2, \ldots, i_d\rangle}$.

Eq7. $C\_OUT^P_{\langle i_1, i_2, \ldots, i_d\rangle} = C^{S_s}_{\langle i_1, i_2, \ldots, i_d\rangle} \cup M^{S_s}_{\langle i_1, i_2, \ldots, i_d\rangle}$.

Eq8. $C\_IN^P_{\langle i_1, i_2, \ldots, i_d\rangle} \subseteq C\_OUT^P_{\langle i_1, i_2, \ldots, i_d\rangle}$.

Under the present assumption that a DO loop has one exit only, we insert a single exit node, X, in L_d. $C\_OUT^X_{\langle i_1, i_2, \ldots, i_d\rangle} = C\_IN^X_{\langle i_1, i_2, \ldots, i_d\rangle}$ is the set of the A elements that must be defined within iteration $\langle i_1, i_2, \ldots, i_d\rangle$.

Definition The *past-modify set* of loop L_d in iteration $\langle i_1, i_2, \ldots, i_d\rangle$, denoted by $\tilde{M}^{L_d}_{\langle i_1, i_2, \ldots, i_d\rangle}$, is the set of A elements defined in the iterations from $\langle i_1, i_2, \ldots, l_d\rangle$ through $\langle i_1, i_2, \ldots, i_d - 1\rangle$. This set is empty if $i_d = l_d$.

Claim 3 *In DO loops $L_1, L_2, \ldots, L_n$, the past-modify sets are determined by the equation*

$$\tilde{M}^{L_d}_{\langle i_1, i_2, \ldots, i_d\rangle} = \bigcup_{l_d \le I_d \le i_d - 1} C\_OUT^{X_d}_{\langle i_1, i_2, \ldots, i_{d-1}, I_d\rangle}. \quad (1)$$

The must-modify sets are determined by the equation

$$M^{L_d}_{\langle i_1, i_2, \ldots, i_{d-1}\rangle} = \bigcup_{l_d \le I_d \le u_d} C\_OUT^{X_d}_{\langle i_1, i_2, \ldots, i_{d-1}, I_d\rangle}, \quad (2)$$

where u_d is the upper bound of L_d. The cover sets of statements are determined by the equation

$$\begin{aligned} C^S_{\alpha}|_d \;=\; & C^S_{\alpha}|_n \cup (C\_IN^{L_{d+1}}_{\langle i_1, i_2, \ldots, i_d\rangle} \cup \tilde{M}^{L_{d+1}}_{\langle i_1, i_2, \ldots, i_{d+1}\rangle}) \\ & \cup (C\_IN^{L_{d+2}}_{\langle i_1, i_2, \ldots, i_{d+1}\rangle} \cup \tilde{M}^{L_{d+2}}_{\langle i_1, i_2, \ldots, i_{d+2}\rangle}) \\ & \cup \ldots \\ & \cup (C\_IN^{L_n}_{\langle i_1, i_2, \ldots, i_{n-1}\rangle} \cup \tilde{M}^{L_n}_{\langle i_1, i_2, \ldots, i_n\rangle}). \end{aligned}$$

If a DO loop L_d has exits due to GOTO, the above equations need modification. First of all, we insert an exit node in G_d for each exit. The exit for the normal termination of L_d is denoted by $X^{(0)}_d$, while the other exits are denoted by $X^{(1)}_d$, $X^{(2)}_d$, and so on. In graph G_{d-1} at the upper level, suppose L_d is represented by a condensed node P. We make a copy of P in G_{d-1} for every GOTO exit in L_d. We draw an edge from each predecessor of P to each copy of P. Suppose an exit jumps to a statement in L_{d-1}. That statement must be the header in a node, Q, in G_{d-1}. We draw an edge from each copy of P to the corresponding target Q. If an exit of L_d jumps outside L_{d-1}, then we treat the corresponding copy of P as an exit node in G_{d-1} and repeat the above process on the new exit node.

For GOTO exits, Claim 3 should be modified as follows. The past-modify set is computed for $X^{(0)}$ only, i.e.

$$\tilde{M}^{L_d}_{\langle i_1,i_2,\ldots,i_d\rangle} = \bigcup_{l_d \le I_d \le i_d - 1} C\_OUT^{X_d^{(0)}}_{\langle i_1,i_2,\ldots,i_{d-1},I_d\rangle}. \quad (3)$$

The must-modify set for the original P (corresponding to the normal exit) is computed in the same way as in Claim 3. Suppose the copies of P are denoted by $P^{(j)}$, $1 \le j \le m$, corresponding to GOTO exits $X_d^{(j)}$. The must-modify set of each copy is computed by

$$M^{P^{(j)}}_{\langle i_1,i_2,\ldots,i_{d-1}\rangle} = C\_OUT^{X_d^{(j)}}_{\langle i_1,i_2,\ldots,i_{d-1},l_d\rangle}. \quad (4)$$

In the above, we assumed conservatively that a GOTO exit may be taken as early as in the first iteration. This may not be true in some cases. However, since our analysis is insensitive to the exact content of an IF condition, the assumption is necessary.

After the above treatment, GOTO exits no longer affect our further discussion except in trivial details. For convenience, we will assume in the rest of the paper that GOTO exits do not exist.

Based on the equations developed so far, we present in Figure 4 the main algorithm for determining the existence of nonprivatizable definitions. A compiler may apply the algorithm to a DO loop at any loop level. The algorithm examines array privatizability for that loop as well as the inner loops (immediately nested or otherwise). We assume that all subroutine calls are in-lined so that no interprocedural propagation is necessary.

3.4 Traversal of the flow graphs

In this subsection, we discuss how to propagate cover sets through the flow graphs. Certain properties of cover sets allow us to simplify the propagation considerably. Most noticeably, we may break cycles in a condensed control flow graph before its traversal.

Definition If $\langle P_2, P_1\rangle$ is an edge in a control flow graph G such that P_1 dominates P_2, $\langle P_2, P_1\rangle$ is called a *back edge* in G [ASU86].

Claim 4 *If P_1 dominates P_2 in a condensed control flow graph G of the body of a DO loop at level d, then $C\_OUT^{P_1}_{\langle i_1,i_2,\ldots,i_d\rangle} \subseteq C\_IN^{P_2}_{\langle i_1,i_2,\ldots,i_d\rangle}$.*

Algorithm 1

Given: (1) DO loop L and all its inner loops (immediately nested or otherwise). Let $\mathcal{L}$ denote the set of these loops. (2) The index variables and the bounds of the outer loops of L, if any.

Output: For each loop in $\mathcal{L}$, an answer to the question whether there exist nonprivatizable definitions of A.

1. Call *Compute-Block-Sets*(L) (Figure 5) which recursively constructs the incoming-cover-sets, the outgoing-cover-sets, the past-modify sets and the must-modify sets in L and the inner loops.
2. **for** each DO loop L' in $\mathcal{L}$, **do**
   (a) **for** each (non-DO) statement S within L', **do**
   Compute the cover set $C^S_{\alpha}|_d$ according to Claim 3, where $\alpha = \langle i_1, i_2, \ldots, i_n\rangle$ is the index vector of the DO loops enclosing S and d is the loop level of L'.
   (b) Compute $UE_{\langle i_1,i_2,\ldots,i_d\rangle}$, the set of the upward exposed A elements in L_d, as prescribed in Claim 2.
   (c) Determine whether nonprivatizable A definitions exist in L_d as prescribed in Claim 1.

Figure 4: The main algorithm

Claim 5 *If $\langle P_2, P_1\rangle$ is a back edge in G, then $C\_IN^{P_1}_{\langle i_1,i_2,\ldots,i_d\rangle}$ remains the same if $\langle P_2, P_1\rangle$ is deleted from G.*

Our traversal algorithm (Figure 6) first prunes G according to Claim 5 and then propagates cover sets through the pruned graph. If G is *reducible* [ASU86], the pruned graph will be acyclic, in which each node needs to be visited only once. If G is irreducible, the traversal algorithm partitions the pruned graph into maximum strong components (MSC) and then visits the MSCs in a topsort order. The nodes in each MSC, Ω, are traversed iteratively. Each node will be visited $\#(\Omega)$ times. For a sparsely connected MSC, many of these visits could be avoided. However, we will not pursue the details.

4 The Live Array Analysis

As mentioned in Section 2, live array analysis is useful in dealing with the copy-out problem. The purpose of the analysis is to determine whether the self dependent definitions (SDDs) in a loop are live outside the loop, i.e. whether they reach any uses outside the loop.

Procedure Compute-Block-Sets(L)

Parameters: L, a DO loop nested in $L_1, L_2, \ldots, L_{d-1}$ whose index variables are $i_1, i_2, \ldots, i_{d-1}$, respectively. The index variable of L is i_d.

1. For each DO loop, L', immediately nested in L, call *Compute-Block-Sets*(L').
2. Construct the condensed control flow graph, G, for the loop body of L.
3. Initialize $C\_IN^T_{\langle i_1,i_2,\ldots,i_d\rangle} = C\_OUT^T_{\langle i_1,i_2,\ldots,i_d\rangle}$ to empty sets, where T is the start node in G.
4. Traverse G according to Algorithm 2 (in the next subsection) and compute $C\_IN^P_{\langle i_1,i_2,\ldots,i_d\rangle}$ and $C\_OUT^P_{\langle i_1,i_2,\ldots,i_d\rangle}$ for every node P in G.
5. Compute the past-modify set $\tilde{M}^L_{\langle i_1,i_2,\ldots,i_d\rangle}$ and the must-modify set $M^L_{\langle i_1,i_2,\ldots,i_{d-1}\rangle}$ according to Claim 3.

Figure 5: Visit loops bottom-up

The merit of such information is twofolds. First, if no SDDs are live, then we are not concerned about the last defining definitions, because no copy-out is necessary. Second, if we can limit the copied-out elements to a minimum, run time overhead will be reduced. However, we want to avoid a full analysis of reaching definitions. Recall that the information we need is quite limited. We only need to know whether SDDs reach *any* outside uses and do not need to identify the reached uses. Moreover, we perform the live array analysis for the privatizable arrays only. We describe one scheme for the live array analysis in this paper. Two other schemes are described in [Li92].

The UEE scheme

Consider privatizable SDDs of array A in loop L_{d+1} at loop level $d+1$. L_{d+1} is represented by a condensed node in G_d, where G_d is the condensed flow graph at the d-th level as defined in Section 3. We use G_0 to denote the condensed control flow graph whose condensed nodes include all outermost DO loops in the program. G_0 is thus the flow graph at the highest level. Let $SM^{L_{d+1}}_{\langle i_1,i_2,\ldots,i_d\rangle}$ denote $\bigcup_{l_d \le k \le u_d} D_{\langle i_1,i_2,\ldots,i_d,k\rangle}$ which is the set of A elements defined by SDDs in L_{d+1}.

In the UEE scheme, we examine the set of the upward exposed elements of any condensed node L in G_d, which is denoted by $UEE^L_{\langle i_1,i_2,\ldots,i_d\rangle}$. The set is determined by the following equation.

$$UEE^L_{\langle i_1,i_2,\ldots,i_d\rangle} = \bigcup_{l_{d+1} \le k \le u_{d+1}} (\tilde{M}^L_{\langle i_1,i_2,\ldots,i_d,k\rangle} \cap UE_{\langle i_1,i_2,\ldots,i_d,k\rangle}) \quad (5)$$

where $\tilde{M}^L_{\langle i_1,i_2,\ldots,i_d,k\rangle}$ is the past-modify set of L as determined in Claim 3, and $UE_{\langle i_1,i_2,\ldots,i_d,k\rangle}$ is the set of the upward exposed elements in the loop body of L, as determined in Claim 2. Note that these sets are already computed before the live array analysis. We also compute $UEE^B_{\langle i_1,i_2,\ldots,i_d\rangle}$, the upward exposed elements in each regular node B in G_d, which is straightforward.

We now compute the UEE set for every node in G_k that is reachable from L_{k+1}, where $0 \le k \le d$. We then intersect the set $SM^{L_{d+1}}_{\langle i_1,i_2,\ldots,i_d\rangle}$, defined above, with each of the UEE sets. If every intersection is empty, then we are sure that no copy-out is necessary. Otherwise, we conservatively assume that copy-out is necessary.

The motivation behind the UEE scheme is a hypothesis that if the SDDs in a DO loop do not reach any outside uses, then the array either disappears outside the loop or the array, as a temporary, is reinitialized in different places. In the latter case, any use of the array outside the loop will likely read a value that is "locally" defined. The scheme is conservative because

Algorithm 2

Given: (1) A DO loop, L, at level d. (2) The condensed flow graph, G, of the loop body. (3) The dominance relations in G.

Output: The incoming-cover-set and the outgoing-cover-set of each node in G.

1. Delete all back edges from G and obtain the *pruned* graph, G'.
2. For each node in G', compute its must-modify set.
3. Find the maximum strong components (MSCs) in G' and construct the *reduced* graph G'', which is acyclic. Each node in G'' represents an MSC in G'.
4. Traverse G'' in a topsort order. **for** each node visited, **do**
   (a) If the node corresponds to a single node P in G', then compute the incoming-cover-set and the outgoing-cover-set of P according to the basic flow equations Eq1 and Eq2.
   (b) If the node corresponds to an MSC, Ω, of several nodes in G', then call procedure *Iterate*(Ω).

Figure 6: The traversal algorithm

Procedure Iterate(Ω)

for each P in Ω, **do** /* initialize the cover sets */

- Suppose P_1, P_2, ..., P_m are the predecessors of P ***outside*** Ω, initialize $C\_IN^P_{(i_1,i_2,..,i_d)}$ to $\bigcap_{j=1,m} C\_OUT^{P_j}_{(i_1,i_2,\ ,i_d)}$.
- If P has no predecessors outside Ω, then initialize $C\_IN^P_{(i_1,i_2,...,i_d)}$ to $\top$, which is the set of *all* A elements.
- Initialize $C\_OUT^P_{(i_1,i_2,...,i_d)}$ to $C\_IN^P_{(i_1,i_2,...,i_d)} \cup M^P_{(i_1,i_2,\ ..,i_d)}$.

for each P in Ω, **do** /* propagate the cover sets */

1. $SnowBall[P] := C\_OUT^P_{(i_1,i_2,\ .\ ,i_d)}$.
2. $Givers := \{P\}$.
3. $Idle := \{$All nodes in Ω but $P\}$.
4. **while** *Idle* is nonempty, **do**
   for each Q in *Givers*, **do**
   (a) $Receivers := \{ R \mid R \in Idle, \langle Q, R\rangle$ is an edge in $\Omega\}$.
   (b) $Idle := Idle - Receivers$.
   (c) **for** each node R in *Receivers*, **do**
   if $C\_IN^R_{(i_1,i_2,\ ,i_d)} \not\supseteq SnowBall[Q]$
   then $C\_IN^R_{(i_1,i_2,\ ,i_d)} := C\_IN^R_{(i_1,i_2,\ ,i_d)} \cap SnowBall[Q]$.
   $SnowBall[R] := C\_OUT^R_{(i_1,i_2,\ ,i_d)} := C\_IN^R_{(i_1,i_2,\ .,i_d)} \cup M^R_{(i_1,i_2,\ ,i_d)}$.
   $Givers := Receivers$.

Figure 7: Traversal of an MSC

even if the intersection of SM and an UEE (of node P) is nonempty, it is possible that the elements in the intersection are killed in every path from L_{d+1} to P.

The UEE scheme works well with the programs in Table 2. In TRACK and MDG, the privatizable arrays are local variables of subroutines. Within each subroutine, there are no references to the privatizable arrays beyond the loop nest. In OCEAN, a privatizable array CWORK is used in all three loops listed in Table 2. CWORK is also passed to a few subroutines called within those loops. However, CWORK is not upward exposed to the outside of any of those loops. The UEE scheme will hence report the definitions of CWORK as dead. Therefore, no copy-out is necessary. In TRFD, two privatizable arrays, XIJ and XRSIQ, are subroutine parameters. The uses of the two arrays outside the subroutines involve array subscripts that have complicated symbolic terms. The difficult subscripts, not the UEE scheme, force a conservative decision to copy out the two privatized arrays.

5 Summary

We have presented compiler algorithms for array privatization, a program transformation technique that is critical in the successful program parallelization in recent experiments. Where appropriate, we also report the behavior in real programs that we have examined. Although the analysis for array privatization is more complicated than commonly known data dependence analysis, the significant performance improvement it brings seems to well justify the additional compile time.

A review of the algorithms in Section 3 yields the following time complexity analysis. The time consumed by the algorithms can be divided into two parts. The first part is spent on constructing the condensed flow graphs and partitioning the graphs into maximum strong components. This part is proportional to the number of basic blocks in the program. The second part is spent on performing symbolic set operations to derive the cover sets and the modify sets. For a program whose flow graph is reducible, the number of such operations is proportional to the number of statements multiplied by the maximum number of loop levels, assuming the number of predecessors of each node in the flow graph is bounded by a small constant. If a program has components whose flow graphs are irreducible, an extremely rare case, then the second part is further multiplied by the maximum number of graph nodes in such components. The time for each symbolic set operation depends on the complexity of array references. Set representations are discussed in [Li92]. Due to lack of space, we do not explore further. In the loops listed in Table 2, array references are quite simple. Set operations are therefore quite simple. However, the compiler does need machineries that can manipulate symbolic expressions in the subscripts. Interprocedural analysis is also often required.

We summarize the practical aspects in array privatization as follows. (1) The UEE algorithm in Section 4 seems adequate for live array analysis in practice. (2) The storage allocation scheme in Section 2 is more than what we need for the programs examined so far, because in practice, we have found privatizable arrays at one loop level only. (3) The last defining iterations are easy to determine in our experience. (4) The flow graphs of the loops encountered are all reducible. Therefore, Procedure Iterate (cf. Figure 7) may be unnecessary. (5) The set computations described in Section 3 seem adequate. Unioning and intersection of the sets do occur over control paths. Further, array definitions and uses may interleave in the statements. Therefore, a simple summary of the references over a whole loop is insufficient. (6) The privatizable arrays range from one-dimensional to three-dimensional, and the array subscripts may be constants or may contain loop indices and other symbolic terms. (7) We do not consider the exact contents of IF conditions here. But in at least two programs, we have found the contents important.

We are currently building an interprocedural analyzer to experiment on aggressive transformations, including array privatization. We adopt a hierarchical approach to dealing with complexity of data flows in large programs. (A similar approach is proposed by Rosen in [Ros77] for scalar analysis.) This approach takes advantage of structures in high level languages, which makes data flow analysis and dependence analysis efficient. Array privatization fits naturally in this approach, because a condensed node is just one example of using structures. The algorithms presented here will be tested in our experimental compiler. Many efficiency vs. precision issues raised in this paper will be explored through experiments.

6 Acknowledgement

The author is grateful to his former compiler group colleagues at CSRD: Rudy Eigenman, Jay Hoeflinger, and Dave Padua. The group performed hand analysis and transformation on several programs, which lead to the cited paper [EHLP91] and eventually motivated the author to pursue the study in this paper. The practical cases cited here constitute only a small part in that tremendous effort. The author takes the sole responsibility for any potential errors in the description of those cases. The author also thanks the reviewers who suggested to include practical cases in this paper.

References

[ABC+88] F. Allen, M. Burke, R. Cytron, J. Ferrante, W. Hsieh, and V. Sarkar. A framework for determining useful parallelism. In *Proc. of the 1988 ACM Int'l Conf. on Supercomputing*, pages 207–215, July 1988.

[All70] F. E. Allen. Control flow analysis. *ACM SIGPLAN Notices*, 5(7):1–19, 1970.

[ASU86] A.V. Aho, R. Sethi, and J.D. Ullman. *Compilers: Principles, Techniques, and Tools*. Addison-Wesley, Reading, Mass., 1986.

[Ban88] U. Banerjee. *Dependence Analysis for Supercomputing*. Kluwer Academic Publishers, New York, 1988.

[BT82] T. Belytschko and C. S. Tsay. Whamse: A program for three-dimensional nonlinear nonlinear structural dynamics. Tech. Rept. No. NP-2250, Dept. of Civil Engin., Northwestern Univ, Evanston, IL, Feb. 1982.

[CF87] R. Cytron and J. Ferrante. What's in a name? or the value of renaming for parallelism detection and storage allocation. In *Proc. of the 1987 Int'l Conf. on Parallel Processing*, pages 19–27, August 1987.

[Coc70] J. Cocke. Global common subexpression elimination. *ACM SIGPLAN Notices*, 5(7):20–24, 1970.

[EB91] R. Eigenmann and W. Blume. An effectiveness study of parallelizing compiler techniques. In *Proc. of the Int'l Conf. on Parallel Processing*, August 1991.

[EHJ+91] R. Eigenmann, J. Hoeflinger, G. Jaxon, Z. Li, and D. Padua. Restructuring fortran programs for cedar. In *Proc. of the 1991 Int'l Conf. on Parallel Processing*, August 1991.

[EHLP91] R. Eigenmann, J. Hoeflinger, Z. Li, and D. Padua. Experience in the automatic parallelization of four perfect-benchmark programs. In *Proc. of the 4-th Workshop on Languages and Compilers for Parallel Computing*. also available as CSRD Tech. Rept No. 1114, Univ. of Illinois at Urbana-Champaign, August 1991.

[Fea88] P Feautrier. Array expansion. In *Proc. of the 1988 ACM Int'l Conf. on Supercomputing*, pages 429–441, July 1988.

[GS90] T. Gross and P Steenkiste. Structured dataflow analysis for arrays and its use in an optimizing compiler. *Software – Practice and Experience*, 20(2):133–155, February 1990.

[Li92] Z. Li. Array privatization: A loop transformation for parallel execution. Tech. Rept. No. 9226, Dept. of Computer Science, Univ. of Minnesota, April 1992.

[LT88] A. Lichnewsky and F. Thomasset. Introducing symbolic problem solving techniques in the dependence testing phases of a vectorizer. In *Proc. of the 1988 Int'l Conf. on Supercomputing*, pages 396–405, July 1988.

[PER89] M. berry et al. the PERFECT club benchmarks: Effective performance evaluation of supercomputers. *International Journal of Supercomputing Applications*, 3(3):5–40, 1989.

[Ros77] B. K. Rosen. High-level data flow analysis. *Communication of the ACM*, 20(10):712–724, 1977.

[TIF86] R. Triolet, F. Irigoin, and P Feautrier. Direct parallelization of CALL statements. In *Proc. of SIGPLAN '86 Symp. Compiler Construction*, pages 176–185, July 1986.

Increasing the Instruction Fetch Rate via Multiple Branch Prediction and a Branch Address Cache

Tse-Yu Yeh, Deborah T. Marr, Yale N. Patt
Department of Electrical Engineering and Computer Science
The University of Michigan
Ann Arbor, Michigan 48109

Abstract

High performance computer implementation today is increasingly directed toward parallelism in the hardware. Superscalar machines, where the hardware can issue more than one instruction each cycle, are being adopted by more implementations. As the trend toward wider issue rates continues, so too must the ability to fetch more instructions each cycle. Although compilers can improve the situation by increasing the size of basic blocks, hardware mechanisms to fetch multiple possibly non-consecutive basic blocks are also needed. Viable mechanisms for fetching multiple non-consecutive basic blocks have not been previously investigated.

We present a mechanism for predicting multiple branches and fetching multiple non-consecutive basic blocks each cycle which is both viable and effective. We measured the effectiveness of the mechanism in terms of the IPC_f, the number of instructions fetched per clock for a machine front-end. For one, two, and three basic blocks, the IPC_f of integer benchmarks went from 3.0 to 4.2 and 4.9, respectively. For floating point benchmarks, the IPC_f went from from 6.6 to 7.1 and 8.9.

1 Introduction

Recent advances in computer architecture have focused on increasing the parallelism of the hardware in order to exploit instruction-level parallelism in the dynamic instruction stream. As these architectures become increasingly parallel, it is important to fetch more and more instructions each cycle. This can be done either by increasing basic block size and fetching the entire block in a single cycle, or by fetching multiple basic blocks per cycle. The optimal solution may be to combine both. The first alternative is being researched and implemented in today's advanced compilers. One approach is to enlarge the basic block into traces [3] or into superblocks [11]. Another approach is to exploit predicate execution to schedule instruction execution along multiple execution paths [4]. The disadvantage of predicate execution is that execution bandwidth is wasted on instructions whose results are discarded, and instruction fetch bandwidth is wasted on instructions which will not be executed.

Here we propose a scheme which allows us to fully utilize the fetch and execution bandwidth with useful instructions from a dynamically predicted path.

There are three essential components to providing the ability to fetch multiple basic blocks each cycle:

- Predicting the branch paths of multiple branches each cycle.
- Generating fetch addresses for multiple and possibly non-consecutive basic blocks each cycle.
- Designing an instruction cache with enough bandwidth to supply a large number of instructions from multiple, possibly non-consecutive basic blocks.

This paper provides an integrated solution for these problems. We introduce a highly accurate branch prediction algorithm capable of making predictions for multiple branches in a single cycle, a branch address cache to provide the addresses of the basic blocks to which the branches direct the instruction flow, and an instruction cache configuration with a suitably high bandwidth. Although hardware intensive, these solutions are not excessively so for the coming generation of processor implementations.

If we can correctly predict two to three branch paths every cycle and if the average basic block size is five instructions, then the average fetch size is 10 to 15 instructions. Many non-numeric applications today have an average basic block size of 5 instructions, and floating point applications tend to be much larger. The ability to fetch multiple basic blocks per cycle coupled with compiler technology to increase basic block size can result in significant performance gains. This paper shows that just providing the ability to fetch multiple instructions without specific compiler optimizations already increases the useful instruction fetch capacity of a machine by 40% and 63% when 2 and 3 basic blocks can be fetched each cycle, respectively, for integer benchmarks. For floating point benchmarks, the improvement is 8% and 35%.

This paper is organized in 6 sections. Section 2 summarizes some related work. Our multiple branch prediction algorithm is based on the Two-level Adaptive Branch Predictor [6, 7, 10]. The Two-level Adaptive

ICS-7/93 Tokyo, Japan
© 1993 ACM 0-89791-600-X/93/0007/0067...$1.50

Branch Predictor achieves an average of 97% accuracy for a single branch prediction. Also, an instruction supply mechanism [9] to do back-to-back branch predictions and supply up to one basic block per instruction cache fetch is briefly reviewed.

Section 3 provides an overview of the multiple basic block supply mechanism. Section 3.1 describes the multiple branch prediction algorithm. Section 3.2 presents the structure and operation of the branch address cache. Section 3.3 discusses the instruction cache design issues. Section 4 describes the simulation model, and the benchmarks used, and Section 5 shows our simulation results. Finally, Section 6 concludes the paper.

2 Related Work

2.1 Two-level Adaptive Branch Predictor

Yeh and Patt [6, 7, 10] introduced several implementations of the Two-level Adaptive Branch Predictor, each with somewhat different cost vs. prediction accuracies. The average prediction accuracy on the SPEC89 benchmarks was shown to be 97 percent. One important result was that each of the different Two-level Adaptive Branch Prediction schemes can achieve the same accuracy by varying its configuration. The following is a brief overview of a few schemes. The interested reader is referred to [6, 7, 10] for more details.

The Two-level Adaptive Branch Predictor uses two structures, a *Branch History Register* (BHR) and a *Pattern History Table* (PHT), as shown in Figure 1. The Branch History Register is used to record the history of taken and not taken branches. For example, if the recent history of the branch behavior is: taken twice, not taken, and taken again, the BHR would contain the *pattern* 1101, where 1 indicates taken, and 0 indicates not taken.

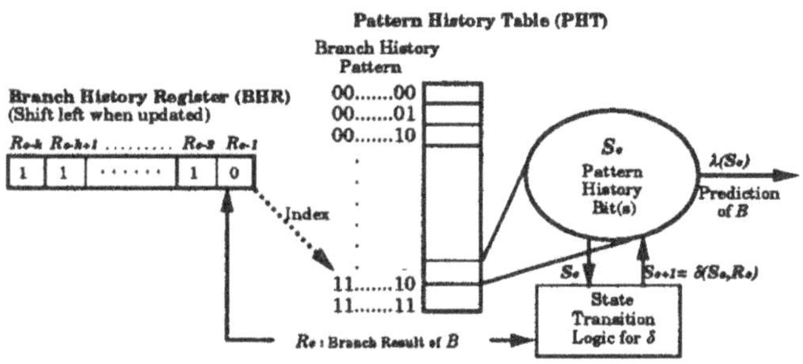

Figure 1: Basic structure of Two-level Adaptive Branch Prediction.

In addition, for each possible pattern in the BHR, a pattern history is recorded in the PHT. If the BHR contains k bits to record the history of the last k branches, then there are 2^k possible patterns in the BHR. Therefore the PHT has 2^k entries, each entry containing a 2-bit up-down saturating counter to record the execution history of the last several times the corresponding pattern occurred in the BHR. [7] showed that the 2-bit up-down saturating counter was sufficient in keeping pattern history to give highly accurate branch predictions. Prediction decision logic interprets the two pattern history bits to make a branch prediction. When the 2-bit up-down saturating counter is used, the prediction is based on the high-order bit of the counter value.

For example, if the BHR were 4 bits wide, the Pattern History Table would have $2^4 = 16$ entries. Suppose that each entry in the Pattern History Table contains 2 bits with initial value of 01, and that the last two times the pattern 1101 showed up the BHR, the branch was taken. Then the 1101_2-th entry of the Pattern History Table will contain 11 and the next prediction when the BHR has the pattern 1101 will be predicted as taken.

Based on the source of the first-level branch history, Two-level Adaptive Branch Prediction has three classes of variations: global history schemes, per-address history schemes, and per-set history schemes. Global history schemes (also called Correlation Branch Prediction [8]) use a single Global BHR to record the history of all branches. The pattern in the Global BHR is used to index into the PHTs. The prediction of a conditional branch is influenced by the history of other branches. Per-address history schemes use one BHR per static branch; therefore, multiple BHRs are used in the scheme. The prediction of a conditional branch is influenced by the history of the branch itself. Per-set history schemes use one BHR to record the history of a set of adjacent static branches. The prediction of a conditional branch is influenced by the history of the branches in the same set, not just the branch itself.

2.2 Instruction Supply

In [9] an instruction supply mechanism was introduced where up to one basic block per cycle can be fetched by predicting branch targets in back-to-back cycles. We summarize a few details of the mechanism in this section, but the interested reader is referred to [9] for more details.

We will use the term *fetch address* to be the address used to fetch a sequence of instructions from the instruction cache. Three things are done at the same time: the instruction cache access, the branch address cache access, and the branch path prediction. The fetch address is used for both the instruction cache access and the branch address cache access from which a fall-through address, target address, and branch type are retrieved.

If the instructions fetched include a branch, those instructions up to and including the branch instruction comprise one basic block. Instructions after the branch are not issued to the processor until the next branch prediction is made.

If the fetch address misses in the branch address cache, then either there is no branch in the sequence of instructions fetched, or the sequence is being fetched for the first time. In either case, the fetch address is incremented by the fetch size, and the hardware continues fetching the next sequential block of instructions. In the event that a branch instruction is discovered after the instructions are decoded, the fall-through address, target address, size, type of branch, and branch path are recorded in the branch address cache.

If the fetch address hits in the branch address cache, then we know that there is a branch somewhere in the sequence of instructions just fetched. Since the information from the branch address cache is available at the same time that the instructions are fetched from the instruction cache, a new fetch address (either the fall-through address or the taken address) can be determined immediately. The next instruction cache and branch address cache accesses begin on the next cycle.

3 Fetching Multiple Basic Blocks Each Cycle

The performance of the mechanism described in [9] and summarized in Section 2.2 limited the fetch capacity to one basic block per cycle. Since only one branch path prediction and only one set of consecutive instructions could be fetched from the instruction cache per cycle, instruction fetch stopped when a branch was encountered. This was due to the limitation of a single prediction per cycle and limitations in the instruction cache configuration.

Fetching multiple basic blocks each cycle requires more a multiple branch prediction algorithm. At the same time that multiple branch paths are being predicted, the addresses of the basic blocks following those branches must be determined. In addition, the instruction cache must be able to supply multiple nonconsecutive blocks of instructions in a single cycle. Our solutions to these issues are:

- The Multiple Branch Two-level Adaptive Branch Predictor which provides highly accurate predictions for multiple branch paths.
- The Branch Address Cache (BAC) which is a hardware structure to provide multiple fetch addresses of the basic blocks following each branch.
- An instruction cache with enough bandwidth to supply a large number of instructions from nonconsecutive basic blocks.

For this paper we will describe the mechanisms for fetching two and three basic blocks each cycle. The mechanisms described can be easily extended to more than three branches, but the hardware cost increases exponentially with each additional basic block.

3.1 The Multiple Branch Two-Level Adaptive Branch Predictor

The prediction algorithm for a single branch per cycle described in Section 2.1 can be extended to two branch predictions per cycle. We will henceforth identify the first branch as the *primary branch*, the second branch as the *secondary branch*, and the third branch as the *tertiary branch*.

The *primary basic block* is the basic block dynamically following the primary branch (i.e. the basic block containing a secondary branch). There are two possibilities for the primary basic block: the target and the fall-through basic blocks of the primary branch. These will be denoted as T or N, depending on whether the primary branch was taken or not taken. The *secondary basic block* is the basic block following the secondary branch. The secondary basic block can be one of up to 4 different blocks depending on the direction of the primary and the secondary branches. These will be denoted TT, TN, NT, or NN, depending on whether the primary and secondary branches were taken-taken, taken-not taken, not taken-taken, or not taken-not taken, respectively. Finally, the *tertiary basic block* is the one following the tertiary branch. The tertiary basic block can be one of 8 different blocks depending on the outcome of the primary, secondary, and tertiary branch paths, and its denotations are TTT, TTN, TNT, etc.

Figure 2 shows the primary and secondary branches and the primary and secondary basic blocks for the case when two predictions are made per cycle. If the darker branch paths are predicted, the darker basic block boxes are fetched.

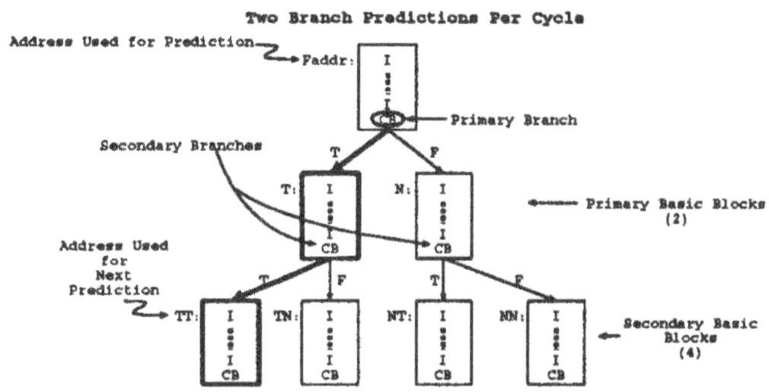

Figure 2: Identification of the primary and secondary branches, and the primary and secondary basic blocks.

The multiple branch prediction algorithm introduced in this paper is modified from the global history schemes of Two-Level Adaptive Branch Prediction described in [10] and summarized in Section 2.1. The modified global history schemes not only make the prediction of the immediately following branch but also extrapolate the predictions of subsequent branches. The per-address history and per-set history schemes of Two-Level Adaptive Branch Prediction, on the other hand, require more complicated BHT accessing logic for making multiple branch predictions in each cycle because they use may different branch history to make predictions for different branches. In order to simplify the BHT design, we consider only the global history schemes in this paper.

The first multiple branch prediction variation is called *Multiple Branch Global Two-Level Adaptive Branch Prediction using a Global Pattern History Table* (MGAg). This scheme uses a global history register of k bits and a global pattern history table of 2^k entries, each entry containing 2 bits. The k bits in the history register record the outcome of the last k branches. The history register is updated speculatively with the predicted branch outcomes and corrected later in the event of an incorrect prediction because the prediction accuracy is expected to be high. The right-most bit corresponds to the prediction of the most recent branch, and the leftmost bit corresponds to the prediction of the oldest branch. As shown in Figure 3, all k bits in the

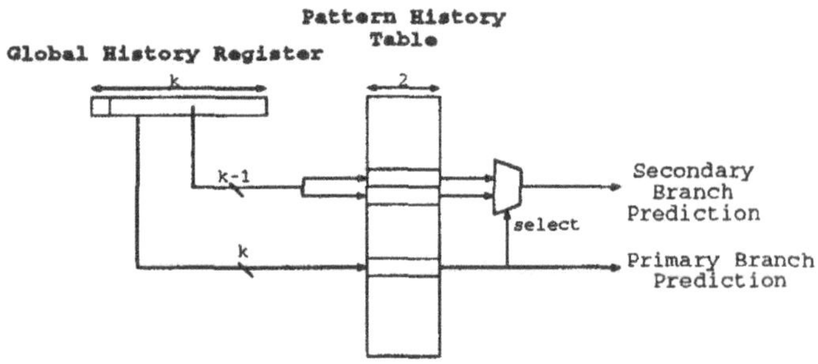

Figure 3: Algorithm to make 2 branch predictions from a single branch history register.

history register are used to index into the pattern history table to make a primary branch prediction. The 2-bit counter value read from the pattern history table entry is used to make the prediction.

To predict the secondary branch, the right-most $k-1$ branch history bits are used to index into the pattern history table. $k-1$ bits address 2 adjacent entries, $BHR_{k-1..0}0$ and $BHR_{k-1..0}1$, in the pattern history table. The primary branch prediction is used to select one of the entries to make the secondary branch prediction. Finally, the tertiary prediction uses the right-most $k-2$ history register bits to address the pattern history table and access 4 adjacent entries. The primary and secondary predictions are used to select one of the 4 entries for the tertiary branch path prediction. This algorithm allows each of the multiple branch path predictions to take full advantage of k bits of branch history. Longer history registers increase the prediction accuracy, and as multiple branches are predicted, the accuracy becomes increasingly important.

The second multiple branch prediction variation is called *Multiple Branch Global Two-Level Adaptive Branch Prediction using Per-set Pattern History Tables* (MGAs). It differs from the previous scheme in that there are multiple pattern history tables. The pattern history tables are associated with the primary branches. Similar to MGAg, all k bits are used to index into a pattern history table to make a prediction for the primary branch. The pattern history table is selected based on the fetch address corresponding to the primary branch. The second prediction is made from the same pattern table since the address of the secondary branch is not known at the time of the prediction. This scheme attempts to limit the amount of pollution in the pattern history tables by different branches, but may result in less accurate secondary and tertiary branch predictions.

The extreme case of the MGAs scheme is when there is a separate pattern history table associated with each branch. This scheme is called *Multiple Branch Global Two-Level Adaptive Branch Prediction using Per-address Pattern History Tables* (MGAp).

The pattern table entries are updated after the branch instructions are resolved, which could take several cycles. Therefore the pattern table entries are always somewhat out-of-date. This is likely to degrade the accuracy of the multiple branch prediction algorithm more than the accuracy of a single branch prediction algorithm. The reason the branch may take several cycles to resolve is that it may have to wait for a condition to be evaluated or an address to be computed which may take several cycles due to data dependencies.

Since the branch predictions are done at the same time the instructions are fetched, the determination of whether there is a branch in a fetch sequence is done through the Branch Address Cache which is described in detail in the next section. If the fetch address hits in the Branch Address Cache, then there is a branch in the sequence being fetched. Otherwise no branch is assumed and the instruction fetch mechanism fetches down the sequential stream.

The branch path predictions made with the Multiple Branch Two-level Adaptive Branch Predictor are done at the same time the Branch Address Cache and instruction cache are accessed. These branch path prediction bits are used to select the fetch addresses that are needed for the next cycle from the possible fetch addresses provided by the Branch Address Cache. For now, we will merely state that if two predictions are made, then two fetch addresses are selected. If three predictions are made, then three fetch addresses are selected.

Multiple predictions might not be made every cycle for several reasons. The first case is when a basic block is very large, so the entire instruction cache bandwidth may be devoted to fetching the basic block. Fetching the primary basic block has higher priority than fetching secondary or tertiary basic blocks. Therefore if we cannot fetch one basic block in its entirety with its instruction cache bandwidth quota, then we allow it to usurp the bandwidth quota from a subsequent block.

If a secondary or tertiary basic block's bandwidth is usurped, the prediction of the branch in that basic block is delayed until the cycle when it is actually being fetched. At that point it becomes the primary branch and a (different) secondary and tertiary branch may be predicted along with it.

The other case when multiple branch path predictions are not made is when the branch is a return instruction. The return instruction's predicted target address is obtained from the return address stack. The next branch is difficult to predict because the return may direct the instruction stream to any number of locations.

3.2 The Branch Address Cache (BAC) Design

With each of the MGAg, MGAs, and MGAp algorithms, we use a Branch Address Cache (BAC) to store the addresses to which the branches may direct the instruction flow. Recall that with the single basic block instruction supply algorithm summarized in Section 2.2 the branch address cache is indexed by the fetch address, from which two potential fetch addresses are obtained (one for the target block and one for the fall-through block). The branch prediction chooses between the two addresses.

The *multiple* basic block supply algorithms use a similar BAC. The fetch address is used to access the BAC. This is done in parallel to the instruction cache access. Although there may be two or three fetch addresses accessing the instruction cache simultaneously, only *a single fetch address is used to accessed the BAC.* If only one basic block is being fetched, that fetch address is used. If two basic blocks are being fetched simultaneously, the second fetch address is used to access the BAC. If three basic blocks are fetched, the third fetch address is used.

If the fetch address hits in the BAC, there is a branch in the sequence of instructions just fetched. The BAC entry records the branch type (conditional, unconditional, or return) and the target and fall-through basic block starting addresses of the primary branch. The same entry also contains the branch type and fetch addresses of basic blocks for each of the expected number of branches we will make predictions for, and all the known potential fetch addresses of their targets. If the number of basic blocks predicted and fetched per cycle is limited to 2, we get 6 fetch addresses; 2 for the two primary basic block addresses, and 4 for the four possible secondary basic blocks. If the basic block prediction and fetch limit is 3, we get 14 possible fetch addresses; 2 for the primary basic blocks, 4 for the secondary, and 8 for the tertiary basic blocks.

Each entry in a 512-entry, 4-way set associative Branch Address Cache which supports two branch predictions per cycle has the following fields: TAG, P_valid, P_type, Taddr, Naddr, ST_valid, ST_type, TTaddr, TNaddr, SN_valid, SN_type, NTaddr, NNaddr where each field contains:

- TAG field — The 23 high-order bits of the primary fetch address. A "BAC Hit" occurs if the tag matches with the upper address bits of the current fetch address and the primary branch is valid.

- valid bits — The valid bits for the corresponding branch entries. P refers to the primary branch, ST refers to the secondary branch if the primary branch is taken, and SN is the secondary branch if the primary branch is not taken.

- type fields — The branch type of the corresponding branch. The type can be conditional, unconditional, or return. Each type field consists of 2 bits.

- addr fields — The address of the corresponding basic block. Each address field consists of 30 bits.

A BAC supporting two branch predictions per cycle would have a total of 212 bits per entry. A BAC supporting three branches would have an additional eight address fields and four additional valid bits for the four possible tertiary branches, making each entry 464 bits wide. We are investigating several possible ways of reducing the number of fields needed per entry, such as storing only the addresses of more likely-taken path(s).

When a fetch address misses in the BAC, a large basic block is assumed and the entire instruction cache bandwidth is devoted to fetching sequential instructions. If a branch is discovered once the instructions are decoded and the branch is predicted taken or is an unconditional branch, the prefetched instructions after the branch are discarded. The address of the fall-through and target addresses are calculated in the cycle after decode. The branch is then allocated a primary branch entry in the BAC. The higher order bits of the fetch address are entered in the tag field, the primary branch valid bit is set, the secondary (and tertiary) branch valid bits are cleared, and primary fall-through and target addresses are entered. If the branch is an indirect branch, however, the target address is not calculated until the operands are ready, and the valid bit is not set until that time.

The branch will also be entered as a secondary branch in the BAC entry of the previous branch if:

- the previous fetch address had a valid primary branch entry in the BAC but did not predict a secondary branch *and*

- the basic block of the previous fetch address was not oversized (i.e. there was enough instruction cache bandwidth for another basic block fetch) *and*

- the previous branch was not a return.

3.3 The Instruction Cache

The ability of the instruction cache to provide enough instructions becomes critical when multiple possibly non-consecutive basic blocks are fetched each cycle. The instruction cache must have high bandwidth, low miss rate, and the ability to fetch from multiple addresses in parallel.

To satisfy the high bandwidth requirement, the cache must either have a large number of banks, or have wide banks. Also, due to off-chip bandwidth and pin limitations, the instruction cache should be on-chip.

The ability to fetch from multiple addresses in parallel implies a cache with either interleaved or multi-ported banks, or both. With interleaved banks, each independently addressable, multiple fetch addresses can access the instruction cache simultaneously provided that their accesses are not to the same bank. If there is a bank conflict, priority is given to the earlier (relative to the dynamic instruction stream) fetch address. Therefore it is important to have enough banks to make the probability of bank conflicts low.

A multi-ported cache eliminates the bank conflict problem. For example, a dual-ported cache allows the simultaneous access of two fetch addresses, and a tri-ported cache allows the simultaneous access of three fetch addresses. Unfortunately, multi-ported memories are expensive in terms of semiconductor chip area.

It is critical for the instruction cache miss rate to be low. Each instruction cache miss stalls the fetch sequence. Since multiple basic blocks can be fetched each cycle, the opportunity cost can be (up to) the number of cycles it takes to service the miss multiplied by the number of instructions we could have fetched during those idle fetch cycles. Also, since more instructions are fetched each cycle, there are fewer cycles between instruction cache misses. Therefore more time is spent waiting for instruction cache misses to be satisfied. Commonly used ways to minimize instruction cache miss rates are to increase the associativity, to increase the size of the cache, and to prefetch instructions.

We chose several cache configurations which gave us reasonably high bandwidth, the ability to fetch multiple addresses in parallel, and a relatively low miss rate. Most of our simulations were done with a 32K cache which was 2-way set associative with 8 interleaved single-ported banks, each bank having a line size of 16 bytes. Each fetch address can access two banks so that we guarantee between 5 and 8 instructions per fetch address (due to basic block alignment). This configuration and several others were compared in Section 5.

4 Simulation Methodology

4.1 Simulation Environment

We used a trace-driven simulator to evaluate the performance of a machine front-end which implements the Multiple Branch Two-level Adaptive Branch Predictor, a 512-entry 4-way set associative Branch Address Cache (BAC), and a high-bandwidth instruction cache. Unless otherwise specified, the instruction cache configuration used was 32K bytes, 2-way set associative, 8-way interleaved, single-ported, and with a line size of 16 bytes (4 instructions).

For the multiple basic block mechanisms, we can fetch two cache lines (a maximum of 8 instructions) per basic block fetch address because most basic blocks contain 4 to 8 instructions. In order to do a fair comparison, we allow the single basic block prediction and fetch algorithm to fetch up to 4 cache lines. The maximum number of instructions issued, passed to the back-end of the machine, is constrained to 16 instructions per cycle.

The benchmarks written in C were compiled with the Motorola Apogee C compiler for the Motorola 88100 instruction set and the ones written in Fortran where compiled with the Green Hill Fortran compiler. A Motorola 88100 instruction level simulator generated the instruction traces. The first 50 million instructions from each trace were used rather than the entire trace due to simulation time constraints.

Nine benchmarks were selected from the SPEC89 benchmark suite. These included 4 integer and 5 floating point benchmarks. The integer benchmarks are *li*, *gcc*, *eqntott*, and *espresso*. The floating point benchmarks are *doduc*, *fpppp*, *matrix300*, *spice2g6*, and *tomcatv*. The figures included in the result section have the abbreviations listed in Table 1 for the various benchmarks. Table 1 also shows the average basic block size of the first 50 million instructions of each benchmark.

The MGAg, MGAs, and MGAp are parameterized according to the history register length and the number of Pattern History Tables. These parameters will be given as: HhPp, where h is the number of bits in the Global History Register, and p is the number of pattern history tables.

4.2 Performance Metric

Since the simulator only models the front end of a machine, we use a new metric, IPC_f, to evaluate the performance of an instruction fetch mechanism. IPC_f stands for the number of effective instructions fetched per cycle by an instruction fetch mechanism. To derive IPC_f, we assume the machine stalls or wastes cycles for various reasons from the instruction fetch mechanism but not from the rest of the machine, so the instructions issued can be executed without stalling the machine front end. Moreover, only effective instructions are counted; instructions fetched down the incorrectly predicted paths are not counted. The machine front end could waste cycles due to the following reasons:

Benchmark	Abbreviation	Average Basic Block Size
eqntott	eq	4.76
espresso	es	3.41
gcc	gc	4.94
li	li	4.14
doduc	dd	10.46
fpppp	fp	57.01
matrix300	mt	28.20
spice2g6	sp	5.36
tomcatv	tc	26.33

Table 1: Benchmark list and their average basic block size.

- Instruction cache misses
- Incorrect branch predictions which include incorrect branch path predictions and incorrect fetch address predictions
- Branch Address Cache misses on taken branches

Since we do not simulate the rest of the machine, the exact mispredicted branch penalty is approximated. A 6 cycle mispredicted branch penalty is assumed; therefore, the instructions following an incorrectly-predicted branch will not be fetched until 6 cycles after the branch is fetched. The I-cache miss penalty is assumed to be 10 cycles. We also show how the machine performance changes as the branch misprediction penalty and I-cache miss penalty are varied.

5 Simulation Results

5.1 Effect on Prediction Accuracy and IPC_f of History Register Length

Figure 4 shows how the prediction accuracy changes as we increase the number of bits in the global history register of the MGAg scheme for two branch predictions per cycle. The prediction accuracy is the number of correctly predicted branches over the total number of branches in the dynamic instruction stream. Longer branch histories give better prediction accuracy which is reflected in the rising curves. The hardware cost goes up exponentially with the number of history bits due to the number of pattern history table (PHT) entries required.

The prediction accuracies varied between 91.5 and 98.4% for a branch history register (BHR) length of 14 bits, and between 93.5 and 98.7% for a history register length of 16 bits. The knees of the curves for most benchmarks are reached at a BHR length of 14-bits.

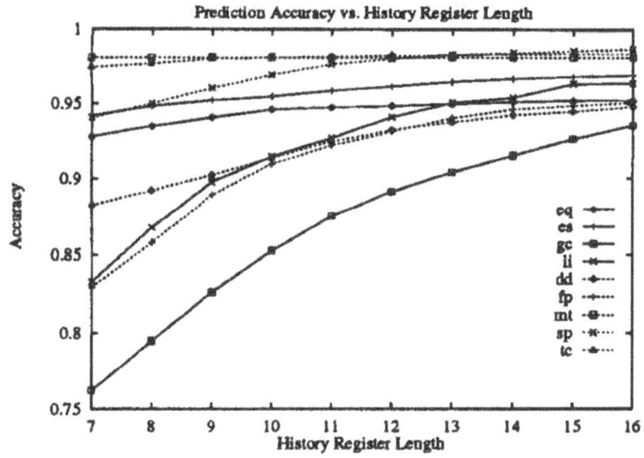

Figure 4: Variation of the size of the global branch history register.

We used a 14-bit BHR length for the other experiments reported in this paper. A 14-bit BHR length means that a PHT has $2^{14} \times 2$ bits, or 32K bits.

5.2 Tradeoff between the Number of Pattern History Tables and History Register Length

We simulated several MGAg, MGAs, and MGAp configurations to determine how the performance accuracy changes with the number of PHTs for two branch predictions per cycle. Figure 5 for integer benchmarks and Figure 6 for floating point benchmarks show the IPC_f for 1 to 512 PHTs. Each configuration shown has the same hardware cost, which was achieved by decreasing the number of entries in each PHT as the number of PHTs is increased. Since the entries in the PHTs are addressed by the BHR, the BHR length is reduced when we decrease the number of entries in each PHT.

The PHT used to make the predictions is determined by the primary branch address. The experiments shown in Figures 5 and 6 used the branch address starting at bit 10 to select a PHT. This allows branches within the same 256-instruction block in the static code to map to the same PHT.

The prediction accuracies shown in Figures 5 and 6 tend to be higher for configurations with one to eight pattern history tables, then decreases when the number of pattern history tables is increased beyond 8. Longer branch history helps to increase the prediction accuracy. Increasing the number of PHTs reduces the interference between branches, but since the second branch is predicted using the PHT of the first branch, the probability of mapping two branches predicted together into different PHTs is higher when more PHTs are used.

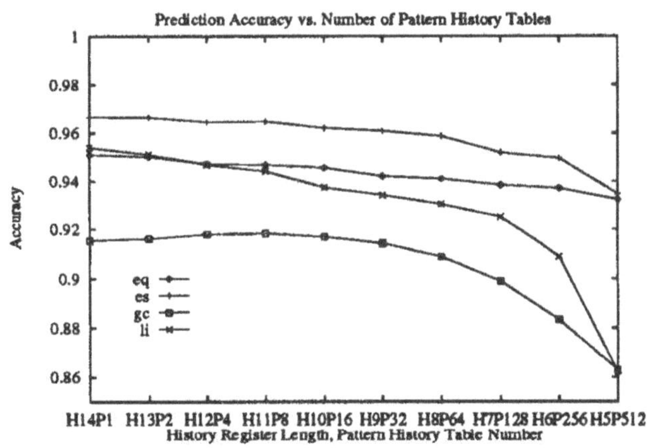

Figure 5: Variation of the number of the PHTs with the hardware cost held constant, for *integer* benchmarks.

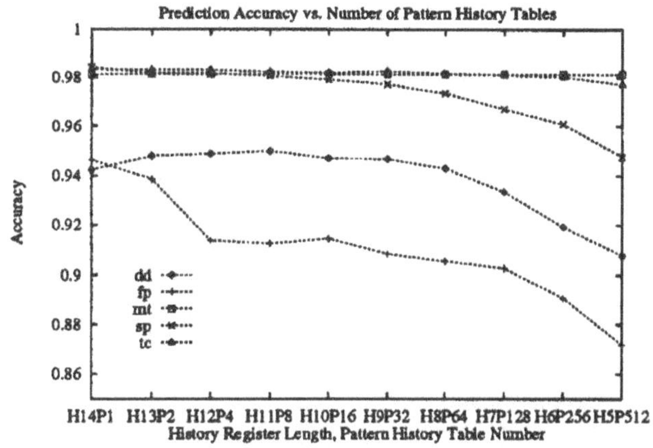

Figure 6: Variation of the number of the PHTs with the hardware cost held constant, for *floating point* benchmarks.

5.3 Number of Branch Predictions per Cycle

Figure 7 shows the IPC_f increase with the number of branch predictions per cycle. The number of opportunities for multiple branch prediction is quite high despite the greater likelihood of bank conflicts in the instruction cache when three basic blocks are fetched.

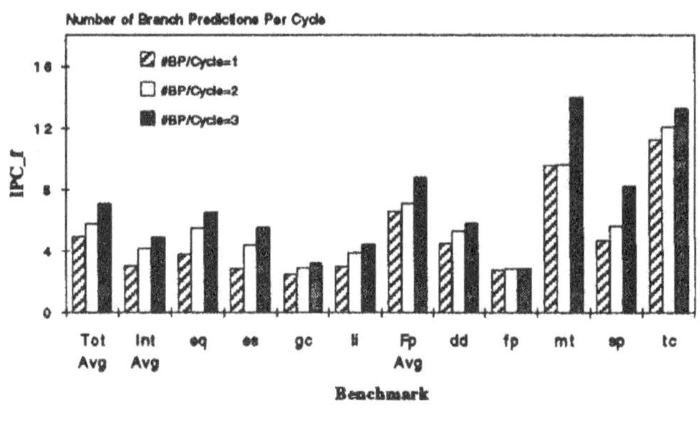

Figure 7: Instructions per cycle when 1, 2, and 3 branches are predicted each cycle.

The average IPC_f when one basic block is predicted and fetched per cycle is 3.0, and 6.6 for integer and floating point benchmarks, respectively. Two predictions per cycle increases this to 4.2 for integer and 7.1 for floating point. Three predictions per cycle increases IPC_f further to 4.9 for integer and 8.9 for floating point.

For the one and two predictions per cycle experiments we allowed a maximum of 16 instructions to be fetched from the instruction cache per cycle. For the three predictions per cycle experiments we increased the instruction cache bandwidth to 24 instruction in order to accommodate the 3 fetch addresses. To cap the number of instructions issued, we constrained the issue width to 16 instructions for all three cases. The larger instruction cache bandwidth allows more instructions to be fetched per cycle, which affects the performance of floating point programs more than integer programs because of the high branch prediction accuracy and large basic block size of floating point benchmarks. This effect results in the significant floating point performance increase when going from two to three predictions per cycle.

fpppp does not show significant performance increase when going from one to two to three predictions per cycle due to the repeated execution of an extremely long sequential code segment which causes the instruction cache to thrash. The instruction cache miss penalty dominates its performance.

Integer programs show noticeable performance increase except for *gcc* which is dominated by incorrect branch predictions.

Figure 8 shows the IPF, instructions per fetch, for the benchmarks as the number of branch predictions and basic block fetches of 1, 2, and 3 per cycle. An efficient instruction fetch mechanism should attain an IPC_f as close to the IPF as possible. The discrepancy between IPF and IPC_f is due to the branch misprediction penalty, BAC misses, and instruction cache miss penalty.

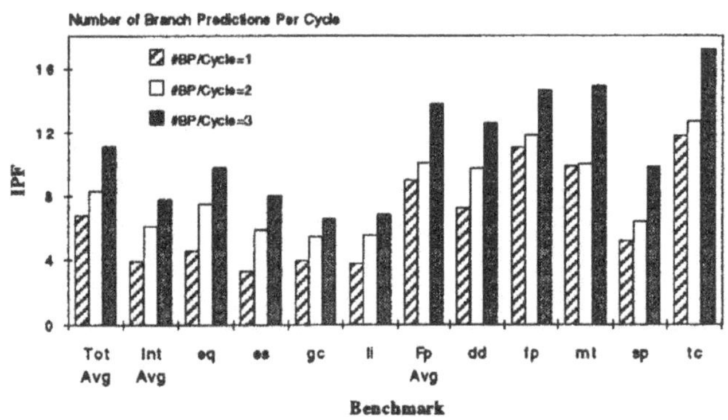

Figure 8: Instructions per fetch when 1, 2, and 3 branches are predicted each cycle.

5.4 Branch Prediction Efficiency

The multiple branch prediction utilization when 2 basic blocks can be predicted and fetched each cycle is shown in Table 2, where we counted the percentage of cycles when zero, one, and two branches were predicted. Zero branches are predicted if we are fetching a long sequential segment of code, or if the fetch address misses in

Bench-mark	No Prediction	One Prediction Oversized	One Prediction Return	Two Predictions
eq	0.0839	0.1231	0.0272	0.7528
es	0.0364	0.1125	0.0145	0.8317
gc	0.1843	0.3634	0.0522	0.3840
li	0.0939	0.2518	0.1213	0.5244
dd	0.3335	0.2580	0.0602	0.3364
fp	0.7415	0.1909	0.0120	0.0550
mt	0.3386	0.3335	0.0042	0.3236
sp	0.2145	0.2142	0.1613	0.4081
tc	0.5893	0.3337	0.0006	0.0751

Table 2: Branch prediction utilization of an instruction fetch mechanism which is able to provide fetch addresses of two basic blocks in each cycle.

the Branch Address Cache, ***and*** a branch is found in the sequence of instructions after the instructions are decoded. Fpppp has a high percentage of cycles with no predictions due to the extremely long sequential code segment which is repeatedly executed. The percentage of cycles when zero predictions were done per cycle is 10% per cycle for integer and 44% for floating point.

Only a single branch is predicted when the primary branch is a return, or the primary basic block is large (oversized) in which case the instruction fetch bandwidth of the secondary basic block is usurped. About 24% of the single basic block fetches are due to oversized basic blocks, and about 5% are due to the primary branch being a return. Two branch predictions are made and two basic blocks are fetched 62% of the time for integer and 24% of the time for floating point benchmarks.

Table 3 shows the percentage of fetches that cause the machine front-end to stall. The machine front-end stalls only due to instruction cache misses, mispredicted branches, and branch decode penalties.

Bench-mark	No Delay	Decode Delay	Incorrect Branch Prediction	I-cache Miss	Bank Conflict
eq	0.8924	0.0004	0.0679	0.0001	0.0392
es	0.9207	0.0063	0.0565	0.0001	0.0164
gc	0.7674	0.0708	0.0980	0.0288	0.0351
li	0.8753	0.0202	0.0645	0.0060	0.0340
dd	0.8678	0.0110	0.0452	0.0632	0.0128
fp	0.6357	0.0003	0.0091	0.3508	0.0041
mt	0.6805	0.0000	0.0065	0.0001	0.3129
sp	0.9706	0.0068	0.0150	0.0034	0.0042
tc	0.9905	0.0006	0.0085	0.0001	0.0003

Table 3: Percentage of fetches causing the instruction fetch mechanism to stall.

No_Delay cause no stalls in instruction fetching. Bank_Conflicts to the same cache line do not stall instruction fetch, but conflicts to different cache lines within the same bank do stall instruction fetch. Therefore 84 to 90% of the fetches do not cause any instruction fetch stall. If a taken branch is not detected in a fetched instruction sequence (via a Branch Address

Configuration No.	Number of Interleaved Banks	Number of Read Ports	Set Associativity	Line Size	Fetch Size
0	8	1	2	16	2
1	8	1	1	16	2
2	4	1	2	16	2
3	8	1	4	16	2
4	8	1	2	32	1
5	8	2	2	16	2

Table 4: Instruction cache configurations.

Cache miss), a branch decode penalty is taken. Branch Decode penalties occur in approximately 2.4% and 0.4% of the fetch cycles for integer and floating point benchmarks, respectively. An incorrect branch path prediction requires a full branch penalty to be incurred. This happens about 7.2% and 1.7% of the time for integer and floating point.

5.5 Instruction Cache Configuration

We simulated six instruction cache configurations with various numbers of read ports, degrees of interleaving, set associativities, and line sizes. These configurations are listed in Table 4. Configuration 0 was used for most of our experiments. Fetch size refers to the number of cache lines each fetch address can access.

Figures 9 and 10 show the performance with the various instruction cache configurations. *Gcc* and *fpppp* were chosen because they have more significant instruction cache miss rates. Each curve represents a different cache size. More read ports and more banks reduce bank conflicts but result in only a minimal performance increase. Higher set associativity significantly improves performance. However, *fpppp* actually has better performance with either direct-mapped or 4-way set associative caches due to the large sequential code segment. 32-byte line size degrades the performance a little because some bandwidth is wasted due to basic block alignment.

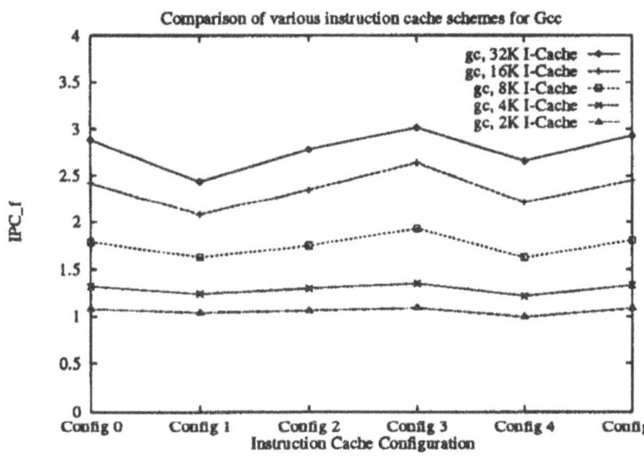

Figure 9: Machine performance of various instruction cache configurations on *gcc*.

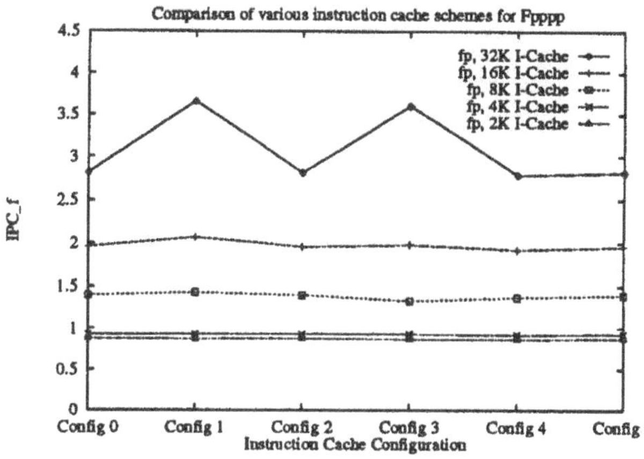

Figure 10: Machine performance of various instruction cache configurations on *fpppp*.

5.6 Effect of Branch Misprediction Penalty

To investigate the effect of branch misprediction penalty on machine performance, we varied the time to resolve a branch from 4 cycles to 12 cycles. Floating point programs have flatter curves because they contain fewer branches and the prediction accuracy of those branches is higher. The performance degradation when the branch resolution time is increased from 4 cycles to 12 cycles is less than 10%. Integer programs have about 20% to 30% performance degradation.

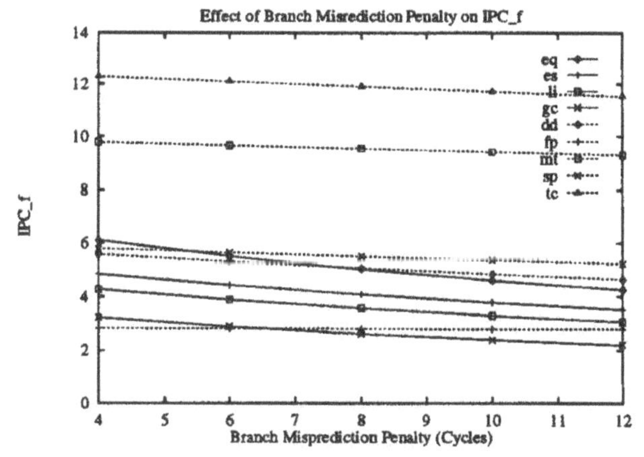

Figure 11: Effect of branch misprediction penalty on machine performance.

5.7 Effect of Instruction Cache Miss Penalty

We varied the instruction cache miss penalty from 4 cycles to 12 cycles. Configuration 0 of Table 4 is used. Among the nine benchmarks, *fpppp*, *doduc*, and *gcc* have lower cache hit rates, as listed in the legend of Figure 12. When the instruction cache miss penalty is increased from 4 cycles to 12 cycles, *Doduc*'s performance degrades by about 20%. *Fpppp*'s performance degrades by about 50%. The other benchmarks showed minimal

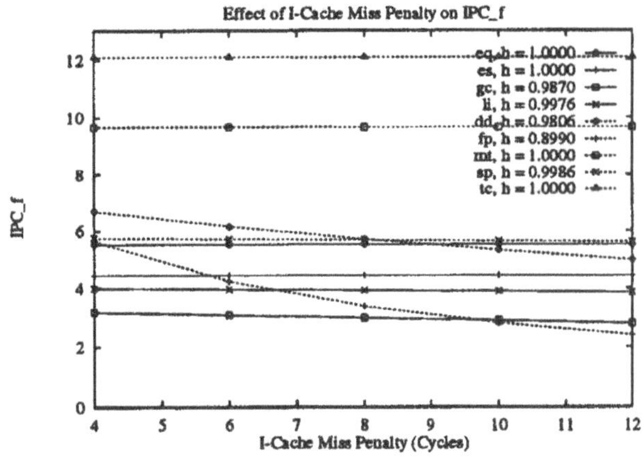

Figure 12: Effect of instruction cache miss penalty on machine performance.

performance degradation due to their low instruction cache miss rates.

6 Conclusion

The trend towards increasingly complex and parallel hardware mechanisms to extract instruction level parallelism from sequential code is advancing at an accelerated rate. Much research has gone into compiler technology to increase basic block size in order to fetch more and more instructions at a time. Increasing basic block size is not enough, however. We propose in this paper a hardware mechanism to fetch multiple basic blocks simultaneously.

We demonstrate in this paper the viability of such schemes by identifying the three essential problems and presenting solutions to each of these. The Multiple Branch Two-level Adaptive Branch Predictor provides the capability of predicting multiple branches each cycle, the Branch Address Cache supplies the starting addresses of basic blocks following the multiple predicted branches, and an instruction cache with interleaved banks provides sufficient bandwidth for fetching multiple non-consecutive basic blocks without the hardware cost of multiple read ports.

In addition, we have presented simulation results indicating that significant performance improvements can be achieved even without specific compiler optimizations. When going from one to two to three branch predictions and basic block fetches per cycle, we saw the IPC_f (instructions fetched per cycle for a machine front-end) improve from 3.0 to 4.2 and 4.9, respectively for integer benchmarks. For floating point benchmarks, the IPC_f went from 6.6 to 7.1 and 8.9. These improvements were achieved by providing the hardware mechanisms to predict and fetch multiple basic blocks without specific compiler optimizations.

Acknowledgement

This paper is one result of our ongoing research in high performance computer implementation at the University of Michigan. The support of our industrial partners: Intel, Motorola, NCR, HaL, Hewlett-Packard, and Scientific and Engineering Software is greatly appreciated. In addition, we wish to gratefully acknowledge the other members of our HPS research group for the stimulating environment they provide, and in particular, for their comments and suggestions on this work. We are particularly grateful to Intel and Motorola for technical and financial support, and to NCR for the gift of an NCR 3550, which is a useful compute server in much of our work.

References

[1] J.E. Smith, "A Study of Branch Prediction Strategies", *Proceedings of the 8th International Symposium on Computer Architecture*, (May 1981), pp.135-148.

[2] J. Lee and A. J. Smith, "Branch Prediction Strategies and Branch Target Buffer Design", *IEEE Computer*, (Jan. 1984), pp.6-22.

[3] R. Colwell, R. Nix, J. O'Donnell, D. Papworth, and P. Rodman, "A VLIW Architecture for a Trace Scheduling Compiler," *Proc of the 2nd Intl Conf on Architectural Support for Programming Languages and Operating Systems*, (Oct. 1987), pp. 180-192.

[4] B.R. Rau, D. Yen, W. Yen, and R. Towle, "The Cydra 5 Departmental Supercomputer - Design Philosophies, Decisions, and Trade-offs," *IEEE Computer*, (Jan. 1989), pp. 12-35.

[5] M. Butler, T-Y Yeh, Y.N. Patt, M. Alsup, H. Scales, and M. Shebanow, "Instruction Level Parallelism is Greater Than Two", *Proceedings of the 18th International Symposium on Computer Architecture*, (May 1991), pp. 276-286.

[6] T-Y Yeh and Y.N. Patt, "Two-Level Adaptive Branch Prediction", *The 24th ACM/IEEE Intl Sym and Workshop on Microarchitecture* , (Nov. 1991), pp. 51-61.

[7] T-Y Yeh and Y.N. Patt "Alternative Implementations of Two-Level Adaptive Branch Prediction," *Proceedings of the 19th International Symposium on Computer Architecture*, (May 1992), pp. 124-134.

[8] S-T Pan, K. So, and J.T. Rahmeh, "Improving the Accuracy of Dynamic Branch Prediction Using Branch Correlation," *Proceedings of the 5th International Conference on Architectural Support for Programming Languages and Operating Systems*, (Oct. 1992), pp. 76-84.

[9] T-Y Yeh and Y.N. Patt "A Comprehensive Instruction Fetch Mechanism for a Processor Supporting Speculative Execution," *Proc of the 25th International Symposium on Microarchitecture*, (Dec. 1992), pp. 129-139.

[10] T-Y Yeh and Y.N. Patt "A Comparison of Dynamic Branch Predictors that use Two Levels of Branch History," *Proceedings of the 20th International Symposium on Computer Architecture*, (May 1993).

[11] W. Hwu, S. Mahlke, W. Chen, P. Chang, N. Warter, R. Bringmann, R. Ouellete, R. Hank, T. Kiyohara, G. Haab, J. Holm, and D. Lavery, "The superblock: An effective technique for VLIW and superscalar compilation," *The Journal of Supercomputing*, January 1993.

Anatomy of a Message in the Alewife Multiprocessor

John Kubiatowicz and Anant Agarwal
Laboratory for Computer Science, NE43–633
Massachusetts Institute of Technology
Cambridge, MA 02139

Abstract

Shared-memory provides a uniform and attractive mechanism for communication. For efficiency, it is often implemented with a layer of interpretive hardware on top of a message-passing communications network. This interpretive layer is responsible for data location, data movement, and cache coherence. It uses patterns of communication that benefit common programming styles, but which are only heuristics. This suggests that certain styles of communication may benefit from direct access to the underlying communications substrate. The Alewife machine, a shared-memory multiprocessor being built at MIT, provides such an interface. The interface is an integral part of the shared memory implementation and affords direct, user-level access to the network queues, supports an efficient DMA mechanism, and includes fast trap handling for message reception. This paper discusses the design and implementation of the Alewife message-passing interface and addresses the issues and advantages of using such an interface to complement hardware-synthesized shared memory.

1 Introduction

Given current trends in network and systems design, it should come as no surprise that most distributed shared-memory machines are built on top of an underlying message-passing substrate [1, 2, 3]. Architects of shared-memory machines often obscure this topology with a layer of hardware that implements their favorite memory coherence protocol and that insulates the processor entirely from the interconnection network. In such machines, communication between processing elements can occur *only* through the shared-memory abstraction. It seems natural, however, to expose the network directly to the processor, as shown in Figure 1, thereby gaining performance in situations for which the shared-memory paradigm is either unnecessary or inappropriate.

For example, consider a thread dispatch operation to a remote node. This operation requires a pointer to the thread's code and any arguments to be placed atomically on the task queue of another processor. The task queue resides in the portion of distributed memory associated with the remote processor. To do so via shared-memory, the invoking processor must first acquire the remote task queue lock, and then modify and unlock the queue using shared-memory reads and writes, each of which can require multiple network messages. As depicted in Figure 2, a message-based implementation is substantially simpler: all the information necessary to invoke the thread is marshalled into a single message which is unmarshalled and queued atomically by the receiving processor. In this manner, synchronization and data transfer are combined in a single message.

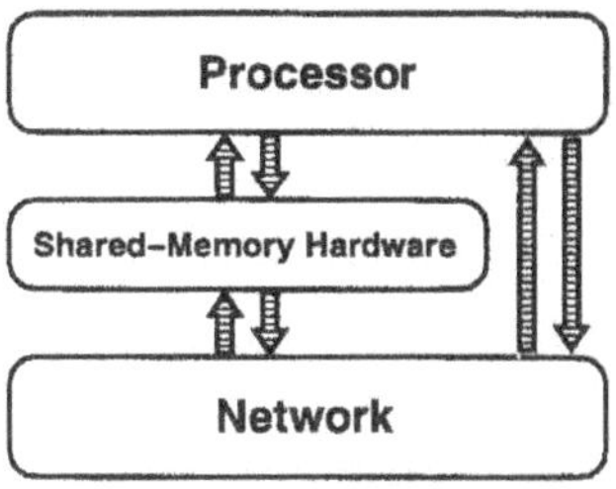

Figure 1: Alewife's integrated interface.

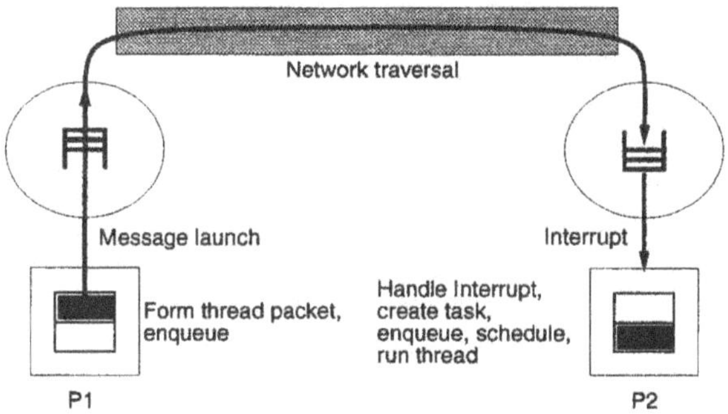

Figure 2: A thread dispatch to a remote node.

The message-passing implementation yields substantial performance gains over a pure shared-memory implementation. We characterize the performance of these two implementation schemes by measuring two intervals: $T_{invoker}$, the time from when the invoking processor begins the operation until it is free to proceed with other work, and $T_{invokee}$, the time from when the invoking processor begins the operation until the invoked thread begins running. With our best shared-memory implementation, these times are 10.7 and 24.4 μsec, respectively. With the message-based implementation, both times are reduced drastically, to 0.5 and 7.4 μsec, respectively. These numbers were derived from a cycle-by-cycle simulation of the Alewife machine, assuming a 33 MHz clock.

While supporting an efficient message interface is advantageous, we believe it is important to provide support for the shared-memory abstraction because of the simplicity it affords those programs where communication patterns cannot be determined statically. Furthermore, shared-memory mechanisms are superior to message-passing mechanisms for operations that require fine-grain communication and computation.

Accordingly, Alewife provides support for both styles of communication. It implements support for coherent shared memory, which implies mechanisms for automatic renaming of memory locations on loads and stores (whether they are local in the cache, in local memory, or in remote memory), automatic local copying of data blocks and coherence checks.

Alewife integrates direct network access with the shared-memory framework. The message-passing mechanisms include direct processor access via loads and stores to the input and output queues of the network, a DMA mechanism, and a fast trap mechanism for message handling. With the integrated interface in Alewife, a message can be sent with just a few user-level instructions. A processor receiving such a message will trap and respond either by rapidly executing a message handler or by queuing the message for later consideration. Scheduling and queuing decisions are made entirely in software.

The challenge in implementing such a streamlined interface to the interconnection network is to achieve a performance that rivals that of purely message passing machines, while at the same time coexisting with the shared memory hardware.

The integration of shared memory and message passing in Alewife is kept simple through a design discipline that provides a *single, uniform interface* to the interconnection network. This means that the shared memory protocol packets and the packets produced by the message passing facilities use the same format and the same network queues and hardware.

The message interface itself follows a similar design discipline: provide a single, uniform communications interface between the processor and the interconnection network. This uniformity is achieved by using a single packet format and by treating all message packets destined to the processor in a uniform way. Specifically, all (non-protocol) messages interrupt the processor. The processor looks at the packet header and initiates an action based on the header. Possible actions include consuming the data into its registers directly, or issuing a command to storeback data via DMA.

The major contributions of this work include: (1) the design of the streamlined and uniform packet interface into the interconnection network, and (2) the mechanisms used to support its integration with the shared-memory hardware. The mechanisms required to integrate the message passing interface with the shared memory hardware include support for coherence on message data, high-availability interrupts, and restrictions placed on message handlers.

This paper describes the design and implementation of the message-passing interface, focusing on the issues related to its integration with the shared-memory layer. Section 3 provides an overview of the message interface. Section 4 outlines the mechanisms provided and presents the rationale behind our design decisions. Section 5 focuses on the mechanisms needed to support the integration with shared memory, and Section 6 describes the opportunities afforded by an integrated interface. Section 7 highlights issues encountered during the implementation of the Alewife machine and discusses the status of this implementation. Section 8 presents empirical evidence of the benefits of implementing an integrated interface. Section 9 discusses related work and Section 10 presents the status of the design and summarizes the major points in this paper.

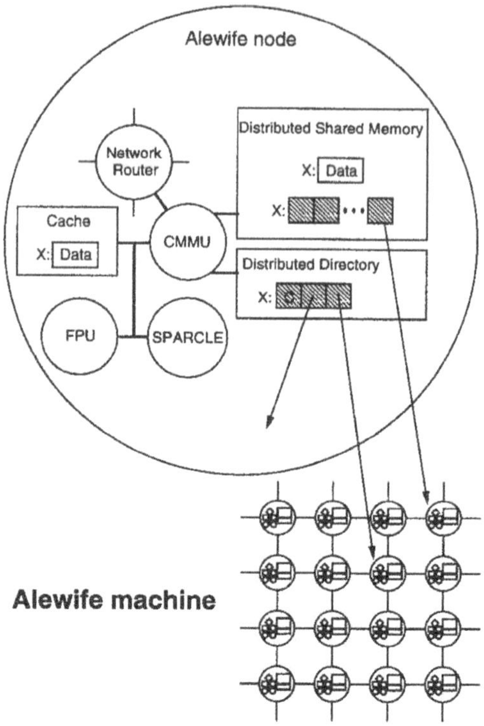

Figure 3: An Alewife processing node.

2 The Alewife Machine

Alewife is a large-scale multiprocessor with distributed shared memory. The machine, organized as shown in Figure 3, uses a cost-effective mesh network for communication. This type of architecture scales in terms of hardware cost and allows the exploitation of locality.

An Alewife node consists of a 33 MHz Sparcle processor, 64K bytes of direct-mapped cache, 4M bytes of globally-shared main memory, and a floating-point coprocessor. Both the cache and floating-point units are SPARC compatible [4]. The nodes communicate via messages through a direct network [5] with a mesh topology using wormhole routing [6]. A single-chip Communications and Memory Management Unit (CMMU) on each node holds the cache tags and implements the cache coherence protocol by synthesizing messages to other nodes. This chip also implements the message interface.

A unique feature of Alewife is its *LimitLESS* directory coherence protocol [7]. This scheme implements a full-map directory protocol [8] by trapping into software for widely shared data items. As discussed in Section 6.1, the Alewife message interface is necessary for implementing LimitLESS.

3 Overview of the Message Interface

Alewife's communications interface is unique for two reasons: first, it integrates message passing with a shared-memory interface, and second, the interface is highly efficient and uses a uniform packet structure. This section provides an overview of this interface and discusses the rationale behind the design.

3.1 A Uniform Message Interface

The message-passing interface in the Alewife machine is designed around four primary observations:

1. Header information for messages is often derived directly from processor registers at the source and, ideally, delivered directly to processor registers at the destination. Thus, efficient messaging facilities should permit direct transfer of information from registers to the network interface. Direct register-to-register transmission has been suggested by a number of architects [9, 10, 11, 12].
2. Blocks of data that reside in memory often accompany such header information. Consequently, efficient messaging facilities should allow direct memory access (DMA) mechanisms to be invoked inexpensively, possibly on multiple blocks of data. This is important for a number of reasons, including rapid task dispatch (where a task-frame or portion of the calling stack may be transmitted along with the continuation) [13] and distributed block I/O (where both a buffer-header structure and data may reside in memory).
3. Some modern processors, such as the Alewife's Sparcle processor [14], MOSAIC [15], and the MDP [10], can respond rapidly to interrupts. In particular, vectored interrupts permit dispatch directly to appropriate code segments, and reserved hardware contexts can remove the need for saving and restoring registers in interrupt handlers. This couples with efficient DMA to provide another advantage: virtual queuing. Here, a thin layer of interrupt-driven operating system software can synthesize an arbitrary network queueing structure in software, although possibly at the cost of extra memory-to-memory copies.
4. Permitting compilers (or users) to generate network communications code can have a number of advantages [11, 9, 16], but requires user-level access to the message interface.

Accordingly, the Alewife machine provides a uniform network interface with the following features:

- Sending a message is an *atomic*, *user-level*, two-phase action: describe the message, then launch it. The sending processor describes a message by writing into coprocessor registers over the cache bus. The resulting descriptor contains either explicit data from registers, or address-length pairs for DMA-style transfers. Because multiple address-length pairs can be specified, the send can *gather* data from multiple memory regions.
- Message receipt is signalled with an interrupt to the receiving processor. Alternatively, the processor can mask interrupts and poll for message arrival. On entering a message reception handler, the processor examines the packet header and can take one of several actions depending on the header. Actions include discarding the message, transferring the message contents into processor registers, or instructing the CMMU to initiate a storeback of the data into one or more regions of memory (*scatter*).
- Mechanisms for *atomicity* and *protection* are provided to permit user and operating system functions to use the same network interface.

3.2 Integration of Shared Memory and Message Passing

Integration of message passing with shared memory is challenging because of their different semantics. The shared-memory interface (as depicted in Figure 1) accepts read and write requests from the processor and converts them into messages to other nodes if the desired data is neither present in the cache nor in the local memory of the requesting node. The Alewife memory system is sequentially consistent.

However, allowing the processor direct access to the interconnection network bypasses the shared-memory hardware, and permits the processor to transmit the contents of its registers or regions of memory to other processors. The direct transmission of memory data through messages interacts with the implicit transmission of (potentially the same) data through loads and stores. The interactions must be designed and specified in such a way that compilers and runtime systems can make use of the two classes of mechanism within the same application, while minimizing implementation complexity.

The following are the important issues that arise when integrating shared memory with message passing:

- The interaction between messages using DMA transfer and cache-coherence. Our solution (as discussed in detail in Section 5.3) guarantees local and remote coherence. This means that data at the source and destination are coherent with respect to local processors. If global coherence is desired, it can be achieved through a two-phase software process. Guaranteeing only local and remote coherence significantly reduces implementation complexity, while still optimizing for common-case operations.
- The need for *high-availability interrupts*. Consider a processor that has issued multiple shared-memory requests and is currently blocked waiting for the return of data. If non-shared-memory messages precede the arrival of the requested data and occupy the head of the message queue, then the processor must trap and dispose of these messages before it can make forward progress.

  To address the above issues, Alewife supports high-availability interrupts. This support allows the Alewife processor to service external messages in the middle of a pending load or store operation.
- Special restrictions on global accesses by message handlers. As discussed in Section 5.3, global shared-memory accesses

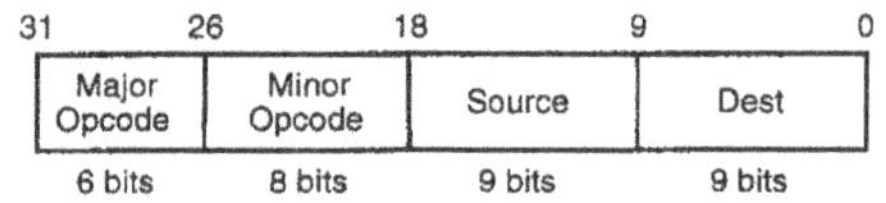

Figure 4: A uniform packet header format. The major opcode distinguishes between protocol, system, and user messages.

made by critical message handlers can lead to harmful interactions.

4 Mechanisms

This section describes the architectural mechanisms supported by Alewife's communications interface. A detailed programmer's interface is given in [17]. We first present the basic messaging facilities, then follow with a discussion of features necessary for user-level messaging.

4.1 Basic Messaging Facilities

Uniform Packet Header Format As a starting point for the integration of message-passing and shared memory, the Alewife machine employs a uniform packet structure for all classes of messages. All packets in the network must have the single, uniform header format shown in Figure 4 as their first word. The three packet classes - *coherence-protocol packets*, *system-level messages*, and *user-level messages* – are distinguished by ranges of the *major opcode*, also shown in this figure. The *minor opcode* contains unrestricted supplementary information, while the *source* and *destination* fields contain, respectively, the node-numbers for the source and destination processors. Only coherence-protocol packets are directly interpreted by hardware; such packets provide coherent shared-memory.

Output Interface Messages in the Alewife machine are sent through a two phase process: first *describe*, then *launch*. A message is described by writing directly to an array of registers in the CMMU, called the *output descriptor array*. Although this array is memory-mapped, the addresses fit into the offset field of a special store instruction called `stio`, as described in Table 1[1]. Consequently, the compiler can generate instructions which perform direct register-to-register moves from the processor into this array. These moves proceed at the speed of the *cache bus*.

Alewife packet descriptors for register-to-register or memory-to-memory transfers have the common structure shown in Figure 5 and consist of one or more 64-bit double-words. The descriptor consists of zero or more pairs of explicit *operands*, followed by zero or more *address-length pairs*. The address-length pairs describe blocks of data which will be fetched from memory via DMA; thus, requests for DMA are an inexpensive and integral aspect of packet description. Packet transmission begins with the operands and finishes with data from each of the requested blocks. The CMMU interprets the first operand (or first word in memory if no operands

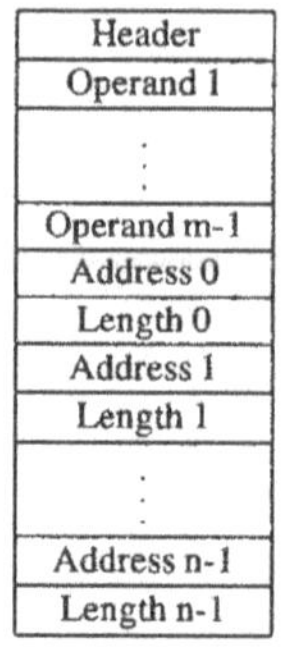

Figure 5: Packet descriptor format. The Header is Operand 0.

are present) as a packet header. The packet descriptor can be up to eight (8) double-words long.

Once a packet has been described, it can be launched via an *atomic*, single-cycle, launch instruction, called `ipilaunch`. (IPI stands for interprocessor-interrupt). As shown in Table 1, the opcode fields of an `ipilaunch` specify the number of explicit operands (in double-words) and the total descriptor length (also in double-words). Consequently, the format of a packet must be known at compile-time. The execution of a launch instruction atomically commits the message to the network. Until the time of the launch, the description process can be aborted, or aborted and restarted without leaving partial packets in the network. After a launch, the descriptor array may be modified without affecting previous messages[2]. The `ipilaunch` and other instructions in Sparcle provide a tight coupling between the processor and the network.

Since requested DMA operations occur in parallel with processor execution, data blocks which are part of outgoing messages should not be modified until after the DMA mechanism has finished with them. Consequently, we provide a second flavor of launch instruction, `ipilaunchi`, which requests the generation of an interrupt as soon as all data has been retrieved from memory and committed to network queues. This *transmission completion* interrupt can be used to free outgoing data blocks or perform other post-transmission actions.

If the output network is blocked due to congestion, then it is possible that the CMMU has insufficient resources to launch the next message. This information is handed to the processor in one of two ways. First, the *space-avail* register in the CMMU indicates the maximum packet descriptor which can be generated at the time it is read. Second, if the processor attempts to store beyond this point in the descriptor array, then the offending `stio` instruction is blocked until resources are available[3]. Since the availability of resources is verified during the description process, launch instructions always complete.

Rather than blocking on insufficient descriptor resources, the software can optionally request that the CMMU generate a *space-request* interrupt when a specified number of double-words of descriptor space are available.

[1]Note that this store instruction differs from normal store instructions only in the value that it produces for the SPARC *alternate space indicator* (ASI) field [4].

[2]In fact, descriptor contents are not preserved across a launch. See Section 7.

[3]An `stio` that is blocked under such circumstances may be faulted during network overflow, as described later.

Instruction		Description
`ldio`	`Ra+AddrOffset, Rd`	Load from CMMU register space.
`stio`	`Rs, Ra+AddrOffset`	Store to CMMU register space.
`ipilaunch(i)`	`Numops, Length`	Launch packet from descriptor. Optionally, generate an interrupt when finished.
`ipicst(i)`	`Skip, Length`	Discard/storeback input packet. Optionally, generate an interrupt when finished.

Table 1: Network instructions

Interrupt	Event that it signals
Reception	Arrival of data. Separate vectors are provided for user and system packets.
Storeback	Latest `ipicsti` has completed.
Transmission	Latest `ipilaunchi` has completed.
Space Request	Requested descriptor space exists.
Network Overflow	Network output queue has been clogged for an extended period.

Table 2: Network Interrupts

Register	Description
`space-avail`	Output descriptor space available
`space-request`	Output descriptor space requested
`desc-length`	Current descriptor length
`storeback-addr`	Address for next DMA storeback
`window-length`	Number of double-words in input window
`net-ovf-cnt`	Network overflow count in cycles

Table 3: Network registers. Sizes are in double-words.

Table 2 lists the interrupts associated with the message interface. These interrupts are maskable and may be individually enabled or disabled. The processor can poll for disabled interrupts by examining a CMMU status register. Table 3 lists the CMMU registers that participate in message sending and receiving.

Input Interface Efficient receipt of messages and dispatching to appropriate handlers is facilitated by an efficient interrupt interface. Upon reception of the first double-word of a packet, the CMMU generates one of two *reception* interrupts, depending upon whether the message is a user message or a system/coherence message[4]. The processor can begin flushing its pipeline and vectoring to the interrupt handler in parallel with reception of the remainder of the message. Upon entering the interrupt handler, the processor can examine the first 8 double-words of the packet through the *packet input window*. As with the descriptor array, the packet input window is memory mapped with short addresses and accessed through a special load instruction, `ldio`. Consequently, the compiler can generate register-to-register moves from the input window to the processor registers that proceed at the speed of the cache bus. If the processor attempts to access data that is not yet present, then the CMMU will block the processor until this data arrives. Portions of the message that are outside the packet input window are invisible to the processor. If a packet is longer than eight (8) double-words, then only the first eight double-words appear in the window. The remainder of the packet is invisible to the processor, possibly stretching into the network.

Once the processor has examined the head of the packet, it invokes a single-cycle storeback instruction, called `ipicst` (for IPI coherent storeback). As shown in Table 1, this instruction has two opcode fields, *skip* and *length*. The skip field specifies the number of double-words that are discarded from the head of the packet, while the length field specifies the number of double-words (following those discarded) that should be stored to memory via DMA. Either of these fields can contain a reserved "infinity" value that denotes "until the end of the packet". When invoking DMA, the processor must write the starting address for DMA to the *storeback-address* register before issuing the storeback instruction. If the sum of the skip and length fields is shorter than the length of the packet, then the remainder of the packet will appear at the head of the packet input window and another reception interrupt will be generated. Multiple storeback instructions can be issued for a single input message to scatter its data to memory (the Alewife CMMU can permit two `ipicst` instructions to issue without blocking).

A second version of the storeback instruction, called `ipicsti` requests a *storeback completion* interrupt upon completion of the storeback operation. This signals the completion of input DMA, and can be used to export blocks of data to higher levels of software.

[4]The LimitLESS coherence protocol invokes software in certain "rare" circumstances (such as wide spread sharing of read-only data). In these cases, coherence protocol messages are passed directly to the software.

4.2 User-Level Messaging

There are numerous advantages to exporting a fast message interface to user code. The Alewife messaging interface has many aspects that can be directly exploited by the compiler, including direct construction of the descriptor and the format of packets themselves. This suggests that unique send and receive code might be generated for each type of communication, much in the flavor of active messages [11]. Further, when a message can be launched in less than ten cycles, the time to cross a protection barrier can easily double or triple the cost of sending that message.

In the Alewife machine, support for user-level messaging includes *atomicity* and *protection* mechanisms, which are described below:

Atomicity User code executes with interrupts enabled. This is necessary since interrupts represent time-critical events that may adversely affect forward-progress or correctness if not handled promptly. Unfortunately, message construction represents a multi-cycle operation that can yield incorrect results if interrupted at the wrong time. Thus, some method of achieving atomicity is necessary.

One solution would be to allow the user to enable and disable interrupts. This is undesirable, however, since user code should not, in general, be allowed to perform actions that may crash or compromise the integrity of the machine. Alternately, we could provide separate output interfaces for the user and supervisor. This solution is also undesirable: on the one hand, it is overkill, since the chance that both the user and supervisor will attempt to send messages simultaneously is very low. On the other hand, the division between user and supervisor is somewhat arbitrary; we may have multiple levels of interrupts.

Consequently, the Alewife machine adopts a more general mechanism. It is designed with the assumption that collisions are rare, but that the highest priority interrupt should always have access to the network. To accomplish this, we start with an *atomic message-send*, as described above. Then, since message launching is atomic, interrupts are free to use the network providing that they restore any partially-constructed message descriptors before returning. Thus, the mechanism is the familiar "callee-saves" mechanism applied to interrupts.

Since the implementation described in Section 7 does not guarantee the contents of the descriptor array after launch, one additional mechanism is provided. This is the *desc-length* register of the CMMU. Whenever the output descriptor array is written, desc-length is set to the maximum of its current value and the array index that is being written. It is zeroed whenever a packet is launched. Consequently, this register indicates the number of entries in the descriptor array that must be preserved. It is non-zero only during periods in which packets are being described.

Protection Historically, there has been tension between protection mechanisms and rapid access to hardware facilities. The Alewife network interface is no different. Protection in the Alewife machine is not intended to hide information, but rather to protect the machine from errant user-code. Such protection is as follows:

- The user is not allowed to send system or coherence messages. To enforce this restriction, we require the user to construct messages with explicit headers (i.e. one or more operands). In this fashion, the opcode can be checked at the time of launch. If a violation occurs, then the `ipilaunch` instruction is faulted.
- The user is not allowed to issue storeback instructions if the message at the head of the queue is a system or coherence message.
- The user is not allowed to store data into kernel space. This rule is enforced by checking the storeback address register at the time that an `ipicst` is issued.

These protection mechanisms are transparent to both user and operating system under normal circumstances[5].

[5] Along the same lines, message hardware in a multiuser system could automatically append the current process identifier (PID) to outgoing packets. At the destination, either hardware or interrupt software could then check this PID and deliver messages to an appropriate user message handler. This is beyond the scope of this paper, however.

5 Interactions Between Shared Memory and Message-Passing

In this section we present three issues that arise when integrating message-passing with cache-coherent shared memory. These issues are the need for high-availability interrupts, special restrictions on message handlers, and data coherence for the DMA mechanism. To some extent, these interactions arise from the fact that the network provides a single logical input and output port to the memory controller. While networks with multiple channels are possible to implement, they are invariably more expensive.

5.1 High-Availability Interrupts

The need for *high-availability interrupts* [18] arises because shared-memory introduces a dependence between instruction execution and and the interconnection network. "Normal" asynchronous interrupts, which occur only at instruction boundaries, are effectively disabled when the processor pipeline is frozen for a remote read or write request. Unfortunately, as shown in Figure 6, the requested data may never arrive if it is blocked behind other messages. This figure illustrates a situation in which the processor has issued multiple shared-memory requests and is currently blocked waiting for the return of data. Unfortunately, several non-shared-memory messages have entered the network input queue ahead of the desired response. Unless the processor traps and disposes of these messages, it will never receive its desired data. Thus, the successful completion of a spinning load or store to memory may require faulting the access in progress so that a network interrupt handler can dispose of the offending messages. The term *high-availability interrupt* is applied to such externally initiated pipeline interruptions.

High-availability interrupts introduce an associated problem: when a load or store is interrupted by a high-availability interrupt, it is possible for its data to arrive *and* to be invalidated while the interrupt handler is still executing. The original request must then be reissued when the interrupt finishes. In unfortunate situations, systematic thrashing can occur. This is part of a larger issue, namely the *window of vulnerability*, discussed in [18]. For a single-threaded processor, the simplest solution is to defer the invalidation until after the original load or store commits.

5.2 Restrictions on Message Handlers

A second issue is the interaction between message handlers and shared memory. When an interrupt handler is called in response to an incoming message, the interrupt code must be careful to ensure the following before accessing global-shared memory:

- The network overflow interrupt must be enabled. (The network overflow handling mechanism is discussed in the next section.)
- The input packet must be *completely* freed and network interrupts must be reenabled.
- There must be no active low-level hardware locks that will defer invalidations in the interrupted code.

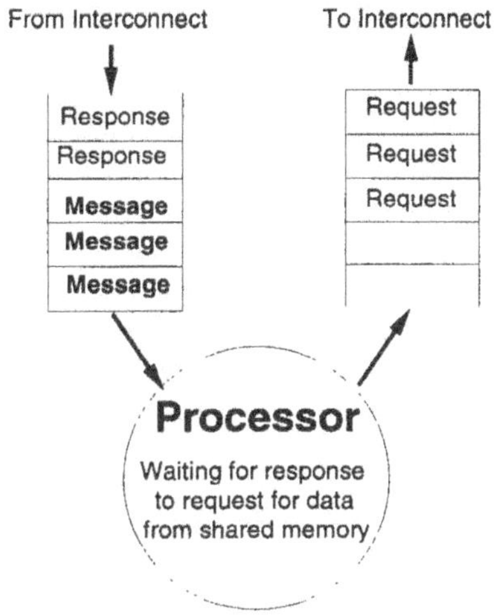

Figure 6: The need for high-availability interrupts.

The first of these conditions arises because all global accesses potentially require use of the network. Consequently, they can be blocked indefinitely if the network should overflow. The second arises for the same reason that high-availability interrupts were introduced into the picture: any global data that is accessed may be stuck behind other messages in the input queue. The last condition prevents deadlocks in the thrash elimination mechanism. See [18] for details.

5.3 Local Coherence for DMA

Since Alewife is a cache-coherent, shared-memory multiprocessor, it is natural to ask which form of data coherence should be supported by the DMA mechanism. Three possibilities present themselves:

1. Non-Coherent DMA: Data is taken directly from memory at the source and deposited directly to memory at the destination, regardless of the state of local or remote caches.
2. Locally-Coherent DMA: Data at the source and destination are coherent with respect to local processors. This means that source data is retrieved from the cache at the source, if necessary. It also means that destination memory lines are invalidated or updated in the cache at the destination, if necessary.
3. Globally-Coherent DMA: Data at the source and destination are coherent with respect to all nodes. Source memory lines that are dirty in the caches of remote nodes are fetched during transmission. Destination memory lines are invalidated or updated in caches which have copies, ensuring that all nodes have a coherent view of incoming data.

For reasons described below, the Alewife machine supports locally-coherent DMA.

Both locally-coherent DMA and non-coherent DMA have appeared on numerous uniprocessors to date. Local coherence gives the programmer more flexibility to send and receive data structures that are in active use, since it removes the need to explicitly flush data to memory. In addition, it is relatively straightforward to implement in a system that already supports a cache invalidation mechanism. Section 7.3 discusses this point. Non-coherent DMA can give better performance for messages that are not cached (such as certain types of I/O), since it does not produce cache invalidation traffic. However, it is less flexible.

Globally-coherent DMA, on the other hand, is an option only in cache-coherent multiprocessors. Globally-coherent DMA can assist in the improvement of locality by allowing globally-shared data items to be easily migrated between phases of a computation or during garbage-collection. This has a particular appeal for machines, such as Alewife, that physically distribute their global address space.

However, while attractive as a "universal mechanism," globally-coherent DMA is not a good mechanism to support directly in hardware. There are a number of reasons for this. First, it provides far more mechanism than is actually needed in many cases. As Section 8 demonstrates, message passing is useful as a way of *bypassing* the coherence protocol. In fact, many of the applications of message-passing discussed in [13] do not require a complete mechanism.

Second, a machine with a single network port cannot fetch dirty source data while in the middle of transmitting a larger packet since this requires the sending of messages. Even in a machine with multiple logical network ports, it is undesirable to retrieve dirty data in the middle of message transmission because the network resources associated with the message can be idle for multiple network round-trip times. Thus, a monolithic DMA mechanism would have to scan through the packet descriptor twice; once to collect data, and once to send data. This adds unnecessary complexity.

Third, globally-coherent DMA complicates network overflow recovery. While hardware can be designed to invalidate or to update remote caches during data arrival (using both input and output ports of the network simultaneously), this introduces a dependence between input and output queues that may prevent the simple "divert and relaunch" scheme described in Section 6.2 for network overflow recovery: input packets that are in the middle of a globally-coherent storeback block the input queue when the output queue is clogged.

In the light of these discussions, the Alewife machine supports a locally-coherent DMA mechanism.

Synthesizing Global Coherence We have argued above against a monolithic, globally-coherent DMA mechanism. However, globally-coherent DMA can be accomplished in other ways. The key is to note that software desiring such semantics can employ a two-phase "collect" and "send" operation at the source and a "clean" and "receive" operation at the destination.

Thus, a globally-coherent send can be accomplished by first scanning through the source data to collect values of outstanding dirty copies. Then a subsequent DMA send operation only needs to access local copies. With the send mechanism broken into these two pieces, we see that the the collection operation can potentially occur in parallel: by quickly scanning through the data and sending invalidations to all caches which have dirty copies.

At the destination, the cleaning operation is similar in flavor to collection. Here the goal of scanning through destination memory blocks is to invalidate all outstanding copies of memory lines before using them for DMA storeback. To this end, some method of marking blocks as "busy" until invalidation acknowledgments have returned is advantageous (and provided by Alewife); then, data can be stored to memory in parallel with invalidations.

It is an open question whether the collection and cleaning operations should be assisted by hardware, accomplished by performing multiple non-binding prefetch operations, or accomplished by scanning the coherence directories and manually sending invalidations[6]. If globally-coherent DMA operations are frequent, then a hardware assist is probably desirable. At this time, however, the Alewife machine provides no hardware assistance for these operations.

6 Opportunities From Integration

In this section, we touch on two unique opportunities, over and above the software advantages mentioned earlier, which arise from the inclusion of a fast message interface in a shared-memory multiprocessor. These are the LimitLESS cache-coherence protocol, and network overflow recovery.

6.1 The LimitLESS Cache Coherence Mechanism

One opportunity that arises from integrating message-passing and shared memory, is the ability to extend the hardware cache-coherence protocol in software. Permitting software to send and receive coherence-protocol packets requires no additional mechanism over and above the basic messaging facilities of Section 4. In Alewife, the memory system implements a set of pointers, called *directories*. Each directory keeps track of the cached copies of a corresponding memory line. In our current implementation, the size of the directory can be varied from zero to five pointers. The novel feature of the LimitLESS scheme [7] is that when there are more cached copies than there are pointers, the system traps the processor for software extension of the directory into main memory[7]. The processor can then implement an algorithm of its choice in software to handle this situation.

The LimitLESS scheme leaves ample opportunity for designing custom protocols which are invoked on a per-memory-line basis. Individual directories can be set to interrupt on all references. Then, all protocol messages which arrive for these memory-lines are automatically forwarded to the message input queue for software handling. In fact, our runtime system makes use of several extended applications of the LimitLESS interface, such as FIFO queue locks, fetch-and-op style synchronizations, and fast barriers.

6.2 Recovery from Network Overflow

Cache-coherence protocols introduce a dependence between the input and output queues of a memory controller, since they process read and write requests by returning data. This leads to a possibility for *protocol deadlock*, since it introduces a circular dependence between the network queues of two or more nodes. Architectures such as DASH [19] have avoided this problem by introducing independent networks for request and response messages. However, the existence of separate request and response networks is not sufficient in a general messaging environment since it can only prevent deadlock for a restricted class of request-response communication. Since protocol deadlock results from insufficient network queue space, we can correct this problem in a different fashion by *augmenting the hardware queues in software*, when a potential for deadlock is detected. We refer to this as *network overflow recovery*. Note that this technique does not require multiple logical networks.

The heuristic that we use to detect protocol deadlock is to initialize a hardware timer with a preset value. Then, whenever the network output queue is full and blocked, the timer begins counting down from the preset value, generating a *network-overflow* trap if it ever reaches zero. This counter affords some hysteresis for overflow detection, since protocol deadlock is a rare event and some queue blockage is expected.

The network overflow handler places the network in "divert mode," diverting all packets from the network *input* queue to the IPI input queue. It then uses DMA to store all incoming packets into a special queue-overflow region of local memory. This process continues until the network output queue has drained sufficiently (a controller status bit indicates that the output queue is half full). As a final phase of recovery, the diverted packets are relaunched with the IPI output interface. A low interrupt priority is used by the relaunch code, to permit normal message processing and network interrupts on relaunched packets.

Consequently, to permit network overflow recovery, we supplement the mechanisms of Section 4 with four additional mechanisms:

1. A countdown timer which can be used detect that the network output queue has been clogged for a "long" time.
2. The ability to force all incoming packets to be diverted to the IPI input queue, rather than being processed by the shared-memory controller. Note that we have only added the ability to force this switch. The data path must already be present to permit both shared memory and message passing to coexist. See Section 7.
3. A flag which indicates that the hardware output queue is empty or half full.
4. An internal loopback path from the IPI output mechanism back to the controller input, which permits packets to be relaunched to the hardware during recovery without routing through the network hardware.

Note that the fourth mechanism is not strictly necessary, but desirable since the network is backed up during network overflow processing. Section 7 shows a diagram of the network queue structure. A final requirement is more a design philosophy than anything else:

- All controller state machines must be designed such that they never attempt to start operations which have insufficient queue resources to complete. In this context, DMA requests are broken into a series of short atomic memory operations.

Adherence to this philosophy is simpler than attempting to abort operations during network overflow.

[6] An option that is uniquely available with Alewife.

[7] A trap bit in main memory associated with each block of data indicates whether accesses of this location must interrupt the processor for software extension.

Component	Size
Coprocessor Pipeline	1589 gates
Asynchronous Network Input	1126 gates
Asynchronous Network Output	1304 gates
Network Control and Datapath	2632 gates
Network Input Queue (1R/1W)	32×65 bits
Network Output Queue (1R/1W)	32×65 bits
IPI Input Queue (2R/1W)	8×64 bits
IPI Output (descriptor) Queue (2R/1W)	8×64 bits
IPI Output Local Queue (1R/1W)	8×65 bits
IPI Input Invalidation Queue (2 entries)	1610 gates
IPI Output Invalidation Queue (2 entries)	1306 gates
IPI Input Interface	4181 gates
IPI Output Interface	3393 gates

Table 4: Module sizes in gates or bits.

7 Implementation and Status

The Alewife message interface is implemented in two components, the Sparcle processor [20] and the A-1000 Communications and Memory Management Unit (CMMU). The Sparcle processor includes the special `ldio` and `stio` instructions for direct access to the IPI output descriptor queue and the IPI input window. In addition, a SPARC-like coprocessor interface enables pipelining of message sends and storeback requests. This processor has been operational since March 1992.

The A-1000 CMMU attaches to the cache bus of the Sparcle processor and integrates both coherent shared-memory and message-passing. It consumes roughly 80,000 gates and 100K-bits of SRAM (for cache tags and network queues) in the LEA 300K hybrid gate-array process from LSI Logic. Most of the logic is implemented in a high-level synthesis language provided by LSI and optimized with the Berkeley SIS tool set. By the time of publication, this chip will have gone to LSI for fabrication.

Table 4 gives a rough breakdown of the sizes of major components of the network interface. All data paths are 64 bits. Note that edge-triggered flip-flops are relatively expensive in this logic, at nine (9) gates per bit (this includes scan).

The Coprocessor Pipeline supplements the basic Sparcle instruction set with a number of instructions, including `ipilaunch` and `ipicst`. The IPI Input Interface and IPI Output Interface include all the launching, storeback, and DMA logic. The Invalidation queues permit locally coherent DMA and include the double-queue structures described below. Together, the logical components of the IPI interface (invalidation queues and interface logic) consume roughly 12% of the controller area. What these numbers do not indicate is the additional logic within the cache and memory controllers to support requests for invalidations and data from the DMA control mechanisms. The size of this logic is difficult to estimate, but appears to be a small fraction of the total logic for cache and memory control.

7.1 Network Queue Structure

Figure 7 shows the network queue structure of the Alewife CMMU. All datapaths are 64 bits. The *IPI output descriptor queue* and *IPI input queue* are visible to the processor and are mapped directly to the output descriptor array and packet input window of section 4.1. The remaining queues are internal queues and not visible to the programmer.

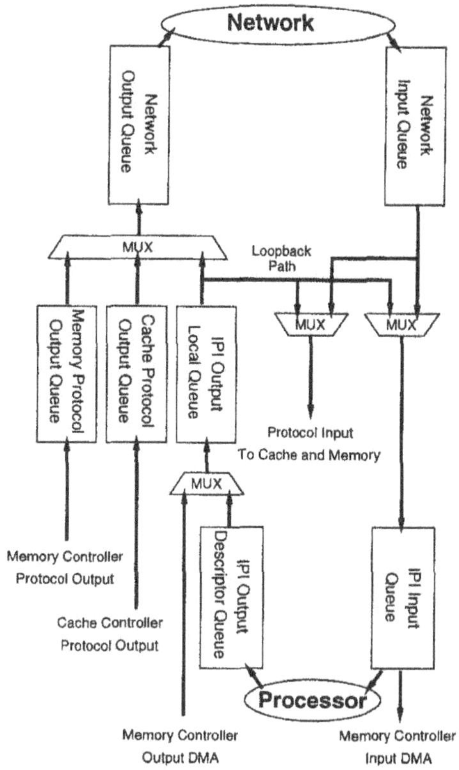

Figure 7: Network queue structure for the Alewife CMMU

7.2 Programmer Visible Queues

`Stio` operations to the descriptor array write *directly* into the circular output descriptor queue, using a hardware tail pointer as the base. The atomic action of an `ipilaunch` instruction moves this tail pointer and records information about the size and composition of the descriptor. Consequently, description of subsequent packets is allowed to begin immediately after an `ipilaunch`, provided that data from pending launches is not overwritten. Queue space becomes available again as descriptors are consumed by the IPI output mechanism. This implementation, while reasonably simple, does not preserve the contents of message descriptors after a launch has occurred.

As shown in Figure 8, messages are committed atomically in the writeback stage of the *ipilaunch* instruction. Here, message throughput is limited by the two-cycle latency of Sparcle stores and the lack of an instruction cache. More aggressive processor implementations would not suffer from these limitations. In addition, the use of DMA on message output adds additional cycles (not shown here) to the network pipeline.

`Ldio` operations from the packet input window receive data directly from the circular IPI input queue, using the current processor head pointer as a base. The effect of an `ipicst` instruction is

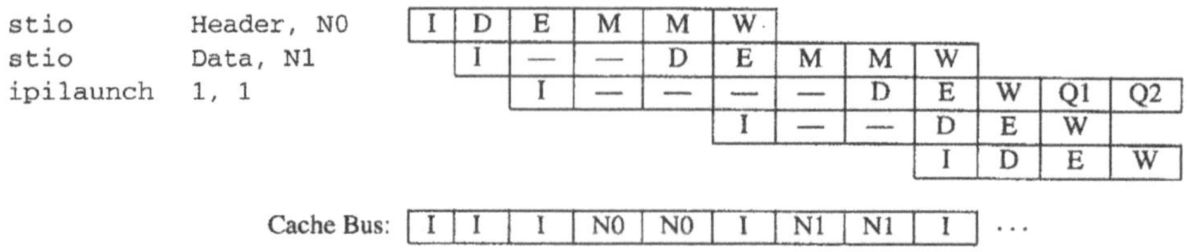

Figure 8: Pipelining for transmission of a message with a single data word. Sparcle pipeline stages are Instruction fetch, Decode, Execute, Memory, and Writeback. Network messages are committed in the Writeback stage. Stages **Q1** and **Q2** are network queuing cycles. The message data begins to appear in the network after stage **Q2**.

to move this head pointer and to initiate DMA actions on the data which has been passed. A separate queue (not shown) holds issued *ipicst* instructions until they can be processed.

7.3 Local Coherence

As mentioned in the discussion on DMA coherence (Section 5.3), supporting locally-coherent DMA is straightforward in a machine with an invalidation-style cache-coherence protocol. In the CMMU, we coordinated the invalidation processes by using double-headed invalidation queues. The DMA controllers generate addresses and place *requests* on these queues as fast as possible (moving the tail of the queue). As soon as requests are written, the cache controller sees them, causes appropriate invalidations, and moves its head pointer. The memory has a second head pointer which lags behind the head pointer of the cache controller. Whenever the two pointers differ, the memory machine knows that it can satisfy the DMA request at its head, since the corresponding invalidation has already occurred. When the memory machine moves its head pointer beyond an entry, that entry is freed. Each of the invalidation queues have two, double-cache-line entries.

Care must be taken with the input interface so that the processor cannot re-request a memory-line after it has been invalidated but before the data has been written to memory. This situation can arise from the pipelining of DMA requests and would represent a violation of local coherence. The difference in area between the input and output invalidation queues (see Table 4) results from address-matching circuitry that serves as an interlock to prevent this "local coherence hole".

7.4 Network Overflow

The *memory protocol output queue* and the *cache protocol output queue* handle protocol traffic from the memory and cache, respectively. While such queues are important for performance reasons, they are also important for a more subtle reason: they simplify the checking of network resources. To allow network overflow recovery, controller state machines must check that all operations have sufficient resources to complete *before* they are initiated (Section 6.2). These two queues simplify this task, since resource checking can be done locally, without arbitrating for the output queue.

Note also that the style of network overflow recovery described in this paper requires the input and output DMA controllers to be independent of each other. This independence is necessary since we relaunch packets from memory (output DMA) which may require storeback operations during processing (input DMA).

8 Results

This section summarizes results comparing the performance of the shared-memory and integrated implementations of several library routines and applications; for a detailed discussion of our experience with this integrated interface see [13]. The results are obtained on a detailed, cycle-by-cycle machine simulator, using Alewife's run-time system based on *lazy task creation* [21] for load-balancing and dynamic partitioning of programs. Our results include a comparison of the performance of purely shared memory and integrated versions of several application kernels.

The applications include a thread scheduler with a synthetic fine-grain tree-structured application, barrier synchronization using combining trees, remote thread invocation, bulk data transfer, and Successive Over-Relaxation (SOR). Each application is implemented both using pure shared memory and using a hybrid system. The thread scheduler uses message sends when searching for work, migrating and invoking remote tasks, and performing certain types of synchronization. The applications run on 64 processors.

The hybrid version yielded substantial improvements over the shared-memory version for the thread scheduler. For very small grain sizes, the run time is almost twice as fast under the hybrid implementation. The barrier synchronization with message passing takes only 20 μsec, while the best shared memory version runs in 50 μsec. Comparable software implementations (e.g. Intel DELTA and iPSC/860, Kendall Square KSR1) take well over 400 μsec [2]. These numbers can also be compared with hardware-supported synchronization mechanisms, such as on the CM5, that take only 2 or 3 μsec but that require separate, log-structured (and potentially less-scalable) synchronization networks.

As described in Section 1, a remote thread invocation using messages reduces the invoker's overhead over a purely shared-memory implementation by a factor of 20 and that of the invokee by a factor of three. Memory-to-memory copy of data for 256-byte blocks is faster than shared-memory copy without prefetching by 2.4, and faster than shared-memory copy with prefetching by 1.5.

These results should not suggest that shared memory is unnecessary or expensive. For programs that have unpredictable, highly data-dependent access patterns, message passing implementations resort to implementing much of the shared-memory interpretive layer in software (for data location and data movement), with a corresponding loss in performance. In other cases, such as SOR, a simple block-partitioned Jacobi SOR solver, we observe little difference between well coded shared-memory and message-passing implementations.

9 Related Work

The CM5 provides a message passing interface and uses SPARCs as its processing nodes. The message interface is implemented using register reads and writes into the network interface (NI) chip. Because the reads and writes are implemented over the main memory bus, they are slower than network register reads and writes in Alewife, which are implemented over the processor cache bus. The CM5 interface does not provide support for DMA or shared memory and requires the processor to be involved in emptying out the message queue. The processor in the CM5 can be notified on message arrival either through an interrupt or by polling [22].

Our interface is different from that provided by the message passing J-machine [10] in that our processor is always interrupted on the arrival of a message, allowing the processor to examine the packet header, and to decide how to deal with the message. Messages in the J-machine are queued and handled in sequence. (The J-machine, however, allows a higher priority message to interrupt the processor.) The J-machine does not provide DMA transfer of data. Finally, message sends in Alewife are atomic in that correct execution is supported even if the processor is interrupted while writing into the network queue.

Somewhat in the flavor of the Alewife machine, the J-machine generates a *send fault* when the network output queue overflows. In addition, a *queue overflow fault* is generated when the input queue overflows. These faults can be used to trigger network overflow recovery similar to that of Section 6.2. Additionally, the J-machine network includes a second level of network priority which can be used to shuffle excess data to other nodes, should local memory for supplementary queue space be unavailable. Unfortunately, the J-machine mechanisms are extremely pessimistic, trapping as soon as local queue space is exhausted. In contrast, Alewife's network overflow mechanism provides hysteresis to ignore temporary network blockages. Further, the lack of message atomicity in the J-machine complicates the functionality of network overflow handlers.

Support for multiple models of computation has been identified as a promising direction for future research. For example, the iWarp [9] integrates systolic and message passing styles of communications. Their interface supports DMA-style communication for long packets typical in message passing systems, while at the same time supporting systolic processor-to-processor communication. In the latter style, a processor could be producing data and streaming it to another, while the receiving processor could be consuming the data using an interface that maps the network queue into a processor register.

To our knowledge, there are no existing machines that support both a shared-address space and a general fine-grain messaging interface in hardware. In some cases where we argue messages are better that shared-memory, such as the barrier in Section 8, a similar effect could be achieved by using shared-memory with a weaker consistency model. For example, the Dash multiprocessor [3, 23] has a mechanism to deposit a value from one processor's cache directly into the cache of another processor, avoiding cache coherence overhead. This mechanism might actually be faster than using a message because no interrupt occurs, but a message is much more general.

Some shared-memory machines have implemented message-like primitives in hardware. For example, Beck, Kasten, and Thakkar [24] describe the implementation of SLIC—a system link and interrupt controller chip—for use with the Sequent Balance system. Each SLIC chip is coupled with a processing node and communicates with the other SLIC chips on a special SLIC bus that is separate from the memory system bus. The SLIC chips help distribute signals such as interrupts and synchronization information to all processors in the system. Although similar in flavor to this kind of interface, the Alewife messaging interface is built to allow direct access to the same scalable interconnection network used by the shared-memory operations.

Another example of a shared-memory machine that also supports a message-like primitive is the BBN Butterfly. This machine provides both hardware support for block transfers and the ability to send remote "interrupt requests." Nodes in the Butterfly are able to initiate DMA operations for blocks of data which reside in remote nodes. In an implementation of distributed shared memory on this machine, Cox and Fowler [25] conclude that an effective block transfer mechanism was critical to performance. They argue that a mechanism that allows more concurrency between processing and block transfer would make a bigger impact. It turns out that Alewife's messages are implemented in a way that allows such concurrency when transferring large blocks of data. Furthermore, the Butterfly's block transfer mechanism is not suited for more general uses of fine-grain messaging because there is no support in the processor for fast message handling.

10 Conclusion

This paper discussed the design of a streamlined message interface that is integrated within a shared-memory substrate. The integration of message passing with shared memory introduces many interesting issues including the need for high-availability interrupts, the need for special restrictions on message handlers, and data coherence requirements for the DMA mechanism. An interface that addresses these needs has been implemented in the Alewife machine's CMMU.

The integration of message passing mechanisms with shared memory affords higher applications performance than either a pure message passing interface or a shared memory interface. In addition, it provides unique opportunities, over and above the software advantages of multimodel support, including the LimitLESS cache-coherence protocol and network overflow recovery.

11 Acknowledgments

Many thanks to David Chaiken for the cycle-by-cycle Alewife simulator and LimitLESS protocol design. Discussions with David Kranz and Beng-Hong Lim provided invaluable feedback on the convenience of some of the more subtle aspects of the network interface and user-level messaging. Further thanks to Beng-Hong Lim, Kirk Johnson, and David Kranz for the applications results and runtime systems work. Finally, many thanks to those involved with testing the A-1000 CMMU, in particular Ken Mackenzie, John Piscitello, David Kranz, Arthur Altman, Beng-Hong Lim, David Chaiken, Jonathan Babb, and Donald Yeung. Many people read earlier drafts of this paper; their feedback and criticism was much appreciated.

The research reported in this paper is funded by NSF grant # MIP-9012773 and DARPA contract # N00014-87-K-0825.

References

[1] Anant Agarwal, David Chaiken, Godfrey D'Souza, Kirk Johnson, David Kranz, John Kubiatowicz, Kiyoshi Kurihara, Beng-Hong Lim, Gino Maa, Dan Nussbaum, Mike Parkin, and Donald Yeung. The MIT Alewife Machine: A Large-Scale Distributed-Memory Multiprocessor. In *Proceedings of Workshop on Scalable Shared Memory Multiprocessors*. Kluwer Academic Publishers, 1991. An extended version of this paper has been submitted for publication, and appears as MIT/LCS Memo TM-454, 1991.

[2] Thomas H. Dunigan. Kendall Square Multiprocessor: Early Experiences and Performance. Technical Report ORNL/TM-12065, Oak Ridge National Laboratory, March 1992.

[3] D. Lenoski, J. Laudon, K. Gharachorloo, W. Weber, A. Gupta, J. Hennessy, M. Horowitz, and M. Lam. The Stanford Dash Multiprocessor. *IEEE Computer*, 25(3):63–79, March 1992.

[4] SPARC Architecture Manual, 1988. SUN Microsystems, Mountain View, California.

[5] Charles L. Seitz. Concurrent VLSI Architectures. *IEEE Transactions on Computers*, C-33(12):1247–1265, December 1984.

[6] William J. Dally. *A VLSI Architecture for Concurrent Data Structures*. Kluwer Academic Publishers, 1987.

[7] David Chaiken, John Kubiatowicz, and Anant Agarwal. LimitLESS Directories: A Scalable Cache Coherence Scheme. In *Fourth International Conference on Architectural Support for Programming Languages and Operating Systems (ASPLOS IV)*, pages 224–234. ACM, April 1991.

[8] Anant Agarwal, Richard Simoni, John Hennessy, and Mark Horowitz. An Evaluation of Directory Schemes for Cache Coherence. In *Proceedings of the 15th International Symposium on Computer Architecture*, New York, June 1988. IEEE.

[9] Shekhar Borkar et al. iWarp: An Integrated Solution to High-Speed Parallel Computing. In *Proceedings of Supercomputing '88*, November 1988.

[10] William J. Dally et al. The J-Machine: A Fine-Grain Concurrent Computer. In *Proceedings of the IFIP (International Federation for Information Processing), 11th World Congress*, pages 1147–1153, New York, 1989. Elsevier Science Publishing.

[11] Thorsten von Eicken, David Culler, Seth Goldstein, and Klaus Schauser. Active messages: A mechanism for integrated communication and computation. In *19th International Symposium on Computer Architecture*, May 1992.

[12] Dana S. Henry and Christopher F. Joerg. A Tightly-Coupled Processor-Network Interface. In *Fifth Internataional Architectural Support for Programming Languages and Operating Systems (ASPLOS V)*, Boston, October 1992. ACM.

[13] David Kranz, Kirk Johnson, Anant Agarwal, John Kubiatowicz, and Beng-Hong Lim. Integrating Message-Passing and Shared-Memory; Early Experience. In *To appear in Proceedings of Practice and Principles of Parallel Programming (PPoPP) 1993*, New York, NY, May 1993. ACM. Also as MIT/LCS TM-478, January 1993.

[14] *MIT-SPARCLE Specification Version 1.1 (Preliminary)*. LSI Logic Corporation, Milpitas, CA 95035, 1990. Addendum to the 64811 specification.

[15] C.L. Seitz, N.J. Boden, J. Seizovic, and W.K. Su. The Design of the Caltech Mosaic C Multicomputer. In *Research on Integrated Systems Symposium Proceedings*, pages 1–22, Cambridge, MA, 1993. MIT Press.

[16] Mark D. Hill, James R. Larus, Steven K. Reinhardt, and David A. Wood. Cooperative Shared Memory: Software and Hardware for Scalable Multiprocessors. In *Fifth International Conference on Architectural Support for Programming Languages and Operating Systems (ASPLOS V)*, Boston, October 1992. ACM.

[17] John Kubiatowicz. User's Manual for the A-1000 Communications and Memory Management Unit. ALEWIFE Memo No. 19, Laboratory for Computer Science, Massachusetts Institute of Technology, January 1991.

[18] John Kubiatowicz, David Chaiken, and Anant Agarwal. Closing the Window of Vulnerability in Multiphase Memory Transactions. In *Fifth International Conference on Architectural Support for Programming Languages and Operating Systems (ASPLOS V)*, pages 274–284, Boston, October 1992. ACM.

[19] D. Lenoski, J. Laudon, K. Gharachorloo, A. Gupta, and J. Hennessy. The Directory-Based Cache Coherence Protocol for the DASH Multiprocessor. In *Proceedings 17th Annual International Symposium on Computer Architecture*, pages 148–159, New York, June 1990.

[20] Anant Agarwal, John Kubiatowicz, David Kranz, Beng-Hong Lim, Donald Yeung, Godfrey D'Souza, and Mike Parkin. Sparcle: An Evolutionary Processor Design for Multiprocessors. *To appear in IEEE Micro*, June 1993.

[21] E. Mohr, D. Kranz, and R. Halstead. Lazy Task Creation: A Technique for Increasing the Granularity of Parallel Programs. *IEEE Transactions on Parallel and Distributed Systems*, 2(3):264–280, July 1991.

[22] *The Connection Machine System: Programming the NI*. Thinking Machines Corporation, March 1992. Version 7.1.

[23] K. Gharachorloo, D. Lenoski, J. Laudon, P. Gibbons, A. Gupta, and J. Hennessy. Memory Consistency and Event Ordering in Scalable Shared-Memory Multiprocessors. In *Proceedings 17th Annual International Symposium on Computer Architecture*, New York, June 1990. IEEE.

[24] Bob Beck, Bob Kasten, and Shreekant Thakkar. VLSI Assist for a Multiprocessor. In *Proceedings Second International Conference on Architectural Support for Programming Languages and Operating Systems (ASPLOS II)*, Washington, DC, October 1987. IEEE.

[25] A. Cox and R. Fowler. The Implementation of a Coherent Memory Abstraction on a NUMA Multiprocessor: Experiences with PLATINUM. In *Proceedings of the 12th ACM Symposium on Operating Systems Principles*, pages 32–44, December 1989. Also as a Univ. Rochester TR-263, May 1989.

Compilation Techniques for Block-Cyclic Distributions

Seema Hiranandani
Ken Kennedy
John Mellor-Crummey
Ajay Sethi
Department of Computer Science
Rice University
Houston, TX 77251-1892
[seema,ken,johnmc,sethi]@rice.edu

Abstract

Compilers for data-parallel languages such as Fortran D and High-Performance Fortran use data alignment and distribution specifications as the basis for translating programs for execution on MIMD distributed-memory machines. This paper describes techniques for generating efficient code for programs that use block-cyclic distributions. These techniques can be applied to programs with symbolic loop bounds, symbolic array dimensions, and loops with non-unit strides. We present algorithms for computing the data elements that need to be communicated among processors both for loops with unit and non-unit strides, a linear-time algorithm for computing the memory access sequence for loops with non-unit strides, and experimental results for a hand-compiled test case using block-cyclic distributions.

1 Introduction

Data parallel languages such as High-Performance Fortran (HPF) [11, 18] and Fortran D [15] have attracted considerable attention as promising languages for writing portable parallel programs. These languages support an abstract model of parallel programming in which users annotate a single-threaded program with data alignment and distribution directives. Compilers for MIMD distributed-memory machines use these directives to partition the program's computation as the basis for deriving a SPMD program to be executed on each node of the parallel machine.

HPF and Fortran D support three principal types of data distribution directives for partitioning arrays among the processors in a parallel machine: block, cyclic, and block-cyclic. A distribution directive is associated with a particular axis of an array, indicating how the array will be partitioned along that axis. A block distribution along an array axis indicates that the array will be partitioned along that axis into a set of equal length intervals, one for each processor assigned to the array axis. Block distributions are the distribution of choice for nearest neighbor stencil-based computations. A cyclic distribution along an array axis indicates that the data will be partitioned into unit intervals which are assigned to processors in a round-robin fashion. Block and cyclic distributions are just common cases of the more general block-cyclic distribution which specifies the length of the intervals into which an array axis will be partitioned. A more precise definition of these distributions is given in section 3. Cyclic and block-cyclic distributions are useful for writing efficient and load-balanced dense matrix algorithms on distributed-memory machines [5].

Previous research has focused on compilation strategies for handling block and cyclic distributions efficiently [19, 17]. Block-cyclic distributions have only been studied in detail recently. Chatterjee *et. al.* [4] present a general solution for generating local addresses and communication sets for data-parallel programs with block-cyclic distributions. Stichnoth *et. al.* [22] look at the problem of generating communication sets for block-cyclically distributed arrays. Gupta *et. al.* [7] compute the communication and local index sets using *virtual processor approach*. In this paper, we present faster and conceptually more intuitive algorithms for generating communication sets, a linear-time algorithm for computing the memory access sequence for loops with non-unit strides, and a list of formulae useful for compiling programs with block-cyclic distributions.

The structure of the paper is as follows. Section 2 briefly reviews the organization of the Rice Fortran 77D compiler which we use as a vehicle explaining our techniques. Section 3 introduces the terminology and notation used throughout the rest of the paper. Sections 4 and 5 present algorithms and analyses to compile Fortran D programs with block-cyclic distributions. Sections 6 presents a hand-compiled Gaussian elimination example and experimental results that show the impact of using block-cyclic distributions with different block sizes. The paper concludes with a brief summary of our contributions.

2 Fortran D Compiler

To compile Fortran D for MIMD distributed-memory machines, the Rice Fortran 77D compiler uses data alignment and distribution directives to partition the data and computation among the available processors, and then introduces communication operations to transfer values as necessary. By using aggressive compile-time analysis and optimization to statically partition the computation and schedule communication, the Fortran 77D compiler can generate programs that are far more efficient than other compilers that rely on *run-time resolution* to explicitly calculate the ownership and communication for each reference at run time [3, 20, 23].

CS 94 - 7/94 Manchester, U. K.
© 1994 ACM 0-89791-665-4/94/0007..$3.50

```
REAL A(n), B(n)
DISTRIBUTE A(BLOCK_CYCLIC(3)), B(BLOCK_CYCLIC(5))
do i = 1, 45
    A(i) = F(B(i))
enddo
```

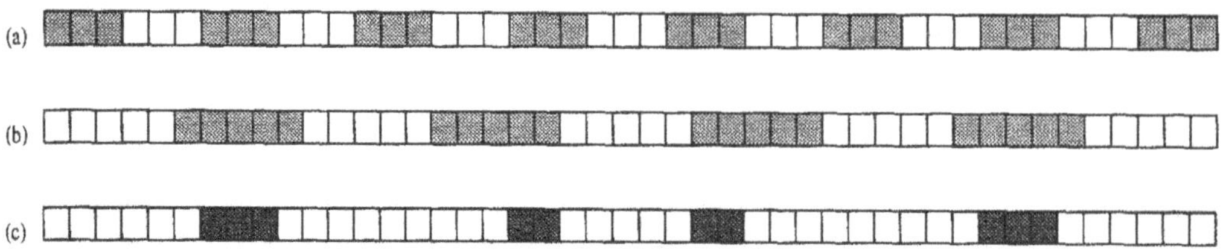

(a) Elements of A owned by processor 0 ≡ elements of B needed by processor 0
(b) Elements of B owned by processor 1
(c) Elements which processor 1 needs to send to processor 0 ≡ (a) ∩ (b)

Figure 1: Data ownership and communication for a block-cyclic data distribution.

Below, we briefly review the sequence of steps performed by the Rice Fortran 77D compiler; details of the compilation process are described elsewhere [13, 14].

1) Analyze program The compiler performs scalar dataflow analysis, symbolic analysis, and dependence testing to determine the type and level of all data dependencies [16].

2) Partition data The compiler determines the decomposition of each array and uses alignment and distribution statements to calculate the array section owned by each processor.

3) Partition computation The compiler uses the "owner computes" rule to partition the computation among the processors. Each processor only computes values of data it owns [3, 20, 23]. The left-hand side (*lhs*) of each assignment statement in a loop nest is used to calculate the set of loop iterations that cause a processor to assign to local data. This iteration set represents the work that must be performed by the processor.

4) Analyze communication The compiler uses the computation partition to calculate the non-local data accessed by each processor for each right-hand side (*rhs*) reference to a distributed array. References that cause non-local accesses are marked since they require insertion of communication.

5) Optimize communication The compiler examines each marked non-local reference and uses results of data decomposition, symbolic and dependence analysis to determine the legality of optimizations to reduce communication costs. *Regular section descriptors* (RSDs) are built for the sections of data to be communicated. RSDs compactly represent rectangular array sections and their higher dimension analogs [10].

6) Manage storage The compiler identifies the extent and type of non-local data accesses represented by RSDs to calculate the storage required for non-local data. For RSDs representing array elements contiguous to the local array section, the compiler reserves storage using *overlaps* created by extending the local array bounds [6]. Otherwise, temporary buffers or hash tables are used for storing non-local data.

7) Generate code The compiler uses the results of previous stages to generate a SPMD message-passing program for nodes of a MIMD distributed-memory machine. To accomplish this, the compiler reduces array and loop bounds, introduces guards to instantiate the data and computation partitions, uses RSDs representing non-local data accesses to generate calls to data-buffering routines and to insert calls *send* and *recv* or collective communication routines as appropriate. The compiler inserts code to use run-time resolution to determine work and communication partitions when complex subscript expressions defy compile-time analysis.

3 Terminology

Here, we briefly review some terminology and notation that is used throughout the remainder of the paper. We use P to denote the number of processors, numbered 0 through $P-1$. For the following canonical loop nest,

$$\text{do } \vec{i} = \vec{l} \text{ to } \vec{u} \text{ by } \vec{s}$$
$$A(g(\vec{i})) = B(f(\vec{i}))$$
$$\text{enddo}$$

we define the following sets; formal definitions of these sets are presented elsewhere [14].

- $image\_set_B(p)$ is the set of indices of array B that are owned by processor p.
- $iter\_set_A(p)$ is the set of loop iterations that cause reference A to access data owned by processor p.
- $index\_set_B(p)$ is the set of indices of array B referenced by processor p on loop iterations contained in $iter\_set_A(p)$.
- $send\_p\_set_B(p)$ is the set of processors to whom p must send local elements of array B.
- $receive\_p\_set_B(p)$ is the set of processors from whom p must receive values of non-local elements of array B.
- rsd_set_B is the set of indices of array B that are referenced in the loop nest.

```
REAL A(n,n)
DISTRIBUTE A(:, BLOCK_CYCLIC(8))
DISTRIBUTE B(:, BLOCK_CYCLIC(8))
do k = 1, n
    do i = k+1, n
S1      A(i,k) = F(B(i,k))
    enddo
    do j = k+1, n
        do i = k+1, n
S2          A(i,j) = G(A(i,j), A(i, k))
        enddo
    enddo
enddo
```

Figure 2: Code fragment with block-cyclic distributions.

As a convenient notation for describing sequences of indices that arise with block-cyclic distributions, we use a quadruplet [l:u:b:c] inspired by the Fortran 90 triplet notation. The components are, respectively, the lower bound, upper bound, block width, and the cycle length which is equal to the product $b * P$.

The elements of a 1D distributed array owned by a particular processor can be represented using a quadruplet. Figure 1(a) shows a 1D array A partitioned among two processors. Processor 0 owns elements [1:3], [7:9], [13:15], and so on; this can be represented as [1:n:3:6] in quadruplet notation. The quadruplet notation also can represent block and cyclic distributions by setting $c = n$ and $b = \lceil \frac{n}{P} \rceil$ for a block distribution and $c = P$ and $b = 1$ for a cyclic distribution. For the sake of convenience we continue to represent contiguous ranges as [l:u]. Sections of multi-dimensional arrays can be represented using an instance of the [l:u:b:c] or [l:u] sequence notation for each array dimension.

Clearly, the quadruplet notation is insufficient to represent the sequence of data accessed on a processor for loops with non-unit stride since the memory access gap is non-constant (details of how this case is handled are presented in section 5). Despite the incomplete expressiveness of the quadruplet notation, we use it for the sake of convenience with the understanding that the compiler will handle cases outside the scope of this simple notation by using appropriate data-structures.

4 Program Analysis

In this section, we describe how to synthesize the analysis results needed to compile data parallel programs in presence of block-cyclic distributions. Before getting into the details of the analysis phases, we illustrate the compilation steps using a simple example.

The program fragment shown in Figure 2 is similar to Gaussian Elimination with pivoting but without a loop-carried dependence from S_2 to S_1. Statement S_1 corresponds to the computation of the pivot while statement S_2 corresponds to row elimination with column indexing. Performing partition and communication analysis (refer to [12] for details) yields the following sets for statement S_2:

$$image\_set_A(p) = [1:n][p*8+1:n:8:P*8]$$
$$iter\_set_A(p) = [1:n][lb:n:8:P*8][k+1:n]$$
$$index\_set_A(p) = [k+1:n][1:n]$$

The image set indicates that the columns of B described by the quadruplet $[p*8+1 : n : 8 : P*8]$ in rows 1 through n are owned by processor p. The iteration set follows from the loop nesting order, resulting in an index domain spanning $[range\ of\ k][range\ of\ j][range\ of\ i]$; the formula for computing lb, the lower bound, is described in Section 4.1. To simplify presentation, we have shown only the index set for the reference A(i,k) since all we are really interested in is $(index\_set_A \setminus image\_set_A)$, the set difference. This set difference indicates the columns not owned by the processor. In this case, the difference is non-empty and each processor needs to receive all the columns owned by other processors. In other words, each processor needs to *broadcast* its columns. Since there exists a dependence from the statement S_1 to S_2, the processor which computes the k*th* column needs to perform a *broadcast* after executing the loop containing statement S_1. Figure 3 shows a hand-compiled version of the source fragment shown in Figure 2 that was translated using this strategy.

```
do kk = 1, n, 8
  do k = kk, min(kk+7, n)
    k$ = ...
    if (my$p owns the kth column) then
      do i = k+1, n
        A(i,k$) = F(B(i,k$))
      enddo
      broadcast A(k+1:n, k$)
    else
      receive A(k+1:n, k$)
    endif
    lb$1 = ...
    ub$1 = ...
    do j = lb$1, ub$1
      do i = k+1, n
        A(i,j) = G(A(i,j), A(i,k$))
      enddo
    enddo
  enddo
enddo
```

Figure 3: Hand-compiled block-cyclic example.

The block-cyclic distribution enables an optimization. Since each processor owns a block of columns, it can compute the pivot for one whole (or part) block of columns it owns. Instead of sending a separate message for each column, a processor can send one message for each sub-block of a block of columns. Since current distributed memory machines have high communication costs, reducing the number of messages with this optimization has the potential to improve performance over that attainable using a cyclic distribution. Figure 4 shows hand-compiled version of the source fragment shown in Figure 2 that was translated using this blocking strategy to vectorize of broadcasts.

4.1 Loop Indices and Bounds Generation

Consider the program fragment shown in the top half of Figure 5. The bottom half of the figure shows its corresponding SPMD node program using the functions *LowerLoopBound*, *UpperLoopBound*, *LocalLoopIndex*, *GlobalLoopIndex* and *Owner*. These formulae to compute these quantities are given below. The functions are specific to the example in the figure since they assume unit loop strides and the free variables L, b, and P in the functions refer to the lower bound of the X array, the block size for the block-cyclic distribution, and the number of processors, respectively. Note that the lower bound of the array in the SPMD code is 1.

```
do kk = 1, n, 8
if (my$p owns columns kk to kk+7) then
  do k = kk, min(kk+7, n)
    k$ = ...
    do i = k+1, n
      A(i,k$) = F(B(i,k$))
    enddo
    buffer A(k+1:n, k$)
  enddo
  broadcast buffer
else
  receive buffer
endif
do k = kk, min(kk+7, n)
  k$ = ...
  lb$1 = ...
  ub$1 = ...
  do j = lb$1, ub$1
    do i = k+1, n
      A(i,j) = G(A(i,j), buffer(...))
    enddo
  enddo
enddo
enddo
```

Figure 4: Hand-compiled code with vectorized broadcasts.

$Owner(X(i)) \equiv \lfloor \frac{i-L}{b} \rfloor \bmod P$

$LocalLoopIndex(i) \equiv \lfloor \frac{i-L}{b*P} \rfloor b + ((i-L) \bmod b) + 1$

$GlobalLoopIndex(i\$,p) \equiv$

$\lfloor \frac{i\$-1}{b} \rfloor (P*b) + p*b + ((i\$-1) \bmod b) + L$

$LowerLoopBound(L_j,p) \equiv$

```
l1 = Lj - L
if (p < ⌊l1/b⌋ mod P) then
    return ⌈l1/(b*P)⌉ * b + 1
else if (p > ⌊l1/b⌋ mod P) then
    return ⌊l1/(b*P)⌋ * b + 1
else
    return ⌊l1/(b*P)⌋ * b + (l1 mod b) + 1
endif
```

$UpperLoopBound(U_j,p) \equiv$

```
u1 = Uj - L
if (p < ⌊u1/b⌋ mod P) then
    return ⌈u1/(b*P)⌉ * b
else if (p > ⌊u1/b⌋ mod P) then
    return ⌊u1/(b*P)⌋ * b
else
    return ⌊u1/(b*P)⌋ * b + (u1 mod b) + 1
endif
```

If the number of processors and the loop bounds are known at compile time, then the loop bounds formulae can be evaluated at compile time. If these quantities are symbolic variables, then the formulae would require run-time evaluation. In experiments that measured the overhead of performing similar calculations at run time in shared virtual memory systems, the overhead of these calculations was found to be insignificant [2].

We present the techniques to handle loops with non-unit strides and more complex array subscripts in Section 5.

```
     {* Original Program *}
     REAL X(L:U)
     DISTRIBUTE X(BLOCK_CYCLIC(b))
     do i = Li,Ui
S1     X(i) = F1(i)
       do j = Lj,Uj
S2       X(j) = F2(j)
       enddo
     enddo

     {* SPMD Node Program *}
     REAL X(1:⌈(U - L + 1)/P⌉)
     lb$ = LowerLoopBound(Lj)
     ub$ = UpperLoopBound(Uj)
     do i = Li,Ui
       i$ = LocalLoopIndex(i)
       if (p .eq. Owner(X(i))) X(i$) = F1(i)
       do j = lb$,ub$
         j$ = GlobalLoopIndex(j, p)
         X(j) = F2(j$)
       enddo
     enddo
```

Figure 5: Loop indices and bounds generation.

4.2 Partitioning Analysis

We now describe the analysis required to compute iteration sets in the presence of symbolic loop bounds, array dimensions and number of processors. These iteration sets are used in two ways by the code generation phase: first, to reduce loop bounds so that each processor iterates only over the portion of the iteration space that causes it to reference data elements that it owns, and second to introduce guards to handle cases in which iteration sets are not identical for all processors.

4.2.1 Symbolic Iteration Sets

For each assignment statement in a loop nest, the compiler must compute an iteration set, parameterized by processor number, that represents the set of loop iterations that cause the processor to access the data it owns. Our discussion of iteration set construction will be based on the canonical loop nest shown below, which is the same as the loop given in Section 3.

```
Given:
  REAL A(l1 : u1, ..., ln : un), B(l1 : u1, ..., ln : un)
  DECOMPOSITION D(l1 : u1, ..., ln : un)
  ALIGN A(..., m, ...), B(..., m, ...) WITH D(..., m, ...)
  DISTRIBUTE D(d1, ..., BLOCK_CYCLIC(b), ..., dn)
Loop nest:
  DO i1 = lb1, ub1
   ...
    DO in = lbn, ubn
     ...
S1    A(..., g(ik), ...) = B(..., f(il), ...)
    ENDDO
   ...
  ENDDO
```

Note that in the loop given above the kth dimension of A, the lth dimension of B are aligned with the mth dimension of D (which is distributed block-cyclically). To determine a processor's iteration set for an assignment statement in a loop nest, the compiler examines the subscripted array reference on the left-hand side of the assignment, the array's alignment with its associated decomposition, and the distribution specification for the decomposition that reaches the assignment statement. Computing the iteration set involves reducing the index variable bounds for each distributed dimension of the decomposition corresponding to the lhs term. This problem of reducing the bounds is independent for each distributed dimension. For presentation purposes, we assume that only one dimension, d_m, is (block-cyclically) distributed. For arrays with more than one distributed dimension, the iteration set can be computed by intersecting the solutions for each singly-distributed dimension sub-problem.

In the above loop nest, it is assumed that the subscript function $g(i_k)$ has been simplified. In the cases where $g(i_k)$ is a constant, an induction variable, or a linear function of a single index variable, the iteration set can be computed at compile-time. For more complex subscript expressions, the compiler defers the computation of the iteration set to run time. In the following formulae, the functions *GlobalLowerLoopBound* and *GlobalUpperLoopBound* return the reduced lower and upper bounds for the loop in global indices. These functions are similar to the *LowerLoopBound* and *UpperLoopBound* functions given in Section 4.1.

- **Constant:** $g(i_k) \equiv c_k$

  if $Owner(A(\ldots, c_k, \ldots)) = p$ then
  $\quad iter\_set(p) = (lb_1 : ub_1, \ldots, lb_k : ub_k, \ldots, lb_n : ub_n)$
  else
  $\quad iter\_set(p) = \emptyset$
  endif

- **Induction Variable Only:** $g(i_k) \equiv i_k$

  $lb_{k1} = GlobalLowerLoopBound(lb_k)$
  $ub_{k1} = GlobalUpperLoopBound(ub_k)$
  $iter\_set(p) = (lb_1 : ub_1, \ldots, lb_{k1} : ub_{k1} : b : b * P, \ldots, lb_n : ub_n)$

- **Simple Linear Expression:** $g(i_k) \equiv i_k + c$

  $lb_{k1} = GlobalLowerLoopBound(lb_k - c)$
  $ub_{k1} = GlobalUpperLoopBound(ub_k - c)$
  $iter\_set(p) = (lb_1 : ub_1, \ldots, lb_{k1} : ub_{k1} : b : b * P, \ldots, lb_n : ub_n)$

- **Linear Expression:** $g(i_k) \equiv c_1 * i_k + c_0$
  To compute the iteration set, the subscript with linear expression is converted into an *induction variable only* subscript by changing the loop parameters. For example, if the original upper and lower loop bounds and the step are lb_k, ub_k and 1 respectively, then the transformed upper and lower loop bounds and step are $lb_k * c_1 + c_0$, $ub_k * c_1 + c_0$ and c_1 respectively.

  To compute the iteration set, the first iteration assigned to the processor needs to be determined. This is equivalent to finding the smallest non-negative integer j such that

  $$Owner(A(lb_k * c_1 + c_0 + c_1 * j)) = p$$

  This equation gives a set of linear Diophantine equations. The solution to a similar set of equations is given in Section 5.

4.3 Communication Analysis

4.3.1 Index Sets

Index sets are built for each distributed right-hand side array reference and contain the section of data accessed by a processor. They are used to determine the resulting communication.

From the previous section, observe that the iter_set(p) could either be $\emptyset$, $(lb_1 : ub_1, \ldots, lb_k : ub_k, \ldots, lb_n : ub_n)$ or $(lb_1 : ub_1, \ldots, lb_k : ub_k : b : b * P, \ldots, lb_n : ub_n)$. The index sets can be computed by substituting the value of iter_set(p) in the *rhs* subscript function f(u). Note that the index set is independent of the distribution of the referenced *rhs* array. If the iter_set(p) cannot be determined at the compile time, the index set computation needs to be done at the run time.

4.3.2 Communication Classification

Communication classification is a crucial step in the compilation process since it allows the compiler to insert calls to fast collective communication primitives in the output program and optimize the communication. Each non-local reference is classified as resulting in Single Send/Receive, Shift, Broadcast, Gather, All-to-All, Inspector/Executor or Run-time Resolution type of communication. The details of the algorithm can be found in [12].

4.4 Send and Receive Sets

To compute the send and receive sets (out_index_set and in_index_set, respectively), the compiler needs to find out, in the most general case, the intersection of two block-cyclically distributed arrays. However, as the example in Figure 1 demonstrates, block-cyclic sets are not closed under intersection.

Stichnoth *et. al.* [22] treat the block-cyclic sets as a union of disjoint cyclic sets. Since the cyclic sets are closed under intersection, the intersection of the two block-cyclic sets can be determined by intersecting all possible pairs of the cyclic sets. An advantage of using this technique is that the cost of translation from global index space to local index needs to be incurred only once for the lower and upper bound and stride of each section. A more general approach, the *virtual processor approach*, is taken by Gupta *et. al.*[8, 7]. Using this approach, a block-cyclic distribution can be viewed as a cyclic (or block) distribution on a set of virtual processors, which are block-wise (or cyclically) mapped to physical processors. With the virtual processor approach, explicit local-to-global and global-to-local translations are not needed for every index element communicated among the processors.

Mostly, the compiler needs to intersect two block-cyclic sets only once: to compute in_index_set and out_index_set. An efficient approach which avoids the overheads of computing *mods, ceilings, etc.* while computing the intersection, is to treat each block-cyclic set as an array sorted in ascending order. The intersection can then be computed by a simple linear-time algorithm similar to the merge sort algorithm. For example, processor 1 needs to send [1:45:3:6] ∩ [6:45:5:10] elements to processor 0. In other words, the compiler needs to find the intersection

$$\{1, 2, 3, 7, 8, 9, 13, 14, 15, 19, 20, 21, \ldots, 43, 44, 45\} \cap$$
$$\{6, 7, 8, 9, 10, 16, 17, 18, 19, 20, \ldots, 36, 37, 38, 39, 40\}$$

Of course, the intersection can be computed without looking at all the array elements because the pattern repeats after LCM(Block-size(A),Block-size(B))*P (= LCM(3,5)*2

```
Input : Arrays A and B as the lhs and the rhs array
    respectively The sender processor s, the destination
    processor d and the block sizes bsize1 and bsize2
    We assume the presence of a function "next_elem"
    that uses the current location and the block-size
    to increment the index pointer to the next array
    element owned by the processor.
Output : The set of elements of array B which need
    to be sent from s to d.
Method :
s_index = first_elem(image_set_B(s));
d_index = first_elem(index_set_B(d)),
while (s_index ≤ LCM(bsize1, bsize2) * P and
        d_index ≤ LCM(bsize1, bsize2) * P) do
    if (s_index < d_index) then
        next_elem(s_index, bsize1),
    else if (s_index > d_index) then
        next_elem(d_index, bsize2),
    else
        buffer(s_index);
        next_elem(s_index, bsize1),
        next_elem(d_index, bsize2),
    endif
endwhile
Using the elements belonging to the intersection (as
computed above) and the periodicity, buffer the rest
of the elements which need to be sent
```

Figure 6: Algorithm for computing the intersection.

= 30, in this case) elements. Hence the time required to compute the intersection is $\mathcal{O}$(LCM(Block-size(A), Block-size(B))*P) which is better than the time complexity of the method suggested in [22]. Note that both the sender and receiver compute the intersection using the global indices. To pack and unpack the message, both the processors need to translate the global indices to local indices. However, by substituting in the value in the formula for *LocalLoopIndex* given in Section 4.1, we get
*LocalLoopIndex(i+LCM(Block-size(A),Block-size(B))*P) = LocalLoopIndex(i) + LCM(Block-size(A),Block-size(B)).*
Therefore, we can use the repetitive pattern to perform address translation for LCM(Block-size(A),Block-size(B))*P index elements only.

In case the number of processors or the loop bounds are unknown at compile time, the compiler needs to perform the intersection at run time. Figure 6 gives the algorithm for computing the array elements which need to be sent from one processor to another. The algorithm for computing the receive set is similar to that for the send set.

In practice, though, we do not expect to find arbitrary block sizes (like 3 and 5 in the Figure 1). Since the block sizes also affect the locality of the array accesses, and hence the memory hierarchy optimizations, we expect the arrays to have the same block sizes or block sizes which are powers of 2. In these cases our algorithm would provide the most benefits. In the case of perfectly aligned arrays, the intersection would still be a block-cyclic set with block size equal to the smaller of the two original block sizes. The in_index_set and out_index_set sets can be computed trivially in this case.

5 Loops with Non-unit Stride

As mentioned earlier, in the presence of block-cyclic distributions, closed-form expressions for iter_set, in_index_set and out_index_set cannot be written. In this section we will describe algorithms to construct these sets in the presence of loops with non-unit strides and/or non-unit array subscripts. We have identified two cases of data access patterns for which we provide fast solutions for computing the sets. If the data access pattern does not fit either form then we resort to the algorithms proposed by Chatterjee *et. al.*[4]. In the case of non-unit stride and/or non-unit array subscript, the data accessed in a processor's local memory results in a non-constant stride pattern. In the example below,

Processor 0				Processor 1				Processor 2				Processor 3			
1	2	3	4	5	6	7	8	9	10	11	12	13	14	15	16
17	18	19	20	21	22	23	24	25	26	27	28	29	30	31	32
33	34	35	36	37	38	39	40	41	42	43	44	45	46	47	48
49	50	51	52	53	54	55	56	57	58	59	60	61	62	63	64
65	66	67	68	69	70	71	72	73	74	75	76	77	78	79	80
81	82	83	84	85	86	87	88	89	90	91	92	93	94	95	96

Figure 7: Block-cyclic distribution with non-unit stride.

```
REAL A(5,96), B(5, 96)
PARAMETER(N$PROC = 4)
DECOMPOSITION D(5, 96)
ALIGN A with D
DISTRIBUTE D(:, BLOCK_CYCLIC(4))
DO 10 i = 1, 5
  DO 10 j = 1, 96, 5
    A(i,j) = ...
10 continue
```

the second dimension of array A is distributed block-cyclically among 4 processors, with a block size of 4. The layout of array A in processor memories is depicted in Figure 7. As illustrated by Chatterjee *et. al.*, the layout of the array in memory can be visualized as an array of courses and offsets. The offset of an array element is its offset within the course. As an example, $A(3)$ resides in course 1, offset 3 in Processor 0's memory. Figure 7 also illustrates the elements of array a that are referenced in the loop nest. For instance, Processor 0 accesses elements A(1), A(36), A(51), ...and so on. The access *stride* for a given array reference on a processor is distance in local memory between each access. For example, the *stride* for array reference $A(i,j)$ on processor 0 is (11, 3, 3, 3).

The key insight, as noted in [4], is that the offset of an element determines the offset of the next element on the same processor. Since the offsets range between 0 and (block-size-1), by pigeon hole principle, at least two of the first (block-size+1) local memory locations on any particular processor must have the same offset. Moreover, since the offset of the next element depends only on the offset of the current array element, we conclude that there exists a cycle of memory access gaps.

Suppose we wish to find the first element (if any) of the array section that resides on a processor. This is equivalent to finding the smallest non-negative integer j such that

$$\left\lfloor \frac{(L_i + s * j - L) \bmod (P * b)}{b} \right\rfloor = p$$

where L_i = lower loop bound, L = array lower bound, s = step size and b is the block size.
The above equation is equivalent to

$$b * p \leq (L_i + s * j - L) \bmod (P * b) \leq b * (p + 1) - 1$$

which is equivalent to finding an integer q such that

$$b * p - L_i + L \leq s * j - q * P * b \leq b * (p + 1) - L_i + L - 1$$

```
do l = 1, n
  ...
  ipnt = ipntp
  ipntp = ipntp+il
  ...
  do k = ipnt+2, ipntp, 2
    i = i + 1
    X(i) = X(k) - V(k)*X(k-1) - V(k+1)*X(k+1)
  enddo
  ...
enddo
```

Figure 8: Livermore kernel 2 (ICCG excerpt).

The above inequality can be written as a set of b linear Diophantine equations in the variables j and q,

$$\{s*j - q*P*b = \lambda | b*p - L_i + L \leq \lambda \leq b*(p+1) - L_i + L - 1\}$$

The equations can be solved independently (solutions exist for an individual equation if and only if λ is divisible by GCD(s, b*P)). The general solution of a linear Diophantine equation can be found using the extended Euclid algorithm.

The extended Euclid algorithm gives not only the first such memory location, but a list of all the locations (array elements). We could then sort this list based on the array elements accessed by a processor and thereby compute the memory access gap sequence. Using this idea, Chatterjee *et. al.*give algorithms for computing the memory access gap sequence for loops with arbitrary array alignments and step size. The running time of the algorithm using this approach is $\mathcal{O}(\log min(s, P*b) + b\log b)$ which reduces to $\mathcal{O}(min(b\log b + \log s, b\log b + \log P))$.

In the following section, we present linear time algorithms for two cases. In the first case, the access stride, s, is less than the block size. In practice, this is the most commonly occurring case. As an example, consider the stripped down version of the loop (Figure 8) which appears in the Kernel 2 (Incomplete Cholesky-Conjugate Gradient) of the Livermore benchmark suite.

For the purpose of illustration, the access pattern corresponding to this case is depicted in Figure 9, where the access stride is 3. The Fortran D loop corresponding to such an access pattern is shown below :

```
REAL A(80)
PARAMETER(N$PROC = 5)
DECOMPOSITION D(80)
ALIGN A with D
DISTRIBUTE D(BLOCK_CYCLIC(4))
DO 10 i = 1, 80, 3
   A(i) = ...
10 continue
```

The second case, though not as common as the first one, has the access stride s with the constraint : $(s \mod (b*P)) < b$. This would occur, for example, when s is equal to the array column size and $b*P$ divides the column size. This occurs in linear algebra codes when one wants to access the consecutive row elements (instead of the column elements) of a linearized array. The access pattern, for case II, is depicted in Figure 10. The access stride is 23 and the total number of memory locations is 500.

Note that the second case subsumes the first one (because $(s \mod (b*P)) < b$ implies $s < b$). However, we are able to exploit the constraint that $s < b$ to achieve a simpler

Processor 0				Processor 1				Processor 2				Processor 3				Processor 4			
1	2	3	**4**	5	6	**7**	8	9	**10**	11	12	**13**	14	15	**16**	17	18	**19**	20
21	**22**	23	24	**25**	26	27	**28**	29	30	**31**	32	33	**34**	35	36	**37**	38	39	**40**
41	42	**43**	44	45	**46**	47	48	**49**	50	51	**52**	53	54	**55**	56	57	**58**	59	60
61	62	63	**64**	65	66	**67**	68	69	**70**	71	72	**73**	74	75	**76**	77	78	**79**	80

Figure 9: Example for case I (step = 3).

algorithm and we present it first. The algorithm for case II works almost identically to case I by treating $s \mod (b*P)$ as the step size (which is less than b). However, in this case, the algorithm also keeps track of the number of skipped rows to compute the memory gaps correctly.

The important property satisfied by both $s < b$ (Case I) and $s \mod b*P < b$ (Case II) is that if processor p executes the *ith* iteration then the (i+1)*th* iteration would be executed either by processor p itself or by processor $(p+1) \mod P$. This fact is used to achieve the linear-time algorithm by computing the offsets (and the memory access gaps) without actually solving the Diophantine equations.

5.1 Algorithms to Calculate the Memory Access Sequence

We now present algorithms to compute the local-memory access sequence for loops with non-unit stride. It is assumed that the data distribution is aligned perfectly with the decomposition. Otherwise, if the data distribution is aligned to the decomposition using an affine alignment, then we would need two applications of the following algorithms to get the memory access sequence.

Figure 11 gives the algorithm for Case I. Given an offset for an index element on processor p and a step size s, first, the number of iterations executed within the same course (= numLocalHops) is computed. Next, we step through the course using the stride s and store the memory access gap (which is simply s for these index elements) in $\Delta\mathcal{M}$ table. Using the location of the last index element accessed in the course (= lastLoc), we can compute the number of elements needed to be stepped through before reaching processor p again (which is e = (P-1)*b + (b-lastLoc)). e mod s then gives the number of array elements left after the last iteration on the $(p-1)$ mod P processor. Therefore, nextOffset = $s - e$ mod $s - 1$ is the offset (within the next course) of the next index element accessed by p. Note that since $s < b$, the next element would lie in the next course and, therefore, local-memory access gap = b - lastLoc + nextOffset + 1. The algorithm iterates till it finds a cycle of memory access gaps.

As mentioned before, for case II, the algorithm works almost identically to that of case I by treating $s \mod (b*P)$ as the step size and keeping track of the number of skipped rows to compute the memory gaps correctly. We illustrate the algorithm for case II (given in Figure 12) using our example (Figure 10). In Figure 10, $s \mod (b*P)$, the horizontal displacement of the current index element from the index element accessed in the previous iteration, is 3 (for example, on Processor 0, element 24 has offset 3 w.r.t. the beginning of the course, while element 1 has offset 0. Therefore, the horizontal displacement from 1 to 24, G = 3). numLocalHops gives the number of consecutive iterations which access data on the same processor. In case consecutive iterations

Processor 0				Processor 1				Processor 2				Processor 3				Processor 4			
1	2	3	4	5	6	7	8	9	10	11	12	13	14	15	16	17	18	19	20
21	22	23	**24**	25	26	27	28	29	30	31	32	33	34	35	36	37	38	39	40
41	42	43	44	45	46	**47**	48	49	50	51	52	53	54	55	56	57	58	59	60
61	62	63	64	65	66	67	68	69	**70**	71	72	73	74	75	76	77	78	79	80
81	82	83	84	85	86	87	88	89	90	91	92	**93**	94	95	96	97	98	99	100
101	102	103	104	105	106	107	108	109	110	111	112	113	114	115	**116**	117	118	119	120
121	122	123	124	125	126	127	128	129	130	131	132	133	134	135	136	137	138	**139**	140
141	142	143	144	145	146	147	148	149	150	151	152	153	154	155	156	157	158	159	160
161	**162**	163	164	165	166	167	168	169	170	171	172	173	174	175	176	177	178	179	180
181	182	183	184	**185**	186	187	188	189	190	191	192	193	194	195	196	197	198	199	200
201	202	203	204	205	206	207	**208**	209	210	211	212	213	214	215	216	217	218	219	220
221	222	223	224	225	226	227	228	229	230	**231**	232	233	234	235	236	237	238	239	240
241	242	243	244	245	246	247	248	249	250	251	252	253	**254**	255	256	257	258	259	260
261	262	263	264	265	266	267	268	269	270	271	272	273	274	275	276	**277**	278	279	280
281	282	283	284	285	286	287	288	289	290	291	292	293	294	295	296	297	298	299	**300**
301	302	303	304	305	306	307	308	309	310	311	312	313	314	315	316	317	318	319	320
321	322	**323**	324	325	326	327	328	329	330	331	332	333	334	335	336	337	338	339	340
341	342	343	344	345	**346**	347	348	349	350	351	352	353	354	355	356	357	358	359	360
361	362	363	364	365	366	367	368	**369**	370	371	372	373	374	375	376	377	378	379	380
381	382	383	384	385	386	387	388	389	390	391	**392**	393	394	395	396	397	398	399	400
401	402	403	404	405	406	407	408	409	410	411	412	413	414	**415**	416	417	418	419	420
421	422	423	424	425	426	427	428	429	430	431	432	433	434	435	436	437	**438**	439	440
441	442	443	444	445	446	447	448	449	450	451	452	453	454	455	456	457	458	459	460
461	462	463	464	465	466	467	468	469	470	471	472	473	474	475	476	477	478	479	480
481	482	483	**484**	485	486	487	488	489	490	491	492	493	494	495	496	497	498	499	500

Figure 10: Example for case II (step = 23).

Input: Offset of a valid iteration for processor 0 (offset_0), Block size (b), step (s), processor number (p), number of processors (P).

Output: The $\Delta\mathcal{M}$ table. The algorithm can also be used to record the starting memory location and the length of the table.

Method:

```
ΔM[i] = NOT_DEFINED, i=0,...,b-1;
offset = s - (p*b - (offset_0 + ⌊(p*b-(offset_0+1))/s⌋*s));
while (true) do
    if (ΔM[offset] ≠ NOT_DEFINED) break;
    numLocalHops = ⌊(b-(offset+1))/s⌋;
    for (i=1; i <= numLocalHops; i++) do
        ΔM[offset] = s;
        offset = offset + s;
    endfor
    lastLoc = offset + 1;
    nextOffset = s - [(P-1)b + (b-lastLoc)] mod s - 1;
    ΔM[offset] = b - offset + nextOffset;
    offset = nextOffset;
endwhile
```

Figure 11: Algorithm for case I (s < b).

access data on the same processor (like the first and the second iterations which access elements 1 and 24, respectively), R gives the number of rows which are skipped between the two index elements. In our example, R = $\lfloor \frac{23}{4*5} \rfloor = 1$ and since block size, b, = 4 and G = 3, depending on the offset of the current index element, numLocalHops would be 0 or 1. Lastly, note that the index element accessed on Processor 0 after 24 is 162. T, the total number of rows skipped between any two such iterations, is computed using G, R and the number of elements which need to be stepped through (in other words, the total horizontal displacement required) after the last index element on the current processor. In Figure 10, for index element 24, T = $(\lfloor \frac{16}{3} \rfloor + 1) * 1 = 6$, which is the number of courses skipped on Processor 0 between index elements 24 and 162. Using these values, we can compute the local-memory access gaps.

Given the loop lower bound L and the array lower bound L_A, for case I :

$$\text{offset}_0 = \begin{cases} (L - L_A) \bmod s, & if\ (L - L_A) \bmod s \neq 0 \\ s, & if\ (L - L_A) \bmod s = 0 \end{cases}$$

For case II, we need slightly more work :

Let $G = s \bmod (b * P)$, the processor which owns L be $p = \lfloor \frac{(L-L_A) \bmod (b*P)}{b} \rfloor$, the offset of L within its course be $o = (L - L_A) \bmod b$. Therefore, the number of elements left in the row, $e = b - (o + 1) + (P - p) * b$ and the number of elements left after the last iteration (in the sense that the next iteration would be executed by Processor 0) in the sequence (refer to Figure 10), $l = e \bmod g$. Now, $\text{offset}_0 = g - l - 1$.

An interesting fact which could be used to further speed up the algorithms is that the length of the memory access gap sequence cycle divides the block size. Others tricks like treating multiplications and divisions as shifts in case of step size or block size being powers of 2 can also be used to improve the running time of the algorithms.

Input: Offset of a valid iteration for processor 0 ($offset_0$), Block size (b), step (s), processor number (p), number of processors (P).

Output: The $\Delta\mathcal{M}$ table. The algorithm can also be used to record the starting memory location and the length of the table.

Method:

```
ΔM[i] = NOT_DEFINED, i=0,...,b-1;
G = Horizontal Displacement = s mod (b * P);
R = Rows Skipped = ⌊s/(b*P)⌋;
T = Total Rows Skipped
offset = G - (p*b - (offset0 + ⌊(p*b-(offset0+1))/G⌋*G));
while (true) do
    if (ΔM[offset] ≠ NOT_DEFINED) break;
    numLocalHops = ⌊(b-(offset+1))/G⌋;
    bf for (i=1; i ≤ numLocalHops; i++) do
        ΔM[offset] = b*R + G;
        offset = offset + G;
    endfor
    lastLoc = offset + 1;
    ElementsLeft = b * P - lastLoc;
    T = (⌊ElementsLeft/G⌋ + 1) * R;
    GlobalElemsLeft = ElementsLeft mod G;
    nextOffset = G - GlobalElemsLeft - 1;
    ΔM[offset] = b * T + (b-(offset+1)) + (nextOffset+1);
    offset = nextOffset;
endwhile
```

Figure 12: Algorithm for case II (s *mod* b*P < b).

Complexity: Each element of the array $\Delta\mathcal{M}$ is filled at most once by the algorithm. As soon as an already filled array element is encountered, the algorithm stops. Therefore, the while loop (together with the inner for loop) iterates at most b times and hence it is an $\mathcal{O}(b)$ algorithm. Therefore, as compared to the method suggested in [4], not only is our approach conceptually more intuitive, the algorithms given above are an $\mathcal{O}(b)$.

5.2 Send and Recv Sets

Once we have computed the memory access sequence for an array access, the computation of the send and receive sets is comparatively easier. Consider the following example :

```
REAL A(n)
DISTRIBUTE A(BLOCK_CYCLIC(4))
do i = 1, N, 5
    A(i) = F(A(i-1), A(i), A(i+1))
enddo
```

If P=4, then we would get the same memory access sequence as shown in Figure 7. Only those iterations which assign to the array elements A(i) s.t. its offset is 0 or 3 (= the block-size - 1) need to receive some data (corresponding to A(i-1) and A(i+1), respectively).

In general, in case of communication required because of *shifts*, we can find both the processors that need to send the data and the location of the array element within the owner processor [4] . Note that, in case of shifts, a processor communicates with at most two processors.

Suppose that element A(i) is located on processor p with offset o. We want to find the processor and local memory location of A(i-d). Let d = q(P*b)+r and $\Delta\mathcal{P} = \lceil (r-o)/b \rceil$, where b is the block size. Then the owner processor of A(i-d) is $(p-\Delta\mathcal{P}+P)$ mod P. Since $0 \le o \le$ b, ΔP can assume only two values.

The location of A(i-d) (say $\mathcal{M}'$) can be computed from the location of A(i) (say $\mathcal{M}$) as follows. We define $\Delta\mathcal{L}$ such that $\mathcal{M}' = \mathcal{M} + \Delta\mathcal{L}(o)$.

$$\Delta\mathcal{L}(o) = ((o - r) \bmod b) - o - bq - \eta,$$
$$\eta = \begin{cases} b & if\ (p * b - r + o) < 0, \\ 0 & otherwise. \end{cases}$$

Since the memory access sequence algorithm can compute offsets also, we can determine the iterations that need communication as well as the elements that need to be sent without any extra work.

In the case of block-cyclic distributions with different block sizes, the send and receive sets can be computed by computing the local index sets, local iteration sets, etc. For more complicated patterns, for example in case of stride changes, there does not exist any simple lookup technique for generating the communication sets because the pattern of destination processors can have period longer than the block size b. In such cases, we resort to the inspector-executor model [21, 9] for irregular loops.

6 Example and Experimental Results

To explore the effects of block-cyclic data distributions, we experimented with the DGEFA subroutine from Linpack. DGEFA is a key subroutine which performs Gaussian elimination with partial pivoting. Since the subroutine contains a triangular loop, a cyclic or block-cyclic distribution is desirable for maintaining good load balance.

Figure 13 shows the original program as well as the hand-compiled Fortran D program that uses a column block-cyclic distribution of width b which distributes blocks of columns in a round-robin fashion across the processors.

Table 1 shows timings for DGEFA benchmark on an Intel iPSC/860 for various block sizes, numbers of processors and problem sizes. The results in the table show that non-unit block sizes provide the best performance in some cases, reducing execution time by 10% or more. Figure 14 shows an alternate view of these results, plotting measured speedups for different problem and block sizes. Improvements measured here for block-cyclic distributions are related to the following observations. If an array is distributed cyclically then for each column, $(P-1)$ processors have to wait for the processor which owns that column to find the maximum element and broadcast it to others. On the other hand, with a block-cyclic distribution, processors own a block of adjacent columns and once a processor begins computing a sequence of pivots it can execute b iterations without waiting for a message. This results in some overlap of communication and computation which reduces the message latency seen by other processors.

From these experiments we conclude that block-cyclic distributions are potentially useful for DGEFA. Clearly, experience with a wider range of codes will be necessary to draw stronger conclusions about the overall effectiveness of block-cyclic distributions.

```
{* Original Fortran D Program *}
SUBROUTINE DGEFA(n,a,ipvt)
  INTEGER n,ipvt(n),j,k,l
  DOUBLE PRECISION a(n,n), al, t
  DISTRIBUTE a(:,BLOCKCYCLIC(b))
  do k = 1, n-1
    {* Find max element in a(k:n,k) *}
S1  l = k
S2  al = dabs(a(k, k))
    do i = k + 1, n
      if (dabs(a(i, k)) .GT. al) then
S3      al = dabs(a(i, k))
S4      l = i
      endif
    enddo
    ipvt(k) = l
    if (al .NE. 0) then
      if (l .NE. k) then
        t = a(l,k)
        a(l,k) = a(k,k)
        a(k,k) = t
      endif
      {* Compute multipliers in a(k+1:n,k) *}
      t = -1.0d0/a(k,k)
      do i = k+1, n
        a(i, k) = a(i, k) * t
      enddo
      {* Reduce remaining submatrix *}
      do j = k+1, n
        t = a(l,j)
        if (l .NE. k) then
          a(l,j) = a(k,j)
          a(k,j) = t
        endif
        do i = k+1, n
S5        a(i, j) = a(i, j) + t * a(i, k)
        enddo
      enddo
    endif
  enddo
  ipvt(n) = n
end
```

```
{* Hand Compiled Output for 4 Processors *}
SUBROUTINE DGEFA(n,a,ipvt)
  INTEGER n,ipvt(n),j,k,l
  DOUBLE PRECISION a(n,n/4), al, t, dp$buf1(n)
  do k = 1, n-1
    owner$proc = MOD((k-1), (b*n$p))/b
    k$ = ((k - 1)/(b*n$p))b + MOD(MOD((k-1), b*n$p), b) + 1
    {* Find max element in a(k:n,k$) *}
    if (my$p .EQ. owner$proc) then
      l = k
      al = dabs(a(k, k$))
      do i = k + 1, n
        if (dabs(a(i, k$)) .GT. al) then
          al = dabs(a(i, k$))
          l = i
        endif
      enddo
      broadcast l, al
    else
      recv l, al
    endif
    ipvt(k) = l
    if (al .NE. 0) then
      if (my$p .EQ. owner$proc) then
        if (l .NE. k) then
          t = a(l,k$)
          a(l,k$) = a(k,k$)
          a(k,k$) = t
        endif
        {* Compute multipliers in a(k+1:n,k$) *}
        t = -1.0d0/a(k,k$)
        do i = k+1, n
          a(i, k$) = a(i, k$) * t
        enddo
      endif
      {* Reduce remaining submatrix *}
      if (my$p .EQ. owner$proc) then
        buffer a(k+1:n, k$) into dp$buf1
        broadcast dp$buf1(1:n-k)
      else
        recv dp$buf1(1:n-k)
      endif
      lb$1 = LowerLoopBound(k+1)
      do j = lb$1, n/4
        t = a(l,j)
        if (l .NE. k) then
          a(l,j) = a(k,j)
          a(k,j) = t
        endif
        do i = k+1, n
          a(i, j) = a(i, j) + t * dp$buf1(i-k)
        enddo
      enddo
    endif
  enddo
  ipvt(n) = n
end
```

Figure 13: DGEFA: Gaussian elimination with partial pivoting.

Program	Problem Size	Proc	Block Size (time in secs) 1	2	4	8	16	32	64	128
Gauss	256 × 256	1	*sequential time = 2.200*							
		2	0.974	0.990	0.985	0.982	0.992	1.003	1.084	1.198
		4	0.629	0.619	0.613	0.621	0.644	0.692	0.683	0.783
		8	0.537	0.505	0.485	0.481	0.490	0.598	0.825	1.348
		16	0.627	0.593	0.577	0.580	0.627	0.687	0.892	1.389
		32	0.756	0.717	0.702	0.725	0.728	0.808	0.997	1.495
	512 × 512	1	*sequential time = 17.53*							
		2	7.328	7.364	7.366	7.396	7.471	7.634	7.962	8.616
		4	4.043	4.022	4.035	4.094	4.208	4.440	4.857	5.459
		8	2.462	2.419	2.418	2.460	2.555	2.739	3.133	5.512
		16	2.106	2.010	1.966	1.957	2.058	2.444	3.328	5.627
		32	2.505	2.413	2.371	2.389	2.540	2.839	3.625	5.820
	1K × 1K	1	*estimated sequential time = 140*							
		2	65.69	65.71	65.75	66.10	66.23	66.97	68.59	71.53
		4	34.07	34.09	34.20	34.62	34.99	36.09	38.20	41.96
		8	18.14	18.14	18.26	18.55	19.16	20.34	22.44	24.99
		16	10.46	10.47	10.54	10.78	11.26	12.14	14.31	25.32
		32		8.791	8.695	8.854	9.547	11.32	15.19	25.79

Table 1: Intel iPSC/860 execution times for Gaussian elimination with BLOCK-CYCLIC distribution.

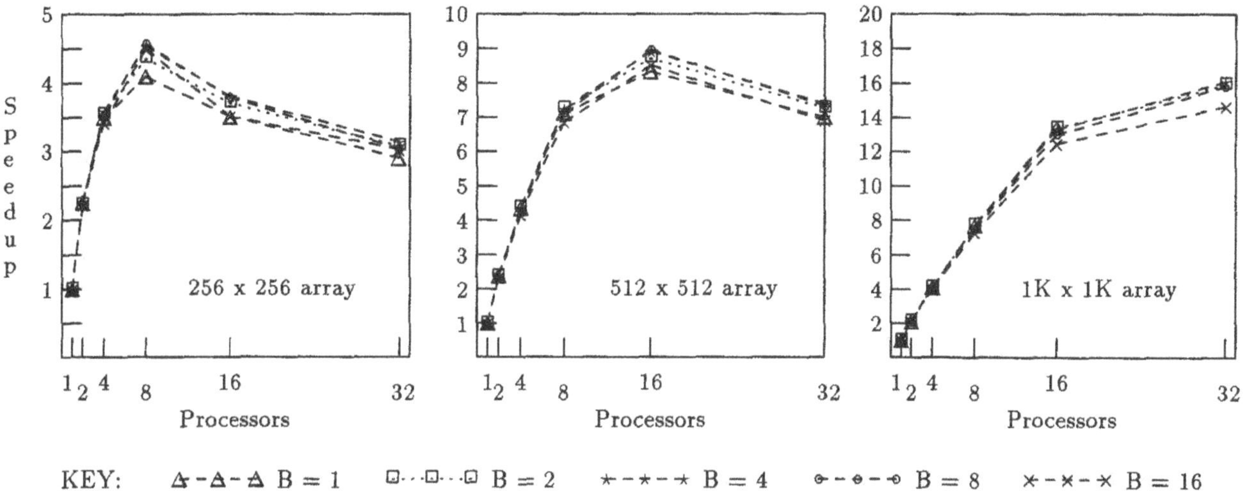

Figure 14: Gaussian elimination speedup results for different problem and block sizes.

7 Conclusions

A usable yet efficient machine-independent parallel programming model is needed to make large-scale parallel machines useful for scientific programmers. We believe that data-placement languages, such as Fortran D and HPF, can provide such a portable data-parallel programming model. The key to achieving good performance with data parallel languages is applying advanced compiler analysis and optimization to automatically exploit parallelism and manage communication. This paper describes techniques that will enable compilers for data parallel languages to handle block-cyclic distributions, extending the class of problems for which good performance can be achieved.

We described the analysis required to compile data parallel programs with block-cyclic distributions in the presence of symbolic loop bounds and array sizes, non-unit loop strides and variable number of processors. We also gave algorithms for computing the data elements that need to be communicated both for the loops with unit and non-unit strides, and presented a linear-time algorithm for computing non-constant local memory access pattern for loops with non-unit stride.

In our experimental results evaluating the effectiveness of block-cyclic distributions for DGEFA, using non-unit block sizes provided some improvements in performance in particular cases. However, larger improvements in performance could be realized if the number of messages could be reduced. In section 4, we described how message vectorization could be used with a block-cyclic distribution to reduce the number of messages. The DGEFA code shown in Figure 13 contains a loop-carried dependence from S_5 to S_2/S_3 that complicates application of message vectorization. To employ message vectorization in this case, the compiler would need to restructure the computation. Since the pivot for a particular column does not depend on the columns occurring after it, the compiler could minimize the computation that needs to be done before broadcasting the pivots for a block of columns by deferring executing of statement S_5 for columns outside the current block until after the broadcast. To increase the computation and communication overlap, the processor also could initially compute and broadcast the pivot for only the first column in a block and then compute and broadcast the pivots for the rest of the columns in the block in a second message. By broadcasting the first pivot as soon as possible, other processors can perform elimination steps while the other processor computes the pivots for the rest of the columns. This optimization would maximize the communication and computation overlap. A similar optimization was discussed by Adve, *et. al.* [1] in the context of cyclic distributions.

To evaluate the potential benefits of block-cyclic distributions for data parallel codes, it is clear that further work is necessary. The techniques we have presented here provide a foundation for that work.

8 Acknowledgments

The authors wish to thank Reinhard von Hanxleden, Uli Kremer and Chau-Wen Tseng for their assistance, and Elana Granston and the referees for providing detailed comments and suggestions. This research was supported in part by the IBM corporation, the Center for Research on Parallel Computation (CRPC) through NSF Cooperative Agreement Number CCR-9120008, and ARPA under contract #DABT63-92-C-0038. Use of the Intel iPSC/860 was provided by the CRPC NSF Cooperative Agreement Nos. CCR-8809615 and CDA-8619893 with support from the Keck Foundation.

References

[1] V.S. Adve, C. Koelbel, and J.Mellor-Crummey. Performance analysis of data parallel programs. *Submitted to Supercomputing '94*, April 1994.

[2] F. Bodin, E.D. Granston, and T. Montaut. Experiences reducing false sharing in shared virtual memory systems (*under preparation*). Technical report, Center for Research on Parallel Computation, Rice University, 1994.

[3] D. Callahan and K. Kennedy. Compiling programs for distributed-memory multiprocessors. *Journal of Supercomputing*, 2:151–169, October 1988.

[4] S. Chatterjee, J. Gilbert, F. Long, R. Schreiber, and S. Teng. Generating local addresses and communication sets for data-parallel programs. In *Proceedings of the Fourth ACM SIGPLAN Symposium on Principles and Practice of Parallel Programming*, San Diego, CA, May 1993.

[5] J. Dongarra, R. van de Geijn, and D. Walker. A look at scalable dense linear algebra libraries. In *Proceedings of the 1992 Scalable High Performance Computing Conference*, pages 372–379, Williamsburg, VA, April 1992.

[6] M. Gerndt. Updating distributed variables in local computations. *Concurrency: Practice & Experience*, 2(3):171–193, September 1990.

[7] S.K.S. Gupta, S.D. Kaushik, S. Mufti, S. Sharma, C.-H. Huang, and P. Sadayappan. On compiling array expressions for efficient execution on distributed-memory machines. In *Proceedings of the 1993 International Conference on Parallel Processing*, volume II, pages 301–305, 1993.

[8] S.K.S. Gupta, S.D. Kaushik, S. Mufti, S. Sharma, C.-H. Huang, and P. Sadayappan. On compiling array expressions for efficient execution on distributed-memory machines. Technical report OSU-CISRC-4/94-TR19, Department of Computer and Information Science, Ohio State University, Columbus, OH, March 1994.

[9] R. v. Hanxleden. Handling irregular problems with fortran d – a preliminary report. Technical Report CRPC-TR93339-S, Center for Research on Parallel Computation, Rice University, October 1993.

[10] P. Havlak and K. Kennedy. An implementation of interprocedural bounded regular section analysis. *IEEE Transactions on Parallel and Distributed Systems*, 2(3):350–360, July 1991.

[11] High Performance Fortran Forum. High Performance Fortran language specification. *Scientific Programming*, 2(1-2):1–170, 1993.

[12] S. Hiranandani, K. Kennedy, J. Mellor-Crummey, and A. Sethi. Advanced compilation techniques for fortran d. Technical Report CRPC-TR93338, Center for Research on Parallel Computation, Rice University, October 1993.

[13] S. Hiranandani, K. Kennedy, and C. Tseng. Compiler optimizations for Fortran D on MIMD distributed-memory machines. In *Proceedings of Supercomputing '91*, Albuquerque, NM, November 1991.

[14] S. Hiranandani, K. Kennedy, and C. Tseng. Compiler support for machine-independent parallel programming in Fortran D. In J. Saltz and P. Mehrotra, editors, *Languages, Compilers, and Run-Time Environments for Distributed Memory Machines*. North-Holland, Amsterdam, The Netherlands, 1992.

[15] S. Hiranandani, K. Kennedy, and C. Tseng. Compiling Fortran D for MIMD distributed-memory machines. *Communications of the ACM*, 35(8):66–80, August 1992.

[16] K. Kennedy, K. S. McKinley, and C. Tseng. Analysis and transformation in the ParaScope Editor. In *Proceedings of the 1991 ACM International Conference on Supercomputing*, Cologne, Germany, June 1991.

[17] C. Koelbel. Compile-time generation of regular communications patterns. In *Proceedings of Supercomputing '91*, pages 101–110, Albuquerque, NM, November 1991.

[18] C. Koelbel, D. Loveman, R. Schreiber, G. Steele, Jr., and M. Zosel. *The High Performance Fortran Handbook*. The MIT Press, Cambridge, MA, 1994.

[19] C. Koelbel and P. Mehrotra. Compiling global name-space programs for distributed execution. ICASE Report 90-70, Institute for Computer Application in Science and Engineering, Hampton, VA, October 1990.

[20] A. Rogers and K. Pingali. Process decomposition through locality of reference. In *Proceedings of the SIGPLAN '89 Conference on Program Language Design and Implementation*, Portland, OR, June 1989.

[21] J. Saltz, K. Crowley, R. Mirchandaney, and H. Berryman. Run-time scheduling and execution of loops on message passing machines. *Journal of Parallel and Distributed Computing*, 8(4):303–312, April 1990.

[22] J. Stichnoth, D. O'Hallaron, and T. Gross. Generating communication for array statements: Design, implementation, and evaluation. In *Proceedings of the Sixth Workshop on Languages and Compilers for Parallel Computing*, Portland, OR, August 1993.

[23] H. Zima, H.-J. Bast, and M. Gerndt. SUPERB: A tool for semi-automatic MIMD/SIMD parallelization. *Parallel Computing*, 6:1–18, 1988.

A Data Cache with Multiple Caching Strategies Tuned to Different Types of Locality

Antonio González, Carlos Aliagas and Mateo Valero

Universitat Politècnica de Catalunya
Departamento de Arquitectura de Computadores
Campus Nord - Módulo D6
c/ Gran Capitán, s/n
E-08071 - Barcelona (Spain)

E-mail: antonio@ac.upc.es

Abstract

Current data cache organizations fail to deliver high performance in scalar processors for many vector applications. There are two main reasons for this loss of performance: the use of the same organization for caching both spatial and temporal locality and the "eager" caching policy used by caches. The first issue has led to the well-known trade-off of designing caches with a line size of a few tens of bytes. However, for memory reference patterns with low spatial locality a significant pollution is introduced. On the other hand, when the spatial locality is very high, larger lines could be more convenient. The eager caching policy refers to the fact that data that miss in the cache and is required by the processor is always cached (excepting writes in a no write allocate cache). However, it is common in numerical applications to have large working sets (large vectors, larger than the cache size), that result on a swept of the cache without any opportunity to exploit temporal locality. In addition, they replace some other data that may be required later.

In this paper, a novel data cache organization, called *dual data cache*, is presented. To our knowledge, this is the first time a cache with independent parts for managing spatial and temporal locality is proposed. In this way, both types of locality can be more efficiently exploited. In addition, the dual data cache implements a lazy caching policy, which tries not to cache something until a benefit (in terms of spatial or temporal locality) can be predicted. For both purposes, the dual data cache makes use of a *locality prediction table*, which is a history table with information about the most recently executed load/store instructions. In addition, a simplified implementation of the dual data cache, which is called *selective cache* is also presented.

Keywords

Cache memory, data locality, cache organization.

1. Introduction

Many real programs, in particular numerical applications, make use of vector data. Vector processors, are aware of this data type and include some instructions that manipulate vectors. However, this is not the case of scalar processors, which usually do not have any specific instruction for vectors. In such processors, operations on vectors are performed by means of a sequence of scalar operations that manipulate individual elements of vectors. Although the computation power of current superscalar processors may be very effective for performing such operations, the processor performance is usually degraded by the low efficiency of the data cache memory.

In the context of this document, a vector is a number of elements identified by its initial address and a constant stride (distance between successive elements of the vector).

The poor performance of current data cache organizations for dealing with vector data is mainly due to the following reasons:

- Vector data usually require very large working sets which result in a swept of the cache without any chance to exploit temporal locality.
- In some cases, vectors are accessed with a stride not equal to one. In those cases, the ability of a cache to exploit spatial locality is significantly reduced. Because conventional cache memories deal with lines of consecutive data, these strides cause a significant cache pollution. This negative effect increases as the stride is higher, and at the worst, it could end up with just one useful data element in every cache line.
- Finally, when the stride measured in cache lines and the number of sets in the cache are not coprime, not all the sets are used to store the elements of the vector, which in turn aggravates the problem caused by large working sets. For instance, suppose a direct mapped cache with 512 lines and a line size equal to the size of a vector element. Then, it can store a vector with stride 3 and length 512. However, if the stride is 2, the length of the vector can not be greater than 256. In other words, some strides make the vector accesses to interfere with themselves, even if the vector is smaller than the cache size.

On the other hand, if the stride is constant, accesses to vector elements are quite easy to predict and therefore it is possible to implement a prefetch mechanism to take advantage of this fact.

We can find in the literature different proposals to deal with some of the above mentioned issues. However, to our knowledge, there is no proposal trying to deal with the four issues (large working sets, strides different to one, interferences and prefetching) at the same time. In this paper, we present a novel cache organization that incorporates some features to exploit the characteristics of vector as well as scalar data. In particular, our cache organization tries to avoid the swept effect of large vectors, reduces the pollution caused by non unit strides, decreases the penalty caused by self-interferences due to strides coprime with the number of lines, and can take advantage of prefetching of vector elements.

The proposed data cache organization, called *dual data cache*, can be used in any (super)scalar processor since it does not require any particular feature in the instruction set architecture. In addition, a simplified implementation of the dual data cache, which is called *selective cache* is also proposed.

The performance of the dual data cache and the selective cache has been evaluated for a set of benchmarks by means of simulation. The results show a significant performance improvement when compared with a conventional cache organization with similar hardware cost.

The rest of this paper is organized as follows. Section 2 summarizes the work related with the topic of this paper. Then, the proposed cache organization is described in section 3. Section 4 presents a qualitative analysis of the performance of the proposed mechanism. Results obtained by simulation are discussed in section 5. Finally, section 6 presents some concluding remarks.

2. Related Work

As described in the previous section, there are four main issues to be considered when designing a data cache for a (super)scalar processor in order to achieve high performance when the processor is using vector data:

- *Large working sets.*
- *Pollution* due to non-unit strides.
- *Interferences* when the stride and the number of sets are not coprime.
- *Prefetching.*

In this section we summarize the most important solutions proposed in the literature to deal with individual or a subset of these four issues.

Block algorithms [12,19] is a technique that tries to reduce the negative effect of large working sets. Block algorithms can be developed by the programmer or, as claimed by several authors ([4] among others), it may be preferable to leave this task to the compiler. In any case, blocking requires a detailed analysis of data dependencies, but in some cases it is very difficult or even impossible to identify some dependencies at compile time. In these cases, the programer or compiler must generate a conservative code that may reduce the possibilities of applying blocking. The cache organization we propose does not exclude the use of block algorithms. Blocking is a software technique that can be used for any cache memory in order to increase the locality of the algorithm, so it can also be applied in the presence of a dual data cache or a selective cache. In addition, the dual data cache implements mechanisms that avoid the swept effect that large working sets would cause when blocking is not satisfactory.

The pollution caused by non-unit strides can be avoided in some cases by means of copying [16]. The main idea of this technique is to copy the elements of non-unit stride vectors into auxiliary vectors with stride one and then performing all the operations using the latter vectors. The main problem with copying is that its overhead may be high when the data is not much reutilized. In addition, the effectiveness of copying is constrained by the fact that the compiler has a limited knowledge of the program.

The performance degradation caused by interferences has been studied by Q. Yang and L.Y. Yang in [20]. However, their proposal focuses on vector processors whereas the present work concentrates on scalar processors. They proposed a direct-mapped cache using Mersenne numbers. A Mersenne number is of the form $2^x - 1$ for some x that makes it a prime. Due to the properties of such numbers, the modulo operation required by the mapping function can be done quite effectively in the context of vector processors. However, it would be very costly if we used it in scalar processors since every cache request would require to perform the modulo operation which requires several additions and therefore would considerably slow down the processor. Many other proposals to reduce the negative effect of interferences have recently appeared in the literature. Some of the most representative are: the victim cache [10], the skewed-associative cache [14], the column-associative cache [2], the dynamic exclusion replacement policy [13], the Half-and-Half cache [17] and the PA7200 Assist cache [11].

Different prefetching techniques have been proposed in the literature. Software techniques are managed by the compiler and usually make use of non-blocking caches in order to issue memory requests in advance. They require very simple hardware support and rely on compile-time information in order to predict future memory requests [6]. Hardware techniques for prefetching vector data require some mechanism to recognize references to vector data. Since the processor does not have vector instructions, this is usually done by means of a history table that keeps informations about load/store instructions. When successive executions of the same load/store instruction are found to generate addresses separated by a constant stride, one can assume that a vector is being accessed. In that case, the computed stride can be used to predict future data accesses to the same vector. The cache is first searched for these data and, in case of miss, a request to the external memory may be issued.

Three of the most significant contributions in the area of hardware prefetching are the *Preloading Scheme* proposed by J-L. Baer and T. F. Chen [3], the *Speculative Prefetching* proposed by Y. Jegou and O. Temam [9], and the *Stride Directed Prefetching* developed by J.W. Fu, J.H. Patel and B.L. Janssens [7].

The Preloading Scheme is based on having two program counters. The first one points to the instruction currently in execution while the other one points to several instructions ahead. When the look-ahead PC finds a load/store instruction, the history table (called reference prediction table by the authors) is checked and the address of this new reference is predicted using past information. If the predicted reference is not in cache, then a request to the external memory is issued. This mechanism requires a considerable amount of hardware since, in addition to the history table, a branch prediction table is needed in order to allow the look-ahead PC to bypass branches. The performance is quite dependent on the branch prediction accuracy which in turn is strongly dependent on the distance between the PC and the look-ahead PC.

The Speculative Prefetching is simpler since it does not make use of any branch prediction mechanism. It uses a history table similar to that of the Preloading Scheme but the prefetching is done at the same time a load/store instruction is executed. That is, when the processor executes a load/store instruction it tries to predict and prefetch, using the history table, the memory reference that will be generated in the next execution (or after n executions) of the same instruction. An appropriate choice of the prefetch distance, n, is crucial for the performance of the mechanism.

The Stride Directed Prefetching is conceptually similar to the previous schemes. It tries to predict future references to a vector by identifying successive memory references separated by a constant stride.

Another hardware prefetching mechanism is the Stream Buffer [10], which is targeted to benefit from references with unit stride.

A combination of hardware and software support for prefetching has been proposed by other authors, [15, 1, 11] among others.

3. The Dual Data Cache

We assume that the processor, like most current microprocessors, has separate instruction and data caches. Here, we center on the design of the data cache. The proposed data cache organization comes from the observation that different types of data usually exhibit different locality properties when they are referenced. In particular:

- Scalar variables exhibit a moderate degree of spatial locality. Two variables that are stored next to each other in memory are not always referenced close in time. However, its temporal locality usually is high (counters, vector indices, etc., are used repeatedly in many cases). Therefore, for such variables the stress should be put on exploiting temporal locality.
- Vectors with a large stride have a poor spatial locality and the temporal locality may or may not be high. However, since vectors may be very large, temporal locality should be exploited only for those vectors that not exceed the cache storage capacity. Otherwise, the above mentioned swept effect would cause a loss of performance.
- Vectors with a small stride exhibit a very high spatial locality. This spatial locality can be exploited no matter the length of the vector. For the temporal locality the same remarks as in the previous paragraph apply here.
- Random accesses (i.e., sparse matrix computations) do not exhibit in general any type of locality.

In consequence, there is a type of data (scalars and not very large vectors with a large stride) for which it seems most appropriate to spend the hardware resources to exploit just temporal locality, another type of data (not very large vectors with a small stride) for which the hardware should be dedicated to exploit both spatial and temporal locality, a third type of data (very large vectors with a small stride) for which the exploitation of just spatial locality is rewarding, and a last type of data (very large vectors with a large stride and random accesses) for which the most effective decision should be not to cache them.

The proposed data cache, which is called *dual data cache*, consists of two independent memories, or subcaches. One is called the *spatial cache* because it is designed to exploit spatial locality, in addition to temporal locality. The other is called *temporal cache* since it is targeted to exploit just temporal locality. Both subcaches work independently and in parallel. Figure 1 depicts the main parts of the dual data cache.

When the processor issues a memory reference, both caches are looked up at the same time and, depending on the result, one of the following actions is taken:

- If the required data is only in one of the subcaches, the data is read or written in that subcache. This is a cache hit

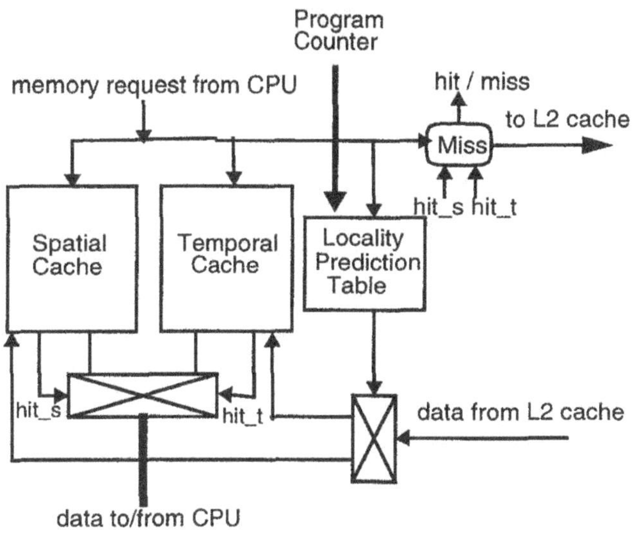

Figure 1: Block diagram of the dual data cache.

- If the required data is found in both subcaches, it is read from the temporal cache or written into both two in parallel. This is again a cache hit.
- If the required data is not in any subcache, a cache miss occurs. In this case, the processor is stalled and the required data is brought from the next level of the memory hierarchy. This data may be placed in just one of the two subcaches or may be not cached anywhere, depending on predicted type of locality for this memory access. This prediction is made by means of a history table, which is called *locality prediction table*, whose operation is explained later on. If spatial locality is predicted for this memory reference, then the missed data is placed in the spatial cache. If temporal locality is predicted and the referenced element is an scalar or if it belongs to a vector that will not cause self-interference in the temporal cache, the data is placed in that cache. Otherwise, it is not cached anywhere. Even if a vector exhibits temporal locality (but not spatial locality), caching it would be detrimental if it interfered with itself.

Both the spatial and temporal caches have the same organization as conventional caches with the characteristic that the line size of the spatial cache is large (several tens of bytes or more) whereas the temporal cache has a small line size (a few bytes). In this way, the spatial cache can exploit both spatial and temporal locality whereas the temporal cache exploits just temporal locality.

The predicted locality for a memory reference is based on guessing whether the accessed data is an scalar, or an element of a vector, and in the latter case, it also depends on the stride and the size of the vector. These attributes are estimated by means of the locality prediction table. The locality prediction table is based on the history table that was proposed by Baer and Chen [3], Fu, Patel and Janssens [7], and Jegou and Temam [9] as part of a hardware mechanism for prefetching vector data. The locality prediction table has a moderate number of entries (it is suggested in [9] that a number about 256 could be sufficient to catch most of the references). Each entry contains information about a recently executed load/store instruction. This information consists of the following fields:

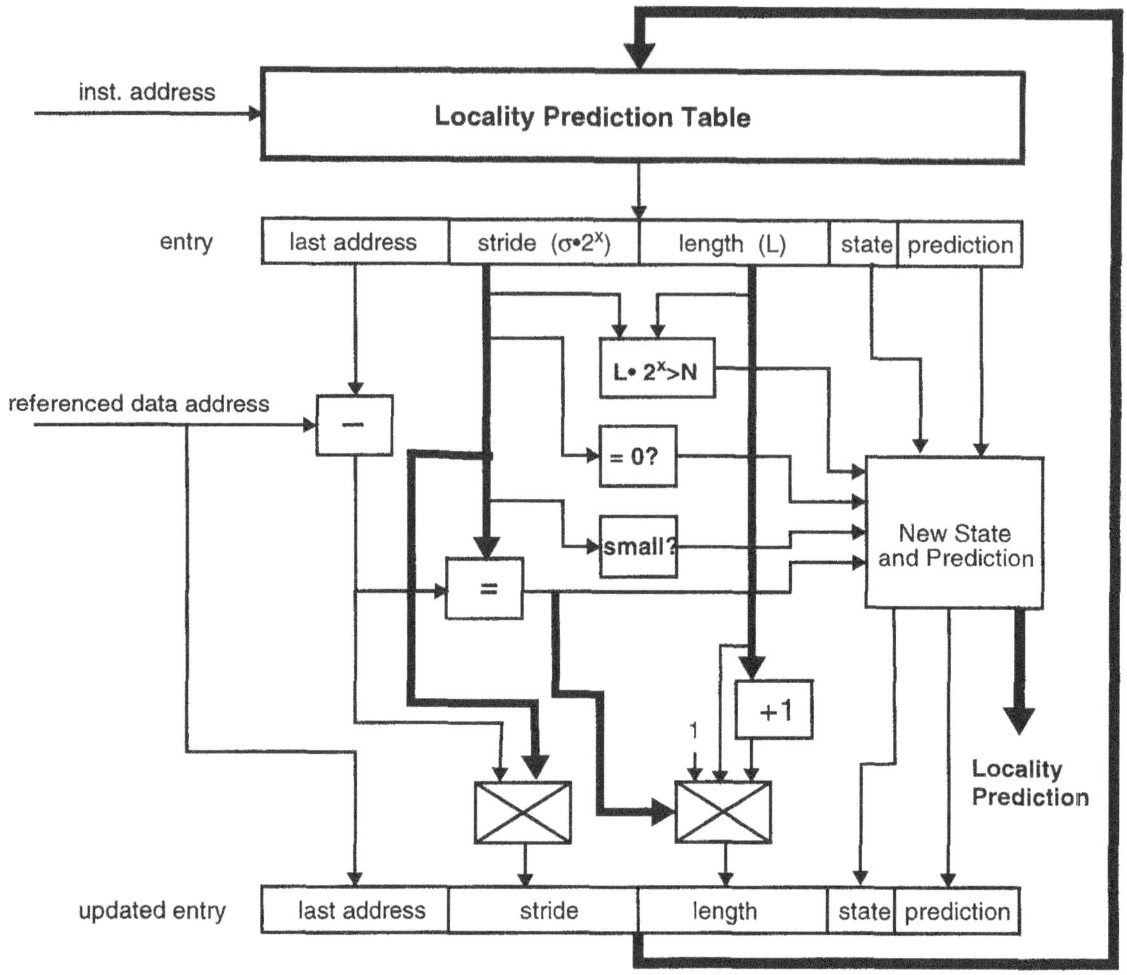

Figure 2: Hardware to update the locality prediction table.

- *Instruction address*: The address of the load/store instruction. This field is the identifier of the entry.
- *Last address*: The last data address referenced by that instruction.
- *Stride*: The difference between the last address and the second last address referenced.
- *Length*: The number of consecutive elements accessed by this load/store instruction with the same stride.
- *State*: This field keeps information about the past behavior of this load/store instruction regarding its stride.
- *Prediction*: This field keeps information about the past behavior of this load/store instructions regarding its prediction.

For every cache miss, the locality prediction table decides where the missed data is cached. The locality prediction table is accessed at the same time as the cache memory. If the load/store instruction that caused the cache miss is not in the locality prediction table, the missed reference is stored in the default subcache (it could be spatial or temporal; we have experimentally checked that the most suitable default value is temporal) once it is brought from the next level of the memory hierarchy. Otherwise, when the load/store instruction is found in the locality prediction table, the information in the state and prediction fields, after being updated, are used to predict the expected type of locality for such reference and therefore, it determines the place where the missing data will be placed. The prediction can be: *spatial* (i.e., in case of miss, the data is placed in the spatial cache), *temporal* (i.e., in case of miss, the data is placed in the temporal cache) or *bypass* (i.e., in case of miss, the data is not cached anywhere).

Figure 2 shows the required hardware to implement the locality prediction table. The hardware mainly consists of a table, two adders, two full comparators, two equality comparators, a shifter and several multiplexers.

The locality prediction table is managed as a cache. It may be direct mapped, set associative or fully associative. Every time a load/store instruction is executed, the locality prediction table is looked up. If the instruction address is not in the table, one of the entries of the table is allocated to this instruction and it is initialized as follows: a) the address of the instruction, b) the address of the

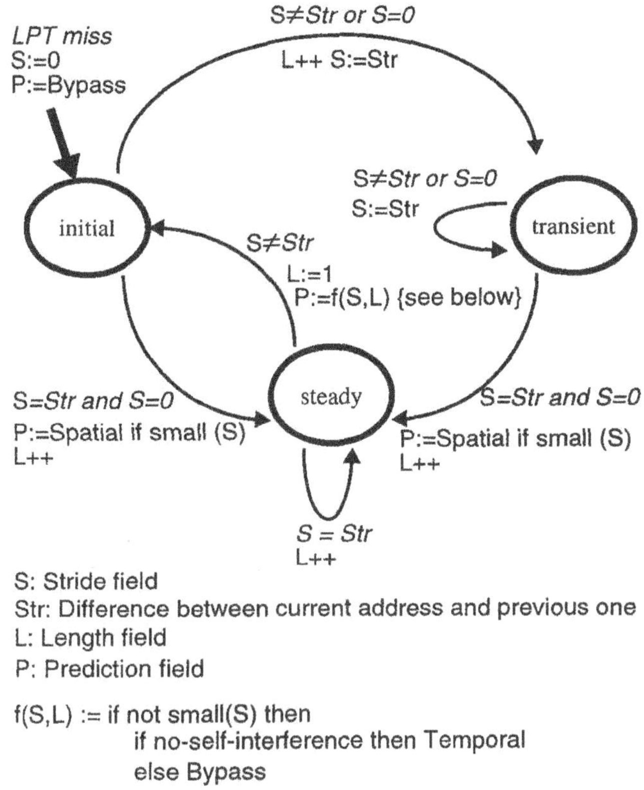

Figure 3: State transitions. In italics the condition that fires the corresponding transition. The rest shows how the LPT entries are updated.

referenced data, c) stride equal to zero, d) length equal to one, e) state equal to initial, and e) prediction equal to bypass. The instruction address will be used as the tag to identify the entry and therefore it will maintain the same value as long as the entry remains in the table. The last address is always updated with the last referenced address. The other fields may vary every time the same load/store instruction is executed, as it is explained below. Figure 3 illustrates how these fields are updated.

The stride field may be either updated with the difference between the previous referenced address and the current one or left unchanged. The length may be incremented by one, reset to 1 or left unchanged.

As it is shown in figure 3, the state field can take one out of three different values:

- *Initial*: This state is reached after the first reference to a vector. In this case the locality prediction is the default value.
- *Transient*: The entry has this state as long as two consecutive references have different stride. In this case the prediction is also the default value.
- *Steady*: This state indicates that successive strides are equal. In this state the prediction is given by the updated value of the prediction field.

Once in the initial state, the update of a locality prediction table entry proceeds as follows. If the current stride (Str in figure 3) is equal to the previous one (S) and they are different from zero, the updated state is steady and the length is incremented. The prediction field becomes spatial if the stride is small (in the experiments presented later, it is assumed that a stride is small when it is lower than the spatial line size); otherwise it maintains the same value. If the current stride is different from the previous one or the latter is equal to zero, the new state is transient, the length is incremented and the stride field is updated.

The entry is kept in the transient state as long as the stride varies or it is equal to zero. In these cases, the stride field is updated for every execution of the corresponding load/store instruction. When the previous conditions does not hold, the state becomes steady. In this case, the length is incremented and the prediction is updated with spatial if the stride is small.

The entry remains in the steady state as long as the stride does not vary. Every time the corresponding load/store instruction is executed, the length is incremented. When eventually the stride varies, the state shifts to initial and the length is reset to one. At this moment, if the stride field is "large" (in the experiments this means greater than the spatial line size), the prediction field is updated depending on the vector length and the family to which the value of the stride field belongs as explained below. The stride family defined by x is the set of strides $\sigma \cdot 2^x$ with σ odd. All the strides belonging to the same family (e.g., $12=3 \cdot 2^2$ and $20=5 \cdot 2^2$ belong to family 2) have the same behavior from the point of view of self-interference [8, 18]. If the value in the stride field is "small" the prediction does not vary (it remains spatial). Otherwise, if the vector length multiplied by 2^x is not higher than the size of the temporal cache, the prediction is temporal; if it is higher, the prediction is bypass, since the vector would interfere with itself.

Finally, the proposed scheme could also incorporate speculative prefetching [9], stride directed prefetching [7] or preloading [3] at a very low additional hardware cost, since the reference prediction table required by these schemes is contained in the locality prediction table. Nevertheless, in the figures presented in section 5, a simpler prefetching scheme has been assumed. Whenever there is a cache miss whose prediction is spatial, in addition to the missing line, p successive lines are also brought into the spatial cache. The optimal value of p has experimentally been determined to be equal to 1.

Note that in some cases the same data element can reside in both caches at the same time. Suppose that a data element d is read into the temporal cache and then modified. Due to the copy-back policy the higher memory level is not immediately updated. Suppose that later on, a nearby data element that causes a cache miss is referenced. If the prediction for such reference is spatial, it may happen that an old copy of d is brought into the spatial cache. To solve this consistency problem, when a data is found in both subcaches, it is always selected the one from the temporal cache. In addition, whenever a dirty line of the temporal cache is replaced and it is also present in the spatial cache, the spatial cache is updated.

3.1. The Selective Cache

A selective cache is a simplified version of the dual data cache. This cache consists of the same locality prediction table but it only has one memory unit like conventional caches. The locality prediction table behaves in the same way with the difference that now, there is not distinction between spatial and temporal caches. That is, everything that must be cached is brought to the same memory unit.

Notice that a selective cache behaves as a conventional cache with a selective caching policy. Only data with spatial locality or data with temporal locality that is guaranteed not to self-interfere is cached.

4. A Qualitative Analysis of the Performance

In this section, the rationale for the design of the dual data cache is explained. The benefits of the dual data cache are illustrated by analyzing its performance for several usual patterns of memory references:

- References to scalars.
- References to vectors with a constant stride.
- References to "random" elements of a vector.

The objective of this analysis is to justify the chosen design. A detailed performance analysis is presented in the next section.

4.1. Scalars

Scalars are cached in the default cache since the first time they are accessed, they miss in the locality prediction table and therefore the prediction is the one assumed by default. It is not clear whether it is convenient to exploit just temporal or spatial and temporal locality for scalars. If the same scalar is referenced repeatedly the new stride for this load/store will always be zero, and therefore, the corresponding entry in the locality prediction table will remain in the transient state in which the locality prediction is again the default value. As previously mentioned, the simulations showed that the most effective default value is temporal.

4.2. Vectors with Constant Stride

When a load/store instruction is used to access a sequence of elements separated by a constant stride, the first element will be cached in the default cache because it will miss in the locality prediction table. At that time we do not have enough information about the memory reference patterns generated by that instruction.

The reference to the second element will have a stride different from zero and thus, different from the previous stride which was initialized to zero. Then, the state of the corresponding entry shifts from initial to transient and therefore the locality prediction is again given by the default value. At that time it is not known whether the stride found between the first two accesses is going to be constant or this load/store instruction is accessing "random" elements.

The third and following accesses will find a constant stride. If the stride is "small" they will be cached in the spatial cache in order to exploit spatial locality and eventually temporal locality. If the stride is "large" they will not be cached anywhere. If the same vector is referenced again, the prediction will remain spatial if the stride is small, and it will depend on the vector length and the stride family otherwise. If it can be assured that the vector is not going to interfere with itself (i.e., the number of elements times 2^{family} is not higher than the number of temporal cache lines) the prediction will become temporal. If not, it will not be cached anywhere, since it does not exhibit spatial locality and temporal locality cannot be exploited due to self-interference.

Note that delaying the caching of a vector with poor spatial locality until the second time it is accessed has the additional benefit of avoiding the pollution of cache memory for vectors that are accessed only once (e.g., the matrix in a matrix by vector algorithm, if it is traversed with a large stride). On the other hand, it has the disadvantage that if the vector is used several times and it fits into the cache, every element will be brought from memory twice. The negative effect of this additional penalty decreases as the number of times the vector is reused increases.

4.3. Random Accesses

This third scenario refers to the case when successive executions of the same load/store instruction reference memory locations that are not at a constant distance. This happens for instant in the algorithm that multiplies a sparse matrix by a vector. The accesses to the vector elements do not follow any pattern.

Consecutive random accesses will usually have a variable stride and therefore, the corresponding entry will remain in the transient state where the prediction is given by the default value.

5. Performance Evaluation

The performance of the dual data cache and the selective cache has been evaluated for a set of benchmarks and compared with the performance of a conventional cache with similar hardware cost. The benchmarks were compiled and executed on a DEC workstation with an Alpha 21064 microprocessor. Those benchmarks written in Fortran were compiled with the DEC Fortran 77 compiler using the most aggressive optimizations (-O5). Those written in C were compiled with the DEC C compiler again using all the optimizations (-O5). A trace of the execution were obtained using the *atom* instrumentation tool. This trace was fed into a simulator of a conventional data cache memory, a simulator of a dual data cache and a simulator of a selective cache.

In addition to compute the miss ratio, the simulators also keep track of the delay caused by data memory references which allows us to compute the execution time of the simulated programs and the average memory access time.

5.1. Simulation Parameters

All the caches are assumed to be direct-mapped with a copy-back and write allocate policy. The cache memory is connected to the next level of the memory hierarchy by means of a 8 byte bus. The first word (8 bytes) of a request to the next memory level arrives after 10 cycles and then, successive words arrive at the rate of one per cycle.

In order to compare different configurations with similar hardware cost, a conventional cache of size S is compared with a dual data cache with a temporal cache of size S/4 and a spatial cache of size S/2. After taking into account the amount of memory required by the tags, the remaining amount of storage (less than S/4) is dedicated to the locality prediction table. In consequence, depending on the value of S and the line size, a different number of entries has been assumed for such table (between 128 and 512 for the results presented later on). The selective cache is assumed to have the same size and configuration as a conventional cache and in addition it has a very small locality prediction table (16 entries for a 16 Kbyte cache memory and 32 entries for a 32 Kbyte cache memory). Unlike the dual data cache, in this case the increase in hardware required by the locality prediction table is not compensated with a reduction in the cache capacity because it is much simpler than that of the dual data cache. This should be taken into account when comparing the performance results.

For the dual data cache, the line size of the temporal cache is 8 bytes and the line size of the spatial cache is either 16 or 32 bytes.

5.2. Benchmarks

The performance of the dual data cache has been evaluated for both vectorizable and non-vectorizable code. Three different types of benchmarks have been used: synthetic benchmarks, kernels and some benchmarks from the SPEC 92 suite. For the latter benchmarks, 5 million of memory references were simulated after discarding the first 10 million.

5.2.1. Synthetic benchmarks

The synthetic benchmarks consist of a set of loops that deal with vectors of different size and stride. Each loop makes use of either one or two vectors and traverse it/them ten times incrementing every element at each iteration. The objective is to consider all possible scenarios regarding temporal and spatial locality and interferences for a data cache of 32 Kbytes. Table 1 lists the characteristics of the benchmarks that use only one vector and table 2 shows the same information for the benchmarks that use two vectors.

The columns of the tables have the following meaning:

- *Length*: The number of elements of the vector that are referenced.
- *Stride*: The stride when accessing the vector.
- *S-Loc*: The amount of spatial locality that will be exploited by the conventional cache. A value of *x/y* means that *x* out of *y* loads will result in a hit due to spatial locality.
- *SS-Loc*: Idem for the spatial subcache of the dual data cache.
- *T-Loc*: The amount of temporal locality that will be exploited by the conventional cache. A value of *x* means that *x*% of the vector elements will remain in cache memory (not replaced by further references) once they have been accessed by the first time.
- *TS-Loc*: Idem for the spatial subcache of the dual data cache.
- *TT-Loc*: Idem for the temporal subcache of the dual data cache.

Bench.	Length	Stride	S-Loc	T-Loc	SS-Loc	TS-Loc	TT-Loc
v1	2000	1	3/4	100	3/4	100	-
v2	4000	1	3/4	100	3/4	2	-
v3	15000	1	3/4	0	3/4	0	-
v4	1000	5	0	100	-	-	100
v5	1000	15	0	13	-	-	100
v6	2500	6	0	0	-	-	0
v7	1000	12	0	100	-	-	0

Table 1: Synthetic benchmarks dealing with one vector

In table 2, every benchmark has two values for each entry. Each of these values correspond to one of the two vectors used by the benchmark.

Note that in these benchmarks each load is followed by a store to the same location. This store will always result in a cache hit in the conventional cache due to temporal locality. However, this is not the case of the dual data cache because some data may be not cached. In other words, this sequence of load-store will benefit most to the conventional cache.

5.2.2. Kernels

The kernels are a set of routines frequently found in numerical applications:

- *fft*: A Fast Fourier Transform of a 2^{19} element input vector. This is a vectorizable code with strides power of 2.
- *mm*: A matrix by matrix multiplication. A vectorizable code with unit and non-unit strides
- *mmb*: A block algorithm for matrix by matrix multiplication, optimized to make an optimal use of a 16 Kbyte conventional cache.
- *smv*: A sparse matrix by vector multiplication. A non-vectorizable code.
- *tri*: A triangular matrix multiplication.

Benchm.	Length	Stride	S-Loc	T-Loc	SS-Loc	TS-Loc	TT-Loc
v11	1000	1	3/4	100	3/4	100	-
	1000	1	3/4	100	3/4	100	-
v22	2000	1	3/4	50	3/4	2	-
	2000	1	3/4	50	3/4	2	-
v23	2000	1	3/4	14	3/4	100	-
	1000	5	0	52	-	-	100
v24	2000	1	3/4	0	3/4	0	-
	15000	1	3/4	0	3/4	0	-
v25	2000	1	3/4	0	3/4	100	-
	2200	7	0	0	-	-	0
v33	500	15	0	22	-	-	100
	500	15	0	22	-	-	100
v34	1000	5	0	0	-	-	100
	15000	1	3/4	0	3/4	0	-
v35	1000	5	0	0	-	-	100
	2200	7	0	0	-	-	0
v44	15000	1	3/4	0	3/4	0	-
	15000	1	3/4	0	3/4	0	-
v45	15000	1	3/4	0	3/4	0	-
	2200	7	0	0	-	-	0
v55	2200	7	0	0	-	-	0
	2200	7	0	0	-	-	0

Table 2: Synthetic benchmarks dealing with two vectors

5.2.3. SPEC 92 benchmarks

The following benchmarks from the SPEC 92 benchmark suite have also been used: *compress*, *eqntott* and *espresso* (from SPECint92) and *alvinn, hydro2d, mdljdp2, mdljsp2* and *swm256* (from SPECfp92). We will refer to them as *com, eqn, esp, alv, hyd, mdd, mds* and *swm* respectively.

5.3. Performance figures

5.3.1. Line Size of the Conventional Cache

Figure 4 shows the average memory access time in cycles of a conventional cache with line size of 32 and 64 bytes. Two different cache sizes have been considered: 16 and 32 Kbytes. From these graphs we can conclude that in general a 32 byte line size is more efficient. In consequence, in the following experiments, a dual data cache and a selective cache will be compared with a conventional cache with such line size.

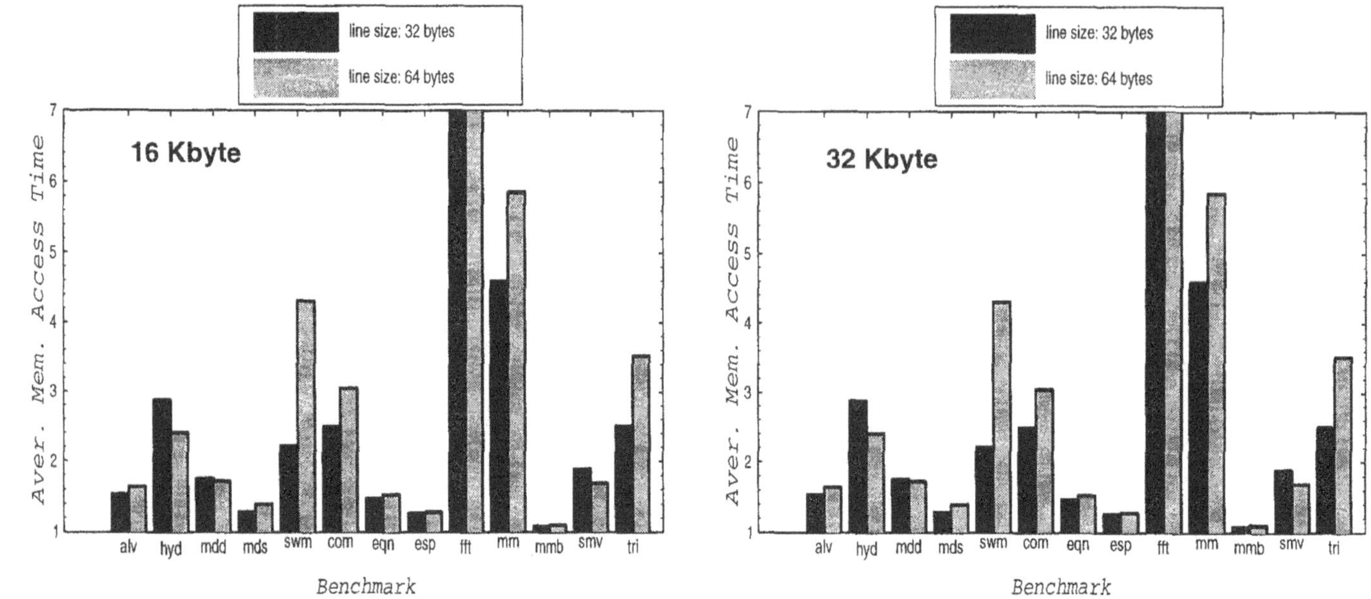

Figure 4: Performance of a 16/32 Kbyte conventional cache for different values of the line size. The average memory access time corresponding to *fft* is 17.5 for a line of 32 bytes and 23 cycles for a line of 64 bytes.

5.3.2. Synthetic Benchmarks

Figure 5 compares the average memory access time of a conventional cache, a selective cache and a dual data cache for the synthetic benchmarks. The dual data cache is assumed to have 1024 lines of 8 bytes in the temporal cache and 512 of 32 bytes in the spatial cache. The conventional and selective caches have 1024 lines of 32 bytes.

The performance figures show that the dual data cache significantly outperforms the conventional cache for almost all the benchmarks. For the benchmarks listed in tables 1 and 2, the dual data cache has a worse performance only in two cases (*v7* and *v2*). For *v7*, the vector is traversed with a stride 12 elements, that is 3 lines. Since 3 belongs to the family 0, the conventional cache does not have any self-interference as long as the number of referenced elements is not higher than the number of lines. In this case, the number of elements is 1000 and the number of lines is 1024, so the vector fits in the conventional cache. The dual data cache does not cache this vector in any of its two subcaches. This is because the stride is large which makes it a good candidate for the temporal subcache. However, the stride 24 belongs to the family 3 and the temporal cache has 1024 lines. This implies that if the vector has more than $1024/2^3=256$ elements, it will interfere with itself. Because this is the case, the dual data cache decides not to cache this vector.

In the case of *v2*, this is a vector that exhibits temporal and spatial locality so, it is placed in the spatial cache. However, it fits into the conventional cache but not into the spatial cache of the dual data cache since its size has been halved.

Notice that in many of the remaining cases, the dual data cache is much better than the conventional cache. One of the highest differences is for *v33*. In this case, the program traverses two vectors with stride 15. Although only 500 elements of each vector are used, which is quite less than the capacity of the cache, the conventional cache can only exploit a small percentage of the temporal locality due to the pollution introduced by a stride greater than one. In this case, every cache line has only one useful element. Spatial locality cannot be exploited neither because the stride is greater than the line size. On the other hand, the dual data cache can exploit temporal locality placing both vectors in the temporal cache. Since the line size of this cache is one element, there is no pollution. In addition, there are not interferences because the stride belongs to the family 0.

Finally, it can be observed that the selective cache has a performance similar to the dual data cache except in two cases: *v4* and *v33*. The reason is that in these two scenarios the selective cache decides not to cache the vectors since it assumes that they would cause self-interferences in the cache. However, the dual data cache can cache the vectors in the temporal cache.

5.3.3. Kernels and SPEC Benchmarks

Figures 6 and 7 depict the performance of the conventional cache, the selective cache and the dual data cache for the kernels and SPEC benchmarks.

We can observe that for those cases when the conventional cache is quite good (see *mmb, esp, mds, alv*), the dual data cache and the selective cache are also very effective, in most cases they are even better than the conventional cache. *bmm* deserves a special mention. This is a program that has been designed in order to exploit the locality of the algorithm as much as possible using a conventional cache of 16 Kbytes. This required some transformations of the original matrix multiply program (blocking and copying). Nowadays there is a huge effort in investigating how these transformations can be automated and applied by the compiler. However, the effectiveness of such transformations depends on the characteristics of the algorithm. It could be relatively straightforward for perfect loop nests with uniform dependencies, but rather limited in other cases. The selective cache behaves not very well for a 16 Kbyte cache. This is due to the pollution introduced by prefetching. This pollution does not degrade performance with a 32 Kbyte cache since the block size has been designed in order to fit into 16 Kbytes and therefore there is much space left in cache.

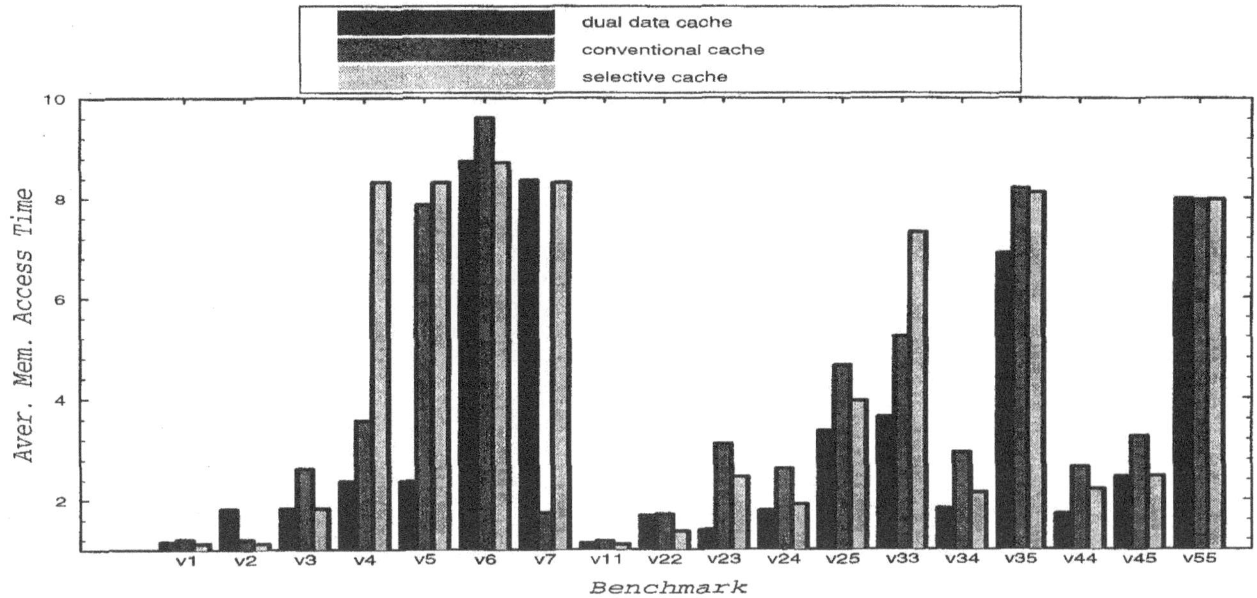

Figure 5: Synthetic benchmarks with a 32 Kbyte cache.

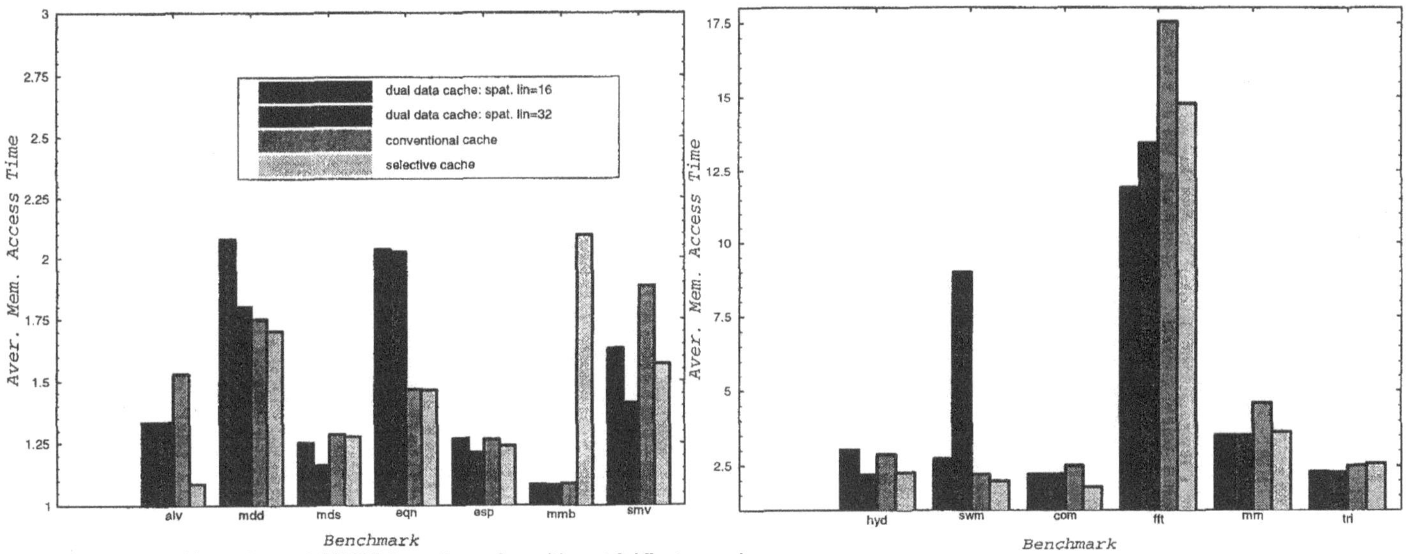

Figure 6: Kernels and SPEC benchmarks with a 16 Kbyte cache.

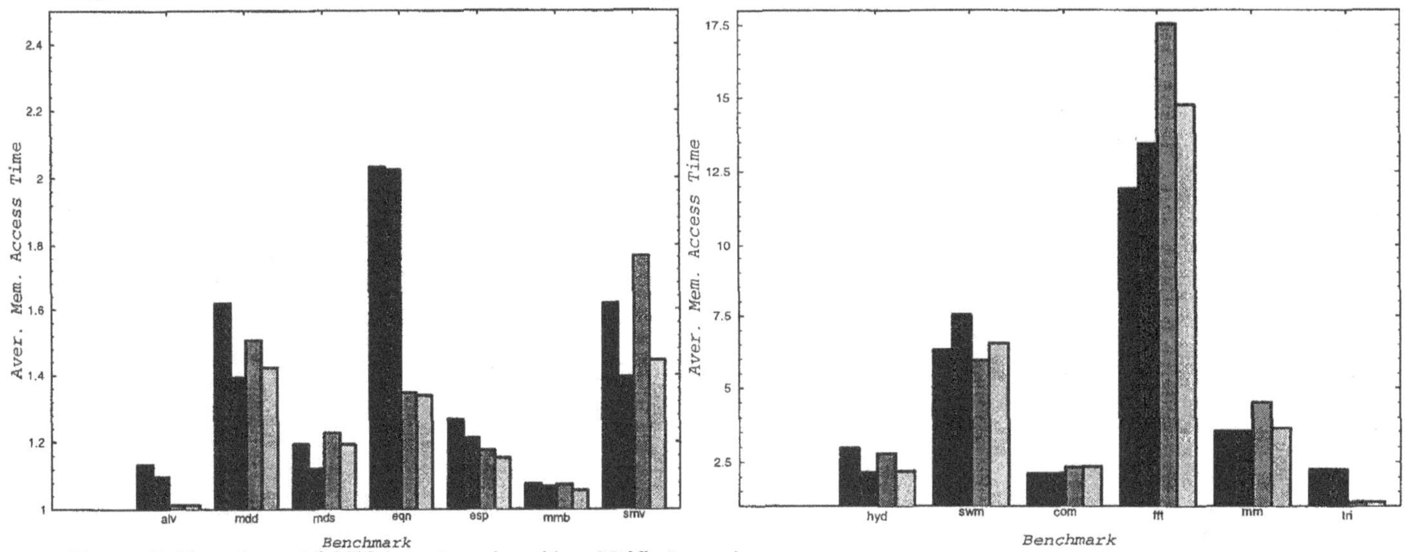

Figure 7: Kernels and SPEC benchmarks with a 32 Kbyte cache.

For the *FFT* benchmark, the dual data cache has much better performance than a conventional cache. This benchmark makes vector accesses with strides that are powers of 2. If the stride is equal to 2^s, a cache with capacity for 2^c elements will cause self-interferences for any vector with more than 2^{c-s} elements. In other words, a power-of-two stride reduces the effective capacity of the cache in a factor equal to the stride. Because many of the vectors are quite large, the conventional cache undergoes many interferences. On the other hand, the dual data cache do not cache those vectors that are going to interfere and then it benefits from the shorter miss penalty due to the shorter line size.

The dual data cache may have a worse performance than a conventional cache for some memory reference patterns. This happens when almost all memory references exhibit spatial locality. In this case, almost all the data is cached into the spatial cache. Since it has a lower number of lines than the conventional cache, more interferences will occur and then the performance will be degraded. This is the case of the *swm* benchmark.

We can also see in figures 6 and 7 that for the non-vectorizable benchmarks (*com* and *smv*), the dual data cache and the selective cache have a slightly better performance than a conventional cache.

In some other cases, the dual data cache is a little bit worse than the conventional cache (*eqntott* always; *alv, mdd* and *esp* for some configurations). However, it is remarkable the good performance of the selective cache, which is always better than the conventional cache with a very few exceptions.

6. CONCLUSIONS

A novel data cache design for superscalar processors has been presented. The proposed data cache, called dual data cache, has two independent parts: the spatial cache, which has been designed to exploit both spatial and temporal locality, with the emphasis in the former, and the temporal cache which exploits only temporal locality. In other words, the proposed scheme is a way of having large lines, which are convenient to exploit spatial locality, and small lines, which are more suitable if spatial locality is not present, in the same cache memory.

A simplified version of the dual data cache, called the selective cache has also been presented.

The performance figures obtained for a set of benchmarks show that the dual data cache outperforms in many cases a conventional cache. It is even more remarkable the good performance of the selective cache, which consists of an ordinary cache plus a locality prediction table with a very few entries.

We have also shown that for those cases where software techniques can be applied to improve the locality of a given algorithm (blocking and copying), the performance of the dual data cache is not degraded. For instance, in the case of matrix multiply with blocking and copying, the performance of the dual cache is about the same as that of a conventional cache.

Acknowledgments

This work has been supported by the Ministry of Education and Science of Spain (CICYT TIC-95/0429, TIC-92/880 and TIC-91/1036).

7. REFERENCES

[1] S G. Abraham et al.
Predictability of Load/Store Instruction Latencies
in *Proc. of MICRO-26*, pp 139-152, 1993

[2] A. Agarwal and S.D. Pudar
Column-Associative Caches: A Technique for Reducing the Miss Rate of Direct-Mapped Caches
in *Proc of the 20th. Int. Symp Comp. Architecture*, pp. 179-190, 1993.

[3] J-L. Baer and T-F. Chen
An Effective On-Chip Preloading Scheme to Reduce Data Access penalty,
in *Proc of Supercomputing'91 Conference*, pp. 176-186, 1991.

[4] S Carr and K. Kennedy,
Compiler Blockability of Numerical Algorithms,
in *Proc of the Supercomputing'92 Conference*, pp 114-124, 1992.

[5] A. Chang,
Application of Sparse Matrix Methods in Electric Power System Analysis,
in *Proc. of the Symp. on Sparse Matrices and their Applications*, pp. 113-122, 1969.

[6] T-F. Chen and J-L. Baer,
A Performance Study of Software and Hardware Data Prefetching Schemes,
in *Proc of the 21th. Int. Symp. Comp. Architecture*, pp. 223-232, 1994.

[7] J.W. Fu, J.H. Patel and B.L. Janssens,
Stride Directed Prefetching in Scalar Processors,
in *Proc of the 25th. Int. Symp on Microarchitecture (MICRO-25)*, pp. 102-110, 1992.

[8] D.T Harper III and D.A. Linebarger,
A Dynamic Storage Scheme for Conflict Free Vector Access,
in *Proc of the 14th. Int. Symp. Comp. Architecture*, pp. 72-77, 1987.

[9] Y Jegou and O. Temam,
Speculative Prefetching
in *Proc. of the 1993 Int. Conf. on Supercomputing*, pp. 57-66, 1993.

[10] N.P. Jouppi,
Improving Direct-Mapped Cache Performance by the Addition of a Small Fully-Associative Cache and Prefetch Buffers
in *Proc of the 17th. Symp. Comp. Architecture*, pp. 364-373, 1990.

[11] G. Kurpanek et al.
PA7200. A PA-RISC Processor with Integrated High Performance MP Bus Interface
in *Proc. of CompCon94*, pp. 375-382, 1994.

[12] M.S Lam, E.E. Rothberg and M.E. Wolf,
The Cache Performance and Optimization of Blocked Algorithms
in *Proc. of ASPLOS 1991*, pp. 67-74, 1991.

[13] S. McFarling
Cache Replacement with Dynamic Exclusion
in *Proc of the 19th. Int. Symp. Comp. Architecture*, pp. 191-200, 1992.

[14] A. Seznec
A Case for Two-Way Skewed-Associative Caches
in *Proc of the 20th. Int. Symp. Comp. Architecture*, pp. 169-178, 1993

[15] O. Temam and N. Drach,
Software Assistance for Data Caches
in *Proc. of the 1st. Int. Symp. on High-Performance Computer Architecture*, pp. 154-163, 1995.

[16] O. Temam, E.D. Granston, W. Jalby,
To Copy or not to Copy: A Compile-time Technique for Assesing when Data Copying Should be Used to Eliminate Cache Conflicts,
in *Proc. of Supercomputing'93 Conference*, pp. 410-419, 1993.

[17] K B. Theobald, H.J. Hum and G R. Gao
A Design Framework for Hybrid-Access Caches
in *Proc of the 1st. Int Symp. on High-Performance Computer Architecture*, pp. 144-153, 1995.

[18] M. Valero et al.
Increasing the Number of Strides for Conflic-Free Vector Access,
in *Proc of the 19th. Int. Symp Comp Architecture*, pp. 372-381, 1992.

[19] M. Wolfe,
Iteration Space Tiling for Memory Hierarchies,
in *Proc of the Third SIAM Conference on Parallel Processing for Scientific Computing*, Dec. 1987.

[20] Q Yang and L.W. Yang,
A Novel Cache Design for Vector Processing
in *Proc of the 19th. Int. Symp. Comp. Architecture*, pp. 362-371, 1992

Optimum Modulo Schedules for Minimum Register Requirements

Alexandre E. Eichenberger and Edward S. Davidson

Advanced Computer Architecture Laboratory
EECS Department, University of Michigan
Ann Arbor, MI 48109-2122
alexe,davidson@eecs.umich.edu

Santosh G. Abraham

Hewlett Packard Laboratories
1501 Page Mill Road
Palo Alto, CA 94304
abraham@hpl.hp.com

Abstract

Modulo scheduling is an efficient technique for exploiting instruction level parallelism in a variety of loops, resulting in high performance code but increased register requirements. We present a combined approach that schedules the loop operations for the highest steady state throughput and minimum register requirements. Our method determines optimal register requirements for machines with finite resources and for general dependence graphs. We compare the performance of this and other modulo schedulers for a benchmark of 629 loops from the Perfect Club, SPEC-89, and the Livermore Fortran Kernels. Measurements demonstrate the potential of register-sensitive modulo schedulers, which will be useful in evaluating the performance of register-sensitive modulo scheduling heuristics.

KEYWORDS: Register-sensitive modulo scheduling, software pipelining, loop scheduling, instruction level parallelism, VLIW, superscalar.

1 Introduction

Current research compilers for VLIW and superscalar machines focus on exposing more of the inherent parallelism in an application to obtain higher performance by better utilizing wider issue machines and reducing the schedule length of a code. There is generally insufficient parallelism within individual basic blocks and higher levels of parallelism can be obtained by also exploiting the instruction level parallelism among successive basic blocks. Software pipelining is a technique that exploits the instruction level parallelism present among the iterations of a loop by overlapping the execution of consecutive loop iterations. With sufficient overlap, some machine resources can be fully utilized, resulting in a schedule with maximum steady state throughput.

Modulo scheduling [1][2][3] is a software pipelining technique that results in high performance code while requiring only modest compilation time by restricting the scheduling space. It uses the same schedule for each iteration of a loop and it initiates successive iterations at a constant rate, i.e. one *Initiation Interval* (II clock cycles) apart. This restriction is known as the *modulo scheduling constraint* and forces a resource to be used by one iteration no more than once within each set of times that are congruent modulo II.

The scope of modulo scheduling has been widened to a large variety of loops. Loops with conditional statements are handled using hierarchical reduction [4] or IF-conversion [5]. Modulo scheduling has also been extended to a large variety of loops with early exits, such as while loops [6][7]. Furthermore, the code expansion due to modulo scheduling can be eliminated by using special hardware, such as rotating register files and predicated execution [8].

Since modulo scheduling exploits high levels of parallelism, it results in higher register requirements because more values are needed to support more concurrent operations. This effect is inherent to parallelism and will be exacerbated by wider machines and higher latency pipelines [9]. As a result, developing scheduling techniques that exploit instruction level parallelism while containing the register requirements is crucial to the performance of future machines. Our research aims at understanding the fundamental relationship between instruction level parallelism and register requirements for a set of benchmarks under realistic assumptions.

In this paper, we present a register-sensitive modulo scheduling method that finds a schedule with the highest steady state throughput over all modulo schedules, and the minimum register requirements among such schedules. This method applies for loop iterations that consist of a single basic block with a general dependence graph. Loop iterations with multiple basic blocks are IF-converted; however, predicates are ignored when evaluating the register requirements of a schedule. Our scheduling method satisfies arbitrary resource and dependence constraints and minimizes MaxLive [3], the minimum number of registers required to generate spill-free code. *MaxLive* corresponds to the maximum number of live values at any single cycle of the loop schedule.

To improve the execution time of register-sensitive modulo schedulers, we propose a technique that removes redundant edges of the dependence graph. We demonstrate the conditions under which scheduling edges as well as register edges may safely be removed from the dependence graph of a loop. This technique is applicable to any modulo scheduler. Also, we demonstrate that the search space for modulo schedules is bounded and we use this bound to improve the execution time of our modulo scheduler.

This paper contributes an optimum solution for register-sensitive modulo scheduling of loops with arbitrary dependence graphs on machines with arbitrary resource constraints.

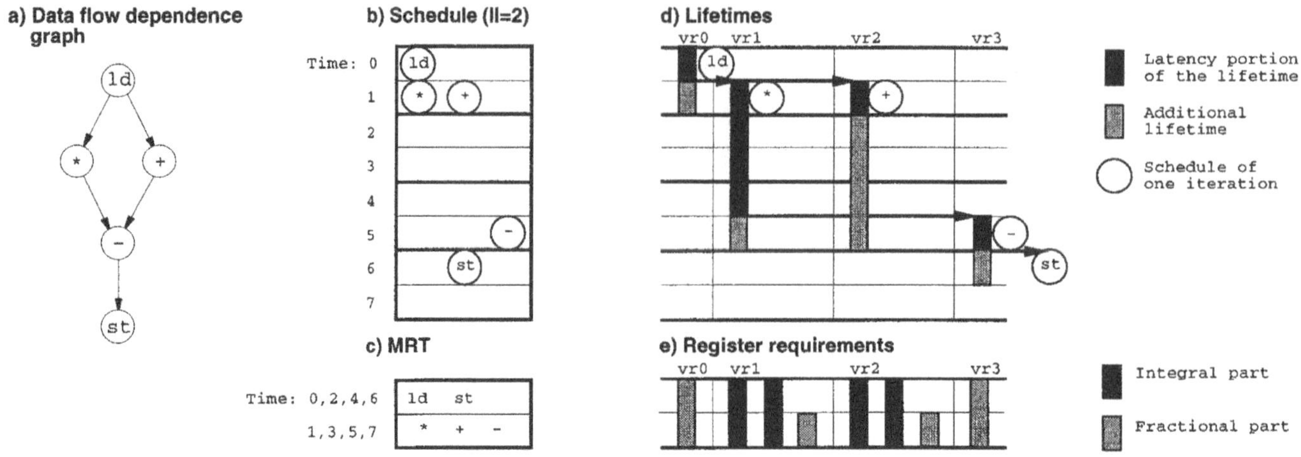

Figure 1: Modulo schedule for the kernel `y[i] = x[i]`^{2}`-x[i]-a` with minimum buffer requirements.

We compare the performance of this and other modulo schedulers for a benchmark of 629 loops from the Perfect Club, SPEC-89, and the Livermore Fortran Kernels for the Cydra 5 machine, a machine with complex resource usage [10]. Though the general algorithm presented in this paper may be too expensive to be integrated in a compiler, the improvements obtained in register requirements motivate the development of better heuristics for combined scheduling and register allocation for modulo-scheduled loops. This method is thus useful in assessing the performance of modulo-scheduling heuristics.

This work builds upon the modulo scheduling algorithm proposed by Govindarajan, Altman, and Gao [11] in which the entire modulo scheduling space is searched to find a schedule with minimum buffer requirements. This algorithm produces schedules for machines with finite heterogeneous functional units. Our work extends this algorithm in that we do not approximate registers by conceptual FIFO buffers that are reserved for an interval of time that is a multiple of II. Because of its accurate modeling of the register requirements, our method results in lower register requirements in 25% percent of the loops in our benchmark.

This work generalizes our previous work on optimizing an existing modulo schedule for a given loop to reduce its register requirements [12]. Although our previous work also modeled the register requirements of a loop accurately, a schedule with minimum register requirements was not sought over the entire search space of valid modulo schedules. Instead, our previous work considered only schedules in which operations of an existing schedule where displaced by multiples of II cycles. Also, our previous work did not present any experimental results. Because of its increased search space, the new method of this paper results in lower register requirements in 11% percent of the loops in our benchmark.

This work also generalizes the linear-time algorithm for determining minimum register requirements by Mangione-Smith *et al* [9], which requires that each virtual register be used no more than once. Our scheduling method handles general dependence graphs, including loop-carried dependence and common sub-expressions.

This work complements the register allocation algorithm presented by Rau, Lee, Tirumalai, and Schlansker [8], which achieves register allocations that are within one register of the MaxLive bound for the vast majority of modulo-scheduled loops on machines with rotating register files and predicated execution to support modulo scheduling. For machines without hardware support, their algorithm typically achieves register allocations that are within four registers of the MaxLive bound, after loop unrolling and consequent code expansion.

Finally, in contrast to the work by Ning and Gao [13] and Ramanujam [14], we allow finite machine resource constraints. Moreover, we do not approximate the register pressure by minimizing the average number of live values over all cycles, but rather we explicitly minimize the maximum number of live values at any single cycle of the loop.

In this paper, we present the impact of modulo scheduling on register requirements in Section 2. We develop an integer linear programming model that minimizes the register requirements for a given initiation interval in Section 3. We present an algorithm that finds a schedule with the highest steady state throughput over all modulo schedules, and the minimum register requirements among such schedules in Section 4. We propose a technique that removes redundant edges of the dependence graph to improve the execution time of modulo schedulers in Section 5. We demonstrate that the search space of modulo schedules is bounded in Section 6. We compare the performance of this and other modulo schedulers for a benchmark of 629 loops in Section 7. Conclusions are presented in Section 8.

2 Register Requirements

In this section, we present the impact of scheduling on the register requirements of a modulo scheduled loop. The example target machine is a hypothetical processor with three fully-pipelined general-purpose functional units. The memory latency and the add/sub latency is one cycle, the `mult` latency is four cycles, and the `div` latency is eight cycles. We selected these values to obtain concise examples; however, our method works independently of the numbers of functional units, resource constraints, and latencies.

Example 1 This example [12] illustrates how to compute the register requirements of a modulo-scheduled loop. This kernel is: `y[i] = x[i]`^{2}`- x[i]- a`, where the value of `x[i]` is read from memory, squared, decremented by `x[i]+a`, and stored in `y[i]`, as shown in the dependence graph of Figure 1a.

The vertices of the dependence graph correspond to operations and the edges correspond to virtual registers. The value of each *virtual register* is defined by a unique opera-

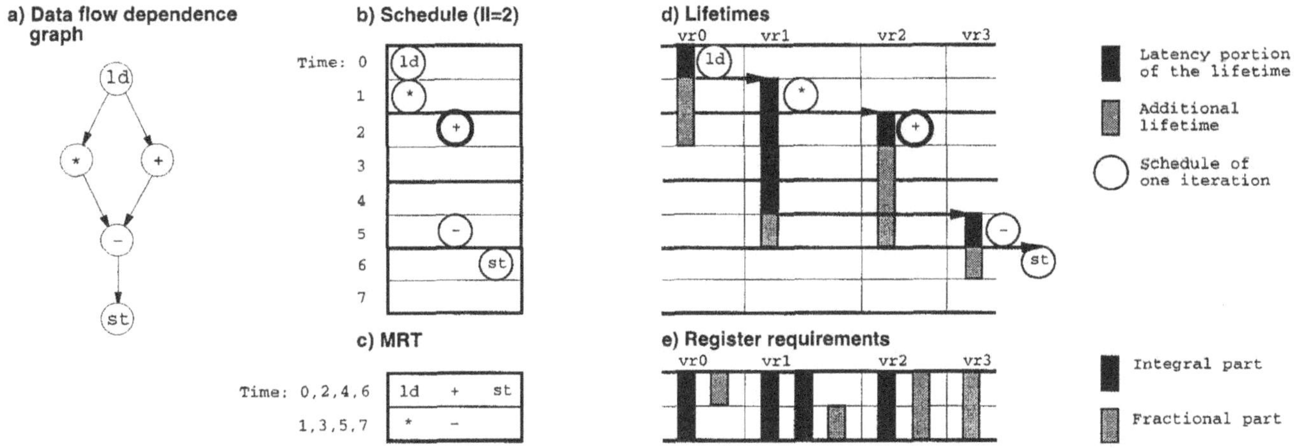

Figure 2: Modulo schedule for the kernel `y[i] = x[i]`^{2}`-x[i]-a` with minimum register requirements.

tion and once its value has been defined, it may be used by several operations. In this paper, a virtual register is reserved in the cycle where its define operation is scheduled, and remains reserved until it becomes free in the cycle following its last-use operation. In our machine model, the additional reserved time beyond the last-use operation cycle is one clock cycle. Other machines may have an additional reserved time which is operation dependent. The *lifetime* of a virtual register is the set of cycles during which it is reserved.

The scheduler places each operation of an iteration so that both resource constraints and dependence constraints are fulfilled. Figure 1b illustrates a schedule with an *II* of 2 for the kernel of Example 1 on the target machine. In this schedule, the `load`, `mult`, `add`, `sub` and `store` operations of the iteration starting at time 0 are respectively scheduled at time 0, 1, 1, 5, and 6.

The *modulo reservation table* (MRT) associated with a schedule is obtained by collapsing the schedule for an iteration to a table of *II* rows, using wraparound. Figure 1c illustrates the MRT associated with the schedule of Figure 1b. The resource constraints of a modulo schedule are satisfied if and only if the packing of the operations within the *II* rows of the MRT does not exceed the resources of the machine. For our target machine, the resource constraints allow up to 3 operations of any kind to be issued in each row of the MRT. The MRT can also model specialized resources by allowing only certain types of operations in each column.

The virtual register lifetimes associated with this iteration are presented in Figure 1d. The black bars correspond to the initial portion of the lifetime that minimally satisfies the latency of the defining functional unit; the grey bars show the additional lifetime of each virtual register. Ideally, the additional lifetime should not be longer than one cycle; but, because of resource constraints, it is not always possible to schedule each use operation immediately after its input operand latencies expire. The dependence constraints are satisfied if and only if no operation is placed during the portion of the lifetime that overlaps with the black bar of a virtual register that it uses.

Formal Problem Definition: Among all modulo schedules that employ the smallest feasible initiation interval and satisfy all resource constraints, find one that minimizes MaxLive.

Because of the modulo constraint, MaxLive can be quickly computed, as illustrated in Figure 1e. Figure 1e shows the number of live virtual registers in each of the *II* cycles of a steady-state loop execution and is constructed by replicating Figure 1d with a shift of *II* cycles between successive copies until the pattern in *II* successive rows repeats indefinitely. Figure 1e then displays these *II* rows in a compact form. Figure 1e can be constructed quickly by collapsing Figure 1d to *II* rows, with wraparound. In Figure 1e, we see that exactly six virtual registers are live in the first row and eight in the second, resulting in a MaxLive of eight.

Figure 1e distinguishes between two distinct contributions to each virtual register lifetime: the fractional and the integral part. For virtual registers with several uses, only the last use is considered. In our machine model, the additional reserved time is one clock cycle and is included, for simplicity, in the fractional part. The *fractional part* thus spans the rows in the MRT inclusively from the def operation row forward with wraparound through the last-use operation row. Its length ranges from 1 to *II* and is equal to 1 plus the modulo *II* distance between these rows, as shown in Figure 1e. The *integral part* spans the entire MRT exactly *s* times, where *s* corresponds to the number of times the row number of the last-use operation appears in the time interval starting inclusively from the def operation schedule time until, but not including, the last-use operation schedule time.

The *integral MaxLive* is defined as the number of integral bars in a row, summed over all virtual registers. Similarly, the *fractional MaxLive* is the number of fractional part bars in the row with the most fractional part bars. Finally, *MaxLive* is the sum of fractional and integral MaxLives.

The schedule presented in Figure 1b is a schedule that results in the minimum buffer requirements for this kernel and target machine, as presented by Govindarajan *et al* [11]. In their study, registers are approximated by conceptual FIFO buffers which are reserved for a time interval that is a multiple of II. It thus corresponds to searching for a schedule that minimizes integral MaxLive. However, minimizing integral MaxLive does not in general result in a schedule with minimal MaxLive.

For example, Figure 2 presents a schedule for the same kernel, resulting in the same integral MaxLive but resulting in a lower total MaxLive. The schedule of Figure 2b differs only by the schedule time of the add operation, which is delayed by one cycle from time 1 to time 2. The register requirements associated with this schedule are shown in Figure 2e. Comparing the register requirements of this schedule to the one of Figure 1e, we see that both have an integral MaxLive of four. However, this schedule results in a lower fractional MaxLive as fractional parts are more evenly distributed among the II rows. As a result, MaxLive decreases from eight to seven.

3 Scheduling for Minimum MaxLive

In this section, we present an integer linear programming model that schedules the operations of an innermost loop while minimizing MaxLive. The definition of the schedule search space used in this section is similar to the one presented by Govindarajan *et al* [11]. All variables of the model presented in this section are summarized in Table 2.

We represent a loop by a dependence graph $G = \{V, E_{sched}, E_{reg}\}$, where the set of vertices V represents operations and the sets of edges E_{sched} and E_{reg} correspond, respectively, to the scheduling dependences and the register dependences among operations. A scheduling edge enforces a temporal relationship between dependent operations or between any operations that cannot be freely reordered, such as load and store operations to ambiguous memory locations. A scheduling edge from operation i to operation j, w iterations later, is associated with a latency $l_{i,j}$ and a dependence distance $\omega_{i,j} = w$. A register edge corresponds to a data flow dependence carried in a register. Initially (until Section 5), each register edge is also a scheduling edge. However, there are scheduling edges that have no corresponding register edge, e.g. the dependence between a store and a load to an ambiguous memory (or the same) location results in a scheduling edge but not in a register edge.

Consider a loop with N operations and an initiation interval of II. We represent a schedule for this loop by a $II \times N$ binary matrix, called A, where $a_{r,i} = 1$ if and only if operation i is scheduled in row r and 0 otherwise. Valid modulo schedules must satisfy two sets of conditions. First, each operation must be scheduled exactly once per iteration:

$$\sum_{r=0}^{II-1} a_{r,i} \quad = \quad 1 \qquad \forall i \in [0, N-1] \tag{1}$$

Second, the resource constraints of the target machine must be satisfied in each row of the MRT. Consider an operation i which consumes a resource q for one cycle exactly c cycles after being issued. A resource q is consumed in row r if operation i is scheduled c cycles earlier, namely if $a_{(r-c) \bmod II, i} = 1$. For a machine with M_q machine resources of type q, the resource constraint for row r and resource q simply states that no more than M_q resources can be consumed concurrently among all operations, namely

$$\sum_{i=0}^{N-1} \sum_{c \in Res_{i,q}} a_{(r-c) \bmod II, i} \le M_q \qquad \forall q, \forall r \in [0, II-1] \tag{2}$$

where $c \in Res_{i,q}$ indicates that operation i uses the resource of type q for one cycle exactly c cycles after being issued.

We now introduce two definitions that characterize the row and the time at which each operation is scheduled:

row_i	row number in which operation i is scheduled (from 0 to $II-1$).
$time_i$	time at which operation i is scheduled

Using matrix A, we may write the row number in which operation i is scheduled as:

$$row_i \quad = \quad \sum_{r=1}^{II-1} r * a_{r,i} \tag{3}$$

A modulo schedule also defines the *stage* in which each operation is scheduled. We represent the stage number by k, an integer vector of dimension N, where k_i is the stage number in which operation i is scheduled. Matrix A and vector k uniquely define the cycle in which operations are scheduled. The schedule time of operation i is equal to:

$$time_i = k_i * II + row_i \tag{4}$$

A modulo schedule must enforce all the dependences of its dependence graph. A dependence between operation i and operation j, $\omega_{i,j}$ iterations later, is fulfilled if operation j is scheduled at least $l_{i,j}$ cycles after operation i:

$$(time_j + \omega_{i,j} * II) - time_i \ge l_{i,j} \qquad \forall (i,j) \in E_{sched} \tag{5}$$

Equations (1), (2), and (5) represent, respectively, the modulo constraints, the resource constraints, and the dependence constraints of a modulo schedule. These constraints define the space of valid modulo schedules for that initiation interval II, target machine, and dependence graph G with dependence distance ω and dependence latency l.

We must now define the register requirements associated with a modulo schedule. Since we are minimizing MaxLive, we must compute the precise number of live virtual registers in each of II consecutive cycles. We define a new $II \times N$ integer matrix, called V, where $v_{r,i}$ corresponds to the number of live virtual registers generated by operation i in row r. Matrix V is defined as follows:

$$\sum_{z=0}^{r} a_{z,i} - \sum_{z=0}^{r-1} a_{z,j} + (k_j + \omega_{i,j}) - k_i \le v_{r,i}$$
$$\forall (i,j) \in E_{reg}, \qquad \forall r \in [0, II-1] \tag{6}$$

Equation (6) quantifies the register requirements in row r generated by the register dependence (i,j), from the def operation i to the use operation j.

To demonstrate the validity of Equation (6), we compute the fractional and integral parts of the lifetime associated with a register edge (i,j), namely:

$frac_{r,i,j}$	fractional part of the lifetime in row r associated with a register edge (i,j).
$int_{i,j}$	integral part of the lifetime associated with a register edge (i,j).

We will demonstrate that their sum is exactly equal to $v_{r,i}$ if operation j is the last-use of the operation i result. We introduce three definitions specific to def operation i and use operation j:

$$d_r = \sum_{z=0}^{r} a_{z,i} \qquad u_r = \sum_{z=0}^{r-1} a_{z,j}$$

$$x = \begin{cases} 1 & \text{if } row_i > row_j \\ 0 & \text{otherwise} \end{cases} \tag{7}$$

Recall that only one $a_{z,i}$ is non zero for a given operation i among all rows. As a result, both d_r and u_r are non-decreasing functions, with minimal value 0 and maximal value 1. As defined in Equation (7), d_r becomes 1 exactly in the row z where def operation i is scheduled ($a_{z,i} = 1$). Similarly, u_r becomes 1 exactly in the row z following the

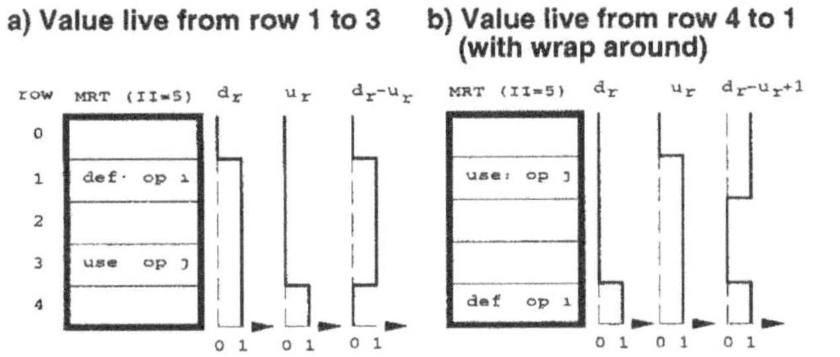

Figure 3: Determining the fractional and integral part of a lifetime.

row where use operation j is scheduled ($a_{z-1,j} = 1$). Once d_r or u_r become 1, they remain 1 through row $II - 1$.

When computing the fractional part of the lifetime associated with the def operation i and the use operation j, two cases must be considered. In the first case, row_i is no greater than row_j. Therefore, the initial value of the term $d_r - u_r$ is initially 0, becomes 1 in the row of the def operation, and returns to 0 in the row after the row of the use operation. As a result, the term $d_r - u_r$ is 1 exactly where the fractional part of the lifetime associated with (i, j) would contribute to the register requirements if operation j is the last use; otherwise, $d_r - u_r$ is 0. In Figure 3a for example, the def operation i is scheduled in row 1 ($a_{1,i} = 1$) and the use operation j is scheduled in row 3 ($a_{3,j} = 1$). The plots of d_r, u_r, and $d_r - u_r$ are also shown in Figure 3a. Notice that the fractional part of this lifetime is correctly determined to be live in rows 1, 2 and 3.

In the second case, row_i is larger than row_j. The initial value of the term $d_r - u_r + 1$ is 1, becomes 0 in the row following the row of the use operation, and returns to 1 in the row of the def operation. As a result, the term $d_r - u_r + 1$ is 1 exactly where the fractional part of the lifetime associated with (i, j) would contribute to the register requirements if operation j is the last use; otherwise, $d_r - u_r + 1$ is 0. In Figure 3b for example, the def operation i is scheduled in row 4 ($a_{4,i} = 1$) and the use operation j is scheduled in row 1 ($a_{1,j} = 1$). The plots of d_r, u_r, and $d_r - u_r + 1$ are shown in Figure 3b. We see that the fractional part of this lifetime is correctly determined to be live in rows 4, 0, and 1.

Using the definitions of Equation (7), we can express the fractional part of the lifetime associated with operations i and j in row r as:

$$frac_{r,i,j} = d_r - u_r + x \tag{8}$$

where $frac_{r,i,j}$ is 1 if and only if row r contributes to the fractional part of the lifetime associated with operations i and j.

To compute the integral part of the lifetime associated with operations i and j, we must also consider two cases. In the first case, row_i is no greater than row_j, and the integer part corresponds directly to the difference between the stage numbers of the use and the def operations, namely $(k_j + w_{i,j}) - k_i$. In Figure 3a, the integral part is 0 when $k_i = k_j$ and $\omega_{i,j} = 0$. If the use operation was delayed by II cycles, k_j would increase by 1 and so would the integral part.

In the second case, row_i is larger than row_j, and the integer part corresponds directly to $(k_j + w_{i,j}) - k_i - 1$, where the -1 term is introduced to counterbalance the wraparound effect. In Figure 3b, the integral part is 0 when $k_i = k_j + 1$ and $\omega_{i,j} = 0$. Again, delaying the use operation by II cycles would increase the integral part by 1.

As a result, we can express the integral part of the lifetime associated with operations i and j as:

$$int_{i,j} = k_j + w_{i,j} - k_i - x \tag{9}$$

By summing the fractional and integral parts of the lifetime, as defined in Equations (8) and (9), the x terms cancel each other, resulting in the left hand side of Equation (6). Finally, the register requirement contribution of an operation i in row r corresponds to the maximum register requirements among all uses of operation i.

Using the previous result, MaxLive is defined as the sum of the fractional and integral part of each virtual register in the row with the largest fractional plus integral part:

$$\sum_{i=0}^{N-1} v_{r,i} \leq MaxLive \qquad \forall r \in [0, II-1] \tag{10}$$

This completes the description of the objective function and we can now present the algorithm that will schedule an iteration for maximal throughput and minimum register requirements.

4 Optimum Modulo Schedules

We present in this section an algorithm that finds a schedule with the highest steady state throughput over all modulo schedules and the minimum register requirements among such schedules. The model, from Equation (1), (2), (5), and (6), and its variables are respectively summarized in Figure 4 and Table 2. Note that the model finds a schedule with minimum MaxLive for a given initiation interval. Therefore, a schedule with minimum register requirements for the smallest feasible initiation interval is obtained by solving a series of problems, starting with the minimum initiation interval.

Algorithm 1 (MinReg Modulo Scheduler) *Consider a machine description M_q, $Res_{i,q}$, and $l_{i,j}$ and consider a data dependence graph $G = \{V, E_{sched}, E_{reg}\}$ and $\omega_{i,j}$. The following algorithm finds a schedule with the highest steady state throughput over all modulo schedules, and the minimum register requirements among such schedules:*

1. *Compute the Minimum Initiation Interval (MII) [3] and set the tentative II to MII.*
2. *Build the integer linear programming system as indicated in Figure 4 and search for a solution.*
3. *If the system built in Step 2 fails to find a feasible solution, increase II by one and return to Step 2. Otherwise, an solution found is optimal.*

Minimize	Variables	Fundamental Constraints
Int MaxLive	$N(II+2)$	$N + m * II + e_{reg} + e_{sched}$
Tot MaxLive	$N(2II+1)$	$N + m * II + (e_{reg}+1)II + e_{sched}$
Increase	$N * (II-1)$	$(e_{reg}+1)II - e_{reg}$

Table 1: Minimizing integral versus total MaxLive.

For comparison purposes, we also investigated a model minimizing integral MaxLive. This integer programming model differs from the model of Figure 4 in that the equations labeled Lifetimes and MaxLive are replaced by an equation defining the number of FIFO buffers needed to

Minimize:	$MaxLive$	
Subject to:		
MRT:	$\sum_{r=0}^{II-1} a_{r,i} = 1$	$\forall i \in [0, N-1]$
Resources:	$\sum_{i=0}^{N-1} \sum_{c \in Res_{i,q}} a_{(r-c) \bmod II, i} \leq M_q$	$\forall q, \forall r \in [0, II-1]$
Dependences:	$time_j + \omega_{i,j} * II - time_i \geq l_{i,j}$	$\forall (i,j) \in E_{sched}$
Lifetimes:	$\sum_{z=0}^{r} a_{z,i} - \sum_{z=0}^{r-1} a_{z,j} + k_j + \omega_{i,j} - k_i \leq v_{r,i}$	$\forall r \in [0, II-1], \forall (i,j) \in E_{reg}$
MaxLive:	$\sum_{i=0}^{N-1} v_{r,i} \leq MaxLive$	$\forall r \in [0, II-1]$
Definitions:	$time_i = \sum_{r=1}^{II-1} r * a_{r,i} + k_i * II$	
	$MaxLive,\ a_{r,i},\ v_{r,i},\ k_i$: integer, ≥ 0	

Figure 4: Scheduling for minimum MaxLive

Machine:	(input)	Schedule:	(input)
$l_{i,j}$	latency between operation i and operation j.	II	initiation interval (constant in the integer programming model).
M_q	number of resources of type q.		
$Res_{i,q}$	set of cycles in which operation i uses resource q.		
Graph:	(input)	Results:	(output)
$G = \{V, E_{sched}, E_{reg}\}$	dependence graph with scheduling edge and register edge set.	$a_{r,i}$	binary matrix where $a_{r,i} = 1$ if operation i is scheduled in row r.
N	number of operations in graph G.	k_i	stage number of operation i.
$\omega_{i,j}$	dependence distance between operation i and operation j (in iteration).	$v_{r,i}$	number of live virtual registers in row r generated by operation i.

Table 2: Variables for the modulo scheduling model.

store the result of operation i, as proposed by Govindarajan *et al* [11]. Algorithm 1 is directly applicable to this integer programming model as well.

The complexity of these models, in number of variables and fundamental constraints, is shown in Table 1 for a loop with N operations, an initiation interval of II, e_{reg} register dependence edges, e_{sched} scheduling dependence edges, and a machine with m kinds of machine resources. The major complexity increase, when minimizing MaxLive instead of integral MaxLive, is that $N * II$ variables are needed to keep track of the register requirements of each operation in each row of the MRT instead of N variables for each operation over the entire MRT. We will subsequently refer to a modulo scheduler minimizing total MaxLive as *MinReg Scheduler* and a modulo scheduler minimizing integral MaxLive as *MinBuf Scheduler*.

5 Removing Redundant Edges

The dependence graph, as defined in Section 3, may contain edges that result in redundant constraints. Removing these redundant constraints is important because while they do not restrict the search space, they consume a significant amount of time to verify them. In this section, we present a technique that removes redundant edges, i.e. those whose removal does not expand the space of modulo schedules. This technique is applicable to any modulo scheduler.

Typically, it is known that transitive scheduling edges of a single basic block can be ignored when scheduling that basic block. In this section, we extend this result in two directions. First, we handle dependence graphs with arbitrary dependence distances. Second, we remove redundant scheduling edges and redundant register edges. Removing redundant register edges is particularly important since excluding one register edge results in II fewer redundant constraints, as indicated in Table 1.

Formally, we remove redundant edges of the original graph $G = \{V, E_{sched}, E_{reg}\}$ to get a new graph $G' = \{V, E'_{sched}, E'_{reg}\}$, with fewer redundant edges. Edges are removed from G' if and only if we can prove that scheduling for G or G' is guaranteed to result in defining the same scheduling search space with the same register requirements. While E_{reg} was defined as a subset of E_{sched}, this inclusion property does not hold in G', as some edges may be removed only from E'_{reg} or E'_{sched}.

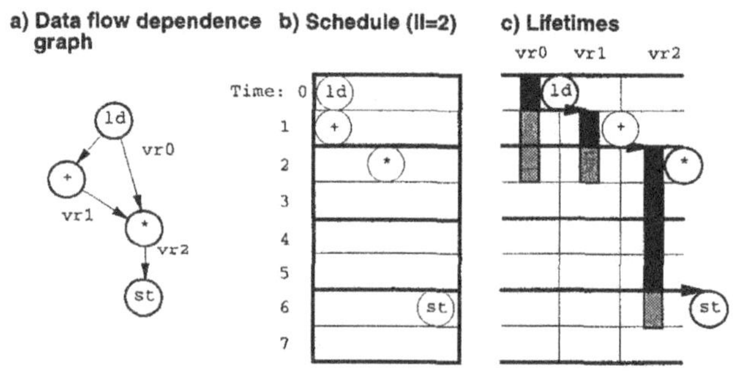

Figure 5: Modulo schedule for Example 2.

Example 2 This example illustrates a case where two redundant edges can safely be removed from G'. This kernel is: `y[i] = x[i] *(x[i] +a)` as shown in the dependence graph

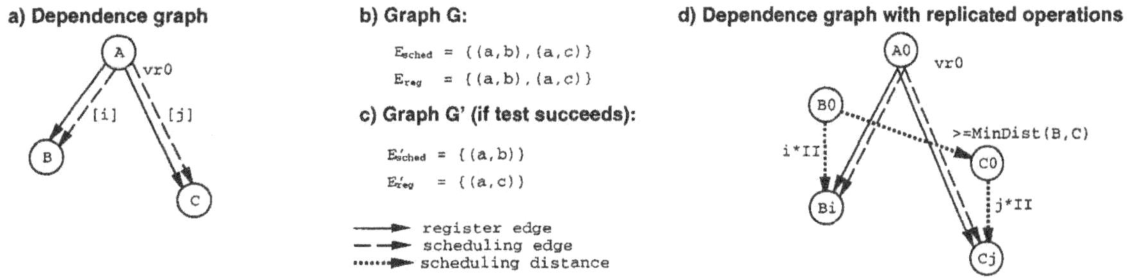

Figure 6: Removing edges.

of Figure 5a. This example is a basic block with no loop-carried dependence. In this example, the `mult` operation is guaranteed to be scheduled no earlier than one cycle after the `add` operation. As a result, the scheduling edge (`load`, `mult`) can be safely removed from E'_{sched} because enforcing the dependence constraints of scheduling edges (`load`, `add`) and (`add`, `mult`) is necessarily more constraining than enforcing the dependence constraints of scheduling edge (`load`, `mult`). Similarly, the register edge (`load`, `add`) can be removed from E'_{reg} since the `mult` is the last-use operation of `vr0` which implies that the register lifetime generated by the (`load`, `add`) edge is necessarily included in the lifetime generated by the register edge (`load`, `mult`).

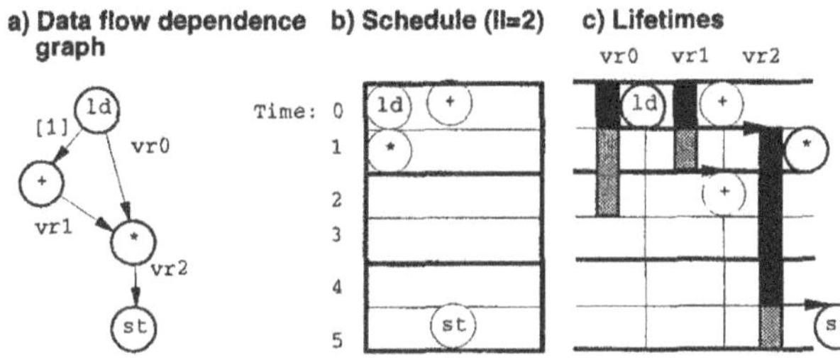

Figure 7: Modulo schedule for Example 3.

Example 3 This example shows that the notion of transitive edges cannot be extended directly to dependence graphs with loop-carried dependences. This kernel is: `y[i] = x[i] *(x[i-1] +a)` as shown in the data flow dependence graph of Figure 7a. This example differs from Example 2 only by the dependence of distance 1 associated with the edge (`load`, `add`). Figure 7b presents a schedule for this kernel where the `add` operation is scheduled at time 0, a valid schedule since the `add` operation input is generated by the `load` operation of the previous iteration. Figure 7c illustrates the lifetimes associated with this schedule. Since the result of the `load` operation is used both by the `mult` operation (time 1) and the `add` operation of the next iteration, (time $0 + II = 2$), the lifetime of $vr0$ lasts through time 2. This schedule shows that the lifetime associated with the register edge (`load`, `add`) is not necessarily included in the lifetime associated with the register edge (`load`, `mult`), even in presence of a scheduling edge from the `add` operation to the `mult` operation. As a result, the register edge (`load`, `add`) cannot be removed from G'.

To determine the conditions under which edges can be safely removed, we introduce the $MinDist$ relation as proposed by Huff [15]. $MinDist(x, y)$ represents the minimum number of cycles, possibly negative, that must occur between the time operation X is scheduled until the time operation Y is scheduled, if there is a path in the dependence graph from X to Y. Otherwise, $MinDist(x, y)$ is defined as minus infinity. Computing $MinDist$ is an all-pairs longest-path problem where each dependence edge (i, j) is assigned a cost of $l_{i,j} - \omega_{i,j} * II$, the minimum schedule distance as defined in Equation (5). $MinDist$ is guaranteed to converge to a solution because II is chosen such that all cycles in the dependence graph have nonpositive costs [15].

Theorem 1 (Edge Removal Test) *Consider the operations A, B, and C in V with edges (a, b) and (a, c) in E_{sched} and E_{reg} of G. When the following inequality holds:*

$$(\omega_{a,c} - \omega_{a,b}) * II + MinDist(b, c) \;\geq\; 0$$

we can guarantee that if the edge (a, b) is a scheduling edge in graph G', the edge (a, c) can be removed from the scheduling edge set of graph G'. Similarly, we can guarantee that if the edge (a, c) is a register edge in graph G', the edge (a, b) can be removed from the register edge set of graph G'.

Figure 6a illustrates Theorem 1. In this partial dependence graph, the value produced by operation A is used i iterations later by operation B ($\omega_{a,b} = i$) and j iterations later by operation C ($\omega_{a,c} = j$). The sets of edges associated with this dependence graph are presented in Figure 6b. When the inequality of Theorem 1 holds, the sets of edges shown in Figure 6c are guaranteed to result in defining the same scheduling search space with the same register requirements.

Proof: Consider the dependence graph with replicated operations shown in Figure 6d, which corresponds to the same dependence graph as illustrated in Figure 6a. In this graph, operations $A0$, $B0$, and $C0$ are operations of the first iteration, operation Bi is an operation of iteration i, and operation Cj is an operation of iteration j. As defined in Figure 6a, the result of operation $A0$ is used by operations Bi and Cj.

Several scheduling distances can be inferred from Figure 6d. First, the modulo constraint guarantees that operation Bi is scheduled exactly $i * II$ cycles after $B0$. Similarly, operation Cj is guaranteed to be scheduled $j * II$ cycles after $C0$. We can also use the minimum distance relation to assert that operation $C0$ must be scheduled at least $MinDist(b, c)$ cycles after operation $B0$.

We now demonstrate the conditions that must hold to guarantee that operation Cj is scheduled no earlier than operation Bi. Without loss of generality, we state that operation Bi is scheduled at time $t_{B0} + i * II$. Summing the scheduling distance from operation $B0$ to Cj, we can guarantee that operation Cj can be scheduled no earlier than $t_{B0} + MinDist(b, c) + j * II$. Using these results, we conclude that operation Cj is scheduled no earlier than operation Bi if the difference of their schedule times is nonnegative, namely if $(t_{B0}+MinDist(b,c)+j*II)-(t_{B0}+i*II) \geq 0$. Simplifying the t_{B0} terms and substituting $\omega_{a,b}$ and $\omega_{a,c}$ for i and j, respectively, we obtain the inequality of Theorem 1. Note that this inequality is independent of t_{B0}, the time at which operation $B0$ is scheduled.

When operation Cj is guaranteed by the edge-removal test to be scheduled no earlier than operation Bi, we know that the scheduling edge (a, c) is guaranteed to be fulfilled and can therefore be removed. Similarly, we know that the register requirements of edge (a, b) are satisfied by register edge (a, c). □

Algorithm 2 (Edge Removal) *For a given dependence graph $G = \{V, E_{sched}, E_{reg}\}$ and initiation interval II, we construct an equivalent graph $G' = \{V, E'_{sched}, E'_{reg}\}$ that is guaranteed to result in defining the same scheduling search space with the same register requirements and fewer edges as follows:*

1. *Initialize $G' = G$ and compute the $MinDist$ matrix for the given II.*
2. *Apply Theorem 1 to each pair of outgoing edges of a vertex v, removing redundant edges in both E'_{sched} and E'_{reg} when feasible.*
3. *Repeat Step 2 for each vertex of the graph.*

6 Bounding the Schedule Space

As presented in Figure 4, the integer linear programming search space is unbounded because there is no limit on the k_i values and hence on the maximal schedule length. To bound the schedule length of an iteration and thereby significantly improve the efficiency of the integer programming solver, we introduce two pseudo operations in the dependence graph: `start` is a predecessor of every operation in the graph, and `stop` is a successor to every operation in the graph. The latency and dependence distance of the outgoing edges from `start` and of the incoming edges to `stop` are 0. Using the methodology presented by Huff [15], the $MinDist$ relation can be used to determine a lower bound and an upper bound on the schedule time of each operation. We know that an operation i cannot be scheduled earlier than $MinDist(start, i)$ cycles after the `start` pseudo operation. Similarly, we know that an operation i cannot be scheduled earlier than $MinDist(i, stop)$ cycles before the `stop` pseudo operation.

To bound the search space of the integer linear programming solver, we must relate the schedule time of these two pseudo operations to one another. Without loss of generality, we define the maximal schedule length of a schedule to be $MinDist(start, stop) + S$ where S is a nonnegative integer value. Using this result, we bound the schedule time of operation i as follows:

$$MinDist(start, i) \leq time_i$$

$$time_i \leq MinDist(start, stop) + S - MinDist(i, stop) \quad (11)$$

where S represents the *schedule slack* or degree of freedom given to the scheduler.

Theorem 2 *Let R_S be the minimum MaxLive for a dependence graph G and initiation interval II among all schedules of schedule length no greater than $MinDist(start, stop) + S$. The minimum MaxLive values are bounded as follows:*

$$R_0 \geq R_1 \geq \ldots \geq R_{y-1} \geq R_y = R_{y+1} = \ldots = R_\infty, \text{ where}$$

$$y = (N-1)*(l_{max} + II - 1) + 1 - MinDist(start, stop)$$

where l_{max} corresponds to the longest minimal schedule distance among pairs of adjacent operations.

Proof: Since the set of schedules of length no greater than $MinDist(start, stop) + S + 1$ necessarily contains all the schedules of length no greater than $MinDist(start, stop) + S$, we can guarantee that the relation on the minimum MaxLive $R_S \geq R_{S+1}$ holds for any schedule slack S.

Consider now a schedule of length $z > (N-1)*(l_{max} + II - 1) + 1$. We can guarantee that there is a shorter schedule of length $z - II$ that still fulfills both resource and dependence constraints and results in lower register requirements. The proof is based on the pigeonhole principle.

Consider the operations scheduled at time t_i and select the operations scheduled at time $t_j > t_i$ such that there are no operations scheduled in the time interval (t_i, t_j). Since there are N vertices, there are at most $N-1$ such intervals. Because the length of the schedule, z, is larger than $(N-1)*(l_{max} + II - 1) + 1$, there must be at least one interval of length larger than $l_{max} + II - 1$. Consider (t_i, t_j) to be such an interval. In this case, we can trivially reschedule all operations scheduled strictly after t_i, II cycles earlier without violating any dependence constraints. Moreover, rescheduling operations II cycles earlier is guaranteed to fulfill the resource constraints as the MRT is unchanged by the new schedule. Consequently, interval (t_i, t_j) is reduced by II. By finite induction, we can get $z \leq (N-1)*(l_{max} + II - 1) + 1$.

Furthermore, reducing the schedule length by II is guaranteed to result in lower register requirements because it reduces all the lifetimes that span the interval (t_i, t_j) by II. Therefore, limiting the schedule length to $(N-1)*(l_{max} + II - 1) + 1$, i.e. limiting the scheduling slack to $y = (N-1)*(l_{max} + II - 1) + 1 - MinDist(start, stop)$, does not preclude any optimal solutions. □

7 Measurements

In this section, we investigate the register requirements of four modulo scheduling algorithms. For the purpose of comparison, we also present the register requirements of an efficient modulo scheduling algorithm that presently does not attempt to minimize the register requirements. Unfortunately, we are unable to provide a comparison with Huff's scheduling algorithm [15] since his machine model differs slightly from ours and his latest scheduler, presented in [15], was not available to us.

MinReg Scheduler: This scheduler minimizes MaxLive over all valid modulo schedules using the integer programming model developed in Section 3 and summarized in Figure 4. The resulting schedule has the lowest register requirements of any modulo schedule for the given machine, loop, and initiation interval.

MinBuf Scheduler: This scheduler minimizes Integral MaxLive over all valid modulo schedules using an integer programming model similar to the one proposed by Govindarajan [11]. The resulting schedule has the lowest buffer requirements of any modulo schedule for the given machine, loop, and initiation interval. Buffers, as opposed to registers, must be reserved for a time interval that is a multiple of II. We present here the register requirements associated with these schedules in our comparisons.

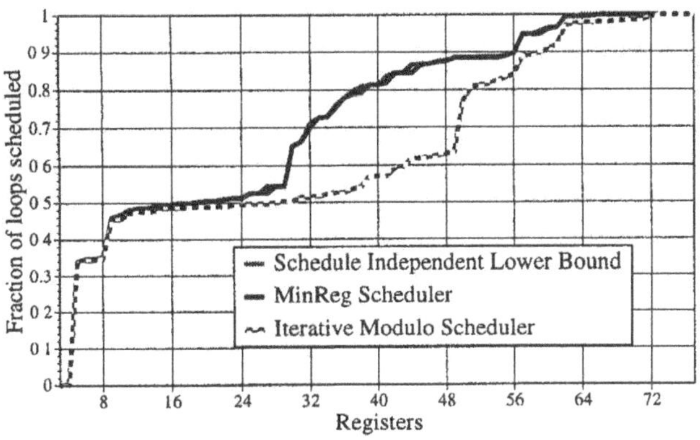

Figure 8: MaxLive.

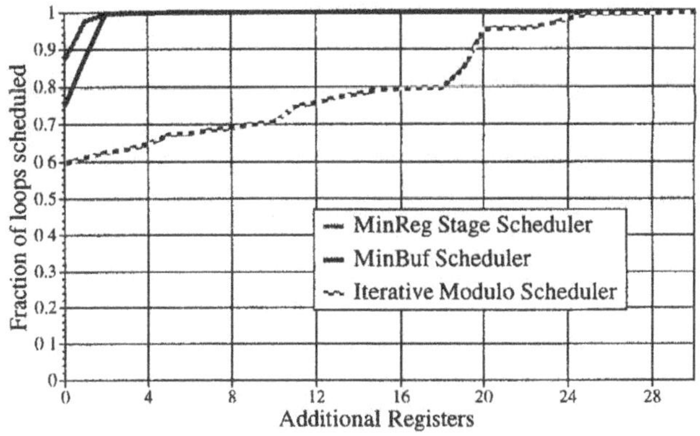

Figure 9: MaxLive increase over the MinReg Scheduler.

MinReg Stage Scheduler[12]: This scheduler minimizes MaxLive over all valid modulo schedules that share a given MRT. This scheduler can only select the stage in which each operation is scheduled[1]; however, it can generate a schedule in linear time for loops with acyclic underlying dependence graphs and in polynomial time otherwise. The resulting schedule has the lowest achievable register requirements for the given machine, loop, and MRT.

Iterative Modulo Scheduler[3]: This scheduler has been designed to deal efficiently with realistic machine models while producing schedules with near optimal steady state throughput. Experimental findings show that this algorithm requires the scheduling of only 59% more operations than does acyclic list scheduling while resulting in schedules that are optimal in II for 96% of loops in their benchmark [3]. In its current form, it does not attempt to minimize the register requirements of its schedules; however, preliminary investigations show that the register requirements of its schedules may be reduced significantly by simple heuristics.

In this section, we use a benchmark of loops obtained from the Perfect Club [16], SPEC-89 [17], and the Livermore Fortran Kernels [18]. Our benchmark consists exclusively of innermost loops with no early exits, no procedure calls, and fewer than 30 basic blocks, as compiled by the Cydra 5 Fortran77 compiler [19]. The input to the four scheduling algorithms consists of the Fortran77 compiler intermediate representation after load-store elimination, recurrence back-substitution, and IF-conversion. Of the 1327 loops successfully modulo scheduled by the Cydra 5 Fortran77 compiler, we selected all the loops with up to 12 operations and with II up to 5, resulting in a benchmark of 629 loops. The cutoff limit was selected such that all scheduling algorithms ran to completion in a reasonable amount of time[2].

The machine model used in these experiments corresponds to the Cydra 5 machine. This choice was motivated by the availability of quality code for this machine. Also, the resource requirements of the Cydra 5 machine are complex [10], thus stressing the importance of good and robust scheduling algorithms. In particular, the machine configuration is the one used in [3].

Redundant edges were removed from the dependence graph of each loop to reduce the execution time of the modulo schedulers. For the MinReg Scheduler and the MinBuf Scheduler, the scheduling slack presented in Theorem 2 was used to bound the search space. The Iterative Modulo Scheduler was used to generate the required MRT input for the MinReg Stage Scheduler. All scheduling algorithms used the same initiation interval as the one generated by the Iterative Modulo Scheduler, which turned out to be optimal for all the 629 loops of the benchmark.

We first investigated the register requirements of the MinReg Scheduler which results in the lowest register requirements over all valid modulo schedules. Figure 8 presents the fraction of the loops in our benchmark that can be scheduled for a machine with any given number of registers without spilling and without increasing II. In this graph, the X-axis represents MaxLive and the Y-axis represents the fraction of loops scheduled. This graph presents three curves. The first curve, labeled "Schedule independent lower bound," corresponds to [15] and is representative of the register requirements of a machine without any resource conflicts. The second curve presents the register requirements of the schedules generated by the MinReg Scheduler. The fact that these two first curves are nearly identical indicates that the complex resource requirements of the Cydra 5 machine does not significantly impact the register requirements of the optimal schedules for the benchmark considered. The third curve presents the register requirements of the Iterative Modulo Scheduler, which presently does not attempt to minimize the register requirements. The gap between the two last curves is indicative of the degree of improvement that is possible with register sensitive modulo scheduling algorithms.

The next graph illustrates the number of additional registers needed when the other scheduling algorithms are used instead of the MinReg Scheduler. The X-axis of Figure 9 represents the number of additional registers and the Y-axis represents the fraction of loops that can be scheduled with this number. The curves represent the additional register requirements for the MinReg Stage Scheduler, the MinBuf Scheduler, and the Iterative Modulo Scheduler. It is interesting to note that in 89% of the loops, the MinReg Stage Scheduler finds a schedule with no additional register requirements, even though it can only choose the stage for each operation. The MinBuf Scheduler finds an optimal schedule in 75% of the loops. This result implies that in 25% of the loops, minimizing Integral MaxLive does not result in a schedule with minimum MaxLive. This result also implies that for this benchmark, MinReg Stage Scheduler performs better than MinBuf Scheduler. In other words, minimizing MaxLive for the MRT selected by the Iterative Modulo

[1] In the notation presented in Section 3, this corresponds to minimizing the register requirements for a search space with a fixed matrix A but variable stage vector k.

[2] The cumulative time to solution for the integer programming solver was 11 minutes and 30 minutes, respectively, for the MinBuf Scheduler and the MinReg Scheduler.

Scheduler results on average in lower register requirements than minimizing integral MaxLive among all MRTs. Finally, the Iterative Modulo Scheduler results in a schedule with minimum register requirements in 60% of the loops, a surprisingly high percentage for a heuristic that does not attempt to minimize the lifetimes. However, the overall performance of the Iterative Modulo Scheduler is severely degraded by a few loops that require up to 31 additional registers.

8 Conclusion

Modulo scheduling is an efficient technique for exploiting instruction level parallelism in a variety of loops. It results in high performance code, but increases the register requirements. As the trend toward higher concurrency continues, whether due to using and exploiting machines with faster clocks and deeper pipelines, wider issue, or a combination of both, the register requirements will increase even more. As a result, scheduling algorithms that reduce register pressure while scheduling for high throughput are increasingly important.

This paper presents an approach that schedules the loop operations to achieve the minimum register requirements for the smallest initiation interval. We compare the performance of this and other modulo schedulers for a benchmark of 629 loops from the Perfect Club, SPEC-89, and the Livermore Fortran Kernels for the Cydra 5 machine, a machine with complex resource usage. Our empirical findings show that the complex resource requirements of the Cydra 5 machine does not significantly impact the register requirements of a modulo schedule with minimal MaxLive in the benchmark considered. Also, our findings show that the Iterative Modulo Scheduler [3] which does not attempt to minimize registers nevertheless achieves the minimum MaxLive in 60% of the loops and uses an average of 14.03 additional registers over the remaining loops. The MinBuf Scheduler [11] finds a schedule with minimum MaxLive in 75% of the loops and uses an average of 1.52 additional registers over the remaining loops. The MinReg Stage Scheduler [12] finds a schedule with minimum MaxLive in 89% of the loops and uses an average of 1.45 additional registers over the remaining loops.

This paper demonstrates that selecting a good schedule results in lower register requirements. Though the optimal algorithm may be too expensive for general use in a compiler it may be extremely useful in special situations. This algorithm is also useful in evaluating the performance of register-sensitive modulo scheduling heuristics.

Acknowledgements

This work was supported in part by the Office of Naval Research under grant number N00014-93-1-0163 and by Hewlett-Packard. The authors would like to thank Bob Rau for his many useful suggestions and for providing the input data set. We are grateful to Vinod Kathail for his explanation of the resource constraints of the Cydra 5 machine.

References

[1] B. R. Rau and J. A. Fisher. Instruction-level parallel processing: History, overview, and perspective. In *The Journal of Supercomputing*, volume 7, pages 9–50, Boston, July 1993. Kluwer Academic Publishers.

[2] P. Y. Hsu. *Highly Concurrent Scalar Processing*. PhD thesis, University of Illinois at Urbana-Champaign, 1986.

[3] B. R. Rau. Iterative Modulo Scheduling: An algorithm for software pipelining loops. *Proceedings of the 27th Annual International Symposium on Microarchitecture*, pages 63–74, November 1994.

[4] M. Lam. Software pipelining: An effective scheduling technique for VLIW machines. *Proceedings of the ACM SIGPLAN'88 Conference on Programming Language Design and Implementation*, pages 318–328, June 1988.

[5] N. J. Warter, G. E. Haab, and J. W. Bockhaus. Enhanced Modulo Scheduling for loops with conditional branches. *Proceedings of the 25th Annual International Symposium on Microarchitecture*, December 1992.

[6] M. S. Schlansker, V. Kathail, and S. Anik. Height reduction of control recurrences for ILP processors. *Proceedings of the 27th Annual International Symposium on Microarchitecture*, pages 40–51, November 1994.

[7] P. P. Tirumalai, M. Lee, and M. S. Schlansker. Parallelization of loops with exits on pipelined architectures. *Proceedings of Supercomputing '90*, pages 200–212, November 1990.

[8] B. R. Rau, M. Lee, P. P. Tirumalai, and M. S. Schlansker. Register allocation for software pipelined loops. *Proceedings of the ACM SIGPLAN'92 Conference on Programming Language Design and Implementation*, pages 283–299, June 1992.

[9] W. Mangione-Smith, S. G. Abraham, and E. S. Davidson. Register requirements of pipelined processors. *Proceedings of the International Conference on Supercomputing*, pages 260–271, July 1992.

[10] G. R. Beck, D. W. L. Yen, and T. L. Anderson. The Cydra 5 mini-supercomputer: Architecture and implementation. *The Journal of Supercomputing*, 7:143–180, May 1993.

[11] R. Govindarajan, E. R. Altman, and G. R. Gao. Minimizing register requirements under resource-constrained rate-optimal software pipelining. *Proceedings of the 27th Annual International Symposium on Microarchitecture*, pages 85–94, November 1994.

[12] A. E. Eichenberger, E. S. Davidson, and S. G. Abraham. Minimum register requirements for a modulo schedule. *Proceedings of the 27th Annual International Symposium on Microarchitecture*, pages 75–84, November 1994.

[13] Q. Ning and G. R. Gao. A novel framework of register allocation for software pipelining. *Twentieth Annual ACM SIGPLAN-SIGACT Symposium on Principles of Programming Languages*, pages 29–42, 1993.

[14] J. Ramanujam. Optimal software pipelining of nested loops. *Proceedings of the International Parallel Processing Symposium*, pages 335–342, June 1994.

[15] R. A. Huff. Lifetime-sensitive modulo scheduling. *Proceedings of the ACM SIGPLAN'93 Conference on Programming Language Design and Implementation*, pages 258–267, June 1993.

[16] M. Berry et al. The Perfect Club Benchmarks: Effective performance evaluation of supercomputers. *The International Journal of Supercomputer Applications*, 3(3):5–40, Fall 1989.

[17] J. Uniejewski. SPEC Benchmark Suite: Designed for today's advanced system. *SPEC Newsletter*, Fall 1989.

[18] F. H. McMahon. The Livermore Fortran Kernels: A computer test of the numerical performance range. Technical Report UCRL-53745, Lawrence Livermore National Laboratory, Livermore, California, 1986.

[19] J. C. Dehnert and R. A. Towle. Compiling for the Cydra 5. *The Journal of Supercomputing*, 7:181–227, May 1993.

Counting Solutions to Linear and Nonlinear Constraints through Ehrhart polynomials: Applications to Analyze and Transform Scientific Programs

Philippe CLAUSS
ICPS, Université Louis Pasteur, Strasbourg,
Pôle API, Bd Sébastien Brant,
67400 Illkirch France
clauss@icps.u-strasbg.fr
http://icps.u-strasbg.fr/people/philippe.html

Abstract

In order to produce efficient parallel programs, optimizing compilers need to include an analysis of the initial sequential code. When analyzing loops with affine loop bounds, many computations are relevant to the same general problem: counting the number of integer solutions of selected free variables in a set of linear and/or nonlinear parameterized constraints. For example, computing the number of flops executed by a loop, of memory locations touched by a loop, of cache lines touched by a loop, or of array elements that need to be transmitted from a processor to another during the execution of a loop, is useful to determine if a loop is load balanced, evaluate message traffic and allocate message buffers.

The objective of the presented method is to evaluate symbolically, in terms of symbolic constants (the size parameters), this number of integer solutions. By modeling the considered counting problem as a union of rational convex polytopes, the number of included integer points is expressed by particular polynomials where the free variables are the size parameters, commonly called *Ehrhart polynomials.* The paper is illustrated by many examples dealing with parallel program optimizations.

1 Introduction

In order to produce efficient parallel programs, optimizing compilers need to include an analysis of the initial sequential code involving the computation of some determinant values. For example, computing the number of flops executed by a loop, of memory locations touched by a loop, of cache lines touched by a loop, or of array elements that need to be transmitted from a processor to another during the execution of a loop, is useful to determine if a loop is load balanced, evaluate message traffic and allocate message buffers. Such computations are relevant to the same general problem: counting the number of integer solutions of selected free variables in a set of linear and/or nonlinear constraints.

This set of constraints depends on some positive integral size parameters. Any constraint C_k is of the form

$$C_k : \sum_i a_i\alpha_i \leq \sum_j b_j n_j + c$$

where the a_i's, b_i's and c are rational constants, the n_j's are the size parameters and the α_i's can be of the form

$$x_i \quad (x_i \bmod d_i) \quad \lfloor \tfrac{x_i}{d_i} \rfloor \quad \lceil \tfrac{x_i}{d_i} \rceil \quad (d_i | x_i)$$

where d_i is an integral constant, $(d_i|x_i)$ means that d_i evenly divides x_i and x_i is any rational linear combination of the free variables. When the form of any α_i yields a nonlinear constraint, this can easily be transformed into a linear one through some elementary transformations, as those presented by W. Pugh in [16]:

• If a term $\lfloor \frac{x_i}{d_i} \rfloor$ appears in C_k, a free variable z is added to the set of free variables, and constraint C_k is replaced with $\{d_i z \leq x_i < d_i(z+1), C'_k\}$ where C'_k is C_k with $\lfloor \frac{x_i}{d_i} \rfloor$ replaced with z.

• If a term $\lceil \frac{x_i}{d_i} \rceil$ appears in C_k, a free variable z is added to the set of free variables, and constraint C_k is replaced with $\{d_i(z-1) < x_i \leq d_i z, C'_k\}$ where C'_k is C_k with $\lceil \frac{x_i}{d_i} \rceil$ replaced with z.

• If a term $(x_i \bmod d_i)$ appears in C_k, a free variable z is added to the set of free variables, and constraint C_k is replaced with $\{d_i z \leq x_i < d_i(z+1), C'_k\}$ where C'_k is C_k with $(x_i \bmod d_i)$ replaced with $x_i - z$.

• A constraint $(d_i|x_i)$ is equivalent to $(x_i \bmod d_i = 0)$ and the precedent rule can be applied.

• If a term of the form $\lfloor \frac{U}{u} \rfloor$ appears in the right side of the constraint C_k, since rational constraints are considered by our method, the floor can be avoided and the whole constraint is multiplied by u.

The objective is to evaluate, in terms of symbolic constants (the size parameters), the number of integer solutions of a combination of linear and nonlinear constraints C_k. This number is expressed by polynomials where the free variables are the size parameters.

As said before, there are a lot of applications of such a counting, in the area of analysis and transformation of scientific programs expressed as loops with affine loop bounds. The polynomials may count the flops executed by a loop, the memory locations touched by a loop, the cache lines touched by a loop, the array elements that need to be transmitted from a processor to another during the execution of a loop, the maximum parallelism induced by a loop from a given time-schedule, the number of processors needed from a given mapping function, the amount of communications from a given loop and data partitionning, the number of

ICS'96, Philadelphia, PA,USA
© 1996 ACM 0-89791-803-7/96/05..$3.50

cache misses from a given loop and data partitioning (size of the footprints [18]).

Such informations can be determinant to estimate the execution time of a code segment, compare the memory bandwidth requirements vs. the flop counts of a code segment [16], determine which loops will flush the cache, and then calculate the cache miss rate [9], determine whether a parallel loop is load balanced, i.e., does each iteration perform the same number of flops [22], given an unbalanced loop, assign different number of iterations to each processor so that each processor gets the same total number of flops (balanced chunk-scheduling, [11]), quantify message traffic, allocate space for message buffers, exploit maximum parallelism, optimize the number of needed processors, optimize the loop and data partioning.

A system of constraints defines a combination of convex polytopes in a lattice of rational points. Hence, the initial problem is equivalent to counting the number of lattice points included in polytopes.

This number can be expressed as a symbolic sum, which is not generally an easy transformation. Some symbolic mathematical packages, such as Maple or Mathematica, compute such symbolic sums, but they assume that the lower bound is never greater than the upper bound. Therefore, their answer is wrong if this assumption is violated. For example, Mathematica computes that

$$\sum_{i=1}^{n}\sum_{j=i}^{m} 1 = \frac{n(2m-n+1)}{2}$$

This answer is valid only if $n \leq m$. Another answer is necessary in the case $n > m$ which is $\frac{m(m+1)}{2}$. It comes that in the general case, the symbolic number of integer solutions of a combination of constraints must by given at domains depending on the related values of the size parameters. This fact was already pointed out by the mathematician E. Ehrhart in 1977 [8]:

Conjecture 1 (Ehrhart's conjecture) *For any significant diophantine linear system of any dimension, linearly dependent of several positive integral parameters, the symbolic number of integer solutions depending on these parameters is expressed at different domains by different pseudo-polynomials.*

A *pseudo-polynomial* is a polynomial where the constant coefficients are varying relatively to the modulos of the size parameters. A more formal definition is given in the next section. E. Ehrhart has shown that the values of these coefficients are closely related to the vertices of the polytopes. Hence, the validity domains associated with the pseudo-polynomials are those associated with the parametric values of the vertices. So, this needs to determine the vertices of parameterized polytopes. To solve this problem, the new parametric vertices finding algorithm of Loechner and Wilde, fully detailed in [13], can be used. Such an algorithm allows to get all the useful informations to generalize Ehrhart's results, and to constitute a systematic method which is entirely computable.

In order to introduce the main results of this paper, we first present the so-called *polytope model*, by giving some geometric and arithmetic definitions and some useful Ehrhart's contributions. They are dealing with the computation of the polynomials, commonly called *Ehrhart polynomials*, associated with the number of lattice points included in a particular combination of convex polytopes called *normal polyhedron*. Ehrhart's results deal with convex polytopes or unions of convex polytopes, defined by linear constraints. Finally, it is shown in section 3 how these results can apply to determine useful values in analysis and transformation of scientific programs: they are illustrated with many examples and compared with related works [9, 22, 11, 12, 21, 16].

2 The polytope model

2.1 Definitions and assumptions

We first recall some basic notions dealing with geometry of numbers [10, 17] and enumerative combinatorics [19, 20]. Then some more specific concepts, closely dedicated to the scope of the paper, are introduced.

In the following, Q denotes the set of rational numbers. A *convex polyhedron* P is a subset of Q^d that is the intersection of a finite number of closed halfspaces. A bounded convex polyhedron is called a *convex polytope*. The *affine span* of P is the smaller affine subspace of Q^d entirely containing P. The *dimension*, dim$P$, of a polyhedron P is the dimension of its affine span, and a k-dimensional polyhedron is called a k-polyhedron for brevity.

A lattice is the set of points $\mathcal{L}^d = \{\alpha_1\vec{g}_1 + ... + \alpha_d\vec{g}_d \mid \alpha_1, ..., \alpha_d \in \mathcal{Z}\}$ where $\vec{g}_1, ..., \vec{g}_d$ are linearly independent vectors of Q^d, called a basis for the lattice. The set of all the integral points is called *standard lattice* denoted by $\mathcal{Z}^d$. Let G be the matrix whose columns are the vectors $\vec{g}_1, ..., \vec{g}_d$, called the *dilatation matrix*. Any lattice $\mathcal{L}^d$ consists of the points $G \cdot z$, $z \in \mathcal{Z}^d$, i.e. $\mathcal{L}^d = G \cdot \mathcal{Z}^d$. So we get the most general lattice $\mathcal{L}^d$ by subjecting the standard lattice $\mathcal{Z}^d$ to an arbitrary non-singular transformation G [10]. Hence, without loss of generality, only the standard lattice $\mathcal{Z}^d$ is considered in the following. The *enumerator* of any set S is the number of points of $S \cap \mathcal{L}^d$.

The intersection between a lattice $\mathcal{L}^d$ and the convex hull of a finite number of points $z_1, \ldots, z_{m+1}$ in Q^d is called a lattice polytope P of $\mathcal{L}^d$. It is then homeomorphic to a ball B^k. We write $k = \dim P$ and call P a k-polytope. If $z_1, \ldots, z_{m+1}$ are affinely independent points of Q^d, which means that $z_2 - z_1, z_3 - z_1, \ldots, z_{m+1} - z_1$ are linearly independent, then the convex hull of $z_1, \ldots, z_{m+1}$ is called a m-dimensional lattice simplex S of $\mathcal{L}^d$ with vertices $z_1, \ldots, z_{m+1}$. A lattice polytope or a lattice simplex is then defined by a set of linear inequalities of the form $\{z \in \mathcal{L}^d \mid A \cdot z \leq b\}$ where A is a $m \times d$ rational matrix and b a m-dimensional rational vector.

If $\vec{c}$ is a nonzero vector and γ is defined by

$$\gamma = MAX\{\vec{c} \cdot z \mid A \cdot z \leq b\}$$

the affine hyperplane $\{z \mid \vec{c} \cdot z = \gamma\}$ is called a supporting hyperplane of P. The *faces* of P are $\emptyset$, P, and the intersections of P with its supporting hyperplanes. Each face of P is itself a polyhedron. If P is a k-polyhedron, faces of P of dimension 0, 1 and $k-1$ are called *vertices*, *edges* and *facets*, respectively.

In this work, we consider lattice polyhedra which may be non-convex, called *normal polyhedra*, according to the following definition. This definition corresponds to the one given by Ehrhart in [6] and [8, p. 47].

Definition 1 (normal polyhedron) *A normal polyhedron P is a closed polyhedron which admits a finite rectilinear simplicial subdivision.*

A lattice polyhedron P of $\mathcal{L}^d$ is a $\mathcal{L}^d$-polyhedron if all its vertices are in $\mathcal{L}^d$. If $\mathcal{L}^d = \mathcal{Z}^d$, P is an *integral polyhedron*. If some vertex of P do not belong to $\mathcal{L}^d$ and have rational coordinates, P is a *rational* polyhedron. Since by definition, any lattice $\mathcal{L}^d$ can be deduced from $\mathcal{Z}^d$ by a non-singular transformation G, any $\mathcal{L}^d$-polyhedron is affinely equivalent to an integral polyhedron. Hence, results given in the following and concerning integral polyhedra, can be directly extended to $\mathcal{L}^d$-polyhedra. From now on and without loss of generality, the generic term of integral polyhedra will be used.

Many scientific methods and applications are defined parametrically in order to reach any size of the considered items. Implementations of these methods yields programs including loops with parameterized affine loop bounds. When modeling such loops with convex polytopes, parameterized polytopes have to be considered. Such polytopes were defined by E. Ehrhart as *homothetic* and *bordered systems* [6, 7], since his most elaborated results handle only polytopes depending on one size parameter:

Definition 2 (Ehrhart's homothetic system) *A system is homothetic if its relations are of the form* $\sum a_i z_i = bn$, $\sum a_i x_i < bn$, $\sum a_i x_i \leq bn$, *where the* a_i*'s and* b *are given integers, the* x_i*'s are free variables and* n *is a positive integral parameters. Such a system* H_n *is significant if and only if* H_1 *defines a polyhedral domain* P_1 *(obviously convex)*[1]. *In this case,* H_n *defines the domain* P_n, *which corresponds to* P_1 *by the n-homothetic transformation of center O.* P_1 *is called the primitive domain of* H_n.

The properties of such homothetic polyhedra yield a main mathematical result in the following. However this definition has to be extended to *bordered polytopes* in order to handle polytopes modeling loops with *affine* loop bounds.

Definition 3 (Ehrhart's bordered system) *A system* B_n *is bordered if its relations are of the form* $\sum a_i x_i = bn + c$, $\sum a_i x_i < bn + c$, $\sum a_i x_i \leq bn + c$, *where the* a_i*'s and the* b*'s are given integers, the* c*'s are rationals or not, the* x_i*'s are free variables and* n*'s is a positive integral parameter.*

By deleting all the c*'s, an homothetic system* H_n *defining the domain* P_n *is obtained. By adding a parallel hyperplane of the same dimension* $(k-1)$ *to each facet of* P_n, *at a rational distance or not, independently of the parameter* n, *but which may depend on the facet, it is obtained the bordered polytope* P'_n *whose kernel is* P_n.

In a general way, a parameterized polyhedron is homothetic or bordered at different domains depending on the values of its size parameters. In the following, we consider any k-polyhedron P_N defined by a union of homothetic or bordered systems of the form $\{z \in \mathcal{L}^d \mid A \cdot z \leq BN + C\}$, where $N = (n_1, \ldots, n_q)$, since any equality $\sum a_i z_i = \sum b_j n_j + c$ is equivalent to the two inequalities $\sum -a_i z_i \leq -\sum b_j n_j - c$ and $\sum a_i z_i \leq \sum b_j n_j + c$.

In the following, we denote by j_N the enumerator of P_N. It will be determined by *polynomials* and *pseudo-polynomials* according to the following definitions. We extend Ehrhart's definition of periodic numbers [8] to any dimension.

Definition 4 (periodic number) *A one-dimensional periodic number* $u(n) = [u_1, u_2, \ldots, u_p]_n$ *is equal to the item whose rank is equal to* n *mod* p, p *is called the period of* $u(n)$.

$$u(n) = \begin{cases} u_1 & if\ n = 1\ mod\ p \\ u_2 & if\ n = 2\ mod\ p \\ \ldots & \\ u_p & if\ n = 0\ mod\ p \end{cases}$$

Let $N = (n_j)$ *be a q-dimensional vector,* $j \in [1 \ldots q]$. *A q-periodic number* $u(N)$ *is defined by a q-dimensional array* $(u_I)_N$, $I = (i_1, i_2, \ldots, i_q)$, *of size* $p_1 \times p_2 \times \ldots \times p_q$ *such that*

$$u(N) = u_I\ if\ \forall j \in [1 \ldots q],\ n_j = i_j\ mod\ p_j$$

The vector $p = (p_j)$ *is called the multi-period of* $u(N)$ *and the lowest common multiple of the* p_i*'s is called the period of* $u(N)$.

Ehrhart in [8] gives the basic properties of one-dimensional periodic numbers which can be easily extended to multi-dimensional ones:

Let $u(N)$ and $u'(N)$ be q-periodic numbers of multi-period p and p' respectively. They can be reduced to the same multi-period $m = (m_i)$, where $m_i = p_i\alpha = p'_i\beta$ is the lowest common multiple of p_i and p'_i, by repeating α times (respectively β times) the sequence of items in the ith dimension of $u(N)$ (respectively $u'(N)$). Since $u(N)$ and $u'(N)$ are reduced to the same period, $u(N) + u'(N) = (u_I + u'_I)_N$ and $u(N)u'(N) = (u_I u'_I)_N$.

Hence, we also extend Ehrhart's definition on pseudo-polynomials.

Definition 5 (pseudo-polynomial) *A polynomial* $f(N)$ *is a pseudo-polynomial if some of its coefficients are periodic numbers instead of being constants. The lowest common multiple of the periods of its periodic coefficients is the pseudo-period of* $f(N)$. *So a pseudo-polynomial has two characteristics, its degree and its pseudo-period.*

The results presented in the next section are those of E. Ehrhart which are limited to homothetic or bordered polyhedra of only one parameter n. We will present general extensions of these results to the case of any number of parameters in further works. Nevertheless an example is already given in section 3, showing clearly that the extension is straightforward.

2.2 The Ehrhart polynomial on normal polyhedra

We recall in this section some results due to E. Ehrhart who made a study of the enumeration of lattice points in polyhedra, by means of polynomials in the way of Euler. All the proofs can be found in [5, 6, 7, 8]. Some aspects of Ehrhart's work were corrected, streamlined, and expanded by I. G. Macdonald [14, 15] and R. P. Stanley [19, 20].

Definition 6 (denominator) *The denominator of a rational point is the lowest common multiple of the denominators of its coordinates. The denominator of a rational polyhedron is the lowest common multiple of the denominators of its vertices.*

Theorem 1 (fundamental theorem) *The enumerator* j_n *of any homothetic or bordered k-polyhedron* P_n *is a polynomial in n of degree k if* P_n *is integral, and it is a pseudo-polynomial in n of degree k whose pseudo-period is the denominator of* P_n *if* P_n *is rational.*

When considering integral polyhedra, the following results can be used, which allow to determine the polynomials of the enumerator from k of its initial values.

Theorem 2 (Ehrhart polynomial) *For any integral k-polyhedron* P_n, *the enumerator verifies the following identities:*

$$\{(j - j_0)^{k+1}\} = 0 \quad j_n = \sum_{q=1}^{k} C_n^q (j - j_0)^q + j_0 \quad j^r \sim j_r$$

where $j^r \sim j_r$ *means that in the expansion of any symbolic power, any power* j^r *must be replaced by* j_r.

$$j_n = \frac{n(n-1)\ldots(n-k)}{k!}(j - j_0)^k \quad j^r \sim \frac{j_r}{n-r}$$

where $j^r \sim \frac{j_r}{n-r}$ *means that in the expansion of any symbolic power, any power* j^r *must be replaced by* $\frac{j_r}{n-r}$.

In the general case of a rational lattice polyhedron, the determination of the pseudo-polynomial of the enumerator needs the use of some more Ehrhart's results.

[1] The term *significant* means that P_1 defines a bounded polyhedral domain.

Theorem 3 *Let P_n be a rational k-polyhedron and let the Ehrhart pseudo-polynomial be*

$$j_n = c_k(n)n^k + c_{k-1}(n)n^{k-1} + \ldots + c_0(n)$$

where $c_0, \ldots, c_k$ are periodic numbers of n. If for some $q \in [0, k]$, the affine span of every q-dimensional face of P_1 contains a lattice point, then for any $p \geq q$, $c_p(n)$ is constant, i.e. of period one.

Computing the coefficients in the Ehrhart polynomial can be done through several approaches. For example, Barvinok[2] in [2] proposes a complexity study of the computation of these coefficients in terms of computation of the volumes of faces, since any coefficient can be related to volumes or surface areas of P_n. But since the problem of volume computation is NP-hard [4], results given by Barvinok step on the strong assumption of a *Volume Computation Oracle.*

We rather choose a more computable method. Due to this last theorem, the periodic coefficients are known. Since the period is equal to the denominator of the k-polyhedron P_n and the degree is equal to k, the determination of the Ehrhart pseudo-polynomial can be done by simply resolving a system of rational linear equations. Since the number of equations ne of the system must be equal to the number of unknown values, the complexity depends on the structure of P_n, its dimension, and on the size of its denominator. Moreover, ne initial values of the enumerator have to be counted.

All these results concern normal polyhedra defined by a combination of linear constraints. When considering some nonlinear ones, the transformation rules given in introduction have to be applied first.

3 Applications to the analysis of scientific programs

3.1 The general problem

The use of Ehrhart's results needs first the computation of the vertices of the considered normal polyhedron P_n. We use the algorithm of Loechner and Wilde [13] which determines the parametric coordinates of the vertices of any convex polytope and their associated definition domains. This algorithm is connected to a software package called *polyhedron* [23] which eliminates redundant constraints. Two particular problems have to be considered:

- P_n has to be homothetic (or bordered) according to definitions 2 and 3, i.e. P_n (or its kernel) can be deduced from P_1 (or the kernel of P_1) by the n-homothetic transformation. But in practice, P_1 does not correspond to the lowest possible size of P_n, since the initial value of n is depending on the constraints C_k and on some definition domains of these constraints. For example, let us consider the set of constraints defined by $\{4 \leq i \leq 2n, i \leq n+10, 1 \leq j \leq i\}$. The Loechner/Wilde algorithm computes the following answer:
  - if $n \geq 2$ and $n \leq 10$, the vertices are $(2n, 1)$, $(2n, 2n)$, $(4, 1)$, $(4, 4)$.
  - if $n > 10$, the vertices are $(n+10, 1)$, $(n+10, n+10)$, $(4, 1)$, $(4, 4)$.

  This result shows that the lowest value of n is 2 and hence, P_1 is undefined. This problem can be avoided by simply substituting n with $m = n - 1$ and considering $P_m = \{4 \leq i \leq 2m+2, i \leq m+11, 1 \leq j \leq i\}$. Moreover, this example shows that generally, several definition domains of n have to be considered.

- Due to the geometric modeling, as illustrated in the next section, non-convex polytopes have to be considered in some cases. Since this non-convexity is closely related to the kind of handled problem, a convexity test is unuseful. In such a case, the Loechner/Wilde algorithm has to be extended in order to consider unions of convex polytopes $P_n^1, P_n^2, \ldots$ This extension consists in the following heuristic procedure:
  - Compute all the vertices of each rational polytope P_n^i.
  - For each found vertex v, v is a vertex of P_n if and only if it is a vertex of a polytope P_n^i and it does not belong to any other $P_n^j, j \neq i$, unless it is also a vertex of $P_n^j, j \neq i$.
  - Compute all the vertices of each intersection $P_n^i \cap P_n^j, j \neq i$.
  - For each found vertex v, v is a vertex of P_n if and only if it is not a vertex of any P_n^i.

[2]Barvinok also proposed in [1] a polynomial-time algorithm for counting integral points in non-parametric polyhedra, i.e. when the dimension is fixed.

3.2 Examples and related work

All the examples considered in this section come from several related works [11, 12, 22, 21, 9, 16] and were also handled by W. Pugh in [16], except example 8 whose aim is to show the generality of our method.

Example 1 M. Haghighat and C. Polychronopoulos present in [11, 12] a method for volume computation. Their first example is $\sum_{i=1}^{n}\sum_{j=3}^{i}\sum_{k=j}^{5} 1$. This sum defines a set of linear constraints $\{1 \leq i \leq n, 3 \leq j \leq i, j \leq k \leq 5\}$. The Loechner/Wilde algorithm computes the following vertices for the so-defined polytope P_n:

- (1) if $3 \leq n \leq 5$, the vertices are $(3,3,5)$, $(3,3,3)$, $(n,3,5)$, $(n,3,3)$, $(n,n,5)$, (n,n,n).
- (2) if $n > 5$, the vertices are $(3,3,5)$, $(3,3,3)$, $(n,3,5)$, $(n,3,3)$, $(5,5,5)$, $(n,5,5)$.

Hence, P_n is an integral 3-polytope and the associated Ehrhart polynomial $j_n = c_1 n^2 + c_2 n + c_3$ is computed on each definition domain (1) and (2):

From $n = 3$ to 5 we count $j_n = 3, 8, 14$.

$$(1)\begin{cases} 9c_1 + 3c_2 + c_3 & = j_3 = 3 \\ 16c_1 + 4c_2 + c_3 & = j_4 = 8 \\ 25c_1 + 5c_2 + c_3 & = j_5 = 14 \end{cases}$$

This system results in $j_n = \frac{1}{2}n^2 + \frac{3}{2}n - 6$. This first polynomial is defined at three points instead of two as computed by Pugh in [16]. That is the reason why his symbolic result is different.

From $n = 6$ to 8 we count $j_n = 20, 26, 32$.

$$(2)\begin{cases} 36c_1 + 6c_2 + c_3 & = j_6 = 20 \\ 49c_1 + 7c_2 + c_3 & = j_7 = 26 \\ 64c_1 + 8c_2 + c_3 & = j_8 = 32 \end{cases}$$

This system results in $j_n = 6n - 16$, which is the same result as W. Pugh. M. Haghighat and C. Polychronopoulos derive an answer of

$$\mu(min(n-2,3))(-(min(n,5))^3 + 15(min(n,5))^2 \\ -38min(n,5) + 24)/6 + 6max(n-5,0)$$

where $\mu(x)$ is defined to be 1 if x is positive and 0 otherwise. The answer they derive gives the same values as ours, but the form is quite different because of the *min* and *max* expressions they introduce. The results tend to be much more complicated. Anyway, our method does not generate *min*'s and *max*'s. □

Example 2 The second example in [11, 12] is

$$\sum_{i=1}^{2n}\sum_{j=1}^{min(i,2n-i)} 1$$

This sum defines a set of linear constraints $\{1 \le i \le 2n, 1 \le j \le i, i+j \le 2n\}$. The Loechner/Wilde algorithm computes the following vertices for the so-defined polytope P_n: if $n \ge 1$, the vertices are $(n,n),(2n-1,1),(1,1)$. Hence, P_n is an integral 2-polytope and the associated Ehrhart polynomial $j_n = c_1 n^2 + c_2 n + c_3$ is computed:
From $n=1$ to 3 we count $j_n = 1,4,9$.

$$\begin{cases} c_1 + c_2 + c_3 & = j_1 = 1 \\ 4c_1 + 2c_2 + c_3 & = j_2 = 4 \\ 9c_1 + 3c_2 + c_3 & = j_3 = 9 \end{cases}$$

This system results in $j_n = n^2$, which is the same result as W. Pugh. In [11, 12], Haghighat and Polychronopoulos do not describe their technique in detail. They define a number of rules in order to transform expressions, but nothing is said on how to decide which rule has to be applied and when. As in [22], they assume the summation must be performed in a predetermined order. □

Example 3 We now handle Pugh's "more elaborate" example of [16], and show that our method does not meet any particular difficulty, while Pugh introduces some additional techniques which are not elaborated in his paper. This example is the set of linear constraints $\{1 \le i, j \le n, 2i \le 3j\}$.

The Loechner/Wilde algorithm computes the following vertices for the so-defined polytope P_n: if $n \ge \frac{2}{3}$, the vertices are $(\frac{3n}{2}, n), (1, \frac{2}{3}), (1, n)$. Hence, P_n is a rational 2-polytope and the associated Ehrhart polynomial is a pseudo-polynomial of period 6. Since it is evident that the affine span of P_n contains at least one integral point ((1,1) for example), theorem 3 can be used in order to reduce the number of unknown coefficients: According to theorem 3, the coefficient of n^2 is constant, i.e. $j_n = c_1 n^2 + [c_2, c_3, c_4, c_5, c_6, c_7]n + [c_8, c_9, c_{10}, c_{11}, c_{12}, c_{13}]$.

From $n=1$ to 13 we count $j_n =$ 1, 4, 8, 14, 21, 30, 40, 52, 65, 80, 96, 114, 133.

$$\begin{cases} c_1 + c_2 + c_8 & = j_1 = 1 \\ 4c_1 + 2c_3 + c_9 & = j_2 = 4 \\ 9c_1 + 3c_4 + c_{10} & = j_3 = 8 \\ 16c_1 + 4c_5 + c_{11} & = j_4 = 14 \\ 25c_1 + 5c_6 + c_{12} & = j_5 = 21 \\ 36c_1 + 6c_7 + c_{13} & = j_6 = 30 \\ 49c_1 + 7c_2 + c_8 & = j_7 = 40 \\ 64c_1 + 8c_3 + c_9 & = j_8 = 52 \\ 81c_1 + 9c_4 + c_{10} & = j_9 = 65 \\ 100c_1 + 10c_5 + c_{11} & = j_{10} = 80 \\ 121c_1 + 11c_6 + c_{12} & = j_{11} = 96 \\ 144c_1 + 12c_7 + c_{13} & = j_{12} = 114 \\ 169c_1 + 13c_2 + c_8 & = j_{13} = 133 \end{cases}$$

This system results in

$$j_n = \frac{3}{4}n^2 + \left[\frac{1}{2}, \frac{1}{2}, \frac{1}{2}, \frac{1}{2}, \frac{1}{2}, \frac{1}{2}\right] n + \left[-\frac{1}{4}, 0, -\frac{1}{4}, 0, -\frac{1}{4}, 0\right]$$

which can be directly simplified to

$$j_n = \frac{3}{4}n^2 + \frac{1}{2}n + \left[-\frac{1}{4}, 0\right]$$

Pugh in [16] derives through his techniques an answer of

$$\begin{cases} \frac{(n + n \bmod 2)(3n + 3(n \bmod 2) - 2)}{8} & if\ 1 \le n \\ \frac{3(n - n \bmod 2)(n - n \bmod 2 + 2)}{8} & if\ 2 \le n \end{cases}$$

This expression is then intuitively simplified to $\frac{3n^2+2n-n \bmod 2}{4}$ giving the same answers as our Ehrhart polynomial. This example shows that Pugh's technique tends to complicated answers when considering rational polytopes, and hence, does not allow to consider systematically any set of rational linear constraints. Our method, without being too complicated, handles any set of rational linear constraints without any restriction, through underlying tools dealing with improved results on polyhedral combinatorics and linear programming.

The method described by Pugh in [16] consists in a set of techniques, each dedicated to simplify the initial set of constraints. Applying all these tools would be expensive for important sets of constraints with rational coefficients. Moreover, their application is often intuitive: it consists in some cases in adding auxiliary variables, and needs the use of standard formulas for sums of powers (the author expects it will be sufficient to hard code the formulas for powers up to 10). All these facts clearly show some limits in the general use of these techniques. □

Example 4 Ferrante, Sarkar and Thrash in [9] present methods for computing the number of distinct memory locations and cache lines accessed by a loop nest. This information is useful in evaluating cache effectiveness. Their first example consists in calculating the number of distinct memory locations touched by

```
for i := 1 to 8 do
    for j := 1 to 5 do
        a(6i+9j-7) = a(6i+9j-7) + 5
```

This loop nest is not parametric and hence we prefer transforming it as a parametric loop nest

```
for i := 1 to n+3 do
    for j := 1 to n do
        a(6i+9j-7) = a(6i+9j-7) + 5
```

The number of distinct memory locations touched by the first form is then given with $n = 5$. This problem is equivalent to counting the number of distinct values of `6i+9j-7` s.t. $1 \le i \le n+3$ and $1 \le j \le n$. From a geometrical point of view, all the couples (i,j) resulting in the same value of $6i + 9j - 7$ all belong to a line generated by the vector $\binom{3}{-2}$. Hence, the initial problem is equivalent to counting the number of points resulting from the linear projection of all the (i,j)'s along this vector. The same type of resolution occurs when counting the number of needed processors from a linear mapping function, as shown in [3]. The used geometrical model is fully detailed in [3]. A short description is given in the following.

When projecting a convex polytope along a vector $\vec{p}$, the number of resulting points is equal to the number of extreme points on one of the extremities of each line segment generated by $\vec{p}$ on the polytope. These extreme points describe what we call *thick facets* of the polytope, which are also convex polytopes. The union of all these thick facets is not generally convex, but is a normal polyhedron, and our method can apply. Counting the number of points in this union of thick facets gives the number of points resulting from the projection along $\vec{p}$.

The vector $\vec{p} = \binom{3}{-2}$ defines two thick facets, which can be automatically determined [3], $P_n^1 = \{(i,j) \in \mathcal{Z}^2 | 1 \le i \le 3, 1 \le j \le n\}$ and $P_n^2 = \{(i,j) \in \mathcal{Z}^2 | 1 \le i \le n+3, n-1 \le j \le n\}$. The parametric vertices of $P_n^1 \cup P_n^2$ are computed by using the heuristic procedure described in subsection 3.1. It gives the following results: $(1,1)$, $(1,n)$, $(n+3,n)$, $(n+3,n-1)$, $(3,n-1)$ and $(3,1)$. Hence, $P_n^1 \cup P_n^2$ is an integral 2-polytope and the associated Ehrhart polynomial $j_n = c_1 n^2 + c_2 n + c_3$ is computed:
From $n=3$ to 5 we count $j_n = 15, 20, 25$.

$$\begin{cases} 9c_1 + 3c_2 + c_3 & = j_3 = 15 \\ 16c_1 + 4c_2 + c_3 & = j_4 = 20 \\ 25c_1 + 5c_2 + c_3 & = j_5 = 25 \end{cases}$$

This system results in $j_n = 5n$ giving the same answer as Pugh for $n = 5$. □

Example 5 The second example in [9] is to calculate the number of memory locations touched in a Successive Over-Relaxation (SOR) code:

```
for i := 2 to n-1 do
  for j := 2 to n-1 do
      a(i,j) = (2*a(i,j) + a(i-1,j) + a(i+1,j)
                + a(i,j-1) + a(i,j+1)) / 6
```

The elements of a touched by this loop are

$$\begin{array}{ll} & \{(i,j)|2 \le i,j \le n-1\} \\ \cup & \{(i-1,j)|2 \le i,j \le n-1\} \\ \cup & \{(i+1,j)|2 \le i,j \le n-1\} \\ \cup & \{(i,j-1)|2 \le i,j \le n-1\} \\ \cup & \{(i,j+1)|2 \le i,j \le n-1\} \\ & \\ = & \{(i,j)|2 \le i,j \le n-1\} \\ \cup & \{(i,j)|1 \le i \le n-2, 2 \le j \le n-1\} \\ \cup & \{(i,j)|3 \le i \le n, 2 \le j \le n-1\} \\ \cup & \{(i,j)|2 \le i \le n-1, 1 \le j \le n-2\} \\ \cup & \{(i,j)|2 \le i \le n-1, 3 \le j \le n\} \end{array}$$

The parametric vertices of this union of polytopes P_n are computed by using the heuristic procedure described in subsection 3.1. It gives the following results: $(1,2)$, $(2,1)$, $(1,n-1)$, $(2,n)$, $(n-1,n)$, $(n,n-1)$, $(n-1,1)$ and $(n,2)$. Hence, it is an integral 2-polytope and the associated Ehrhart polynomial $j_n = c_1 n^2 + c_2 n + c_3$ is computed:

From $n = 4$ to 6 we count $j_n = 12, 21, 32$.

$$\left\{ \begin{array}{ll} 16c_1 + 4c_2 + c_3 & = j_4 = 12 \\ 25c_1 + 5c_2 + c_3 & = j_5 = 21 \\ 36c_1 + 6c_2 + c_3 & = j_6 = 32 \end{array} \right.$$

This system results in $j_n = n^2 - 4$ giving the same answer as Pugh.

To calculate the number of cache lines touched, we need a mapping from array elements to cache lines. We choose the same simple mapping as Pugh, which is to state that a reference to element $a(i,j)$ of an array references cache line $((i-1) \div 16, j)$. Hence, the problem consists in counting the number of distinct values of $((i-1) \div 16, j)$ for all the $a(i,j)$'s touched by the loop.

In such a case, the way of using our method is to model these different values by a union of polytopes U_n, deduced from the union of polytopes defining the elements touched by the loop P_n, and by computing the Ehrhart polynomial of U_n in a lattice $\mathcal{L}^2 \neq \mathcal{Z}^2$. This is done by transforming U_n through G^{-1}, where G is the dilatation matrix of $\mathcal{L}^2$, and then by computing the Ehrhart polynomial of $(G^{-1} \cdot U_n)$ in $\mathcal{Z}^2$.

On the affine span of the initial union of polytopes, the final result can be given by counting some points characterized by $(i-1)\ mod\ 16 = 0$, and such that $\exists \alpha \in [0..15]$, $\exists j$, $(i+\alpha, j) \in P_n$. All these points belong to the lattice defined by $\mathcal{L}^2 = \{\alpha_1 \binom{16}{0} + \alpha_2 \binom{0}{1} | \alpha_1, \alpha_2 \in \mathcal{Z}\}$.

Let $G = \begin{pmatrix} 16 & 0 \\ 0 & 1 \end{pmatrix}$. By moving P_n along the vector $\binom{-1}{0}$ and by applying G^{-1} to P_n, it is obtained a new union of polytopes containing only these interesting points (moved and transformed by G^{-1}), excepting those points of P_n characterized by $(i-1)\ mod\ 16 \neq 0$ and $\forall j$, $(i - ((i-1)\ mod\ 16), j) \notin P_n$. In order to get the whole union of polytopes U_n, points of the form $(i - ((i-1)\ mod\ 16), j)$ for all $(i,j) \in P_n$ have to be added to P_n. Hence, the definition of P_n is extended to U_n:

$$\begin{array}{ll} & \{(i,j)|2 \le i,j \le n-1\} \\ \cup & \{(i,j)|1 \le i \le n-2, 2 \le j \le n-1\} \\ \cup & \{(i,j)|3 \le i \le n, 2 \le j \le n-1\} \\ \cup & \{(i,j)|2 \le i \le n-1, 1 \le j \le n-2\} \\ \cup & \{(i,j)|2 \le i \le n-1, 3 \le j \le n\} \\ \cup & \{(i - ((i-1)\ mod\ 16), j)|(i,j) \in P_n\} \end{array}$$

In order to compute the Ehrhart polynomial of $(G^{-1} \cdot U_n)$, just its vertices have to be determined. So there is no need to compute its constraints definition. It is sufficient to apply G^{-1} to the vertices of U_n to get the ones of $(G^{-1} \cdot U_n)$, since any polytope is entirely defined by its vertices.

$$\left\{ \begin{array}{ll} 16c_1 + 4c_5 + c_{21} & = j_4 = 4 \\ 25c_1 + 5c_6 + c_{22} & = j_5 = 5 \\ 36c_1 + 6c_7 + c_{23} & = j_6 = 6 \\ 49c_1 + 7c_8 + c_{24} & = j_7 = 7 \\ 64c_1 + 8c_9 + c_{25} & = j_8 = 8 \\ 81c_1 + 9c_{10} + c_{26} & = j_9 = 9 \\ 100c_1 + 10c_{11} + c_{27} & = j_{10} = 10 \\ 121c_1 + 11c_{12} + c_{28} & = j_{11} = 11 \\ 144c_1 + 12c_{13} + c_{29} & = j_{12} = 12 \\ 169c_1 + 13c_{14} + c_{30} & = j_{13} = 13 \\ 196c_1 + 14c_{15} + c_{31} & = j_{14} = 14 \\ 225c_1 + 15c_{16} + c_{32} & = j_{15} = 15 \\ 256c_1 + 16c_{17} + c_{33} & = j_{16} = 16 \\ 289c_1 + 17c_2 + c_{18} & = j_{17} = 32 \\ 324c_1 + 18c_3 + c_{19} & = j_{18} = 36 \\ 361c_1 + 19c_4 + c_{20} & = j_{19} = 38 \\ 400c_1 + 20c_5 + c_{21} & = j_{20} = 40 \\ 441c_1 + 21c_6 + c_{22} & = j_{21} = 42 \\ 484c_1 + 22c_7 + c_{23} & = j_{22} = 44 \\ 529c_1 + 23c_8 + c_{24} & = j_{23} = 46 \\ 576c_1 + 24c_9 + c_{25} & = j_{24} = 48 \\ 625c_1 + 25c_{10} + c_{26} & = j_{25} = 50 \\ 676c_1 + 26c_{11} + c_{27} & = j_{26} = 52 \\ 729c_1 + 27c_{12} + c_{28} & = j_{27} = 54 \\ 784c_1 + 28c_{13} + c_{29} & = j_{28} = 56 \\ 841c_1 + 29c_{14} + c_{30} & = j_{29} = 58 \\ 900c_1 + 30c_{15} + c_{31} & = j_{30} = 60 \\ 961c_1 + 31c_{16} + c_{32} & = j_{31} = 62 \\ 1024c_1 + 32c_{17} + c_{33} & = j_{32} = 64 \\ 1089c_1 + 33c_2 + c_{18} & = j_{33} = 97 \\ 1156c_1 + 34c_3 + c_{19} & = j_{34} = 102 \\ 1225c_1 + 35c_4 + c_{20} & = j_{35} = 105 \\ 1296c_1 + 36c_5 + c_{21} & = j_{36} = 108 \end{array} \right.$$

Figure 1: the linear equations system of example 5

The parametric vertices of U_n are computed: $(0,1)$, $(0,n)$, $(n-2,n)$, $(n-1,n-1)$, $(n-2,1)$ and $(n-1,2)$, which are transformed through G^{-1}, resulting in the parametric vertices of $(G^{-1} \cdot U_n)$: $(0,1)$, $(0,n)$, $(\frac{n-2}{16}, n)$, $(\frac{n-1}{16}, n-1)$, $(\frac{n-2}{16}, 1)$ and $(\frac{n-1}{16}, 2)$. Hence, it is a rational 2-polytope and the associated Ehrhart polynomial is a pseudo-polynomial of period 16. Theorem 3 is used to reduce the number of unknown coefficients:

$$\begin{array}{ll} j_n & = c_1 n^2 \\ & +[c_2, c_3, c_4, c_5, c_6, c_7, c_8, c_9, c_{10}, c_{11}, c_{12}, c_{13}, c_{14}, c_{15}, \\ & c_{16}, c_{17}]n \\ & +[c_{18}, c_{19}, c_{20}, c_{21}, c_{22}, c_{23}, c_{24}, c_{25}, c_{26}, c_{27}, c_{28}, c_{29}, \\ & c_{30}, c_{31}, c_{32}, c_{33}] \end{array}$$

From $n = 4$ to 36 we count $j_n = 4$, 5, 6, 7, 8, 9, 10, 11, 12, 13, 14, 15, 16, 32, 36, 38, 40, 42, 44, 46, 48, 50, 52, 54, 56, 58, 60, 62, 64, 97, 102, 105, 108. The system, which is shown on figure 1, results in

$$\begin{array}{ll} j_n & = \frac{1}{16} n^2 \\ & +[\frac{15}{16}, \frac{7}{8}, \frac{13}{16}, \frac{3}{4}, \frac{11}{16}, \frac{5}{8}, \frac{9}{16}, \frac{1}{2}, \frac{7}{16}, \frac{3}{8}, \frac{5}{16}, \frac{1}{4}, \frac{3}{16}, \frac{1}{8}, \frac{1}{16}, 0]n \\ & +[-2, 0, 0, 0, 0, 0, 0, 0, 0, 0, 0, 0, 0, 0, 0, 0] \end{array}$$

Pugh in [16] derives an answer, giving the same results as ours: $(\sum : n \geq 3 : n(1+(n-2) \div 16)) + (\sum : n\ mod\ 16 = 1 \wedge n \geq 17 : n-2)$, which means in a more common expression:

- if $n \geq 17$ and $n\ mod\ 16 = 0$, $j_n = n(1+(n-2) \div 16) + n - 2$
- if $n \geq 3$, $j_n = n(1 + (n-2) \div 16)$

whose symbolic determination is not detailed in the paper. The method described in [9] by Ferrante et al., cannot handle unions of polytopes, does not compute symbolic answers, often computes only an approximation and uses expensive methods to handle the cache lines touched by a set of references. □

Example 6 An extension of our method to several size parameters is currently developped. It is applied to an example handled by Tawbi in [21] which is $\sum_{i=1}^{n} \sum_{j=1}^{i} \sum_{k=j}^{m} 1$. This sum defines a set of linear constraints $\{1 \le i \le n, 1 \le j \le i, j \le k \le m\}$. The Loechner/Wilde algorithm computes the following vertices for the so-defined polytope $P_{n,m}$:

- (1) if $1 \le n \le m$, the vertices are $(1,1,m)$, $(1,1,1)$, $(n,1,m)$, $(n,1,1)$, (n,n,m), (n,n,n).

- (2) if $1 \le m \le n$, the vertices are $(1,1,m)$, $(1,1,1)$, $(n,1,m)$, $(n,1,1)$, (m,m,m), (n,m,m).

Hence, $P_{n,m}$ is an integral 3-polytope and the associated Ehrhart polynomial is of the form $j_{n,m} = \sum_{i=0}^{3}\sum_{j=0}^{3} c_{ij} n^i m^j$ and has to be computed on each definition domain (1) and (2). Our method, applied with several size parameters, uses a symbolic resolution by first considering the polynomial $j_n = d_1 n^3 + d_2 n^2 + d_3 n + d_4$ where:

$$\begin{array}{lcl} d_1 & = & c_{33}m^3 + c_{32}m^2 + c_{31}m + c_{30} \\ d_2 & = & c_{23}m^3 + c_{22}m^2 + c_{21}m + c_{20} \\ d_3 & = & c_{13}m^3 + c_{12}m^2 + c_{11}m + c_{10} \\ d_4 & = & c_{03}m^3 + c_{02}m^2 + c_{01}m + c_{00} \end{array}$$

It follows the symbolic resolution:

$$\left\{ \begin{array}{ll} 64d_1 + 16d_2 + 4d_3 + d_4 & = j_4 = j_{4,m} \\ 125d_1 + 25d_2 + 5d_3 + d_4 & = j_5 = j_{5,m} \\ 216d_1 + 36d_2 + 6d_3 + d_4 & = j_6 = j_{6,m} \\ 343d_1 + 49d_2 + 7d_3 + d_4 & = j_7 = j_{7,m} \end{array} \right.$$

This system results in

$$\begin{array}{rl} j_n = & \frac{j_{7,m} - 3j_{6,m} + 3j_{5,m} - j_{4,m}}{6} n^3 \\ & + \frac{-5j_{7,m} + 16j_{6,m} - 17j_{5,m} + 6j_{4,m}}{2} n^2 \\ & + \frac{74j_{7,m} - 249j_{6,m} + 282j_{5,m} - 107j_{4,m}}{6} n \\ & -20j_{7,m} + 70j_{6,m} - 84j_{5,m} + 35j_{4,m} \end{array}$$

In order to evaluate these symbolic coefficients, $j_{4,m}$, $j_{5,m}$, $j_{6,m}$ and $j_{7,m}$ have to be computed on each definition domain (1) and (2):

For $n = 4$ and from $m = 4$ to 7, we count $j_{n,m} = 30, 40, 50, 60$.

$$\left\{ \begin{array}{ll} 64c_1 + 16c_2 + 4c_3 + c_4 & = j_{4,4} = 30 \\ 125c_1 + 25c_2 + 5c_3 + c_4 & = j_{4,5} = 40 \\ 216c_1 + 36c_2 + 6c_3 + c_4 & = j_{4,6} = 50 \\ 343c_1 + 49c_2 + 7c_3 + c_4 & = j_{4,7} = 60 \end{array} \right.$$

This system results in $j_{4,m} = 10m - 10$. In the same way, we compute $j_{5,m} = 15m - 20$, $j_{6,m} = 21m - 35$ and $j_{7,m} = 28m - 56$.

Hence, d_1, d_2, d_3 and d_4 can be computed as being: $d_1 = -\frac{1}{6}$, $d_2 = \frac{m}{2}$, $d_3 = \frac{3m+1}{6}$ and $d_4 = 0$. Finally, $j_{n,m}$ is evaluated for domain (1), i.e. $1 \le n \le m$, as being:

$$\begin{array}{rcl} j_{n,m} & = & -\frac{1}{6}n^3 + \frac{m}{2}n^2 + \frac{3m+1}{6}n + 0 \\ & = & -\frac{n^3}{6} + \frac{n^2 m}{2} + \frac{nm}{2} + \frac{n}{6} \end{array}$$

The same work is done for domain (2), i.e. $1 \le m \le n$, resulting in $j_{n,m} = -\frac{m^3}{6} + \frac{m^2 n}{2} + \frac{mn}{2} + \frac{m}{6}$, which is the same result as Pugh. Our method can be applied in the same way when considering several size parameters in the case of rational polytopes, case which is not systematically handled by Pugh's techniques (example 5). Tawbi in [22, 21] first uses a polyhedral splitting technique to characterize the definition domains, and an elimination of the variables in a predetermined order. However, her method does not allow to compute systematically exact answers as ours. □

Example 7 We propose a more elaborate example, requiring to utilize entirely the method we have described. This example involves rational parameterized polytopes depending on three size parameters. Let us consider the following loop nest:

```
for i := 0 to n do
  for j := 0 to i + m/2 do
    for k := 0 to i - n + p do
      a(i,j,k) = a(i,j,k-1) + a(k,j,k)*a(i,k,k)
```

We want to compute the number of flops in order to evaluate the execution time of this code segment. This loop nest is modeled by the convex polytope $P_N = \{z \in \mathcal{Z}^3 \mid A \cdot z \le BN + C\}$ where

$$A = \begin{pmatrix} -1 & 0 & 0 \\ 1 & 0 & 0 \\ 0 & -1 & 0 \\ -2 & 2 & 0 \\ 0 & 0 & -1 \\ -1 & 0 & 1 \end{pmatrix} \quad B = \begin{pmatrix} 0 & 0 & 0 \\ 1 & 0 & 0 \\ 0 & 0 & 0 \\ 0 & 1 & 0 \\ 0 & 0 & 0 \\ -1 & 0 & 1 \end{pmatrix} \quad N = \begin{pmatrix} n \\ m \\ p \end{pmatrix} \quad C = 0$$

The Loechner/Wilde algorithm computes the following vertices for the so-defined polytope P_N:

- (1) if $n > p$: $(n-p, \frac{2n+m-2p}{2}, 0)$, $(n-p, 0, 0)$, $(n, \frac{2n+m}{2}, p)$, $(n, \frac{2n+m}{2}, 0)$, $(n, 0, p)$, $(n, 0, 0)$.
- (2) if $n = p$: $(0, \frac{m}{2}, 0)$, $(n, 0, p)$, $(0,0,0)$, $(n, \frac{2n+m}{2}, 0)$, $(n, 0, 0)$, $(n, \frac{2n+m}{2}, p)$.
- (3) if $n < p$: $(0, \frac{m}{2}, -n+p)$, $(0, \frac{m}{2}, 0)$, $(0, 0, -n+p)$, $(0,0,0)$, $(n, \frac{2n+m}{2}, p)$, $(n, \frac{2n+m}{2}, 0)$, $(n, 0, p)$, $(n, 0, 0)$.

As an example, we now compute the Ehrhart polynomial on the first definition domain.

The denominator of P_N is 2. We count $((k+1)d)^q = 512$ initial values of $j(n,m,p)$. The lowest initial value of n is 9 since we consider the first definition domain ($n > p$) and since for any initial value of n, 8 initial values of p have to be considered. For example, with $n = 9$ we get the following initial countings:

m \ p	1	2	3	4	5	6	7	8
1	29	56	90	130	175	224	276	330
2	32	62	100	145	196	252	312	375
3	32	62	100	145	196	252	312	375
4	35	68	110	160	217	280	348	420
5	35	68	110	160	217	280	348	420
6	38	74	120	175	238	308	384	465
7	38	74	120	175	238	308	384	465
8	41	80	130	190	259	336	420	510

Each line of such arrays allows to resolve a system of equations to determine $j(x,y,p)$, for all $x \in [9..16]$ and $y \in [1..8]$. For example, the first system dedicated to the determination of $j(9,1,p) = [c_1,c_2]_p\, n_3^3 + [c_3,c_4]_p\, n_3^2 + [c_5,c_6]_p\, n_3 + [c_7,c_8]_p$ is

$$\left\{ \begin{array}{ll} c_1 + c_3 + c_5 + c_7 & = 29 \\ 8c_2 + 4c_4 + 2c_6 + c_8 & = 56 \\ 27c_1 + 9c_3 + 3c_5 + c_7 & = 90 \\ 64c_2 + 16c_4 + 4c_6 + c_8 & = 130 \\ 125c_1 + 25c_3 + 5c_5 + c_7 & = 175 \\ 216c_2 + 36c_4 + 6c_6 + c_8 & = 224 \\ 343c_1 + 49c_3 + 7c_5 + c_7 & = 276 \\ 512c_2 + 64c_4 + 8c_6 + c_8 & = 330 \end{array} \right.$$

resulting in $j(9,1,p) = -\frac{1}{6}p^3 + \frac{9}{2}p^2 + \frac{44}{3}p + 10$.

All these last polynomials allows to resolve systems to determine $j(x,m,p)$, for all $x \in [9..16]$. For example, the first system dedicated to the determination of $j(9,m,p) = [c_1,c_2]_m\, m^3 + [c_3,c_4]_m\, m^2 + [c_5,c_6]_m\, m + [c_7,c_8]_m$ is,

$$\left\{ \begin{array}{ll} c_1 + c_3 + c_5 + c_7 & = -\frac{1}{6}p^3 + \frac{9}{2}p^2 + \frac{44}{3}n_3 + 10 \\ 8c_2 + 4c_4 + 2c_6 + c_8 & = -\frac{1}{6}p^3 + 5p^2 + \frac{97}{6}p + 11 \\ 27c_1 + 9c_3 + 3c_5 + c_7 & = -\frac{1}{6}p^3 + 5p^2 + \frac{97}{6}p + 11 \\ 64c_2 + 16c_4 + 4c_6 + c_8 & = -\frac{1}{6}p^3 + \frac{11}{2}p^2 + \frac{53}{3}p + 12 \\ 125c_1 + 25c_3 + 5c_5 + c_7 & = -\frac{1}{6}p^3 + \frac{11}{2}p^2 + \frac{53}{3}p + 12 \\ 216c_2 + 36c_4 + 6c_6 + c_8 & = -\frac{1}{6}p^3 + 6p^2 + \frac{115}{6}p + 13 \\ 343c_1 + 49c_3 + 7c_5 + c_7 & = -\frac{1}{6}p^3 + 6p^2 + \frac{115}{6}p + 13 \\ 512c_2 + 64c_4 + 8c_6 + c_8 & = -\frac{1}{6}p^3 + \frac{13}{2}p^2 + \frac{62}{3}p + 14 \end{array} \right.$$

In this case, the following result is obtained:

$$\begin{array}{l} j(9,m,p) = \frac{1}{4}mp^2 + \frac{3}{4}mp + \frac{1}{2}m - \frac{1}{6}p^3 + \left[\frac{17}{4}, \frac{9}{2}\right]_m p^2 \\ \qquad + \left[\frac{167}{12}, \frac{44}{3}\right]_m p + \left[\frac{19}{2}, 10\right]_m \end{array}$$

Finally, $j(n,m,p)$ is determined by resolving the system shown on figure 2. The following result is obtained, giving the number of flops executed by the loop nest when $n > p$:

$$\begin{array}{l} j(n,m,p) = \frac{1}{2}np^2 + \frac{3}{2}np + n + \frac{1}{4}mp^2 + \frac{3}{4}mp \\ + \frac{1}{2}m - \frac{1}{6}p^3 + \left[-\frac{1}{4}, 0\right]_m p^2 + \left[\frac{5}{12}, \frac{7}{6}\right]_m p + \left[\frac{1}{2}, 1\right]_m \end{array} \quad \square$$

$$
\left\{
\begin{array}{l}
729c_1 + 81c_3 + 9c_5 + c_7 \\
= \frac{1}{4}mp^2 + \frac{3}{4}mp + \frac{1}{2}m - \frac{1}{6}p^3 + [\frac{17}{4}, \frac{9}{2}]_m p^2 + [\frac{167}{12}, \frac{44}{3}]_m p + [\frac{19}{2}, 10]_m \\
1000c_2 + 100c_4 + 10c_6 + c_8 \\
= \frac{1}{4}mp^2 + \frac{3}{4}mp + \frac{1}{2}m - \frac{1}{6}p^3 + [\frac{19}{4}, 5]_m p^2 + [\frac{185}{12}, \frac{97}{6}]_m p + [\frac{21}{2}, 11]_m \\
1331c_1 + 121c_3 + 11c_5 + c_7 \\
= \frac{1}{4}mp^2 + \frac{3}{4}mp + \frac{1}{2}m - \frac{1}{6}p^3 + [\frac{21}{4}, \frac{11}{2}]_m p^2 + [\frac{203}{12}, \frac{53}{3}]_m p + [\frac{23}{2}, 12]_m \\
1728c_2 + 144c_4 + 12c_6 + c_8 \\
= \frac{1}{4}mp^2 + \frac{3}{4}mp + \frac{1}{2}m - \frac{1}{6}p^3 + [\frac{23}{4}, 6]_m p^2 + [\frac{221}{12}, \frac{115}{6}]_m p + [\frac{25}{2}, 13]_m \\
2197c_1 + 169c_3 + 13c_5 + c_7 \\
= \frac{1}{4}mp^2 + \frac{3}{4}mp + \frac{1}{2}m - \frac{1}{6}p^3 + [\frac{25}{4}, \frac{13}{2}]_m p^2 + [\frac{239}{12}, \frac{62}{3}]_m p + [\frac{27}{2}, 14]_m \\
2744c_2 + 196c_4 + 14c_6 + c_8 \\
= \frac{1}{4}mp^2 + \frac{3}{4}mp + \frac{1}{2}m - \frac{1}{6}p^3 + [\frac{27}{4}, 7]_m p^2 + [\frac{257}{12}, \frac{133}{6}]_m p + [\frac{29}{2}, 15]_m \\
3375c_1 + 225c_3 + 15c_5 + c_7 \\
= \frac{1}{4}mp^2 + \frac{3}{4}mp + \frac{1}{2}m - \frac{1}{6}p^3 + [\frac{29}{4}, \frac{15}{2}]_m p^2 + [\frac{275}{12}, \frac{71}{3}]_m p + [\frac{31}{2}, 16]_m \\
4096c_2 + 256c_4 + 16c_6 + c_8 \\
= \frac{1}{4}mp^2 + \frac{3}{4}mp + \frac{1}{2}m - \frac{1}{6}p^3 + [\frac{31}{4}, 8]_m p^2 + [\frac{293}{12}, \frac{151}{6}]_m p + [\frac{33}{2}, 17]_m
\end{array}
\right.
$$

Figure 2: the linear equations system of example 7

4 Conclusion

We have presented a general method, based on the vertices of parameterized polytopes and Ehrhart polynomials, which allows to compute the number of integer solutions of selected free variables in a set of linear and/or nonlinear contraints. Our answers are given symbolically, in terms of size parameters, having many applications in the analysis and transformation of scientific programs. This method is quite simple and handles any set of rational linear constraints without any restriction, through underlying tools dealing with improved results on polyhedral combinatorics and linear programming. Moreover, the method gives systematically exact answers. It is entirely computable and will be soon implemented to be connected to the parametric vertices finding algorithm of Loechner and Wilde [13]. A first application of our method, to the computation of the potential parallelism of a given parallel loop, and the number of needed processors from a linear mapping function, was already presented in [3]. Compared with methods which ensure more limited capabilities [22, 11, 16], this paper allows some important observations:

- summations over several variables should not presume an order in which to perform the summation (as pointed out by Pugh in [16]),
- a general technique must consider rational polytopes too, since the nested loops model yields rational affine loop bounds, and since it is useful to handle systematically a wide variety of applications in the parallelization of scientific programs.
- in order to be simple, the answers gain to be expressed without any complex function as *min*'s, *max*'s, *mod*'s, floors or ceilings. In this way, periodic numbers introduced by Ehrhart [8] are a good answer, and can undoubtly be used in some other context.

References

[1] A. I. Barvinok. A polynomial-time algorithm for counting integral points in polyhedra when the dimension is fixed. In *Proc. of the 34th Symp. on the Foundations of Computer Science (FOCS'93)*, pages 566-572. IEEE Computer Society Press, New York, 1993.

[2] A. I. Barvinok. Computing the Ehrhart Polynomial of a Convex Lattice Polytope. *Discrete Comput. Geom.*, 12:35-48,1994.

[3] Ph. Clauss. The volume of a lattice polyhedron to enumerate processors and parallelism. Research Report ICPS 95-11, Submitted to publication, 1995. `http://icps.u-strasbg.fr/pub-95/pub-95-11.ps.gz`

[4] M. Dyer and A. M. Frieze. On the complexity of computing the volume of a polyhedron. *SIAM J. Comput.*, 17(5):967-974, 1988.

[5] E. Ehrhart. Sur les polyèdres rationnels homothétiques à *n* dimensions. *C.R. Acad. Sci. Paris*, 254:616-618, 1962.

[6] E. Ehrhart. Sur un problème de géométrie diophantienne linéaire I. *J. Reine Angew. Math.*, 226:1-29, 1967.

[7] E. Ehrhart. Sur un problème de géométrie diophantienne linéaire II. *J. Reine Angew. Math.*, 227:25-49, 1967.

[8] E. Ehrhart. *Polynômes arithmétiques et Méthode des Polyèdres en Combinatoire.* International Series of Numerical Mathematics, vol.35, Birkhäuser Verlag, Basel/Stuttgart, 1977.

[9] J. Ferrante, V. Sarkar and W. Thrash. On estimating and enhancing cache effectiveness. *Advances in Languages and Compilers for Parallel Processing*, pages 328-343. The MIT Press, 1991.

[10] P.M. Gruber and C.G. Lekkerkerker. *Geometry of Numbers.* North-Holland, Amsterdam, 1987.

[11] M. Haghighat and C. Polychronopoulos. Symbolic analysis: A basis for parallelization, optimization and scheduling of programs. *U. Banerjee et al., ed., Languages and Compilers for Parallel Computing.* Springer-Verlag, Aug. 1993. LNCS 768, *Proc. of the 6th annual worshop on Programming Languages and Compilers for Parallel Computing.*

[12] M. Haghighat and C. Polychronopoulos. Symbolic analysis: A basis for parallelization, optimization and scheduling of programs. Technical Report 1317, CSRD, Univ. of Illinois, Aug. 1993.

[13] V. Loechner and D. K. Wilde. Parameterized polyhedra and their vertices. Research Report ICPS 95-16, Submitted to publication, 1995. `http://icps.u-strasbg.fr/pub-95/pub-95-16.ps.gz`

[14] I. G. Macdonald. The volume of a lattice polyhedron. *Proc. Camb. Phil. Soc.*, 59:719-726, 1963.

[15] I. G. Macdonald. Polynomials associated with finite cell-complexes. *J. London Math. Soc.*, 4(2):181-192, 1971.

[16] W. Pugh. Counting Solutions to Presburger Formulas: How and Why. *Proc. of the 1994 ACM SIGPLAN Conf. on Programming Language Design and Implementation*, 1994.

[17] A. Schrijver. *Theory of Linear and Integer Programming.* Wiley, New York, 1986.

[18] H. S. Stone and D. Thiebaut. Footprints in the cache. *Proc. ACM SIGMETRICS 1986*, pp. 4-8, May 1986.

[19] R. P. Stanley. *Combinatorics and Commutative Algebra.* Birkhäuser, Boston, 1983.

[20] R. P. Stanley. *Enumerative Combinatorics Volume I.* Wadsworth & Brooks/Cole, Monterey, California, 1986.

[21] N. Tawbi. Estimation of nested loop execution time by integer arithmetics in convex polyhedra. *Proc. of the 1994 Int. Parallel Processing Symp.*, Apr. 1994.

[22] N. Tawbi and P. Feautrier. Processor allocation and loop scheduling on multiprocessor computers. *Proc. of the 1992 Int. Conf. on Supercomputing*, pages 63-71, July 1992.

[23] D. K. Wilde. A library for doing polyhedral operations. *Master's thesis*, Oregon State Univ., Corvallis, Oregon, december 1993. Also published as IRISA technical report PI 785, Rennes, France, dec. 1993.

Improving Data Cache Performance by Pre-executing Instructions Under a Cache Miss

James Dundas and Trevor Mudge
Department of Electrical Engineering and Computer Science
The University of Michigan
Ann Arbor, Michigan 48109-2122
{dundas, tnm}@eecs.umich.edu

Abstract

In this paper we propose and evaluate a technique that improves first level data cache performance by pre-executing future instructions under a data cache miss. We show that these pre-executed instructions can generate highly accurate data prefetches, particularly when the first level cache is small. The technique is referred to as *runahead* processing. The hardware required to implement runahead is modest, because, when a miss occurs, it makes use of an otherwise idle resource, the execution logic. The principal hardware cost is an extra register file. To measure the impact of runahead, we simulated a processor executing five integer Spec95 benchmarks. Our results show that runahead was able to significantly reduce data cache CPI for four of the five benchmarks. We also compared runahead to a simple form of prefetching, sequential prefetching, which would seem to be suitable for scientific benchmarks. We confirm this by enlarging the scope of our experiments to include a scientific benchmark. However, we show that runahead was also able to outperform sequential prefetching on the scientific benchmark. We also conduct studies that demonstrate that runahead can generate many useful prefetches for lines that show little spatial locality with the misses that initiate runahead episodes. Finally, we discuss some further enhancements of our baseline runahead prefetching scheme.

1. Introduction

Prefetching data into the data cache is one well-established approach to reducing the detrimental effects memory latency has on processor performance. Prefetching can be accomplished via software, hardware, or a combination of both. Typical software prefetching methods [1][2][3] allow a compiler to use its static knowledge of a program's behavior to generate prefetch instructions. Typical hardware prefetching methods can observe the dynamic nature of a program, and work by either exploiting spatial locality [4][5], or by keeping track of the access patterns for earlier accesses [6][7].

Confining prefetching to software approaches means that the hardware can be kept simple and fast, but prefetch instructions may cause code bloat, and increase register pressure. Existing programs may have to be recompiled to exploit software prefetching. Furthermore, the compiler cannot observe, or take advantage of, the dynamic behavior of programs.

Hardware prefetching can take advantage of information created at run-time and execute existing binaries, however, they can require a significant amount of hardware in order to be effective. The stride and reference prediction tables in [6][7], are a case in point. The hardware requirements can be reduced if the table entries are allocated by the software. This hybrid hardware-software technique was presented in [8]. Their instruction stride table (IST) selectively generates cache miss initiated prefetches for accesses chosen beforehand by the compiler. This resulted in multiprocessor performance for scientific benchmarks comparable in some cases to software prefetching, with an instruction stride table as small as 4 entries. The IST concept was subsequently combined with the prefetch predicates of [2] in [9]. Another hardware prefetching scheme that avoids the need for significant amounts of hardware is the "wrong path" prefetching described in [10]. This actually prefetches instructions from the not-taken path, in the expectation that they will be executed during a later iteration.

Most prefetching techniques, software- or hardware-based, tend to perform poorly on an important class of applications having recursive data structures such as linked-lists. A software technique that overcomes this limitation was presented recently in [11], in which software prefetches were inserted at subroutine call sites that passed pointers as arguments. Another pointer-based approach was described in [12]. This approach uses pointers stored within the data structures to generate software prefetches.

The runahead prefetching approach presented in this paper is a hardware approach, that requires only a modest amount of hardware, because, when a miss occurs, it makes use of an otherwise idle resource, the execution logic. The principal hardware cost is an extra register file. Unlike most of the proposed hardware methods it does not rely on any spatial locality of the data or on the history of previous accesses. It attempts to generate accurate data prefetches by pre-executing future instructions while data cache misses are outstanding. Cache misses resulting from pre-executed loads and stores create the prefetches into the data cache. Because their pre-execution is simply a preview of their actual execution any resulting cache misses are highly accurate, although not perfect as we shall see. The cache misses generated during runahead are placed in a data memory access queue, DMAQ.

We examine two variants of runahead, a conservative method which allows pre-execution to continue only up to the point where branches and jumps cannot be resolved, and an aggressive method which assumes branches and jumps are correctly resolved during runahead. In either case, stores are used as cache touch instructions. They are not allowed to complete and write into memory during runahead.

By waiting until cache misses occur before generating prefetches, runahead adds a highly responsive feedback component to the memory hierarchy: the greater the cache miss penalty, the more opportunities there are for prefetching, which tend to reduce the frequency of future cache misses. Conversely, if an application enters a phase where its hit rate is high, few prefetches are generated.

The paper is organized as follows. The next section provides more details on the mechanism of runahead prefetching. Section 3 discusses the simulator, benchmarks, and experimental results. Sec-

ICS 97 Vienna Austria

tion 4 presents some concluding remarks and discussion of future work.

2. How Runahead Works

When the processor detects an L1 data cache miss it records the instruction address of the faulting load or store instruction and enters runahead mode. It also checkpoints the register file, RF, by copying it to a backup register file BRF. The processor then pre-executes subsequent instructions while the cache miss is serviced. Because the value returned from a cache miss cannot be known ahead of time, it is possible for pre-executed instructions to be dependent upon invalid data. Rather than terminating runahead we allow registers and data cache values to have an explicit "invalid" state during runahead. Denoting this value, INV, requires an extra bit associated with each register in RF as well as with each word in the L1 data cache line (if byte addressing is allowed, each byte requires an invalid bit). Pre-execution of most instructions consists of the usual steps of fetch, decode, and execute, with some changes to deal with invalid data. Also stores are treated slightly differently. The actions associated with pre-execution can be summarized by instruction type as follows:

1. **register-to-register** instructions mark their destination register INV if any of their source registers contain an INV. They can also replace an INV value in their destination if all sources are valid.
2. **load** instructions mark their destination register INV if either of three cases arises:
   i. if the base register used to form the effective address is marked INV, or
   ii. if the base register is not INV but the load causes a cache miss, or
   iii. if the base register is not INV and a cache miss does not occur but the target word in the cache is marked INV as a result of a preceding store during the same runahead episode (see next case).

   They can also replace an INV value in their destination if none of the preceding three cases apply.
3. **store** instructions do not write data into the cache or main memory. They do, however, mark the referenced L1 data cache item INV, if the base register used in address calculation is not INV and a cache miss does not occur.
4. **conditional branch** instructions are resolved normally if their branch condition is not INV. If it is, the outcome is determined by whatever branch prediction strategy the processor employs.
5. **jump register indirect** instructions (the target of the jump is obtained from a register) in which the register contains an INV value assume that the return stack contains the address of the next instruction.

The above actions were formulated from straightforward considerations of read-after-write dependencies, however they do not always accurately anticipate what occurs during actual execution. Action 3 does not account for the case when stores cause a cache miss or cannot compute their target addresses because their base register has an INV value. Such stores cannot mark their destination word INV. It thus follows that subsequent loads have a small possibility of introducing apparently valid data into the RF, which should have been marked INV. Action 4 does not account for the case when an unresolvable conditional branch is mispredicted. Finally, action 5 does not account for the case when jump indirects are used to provide dynamically relocatable subroutine call linking rather than subroutine return linking.

To summarize, the above runahead pre-execution actions result in values in the RF that cannot be trusted with certainty during runahead: there is a small possibility that a valid register should be marked INV and vice versa. Because the values in RF during runahead are only used to create runahead data prefetches, they do not affect the sequential state of the processor. The worst thing that can happen is that some number of useless prefetches can be generated.

After the cache miss that started runahead mode is serviced the processor resumes execution at the faulting instruction, and RF is restored from its backup, BRF. Each register in the BRF need only be connected to the one RF register that it shadows. No read or write ports connect to the BRF, simplifying its implementation, keeping it off of the critical path, and allowing the RF $\leftrightarrow$ BRF transfers to be done via two global signals. At most a cycle will be added to the miss penalty. Load and store instructions, that can compute their target addresses with valid registers, can generate prefetch requests if their target lines are not in the L1 data cache. The valid bits in RF and the cache are set to the valid state when the processor leaves runahead.

2.1 Two runahead policies

We consider two runahead policies in this paper: a conservative policy and an aggressive one. If a conditional branch or jump is pre-executed that is dependent upon an invalid register, the processor can do one of two things.The conservative policy halts runahead until the runahead-initiating miss is serviced. The aggressive policy assumes that the branch prediction or subroutine call return stack is good enough to accurately resolve the branch or jump. The conservative policy should generate fewer useless prefetches, but the aggressive policy can potentially deliver superior performance if it can continue to pre-execute the proper instructions past unresolvable branches and jumps. Our simulations of the aggressive runahead policy assume that the processor always stays on the proper path of execution during runahead.

3. Experiments

The simulator was created using ATOM [13]. The simulated processor fetches, decodes, and executes one instruction per cycle. It did not model pipeline stalls or penalties due to instruction cache misses, just the effects of data cache misses and any resulting prefetching. Thus the CPI figures obtained in the experiments is simply the contribution due to data cache effects, dcache-CPI, plus one. Effects such as page faults and context switches were not modeled, and the data caches were cold started.

A total of six benchmarks from the Spec95 suite were simulated, and are described in Table 1. All of the benchmarks were compiled using version 2.7.2 of gcc with the -O optimization level.

In the simulations an 8 entry DMAQ is used to send miss and prefetch requests, as well as store-throughs, from an on-chip L1 data cache to an off-chip L2 data cache strictly in the order in which they were generated. The DMAQ thus provides the functionality of a store queue, outstanding request list [6], and miss status holding registers [14]. It is further assumed that the DMAQ cannot coalesce store-throughs, or allow demand fetches or store-throughs to either pass or squash outstanding prefetches. The processor stalls for store throughs and demand fetches when the DMAQ is full, while prefetches that are generated when the DMAQ is full are dropped. In summary, we simulate a model of the interface to the off-chip memory hierarchy that is both simple and conservative. A description of the data memory hierarchy is given in Table 2.

3.1 Results of using runahead for data prefetching

Plots of data memory CPI versus L1 data cache size are shown in Figure 1 through Figure 5. These simulations were allowed to run for the first 500 million instructions of each benchmark.

There are three data sets shown in each of the figures. No prefetch corresponds to the simulated processor without any data prefetching. The other two data sets correspond to the conservative and aggressive runahead policies. The percentage reduction of dcache-CPI from that of the no-prefetch scheme is provided next to each data point. (Recall that the data memory portion of the CPI figure is simply one less than the overall CPI that was measured.)

Conservative runahead reduced performance by 4% (0.016 CPI) for the larger 8KB L1 data cache on the Compress benchmark (Figure 1). This can be attributed to the simple model assumed for the memory interface which allows store-throughs, demand fetches, and a small number of runahead prefetches to compete for DMAQ entries on an equal basis. Interestingly, while the aggressive runahead strategy was able to consistently improve performance over the entire range of cache sizes, conservative runahead was able to outperform aggressive runahead for the 1KB L1 data cache size. The small cache results in increased opportunities for prefetching, particularly for aggressive runahead, resulting in more competition for DMAQ entries. Conservative runahead generates fewer prefetches, resulting in less competition. A more advanced interface to the off-chip memory hierarchy which prioritizes the off-chip memory references would improve performance by reducing the competition between prefetches, demand fetches, and store-throughs.

The rest of the benchmarks were able to benefit significantly from runahead prefetching. Note that the dcache-CPI for the no prefetch scheme is significant: all of the simulations have a dcache-CPI of about 2 for a 4KB L1 data cache, with the exception of Ijpeg. Go (Figure 2) benefited the most from the aggressive runahead scheme, with reductions in dcache-CPI of 58 to 43% for the aggressive runahead scheme. The conservative runahead scheme delivered performance reductions half that of the aggressive runahead scheme, indicating that a significant number of unresolvable branches and jumps were encountered. Perl (Figure 3)had reductions of dcache-CPI of 49 to 22% for the aggressive scheme and 35 to 15% for the conservative scheme. The dcache-CPI reductions for Vortex (Figure 4) were similar with 47 to 26% for the aggressive scheme, and 33 to 18% for the conservative scheme. Ijpeg (Figure 5) was perhaps the most interesting of the integer benchmarks, with reductions of dcache-CPI of 44 to 31% for the aggressive scheme, and nearly identical reductions of 43 to 30% for the conservative scheme. This indicates that virtually all of the branches and jumps encountered during runahead could be resolved with valid registers.

3.2 Comparison with sequential prefetching

The following simulations were performed with the L1 data cache size fixed at 4KB, and were only simulated for the first 100 million instructions of each benchmark.

Simulations of the *prefetch-on-miss* and *always-prefetch* sequential prefetching techniques described in [4] were performed. Prefetch-on-miss generates a prefetch for line $i+1$ whenever an access of line i misses in the L1 data cache. Always-prefetch generates a prefetch for line $i+1$ whenever line i is accessed. Both techniques were also simulated with the ability to generate prefetches for line $i+2$ in addition to line $i+1$, giving us a total of 4 sequential prefetching schemes. Prefetches that hit in the L1 data cache were dropped.

Bar graphs are shown in Figure 6 through Figure 11, which compare the dcache-CPI reducing ability of the four types of sequential prefetching to that of aggressive and conservative runahead prefetching. The percentage reduction of dcache-CPI over the baseline no-prefetch scheme is provided on top of each bar. Performance degradation is indicated by enclosing the percentage in parentheses. In general, sequential prefetching works well for scientific benchmarks but poorly for integer benchmarks. Because the benchmarks we are using are integer benchmarks, we added a scientific benchmark, Tomcatv, to provide a comparison with at least one benchmark for which sequential prefetching schemes generally work well.

Figure 6 shows results for Ijpeg. This is the one case where both prefetch-on-miss schemes were able to improve performance to a small extent (dcache-CPI decreased by 7 and 3%), however, this was greatly overshadowed by that of conservative and aggressive runahead prefetching where the dcache-CPI was decreased by 26 and 27%, respectively. The always-prefetch schemes significantly degraded performance (dcache-CPI increased by 34 and 49%).

As we expected, Tomcatv (Figure 7) benefited from sequential prefetching. The always-prefetch and prefetch-on-miss schemes were able to improve performance (dcache-CPI decreased by 7 and 8%) when prefetches were generated for only the immediately sequential line. When up to two lines could be prefetched, performance was reduced for both always-prefetch and prefetch-on-miss (dcache-CPI increased by 28 and 25%). The conservative and aggressive runahead schemes were able to reduce data dcache-CPI significantly (dcache-CPI decreased by 25 and 24%), outperforming all of the sequential prefetching schemes.

In the remainder of the benchmarks (Figure 8 through Figure 11) the conservative and aggressive runahead schemes were able to reduce dcache-CPI significantly, with the exception of compress where gains were modest. Sequential prefetching resulted in reduced performance for all of these benchmarks.

3.3 Measurements of miss-prefetch spatial locality

In order to get a better picture of why runahead is effective for integer benchmarks we measured the miss-prefetch spatial locality provided by runahead for our benchmarks. Again our simulations ran for the first 100 million instructions of each benchmark with the L1 data cache fixed at 4 KB.

Plots of the miss-prefetch spatial locality for the aggressive runahead policy are shown in Figure 12 through Figure 17. The $x = 0$ point on the x-axis represents the cache line address of each runahead-initiating L1 data cache miss. The other points on the x-axis represent the distance in cache lines between the address of each runahead-initiating miss and any runahead prefetches that are generated during the corresponding runahead episode. For example, $x = 1$ represents the address of the next sequential line after the address that caused the runahead-initiating miss. The y-axis is a cumulative value. Its value at a particular x, say 35, represent the fraction of all runahead prefetches that result from pre-executed accesses to any of the 35 sequential line addresses after the address causing the miss that initiated runahead. The negative part of the x-axis represents addresses before the runahead-initiating miss. The extreme data points at x = +/- 1000 lines represent the fraction of runahead prefetches whose addresses correspond to lines that are at least 1000 lines distant from their corresponding runahead-initiating misses. The plots in Figure 12 through Figure 17 are aggregates of all the runahead prefetches that are generated over the course of running each benchmark.

For example, by looking at the data points for positive x close to $x = 0$ in Figure 12, one can see that 18% of all runahead prefetches generated for Vortex are for the 12 immediately sequential cache lines after their runahead-initiating misses. Similarly, 8% are generated for the 12 lines preceding their runahead-initiating misses. The cumulative distributions are relatively flat until they reach x = 1000, at which point there are lage spikes. The spike at x = +1000 indicates that 27% of the runahead prefetches are generated for lines whose addresses are more than 1000 lines ahead of their runahead-initiating misses. Another 38% are generated for lines whose addresses are more than 1000 lines before their runahead-initiating miss.

Go (Figure 13) exhibited even less miss-prefetch spatial locality than Vortex. Only 15% of the runahead prefetches are generated for addresses within 100 lines of their runahead-initiating miss, and only 29% of the runahead prefetches are within 999 lines. The majority of the prefetches are for lines far removed from their runahead-initiating misses. Perl (Figure 14) exhibited somewhat more miss-prefetch spatial locality than that for Go. 16% of the runahead prefetches are for lines within 10 lines their runahead-initiating misses, two-thirds of which are for lines located before their corresponding misses. The overwhelming majority of the prefetches, 73%, are for lines far removed from their runahead-initiating misses. Compress (Figure 15) exhibited by far the best miss-prefetch spatial locality of the benchmarks that we examined, with 85% of the prefetches within 25 lines of their runahead-initiating misses. Note that two-thirds of these prefetches were for lines immediately preceding their runahead-initiating misses. Ijpeg (Figure 16) exhibited the least miss-prefetch spatial locality of the benchmarks that we examined, with very few prefetches generated close to their runahead-initiating misses. However, 85% of the prefetches were generated within 500 lines.

Tomcatv (Figure 17) shows somewhat more miss-prefetch spatial locality than Ijpeg for lines close to their runahead-initiating misses. The majority of the prefetches generated for Tomcatv were for lines far removed from their runahead-initiating misses.

These results indicate that runahead is very effective at generating cache-miss initiated prefetches that exhibit little spatial locality with respect to their prefetch-initiating misses. Sequential prefetching can only generate prefetches for lines that exhibit spacial locality.

3.4 What happens to potential prefetches

Many of the pre-executed load and store instructions that would otherwise miss in the L1 data cache are unable to generate prefetches for a variety of reasons:

- a demand fetch or prefetch for the missing line is already in progress, or
- the pre-executed load or store instruction could not generate its target address with valid registers, or
- the DMAQ was full, causing what would have been a useful prefetch to be dropped.

A bar graph illustrating what happened to the potential prefetches for each benchmark is shown in Figure 18. Only the aggressive runahead policy is shown. The numbers on top of each bar represent the total number of potential runahead prefetches (pre-executed loads and stores whose actual target addresses would cause a miss in the L1 data cache) for the benchmark in question. Note that since instructions can be pre-executed multiple times in successive runahead episodes it is possible for the number of potential prefetches to exceed the number of instructions actually executed in the simulation (100 million).

From the figure it can be seen that 23 to 46% of the potential runahead prefetches were for lines that were already being fetched by an earlier prefetch or runahead-initiating miss. Another 12 to 37% of the potential runahead prefetches could not compute their target addresses with valid registers. Of the remaining potential prefetches, up to 38% were dropped due to a lack of available DMAQ entries. The remainder of the potential runahead prefetches, 19 to 40%, were actually able to become useful runahead prefetches. This strongly suggests that separate queues are needed for runahead prefetches and store-throughs, and that a runahead processor should avoid dropping prefetches, perhaps with a longer prefetch queue.

The benchmarks that had the most potential runahead prefetches (Vortex, Perl, and Tomcatv) also lost the largest proportion of them to a lack of DMAQ entries. The rest of the benchmarks lost very few potential prefetches in this way. Tomcatv also lost the smallest fraction of its potential prefetches to invalid registers, with just over 33 million prefetches generated during the first 100 million instructions of the benchmark. This huge number of prefetches for Tomcatv caused by far the largest absolute reduction in dcache-CPI among the benchmarks that we examined. This suggests that runahead may be very effective for both integer and scientific benchmarks in general.

3.5 The effect on off-chip fetch traffic

Off-chip fetch traffic can lead to performance problems if the memory hierarchy does not have adequate bandwidth to service the requests in a timely fashion, or if a significant fraction of the fetch traffic is composed of useless prefetches. Runahead prefetches are by nature quite accurate, so any performance degradation attributable to runahead is likely to arise from the sheer quantity of additional fetch traffic that may occur. A bar chart is shown in Figure 19, which depicts the number of fetches that are generated during the simulation of the first 100 million instructions of each benchmark. The number of fetches for each benchmark is broken down into three bars, which depict the number of fetches for the no-prefetch, conservative runahead, and aggressive runahead schemes. Each bar is broken down further into demand fetches (those that are the result of a conventional load or store miss) and runahead prefetches.

The percentage increase in fetch traffic for each runahead scheme over that of no-prefetch is indicated as a number on top of each bar. Note that all of the integer benchmarks incurred small increases in fetch traffic due to runahead. Only one of the integer benchmarks, Perl, suffered an increase in fetch traffic of more than three percent for either of the runahead prefetching schemes. Furthermore, the number of demand fetches was significantly reduced for most of the benchmarks when runahead was employed.

The only scientific benchmark that we simulated, Tomcatv, incurred large increases in overall fetch traffic as a result of runahead (112.6 and 114.3%). However the number of demand fetches was dramatically reduced, and Tomcatv was able to derive the largest absolute reduction in dcache-CPI of all the benchmarks that we examined.

4. Concluding Remarks

In this paper we present runahead pre-execution, a new method of improving several aspects of processor performance. Our simulations indicate that runahead data prefetching is effective at improving the performance of integer benchmarks. Simulations of a scientific benchmark, Tomcatv, indicate that runahead data prefetching may also be effective for benchmarks that work well with traditional hardware and software data prefetching methods. The experiments were conducted for a range of L1 data cache sizes that are quite small, as this was the range that we were interested in as part of our studies of the design of a very high-clock rate GaAs processor. Clearly, experiments need to be done for L1 caches larger than 8 KB.

There are a number of areas where runahead has the potential to improve performance that were not examined in this study. For example, runahead can improve branch prediction performance by pre-executing conditional branches. A shift register can be used to record the outcomes of pre-executed conditional branches. A count register is needed to keep track of how many valid outcomes are in the shift register. A second count register and two bits of state are needed to determine when to allow the processor to add or remove outcomes to or from the shift register. When the processor leaves runahead mode any outcomes that were recorded in the shift register are used as branch predictors by shifting them out one at a time for each conditional branch that is encountered. A similar approach can be used to record pre-executed indirect jump targets. Pre-executed conditional branch outcomes can also be used to train a traditional dynamic branch prediction scheme during runahead episodes, which is used to predict conditional branches when the shift register is empty.

Some preliminary runahead branch prediction simulation results were reported in [15]. Although the initial results were encouraging, the fact that the simulator could not explore wrong paths during runahead meant that the results were somewhat optimistic. We will present more accurate results once we have a simulator that can explore wrong paths.

Some performance is lost since runahead stores cannot modify the L1 data cache, which can cause read-after-write dependencies with subsequent loads during the same runahead episode. A small fully associative store data cache may be used to capture store data in runahead, which could then be used by subsequent runahead loads. This cache can be quite small yet still deliver a noticeable improvement in performance. This approach would be most useful when runahead crosses procedure boundaries or whenever registers are spilled, both of which can cause a significant number of stack-based loads and stores.

Finally, a runahead processor needs a steady supply of instructions to pre-execute in order to be effective. Although instruction cache misses that are detected during runahead are desirable in the sense that they become instruction stream prefetches, it may be possible to obtain additional performance by continuing to pre-execute instructions after an instruction cache miss is detected, or by initiating runahead on an instruction cache miss. We leave this for future work.

5. References

[1] D. Callahan, K. Kennedy, and A. Porterfield, "Software Prefetching," In the Proceedings of the Fourth International Conference on Architectural Support for Programming Languages and Operating Systems, April 1991.

[2] T.C. Mowry, M.S. Lam, and A. Gupta, "Design and evaluation of a compiler algorithm for prefetching," In the Proceedings of the Fifth International Conference on Architectural Support for Programming Languages and Operating Systems, October 1992.

[3] A.C. Klaiber and H.M. Levy, "An Architecture for Software-Controlled Data Prefetching," In the Proceedings of the 18th Annual International Symposium on Computer Architecture, 1991.

[4] A.J. Smith, "Cache Memories," ACM Computing Surveys, vol. 18, num. 3, September 1982.

[5] N.P. Jouppi, "Improving direct-mapped cache performance by the addition of a small fully-associative cache and prefetch buffers," In the Proceedings of the 17th Annual International Symposium on Computer Architecture, May 1990.

[6] J.L. Baer and T.F. Chen, "An Effective On-Chip Preloading Scheme To Reduce Data Access Penalty," In the Proceedings of Supercomputing, 1991.

[7] J.W.C. Fu and J.H.Patel, "Stride directed prefetching in scalar processors," In the Proceedings of the 25th International Symposium on Microarchitecture, December 1992.

[8] R. Bianchini and T.J. LeBlanc, "A Preliminary Evaluation of Cache-Miss-Initiated Prefetching Techniques in Scalable Multiprocessors," University of Rochester Computer Science Department Technical Report 515, May 1994.

[9] T.F. Chen, "An Effective Programmable Prefetch Engine for On-Chip Caches," In the Proceedings of the 28th International Symposium on Microarchitecture, 1995.

[10] J. Pierce and T. Mudge, "Wrong-Path Instruction Prefetching," In the Proceedings of the 29th International Symposium on Microarchitecture, 1996.

[11] M. Lipasti, W. Schmidt, S. Kunkel, and R. Roediger, "SPAID: Software Prefetching in Pointer- and Call-Intensive Environments," In the Proceedings of the 28th International Symposium on Microarchitecture, 1995.

[12] C.K. Luk and T.C. Mowry, "Compiler-Based Prefetching for Recursive Data Structures," In the Proceedings of the Seventh International Conference on Architectural Support for Programming Languages and Operating Systems, October 1996.

[13] A. Eustace and A. Srivastava, "ATOM: A Flexible Interface for Building High Performance Program Analysis Tools," Digital Equipment Corporation Western Research Laboratory Technical Note TN-44, July 1994.

[14] D. Kroft, "Lockup-Free Instruction Fetch/Prefetch Cache Organization," In the Proceedings of the 8th International Symposium on Computer Architecture, May 1981.

[15] J. Dundas and T. Mudge, "Using Stall Cycles to Improve Microprocessor Performance," University of Michigan Department of Electrical Engineering and Computer Science Technical Report CSE-TR-301-96, September 1996.

Benchmark (Spec95)	Data Set	Load/Store Data References		Description
		First 100M Instr.	First 500M Instr.	
Vortex	reference	23.4M/17.7M	121.3M/85.9M	Database program
Go	play = 10 board = 13	30.1M/6.4M	159.8M/36.6M	Artificial intelligence program that plays Go
Ijpeg	reference	20.0M/10.7M	91.4M/36.4M	Image compression and decompression
Perl	reference	24.2M/12.6M	120.7M/62.6M	Manipulates strings and prime numbers using Perl
Compress	reference	24.8M/10.9M	124.0M/54.9M	Compresses and decompresses a file in memory
Tomcatv	reference	22.9M/10.9M	Not simulated	Mesh generation (scientific benchmark)

Table 1 Benchmark Descriptions

Policy	L1 Data Cache	L2 Data Cache	Main Memory
Placement	direct-mapped	direct-mapped	N.A.
Store-hit	write-through (up to 8 outstanding)	write-back	N.A.
Store-miss	write-allocate	write-allocate	N.A.
Line / transfer size	32 B	32 B	32 B
Size	4 KB	1 MB	N.A.
Blocking	Non-blocking (up to 8 outstanding)	Hit-under-miss only	N.A.
Maximum throughput	1 accesses/cycle	0.2 accesses/cycle	0.01 accesses/cycle
Latencies (cycles)	Hit: 0 (covered by pipeline model) Miss: 24 + time in DMAQ	Hit: 0 (covered by L1 miss) Miss: additional 100 (200 if Dirty)	0 cycles (covered by L2 miss and dirty WB)

Table 2 Data Memory Hierarchy Parameters

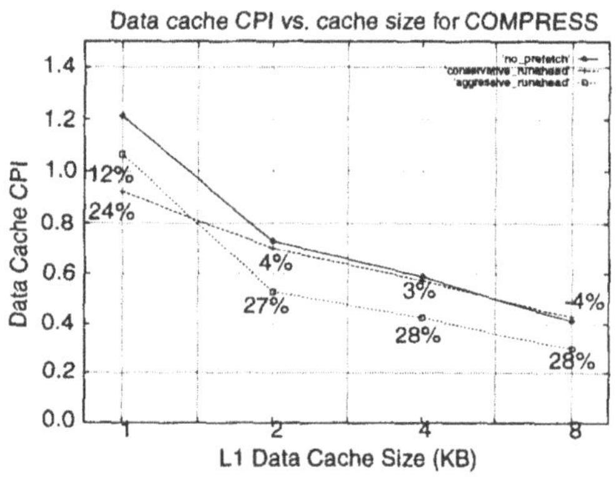

Figure 1

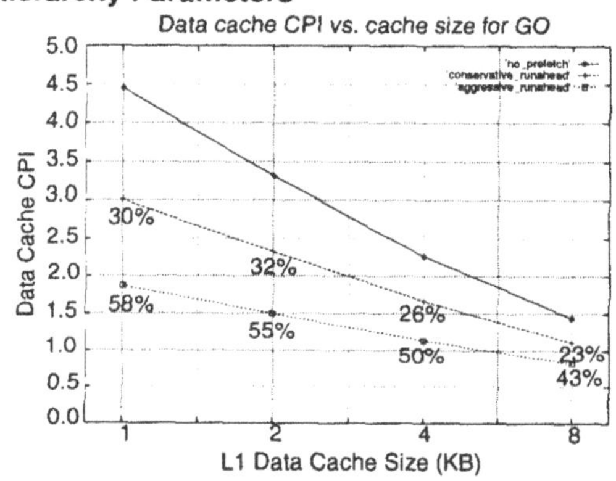

Figure 2

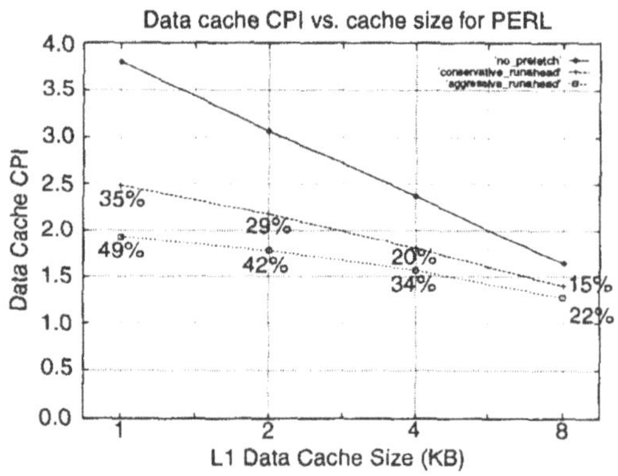

Figure 3

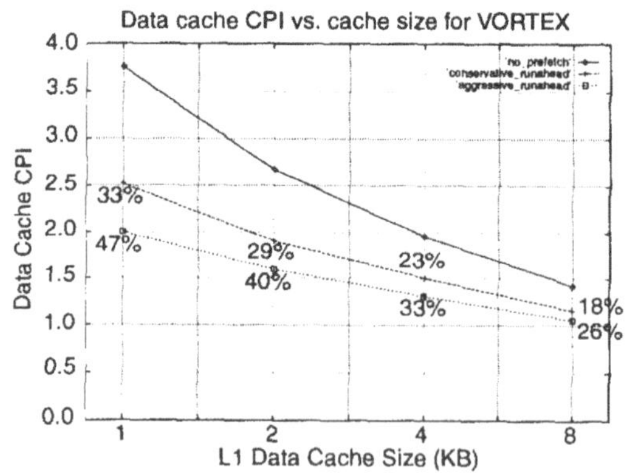

Figure 4

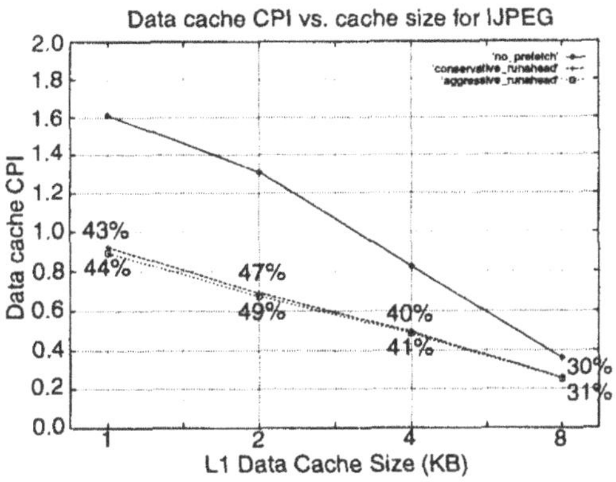

Figure 5

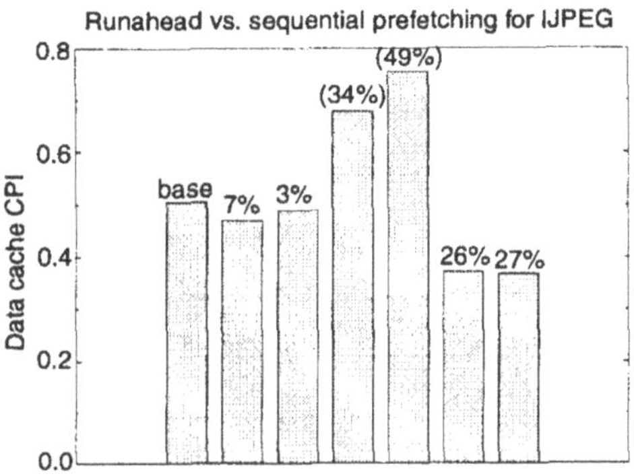

Figure 6

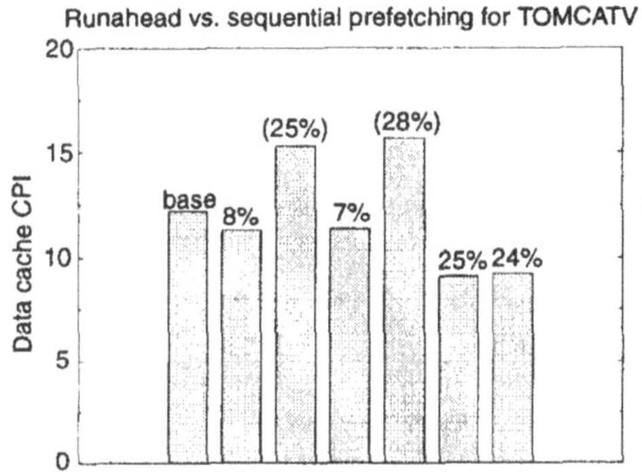

Figure 7

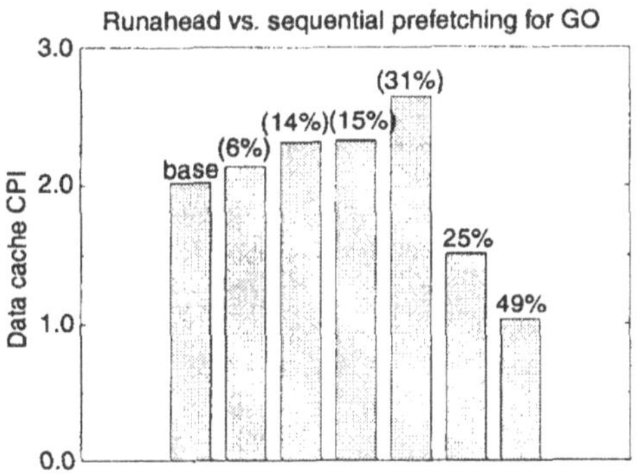

Figure 8

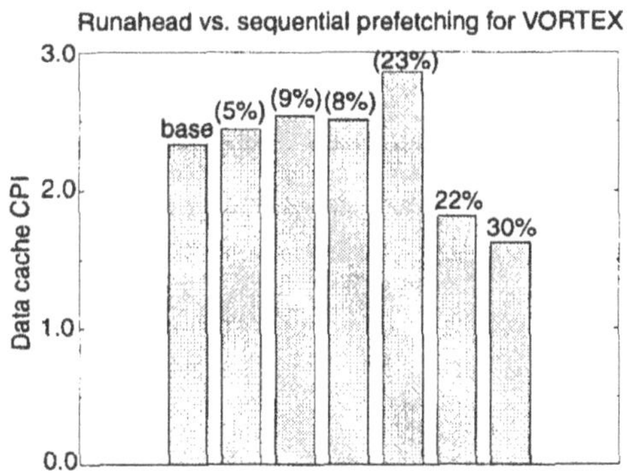

Figure 9

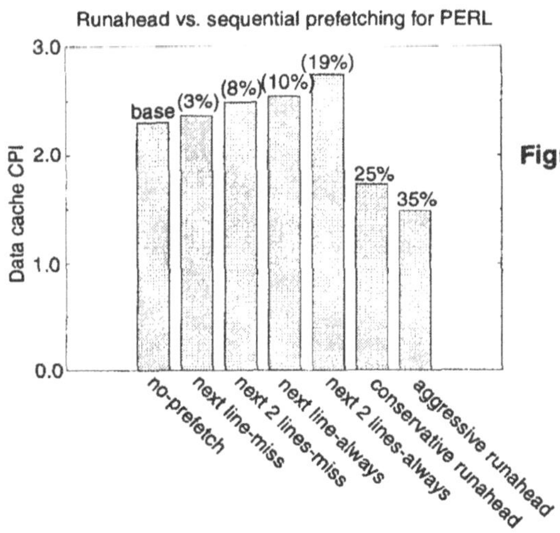

Figure 10

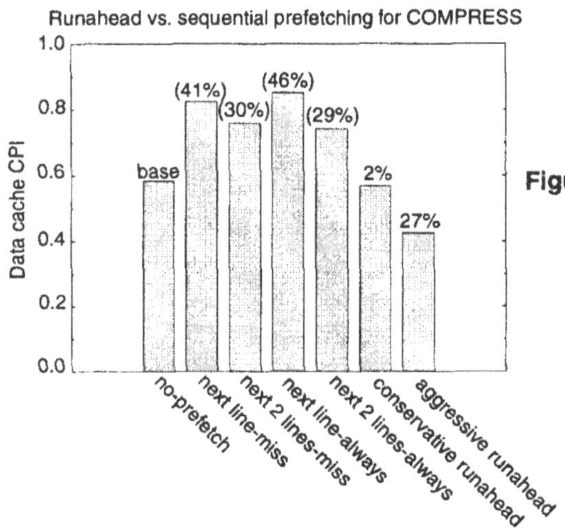

Figure 11

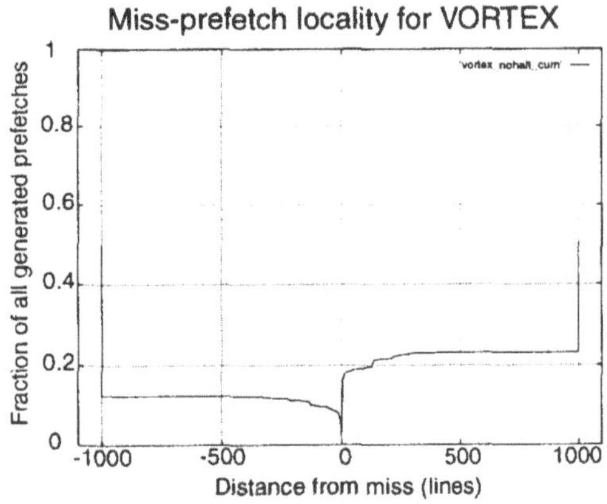

Figure 12

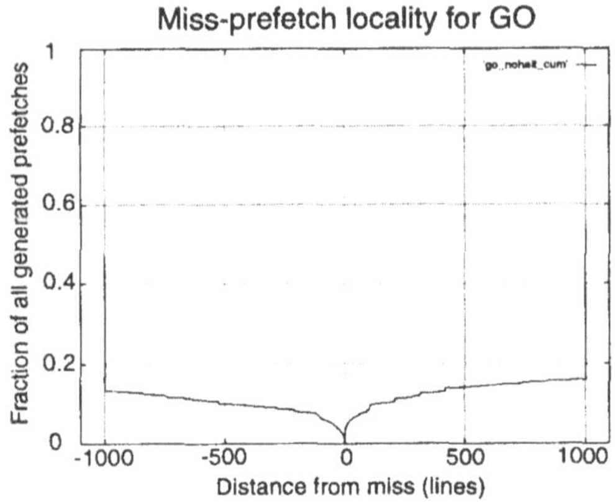

Figure 13

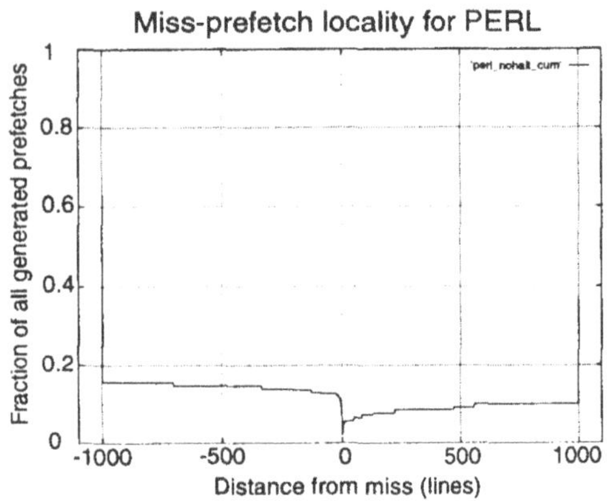

Figure 14

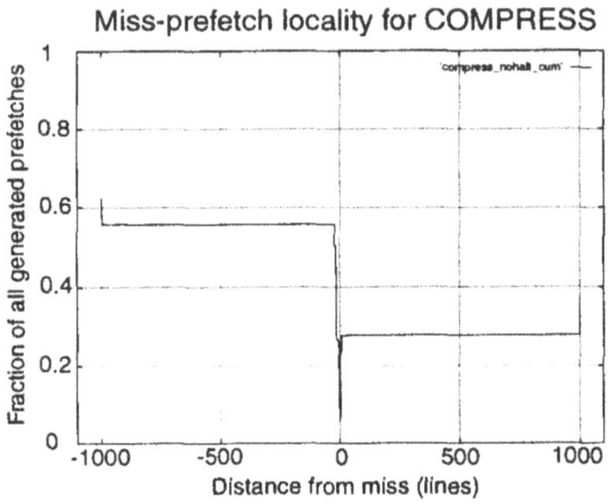

Figure 15

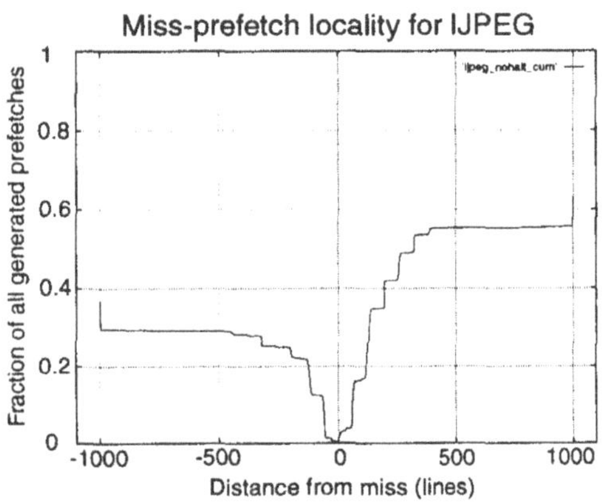

Figure 16

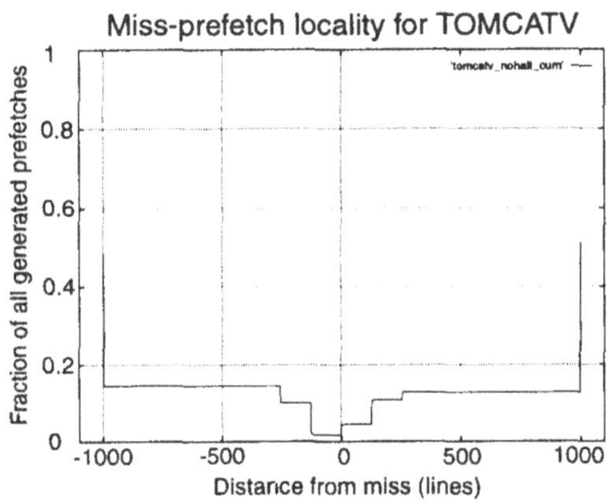

Figure 17

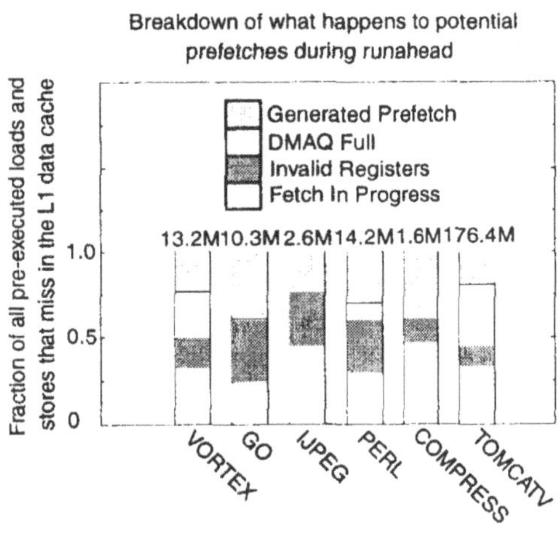

Figure 18

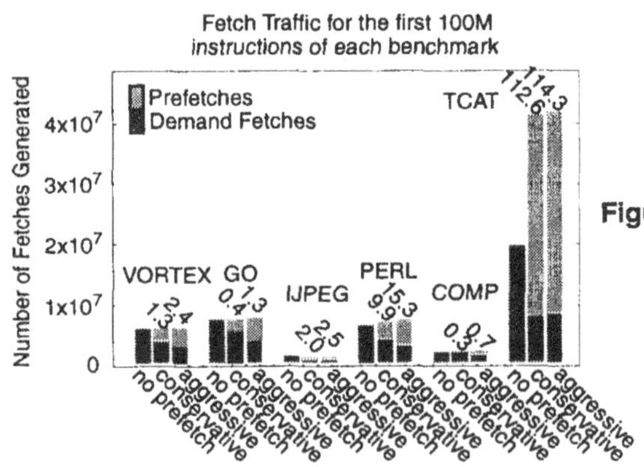

Figure 19

Optimizing Matrix Multiply using PHiPAC: a Portable, High-Performance, ANSI C Coding Methodology

Jeff Bilmes*, Krste Asanović†, Chee-Whye Chin‡, Jim Demmel§
{bilmes,krste,cheewhye,demmel}@cs.berkeley.edu

CS Division, University of California at Berkeley
Berkeley CA, 94720

International Computer Science Institute
Berkeley CA, 94704

Abstract

Modern microprocessors can achieve high performance on linear algebra kernels but this currently requires extensive machine-specific hand tuning. We have developed a methodology whereby near-peak performance on a wide range of systems can be achieved automatically for such routines. First, by analyzing current machines and C compilers, we've developed guidelines for writing Portable, High-Performance, ANSI C (PHiPAC, pronounced "fee-pack"). Second, rather than code by hand, we produce parameterized code generators. Third, we write search scripts that find the best parameters for a given system. We report on a BLAS GEMM compatible multi-level cache-blocked matrix multiply generator which produces code that achieves around 90% of peak on the Sparcstation-20/61, IBM RS/6000-590, HP 712/80i, SGI Power Challenge R8k, and SGI Octane R10k, and over 80% of peak on the SGI Indigo R4k. The resulting routines are competitive with vendor-optimized BLAS GEMMs.

*CS Division, University of California at Berkeley and the International Computer Science Institute. The author acknowledges the support of JSEP contract F49620-94-C-0038.

†CS Division, University of California at Berkeley and the International Computer Science Institute. The author acknowledges the support of ONR URI Grant N00014-92-J-1617.

‡CS Division, University of California at Berkeley. The author acknowledges the support of ARPA contract DAAL03-91-C-0047 (University of Tennessee Subcontract ORA4466.02).

§CS Division and Mathematics Dept., University of California at Berkeley. The author acknowledges the support of ARPA contract DAAL03-91-C-0047 (University of Tennessee Subcontract ORA4466.02), ARPA contract DAAH04-95-1-0077 (University of Tennessee Subcontract ORA7453.02), DOE grant DE-FG03-94ER25219, DOE contract W-31-109-Eng-38, NSF grant ASC-9313958, and DOE grant DE-FG03-94ER25206.

ICS 97 Vienna Austria

1 Introduction

The use of a standard linear algebra library interface, such as BLAS [LHKK79, DCHH88, DCDH90], enables portable application code to obtain high-performance provided that an optimized library (e.g., [AGZ94, KHM94]) is available and affordable.

Developing an optimized library, however, is a difficult and time-consuming task. Even excluding algorithmic variants such as Strassen's method [BLS91] for matrix multiplication, these routines have a large design space with many parameters such as blocking sizes, loop nesting permutations, loop unrolling depths, software pipelining strategies, register allocations, and instruction schedules. Furthermore, these parameters have complicated interactions with the increasingly sophisticated microarchitectures of new microprocessors.

Various strategies can be used to produced optimized routines for a given platform. For example, the routines could be manually written in assembly code, but fully exploring the design space might then be infeasible, and the resulting code might be unusable or sub-optimal on a different system.

Another commonly used method is to code using a high level language but with manual tuning to match the underlying architecture [AGZ94, KHM94]. While less tedious than coding in assembler, this approach still requires writing machine specific code which is not performance-portable across a range of systems.

Ideally, the routines would be written once in a high-level language and fed to an optimizing compiler for each machine. There is a large literature on relevant compiler techniques, many of which use matrix multiplication as a test case [WL91, LRW91, MS95, ACF95, CFH95, SMP+96][1]. While these compiler heuristics generate reasonably good code in general, they tend not to generate near-peak code for any one operation. A high-level language's semantics might also obstruct aggressive compiler optimizations. Moreover, it takes significant time and investment before compiler research appears in production compilers, so these capabilities are often unavailable. While both microarchitectures and compilers will improve over time, we expect it will

[1] A longer list appears in [Wol96].

be many years before a single version of a library routine can be compiled to give near-peak performance across a wide range of machines.

We have developed a methodology, named PHiPAC, for developing Portable High-Performance linear algebra libraries in ANSI C. Our goal is to produce, with minimal effort, high-performance linear algebra libraries for a wide range of systems. The PHiPAC methodology has three components. First, we have developed a generic model of current C compilers and microprocessors that provides guidelines for producing portable high-performance ANSI C code. Second, rather than hand code particular routines, we write parameterized generators [ACF95, MS95] that produce code according to our guidelines. Third, we write scripts that automatically tune code for a particular system by varying the generators' parameters and benchmarking the resulting routines.

We have found that writing a parameterized generator and search scripts for a routine takes less effort than hand-tuning a single version for a single system. Furthermore, with the PHiPAC approach, development effort can be amortized over a large number of platforms. And by automatically searching a large design space, we can discover winning yet unanticipated parameter combinations.

Using the PHiPAC methodology, we have produced a portable, BLAS-compatible matrix multiply generator. The resulting code can achieve over 90% of peak performance on a variety of current workstations, and is sometimes faster than the vendor-optimized libraries. We focus on matrix multiplication in this paper, but we have produced other generators including dot-product, AXPY, and convolution, which have similarly demonstrated portable high performance.

We concentrate on producing high quality uniprocessor libraries for microprocessor-based systems because multiprocessor libraries, such as [CDD+96], can be readily built from uniprocessor libraries. For vector and other architectures, however, our machine model would likely need substantial modification.

Section 2 describes our generic C compiler and microprocessor model, and develops the resulting guidelines for writing portable high-performance C code. Section 3 describes our generator and the resulting code for a BLAS-compatible matrix multiply. Section 4 describes our strategy for searching the matrix multiply parameter space. Section 5 presents results on several architectures comparing against vendor-supplied BLAS GEMM. Section 6 describes the availability of the distribution, and discusses future work.

2 PHiPAC

By analyzing the microarchitectures of a range of machines, such as workstations and microprocessor-based SMP and MPP nodes, and the output of their ANSI C compilers, we derived a set of guidelines that help us attain high performance across a range of machine and compiler combinations [BAD+96].

From our analysis of various ANSI C compilers, we determined we could usually rely on reasonable register allocation, instruction selection, and instruction scheduling. More sophisticated compiler optimizations, however, including pointer alias disambiguation, register and cache blocking, loop unrolling, and software pipelining, were either not performed or not very effective at producing the highest quality code.

Although it would be possible to use another target language, we chose ANSI C because it provides a low-level, yet portable, interface to machine resources, and compilers are widely available. One problem with our use of C is that we must explicitly work around pointer aliasing as described below. In practice, this has not limited our ability to extract near-peak performance.

We emphasize that for both microarchitectures and compilers we are determining a *lowest common denominator*. Some microarchitectures or compilers will have superior characteristics in certain attributes, but, if we code assuming these exist, performance will suffer on systems where they do not. Conversely, coding for the lowest common denominator should not adversely affect performance on more capable platforms.

For example, some machines can fold a pointer update into a load instruction while others require a separate add. Coding for the lowest common denominator dictates replacing pointer updates with base plus *constant offset addressing where possible*. In addition, while some production compilers have sophisticated loop unrolling and software pipelining algorithms, many do not. Our search strategy (Section 4) empirically evaluates several levels of explicit loop unrolling and depths of software pipelining. While a naive compiler might benefit from code with explicit loop unrolling or software pipelining, a more sophisticated compiler might perform better without either.

2.1 PHiPAC Coding Guidelines

The following paragraphs exemplify PHiPAC C code generation guidelines. Programmers can use these coding guidelines directly to improve performance in critical routines while retaining portability, but this does come at the cost of less maintainable code. This problem is mitigated in the PHiPAC approach, however, by the use of parameterized code generators.

Use local variables to explicitly remove false dependencies.

Casually written C code often over-specifies operation order, particularly where pointer aliasing is possible. C compilers, constrained by C semantics, must obey these over-specifications thereby reducing optimization potential. We therefore remove these extraneous dependencies.

For example, the following code fragment contains a false Read-After-Write hazard:

```
a[i] = b[i]+c;
a[i+1] = b[i+1]*d;
```

The compiler may not assume `&a[i] != &b[i+1]` and is forced to first store `a[i]` to memory before loading `b[i+1]`. We may re-write this with explicit loads to local variables:

```
float f1,f2;
f1 = b[i]; f2 = b[i+1];
a[i] = f1 + c; a[i+1] = f2*d;
```

The compiler can now interleave execution of both original statements thereby increasing parallelism.

Exploit multiple integer and floating-point registers.

We explicitly keep values in local variables to reduce memory bandwidth demands. For example, consider the following 3-point FIR filter code:

```
while (...) {
   *res++ = filter[0]*signal[0] +
            filter[1]*signal[1] +
            filter[2]*signal[2];
  signal++; }
```

The compiler will usually reload the filter values every loop iteration because of potential aliasing with `res`. We can remove the alias by preloading the filter into local variables that may be mapped into registers:

```
float f0,f1,f2;
f0=filter[0];f1=filter[1];f2=filter[2];
while ( ... ) {
  *res++ = f0*signal[0]
         + f1*signal[1] + f2*signal[2];
  signal++;   }
```

Minimize pointer updates by striding with constant offsets.

We replace pointer updates for strided memory addressing with constant array offsets. For example:

```
f0=*r8;r8+=4;f1=*r8;r8+=4;f2=*r8;r8+=4;
```

should be converted to:

```
f0 = r8[0]; f1 = r8[4]; f2 = r8[8]; r8 += 12;
```

Compilers can fold the constant index into a register plus offset addressing mode.

Hide multiple instruction FPU latency with independent operations.

We use local variables to expose independent operations so they can be executed independently in a pipelined or superscalar processor. For example:

```
f1=f5*f9;f2=f6+f10;f3=f7*f11;f4=f8+f12;
```

Balance the instruction mix.

A balanced instruction mix has a floating-point multiply, a floating-point add, and 1–2 floating-point loads or stores interleaved. It is not worth decreasing the number of multiplies at the expense of additions if the total floating-point operation count increases.

Increase locality to improve cache performance.

Cached machines benefit from increases in spatial and temporal locality. Whenever possible, we arrange our code to have predominantly unit-stride memory accesses, and try to reuse data once it is in cache. See Section 3.1, for our blocked matrix multiply example.

Convert integer multiplies to adds.

Integer multiplies and divides are slow relative to integer addition. Therefore, we use pointer updates rather than subscript expressions. Rather than:

```
for (i=...) {row_ptr=&p[i*col_stride];...}
```

we produce:

```
for (i=...) {...row_ptr+=col_stride;}
```

Minimize branches, avoid magnitude compares.

Branches are costly, especially on modern superscalar processors. Therefore, we unroll loops to amortize branch cost and use C `do {} while ();` loop control whenever possible to avoid any unnecessary compiler-produced loop head branches.

Also, on many microarchitectures, it is cheaper to perform equality or inequality loop termination tests than magnitude comparisons. For example, instead of:

```
for (i=0,a=start_ptr;i<ARRAY_SIZE;i++,a++)
    { ... }
```

we produce:

```
end_ptr = &a[ARRAY_SIZE]; a = start_ptr;
do { ... a++; } while (a != end_ptr);
```

This also removes one loop control variable.

Loop unroll explicitly to expose optimization opportunities.

We unroll loops explicitly to increase opportunities for other performance optimizations. For example, our 3-point FIR filter example above may be further optimized as follows:

```
float f0,f1,f2,s0,s1,s2;
f0=filter[0];f1=filter[1];f2=filter[2];
s0=signal[0];s1=signal[1];s2=signal[2];
*res++=f0*s0+f1*s1+f2*s2;
do {
   signal+=3;
   s0=signal[0];res[0]=f0*s1+f1*s2+f2*s0;
   s1=signal[1];res[1]=f0*s2+f1*s0+f2*s1;
   s2=signal[2];res[2]=f0*s0+f1*s1+f2*s2;
   res += 3;
} while ( ... );
```

In the inner loop, there are now only two memory access per five floating point operations whereas in our unoptimized code, there were seven memory accesses per five floating point operations.

3 Matrix Multiply Generator

`mm_gen` is a generator that produces C code, following the PHiPAC coding guidelines, for one variant of the matrix multiply operation $C = \alpha op(A)op(B) + \beta C$ where $op(A)$, $op(B)$, and C, are respectively M×K, K×N, and M×N matrices, α and β are scalar parameters, and $op(X)$ is either $transpose(X)$ or just X. Our individual procedures have a lower level interface then a BLAS GEMM and have no error checking. For optimal efficiency, error checking should be performed by

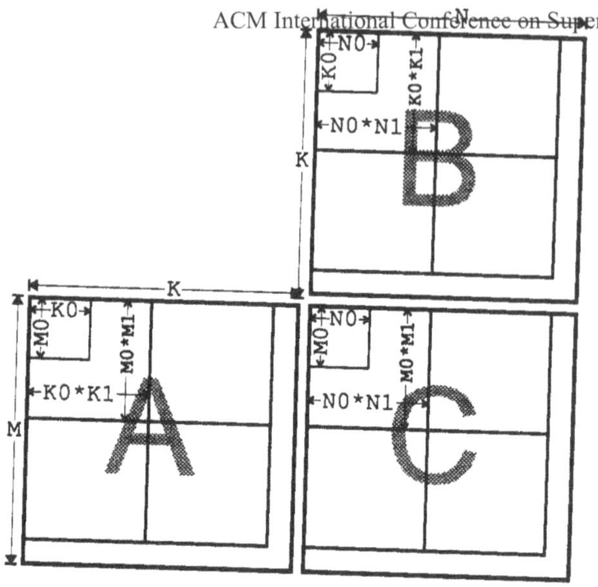

Figure 1: Matrix blocking parameters

the caller when necessary rather than unnecessarily by the callee. We create a full BLAS-compatible GEMM, by generating all required matrix multiply variants and linking with our GEMM-compatible interface that includes error checking.

mm_gen produces a cache-blocked matrix multiply [GL89, LRW91, MS95], restructuring the algorithm for unit stride, and reducing the number of cache misses and unnecessary loads and stores. Under control of command line parameters, **mm_gen** can produce blocking code for any number of levels of memory hierarchy, including register, L1 cache, TLB, L2 cache, and so on. **mm_gen**'s code can also perform copy optimization [LRW91], optionally with a different accumulator precision. The latest version can also generate the innermost loop with various forms of software pipelining.

A typical invocation of **mm_gen** is:

```
mm_gen -cb M0 K0 N0 [ -cb M1 K1 N1 ] ...
```

where the register blocking is M_0, K_0, N_0, the L1-cache blocking is M_1, K_1, N_1, etc. The parameters M_0, K_0, and N_0 are specified in units of matrix elements, i.e., single, double, or extended precision floating-point numbers, M_1, K_1, N_1 are specified in units of register blocks, M_2, K_2, and K_2 are in units of L1 cache blocks, and so on. For a particular cache level, say i, the code accumulates into a C destination block of size $M_i \times N_i$ units and uses A source blocks of size $M_i \times K_i$ units and B source blocks of size $K_i \times N_i$ units (see Figure 1).

3.1 Matrix Multiply Code

In this section, we examine the code produced by **mm_gen** for the operation `C = C + A*B` where A (respectively B, C) is an M×K (respectively K×N, M×N) matrix. Figure 2 lists the L1 cache blocking core code comprising the 3 nested loops, M, N, and K. **mm_gen** does not vary the loop permutation [MS95, LRW91] because the resulting gains in locality are subsumed by the method described below.

The outer M loop in Figure 2 maintains pointers **c0** and **a0** to rows of register blocks in the A and C matrices. It also maintains end pointers (**ap0_endp** and **cp0_endp**) used for loop termination. The middle N loop maintains a pointer **b0** to columns of register blocks in the B matrix, and maintains a pointer **cp0** to the current C destination register block. The N loop also maintains separate pointers (**ap0_0** through **ap0_1**) to successive rows of the current A source block. It also initializes a pointer **bp0** to the current B source block. We assume local variables can be held in registers, so our code uses many pointers to minimize both memory references and integer multiplies.

The K loop iterates over source matrix blocks and accumulates into the same $M_0 \times N_0$ destination block. We assume that the floating-point registers can hold a $M_0 \times N_0$ accumulator block, so this block is loaded once before the K loop begins and stored after it ends. The K loop updates the set of pointers to the A source block, one of which is used for loop termination.

The parameter K_0 controls the extent of inner loop unrolling as can be seen in Figure 2. The unrolled core loop performs K_0 outer products accumulating into the C destination block. We code the outer products by loading one row of the B block, one element of the A block, then performing N_0 multiply-accumulates. The C code uses $N_0 + M_0$ memory references per $2N_0M_0$ floating-point operations in the inner K loop, while holding $M_0N_0 + N_0 + 1$ values in local variables. While the intent is that these local variables map to registers, the compiler is free to reorder all of the independent loads and multiply-accumulates to trade increased memory references for reduced register usage. The compiler also requires additional registers to name intermediate results propagating through machine pipelines.

The code we have so far described is valid only when M, K, and N are integer multiples of M_0, K_0, and N_0 respectively. In the general case, **mm_gen** also includes code that operates on power-of-two sized fringe strips, i.e., 2^0 through $2^{\lfloor \log_2 L \rfloor}$ where L is M_0, K_0, or N_0. We can therefore manage any fringe size from 1 to L−1 by executing an appropriate combination of fringe code. The resulting code size growth is logarithmic in the register blocking (i.e., $O(\log(M_0)\log(K_0)\log(N_0))$) yet maintains good performance. To reduce the demands on the instruction cache, we arrange the code into several independent sections, the first handling the matrix core and the remainder handling the fringes.

The latest version of the generator can optionally produce code with a software-pipelined inner loop. Each outer product consists of a load, a multiply, and an accumulate section. We group these sections into three software pipelined code variants: two two-stage pipes with stages [load-multiply, accumulate] and [load, multiply-accumulate], and a three-stage pipe with stages [load, multiply, accumulate]. Recent results show that this software pipelining can result in an appreciable speedup.

Because of the separation between matrix dimension and matrix stride, we can implement higher levels of cache blocking as calls to lower level routines with appropriately sized sub-matrices.

```
mul_mfmf_mf(const int M,const int K,const int N,
const float*const A,const float*const B,float*const C,
const int Astride,const int Bstride,const int Cstride)
{
   const float *a,*b; float *c;
   const float *ap_0,*ap_1; const float *bp; float *cp;
   const int A_sbs_stride = Astride*2;
   const int C_sbs_stride = Cstride*2;
   const int k_marg_el = K & 1;
   const int k_norm = K - k_marg_el;
   const int m_marg_el = M & 1;
   const int m_norm = M - m_marg_el;
   const int n_marg_el = N & 1;
   const int n_norm = N - n_marg_el;
   float *const c_endp = C+m_norm*Cstride;
   register float c0_0,c0_1,c1_0,c1_1;
   c=C;a=A;
   do { /* M loop */
      const float* const ap_endp = a + k_norm;
      float* const cp_endp = c + n_norm;
      const float* const apc_1 = a + Astride;
      b=B;cp=c;
      do {  /* N loop */
         register float _b0,_b1;
         register float _a0,_a1;
         float *_cp;
         ap_0=a;ap_1=apc_1;bp=b;
         _cp=cp;c0_0=_cp[0];c0_1=_cp[1];
         _cp+=Cstride;c1_0=_cp[0];c1_1=_cp[1];
         do { /* K loop */
            _b0 = bp[0]; _b1 = bp[1];
            bp += Bstride; _a0 = ap_0[0];
            c0_0 += _a0*_b0; c0_1 += _a0*_b1;
            _a1 = ap_1[0];
            c1_0 += _a1*_b0; c1_1 += _a1*_b1;

            _b0 = bp[0]; _b1 = bp[1];
            bp += Bstride; _a0 = ap_0[1];
            c0_0 += _a0*_b0; c0_1 += _a0*_b1;
            _a1 = ap_1[1];
            c1_0 += _a1*_b0; c1_1 += _a1*_b1;

            ap_0+=2;ap_1+=2;
         } while (ap_0!=ap_endp);
         _cp=cp;_cp[0]=c0_0;_cp[1]=c0_1;
         _cp+=Cstride;_cp[0]=c1_0;_cp[1]=c1_1;
         b+=2;cp+=2;
      } while (cp!=cp_endp);
      c+=C_sbs_stride;a+=A_sbs_stride;
   } while (c!=c_endp);
}
```

Figure 2: $M_0 = 2$, $K_0 = 2$, $N_0 = 2$ matrix multiply L1 routine for $M \in \{2m : m \geq 1\}, K \in \{2k : k \geq 1\}, N \in \{2n : n \geq 1\}$. Within the K-loop is our fully-unrolled $2 \times 2 \times 2$ core matrix multiply. The code is not unlike the register code in [CFH95]. In our terminology, the leading dimensions LDA, LDB, and LDC are called `Astride`, `Bstride`, and `Cstride` respectively. The four local variables `c0_0` through `c1_1` hold a complete C destination block. Variables `ap_0` and `ap_1` point to successive rows of the A source matrix block, and variable `bp` points to the first row of the B source matrix block. Elements in A and B are accessed using constant offsets from the appropriate pointers.

4 Matrix Multiply Search Scripts

The search script take parameters describing the machine architecture, including the number of integer and floating-point registers and the sizes of each level of cache. For each combination of generator parameters and compilation options, the matrix multiply search script calls the generator, compiles the resulting routine, links it with timing code, and benchmarks the resulting executable.

To produce a complete BLAS GEMM routine, we find separate parameters for each of the three cases $A \times B$, $A^T \times B$, and $A \times B^T$ ($A^T \times B^T$ has code identical to $A \times B$). For each case, we first find the best register (or L0) parameters for in-L1-cache matrices, then find the best L1 parameters for in-L2-cache matrices, etc. While this strategy is not guaranteed to find the best L0 core for out-of-L1-cache matrices, the resulting cores have performed well in practice.

4.1 Register (L0) Parameter Search

The register block search evaluates all combinations of M_0 and N_0 where $1 \leq M_0 N_0 \leq \mathrm{NR}$ and where NR is the number of machine floating-point registers. We search the above for $1 \leq K_0 \leq K_0^{max}$ where $K_0^{max} = 20$ but is adjustable. Empirically, $K_0^{max} > 20$ has never shown appreciable benefit.

Our initial strategy [BAD+96] benchmarked a set of square matrices that fit in L1 cache. We then chose the L0 parameters that achieved the highest performance. While this approach gave good performance, the searches were time consuming.

We noted that that the majority of the computation, especially for larger matrices, is performed by the core $M_0 \times K_0 \times N_0$ register blocked code. Our newer search strategy, therefore, produces code containing only the core, which decreases compile time, and for each L0 parameter set, we benchmark only a single matrix multiply with size $M = M_0$, $N = N_0$, and $K = kK_0$. The parameter k is chosen such that the three matrices are no larger than L1 cache (we call this a "fat" dot-product). While this case ignores the cost of the M- and N-loop overhead, we have so far found this approach to produce comparable quality code in much less time than the previous strategy (e.g., 5 hours vs. 24 hours on the SGI Indigo R4K).

We initially thought the order in which we searched the L0 parameter space could have an effect on search time and evaluated orders such as i-j-k, random, best-first, and simulated annealing. We found, however, that the added search complexity outweighed any benefit so we settled on a random strategy.

4.2 Cache Block Search

We perform the L1 cache blocking search after the best register blocking is known. We would like to make the L1 blocks large to increase data reuse but larger L1 blocks increase the probability of cache conflicts [LRW91]. Tradeoffs between M- and N- loop overheads, memory access patterns, and TLB structure also affect the best L1 size. We currently perform a relatively simple search of the L1 parameter space. For the D×D square case, we search the neighborhood centered at $3D^2 = L1$ where $L1$ is the L1 cache size in elements. We set M_1 to the values $\lfloor \phi D/M_0 \rfloor$ where $\phi \in \{0.25, 0.5, 1.0, 1.5, 2.0\}$ and $D = \sqrt{L1/3}$. K_1 and N_1 are set similarly. We benchmark the resulting 125 combinations with matrix sizes that either fit in L2 cache, or are within some upper bound if no L2 cache exists. The L2 cache blocking search, when necessary, is performed in a similar way.

5 Results

We ran the search scripts to find the best register and L1 cache blocking parameters for six commercial workstation systems. These systems have different instruction set architectures and widely varying microarchitectures and memory hierarchies. The results are summarized in Table 1.

The SGI R8K and R10K searches used the newer version of the code generator and search scripts, while other results were obtained with the alpha release. Figures 3–6 plot the performance of the resulting routines for all square matrices $M = K = N = D$, where D runs over powers of 2 and 3, multiples of 10, and primes, up to a maximum of 300. We compare with the performance of a vendor-optimized BLAS GEMM where available. In each case, PHiPAC yields a substantial fraction of peak performance and is competitive with vendor BLAS. Due to limited availability, we could only perform an incomplete search on the R8K and R10K, and so these are preliminary performance numbers. There is also potential for improvement on the other machines when we rerun with the newer version. For completeness, we also show the poor performance obtained when compiling a simple three nested loop version of GEMM with FORTRAN or C optimizing compilers.

The PHiPAC methodology can also improve performance even if there is no scope for memory blocking. In Figure 9 we plot the performance of a dot product code generated using PHiPAC techniques. Although the parameters used were obtained using a short manual search, we can see that we are competitive with the assembly-coded SGI BLAS SDOT.

In some of the plots, we see that PHiPAC routines suffer from cache conflicts. Our measurements exaggerate this effect by including all power-of-2 sized matrices, and by allocating all regions contiguously in memory. For matrix multiply, we can reduce cache conflicts by copying to contiguous memory when pathological strides are encountered [LRW91]. Unfortunately, this approach does not help dot product. One drawback of the PHiPAC approach is that we can not control the order compilers schedule independent loads. We've occasionally found that exchanging two loads in the assembly output for dot product can halve the number of cache misses where conflicts occur, without otherwise impacting performance.

6 Status, Availability, and Future Work

This paper has demonstrated our ability to write portable, high performance ANSI C code for matrix multiply using parameterized code generators and a timing-driven search strategy.

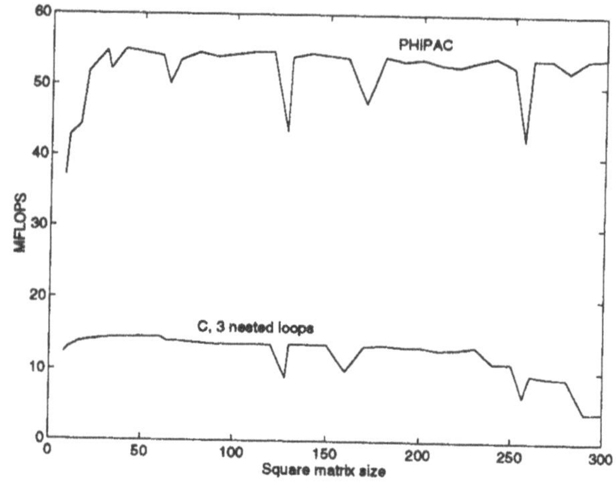

Figure 3: Performance of single precision matrix multiply on a Sparcstation-20/61.

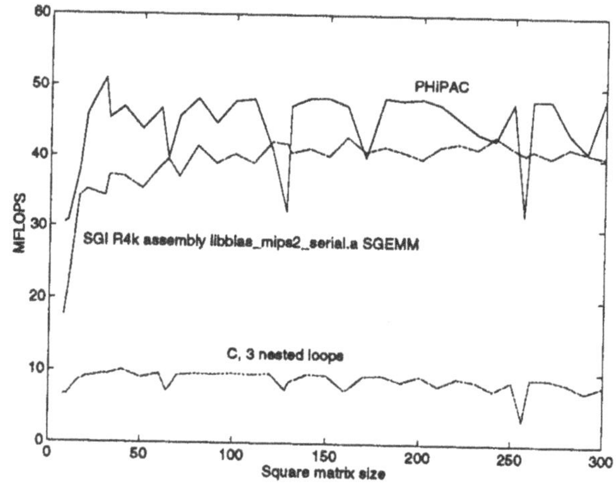

Figure 4: Performance of single precision matrix multiply on a 100 MHz SGI Indigo R4K. We show the SGEMM from SGI's `libblas_mips2_serial.a` library.

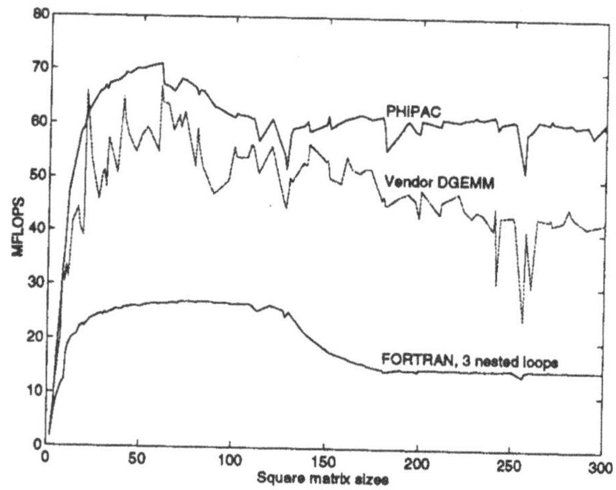

Figure 5: Performance of double precision matrix multiply on a HP 712/80i. We show DGEMM from the `pa1.1` version of `libvec.a` in HP's compiler distribution.

	Sun Sparc-20/61	HP 712/80i	IBM RS/6000-590	SGI Indigo R4K	SGI Challenge	SGI Octane
Processor	SuperSPARC+	PA7100LC	RIOS-2	R4K	R8K	R10K
Frequency (MHz)	60	80	66.5	100	90	195
Max Instructions/cycle	3	2	6	1	4	4
Peak MFLOPS (32b/64b)	60/60	160/80	266/266	67/50	360/360	390/390
FP registers (32b/64b)	32/16	64/32	32/32	16/16	32/32	32/32
L1 Data cache (KB)	16	128	256	8	-	32
L2 Data cache (KB)	1024	-	-	1024	4096	1024
OS	SunOS 4.1.3	HP-UX 9.05	AIX 3.2	Irix 4.0.5H	IRIX6.2	IRIX6.4
C Compiler	Sun acc 2.0.1	HP c89 9.61	IBM xlc 1.3	SGI cc 3.10	SGI cc	SGI cc
Search results						
PHiPAC version	alpha	alpha	alpha	alpha	new	new
Precision	32b	64b	64b	32b	64b	64b
M_0,K_0,N_0	2,4,10	3,1,2	2,1,10	2,10,3	2,4,14	4,2,6
M_1,K_1,N_1	26,10,4	30,60,30	105,70,28	30,4,10	200,80,25	12,24,9
CFLAGS	-fast	-O	-O3 -qarch=pwr2	-O2 -mips2	-n32 -mips4 -O3	

Table 1: Workstation system details and results of matrix multiply parameter search.

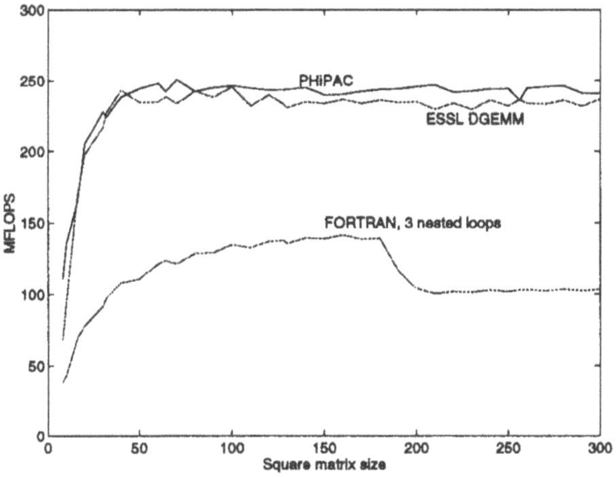

Figure 6: Performance of double precision matrix multiply on an IBM RS/6000-590. We show the DGEMM from IBM's POWER2-optimized ESSL library.

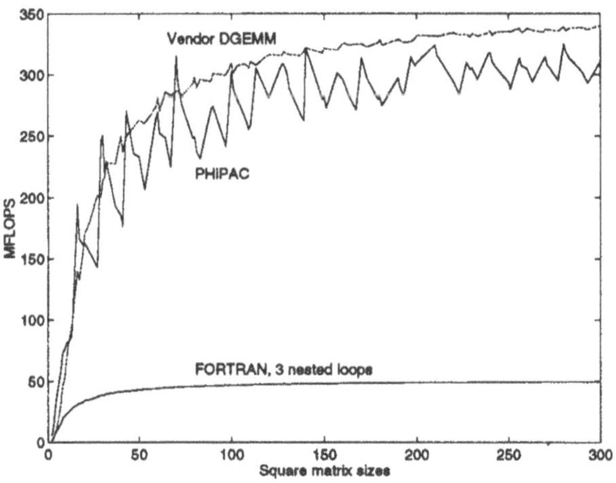

Figure 7: Preliminary performance of double precision matrix multiply on an SGI R8K Power Challenge. We show the DGEMM from SGI's R8K-optimized libblas.

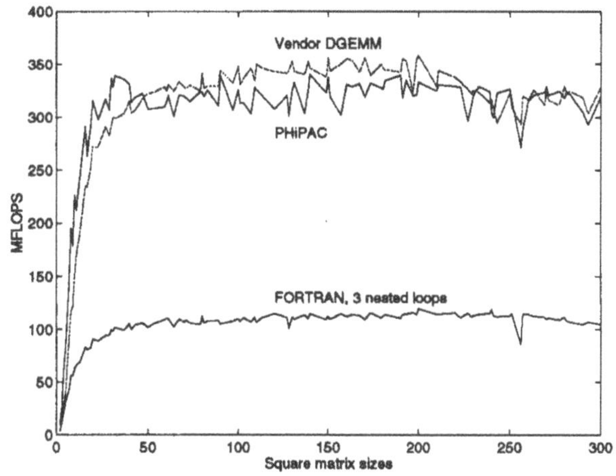

Figure 8: Preliminary performance of double precision matrix multiply on an SGI R10K Octane. We show the DGEMM from SGI's R10K-optimized libblas.

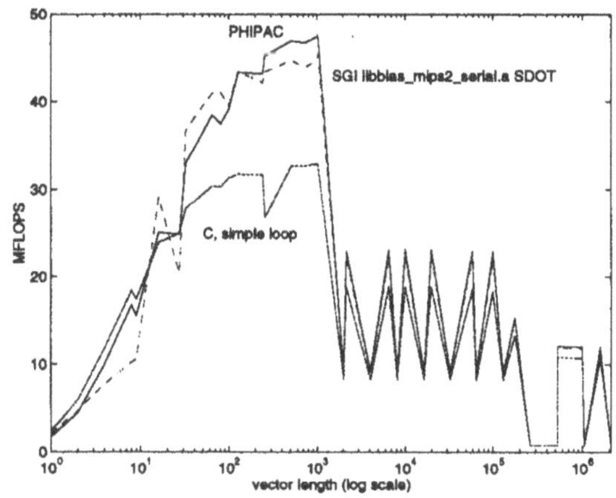

Figure 9: Performance of single precision unit-stride dot-product on a 100 MHz SGI R4K.

The PHiPAC alpha release contains the matrix multiply generator, the naive search scripts written in `perl`, and our timing libraries. We have created a Web site from which the alpha release is available and on which we plan to list blocking parameters for many systems [BAD+]. We are currently working on a better L1 blocking strategy and accompanying methods for search based on various criteria [LRW91]. The PHiPAC GEMM can be used with Bo Kågström's GEMM-based BLAS3 package [BLL93] and LAPACK [ABB+92].

We have also written parameterized generators for matrix-vector and vector-matrix multiply, dot product, AXPY, convolution, and outer-product, and further generators, such as for FFT, are planned.

We wish to thank Ed Rothberg of SGI for help obtaining the R8K and R10K performance plots. We also wish to thank Nelson Morgan who provided initial impetus for this project and Dominic Lam for work on the initial search scripts.

References

[ABB+92] E. Anderson, Z. Bai, C. Bischof, J. Demmel, J. Dongarra, J. Du Croz, A. Greenbaum, S. Hammarling, A. McKenney, S. Ostrouchov, and D. Sorensen. LAPACK users' guide, release 1.0. In *SIAM*, Philadelphia, 1992.

[ACF95] B. Alpern, L. Carter, and J. Ferrante. Space-limited procedures: A methodology for portable high-performance. In *International Working Conference on Massively Parallel Programming Models*, 1995.

[AGZ94] R. Agarwal, F. Gustavson, and M. Zubair. *IBM Engineering and Scientific Subroutine Library, Guide and Reference*, 1994. Available through IBM branch offices.

[BAD+] J. Bilmes, K. Asanović, J. Demmel, D. Lam, and C.W. Chin. The PHiPAC WWW home page. `http://www.icsi.berkeley.edu/~bilmes/phipac`.

[BAD+96] J. Bilmes, K. Asanović, J. Demmel, D. Lam, and C.W. Chin. PHiPAC: A portable, high-performance, ANSI C coding methodology and its application to matrix multiply. LAPACK working note 111, University of Tennessee, 1996.

[BLL93] B.Kågström, P. Ling, and C. Van Loan. Portable high performance GEMM-based level 3 BLAS. In R.F. Sincovec et al., editor, *Parallel Processing for Scientific Computing*, pages 339–346, Philadelphia, 1993. SIAM Publications.

[BLS91] D. H. Bailey, K. Lee, and H. D. Simon. Using Strassen's algorithm to accelerate the solution of linear systems. *J. Supercomputing*, 4:97–371, 1991.

[CDD+96] J. Choi, J. Demmel, I. Dhillon, J. Dongarra, S. Ostrouchov, A. Petitet, K. Stanley, D. Walker, and R.C. Whaley. ScaLAPAC: A portable linear algebra library for distributed memory computers - design issues and performance. LAPACK working note 95, University of Tennessee, 1996.

[CFH95] L. Carter, J. Ferrante, and S. Flynn Hummel. Hierarchical tiling for improved superscalar performance. In *International Parallel Processing Symposium*, April 1995.

[DCDH90] J. Dongarra, J. Du Croz, I. Duff, and S. Hammarling. A set of level 3 basic linear algebra subprograms. *ACM Trans. Math. Soft.*, 16(1):1–17, March 1990.

[DCHH88] J. Dongarra, J. Du Cros, S. Hammarling, and R.J. Hanson. An extended set of FORTRAN basic linear algebra subroutines. *ACM Trans. Math. Soft.*, 14:1–17, March 1988.

[GL89] G.H. Golub and C.F. Van Loan. *Matrix Computations.* Johns Hopkins University Press, 1989.

[KHM94] C. Kamath, R. Ho, and D.P. Manley. DXML: A high-performance scientific subroutine library. *Digital Technical Journal*, 6(3):44–56, Summer 1994.

[LHKK79] C. Lawson, R. Hanson, D. Kincaid, and F. Krogh. Basic linear algebra subprograms for FORTRAN usage. *ACM Trans. Math. Soft.*, 5:308–323, 1979.

[LRW91] M. S. Lam, E. E. Rothberg, and M. E. Wolf. The cache performance and optimizations of blocked algorithms. In *Proceedings of ASPLOS IV*, pages 63–74, April 1991.

[MS95] J.D. McCalpin and M. Smotherman. Automatic benchmark generation for cache optimization of matrix algorithms. In R. Geist and S. Junkins, editors, *Proceedings of the 33rd Annual Southeast Conference*, pages 195–204. ACM, March 1995.

[SMP+96] R. Saavedra, W. Mao, D. Park, J. Chame, and S. Moon. The combined effectiveness of unimodular transformations, tiling, and software prefetching. In *Proceedings of the 10th International Parallel Processing Symposium*, April 15–19 1996.

[WL91] M. E. Wolf and M. S. Lam. A data locality optimizing algorithm. In *Proceedings of the ACM SIGPLAN'91 Conference on Programming Language Design and Implementation*, pages 30–44, June 1991.

[Wol96] M. Wolfe. *High performance compilers for parallel computing.* Addison-Wesley, 1996.

Software Trace Cache *

Alex Ramírez Josep-L. Larriba-Pey Carlos Navarro Josep Torrellas†
Mateo Valero

Computer Architecture Department
Universitat Politècnica de Catalunya
Jordi Girona 1-3, Module D6
08034 Barcelona (Spain)
{aramirez,larri,cnavarro,mateo}@ac.upc.es

bstract

n this paper we address the important problem of instruc-on fetch for future wide issue superscalar processors. Our pproach focuses on understanding the interaction between oftware and hardware techniques targeting an increase in ne instruction fetch bandwidth. That is the objective, for stance, of the Hardware Trace Cache (HTC).

We design a profile based code reordering technique which rgets a maximization of the sequentiality of instructions, hile still trying to minimize instruction cache misses. We all our software approach, *Software Trace Cache (STC)*.

We evaluate our software approach, and then compare with the HTC and the combination of both techniques. ur results show that for large codes with few loops and eterministic execution sequences like databases and some PEC-INT codes, the STC offers similar, or better, results nan a HTC. Moreover, when combining the software and ardware approaches, we obtain encouraging results: the TC and a small HTC offer similar performance to a much rger HTC alone.

Introduction

nstruction fetch bandwidth may become a major limiting ctor for future aggressive wide-issue superscalars. Conse-uently, it is crucial to develop software and hardware tech-iques that interact to deliver multiple basic blocks to the rocessor every cycle.

Unfortunately, for many important codes, this is hard to o. For instance, database codes and several integer SPEC applications have frequent control flow transfers and high instruction-cache miss rates. These characteristics make supplying a high number of useful instructions a difficult task, even in the presence of aiding devices like the Hardware Trace Cache (HTC) [4, 12].

On the software side, it is possible to reorder the code in memory so that it is easier to supply useful instructions to the execution unit. Code reordering can target the elimination of cache conflicts [5, 6, 8, 7, 10, 13]. In addition, it can also map sequentially-executed basic blocks in consecutive memory positions [7, 10, 13]. Both aspects may increase the number of useful instructions fetched per access for future wide-issue superscalars.

In this paper, we focus on the interaction between hardware and software to provide a high instruction bandwidth. We start presenting a fully-automated, compile-time code reordering technique that focuses on maximizing the sequentiality of instructions, while still trying to minimize instruction cache misses. We call our technique *Software Trace Cache (STC)*.

We compare the results obtained with the STC to those obtained with a HTC alone and to the combination of both techniques. The results are obtained for the PostgreSQL database, an arcade game, and the SPEC'95 benchmark.

Our results show that for large codes with few loops and deterministic execution sequences like the Postgres95 database management system, the STC offers similar, or better, results than a HTC. Moreover, if we combine the STC and the HTC, we obtain very encouraging results. Specifically, the number of fetched instructions per cycle obtained with a combination of the STC and a small HTC is comparable to that of a HTC of double size alone. Finally, the STC can be useful even in combination with a large HTC due to the instruction cache miss rate reduction.

This paper is structured as follows: Section 2 describes the fetch mechanism and the HTC; Section 3 describes the STC technique; Section 4 characterizes the instruction reference stream for a variety of workloads; Section 5 uses simulations to evaluate various combinations of the STC and the HTC; Section 6 discusses related work; and in Section 7 we draw some final remarks.

2 The Fetch Mechanism

We simulate an aggressive sequential fetch unit similar to that described in [12]. As shown in Figure 1, our core fetch unit model is composed of an interleaved instruction cache (i-cache), a multiple branch predictor (BP), an in-

*This research has been supported by CICYT grant TIC-0511- (UPC authors), the Generalitat de Catalunya grants ACI 97- (Josep L. Larriba-Pey and Josep Torrellas) and 1998FI-00306-PTIND (Alex Ramírez), the Commission for Cultural, Educational d Scientific Exchange between the United States of America and pain (Josep L. Larriba-Pey, Josep Torrellas and Mateo Valero), SF grant MIP-9619351 (Josep Torrellas) and CEPBA. Alex Ramírez ants to thank all his fellow PBC's for their time and efforts. The thors want to thank Xavi Serrano for all his help setting up and alyzing PostgreSQL.

†University of Illinois at Urbana Champaign, USA. orrella@cs.uiuc.edu)

terleaved branch target buffer (BTB) and a return address stack (RAS). This fetch unit is designed to fetch as many contiguous instructions as possible. The limits are posed by the width of the data path and the branch predictor throughput. In this work, we will assume a limit of 16 instructions and 3 branches per cycle.

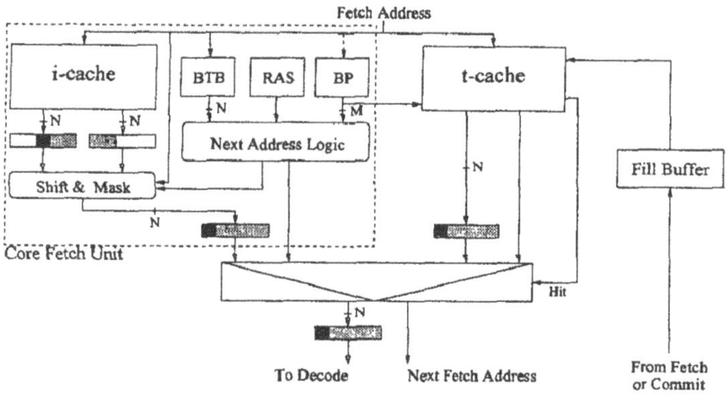

Figure 1: Fetch unit model used for simulation, complete with the Hardware Trace Cache mechanism. In our simulations N=16 and M=3.

Two consecutive i-cache lines are accessed per cycle, allowing us to fetch sequential code crossing the cache line boundary. The BTB is accessed in parallel with the i-cache, and is used to predict the address of indirect jumps and subroutine calls. The return address of subroutines can be accurately predicted using the RAS. It is assumed that instructions will be pre-decoded, allowing branches and other control transfers to be detected. The target of PC-relative branches is calculated, not obtained from the BTB. Using the outputs from the BP, the BTB and the information regarding which instructions represent control transfers, we obtain an instruction mask to select the valid instructions from the fetched i-cache lines, and generate the fetch address for the next cycle.

We do not allow our fetch unit to stop at indirect jumps if those do not break the execution sequence. We add a *breaking* bit to the BTB, which informs the fetch unit when the predicted jump address will break the sequence.

Summarizing, instruction fetch stops in one of these conditions:

- 16 instructions are fetched
- 3 branches are fetched
- A branch is predicted taken
- An indirect jump is predicted to break the execution sequence
- A system call is fetched
- On any misprediction or BTB miss

For high branch prediction accuracy we use a 4KB GAg correlated branch predictor, with 14-bit history length, extended to allow multiple branches to be predicted in a single cycle, a 256-entry BTB enhanced with the *breaking* bit, and a 256-entry RAS.

We also simulated our core fetch unit in conjunction with the basic trace cache model described in [12]. The complete fetch unit, with a trace cache (t-cache), is what we call the Hardware Trace Cache (HTC). The fill buffer reads instructions from either the fetch unit (speculative trace co struction) or from the commit stage (non-speculative tra construction) and stores them in a special purpose buff When a trace is completed, it is stored in the t-cache conjunction with the branch outcomes that led to that struction sequence. If the same leading instruction and t same branch outcomes are encountered in the future, trace is fed directly from the t-cache to the decode ur The fill buffer stops building a trace on the same conditio as the core fetch unit, except for the case of sequence brea as the t-cache is able to store non-contiguous instructions contiguous memory positions.

3 The Software Trace Cache

The number of useful instructions per cycle provided to processor is broadly determined by three factors: bra prediction accuracy, instruction cache miss rate and the ecution of non-contiguous basic blocks. To deal with last two problems, we propose a code reordering technic which uses the whole memory space as a *Software Tr Cache* to store the most popular sequences of basic bloc In order to avoid sequence breaks we will reorder the ba blocks in a program to change taken branches to non-tal ones, moving unused basic blocks out of the execution pa and inlining basic blocks from the most popular functio To reduce the instruction cache miss rate we map the m popular traces in a reserved area of the i-cache.

Our algorithm is based on profile information. T means that the results obtained will depend on the repres tativity of the training inputs. The most popular execut paths for a given input set do not need to be related to execution paths of a different input set.

Running the training set on each benchmark, we obt a directed graph of basic blocks with weighted edges. edge connects two basic blocks p and q, if q is executed af p. The weight of an edge $W(pq)$ is equal to the total numb of times q has been executed after p. The weight of a ba block $W(p)$ can be obtained by adding the weight of outgoing edges. The branch probability of an edge $B(pq)$ obtained as $W(pq)/W(p)$. All unexecuted basic blocks pruned from the graph.

Next we describe how we select the *seeds* or starti basic blocks for our code sequences, the algorithm wh builds the basic block traces from the selected seeds, and mapping algorithm used to allocate these traces minimizi instruction cache misses.

3.1 Seed selection

We obtain an ordered list of seeds by sorting the entry poi of all functions in decreasing frequency of execution. T tries to expose the maximum temporal locality, as the fi traces built will start on the most frequently referenced fu tions.

It is possible to obtain better results with a seed sel tion based on the internal structure of the code, as we sh in [11]. However, access to the source code of applicatio is not always granted, and gaining such deep understand of the code is a time consuming task, which may not of an improvement large enough to compensate for the effo

3.2 Trace building

Using the weighted graph obtained running the training s and starting from the selected seeds, we implement a gree gorithm to build our basic block traces targeting an in- ·ease in the code sequentiality. Given a basic block, the al- ›rithm follows the most frequently executed path out of it. his implies visiting a subroutine called by the basic block, : following the control transfer with the highest probability ; being used. All the other valid transitions from the basic lock are noted for future examination.

For this algorithm we use two parameters called *Exec 'hreshold*, and *Branch Threshold*. The trace building algo- thm stops when all the successor basic blocks have been isited or have a weight lower than the Exec Threshold, or ll the outgoing arcs have a branch probability less than the ranch Threshold. In that case, we start again from the ext acceptable transition, as we noted before, building sec- ndary execution paths for the same seed. Once all basic locks reachable from the given seed have been included in ıe main or secondary sequences, we proceed to the next ›ed.

Figure 2.a shows an example of the weighted graph and igure 2.b shows the resulting sequences. We use an Exec- 'hresh of 4 and a BranchThresh of 0.4. Starting from seed .1 and following the most likely outgoing edge from each ba- c block we build the sequence $A1 \rightarrow A8$ (Figure 2.b). The ·ansitions to $B1$ and $C5$ are discarded due to the Branch 'hreshold. We noted that the transition from $A3$ to $A5$ is valid transition, so we start a secondary trace with $A5$, ut all its successors have been already visited, so the se- uence ends there. We do not start a secondary trace from .6 because it has a weight lower than the Exec Threshold.

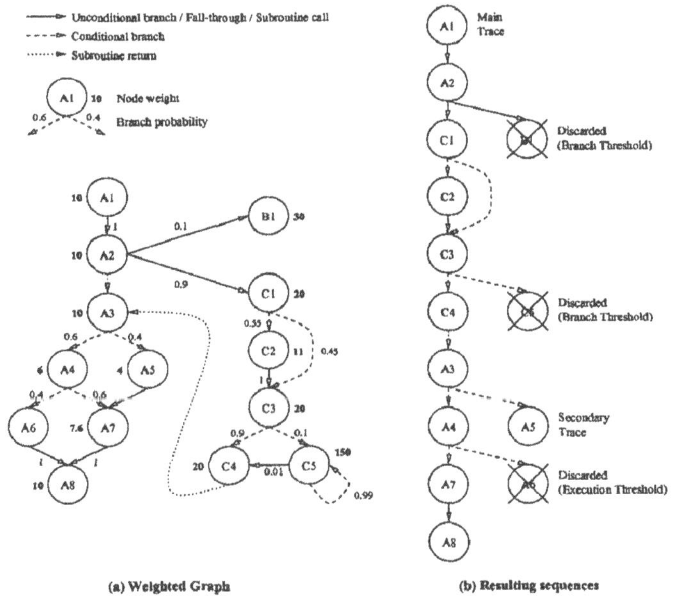

Figure 2: Trace building example.

:ode replication

n order to increase code sequentiality, we introduce a lim- :ed form of code replication in out method. We allow the ıain execution path of each subroutine to be replicated at ll call points.

We introduce two new threshold values, the *ExecRep* nd *BranchRep* Thresholds to control the amount of code re are replicating. A sequence will be replicated if the call ›robability passes the BranchRep threshold and the starting ›asic block for that sequence passes the ExecRep Threshold.

In the example from Figure 2, if we found a new call to $C1$ from, say $A7$, we would replicate the sequence $C1 \rightarrow C4$ and include it between $A7$ and $A8$ in the main execution path.

Threshold selection

We have a loop in our algorithm that repeatedly selects a set of values for the four thresholds and generates the resulting traces for each pass. The basic blocks included in previous passes are pruned from the newly formed traces, further limiting the amount of code replicated in each pass. By iteratively selecting less and less restrictive values for the thresholds, we build our traces grouped in passes of decreasing frequency of execution.

The values selected for the Exec and Branch threshold will determine the number of basic blocks included in each pass of the algorithm, generating larger or smaller groups of traces. The target is to pack in a given pass those traces with a similar popularity, while keeping the total number of instructions under control. For this paper we selected our Exec Threshold so that each pass contained approximately 4KB of not replicated code. To maximize the effect of the code replication we used the least restrictive ExecRep and BranchRep thresholds.

3.3 Trace mapping

As shown in Figure 3, we map our code sequences in decreasing order of popularity, concentrating the most likely used code in the first memory pages and mapping popular sequences close to other equally popular ones, reducing conflict misses among them. Also, the most popular sequences will map to a reserved area of the cache, leaving gaps to create a Conflict Free Area (CFA), shielding the most popular traces from interference with any other code.

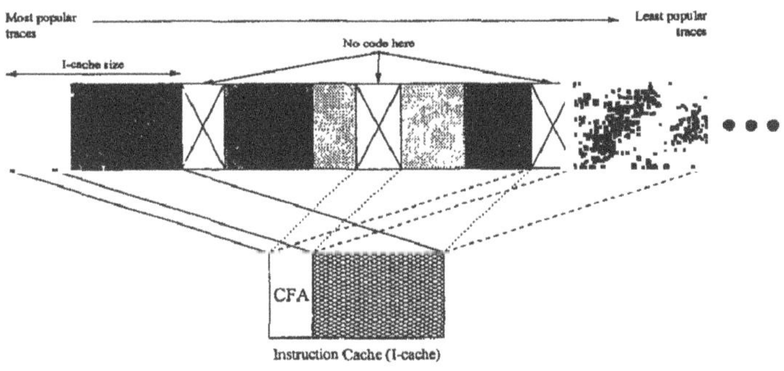

Figure 3: Trace mapping for a direct mapped instruction cache.

The same mapping algorithm can be applied to set associative cache with minor modifications. A complete study of the different factors which determine the instruction cache miss reduction offered by this mapping of code sequences, and a comparison with other code mapping algorithms for the PostgreSQL database can be found in [11].

4 Locality Study

The objective of the STC is to build at compile time the most popular traces that are built at run time by the HTC. Also, the STC targets a minimization of the i-cache miss rate at the same time. We analyze the instruction reference stream for a wide set of workloads, characterizing instruction locality and execution path determinism, which affect the performance offered by the STC. With this information we intend to predict the performance increase we can expect when using the STC for each workload. The reference locality will affect the i-cache miss rate reduction offered by our technique, and the basic block size, the number of loops and the determinism of program execution will influence the increase in code sequentiality accomplished by the basic block reordering.

4.1 Workloads

We have used four classes of workloads, trying to cover a wide range of applications: common integer and floating point codes, commercial workloads, and arcade games.

Recent studies have shown that commercial workloads do not behave like common integer codes, like the SPEC-INT set. Also, it is well known that floating point codes have a different behavior than integer codes. Our workloads include the whole SPEC 95 benchmarks. We use the PostgreSQL 6.3.2 database management system as our commercial workload and XBlast 2.2, an arcade game, as an example of a little studied workload.

All the executions and simulations needed to develop this work, have been done using the Alpha 21164 processor, DEC ATOM, and trace driven simulation. We used different input sets to obtain the profile information and to obtain the simulation results to ensure that the improvements were valid for inputs other than the profiled ones. All benchmarks were run to completion for both training and simulation.

4.2 Code Analysis

Examining the profile information obtained running the training set, we classify the workloads attending to those characteristics that affect the performance of our technique: code locality, the amount of loops, conditional branches and subroutine calls, the basic block size and the number of sequence breaks.

To examine code locality, we determine the number of static instructions needed to gather 75, 90 and 99% of the dynamic instruction references as shown in Table 1. The total code size for each benchmark and the CFA size we selected for 32 and 64KB instruction caches are also shown in Table 1. We observe that some codes have very large working sets, like *applu*, *apsi*, *fpppp*, *gcc* and *postgres* which do not fit even in 32KB caches. Furthermore, some codes exhibit very little temporal locality, like *gcc*, which can not fit 75% of the references in a 32KB cache.

We select the CFA size so that it gathers between 75 and 90% of the instruction references, while still leaving reasonable space for the rest of the code. Obviously, larger caches allow a larger CFA and more code replication. For example, *xblast* concentrates 90% of the dynamic references in 2362 instructions (9448 bytes) which almost fit in an 8KB CFA, which we will use for a 32KB instruction cache, but for a 64KB cache we will allow the CFA to grow to 16KB.

Next, we examine the code sequentiality for the original layout. We observe that all floating point benchmarks have very large basic blocks (35 instructions average), leading to large code sequences (57 consecutive instructions average). Meanwhile, the average sequence length for the integer benchmarks is usually under 12 instructions, as less than 2 consecutive basic blocks are executed, and the typical basic block size is around 5–7 instructions.

Benchmark	Dynamic references			Code	CFA size	
	75%	90%	99%	size	32KB	64K
101.tomcatv	223	308	1328	108237	8	8
102.swim	148	232	763	110350	4	4
103.su2cor	979	1839	4197	129741	8	1
104.hydro2d	1223	1977	5371	125946	8	1
107.mgrid	147	218	1029	112421	4	4
110.applu	2407	5060	10509	132803	16	2
125.turb3d	1065	1771	2828	121181	8	8
141.apsi	3099	5694	9883	156479	16	2
145.fpppp	8985	8985	9879	124970	8	3
146.wave5	1116	1919	5506	154987	8	2
124.m88ksim	458	1006	2863	51341	8	1
126.gcc	9595	22098	57878	349382	8	1
129.compress	243	338	525	21991	4	8
130.li	325	563	1365	38126	8	8
132.ijpeg	862	1489	3271	67646	8	1
134.perl	987	1582	3006	108227	8	1
147.vortex	751	1486	5128	172690	8	2
postgres	2716	5221	11748	374399	16	1
xblast	1100	2362	6326	430664	8	1

Table 1: Number of static instructions needed to accumula 75, 90 and 99% of the dynamic references, and the total co size, including unreferenced instructions. Selected CFA si for 32 and 64KB instruction caches.

Finally, we examined a classification of the dynamic ba blocks executed by each benchmark. The different types basic block considered are shown in Table 2. The percenta of basic blocks of each type executed is shown in Table The last two columns show the percentage of branch a loop basic blocks which behave in a fixed way (FB,FL), th is, they are always taken or always not taken. A low propo tion of fixed loop branches means that each loop execut few iterations (less than 20).

BB Type	Description	Target
F	Fall-through	Next instruction
J	Unconditional branches	PC relative
j	Unconditional branches	Indirect
B	Conditional branches	PC relative
L	Loop branches	PC relative
S	Subroutine call	PC relative
s	Subroutine call	Indirect
R	Subroutine returns	Indirect

Table 2: Basic block types considered.

By changing the order of the basic blocks in a progra we can reduce the number of unconditional branches, ar change taken conditional branches for not taken ones. Als by inlining the most popular functions we can eliminate su routine calls and returns, and increment the number of s quentially executed instructions. Note that the number sequence breaks due to loop branches and unpredictable co ditional branches does not depend on the organization of t code.

We consider the indirect jumps in a separate way b cause they can not be eliminated, as the target address unknown, and may jump to an unexpected address. Ho ever, we can reorder the code so that the most freque target address does not break the execution sequence.

To reduce the number of loops, compiler optimizatio like loop unrolling can be used, but it is not yet includ in our work. Consequently, the STC as it is now will off little advantage to codes with lots of loops and few fix conditional branches.

Also, codes with few subroutine calls will not benefit ›m the fact that the STC builds its execution sequences ›ssing procedure calls.

The number of predictable basic block transitions is de- rmined by fall-through basic blocks, PC-relative uncondi- nal branches, conditional branches with a fixed behavior .d subroutine calls. The percentage of fall-through basic ocks is around 10–20% for most codes, so STC perfor- ance will be determined by the rest of the basic block asses, mainly by the percentage of loop basic blocks.

With this criteria, we expect *postgres*, with only a 3.4% loop basic blocks, 12.8% of subroutine calls and 43% of nditional branches (76.2% of which behave in a fixed way) be the one which will benefit the most from the STC. On e other hand, 32% of the basic blocks executed by *ijpeg* .d with a loop branch, and barely 30% of its conditional anches behave in a fixed way, which makes it difficult to large the execution sequences. Among the FP codes, *apsi* oks as the best candidate, with a large proportion of fixed nditional branches and few loops but few subroutine calls.

Simulation results

fter selecting an appropriate CFA size for each bench- ark, we measured the increase in the number of instruc- ›ns executed between two sequence breaks obtained with e STC. Table 4 shows the percentage of basic block tran- ;ions which break the sequence, and the average number consecutive instructions executed for each benchmark for ›th the original code and our proposed layout, measured .nning the Test set.

The number of consecutive instructions executed repre- nts the performance limit of a sequential fetch unit. Even we were not limited by the bus width, the branch predic- r throughput, and branch mispredictions, we would still limited by taken branches. Table 4 shows how the STC nproves this performance limit.

3enchmark	Average BB size	Original		Reordered	
		%breaks	Seq len.	%breaks	Seq len.
omcatv	44.0	80	55.2	72	61.4
wim	48.7	99	49.2	99	49.1
u2cor	19.8	52	37.7	49	40.1
ydro2d	14.9	69	21.6	53	28.3
ngrid	62.0	89	70.0	90	68.8
pplu	23.4	50	46.5	58	40.7
urb3d	21.9	47	46.7	36	60.6
psi	26.3	55	48.0	44	59.4
pppp	69.1	43	162.5	40	171.6
vave5	24.6	62	39.5	61	40.4
Average	35.5	65	57.7	60	62.0
n88ksim	4.82	61	7.9	27	17.8
cc	5.33	55	9.8	40	13.4
ompress	6.77	58	11.7	62	10.9
i	4.20	49	8.5	37	11.2
jpeg	16.7	68	24.4	65	25.9
erl	5.36	54	10.0	38	13.9
ortex	4.76	55	8.7	27	17.6
Average	6.85	57	11.6	42	15.8
ostgres	4.58	51	9.0	25	18.3
blast	5.25	62	8.4	27	19.5

ıble 4: Percentage of basic block transitions and average ımber of consecutive instructions executed for the original ıd the reordered code. The average BB size is the same r both code layouts.

As expected, the FP benchmarks barely reduce the per- centage of sequence breaks. The best results are obtained by *hydro2d* and *apsi*, with reductions between 20–25%, which translate to sequence length increases of 24–31%. This was to be expected due to the reduced proportion of loops executed. On the other hand, *mgrid* actually increased the percentage of sequence breaking BB transitions from 89% to 90%. It is the FP benchmark with a higher proportion of loop basic blocks executed.

For the integer codes, we obtain sequence length increases above 100% for *m88ksim*, *vortex*, *postgres* and *xblast*. Meanwhile, *ijpeg* did not experience any noticeable improvement. This roughly corresponds to what we expected from Section 4.

In general terms, most integer codes experience significant reductions in the percentage of sequence breaking BB transitions. After reordering, most codes execute 2–3 consecutive basic blocks, raising the average performance limit to 15.8 instructions.

5.1 Fetch unit simulation

Table 5 shows simulation results for the fetch unit described in Section 2, using a 32KB instruction cache (i-cache). We simulated both code layouts on the core fetch unit, and in combination with trace caches (t-cache) of 16 and 32KB. The code layout is either the original code (Base), or the optimized layout corresponding to a CFA of xKB (CFA_x).

We present the number of Fetched Instructions per Access (FIPA) as three separate results, the average number of instructions the core fetch unit (i-cache) provides, the average number of instructions the t-cache provides, and the average global performance. If no t-cache is present, the core fetch unit is the same as the global performance.

Also, separate i-cache and t-cache miss rates are presented in terms of misses per line access. There are two i-cache line accesses and one t-cache line access for each fetch unit access.

We also present the branch misprediction rate.

The final performance metric is the number of Fetched Instructions per Cycle (FIPC). The FIPC was obtained dividing the FIPA for an estimated number of cycles per access (CPA). Instruction cache misses cause the fetch engine to stall, increasing the CPA, and branch mispredictions cause the fetch unit to fetch instructions from the wrong execution path, effectively wasting fetch cycles.

We used a fixed number of cycles for each i-cache miss, and assumed that if both i-cache lines missed, they could be served simultaneously. We also assumed an average number of penalty cycles for each branch misprediction. As i-cache miss penalties we used 3 and 6 cycles, and branch misprediction penalties of 4, 8 and 12 cycles, as it will depend on the execution core of the processor.

Software Trace Cache

The main effects of the STC are an increase in the FIPA provided by the core fetch unit and a reduction of the i-cache miss rate. Some codes show large improvements in one or both numbers, while others seem unaffected. We found some unexpected side effects on the branch prediction accuracy.

For example, reordering the code for *postgres* increases the FIPA for the core fetch unit from 7.5 to 10.3 instructions. These 10.3 instructions per access are still far away from the 18.3 shown in Table 4, but that is a performance limit. Here we are limited by the bus width and the branch predictor throughput and accuracy, not only by taken branches.

Benchmark	Basic Block Type								Fixed branches	
	F	J	j	B	L	S	s	R	FB	FL
101.tomcatv	3.3	4.1	3.1	28.2	59.0	0.2	1.0	1.2	92.0	49.3
102.swim	7.1	5.9	2.0	19.4	57.5	0.0	3.9	3.9	54.7	100.0
103.su2cor	11.8	5.9	2.0	44.4	25.3	0.1	5.2	5.3	65.9	92.4
104.hydro2d	9.8	1.6	0.6	46.3	39.1	0.1	1.3	1.3	66.5	88.1
107.mgrid	5.2	0.1	0.1	13.2	81.1	0.0	0.1	0.1	81.1	0.0
110.applu	11.1	0.0	0.0	43.3	45.4	0.0	0.0	0.0	58.8	13.0
125.turb3d	11.8	6.4	0.4	46.9	29.3	2.2	0.4	2.6	81.5	14.8
141.apsi	17.8	2.9	0.0	44.7	23.7	3.2	2.2	5.4	77.9	18.8
145.fpppp	19.8	2.7	2.7	56.3	9.6	0.0	4.5	4.5	46.2	16.9
146.wave5	15.2	1.7	0.8	35.2	31.9	2.5	5.1	7.6	90.5	88.3
124.m88ksim	11.7	6.9	0.4	47.3	9.4	2.0	10.2	12.2	62.7	53.6
126.gcc	9.5	4.2	2.2	58.8	11.3	4.0	3.0	7.0	39.9	21.7
129.compress	12.3	5.9	0.0	37.0	16.5	14.1	0.0	14.1	48.2	44.7
130.li	21.1	3.2	1.9	39.8	11.6	7.3	3.9	11.2	44.4	50.8
132.ijpeg	13.8	5.0	0.0	43.7	32.1	1.6	1.1	2.7	29.8	35.1
134.perl	21.1	3.6	2.6	45.9	9.2	2.1	6.7	8.8	69.0	53.4
147.vortex	16.0	6.2	0.5	44.4	17.8	0.1	7.5	7.6	63.7	32.6
postgres	22.1	2.5	1.2	43.4	3.4	12.8	0.9	13.6	76.2	26.3
xblast	20.8	1.0	0.1	50.1	11.2	2.2	6.2	8.4	65.1	13.5

Table 3: Percent of the dynamic basic blocks of each type for each workload. Percent of conditional and loop branches w a fixed behavior.

This increase causes the global FIPA performance of the STC alone to come quite close to the HTC for some codes. For example, the core fetch unit provides 10.1 instruction per access with the reordered *xblast*, while using a 16KB t-cache with the original code obtains 10.8 instructions per access.

We also observe that the STC drastically reduces the i-cache miss rate for both the FP and the integer codes. Large codes like *apsi*, *xblast* and *postgres* obtain miss rate reductions around 90%, and a final i-cache miss rate around 1% on a 32KB cache.

The branch misprediction rate increases slightly with the reordered code. It is so because the reordered code reduces the number of taken branches, introducing more zeroes in the history register of the GAg predictor, leading to a worse utilization of the history table. For example, the branch misprediction rate for *m88ksim* increases from 4.9% to 7.9% when the code is reordered, mainly due to the reduction of sequence breaks from 61% to 27% (see Table 4).

Hardware Trace Cache

The fact that the traces provided by the t-cache are built in the fill buffer makes the FIPA provided from the t-cache independent of the t-cache geometry. Also, reading the instructions form the dynamic stream, makes the traces independent of the code layout.

The t-cache miss rate does not seem to depend on the code layout, but on the t-cache size itself. In order to reduce the t-cache miss rate, techniques like *Partial matching* [4] have been proposed, which also reduce the number of instruction provided. The HTC mechanism assumes that the t-cache will always be able to provide more instructions than the core fetch unit. This statement may not be true if we consider the increased FIPA performance of the STC and the reduced trace length caused by such techniques. It may not be worth adding such functionality to the HTC, as a compile-time optimization can obtain similar results.

The HTC does not have a visible impact on the branch prediction accuracy.

STC and HTC interaction

The best results are obtained when combining both S and HTC, as the core fetch unit will be able to provide m instructions on a t-cache miss and a lower i-cache miss r. For example, a combination of STC and 16KB t-cache *vortex* provides 12.2 instructions per access, while a HT(32KB provides only 11.3.

For the larger codes, the t-cache can not remember the executed code sequences, and the core fetch unit is u extensively. It is in these cases, like *gcc*, where the S proves more useful, combining with a small t-cache to p vide better results than a t-cache of double size alone. C bining a STC with a large t-cache still improves the res for the larger codes, but the FIPA increase is minimum the small ones.

Both the STC and the HTC improve the FIPA, but STC also targets a reduction of the CPA by minimizin cache misses. For small codes, like *hydro2d* which alre have a very low i-cache miss rate, the STC is not too use with the HTC providing much better performance. In sc cases, like *li*, the increased branch misprediction rate actually hinder the performance of the HTC.

On the other hand, for the largest codes, like *post* and *xblast*, the STC alone can offer similar, or better res than a HTC alone. In these cases, combining the comp time and the run-time techniques offers the best results, r ing the FIPC from 5.9 with the STC, or 4.6 with the 16 HTC, to 6.5 with a combination of both. In most ca using a combination of STC and a small HTC offers sim or better results than a HTC of double size.

The benefits of the STC are more obvious when th cache miss penalty increases and the branch mispredict penalty is small, while the HTC proves most useful w the i-cache miss penalty is low.

We conclude that for large codes with few loops, the S can provide better results than the HTC alone, and th combination of the STC with a small HTC provides sim or better results than a much larger HTC alone. When c bined with a large t-cache, the STC is still able to prov performance improvements, due to the reduced i-cache r rate.

Bench.	Setup		FIPA			Miss rate (%)		Branch	FIPC [miss pen,br pen]			
	t-cache	Layout	i-cache	t-cache	global	i-cache	t-cache	mispr. (%)	6/8	6/12	3/8	6/4
hydro2d	0	Base	11.7	—	11.7	0.08	—	0.3	11.5	11.4	11.5	11.6
	0KB	CFA_8	12.2	—	12.2	0.01	—	0.4	11.9	11.8	11.9	12.0
	16KB	Base	11.4	15.5	15.4	0.09	3.3	0.3	15.0	14.8	15.0	15.2
	16KB	CFA_8	11.1	15.5	15.5	0.01	3.9	0.4	15.0	14.8	15.0	15.2
	32KB	Base	9.1	15.5	15.5	0.08	0.5	0.3	15.0	14.8	15.1	15.2
	32KB	CFA_8	9.9	15.5	15.5	0.01	0.7	0.4	15.0	14.8	15.0	15.2
apsi	0KB	Base	13.8	—	13.8	1.3	—	2.8	11.8	11.4	12.4	12.3
	0KB	CFA_{16}	14.2	—	14.2	0.2	—	3.3	12.8	12.2	12.8	13.4
	16KB	Base	13.5	15.9	15.3	1.5	23.1	2.8	12.9	12.4	13.5	13.4
	16KB	CFA_{16}	13.7	15.9	15.4	0.2	21.0	3.3	13.7	13.1	13.8	14.4
	32KB	Base	13.3	15.9	15.5	1.4	16.5	2.8	13.0	13.5	13.7	13.6
	32KB	CFA_{16}	13.7	15.9	15.5	0.2	16.5	3.3	13.8	13.2	13.9	14.5
m88ksim	0KB	Base	6.9	—	6.9	11.6	—	4.9	3.2	3.0	4.1	3.5
	0KB	CFA_8	10.0	—	10.0	0.06	—	7.9	5.5	4.5	5.5	7.1
	16KB	Base	6.5	13.8	11.1	14.5	36.9	4.9	4.4	4.0	5.7	5.0
	16KB	CFA_8	8.8	13.7	11.6	0.06	42.7	7.9	6.0	4.8	6.0	7.9
	32KB	Base	6.4	13.7	11.9	13.5	25.4	4.9	4.7	4.2	6.1	5.4
	32KB	CFA_8	8.1	13.8	12.0	0.06	31.5	7.9	6.1	4.9	6.1	8.1
gcc	0KB	Base	7.7	—	7.7	10.2	—	10.0	3.2	2.7	3.7	3.8
	0KB	CFA_8	8.8	—	8.8	7.3	—	11.8	3.4	2.8	3.9	4.3
	16KB	Base	7.1	13.6	9.8	12.4	59.4	10.0	3.5	2.9	4.2	4.2
	16KB	CFA_8	8.2	13.3	10.5	8.3	56.0	11.8	3.7	3.0	4.2	4.7
	32KB	Base	6.9	13.6	10.1	12.4	51.6	10.0	3.6	3.0	4.2	4.4
	32KB	CFA_8	8.0	13.3	10.7	8.3	48.6	11.8	3.7	3.0	4.2	4.8
li	0KB	Base	7.4	—	7.4	0.1	—	5.0	5.3	4.6	5.3	6.1
	0KB	CFA_4	8.4	—	8.4	0.1	—	5.8	5.5	4.7	5.6	6.6
	16KB	Base	6.4	13.5	10.6	0.2	40.4	5.0	6.8	5.8	6.8	8.2
	16KB	CFA_4	7.3	13.2	11.1	0.2	36.4	5.8	6.6	5.5	6.6	8.2
	32KB	Base	6.1	13.4	11.1	0.2	32.0	5.0	7.0	5.9	7.0	8.5
	32KB	CFA_4	6.8	13.4	11.5	0.2	29.0	5.8	6.8	5.6	6.8	8.5
ijpeg	0KB	Base	11.7	—	11.7	0.07	—	9.7	8.3	7.2	8.3	9.7
	0KB	CFA_8	11.6	—	11.6	0.01	—	10.1	8.2	7.1	8.2	9.6
	16KB	Base	9.7	15.5	14.5	0.1	17.4	9.7	9.6	8.2	9.6	11.4
	16KB	CFA_8	10.3	15.4	14.5	0.01	18.4	10.2	9.5	8.1	9.5	11.5
	32KB	Base	8.8	15.5	14.5	0.1	14.4	9.7	9.6	8.2	9.6	11.5
	32KB	CFA_8	9.0	15.4	14.6	0.01	14.6	10.1	9.5	8.1	9.6	11.5
vortex	0KB	Base	7.6	—	7.6	7.8	—	7.4	3.5	3.1	4.2	4.1
	0KB	CFA_8	10.2	—	10.2	1.1	—	6.2	5.9	5.0	6.1	7.2
	16KB	Base	6.7	13.8	10.8	8.1	42.1	7.4	4.6	3.9	5.3	5.5
	16KB	CFA_8	9.2	13.8	12.2	1.3	34.0	6.2	6.5	5.4	6.7	8.2
	32KB	Base	6.7	13.7	11.3	8.2	34.7	7.4	4.7	4.0	5.4	5.7
	32KB	CFA_8	8.6	13.8	12.3	1.3	27.7	6.2	6.5	5.4	6.8	8.2
postgres	0KB	Base	7.5	—	7.5	9.3	—	3.0	4.1	3.9	5.2	4.3
	0KB	CFA_{16}	10.3	—	10.3	1.0	—	8.4	5.7	4.8	5.9	7.2
	16KB	Base	7.2	14.2	10.6	10.0	51.8	3.0	5.3	5.0	6.8	5.7
	16KB	CFA_{16}	9.7	14.0	11.9	1.1	49.6	8.4	6.2	5.1	6.4	7.9
	32KB	Base	7.0	14.2	11.6	9.9	35.7	3.0	5.8	5.4	7.4	6.2
	32KB	CFA_{16}	8.9	14.1	12.3	1.2	33.7	8.4	6.3	5.2	6.5	8.1
xblast	0KB	Base	7.1	—	7.1	4.8	—	7.7	3.9	3.4	4.4	4.5
	0KB	CFA_8	10.1	—	10.1	0.6	—	7.9	5.7	4.8	5.8	7.2
	16KB	Base	7.0	13.7	10.8	6.8	43.4	7.7	4.9	4.2	5.6	5.9
	16KB	CFA_8	9.2	13.7	11.5	1.5	48.7	8.8	5.8	4.8	6.0	7.4
	32KB	Base	6.8	13.7	11.1	7.2	37.9	7.9	4.9	4.2	5.6	5.9
	32KB	CFA_8	8.6	13.8	12.1	0.9	33.1	7.8	6.4	5.2	6.5	8.2

Table 5: Simulation results for a 32KB instruction cache.

Related Work

here has been much work on code mapping algorithms to ›timize the instruction cache miss rate. These works were rgeted at less aggressive processors, which do not need to tch instructions from multiple basic blocks per cycle.

Hwu and Chang [7] use function inline expansion, and oup into traces those basic blocks which tend to execute sequence as observed on a profile of the code. Then, they ap these traces in the cache so that the functions which e executed close to each other are placed in the same page.

Pettis & Hansen [10] propose a profile based technique reorder the procedures in a program, and the basic blocks ithin each procedure. Their aim is to minimize the concts between the most frequently used functions, placing nctions which reference each other close in memory. They so reorder the basic blocks in a procedure, moving unused sic blocks to the bottom of the function code, even splitng the procedures in two, and moving away the unused sic blocks.

Torrellas *et al* [13] designed a basic block reordering al›rithm for Operating System code, running on a very conrvative vector processor. They map the code in the form sequences of basic blocks spanning several functions, and ep a section of the cache address space reserved for the ost frequently referenced basic blocks. A comparison between the STC, the Pettis & Hansen method and the Torrellas *et al* method can be found in [11].

Gloy *et al.* [5] extend the Pettis & Hansen placement algorithm at the procedure level to consider the temporal relationship between procedures in addition to the target cache information and the size of each procedure. Hashemi *et al* [6] and Kalamaitianos *et al* [8] use a cache line coloring algorithm inspired in the register coloring technique to map procedures so that the resulting number of conflicts is minimized.

Techniques developed for VLIW processors, like Trace Scheduling [3] also identify the most frequent execution paths in a program. But these techniques are trying to optimize the scheduling of instructions in the execution core of the processor, not the performance of the instruction fetch engine. Individual instructions are moved up and down, crossing the basic block boundary, to optimize ILP in the execution core of the processor, inserting *compensation code* to undo what wrongly placed instructions did when the wrong path is taken. The traces they define are logical, the basic blocks need not be actually moved in order to obtain the desired effect. In that sense, these techniques and the STC may be complementary, one optimizes instruction fetch while the other optimizes instruction scheduling, both using the same profile information.

On the hardware side, techniques like the Branch Address Cache [14], the Collapsing Buffer [2] and the Trace Cache [4, 12] approach the problem of fetching multiple, non-contiguous basic blocks each cycle. The Branch Address Cache and the Collapsing Buffer access non-consecutive cache lines from an interleaved i-cache each cycle and then merge the required instructions from each accessed line. The Trace Cache does not require fetching of non-consecutive basic blocks from the i-cache as it stores dynamically constructed sequences of basic blocks in a special purpose cache. These techniques require hardware extensions of the fetch unit, and do not target an i-cache miss rate reduction, relying on other techniques for it.

Some other works have examined the interaction of run-time and compile-time techniques regarding the instruction fetch mechanism. Chen *et al.* [1] examined the effect of the code expanding optimizations (loop unrolling and function inlining) on the instruction cache miss rate. Also, as an example of software and hardware cooperation, Patel *et al* [9] identify branches with a fixed behavior and avoid making prediction on them, increasing the potential of the Trace Cache.

7 Conclusions

In this paper we present a profile based code reordering technique which targets an optimization of the instruction fetch performance in the more aggressive wide superscalar processors.

By carefully mapping the basic blocks in a program we can store the more frequently executed traces in memory, using the instruction cache as a *Software Trace Cache* (STC), obtaining better performance of a sequential fetch unit, and complementing the Hardware Trace Cache (HTC) mechanism with a better failsafe mechanism.

Our results show that for large codes with few loops and deterministic execution sequences, like database applications, the STC can offer similar, or better, results than the HTC alone. However, optimum results come from the combination of both the software and the hardware approaches. The number of fetched instructions per cycle obtained with a combination of the STC and a small trace cache is comparable to that of a HTC of double size alone.

The storage of the most popular traces in the instruction cache leads to a new view of the fetch unit, where the trace cache is more tightly coupled with the contents of the instruction cache. Some traces are being redundantly stored in both caches, effectively wasting space, and displacing potentially useful traces from the trace cache. It is yet another example of the need for the software and the hardware to work together in order to obtain optimum performance with the minimum cost.

References

[1] W. Y. Chen, P. P. Chung, T. M. Conte, and W.-M. Hwu. The effect of code expanding optimizations on instruction cache design. *IEEE Transactions on Computers*, 42(9):1045–1057, Sept. 1993.

[2] T. Conte, K. Menezes, P. Mills, and B. Patell. Optimization of instruction fetch mechanism for high issue rates. *Proceedings of the 22th Annual Intl. Symposium on Computer Architecture*, pages 333–344, June 1995.

[3] J. A. Fisher. Trace scheduling: A technique for global microcode compaction. *IEEE Transactions on Computers*, 30(7):478–490, July 1981.

[4] D. H. Friendly, S. J. Patel, and Y. N. Patt. Alterna fetch and issue techniques from the trace cache me nism. *Proceedings of the 30th Anual ACM/IEEE Symposium on Microarchitecture*, Dec. 1997.

[5] N. Gloy, T. Blackwell, M. D. Smith, and B. Cal Procedure placement using temporal ordering infor tion. *Proceedings of the 30th Anual ACM/IEEE Symposium on Microarchitecture*, pages 303–313, 1997.

[6] A. H. Hashemi, D. R. Kaeli, and B. Calder. Effic procedure mapping using cache line coloring. *P ACM SIGPLAN'97 Conf. on Programming Lang Design and Implementation*, pages 171–182, June 1

[7] W.-M. Hwu and P. P. Chang. Achieving high inst tion cache performance with an optimizing comp *Proceedings of the 16th Annual Intl. Symposium Computer Architecture*, pages 242–251, June 1989.

[8] J. Kalamaitianos and D. R. Kaeli. Temporal-based cedure reordering for improved instruction cache per mance. *Proceedings of the 4th Intl. Conference on Performance Computer Architecture*, Feb. 1998.

[9] S. J. Patel, M. Evers, and Y. N. Patt. Improving t cache effectiveness with branch promotion and t packing. *Proceedings of the 25th Annual Intl. Sym sium on Computer Architecture*, pages 262–271, J 1998.

[10] K. Pettis and R. C. Hansen. Profile guided code p tioning. *Proc. ACM SIGPLAN'99 Conf. on Progr ming Languaje Design and Implementation*, pages 27, June 1990.

[11] A. Ramírez, J. L. Larriba-Pey, C. Navarro, X. Serr J. Torrellas, and M. Valero. Code reordering of d sion support systems for optimized instruction fe Technical Report UPC-DAC-1998-56, Universitat litecnica de Catalunya, Dec. 1998.

[12] E. Rottenberg, S. Benett, and J. E. Smith. Trace ca a low latency aprroach to high bandwith instruc fetching. *Proceedings of the 29th Anual ACM/I Intl. Symposium on Microarchitecture*, pages 24 Dec. 1996.

[13] J. Torrellas, C. Xia, and R. Daigle. Optimizing inst tion cache performance for operating system inten workloads. *Proceedings of the 1st Intl. Conference High Performance Computer Architecture*, pages 3 369, Jan. 1995.

[14] T. Y. Yeh, D. T. Marr, and Y. N. Patt. Increa the instruction fetch rate via multiple branch predic and a branch address cache. *7th Intl. Conference Supercomputing*, pages 67–76, July 1993.

Application Level Scheduling of Gene Sequence Comparison on Metacomputers*

Neil Spring
Rich Wolski†

Abstract

This paper investigates the efficacy of Application-Level Scheduling (AppLeS) [3] for a parallel gene sequence library comparison application in production metacomputing settings. We compare an AppLeS-enhanced version of the application to an original implementation designed and tuned to use the native scheduling mechanisms of Mentat [6] – a metacomputing software infrastructure. The experimental data shows that the AppLeS versions outperform the best Mentat versions over a range of problem sizes and computational settings.

The structure of the AppLeS we have defined for this application does not depend on the scheduling algorithms that it uses. Instead, the AppLeS scheduler considers the uncertainty associated with the information it uses in its scheduling decisions to choose between the static placement of computation, and the dynamic assignment of computation during execution. We propose that this framework is general enough to represent the class of metacomputing applications that are organized as a master and set of parallel slaves, in which the master distributes uncomputed work.

1 Introduction

Recent advances in network technology have made it possible for parallel applications to use ensembles of distributed computers to achieve high-performance. Typically, however, it is difficult or impossible to dedicate large-scale, widely dispersed resources to a single application at a single time: applications must be able to execute efficiently using heterogeneous sets of resources that are shared by other users and applications. Since computing in this form involves the interoperation of complete computer systems (including the resident operating systems, languages and language libraries, storage devices, etc. on each) it is often termed *metacomputing* [4, 8, 15, 3].

To take the fullest advantage of the shared, heterogeneous resources of a high-performance metacomputer, a parallel application's components (tasks, inter-task communication, I/O) must be carefully scheduled. However, because the resources at hand may be administered by different organizations (although linked by a network) it is difficult to institute a single, system wide scheduler that would be capable of effectively coordinating execution across all domains. Moreover, since the resources are shared, the fraction of maximum performance each can deliver to an application varies over time as a result of contention between competing applications. Resource heterogeneity adds an additional complication since the way in which an application uses a particular resource or resource type dramatically affects the performance that resource can actually deliver to the application.

Application Level Scheduling (AppLeS) [3] is an approach to metacomputer application scheduling in which each application is integrated with a customized scheduler. Using application-specific performance models and dynamically gathered system information, the AppLeS scheduler attempts to make the best use of the resources that are available to its application at the time the application executes. Each resource is viewed by the scheduler strictly in terms of the potential performance it can deliver. Both the type of the resource and its expected load at the time the application will use it are considered when a schedule is determined. Together, the application and the scheduler form a "resource aware" program that seeks to optimize its own performance using the resources made available to it by the metacomputing system.

In this paper, we describe an application level scheduler designed for a parallel gene sequence library comparison application written for the Mentat [6] prototype metacomputing system. By default, Mentat employs a variant of workstealing [7], to schedule all applications that execute within its environment. We contrast the performance of this system-provided default method with an AppLeS-determined static schedule derived at runtime, and an AppLeS hybrid method based on a combination of runtime scheduling and workstealing. This comparison is important for two reasons. First, the sequential tasks that compose most parallel gene sequence comparison applications have data-dependent execution profiles. Since the duration of each task varies as a function of its inputs, it is difficult to predict ahead of time. As a result, workstealing

*Supported by NSF grant ASC-9308900 and Advanced Research Projects Agency/ITO, Distributed Object Computation Testbed, ARPA order No. D570, Issued by ESC/ENS under contract #F19628-96-C-0020.

†email: nspring@cs.ucsd.edu, rich@cs.ucsd.edu

type dynamic scheduling techniques are typically employed for such applications. Idle workers "steal" work from busy ones thereby ensuring good resource utilization. We wished to compare the AppLeS approach (based on application-derived information and dynamically generated resource performance forecasts) to the common approach for a parallel application with hard-to-predict task execution times.

The second goal of this work was to investigate a general framework for master/slave computations in which the master process is responsible for distributing work to a set of parallel slaves, either on-demand or proactively. We believe the Mentat implementation we examined (called *complib* which is described more fully in Section 3) constitutes a reasonable exemplar in terms of its performance characteristics for this application class. As such, *complib* was designed assuming that the default Mentat method would yield the best performance in a metacomputing setting.

In Section 2, we describe the problem of comparing biological sequence libraries. In Section 3, we describe the implementation structure of the *complib* sequence library comparison application. In Section 4, we describe the AppLeS algorithm we chose for *complib*, and in Section 5, we present the performance of the application in different environments executing with different problem sizes. We conclude in Section 6 with an evaluation of the AppLeS methodology, and a description of future work.

2 Biological Sequence Library Comparison

Determining the structure and function of biological sequences, like proteins and DNA, is an important problem in molecular biology. The primary structure of proteins consists of sequences of amino acids. Similarly, DNA analysis focuses on the identification of base-pair sequences within the molecule itself. Determining these sequences, a process known as sequencing, has become efficient enough that it is commonplace for scientists to sequence as a first step toward determining the structure and function of a protein. Newly discovered sequences can be compared to all known sequences to find others with potentially similar structure, function, and origin.

The desire to compare new sequences against large sequence databases creates a demand for computational resources. The *complib* application implements biological sequence library comparison in a metacomputing environment. Individual sequences are compared using the FASTA sequential algorithm, described below. Many individual sequence comparisons are executed during library comparison, (described in Section 2.2) and since they are independent, the entire set of comparisons may be done in parallel.

2.1 Sequence Comparison

Sequence comparison is a type of substring matching operation where sequence similarity is scored based on biological criteria. Pairs of sequences that match with a higher score are considered to be more similar, potentially sharing common function and origin. The score of a sequence match increases for each matching item, known as an identity, and decreases when elements are substituted, inserted, or removed.

The score associated with each substring pair is a function of biological interaction based on mutation and not necessarily minimal structural difference. For example, without using knowledge of the English language, the words *friend* and *fiend* would seem quite similar, and the words *friend* and *friendly* less so. Simple rules based on minimum structural difference would make the comparison of *friend* and *fiend* yield a higher score than *friend* and *friendly*. Using rules based on the semantics of the words, a better scoring is possible. Such rules exist for comparing proteins. One of these rules is based on a table called a Point Accepted Mutation (PAM) matrix. This matrix describes the the likelihood of substitution of one amino acid by another, and was derived by examination of the small variations between known related sequences. This matrix is then used to determine the scoring penalty for a mismatched element.

It is likely that many of the matching pairs of sequences share little function or origin, and attempting to separate these from relevant matches by parameter tuning is generally worthwhile. FASTA is just one fast heuristic method used to compare sequences. Others include Smith-Waterman [and BLAST [1]. Choosing a particular algorithm and tuning its parameters effects the tradeoff between *sensitivity* (finding distantly related sequences), *selectivity* (discriminating unrelated sequences), and *speed*.

2.2 Library Comparison

Gene sequence library comparison consists of many individual sequence comparisons. Each sequence of amino acids or base pairs in a "source" library is compared to every sequence in the "target" library. We visualize the computation space in Figure 1. Source and target libraries are stored as lists of variable-length sequence structures. Result structures have a statically defined size and contain only the score of the match. Since each sequence comparison is independent, the entire library comparison may be performed in parallel. *Complib*, the library-comparison implementation we discuss in the next section, exploits this parallelism for performance.

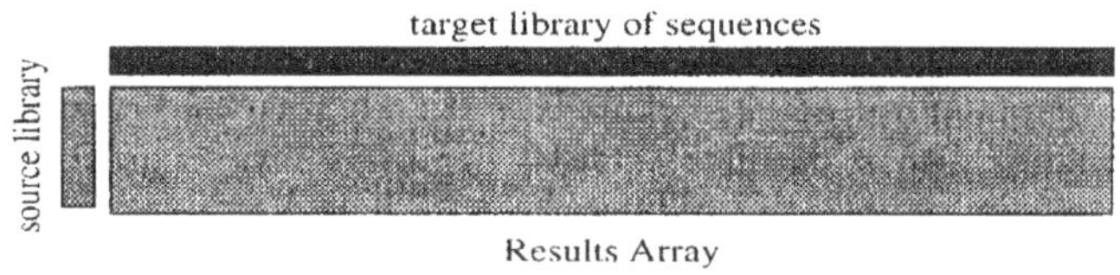

Figure 1. Comparison space. Each sequence in the "source" and "target" arrays must be compared to form a two dimensional array of results structures.

3 Complib

Complib is a metacomputer application for comparing biological sequence libraries using the FASTA algorithm, written in Mentat [6, 5]. Mentat is both a run-time system for metacomputer resource management and a programming language based on C++. Parallel tasks in this object-oriented system are contained within Mentat objects, and these Mentat objects are distributed on the different machines in the metacomputer. Communication is accomplished in this object oriented system by passing parameters and return values.

The *complib* application distributes chunks of the source and target libraries to different machines in a metacomputer, so that sequence comparison takes place in parallel. Individual machines compare these chunks of the libraries using the sequential FASTA algorithm.

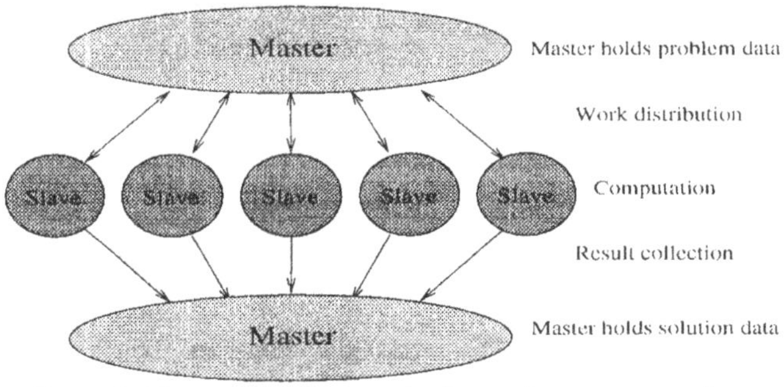

Figure 2. Master-slave communication and structure template.

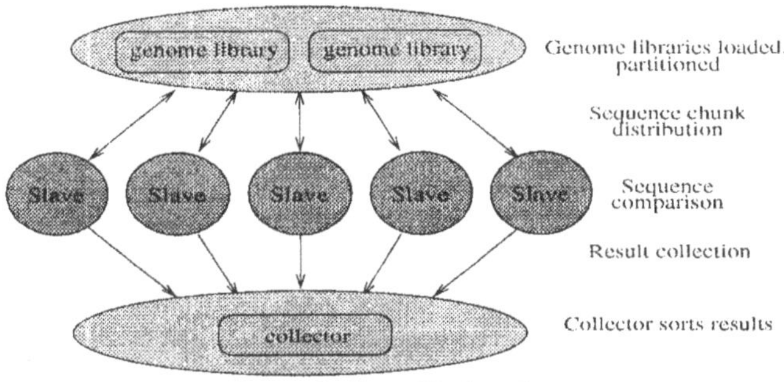

Figure 3. Complib data flow.

3.1 Master-Slave Paradigm

This application is structured using the master-slave paradigm shown in Figure 2. Metacomputers are well suited to applications with this structure since its large computation-to-communication ratio yields performance even with slow networks. A master process distributes work to slave processes which return the results of the computation to the master.

Work may be placed by the master, as shown by the downward arrows in the work distribution phase of Figure 2, or requested by idle slaves, as shown by the upward arrows. Downward arrows imply *placement*, where a scheduler has knowledge of the slave's performance and can determine an appropriate piece of work to allocate. Upward arrows imply workstealing or *replacement*, where idle slaves request work. Placement generally incurs lower overhead since it is done once just after execution begins, while replacement can be accomplished with very little scheduling complexity.

3.2 Program Architecture

There are three classes of complib object: libraries, workers, and collectors, shown in Figure 3. Genome library objects load sequence libraries from disk, then disseminate chunks of these libraries to the worker objects. There are two library objects during execution: one for the source library, and another for the target.

In this object-oriented system, computation takes place as the result of method invocation. In this case, the worker objects export a sequence comparison function that accepts library chunks as parameters and returns a two dimensional array of result structures. These result structures consist of the scores generated by the sequence comparison algorithm, and are forwarded to the collector object. The results are then sorted according to score by the collector object.

Although there are two genome library objects, only the target genome library handles the startup of worker objects and the allocation of sequences. Logically, these two library objects represent the master process for work distribution, and the collector object represents the master for the purpose of result collection.

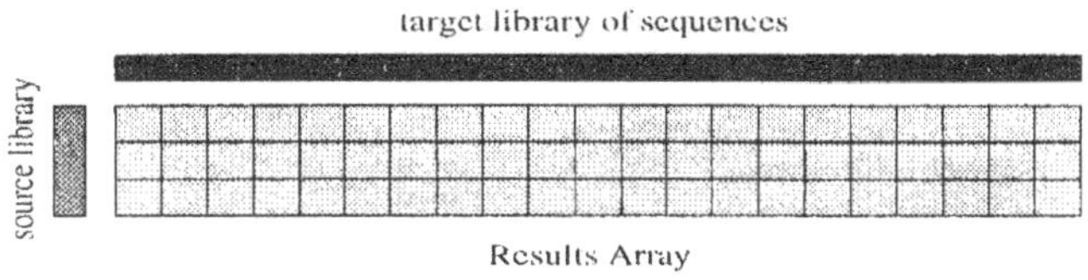

Figure 4. Default block distribution of data. Block size is configurable and affects application runtime.

Worker objects are a type of *regular* Mentat object, which allows the system to determine where and how many objects will be started. *Persistent* Mentat objects can reside on a specified host, and are created one at a time at the application level. Library and collector objects are both persistent, since they both store state between method invocations. The collector object stores a partially assembled array of results between functions, and the library objects store the genome library to be distributed.

3.3 Mentat System Scheduling Policy

Currently, *complib* relies on the Mentat scheduler [7]. Chunks of a parameterizable maximum size are placed on a system-managed queue. This block-style data distribution is shown in Figure 4. Effectively, when objects run out of work, they request a pair of chunks, one from the source library and another from the target from this queue. Since worker objects are members of a *regular* Mentat class, the Mentat scheduler chooses where worker objects will be started, and will start as many worker objects as necessary.

4 AppLeS

Application Level Scheduling (AppLeS) combines dynamic system performance information with application specific models and user specified parameters in order to produce better schedules [3]. "Better" is defined by the user, but in this case will be taken to mean decreased run time. In this section, we will describe the application model used, and how the scheduler can improve application performance during each phase of execution. We also present a framework for scheduling master-slave applications in a shared, heterogeneous environment.

4.1 Complib Application Model

The *complib* application model can be split into three overlapping phases. First, the workers are started and given gene sequence library chunks to compare. Second, the workers compare each sequence in the "source" chunk to each sequence in the "target" chunk. Finally, the workers return results to the collector. These activities are shown in Figure 5. This model does not assume the block decomposition shown in Figure 4. Instead, single data chunks are allocated to each worker, in order to reduce communication overhead.

Each of the AppLeS scheduled worker objects is a Mentat persistent object. We use persistent objects because, in Mentat[1], persistent objects are the only way to allow application-controlled placement. Persistent Mentat objects, however, can only be started one at a time. This creates significant startup overhead which the AppLeS must consider.

[1]Legion, the successor to Mentat unavailable when our AppLeS was being constructed, fixes this problem.

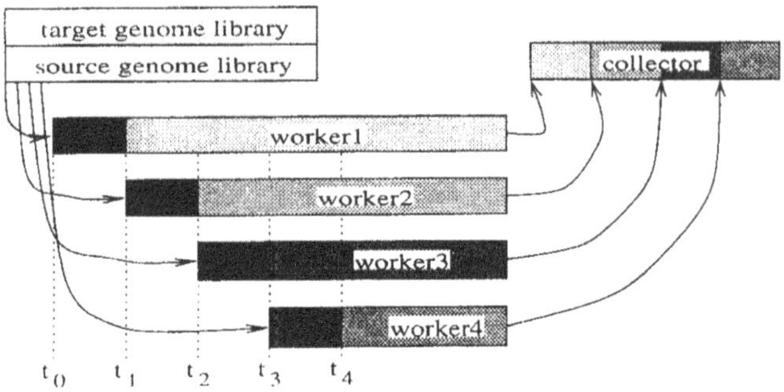

Figure 5. Basic complib application model. Black areas show startup overhead. Arrows indicate data flow.

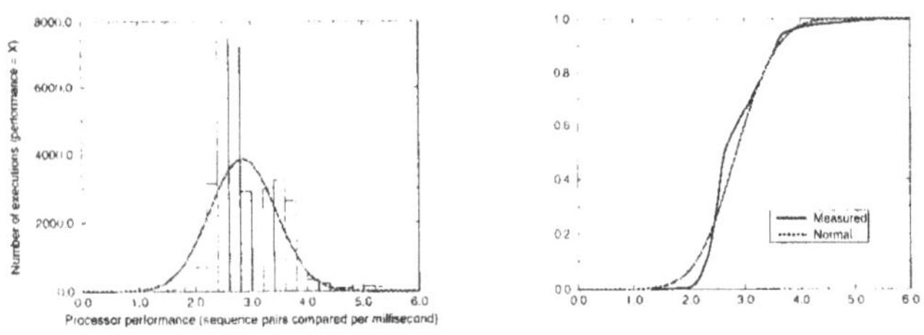

Figure 6. Distribution of execution performance. Shown on the left is a histogram of average execution performance for one of the Sun HPC servers, measured in sequence pairs compared per millisecond. Superimposed on the histogram is the bell curve of a normal distribution with the same mean and standard deviation. On the right is the same information shown as a cumulative distribution.

Note that since regular objects are not application schedulable, the AppLeS approach must be able to improve execution enough to recover the additional overhead (imposed by Mentat) associated with using persistent objects.

The startup behavior of persistent objects is shown in Figure 5. At time t_0, worker1 is started. The black area is a combination of the time to load the worker's binary code from an NFS mounted file system, and the time to receive genome library chunks. As soon as worker1 begins actual execution, at time t_1, worker2 is started. This pattern continues through t_4, when all the workers are executing.

The time to compare source and library chunks is modeled using two parameters:

- a benchmark execution time of a worker task on each possible host in dedicated mode, and
- a predicted measure of percentage CPU availability generated by the Network Weather Service.

By dividing the expected execution time of a worker task on a dedicated host by the expected percentage of the time the task will be able to occupy the host's CPU, we can obtain an expected execution time for the task that accounts for CPU contention. We obtain the benchmark information by using operating system provided CPU-time accounting information. This provides an estimate of the dedicated time required to compare a pair of sequences on each host. In Figure 6, we show a histogram and cumulative distribution of execution times for the FASTA implementation within *complib* over a sample from the GenBank data. As shown in Figure 6, while the histogram does not appear to be modeled well by a normal distribution, note that the cumulative distribution tracks the normal well above the 70th quantile.

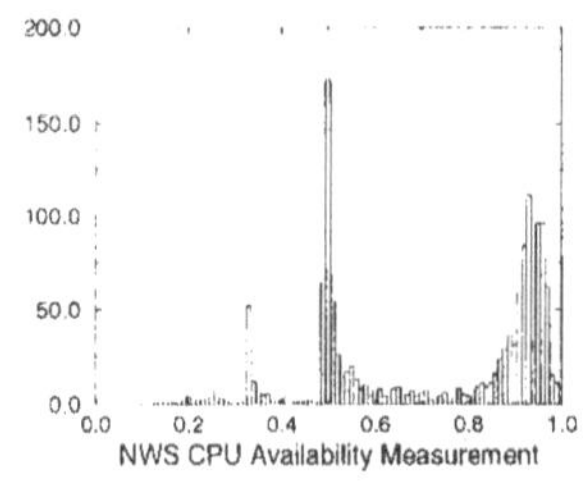

Figure 7. Histogram of CPU availability values on a single workstation provided by the Network Weather Service. This distribution is multimodal. Availability refers to the fraction of the CPU a new application to be executed can expect to receive.

The scheduling algorithm we describe in Section 4.3.1 relies on the ability to determine a *dependability threshold* on execution time prediction. Based on the relationship between the observed data and the normal quantiles, we chose to use a normal distribution to model the dedicated execution time of FASTA. Expected CPU availability, however, is not normally distributed [9] as shown in Figure 7.

To predict the percentage of available CPU occupancy that will be possible for each worker task, we use the Network Weather Service (NWS) [17, 18]. The NWS is a distributed performance monitoring and forecasting facility designed to provide schedulers with predictions of the deliverable performance of resources to applications. Currently, the NWS provides CPU availability forecasts, and available network bandwidth and latency predictions to the scheduler. For this application, we are most concerned with the fraction of the CPU that the NWS predicts will be available at the time the application will execute.

The following formula is used to model the execution time of a worker process in the implementation of *complib*:

$$T_{compare} = \frac{\text{Source chunk size * Target chunk size}}{\text{Benchmark seq. pairs/ms * NWS CPU Avail}}$$

After comparison, workers pass their results to the collector object. The size of a result structure scales in proportion to the product of source chunk size and target chunk size, and can reach 10 megabytes. Transfer time for result structures of this size is significant, and takes place sequentially.

Although further performance improvements may be gained by scheduling the I/O and collection phases of the program, we chose to focus on the computational phase first as it constitutes the largest fraction of overall execution time. Moreover, substantial structural changes to the existing *complib* application would be necessary to allow such scheduling. In this work, we wished to investigate the effect of AppLeS scheduling techniques in comparison with the existing Mentat scheduling method (which was conjectured to be the "best" methodology for the application as it was written). As such, we did not wish to change the structure of the implementation in a way which might favor AppLeS.

4.2 Startup Phase & Resource Selection

Given the behavior of persistent objects in Mentat, it is necessary to limit the number of processors used, and choose the best processors available. Not all resources are useful because of the large startup delay. Note, however, that AppLeS can consider the delay associated with different object-to-host mappings, and choose only those resources (and the time at which they should be used) so that the execution time of the program is optimized. To decide on a schedule, the AppLeS employs a time-balancing heuristic [3] which attempts to make all worker tasks finish simultaneously. In this work, we extend time-balancing to include the notion of start-up delay so that the AppLeS scheduler may consider the start-up cost associated with Mentat persistent objects.

4.2.1 Library and Collector Placement

Library placement is the process of determining where the library objects will reside. These hosts should be *close* to both data storage and the processors where workers will be run. The term "close" in this context refers to the relative bandwidth performance of the network linking two computational sites. Two hosts are close if the relative bandwidth linking them is high. Potential library locations are scored based on the sum of the products of processor power and bandwidth to each host.

$$\text{Library Placement Score} = \Sigma(P_{processor} * BW_{toprocessor})$$

The host with the highest score is allocated the target library, and the second highest score is allocated the source library and collector object. Library objects are placed on different hosts to promote even memory consumption, while the collector object can reside on the same host with the source library since these objects are active during different phases of the execution of the application.

4.2.2 Worker Placement

To select an appropriate subset of resources to use, the scheduler starts by sorting the available hosts by their relative abilities to run the FASTA algorithm on a representative problem size (processor power).

$$P_{processor} = \text{NWS CPU Avail} * \text{Benchmark}$$

Since the processors are sorted by power, the most powerful processor will be started first, thus maximizing our use of the best processor resources that are available.

The next step is to determine the maximum number of processors that should be used to decrease the overall runtime. Startup cost is modeled as a static 1.5 seconds plus a communication cost, which was a reasonable approximation in our environment. This communication portion of the startup cost is calculated using the following formula:

$$t_{xfer} = \frac{PartitionSize * AvgSeqLength}{BandwidthPrediction} + 3 * LatencyPrediction$$

The latency prediction is multiplied by three, as an estimate of the number of message transfers between libraries and worker at startup.[2] *PartitionSize* * *AvgSeqLength* represents the size of the partition being transferred. Since the lengths of sequences in a chunk are not known until the chunk is assembled, a representative measure of sequence length must be used, in this case, we chose an average. The *AvgSeqLength* from the GenBank protein database described in Section 2 was 243 bytes. A similar formula is used to estimate the communication cost involved in transferring the result structures back to the collector, which is not as important at this phase. The scheduler chooses the number of processors that yields the lowest expected execution time by considering successively larger subsets of the sorted processor set in sorted order.

[2]Due to the object-oriented macro data flow model used in Mentat, the number of actual message transactions is hidden from the application.

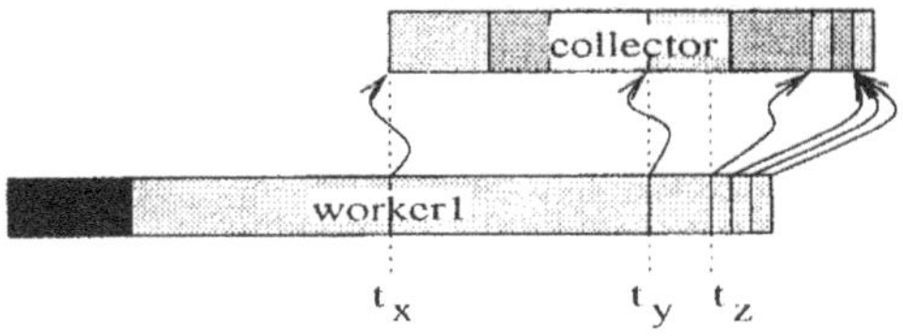

Figure 8. Single worker object's partitions. At time t_x, work on the second half-partition begins. Time t_y is the boundary between placement and replacement, as the worker begins using some dynamic technique such as GSS or workstealing. At time t_z, the worker executes a second dynamically determined partition.

4.3 Comparison Phase & Hybrid Vigor

The performance improvements gained using a static placement strategy (determined at runtime just before execution begins) depend on the quality of the information used. Incorrect benchmarks or poor performance predictions from the Network Weather Service can cause the scheduler to make the wrong decisions. These wrong decisions result in costly load imbalance. There are many factors, both operating system and algorithm dependent, that influence the time it will take to compare sequences. In the general case, even the most refined benchmarks and best predictions of available performance will have an associated uncertainty, and this uncertainty equates to a variance in execution time of the worker processes.

The goal of the scheduler, then is to avoid load imbalance while still enjoying the advantages of static placement. To do so, the scheduling model can be separated into two phases: *placement* and *replacement*. *Placement* is the process of allocating work to processors once, before execution begins, using the best performance estimates that are available. *Replacement* is the allocation of the remaining work using a dynamic technique, in this case, Guided Self-Scheduling (GSS) [12]. This strategy is shown in Figure 8 for comparison with Figures 5 and ??. GSS allocates successively smaller chunks of the computation in order to avoid overhead early on, while still providing parameterizably even finishing time.

It is the scheduler's job to choose the *demarkation point* between static placement and dynamic allocation so that the load imbalance that might result from a bad placement is mitigated by the dynamic technique. Simultaneously, the scheduler must try and make the statically placed tasks as large as possible to reduce execution time overhead associated with dynamic scheduling. Note that this scheduling model is general enough to include most master/slave implementations in which the master can dole out the work on demand. To determine the demarkation point the scheduler must consider the uncertainty associated with each execution time estimate. If the estimates are relatively accurate, the scheduler can profitably assign more work using static placement and less work using a dynamic technique. If the uncertainties are high, the reverse is true.

The algorithms used for placement and replacement, however, are not specified by the model. Much work, for example, has been done to improve dynamic scheduling techniques [11, 2, 12, 10]. The scheduler need only be able to consider the non-amortizable overhead cost of each in order to determine its benefit relative to a given placement algorithm. Similarly, a variety of static placement algorithms such as time-balancing or recursive bisection may be employed. In this work, we chose time-balancing and GSS to

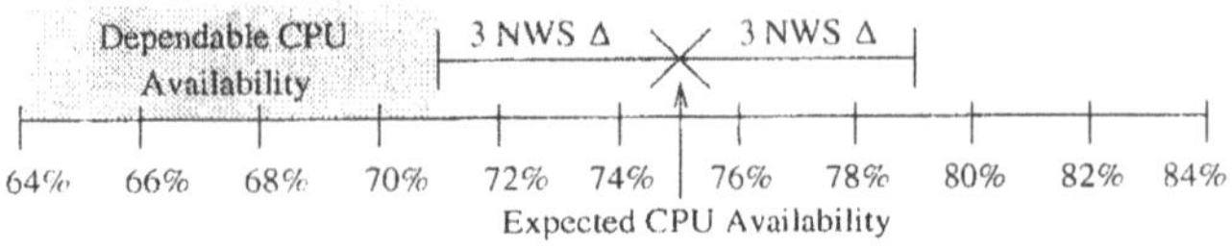

Figure 9. Dependable and Expected CPU Availability. In this case, the Network Weather Service predicts that 75% of the processor will be available with a mean percentage error (Δ) of 1.3%.

instantiate the model as both have demonstrated their ability to achieve high-performance levels in a variety of settings. We combine the time-balancing algorithm for placement, with a weighted adaptation of GSS to allocate the remaining computation.

4.3.1 Boundary Placement

In order to take the best advantage of the low overhead of placement, the boundary should be chosen so that placement is used for as much of the data as possible. We estimate how much of the work can be placed by estimating the variance in execution time as a function of the variance in CPU availability. Execution time also varies as a function of the sequences being compared. The distribution of CPU time required per sequence compared (averaged over chunks of at least 1000 sequence comparisons) is shown in Figure 6. The boundary is chosen on a per-object basis so that a maximal portion of the work that can dependably be completed is placed. After an object's dependable portion of the work is complete, it requests additional work as part of the replacement phase.

Since the distribution of CPU availability values is often multimodal, (see Figure 7) we do not assume normality, but rather use an estimate of variance provided by the NWS prediction modules [16]. The NWS tracks the error associated with each of the predictions of resource performance it supplies. We incorporate that information into the calculation of the placement/replacement boundary by using a multiple of the mean percent prediction error as a confidence interval about the prediction. Empirically, 3 times the mean percent prediction error generated an appropriate interval. That is, the scheduler assumes that the performance that the application will eventually receive will fall reliably within the interval provided by the NWS. It can therefore count on receiving at least as much resource performance as indicated by the leading edge of the interval. The calculation of dependable CPU performance is shown graphically in Figure 9, and as an equation below.

$$\begin{aligned} ExpectedPerf &= \text{NWS CPU Avail} * \text{Benchmark} \\ DependableCPU &= \text{NWS CPU Avail} - \\ &\quad 3 * \text{NWS CPU } \Delta \\ DependablePerf &= DependableCPU * \text{Benchmark} \end{aligned}$$

The number of sequences proportional to the fraction

$$\frac{ExpectedPerf - DependablePerf}{ExpectedPerf}$$

is held in reserve for replacement. This calculation takes place for each machine, so that machines with high load variance are allocated a smaller portion of the problem and contribute more to the replacement work pool.

Sequences allocated through placement are shown in Figures 10 and 11. In Figure 10, the difference between *expected* and *dependable* performance is shown. Regions shaded in black represent the difference between these, to be held in reserve. In actual implementation, sequences are allocated contiguously, and the reserved work actually represents the last set of sequences, as shown in Figure 11.

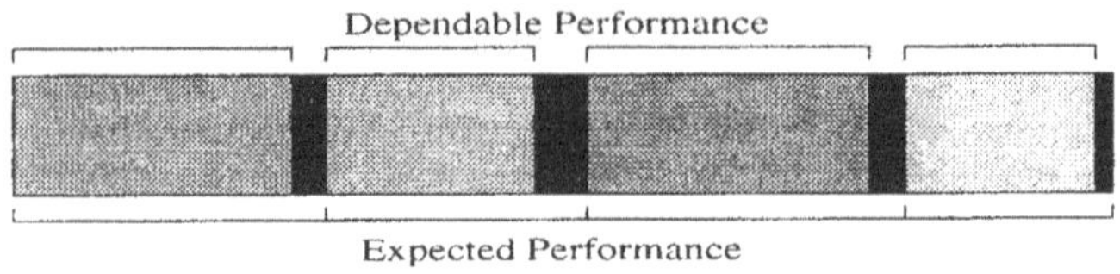

Figure 10. Conceptual view of expected and dependable performance. Sequences are placed based on the dependable performance of a processor. Sequences to be compared are held in reserve based on the difference between expected and deliverable performance.

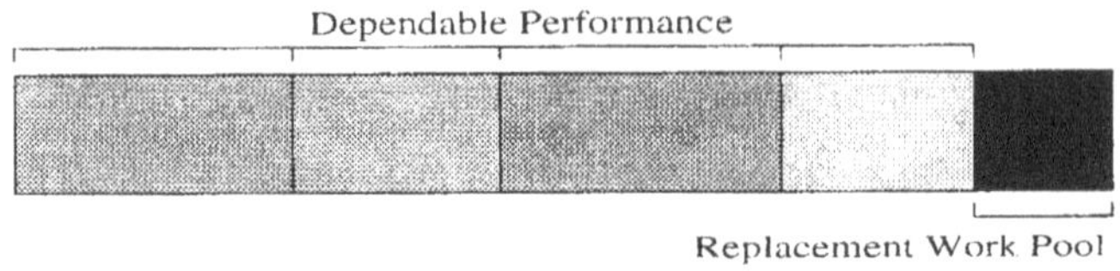

Figure 11. Implementation view of expected and dependable performance. Sequences are allocated in contiguous blocks. Work kept in reserve can be allocated to any worker object that requests more work, and is not tied to any individual machine.

5 Results

In this section, we compare the execution time of the original Mentat implementation of *complib* with that of an AppLeS-enhanced version. In all experiments, we execute both versions back-to-back multiple times on non-dedicated machines and networks, and report the range of execution times along with the average. Since the overheads are not invariant with respect to problem size, we compare executions using three different representative sequence libraries: one small, one medium, and one large. Similarly, we wish to reflect different possible metacomputing settings, so we use clusters of resources representing small, medium, and large levels of geographic dispersion, the largest of which employs resources located on opposite coasts of the United States.

Since application run-times for the original *complib* depend upon the size of the library chunk-size, we attempted to determine the best chunk size for each cluster empirically. That is, we conducted several hundred runs of the Mentat *complib* on each cluster, using different blocking factors. In all of the experiments shown below, we report the performance of the original Mentat *complib* using the chunk-size we observed to perform best on each cluster size. In contrast, the AppLeS-enhanced version chooses its own partitioning automatically based on performance forecasts.

5.1 Heterogeneous Platforms

We chose three different platforms so that scheduling methodologies could be compared in different environments. The small cluster is intended to show machines on a local area network, the medium adds machines in another building reflecting metacomputing at an organizational or enterprise-scale, and the large adds a machine across the country. All resources in each cluster, during each run, were operating in a non-dedicated production computing mode. Each *complib* execution had to compete with potentially contending applications and had to use shared networks.

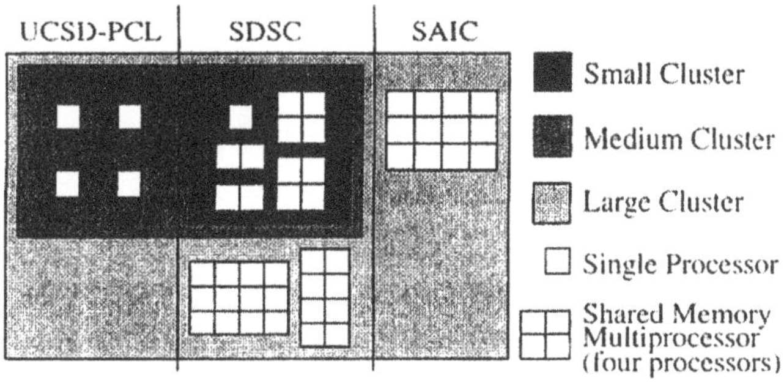

Figure 12. Cluster sizes chosen. Workstations and servers from UCSD's Parallel Computation Lab (PCL), the San Diego Supercomputer Center (SDSC), and Science Applications International Corporation (SAIC) in Virginia were used.

The small cluster consists of five machines, all located at the San Diego Supercomputer Center. These include two four processor Sun HPC servers, two two-processor Sun Ultra workstations, and one Sun Sparc-4 workstation, to total eleven processors. The network configuration is also heterogeneous: the HPC servers are connected to each other by fast (100 megabit) ethernet, other machines are connected by 10 megabit ethernet, and the processors within each multiprocessor machine communicate via shared memory.

The medium cluster adds four single processor machines from the Parallel Computation Lab (PCL) at UCSD. There are two Sun Ultra workstations, one Sun Sparc-5 and one Sun Sparc-10. These four machines are connected by a slow ethernet serving the rest of the PCL resources, and over the shared campus backbone to SDSC, a total of fifteen processors. The large cluster adds a 12 processor Sun CS-6400 at SAIC in Virginia, connected via a national ATM internet, and two additional multiprocessor Sun HPC servers at SDSC, a total of 47 processors.

We also compare two different AppLeS scheduling techniques to the Mentat-scheduled version of *complib* in each setting, for each problem size. The first uses an AppLeS to determine a static *placement* only of the computations. The placement is determined at run-time just before execution begins, all sequence comparisons are assigned, and no *replacement* phase is executed. The second AppLeS uses a hybrid combination of static, run-time *placement* and dynamic *replacement* based on Guided Self-Scheduling. The boundary between these two phases is determined by the prediction accuracy reported for each resource by the NWS as a quantitative measure of that prediction's quality. Use of such *Quality of Information* or *QoIn* metrics is the subject of other, on-going research efforts within the AppLeS research group at UCSD [13].

5.2 Complib Execution Performance

The largest performance improvement provided by application level scheduling of *complib* was seen on the medium problem size on the medium sized cluster (Figure 14). AppLeS run-time static scheduling ran an average of 59.7% (63.8 s) faster than Mentat *complib*. Using the hybrid approach increased that performance gain to 69% (74.0 s).

The largest difference between the two AppLeS approaches (AppLeS run-time static and the hybrid combination of *placement* and *replacement* strategies) was seen at the small cluster size and large data size (Figure 13). The hybrid was 34.4% (9.3 s) faster than the run-time static. The reason for this performance difference is that that the accuracy of the run-time static prediction degrades over time. A prediction made at the beginning of a short execution run is more accurate for the duration of the run, than for a long execution run. The hybrid approach considers the effect of this inaccuracy and compensates for it by using dynamic Guided Self-Scheduling when prediction inaccuracy would cause a load imbalance.

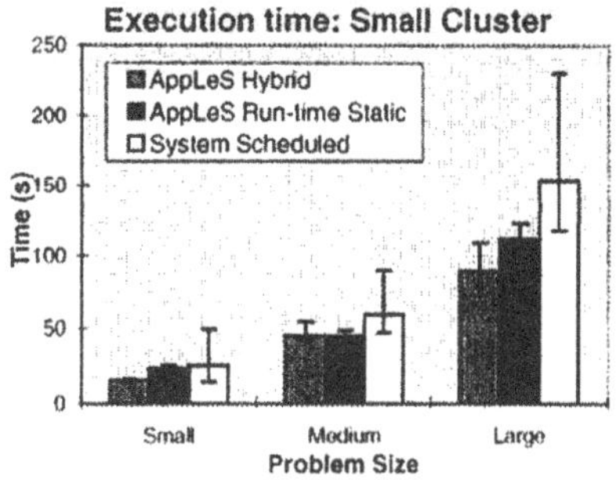

Figure 13. Execution times for small cluster. Bar height is the average of 30 execution times. Error bars cover the range.

Our hybrid approach provided the worst performance on the small cluster with the medium data size (Figure 14). The hybrid actually ran 1.1% slower than static partitioning alone. It is likely that this is a result of very little contention on the machines at the time these were executed: workstealing simply was not necessary to provide balanced load. We had hoped that the AppLeS would automatically recognize this condition and use only static *placement* in response. Since the performance penalty was small, however, we did not attempt to tune the AppLeS further to eliminate this discrepancy.

In general, however, the AppLeS improvement over the original Mentat scheduling method increases with both problem size and cluster size. Similarly, the improvement of hybrid *placement* and *replacement* over run-time static AppLeS scales with problem and cluster size. As metacomputing becomes more prevalent, we believe that these AppLeS based techniques will offer even greater performance advantages.

6 Conclusion

The goal of this work was to investigate the comparison of application-level scheduling techniques with a commonly used dynamic scheduling method (dynamic workstealing) using an application that was designed and tuned to work with this common method. In addition, we wished to define a general framework for scheduling master-slave parallel applications with data dependent execution profiles in a shared, heterogeneous environment.

To do so, we chose a biological sequence comparison application based on the FASTA algorithm implemented for Mentat called *complib*. The implementation of *complib* was specifically designed to work with the native Mentat workstealing scheduler. We attempted to fit this implementation with an AppLeS (application-level scheduler) without rewriting it to favor and the implementation of the the AppLeS. That is, we wished to compare the best possible Mentat implementation with a simple application of the AppLeS techniques, favoring the Mentat implementation whenever

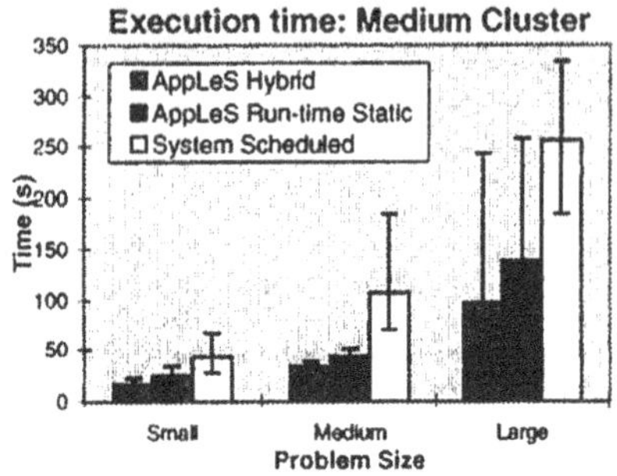

Figure 14. Execution times for medium cluster. Bar height is the average of 30 execution times. Error bars cover the range.

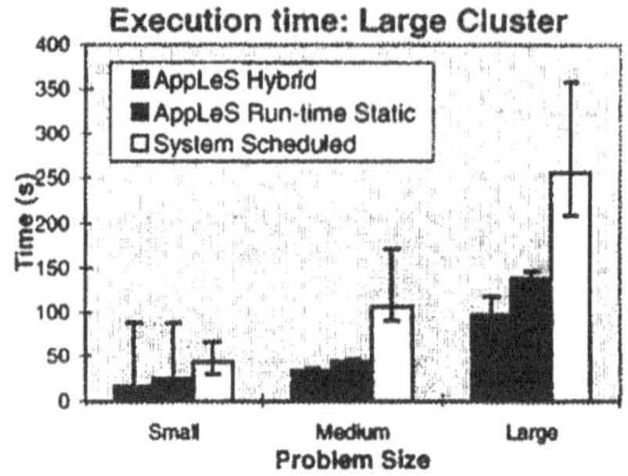

Figure 15. Execution times for large cluster. Bar height is the average of 30 execution times. Error bars cover the range.

possible.

In the experiments we conducted, the AppLeS-enhanced version of *complib* outperformed the original Mentat version in production metacomputing settings by as much as 69%. Moreover, the relative performance improvements of the AppLeS-enhanced versions scale with problem size and the size of the metacomputing resource pool leading us to believe that AppLeS will become an even more effective approach as metacomputing matures.

The most effective technique we have demonstrated combines static, run-time determined *placement* of some fraction of the work with dynamic *replacement* of the uncomputed fraction to ensure load balance. Controlling the balance between *placement* and *replacement* requires the AppLeS scheduler to evaluate the *Quality of Information* associated with each prediction. The function of the AppLeS itself does not depend on a specific *placement* or *replacement* algorithm. In the experiments, we used time-balancing and Guided Self-Scheduling, but other static and dynamic techniques could be used instead. As such, we believe that this technique represents a general framework for master/slave parallel metacomputing computations in which the master distributes uncomputed work to the slaves. As part of our future research efforts, we plan to investigate different applications from this application class as well as different static *placement* and dynamic *replacement* algorithms within the context of this framework.

Acknowledgements

We thank Mark Hyett, John Karpovich, and the rest of the Legion team for their assitance with Mentat and the complib application, Francine Berman and Allen Downey for informative scheduling and statistics discussions, Jennifer Schopf for comments on a previous draft of this paper, and Reagan Moore at SDSC for access to hardware and office space.

References

[1] S. Altschul, W. Gish, W. Miller, E. Myers, and D. Lipman. Basic local alignment search tool. *Journal of Molecular Biology*, 215:403–10, 1990.

[2] I. Banicescu and S. F. Hummel. Balancing processor loads and exploiting data locality in irregular computation. Technical Report RC 19934, IBM, 1995.

[3] F. Berman, R. Wolski, S. Figueira, J. Schopf, and G. Shao. Application level scheduling on distributed heterogeneous networks. In *Proceedings of Supercomputing 1996*, 1996.

[4] I. Foster and C. Kesselman. Globus: A metacomputing infrastructure toolkit. *International Journal of Supercomputer Applications*, 1997.

[5] A. Grimshaw. The mentat run-time system: Support for medium grain parallel computation. In *Proceedings of the Fifth Distributed Memory Computing Conference*, pages 1064–1073, April 1990.

[6] A. Grimshaw. Easy-to-use object-oriented parallel programming with mentat. *IEEE Computer*, May 1993.

[7] A. Grimshaw and V. Vivas. Falcon: A distributed scheduler for mimd architectures. In *Proceedings of the Symposium on Experiences with Distributed and Multiprocessor Systems*, pages 149–163, March 1991.

[8] A. S. Grimshaw, W. A. Wulf, J. C. French, A. C. Weaver, and P. F. Reynolds. Legion: The next logical step towrd a nationwide virtual computer. Technical Report CS-94-21, University of Virginia, 1994.

[9] M. Harchol-Balter and A. Downey. Exploiting process lifetime distributions for dynamic load balancing. In *Proceedings of the 1996 ACM Sigmetrics Conference on Measurement and Modeling of Computer Systems*, 1996.

[10] S. Hummel, J. Schmidt, R. Uma, and J. Wein. Load-sharing in heterogeneous systems via weighted factoring. In *Proc. 8th ACM Symp. on Parallel Algorithms and Architectures*, pages 318–328, 1996.

[11] S. Lucco. *Adaptive Parallel Programs*. PhD thesis, University of California, Berkeley, August 1994.

[12] C. Polychronopoulos and D. Kuck. A practical scheduling scheme for parallel computers. *IEEE Transactions on Computers*, C-36(12):1425–1439, December 1987.

[13] J. M. Schopf and F. Berman. Performance prediction in production environments. In *Proceedings of IPPS/SPDP '98*, 1998. to appear.

[14] T. Smith and M. Waterman. Identification of common molecular subsequences. *Journal of Molecular Biology*, 147:195–197, 1981.

[15] T. Tannenbaum and M. Litzkow. The condor distributed processing system. *Dr. Dobbs Journal*, February 1995.

[16] R. Wolski. Dynamically forecasting network performance to support dynamic scheduling using the network weather service. In *Proc. 6th IEEE Symp. on High Performance Distributed Computing*, August 1997.

[17] R. Wolski. Dynamically forecasting network performance using the network weather service. *Cluster Computing*, 1998. available from http://www.cs.ucsd.edu/users/rich/publications.html.

[18] R. Wolski, N. Spring, and C. Peterson. Implementing a performance forecasting system for metacomputing: The network weather service. In *Proceedings of Supercomputing 1997*, November 1997.

Improving the Performance of Speculatively Parallel Applications on the Hydra CMP

Kunle Olukotun, Lance Hammond and Mark Willey
Computer Systems Laboratory
Stanford University
Stanford, CA 94305-4070
http://www-hydra.stanford.edu/

ABSTRACT

Hydra is a chip multiprocessor (CMP) with integrated support for thread-level speculation. Thread-level speculation provides a way to parallelize sequential programs without the need for data dependence analysis or synchronization. This makes it possible to parallelize applications for which static memory dependence analysis is difficult or impossible. While performance of the baseline Hydra system on applications with medium to large grain parallelism is good, the performance on integer applications with fine-grained parallelism is unimpressive. In this paper, we describe a collection of software and hardware techniques for improving speculation performance over the baseline speculative Hydra CMP. These techniques focus on reducing the overheads associated with speculation and improving the speculation behavior of the applications using code restructuring. When these techniques are applied to a set of eleven integer, multimedia and floating-point benchmarks, significant performance improvements result. In particular, the overall performance of the integer benchmarks is improved by seventy-five percent.

Keywords

Chip multiprocessor, data speculation, multithreading, performance evaluation, parallel programming, feedback-driven optimization.

1. INTRODUCTION

Hardware support for speculative thread parallelism makes it possible to parallelize sequential applications without worrying about data dependencies at compile time. Even if there are dependencies between speculative threads, the hardware support guarantees correct program execution. This support significantly increases the scope of applications that can be automatically parallelized, because there are many applications that have thread-level parallelism, but whose memory dependencies cannot be analyzed at compile time. The Multiscalar architecture was the first architecture to include this support [18]. More recently, there have been proposals to add support for speculative thread parallelism to a chip multiprocessor (CMP) [15] [19]. In this paper, we focus on improving performance with speculative thread support on the Hydra CMP [7].

To generate code for a speculative thread architecture, the program must be broken into threads. A program can be partitioned into arbitrary threads, but to minimize the effect of control hazards it is desirable to pick threads that are either control independent or whose control dependencies are easy to predict. Loop and procedure program constructs provide good candidates for speculative threads [16]. With loops the speculative threads are the loop iterations, while with procedures the speculative threads are the procedure call and the code following the procedure call.

Given a sequence of speculative threads, it is the job of the Hydra hardware to execute these threads correctly. The hardware accomplishes this using data speculation support in the memory system, which records speculatively executed memory references so that they can be squashed when necessary. Speculative threads are executed in parallel, but commit in sequential order. Committing a speculative thread requires the thread to write out any speculative data that was created during the execution of the thread to the sequential state of the machine. At any point before a thread is committed, it may be forced to restart due to a data dependency violation with a less speculative thread, which occurs when a speculative thread reads a data memory location before it has been written by the less speculative thread. The simplest way to deal with violations is to discard the speculative state and restart the speculative region from the first instruction in the thread.

Unfortunately, hardware support for speculation is not sufficient to guarantee good parallel performance for all applications. There are several reasons why parallel performance with speculative threads may be limited for a particular application. The most fundamental limit is a lack of parallelism in the application. This manifests itself as low parallel coverage (the fraction of the sequential execution time that can be parallelized using speculative threads) or reasonable coverage but low performance due to true data dependencies in the parallel portion of the program that continually cause violations. These data dependencies may be inherent to the algorithm, or they may just be an unfortunate programming choice that worked well in sequential execution but causes unnecessary dependencies when the program is speculatively parallelized. Less fundamental performance limits are due to the software overheads associated with managing speculative threads, the increased latency of inter-thread communication through memory (instead of registers), and the amount of wasted work that must be reexecuted when violations occur.

The performance of speculatively parallelized applications can be improved by optimizing the applications themselves and/or the speculation support software and hardware. Performance can be

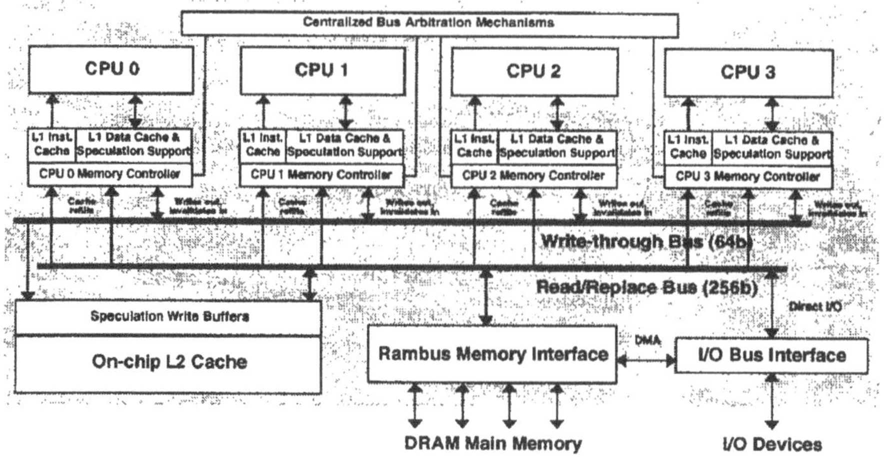

Figure 1. The main datapaths in the Hydra CMP.

improved by selectively choosing threads that have more parallelism. Furthermore, compiler and manual optimization can be used to rearrange code to reduce the likelihood of violations. Speculation runtime software can be optimized to reduce the overheads of managing speculative threads and a combination of hardware and software can be used to minimize the performance losses from violations. In this paper we show how many of these techniques can be combined to improve the performance of speculatively parallel applications on the Hydra CMP.

The rest of this paper describes the Hydra system and shows how the performance of Hydra on speculatively parallelized applications can be improved using both software and hardware. In the next section, we describe previous work in thread speculation. In Section , we briefly describe the Hydra chip multiprocessor and the software support required for speculation. In Section 4, we present and explain the performance of the baseline Hydra system on eleven benchmarks. In Section 5, we describe how the model used to divide the program into threads can be extended to expose more speculative parallelism and explain how violation statistics collected from previous runs of a speculative program can be used to find and eliminate unnecessary dependencies. We also describe how the base support for speculation in the memory system can be improved to reduce the effects of data dependence violations, which provides further performance gains. In Section 6, we present speculation performance results using these software and hardware enhancements. We conclude in Section 7.

2. PREVIOUS WORK

The first mention of speculative threads was in the work of Knight in the context of LISP [10]. However, the Multiscalar paradigm [3] [18] has most directly influenced the Hydra research. The Multiscalar paradigm takes a hardware-centric approach to extracting fine-grained parallelism from sequential integer programs. The hardware required includes processing units whose register files are connected by a ring and a shared primary data cache with speculative memory support provided by an address resolution buffer (ARB) [4]. More recently, the speculative versioning cache work has eliminated the requirement of the shared primary data cache using extensions to a multiprocessor cache coherency protocol [5]. The Multiscalar group has observed that blind speculation on all data dependencies can severely impact performance when the speculation is wrong and that dynamic data dependence prediction techniques can be used to improve performance over blind speculatio [13]. Following on the Multiscalar work other researchers have pr posed adding speculative data support to a chip multiprocessor [1 [19]. Here the goal is to simplify the task of creating parallel pr grams for a multiprocessor. The assumption in these proposals that the processing units are less tightly coupled than in the Mult scalar architecture and so the focus of the CMP work is on extrac ing and exploiting coarser-grain parallelism.

3. THE HYDRA CMP

Hydra is a chip multiprocessor with data speculation support. W briefly describe the Hydra architecture and software support env ronment here in sufficient detail to understand the remainder of th paper, but the Hydra system is more completely described in [and [7].

3.1 Architecture

The Hydra architecture consists of 4 MIPS processors, each with pair of private data caches, attached to an integrated on-chip se ondary cache using separate read and write busses, as shown in Fi ure 1. The processors use data caches with a write-through policy simplify the implementation of cache coherence. All writes prop gate through to the write back secondary cache using the dedicate *write bus*. In order to ensure coherence, the other processors' da caches watch this bus — using a second set of cache tags — an invalidate lines when necessary to maintain cache coherence. O chip communication among the caches and the external ports, suc as data cache refills, are supported by the cache-line-wide *read bu* Both buses are fully pipelined to maintain single-cycle occupanc for all accesses. Off-chip accesses are handled using dedicate main memory and I/O buses. For the applications evaluated in th paper, the bandwidth of these buses is not a performance bottl neck. A summary of the pertinent characteristics of the Hydra CM memory system appears in Table 1.

Thedata speculation support in Hydra allows threads to execute parallel but ensures that they commit in sequential order. The har ware guarantees that no speculative thread can change the seque tial state of the processor, which is kept in the secondary cache ar main memory, until the thread commits. Executing threads in para lel causes memory data hazards. Hydra deals with WAR and WA hazards using the implicit memory location renaming that occu

	L1 Cache	L2 Cache	Main Memory
Configuration	Separate I & D SRAM cache pairs per CPU	Shared, on-chip SRAM cache	Off-chip DRAM
Capacity	16KB each	2 MB	128 MB
Bus Width	32-bit connection to CPU	256-bit read bus and 64-bit write bus	32-bit wide Rambus connection at full CPU speed
Access Time	1 CPU cycle	5 CPU cycles	at least 50 cycles
Associativity	4-way	4-way	N/A
Line Size	32 bytes	64 bytes	4 KB pages
Write Policy	Writethrough, no write allocate	Writeback, allocate on writes	"Writeback" (virtual memory)
Inclusion	N/A	Inclusion enforced on L1	Includes all cached data

Table 1. Hydra memory hierarchy characteristics.

	Application	Source	Data Set
General Integer	compress	SPEC95	train
	eqntott	SPEC92	reference
	grep	UNIX utility [8]	190 line file
	m88ksim	SPEC95	test
	wc	UNIX utility	10,000 character file
Multimedia Integer	ijpeg(compression)	SPEC95	train
	mpeg-2(decoding)	MediaBench [12]	test.m2v
Floating Point	alvin	SPEC92	reference
	cholesky	Num. Recipes [17]	100×100
	ear	SPEC92	reference
	simplex	Num. Recipes [17]	40 variables

Table 2. Benchmark summary.

when a processor has speculative data in its data cache. This memory renaming avoids the need to stall speculative threads for these memory hazards. RAW hazards caused by true data dependencies result in violations that force the violating processor to back up and start again from the beginning of the speculative region it is currently processing. However, using the write bus to forward speculative data between threads running on different processors reduces the occurrence of these violations.

Data speculation support in Hydra consists of a set of new coprocessor instructions, extra tag bits which are added to the processor data caches, and a set of secondary cache write buffers. The coprocessor instructions are provide an interface to the thread speculation control hardware, the tag bits are used to detect data dependency violations between threads, and the write buffers are used to buffer speculative data until it can be safely committed to the secondary cache or discarded.

3.2. Software Support

There is both compiler and run-time system software support for speculation in the Hydra architecture. A source to source compiler (*hydracat*) is used to transform C `for` and `while` loops into speculative `for` and `while` loops. Currently, the loops are selected by the programmer by designating candidate loops using the `pfor` and `pwhile` keywords. The compiler then automatically transforms these loops to their speculative versions by outlining the loop as a procedure and by analyzing the dataflow in the loop body so that any local variables that have the potential to create loop-carried dependencies are globalized

The other component of the software support for speculation is the runtime system. The runtime system is used to control speculative threads through the coprocessor interface and stores to special I/O locations. This collection of small software control routines is used to control the speculative threads currently active in the system. In our baseline system, these routines control threads created in two different ways: loop iterations and procedure calls. When a procedure call is encountered, the runtime system forks off a thread to speculatively execute the code following the return from the call, while the original thread executes the code within the procedure itself. If the return value from the procedure is predictable, and if no memory referenced as a side effect by the procedure is read immediately following the procedure return, then the two threads may run in parallel. Similarly, when a `pfor` or `pwhile` loop is encountered, the system starts threads on all of the processors to handle iterations of the loop, which are then distributed among the new threads in a round-robin fashion. The routines must also track the order of all speculative threads in the system in order to properly forward data between threads and to signal data dependency violations, which trigger exception routines that squash and restart the violating thread and all threads that are more speculative. See [7] for further details.

4. BASE SPECULATION PERFORMANCE

4.1. Benchmarks and Simulation Methodology

To evaluate our speculative system and identify potential areas for improvement, we used eleven representative benchmarks that cover a significant portion of the general-purpose application space. These benchmarks are listed in Table 2. The speculative versions of the benchmarks were created using Hydracat. The binaries were generated using GCC 2.7.2 with optimization level -O2 on an SGI workstation running IRIX 5.3. Currently, Hydracat only works on C programs. This prevents us from experimenting with any of the SPEC95 floating-point benchmarks, which are all written in FORTRAN. However, from the point of view of extracting parallelism, the C SPEC92 floating point benchmarks are more challenging than the SPEC95 floating point benchmarks, so we would expect the performance on SPEC95 benchmarks to be similar or better.

All the performance results we present are obtained by executing the benchmarks on a detailed, cycle-accurate simulator that models the Hydra architecture described in Section 3.1. The execution time of the speculative binaries includes the time spent in the run-time system. Our simulation environment can switch back and forth between execution using the cycle-accurate simulator and execution directly on the real machine. Switching to the real machine allows us to run entire applications on the simulator by quickly executing initialization code and redundant executions of kernels. However, code representing at least 95% of the original sequential execution time is run on the cycle-accurate simulator to ensure that the simulations are representative.

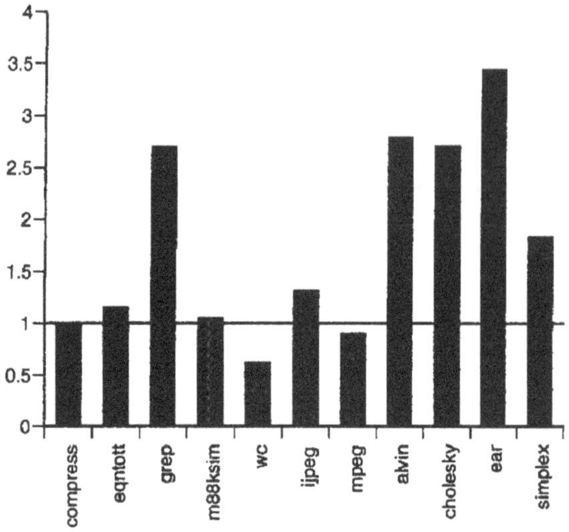

Figure 2. Baseline speculation speedup.

4.2. Baseline Performance

The performance of the base Hydra CMP is shown in Figure 2. The speedups represent the execution time of one of the processors in Hydra running unmodified C code divided by the execution time of the speculative Hydra CMP running speculatively parallelized C code. We see that the performance is highly dependent on the application and varies from 0.6 to 3.4. To understand the performance profile in more detail, we explain how each benchmark was parallelized and what limits the speculative parallel performance on the benchmark.

compress(compression): Thisbenchmarkcompressesaninputfile using entropy encoding. Compress is dominated by a single small loop (about 100 instructions, on average) that has complex control flow. As observed in [18] and contrary to the analysis in [19] there is a loop-carried dependency that limits the parallelism in this loop. However, there are opportunities to overlap the I/O routines of separate loop iterations. The limited parallelism and small thread size in compress are overwhelmed by the speculation software overheads on the baseline system.

eqntott: This benchmark performs logic minimization on a set of input equations. Unlike the other benchmarks, we did not parallelize the loops in this application, because the only good candidate loop (in the *cmppt* function) is too small to be effectively parallelized on Hydra without significant programmer help. As a result, we used procedure-call based speculation. Despite a reasonable amount of parallelism in the recursive *quicksort* procedure, the speculation software overheads and squashing of non-parallel procedures limit speedup.

grep: This benchmark is the well-known regular expression tool that matches a regular expression to each line of an input file and prints those lines that contain matching strings. The main loop of the program iterates over all the lines of the input file. The speculative thread version of this loop performs very well because the only dependencies that occur are during file input and when a match is found. However, most lines do not match the expression and so once they have been read from the input file they are processed completely in parallel.

m88ksim: This program performs simulates a Motorola 8800(RISC CPU on a cycle-by-cycle basis. It consists of a single, larg instruction execution loop that is potentially parallel, but unfortu nately also accesses several global variables that tend to exhibit tru dependencies in a manner that is very difficult for a compiler t statically analyze. In the speculative version of m88ksim, accesse to these global variables cause a considerable number of violations The execution time that is lost when these violations occur limit speedup.

wc: This is the UNIX word count utility, which counts the numbe of characters, words, and lines in an input file. It primarily consist of a single character processing loop that is very small — loop iter ations have only 20-40 instructions, on average. In addition, ther are loop-carried dependencies, such as the file pointer and *in a wor* indicator. The speculative version of this tiny loop is slowed dow by the speculation software overheads and the relatively high inter processor communication latencies, caused by communicatin through memory instead of registers. Consequently, wc slows dow by a considerable amount.

ijpeg (compression): This is an integer, multimedia benchmar that compresses an input RGB color image to a standard JPEG file using a lossy algorithm consisting of color conversion, downsam pling, and DCT steps. The multiple loops in these steps posses large amount of inherent parallelism, but were originally coded s that the parallelism is often obscured by existing program seman tics, such as numerous pointers, poor code layout, and odd loo sizes. The speculatively parallel version of ijpeg exposes this paral lelism, but performance is limited by parallel coverage and specula tion software overheads.

mpeg (decoding): This is a benchmark from the Mediabenc suite [12] that decodes a short MPEG-2 video sequence to an RGI frame buffer. Parallelization occurs at the macro block level, wher the variable-length decoding (VLD) is performed. The VLD step i completely serial, but speculation is able to overlap the processin performed during the other, more parallel stages of decodin (IDCTs and motion estimation) with the serial VLD step of late macroblocks. This parallelization technique is described in greate detail for a hand-parallelized version of mpeg in [9]. Despite a sig nificant amount of potential parallelism, MPEG-2 decoding slow down because of a loop-carried dependency that unnecessarily seri alizes execution.

alvin: This is a neural network training application for autono mous land vehicle navigation. It is composed of four key proce dures which are dominated by doubly-nested loops. Although thes loops are parallel, the parallelism is obscured by the way in whic the application is coded with pointer variables. However, thes loops are easily speculatively parallelized and result in good paral lel performance.

cholesky: Cholesky decomposition and substitution is a well known matrix kernel. The multiply nested loops in the decomposi tion procedure have significant amounts of parallelism, but the also contain loop-carried dependencies that occur infrequently. I conventional parallelization, these dependencies would have to b detected and synchronized, but with speculation we can obliviousl parallelize them. The loops in the substitution routine are also pa allel, but here each loop is written in so that a loop-carried depen dency serializes the speculative loop. Fortunately th decomposition procedure dominates the sequential execution tim and speedup is still quite good.

Application	Coverage (%)	Restarts per thread	CPU utilization (%)	Maximum write state
compress	100	6.4	28	24
eqntott	93	12.1	32	40
grep	90	1.1	75	11
m88ksim	94	15.5	29	28
wc	100	4.6	69	8
ijpeg	60	2.35	42	32
mpeg	92	1275	25	56
alvin	96	0.31	81	158
cholesky	91	0.88	74	4
ear	96	0.32	97	82
simplex	86	0.14	60	14

Table 3. Speculation performance characteristics. The speculative write state is presented in terms of 32 byte cache lines.

ar: This benchmark simulates the propagation of sound in the uman inner ear. The conventional wisdom is that the structure of his program is a sequential outer loop and a sequence of parallel nner loops [11]. The parallel inner loops are extremely fine grained nd therefore are not good candidates for speculative threads on the Hydra CMP. However, the outer loop can be speculatively parallel-zed and achieves very good speedup. The dependent outer loop pipelines across the processors quite well because each iteration is only dependent on the previous iteration in a way that allows much of the computation to be overlapped. Memory renaming ensures hat, even though each iteration of the outer loop uses the same data structures, each processor dynamically gets a private copy.

implex: This kernel solves problems in linear programming. The hree procedures in this kernel have a number of small loops. The lependences between the iterations of these loops are not at all obvious. The speculative parallelization of these loops achieves good speedup, but less than the other numerical benchmarks. This s mainly due to the speculation software overheads that dominate he short running loops.

Table 3 shows some key performance characteristics for the specu-ative versions of the eleven benchmarks. Except for the results from the eqntott benchmark, the data for this table was collected vith the speculation control software optimizations to be discussed n Section 5.1 (but without the other optimizations discussed in Section 5). Except for the ijpeg and simplex benchmarks, more than 90 percent of each benchmark can be speculatively parallelized. However, high coverage does not guarantee good performance vhen there are a significant number of violations. The number of estarts per committed thread (restart rate) gives a good indication of the inherent parallelism in an application. As expected, the benchmarks fall into two main classes: integer benchmarks with estart rates that are much greater than one and numerical bench-narks with restart rates less than one. The combination of the cov-erage, the restart rate, the amount of work that is lost due to the estarts, and the speculation software overheads determines the fraction of the time the processors are doing useful work (CPU uti-ization), which ultimately determines performance.

A key architectural metric is the size of the speculative write state. This metric is important because it indicates the feasibility of mplementing a Hydra CMP architecture with reasonably sized speculative write buffers that achieves good performance. Table 3 ists the number of 32 byte cache line buffers required to hold the maximum size write state for the eleven benchmarks. The results indicate that a buffer size of 64 lines (2KB) per processor is suffi-cient for all but the alvin and ear benchmarks. These two applica-tions would require 8KB write buffers for maximum performance. However, it would be possible to reduce the memory requirements of the alvin benchmark to an arbitrary degree simply by using loop iteration chunking on the inner loop of alvin, as described in Sec-tion 5.2.3, instead of our original scheme of speculating on the outer loop. Lastly, the Hydra memory system is capable of handling overflows simply by temporarily halting execution on the specula-tive processor that experiences the buffer overflow. Thus, it may be possible to capture the write state from most iterations using a smaller buffer, as we showed in [7].

5. IMPROVING SPECULATION PERFORMANCE

There are four key problems that need to be addressed to improve speculation performance: 1) reducing the performance losses from the speculation software overheads, 2) reducing the performance impact of inter-thread communication through memory, 3) increas-ing the amount of parallelism in the program that is exposed to the speculation system, and 4) reducing both the number of violations and the work lost when violations occur. We propose a simple solu-tion to the first problem in Section 5.1. Section 5.2 outlines code motion techniques that help attack both the third and fourth prob-lems. Finally, hardware techniques to address the fourth are pre-sented in Section 5.3. The second problem requires fundamental changes to the underlying interprocessor communication mecha-nism which are beyond the scope of this paper.

5.1. Loop-only Speculation

The protocol software required to handle loops is much simpler than the protocol software for procedure calls. As soon as a loop starts, its iterations are distributed among the processors in a sim-ple, round-robin fashion. In contrast, procedure calls occur one at a time, on arbitrary processors, in an unpredictable pattern. As a result, the control software must be able to handle a complex, dynamically changing list of speculative threads. This complexity does not lend itself to simple, fast software control routines, as the routines must maintain a dynamic list of threads. Being able to do both loops and procedures simultaneously increases the complexity

	Routine	Use	Procedure and Loops Overhead	Loop-only Overhead
Procedures	Start Procedure	Forks off the code following a procedure call to another processor	~70	—
	End Procedure	Completes processing for a procedure that has forked off its completion code, and starts running another speculative task on the CPU	~110	—
Loops	Start Loop	Prepares the system to speculatively execute loop iterations	~70	~30
	End of each loop iteration	Completes the current loop iteration, and then attempts to run the next loop iteration (or speculative procedure thread, if present)	~80	12
	Finish Loop	Completes the current loop iteration, and then shuts down the loop	~80	~22
Support	Violation: Local	Handles a RAW violation	~25	7
	Violation: Receive from another CPU	Restarts the current speculative thread on this processor, when another, less speculative processor needs it	~80	7
	Hold: Buffer Full	Temporarily halts execution if a processor is out of speculative buffers	15	12
	Hold: Exception	Pauses the processor following a SYSCALL instruction, until it is the "head," nonspeculative processor	25 + OS time	17 + OS time

Table 4. Overheads of key speculation software routines.

of both, slowing down the system even more. By limiting speculation to loops alone, we can dramatically simplify the control routines so they require many fewer instructions. Table 4 shows the overhead reductions we were able to obtain by simplifying several key loop-control routines so that they would only work in an environment without procedure speculation. The savings obtained by simplification of the routine that must be called at the end of each loop iteration and the violation-processing routines have the most impact on overall performance.

5.2. Using Feedback From Violation Statistics

Our simulator produces output that explicitly identifies loads and stores in the application that cause violations. In a real system, similar feedback could be obtained by adding speculative load PC memory to each processor, broadcasting store PCs along with data on the write bus, and then interpreting the results from these hardware structures using instrumentation code built into the speculation software routines (at profiling time only — normally the overhead imposed by such code could be eliminated). We developed a tool to translate the load and store addresses produced by the simulator to source code locations, for easier analysis. Armed with this information, we attempted to reduce the number of violations caused by the most critical dependencies using synchronization, code motion, and loop transformations. While we used the feedback information from the violation statistics to make manual modifications to our benchmarks, many of these modifications could be performed using a feedback-directed compiler targeted to a speculatively parallel architecture.

5.2.1. Explicit Synchronization

The first technique we used to minimize effects from these critical data dependencies was to add explicit synchronization to cause the dependent thread to stall instead of causing a dependency violation. This was achieved simply by adding a way to issue a non-speculative load instruction even while the processor is executing speculatively. As depicted in Figure 3, this special load may be used to test lock variables that protect the critical regions of code in which pairs of loads and stores exist that cause frequent dependency violations. Before entering a critical region, synchronizing code spins on the lock variable until the lock is released by another processor. Because the special load is non-speculative, a violation does not

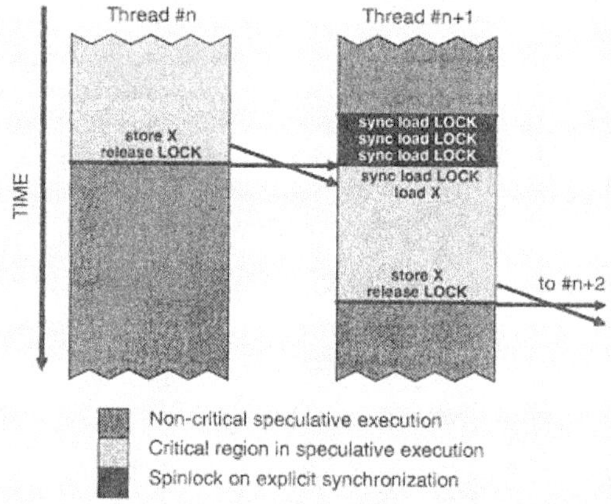

Figure 3. Explicit synchronization.

occur when the lock is released by a store from another process Once the lock is freed, the speculative processor may perform t load at the beginning of the critical region. Finally, when a proce sor has performed the store at the end of the region, it updates t lock so that the next processor may enter the critical region. Th process eliminates all restarts caused by dependent load-store pa in the critical region, at the expense of forcing the speculative pr cessors to serialize through the critical regions, eliminating a possibility of finding parallelism there. The lock handling code al adds a small software overhead to the program.

Similar synchronization mechanisms have been proposed before. [19], special loads and stores were used to pass data between pr cessors directly and perform explicit synchronization at the sa time. This method avoided the overhead of extra synchronizati code, but required more complex hardware synchronization mech nisms to handle the special loads and stores. An all-hardware da dependence prediction and synchronization technique was explor in [13] for use with the Multiscalar architecture. Special hardwa structures tracked dependencies and then automatically used sy chronizing hardware to prevent restarts due to dependent load-stc pairs. This hardware-based technique allows a limited degree automatic synchronization even without programmer interventio and it would be adaptable for use on a Hydra-like architecture. alternative design for a superscalar architecture that tracks sets stores that commonly supply data to a following, dependent lo vas proposed in [2]. Finally, we presented some preliminary results n the use of synchronization with the compress benchmark in [7].

.2.2. *Code Motion*

Vhile explicit synchronization prevents critical dependencies from ausing violations, it also forces the speculative processors to seri- lize their execution. For small critical regions, this is perfectly cceptable, but for large ones it can easily eliminate all of the paral- elism that speculative threads are attempting to exploit. To avoid his situation the second technique we use to improve speculation erformance is to manually move source code lines with dependent oads and stores in order to shrink the critical path between fre- uently violating load-store pairs. This makes it possible to reduce he number of violations and often increases the inherent parallel- sm in the program by lengthening the sections of code that could e overlapped on different processors without causing violations.

'his works in two ways. At the tops of critical regions, loads can ometimes be delayed by rearranging code blocks in order to move ode without critical dependencies higher up in the loop body. Iowever, this is usually only possible in large loops built up from everal non-dependent sections of code that can be interchanged reely. More importantly, we were frequently able to rearrange code o make stores to shared variables occur earlier. Induction variables re an obvious target for early stores. Since the store that updates he induction variable is not dependent upon any computation vithin the loop, these can safely be moved to the top of the loop ody. When this is done, a "local" copy of the old value is made at he same time, with a small amount of additional code, and this ocal copy is used throughout the remainder of the loop body while he "global" variable is used by other processors starting their own oop iterations. Other variables, that *do* depend upon results calcu- ated in a loop iteration, will not be improved as dramatically by cheduling their critical stores early, but performance can often still e improved significantly over unmodified code using these tech- iques.

t should also be noted that code motion on a speculative processor s somewhat different from that on a conventional multiprocessor, ince only the most critical loads and stores of variables need to be noved to reduce the potential for restarts. For example, variables hat often — but not always — act like induction variables can be peculatively treated like induction variables at the top of the loop. hould they later act differently, the variable may be re-written, robably causing restarts on the more speculative processors. How- ver, as long as the value computed and written early is used most f the time, the amount of available parallelism in the program may e vastly increased.

'or the measurements taken in this paper, we did all code motion by and based on violation statistics provided by our simulator. How- ver, while synchronization may easily slow down a program if mplemented in an improper fashion, code motion will rarely egrade performance. Hence, a feedback-directed compiler could erform this job almost as well as a human programmer by aggres- ively moving references that frequently cause violations within peculative code, up to the limits imposed by existing data and con- 'ol dependencies, in order to reduce the critical path between ependent load-store pairs.

.2.3. *Loop Body Slicing and Chunking*

Aore radical forms of code motion and thread creation are possible y breaking up a loop body up into smaller chunks that execute in parallel or its converse, combining multiple speculative threads together into a single thread. With the former technique, loop slicing, a single loop body is spread across several speculative iterations running on different processors, instead of running only as a single iteration on a single processor. In the latter case, loop chunking, multiple loop iterations may be chunked together into a single, large loop body. Loop bodies that were executed on several processors are combined and run on one. This generally only results in better performance if there are no loop-carried dependencies besides induction variables, which limits the versatility of loop chunking. However, if a parallel loop can be found, chunking can allow one to create speculative threads of nearly optimal size for the speculative system. Figure 4 shows conceptually how slicing and chunking work.

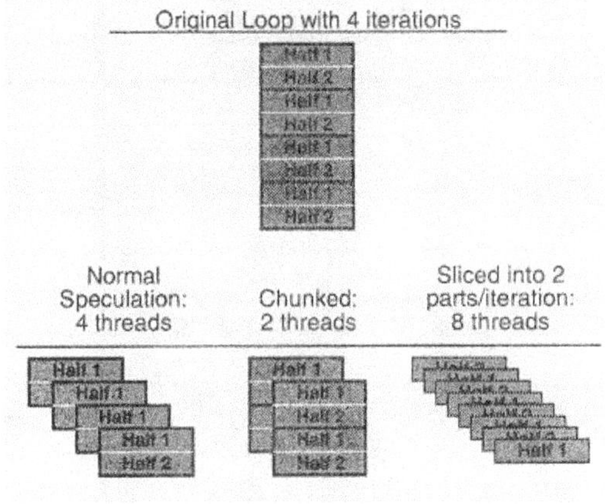

Figure 4. Loop body chunking and slicing.

While loop chunking only needs to be performed if the body of the loop is so small that the execution time is dominated by speculation overheads, the motivation for loop slicing are more complex. The primary reason is to break down a single, large loop body, made up of several fairly independent sections, into smaller parts if they are more optimally sized for speculation. In a very large loop body a single memory dependence violation near the end of the loop can result in a large amount of work being discarded. Also, the large loop body may overflow the buffers holding the speculative state. Buffer overflow prevents a speculative processor from making forward progress until it becomes the head, non-speculative processor, so this should normally be avoided whenever possible. Loop slicing is also a way to perform code motion to prevent violations. If there is code in the loop body that calculates values that will be used in the next loop iteration and this code is not *usually* dependent upon values calculated earlier in the same loop iteration, then this code may be sliced off of the end of the loop body and assigned to its own speculative thread. In this way, the values calculated in the sliced-off region are essentially "precomputed" for later iterations, since they are produced in parallel with the beginning of the loop iteration. The advantage of slicing over normal code motion is that no data dependency analysis is required to ensure it is legal to perform the code motion, since the violation detection mechanism will still enforce all true dependencies that may exist.

Loop chunking may be implemented in a compiler in a similar manner to the way loop unrolling is implemented today, since both are variations on the idea of combining loop iterations together. In fact, the two operations may be merged together, so that a loop is unrolled as it is chunked into a speculative thread. As a result, adding this capability to current compilers should not be difficult. Effective slicing, however, will require more knowledge about the

	Application	Procedures and Loops	Loops Only	After SW Optimization	With HW Checkpoints
General Integer	compress	1.00	1.42	1.57	1.71
	eqntott	1.15	—	1.75	1.8
	grep	2.65	2.86	—	2.85
	m88ksim	1.05	1.13	1.45	1.56
	wc	0.62	1.57	—	1.64
Multimedia Integer	ijpeg (compression)	1.31	1.56	—	1.6
	mpeg (decoding)	0.90	0.96	2.14	2.14
Floating Point	alvin	2.79	3.02	—	—
	cholesky	2.71	2.85	3.16	3.25
	ear	3.44	3.87	—	3.88
	simplex	1.83	2.67	—	2.72

Table 5. Performance with the various system enhancements.

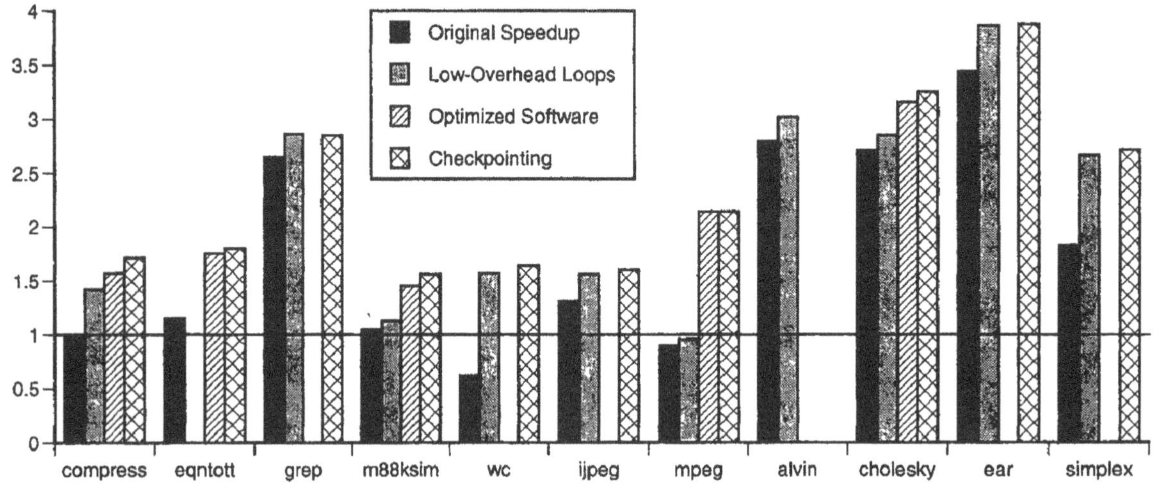

Figure 5. A performance comparison of the baseline system and the enhanced systems.

execution of a program than loop unrolling, although the ability to analyze the control structure of the application combined with violation statistics should be sufficient. Slicing should not be performed indiscriminately because it may allow speculative overheads to become significant and/or it may result in significant load imbalance among the processors if some slices are much larger than others. The former problem will obviously slow the system down, while the latter problem will degrade performance in the current Hydra design, since a speculative processor that completes its assigned thread must stall until it becomes the head processor, wasting valuable execution resources in the process. This problem can only be overcome by making the speculation system allow multiple speculative regions within each CPU, so that a processor that completes a speculative region may immediately go on to another while it waits to commit the results from the first. However, implementing this capability has significant hardware overheads [7].

5.3. Hardware Checkpointing

Another technique to prevent large quantities of work from being discarded after violations is to provide a mechanism for taking extra checkpoints in the middle of loop iterations. The basic speculation system takes a checkpoint of the system state only at the beginning of a speculative thread, and must return to that checkpoint aft every violation. A possible technique to save time on restarts is take an extra checkpoint whenever a violation-prone load actual occurs. That way, if the load really does cause a violation later, t work done by the speculative processor before the bad load doesn need to be discarded, because the processor will be able to return the machine state just before the load.

Hardware checkpointing requires four key mechanisms. First, hardware mechanism must be installed to track the PCs of loa that tend to cause violations. When one of these loads is encou tered, the mechanism must signal the speculative hardware to take checkpoint. If load PCs are already recorded in order to allow viol tion statistics tracking, as described in Section 5.2, this will be fairly minor addition. The other three items are necessary to ta the checkpoints themselves. Backup copies of the register file a necessary to hold the register file state at the checkpoint. The backups are not normally necessary, since checkpoints are usual made during speculation software routines, when the register file in a well-known state. However, checkpoints made at violati loads may come at arbitrary times, when the register file is in arbitrary state. From a hardware point of view, this addition is t most troublesome, since it requires modifications to the existi ocessor's register file, where many high-speed signals may be fected. Less problematic are additional sets of bits in the primary che to indicate that words have been loaded ("read" bits) and lditional, smaller store buffers before the secondary cache. For *ch* checkpoint, a new set of "read" bits and store buffers are eded to track the speculative state. The other speculation control ts in the primary cache may be safely shared among all the check-ints, to reduce the hardware requirements. The store buffers do t need to grow significantly in overall memory size, because each iginal monolithic speculative thread now has its stores scattered er several smaller checkpoint store buffers. Only a relatively nall overall size increase is necessary to handle the inevitable load balance that will occur among the different checkpoints.

. IMPROVED SPECULATION PERFORMANCE

fter applying the software optimizations to the benchmarks and e hardware enhancements to the Hydra simulator, we collected a w set of performance results. Table 5 These results are shown in d Figure 5. From these results it is clear that the lower overheads loop-only speculation provide significant performance improve-ents for most benchmarks. The most dramatic improvement is en with the wc benchmark, whose performance more than dou-es. This is consistent with wc's small loop body, that was com-etely dominated by the speculation software overheads in the base n-time system.

e were able to optimize five (compress, eqntott, m88ksim, mpeg, d cholesky) of the eleven benchmarks using the optimizations scribed in Section 5.2.

compress: Synchronization was added to compress to prevent the key loop-carried dependency from causing violations. This reduced the number of restarts by a factor of 3 (to 2.1 per iteration), allowing a greater speedup.

eqntott: The optimization of eqntott is a actually a change to the speculation software. Instead of speculating on all procedure calls, we modified the system so that only calls to the recursive *quicksort* procedure generate new speculative threads. This eliminates the performance losses from blind procedure speculation of procedures with little parallelism.

m88ksim: The large loop body in m88ksim was sliced to expose parallelism within the loop body and to allow code motion for a data value that is read early in each iteration, but is normally computed late in the previous iteration. This code motion decreased the number of restarts by a factor of 5 (to 3.1 per iteration), as the amount of available parallelism was dramatically increased.

mpeg: The performance of the mpeg-2 benchmark is improved substantially by moving an induction-like variable update from the end of the loop body to before the time-consuming DCT step. This code motion makes it possible for DCTs of multiple macroblocks to overlap. The same performance improvement was also achieved with slicing. As with m88ksim, the additional parallelism exposed by these modifications reduced the number of restarts by a factor of 5 (to 280 per iteration). Our speculatively parallel version of this code was actually faster than the macroblock-based hand-parallelized version in [9], because the speculative system does not have to synchronize between processors in a conservative fashion.

Category	Procedures and Loops	Loops Only	W/ better software	W/ optimal hardware
General Integer	1.04	1.45	1.73	1.81
Multimedia Integer	1.07	1.19	1.80	1.80
Floating Point	2.56	3.04	3.12	3.15
Total	1.33	1.71	2.10	2.14

Table 6. Harmonic mean summaries of results.

cholesky: In the cholesky substitution program stage, the direction of the inner loop is reversed so that the loop carried dependency occurs on the last loop iteration, instead of the first. This allows the inner loop iterations from consecutive outer loop iterations to overlap.

These modifications resulted in significant performance improvements in these benchmarks, as is shown in Table 5. In particular, we were able to achieve a speedup of 2.14 on mpeg, whereas the baseline system slowed down.

With eight hardware checkpoints per processor, the performance improvements from hardware checkpointing on the optimized software are quite modest. Furthermore, mixing explicit software synchronization and hardware checkpointing is not useful, based on our observations with the compress benchmark. In effect, hardware checkpointing is an optimistic form of synchronization — a form of "wait-free" synchronization. As a result, software synchronization just provides additional overhead, slowing down the system while supplying little or no benefit, as it is redundant.

Table 6 summarizes the gains from these improvements for each of the major application classes using the harmonic means

7. CONCLUSIONS

In this paper, we have shown that a few simple optimization techniques can dramatically improve the performance of the Hydra CMP on sequential programs executed as a sequence of speculative threads. We achieved a 60 percent overall performance improvement on the eleven benchmarks and a 75 percent performance improvement on general integer benchmarks.

We began with our baseline architecture from [7], which extracts speculative parallelism from procedures and loops. This architecture is effective at exploiting speculative parallelism when large amounts of parallelism are present in the application, as our results for the floating point benchmarks demonstrate. However, it has difficulty extracting parallelism from conventional integer applications, sometimes slowing the applications down. A key problem with the baseline Hydra speculation implementation is the high overhead incurred by the speculation software to properly handle both procedures and loops. This problem is especially acute with integer applications because the number of overhead-incurring restarts is higher due to a larger number of dependencies between loop iterations and among procedures. Lastly, procedures typically degrade performance because too much time is spent starting speculative threads for procedures that turn out to have little parallelism.

As an initial optimization technique, we eliminated procedures and focused on making loop iteration speculation run as quickly as possible, with much lower speculation software overheads. This effort was very successful and resulted in significant speedups on most of our applications. Violation statistic gathering mechanisms allowed us to identify data-dependent pairs of loads and stores in the benchmarks that frequently resulted in violations. On half of our applications, we were able to use this information to guide several software optimization techniques that modified parts of the original source code. These modifications also improved performance significantly. Finally, we implemented a hardware checkpointing scheme that provides nearly optimal performance by eliminating most of the delay caused by frequently violating loads. The performance gains that we were able to achieve with hardware checkpointing would probably not justify the investment in hardware required to implement this technique.

Eqntott was the only benchmark that whose performance was not improved by the software optimization techniques. Much of the execution time in eqntott is dominated by a recursive quicksort procedure call instead of an iterative loop of reasonable size, and so our loop-based techniques were of little use. However, by manually limiting procedure speculation to the key quicksort routine, instead of speculating throughout the program, we were able to get a significant improvement. This strongly indicates that procedure speculation is still a viable alternative for environments where it can be used judiciously (Java is one such environment [1]). This will be especially true if the overheads can be reduced through the addition of specialized hardware to accelerate the procedure speculation software.

Overall, our results demonstrate that there is a promising migration path from our current, simple sequential-to-speculatively parallel conversion tools, such as hydracat, to more sophisticated compilation tools that can optimize code for a speculatively parallel architecture. Today, these optimizations still require programmer intervention, but it should be possible to automate them significantly, allowing a speculatively parallel CMP to be competitive with a conventional wide-issue out-of-order machine on many integer applications [14]. At the same time, the CMP should be able to achieve higher performance on inherently parallel applications, such as floating point numerical code and multimedia applications, than a comparable cost superscalar architecture.

8. ACKNOWLEDGMENTS

This work was supported by DARPA contracts DABT 63-95-C-0089 and MDA 904-98-C-A933.

9. REFERENCES

[1] M. Chen and K. Olukotun, "Exploiting method-level parallelism in single-threaded Java programs," *Proceedings of Parallel Architectures and Compilation Techniques (PACT 98)*, pp. 176–184, Paris, France, October 1998.

[2] G. Z. Chrysos and J. S. Emer, "Memory dependence prediction using store sets," *Proceedings of 25th Annual International Symposium of Computer Architecture*, pp. 142–153, Barcelona, Spain, June 1998.

[3] M. Franklin and G. S. Sohi, "The expandable split window paradigm for exploiting fine-grain parallelism," *Proceedings of the 19th Annual International Symposium on Computer Architecture*, pp. 58–67, Gold Coast, Australia, May 1992.

[4] M. Franklin and G. Sohi, "ARB: A hardware mechanism for dynamic reordering of memory references," *IEEE Transactions on Computers*, vol. 45, no. 5, pp. 552–571, May 1996.

[5] S. Gopal, T. N. Vijaykumar, J. E. Smith, and G. S. Sc "Speculative versioning cache," *Proceedings of the Fou International Symposium on High-Performance Compu Architecture (HPCA-4)*, Las Vegas, NV, February 1998.

[6] L. Hammond and K. Olukotun, *Considerations in the Des of Hydra: a Multiprocessor-on-a-Chip Microarchitectu* Stanford University Computer Systems Laboratory, Techni Report No. CSL-TR-98-749, Stanford University, Febru 1998.

[7] L. Hammond, M. Willey, and K. Olukotun, "Data speculat support for a chip multiprocessor," *Proceedings of Eig International Conference on Architectural Support Programming Languages and Operating Systems (ASPL VIII)*, pp. 58–69, San Jose CA, October 1998.

[8] B. Kernighan and R. Pike, The Practice of Programmi Reading, Massachusetts: Addison-Wesley, 1999.

[9] E. Iwata and K. Olukotun, *Exploiting coarse-gr parallelism in the MPEG-2 Algorithm*, Stanford Univer Computer Systems Laboratory, Technical Report CSL-T 98-771, September 1998.

[10] T. Knight, "An architecture for mostly functional language *Proceedings of the ACM Lisp and Functional Programm Conference*, pp. 500–519, August 1986.

[11] S. Keckler, W. Dally, D. Maskit, N. Carter, A. Chang, and Lee, "Exploiting fine-grain thread level parallelism on MIT multi-ALU processor," *Proceedings of 25th Ann International Symposium on Computer Architecture*, pp. 3(317, Barcelona, Spain, June 1998.

[12] C. Lee, M. Potkonjak, and W. Mangione-Sm "MediaBench: A tool for evaluating and synthesiz Multimedia and communications systems," *Proceedings 30th Annual International Symposium on Microarchitectu* Research Triangle Park, NC, December 1997.

[13] A. Moshovos, S. E. Breach, T. N. Vijaykumar, and G. S. S("Dynamic speculation and synchronization of d dependences," *Proceedings of 24th Annual Int. Sy Computer Architecture*, pp. 181–193, Denver, CO, June 19

[14] K. Olukotun, K. Chang, L. Hammond, B. Nayfeh, and Wilson, "The case for a single chip multiprocess *Proceedings of the 7th Int. Conf. for Architectural Support Programming Languages and Operating Systems (ASPL VII)*, pp. 2–11, Cambridge, MA, 1996.

[15] J. Oplinger, D. Heine, S.-W. Liao, B. A. Nayfeh, M. S. L and K. Olukotun, *Software and Hardware for Exploit Speculative Parallelism in Multiprocessors*, Stanf University Computer Systems Laboratory Technical Re CSL-TR-97-715, Stanford University, February 1997.

[16] J. Oplinger, D. Heine, M. Lam, and K. Olukotun, *In Searc Speculative Thread-Level Parallelism*, Stanford Univer Computer Systems Laboratory Technical Report CSL-TR- 765, July 1998.

[17] W. H. Press, S. A. Teulosky, W. T. Vetterling, and B. Flannery, *Numerical Recipes in C: The Art of Scien Computing*. Cambridge: Cambridge University Press, 199

[18] G. Sohi, S. Breach, and T. Vijaykumar, "Multisc processors," *Proceedings of the 22nd Annual Internatio Symposium on Computer Architecture*, pp. 414–425, Lig Italy, June 1995.

[19] J. G. Steffan and T. Mowry, "The potential for using thre level data speculation to facilitate automatic parallelizatic *Proceedings of the Fourth International Symposium on H Performance Computer Architecture (HPCA-4)*, Las Ve NV, February 1998.

Characterizing Processor Architectures for Programmable Network Interfaces

Patrick Crowley, Marc E. Fiuczynski, Jean-Loup Baer, and Brian N. Bershad*
Department of Computer Science & Engineering
University of Washington
Seattle, WA 98195
{pcrowley,mef,baer,bershad}@cs.washington.edu

Abstract

The rapid advancements of networking technology have boosted potential bandwidth to the point that the cabling is no longer the bottleneck. Rather, the bottlenecks lie at the crossing points, the nodes of the network, where data traffic is intercepted or forwarded. As a result, there has been tremendous interest in speeding those nodes, making the equipment run faster by means of specialized chips to handle data trafficking. The *Network Processor* is the blanket name thrown over such chips in their varied forms. To date, no performance data exist to aid in the decision of what processor architecture to use in next generation network processor. Our goal is to remedy this situation. In this study, we characterize both the application workloads that network processors need to support as well as emerging applications that we anticipate may be supported in the future. Then, we consider the performance of three sample benchmarks drawn from these workloads on several state-of-the-art processor architectures, including: an aggressive, out-of-order, speculative super-scalar processor, a fine-grained multithreaded processor, a single chip multiprocessor, and a simultaneous multithreaded processor (SMT). The network interface environment is simulated in detail, and our results indicate that SMT is the architecture best suited to this environment.

1. Introduction

As networks have evolved and expanded technologically, their role and importance have also increased considerably. The role of the network interface (NI), which allows a computer system to exchange messages with other systems connected to the network, has grown accordingly. To meet the functionality and performance requirements of present and emerging network applications, the current trend is to use *programmable* microprocessors on *network interfaces* (PNI) that can be customized with domain-specific software. This trend has created the so-called *network processor* market niche that many vendors, including Intel, IBM, and numerous start-ups, are eager to fill with chip architectures designed specifically to match the network application workload of PNIs. Although the architectural design of the various network processors often differs significantly, all are optimized to match the inherent parallelism present in network workloads. To date, though, there exists little performance data that allow fair comparisons between the various options. Our goal, in this paper, is to remedy this situation.

To evaluate different network processor architectures, we consider the following three questions: what workloads must the processor architecture support, what level of performance is required, and what type of architecture provides the required level of performance. In this study, we characterize both the application workloads that network processors need to support as well as emerging applications that we anticipate may be supported in the future. Then, we consider the performance of three sample benchmarks drawn from these workloads on several state-of-the-art processor architectures, including: an aggressive, out-of-order, speculative super-scalar processor (SS), a fine-grained multithreaded processor (FGMT), a single chip multiprocessor (CMP) [11], and a simultaneous multithreaded processor (SMT) [17]. After considering the benchmarks as individual standalone workloads, we then investigate the performance of each of these architectures when the applications run under an operating system designed specifically for managing programmable network interfaces [6]. In all of these performance evaluations, the key metric is the *number of messages per second* that a given architecture can support for a given workload, which translates directly into the network speeds that are enabled by the different architectures.

All of our performance evaluation is done within the context of a simulator that is cycle accurate with respect to instruction issue and execution, cache accesses, memory bandwidth and latency, as well as to memory contention between the processor and DMA transfers caused by network send and receive operations. As a result, we are able to accurately simulate and measure the performance of the aforementioned processor architectures in the context of a programmable network interface.

The contributions of this work are as follows. First, we identify a number of applications that can be used as components of a workload suite to assess the performance of PNIs. Second, we show the maximal performance attainable on these workloads (i.e., the maximum sustainable link-rate) for four high-performance processor architectures. As expected, architectures

* This work was supported in part by NSF Grant MIP-9700970, in part by DARPA Grant F30602-97-2, and by a gift from Intel Corporation.

designed for a high-degree of thread-level parallelism perform best for these workloads. Lastly, we characterize the overall performance of these processor architectures in the context of a programmable network interface.

The remainder of the paper is organized as follows. The next section presents background and other work related to programmable network interfaces. PNI workloads, including the benchmarks used in this study, and our experimental methodology are discussed in Section 3. Section 4 describes the high performance processor architectures evaluated in this paper. Experiment descriptions and results are given in Section 5. Finally, Section 6 concludes and proposes future work.

2. Background & Motivation

The rapid advancements of networking technology have boosted potential bandwidth to the point that the cabling is no longer the bottleneck. Rather, the bottlenecks lie at the crossing points, the nodes of the network, where data traffic is intercepted or forwarded. As a result, there has been tremendous interest in speeding those nodes, making the equipment run faster by means of specialized chips to handle data trafficking. The *Network Processor* is the blanket name thrown over such chips in their varied forms.

Network processors are used both in the "middle" of the network, at nodes composing the backbone of the Internet, as well as at the "edges" of the network in enterprise class routers, switches, and host network interfaces. The conventional application workload of such communication devices used to consist of simple packet forwarding and filtering algorithms based on the addresses found in layer-2 or layer-3 protocol packets. Today, however, the role of such devices is changing from simple packet forwarders to general-purpose computing/communications systems processing packets at layer-3 and above [13]. The application workloads used today include traffic shaping, network firewalls, network address and protocol translations (NAT), and high-level data transcoding (e.g., to convert a data stream going from a high-speed link to a low-speed link). Additionally, with the tremendous growth and popularity of the Web, many network equipment manufacturers are touting devices that can transparently load balance HTTP client requests over a set of WWW servers to increase service availability [1].

These emerging applications require significant processing capacity per network connection. Further, the processing requirements within these domains are unique in that, generally speaking, performance must be sustained at a level equivalent to the speed of the network itself. Unfortunately, while the speed of high-performance processors is increasing every year, the rate of increase is not as fast as that of the data rate in the middle of the network; hence the need to lookg at enhanced processor architectures.

The basic observation is that workloads for network processors have an inherent characteristic: network packets or messages, which are the basic unit of work for these applications, are often independent and may be processed concurrently. It is this packet-level parallelism that can be exploited at the architectural level to achieve the sustained high-performance demanded by fast networks. Thus, it is no big surprise that network processor parts, such as Intel's IXP1200 [10], IBM's Rainier [9], and those from various startup companies, use parallel architectures, such as multiple processor cores on a single chip or fine-grain multithreaded processors, to match this packet-level parallelism.

Unfortunately, there exists little data that identifies which processor architecture is best suited for the application workload used by the next generation communication devices. This lack of data and the uniqueness of the workloads motivated us to conduct this study.

3. Workloads & Methodology

This section identifies the application workloads used by network nodes, describes the evaluation methodology used to compare the performance that each processor architecture yields for these workloads, and details the execution environment that these applications are run within, which is markedly different from that of traditional operating system environments.

3.1 Workloads

There are currently three main application domains for programmable NIs, which can be roughly categorized into *Server* NI software, *Web Switching* software [1], and *Active Networking* software [15, 18]. The first two are product niches in their own right and are driving the development of programmable NIs. The latter is a research area that is pursuing the ability to dynamically deploy innovative network services rapidly and securely. With computation becoming less expensive, other NI resident applications are emerging as well.

In the context of these application domains we have identified a set of application-specific packet processing (ASPP) routines that are representative of workloads in the context of a PNI execution environment. Table 1 briefly describes present and emerging ASPPs in ascending order of per packet processing requirements.

The applications in Table 1 can be divided into two categories according to the amount of the packet that is processed. The first six applications process a limited amount of data within the protocol headers of the packet, and their processing requirements are independent of the packet's overall size. However, these applications tend to maintain state tables in complex data structures that need to be searched or accessed on a per packet basis. In contrast, the last three applications listed in Table 1 compute over all of the data contained in a packet, and therefore require a significant amount of processing capacity to process packets at the network link rate. As mentioned earlier, in these applications the processing of one packet is largely, and usually entirely, independent of the processing of any other packet. Consequently, packets may be processed in parallel.

We have selected three benchmarks from this set of workloads, namely, IP forward*, hereafter denoted ip4, and two components of IP security, MD5 and 3DES. The first benchmark, ip4, performs address-based packet lookups in a tree data structure and is a component of conventional layer-3 switches and routers. In test runs of ip4 we perform lookups into a routing table of 1000 entries, a size representative of a large corporate (or campus) network. MD5 is a message digest application used to uniquely identify messages. MD5 computes a unique signature over the data in each packet and is used for authentication. Finally, 3DES

* We used algorithms for forwarding table compression and fast IP lookup described in [12].

Applications	Description
Packet Classification/Filtering	Claim/forward/drop decisions, statistics gathering, and firewalling.
IP Packet Forwarding	Forward IP packets based on routing information.
Network Address Translation (NAT)	Translate between globally routable and private IP packets. Useful for IP masquerading, virtual web server, etc.
Flow management	Traffic shaping within the network to reduce congestion and enforce bandwidth allocation.
TCP/IP	Offload TCP/IP processing from Internet/Web servers to the network interface.
Web Switching[1]	Web load balancing and proxy cache monitoring.
Virtual Private Network IP Security (IPSec)	Encryption (3DES) and Authentication (MD5)
Data Transcoding[2]	Converting a multimedia data stream from one format to another within the network.
Duplicate Data Suppression[3]	Reduce superfluous duplicate data transmission over high cost links.

Table 1. Representative application specific packet processing routines. [1] [1], [2] [7], [3] [14]

is an encryption routine that is used here to encrypt the full payload of a packet.

Dynamic instruction characterization for these benchmarks is presented in Table 2. An examination of the instruction and data cache performance for ip4, MD5 and 3DES indicates that these applications are compute bound as both the instruction and data working sets fit within L1 caches of size 32K and greater (miss rates generally less than 1%). While none of our applications tax the memory hierarchy in isolation, it is likely that cache performance and organization will be important when more than one program is running concurrently. As noted later, we will consider this fact as we evaluate the simultaneous execution of these workloads in future work.

3.2 Evaluation Methodology

As previously noted, our approach is to use the benchmarks in Table 2 to evaluate and compare the performance achieved by a number of different architectures for programmable network interfaces. Figure 1 depicts the basic components of a PNI. To drive applications during experiments, our simulator uses an IP packet trace collected from our local network to provide realistic network packet delivery to the PNI. Packets are delivered to the NI via either the host controller (out-bound packets) or the network controller (in-bound packets) and, upon message arrival, the processor is signaled. As described in the next section, the network processor then stores (into buffer memory) and processes the packet. At this point, packets may be redirected, modified, dropped or measured in some way dependent upon the target application. Since the emphasis of this study is to consider the programmability and performance of these PNI's, we focus on the network processor and its interaction with buffer memory.

To do this, we have assembled a simulation environment capable of simulating: several processor organizations (based on the SMT simulator [17], itself based on the Alpha 21x64 ISA), a full memory hierarchy including caches and main (buffer) memory, and DMA/packet transfers between main memory and a physical network link. With our simulation infrastructure, we are able to measure overall PNI system performance, in terms of packets per second, as well as many other lower level performance metrics including instructions-per-cycle (IPC), cache miss rates, prediction rates, and contention for resources such as functional units (FUs) and busses. Our simulation infrastructure provides a cycle accurate simulation of a modern high-performance, out-of-order, superscalar microprocessor core and memory system. By varying the microprocessor and memory system configurations, we can investigate a number of architectural alternatives.

3.3 Execution Environment

The execution environment for a PNI can be characterized as having a basic store-process-forward structure. The *store* and *forward* stages simply transfer message data into and out of the NI's buffer memory. The *process* stage invokes application-specific handlers based on some matching criteria applied to the message. Figure 2 illustrates this structure as a pipeline of stages.

As messages arrive on the input channel, as depicted in Figure 2, they are first *stored* in the NI's buffer memory. Messages are then classified and dispatched to some application-specific handler function to be *processed*. Finally, the messages may then be *forwarded* on to an output channel. To achieve high throughput and low latency it is important that messages be pipelined through these stages. Thus, the goal is to sustain three forms of concurrent operation: message reception from the input

Application	Insts Executed per Message	Loads/Stores (%)	Ctrl Flow (%)	Other (%)
IP forward	~200	25.4	12.7	61.9
MD5	~2000	10.7	2.8	86.5
3DES	~40000	17.8	1.2	81.0

Table 2. Benchmark characteristics.

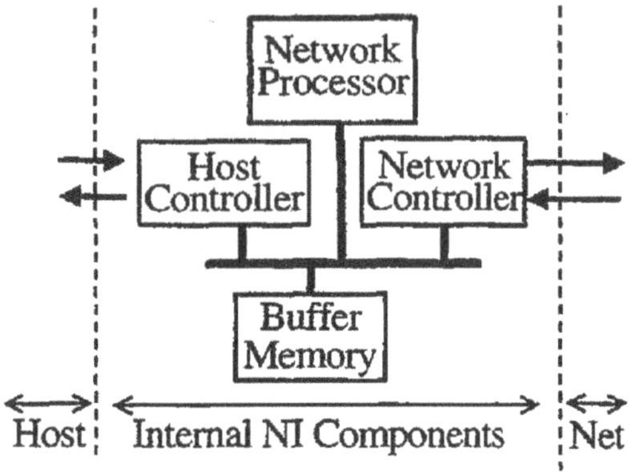

Figure 1. Generic Programmable Network Interface Architecture

channel, message processing on the NI, and message transmission to the output channel. It is the task of the system software to schedule these concurrent operations such that each pipeline stage is occupied. Varying degrees of programmability may be used to implement each of these stages. Much work has been done to design packet classifiers in both hardware [2, 8] and software [3, 5, 16]. For this study, we assume that all packet classification is performed in dedicated hardware that is ideal in the sense that it is never the performance bottleneck in the system. The experiments discussed in this paper consider both hardware and software implementations of the packet storage stage. These implementations are generally applicable to the forward stage as well, although our benchmarks do not exercise this stage. That is, in our experiments, the PNI always acts as a consumer, or observer, of packets. From our perspective, the creation or forwarding of packets will only increase demand on the busses connecting processor, memory, and controllers. We will consider these effects in our future work.

We have designed and implemented an execution environment for a PNI with the above-mentioned properties for both uniprocessor and multiprocessor configurations. Fiuczynski et al. [6] describes this execution environment in more detail.

Instruction type	Latency
ALU	1
Multiply	8 & 16
Divide	16
Branch	2
Load	1
Store	1
Synchronization	4

Table 3. Instruction latencies.

4. Processor Architectures

In this section, we briefly describe the four high-performance processor architectures that we consider in this study. Unless specified otherwise, all processors may be assumed to have instruction latencies as depicted in Table 3. Their instruction set is an extension of the Alpha ISA with support for byte and 16-bit word load/store operations. The functional units in each processor are capable of executing each of the instruction types found in Table 3. Table 4 details the general characteristics of the four processor architectures most relevant for this study. As indicated, some of these parameters are varied in the following experiments. Our intention is to make fair comparisons between architectures possessing roughly equal resources. Therefore, to keep resources approximately equal as we scale, we provision each architecture with an equivalent amount of the primary resource, namely, the total number of functional units.

4.1 Processor Descriptions

Superscalar (SS). The SS out-of-order processors we simulate in this study have a deep pipeline (7 stages) and use scoreboarding and register renaming to resolve dynamic dependencies. The maximum number of instructions that can be issued each cycle (issue width) is equal to n, the number of functional units, which is a parameter varied in our experiments.

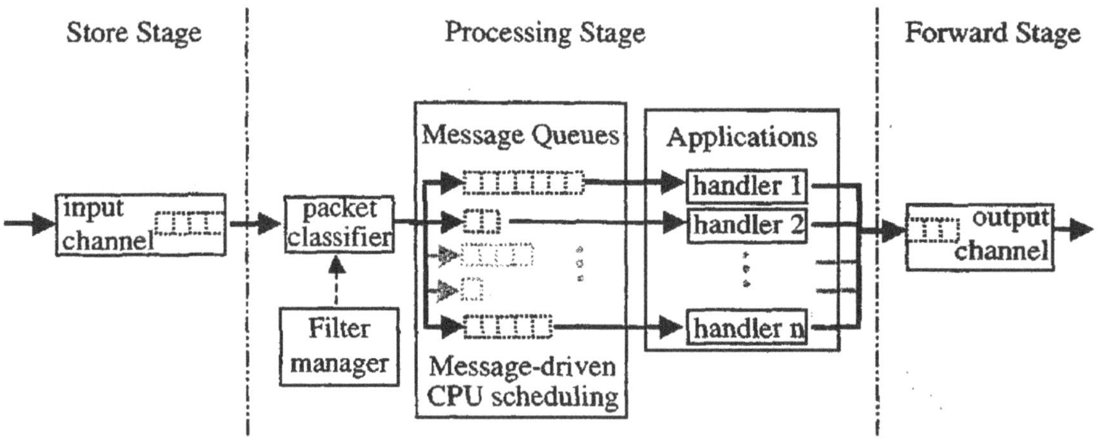

Figure 2. The Store-Process-Forward stages of messages flowing through a programmable NI.

Property	Superscalar n-way	FGMT n-way m thread contexts	CMP p processors, each 1-way	SMT n-way m thread contexts
# of CPUS	1	1	p	1
Total issue width	n	n	p	n
Total fetch width	n	n	p	n
# of architectural registers	32	32	32*p	32
# of physical registers	100	100*m	32*p	100
# of integer FUs	min 1/max 8	min 1/max 8	p	min 1/max 8
BTB entries	256	256	256	256
Return stack size	12	12	12*p	12
Instruction queue size	32	32	8*p	32
I cache (size/assoc/banks)	32K/2/8	32K/2/8	32K/2/8	32K/2/8
D cache (size/assoc/banks)	32K/2/8	32K/2/8	32K/2/8	32K/2/8
L1 hit time (cycles)	1	1	1	1
Shared L2 cache (size/assoc/banks)	512K/1/1	512K/1/1	512K/1/1	512K/1/1
L2 hit time (cycles)	10	10	10	10
Memory latency (cycles)	68	68	68	68
Thread fetch width	1	1	p	2
Cache line Size (bytes)	64	64	64	64
L1-L2 bus width (bytes)	32	32	32	32
Memory bus width (bytes)	16	16	16	16

Table 4. Architectural details. Cache write policies: L1 write-through, L2 write-back, no write-allocate.

Fine-Grain Multithreaded (FGMT). The multithreading support extends the core out-of-order, superscalar microprocessor by adding support for multiple hardware thread contexts. In an FGMT architecture, instructions may be fetched and issued from a different thread of execution *each cycle*. The FGMT architecture attempts to find and exploit all available ILP within a thread of execution, but can also mitigate the effects of a stalled thread by quickly switching to another thread. In this way, ideally, overall system throughput is increased. The architecture simulated here uses a round-robin thread fetch and issue policy among runnable threads (i.e., those threads in a valid state and not blocked on a synchronization event).

Chip-Multiprocessor (CMP). A CMP partitions chip resources rigidly in the form of multiple processors [11]. As an example, a 4 processor CMP has 4 separate execution pipelines, 4 separate register files, 4 separate fetch units, etc. CMP has the benefit of permitting multiple threads to execute completely in parallel. However, CMP has the drawback of restricting the amount of total chip resources a given thread may utilize to those resources found within its local processor. In the experiments described in this study, each processor will have only one functional unit, and, hence, an issue width of one (therefore, the CMP will exploit no ILP). Each processor has a private L1 (both data and instruction), while a single L2 is shared amongst all processors. These caches are as described in Table 4. The L1 caches are kept coherent using an invalidation protocol similar to the one described in [11].

Simultaneous Multithreaded (SMT). An SMT architecture [17] has hardware support for multiple thread contexts and extends instruction fetch and issue logic to allow instructions to be fetched and issued from multiple threads each cycle. As a result, overall instruction throughput can be increased according to the amount of ILP available *within* each thread and the amount of thread-level parallelism (TLP) available *between* threads. The SMT architectures we simulate in this study fetch eight instructions each cycle from a maximum of two threads.

5. Experimental Results

The experiments in this study consider the performance of each architecture while executing the benchmarks both with and without an operating system. The following subsections describe and discuss our three sets of experiments: standalone application performance, standalone operating system overhead, and OS-governed application performance.

5.1 Single Application Performance

Our first set of experiments considers the performance of each benchmark in isolation on each type of processor. Furthermore, we initially operate under the assumption that our network interface possesses "ideal" hardware for packet handling and delivery. This means that the processor will not be concerned with handling DMA requests for moving packets into and out of main (buffer) memory; this task is managed in hardware. Instead, the processor is provided with a set of buffers in memory, which are filled with packets that require application specific processing.

The processor fully commits its resources to processing those packets.

5.1.1 *Dynamic discovery of ILP: aggressive superscalar*

We first consider the performance of the aggressive superscalar processor. In this experiment, as in the others, we scale a number of architectural parameters, including clock rate and number of functional units (i.e., issue width). We scale issue width (and functional units) to show the limits of available ILP within a single thread of execution for these workloads. The overall system performance, expressed in packets processed per second, achieved by this architecture for each of our benchmarks is shown in Figure 3.

There are a number of observations to be made. First, performance for all benchmarks scales reliably with clock rate, as we expect to find with compute bound workloads. Secondly, we note that these benchmarks exhibit differing degrees of ILP, as evidenced by the fact that ip4 benefits from the addition of functional units up to the sixth, while MD5 and 3DES peak at around two and three functional units, respectively. Indeed, the aggressive SS achieved, with a maximum issue width of eight, an IPC of 2.79, 1.29, and 2.72 for ip4, MD5, and 3DES, respectively. Dramatically increasing other processor resources such as instruction queue length and renaming registers did nothing to improve performance. Hence, we may conclude that these ILP limits are properties of the workloads themselves. Given an average packet size of 128 bytes, the peak throughput of the SS architecture at 500 Mhz corresponds to network rates of 12 Gbps, 330 Mbps, and 32 Mbps for ip4, MD5 and 3DES, respectively.

These results demonstrate, and later experiments will confirm, that discovering ILP, alone, within a single thread of execution does not hold much promise towards achieving scalable, high performance.

5.1.2 *Tolerating blocked threads: FGMT*

We next consider the performance of the FGMT architecture while executing these benchmarks. An important distinction exists between this experiment and the previous one. With FGMT (and likewise for SMT and CMP), we use multithreaded versions of our benchmarks. In the SS case, the application was organized as a single thread of execution since the use of software-based threads is a detriment to performance for compute bound workloads such as ours. Our multithreaded benchmarks are symmetric in the sense that each thread executes the same code. Figure 4 graphs the performance of the FGMT architecture on each of our benchmarks. Note that in this figure, both issue width and number of thread contexts are scaled along the x-axis. We are scaling issue width just as we did in the SS case, and we are in addition adding thread contexts, i.e., $m = n$ in Table 4.

We see only a modest performance improvement over SS on MD5, while performance is nearly unchanged for ip4 and 3DES. Since there is sufficient ILP in ip4 and 3DES there is no need to hide the sorts of latencies that FGMT can help mitigate. Fine-grained thread switching was able to tolerate some of this type of delay with MD5, hence the slightly improved performance, but it did nothing to help in finding greater parallelism since at each cycle only one thread may issue. Hence, in the absence of long latency operations, performance for FGMT is limited by the ILP within a single thread and, therefore, essentially equivalent to SS performance.

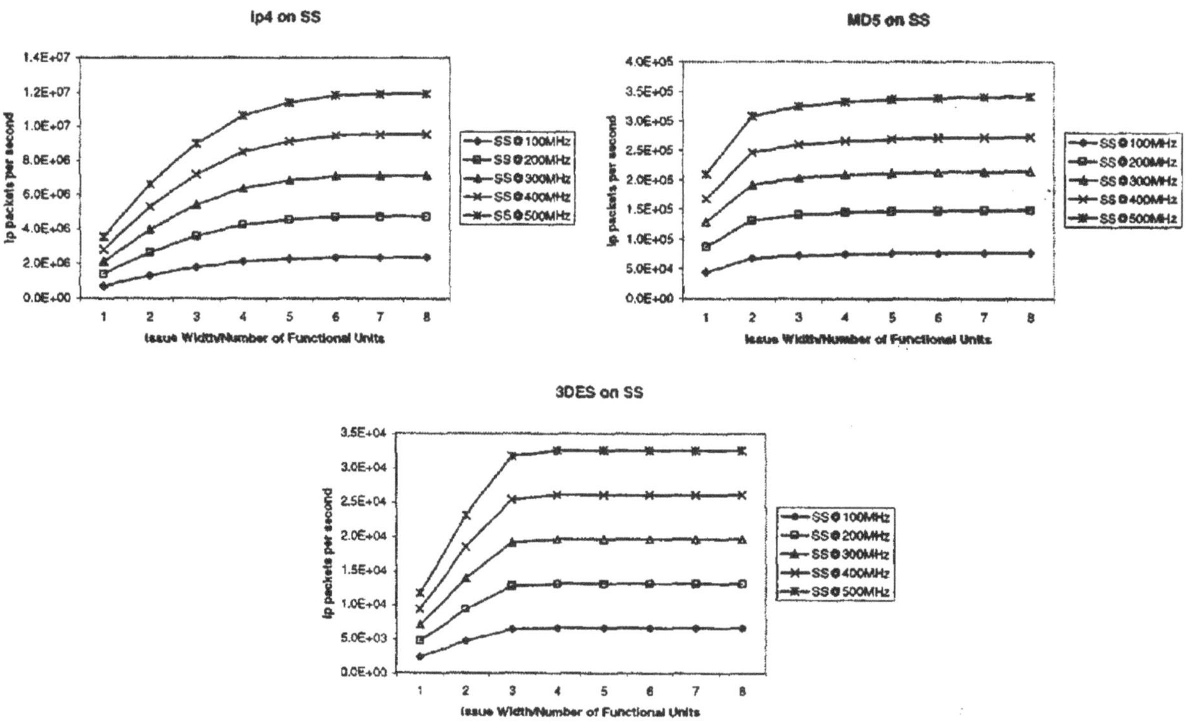

Figure 3. IP packet throughput achieved with each benchmark on a SS processor.

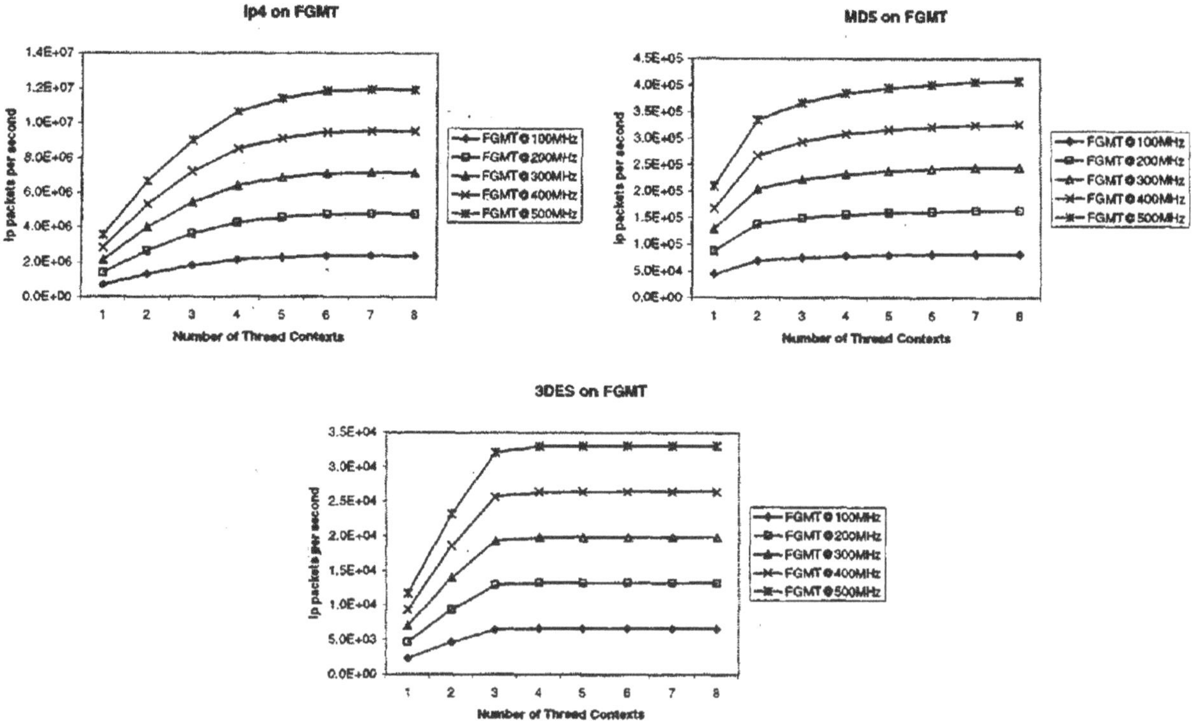

Figure 4. IP packet throughput achieved with each benchmark on a FGMT processor.

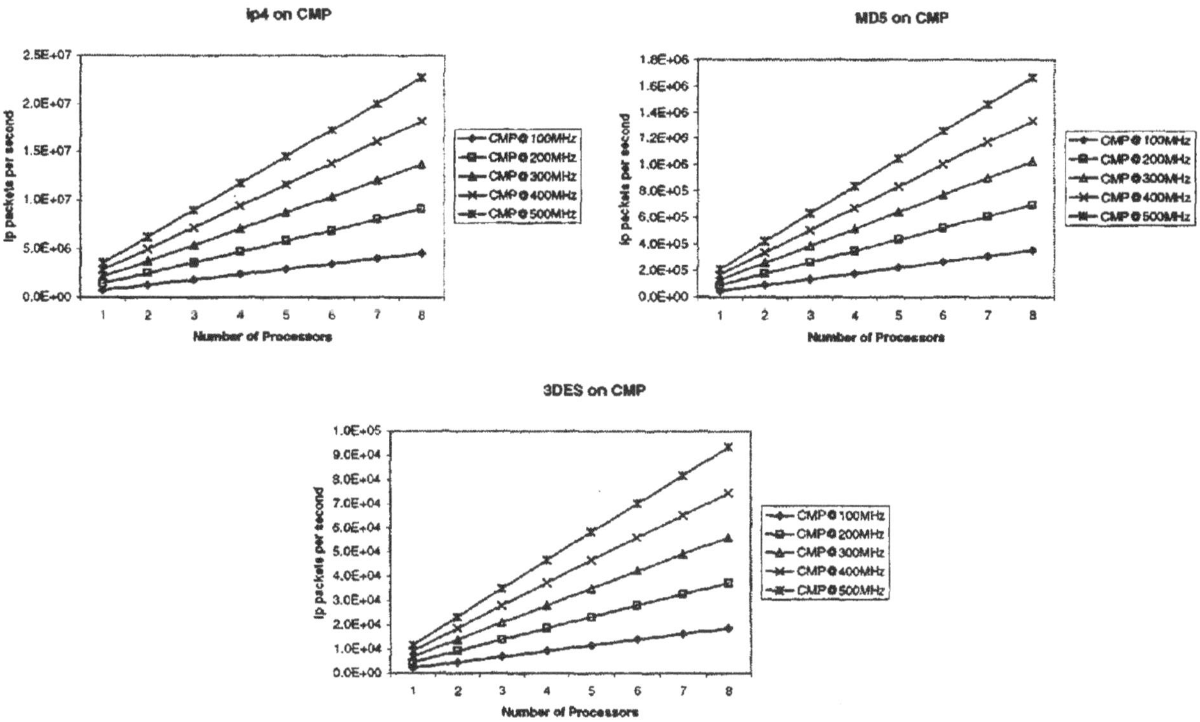

Figure 5. IP packet throughput achieved with each benchmark on a CMP.

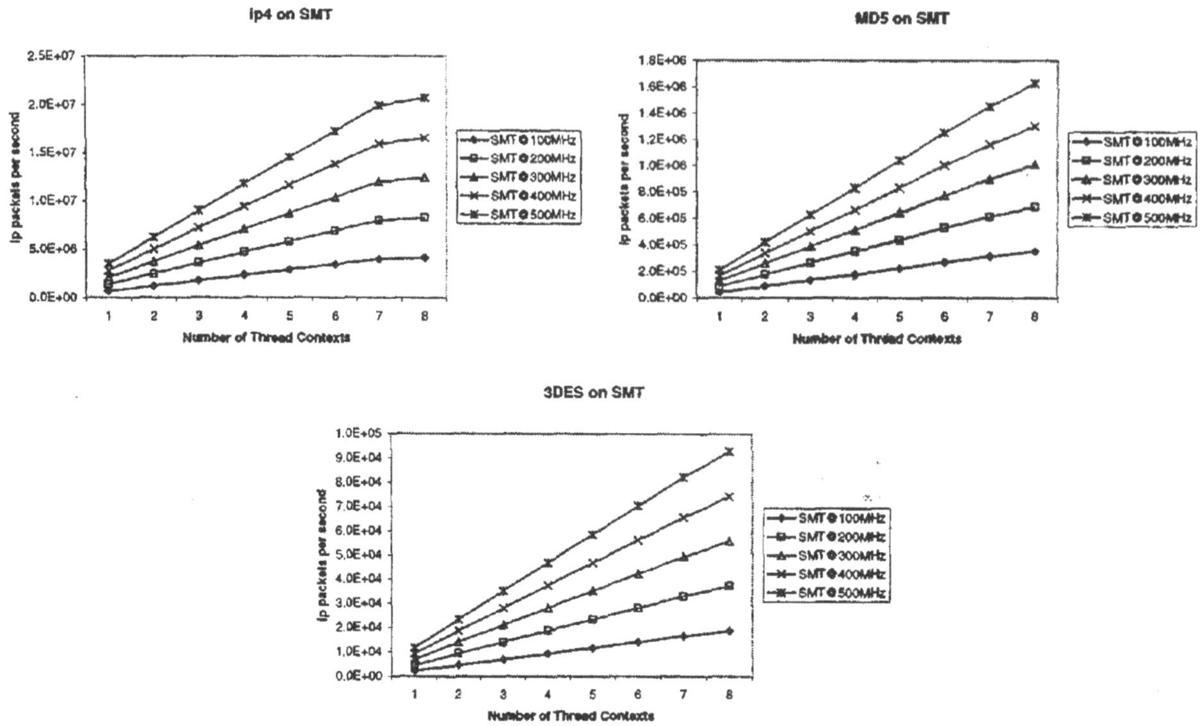

Figure 6. IP packet throughput achieved with each benchmark on an SMT processor.

5.1.3 Simple replication: CMP

An alternative approach for increasing overall IPC is to replicate the processor core on the chip, as opposed to devoting hardware resources to thread support. In our experiments regarding CMP, the processor core that we replicate has an issue width of one (a single FU) and, in the graphs, we scale the number of processor cores along the x-axis. It is important to note that we are *not* scaling the issue width of each processor core individually, but, rather, we are increasing the total chip issue width by scaling the number of single-issue processor cores. Not surprisingly, CMP performance scales linearly with the number of processors as shown in Figure 5. Despite the fact that each processor core is somewhat under-provisioned (that is, there is more ILP available in each thread of execution than the single issue core can accommodate), by replicating cores, the CMP achieves linear speedups by issuing from multiple threads simultaneously. With 8 processors, CMP achieves throughput between 2 and 4 times greater than SS.

5.1.4 ILP & Thread-level Parallelism: SMT

Finally, we consider SMT. By fetching and issuing from multiple threads each cycle, SMT combines the best features of the previous architectures, namely ILP, with thread-level parallelism. Again, in this experiment, we scale both issue width and number of hardware thread contexts. As the graphs in Figure 6 indicate, the performance of each of our benchmarks scales linearly with the number of thread contexts and issue slots. What neither the SS nor the FGMT architecture could find within a single thread of execution, SMT is able to find among all executing threads. Both CMP and SMT, that reach the same level of throughput, see linear performance increases for the same reason: they are each capable of issuing a maximum number of instructions each cycle by finding available work in all threads. It is the same characteristic that enables both, but each architecture has a different mechanism for issuing from multiple threads. Neither of the other two architectures can issue from more than one thread, and, hence, their performance is not as scalable in this manner. However, we can see that performance appears to saturate at the high-rates achieved with ip4. The SMT architecture is still being fine-tuned, and we speculate that this saturation represents contention for a shared hardware resource that has not been scaled in these experiments.

5.1.5 Comparison

These results show that SS and FGMT have basically the same performance for these workloads, and, likewise, CMP and SMT have roughly equivalent performance that is 2 to 4 times greater. For ease of comparison, Figure 7 depicts the results for all architectures clocked at 500 MHz. CMP and SMT, at clock rates of 500 Mhz, are able to sustain peak message rates of roughly 20 million, 1. 5 million, and 90 thousand IP packets per second on ip4, MD5 and 3DES, respectively. Given an average packet size of around 128 bytes, these rates correspond to network speeds on the order of 10, 1, and 0,1 Gbps. While these results clearly indicate that SMT and CMP are architectures better suited to exposing the parallelism inherent in these workloads, one could argue effectively that both the SS processor and the FGMT processor will more easily scale by clock rate, as they are less complex than SMT. This is a valid point. However, no such

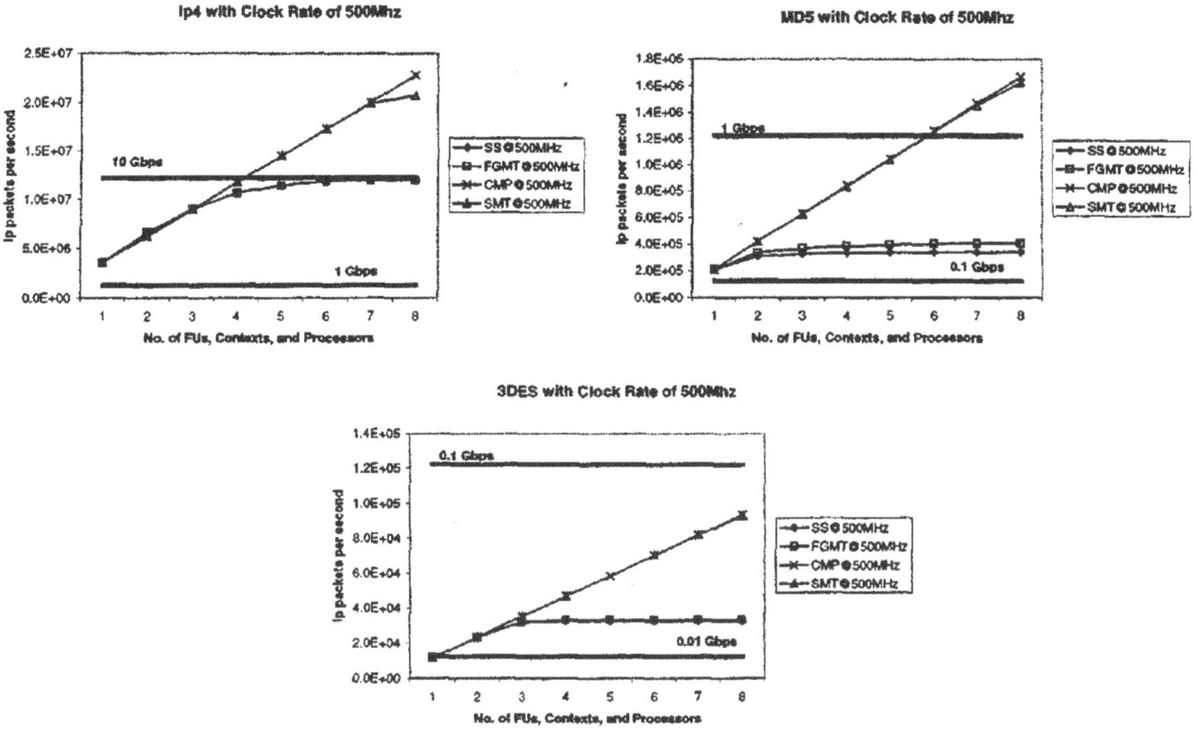

Figure 7. Performance results for all architectures, clocked at 500 MHz, running all benchmarks.

argument may be made against CMP. In the next section of results, we consider how the landscape changes as we transition from ideal packet handling hardware to OS-based packet handling in software.

5.2 Operating System Overhead

The results we have presented to this point executed in a simple test harness and assumed the presence of zero overhead operating system software and networking hardware that managed packet handling, classification, and delivery to the application processes. This section considers overall performance of these processor architectures in the context of a programmable network interface that is similar to the high-speed Myrinet [4] managed by an operating system, called SPINE, designed to enable application specific software to process messages as they stream through the system [6].

Our simulator emulates the register interface of the Myrinet packet interface and its DMA controller. As a result, the same SPINE operating system device driver code can be used either with the simulator or the actual Myrinet network interface hardware. The benefit of using the simulator is that we can study different processor architectures as well as faster network speeds. That said, we have found that the simple DMA controller used in the Myrinet incurs a fair amount of overhead when managed in software, which will become apparent in the following performance evaluation. We are considering a more sophisticated DMA controller model for use in future work to reduce the amount of software overhead incurred by the operating system.

The SPINE operating system executes in the context of a single thread. On a uniprocessor all operating system and application processing is done within that single thread context. For the multiprocessor configurations, one processor is devoted to the operating system for low latency message handling to avoid the overhead of interrupts, while the remaining processors are devoted to application processing. It is transparent to SPINE whether the multiprocessor configuration uses a FGMT, CMP, or SMT processor. A work-list based parallel computation model is used to schedule work (i.e., unprocessed packets) across the "application processors." Each of these application processors runs a single worker thread that waits for available work items, consumes it from the work-list, processes it, and then waits for the next work item, and so on.

The remainder of this section describes our performance results.

5.2.1 *SPINE/OS Performance*

First, we determine the maximum number of packets per second that SPINE is able to deliver—the basic packet delivery rate. To do this, we execute just the operating system on the processor. That is, SPINE consumes packets from the physical network controller as quickly as possible, without dispatching any worker threads for application specific processing. The maximum packet rate SPINE is able to sustain in this situation represents the upper bound on the performance of our system since under no circumstances will worker threads be able to consume more packets than SPINE is able to produce. The results of this experiment, for processors clocked at 500Mhz, are shown in Figure 8.

As indicated, SPINE on the SS, FGMT and SMT architectures delivers packets at roughly the same rate, which is, moreover, well above the packet delivery rate sustained by SPINE on CMP. This is precisely as we would expect. SPINE runs as a single thread of execution, and, hence, has the performance characteristics of a single-threaded program. With a single thread of execution, the SS, FGMT, and SMT architectures are all more or less equivalent. Recall, however, that the CMP processor has a constant number, one, of functional units per processor core. Adding processor cores to CMP, while generally improving multi-threaded performance, does not improve single thread performance. The packet delivery rates shown in Figure 8, approximately 1.4 million packets per second for SS, FGMT, and SMT and about half of that, i.e., 0.7 million packets per second, for CMP, are therefore the performance upper-bounds that our applications are subject to while executing on SPINE.

In the best case, the above results roughly translate to 360 cycles and 720 cycles per packet on average for SS/FGMT/SMT and CMP, respectively, for packets with an average size of roughly 128 bytes. Or in other words, SPINE using a 500 Mhz processor can deliver packets to applications at a sustained rate of roughly 1.4 Gbits per second for SS/FGMT/SMT and approximately half that rate for CMP. Our previous ideal hardware results indicate that this will only be a major bottleneck for ip4, which, in a standalone fashion, processes packets above these ranges in most cases.

5.2.2 Application Performance on SPINE

Having determined a strict upper bound on performance, the next set of experiments will measure the performance of the three applications running on top of an operating system. This experiment differs from our previous single application experiments in that there is now operating system code that will compete with the application code for processor resources. As we have already demonstrated the effect of scaling clock rate, from this point on we report performance results only for processors clocked at 500 Mhz. The performance results for each of our benchmarks on each of the architectures is shown in Figure 9. Incidentally, in all three graphs, the first data point, which corresponds to a single functional unit, thread context, and processor for SS, FGMT & SMT, and CMP, respectively, correctly demonstrates that the architectures are equivalent for these parameter choices. Hence, each architecture's curve begins

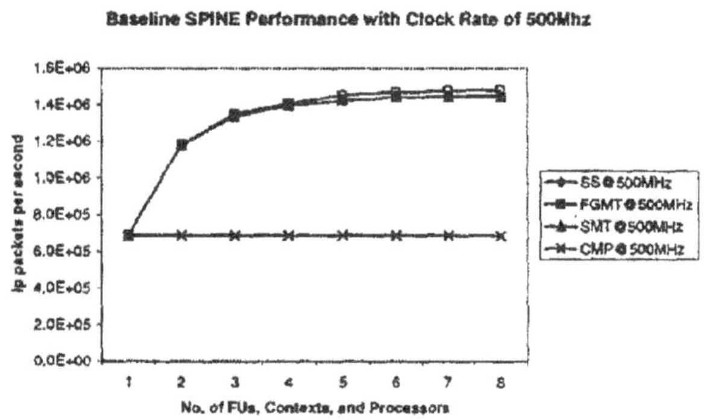

Figure 8. Basic SPINE packet delivery performance test. SS and SMT have coincident curves.

at this point. Let us consider ip4 first.

First note that for ip4, FGMT, SMT and CMP have curves similar to those seen in Figure 8. This suggests that these architectures have rather quickly run into their packet delivery bottlenecks. Further, as noted in Section 5.2.1, the ip4 application processes packets faster than SPINE delivers them. Hence, only one worker thread is ever utilized. These architectures do not achieve the peak performance shown in Figure 8 since the OS and application are now competing for resources. SS, on the other hand, performs around 1.5 times slower than its maximum. Recall that in the SS case, packet handling and application specific packet processing occur within the same thread. Hence, we see diminished results because every packet must be processed before the next one can be retrieved (these activities are overlapped in the other architectures). In many ways, ip4 is the least interesting result since the operating system represents such a severe limit to performance.

With MD5, we have a few more issues to consider. In the second column of data points, when there are two FUs, we see that SS in fact slightly outperforms SMT and CMP, which in turn slightly outperform FGMT. We have already seen that neither SPINE nor MD5 perform well with only a single functional unit. This artifact suggests that the multithreaded implementation of this application is a slightly inferior form of organization compared to the single-threaded one when the architecture is not sufficiently provisioned for *any* of the executing threads. However, we see drastic improvements for the multithreaded implementations when we increase processor resources. In contrast, SS performance settles well below that seen in the non-OS version, in Figure 3, due to the additional overhead of managing packet delivery. FGMT settles slightly below its non-OS version performance (which is considerably lower than the peak packet delivery rate) and, as before, outperforms SS by hiding instruction latencies. CMP once again settles just beneath its peak packet delivery rate. SMT, on the other hand, sees the best performance but suffers as a result of the SPINE packet producer thread competing fiercely with the worker threads. From Figure 3, we know that each MD5 thread of execution can fully utilize 2 functional units; likewise, SPINE can utilize at least 2 functional units. Here however, resources are shared more or less evenly so it may be presumed that each thread is allotted a single FU. Therefore, the performance increase diminishes greatly beyond the packet delivery rate of SPINE with one FU (approximately $7*10^5$ packets per second). It is likely that both FGMT and SMT would benefit from increasing the SPINE thread's execution priority.

With 3DES, SS outperforms the others as resources increase up to the fourth FU for the reasons discussed above regarding MD5: when there are no unused resources, serializing packet handling and processing, as SS does, is better than parallelizing these tasks. CMP and SMT achieve the linear speedups obtained in the non-OS versions shown in Figure 5 and Figure 6 as soon as there are at least two FUs. FGMT, however, exhibits terrible performance and, in fact, converges to SS performance from below. There are two reasons for this. First, performance will never exceed the non-OS result (see Figure 4), which is equivalent to SS performance and is approximately $3.2*10^4$ messages per second. Second, performance will slowly approach this value, and lag behind SS, since resources are wastefully consumed in packet handling when they would be better spent processing packets. In this case, the SPINE thread is consuming its equal share of

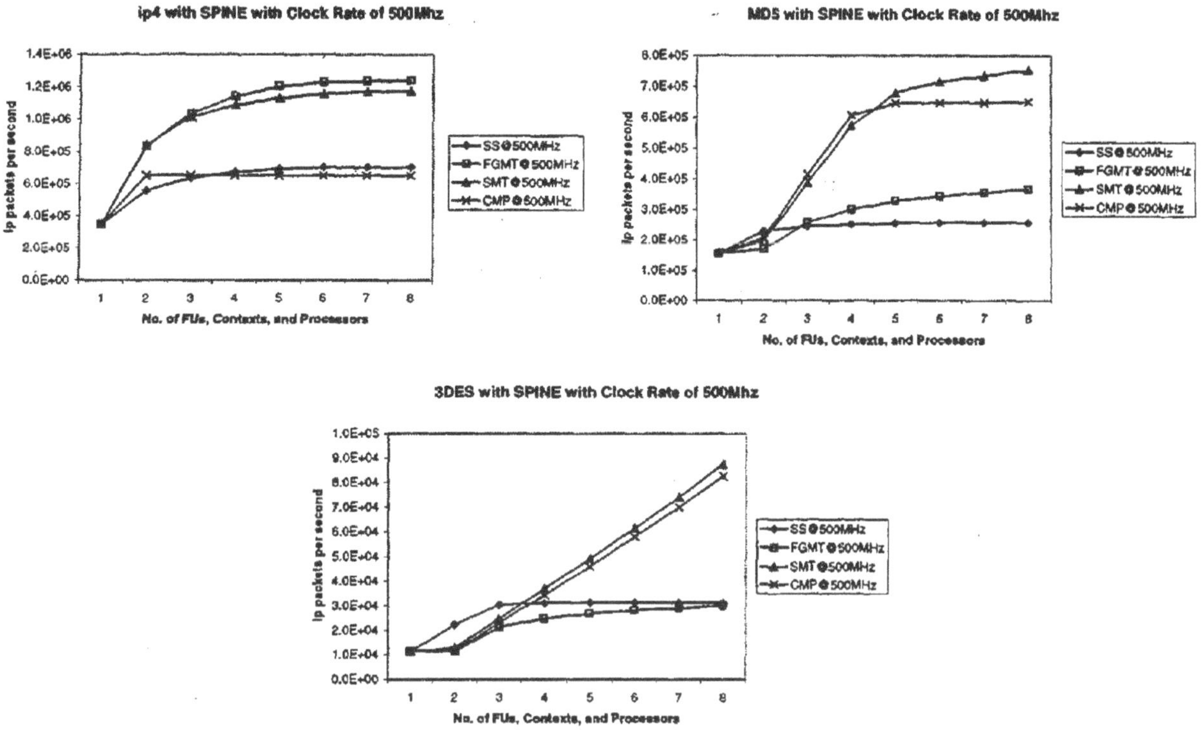

Figure 9. IP packet throughput achieved with each benchmark on each architecture, with all processors clocked at 500Mhz.

resources, as a consequence of the round-robin scheduling policy. Since 3DES is heavily compute bound, a better policy would be to give the worker threads priority over the packet delivery thread so that no resources are wasted managing packets that won't be used until the relatively distant future.

5.3 Summary

In the first set of experiments, CMP and SMT clearly demonstrate their superiority over SS and FGMT in exploiting the packet-level parallelism available within these workloads. In particular, the ability to issue from multiple threads simultaneously is key to this scalable performance. This fact is supported by the performance achieved by CMP, which exploits no ILP.

In the second set of experiments, both the operating system and applications contribute to overall system performance. Managing packet delivery and handling in software only involves a significant decrease in performance for ip4. In this case, ip4 process packets faster than the OS delivers them, hence ip4 performance on SPINE converges to SPINE performance, which is roughly an order of magnitude lower than ip4's standalone performance. MD5 and 3DES, on the other hand, process packets much slower and tend towards the standalone performance. In our simulations, SMT proves to be the architecture best suited to the workload since it is able to exploit both ILP and TLP, as no other architecture can. SPINE performance on CMP is severely limited and under-performs all other architectures since it can exploit no ILP. That said, the generally competitive performance of CMP is somewhat surprising in spite of the simplicity of each processor core.

6. Summary and Future Work

In this study, we have characterized the performance of processor architectures for programmable network interfaces. We have identified a set of benchmarks for network processors, evaluated the performance of a subset of these benchmarks on four high-performance computer architectures, and considered their performance with the added overhead from both operating system management and the underlying networking hardware. We have observed that network processor workloads exhibit a high-degree of parallelism at the packet-level, which represents an opportunity for high performance. Our experimental results suggest that, on the basis of equivalent processor resources, SMT performs better than CMP and more than a factor of two better than FGMT and SS by dynamically exploiting both instruction and thread level parallelism. For simple applications, such as IP forwarding, SMT and CMP can sustain network speeds exceeding 10Gbits/second (e.g., OC12 links). Higher speeds may be attained with better IP forwarding algorithms, such as [16]. For computationally intensive applications, such as MD5, both SMT and CMP sustain network speeds approaching 1Gbits (e.g., gigabit Ethernet).

There are a number of questions we plan to investigate in future work. First, we will augment some of the experimental architectures used in this study. The threaded architectures, FGMT and SMT, will support thread priorities to improve the thread fetch and issue scheduling algorithms. We will consider a more aggressive CMP core, with increased issue width, so that it can exploit some of the ILP available in these workloads. Secondly, we will implement additional benchmarks both from the set of more conventional applications (e.g., flow management) and emerging applications (HTTP load balancing) to round out our network processor workloads. Thirdly, we plan to implement packet classification in software to investigate the performance tradeoffs relative to hardware-based packet classification. That is, assuming that the hardware-based packet classification requires a similar number of transistors relative to a processor core, is it better to perform packet classification in software with N processors or in hardware with N-1 processors? Finally, we realize that network processors in switches/routers and host adapters will need to support some combination of these applications concurrently. Consequently, we believe that the combined behavior of these applications running in the previously described execution environment yields an interesting and compelling workload at both the system software and architectural level. Hence, we plan to measure the performance of these applications as executed in a multi-programmed environment.

References

[1] Alteon. WEBWORKING: Networking with the Web in mind. Alteon WebSystems, White Paper: www.alteon.com/products/white_papers/webworking May 3rd 1999 San Jose, California.

[2] M.L. Bailey, B. Gopal, M.A. Pagels, L.L. Peterson, and P. Sarkar. PATHFINDER: A Pattern-Based Packet Classifier. *Proceedings of the First USENIX Conference on Operating System Design and Implementation (OSDI)*, pp. 115-224. Monterey CA, November 1994.

[3] A. Begel, S. McCanne, and S.L. Graham. BPF+: Exploiting Global Data-Flow Optimization in a Generalized Packet Filter Architecture. *Proceedings of the ACM Communication Architectures, Protocols, and Applications (SIGCOMM '99)*, 1999.

[4] N. Boden and D. Cohen. Myrinet -- A Gigabit-per-Second Local-Area Network. *IEEE Micro*, 15(1):29-36, 1995.

[5] D.R. Engler and M.F. Kaashoek. DPF: Fast, Flexible Message Demultiplexing using Dynamic Code Generation. *Proceedings of the ACM Communication Architectures, Protocols, and Applications (SIGCOMM '96)*, 1996.

[6] M.E. Fiuczynski, R.P. Martin, T. Owa, and B.N. Bershad. SPINE: An Operating System for Intelligent Network Adapters. *Proceedings of the Eighth ACM SIGOPS European Workshop*, pp. 7-12. Sintra, Portugal, September 1998.

[7] A. Fox, S.D. Gribble, E.A. Brewer, and E. Amir. Adapting to Network and Client Variability via On-Demand Dynamic Distillation. *Proceedings of the ASPLOS-VII*, pp. 160-170, Oct. 1996.

[8] P. Gupta and N. McKeown. Packet Classification on Multiple Fields. *Proceedings of the ACM Communication Architectures, Protocols, and Applications (SIGCOMM '99)*, 1999.

[9] IBM. The Network Processor: Enabling Technology for High-Performance Networking. IBM Microelectronics, 1999

[10] LevelOne. IX Architecture Whitepaper. An Intel Company, 1999

[11] B.A. Nayfeh, L. Hammond, and K. Olukotun. Evaluation of Design Alternatives for a Multiprocessor Microprocessor. *Proceedings of the 23rd International Symposium on Computer Architecture*, pp. 67-77, May 1996.

[12] S. Nilsson and G. Karlsson. Fast Address Lookup for Internet Routers. *Broadband Communications: The Future of Telecommunications*, 1998.

[13] L. Peterson, S. Karlin, and K. Li. OS Support for General-Purpose Routers. *Proceedings of the HotOS Workshop*, March 1999.

[14] J. Santos and D. Wetherall. Increasing Effective Link Bandwidth by Suppressing Replicated Data. *Proceedings of the Usenix Annual Technical Conference*, pp. 213-224. New Orleans, Louisiana, June 1998. USENIX.

[15] J.M. Smith, K.L. Calvert, S.L. Murphy, H.K. Orman, and L.L. Peterson. Activating Networks: A Progress Report. IEEE Computer Magazine vol. 32, no. 4, pp. 3-41, April 1999.

[16] V. Srinivasan, S. Suri, and G. Varghese. Packet Classification Using Tuple Space Search. *Proceedings of the ACM Communication Architectures, Protocols, and Applications (SIGCOMM '99)*, 1999.

[17] D. Tullsen, S. Eggers, and H. Levy. Simultaneous Multithreading: Maximizing On-Chip Parallelism. *Proceedings of the 22nd Annual International Symposium on Computer Architecture*, pp. 392-403. Santa Margherita Ligure, Italy, June 1995.

[18] D.J. Wetherall, U. Legedza, and J. Guttag. Introducing New Internet Services: Why and How. IEEE Network Magazine , July/August 1998.

Synthesizing Transformations for Locality Enhancement of Imperfectly-nested Loop Nests

Nawaaz Ahmed, Nikolay Mateev, Keshav Pingali
Department of Computer Science
Cornell University
Ithaca, NY 14853
{nawaaz,mateev,pingali}@cs.cornell.edu

ABSTRACT

We present an approach for synthesizing transformations to enhance locality in imperfectly-nested loops. The key idea is to embed the iteration space of every statement in a loop nest into a special iteration space called the *product space*. The product space can be viewed as a perfectly-nested loop nest, so embedding generalizes techniques like code sinking and loop fusion that are used in ad hoc ways in current compilers to produce perfectly-nested loops from imperfectly-nested ones. In contrast to these ad hoc techniques however, our embeddings are chosen carefully to enhance locality. The product space is then transformed further to enhance locality, after which fully permutable loops are tiled, and code is generated. We evaluate the effectiveness of this approach for dense numerical linear algebra benchmarks, relaxation codes, and the tomcatv code from the SPEC benchmarks.

1. BACKGROUND AND PREVIOUS WORK

Sophisticated algorithms based on polyhedral algebra have been developed for determining good sequences of linear loop transformations (permutation, skewing, reversal and scaling) for enhancing locality in perfectly-nested loops[1]. Highlights of this technology are the following. The iterations of the loop nest are modeled as points in an integer lattice, and linear loop transformations are modeled as nonsingular matrices mapping one lattice to another. A sequence of loop transformations is modeled by the product of matrices representing the individual transformations; since the set of nonsingular matrices is closed under matrix product, this means that a sequence of linear loop transformations can be represented by a nonsingular matrix. The problem of finding an optimal sequence of linear loop transformations is thus reduced to the problem of finding an integer matrix that satisfies some desired property, permitting the full machinery of matrix methods and lattice theory to be applied to the problem of locality-enhancement [2; 4; 23; 17; 21; 3].

[0]This work was supported by NSF grants CCR-9720211, EIA-9726388, ACI-9870687,EIA-9972853.

[1]A perfectly-nested loop is a set of loops in which all assignment statements are contained in the innermost loop.

ICS 2000 Santa Fe New Mexico USA
Copyright ACM 2000 1-58113-270-0/00/5...$5.00

```
for t = 1,T
  for i1 = 2,N-1
    for j1 = 2,N-1
S1:   L(i1,j1) = (A(i1,j1+1) + A(i1,j1-1)
                 + A(i1+1,j1) + A(i1-1,j1)) / 4
    end
  end
  for i2 = 2,N-1
    for j2 = 2,N-1
S2:   A(i2,j2) = L(i2,j2)
    end
  end
end
```

Figure 1: Jacobi

This technology is fairly mature, and it has been incorporated into production compilers, enabling these compilers to produce good code for perfectly-nested loop nests. In most programs however, most loop nests are *imperfectly-nested* because one or more assignment statements are contained in some but not all of the loops of the loop nest. For example, important matrix factorizations like Cholesky, LU and QR factorizations [9] are all imperfectly-nested loop nests. An entire procedure, which usually is a sequence of perfectly- or imperfectly-nested loop nests, can itself be considered to be imperfectly-nested loop nest.

As an example, consider the Jacobi code fragment in Figure 1 which is typical of programs that solve partial differential equations (pde's) by explicit methods. These are called relaxation codes in the compiler literature. They contain an outer loop that counts time-steps; in each time-step, a smoothing operation (stencil computation) is performed on arrays that represent approximations to the solution to the pde. In the Jacobi code, statements `S1` and `S2` touch the same data in each iteration of the `t` loop; instances of these statements in different iterations of the outer loop touch the same data as well. If the arrays do not fit into cache, this reuse will not be exploited. It is possible to exploit the reuse between statements in a given iteration of the `t` loop if the code is rewritten as in Figure 2. This code can be obtained by peeling the first iterations of the `i1`,`j1` loops and the last iterations of the `i2` and `j2` loops, and then fusing the remaining `i1` and `i2` loops as well as `j1` and `j2` loops. Furthermore, reuse between different iterations of the `t`-loop can be exploited by skewing the resulting `i` and `j` loops by `2*t` and then tiling all three loops; if the arrays are stored in column major order, interchanging the `i` and `j` loops allows the

```
for t = 1,T
  for j1 = 2, N-1
    L(2, j1) = (A(2,j1+1) + A(2,j1-1)
              + A(4,j1) + A(1,j1)) / 4
  end
  for i = 3,N-1
    L(i, 2) = (A(i,3) + A(i,1)
              + A(i+1,2) + A(i-1,2)) / 4
    for j = 3,N-1
      L(i,j) = (A(i,j+1) + A(i,j-1)
               + A(i+1,j1) + A(i-1,j1)) / 4
      A(i-1,j-1) = L(i-1,j-1)
    end
    A(i-1,N-1) = L(i-1,N-1)
  end
  for j2 = 2,N-1
    A(N-1,j2) = L(N-1,j2)
  end
end
```

Figure 2: Fused Jacobi

exploitation of spatial locality as well. These variants are not shown here due to their complexity.

A number of approaches have been proposed for enhancing locality of reference in imperfectly-nested loop nests like Jacobi. The performance improvement that can be obtained by transforming only the perfectly-nested loops in such programs can be quite limited [14]. Special purpose techniques for tiling matrix factorization codes have been proposed by Carr and Kennedy [6]; similar work for relaxation codes has been done by Song and Li [22].

A more general approach used by current commercial compilers is to convert an imperfectly-nested loop nest into a perfectly-nested loop nest if possible by applying transformations like *code sinking*, *loop fusion* and *loop fission* [25; 12], and then using locality enhancement techniques for the resulting maximal perfectly-nested loops. For most programs, there are many ways to do this conversion, and the performance of the resulting code may depend critically on how this conversion is done. For example, certain orders of applying these transformations might lead to code that cannot be tiled, while other orders could result in tilable code [13]. A further complication is that loop fission and fusion are themselves useful in improving data locality of loop nests; for example, loop fusion improves inter-loop-nest reuse as in the Jacobi example.

In this paper, we propose a general approach to locality enhancement of imperfectly-nested loops that builds on the standard approach used for perfectly-nested loops. Our strategy is shown in Figure 3. The iteration space of each statement is embedded in a special space called the *product space* using affine embedding functions F_i. These embeddings can be chosen so as to improve reuse in the program, and they generalize transformations like loop fusion and loop fission that have been used in the literature for locality enhancement. Furthermore, the product space itself can be viewed as a perfectly-nested loop nest (although one which has many redundant dimensions as we discuss later in this paper), so locality enhancement techniques such as height reduction [16] can be applied to the resulting loop nest; when possible, this loop nest can also be made fully permutable, enabling it to be tiled. Finally, code is generated after projecting out redundant dimensions, using standard techniques from polyhedral algebra; this code generation process may produce imperfectly-nested loop nests if appropriate.

The rest of this paper is organized as follows. Section 2 describes a framework for locality enhancement of imperfectly-nested loop

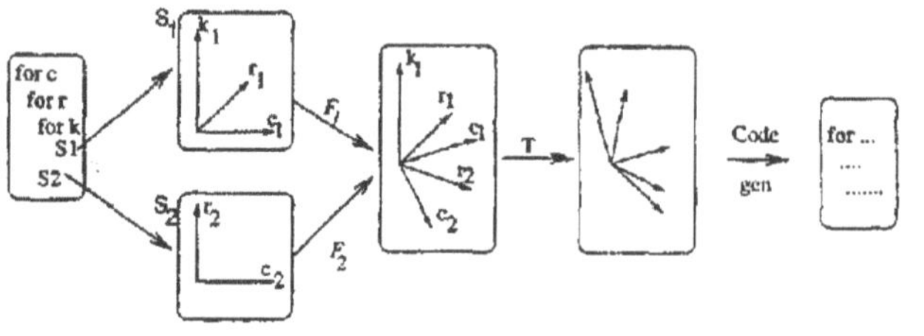

Figure 3: Locality Enhancement of Imperfectly-nested Loop Ne

nests. Section 3 describes the concrete approach to locality e hancement we use in this paper. Because the complete algorithm complicated, we work through an example in Section 4 to highlig important aspects of our approach. Section 5 gives the details of t algorithm. Section 6 evaluates the effectiveness of this algorith in enhancing locality of programs on the SGI Octane workstatio We show in that section that our approach automatically perfor the transformations on the Jacobi code fragment discussed abo Finally, Section 7 compares our approach with other approaches the literature.

2. AN ABSTRACT MODEL OF LOCALIT ENHANCEMENT

This section gives an abstract view of how program transformatio and locality enhancement can be modeled by polyhedral method

2.1 Program Execution Model

A program is assumed to consist of statements contained in a s quence of perfectly and imperfectly-nested loop nests. All lo bounds and array access functions are assumed to be affine fu tions of surrounding loop indices. We will use $S_1, S_2, \ldots, S_n$ name the statements in the program in syntactic order. A *dynam instance* of a statement S_k refers to a particular execution of t statement for a given value of index variables $\vec{i_k}$ of the loops su rounding it, and is represented by $S_k(\vec{i_k})$.

Program execution induces a total order on the dynamic instanc of a statement S_k. This *statement execution order* is modeled the *statement iteration space*, denoted by $\mathcal{S}_k$, as follows:

1. Construct a Cartesian space $\mathcal{S}_k$ of dimension equal to t number of loops surrounding S_k.
2. Map dynamic instances of S_k to $\mathcal{S}_k$ so that the followi conditions are satisfied:
   (a) At most one statement instance is mapped to a point the space $\mathcal{S}_k$.
   (b) If the points in space $\mathcal{S}_k$ are traversed in lexicograp order, and any statement instance mapped to a point executed when that point is visited, the statement ex cution order is reproduced.

The program execution order of a code fragment can be modeled a similar manner by a *program iteration space*, defined as follow

1. Let $\mathcal{P}$ be a p-dimensional Cartesian space for some p.
2. Embed all statement iteration spaces $\mathcal{S}_k$ into $\mathcal{P}$ using emb ding functions $\vec{F_k}$ which satisfy the following constraints:

```
for i1 = 1, N
S1:  x[i1] = a[i1]
for i2 = 1, N
S2:  x[i2] += b[i2]
```

(a) Code Fragment

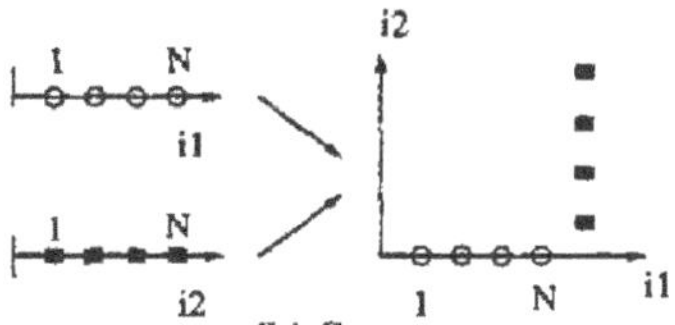

(b) Space

$$F_1(i_1) = \begin{bmatrix} i_1 \\ 0 \end{bmatrix} \quad F_2(i_2) = \begin{bmatrix} N+1 \\ i_2 \end{bmatrix}$$

(c) Embedding Functions

Figure 4: Modeling Program Execution

```
for i = 1, N
S1:  x[i] = a[i]
S2:  x[i] += b[i]
```

(a) Code Fragment

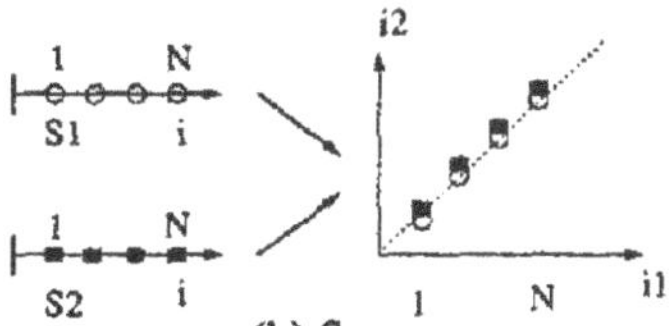

(b) Space

$$F_1(i_1) = \begin{bmatrix} i_1 \\ i_1 \end{bmatrix} \quad F_2(i_2) = \begin{bmatrix} i_2 \\ i_2 \end{bmatrix}$$

(c) Embedding Functions

Figure 5: Reducing Reuse Distances

(a) Each $\vec{F}_k$ must be one-to-one[2].

(b) If the points in space $\mathcal{P}$ are traversed in lexicographic order, and all statement instances mapped to a point are executed in original program order when that point is visited, the program execution order is reproduced.

The program execution order can therefore be modeled by the pair $(\mathcal{P}, \vec{\mathcal{F}} = \{\vec{F}_1, \vec{F}_2, \ldots, \vec{F}_n\})$. For the example, the execution order of the code fragment shown in Figure 4(a) can be represented by mapping the statements to a 2-dimensional space as shown in Figure 4(b). The embedding functions for the two statements are shown in Figure 4(c). We will refer to the program execution order as the *original* execution order.

In a similar way, any other execution order of the program can be represented by an appropriate pair $(\mathcal{P}, \mathcal{F})$. We can therefore optimize programs by transforming the original execution order $(\mathcal{P}, \vec{\mathcal{F}})$ to another execution order $(\mathcal{P}, \mathcal{F})$ that is is somehow "better" for locality and still preserves the semantics of the original program.

2.2 Promoting Data Reuse

Consider the data access patterns of the example in Figure 4. Statement instances `S1(i)` and `S2(i)` *exhibit data reuse* because they touch the same memory location `x(i)`. The number of statement instances executed between them is called the *reuse distance*. In the example, the reuse distance is $N-1$. If we represent the execution order for the example by $(\mathcal{P}, \mathcal{F})$, the reuse distance between `S1(i)` and `S2(i)` is proportional to the number of points in $\mathcal{P}$ with statements mapped to them that lie lexicographically between the points to which `S1(i)` and `S2(i)` are mapped. This is because of the initial one-to-one mapping requirement—there are at most a constant number of statement instances (one from each statement) mapped to each point in the space.

Reducing reuse distance increases the likelihood that the data will be in the cache when the second statement instance tries to access it. For our example, we can reduce the reuse distances from $N-1$ to zero by the embedding shown in Figure 5(c). This corresponds to the code obtained by fusing the two loops as shown in Figure 5(a), and can be shown to preserve the semantics of the original code. In general, there are many embeddings that preserve the correctness of a program. We can enhance the locality of a program by picking embeddings that reduces the reuse distances between statement instances while preserving correctness.

[2]Note that instances of *different* statements may get mapped to a single point of the program iteration space.

2.3 Reuse Classes

Formally, a reuse exists from instance $\vec{i}_s$ of statement S_s (the source of the reuse) to instance $\vec{i}_d$ of statement S_d (the destination) if the following conditions are satisfied:

1. *Loop bounds*: Both the source and destination statement instances lie within the corresponding iteration space bounds. Since the iteration space bounds are affine expressions of index variables, we can represent these constraints as $B_s * \vec{i}_s + b_s \geq 0$ and $B_d * \vec{i}_d + b_d \geq 0$ for suitable matrices B_s, B_d and vectors b_s, b_d.

2. *Same array location*: Both statement instances reference the same memory location. If we restrict memory references to array references, these references can be written as $A_s * \vec{i}_s + a_s$ and $A_d * \vec{i}_d + a_d$. Hence the existence of a reuse requires that $A_s * \vec{i}_s + a_s = A_d * \vec{i}_d + a_d$.

3. *Precedence order*: Instance $\vec{i}_s$ of statement S_s occurs before instance $\vec{i}_d$ of statement S_d in program execution order. If $common_{sd}$ is a function that returns the loop index variables of the loops common to both $\vec{i}_s$ and $\vec{i}_d$, this condition can be written as $common_{sd}(\vec{i}_d) \succeq common_{sd}(\vec{i}_s)$ if S_d follows S_s syntactically or $common_{sd}(\vec{i}_d) \succ common_{sd}(\vec{i}_d)$ if it does not, where $\succ$ is the lexicographic ordering relation. This condition can be translated into a disjunction of matrix inequalities of the form $X_s * \vec{i}_s - X_d * \vec{i}_d + x \geq 0$.

If we express the reuse constraints as a disjunction of conjunctions, each term in the resulting disjunction can be represented as a matrix inequality of the following form.

$$R\begin{bmatrix} \vec{i}_s \\ \vec{i}_d \end{bmatrix} + r = \begin{bmatrix} B_s & 0 \\ 0 & B_d \\ A_s & -A_d \\ -A_s & A_d \\ X_s & -X_d \end{bmatrix}\begin{bmatrix} \vec{i}_s \\ \vec{i}_d \end{bmatrix} + \begin{bmatrix} b_s \\ b_d \\ a_s - a_d \\ a_d - a_s \\ x \end{bmatrix} \geq 0$$

Each such matrix inequality will be called a *reuse class*, and will be denoted by $\mathcal{R}$ with an appropriate subscript.

The above definition applies to *temporal* reuses where the same array location is accessed by the source and the destination. If the cache line contains more than one array element, then we can also consider *spatial reuse* where the same cache line is accessed by the source and the destination of the reuse. Spatial reuse depends on the storage order of the array.

The conditions for spatial reuse are similar to the ones for temporal reuse, the only difference being that instead of requiring both statement instances to touch the same array location, we require that the two statement instances touch *nearby array locations that fit in the same cache line*. We can represent this condition as a matrix inequality by requiring the first[3] row of $A_d * \vec{\imath}_d + a_d - A_s * \vec{\imath}_s - a_s$ to lie between 1 and $c-1$, where c is the number of array elements that fit into a single cache line, instead of being equal to 0.

For the example in Figure 4(a), the temporal reuse existing between $S1(i_1)$ and $S2(i_2)$ can be represented by the reuse class $\mathcal{R}_1 = \{(i_1, i_2) : 1 \le i_1, i_2 \le N, i_1 = i_2\}$. It is straightforward to represent these inequalities as matrix inequalities, but we will not do so to keep the discussion simple. There also exists spatial reuse between these two statements. For a cache line containing 4 array elements it can be represented by the reuse class $\mathcal{R}_2 = \{(i_1, i_2) : 1 \le i_1, i_2 \le N, 1 \le i_2 - i_1 \le 3\}$.

2.4 Legality of Transformations

The original execution order $(\mathcal{P}, \tilde{\mathcal{F}})$ can be legally transformed to another execution order $(\mathcal{P}, \mathcal{F})$ if the latter preserves the semantics of the program. Dependence analysis states that semantics of a program will be preserved if all dependences[4] are preserved under the transformation.

The dependences in a program can be represented by a set of *dependence classes* similar to the reuse classes defined in Section 2.3. Each dependence class captures the constraints between the source ($\vec{\imath}_s$) and destination ($\vec{\imath}_d$) of a dependence that can be represented by a set of linear inequalities $\mathcal{D} : D \begin{bmatrix} \vec{\imath}_s \\ \vec{\imath}_d \end{bmatrix} + d \ge 0$.

Let $\mathcal{F} = \{F_1, F_2, \ldots F_n\}$ be a set of embedding functions for the program. We will say that these embedding functions are *legal* if for every $(\vec{\imath}_s, \vec{\imath}_d)$ in a dependence class, the point that $\vec{\imath}_s$ is mapped to in the program iteration space is lexicographically less than the point that $\vec{\imath}_d$ is mapped to. For future reference, we define this formally.

Definition 1. Let $\mathcal{F} = \{F_1, F_2, \ldots F_n\}$ be embedding functions that embed the statement iteration spaces of a program into a space $\mathcal{P}$. These embedding functions are said to be *legal* if for every dependence class $\mathcal{D}$ of the program,

$$\forall (\vec{\imath}_s, \vec{\imath}_d) \in \mathcal{D} \;\; F_d(\vec{\imath}_d) \succeq F_s(\vec{\imath}_s)$$

We will refer to the vector $F_d(\vec{\imath}_d) - F_s(\vec{\imath}_s)$ as the *difference vector* for $(\vec{\imath}_s, \vec{\imath}_d) \in \mathcal{D}$.

2.5 Minimizing Reuse Distances

Let $\mathcal{F} = \{F_1, F_2, \ldots F_n\}$ be embedding functions that embed the statement iteration spaces of a program into a space $\mathcal{P}$, and let $\mathcal{R}$ be any reuse class for that program. Consider any reuse pair $(\vec{\imath}_s, \vec{\imath}_d) \in \mathcal{R}$. Let $Distance(\vec{\imath}_s, \vec{\imath}_d)$ be the number of points in the space $\mathcal{P}$ with statements mapped to them that lie lexicographically between $F_s(\vec{\imath}_s)$ and $F_d(\vec{\imath}_d)$. As we saw in Section 2.2, the reuse distance between $S_s(\vec{\imath}_s)$ and $S_d(\vec{\imath}_d)$ is proportional to $Distance(\vec{\imath}_s, \vec{\imath}_d)$. We define $ReuseDistances(\mathcal{P}, \mathcal{F})$ to be the vector of $Distance(\vec{\imath}_s, \vec{\imath}_d)$ for all reuse pairs $(\vec{\imath}_s, \vec{\imath}_d)$ in the program under the execution order $(\mathcal{P}, \mathcal{F})$.

Our goal for locality enhancement is to find legal embeddings $\mathcal{F}_{opt}$ that minimize $\|ReuseDistances(\mathcal{P}, \mathcal{F})\|_X$ for a suitable norm $\|\cdot\|_X$.

[3]For Fortran storage order.

[4]*Dependence* is a temporal reuse in which at least one of the statement instances writes to the common location.

```
  for i = 1, N
    for j = 1, N
S1:   c(i,j) = 0
      for k = 1, N
S2:     c(i,j) += a(i,k) * b(k,j)
```

Figure 6: Imperfectly-nested MMM

3. A CONCRETE MODEL OF LOCALITY ENHANCEMENT

We now discuss the simplifications we make to develop a practical algorithm. In Section 3.1, we restrict embedding functions to be affine, and define a special space called the *product space* which we argue is the right space for locality enhancement considerations. In Section 3.2, we present our approach to minimizing reuse distances in the product space.

3.1 Product Spaces and Embedding Functions

We restrict our embedding functions to be *affine* to permit the use of integer linear programming techniques. Affine embedding functions can be decomposed into their linear and offset parts as follows: $F_k(\vec{\imath}_k) = G_k \vec{\imath}_k + g_k$. We allow symbolic constants in the offset part of the embedding functions.

THEOREM 1. *Let $\mathcal{P}$ be any Cartesian space and let $\mathcal{F} = \{F_1, F_2, \ldots, F_n\}$ be a set of affine embedding functions $F_k : S_k \to \mathcal{P}$. Let $F_k(\vec{\imath}_k) = G_k \vec{\imath}_k + g_k$. The number of independent dimensions of the space $\mathcal{P}$ is equal to the rank of matrix $G = [G_1 G_2 \ldots G_n]$.*

Let p be the sum of the number of dimensions in all statement iteration spaces. Theorem 1 tells us that affine embedding functions cannot utilize more than p dimensions. We therefore use a p-dimensional space to model program execution orders.

Definition 2. The *product space* for a program is the Cartesian product of all the statement iteration spaces of the statements in that program. The order in which this product is formed is the syntactic order in which the statements appear in the program.

For the imperfectly-nested matrix multiplication code in Figure 6, the iteration space $\mathcal{S}_1$ of statement S1 is a two-dimensional space $i_1 \times j_1$, while the iteration space $\mathcal{S}_2$ of S2 is a three-dimensional space $i_2 \times j_2 \times k_2$. The product space is the five dimensional space $i_1 \times j_1 \times i_2 \times j_2 \times k_2$.

The relationship between statement iteration spaces and the product space is specified by projection and embedding functions. Suppose $\mathcal{P} = \mathcal{S}_1 \times \mathcal{S}_2 \times \ldots \times \mathcal{S}_n$. Projection functions $\pi_i : \mathcal{P} \to \mathcal{S}_i$ extract the individual statement iteration space components of a point in the product space, and are obviously linear functions. For the imperfectly-nested matrix multiplication code in Figure 6,

$$\pi_1 = \begin{bmatrix} 1 & 0 & 0 & 0 & 0 \\ 0 & 1 & 0 & 0 & 0 \end{bmatrix} = \begin{bmatrix} I_{2\times 2} & 0 \end{bmatrix},$$

$$\pi_2 = \begin{bmatrix} 0 & 0 & 1 & 0 & 0 \\ 0 & 0 & 0 & 1 & 0 \\ 0 & 0 & 0 & 0 & 1 \end{bmatrix} = \begin{bmatrix} 0 & I_{3\times 3} \end{bmatrix}.$$

Definition 3. An *embedding function* F_i maps a point in statement iteration space $\mathcal{S}_i$ to a point in the product space. We consider only those embedding functions $F_i : \mathcal{S}_i \to \mathcal{P}$ that satisfy the condition $\pi_i(F_i(q)) = q$ for all $q \in \mathcal{S}_i$.

```
for i1 = 1, N
 for j1 = 1, N
  for i2 = 1, N
   for j2 = 1, N
    for k2 = 1, N
S1:  if ((i2==i1)&&(j2==j1)&&(k2==1))
       c(i,j) = 0
S2:  if ((i1==i2)&&(j1==j2))
       c(i,j) += a(i,k) * b(k,j)
```

Figure 7: Original Embeddings for MMM

Intuitively, this condition requires that the statement iteration space of a statement S be mapped to itself in the subspace of the product space corresponding to that statement. This restriction keeps the development simple. Each F_i is therefore one-to-one, but points from two different statement iteration spaces may be mapped to a single point in the product space.

3.1.1 *Embedding the Original Code*

We show that there always exists a way of embedding the code in the product space that represents the original program execution order.

As an example, consider the code in Figure 6. It is easy to verify that the code in Figure 7 is equivalent, and has the same execution order. Intuitively, the loops in Figure 7 correspond to the dimensions of the product space; the embedding functions for different statements can be read off from the guards in the loop nest:

$$F_1\left(\begin{bmatrix} i_1 \\ j_1 \end{bmatrix}\right) = \begin{bmatrix} i_1 \\ j_1 \\ i_1 \\ j_1 \\ 1 \end{bmatrix} \quad F_2\left(\begin{bmatrix} i_2 \\ j_2 \\ k_2 \end{bmatrix}\right) = \begin{bmatrix} i_2 \\ j_2 \\ i_2 \\ j_2 \\ k_2 \end{bmatrix}.$$

To preserve the original program execution order, the embedding functions in this example are chosen to satisfy the following conditions: (i) the identity mapping is used for dimensions corresponding to common loops (i and j) in the original code; and (ii) mappings for dimensions corresponding to non-common loops are chosen to preserve the original execution order.

In general, we can embed any code into its product space as follows. Let $F_k : \mathcal{S}_k \to \mathcal{P}$ be the affine function that maps the statement S_k to the product space. The components of F_k that map into the dimensions of the product space corresponding to statement S_j are denoted by $F_{k,j}$. Our initial requirement on embedding functions can be summarized by $F_{k,k}(\vec{\imath}_k) = \vec{\imath}_k$.

In Section 2.3 we defined $common_{kl}$ to be a function that returns the loop index variables of the loops common to both $\vec{\imath}_k$ and $\vec{\imath}_l$. Similarly, we define $noncommon_{kl}$ to return the loop index variables of the rest of the loops in $\vec{\imath}_l$. For the example above, we have $common_{12}((i_1, j_1)^T) = (i_1, j_1)^T$, and $noncommon_{12}((i_1, j_1)^T) = k_2$. Let $\min_{\prec}(\vec{\imath})$ and $\max_{\prec}(\vec{\imath})$ return the lexicographically smallest and largest values of the indices of the loops $\vec{\imath}$. For our example, $\min_{\prec}(k_2) = 1$.

For every statement S_l that occurs syntactically after S_k in the original program (i.e. $l > k$) we define

$$F_{k,l}(\vec{\imath}_k) = \begin{bmatrix} common_{kl}(\vec{\imath}_k) \\ \min_{\prec}(noncommon_{kl}(\vec{\imath}_k)) \end{bmatrix},$$

and for every statement S_l that occurs syntactically before S_k in the original program (i.e. $l < k$) we define

$$F_{k,l}(\vec{\imath}_k) = \begin{bmatrix} common_{kl}(\vec{\imath}_k) \\ \max_{\prec}(noncommon_{kl}(\vec{\imath}_k)) \end{bmatrix}.$$

These embeddings represent the original execution order.

3.1.2 *Redundant Dimensions in Product Space*

The number of dimensions in the product space can be quite large, and one might wonder if it is possible to embed statement iteration spaces into a smaller space without restricting program transformations. For example, in Figure 7, statements in the body of the transformed code are executed only when `i2 = i2`, so it is possible to eliminate the `i2` loop entirely, replacing all occurrences of `i2` in the body by `i1`. Therefore, dimension i_2 of the product space is redundant, as is dimension j_2.

There are transformations, however, that use all dimensions of the product space. For example completely fissioned codes, such as the one in Figure 4, need all dimensions of the product space. Since we do not want to restrict transformations unnecessarily, we work with the full product space. Once all embedding functions are determined, redundant dimensions are easy to identify and our algorithm removes them, so there is no performance penalty in the generated code.

3.2 Enhancing Locality in the Product Space

Consider a reuse class $\mathcal{R}$ and a reuse pair $(\vec{\imath}_s, \vec{\imath}_d) \in \mathcal{R}$. The abstract locality enhancement model in Section 2.5 required the minimization of $Distance(\vec{\imath}_s, \vec{\imath}_d)$, which is the number of points in the space $\mathcal{P}$ with statements mapped to them between $F_s(\vec{\imath}_s)$ and $F_d(\vec{\imath}_d)$. Unfortunately, it is not possible to calculate $Distance(\vec{\imath}_s, \vec{\imath}_d)$ efficiently, since there may be points with no statements mapped to them. Instead, we reduce reuse distances as follows.

Consider the *reuse vector* ($\vec{v}$) for the reuse pair $(\vec{\imath}_s, \vec{\imath}_d)$ for a given choice of embedding functions $\mathcal{F} = \{F_1, F_2, \ldots, F_n\}$; we will refer to the jth entry of this vector as v_j.

$$\begin{bmatrix} v_1 \\ v_2 \\ \vdots \\ v_p \end{bmatrix} = F_d(\vec{\imath}_d) - F_s(\vec{\imath}_s) = \begin{bmatrix} F_{d,1}(\vec{\imath}_d) - F_{s,1}(\vec{\imath}_s) \\ F_{d,2}(\vec{\imath}_d) - F_{s,2}(\vec{\imath}_s) \\ \vdots \\ F_{d,s}(\vec{\imath}_d) - \vec{\imath}_s \\ \vdots \\ \vec{\imath}_d - F_{s,d}(\vec{\imath}_s) \\ \vdots \\ F_{d,n}(\vec{\imath}_d) - F_{s,n}(\vec{\imath}_s) \end{bmatrix}.$$

We say that dimension j *carries reuse* for the reuse pair $(\vec{\imath}_s, \vec{\imath}_d)$ if $v_j \neq 0$. If a dimension carries reuse for some reuse pair in a reuse class $\mathcal{R}$, that dimension is said to carry reuse for that reuse class.

For all reuse pairs $(\vec{\imath}_s, \vec{\imath}_d) \in \mathcal{R}$, entries corresponding to $F_{d,k}(\vec{\imath}_d) - F_{s,k}(\vec{\imath}_s)$ (for $k \neq s, d$) can be made zero simultaneously (e.g. by choosing $F_{d,k}(\vec{\imath}_d) = F_{s,k}(\vec{\imath}_s) = const$). This may not always be possible for the elements $F_{d,s}(\vec{\imath}_d) - \vec{\imath}_s$ and $\vec{\imath}_d - F_{s,d}(\vec{\imath}_s)$ since the appropriate functions $F_{d,s}$ and $F_{s,d}$ may not exist. We try to make these entries zero; if this does not succeed, we can permute these dimensions of the product space so that they are innermost and tile them. This results in the following strategy:

1. We attempt to make all entries v_j of the reuse vector zero by choosing embedding functions appropriately. Since the dimensions of the embedding functions are independent, we can process each dimension separately. If we succeed in making all entries $v_j = 0$, then the reuse distance is also zero.

2. We reorder the dimensions of the product space so that dimensions for which $v_j = 0$ come first, and dimensions with larger entries come later.

3. We reduce reuse distances further by *tiling* all dimensions j for which the entry v_j of the reuse vector is non-zero.

As an example, consider the code in Figure 4(a) and the reuse from statement `S1(i)` to `S2(i)`. The embeddings in Figure 4(c) result in $v_1 \neq 0, v_2 \neq 0$ and reuse distance of $N-1$, while the embeddings in Figure 5(c) make each entry of the reuse vector zero and result in reuse distance of 0.

4. AN EXAMPLE

Before presenting the general locality enhancement algorithm, we illustrate our approach on the program of Figure 6. There are two dependence classes in this example:

1. Dependence class $\mathcal{D}_1 = \{(i_1, j_1, i_2, j_2, k_2) : 1 \leq i_1, j_1, i_2, j_2, k_2 \leq N, i_1 = i_2, j_1 = j_2\}$ is a flow-dependence that arises because statement `S1` writes to a location `c(i,j)` which is then read by statement `S2`.
2. Dependence class $\mathcal{D}_2 = \{(i_2, j_2, k_2, i_2', j_2', k_2') : 1 \leq i_2, j_2, k_2, i_2', j_2', k_2' \leq N, i_2 = i_2', j_2 = j_2', k_2 < k_2'\}$ is a flow-dependence that arises because statement `S2` writes to location `c(i,j)` which is then read by this statement in a later k iteration. This dependence also captures the anti- and output-dependences of statement `S2` on itself.

These two classes also represent reuse classes. The program has other reuse classes arising from spatial locality and input dependences, but these are not shown here for simplicity.
As shown in Figure 3, our locality enhancement algorithm will

1. determine affine embedding functions,
2. transform the product space,
3. eliminate redundant dimensions, and
4. decide which dimensions to tile.

The most difficult steps are (1) and (2), and these are interleaved in the algorithm described in Section 5. To simplify the presentation, let us assume for now that an oracle determines the transformation of the product space in Step (2) (we show in Section 5 that interleaving eliminates the need for such an oracle). Therefore, we are left with the problem of determining affine embedding functions. These are determined one dimension at a time by solving a system of linear constraints on the coefficients of the embedding functions for that dimension. These linear constraints describe the requirements that embeddings should (i) result in a legal program, and (ii) minimize reuse distances.
For the running example, we will assume that the oracle tells us that the transformation is the identity transformation, so the product space is left unchanged. Since the product space for this program is the five dimensional space $i_1 \times j_1 \times i_2 \times j_2 \times k_2$, Definition 3 of embedding functions requires that the embedding functions for this program look like the following:

$$F_1\left(\begin{bmatrix} i_1 \\ j_1 \end{bmatrix}\right) = \begin{bmatrix} i_1 \\ j_1 \\ G^3_{i_1} i_1 + G^3_{j_1} j_1 + g^3_N N + g^3_1 \\ G^4_{i_1} i_1 + G^4_{j_1} j_1 + g^4_N N + g^4_1 \\ G^5_{i_1} i_1 + G^5_{j_1} j_1 + g^5_N N + g^5_1 \end{bmatrix}$$

$$F_2\left(\begin{bmatrix} i_2 \\ j_2 \\ k_2 \end{bmatrix}\right) = \begin{bmatrix} G^1_{i_2} i_2 + G^1_{j_2} j_2 + G^1_{k_2} k_2 + g^1_N N + g^1_1 \\ G^2_{i_2} i_2 + G^2_{j_2} j_2 + G^2_{k_2} k_2 + g^2_N N + g^2_1 \\ i_2 \\ j_2 \\ k_2 \end{bmatrix}$$

The unknowns G and g will be referred to as the *unknown embedding coefficients*.

4.1 First Dimension

We first find embedding coefficients for the first dimension i_1.

Legality

At the very least, these embeddings must not violate legality. Therefore, as discussed in Section 2.4, the embedding coefficients must satisfy the following constraints.

1. $G^1_{i_2} i_2 + G^1_{j_2} j_2 + G^1_{k_2} k_2 + g^1_N N + g^1_1 - i_1 \geq 0$ for all points in $\mathcal{D}_1$, and
2. $G^1_{i_2} i_2' + G^1_{j_2} j_2' + G^1_{k_2} k_2' + g^1_N N + g^1_1 - (G^1_{i_2} i_2 + G^1_{j_2} j_2 + G^1_{k_2} k_2 + g^1_N N + g^1_1) \geq 0$ for points in $\mathcal{D}_2$.

Standard integer linear programming techniques can be used to convert these constraints into the following system of linear inequalities on the unknown embedding coefficients, as described in the appendix.

$$\begin{bmatrix} 1 & 1 & 0 & 1 & 0 \\ 0 & 1 & 0 & 1 & 0 \\ 1 & 1 & 1 & 1 & 1 \\ 1 & 0 & 0 & 1 & 0 \\ 0 & 0 & 0 & 1 & 0 \\ 0 & 0 & 1 & 0 & 0 \end{bmatrix} \begin{bmatrix} G^1_{i_2} \\ G^1_{j_2} \\ G^1_{k_2} \\ g^1_N \\ g^1_1 \end{bmatrix} \geq \begin{bmatrix} 1 \\ 0 \\ 1 \\ 1 \\ 0 \\ 0 \end{bmatrix} \quad (1)$$

Minimizing Reuse Distance

System (1) clearly has many solutions. We need to choose the solution that maximizes reuse. For our running example, consider locality optimization for the reuse that arises because of dependence $\mathcal{D}_1$. To ensure that dimension i_1 does not carry reuse for $\mathcal{D}_1$, we require that

$$G^1_{i_2} i_2 + G^1_{j_2} j_2 + G^1_{k_2} k_2 + g^1_N N + g^1_1 - i_1 = 0$$

for all points $(i_1, j_1, i_2, j_2, k_2) \in \mathcal{D}_1$. This condition too can obviously be converted into a system of inequalities on the unknown coefficients of the embeddings. The conjunction of this system and System (1) results in the following solution:

$$G^1_{i_2} = 1, G^1_{j_2} = 0, G^1_{k_2} = 0, g^1_N = 0, g^1_1 = 0$$

Therefore, the first dimensions of the two embedding functions are $F^1_1(i_1, j_1) = i_1$ and $F^1_2(i_2, j_2, k_2) = i_2$. Intuitively, this solution fuses dimensions i_1 and i_2 of the product space.
Even in our simple example, there are other reuse classes such as $\mathcal{D}_2$. To optimize locality for more than one reuse class, we prioritize the reuse classes heuristically and try to find embedding functions that make entries of the reuse vectors of the highest-priority reuse class equal to zero. Reuse classes are considered in order of priority until all embedding coefficients for that dimension are completely determined. If we assume that reuse class $\mathcal{D}_1$ has highest priority, we see that it completely determines the first dimension of the embedding functions, so no other reuse classes can be considered.

4.2 Remaining Dimensions

The remaining dimensions of the embedding functions are determined successively in a manner similar to the first one. The only difference is that some of the dependence classes may already be satisfied by preceding dimensions; these do not have to be considered for legality but only for reducing reuse distances by tiling.
Let us assume that the first $j-1$ dimenions of the embedding functions $\mathcal{F}^{1:j-1}$ have been determined and that we are currently processing the jth dimension of the product space.

Legality

Generalizing the corresponding notion in perfectly-nested loops, we say that a dependence class $\mathcal{D} : D \begin{bmatrix} \vec{\imath}_s \\ \vec{\imath}_d \end{bmatrix} + d \geq 0$ is *satisfied* by the first $j-1$ dimensions of the embedding functions $\mathcal{F}^{1:j-1}$ if the difference vector $F_d^{1:j-1}(\vec{\imath}_d) - F_s^{1:j-1}(\vec{\imath}_s)$ is lexicographically positive for all $(\vec{\imath}_s, \vec{\imath}_d) \in \mathcal{D}$. This means that this dependence will be respected regardless of how the remaining dimensions of the embedding functions are chosen. Therefore it is sufficient to require that for every pair $(\vec{\imath}_s, \vec{\imath}_d)$ in an *unsatisfied* dependence class $\mathcal{D}$,

$$F_d^j(\vec{\imath}_d) - F_s^j(\vec{\imath}_s) = \begin{bmatrix} -G_s^j & G_d^j \end{bmatrix} \begin{bmatrix} \vec{\imath}_s \\ \vec{\imath}_d \end{bmatrix} + g_d^j - g_s^j \geq 0 \quad (2)$$

In our running example, it can be shown that none of the dependence classes $\mathcal{D}_1, \mathcal{D}_2$ are satisfied by the first dimension of the embedding functions determined above, so both dependence classes must be considered when processing the second dimension.

Minimizing Reuse Distance

Constraining embedding coefficients to minimize reuse distances can be done in an identical manner to the first dimension.

An additional concern in picking coefficients for a dimension other than the first is that we may want to tile that dimension with outer dimensions. Tiling requires that these dimensions be fully permutable. We can ensure this by requiring that the constraint (2) holds even for satisfied dependence classes. If the resulting system has solutions, we can pick one that minimizes reuse distances as discussed for the first dimension (note that minimizing reuse distances before we add the tiling constraints might produce embeddings that do not allow tiling). If the resulting system has no solutions, the current dimension cannot be made permutable with outer dimensions, so constraint (2) is dropped for satisfied dependence classes.

Our algorithm produces the following embeddings for the running example:

$$F_1\left(\begin{bmatrix} i_1 \\ j_1 \end{bmatrix}\right) = \begin{bmatrix} i_1 \\ j_1 \\ i_1 \\ j_1 \\ 0 \end{bmatrix} \qquad F_2\left(\begin{bmatrix} i_2 \\ j_2 \\ k_2 \end{bmatrix}\right) = \begin{bmatrix} i_2 \\ j_2 \\ i_2 \\ j_2 \\ k_2 \end{bmatrix}$$

This embedding allows all five dimensions to be tiled. The code generation algorithm (Section 5.2) determines that i_2 and j_2 are redundant, and tiles the remaining dimensions.

4.3 Putting it All Together

If the transformation on the product space is given, we can obtain embedding coefficients for each dimension successively by constraining them based on (i) legality, (ii) tiling considerations, and (iii) minimizing reuse distances.

The algorithm for formulating legality and tiling constraints for a given dimension q is shown in Figure 8. This algorithm takes the dimension being processed, and the sets of unsatisfied and satisfied dependence classes as input, and returns a linear system L expressing constraints on embedding coefficients.

A small but useful feature of this algorithm is that it supports skewing of a dimension by outer dimensions to enable tiling. Dimension j will be permutable *after skewing* by outer dimensions if the difference vector entries corresponding to the satisfied dependence classes are bounded below by a negative constant. Hence, for every pair $(\vec{\imath}_s, \vec{\imath}_d)$ in all satisfied dependence classes $\mathcal{D}$, we require that

$$\begin{bmatrix} -G_s^j & G_d^j \end{bmatrix} \begin{bmatrix} \vec{\imath}_s \\ \vec{\imath}_d \end{bmatrix} + g_d^j - g_s^j + \alpha \geq 0, \quad \alpha \geq 0,$$

where α is an additional variable introduced into the system. The solution with the smallest α allows us to make dimension j permutable with the outer dimensions using a minimum amount of skewing. If α can be chosen to be 0, the dimension is permutable with outer dimensions without skewing.

Figure 9 shows how such a linear system is further constrained to determine coefficients for good locality. This algorithm assumes that reuse classes have been sorted in decreasing order of priority using some heuristic. In our implementation, we rank reuse classes by estimating the number of reuse pairs in each class.

```
ALGORITHM LegalityConstraints(q, DU, DS ) {
  /*
   q is dimension being processed.
   DU is set of unsatisfied dependence classes.
   DS is set of satisfied dependence classes.
  */

   Construct system Temp constraining the qth dimension
     of every embedding function as follows:

   for each unsatisfied dependence class u ∈ DU
      Add constraints so that each entry in dimension q
        of all difference vectors of u is non-negative;
   for each satisfied dependence class s ∈ DS
      Add constraints so that each entry in dimension q
        of all difference vectors of s + positive α
        is non-negative;

   Use Farkas' lemma to convert system Temp into
     a system L constraining unknown embedding
     coefficients;

   Return L;
 }
```

Figure 8: Formulating Linear System for Legality

```
ALGORITHM PromoteReuse(q,L,RS) {
  /*
   q is dimension being processed.
   L is a system constraining unknown embedding
          coefficients.
   RS is set of prioritized reuse classes.
  */

L' := L
for every reuse class R in RS in priority order
 {
    Z := System constraining unknown embedding function
         coefficients so qth dimension entries of
         all reuse vectors of class R is zero

    if (L' ∩ Z ≠ ∅)
    {
         L' := L' ∩ Z
    }
 }

 return any set of coefficients satisfying L';
}
```

Figure 9: Formulating Linear Systems for Promoting Reuse

```
ALGORITHM LocalityEnhancement

Q  := Set of dimensions of product space;
DU := Set of unsatisfied dependence classes
          (initialized to all dependence classes);
DS := Set of satisfied dependence classes
          (initialized to empty set);
RS := Set of reuse classes of the program
          (sorted by priority);
j  := Current dimension in transformed product space
          (initialized to 1);

while (Q is non-empty)
 {
   for each q in Q
    {
      L = LegalityConstraints(q, DU, DS);
      if system L has solutions
       {  Embedding coefficients for dimension j =
             PromoteReuse(q,L,RS);
          Update DS and DU;
          Delete q from Q;
          j = j + 1;
       }
    }

   // No more dimensions q can be added to current band.
   // Start a new band of fully permutable loops.

   DS := empty set;
 }

Apply Algorithm  DimensionOrdering to the dimensions;
Eliminate redundant dimensions;
Tile permutable dimensions with non-zero ReusePenalty;
```

Figure 10: Algorithm to Enhance Locality

5. ALGORITHM

Figure 10 shows the complete locality enhancement algorithm.

5.1 High-level Structure

Our algorithm interleaves the determination of the transformation for the product space with the determination of embedding coefficients for each dimension, and finds bands of fully permutable dimensions.

Each iteration of the inner `for each` q-loop tries to find a dimension q of the product space which can be permuted into position j of the transformed product space. The legality of this permutation is determined by a call to procedure `LegalityConstraints` in Figure 8 which attempts to find legal embeddings for dimension j which permit this dimension to be permuted with dimensions in the same band. If this procedure succeeds, we call procedure `PromoteReuse` in Figure 9 to choose embeddings with good locality. We drop out of the `for` loop when no more dimensions of the product space can be added to the current fully permutable band. All satisfied dependences are then dropped from further consideration, and a new fully permutable band is started. The algorithm terminates when all dimensions of the product space have been mapped into the transformed space.

Reordering of Dimensions

When constructing bands, the algorithm does not try to optimize the order of dimensions within a band since it adds dimensions to bands in arbitrary order. Since arbitrary order may not be best for locality, we need to reorder dimensions after all embedding coefficients have been determined. This is similar to the problem of choosing a good order for loops in a fully permutable loop nest, and any of the techniques in the literature can be used. Here we present a simple heuristic similar to *memory order* [12]. We reorder dimensions of the product space so that the dimensions with most

```
ALGORITHM DimensionOrdering

RPO  =  {i1, i2, ... ip}  // ReusePenalty order
NRPO =  ∅                 // nearby permutation

m = p   // number of dimensions left to process
k = 0   // number of dimensions processed
while  RPO ≠ ∅
 {
    for dimension j = 1,m
     {
        l = ij ∈ RPO
        Let NRPO = {i1', i2', ... ik'}
        if {i1', i2', ... ik', l} is legal
         {  NRPO = {i1', i2', ... ik', l}
            RPO  = RPO  -  {l}
            m = m - 1
            k = k + 1
            continue while loop
         }
     }
 }
```

Figure 11: Determining Dimension Ordering

unsatisfied reuses come last. For each dimension j of the produc space, we define the *reuse penalty* of that dimension with respect t embedding functions $\{F_1^j, F_2^j, \ldots, F_n^j\}$ to be the number of reus pairs in the classes for which the dimension carries reuse.

$$ReusePenalty(j, \mathcal{F}) = \sum_{\mathcal{R} \text{ unsatisfied}} \|\mathcal{R}\|$$

where $\|\mathcal{R}\|$ is the number of reuse pairs in reuse class $\mathcal{R}$. Clearl sorting dimensions in $ReusePenalty$ order is not always legal Figure 11 shows an algorithm that finds a nearby legal permutation. Intuitively, algorithm `DimensionOrdering` tries to or der dimensions greedily so that the dimension with the smalles $ReusePenalty$ is outermost if that is legal. Otherwise, it check whether the dimension with next smallest $ReusePenalty$ can b placed outermost. Once it finds a dimension to place outermos it repeats the process with the remaining dimensions. It is easy t see that the algorithm will always produce a legal ordering of th dimensions, and that it will pick the $ReusePenalty$ order if that i legal.

For the running example in Figure 6, our algorithm places all fiv dimensions of the product space in a single fully permutable band It then picks the dimension order $j_1 \times j_2 \times k_2 \times i_1 \times i_2$.

5.2 Code Generation

Removing Redundant Dimensions

Let $\mathcal{F} = \{F_1, F_2, \ldots, F_n\}$ be the set of embedding functions an let $F_k(\vec{i}_k) = G_k\vec{i}_k + g_k$. As discussed in Section 3, any dimensio j for which the jth row G^j of the matrix $G = [G_1, G_2, \ldots, G_n$ is linearly dependent on other rows is redundant. Once a good lega ordering of the dimensions is determined, our algorithm identifie all dimensions j for which G^j is linearly dependent on previou dimensions, and eliminates those dimensions.

For our running example, dimensions j_2 and i_2 are redundant a $G^{j_2} = G^{j_1}$ and $G^{i_2} = G^{i_1}$.

Tiling

All dimensions with non-zero $ReusePenalty$ will benefit fro tiling. Each fully permutable band is tiled (after individual dimer sions are skewed by outer loops if necessary).

Heuristics have been proposed for choosing tile sizes for perfectl nested loops [7; 21; 5], and any of them can be used with our fram

```
//tile counter loops
for t1 = 1,N, B
 for t2 = 0, N, B
  for t3 = 1, N, B
    //iterations within a tile
    for j = t1, min(t1+B-1,N)
     for k = t2, min(t2+B-1,N)
      for i = t3, min(t3+B-1,N)
        if (k==0)
          c(i,j) = 0
        c(i,j) += a(i,k) * b(k,j)
```

Figure 12: Locality-optimized MMM before Code Simplification

work. For the running example, j_1, k_2, and i_1 are not redundant and exhibit reuse, therefore we decide to tile all of them. They are all in the same band and do not require skewing. The resulting tiled code is shown in Figure 12. The *min*'s, *max*'s and conditionals within the loop body are removed by the code generation process using standard techniques from polyhedral algebra.

6. EXPERIMENTAL RESULTS

In this section, we present preliminary results from our implementation for three important codes—Cholesky factorization, Jacobi kernel, and the tomcatv SPECfp benchmark. All experiments were run on an SGI Octane workstation based on a R12000 chip running at 300MHz with 32 KB first-level data cache and an unified second-level cache of size 2 MB (both caches are two-way set associative). We present the following performance numbers for each code:

1. Performance of code produced by the SGI MIPSPro compiler (Version 7.2.1) with the "-O3" flag turned on. At this level of optimization, the SGI compiler applies the following set of transformations to the code—it converts imperfectly-nested loop nests to *singly nested loops* (SNLs) by means of fission and fusion and then applies transformations like permutation, tiling and software pipelining inner loops [24].

2. Performance of code produced by an implementation of the techniques described in this paper, and then compiled by the SGI MIPSPro compiler with flags "-O3 -LNO:blocking=off" to disable further tiling by the SGI compiler.

For Cholesky factorization, we also present performance of vendor supplied LAPACK library routine running on top of native BLAS.

Our tile size selection algorithm is still being implemented, so we tiled all codes with a fixed block size of 40. Our experiments show that there are no significant differences in performance for block sizes ranging from 20 to 100. Performance for Cholesky factorization is reported in MFLOPS, counting each multiply-add as 1 Flop. For Jacobi and tomcatv, we did not have hand-coded versions as a comparison; in these cases, we report running time.

The performance numbers presented show the benefits of synthesizing a sequence of locality-optimizing transformations instead of searching for that sequence. Even though the SGI MIPSPro compiler implements all the transformations necessary to optimize our benchmarks, it does not find the right sequence of transformations, so the performance of the resulting code suffers. For Cholesky factorization, the performance of our optimized code approaches the performance of hand-written libraries.

```
for k = 1,N
S1: a(k,k) = sqrt(a(k,k))
     for i = k+1,N
S2:       a(i,k) = a(i,k) / a(k,k)
          for j = k+1,i
S3:            a(i,j) -= a(i,k) * a(j,k)
```

(a) kij-Cholesky Factorization

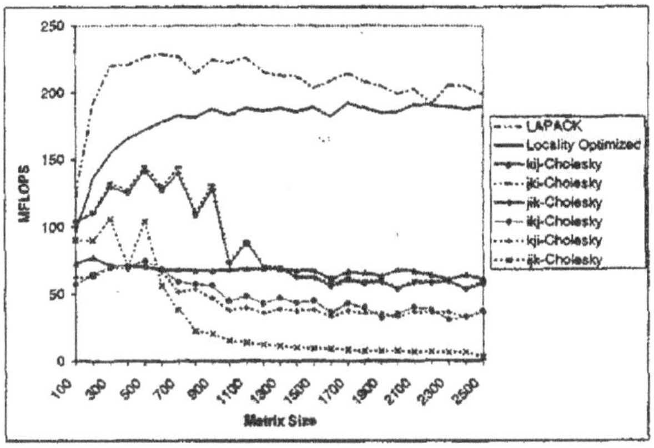

(b) Performance

Figure 13: Cholesky Factorization and its Performance

6.1 Cholesky Factorization

Cholesky factorization is used to solve symmetric positive-definite linear systems. Figure 13(a) shows one version of Cholesky factorization called *kij-Cholesky*; there are five other versions of Cholesky factorization corresponding to the permutations of the i, j, and k loops. Figure 13(b) compares the performance of all six versions compiled by the SGI compiler, the hand-optimized LAPACK library routine, and the code produced by our algorithm starting from *any* of the six versions.

The performance of the compiled code varies widely for the six different versions of Cholesky factorization. The *kij-Cholesky* is SNL and the SGI compiler is able to sink and tile two of the three loops (k and i), resulting in good L2 cache behavior and best performance for large matrices (about 65 MFLOPS) among the compiled codes. In contrast, the compiler is not able to optimize the *ijk-Cholesky* at all, resulting in the worst performance of about 5 MFLOPS for large matrices. The LAPACK library code performs consistently best at about 200 MFLOPS.

Our algorithm produces the same locality optimized code independent on which of the six versions we start with. That is expected as the abstraction that our algorithm uses—statements, statement iteration spaces, dependencies, and reuses—is the same for all six versions of Cholesky factorization.

For the *kij* version shown here, the algorithm picks the following embeddings (after reordering and removing redundant dimensions):

$$F_1([\ k\ ]) = \begin{bmatrix} k \\ k \\ k \end{bmatrix} \quad F_2(\begin{bmatrix} k \\ i \end{bmatrix}) = \begin{bmatrix} k \\ k \\ i \end{bmatrix} \quad F_3(\begin{bmatrix} k \\ i \\ j \end{bmatrix}) = \begin{bmatrix} j \\ k \\ i \end{bmatrix}$$

All three dimensions are tiled without skewing. The same code is obtained starting from any of the six versions of Cholesky factorization, and the line marked "Locality Optimized" in Figure 13(b) shows the performance of that code. The code produced by our approach is roughly 3 to 30 times faster than the code produced by the SGI compiler, and it is within 5% of the hand-written LAPACK library code for large matrices.

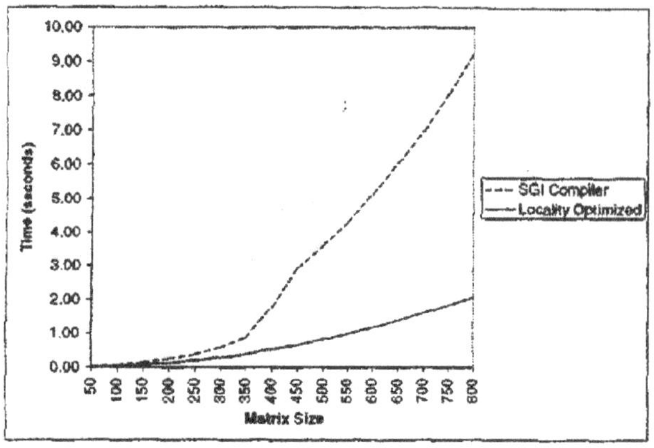

Figure 14: Performance of Jacobi

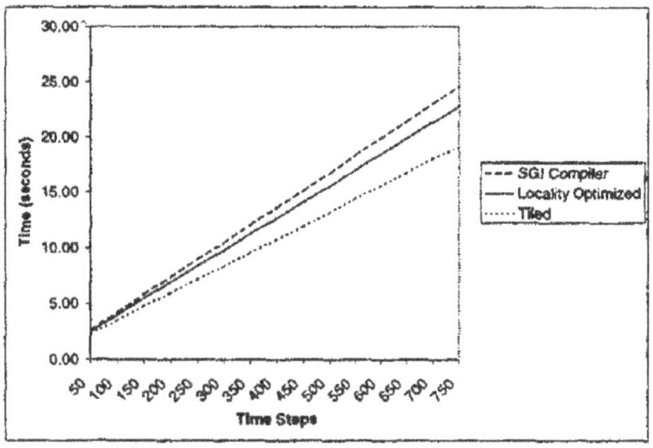

Figure 15: Performance of tomcatv

6.2 Jacobi

Our next benchmark is the Jacobi kernel in Figure 1, which was discussed in Section 1. Our algorithm picks embeddings that perform all the optimization steps discussed in Section 1.

$$F_1(\begin{bmatrix} t \\ i \\ j \end{bmatrix}) = \begin{bmatrix} t \\ j \\ i \end{bmatrix} \quad F_2(\begin{bmatrix} t \\ i \\ j \end{bmatrix}) = \begin{bmatrix} t \\ j+1 \\ i+1 \end{bmatrix}$$

These embeddings correspond to shifting the iterations of the two statements with respect to each other, fusing the resulting `i` and `j` loops respectively, and finally interchanging the `i` and `j` loops. This not only allows us to tile the loops but also benefits the reuses between the two arrays in the two statements, as well as the spatial locality in both statements.

The resulting space cannot be tiled directly, so our implementation chooses to skew the second and the third dimensions by `2*t` before tiling.

Figure 14 shows the execution times for the code produced by our technique and by the SGI compiler for a fixed number of time-steps (100).

6.3 Tomcatv

As a final example, we consider the tomcatv code from the SPECfp benchmark suite. The code consists of an outer time loop `ITER` containing a sequence of doubly- and singly-nested loops which walk over both two-dimensional and one-dimensional arrays. The results of applying our technique are shown in Figure 15 for a fixed array size (253 from a reference input), and a varying number of time-steps. Tomcatv is not directly amenable to our technique b cause it contains an exit test at the end of each time-step. The li marked "Locality Optimized" represents the results of optimizi a single time-step (i.e. the code inside the `ITER` loop) for loc ity. Treating every basic block as a single statement, our algorit produces an embedding which corresponds to fusing some of the loops and all the `I` loops. The exploitation of reuse between diff ent basic blocks results in roughly 8% improvement in performan compared to the code produced by the SGI compiler. If we consic the tomcatv kernel without the exit condition[5], our algorithm ske the fused `I` loop by `2*ITER`, and then tiles `ITER` and the skewec loops. The performance of the resulting code (line marked "Tilec is around 22% better than the original code.

7. RELATED WORK AND CONCLUSION

The mathematical techniques used in this paper have been us by the systolic array community for scheduling statements in lo nests on systolic arrays [15]. These techniques were extended Feautrier in his theory of *schedules* in multi-dimensional time which he used for automatic parallelization; related approaches mappings and affine transforms [10; 18].

For data locality, Kelly and Pugh advocate searching the space legal transformations using cost models that evaluate the mappin produced [11]. They associate a multi-dimensional mapping w each statement but the range of these mappings is not fixed sin there is no analog of our product space. Starting from totally u specified mappings, they propose to explore the tree of partia specified mappings till they completely specify the mapping, ing estimates of the number of cache misses to guide the sear Their estimator targets only reuses with source and destination the same statement. In particular, reuse between different sta ments requiring fusion will not be modeled. Though they repres tiling by means of pseudo-linear functions (using `mod` and `di` they do not include them in their search space of possible tra formations and hence do not necessarily find solutions that can tiled. By using a well-defined space (the product space), we able to target all reuses by representing reuse distances betwe statement instances by reuse vectors which we can then minim dimension by dimension. Furthermore, the product space allo us to impose constraints so that dimensions are permutable—t lets us order the dimensions and tile them to reduce reuse distanc further.

A different approach to locality enhancement in imperfectly-nes loops has been taken in *data-centric approaches* such as data sha ling [13]. The compiler determines an order in which array e ments should be touched, and then schedules code so that all sta ments that touch a given data element are scheduled to exec when that data item is brought into the cache. Integer linear p gramming techniques are used to determine if such a schedule legal. This work has been extended by Pugh and Rosser in th work on iteration space slicing [20]. The data-centric approach be used to generate code for sparse matrix applications as well [1 The framework in this paper can be used to generate data-cen code by adding data dimensions to the product space [1].

In conclusion, we have described a systematic approach to local enhancement of imperfectly-nested loops, and we have shown t it improves performance substantially on codes that are import in practice. Our approach generalizes techniques used in curr compilers for locality enhancement of both perfectly-nested imperfectly-nested loops [4; 23; 17; 25; 24].

[5]The resulting kernel can be tiled speculatively as demonstrated Song and Li [22].

8. REFERENCES

[1] Nawaaz Ahmed, Nikolay Mateev, Keshav Pingali, and Paul Stodghil. Compiling imperfectly-nested sparse matrix codes with dependences. Technical Report TR2000-1788, Cornell University, Computer Science, March 2000.

[2] C. Ancourt and F. Irigoin. Scanning polyhedra with DO loops. In *Principle and Practice of Parallel Programming*, pages 39–50, April 1991.

[3] E. Ayguadé and Jordi Torres. Partitioning the statement per iteration space using nonsingular matrices. In *1993 ACM International Conference on Supercomputing*, pages 407–415, Tokyo, July 1993.

[4] Uptal Banerjee. A theory of loop permutations. In *Languages and compilers for parallel computing*, pages 54–74, 1989.

[5] Pierre Boulet, Alain Darte, Tanguy Risset, and Yves Robert. (Pen)-ultimate tiling? In *INTEGRATION, the VLSI Journal*, volume 17, pages 33–51. 1994.

[6] Steve Carr and K. Kennedy. Compiler blockability of numerical algorithms. In *Supercomputing*, 1992.

[7] Jack Dongarra and Robert Schreiber. Automatic blocking of nested loops. Technical Report UT-CS-90-108, Department of Computer Science, University of Tennessee, May 1990.

[8] Paul Feautrier. Some efficient solutions to the affine scheduling problem - part ii: multi-dimensional time. *International Journal of Parallel Programming*, December 1992.

[9] Gene Golub and Charles Van Loan. *Matrix Computations*. The Johns Hopkins University Press, 1996.

[10] Wayne Kelly and William Pugh. Finding legal reordering transformations using mappings. In *Proceedings of the 7th International Workshop on Languages and Compilers for Parallel Computing*, pages 107–124, Ithaca, New York, August 8–10, 1994. Springer-Verlag.

[11] Wayne Kelly and William Pugh. Selecting affine mappings based on performance estimation. *Parallel Processing Letters*, 4(3):205–209, September 1994.

[12] K. Kennedy and K. S. McKinley. Optimizing for parallelism and data locality. In *1992 ACM International Conference on Supercomputing*, pages 323–334, Washington, D.C., July 1992. ACM Press.

[13] Induprakas Kodukula, Nawaaz Ahmed, and Keshav Pingali. Data-centric multi-level blocking. In *Programming Languages, Design and Implementation*. ACM SIGPLAN, June 1997.

[14] Induprakas Kodukula, Keshav Pingali, Robert Cox, and Dror Maydan. Imperfectly nested loop transformations for memory hierarchy management. In *International Conference on Supercomputing*, Rhodes, Greece, June 1999.

[15] S.Y. Kung. *VLSI Array Processors*. Prentice-Hall Inc, 1988.

[16] W. Li and K. Pingali. Access Normalization: Loop restructuring for NUMA compilers. *ACM Transactions on Computer Systems*, 1993.

[17] Wei Li and Keshav Pingali. A singular loop transformation based on non-singular matrices. *International Journal of Parallel Programming*, 22(2), April 1994.

[18] Amy Lim and Monica Lam. Maximizing parallelism and minimizing synchronization with affine partitions. *Parallel Computing*, 24:445–475, 1998.

[19] Nikolay Mateev, Keshav Pingali, Paul Stodghill, and Vladimir Kotlyar. Next-generation generic programming and its application to sparse matrix computations. In *Proceedings of the 2000 International Conference on Supercomputing*, Santa Fe, New Mexico, May 8–11, 2000. To appear.

[20] William Pugh and Evan Rosser. Iteration space slicing for locality. In *Proc. of 12th International Workshop on Languages and Compilers for Parallel Computing, (LCPC99)*, August 1999.

[21] J. Ramanujam and P. Sadayappan. Tiling multidimensional iteration spaces for multicomputers. *Journal of Parallel and Distributed Computing*, 16(2):108–120, October 1992.

[22] Yonghong Song and Zhiyuan Li. New tiling techniques to improve cache temporal locality. In *SIGPLAN99 conference on Programming Languages, Design and Implementation*, June 1999.

[23] M.E. Wolf and M.S. Lam. A data locality optimizing algorithm. In *SIGPLAN 1991 conference on Programming Languages Design and Implementation*, June 1991.

[24] Michael E. Wolf, Dror E. Maydan, and Ding-Kai Chen. Combining loop transformations considering caches and scheduling. In *MICRO 29*, pages 274–286, Silicon Graphics, Mountain View, CA, 1996.

[25] M. Wolfe. *High Performance Compilers for Parallel Computing*. Addison-Wesley Publishing Company, 1995.

APPENDIX

A. FARKAS' LEMMA

We show how to apply Farkas' Lemma to determine constraints in embeddings.

Consider a dependence class $\mathcal{D} : D \begin{bmatrix} \vec{\imath}_s \\ \vec{\imath}_d \end{bmatrix} + d \geq 0$, and a dependence pair $(\vec{\imath}_s, \vec{\imath}_d) \in \mathcal{D}$. Let F_d and F_s be the embedding functions for the destination and source statements of this dependence, and let the jth dimensions of these functions be $F_d^j = G_d^j \vec{\imath}_d + g_d^j$ and $F_s^j = G_s^j \vec{\imath}_s + g_s^j$.
Suppose that we must choose these unknown coefficients (G, g) so that $F_d^j(\vec{\imath}_d) - F_s^j(\vec{\imath}_s) \geq 0$.
The affine form of Farkas' lemma lets us express the constraints on these coefficients in terms of dependence class coefficients (D, d).

LEMMA 1. *(Farkas' Lemma) Any affine function $f(x)$ which is non-negative everywhere over a polyhedron defined by the inequalities $Ax + b \geq 0$ can be represented as follows:*

$$f(x) = \lambda_0 + \Lambda^T Ax + \Lambda^T b, \quad \lambda_0 \geq 0, \Lambda \geq 0,$$

where Λ is a vector of length equal to the number of rows of A. λ_0 and Λ are called the Farkas multipliers.

Applying Farkas' Lemma to our dependence equations we obtain

$$[\ -G_s^j \quad G_d^j\ ]\begin{bmatrix}\vec{i}_s\\ \vec{i}_d\end{bmatrix} + g_d^j - g_s^j = \lambda_0 + \Lambda^T D\begin{bmatrix}\vec{i}_s\\ \vec{i}_d\end{bmatrix} + \Lambda^T d,$$
$$\lambda_0 \geq 0, \Lambda \geq 0.$$

Equating coefficients of $\vec{i}_s$ and $\vec{i}_d$ on both sides, we get

$$\begin{aligned}[\ -G_s^j \quad G_d^j\ ] &= \Lambda^T D,\\ g_d^j - g_s^j &= \lambda_0 + \Lambda^T d,\\ \lambda_0 \geq 0, &\quad \Lambda \geq 0.\end{aligned}$$

The Farkas multipliers can be eliminated through Fourier-Motzkin projection to give a system of inequalities constraining the unknown embedding coefficients.

As an example, consider the first dimension of the embedding functions for the running example in Section 4. The following conditions must be satisfied:

1. $G_{i_2}^1 i_2 + G_{j_2}^1 j_2 + G_{k_2}^1 k_2 + g_N^1 N + g_1^1 - i_1 \geq 0$ for all points $(i_1, j_1, i_2, j_2, k_2)$ in $\mathcal{D}_1 = \{(i_1, j_1, i_2, j_2, k_2) : 1 \leq i_1, j_1, i_2, j_2, k_2 \leq N, i_1 = i_2, j_1 = j_2\}$, and
2. $G_{i_2}^1 i_2' + G_{j_2}^1 j_2' + G_{k_2}^1 k_2' + g_N^1 N + g_1^1 - (G_{i_2}^1 i_2 + G_{j_2}^1 j_2 + G_{k_2}^1 k_2 + g_N^1 N + g_1^1) \geq 0$ for points $(i_2, j_2, k_2, i_2', j_2', k_2')$ in $\mathcal{D}_2 = \{(i_2, j_2, k_2, i_2', j_2', k_2') : 1 \leq i_2, j_2, k_2, i_2', j_2', k_2' \leq N, i_2 = i_2', j_2 = j_2', k_2 < k_2'\}$.

Let us apply Farkas' lemma to the first condition. We have

$$\begin{aligned}&G_{i_2}^1 i_2 + G_{j_2}^1 j_2 + G_{k_2}^1 k_2 + g_N^1 N + g_1^1 - i_1 =\\ &\quad \lambda_0 + \lambda_1(i_1 - 1) + \lambda_2(N - i_1) + \lambda_3(j_1 - 1)\\ &\quad + \lambda_4(N - j_1) + \lambda_5(i_2 - 1) + \lambda_6(N - i_2) + \lambda_7(j_2 - 1)\\ &\quad + \lambda_8(N - j_2) + \lambda_9(k_2 - 1) + \lambda_{10}(N - k_2)\\ &\quad + \lambda_{11}(i_1 - i_2) + \lambda_{12}(i_2 - i_1) + \lambda_{13}(j_1 - j_2)\\ &\quad + \lambda_{14}(j_2 - j_1),\\ &\lambda_0, \lambda_1, \ldots, \lambda_{14} \geq 0\end{aligned}$$

After equating coefficients on both sides, we get:

$$\begin{aligned}i_1: &\quad -1 &= \lambda_1 - \lambda_2 + \lambda_{11} - \lambda_{12}\\ j_1: &\quad 0 &= \lambda_3 - \lambda_4 + \lambda_{13} - \lambda_{14}\\ i_2: &\quad G_{i_2}^1 &= \lambda_5 - \lambda_6 + \lambda_{12} - \lambda_{11}\\ j_2: &\quad G_{j_2}^1 &= \lambda_7 - \lambda_8 + \lambda_{14} - \lambda_{13}\\ k_2: &\quad G_{k_2}^1 &= \lambda_9 - \lambda_{10}\\ N: &\quad g_N^1 &= \lambda_2 + \lambda_4 + \lambda_6 + \lambda_8 + \lambda_{10}\\ 1: &\quad g_1^1 &= \lambda_0 - \lambda_1 - \lambda_3 - \lambda_5 - \lambda_7 - \lambda_9\end{aligned}$$

Eliminating Farkas multipliers through Fourier-Motzkin projection, we obtain the following constraints on the unknown embedding coefficients:

$$\begin{bmatrix}1&0&1&1&0\\0&1&1&1&0\\0&0&1&1&0\\1&1&0&1&0\\1&1&1&1&0\\0&1&0&1&0\\1&1&1&1&1\\1&0&0&1&0\\0&0&0&1&0\end{bmatrix}\begin{bmatrix}G_{i_2}^1\\G_{j_2}^1\\G_{k_2}^1\\g_N^1\\g_1^1\end{bmatrix} \geq \begin{bmatrix}1\\0\\0\\1\\1\\0\\1\\1\\0\end{bmatrix} \qquad (3)$$

Going through the same steps for the second condition, we get

$$[\ 0\ \ 0\ \ 1\ \ 0\ \ 0\ ]\begin{bmatrix}G_{i_2}^1\\G_{j_2}^1\\G_{k_2}^1\\g_N^1\\g_1^1\end{bmatrix} \geq [\ 0\ ] \qquad (4)$$

Combining conditions (3) and (4), we obtain the system of inequalities shown in Section 4:

$$\begin{bmatrix}1&1&0&1&0\\0&1&0&1&0\\1&1&1&1&1\\1&0&0&1&0\\0&0&0&1&0\\0&0&1&0&0\end{bmatrix}\begin{bmatrix}G_{i_2}^1\\G_{j_2}^1\\G_{k_2}^1\\g_N^1\\g_1^1\end{bmatrix} \geq \begin{bmatrix}1\\0\\1\\1\\0\\0\end{bmatrix}$$

Adaptive Reduction Parallelization Techniques

Hao Yu Lawrence Rauchwerger *
Dept. of Computer Science
Texas A&M University
College Station, TX 77843-311
{h0y8494,rwerger}@cs.tamu.edu

ABSTRACT

In this paper, we propose to adapt parallelizing transformations, more specifically, reduction parallelizations, to the actual reference pattern executed by a loop, i.e., to the particular input data and dynamic phase of a program. More precisely we will show how, after validating a reduction at run-time (when this is not possible at compile time) we can dynamically characterize its reference pattern and choose the most appropriate method for parallelizing it. For this purpose, we develop a library of parallel reduction algorithms, including both previously known and novel schemes, which includes algorithms specialized for different classes of access behavior. In particular, each algorithm in our library has identified strengths related to specific reference pattern characteristics, which are matched, at run-time, with measured characteristics of the actual reference pattern. The matching of algorithm to reference pattern is performed using a decision-tree based selection scheme. The contribution of this work consists in new optimizations for reduction parallelization and in the introduction of a new approach to the optimization of irregular applications: Characteristic based customization.

1. PARALLEL PERFORMANCE IS INPUT DEPENDENT AND NEEDS AUTOMATIC TUNING

Improving performance on current parallel processors is a very complex task which, if done 'by hand' by programmers, becomes increasingly difficult and error prone. Moreover, due to the inherent complexity and human limitations, true optimizations are hard to achieve. During the last decade, programmers have obtained increasingly more help from parallelizing (restructuring) compilers. Such compilers address the need of detecting and exploiting parallelism in sequential programs written in conventional languages as well as parallel languages (e.g., HPF). They also optimize data layout and perform other transformations to reduce and hide memory latency, the other crucial optimization in modern, large scale parallel systems. The success in the 'conventional' use of compilers to automatically optimize code is limited to the cases when performance is independent of the input data of the applications. When the access pattern of the code (e.g., loops) is statically insufficiently defined, either because it is read–in from a file or it is actually computed (and re-computed) during execution, then the compiler cannot use classic analysis techniques, e.g., data dependence analysis. Unfortunately, this precludes traditional static compiler parallelization and latency hiding techniques from being used in the optimization of many important modern applications such as SPICE [8], DYNA–3D [12], GAUSSIAN [7], and CHARMM [1], which have input-dependent and/or computation-dependent memory reference patterns.

*Research supported in part by NSF CAREER Award CCR-9734471, NSF Grant ACI-9872126, NSF Grant EIA-9975018, DOE ASCI ASAP Level 2 Grant B347886 and a Hewlett-Packard Equipment Grant

ICS 2000 Santa Fe New Mexico USA

One of the most important operations in scientific applications is the reduction operation, which is also commonly referred to as an update operation. The parallelization of reductions is crucial to the overall performance of parallel codes. The transformation of reductions for parallel execution requires a data dependence analysis (or equivalent analysis) to prove that indeed the operation is a reduction, and an algorithm substitution because reduction statements have a loop carried flow–dependence, i.e., the original sequential computation of the reduction must be replaced with a parallel algorithm. For example, a sequential summation is a reduction which can be replaced by a parallel prefix, or recursive doubling, computation [5, 6]. For some applications, most notably for SPICE 2G6, the data dependence analysis involved cannot be performed at compile time because the reference pattern is not defined at that time. In the case of irregular, sparse programs the access pattern traversed by the sequential reduction during a loop is also sensitive to the input data and/or computation. Therefore, not all parallel reduction algorithms and/or implementations are equally suited as substitutes for the original sequential algorithm. Each access pattern, though irregular, has its own characteristics and will best be parallelized with an appropriately tailored algorithm or a customized implementation of an existing algorithm.

In this paper, we propose to adapt parallelizing transformations, more specifically, reduction parallelizations, to the actual reference pattern executed by a loop, i.e., to the particular input data and dynamic phase of a program. More precisely we will show how, after validating a reduction at run-time (when this is not possible at compile time) we can dynamically characterize its reference pattern and choose the most appropriate method for parallelizing it. For this purpose, we develop a library of parallel reduction algorithms, including both previously known and novel schemes, which includes algorithms specialized for different classes of access behavior. In particular, each algorithm in our library has identified strengths related to specific reference pattern characteristics, which are matched, at run-time, with measured characteristics of the actual reference pattern. The matching of algorithm to reference pattern is performed using a decision-tree based selection scheme.

In Section 2, we first define more formally the reduction operation, and briefly survey known static and run-time methods for identifying and validating, respectively, reduction operations. Next, in Section 3, we introduce a model for the characterization of reduction access patterns and in Section 4, discuss previous and novel techniques for executing reductions in parallel that are tailored for specific types of reference patterns. Our decision-tree based model for the dynamic matching of the reduction parallelization scheme to the actual memory reference pattern is presented in Section 5. Finally we present experimental results that validate the decisions made by our decision-tree model. The experiments involve several known applications for which we first use our model to predict the best performing reduction algorithm and then show that indeed it was the best choice.

2. ESSENTIALS OF REDUCTION PARALLELIZATION

A special and very frequent case of loop dependence pattern occurs in loops which implement reduction operations. In particular, reductions (also known as updates) are at the core of a very large number of algorithms and applications – both scientific and otherwise – and there is a large body of literature dealing with their parallelization.

A reduction variable is a variable whose value is used in one associative and commutative operation of the form $x = x \otimes exp$, where $\otimes$ is the operator and x does not occur in exp or anywhere else in the loop. A simple example is statement S1 in Fig. 1-(a). The operator $\otimes$ is exemplified by the + operator, the access pattern of array $A(:)$ is *read, modify, write*, The function performed by the loop is to add a value computed in each iteration to the value stored in $A(:)$. This type of reduction is sometimes called an *update*.

There are two tasks required for reduction parallelization: *recognizing the reduction variable*, and *parallelizing the reduction operation*. (In contrast, privatization needs only to recognize privatizable variables by performing data dependence analysis, i.e., it is contingent only on the access pattern and not on the operations.)

In this paper, we assume we are given a known reduction operation, and our goal is to select the best method for performing it in parallel. Here, we briefly describe the available static and run-time techniques for recognizing reduction variables. In the remainder of the paper, we assume such techniques have been used appropriately to identify the reduction variables.

Static reduction recognition. The problem of recognizing reduction statements has usually been handled at compile-time by syntactically pattern matching the loop statements with a template of a generic reduction, and then performing a data dependence analysis of the variable under scrutiny to guarantee that it is not used anywhere else in the loop except in the reduction statement [15].

```
        do i=1, n
          do j = 1, m
S1:         A(j) = A(j) + exp()
          enddo
        enddo
                                (a)

        do i = 1, n
S1:       A(K(i)) = .......
S2:       ........... = A(L(i))
S3:       A(R(i)) = A(R(i)) + exp()
        enddo
                                (b)

        doall i = 1, p
          pA(1:n) = 0
        enddoall
        doall i = 1, n
S1:       A(K(i)) = .......
S2:       ........... = A(L(i))
S3:       pA(R(i)) = pA(R(i)) + exp()
        enddoall
        doall i = 1, p
          A(1:n) = A(1:n) + pA(1:n)
        enddoall
                                (c)
```

Figure 1: (a) Simple example of reduction, (b) Reduction needing run-time validation, (c) Reduction transformed for parallel execution

Run-time reduction validation. In the cases where data dependence analysis cannot be performed at compile time, reductions have to be validated at run-time. For example, although statement S3 in the loop in Fig. 1-(b) matches a reduction statement, it is still necessary to check at run-time that the elements of array A referenced in S1 and S2 do not overlap with those accessed in statement S3. Thus, we will check at run-time that there is no intersection between the references in S3 and those in S1 and/or S2. Of course, all other potential dependences caused by the references in S1 and S2 will have to be checked, because they cannot be analyzed at compile time

The technique we use to verify such reductions at run-time is the LRPD test, which is described in detail in [10] with more implementation guidelines given in [9]. The main idea of the LRPD test with respect to reduction validation is to speculatively execute a loop (including the reduction operation) in parallel and test subsequently if the reduction operation was indeed a valid reduction, i.e., it tests if any data dependences occurred and if the references appearing in the reduction statement were accessed anywhere else in the loop. If the test passes, the *reduction variables*, which were privatized and accumulated on each processor during the speculative execution, will be merged into the shared array after loop termination. If the test fails, the loop is re–executed in a safe manner, e.g., sequentially. To qualify more parallel loops, *array privatization* can also be speculatively applied and its validity tested after loop termination.[1]

In a simplified implementation of this test several shadow arrays are allocated: for marking the write accesses, the read accesses, the non-privatizable elements (those that are read before they are written in an iteration) and non-reduction elements (those elements that are initially assumed to be reductions and are accessed outside the reduction statements). A loop which is speculatively parallelized is first augmented with code that will mark during speculative execution the shadow arrays every time the array under test (the array whose dependences cannot be statically analyzed) is referenced (based on specific rules). After loop execution an analysis of the shadow arrays will verify the initial optimistic assumptions. If the speculation succeeds then the private contribution of all processors to the reduction elements will be combined and the corresponding shared array updated. In practice we need to use at most 3 bits per shadowed element. If the access pattern is sparse, then other data structures besides arrays are used for shadowing references under test [14].

3. ADAPTIVE TECHNIQUE: CHOOSE THE RIGHT METHOD FOR EACH CASE

Memory accesses in irregular programs take a variety of patterns and are dependent on the code itself as well as on their input data. Moreover, some codes are of a dynamic nature, i.e., they modify their behavior during their execution because they usually (not necessarily) simulate position dependent interactions between physical entities.

In this context it is indeed hard to find a reduction parallelization algorithm (or for that matter, other optimizations) that will work well in *all* cases. We propose an adaptive scheme that will detect the type of reference pattern through static (compiler) and dynamic (run-time) methods and choose the most appropriate scheme from a library of already implemented choices. To find the best choice we need to first establish a taxonomy of different access patterns, devise simple, fast ways to recognize them, and model the various old and newly developed reduction methods in order to find the best match.

[1] *Privatization* creates, for each processor cooperating on the execution of the loop, private copies of the program variables.

3.1 A Taxonomy of Memory Reduction Reference Patterns

The characterization of the access pattern is performed at compile time whenever possible, and otherwise, at run-time, during an inspector phase or during speculative execution.

From the point of view of optimizing the parallelization of reductions (i.e., selecting the best parallel reduction algorithm) we recognize the following characteristics of memory references to reduction variables:

Degree of contention measures:

- **C:** The degree of **Contention (C)** of a reduction element is the number of iterations referencing it.
- **CH:** The histogram of C which shows the number of elements referenced by a certain number of iterations. We will use a histogram per processor rather than per iteration because it has more practical effect on performance, which can clearly show how 'bad' the hot spot problem is.
- **CHR:** The ratio of the total number of references (or the sum of the **CH** histogram) and the space needed for allocating replicated arrays across processors (it is equal to the number of processors × dimension of the reduction array). **CHR** measures the percentage of elements that are referenced if replicated arrays are used. In essence it tells us if replicated arrays should be considered or not. We refer to the set of **CHR**s which have a high degree of contention as **HCHR**.
- **CD:** The **contention (C) Distribution (CD)** is the deviation of the spatial distribution of **C** on the address axis (array index range) from a uniform distribution. It is computed for each value of **C** as the standard deviation of the distance between them (on the address axis). **CD** tells, for example, whether the hot spots are clustered in a narrow range of the address space or if they are uniformly dispersed. It can be computed for all **C** values but in practice only the high **C** elements (hot spots) are of interest.

CON: The Connectivity (**CON**) of a loop is a ratio between the number of iterations of the loop and the number of distinct memory elements referenced by the loop. In [4] it is equivalently defined as the number of edges over the number of nodes of a graph. The higher the connectivity, the higher the ratio of computation to communication will be, or, in other words, if **CON** is high, a small number elements will be referenced by many iterations. The **C** measure is related to the **CON** measure: if an element is referenced by many iterations it is quite likely (but not necessarily so) that the loop has many iterations that reference a small number of addresses.

MO: The **Mobility (MO)** per iteration of a loop is directly proportional to the number of distinct elements that an iteration references. We have found that this measure is directly related to the number of reduction statements with different subscripts. The effect of a low iteration Mobility is a constraint with respect to the scheduling of iterations on different processors for the purpose of reducing remote misses and/or reduced duplication if the Local Write scheme is used.

SP: The **Sparsity (SP)** is simply the ratio of referenced elements to the dimension of the array.

R: The **reusability (R)** measures the frequency and degree of change of the access pattern from one instantiation of the reduction loop to the next. If **R** is larger than 1 it means that we can reuse the pattern characterization for **R** consecutive loop invocations. A smaller **R** between 0 and 1 is more or less dynamic. $\mathbf{R} = 0$ means dramatic changes every invocation. If the pattern is static for the whole execution of a program then chances are this can be proven at compile time and does not have to be collected.

DIM: The **DIM** measure gives the ratio between the reduction array dimension and cache size. It indicates whether compaction of the working space (if possible) is necessary and if full scale replication is a good idea.

If the program is dynamic then changes in the access pattern will be collected, as much as possible, in an incremental manner. When the changes are significant enough (a threshold that is tested at run-time) then a re-characterization of the reference pattern is needed.

4. REDUCTION PARALLELIZATION SCHEMES

We believe that the difficulty in dealing with irregular behavior is that no method will perform well for all reference patterns. Our idea is to identify the regular components of each irregular pattern (including uniform distribution), isolate and group them together in space and time, if this is not already the case, and then apply the best reduction parallelization method to each component.

More specifically we will characterize the global reference pattern through the measures defined in Section 3, and then if necessary reorganize it in groups of references that display similar behavior. If, for example, we find that we deal with a pattern that is sparse, has relatively few hot-spots and high mobility we will first compact the references through remapping using hash tables or through an indirection array and schedule iterations to processors so that the average degree of contention is lowered. Then we group the hot-spots together through remapping (modify the subscript array). This new access pattern will then be composed of two 'regular' sections: a dense section whose elements are referenced on most processors and a sparse section whose elements are referenced by only a few processors. Finally we will employ a replicated array section method (on the high contention area) and a linked structure on the low contention side.

We now present techniques for performing reduction operations in parallel. We first briefly describe previously known methods, and then present various novel techniques. Our new techniques were developed for situations, as identified by our reference pattern characterization criteria, that are not adequately covered by the previous techniques. For brevity, we provide only a high level description of the methods.

4.1 Previous Reduction Parallelization Algorithms

We distinguish two major approaches to reduction parallelization: (a) methods that update shared reduction variables during the the original loop execution, and (b) methods that accumulate in private storage during the original loop execution and update the shared variables with each processor's contribution after the loop has finished. In the following, we review three direct update methods (Unordered Critical Sections, Local Write, and Software Coherence Protocols) and one private accumulation and global update method. For each method, we describe its relative advantages and disadvantages.

4.1.1 Direct Update Methods

Unordered critical sections. The original, sequential `do` loop is transformed into a `doall` and the accesses to the reduction variable are enclosed in an **unordered critical section** [3, 15].
Advantages: It is very simple to implement with locks, and works well if contention on reduction elements is low.
Disadvantages: It is not scalable because the penalty due to synchronizations increases with the number of processors. This method is recommended only for low contention reductions.

Local Write is a recently proposed technique [4] which uses a variation of the 'owner compute' method and is mostly employed in the parallelization of irregular codes. The reference pattern is first collected in an inspector loop [13] and is followed by a partitioning of the iteration space based on the *owner-computes* rule. Memory locations referenced across processors will have their iterations replicated so that they access addresses local to each processor.
Advantages: This mechanism works well when contention across iterations, or, a measure called *connectivity* by its authors (the ratio between iterations and distinct elements referenced), is low and thus work (iteration) replication can be kept at a minimum. Because this method eliminates any contention through iteration replication no critical sections are necessary. Another significant advantage of the Local Write method is the fact that it maximizes locality (owner compute) and thus its effect is maximized in distributed memory environments where latency and message passing are quite expensive.
Disadvantages: The inspector phase can be quite expensive because it traverses and collects all references to the reduction array occurring in the loop. The resulting data structure may be quite large and its analysis expensive. Another potential drawback of the method is that for reference patterns with high connectivity, work duplication may be large.

The *applicability of Local Write is limited to that of inspectors.* If the data and address computation form a potential control and/or dependence cycle then a proper inspector (no side-effects and very inexpensive) cannot be extracted – the inspector becomes the loop itself.

Software Coherence Protocols. Another technique employed in software DSM [11] uses a modified coherence protocol which

sends continuous updates to the homes of the various references (in essence a write-through protocol).
Advantages: The method works well if contention is low and locality high.
Disadvantages: It can potentially generate a lot of memory traffic, and is applicable only for software DSM environments.

4.1.2 Private Accumulation and Global Update

A reduction operation is an associative recurrence and can thus be parallelized using a recursive doubling algorithm [5, 6]. In a similar manner, we can privatize the reduction variables and accumulate in private storage the partial results and thus allow the original loop to execute as a `doall`. Then, after loop execution, the partial results are accumulated across processors and the corresponding shared array is updated. As sketched below, there are several possible implementations of this method [16, 17].

Replicated Private Arrays (buffers). In this implementation, the reduction variable is privatized through replicated arrays on all processors and the partial results are accumulated on each processor. After the parallel loop finishes, the final result is obtained by performing the reduction across processors and the update of the shared array.
Advantages: This technique works very well if the access pattern is dense, i.e., if most elements of the replicated arrays are indeed written during execution. The method is very simple to implement and no additional work is generated during loop execution. The final cross-processor update (reduction) is easy to implement (it is fully parallel) and its work increases linearly with the number of processors (more processors implies more private arrays). Individual access to the reduction variables is very fast (array access).
Disadvantages: If the reference pattern is sparse and/or contention is low, then many elements may either not be touched at all or only by a small subset of the processors. Thus, the maximally allocated private space is wasted and can create problems associated with referencing a large data structure (e.g., page misses, TLB misses, etc) during the parallel loop execution. Moreover, the final cross-processor reduction performs a lot unnecessary work: instead of being proportional to the actual number of distinct memory references on each processor it is proportional to the dimension of the private arrays. This makes the scheme not scalable.

4.2 Novel Reduction Parallelization Algorithms

In this section, we describe several novel reduction parallelization algorithms we have developed in order to address the cases not covered by previous algorithms. To illustrate our new techniques we will use throughout this section the loop in Fig. 2. It is an example of a sequential, irregular reduction loop which we want to execute in parallel.

4.2.1 Replicated Buffer With Links

This technique is very similar to the previously described **Replicated Private Arrays** and is in essence a sparse storage scheme that can be processed easily in parallel. Here we also allocate, on all processors, private arrays conformable to the original shared reduction array, but, we also provide an additional *link* to the data. This link is in fact a pointer to the private array of the next processor where it is referenced. After the parallel loop finishes, the cross-processor merging operation can be performed only along the chain of links, thus reducing the number of remote misses to those absolutely necessary. This is useful when the degree of contention is low and only a few processors need to participate in the merging operation.

```
do i=1,6
  ........
  A(B(i)) = A(B(i)) + 1
  ..........
enddo

B(1:6) = (9 110 251 700 251 9)
P = 3 , static scheduling
```

Figure 2: Loop used as example for new techniques

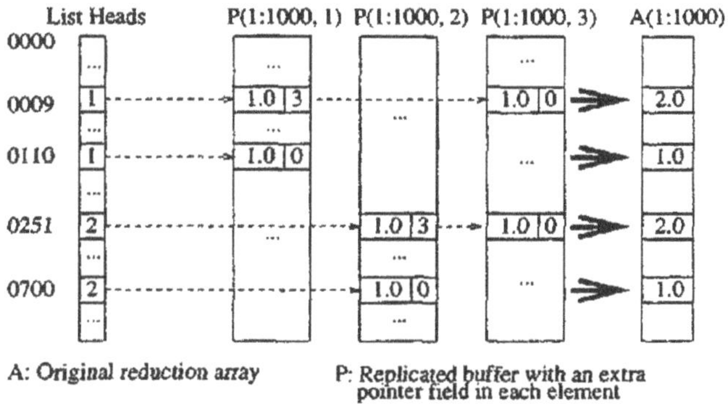

Figure 3: Data Structure for Replicated Buffer with Links.

The data structure needed to implement this method is shown in Fig. 3. Here, referenced elements with the same first index are linked together and are headed by the array `ListHeads`, of the same dimension as that of A (the reduction array). The links are established either during an inspector phase or during a first instantiation of the loop (at its merging phase), when regular replicated arrays are used. When we detect a pattern change we update the linked list structure.
Disadvantage: It requires more memory and a setup phase.

4.2.2 Selective Privatization

For patterns with few hot spots (low **CHR**), high **DIM** and/or are sparse (**SP**), we wish to replicate only those elements that are referenced on most processors. All other elements can be allocated on an as-needed basis, i.e., only where they are actually referenced. The main idea is to first determine which elements are referenced on multiple processors and then allocate for them (and only for them) private storage space. Then we will make a private copy of the indirection array (most applications that we have studied reference their reduction arrays through subscript arrays) and modify the appropriate locations to point to the private storage. In this manner, the execution of the parallel loop will not be slowed down and a lot of space will be saved. In the final merging phase, only the privatized portions of the array will be merged, further improving perfor-

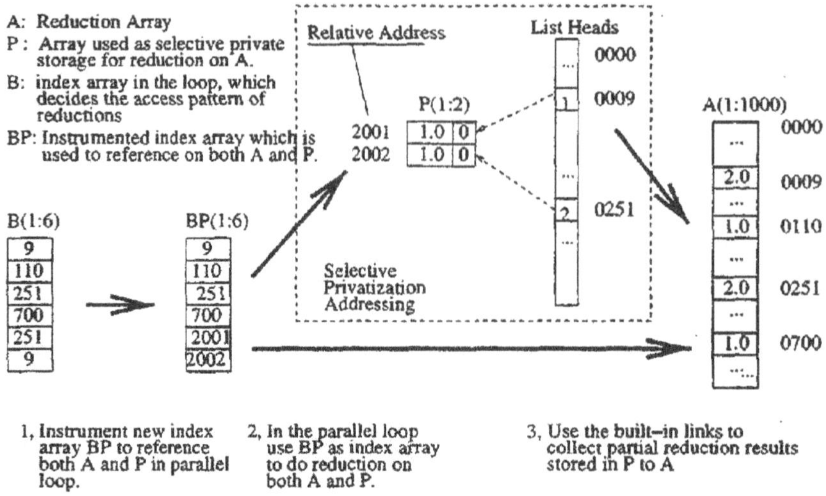

Figure 4: Example for Selective Privatization. A private index array is used to reference reduction elements during the parallelized loop. The final reduction is performed using the linked list.

mance. It should be noted though, that each reference during the merging phase will be more expensive because the private storage may not be conformable and the original indexes have to be stored with the private data and later verified. It is important to take this extra cost into account when deciding when to apply the method, however scalable it may be. This means that a good threshold number for the sparsity measure should be determined (experimentally). The data structure used to implement this method is shown in Fig. 4. The data structure is derived from Fig. 3 by shrinking the privatized space (P) such that only multiply referenced elements of the original replicated buffer remain privatized. The links from Fig. 3 are maintained and used in the cross-processor reduction phase.

Because this technique inherently remaps references it can also be used in tandem with the *replicated buffer* scheme. For high contention elements we use replication and for the rest selective privatization. To improve locality (and later reduce remote misses) the two types of replication can be grouped in contiguous sections through remapping.

Another useful optimization is that we always privatize (whether selective or replicated) the data on all sharing processors *except one* (usually the first). This is because one processor can always write directly to the original shared array without any contention. The benefits may seem small (proportional to 1/p) but if there are only 2 sharers the final merge time is significantly reduced: instead of merging cross-processor we just update the shared array with one private contribution.

A potential disadvantage is the existence of a private index array per processor. Its size is proportional to the number of referenced elements, not necessarily distinct. So the *setup phase* needs to traverse it and modify all positions where private storage has been allocated. This operation can be quite expensive, if it cannot be amortized across many invocations of the loop (low Reusability **R**). An alternative is use the original subscript array and modify it where elements need to be privatized. Each processor will then point to its own space. Because the subscript array may be also used outside the scope of the loop, we need to save the original values before modifications are done and restore them after loop end.

4.2.3 Sparse Reductions with Privatization in Hash Tables

Sparse codes index their reduction operands indirectly. For example, in SPICE, all memory references are indirect and point to the same global array name. Because this array is potentially very large and the compiler cannot evaluate where the 'reduction area' is, the use of privatized arrays is prohibitively expensive, both in terms of space and in traversal time. We have developed a hybrid method that first compacts the reduction references on every processor, through the use of private conformable (across processors) hash tables, and then later uses the collected cross-processor collision information to selectively privatize only those reduction elements that cause contention across processors. Furthermore, this information can be reused during subsequent instantiations of the loop without the need to re-hash the reference pattern.

Phase 1: Hashing Reductions. The first time a loop with reductions is executed all reduction operands are hashed in private, conformable arrays. Let us take the sample loop given in Section 4.2, which performs a reduction on an array A, which is indexed by array B, using 3 processors. First, we allocate 3 private hash tables H pointing into 3 private accumulation arrays P (all of the same dimension). H and P could be also considered as a structure H-P consisting of a key and data and expanded across the 3 processors. After inserting into the H-P table during parallel loop execution, the expanded array P is 'reduced' into the original shared array A. Fig. 5 shows how the contents of the subscript array B are hashed into H and then H is used to accumulate in private storage during parallel execution.

This phase is scalable, uses compact private memory and privatizes all references. Of course, references are hashed and therefore fairly expensive.

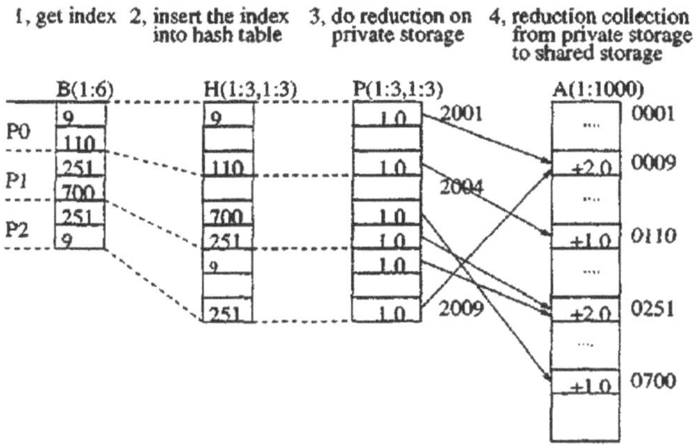

Figure 5: Sparse reductions using private hash tables P and final cross-processor reduction into shared array A.

Phase 2: Selective Privatization and Reference Redirection. In the second instantiation of the loop during the execution of the program, we speculate (or know) that the access pattern of the reduction has not changed and reuse the information collected in the first phase (the first instantiation of the loop). In this case we know exactly which array elements are referenced by more than one processor and need to be privatized. To keep the access time to the reduction elements fast (as opposed to hashing the address) we allocate a private subscript array which contains either the original entries or the entries to the privatized arrays. For 'pure' Fortran this means that 'out of bounds' indexing will occur. We overcome this 'syntactic' problem by allowing the compiler to over-allocate the relevant shared arrays by a sufficient amount beyond their original dimension. This additional 'legal' space will provide the needed private storage.

Fig. 6 shows the needed transformations for parallelizing a sparse reduction with a low degree of cross-processor contention (sharing). In *stage 1* we allocate BP, a private copy of index array B, and modify it only in the positions where privatization was found to be necessary. These positions have been collected in Phase 1 and the additional space has been preallocated at the end of the shared array A in a section named P. The original subscript elements from array B are saved. In *stage 2*, the loop executes in fully parallel mode without contention. In *stage 3*, after the loop finishes, the privately accumulated results are added into the shared array A based on the established map. Finally, we should mention that in this phase the H-P section is much smaller than that used in Phase 1 because it has to hold only the privatized elements (in Phase 1 it holds all references).

Alternatively, we can temporarily modify index array B, use it during the parallel reduction loop and then restore it to its original value for the remainder of the program.

In the application illustrating this technique (SPICE) the access pattern can then be proven to have high reusability.

4.2.4 Rescheduling Iterations

Similarly to the Local Write scheme, we can reorder iterations on the processors in order to obtain some improvements. We reorder the assignment of iterations to reduce the access pattern's C (contention). This in turn will increase locality and reduce the number of privatized elements. However, if mobility (**MO**) is high, this scheme does not bring any improvements and is in fact quite expensive to setup. Our experimental results do not yet reflect the use of this technique.

5. ADAPTIVE CHOICE OF THE ALGORITHM: THE DECISION TREE

So far we have presented some new and some well-known algorithms for reduction parallelization and have ascertained, at least to a certain degree, their suitability for programs (loops) with certain characteristics. We have also introduced some measures for characterizing irregular access patterns. We have shown that we can analyze the reference pattern of such codes first, through compiler analysis and then, at run-time, either with inspectors or speculatively, by adopting a simple 'general purpose' technique at the first instantiation of the loop. The speculation is in fact quite 'benign', in the sense that its only possible negative side-effect is poor performance. The work involved in the actual characterization of the reduction pattern is very simple: some scalar values are inexpensively computed on-the-fly while the references are traversed.

The main goal however is that once the type of pattern is established, the appropriate reduction parallelization algorithm, that is the one which best matches these characteristics, can be chosen and successfully employed. In order to make this choice we need a decision algorithm that takes as input measured, real, code characteristics, and a library of available techniques, and selects an algorithm for the given instance. It is hard to obtain a perfect match because we use very simple reference characteristics. But at the same time it may not pay to put more time in their analysis if the difference in the resulting performance gain is not high enough. In Fig. 7 we have constructed a decision tree based on our reduction pattern measures and our knowledge of the suitability of each reduction method available to us. In Fig. 8, we show the *empirical* thresholds against which the parameters used in the decision making process are compared. They were measured through experimentation by comparing the performance of each reduction technique when presented with various access patterns.

We now give a brief explanation of our decision process. First we will check if the reference pattern is sparse. If **SP** is below the threshold then we will use hash table based privatization for our reduction variables. If the collision histogram ratio (**CHR**) is large then we may have the choice between Local Write and Replicate Buffers. It means that we are frequently accessing many elements. If it is possible to localize all these references without much work duplication (small connectivity, good mobility and large array dimensions) then we can use the Local Write method, and otherwise the the Replicated Buffer method may provide the best performance. If not many distinct elements are referenced then a replicated buffer scheme would be wasteful – the sharing pattern is small enough to warrant a more expensive selective privatization or linked repli-

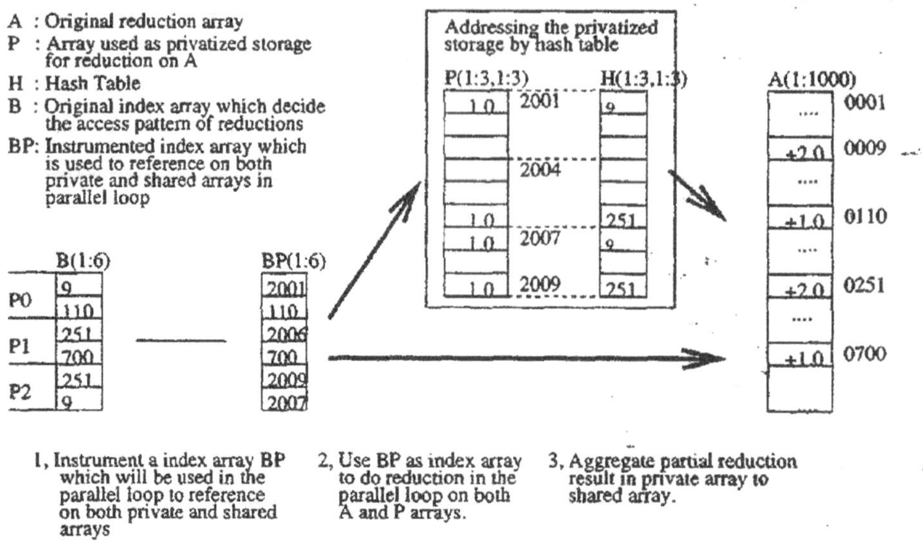

Figure 6: Sparse reductions using selectively privatized reduction references and their cross-processor reduction into shared array A.

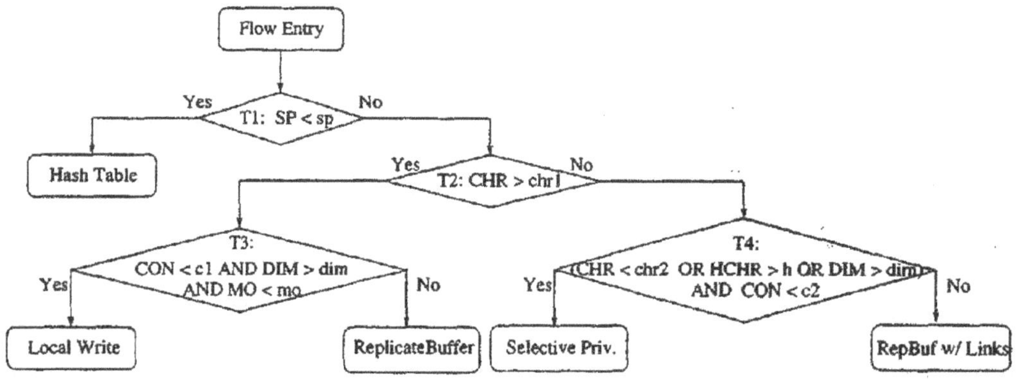

Figure 7: Decision Tree. (SP, CHR, CON, MO, DIM, HCHR are defined in Section 3; sp, chr1, c1, dim, mo, c2, chr2, h are empirical constants used as thresholds.)

cated buffer. Both make use of point to point communication because the references are not dense and are not spread uniformly across processors. The decision between these last two methods depends in essence on the associated cost of the consumption of additional private memory, i.e.,. if we can use Replicate Buffers with Links then that would be a better choice, but only if we can afford its memory requirements.

Symbol	Value	Symbol	Value	Symbol	Value
sp	0.2	chr1	0.4	c1	10
dim	$\frac{CacheSize}{ST}$	mo	2	c2	100
chr2	0.25	h	0.1	mr	2

Figure 8: Empirical constants (ST is the size_of_array_type of the reduction array).

5.1 Experimental Validation of the Model

In this section we evaluate the accuracy and validity of our decision-tree based performance model. To make this analysis simpler, we use the following notation when referring to each decision node in the tree in the table in Fig. 9.

$$T1 = SP < sp$$

$$T2 = CHR > chr1$$

$$T3 = (CON < c1) \wedge (DIM > dim) \wedge (MO < mo)$$

$$T4 = ((CHR < chr2) \vee (HCHR > h) \vee (DIM > dim)) \wedge (CON < c2)$$

In this section we will show performance data (speedups) of reduction loops from several codes which have been parallelized using most of the known and newly introduced reduction techniques and which have been executed with a several different input sets. Their relative performance can be seen in the graphs in Figures 10–11.

At the same time we have used our memory reference pattern characterization to make a hierarchical choice between

APP	MO	DIM	SP	CON	CHR	HCHR	CD	T1	T2	T3	T4	Recom. Scheme	Expe. Result
Irreg do100	2	1000000	2.5	10	0.92	0.88	1.16	F	T	T	T	lw	lw, sel, ll, rep
			1.25	5	0.71	0.36	3.54	F	T	T	T	lw	lw, sel, rep, ll
			0.5	2	0.40	0.017	132.2	F	T	T	T	lw	lw, sel, rep, ll
			0.25	1	0.26	0.0005	6506.	F	F	T	T	sel	lw, sel, ll, rep
Nbf do50	1	128000	12.5	100	0.25	0.0	N/A	F	F	F	T	sel	sel, ll, rep, lw
			6.25	50	0.25	0.0	N/A	F	F	F	T	sel	sel, ll, rep, lw
			3.125	25	0.25	0.0	N/A	F	F	F	T	sel	sel, ll, rep, lw
			1.25	10	0.25	0.0	N/A	F	F	F	T	sel	sel, ll, rep, lw
Moldyn	2	16384	10.75	43	0.41	0.002	1.0	F	T	F	F	rep	ll, rep, sel, lw
		32000	6.75	27	0.36	0.0	N/A	F	T	F	F	rep	ll, rep, sel, lw
		55296	2.25	9	0.33	0.0	N/A	F	F	F	F	ll	ll, rep, sel, lw
		87808	1.5	6	0.29	0.0	N/A	F	F	F	F	ll	ll, rep, sel, lw
Spark98	1	30169	0.625	5	0.18	0.0	N/A	F	F	F	T	sel	sel, ll, rep, lw
		7294	0.6	4.8	0.2	0.0	N/A	F	F	F	T	sel	ll, sel, rep, lw
Charmm do78	2	332288	35.88	17.9	0.14	0.11	2	F	F	F	T	sel	ll, sel, rep, lw
			17.94	8.97	0.15	0.06	2	F	F	F	T	sel	ll, sel, rep, lw
		664576	1.12	4.48	0.13	0.04	2	F	F	T	T	sel	ll, sel, rep, lw
Spice bjt100	28	186943	0.14	0.04	0.125	$\approx 10^{-4}$	0 [2]	T	F	F	T	hash	hash, ll, rep, lw [3]
		99190	0.20	0.06	0.125	$\approx 10^{-4}$	0	T	F	F	T	hash	hash, ll, rep
		89925	0.16	0.05	0.125	$\approx 10^{-4}$	0	T	F	F	T	hash	hash, ll, rep
		33725	0.16	0.05	0.126	$\approx 10^{-4}$	0	T	F	F	T	hash	hash, ll, rep

Figure 9: Modeling Summary. P = 8; MO, DIM, SP, CON, CHR, HCHR, CD are defined in Section 3. *rep, ll, sel, hash, lw* represent Replicated Buffer, Linked-List Replicated Buffer, Selective Privatization, Hash Table Privatization, and Local Write schemes respectively.

the various reduction methods. Finally we have compared the recommendation of our model with the experimental results. While our model has always recommended the correct solution we should hedge this good result with fact that sometimes the performance differences between the various choices were not that important. What is however important is the fact that the trend was always correctly predicted.

5.1.1 Experimental Setup

We have chosen 6 programs from a variety of scientific domains and augmented them with our instrumentation to collect information about the access pattern. This has been done in most cases (for all Fortran codes) automatically using the Polaris compiler [2]. The compiler is capable of extracting the condensed access descriptors of a loop (similar to an inspector loop) and, where it was not possible (SPICE), used our run-time parallelization pass [14] to collect data during actual loop execution. The compiler has inserted calls to a run-time library that compute the various parameters we were interested in. Then we have implemented (by hand) the various reduction algorithms and inserted them one by one for our experiments. We intend to implement this phase automatically by substituting the reduction statements with calls to a run-time library.

The experimental setup for our speedup measurement consisted of a 16 processor HP-V class system with 4Gb memory and 4Mb cache per processor, running the HPUX11 operating system. It is a directory based cache coherent UMA shared memory machine. Due to the limited size of our input sets and constraints on our single user time allocation for this project we have used only 8 processors.

We have chosen the following well known applications which we will briefly describe here in order to make the paper self-contained. Their detailed description can be found elsewhere in the literature. It is important to note that *we have tried, where possible, to use data sets that exercise the entire memory hierarchy of our parallel machine in order to get the performance data of 'real-life' applications.*

Irreg is an iterative PDE solver used in CFD applications. It uses an unstructured mesh to model physical structures. The code uses nodes and edges of a graph to represent its mesh. The time is spent computing the forces that are applied to the end points of its edges. After evaluating the forces at each node the program performs an irregular reduction to update them with the new values. We have used a large input size of 1,000,000 nodes with various degrees of sparsity and connectivity. The actual values can be seen in Fig. 9. Mobility is 2 because there are two updates to different addresses for each iteration of the reduction loop.

Nbf is a widely available kernel from the GROMOS molecular dynamics benchmark. It is typical of N-body simulations in that the code maintains a continuously updated list of its neighbors with which it interacts. At every time step forces are evaluated at each node and applied through a reduction operation across the whole data structure of the program. Because the interaction of the molecules changes the Reusability is variable. For our experiments we have used a data set with 128,000 nodes and various degrees of sparsity and connectivity.

Moldyn is a well-known kernel for the molecular dynamics code CHARMM. It is in a way similar to Nbf in the sense that its nodes interact only with its neighbors. The list of neighbors changes at various times because of the forces applied to them. It is a quite dynamic irregular code for which Reusability is low. We have simulated input sets with a number of nodes between 16,384 and 87,808 and various sparsity and connectivity. Mobility is 2.

Charmm is the original code for Moldyn. We have used other

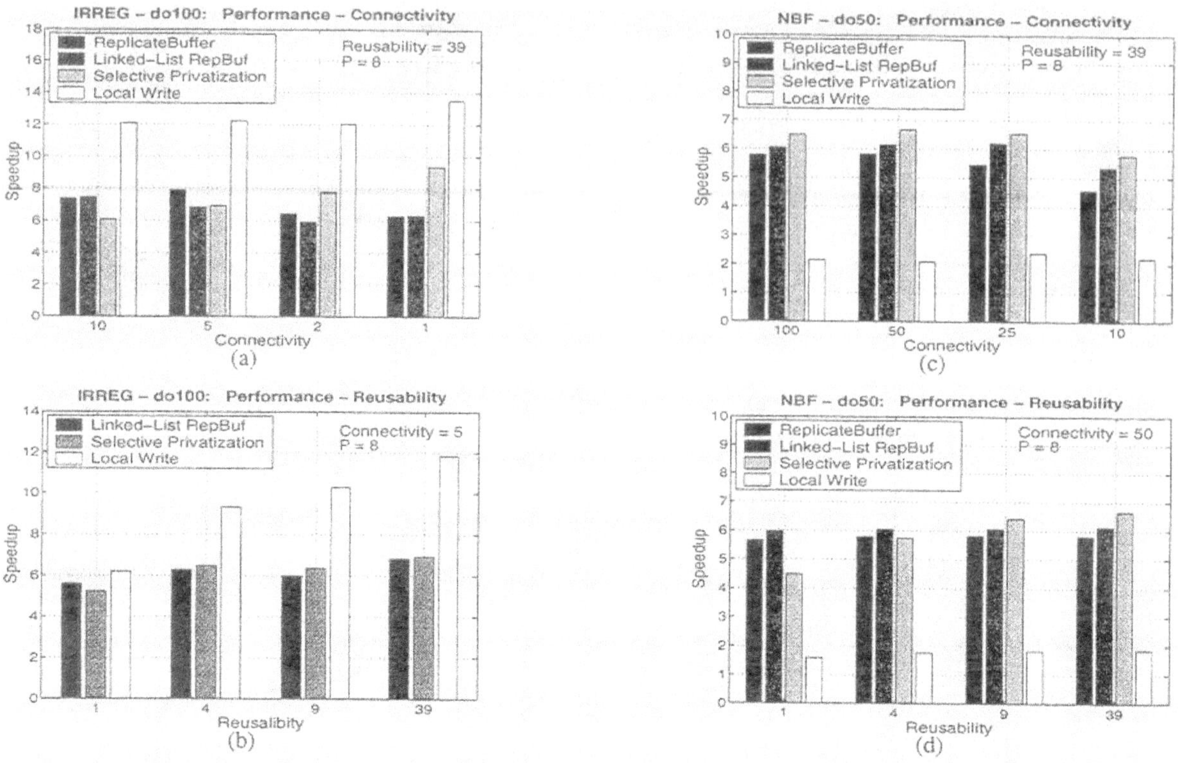

Figure 10: Performance comparisons.

data sets with sizes of 332,288 and 664,576 in order to produce 'real results'. Mobility is 2.

Spark98 is a collection of 10 sparse kernels developed by David O'Hallaron at CMU. The sparse matrices are induced from a pair of three-dimensional unstructured finite element simulations of earthquake ground motion in the San Fernando Valley. Each kernel is a program/mesh pair. There are 5 C programs (smv, lmv, rmv, mmv, hmv) and 2 finite element input data sets (sf10 and sf5). We have chosen the *rmv* kernel which computes irregular reductions. The meshes determine both the size and nonzero structure of the sparse matrices used. We have used the moderate size mesh (because the large one was not available to us) Sf5. It has 30,169 nodes, 410,923 nonzero matrix entries. Reusability is high, mobility is good (1). This code has been transformed by hand because our compiler infra-structure can handle only Fortran code.

SPICE 2G6 is a well-known circuit simulation code written in an older Fortran style. Its main feature is that it does its own memory management inside a statically allocated large array named `Value`. Therefore all references to arrays are through indirection (subscripted subscripts) which makes almost any compiler analysis impossible. We have transformed the code for parallel execution using the run-time techniques described in [14]. For the experiments described in this paper we have chosen the main loop in subroutine BJT. The loop evaluates the device model and updates the Y matrix of the circuit (this is the reduction loop). After solving the linear system the program re-evaluates the device model with the new input data and iterates the process until the error is acceptable. In essence, it iterates a sparse solver to a fixed point. The model evaluation loop takes between 11% and 45% of total execution time depending on the complexity of the devices and circuits being simulated.

Our run-time parallelization technique generates several versions of the loop. We present results for the version proven parallel (after run-time testing) and show how well the reduction parallelization performs. The Mobility is 28, which means that there are 28 distinct reduction statements for each iteration. In the sequential version these take about 33% of the time spent in the loop. The address range taken by the reduction elements for our input file is 143,365. This represents a run-time optimization because the compiler cannot evaluate this range statically - it is collected and later reused at run time. The Replicated Buffer scheme has been applied using this range information. Otherwise the size of the privatized array would have on the order of Mb/processor. The Sparsity is very low and so is Connectivity. In order to reuse the information we have used a technique we have named Global Variance Control. Instead of proving that addresses do not change from one instance of the loop to the other one, we have checked, at run-time, when it does change. In the more global scope of the iteration to a fixed point we have inserted code to flag when a shared integer array is modified. We have taken this event, in a conservative manner, as an address change and then redone our reduction setup phase. Fortunately this address change occurs only 2 times during the whole program execution. We have also implemented a less conservative technique (than checking integer modification), but it is beyond the scope of this paper.

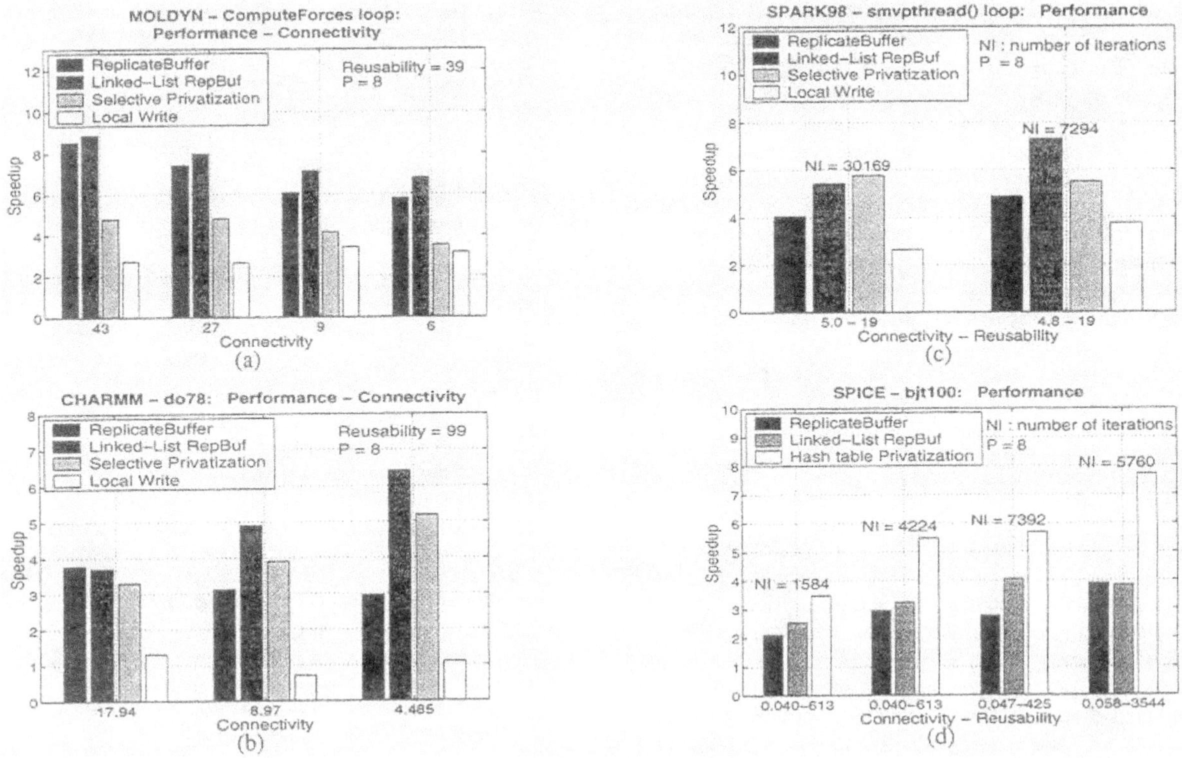

Figure 11: Performance comparisons.

5.1.2 *Discussion*

The table shown in Fig.9 illustrates all experimental data - all memory reference parameters are computed at run-time. The columns labeled T1 through T4 refer to the run-time trace of the decision process using the algorithm described in the previous sections. The result of these decisions is shown in the "Recommended scheme" column. The final column shows the actual experimental speedup obtained with the various reduction schemes which are presented in decreasing order of their speedup. For example, for Irreg, the model recommended the use of Local Write. The experiments confirm this choice: *lw* is listed as having the best measured speedup of all schemes. The Figures 10–11 show a quantitative evaluation of the reduction schemes. The last column in the table uses this data to show the actual performance order.

All speedup graphs include **all** the time associated with setting up the auxiliary data structures used by the various reduction schemes.

While most of the speedup graphs are self-explanatory (speedups with and without reuse of information) some deserve some comments. Irreg works much better with Local Write reductions because it manages to increase locality and break up the working set among processors. So, in spite of some code replication (about 80% more work due to iteration duplication) the code gets a superlinear speedup for the large data sizes used.

In the experiment for the SPICE loop, the hash table reduces the allocated and processed space to such an extent that, although the setup of a hash table is large, the performance improves dramatically. It is the only example where hash table reductions represent the best solution because of the very sparse nature of the references. We believe that codes in C would be of the same nature and thus benefit from it. There are no experiments with the Local Write method because iteration replication is very difficult due to the modification of shared arrays inside the loop body.

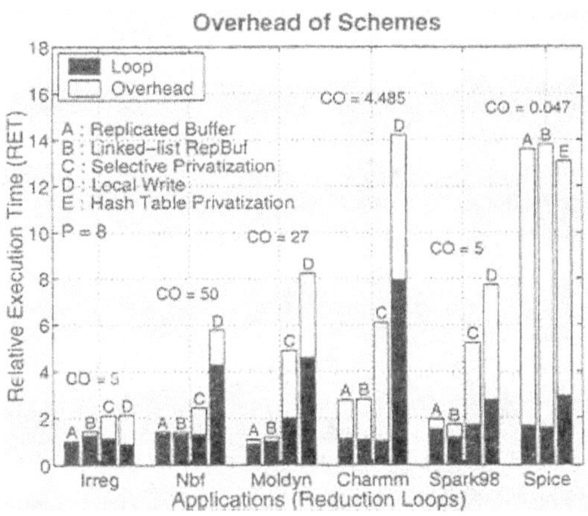

Figure 12: Overhead Comparison. The reduction loops corresponding to the applications are the same as those in figs 10–11.

Figure 12 shows the overhead associated with the various reduction parallelization methods presented previously. The graphs correspond to the reusability parameter set to zero. In order to compare the five schemes across six applications we have computed the Relative Execution Time(RET), defined as $\frac{ActualParallelExecTime \times P}{SequentialExecTime}$. In the legend, *Loop* refers to RET of parallelized reduction loop; *Overhead* refers to RET of the overheads (outside the reduction loop) related to reduction parallelization such as: reduction collection, replicated buffer initialization, Local Write inspector, etc. There are also some reduction parallelization overheads 'hidden' in the *Loop* part such as hash table access for the Hash Table Privatization scheme, work duplication for the Local Write method, etc. In Figure 12, Selective Privatization and Hash Table Privatization have a relative large overhead due to privatized storage reconstruction; Local Write has large overhead due to a time consuming inspector loop and work duplication. For SPICE, overheads for Replicated Buffer and Linked_list Replicated Buffer also are large due to the expensive privatized storage traversal.

6. CONCLUSION AND FUTURE WORK

In this paper we have presented several new techniques for efficiently parallelizing irregular and/or sparse reductions. We have also presented a method for the characterization of irregular access patterns. While it is an empirical method it has served our purposes well - the model extracted from them has allowed us to choose the best scheme from all those available to us. With the information presented here we hope that reductions, a very important activity in scientific codes, will be better optimized in the future. More work needs to be done: We need to fit better the thresholds used in our decision tree and evaluate the model on more programs. Statistical processing of the experimental data may also be helpful.

Another important aspect that needs to be developed more is the adaptation of the schemes to minor changes in the access pattern (R smaller than 1). Some reduction schemes lend themselves better than other ones to be modified on-the-fly and this issue needs to be included in the choice of the best algorithm.

However, we believe that the real importance of this work is to show that we can model program behavior even when it is irregular and customize solutions every time we need to. We have shown this through the example of reduction speedups, but we hope that other optimizations for irregular codes can be done in a similar, run-time adaptive manner.

7. REFERENCES

[1] Charmm: A program for macromolecular energy, minimization, and dynamics calculations. *Journal of Computational Chemistry*, 4(6), 1983.

[2] W. Blume, R. Doallo, R. Eigenmann, J. Grout, J. Hoeflinger, T. Lawrence, J. Lee, D. Padua, Y. Paek, B. Pottenger, L. Rauchwerger, and P. Tu. Advanced Program Restructuring for High-Performance Computers with Polaris. *IEEE Computer*, 29(12):78–82, December 1996.

[3] R. Eigenmann, J. Hoeflinger, Z. Li, and D. Padua. Experience in the Automatic Parallelization of Four Perfect-Benchmark Programs. *Lecture Notes in Computer Science 589. Proceedings of the Fourth Workshop on Languages and Compilers for Parallel Computing, Santa Clara, CA*, pages 65–83, August 1991.

[4] H. Han and C.-W. Tseng. Improving compiler and run-time support for adaptive irregular codes. In *International Conference on Parallel Architectures and Compilation Techniques (PACT'98)*, October 1998.

[5] C. Kruskal. Efficient parallel algorithms for graph problems. In *Proceedings of the 1986 International Conference on Parallel Processing*, pages 869–876, August 1986.

[6] F. Thomson Leighton. *Introduction to Parallel Algorithms and Architectures: Arrays, Trees, Hypercubes*. Morgan Kaufmann, 1992.

[7] M. J. Frisch, et. al. *Gaussian 94, Revision B.1*. Gaussian, Inc., Pittsburgh PA, 1995.

[8] Laurence Nagel. *SPICE2: A Computer Program to Simulate Semiconductor Circuits*. PhD thesis, University of California, May 1975.

[9] D. Patel and L. Rauchwerger. Principles of speculative run-time parallelization. In *Proceedings 11th Annual Workshop on Programming Languages and Compilers for Parallel Computing*. Springer-Verlag, 1998.

[10] Lawrence Rauchwerger and David A. Padua. The LRPD Test: Speculative Run-Time Parallelization of Loops with Privatization and Reduction Parallelization. *IEEE Transactions on Parallel and Distributed Systems*, 10(2), 1999.

[11] A.I. Cox S. Dwardakas, P. Keleher and W. Zwaenopoel. An integrated compile-time/run-time software distributed shared memory system. In *Proceedings of the Eighth International Conference on Architectural Support for Programming Languages and Operating Systems*, 1996.

[12] Robert G. Whirley and Bruce Engelmann. *DYNA3D: A Nonlinear, Explicit, Three-Dimensional Finite Element Code For Solid and Structural Mechanics*. Lawrence Livermore National Laboratory, November, 1993.

[13] J. Wu, J. Saltz, S. Hiranandani, and H. Berryman. Runtime compilation methods for multicomputers. In Dr. H.D. Schwetman, editor, *Proceedings of the 1991 International Conference on Parallel Processing*, pages 26–30. CRC Press, Inc., 1991. Vol. II - Software.

[14] Hao Yu and L. Rauchwerger. Run-time parallelization overhead reduction techniques. In *Proc. of the 9th International Conference on Compiler Construction (CC2000), Berlin, Germany*. Lecture Notes in Computer Science, Springer-Verlag, 2000.

[15] H. Zima. *Supercompilers for Parallel and Vector Computers*. ACM Press, New York, New York, 1991.

[16] William M. Pottenger. Theory, Techniques, and Experiments in Solving Recurrences in Computer Programs. *PhD thesis, Univ. of Illinois at Urbana-Champaign, Center for Supercomputing Res. & Dev.*, May 1997.

[17] Yuan Lin and David A. Padua. On the Automatic Parallelization of Sparse and Irregular Fortran Programs. In *Proc. of 4th Workshop on Languages, Compilers, and Run-time Systems for Scalable Computers (LCR98)*, Pittsburgh, PA, 1998

Analytical Cache Models with Applications to Cache Partitioning

G. Edward Suh, Srinivas Devadas, and Larry Rudolph
Laboratory for Computer Science
Massachusetts Institute of Technology
Cambridge, MA 02139
{suh,devadas,rudolph}@mit.edu

ABSTRACT

An accurate, tractable, analytic cache model for time-shared systems is presented, which estimates the overall cache miss-rate of a multiprocessing system with any cache size and time quanta. The input to the model consists of the isolated miss-rate curves for each process, the time quanta for each of the executing processes, and the total cache size. The output is the overall miss-rate. Trace-driven simulations demonstrate that the estimated miss-rate is very accurate. Since the model provides a fast and accurate way to estimate the effect of context switching, it is useful for both understanding the effect of context switching on caches and optimizing cache performance for time-shared systems. A cache partitioning mechanism is also presented and is shown to improve the cache miss-rate up to 25% over the normal LRU replacement policy.

1. INTRODUCTION

This paper presents an analytical model for the behavior of a cache in a multiprocessing system that can accurately estimate overall miss-rate for any cache size and any time quantum. An evaluation method for miss-rate is essential to optimize cache performance. Traditional cache performance evaluation is done by simulations [25, 16, 12], which provide accurate results, but simulation time is often long. Hardware monitoring can dramatically speed up the process [26], however, it is limited to the particular cache configuration. As a result, both simulations and hardware monitoring can only be used to evaluate the effect of context switches [14, 10]. Moreover, simulations and monitoring rarely provide intuitive understanding making it difficult to improve cache performance. To provide both performance prediction and insight into improving performance, analytical cache models are required.

We use our model to determine the best cache partitioning so as to improve performance. Partitioning is needed to mitigate the effects of conflicts among concurrently executing processes, especially for large caches. In the past, caches were small and it was best to let each process consume the entire cache space, since process footprints were much larger than the cache. In modern microprocessors, caches are much larger; some Level 1 (L1) caches range up to one MB [5], and L2 caches are up to several MB [2, 13]. Large caches allow potential performance improvement by partitioning. Since each process may not need the entire cache space, the effect of context switches can be mitigated by keeping useful data in the cache over context switches. It is crucial for modern microprocessors to minimize inter-process conflicts by proper cache partitioning [21, 9] or scheduling [17, 23].

Our model requires information that is relatively easy to acquire. The characteristics for each process are given by the miss-rate as a function of cache size when the process is isolated, which can be easily obtained either on-line or off-line. The time quantum for each process and cache size are also given as inputs to the model. With this information, the model estimates the overall miss-rate for a given cache size when an arbitrary combination of processes is run. The model provides good estimates for any cache size and any time quantum, and is easily applied to real problems since the input miss-rate curves are both intuitive and easy to obtain in practice. Therefore, we believe that the model is useful for any study related to the effect of context switches on cache memory.

After describing related research in Section 2, Section 3 derives an analytical cache model for time-shared systems. Section 4 discusses cache partitioning based on the model and evaluates the model-based partitioning method by simulations. Finally, Section 5 concludes the paper.

2. RELATED WORK

Several early investigations of the effects of context switches use analytical models. Thiébaut and Stone [20] modeled the amount of additional misses caused by context switches for set-associative caches. Agarwal, Horowitz and Hennessy [1] also included the effect of conflicts between processes in their analytical cache model and showed that inter-process conflicts are noticeable for a mid-range of cache sizes that are large enough to have a considerable number of conflicts but not large enough to hold all the working sets. However, these models work only for long enough time quanta, and require information that is hard to collect on-line.

ICS '01 Sorrento, Italy

Mogul and Borg [14] studied the effect of context switches through trace-driven simulations. Using a timesharing system simulator, their research shows that system calls, page faults, and a scheduler are the main sources of context switches. They also evaluated the effect of context switches on cycles per instruction (CPI) as well as the cache miss-rate. Depending on cache parameters, the cost of a context switch appears to be in the thousands of cycles, or tens to hundreds of microseconds in their simulations.

Stone, Turek and Wolf [18] investigated the optimal allocation of cache memory between two competing processes that minimizes the overall miss-rate of a cache. Their study focuses on the partitioning of instruction and data streams, which can be thought of as multitasking with a very short time quantum. Their model for this case shows that the optimal allocation occurs at a point where the miss-rate derivatives of the competing processes are equal. The LRU replacement policy appears to produce cache allocations very close to optimal for their examples. They also describe a new replacement policy for longer time quanta that only increases cache allocation based on time remaining in the current time quantum and the marginal reduction in miss-rate due to an increase in cache allocation. However, their policy simply assumes the probability for a evicted block to be accessed in the next time quantum as a constant, which is neither validated nor is it described how this probability is obtained.

Thiébaut, Stone and Wolf applied their partitioning work [18] to improve disk cache hit-ratios [21]. The model for tightly interleaved streams is extended to be applicable for more than two processes. They also describe the problems in applying the model in practice, such as approximating the miss-rate derivative, non-monotonic miss-rate derivatives, and updating the partition. Trace-driven simulations for 32-MB disk caches show that the partitioning improves the relative hit-ratios in the range of 1% to 2% over the LRU policy.

Our analytical model and partitioning differ from previous efforts that tend to focus on some specific cases of context switches. Our model works for any specific time quanta, whereas the previous models focus only on long time quanta. Also, our partitioning works for any time quanta, whereas Thiébaut's algorithms only works for very short time quanta. Moreover, the inputs of our model (miss-rates) are much easier to obtain compared to footprints or the number of unique cache blocks that previous models require.

3. ANALYTICAL CACHE MODEL

The analytical cache model estimates the overall cache miss-rate for a multi-processing system. The cache size and the time quantum length for each job is known. The cache size is given by the number of cache blocks, and the time quantum is given by the number of memory references. Both are assumed to be constants (See Figure 1 (a)). In addition, associated with each job is its miss-rate curve, i.e., the number of cache misses as a function of the cache size.

This section explains the development of the model in several steps. Heavy use is made of the individual, isolated miss-rate curve (iimr). This curve is the miss-rate for a process as a function of cache size assuming no other processes are running. There is much information that can be gleaned from this equation. For example, we can compute the miss rate of a process as a function of time (Section 3.2.1) from the miss-rate of a process as a function of space.

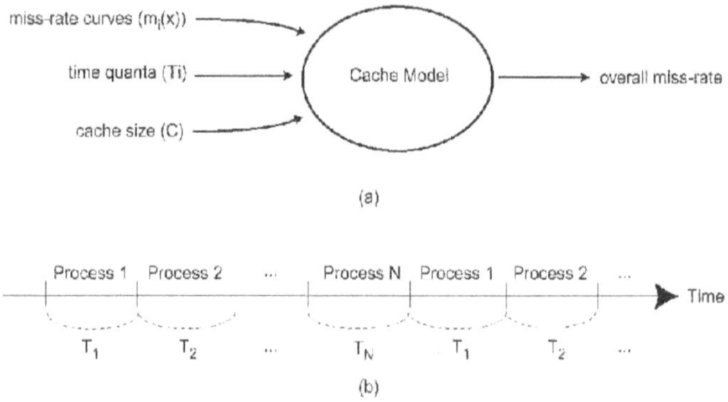

Figure 1: (a) The overview of an analytical cache model. (b) Round-robin schedule.

Observe that as a process executes, it either references an item in the cache, in which case its footprint size remains the same, or it gets a cache miss thereby increasing its footprint size. In other words, we know how much cache is allocated to a process as a function of time: from the iimr curve, we compute the independent, isolated footprint as a function of time (iifp) (Section 3.2.2).

If one knows how much cache is allocated to a process when it begins executing its time quantum and how much more cache it will need during the execution of that time quantum, we can compute how much cache will be left for the next process that is about to begin its time quantum execution. In other words, from the iifp curves of all the concurrent processes, we compute the individual, dependent footprint (dfp) as a function of time (Section 3.2.3).

At each time step, we know how much cache is allocated to the running process (from dfp(t)) and we know the miss rate for that size (from iimr(S)) for the executing process and so we can get the dependent miss rate as a function of time (dmr(t)) (Section 3.2.1).

Finally, integrating or summing the dmr(t) over time, gives the overall average miss rate for a given cache size, given time quantum sizes, and a given set of concurrent processes (Section 3.2.4).

The following subsection gives an overview of our assumptions. The development of the cache model is then presented, following the outline given above. Finally, this section ends with experimental verification of the model.

3.1 Assumptions

The memory reference pattern of each process is assumed to be represented by a miss-rate curve that is a function of the cache size. Moreover, this miss-rate curve is assumed not to change over time. Although real applications do have

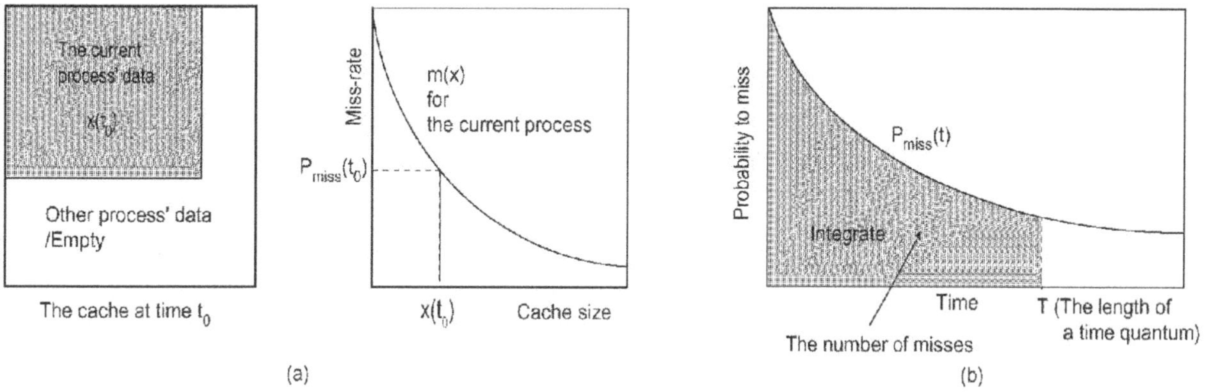

Figure 2: (a) The probability of a miss at time t_0. (b) The number of misses from $P_{miss}(t)$ curve.

dynamically changing memory reference patterns, our results show that, in practice, an average miss-rate function works very well. For abrupt changes in the reference pattern, multiple miss-rate curves can be used to estimate an overall miss-rate.

There is no shared address space among processes. This assumption is true for common cases where each process has its own virtual address space and the shared memory space is negligible compared to the entire memory space that is used by a process.

Finally, a round-robin scheduling policy with a fixed time quantum for each process is assumed (see Figure 1 (b)), an LRU replacement policy is used, and the cache is fully associative. Although most real caches are set-associative, a model for fully-associative caches is very useful for understanding the effect of context switches because the model is simple. Moreover, cache partitioning experiments demonstrate that the fully-associative model can also be applied to set-associative caches in practice (Section 4). Elsewhere, we have extended the model to handle set-associative caches [19]. A model assuming many other scheduling methods and replacement policies can be similarly derived.

We make use of the following notations:

t the number of memory references from the beginning of a time quantum.

$x(t)$ the number of cache blocks that belong to a process after t memory references.

$m(x)$ the steady-state miss-rate for a process with cache size x.

T the number of memory references in a time quantum.

3.2 Cache Model

The goal is to predict the average miss-rate for a multiprocess machine with a given cache size and set of processes.

3.2.1 *Miss rate as function of time*

Given the independent, isolated miss-rate of a process as a function of cache size, we compute its miss-rate as a function of time. Let time t start at the beginning of a time quantum, not at the beginning of execution. Since all time quanta for a process are identical by our assumptions, we consider only one time quantum for each process.

Although the cache size is C, at certain times, it is possible that only part of the cache is filled with the current process' data (Figure 2 (a) shows a snapshot of a cache at time t_0). Therefore, the effective cache size at time t_0 can be thought of as the amount of the current process' data $x(t_0)$ in the cache at that time. The probability of a cache miss in the next memory reference is given by

$$P_{miss}(t_0) = m(x(t_0)). \tag{1}$$

Once we have $P_{miss}(t_0)$, it is easy to estimate the miss-rate over time during that time quantum. The number of misses for the process over a time quantum can be expressed as a simple integral, Figure 2 (b), where the miss-rate is expressed as the number of misses divided by the number of memory references.

$$\text{miss-rate} = \frac{1}{T}\int_0^T P_{miss}(t)dt = \frac{1}{T}\int_0^T m(x(t))dt \tag{2}$$

3.2.2 *Footprint as a function of time*

We now estimate $x(t)$, the amount of a process' data, i.e. its footprint, in a cache as a function of time. Let us begin with the assumption that a process starts executing during a time quantum with an empty cache in order to estimate cache performance for cases when a cache gets flushed for every context switch. Virtual address caches without process ID are good examples of such a case. We show later how to estimate $x(t)$ when the cache is not empty at the start of a time quantum.

Consider $x^\infty(t)$ as the amount of the current process' data at time t for an infinite size cache. We assume that the process starts with an empty cache at time 0. There are two possibilities for $x^\infty(t)$ at time $t+1$. If the $(t+1)^{th}$ memory reference results in a cache miss, a new cache block is brought into the cache. As a result, the amount of the process's cache data increases by one block. Otherwise, the amount of data remains the same. Therefore, the amount of the process' data in the cache at time $t+1$ is given by

$$x^{\infty}(t+1) = \begin{cases} x^{\infty}(t)+1 & (t+1)^{th} \text{ reference misses} \\ x^{\infty}(t) & \text{otherwise.} \end{cases} \quad (3)$$

Since the probability for the $(t+1)^{th}$ memory reference to miss is $m(x^{\infty}(t))$ from Equation 1, the expected value of $x(t+1)$ can be written by

$$\begin{aligned} E[x^{\infty}(t+1)] &= E[x^{\infty}(t)\cdot(1-m(x^{\infty}(t))) \\ &\quad + (x^{\infty}(t)+1)\cdot m(x^{\infty}(t))] \\ &= E[x^{\infty}(t)+1\cdot m(x^{\infty}(t))] \\ &= E[x^{\infty}(t)] + E[m(x^{\infty}(t))]. \end{aligned} \quad (4)$$

Assuming that $m(x)$ is convex[1], we can use Jensen's inequality [3] and rewrite the equation as a function of $E[x^{\infty}(t)]$.

$$E[x^{\infty}(t+1)] \geq E[x^{\infty}(t)] + m(E[x^{\infty}(t)]). \quad (5)$$

Usually, a miss-rate changes slowly. As a result, for a short interval such as from x to $x+1$, $m(x)$ can be approximated as a straight line. Since the equality in Jensen's inequality holds if the function is a straight line, we can approximate the amount of data at time $t+1$ as

$$E[x^{\infty}(t+1)] \simeq E[x^{\infty}(t)] + m(E[x^{\infty}(t)]). \quad (6)$$

We can calculate the expectation of $x^{\infty}(t)$ more accurately by calculating the probability for every possible value at time t [19]. However, calculating a set of probabilities is computationally expensive. Also, our experiments show that the above approximation closely matches simulation results.

If we further approximate the amount of data $x^{\infty}(t)$ to be the expected value $E[x^{\infty}(t)]$, $x^{\infty}(t)$ can be expressed with a differential equation:

$$x^{\infty}(t+1) - x^{\infty}(t) = m(x^{\infty}(t)), \quad (7)$$

which can be easily calculated in a recursive manner.

To obtain a closed form solution, we can rewrite the discrete form of the differential equation 7 to a continuous form:

$$\frac{dx^{\infty}}{dt} = m(x^{\infty}). \quad (8)$$

Solving the differential equation by separating variables, the differential equation becomes

$$t = \int_{x^{\infty}(0)}^{x^{\infty}(t)} \frac{1}{m(x')} dx'. \quad (9)$$

We define a function $M(x)$ as an integral of $1/m(x)$, which means that $dM(x)/dx = 1/m(x)$, and then $x^{\infty}(t)$ can be written as a function of t:

$$x^{\infty}(t) = M^{-1}(t + M(x^{\infty}(0))) \quad (10)$$

where $M^{-1}(x)$ represents the inverse function of $M(x)$.

Finally, for a finite size cache, the amount of data in the cache is limited by the size of the cache C. Therefore, $x^{\phi}(t)$, the amount of a process' data starting from an empty cache, is written by

$$x^{\phi}(t) = MIN[x^{\infty}(t), C] = MIN[M^{-1}(t+M(0)), C]. \quad (11)$$

[1] If a replacement policy is smart enough, the marginal gain of having one more cache block monotonically decreases as we increase the cache size.

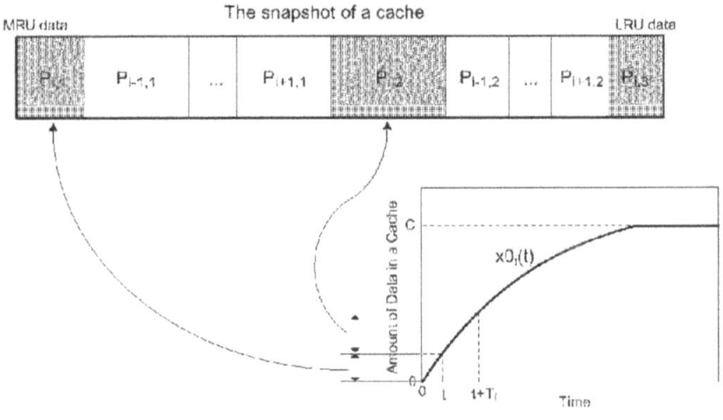

Figure 3: The snapshot of a cache after running Process i for time t.

3.2.3 *Individual, Dependent Footprint as a function of time*

We now compute the amount of a process' data at time t when the cache is not flushed at a context switch, i.e., the dependent case. To distinguish between the processes, a subscript i is used to represent Process i. For example, $x_i(t)$ represents the amount of Process i's data at time t.

The estimation of $x_i(t)$ is based on round-robin scheduling (See Figure 1 (b)) and the LRU replacement policy. Process i runs for a fixed length time quantum T_i. For simplicity, processes are assumed to be of infinite length so that there is no change in the scheduling. Also, the initial startup transient from an empty cache is ignored since it is negligible compared to the steady state.

To estimate the amount of a process' data at a given time, imagine the snapshot of a cache after executing Process i for time t as shown in Figure 3. Note that time is 0 at the beginning of the process' time quantum. In the figure, the blocks on the left side show recently used data, and blocks on the right side show old data. $P_{j,k}$ represents the data of Process j, and subscript k specifies the most recent time quantum when the data are referenced. From the figure, we can obtain $x_i(t)$ once we know the size of all $P_{j,k}$ blocks.

The size of each block can be estimated using the $x_i^{\phi}(t)$ curve from Equation 11, which is the amount of Process i's data when the process starts with an empty cache. Since $x_i^{\phi}(t)$ can also be thought of as the amount of data that are referenced from time 0 to time t, $x_i^{\phi}(T_i)$ is the amount of data that are referenced over one time quantum. Similarly, we can estimate the amount of data that are referenced over k recent time quanta to be $x_i^{\phi}(k\cdot T_i)$. As a result, the size

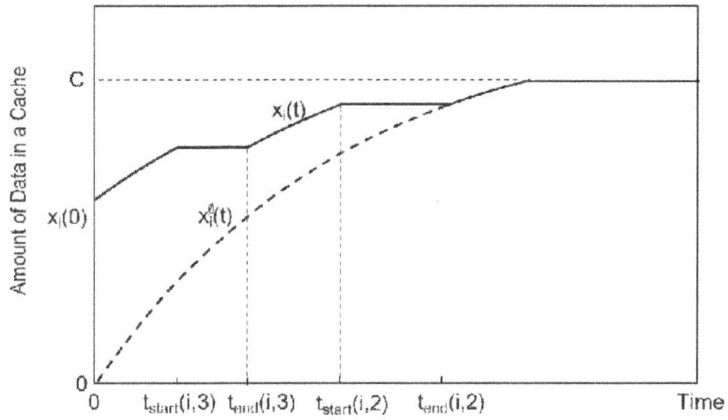

Figure 4: The relation between $x_i^\phi(t)$ and $x_i(t)$. $x_i(0)$ is the amount of Process i's data in the cache when a time quantum starts.

of Block $P_{j,k}$ can be written as

$$P_{j,k} = \begin{cases} x_j^\phi(t+(k-1)\cdot T_j) - x_j^\phi(t+(k-2)\cdot T_j) & \text{if } j \text{ is executing} \\ x_j^\phi(k\cdot T_j) - x_j^\phi((k-1)\cdot T_j) & \text{otherwise} \end{cases} \quad (12)$$

where we assume that $x_j^\phi(t) = 0$ if $t < 0$.

$x_i(t)$ is the sum of $P_{i,k}$ blocks that are inside the cache of size C in Figure 3. If we define $l_i(t)$ as the maximum integer value that satisfies the following inequality, then $l_i(t)+1$ represents how many $P_{i,k}$ blocks are in the cache.

$$\sum_{k=1}^{l_i(t)}\sum_{j=1}^{N} P_{j,k} = x_i^\phi(t+(l_i(t)-1)\cdot T_i) + \sum_{j=1,j\neq i}^{N} x_j^\phi(l_i(t)\cdot T_j) \leq C \quad (13)$$

where N is the number of processes. From $l_i(t)$ and Figure 3, the estimated value of $x_i(t)$ is

$$x_i(t) = \begin{cases} x_i^\phi(t+l_i(t)\cdot T_i) & \text{if } x_i^\phi(t+l_i(t)\cdot T_i) + \sum_{j=1,j\neq i}^{N} x_j^\phi(l_i(t)\cdot T_j) \leq C \\ C - \sum_{j=1,j\neq i}^{N} x_j^\phi(l_i(t)\cdot T_j) & \text{otherwise} \end{cases} \quad (14)$$

Figure 4 illustrates the relation between $x_i^\phi(t)$ and $x_i(t)$. In the figure $l_i(t)$ is assumed to be 2. Unlike the cache flushing case, a process can start with some of its data left in the cache. The amount of initial data $x_i(0)$ is given by Equation 14. If the least recently used (LRU) data in a cache does not belong to Process i, $x_i(t)$ increases the same as $x_i^\phi(t)$. However, if the LRU data belongs to Process i, $x_i(t)$ does not increase on a cache miss since Process i's block gets replaced.

Define $t_{start}(j,k)$ as the time when the kth MRU block of Process j ($P_{j,k}$) becomes the LRU part of a cache, and $t_{end}(j,k)$ as the time when $P_{j,k}$ gets completely replaced from the cache (See Figure 3). $t_{start}(j,k)$ and $t_{end}(j,k)$ specify the flat segments in Figure 4 and can be estimated from the following equations that are based on Equation 12.

$$x_j^\phi(t_{start}(j,k)+(k-1)\cdot T_j) + \sum_{p=1,p\neq j}^{N} x_p^\phi((k-1)\cdot T_p) = C. \quad (15)$$

$$x_j^\phi(t_{end}(j,k)+(k-2)\cdot T_j) + \sum_{p=1,p\neq j}^{N} x_p^\phi((k-1)\cdot T_p) = C. \quad (16)$$

$t_{start}(j,l_j(t)+1)$ would be zero if Equation 15 is satisfied when $t_{start}(j,l_j(t)+1)$ is negative, which means that the $P(j,l_j(t)+1)$ block is already the LRU part of the cache at the beginning of a time quantum.

3.2.4 Overall Miss-rate

This section presents the overall miss-rate calculation. When a cache uses virtual address tags and gets flushed for every context switch, each process starts a time quantum with an empty cache. In this case, the miss-rate of a process can be estimated from the results of Section 3.2.1 and 3.2.2. From Equation 2 and 11, the miss-rate for Process i can be written by

$$\text{miss-rate}_i^\phi = \frac{1}{T_i}\int_0^{T_i} m_i(MIN[M_i^{-1}(t+M_i(0)), C])dt. \quad (17)$$

If a cache uses physical address tags or has a process' ID with virtual address tags, it does not have to be flushed at a context switch. In this case, the amount of data $x_i(t)$ is estimated in Section 3.2.3. The miss-rate for Process i can be written by

$$\text{miss-rate}_i = \frac{1}{T_i}\int_0^{T_i} m_i(x_i(t))dt \quad (18)$$

where $x_i(t)$ is given by Equation 14.

For actual calculation of the miss-rate, $t_{start}(j,k)$ and $t_{end}(j,k)$ from Equation 15 and 16 can be used. Since $t_{start}(j,k)$ and $t_{end}(j,k)$ specify the flat segments in Figure 4, the miss-rate of Process i can be rewritten by

$$\begin{aligned} \text{miss-rate}_i = \frac{1}{T_i}\{ & \int_0^{T_i'} m_i(MIN[M_i^{-1}(t+M_i(x_i(0))), C])dt \\ & + \sum_{k=d_i}^{l_i(t)+1} m_i(x_i^\phi(t_{start}(i,k)+(k-1)\cdot T_i)) \\ & \cdot (MIN[t_{end}(i,k), T_i] - t_{start}(i,k))\} \end{aligned} \quad (19)$$

where d_i is the minimum integer value that satisfies $t_{start}(i,d_i) < T_i$. T_i' is the time that Process i actually grows.

$$T_i' = T_i - \sum_{k=d_i}^{l_i(t)+1} (MIN[t_{end}(i,k), T_i] - t_{start}(i,k)). \quad (20)$$

As shown above, calculating a miss-rate could be complicated if we do not flush a cache at a context switch. If we assume that the executing process' data left in a cache is all in the most recently used part of the cache, we can use the

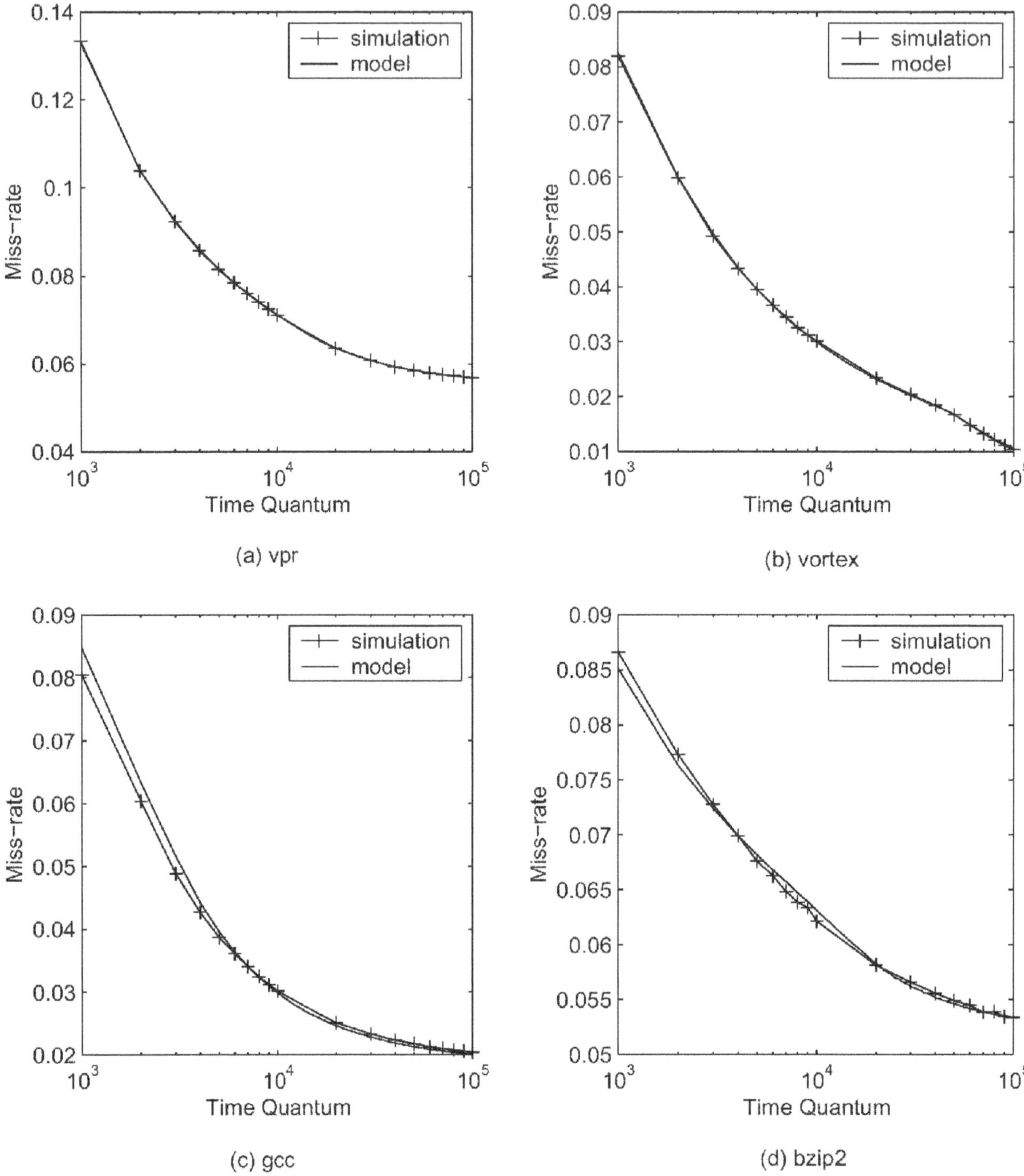

Figure 5: The result of the cache model for cache flushing cases. (a) `vpr`. (b) `vortex`. (c) `gcc`. (d) `bzip2`.

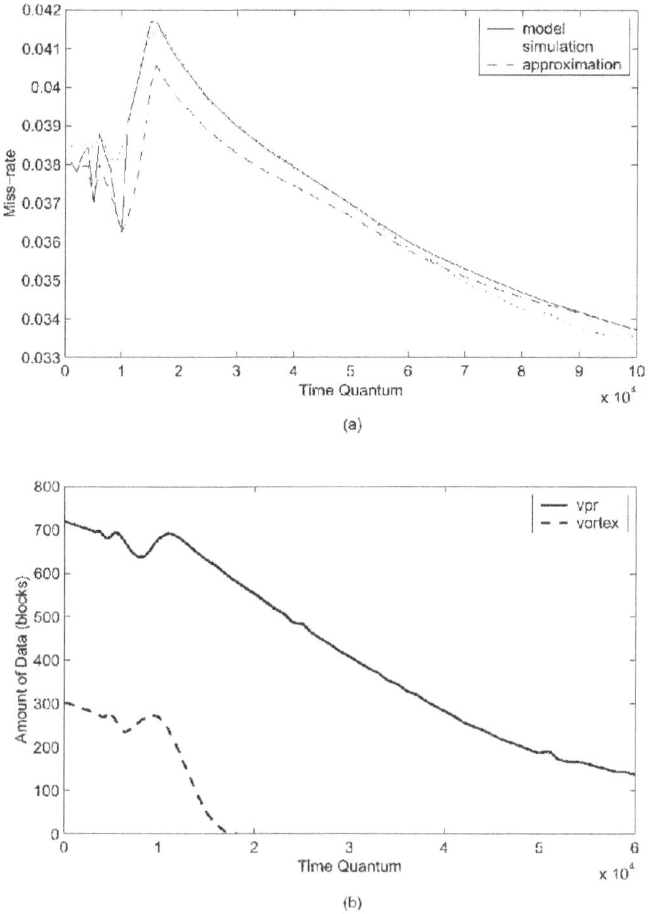

Figure 6: The result of the cache model when two processes (vpr, vortex) are sharing a cache (32 KB fully-associative). (a) the overall miss-rate. (b) the initial amount of data $x_i(0)$.

equation for estimating the amount of data starting with an empty cache. Therefore, the calculation can be much simplified as follows,

$$\overline{\text{miss-rate}_i} = \frac{1}{T_i}\int_0^{T_i} m_i(MIN[M_i^{-1}(t + M_i(x_i(0))), C])dt \qquad (21)$$

where $x_i(0)$ is estimated from Equation 14. The effect of this approximation is evaluated in the experiment section (cf. Section 3.3).

Once we calculate the miss-rate of each process, the overall miss-rate is straightforwardly calculated from those miss-rates.

$$\text{Overall miss-rate} = \frac{\sum_{i=1}^{N} \text{miss-rate}_i \cdot T_i}{\sum_{i=1}^{N} T_i} \qquad (22)$$

3.3 Experimental Verification

Our cache model can be validated by comparing estimated miss-rate predictions with simulation results. Several combinations of benchmarks are modeled and simulated for various time quanta. First, we simulate cases when a cache gets flushed at every context switch, and compare the results with the model's estimation. Cases without cache flushing are also tested. For the cases without cache flushing, both the complete model (Equation 19) and the approximation (Equation 21) are used to estimate the overall miss-rate. Based on the simulation results, the error caused by the approximation is discussed.

3.3.1 Cache Flushing Case

The results of the cache model and simulations are shown in Figure 5 in cases when a process starts its time quantum with an empty cache. Four benchmarks from SPEC CPU2000 [7], which are **vpr**, **vortex**, **gcc** and **bzip2**, are tested. The cache is a 32-KB fully-associative cache with 32-Byte blocks. The miss-rate of a process is plotted as a function of the length of a time quantum, and shows a good agreement between the model's estimation and the simulation result.

As inputs to the cache model, the average miss-rate of each process has been obtained from simulations. Each process has been simulated for 25 million memory references, and the miss-rates of the process for various cache size have been recorded. The simulation results were also obtained by simulating benchmarks for 25 million memory references with flushing a cache every T memory references. As the result shows, the average miss-rate works very well.

3.3.2 General Case

Figure 6 shows the result of the cache model when two processes are sharing a cache. The two benchmarks are **vpr** and **vortex** from SPEC CPU2000, and the cache is a 32-KB fully-associative cache with 32-Byte blocks. The overall miss-rates are shown in Figure 6 (a). As shown in the figure, the miss-rate estimated by the model shows a good agreement with the results of the simulations.

The figure also shows an interesting fact that a certain range of time quanta could be very problematic for cache performance. For short time quanta, the overall miss-rate is relatively small. For very long time quanta, context switches do not matter since a process spends most of its time in the steady state. However, medium time quanta could severely degrade cache miss-rates as shown in the figure. This problem occurs when a time quantum is long enough to pollute the cache but not long enough to compensate for the misses caused by context switches. The problem becomes clear in Figure 6 (b). The figure shows the amount of data left in the cache at the beginning of a time quantum. Comparing Figure 6 (a) and (b), we can see that the problem occurs when the initial amount of data rapidly decreases.

The error caused by our approximation (Equation 21) method can be seen in Figure 6. In the approximation, we assume that the data left in the cache at the beginning of a time quantum are all in the MRU region of the cache. In reality, however, the data left in the cache could be the LRU cache blocks and get replaced before other process' blocks in the cache, although the current process's data are likely to be accessed in the time quantum. As a result, the approximated miss-rate is lower than the simulation result when the initial amount of data is not zero.

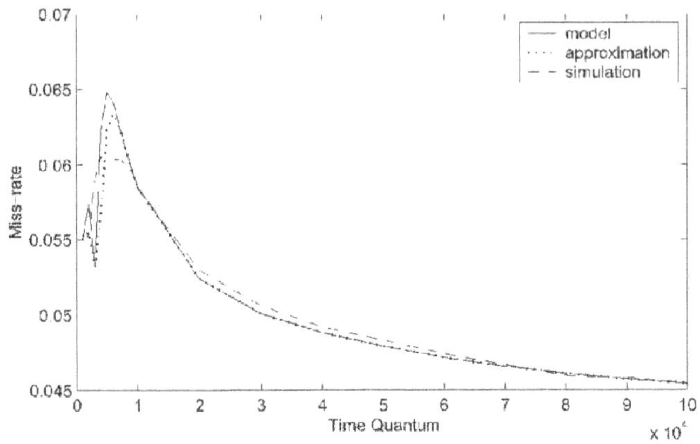

Figure 7: The overall miss-rate when four processes (vpr, vortex, gcc, bzip2) are sharing a cache (32 KB, fully-associative).

A four-process case is also tested in Figure 7. Two more benchmarks, gcc and bzip2, from SPEC CPU2000 [7] are added to vpr and vortex, and the same cache configuration is used as the two process case. The figure also shows a very close agreement between the miss-rate estimated by the cache model and the miss-rate from simulations. The problematic time quanta and the effect of the approximation have changed. Since there are more processes polluting the cache as compared to the two process case, a process experiences an empty cache in shorter time quanta. As a result, the problematic time quanta become shorter. On the other hand, the effect of the approximation is less harmful in this case. This is because the error in one process' miss-rate becomes less important as we have more processes.

4. CACHE PARTITIONING

This section shows how the analytical cache model can be used to dynamically partition the cache. A partitioned cache allocates cache space to particular processes. This space is dedicated to the process and cannot be used to satisfy cache misses by other processes. Using trace-driven simulations, we compare partitioning with the normal LRU. The partitioning is based on the fully-associative cache model. However, simulation results demonstrate that this implementation works for both fully-associative caches and set-associative caches.

4.1 Recording Memory Reference Patterns

The miss-rate curves for each process are generated off-line. We record the miss-rate curve for each process to represent its memory reference pattern. For various cache sizes, a single process cache simulator is applied to each process. This information can be reused for any combination of processes as long as the cache configuration is the same[2].

To incorporate the dynamically changing behavior of a process, a set of miss-rate curves, one for each time period, are produced. At run-time, the miss-rate curve is mapped to the appropriate time quantum.

[2]Note that for our fully-associative model, only the cache block size matters

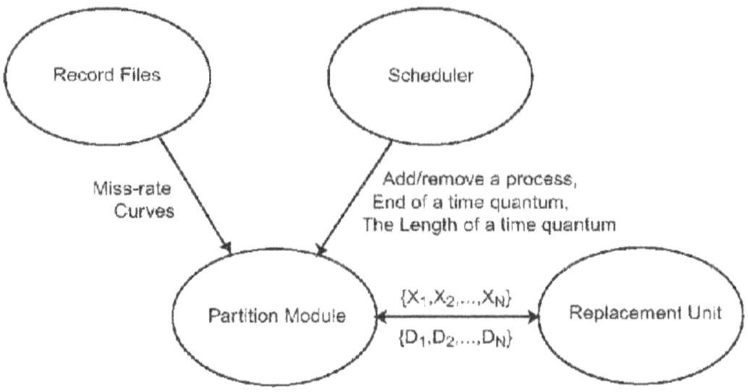

Figure 8: The implementation of on-line cache partitioning.

4.2 The Partitioning Scheme

The overall flow of the partitioning scheme can be viewed as a set of four modules: off-line recording, scheduler information, allocation, and replacement (Figure 8). The scheduler provides the partition module with the set of executing processes and their start/end times. The partition module uses the miss-rate information for the processes to calculate cache partitions at the end of each time quantum. Finally, the replacement unit maps these partitions to the appropriate parts of the cache.

The partition module decides the number of cache blocks that should be dedicated to a process (D_i). The D_i most recently used cache blocks of Process i are kept in the cache over other process' time quanta, and Process i starts its time quantum with those cache blocks in the cache. During its own time quantum, Process i can use all cache blocks that are not reserved for other processes ($S = C - \sum_{j=1, j\neq i}^{N} D_j$).

In addition to LRU information, our replacement decision depends on the number of cache blocks that currently belong to each process (X_i), that is, the number of cache lines in the cache that currently contain memory of that process. The LRU cache block of an active process (i) is chosen if its allocation is larger than its current use ($D_i + S \geq X_i$). Otherwise, the LRU cache block of a dormant overallocated process is chosen. For set-associative caches, there may be no cache block of the desired process in the set. In this case, the LRU cache block of the set is replaced.

For set-associative caches, the fully-associative replacement policy may result in replacing recently used data to keep useless data. Imagine the case when a process starts to heavily access two or more addresses that happen to be mapped to the same set. If the process already has many cache blocks in other sets, our partitioning will allocate only a few cache blocks in the accessed set for the process, causing lots of conflict misses. To solve this problem, we can use better mapping functions [22, 6] or a victim cache [8].

When a Process i first starts, D_i is set to zero since there is no cache block that belongs to the process. At the end

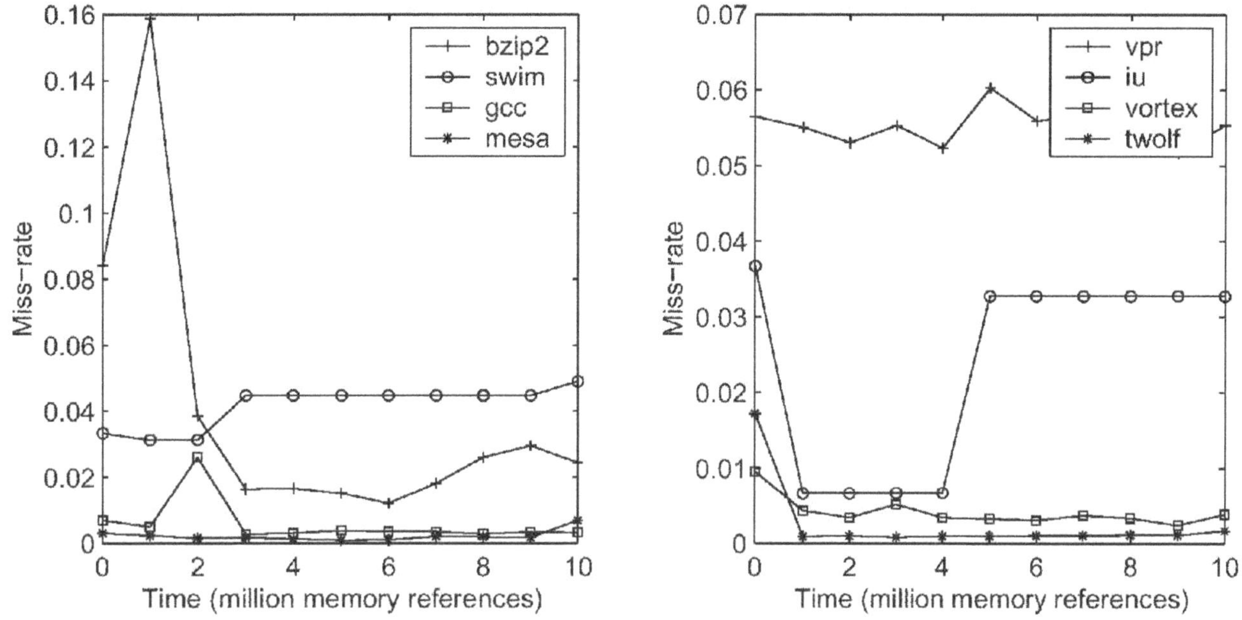

(a)

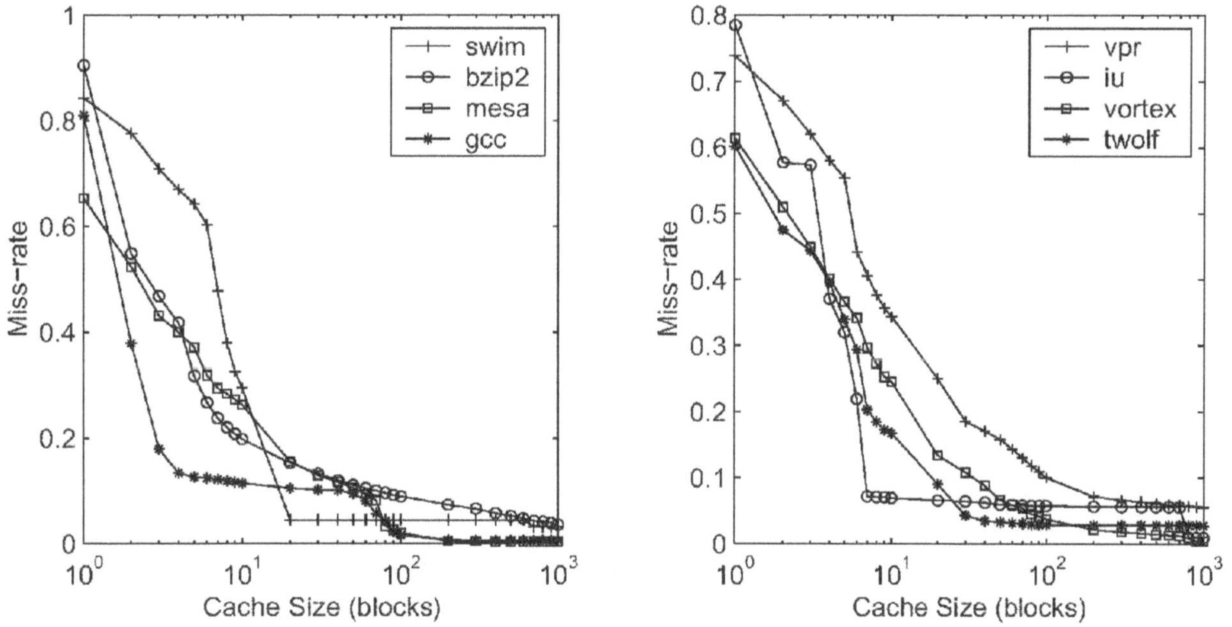

(b)

Figure 9: The characteristics of the benchmarks. (a) The change of a miss-rate over time. (b) The miss-rate as a function of the cache size.

of Process i's time quantum, the partition module updates the information such as the miss-rate curve($m_i(x)$) and the time quantum(T_i). If there is any change, D_i is also updated based on the cache model.

A cache partition specifies the amount of data in the cache at the beginning of a process' time quantum (D_i), and the maximum cache space the process can use ($C - \sum_{j=1,j\neq i}^{N} D_j$). Therefore, the number of misses for a process over one time quantum can be estimated from Equation 21:

$$miss_i = \int_0^{T_i} m_i(MIN[M_i^{-1}(t + M_i(D_i)), C - \sum_{j=1,j\neq i}^{N} D_j])dt \tag{23}$$

where C is cache size, and N is the number of processes sharing the cache.

The new value of D_i is the integer, in the range $[0, X_i]$, that minimizes the total number of misses that is given by the following quantity:

$$\sum_{p=1}^{N} \int_0^{T_p} m_p(MIN[M_p^{-1}(t + M_p(D_p)), C - \sum_{q=1,q\neq p}^{N} D_q])dt. \tag{24}$$

4.3 Experimental Verification

The case of eight processes sharing a 32-KB cache is simulated to evaluate model-based partitioning. Seven benchmarks (bzip2, gcc, swim, mesa, vortex, vpr, twolf) are from SPEC CPU2000 [7], and one (the image understanding program (iu)) is from a data intensive systems benchmark suite [15]. The overall miss-rate with partitioning is compared to the miss-rate only using the normal LRU replacement policy.

The simulations are carried out for fifty million memory references for each time quantum. Processes are scheduled in a round-robin fashion with the fixed number of memory references per time quantum. Also, the number of memory references per time quantum is assumed to be the same for the all eight processes. Finally, two record cycles (P), of ten million and one hundred thousand memory references, respectively, are used for the model-based partitioning. The record cycle represents how often the miss-rate curve is recorded for the off-line profiling. Therefore, a shorter record cycle implies more detailed information about a process' memory reference pattern.

The characteristics of the benchmarks are illustrated in Figure 9. Figure 9 (a) shows the change of a miss-rate over time. The x-axis represents simulation time. The y-axis represents the average miss-rate over one million memory references at a given time. As shown in the figure, bzip2, gcc, swim and iu show abrupt changes in their miss-rate, whereas other benchmarks have very uniform miss-rate characteristics over time. Figure 9 (b) illustrates the miss-rate as a function of the cache size. For a 32-KB fully-associative cache, benchmarks show miss-rates between 1% and 5%.

4.3.1 *Fully-Associative Result*

The results of cache partitioning for a fully-associative cache are shown in Figure 10. In Figure 10 (a), the miss-rates are averaged over 50 million memory references and shown for various time quanta. As discussed in the cache model, the normal LRU replacement policy is problematic for a certain range of time quanta. In this case, the overall miss-rate increases dramatically for time quanta between one thousand and ten thousand memory references. For this problematic region, the model-based partitioning improves the cache miss-rate by lowering it from 4.6% to 3.4%, which is about a 25% improvement. For short time quanta, the relative improvement is about 7%. For very long time quanta, the model-based partitioning shows the exact same result as the normal LRU replacement policy. In general, it is shown by the figure that the model-based partitioning always performs at least as well as or better than the normal LRU replacement policy. Also, the partitioning with a short record cycle performs better than the partitioning with a long record cycle.

In our example of a 32-KB cache with eight processes (Fig-

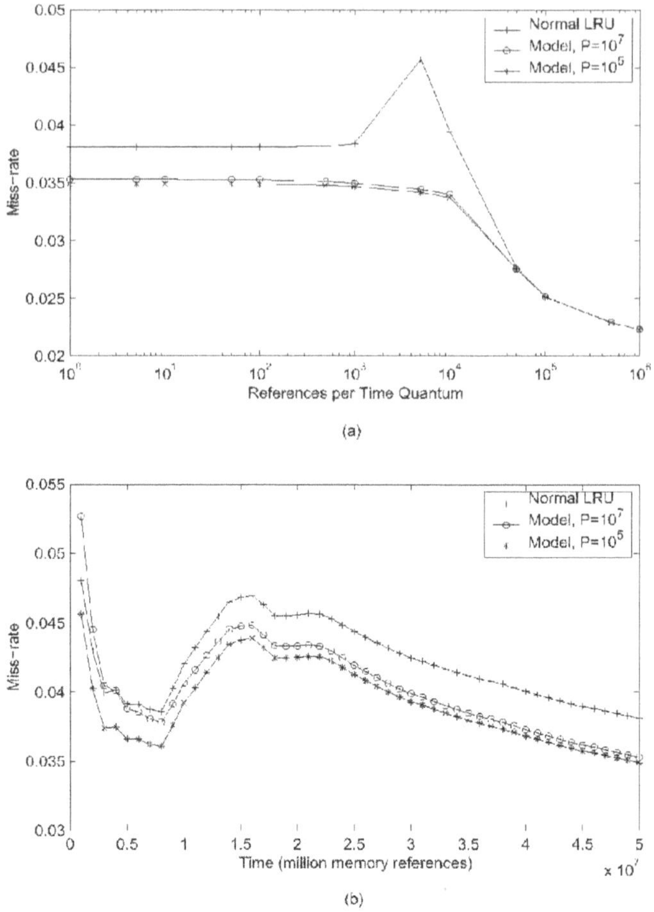

Figure 10: The results of the model-based cache partitioning for a fully-associative cache when eight processes (bzip2, gcc, swim, mesa, vortex, vpr, twolf, iu) are sharing the cache (32 KB, fully associative). (a) the average miss-rate for various time quanta. (b) the change of the miss-rate over time with ten memory references per time quantum.

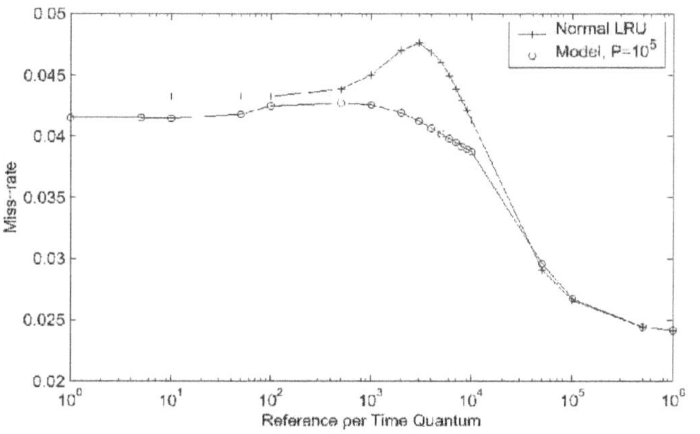

Figure 11: The results of the model-based cache partitioning for a set-associative cache when eight processes (bzip2, gcc, swim, mesa, vortex, vpr, twolf, iu) are sharing the cache (32 KB, 8-way associative).

ure 10), the problematic time quanta are in the order of a thousand memory references, which is very short for modern microprocessors. As a result, only systems with very fast context switching, such as simultaneous multi-threading machines [24, 11, 4], can be improved for this cache size and workload. However, longer time quanta become problematic if a cache is larger. Therefore, conventional time-shared systems with very high clock frequency can also be improved by the same technique if a cache is large.

Figure 10 (b) shows the change of a miss-rate over time rather than an average miss-rate over the entire simulation. It is clear from the figure how the short record cycle helps partitioning. In the figure, the model-based partitioning with the long record cycle ($P = 10^7$) performs worse than LRU at the beginning of a simulation, even though it outperforms the normal LRU replacement policy overall. This is because the model-based partitioning has only one average miss-rate curve for a process. As shown in Figure 9, some benchmarks such as bzip2 and gcc have a very different miss-rate at the beginning. Therefore, the average miss-rate curves for those benchmarks do not work at the beginning of the simulation, which results in worse performance than the normal LRU replacement policy. The model-based partitioning with the short record cycle ($P = 10^5$), on the other hand, always outperforms the normal LRU replacement policy. In this case, the model has correct miss-rate curves for all the time quanta, and partitions the cache properly even for the beginning of processes.

4.3.2 Set-Associative Result

The result of cache partitioning for a set-associative cache is shown in Figure 11. The same set of benchmarks are simulated with a 32-KB 8-way set-associative cache, and the same miss-rate curves generated for a 32-KB fully-associative cache are used. In this case, a 16 entry victim cache is added. In the figure, the model-based partitioning improves the miss-rate about 4% for short time quanta and up to 15% for mid-range time quanta. The figure demonstrates that the model-based partitioning mechanism works reasonably well for set-associative caches.

5. CONCLUSION

An analytical cache model to estimate overall miss-rate when multiple processes are sharing a cache has been presented. The model obtains the information about each process from its miss-rate curve, and combines it with parameters that define the cache configuration and schedule of processes. Interference among processes under the LRU replacement policy is quickly estimated for any cache size and any time quantum, and the estimated miss-rate is very accurate. A more important result is that the model provides not only the overall miss-rate but also a very good understanding of the effect of context switching. For example, the model clearly shows that the LRU replacement policy is problematic for mid-range time quanta because the policy replaces the blocks of least recently executed process that are more likely to be accessed in the near future.

The analytical model has been applied to the cache partitioning problem. A model-based partitioning method has been implemented and verified by simulations. Miss-rate curves are recorded off-line and partitioning is performed on-line according to the combination of processes that are executing. Even though we have used an off-line profiling method to obtain miss-rate curves, it should not be hard to approximate the miss-rate curve on-line using a miss-rate monitoring technique. Therefore, a fully on-line cache partitioning method can be developed based on the model.

Only the cache partitioning problem has been studied in this paper. However, as shown by the study of cache partitioning, our model can be applied to any cache optimization problem that is related to the problem of context switching. For example, it can be used to determine the best combination of processes that can be run on each processor of a multi-processor system. Also, the model is useful to identify areas in which further research in improving cache performance would be fruitful since it can easily provide the maximum improvement we can expect in the area.

6. ACKNOWLEDGMENTS

Funding for this work is provided in part by the Defense Advanced Research Projects Agency under the Air Force Research Lab contract F30602-99-2-0511, titled "Malleable Caches for Data-Intensive Computing". Thanks also to E. Peserico, D. Chiou, and D. Chen for their comments on the cache model.

7. REFERENCES

[1] A. Agarwal, M. Horowitz, and J. Hennessy. An analytical cache model. *ACM Transactions on Computer Systems*, 7(2), May 1989.

[2] Compaq. Compaq AlphaStation family.

[3] T. M. Cover and J. A. Thomas. *Elements of Information Theory*. Wiley, John & Sons, Incorporated, Mar. 1991.

[4] S. J. Eggers, J. S. Emer, H. M. Levy, J. L. Lo, R. L. Stamm, and D. M. Tullsen. Simultaneous multithreading: A platform for next-generation processors. *IEEE Micro*, 17(5), 1997.

[5] C. Freeburn. The hewlett packard PA-RISC 8500 processor. Technical report, Hewlett Packard Laboratories, Oct. 1998.

[6] A. González, M. Valero, N. Topham, and J. M. Parcerisa. Eliminating cache conflict misses through XOR-based placement functions. In *the 1997 international conference on Supercomputing*, 1997.

[7] J. L. Henning. SPEC CPU2000: Measuring CPU performance in the new millennium. *IEEE Computer*, July 2000.

[8] N. Jouppi. Improving direct-mapped cache performance by the addition of a small fully-associative cache and prefetch buffers. In *the 17th Annual International Symposium on Computer Architecture*, 1990.

[9] D. B. Kirk. Process dependent static cache partitioning for real-time systems. In *Real-Time Systems Symposium*, 1988.

[10] H. Kwak, B. Lee, A. R. Hurson, S.-H. Yoon, and W.-J. Hahn. Effects of multithreading on cache performance. *IEEE Transactions on Computers*, 48(2), Feb. 1999.

[11] J. L. Lo, J. S. Emer, H. M. Levy, R. L. Stamm, D. M. Tullsen, and S. J. Eggers. Converting thread-level parallelism to instruction-level parallelism via simultaneous multithreading. *ACM Transactions on Computer Systems*, 15, 1997.

[12] P. Magnusson and B. Werner. Efficient memory simulation in SimICS. In *28th Annual Simulation Symposium*, 1995.

[13] MIPS Technologies, Inc. *MIPS R10000 Microprocessor User's Manual*, 1996.

[14] J. C. Mogul and A. Borg. The effect of context switches on cache performance. In *the fourth international conference on Architectural support for programming languages and operating systems*, 1991.

[15] J. Muoz. *Data-Intensive Systems Benchmark Suite Analysis and Specification*. http://www.aaec.com/projectweb/dis, June 1999.

[16] M. Rosenblum, S. A. Herrod, E. Witchel, and A. Gupta. Complete computer system simulation: The SimOS approach. *IEEE Parallel & Distributed Technology*, 1995.

[17] M. S. Squillante and E. D. Lazowska. Using processor-cache affinity information in shared-momory multiprocessor scheduling. *IEEE Transactions on Parallel and Distributed Systems*, 4(2), Feb. 1993.

[18] H. S. Stone, J. Turek, and J. L. Wolf. Optimal partitioning of cache memory. *IEEE Transactions on Computers*, 41(9), Sept. 1992.

[19] G. E. Suh and L. Rudolph. Set-associative cache models for time-shared systems. Technical Report CSG Memo 433, Massachusetts Institute of Technology, 2001.

[20] D. Thiébaut and H. S. Stone. Footprints in the cache. *ACM Transactions on Computer Systems*, 5(4), Nov. 1987.

[21] D. Thiébaut, H. S. Stone, and J. L. Wolf. Improving disk cache hit-ratios through cache partitioning. *IEEE Transactions on Computers*, 41(6), June 1992.

[22] N. Topham and A. González. Randomized cache placement for eleminating conflicts. *IEEE Transactions on Computers*, 48(2), Feb. 1999.

[23] J. Torrellas, A. Tucker, and A. Gupta. Benefits of cache-affinity scheduling in shared-memory multiprocessors: A summary. In *the 1993 ACM SIGMETRICS conference on Measurement and modeling of computer systems*, 1993.

[24] D. M. Tullsen, S. J. Eggers, and H. M. Levy. Simultaneous multithreading: Maximizing on-chip parallelism. In *22nd Annual International Symposium on Computer Architecture*, 1995.

[25] R. A. Uhlig and T. N. Mudge. Trace-driven memory simulation: A survey. *ACM Computing Surveys*, 29(2), June 1997.

[26] M. Zagha, B. Larson, S. Turner, and M. Itzkowitz. Performance analysis using the MIPS R1000. In *Supercomputing'96*, 1996.

Search and Replication in Unstructured Peer-to-Peer Networks

Qin Lv
Dept. of Computer Science
Princeton University
qlv@CS.Princeton.EDU

Pei Cao
Cisco Systems, Inc.
cao@cisco.com

Edith Cohen
AT&T Labs-Research
edith@research.att.com

Kai Li
Dept. of Computer Science
Princeton University
li@CS.Princeton.EDU

Scott Shenker
ICSI
shenker@icsi.berkeley.edu

ABSTRACT

Decentralized and unstructured peer-to-peer networks such as Gnutella are attractive for certain applications because they require no centralized directories and no precise control over network topology or data placement. However, the flooding-based query algorithm used in Gnutella does not scale; each query generates a large amount of traffic and large systems quickly become overwhelmed by the query-induced load. This paper explores, through simulation, various alternatives to Gnutella's query algorithm, data replication strategy, and network topology. We propose a query algorithm based on multiple random walks that resolves queries almost as quickly as Gnutella's flooding method while reducing the network traffic by two orders of magnitude in many cases. We also present simulation results on a distributed replication strategy proposed in [8]. Finally, we find that among the various network topologies we consider, uniform random graphs yield the best performance.

Categories and Subject Descriptors

H.3.5 [**Information Storage and Retrieval**]: [Online Information Services, Data Sharing]

General Terms

Algorithms, Measurement, Performance, Theory

Keywords

peer-to-peer, search, replication, unstructured

1. INTRODUCTION

The computer science community has become accustomed to the Internet's continuing rapid growth, but even to such jaded observers the explosive increase in Peer-to-Peer (P2P) network usage has been astounding. Within a few months of Napster's [16] introduction in 1999 the system had spread widely, and recent measurement data suggests that P2P applications are having a very significant and rapidly growing impact on Internet traffic [12, 17]. It is important to study the performance and scalability of these P2P networks.

Currently, there are several different architectures for P2P networks:

Centralized: Napster and other similar systems have a constantly-updated directory hosted at central locations (*e.g.*, the Napster web site). Nodes in the P2P network issue queries to the central directory server to find which other nodes hold the desired files. Such centralized approaches do not scale well and have single points of failure.

Decentralized but Structured: These systems have no central directory server, but they have a significant amount of structure. By "structure" we mean that the P2P overlay topology (that is, the set of connections between P2P members) is tightly controlled and that files are placed not at random nodes but at specified locations that will make subsequent queries easier to satisfy. In "loosely structured" systems this placement of files is based on hints; the Freenet P2P network [11] is an example of such systems. In "highly structured" systems both the P2P network topology and the placement of files are precisely determined; this tightly controlled structure enables the system to satisfy queries very efficiently. There is a growing literature on highly structured P2P systems which support a hash-table-like interface; see [18, 23, 20, 26]. Such highly structured P2P designs are quite prevalent in the research literature, but almost completely invisible on the current network. Moreover, it isn't clear how well such designs work with an extremely transient population of nodes, which seems to be a characteristic of the Napster community.

Decentralized and Unstructured: These are systems in which there is neither a centralized directory nor any precise control over the network topology or file placement. Gnutella [13] is an example of such designs. The network is formed by nodes joining the network following some loose rules (for example, those described in [6]). The resultant topology has certain properties, but the placement of files is not based on any knowledge of the topology (as it is in structured designs). To find a file, a node queries its neighbors. The most typical query method is flooding, where the query is propagated to all neighbors within a certain radius [6]. These unstructured designs are extremely resilient to nodes entering and leaving the system. However, the current search mechanisms are extremely unscalable, generating large loads on the network participants.

In this paper, we focus on Gnutella-like decentralized, unstructured P2P systems. We do so because (1) these systems are actively used by a large community of Internet users [24, 7], and (2) these systems have not yet been subject to much serious research, except for empirical studies [21, 22].

The goal of this paper is to study more-scalable alternatives to existing Gnutella algorithms, focusing on the search and replication aspects. We first quantify the poor scaling properties of the flooding search algorithms. We then propose, as an alternative, a k-walker random walk algorithm that greatly reduces the load generated by each query. We also show that active replication (where the files may be stored at arbitrary nodes) produces lower overall query load than non-active node-based replication (*i.e.*, a file is only replicated at nodes requesting the file). Confirming the results in [8], we use simulations to show that path replication, where the file is replicated along the path from the requester to the provider, yields a close-to-optimal replication distribution. Finally, we show that for unstructured networks, power-law random graphs are less desirable than uniform random graphs and so P2P systems should adopt graph-building algorithms that reduce the likelihood of very-high degree nodes.

2. METHODOLOGY

It is impossible to model all the dynamics of an Internet-based P2P system. In this paper, we are not trying to resolve small quantitative disparities between different algorithms, but instead are trying to reveal fundamental qualitative differences. While our simple models do not capture all aspects of reality, we hope they capture the essential features needed to understand the qualitative differences.

2.1 Abstractions

We look at three aspects of a P2P system: P2P network topology, query distribution and replication. By network topology, we mean the graph formed by the P2P overlay network; each P2P member has a certain number of "neighbors" and the set of neighbor connections forms the P2P overlay network. In this paper when we refer to the "network" we are referring to the P2P network, not the underlying Internet. For simplicity, we assume that the P2P network graph does not change during the simulation of our algorithms. By query distribution, we mean the distribution of query frequencies for individual files. Again, we assume that this distribution is fixed during our simulations. By replication, we mean the number of nodes that have a particular file.[1]

[1]We will use replication ratio to mean the *percentage* of nodes having the file.

	#nodes	total #links	avg. node degree	std. dev.	max degree	median degree
PLRG	9230	20599	4.46	27.9	1746	1
Random	9836	20099	4.09	1.95	13	4
Gnutella	4736	13022	5.50	10.7	136	2
Grid	10000	19800	3.96	0.20	4	4

Table 1: Key statistics of the network topologies

Our assumption of fixed network topology and fixed query distributions are obviously gross simplifications. However, for the purpose of our study, if one assumes that the time to complete a search is short compared to the time of change in network topology and in query distribution, results obtained from these settings are still indicative of performance in real systems.

We use four network topologies in our study:

- Power-Law Random Graph (PLRG): this is a 9230-node random graph. The node degrees follow a power-law distribution: when ranked from the most connected to the least connected, the i'th most connected node has ω/i^α neighbors, where ω is a constant. Once the node degrees are chosen, the nodes are connected randomly; see [3]. Many real-life P2P networks have topologies that are power-law random graphs [14].

- Normal Random Graph (Random): a 9836-node random graph generated by a modified version of GT-ITM topology generator [5].

- Gnutella graph (Gnutella): the Gnutella network topology, as obtained in October 2000. The graph has 4736 nodes.[2] Its node degrees roughly follow a two-segment power-law distribution, as shown in Figure 1.

- Two-Dimensional Grid (Grid): a two-dimension (100x 100) grid. We choose this simple graph for comparison purposes.

Node degree information of the four graphs are shown in Figure 1. and are also summarized in Table 1.

We assume that there are m objects of interest. (In this paper we use the terms "file" and "object" interchangeably.) Let q_i be the relative popularity, in terms of the number of queries issued for it, of the i'th object. The values are normalized:

$$\sum_{i=1}^{m} q_i = 1 \tag{1}$$

We investigate the following distributions:

- Uniform: all objects are equally popular.

$$\text{Uniform}: q_i = 1/m \tag{2}$$

- Zipf-like: object popularity follows a Zipf-like distribution. Studies have shown that Napster, Gnutella and Web queries follow Zipf-like distributions [4, 21].

$$\text{Zipf-like}: q_i \propto 1/i^\alpha \tag{3}$$

[2]Cautions are taken when we choose metrics and parameters in our analysis and simulations to account for the difference in network sizes.

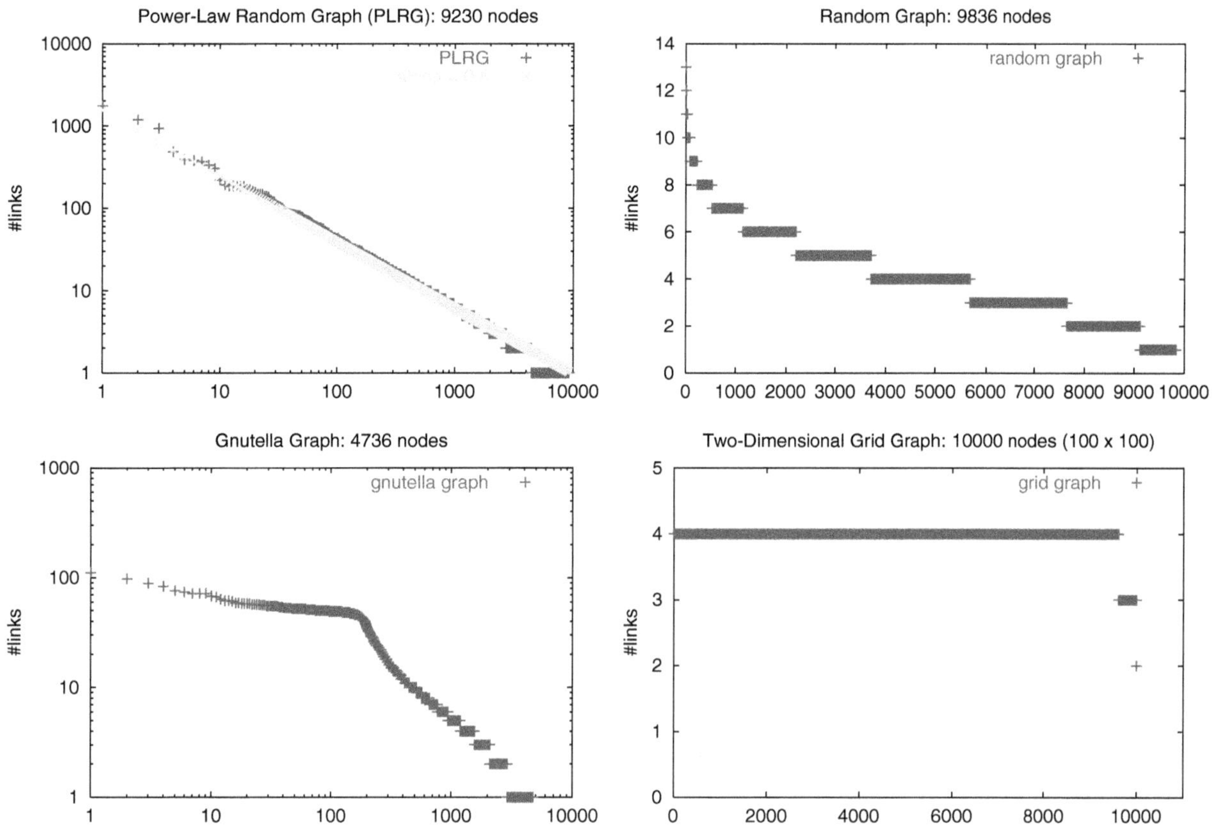

Figure 1: Distribution of node degrees in the four network topology graphs. Note that we use log scale for PLRG and Gnutella, and linear scale for Random and Grid.

We assume each object i is replicated on r_i nodes, and the total number of objects stored in the network is R.

$$\sum_{i=1}^{m} r_i = R \tag{4}$$

We consider several static replication distributions: [3]

- Uniform: all objects are replicated at the same number of nodes.

$$\text{Uniform} : r_i = R/m \tag{5}$$

- Proportional: the replication of an object i is proportional to the query probability of the object. If only nodes requesting an object store the object, then the replication distribution is usually proportional to query distribution.

$$\text{Proportional} : r_i \propto q_i \tag{6}$$

- Square-root: replication of an object i is proportional to the square root of its query probability q_i. The reason for this distribution is discussed in [8] and reviewed in Section 5.

$$\text{Square-root} : r_i \propto \sqrt{q_i} \tag{7}$$

[3]We assume static replication when we study various search methods. We'll look at dynamic replication when we investigate different replication strategies.

A simulation, in the static case, is determined by the combination of query distribution and replication distribution. When the replication is uniform, the query distribution is irrelevant (since all objects are replicated by the same amount, the search times are equivalent). When the query distribution is uniform, all three replication distributions are equivalent. Thus, there are only three relevant combinations of query distribution and replication distribution: uniform/uniform, Zipf-like/proportional, and Zipf-like/square-root.

2.2 Metrics

Performance issues in real P2P systems are extremely complicated. In addition to issues such as load on the network, load on network participants, and delays in getting positive answers, there are a host of other criteria such as success rate of the search, the bandwidth of the selected provider nodes, and fairness to both the requester and the provider. It is impossible for us to use all of these criteria in evaluating search and replication algorithms.

Instead, we focus on efficiency aspects solely, and use the following simple metrics in our abstract P2P networks. These metrics, though simple, reflect the fundamental properties of the algorithms.

- User aspects:
  - Pr(success): the probability of finding the queried object before the search terminates. Different al-

gorithms have different criteria for terminating a search, leading to different probabilities of success under various replication distributions.

  - #hops: delay in finding an object as measured in number of hops. We do not model the actual network latency here, but rather just measure the abstract number of hops that a successful search message travels before it replies to the originator.

- Load aspects:

  - #msgs per node: overhead of an algorithm as measured in average number of search messages each node in the P2P network has to process. The motivation for this metric is that in P2P systems, the most notable overhead tends to be the processing load that the network imposes on each participant. The load, usually interrupt processing or message processing, is directly proportional to the number of messages that the node has to process.

  - #nodes visited: the number of P2P network participants that a query's search messages travel through. This is an indirect measure of the impact that a query generates on the whole network.

  - percentage of message duplication: calculated as (total_#msgs - #nodes visited)/total_#msgs.

  - peak #msgs: to identify hot spots in the network, we calculate the number of messages that the busiest node has to process for a set of queries.

- Aggregate performance: for each of the above measures, which are per-query measures, we calculate an aggregate performance number, which is the performance of each query convoluted with the query probability. That is, if the performance measure for object i is $a(i)$, then the aggregate is $\sum_i q_i * a(i)$.

2.3 Simulation Methodology

For each set of simulations, we first select the topology and the query/replication distributions. For each object i with replication r_i, we generate *numPlace* different sets of random replica placements (each set contains r_i random nodes, on which to place the replicas of object i). For each replica placement, we randomly choose *numQuery* different nodes from which to initiate a query for object i. Then, for each query, we simulate the searching process using the designated search method. We can run the simulation for each query independent of other queries because the object replication is fixed, and hence running all the queries concurrently is the same as running each one separately and then summing the results.

Statistics are collected from the *numPlace* $\times$ *numQuery* queries. For the results we present in this paper, *numPlace = 10* and *numQuery = 100*, resulting in 1000 different queries for each object. This ensures small standard deviation in our results.[4] We then calculate the aggregate results for the above metrics.

[4]Due to space limitation we do not present standard deviations associated with the averages, except to point out that the standard deviation data do not change the conclusions in the paper.

As a final note about our abstractions and metrics, we stress that they omit a lot of issues, including the true dynamics of node coming and going in the network, the message delays in the network, the actual load on a network node for processing and propagating messages, etc. However, these models help us understand the fundamental properties of various search and replication algorithms.

3. LIMITATIONS OF FLOODING

One of the major load issues in P2P networks is the load on individual network participants. Typically, the participants are PCs at home or office, and are used for normal work and entertainment. If a PC has to handle many network interrupts when it joins the P2P network, the user will be forced to take the PC off the P2P network to get "real" work done. This in turn limits the size and the usefulness of the P2P network. Unfortunately, the flooding search algorithm used in Gnutella exacerbates this problem.

Gnutella uses TTL(Time-To-Live) to control the number of hops that a query can be propagated. However, choosing the appropriate TTL is not easy. If the TTL is too high, the node unnecessarily burdens the network. If the TTL is too low, the node might not find the object even though a copy exists somewhere.

Figure 2 shows the probability of success and average per-node message overhead of flooding as TTL increases. The search is for an object that is replicated at 0.125% of the nodes. We can see from the figures that different TTLs are needed in different network topologies. And the values differ for different replication ratios. Unfortunately, since in practice the replication ratio of an object is unknown, users have to set TTLs high to ensure success of the query.

Another problem with flooding is that, there are many duplicate messages introduced by flooding, particularly in high connectivity graphs. By duplicate messages we mean the multiple copies of a query that are sent to a node by its multiple neighbors. Duplicate queries are pure overhead; they incur extra network interrupt processing at the nodes receiving them but do not contribute to increased chance of finding the object. Duplication detection mechanisms are always needed in flood-style search so that duplicate messages are detected and not forwarded. However, even with this duplicate suppression the number of duplicate messages in flooding-style algorithms can be excessive, and the problem worsens as the TTL increases.

Figure 3 shows the percentage of duplicate messages and the number of unique nodes visited as TTL increases. As we can see, when TTL increases, the number of unique nodes visited increases, but the percentage of duplicate messages also increases.

These limitations mean that flooding incurs considerable message processing overhead for each query, increasing the load on each node as the network expands and the query rate increases, to the point that a node can be so loaded that it has to leave the network. Other researchers have also noted the limitations of flooding [19].

Our simulations also show that Power-Law random graphs and Gnutella style graphs are particularly bad with flooding. The presence of highly connected nodes mean that its duplication ratios are much higher than those in the random graph, because many nodes' neighbors overlap. In fact, for flooding, the random graph would be the best topology because in a truly random graph the duplication ratio (likeli-

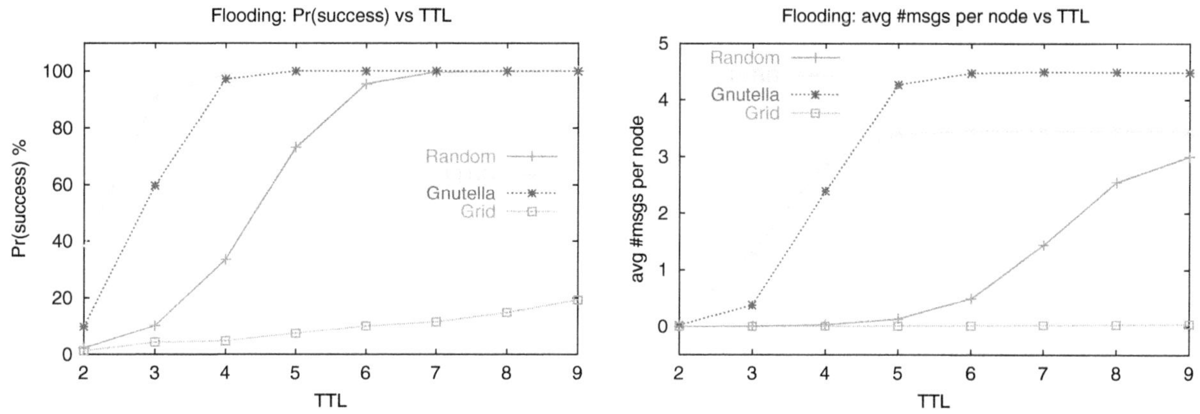

Figure 2: Pr(success) and per-node message overhead under various TTLs.

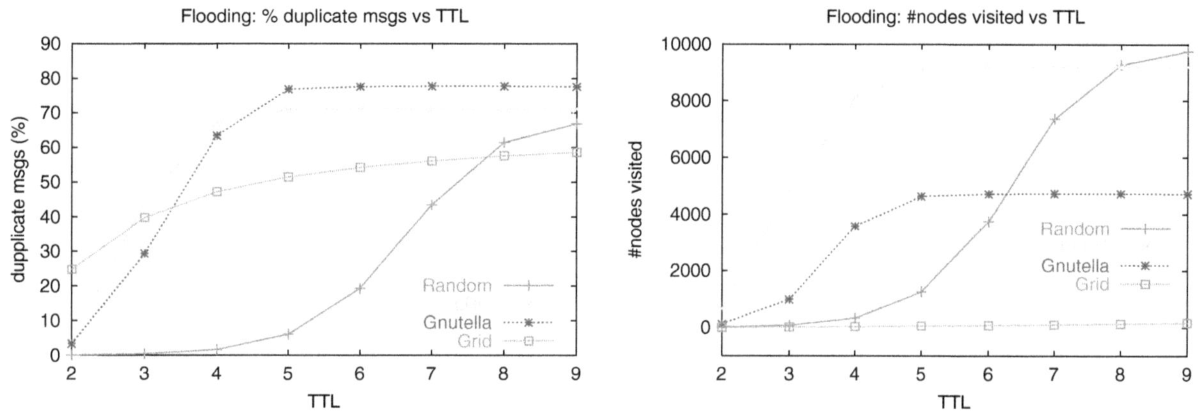

Figure 3: Message duplication percentage and node coverage under various TTLs.

hood that the next node already received the query) is the same as the fraction of nodes visited so far, as long as that fraction is small.

The random graph is also better for load distribution among its nodes. In the random graph, the maximum load on any one node is logarithmic to the total number of nodes that the search visits. In contrast, the high degree nodes in PLRG and Gnutella graphs have much higher load than other nodes. Due to space constraints we omit the data on peak # of messages here.

4. FINDING BETTER SEARCH METHODS

Our first try is to address the TTL selection problem.

4.1 Expanding Ring

One might suggest asking nodes to check with the original requester before forwarding the query to neighbors. However, this approach can lead to message implosion at the requester node. Hence, we do not adopt this approach.

Instead, we can use successive floods with increasing TTLs. A node starts a flood with small TTL, If the search is not successful, the node increases the TTL and starts another flood. The process repeats until the object is found. We expect this method to perform particularly well when hot objects are replicated more widely than cold objects, which is likely the case in practice. This method is called "expanding ring."

To understand how well expanding ring works, we measure the average stopping TTL for searches to objects with increasing replication ratios. In our simulations the expanding ring starts with TTL=1, and expands the TTL linearly by 2 each time. Figure 4 shows the results for various topologies. As we can see, expanding ring successfully reins in the TTL as the object's replication ratio increases. While searches for objects with low replication ratio need TTLs larger than 5, the searches stop at TTL of 1 or 2 when the object replication is over 10%.

We also record the average number of messages a node has to process (Figure 4). Comparing the message overhead between flooding and expanding ring, we can see that, for objects that are replicated at 0.125% of the nodes, even if flooding uses the best TTL for each network topology, expanding ring still halves the per-node message overhead.

To understand the overall impact of expanding rings in a P2P network, we run a large set of simulations as explained in section 2.3. The results are shown in the "expanding ring" column in Tables 2 through 5.

The results show that, despite the successive retries, expanding ring still reduces message overhead significantly compared with regular flooding with a fixed TTL. The savings are obtained across all query and replication distributions.

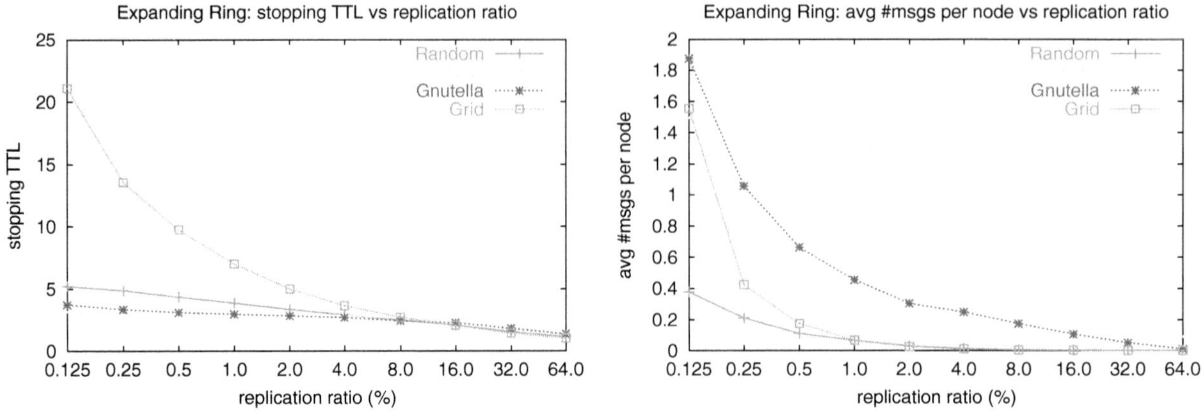

Figure 4: stopping TTL and per-node message overhead for expanding ring under various replication ratios.

The improvements are also more pronounced for Random and Gnutella graphs than for the PLRG graph, partly because the very high degree nodes in PLRG graph reduce the opportunity for incremental retries in expanding ring.

Expanding ring achieves the savings at the expense of slight increase in the delays to find the object. As we can see, for Random, PLRG and Gnutella, the average number of hops only increases from 2 to 4 in flooding to 3 to 6 in expanding ring, which we believe is tolerable for users.

Though expanding ring solves the TTL selection problem, it does not address the message duplication issue inherent in flooding. Inspection of simulation results shows that the duplication contributes significantly to the message overhead, particularly for PLRG and Gnutella graphs. To reduce message duplication, we try a different approach, random walk.

4.2 Random Walks

Random walk is a well-known technique, which forwards a query message to a randomly chosen neighbor at each step until the object is found. We call this message a "walker".

The standard random walk (which uses only one walker) can cut down the message overhead by an order of magnitude compared to expanding ring across the network topologies. However, there is also an order of magnitude increase in user-perceived delay.

To reduce the delay we increase the number of "walkers.". That is, instead of just sending out one query message, a requesting node sends k query messages, and each query message takes its own random walk. The expectation is that k walkers after T steps should reach roughly the same number of nodes as 1 walker after kT steps, and indeed simulations confirm that. Therefore, by using k walkers, we can expect to cut the delay down by a factor of k.

We experimented with different number of walkers. With more walkers, we can find objects faster, but also generate more loads. And when the number of walkers is big enough, increasing it further yield little reduction in the number of hops, but significantly increases the message traffic. Usually, 16 to 64 walkers give good results.

Since multiple-walker random walks require a mechanism to terminate the walks, we experimented with two methods, TTL and "checking.". TTL means that, similar to flooding, each random walk terminates after a certain number of hops. "Checking" means that a walker periodically checks with the original requester before walking to the next node. The checking method still uses a TTL, but the TTL is very large and is mainly used to prevent loops.

Our simulations show that checking is the right approach for terminating searches in random walks. The TTL approach runs into the same TTL selection issue in flooding. Meanwhile, since there are a fixed number of walkers (typically 16 to 64), having the walkers check back with the requester will not lead to message implosion at the requester node. Of course, checking does have overhead; each check requires a message exchange between a node and the requester node. Further experiments show that checking once at every fourth step along the way strikes a good balance between the overhead of the checking messages and the benefits of checking.

Tables 2 through 5 compare the discussed search methods under all combinations of query and replication distributions for the four network topologies. There are two sets of columns in each table; the first set are results of the queries to the top 50% hottest objects, and the second set are results of all queries.

The results show that, compared to flooding, the 32-walker random walk reduces message overhead by roughly *two orders of magnitude* for all queries across all network topologies, at the expense of slight increase in the number of hops (increasing from 2-6 to 4-15). The 32-walker random walk generally outperforms expanding ring as well, particularly in PLRG and Gnutella graphs.

We also studied an improvement to the above approach by asking each node to keep state. Each query has a unique ID and all its k walkers are tagged with that ID. For each ID, a node remembers the neighbors to which it has forwarded queries of that ID, and when a new query with the same ID arrives, the node forwards it to a different neighbor (randomly chosen). This state keeping accelerates the walks because walkers are less likely to cover the same route and hence they visit more nodes. Simulation results, also shown in the tables, confirm the improvement. Compared with random walks without state keeping, random walk with state keeping shows the biggest improvement in Random and Grid graphs, reducing message overhead by up to 30%, and reducing number of hops by up to 30%. However, the improvements for PLRG and Gnutella graphs are small. Hence, de-

distribution model query/replication	metrics	50 % (queries for hot objects) flood	ring	check	state	100 % (all queries) flood	ring	check	state
Uniform / Uniform	#hops	3.40	5.77	10.30	7.00	3.40	5.77	10.30	7.00
	#msgs per node	2.509	0.062	0.031	0.024	2.509	0.061	0.031	0.024
	#nodes visited	9220	536	149	163	9220	536	149	163
	peak #msgs	6.37	0.26	0.22	0.19	6.37	0.26	0.22	0.19
Zipf-like / Proportional	#hops	1.60	2.08	1.72	1.64	2.51	4.03	9.12	6.66
	#msgs per node	1.265	0.004	0.010	0.010	1.863	0.053	0.027	0.022
	#nodes visited	6515	36	33	47	7847	396	132	150
	peak #msgs	4.01	0.02	0.11	0.10	5.23	0.20	0.17	0.14
Zipf-like / Square root	#hops	2.23	3.19	2.82	2.51	2.70	4.24	5.74	4.43
	#msgs per node	2.154	0.010	0.014	0.013	2.308	0.031	0.021	0.018
	#nodes visited	8780	92	50	69	8983	269	89	109
	peak #msgs	5.88	0.04	0.16	0.16	6.14	0.12	0.17	0.16

Table 2: Static simulation results for Random Graph. The first set of columns are results of queries to the top 50% most popular objects; the second set of columns are results of all queries. "flood" is flooding with TTL=8. "ring" is expanding ring. "walk" is 32-walker random walk with checking. "state" is 32-walker random walk with checking and state keeping. #objects m is 100, average replication ratio is 1.0%, and the parameter α in the Zipf-like query distribution is 1.20.

distribution model query/replication	metrics	50 % (queries for hot objects) flood	ring	check	state	100 % (all queries) flood	ring	check	state
Uniform / Uniform	#hops	2.37	3.50	8.95	8.47	2.37	3.50	8.95	8.47
	#msgs per node	3.331	1.325	0.030	0.029	3.331	1.325	0.030	0.029
	#nodes visited	8935	4874	147	158	8935	4874	147	158
	peak #msgs	510.4	132.7	12.3	11.7	510.4	132.7	12.3	11.7
Zipf-like / Proportional	#hops	1.74	2.36	1.81	1.82	2.07	2.93	9.85	8.98
	#msgs per node	2.397	0.593	0.011	0.011	2.850	0.961	0.031	0.029
	#nodes visited	6969	2432	43	49	7923	3631	136	145
	peak #msgs	412.7	58.3	4.9	5.1	464.3	98.9	12.7	11.7
Zipf-like / Square root	#hops	2.07	2.94	2.65	2.49	2.21	3.17	5.37	4.79
	#msgs per node	3.079	0.967	0.014	0.014	3.199	1.115	0.021	0.020
	#nodes visited	8434	3750	62	69	8674	4200	97	103
	peak #msgs	496.0	93.7	6.3	6.3	499.6	111.7	8.9	8.4

Table 3: Static simulation results for Power-Law Random Graph (PLRG). The legends are the same as in Table 2, except that the TTL for "flood" is 5.

distribution model query/replication	metrics	50 % (queries for hot objects) flood	ring	check	state	100 % (all queries) flood	ring	check	state
Uniform / Uniform	#hops	2.39	3.40	7.30	6.11	2.39	3.40	7.30	6.11
	#msgs per node	4.162	0.369	0.051	0.045	4.162	0.369	0.051	0.045
	#nodes visited	4556	933	141	151	4556	933	141	151
	peak #msgs	64.9	6.4	1.3	1.2	64.9	6.4	1.3	1.2
Zipf-like / Proportional	#hops	1.60	2.18	1.66	1.66	2.03	3.05	9.39	7.94
	#msgs per node	2.961	0.109	0.021	0.021	3.548	0.423	0.058	0.051
	#nodes visited	3725	357	49	60	4137	810	143	153
	peak #msgs	43.8	2.0	0.7	0.8	54.5	7.0	1.6	1.5
Zipf-like / Square root	#hops	1.88	2.70	2.31	2.15	2.10	3.02	4.61	4.12
	#msgs per node	3.874	0.208	0.027	0.026	4.007	0.302	0.038	0.035
	#nodes visited	4404	621	67	80	4479	789	101	114
	peak #msgs	62.5	3.8	0.8	0.9	63.8	5.3	1.1	1.1

Table 4: Static simulation results for Gnutella Graph. The legends are the same as in Table 2, except that the TTL for "flood" is 5.

distribution model		50 % (queries for hot objects)				100 % (all queries)			
query/replication	metrics	flood	ring	check	state	flood	ring	check	state
Uniform / Uniform	#hops	6.52	19.15	27.95	15.20	6.52	19.15	27.95	15.20
	#msgs per node	0.472	0.070	0.068	0.041	0.472	0.070	0.068	0.041
	#nodes visited	1692	128	107	128	1692	128	107	128
	peak #msgs	0.72	0.18	0.30	0.16	0.72	0.18	0.30	0.16
Zipf-like / Proportional	#hops	1.70	2.32	1.95	1.77	4.71	19.04	33.78	15.14
	#msgs per node	0.321	0.003	0.011	0.010	0.392	0.120	0.082	0.040
	#nodes visited	1398	14	22	28	1533	118	111	121
	peak #msgs	0.57	0.02	0.07	0.06	0.64	0.25	0.26	0.16
Zipf-like / Square root	#hops	2.77	4.64	4.60	3.32	4.31	10.66	15.53	8.22
	#msgs per node	0.437	0.008	0.018	0.015	0.450	0.034	0.041	0.025
	#nodes visited	1647	31	34	42	1656	70	67	77
	peak #msgs	0.68	0.04	0.10	0.08	0.68	0.10	0.19	0.12

Table 5: Static simulation results for Grid Graph. The legends are the same as in Table 2, except that the TTL for "flood" is 32.

pending on the implementation overhead of state keeping, each P2P network should decide separately whether state keeping is worthwhile.

4.3 Principles of Scalable Search in Unstructured Networks

Our results show that the k-walker random walk is a much more scalable search method than flooding. However, perhaps more important than this conclusion is the understanding we have gained from this exercise. The key to scalable searches in unstructured network is to cover the right number of nodes as quickly as possible and with as little overhead as possible. In unstructured network, the only way to find objects is to visit enough nodes so that, statistically speaking, one of the nodes has the object. However, in reaching the required node coverage, one must pay attention to the following:

- *Adaptive termination is very important.* TTL-based mechanism does not work. Any adaptive/dynamic termination mechanism must avoid message implosion at the requester node. The checking method described above is a good example of adaptive termination.

- *Message duplication should be minimized.* Preferably, each query should visit a node just once. More visits are wasteful in terms of the message overhead.

- *Granularity of the coverage should be small.* Each additional step in the search should not significantly increase the number of nodes visited. This is perhaps the fundamental difference between flooding and multiple-walker random walk. In flooding, an additional step could exponentially increase the number of nodes visited; in random walk, it increases only by a constant.

5. REPLICATION: THEORY

Our study in the previous section examined how one should search for an object, assuming that it is replicated at some random locations in the network. In certain P2P systems such as Gnutella, only nodes that request an object make copies of the object. Other P2P systems such as Freenet allow for more proactive replications of objects, where an object may be replicated at a node even though the node has not requested the object. For such systems, we must answer the question: how many copies of each object should there be so that the search overhead for the object is minimized, assuming that the total amount of storage for objects in the network is fixed? Answers to this question have implications to non-proactive replication systems as well, because the information of an object's location could be proactively replicated to expedite the searches.

This question has been addressed in great theoretical detail in [8]. Here we review those results and evaluate the resulting algorithms via simulation. Consider the simple model used in [8] where there are m objects and n sites(nodes). Each object i is replicated at r_i random (distinct) sites (recall that $R = \sum_i r_i$), and that object i is requested with relative rates q_i, where we normalize this by setting $\sum_i q_i = 1$. For convenience, we assume that query and replication strategies are such that $1 \ll r_i \leq n$ and that searches go on until a copy is found. The other cases are dealt with in [8], and the conclusions are consistent with, but a bit messier than, what we present here. Search consists of randomly probing sites until the desired object is found. Thus, the probability $Pr(k)$ that the object is found on the k'th probe is given by: $Pr_i(k) = \frac{r_i}{n}(1 - \frac{r_i}{n})^{k-1}$. An object's *average search size* A_i is merely the inverse of the fraction of sites which have replicas of the object: $A_i = \frac{n}{r_i}$. We are interested in the average search size of all the objects: $A = \sum_i q_i A_i = n \sum_i \frac{q_i}{r_i}$. This metric essentially captures the message overhead of efficient searches.

If there were no limit on r_i then clearly the optimal strategy would be to replicate everything everywhere, and all searches become trivial. Instead, we assume that the average number of these replicas per site, $\rho = \frac{R}{n}$, is fixed and less than m. The question is how to allocate these R replicas among the m objects.

The simplest replication strategy is to create the same number of replicas of each object: $r_i = \frac{R}{m}$. We call this *uniform* replication strategy. In this case the average search size $A_{uniform}$ is given by:

$$A_{uniform} = \sum_i q_i \frac{m}{\rho} = \frac{m}{\rho}$$

which is independent of the query distribution.

It is clear that uniformly replicating all objects, even those that are not frequently queried, is inefficient. A more natural policy is to replicate *proportional* to the querying rate: $r_i = Rq_i$. This should reduce the search sizes for the more popular objects. However, a quick calculation reveals that the *average* remains the same:

$$A_{proportional} = n\sum_i \frac{q_i}{Rq_i} = \frac{m}{\rho} = A_{uniform}$$

Thus, the Proportional and Uniform replication strategies yield *exactly* the same average search size, and that average search size is independent of the query distribution.

Another important metric that captures the load balancing ability of a replication strategy is *utilization rate*, $U_i = R\frac{q_i}{r_i}$. That is, the rate of requests that a replica of object i serves (the random probing search process implies that all replicas of the same object have the same utilization rate). Note that the average utilization over all objects $U = \sum_i r_i U_i / R = 1$ is *fixed* for all replication strategies. The maximum utilization $\max_i U_i$, however, varies considerably.

The distributions of average search sizes and utilization rates for an object are quite different between the Uniform and Proportional strategies. For Uniform replication, all objects have the same average search size, but replicas have utilization rates *proportional* to their query rates. Proportional replication achieves perfect load balancing with all replicas having the same utilization rate, but average search sizes vary with more popular objects having smaller average search sizes than less popular ones. Objects whose query rates are greater than average (i.e., greater than $\frac{1}{m}$) do better with Proportional replication, and the other objects do better with Uniform replication. Interestingly, the weighted average of the search sizes over all objects balances out to be unchanged.

Square-Root Replication Given that Uniform and Proportional have the same average search size, a natural question is what is the optimal way to allocate the replicas so that the average search size is minimized? A simple calculation (see [8]) reveals that Square-Root replication is optimal; that is, A is minimized when $r_i = \lambda\sqrt{q_i}$ where $\lambda = \frac{R}{\sum_i \sqrt{q_i}}$. The average search size is

$$A_{optimal} = \frac{1}{\rho}\left(\sum_i \sqrt{q_i}\right)^2$$

Table 6 lists properties of the three replication strategies. Square-Root replication is such that both average search size and utilization rate vary per object, but the variance in utilization is considerably smaller than with Uniform, and the variance in average search size is considerably smaller than with Proportional.

	Uniform	Proportional	Square-Root
A	$\rho^{-1}m$	$\rho^{-1}m$	$\rho^{-1}(\sum_i \sqrt{q_i})^2$
r_i	R/m	$q_i R$	$R\sqrt{q_i}/\sum_j \sqrt{q_j}$
$A_i = n/r_i$	$\rho^{-1}m$	$(\rho q_i)^{-1}$	$\rho^{-1}\sum_j \sqrt{q_j}/\sqrt{q_i}$
$U_i = Rq_i/r_i$	$q_i m$	1	$\sqrt{q_i}\sum_j \sqrt{q_j}$

Table 6: Comparing the three replication strategies

5.1 Truncated Pareto Distribution

Assuming $q_1 \geq q_2 \geq \cdots \geq q_m$, let $R_{m,\alpha}$ be a truncation to m objects of a Pareto distribution with shape parameter α. Thus, $q_i = i^{-\alpha-1}/B_{\alpha+1,m}$ $(i = 1,\ldots,m)$, where $B_{\alpha+1,m}$ is the normalization factor. With Square-Root replication we obtain $r_i/R = i^{(-\alpha-1)/2}/B_{(\alpha+1)/2,m}$, average search size

$$\rho A_{optimal} = (B_{(\alpha+1)/2,m})^2/B_{\alpha+1,m} \approx \begin{cases} 4\alpha m^{1-\alpha}/(1-\alpha)^2 & (\alpha < 1) \\ \ln^2 m & (\alpha = 1) \\ 4\alpha/(\alpha-1)^2 & (\alpha > 1) \end{cases}$$

We then compute *gain factor*, $A_{uniform}/A_{optimal}$, of using Square-Root rather than Uniform or Proportional replication. For Pareto distribution with $\alpha > 1$, the optimal average search size is *constant*. Thus, the gain factor is $\Theta(m)$. The gain factor is $\Theta(m^\alpha)$ for Pareto with $\alpha < 1$ and $\theta(m/\ln^2 m)$ for $\alpha = 1$.

Figure 5 helps visualize the different properties of the three replication strategies. Both Uniform and Square-Root allocate to popular objects less than their "fair share" and to less popular objects more than their "fair share" of replicas, but Square-Root does so to a lesser extent. The variance in average search sizes of different objects with Square-Root is considerably smaller than with Proportional. The maximum utilization rate with Square-Root, is much lower than with Uniform (although larger than Proportional which provides optimal load balancing).

5.2 Achieving Square-Root Replication

Assume that each query keeps track of the search size, each time a query is finished, the object is copied to a number of sites proportional to the number of probes. This means that on average the i'th object will be replicated $c\frac{n}{r_i}$ times each time a query is issued (where c is an arbitrary constant). Thus, the number of copies r_i can be roughly described by the differential equation $\dot{r_i} = q_i c\frac{n}{r_i}$, where $\dot{r_i}$ is the time derivative of r_i.

If we look at the ratio of two objects, ask how the logarithm of this quantity changes, we find that, setting $z_{i,j} = \ln\frac{r_i}{r_j}$, we have $\dot{z} = cn(\frac{q_j}{r_j^2} - \frac{q_i}{r_i^2})$. Thus, Square-Root replication, $r_i = \lambda\sqrt{q_i}$ is a fixed point of this equation. This heuristic calculation suggests that perhaps replicating proportional to the number of sites probed would yield Square-Root replication.

Our analysis above makes some implicit assumptions on the the *deletion of replicas*, that is, replicas disappear over time and new replicas are created. The steady state is achieved when the creation rate equals the deletion rate. To achieve this, the lifetimes of replicas must be *independent* of object identity or query rate. Examples of deletion processes that have this independence are: assigning fixed lifetimes (or lifetimes from a fixed distribution) for each replica, subject replicas at each site to First In First out (FIFO) replacement, or perform random deletions. Usage-based replacement policies such as Least Recently Used (LRU) or Least Frequently Used (LFU) *do not* have this independence property. These policies could *impede* the Square-Root scheme:

Note that unlike Freenet's replication algorithm, the replication strategies studied here do not attempt to cluster certain group of objects in certain regions of the network. In other words, they do not produce any correlation between routing and object locations, or, "structure," in the P2P network.

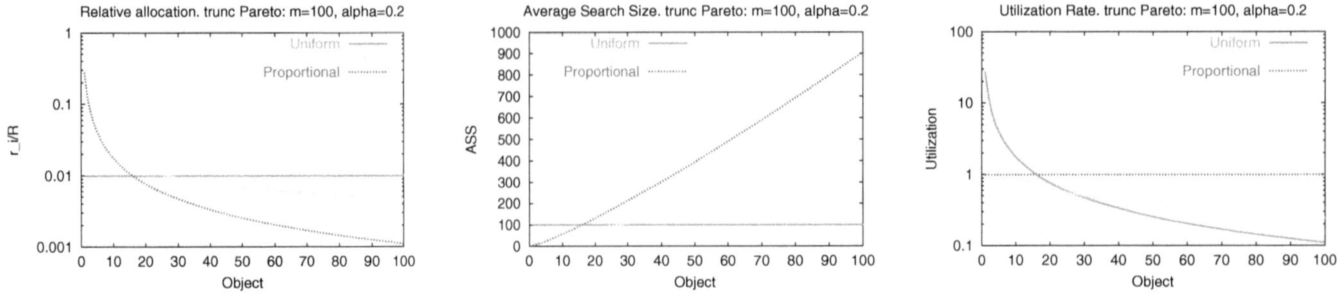

Relative allocation r_i/R — Average search size ρA_i — Utilization rate U_i

Figure 5: Uniform, Proportional, and Square-Root strategies on a truncated Pareto distribution

6. REPLICATION: EVALUATION

We observe that there are two replication strategies that are easily implementable. One is "owner replication", where, when a search is successful, the object is stored at the requester node only. The other is "path replication", where, when a search succeeds, the object is stored at all nodes along the path from the requester node to the provider node. Owner replication is used in systems such as Gnutella. Path replication is used in systems such as Freenet.

The analysis in the previous section suggests that square-root replication distribution is needed to minimize the overall search traffic, and an object should be replicated at the number of nodes that is proportional to the number of probes that the search required. If a P2P system uses the k-walker random walk as the search algorithm, then on average, the number of nodes between the requester node and the provider node is $1/k$ of the total nodes visited. Path replication in this system should result in square-root distribution.

However, path replication tends to replicate objects to nodes that are *topologically* along the same path. To understand how this impacts the overall search traffic, we also study a third replication algorithm, "random replication." In random replication, once a search succeeds, we count the number of nodes on the path between the requester and the provider, p, then randomly pick p of the nodes that the k walkers visited to replicate the object. "Random replication" is harder to implement, but the performance difference between it and path replication highlights the topological impact of path replication.

We design a set of dynamic simulations to study the performance of the three replication strategies in the Random graph network topology. A simulation starts by placing the m distinct objects randomly into the network. Then the *Query Generator* starts to generate queries according to a Poisson process with average generating rate at 5 queries per second. The query distribution among the m objects follows Zipf-like distribution with a given α value. The α value for the results presented here is 1.20. (We also ran simulations with $\alpha = 0.80$ and $\alpha = 2.40$. The results are similar.) For each query, a node (that doesn't have the requested object yet) is randomly chosen to start the query. For the search method, we use the 32-walker random walk with state keeping, with checking at every fourth step. Each node can store at most *objAllow* objects (40 in our simulations). The replacement policy is Random Deletion. "Snapshots" are taken for every 2,000-query chunks. To allow for enough "warming up" process, we run each simulation for

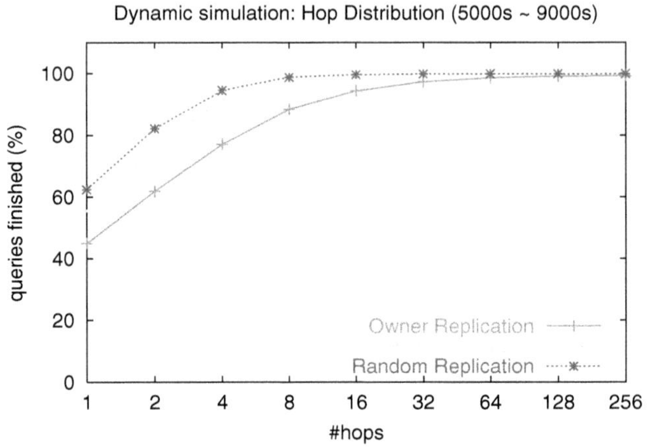

Figure 7: Cumulative distribution of the number of hops under the three replication strategies.

10,000 seconds, and look at the later part of the simulation. For each replication strategy, we examine:

- what kind of replication ratio distribution does the strategy generate?
- what is the average number of messages per node in a system using the strategy?
- what is the distribution of number of hops in a system using the strategy?

Figure 6 shows log-log plots of the distribution of replication ratios under path replication and random replication. We also plot the distribution that is the square root of the query distribution. Confirming our theoretical predictions, the results show clearly that both path replication and random replication generates replication ratios that are quite close to square-root of query ratios.

Table 7 lists the average number of messages a node has to process during the simulation. The result shows clearly the benefit of square-root distribution on reducing search traffic. Path replication and random replication reduces the overall message traffic by a factor of three to four. Hence, proactive replication such as path or random replication can improve the scalability of P2P systems significantly.

Much of the traffic reduction comes from reducing the number of hops it takes to find an object. Figure 7 shows

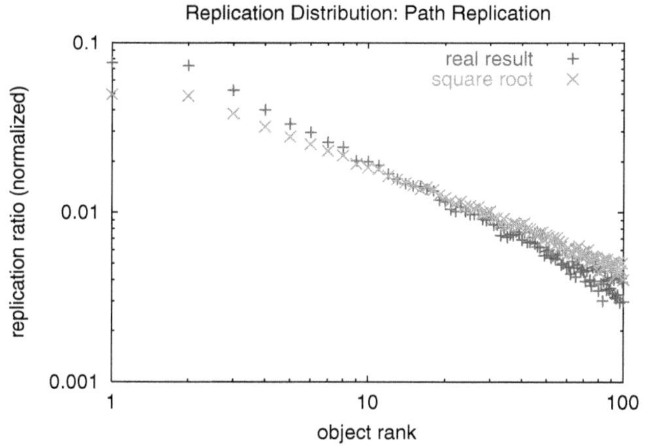

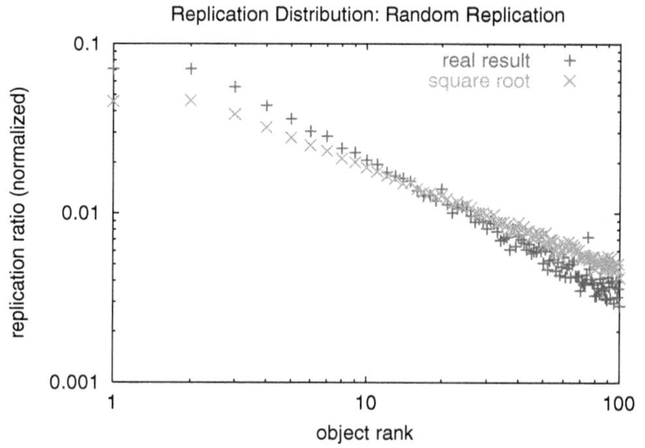

Figure 6: Distribution of replication ratios under Path replication and Random replication.

	Owner Replication	Path Replication	Random Replication
avg #msgs per node	56542.6	19155.5	14463.0
factor of improvement	1	2.95	3.91

Table 7: Message traffic of different replication strategies.

the cumulative hop distribution for all queries under the three replication strategies. Path replication and random replication clearly outperform the owner replication; for example, the percentage of queries that finish within four hops are 71% for owner replication, 86% for path replication and 91% for random replication.

The results also show that random replication improves upon the path replication. Thus, the topological effects of replicating along the path do hurt performance somewhat. Hence, if the implementation is not overly complex, a P2P system should adopt random replication instead of path replication.

7. RELATED WORK

As mentioned in the Introduction, there are several different kinds of P2P networks. The highly structured P2P networks, such as CAN [18], Chord [23], Past [20], and Tapestry [26], all use precise placement algorithms and specific routing protocols to make searching efficient. However these systems have not been widely deployed, and their ability to operate with extremely unreliable nodes has not yet been demonstrated. Moreover, they cannot deal with partial-match queries.

There are also many loosely structured P2P networks. Freenet [11], Free Haven [10], Mojo Nation [15] are but a few examples of this rapidly growing list. Many of them are storage systems that can protect the anonymity of both authors and readers. Some systems, such as Free Haven and Mojo Nation, focus on the trust, reputation management and security issues in Peer-to-Peer systems. Most of these loosely structured P2P networks use either directories or placement hints to improve the scalability of the search process. However, centralized directories don't scale well and placement hints don't handle partial-match queries.

An interesting paper by Adamic *et al.* [1] studies random-walk search strategies in power-law networks, and finds that by modifying walkers to seek out high degree nodes the search performance can be greatly increased. However, such strategies greatly reduce the scalability of the search algorithm, which is our focus and not the subject of [1], because then almost all queries are sent to the very high degree nodes, making them bear the burden of almost the entire query load of the network.

The random walk search style is used in Freenet as well. There, the walk is guided; each node uses hints to help it choose which node to forward the query to. It also uses only one "walker". [9] also studies ways to provide hints by building routing indices. In comparison, our focus is on unstructured network, where hints are not available.

Several search techniques for unstructured networks are discussed in [25]: iterative deepening, directed BFS and local indices. The first scheme is similar to the expanding ring scheme we examine here. Their work focuses on search techniques only and does not study replication strategies.

We found a wealth of information on Gnutella at web sites such as www.openP2P.com and gnutella.wego.com. We are also aware of a number of published research studies on the Gnutella network. For example, the freeloader phenomenon is examined in [2], and the topology and query distribution are studied in [21, 14]. However, none of these papers address the issue of better search algorithms or replication algorithms.

8. CONCLUSIONS AND FUTURE WORK

This paper reports our simulation and modeling studies of several search algorithms and replication strategies for decentralized, unstructured peer-to-peer networks.

From simulation studies, we have learned that scalable search algorithm designs for such networks should consider three properties: adaptive termination, minimizing message duplication, and small granularity of coverage. The flooding algorithm being used in Gnutella does not satisfy any of the properties. We show that it generates a lot of network traffic and does not scale well. The expanding ring approach improves the flooding algorithm by using an adaptive termination mechanism. It can find data reasonably quickly while reducing the network traffic substantially, sometimes by an order of magnitude. The k-walker random walk with checking approach can find data more quickly while reducing the traffic further by another order of magnitude, because it reduces the granularity of coverage by using a fixed number of random walkers.

We reviewed the calculations in [8] that show that, for a fixed average number of replicas per node, square-root replication distribution is theoretically optimal in terms of minimizing the overall search traffic. The simulations presented here demonstrate the effectiveness of the square-root replication policy and illustrated how it can be achieved in practice. We simulated owner, path and random replications, with the k-walker random walk with state keeping. Since path and random replications lead to square-root replication distribution, their overall message traffic is about four times less than the owner replication approach.

We have also learned from our simulation studies that uniformly random graphs are better for searching and data replication. The high degree nodes in power-law random graph and the current Gnutella network bear much higher load than average and introduce more duplication overhead in searches. The results imply that it is better to use P2P network building algorithms that form a uniformly random network topology.

This study is our first step towards understanding the properties of scalable search algorithms, replication strategies, and network topologies for decentralized, unstructured peer-to-peer networks. There are still many open issues to study. It would be useful to model various search algorithms with certain network topologies and study them analytically. The k-walker random walk with checking and state keeping has a lot of rooms to improve. Also, for the various replication strategies, we show that Square-Root replication minimizes the average search size, while Proportional replication achieves optimal load balance. It would be interesting to study the tradeoff between the two metrics, and see how the tradeoff can be achieved in a distributed system.

9. REFERENCES

[1] L. A. Adamic, R. M. Lukose, A. R. Puniyani, and B. A. Huberman. Search in power law networks. In *Phys. Rev. E64*, pages 46135–46143, 2001.

[2] E. Adar and B. A. Huberman. Free riding on gnutella. In *First Monday, http://www.firstmonday.dk/issues/issue5_10/adar/index.html*, Oct. 2000.

[3] W. Aiello, F. Chung, and L. Lu. A random graph model for massive graphs. In *Proceedings of STOC'00*, pages 171–180, 2000.

[4] V. Almeida, A. Bestavros, M. Crovella, and A. de Oliveira. Characterizing reference locality in the www. In *Proceedings of 1996 International Conference on parallel and Distributed Information Systems (PDIS '96)*, Dec. 1996.

[5] K. Calvert and E. W. Zegura. Gt-itm: Georgia tech internetwork topology models. In *http://www.cc.gatech.edu/projects/gtitm/*, 1997.

[6] Clip2.com. The gnutella protocol specification v0.4. In *http://www9.limewire.com/developer/gnutella_protocol_0.4.pdf*, 2000.

[7] Clip2.com. Gnutella: To the bandwidth barrier and beyond. In *http://www.clip2.com/gnutella.html*, 2000.

[8] E. Cohen and S. Shenker. Replication strategies in unstructured peer-to-peer networks. In *Proceedings of ACM SIGCOMM'02*, Aug. 2002.

[9] A. Crespo and H. Garcia-Molina. Routing indices for peer-to-peer systems. In *Proceedings of the 22nd IEEE International Conference on Distributed Computing Systems (ICDCS)*, July 2002.

[10] *Free Haven website.* http://www.freehaven.net.

[11] *Freenet website.* http://freenet.sourceforge.net.

[12] D. Gallagher and R. Wilkerson. Network performance statistics for university of south carolina. In *http://eddie.csd.sc.edu*, Oct. 2001.

[13] *Gnutella website.* http://gnutella.wego.com.

[14] M. A. Jovanovic, F. S. Annexstein, and K. A. Berman. Scalability issues in large peer-to-peer networks - a case study of gnutella. Technical Report http://www.ececs.uc.edu/~mjovanov/Research/paper.html, University of Cincinnati, 2001.

[15] *Mojo Nation*, 2001. http://www.mojonation.net.

[16] *Napster website.* http://www.napster.com.

[17] D. Plonka. Uw-madison napster traffic measurement. In *http://net.doit.wisc.edu/data/Napster*, Mar. 2000.

[18] S. Ratnasamy, P. Francis, M. Handley, R. Karp, and S. Shenker. A scalable content-addressable network. In *Proceedings of ACM SIGCOMM'01*, Aug. 2001.

[19] J. Ritter. Why gnutella can't scale. no, really. In *http://www.darkridge.com/~jpr5/doc/ gnutella.html*, 2001.

[20] A. Rowstron and P. Druschel. Storage management and caching in past, a large-scale, persistent peer-to-peer storage utility. In *Proceedings of SOSP'01*, 2001.

[21] K. Sripanidkulchai. The popularity of gnutella queries and its implications on scalability. In *O'Reilly's www.openp2p.com*, Feb. 2001.

[22] S. D. G. Stefan Saroiu, P. Krishna Gummadi. A measurement study of peer-to-peer file sharing systems. Technical Report UW-CSE-01-06-02, Department of Computer Science & Engineering, University of Washington, 2002.

[23] I. Stoica, R. Morris, D. Karger, F. Kaashoek, and H. Balakrishnan. Chord: A scalable peer-to-peer lookup service for internet applications. In *Proceedings of ACM SIGCOMM'01*, Aug. 2001.

[24] K. Truelove. Gnutella: Alive, well, and changing fast. In *http://www.openp2p.com/pub/a/p2p/2001/01/25/truelove0101.html*, Jan. 2001.

[25] B. Yang and H. Garcia-Molina. Efficient search in peer-to-peer networks. In *Proceedings of the 22nd IEEE International Conference on Distributed Computing Systems (ICDCS)*, July 2002.

[26] B. Y. Zhao, J. Kubiatowicz, and A. Joseph. Tapestry: An infrastructure for fault-tolerant wide-area location and routing. Technical Report UCB/CSD-01-1141, University of California at Berkeley, Computer Science Department, 2001.

Bloom Filtering Cache Misses for Accurate Data Speculation and Prefetching

Jih-Kwon Peir
CISE Department
University of Florida
peir@cise.ufl.edu

Shih-Chang Lai
ECE Department
Oregon State University
laish@ece.orst.edu

Shih-Lien Lu
Jared Stark
Konrad Lai
Microprocessor Research
Intel Labs
shih-lien.l.lu@intel.com

ABSTRACT

A processor must know a load instruction's latency to schedule the load's dependent instructions at the correct time. Unfortunately, modern processors do not know this latency until well after the dependent instructions should have been scheduled to avoid pipeline bubbles between themselves and the load. One solution to this problem is to predict the load's latency, by predicting whether the load will hit or miss in the data cache. Existing cache hit/miss predictors, however, can only correctly predict about 50% of cache misses.

This paper introduces a new hit/miss predictor that uses a Bloom Filter to identify cache misses early in the pipeline. This early identification of cache misses allows the processor to more accurately schedule instructions that are dependent on loads and to more precisely prefetch data into the cache. Simulations using a modified SimpleScalar model show that the proposed Bloom Filter is nearly perfect, with a prediction accuracy greater than 99% for the SPECint2000 benchmarks. IPC (Instructions Per Cycle) performance improved by 19% over a processor that delayed the scheduling of instructions dependent on a load until the load latency was known, and by 6% and 7% over a processor that always predicted a load would hit the cache and with a counter-based hit/miss predictor respectively. This IPC reaches 99.7% of the IPC of a processor with perfect scheduling.

Categories and Subject Descriptors

C.1.1 [**Processor Architectures**]: Single Data Stream Architectures

General Terms

Algorithm, Design, Performance

Keywords

Bloom Filter, Data Cache, Data Prefetching, Instruction Scheduling, Data Speculation

1. INTRODUCTION

To achieve the highest performance, a processor must execute a pair of dependent instructions with no intervening pipeline bubbles. It must arrange for—or schedule—the dependent instruction to begin execution immediately after the instruction it depends on (i. e., the parent instruction) completes execution. Accomplishing this requires knowing the latency of the parent.

Unfortunately, a modern processor schedules an instruction well before it executes, and the latency of some instructions can only be determined by their execution. For example, the latency of a load depends on where in the cache/memory hierarchy its data exists, and can only be determined by executing the load and querying the caches. At the time the load is scheduled, its latency is unknown. At the time its *dependents* should be scheduled, its latency may *still* be unknown. Hence, the timely scheduling of the instructions that are dependent on a load is a problem in modern processors.

The Intel Pentium 4 illustrates this problem. On an Intel Pentium 4 [6, 7], a load is scheduled 7 cycles before it begins execution. Its execution (load-use) latency is 2 cycles. At the time a load is scheduled, its execution will not begin for another 7 cycles. Two cycles after the load is scheduled, if the load will hit the (first-level) cache, its dependent instructions must be scheduled to avoid pipeline bubbles. However, two cycles after the load is scheduled, the load has not yet even started executing, so its cache hit/miss status is unknown. A similar situation exists in the Compaq Alpha 21264 [9]. A load is scheduled 2 cycles before it begins execution, and its execution latency is 3 cycles. If the load will hit the (first-level) cache, its dependents must be scheduled 3 cycles after it has been scheduled to avoid pipeline bubbles. However, the load's cache hit/miss status is still unknown 3 cycles after it has been scheduled.

One possible solution to this problem is to schedule the dependents of a load only after the latency of the load is known. The processor delays the scheduling of the dependents until it knows the load hit the cache. This effectively increases the load's latency to the amount of time between when the load is scheduled and when its cache hit/miss status is known. This solution introduces bubbles into the pipeline, and can devastate processor performance. Our simulations show that a processor using this solution drops 17% of its performance (in Instructions Per Cycle [IPC]) compared to an ideal processor that uses an oracle to perfectly predict load latencies and perfectly schedule their dependents.

A better solution—and the solution that is the focus of this work—is to use *data speculation*. The processor speculates that a load will hit the cache (a good assumption given cache hits rates are generally over 90%), and schedules its dependents accordingly. If the load hits, all is well. If the load misses, any dependents that have been scheduled will not receive the load's result before they begin execution. All these instructions have been erroneously scheduled, and will need to be rescheduled.

Recovery must occur whenever instructions are erroneously scheduled due to data (mis)speculation. Although mis-speculation is rare, the overall penalty for all mis-speculations may be high, as the cost of each recovery can be high. If the processor only rescheduled those instructions that are (directly or indirectly) dependent on the load, the cost would be low. However, such a recovery mechanism is expensive to implement. The recovery mechanism for the Compaq Alpha 21264 simply reschedules all instructions scheduled since the offending load was scheduled, whether they are dependent or not. Although it's cheaper to implement, the recovery cost can be high with this mechanism due to the rescheduling and re-execution of the independent instructions. Regardless of which recovery mechanism is implemented, as processor pipelines grow deeper and issue widths widen, the number of erroneously scheduled instructions will increase, and recovery costs will climb.

To reduce the penalty due to data mis-speculations, the processor can predict whether the load will hit the cache, instead of just speculating that the load will always hit. The load's dependents are then scheduled according to the prediction. As an example of a cache hit/miss predictor, the Compaq Alpha 21264 uses the most significant bit of a 4-bit saturating counter as the load's hit/miss prediction. The counter is incremented by one every time a load hits, and decremented by two every time a load misses. Unfortunately, even with 2-level predictors [15], only about 50% of the cache misses can be correctly predicted.

In this paper, we describe a new approach to hit/miss prediction that is very accurate and space (and hence power) efficient compared to existing approaches. This approach uses a *Bloom Filter (BF)*, which is a probabilistic algorithm to quickly test membership in a large set using hash functions into an array of bits [2]. We investigate two variants of this approach: the first is based on *partitioned-address* matching, and the second is based on *partial-address* matching. Experimental results show that, for modest-sized predictors, Bloom Filters outperform predictors that used a table of saturating counters indexed by load PC. These *table-based* predictors operate just like the predictor for the Compaq Alpha 21264, except they have multiple counters instead of just one. As an example, for an 8K-bit predictor, the Bloom Filter mispredicts 0.4% of all loads, whereas the table-based predictor mispredicts 8% of all loads. This translates to an 7% improvement in IPC over the table-based predictor. Compared to a machine with a perfect predictor, a machine with a Bloom Filters has 99.7% of its IPC.

The remainder of the paper is organized as follows: The next section explains data speculation fundamentals and related work. Section 3 explains BFs and how they can be used as hit/miss predictors. Section 4 describes how the SimpleScalar microarchitecture [3] must be modified to support data speculation using a BF as a hit/miss predictor. Section 5 evaluates the performance of BFs, reporting their accuracy as hit/miss predictors and the performance benefit (in IPC) they can provide. Finally, Section 6 concludes.

2. DATA SPECULATION

2.1 The Fundamentals

To facilitate the presentation and discussion, we consider a baseline pipeline model that is similar to the Compaq Alpha 21264 [9]. In the baseline model, the front-end pipeline stages are: instruction fetch and decode/rename. After decode/rename, the ALU instructions go through the back-end stages: schedule, register read, execute, writeback, and commit. Additional stages are required for executing a load. After decode/rename, loads go through schedule, register read, address generation, two cache access cycles, an additional cycle for hit/miss determination (data access before hit/miss using way prediction [4]), writeback, and commit. Thus, there are a total of 7 and 10 cycles for ALU and load instructions, respectively.

Figure 1 shows the problem in scheduling the instructions that are dependent on a load. For simplicity, the front-end stages are omitted. In this example, the *add* instruction consumes the data produced by the *load* instruction. After the *load* is scheduled, it takes 5 cycles to resolve the hit/miss. However, the dependent *add* must be scheduled the third cycle after the load is scheduled to achieve the minimum 3-cycle load-use latency and allow back-to-back execution of these two dependent instructions. If the processor speculatively schedules the *add* assuming the *load* will hit the cache, the *add* will get incorrect data if *load* actually misses the cache. In this case, the *add* along with any other dependent instructions scheduled within the illustrated 3-cycle speculative window must be canceled and rescheduled.

To show the performance potential of using data speculation for scheduling instructions that are dependent on loads, we simulated the SPECint2000 benchmarks. We compare two scheduling techniques. The first is a *no-speculation* scheme: the dependents are delayed until the hit/miss of the parent load is known. The second uses a *perfect* hit/miss predictor that knows the hit/miss of a load in time to (perfectly) schedule its dependents to achieve minimum load latency. The performance gap (in IPC) between these two extremes shows the performance potential of speculatively scheduling the dependents of loads. Figure 2 shows the results. In these simulations, we modified the SimpleScalar out-of-order pipeline to match our baseline model; and doubled the default SimpleScalar issue width to 8, scaling the other parameters accordingly. A more detailed description of the simulation model is given in Section 5. On average, the IPC for perfect scheduling is 17% higher than the IPC for the no-speculation scheme. Thus, the main focus of this paper is to recover this 17% performance gap, by using mechanisms for efficient load data speculation.

2.2 Related Work

The Compaq Alpha 21264 uses a mini-restart mechanism to cancel and reschedule all instructions scheduled since a mis-speculated load was scheduled [9]. While this mini-restart is less costly than restarting the entire processor pipeline, it is still expensive to reschedule (and re-execute) both the dependent and the independent instructions. To alleviate this problem, the Compaq Alpha 21264 uses the

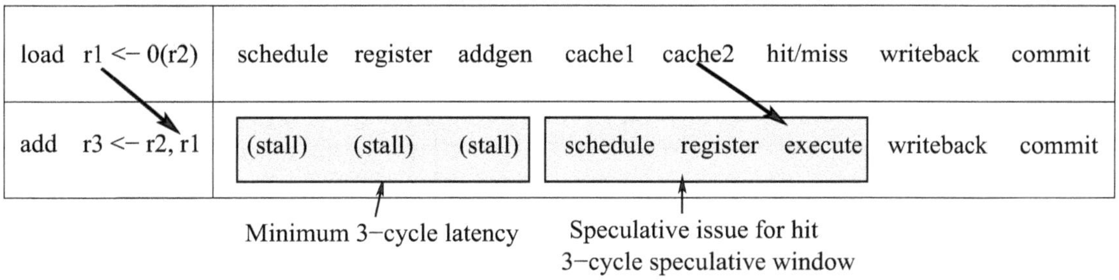

Figure 1: Example of Data Speculation for a Load

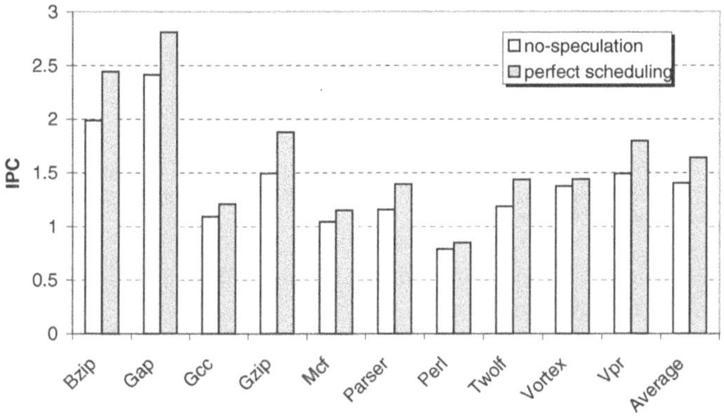

Figure 2: No-Speculation vs. Perfect Scheduling

most significant bit of a 4-bit saturating counter as the load's hit/miss prediction. The counter is incremented by one every time a load hits, and decremented by two every time a load misses. The load's dependents are scheduled according to the prediction. If the prediction is wrong, either the load was predicted to miss and it hit, in which case the execution of the dependents will be unnecessarily delayed; or the load was predicted to hit and it missed, in which case dependents may have been erroneously scheduled and will need to be rescheduled.

Yoaz et al. [15] used 2-level local predictors, 2-level global predictors, and hybrid predictors for cache hit/miss prediction. Their results show that these predictors only correctly identify half of the misses (for SPECint95), leaving the other half predicted as hits. Furthermore, they incorrectly identify a small percentage of the hits as being misses.

The MIPS R10000 speculatively issues instructions that are dependent on a load and reschedules them if the load misses the cache [14].

The Intel Pentium 4 achieves a minimum 2-cycle load-use latency by leveraging the fact that most accesses hit the first-level (L_1) cache. The scheduler issues the dependent micro-operations (called *uops*) before the parent load has finished executing [6, 7]. In most cases, the scheduler assumes the load will hit the L_1 cache. A '*replay*' mechanism is used to handle the case where the load misses the L_1 cache. The replay logic keeps track of the dependent *uops* of each speculative load. When a load misses, all its dependent *uops* are re-executed with the correct data when that data becomes available.

Morancho, Llabería, and Olivé describe a recovery mechanism for load latency misprediction [11]. A recovery buffer retains all speculatively scheduled instructions. After a latency misprediction, the load's dependent instructions can be re-scheduled directly from the recovery buffer as soon as the load data becomes available. The recovery buffer allows the processor to remove instruction from the scheduler early, providing more space for other instructions.

3. BLOOM FILTERS

A *Bloom Filter (BF)* is a probabilistic algorithm to quickly test membership in a large set using multiple hash functions into an array of bits [2]. A BF quickly filters (i. e., identifies) non-members without querying the large set by exploiting the fact that a small percentage of erroneous classifications can be tolerated. When a BF identifies a non-member, it is *guaranteed* to not belong to the large set. When a BF identifies a member, however, it is *not guaranteed* to belong to the large set. To put it more simply, the result of the membership test is either: it is definitely not a member, or, it is probably a member. In this paper, we consider two variants of the BF for filtering cache misses: one based on *partitioned-address* matching, and the other based on *partial-address* matching. To simplify our discussion, we first assume both the BF and the cache use physical addresses. Afterwards, we will describe using virtual addresses.

3.1 Partitioned-Address Bloom Filter

Consider a cache line address with n bits (ignoring the offset bits). A large, direct-mapped array of 2^n bits is required to precisely record whether each cache line address is in the cache. To reduce the space and allow a quick access, a *partitioned-address* BF can be constructed. Instead of using the entire line address, the address can be split into m partitions, with each partition using its own array of bits. The result is m sub-arrays with $2^{n/m}$ bits, each of which records the membership of the respective address partitions of lines stored in the cache. A cache miss is identified when one or more of the address partitions for the address of a requested line does not belong to the respective address partition of any line in the cache. A *filter error* is encountered when a cache miss cannot be identified. This situation happens when the line is not in the cache, but all m partitions of the line's address match address partitions of other cache lines. The *filter rate* represents the percentage of cache misses that can be identified.

Figure 3 illustrates how the *partitioned-address* BF works. A load address is partitioned, in this example, into 4 equally divided groups, *A1, A2, A3*, and *A4*. Each of the four address partitions is used to index separate BF arrays, *BF1, BF2, BF3*, and *BF4*, respectively. Each entry in the BF

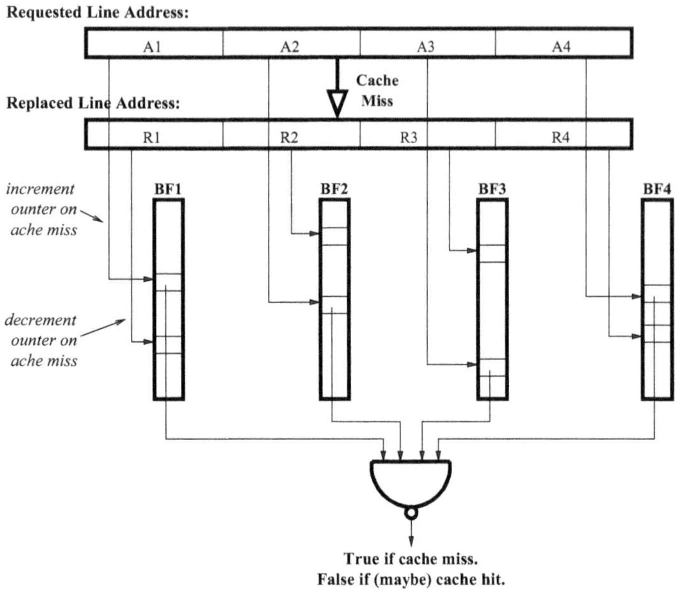

Figure 3: Partitioned-Address Bloom Filter for Cache Miss Detection

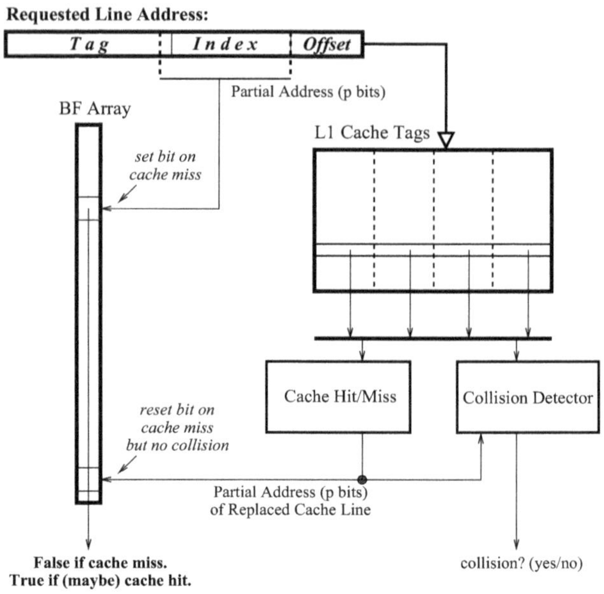

Figure 4: Partial-Address Bloom Filter for Cache Miss Detection

arrays contains the information of whether the address partition belongs to the corresponding address partition of any line in the cache. If any of the 4 BF arrays indicates one of the address partitions is absent from the cache, the requested line is not in the cache. Otherwise, the requested line is probably in the cache, but it's not guaranteed to be.

Given the fact that a single address partition can exist for multiple lines in the cache, the primary difficulty of the *partitioned-address* BF is to maintain the correct membership information. When a line is removed from the cache, an exhaustive search is necessary to check if the address partitions for the address of the removed line still exist for any of the remaining lines. To avoid such a search, each entry in the BF array contains a reference counter that keeps track of the number of cache lines with the entry's corresponding address partition. When a cache miss occurs, each counter for the address partitions for the address of the newly-requested line is incremented, while the counters for the address partitions for the address of the replaced line are decremented. A zero count indicates the corresponding address partition does not belong to any line in the cache. Although accurate, this counter technique requires extra space in the BF arrays for the counters along with adders to handle the updates. A similar idea has been considered to reduce the number of comparators for a set-associative cache [8] and to filter cache-coherence traffic in a multiprocessor environment [12].

3.2 Partial-Address Bloom Filter

The *partial-address* BF uses the least-significant bits of the line address to index a small array of bits. Each bit indicates whether the partial address matches any corresponding partial address of a line in the cache. The array size is reduced to 2^p bits, where p is the number of partial address bits. A *filter error* occurs when the partial address of the requested line matches the partial address of an existing cache line, but the other portion of the line address does not match. We call such cases *collisions*. The least-significant bits are selected rather than more-significant bits to reduce the chance of collisions. Due to memory reference locality, the more-significant line address bits tend to change less frequently. With a sufficient number of low-order partial address bits to represent cache line addresses, collisions are rare [10].

The design of a *partial-address* BF is illustrated in Figure 4. A *BF array* with 2^p bits indicates whether the corresponding partial address matches that of any cache line. The BF array is updated to reflect any cache content change. When a cache miss occurs, except for the caveat described in the paragraph below, the entry in the BF array for the replaced line is *reset* to indicate that the line with that partial address is no longer in the cache. Then, the entry for the requested line is *set* to indicate that a line with that partial address now exists in the cache.

If the partial address is wider than the cache index, when two cache lines share the same partial address, they must be in the same set in a set-associative cache. The BF array indicates which partial addresses exist in the cache, so if one of these lines is replaced, the BF entry for the replaced line should *not* be reset, since the partial address still exists for the line that was not replaced. When a cache line is replaced, the *collision detector* checks the remaining cache lines in the same set as the replaced line to see if any of them have the same partial address as the replaced line. If any do have the same partial address, the BF entry is not reset. Otherwise, the entry is reset. The collision detection is done in parallel with the cache hit/miss detection. The BF array is updated on the detection of a cache miss.

3.3 Bloom Filters using Virtual Addresses

The hit/miss prediction for a load must be done before the scheduling of its dependents. If the physical address is not available in time to perform the prediction, the virtual address must be used. When a virtual address is used to access a BF, it is called a *virtual-address BF*. If the cache is virtually indexed and tagged, the virtual-address BF op-

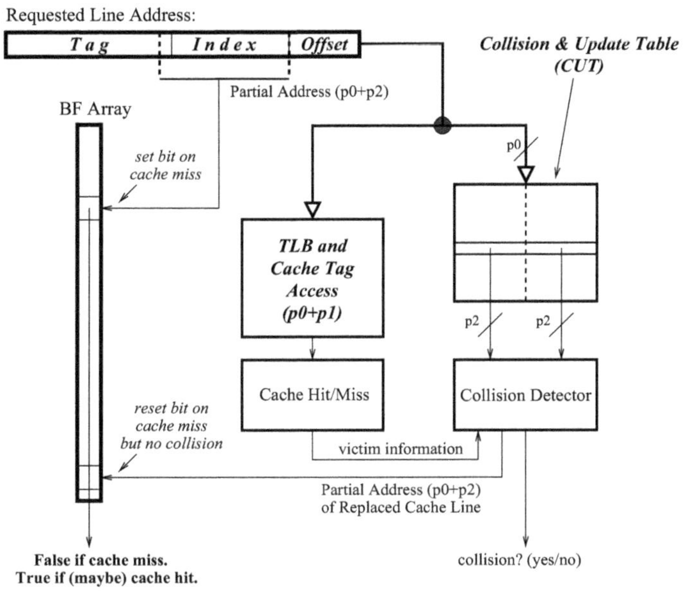

Figure 5: Partial-Virtual-Address Bloom Filter for Cache Miss Detection

erates analogously to the BF and cache that both use only physical addresses. However, if the cache is either virtually-indexed physically-tagged or physically-indexed physically-tagged, the BF array update for the virtual-address BF must be modified. In this section, we describe these modifications.

With virtual addresses, two virtual addresses can map to the same physical address, causing an *address synonym*. With a virtual-address BF, the BF might identify the first address as missing the cache, even though the line is in the cache set identified by the second address. That is, the BF identifies a load as missing the cache even though it hits. This situation can arise regardless of whether the cache is physically or virtually indexed. In this situation, the processor simply delays scheduling the load's dependent instructions. Since cache hits by synonyms are rare, the performance loss caused by the delayed scheduling is minimal. In fact, for some virtually-indexed caches, the load-use latency for a synonym hit is longer than for a non-synonym hit. For scheduling, the processor may initially treat the synonym hit as a cache miss, in which case the BF should identify the synonym hit as a cache miss anyway.

A more essential issue is correctly updating the BF array on cache misses. Let's first focus on the *partial-address* BF shown in Figure 5. To simplify our discussion, assume the cache is physically indexed and tagged with p_0+p_1 index bits, where p_0 bits are within the page offset and p_1 bits are beyond the offset. During a cache access, p_1 bits are translated. Also assume p_0+p_2 partial virtual address bits are used to access the BF, where p_2 bits are beyond the page offset. To correctly update the BF array, the p_2 bits of each cache line are stored in a *Collision and Update Table (CUT)*. When a line is replaced, its p_2 bits are read from the CUT. These p_2 bits are then combined with the requested line's p_0 bits to update the BF array.

The CUT is organized as a two-dimensional array and indexed by the p_0 bits. During each cache access, the set of p_2 bits indexed by p_0 are read from the CUT. If a cache miss is detected, the p_2 bits of the victim (e. g., LRU) line in the accessed cache set are compared to the p_2 bits for the other lines in that CUT set. If the victim's p_2 bits don't match any other line's p_2 bits, there is no collision, and the victim's p_2 bits are used along with the p_0 bits to reset the BF array to indicate that the line with the p_0+p_2 partial address is no longer in the cache. If the victim's p_2 bits do match another line's p_2 bits, the victim and the other line share the same partial address, and there is a collision. In this case, the BF entry for the victim line is left alone. Then, the BF entry for the requested line is set using the partial virtual address of the requested line. Note that when the cache is virtually-indexed physically-tagged, all the cache index bits are used to access the CUT. In this case, only the partial address bits beyond the virtual cache index bits need to be saved in the CUT and compared for collision detection.

Handling a virtual *partitioned-address* BF is straightforward. Virtual address tags must be stored in the cache tag array along with the physical tags. When a line is replaced, the replaced line's virtual address tag is used to update the counter in each partitioned BF.

For the remainder of the paper, we will assume virtual-address BFs. The virtual address needed to access the BF is available after the address generation cycle. Due to its rarity, we will omit discussions of synonym hits. If fact, for our benchmarks there are no synonyms.

4. THE MICROARCHITECTURE

In our baseline model, ALU instructions require a minimum of 7 cycles: instruction fetch (IFE), decode/rename (DEC), schedule (SCH), register read (REG), execute (EXE), writeback (WRB), and commit (CMT). Loads extend the execute stage to 4 cycles: address generation (AGN), two cache access cycles (CA1, CA2), and hit/miss determination (H/M). Assuming a load hits the L_1 cache, there is a 3-cycle speculative window in which the load's dependents and their children are scheduled. When a miss occurs, all of the dependent instructions and their children scheduled in these 3 cycles must be canceled and re-executed using the correct data when it becomes available.

4.1 Predictor Timing and Mini-Restart

If data cache misses can be predicted early enough and accurately enough, the processor's scheduler can avoid inserting pipeline bubbles between a load and its dependent instructions. To be effective, the load's cache hit/miss prediction must be done before its dependents must be scheduled. Thus, there are two basic issues: (1) when, and (2) how fast the hit/miss prediction can be performed. Hit/miss predictors that use saturating counters, like the one used by the Compaq Alpha 21264, can access the counter at the beginning of the pipeline. Since our pipeline has a minimum 3-cycle load latency, the prediction is available before any of the load's dependents need to be scheduled. If a miss is predicted, the dependents are blocked from scheduling until either the data comes back from the outer levels of the memory hierarchy or the prediction is found to be incorrect.

The proposed Bloom Filter approach, on the other hand, requires the load address to accurately identify (filter) misses. This filtering can only be performed after the load address is calculated in the address generation cycle. As shown in Figure 1, the load's dependent instructions must be scheduled the cycle after the load's address generation to avoid pipeline bubbles. By using a small BF, cache misses can be filtered in the cycle after the address generation, which is two cycles before the hit/miss determination. However, it is still one cycle too late to prevent the dependent instructions from scheduling.

To reap the prediction accuracy benefit provided by the BF, the load's dependents are always aggressively scheduled assuming a cache hit. At the end of the cycle the dependents are scheduled, the parent load has finished accessing the BF. If a miss is identified, the dependents are canceled and recovered in the next cycle. Since there is only a single-cycle speculative window, a precise recovery of the load's dependents may be feasible without excessive hardware complexity. This could be achieved by preventing the load's scheduled dependents from broadcasting their tags to their dependents, inhibiting the wakeup of their dependents. All independent instructions scheduled during this single-cycle window would be allowed to continue.

The Compaq Alpha 21264 has a similar precise recovery scheme to handle the dependents of floating-point loads. It also has a 3-cycle minimum load-use latency (1 for address generation and 2 for cache access). The cache hit/miss detection is done in the second cache access cycle, so the speculative window is only 2 cycles. The dependents of floating-point loads are always delayed from scheduling by one cycle. Consequently, the two-cycle speculative window for integer loads is reduced to a one-cycle window for floating-point loads. When the dependents of a floating-point load are being scheduled, the hit/miss detection is being performed in the same cycle. If a miss is detected, the dependents in this one-cycle window are precisely recovered in the next cycle [1]. This recovery should incur minimum penalty, as these dependents have to wait for the load data to return from the outer levels of the memory hierarchy anyway. The only potential adverse impact is that these dependents unnecessarily occupy functional units.

If a load is predicted to hit the cache, and it is later identified by the normal cache access as a miss, all dependent instructions scheduled during the entire 3-cycle speculative window have been or will be incorrectly executed. It is not sufficient to only re-schedule those instructions that directly depend on the load. Descendants of those dependent instructions may have been scheduled, and also need to be canceled and re-scheduled. A simple and workable scheme is to squash all instructions scheduled during the 3-cycle speculative window, as is done by the Compaq Alpha 21264. This simple recovery scheme reduces the hardware complexity needed to track all the dependencies and speculative states. However, both dependent and independent instructions scheduled in this 3-cycle window are canceled and re-scheduled. Independent instructions are rescheduled the cycle after the misprediction is detected. Dependent instructions are rescheduled according to the correct completion time of the load, which in most cases is determined by the level 2 cache access time.

Figure 6 illustrates the recovery mechanism for data misspeculation. Again, the first two pipeline stages are omitted to simplify the figure. When the BF identifies a load as missing the cache, only those dependent instructions scheduled in the same cycle are canceled. The cancellation does not affect any independent instructions scheduled in this cycle, as shown in Part (a) of the figure. When a miss cannot be correctly filtered by the BF, and the miss is detected during

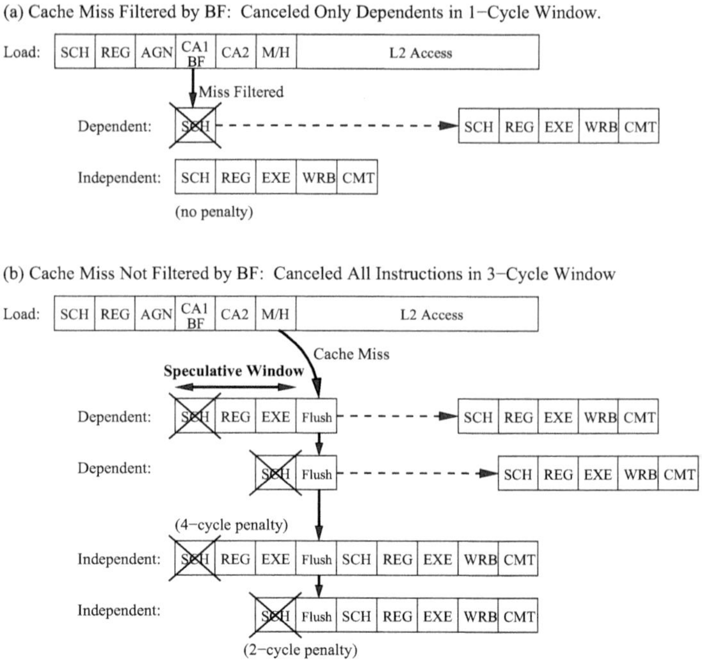

Figure 6: Recovery and Re-execution for: (a) Cache Miss Filtered by BF, and (b) Cache Miss Not Filtered by BF

the regular cache access, all of the instructions that were scheduled during the 3-cycle speculative window are canceled. Cancellation and re-execution involves resetting the canceled instructions' processor state. We assume it takes a separate *flush* cycle before the canceled instructions can be re-scheduled. Although independent instructions can be rescheduled right away, they encounter a minimum 2–4 cycle penalty depending on where they reside in the speculative window. For example, a 4-cycle penalty occurs for those instructions that were scheduled in the first of the three speculative cycles as marked in Part (b) of the figure. Other factors such as data and resource dependencies may further increase the number of penalty cycles.

4.2 Prefetching and Memory Dependencies

Compared with other cache hit/miss predictors, the BF is unique in that misses that are identified must not exist in the L_1 cache. Therefore, once a miss is identified, it is safe to issue a miss request to the second-level cache (L_2). In our pipeline model, this effectively reduces the L_2 cache and memory latencies by two cycles. Although other predictors also allow early L_2 cache access, they may incorrectly identify some L_1 cache hits as being misses, introducing extra penalties and complexity into the processor.

In our simulator, a Load-Store Queue (LSQ) is used to detect and enforce memory dependencies. It also allows loads to fetch data directly from an aliasing store in the LSQ without accessing the cache. The memory dependence is detected after the address of the load is generated (AGN). The load is forced to wait if the address of any potentially aliasing store in the LSQ is unknown. In our processor model, we assume this memory dependence detection is done early and accurately in the pipeline, which we model with a perfect memory dependence predictor. This allows the scheduling

Fetch/Decode/Issue Width	8
Branch Predictor	8K-entry 4-way BTB 16-bit Gshare
RUU/LSQ Size	64
L_1 Inst/Data	16KB 4-way
L_2 Cache	4MB 8-way
Access Latency: L_1/L_2/Mem	2/7/100
Memory Ports	4
Integer Add/Mult ALU	4/2
Floating-P Add/Mult ALU	4/2

Table 1: Simulation parameters

Prediction Method	Array Size (in bits)
Partition-3	15360
Partition-4	4480
Partial-1x	512
Partial-4x	2048
Partial-16x	8192
Partial-64x	32768
Always-hit	0
Counter-1	4
Counter-128	512
Counter-512	2048
Counter-2048	8192
Counter-8192	32768

Table 2: Cache hit/miss predictors and their required storage

of the cache access to be inhibited if the load depends on a store in the LSQ. For the SPECint2000 benchmarks we tested, half of them have a very low percentage (1–3%) of loads which fetch data from the LSQ. However, the other half have higher percentages, indicating the importance of knowing memory dependencies before scheduling a cache access. If memory dependence detection can not be done early enough to avoid pipeline bubbles, cache accesses can be speculatively scheduled before memory dependencies are known. The speculative cache access—and any instructions dependent on the load that were scheduled/executed—are canceled and potentially re-scheduled and re-executed if a memory dependence is later detected. The BF may also be used in conjunction with a memory dependence predictor [5] to provide more accurate scheduling of loads and their dependents. Further discussion in this direction is out of the scope of this paper.

5. PERFORMANCE EVALUATION

To evaluate the potential performance benefit of using a BF as a cache hit/miss predictor, we modified SimpleScalar to support BFs and other hit/miss predictors, and then ran most of the SPECint2000 benchmarks through the simulator. Our evaluation will compare the proposed BF technique to the other hit/miss predictors. Our simulated machine is a general-purpose out-of-order processor capable of issuing 8 instructions per cycle. The branch predictor consists of an 8K entry 4-way set-associative BTB and a 16-bit Gshare predictor. As described in Section 4, the pipeline is a minimum of 7 stages for ALU instructions and 10 stages for loads. A small 64-entry reorder buffer (called the RUU in SimpleScalar) was used for our studies as a larger instruction window may affect the cycle time. We modeled a detailed memory hierarchy, with the size and latency at each level reflecting current trends. We slightly modified the original SimpleScalar L_1 cache: instead of updating the cache tag array when a miss is detected, the tag array is updated when the missed data comes back from the outer levels of the memory hierarchy. This modification more accurately simulates cache misses, since the LRU line is not removed until the new data comes in.

Table 1 summarizes the simulation parameters. We simulated 10 of the SPECint2000 benchmarks using the reference input file. For each benchmark, we skip the first 500 million instructions and collect result statistics on the next 500 million instructions. We collect both prediction accuracy and IPC for the BFs and other cache hit/miss predictors.

We simulated different sizes of the two BF variants. For the *partitioned-address* BF, we simulated three (*Partition-3*) and four (*Partition-4*) equal partitions of the line address (27 bits). Each entry in the BF array maintains a counter capable of counting the entire number of L_1 cache lines. To avoid overflow in our simulations, each counter was 10 bits. For the *partial-address* BF, the BF array size ranges from having only one entry per L_1 cache line (*Partial-1x*) all the way up to having 64 entries per L_1 cache line (*Partial-64x*). In our baseline model, the L_1 data cache is 16KB with a 32-byte line size. We also perform sensitivity studies on cache size.

We also evaluate two previously proposed hit/miss predictors and some simple extensions to them. The first is to always predict cache hit (*Always-hit*). This method does not require any prediction table. The second is the predictor in the Compaq Alpha 21264, which uses a single 4-bit saturating counter (*Counter-1*). We also evaluate using an untagged table of 4-bit saturating counters, indexed by the PC of the load. We vary the size of the table from 128 counters (*Counter-128*) to 8192 counters (*Counter-8192*). Since each counter is 4 bits, the total size of the *Counter-128* predictor matches the size of the *Partial-1x* predictor. For the counter-based predictors, the prediction is performed in the instruction fetch cycle, and the counters are updated after the cache hit/miss status is known. Table 2 summarizes the predictors we simulated and the amount of storage they require. Note that besides the predictor array tables, other logic such as adders and comparators are required to perform predictions.

5.1 Prediction Accuracy

Figure 7 plots the filtering rates of the BFs. Recall the filtering rate is the percentage of misses identified (filtered) by the BF. In general, *partitioned-address* BFs perform poorly. The average filtering rate of *Partition-3* is only about 45%. *Partition-4* (not shown) has a dismal 5% average rate. Due to memory reference locality, the lowest partition of an address provides the most information, with the upper partitions providing almost no information. This is evident when comparing *Partition-3* to *Partial-1x*. The lowest partition of *Partition-3* uses the same 9 bits as *Partial-1x*. Yet the upper two partitions used by *Partition-3* only help to identify an additional 3% of misses. For *partial-address* BFs, the filtering rate improves dramatically as the size of the BF array

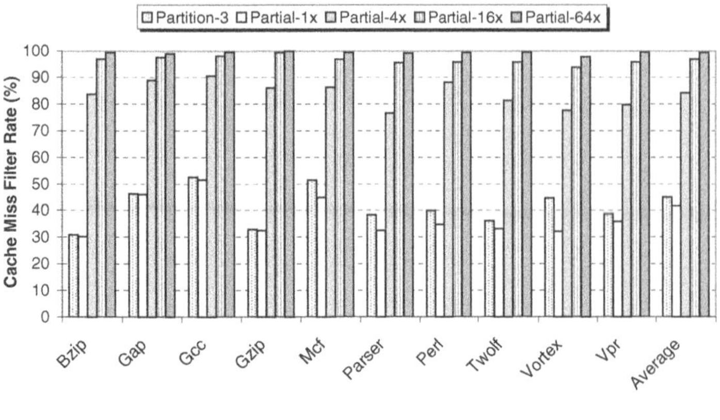

Figure 7: Cache Miss Filter Rate Using Partitioned and Partial Address Bloom Filters

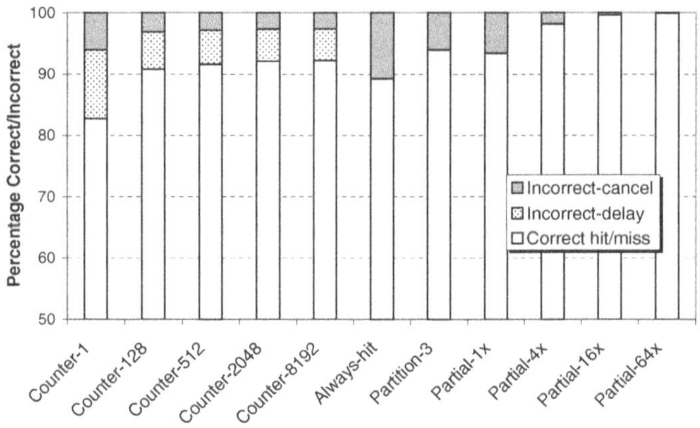

Figure 8: Prediction Accuracies for Different Cache Hit/Miss Predictors

increases. For a modestly sized 8K-bit BF array, the average filtering rate of *Partial-16x* is 97%.

Figure 8 shows the average (over all the benchmarks) correct and incorrect cache hit/miss prediction rates. It shows the prediction accuracy for BFs as well as other predictors. Correct predictions include both predict-hit-actual-hit and predict-miss-actual-miss cases. Incorrect predictions are separated into two groups. *Incorrect-cancel* is the case where a hit is predicted, but the load actually misses the cache. All speculatively scheduled dependents of the load must be canceled and rescheduled. *Incorrect-delay* is the case where a miss is predicted, but the load actually hits the cache. This misprediction unnecessarily delays the scheduling of the load's dependents and hence injects bubbles into the pipeline.

The predictors using saturating counters have a significant percentage of predictions in the *Incorrect-delay* group, and this percentage is insensitive to the predictor size. For *Counter-2048*, 5.2% of predictions are in the *Incorrect-delay* group and 2.7% are in the *Incorrect-cancel* group. The BFs, on the other hand, don't have any predictions in the *Incorrect-delay* group. In addition, the percentage in *Incorrect-cancel* decreases dramatically with larger BFs. The total misprediction rate is only 0.4% for *Partial-16x* using a moderately sized 8K-bit BF array. As expected, the simple *Counter-1* and *Always-hit* predictors have the two highest average misprediction rates.

5.2 IPC Improvement

Figure 9 compares the IPCs for several data speculation methods. In addition to the different types of hit/miss predictors, we include the IPC of a machine that doesn't use any data speculation and of a machine that uses a perfect hit/miss predictor (*Perfect-sch*). Also, the benefit of data prefetching using *Partial-16x* and *Perfect-sch* are shown (labeled with *-DP* in the legend of the figure). We show results for all the individual benchmarks since the IPC improvements are very different among them. *Partial-16x* without data prefetching shows a 17% improvement over *No-speculation* and a 4% improvement over *Always-hit*. Compared to *Counter-1* and *Counter-2048*, the improvements are 9% and 6%. With data prefetching, the improvements rise to 19%, 6%, 11% and 8%, respectively. It is important to point out that *Partial-16x* reaches 99.7% of the IPC of *Perfect-sch*, and *Partial-16x-DP* reaches 99.7% of the IPC of *Perfect-sch-DP*.

Among the benchmarks, *Gcc*, *Perl*, and *Vortex* show little difference between the different data speculation methods. Analysis reveals that these three programs have a large number of L_1 instruction cache (I-cache) misses. The high I-cache miss rate prevents instructions from entering the pipeline, reducing the benefit of data speculation. The lower instruction fetch rate greatly reduces the RUU occupancy, which is measured as the average number of RUU entries occupied. Since the RUU occupancy is much lower, loads and their dependents can stay in the RUU longer without blocking other instructions, so there is less of a difference between *No-speculation* and aggressive speculation such as *Partial-16x*. Table 3 summarizes the performance improvement of *Partial-16x* over *No-speculation* for 3 different I-cache sizes. Note the IPC improvement grows as the I-cache size increases. The IPC improvement for *Always-hit* also grows as I-cache size increases (not shown in the table), but not as quickly as it does for *Partial-16x*.

5.3 Sensitivity Studies

In this section we examine the effect of BFs on processor performance for various data cache sizes, RUU sizes, and different branch predictors.

Figure 10 plots the IPC improvement of *Always-hit*, *Partial-16x*, *Partial-16x-DP*, and *Perfect-sch-DP* over *No-speculation* for four different data cache sizes. We make three observations. First, the bigger the cache, the better the IPC improvement for all 4 data speculation methods. With bigger caches, scheduling becomes more important, because the performance bottleneck caused by data cache misses is reduced. Thus, delaying the scheduling of a load's dependents until after its cache hit/miss status has been determined (as is done by the *No-speculation* method) is a bigger loss of opportunity. Second, the IPC of *Always-hit* improves faster than the other methods as cache size increases. This is because its prediction accuracy is directly tied to the cache hit rate, so it sees the biggest improvement in prediction accuracy as the cache size increases. The IPC improvement of *Partial-16x-DP* over *Always-hit* reduces from 5.9% to 5.4% to 4.9% to 4.3% as the cache size is increased from 8KB to 64KB. Nevertheless, we expect future high-performance processors will use smaller first-level caches to enable higher clock frequencies. Third, due to high accuracy, *Partial-16x-*

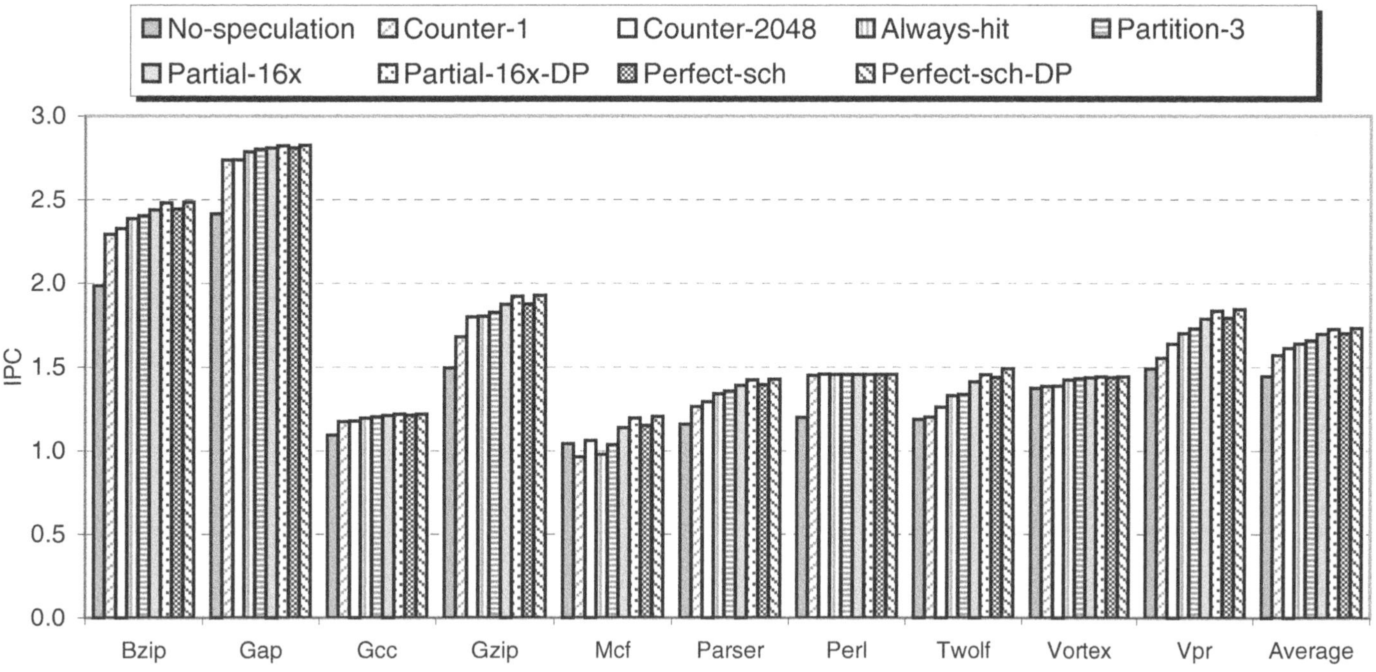

Figure 9: IPC Comparisons for Different Data Speculation Methods

	Gcc			Perl			Vortex		
I-cache	IPC%	I-miss%	RUU-ocu.	IPC%	I-miss%	RUU-ocu.	IPC%	I-miss%	RUU-ocu.
8KB	7.7	6.3	15.5	5.3	8.5	14.3	1.5	10.5	14.7
16KB	10.7	4.2	19.8	7.0	6.0	17.6	4.6	6.9	22.2
32KB	16.3	2.0	27.6	13.6	2.9	26.4	7.9	4.3	30.5

Table 3: Percent IPC improvement, I-cache miss rate, and RUU occupancy for 3 I-cache sizes

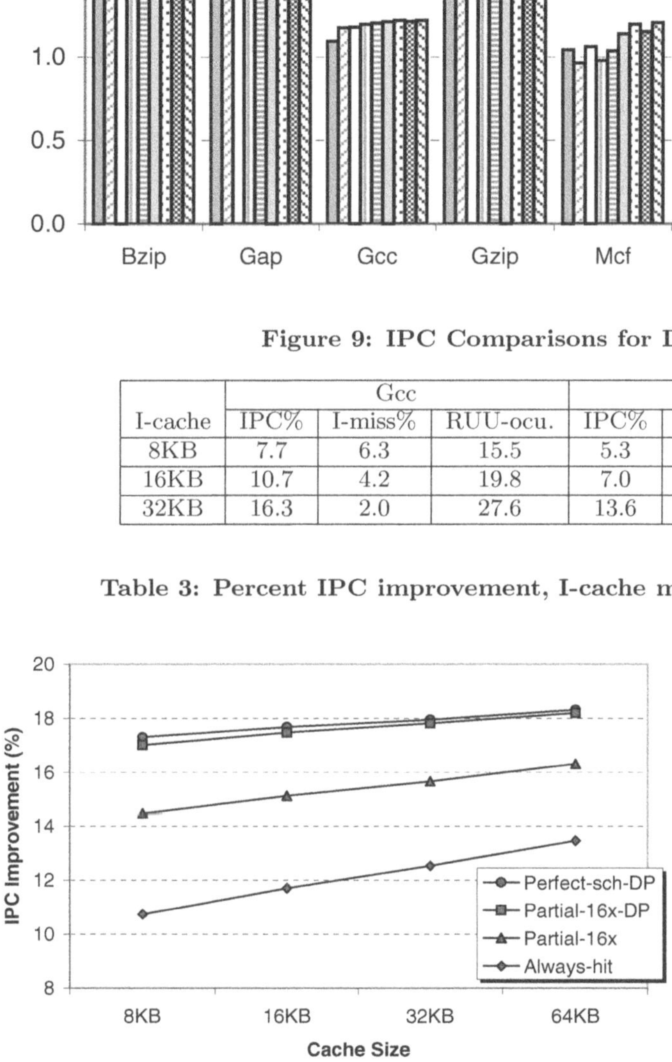

Figure 10: IPC Improvement Over No-speculation for Different Data Cache Sizes

DP achieves 99.9% of the IPC of the machine with a perfect scheduler for large caches.

Figure 11 shows the IPC improvement of *Partial-16x-DP*, *Partial-16x*, and *Always-hit* over *No-prediction* for three RUU sizes: 32, 64, and 128. We make several observations.

First, the IPC improvement is the greatest for the small RUU for all three methods. To achieve high performance with a small RUU, instructions need to flow through the RUU freely. Without data speculation, instructions that are dependent on loads block the flow. Thus, data speculation—even with all the rescheduling of dependent instructions due to mis-speculations—is essential for high performance when the RUU size is small.

Second, immediately prefetching the data when the BF identifies a miss improves IPCs by an additional 2–3%.

Third, the IPC improvement for *Always-hit* drops faster with increasing RUU size than the other two methods. And the performance gap between *Partial-16x* and *Always-hit* widens with bigger RUUs. To better illustrate this behavior, Figure 12 plots the IPC improvement of *Partial-16x-DP* and *Partial-16x* over *Always-hit*. In addition to the default Gshare predictor, the figure plots the performance of the two methods using a perfect branch predictor (labeled with *-perfectBR* in the legend of the figure). The results clearly show that the IPC improvement over *Always-hit* increases for bigger RUUs. Our simulation results show that with a small RUU, *Partial-16x* and *Always-hit* have similar RUU occupancies even though *Always-hit* produces more mispredictions. With a larger RUU, *Partial-16x* produces fewer RUU-full stalls than *Always-hit*. Effectively, *Partial-16x* has a larger instruction window in which to find instruction level

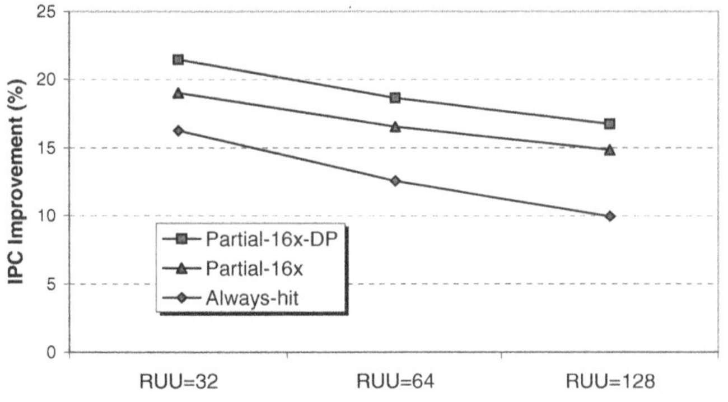

Figure 11: IPC Improvement Over No-speculation for Different RUU Sizes

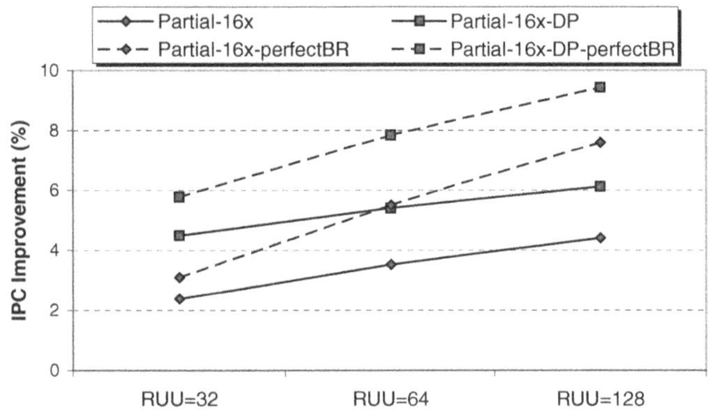

Figure 12: IPC Improvement Over Always-Hit for Different RUU Sizes

parallelism.

Lastly, in Figure 12, the IPC improvement of *Partial-16x* grows faster with increasing RUU size for the perfect branch predictor than for the default Gshare predictor. With a perfect branch predictor, the performance bottleneck due to branch mispredictions is eliminated, and instruction scheduling becomes more important. In addition, RUU occupancy is very high, since there are never any branch mispredictions that flush the RUU. A critical scheduling resource—RUU entries—becomes incredibly scarce. *Partial-16x* makes better use of this critical resource than *Always-hit*, as it cancels and reschedules fewer instructions. For a 128 entry RUU and a perfect branch predictor, the proposed *partial-address* BF improves IPC by more than 9% over the *Always-hit* method. Note that as branch prediction technology improves, the performance characteristics of real processors approach the performance characteristics of processors with perfect branch predictors.

6. CONCLUSION

Data speculation allows instructions that are dependent on a load to be scheduled before the latency of the load is known. A simple approach is to speculate (predict) that the load will always hit the L_1 cache and schedule its dependents accordingly. Unfortunately, whenever a prediction is wrong, the machine must recover all the mis-scheduled dependents, and performance suffers. In this paper we described how a Bloom Filter (BF) can be used to accurately predict cache misses. With a reasonably sized BF, we can correctly predict 99% of all misses. For the SPECint2000 benchmarks running on a modified SimpleScalar out-of-order model, the performance of a machine with a BF improved by 19% over a machine that delayed the scheduling of the load's dependents until the load's hit/miss status was known, and by 6% over a machine that speculated loads always hit the cache. We have also shown that this performance improvement grows as the window size and branch prediction accuracy increase. We expect that our BF technique will have an even greater performance advantage as pipelines deepen and cache latencies increase.

ACKNOWLEDGEMENTS

Jih-Kwon Peir thanks Windsor Hsu at IBM Almaden Research Center for early feedback on this paper. We also thank the anonymous referees for their helpful comments. This work is supported in part by NFS grants MIP-9624498 and EIA-0073473, and by Intel research donations.

REFERENCES

[1] Compaq Computer Corporation. *Alpha 21264 Microprocessor Hardware Reference Manual*, 1999.

[2] B. Bloom. Space/Time Tradeoffs in Hash Coding with Allowable Errors. *Communications of The ACM*, 13(7):422–426, 1970.

[3] D. Burger and T. Austin. The SimpleScalar Tool Set, Version 2.0. Technical Report #1342, CS Department, Univ. of Wisconsin-Madison, June 1997.

[4] B. Calder, D. Grunwald, and J. Emer. Predictive Sequential Associative Cache. *Proc. of 2nd Int'l Symp. on High Performance Computer Architecture*, 1996.

[5] G. Chrysos and J. Emer. Memory Dependence Prediction using Store Sets. *Proc. of 25th Int'l Symp. on Computer Architecture*, 1998.

[6] P. Glaskowsky. Pentium 4 (Partially) Previewed. *Microprocessor Report*, Aug. 2000.

[7] G. Hinton, D. Sager, M. Upton, D. Boggs, D. Carmean, A. Kyker, and P. Roussel. The Microarchitecture of the Pentium 4 Processor. *Intel Technical Journal*, Q1 2001.

[8] R. Kessler, R. Jooss, A. Lebeck, and M. Hill. Inexpensive Implementations of Set-Associativity. *Proc. of 16th Int'l Symp. on Computer Architecture*, 1989.

[9] R. Kessler. The Alpha 21264 Microprocessor. *IEEE Micro*, 19(2):24–36, 1999.

[10] L. Liu. Cache Design with Partial Address Matching. *Proc. of 27th Int'l Symp. on Microarchitecture*, 1994.

[11] E. Morancho, J. Llabería, and A. Olivé. Recovery Mechanism for Latency Misprediction. *Proc. of 10th Int'l Conf. on Parallel Architectures and Compilation Techniques*, 2001.

[12] A. Moshovos, G. Memik, B. Falsafi, and A. Choudhary. Jetty: Filtering Snoops for Reduced Energy Consumption in SMP Servers. *Proc. of 7th Int'l Symp. on High Performance Computer Architecture*, 2001.

[13] D. Papworth. Tuning the Pentium Pro Microarchitecture. *IEEE Micro*, 16(2):8–15, 1996.

[14] K. Yeager. The MIPS R10000 Superscalar Microprocessor. *IEEE Micro*, 16(2):28–41, 1996.

[15] A. Yoaz, M. Erez, R. Ronen, and S. Jourdan. Speculation Techniques for Improving Load Related Instruction Scheduling. *Proc. of 26th Int'l Symp. on Computer Architecture*, 1999.

AEGIS: Architecture for Tamper-Evident and Tamper-Resistant Processing

G. Edward Suh, Dwaine Clarke, Blaise Gassend, Marten van Dijk, Srinivas Devadas
Laboratory for Computer Science
Massachusetts Institute of Technology
Cambridge, MA 02139
{suh,declarke,gassend,marten,devadas}@mit.edu

ABSTRACT

We describe the architecture for a single-chip AEGIS processor which can be used to build computing systems secure against both physical and software attacks. Our architecture assumes that all components external to the processor, such as memory, are untrusted. We show two different implementations. In the first case, the core functionality of the operating system is trusted and implemented in a security kernel. We also describe a variant implementation assuming an untrusted operating system.

AEGIS provides users with tamper-evident, authenticated environments in which any physical or software tampering by an adversary is guaranteed to be detected, and private and authenticated tamper-resistant environments where additionally the adversary is unable to obtain any information about software or data by tampering with, or otherwise observing, system operation. AEGIS enables many applications, such as commercial grid computing, secure mobile agents, software licensing, and digital rights management.

Preliminary simulation results indicate that the overhead of security mechanisms in AEGIS is reasonable.

Categories and Subject Descriptors

C.1 [**Processor Architectures**]: Miscellaneous;
D.4.6 [**Operating Systems**]: Security and Protection

General Terms

Security, Design, Performance

Keywords

Certified execution, software licensing, secure processors

1. INTRODUCTION AND MOTIVATION

It is becoming common to use a multitude of computing devices that are highly interconnected to access public as well as private or sensitive data. On the one hand, users desire open systems for ease-of-use and interoperability, but on the other hand, they require privacy mechanisms that restrict access to sensitive data, and authentication mechanisms that ensure data integrity. With the proliferation and increasing usage of embedded, portable and wearable devices, in addition to protecting against attacks from malignant software, we also have to be concerned with physical attacks that corrupt data, discover private data or violate copy-protection, as well as combinations of physical and software attacks.

Given these trends, computing systems have to achieve several goals in order to be secure. Systems should provide *tamper-evident (TE) environments* where software processes can run in an authenticated environment, such that any physical tampering or software tampering by an adversary is guaranteed to be detected. In *private and authenticated tamper-resistant (PTR) environments*,[1] an additional requirement is that an adversary should be unable to obtain any information about software and data within the environment by tampering with, or otherwise observing, system operation. Ideally, a computing platform should provide a multiplicity of private and authenticated environments wherein each process (or each user) is protected from all other users and potential adversaries.

In this paper we describe the AEGIS processor architecture, which provides multiple mistrusting processes with environments such as those described above, assuming untrusted external memory. We first show an implementation with an untrusted operating system. We also describe a variant implementation of the architecture, that may provide increased flexibility under a different secure computing model, wherein core functionality of the operating system, termed the security kernel, is trusted – the remaining part of the operating system is untrusted, as is external memory.

We believe that these environments will enable a new set of applications. For example, grid computing is a popular way of solving computationally-hard problems (e.g., `SETI@home`, `distributed.net`) in a distributed manner on a huge number of machines with different volunteer owners connected via the Internet. However, maintaining reliability in the presence of malicious volunteers requires significant additional computation to check the results produced by volunteers. The TE and PTR environments provided by

[1]In the remainder of this paper, we may refer to these environments as private tamper-resistant (PTR) environments for brevity.

AEGIS can enable commercial grid computing on multitasking server farms, where computation power can be sold with the guarantee of a compute environment that processes data correctly and privately.

PTR environments can also enable applications where a compute server is used as a trusted third party. For example, a proprietary algorithm owned by party A can be applied to a proprietary instance of a problem owned by party B to produce a certifiable result, ensuring that no information regarding either the algorithm or the problem instance is leaked, and ensuring that the data was processed by the code correctly.[2] PTR environments also enable the copy-protection of software and media content in a wide range of computing systems in a manner that is resistant to software or physical attacks. This will enable strong forms of software licensing and intellectual property protection on portable as well as desktop computing systems. Finally, this PTR platform can enable secure mobile agents to perform electronic transactions on untrusted hosts [5].

The key architectural mechanisms required in an AEGIS processor that assumes an untrusted operating system are memory integrity verification, encryption/decryption of off-chip memory and a secure context manager. In this paper, we describe how these mechanisms are integrated into the AEGIS microarchitecture, and evaluate the performance overheads of these mechanisms. We describe a variant implementation, that assumes a trusted security kernel, wherein some of the hardware functionality can be eliminated. Detailed simulation results indicate that the performance overhead of security mechanisms in AEGIS is reasonable. These mechanisms therefore enable the implementation of a secure computing system with the only trusted component being a single-chip AEGIS processor.

We present our security model in Section 2. The AEGIS architecture is described in Section 3. Section 4 presents two essential mechanisms to protect off-chip memory: integrity verification and encryption. We describe how the architecture can be used for a certified execution application and a simple Digital Rights Management (DRM) application in Section 5. Simulation experiments to evaluate the performance overheads of the various mechanisms are presented in Section 6. Related work is described in Section 7, and we conclude the paper in Section 8.

2. SECURE COMPUTING MODEL

We consider systems that are built around a processing subsystem with external memory and peripherals. Figure 1 illustrates the model. The processor is assumed to be trusted and protected from physical attacks, so that its internal state cannot be tampered with or observed directly by physical means. The processor can contain secret information that identifies it and allows it to communicate securely with the outside world. This information could be a Physical Random Function [7], or the secret part of a public key pair protected by a tamper-sensing environment [9].

In the model of Figure 1, external memory and peripherals are assumed to be untrusted. They may be observed and tampered with at will by an adversary. In general, the operating system (OS) is also untrusted. Software attacks by

[2]By correctly, we do not mean that the code does not have any bugs, but that the code was not tampered with and was correctly executed.

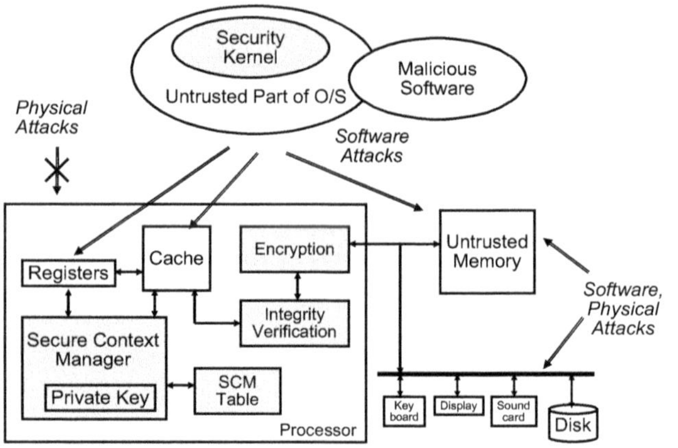

Figure 1: Our secure computing model.

the operating system or from other malicious software are therefore possible. In particular implementations, it may be assumed that there is a trusted part of the operating system, called the *security kernel*, that operates at a higher privilege level than the regular operating system. The processor is used in a multitasking environment, which uses virtual memory, and runs mutually mistrusting processes within TE or PTR environments.

The adversary can attack off-chip memory, and the processor needs to check that it behaves like valid memory. *Memory behaves like valid memory if the value the processor loads from a particular address is the most recent value that it has stored to that address.* If the contents of the off-chip memory have been altered by an adversary, the memory may not behave correctly (like valid memory). We therefore require memory integrity verification [22].

In the case of PTR environments, we have to encrypt data values stored in off-chip memory.

We assume that programs are well-written and do not leak secrets via their memory access patterns. In particular, we do not handle security issues caused by bugs in an application program.

3. THE AEGIS ARCHITECTURE

This section describes a processor architecture with which tamper-evident (TE) and private tamper-resistant (PTR) execution environments can be built. We first focus on the high-level description of our architecture and how the environments are used by application programs. Then, the protection mechanisms to enable this architecture are discussed in more detail.

3.1 Trusted Computing Base: TCB

Our trusted computing base (TCB) consists of a processor chip and optionally a part of an operating system. We refer to the trusted core part of the operating system as the *security kernel (SKernel)*. Unless the entire operating system is trusted, the security kernel operates at a higher protection level than other parts of the operating system in order to prevent attacks from untrusted parts of the operating system such as device drivers.

In the following discussion of the high-level architecture, we do not distinguish between tasks that are accomplished by a security kernel and tasks that are accomplished by the processor. In most cases, the same functionality can be implemented in either one. We simply refer to the TCB when either one is concerned. In Section 3.4, we show how the required functionality can be partitioned between the security kernel and the processor in different ways.

3.2 Tamper-Evident Processing

The TE environment guarantees that any physical or software tampering that can alter the behavior of a program is detected or prevented. In other words, the integrity of a program execution is guaranteed. TE mode does not provide any privacy for code or data; a PTR environment is required for privacy.

The AEGIS architecture provides the following new operations for an application program to enable TE processing:

- `enter_aegis`: Start execution in a TE environment.
- `exit_aegis`: Exit the TE environment and return to a standard processing mode.
- `sign_msg`: Generate a signature of a message and a program hash with the processor's secret key.

Valid Execution. A valid execution of a program on a general-purpose time-shared processor can be guaranteed by securing three potential sources of attacks: *initial state*, *state on interrupts* including context switching, and *on-chip/off-chip memory*.

To enter TE mode, applications use the `enter_aegis` instruction. The instruction specifies a stub region that is used to generate a program hash ($H(Prog)$) that identifies the program. The program hash is stored in protected storage for later use. The stub region starts with the `enter_aegis` instruction and extends over a number of bytes that is specified as an argument to the instruction. The stub code gets executed immediately after the `enter_aegis` instruction, and is responsible for checking any other code and data that the application relies on. It does so by comparing their hashes with hashes that are stored in the stub region. The stub code must also check the sanity of the environment it is running in: processor mode, virtual address of the stub code (if it assumes an absolute entry point), position of the stack, etc. On some architectures such as x86, it is necessary for the TCB to check that the stack pointer is far from the stub code, as the stub would be helpless against an interrupt occurring and writing to the stack before it has a chance to change the stack pointer. This process guarantees that the *initial state* of a program is properly set up.

Once a program starts its execution in TE mode with the `enter_aegis` instruction, the TCB protects the program's state in both on-chip and off-chip memory. In fact, the integrity of the verified code and data should be protected as soon as they are used to compute the program hash $H(Prog)$. The register state of the program is protected and guaranteed to be preserved over an interrupt. The integrity of program instructions and data in the on-chip/off-chip memories is also protected. On-chip caches are secure from physical attacks, thus only need to be protected from malicious or buggy software. Off-chip memory, including pages swapped out to the disk, is vulnerable to both physical and software attacks. The TCB verifies the integrity of a block whenever it is read from off-chip memory.

The integrity verification mechanism (see Section 4.1) ensures that only one program or processor can legally modify a memory location. If the entire memory space is protected, the mechanism does not allow any sharing among different secure processes. Even any legitimate input from a I/O device would be prohibited. Therefore, a program should be able to access a part of memory space without integrity verification.

We handle this problem by using the most significant bit (MSB) of an address to determine whether the integrity of the address should be protected or not. Therefore, the upper half of the virtual memory space is protected and the lower half is not. The program lays out its code and data accordingly. This design allows a very simple implementation of the protection scheme even in hardware. This static division of memory space restricts processes to have only one half of the memory space for secure data. This is not a problem for 64-bit architectures. In the case of small address spaces, a finer granularity might be desirable to avoid wasting virtual address space.

Exporting Results. The protections described above are enough to guarantee the correct execution of a program. However, in practice, there is additional functionality required for the TE mode to be useful; a user should be able to trust the result provided by a system when communication channels from a processor are untrusted.

For this purpose, a program can use the `sign_msg` operation. It returns the signature $\{H(Prog), M\}_{SKp}$ for a message M,[3] where $H(Prog)$ is the hash of the program that was computed when the `enter_aegis` instruction was executed, and SKp is the secret part of a processor's private/public key pair. The TCB signs the message only if the program is in TE mode, and always includes the program hash in the signature. That way, when the user receives a message signed by the processor's secret key SKp, he knows that the message is from a particular program (program authentication) running on a particular processor (system authentication). The signature of a message also prevent adversaries from forging messages (message authentication).

3.3 Private Tamper-Resistant Processing

The TE environment presented in the previous subsection can be extended to a PTR environment to support a private and authenticated execution. Additional protections are needed to ensure the privacy of registers, on-chip caches, and off-chip memory. One new instruction is needed to support this mode:

- `set_aegis_mode`: Enable or disable the PTR environment. Set the static key K_{static} that is used to decrypt *static content* corresponding to instructions and data that are encrypted in the program binary.

To enable or disable privacy from TE mode, programs use the `set_aegis_mode` instruction. The instruction enables the PTR environment and provides the static key encrypted with the processor's public key ($E_{PKp}\{H(Prog), K_{static}\}$), so the static key can be decrypted only by a trusted processor for a particular program. The processor decrypts the key and sets the K_{static} accordingly only if the program hash matches the hash of the executing program. The encryption scheme should be non-malleable so that an adversary cannot

[3]If there is a security kernel within the TCB, `sign_msg` returns $\{H(SKernel), H(Prog), M\}_{SKp}$ so that a user can authenticate the security kernel as well as the processor.

change the encrypted program hash and use the static key with a different program. If there is a security kernel, the operation uses $E_{PKp}\{H(SKernel), H(Prog), K_{static}\}$ to identify the trusted security kernel as well.

In the PTR environment, all the register values are considered private and protected. Whether instructions and data in the memory are private is determined using the second MSB of the address. Data stored to virtual addresses that have the second MSB set has its privacy protected.

Ensuring Privacy. The privacy of registers and on-chip caches should be protected by the TCB from software attacks. When an interrupt occurs, the TCB saves the register values in private storage in the TCB and clears them before an untrusted interrupt handler starts. The TCB also protects on-chip caches so that no process can read other process' private data.

Whenever data that needs to remain private goes off-chip, the TCB encrypts it. Fast symmetric encryption and decryption can be used because the data only needs to be read by the processor that wrote it in the first place. Each process uses a pair of keys, K_{static} and $K_{dynamic}$. The static key K_{static} is used to decrypt instructions and data from the program binary, and obtained from the `set_aegis_mode` instruction. The dynamic key $K_{dynamic}$ is used to encrypt and decrypt data that is generated during the program's execution, and randomly chosen by the TCB when `enter_aegis` is called.

Simply encrypting memory is not sufficient to provide complete opacity of program operation. Information can be leaked via memory access patterns or other covert channels. Here we will assume that programs are well-written and do not leak their secrets via those channels. Techniques exist (e.g., [14, 1]) which can check programs for information leaks and prevent them [9].

3.4 TCB Implementations

The high-level architecture described in the previous subsections can be implemented in many different ways depending on how to partition the required functionality between the security kernel and the processor. In general, relying more on the security kernel provides more flexibility and requires less architectural modification on the processor. On the other hand, putting mechanisms into the processor reduces the trusted code to be verified, and can sometimes result in better performance.

In this subsection, we present two reference implementations of the AEGIS architecture: the *Security Kernel Solution* and the *Untrusted OS Solution*. In the security kernel solution, some core functionality of the operating system is trusted, so that we can construct a secure system with minimal modifications to a conventional processor architecture. The untrusted operating system solution does not trust any part of the operating system (which means there is no security kernel within the TCB), and implements all mechanisms in the processor. Table 1 summarizes the two implementations.

3.4.1 Security Kernel Solution

Security Kernel Start-Up. When a security kernel exists in the TCB, its identity should be verifiable by a user. In order to achieve this goal, the processor computes the hash of the security kernel $H(SKernel)$ when it boots up as in [2, 4]. After that, the integrity of the security kernel code is protected using the same mechanisms for other secure processes: trusted VM management and off-chip integrity verification. A user can identify a TCB with the security kernel hash $H(SKernel)$ and the processor's private/public key pair.

Initial Start-Up and Interrupts. The security kernel manages the start-up of a program and interrupts, thus ensuring that *the initial state* is properly set up and *the states on an interrupt* are correctly restored when a program resumes execution.

Software Attacks on Memory. The security kernel protects both on-chip caches and off-chip memory from software attacks. Indeed, traditional mechanisms such as virtual memory and privilege levels are adequate to protect applications from each other. Therefore, we include the virtual memory manager within the security kernel to properly protect the integrity and the privacy of memory from software attacks.

Physical Attacks on Memory. Because we assume that an adversary cannot tamper with a processor chip, the on-chip caches are secure from physical attacks. To protect the off-chip memory from physical attacks, the hardware memory integrity verification mechanism in Section 4.1 is applied to the *physical memory space*. The mechanism uses hash trees to check if the value the processor loads from a particular address is the most recent value that it stored to that address. The mechanism guarantees that if the memory is written by any entity other than the processor, this tampering is detected.

When the OS swaps a page from memory to disk, the security kernel implements the hash tree scheme in software and protects the page. The hash tree allows the OS to verify the integrity of a page when the page is brought into the memory in the future. We note that it would also be possible to verify the integrity of off-chip RAM with a software checker in the security kernel as long as the integrity verification code always stays on-chip. However, this approach would significantly degrade performance compared to the hardware implementation.

Encryption. The encryption and decryption of memory is done by a hardware engine placed between the integrity checker and the off-chip memory bus, which is detailed in Section 4.2. Although encryption in software is also possible, the hardware engine is chosen for performance.

For the PTR environment, the security kernel implements the `set_aegis_mode` operation. To set the static key for a program, the operation is used with $E_{PKp}\{H(SKernel), H(Prog), K_{static}\}$. The processor provides a special instruction `decrypt_key` for the security kernel. The instruction gets the encrypted key and returns $H(Prog), K_{static}$ only if the hash of the security kernel's matches the $H(SKernel)$ in the instruction. Once the security kernel obtains the decrypted key, it compares the program hash and sets the static key for a program if the hashes match. When context switching between processes, the security kernel is responsible for clearing the static key of the process that is being interrupted and, if appropriate, loading the key for the new process into the processor.

Signing Operation. With a security kernel, the `sign_msg` operation is implemented as a system call. Because the pro-

Problems	Security Kernel Solution	Untrusted OS Solution
SKernel start-up	Processor computes $H(SKernel)$	-
Process start-up	Managed by security kernel - trusted loader - trusted multitasking	Processor computes $H(Prog)$, checks the stack pointer
Registers on interrupts		Processor saves registers, clears the registers (PTR), and restores them on a resume.
On-chip caches	Trusted VM manager,	Secure process ID tags, virtual address for each block,
Off-chip RAM	Processor verifies physical memory	Processor verifies virtual memory
Pages on disk	Security kernel verifies paging	
Encryption (PTR)	Hardware encryption engine	Hardware encryption engine
`sign_msg`	Security kernel system call	Processor instruction

Table 1: Implementing the AEGIS architecture with/without a trusted security kernel in the operating system (OS). (PTR) indicates that the mechanism is only required for the private tamper-resistant environment.

gram hashes are maintained by the security kernel, the operation cannot be done by the processor directly. Instead of a user level `sign_msg` instruction, the processor provides a privileged instruction `sign_kernel_msg` for the security kernel, which returns $\{H(SKernel), M'\}_{SK_P}$ for message M'. Then, the security kernel uses this instruction with $M' = \{H(Prog), M\}$ to implement the `sign_msg` system call, which returns $\{H(SKernel), H(Prog), M\}_{SK_P}$. Note that the $H(SKernel)$ is always included in the signature by the trusted processor so that a malicious security kernel cannot forge a message on behalf of another security kernel.

3.4.2 *Untrusted OS Solution*

The Secure Context Manager. To have a secure execution environment without the security kernel, the processor needs to keep track of the processes that it is running in the AEGIS mode, so that it can securely keep track of their states. We introduce a *secure context manager (SCM)*, which is a specialized component in the processor that ensures proper protection for each secure process. For each secure process, the SCM assigns a non-zero secure process ID (SPID). Zero is used to represent regular processes.

The SCM maintains a table that holds various protection information for each secure process running in AEGIS mode. The table entry for a process consists of a SPID, the program hash ($H(Prog)$), the architectural registers ($Regs$), a hash used for memory integrity verification, a bit indicating whether the process is in the PTR mode, and a pair of keys for encryption (K_{static}, $K_{dynamic}$). We refer to the table as the SCM table. An entry is created by the `enter_aegis` instruction, and deleted by the `exit_aegis` instruction. The operating system can also delete an entry as it has to be able to kill processes; this feature is not a security issue, as it does not allow the operating system to impersonate the application that it killed.

The SCM table can be entirely stored on the processor as in XOM [12], however, this severely restricts the number of secure processes. Instead, we store the table in a virtual memory space that is managed by the operating system and stored in off-chip memory. Memory integrity verification mechanisms prevent the operating system from tampering with the data in the SCM table. A specialized on-chip cache similar in structure to a TLB is used to store the SCM table entries for recent processes. To protect the encryption keys, the processor holds a master key K_M, which can be randomly generated when the system boots, and encrypts the encryption keys and register values in the SCM table when they are moved out to off-chip memory.

Initial Start-Up. To ensure a valid initial start-up, the SCM implements the `enter_aegis` operation as a processor instruction. The SCM computes a hash of essential program code and data (and checks the initial stack pointer on architectures such as x86 to avoid a stack overflow if an interrupt occurs) when the `enter_aegis` instruction is executed. Once the instructions and data are used for the hash computation, they are protected by the on-chip and off-chip memory protection mechanisms, described in the subsequent paragraphs, so that they cannot be tampered with. The program hash is stored in the SCM table.

Registers on an Interrupt. Given that interrupt handling and context switching are rather complicated tasks, we let the untrusted operating system manage all aspects of multitasking. The processor nevertheless has to verify that a TE process' state is correctly preserved when it is not executing. For that reason, the SCM stores all the process' register values in the SCM table when the interrupt occurs, and restores them at the end of the interrupt. For PTR processes, once the register values are stored in the SCM table, the working copy of the registers is cleared so that the interrupt handler cannot see their previous values.

On-Chip Caches. The on-chip caches are protected using tags. Whenever a process accesses a cache block, the block is tagged with the process' SPID. Regular processes are represented by the SPID value of zero. This SPID specifies the ownership of the cache block. Each cache block also contains the corresponding virtual address, which was used by the owner process on the last access to the block.

When a secure process accesses an address that requires integrity protection, the processor verifies a cache block before using it. If the active SPID matches the SPID of the cache block and the accessed virtual address matches the virtual address of the cache block, the access continues. Otherwise, the value of the cache block is verified by the off-chip integrity verification mechanisms, and the SPID and the virtual address of the block is updated.

In PTR mode, if a block's virtual address is in the private region, the block requires additional protection for privacy. Accesses to a private cache block are allowed only if the SPID of the cache block matches the active SPID and the active process is in the PTR mode. Otherwise, the block gets evicted from the cache and reloaded.

Off-Chip Memory. For off-chip memory, we use the hardware memory integrity verification mechanism in Section 4.1. The memory verification algorithm is applied to each secure process' virtual memory space. Each TE process uses a separate hash tree to protect its own virtual memory space. Changes made by a different process are detected as tampering. Because we are protecting virtual memory space, pages are protected both when they are in RAM and when they are swapped to disk.

As described in the high-level architecture, the private cache blocks are encrypted when they are evicted from the L2 cache. Encryption and decryption is done by a hardware engine placed between the integrity checker and the off-chip memory bus (see Section 4.2).

Signing Operation. The SCM implements the `sign_msg` operation as a processor instruction as described in the high-level architecture. The SCM returns $\{H(Prog), M\}_{SK_P}$, which is the signature of the program hash and the message.

3.5 Performance Implication

Most mechanisms that are required for TE processing have marginal overhead on the processor performance. The `enter_aegis` instruction and the `sign_msg` instruction involve cryptographic hash computation and private/public key signing, respectively, which are rather expensive operations. However, these instructions are only used very infrequently; the `enter_aegis` instruction is only for the beginning of a program, and the `sign_msg` instruction is only for exporting trusted results. Thus, the overhead will be amortized over a long execution period.

There are three mechanisms that are frequently used at run-time: register protection on an interrupt, on-chip cache tagging, and off-chip integrity verification. Fortunately, the performance overhead of register protection and cache tagging is negligible. Register protection simply requires storing the register in the SCM table, and the cache tags do not increase cache access time although they occupy additional on-chip storage.

The only significant performance overhead comes from off-chip integrity verification. The integrity verification consumes additional memory bandwidth to access meta-data such as hashes on every memory access, and may also cause additional latency for the `sign_msg` instruction. Therefore, the performance overhead of TE processing can be closely approximated by evaluating the performance overhead of the memory integrity verification.

The PTR processing requires only one additional run-time mechanism over TE processing: off-chip memory encryption. Therefore, the performance overhead of our PTR architecture can be estimated by only considering memory integrity verification and memory encryption. We study this performance impact quantitatively through simulations in Section 6.

4. MEMORY PROTECTION SCHEMES

This section describes two mechanisms to protect off-chip memory: *integrity verification* and *encryption*. The memory integrity verification protects the integrity of off-chip data, and the encryption protects the privacy of the data.

Memory integrity verification mechanisms operate as a layer between the L2 cache and the encryption mechanisms, protecting the plaintext data. Therefore, an encrypted data block from memory is first decrypted and then verified by the integrity verification mechanism. Verifying plaintexts rather than ciphertext eliminates the need to protect the meta-data for encryption such as random vectors because such tampering will be detected by the integrity verification of the decrypted plaintext.

4.1 Integrity Verification

This section briefly summarizes an integrity verification mechanism based on cached hash trees [8], and discusses issues related to applying this scheme to our architecture. We use the hash tree scheme for simplicity, but note that there exists a more efficient scheme that can reduce the performance overhead of memory integrity verification [22].

4.1.1 Cached Hash Trees

Hash trees (or Merkle trees) are often used to verify the integrity of dynamic data in untrusted storage [13]. Figure 2 illustrates a hash tree. The memory space is divided into multiple chunks, denoted by V_1, V_2, etc. The chunks are the leaves of the hash tree. A parent is the hash of the concatenation of its children. In our case, each hash covers one L2 cache block. The root of the tree is stored in the SCM table where it cannot be tampered with.

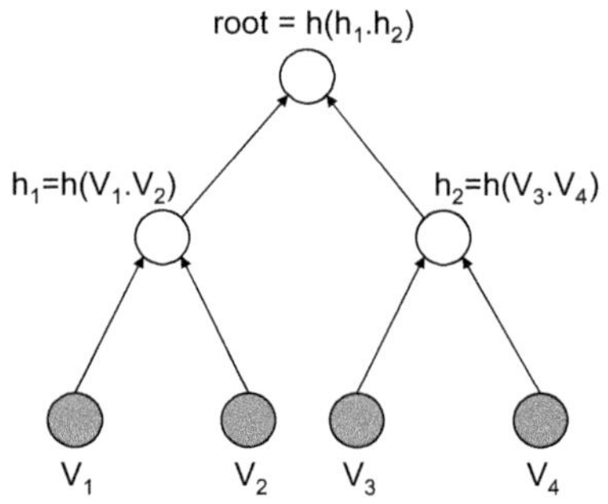

Figure 2: A binary hash tree. Each internal node is a hash of the concatenation of the data in the node's children.

To check the integrity of a node in the tree, the processor (i) reads the node and its siblings from the memory, (ii) concatenates their data together, (iii) computes the hash of the concatenated data, and (iv) checks that the resultant hash matches the hash in the parent. The steps are repeated all the way to the root of the tree.

To update a node, the processor checks its integrity as described in the previous paragraph while it (i) modifies the node, and (ii) recomputes and updates the parent to be the hash of the concatenation of the node and its siblings. These steps are repeated to update the whole path from the node to the root, including the root.

To reduce the performance overhead of the hash tree, we cache the internal hash nodes in the on-chip L2 cache with regular data. The processor trusts data stored in the cache. Therefore, instead of checking the entire path from the chunk to the root of the tree, the processor checks the path from the chunk to the first hash it finds in the cache. This hash is trusted and the processor can stop checking.

When a chunk or hash is ejected from the cache, the processor brings its parent into the cache (if it is not already there), and updates the parent in the cache. Details and variants can be found in [8].

4.1.2 Initialization

To make initialization easier, we have simply attach a valid bit to each hash in the tree to indicate whether the cache line that it covers is actually present in the tree. Initially all the hashes in the tree are marked as invalid. Whenever a hash with a zero valid bit is read during memory checking, the processor automatically initializes it by computing a hash of its child cache line and setting the valid bit. This way, as soon as a virtual address has been accessed once in TE or PTR mode, the data that it contains is protected. Protecting data before that first access would be futile as the data predates the initialization of TE mode, and therefore could have been tampered with before any protection mechanism was activated. With this scheme, there is no need to allocate physical memory for hashes or data until they are used. Hashe in newly allocated pages must have zero valid flags or a memory integrity exception will be raised.

4.1.3 Tree Layout

In order to implement the hash tree scheme, a processor should be able to easily obtain a parent's address from a node's address. By laying out the nodes of the tree in breadth first or depth first manner, the address of a parent node can easily be computed from the address of a child.

When there is a security kernel case, we propose that the physical memory be split into three parts: an unverified region for programs that do not use the secure modes and for DMA accesses, a region for verified data, and a region for the nodes of the hash tree. The nodes of the hash tree should be laid out in depth first manner to make expanding the tree easy. The security determines the size of these regions base on the needs of running applications.

4.1.4 Checking Virtual Memory

When a virtual memory space is authenticated, a processor needs additional support to use the tree layout and determine the physical address of the parent hash for a cache block. In this case, the L2 cache contains virtual addresses, which are also used for on-chip cache protection. From this virtual address, a processor computes the virtual address of the corresponding parent node. We assume that the nodes of the hash tree are laid out in breadth first manner in their own virtual memory space, separate from the user space, so that the entire process virtual space can be utilized by the program. Finally, the processor needs to convert virtual addresses of parent nodes into physical addresses. For this we use a TLB; in practice, we should not use the processor core's standard TLB and should use a second TLB to avoid increasing the latency of the standard TLB. The second TLB is also tagged with process identifier bits which are combined with virtual addresses to translate to physical addresses.

4.1.5 Blocking Instructions

When data is loaded from memory, operations which do not generate a signature or reveal private information are immediately allowed to start using the fetched data. Memory checking is carried out concurrently in the background. This speculative execution on unchecked data is permissible because these operations do not break the security of our system when they are executed on tampered data, as long as an exception is eventually raised when the tampering is detected. Because these exceptions imply either a malicious OS or physical attacks, graceful recovery is not needed, and the exceptions need not be precise. Therefore, integrity checking latency is not directly added to the data access latency seen by the processor.

There are exceptions to this rule. In a TE environment, the processor must wait for integrity checking of all the previous memory accesses to complete before allowing the result of a (`sign_msg`) instruction to be exported outside of the processor. In a PTR environment, besides waiting when there is a signing instruction, the processor must also wait for the integrity checking to complete before executing an instruction that stores plaintext data (i.e., when storing to a non-private memory region).

4.1.6 Untrusted I/O

For untrusted disk, when virtual memory is being protected, pages will already be protected by the integrity verification even when they are stored on disk. For Direct Memory Access (DMA), an unprotected area for use in DMA transfers is set aside in the memory space. When the transfer is done, the process can copy it to protected memory and authenticate the data using some scheme of its choosing.

4.2 Encryption

For off-chip memory encryption, we use a symmetric key encryption algorithm rather than public/private key algorithms. In our case, it is safe to use symmetric keys because the same processor performs both encryption and decryption.

4.2.1 Advanced Encryption Standard

The National Institute of Standards and Technology specifies Rijndael as the Advanced Encryption Standard (AES), which is an approved symmetric encryption algorithm [15]. AES is one of the most advanced symmetric encryption algorithms in terms of both security and performance. While any symmetric key encryption algorithm can be used for our purposes, we base our subsequent discussions on AES as a representative symmetric algorithm.

AES can process data blocks of *128 bits* using cipher keys with lengths of *128*, *192*, and *256 bits*. The encryption and decryption consist of 10 to 16 rounds of four transformations. The critical path of one round consists of one S-box look-up, two shifts, 6-7 XOR operations, and one 2-to-1 MUX. This critical path will take 2-4 ns in 0.13μ technology depending on the implementation of the S-box look-up table. Therefore, encrypting or decrypting one 128-bit data block will take about 20-64 ns depending on the implementation and the key length.

When the difference in technology is considered, this latency is in good agreement with one custom ASIC implementation of the Rijndael in 0.18μ technology [11, 19]. It is reported that the critical path of encryption is 6 ns per round and the critical path of key expansion is 10 ns per round with 1.89 ns latency for the S-box. Their key expansion is identical to two rounds of the AES key expansion because they support 256-bit data blocks. Therefore, the AES implementation will take 5 ns per round for key expansion, which results in a 6 ns cycle per round, for a total of 60-96 ns, depending on the number of rounds.

Given the gate counts in [19], a 128-bit block encryption using AES without pipelining costs approximately 75,000 gates. If we implement AES fully in parallel for the four 128-bit blocks in a 64-B L2 cache block, the module should be duplicated four times. Therefore, in this case, the AES implementation will result in the order of 300,000 gates.

4.2.2 Direct Block Encryption

We encrypt and decrypt off-chip memory on an L2 cache block granularity because memory accesses are carried out with that granularity. Encrypting multiple cache blocks together implies that all the blocks have to be decrypted to access any one of them.

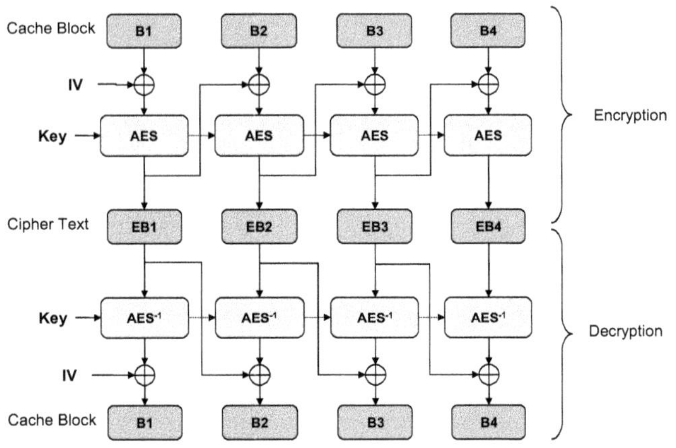

Figure 3: Encryption mechanism that directly encrypts cache blocks with the AES algorithm.

To encrypt a dirty cache block when it gets evicted from the L2 cache, the cache block is used as an input data block of the AES algorithm. For example, a 64-B cache block `B` is broken into 128-bit chunks (`B[1]`, `B[2]`, `B[3]` and `B[4]`), and encrypted by the AES algorithm. Figure 3 illustrates this mechanism with Cipher Block Chaining (CBC) mode. The encrypted cache block `EB = (EB[1], EB[2], EB[3], EB[4])` is generated by `EB[i]` $= AES_K($`B[i]` $\oplus$ `EB[i-1]`$)$, where `EB[0]` is an initial vector `IV`.

The initial vector `IV` consists of the address of the block and a random vector `RV`, and is padded with zeros to be 128 bits. To prevent adversaries from comparing whether two cache blocks are the same or not, `RV` is randomly generated as a non-zero value on each encryption. Zero indicates the block should be decrypted with the static key. After the encryption, the random vector `RV` is stored in the off-chip memory along with the encrypted cache block (`EB`). The random vectors are laid out linearly in memory as an array.

In our experiments, we used a 32-bit random vector for each cache block. Although the encryption is randomized, we note that an adversary may be able to find out that a cache block has the same value at different times if both happen to use the same random vector. To eliminate this information leak, we can replace the random vector by a counter and re-encrypt memory with a new dynamic key whenever the counter reaches its limit. When encryption is combined with the hash tree mechanism, some randomization should be included in the lowest level hashes or else we lose the benefit of randomized encryption. The most convenient way of achieving this is to include `IV` in the hash, though care must taken to ensure that using the same initial vector for the hashes and the encryption does not lead to any unexpected interaction between primitives.

For an L2 cache miss in a private memory space, an encrypted cache block (`EB`) and the corresponding random vector `RV` are read from memory. If the random vector is zero, the initial vector is set to zero and the static key is used for decrypting the block. Otherwise, the initial vector is computed from the address of the block and the random vector, and dynamic key is used. Once the data arrives, the decryption of four chunks (`B[1]`, `B[2]`, `B[3]` and `B[4]`) can be done in parallel, and stored in the L2 cache. Since decryption starts after reading data from off-chip memory, the decryption latency is directly added to the memory latency. For example, if the memory latency is 120 ns and the decryption latency is 40 ns, the processor will see a load latency of 160 ns.

5. APPLICATIONS

We describe two representative applications enabled by the AEGIS processor, Certified Execution and Digital Rights Management.

5.1 Certified Execution

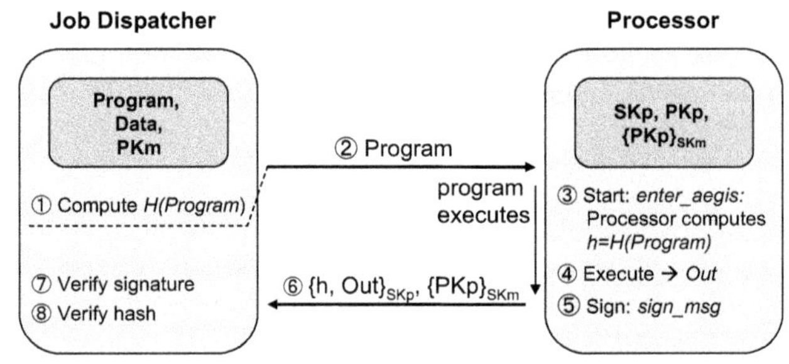

Figure 4: Certified execution for distributed computation.

A typical example of certified execution is grid computing. A number of organizations, such as `SETI@home` and `distributed.net`, are trying to carry out large computations in a highly distributed way. This style of computation is unreliable as the person requesting the computation has no way of knowing that it was executed without any tampering. In order to obtain correctness guarantees, redundant computations can be performed, at the cost of reduced efficiency. Moreover, to detect malicious volunteers, it is assumed that these volunteers do not collude and are continuously malicious [18].

Using a TE environment as described in Section 3, a certificate can be produced that proves that a specific computation was carried out on a specific processor chip. The person requesting the computation can then rely on the trustworthiness of the chip manufacturer who can vouch that he produced the processor chip, instead of relying on the owner of the chip.

Figure 4 outlines a protocol that could be used by a job dispatcher to do certified execution of a program on a remote computer. First (1) the job dispatcher needs to know the hash of the program that it is sending out. For simplicity, we assume that the program encompasses all the necessary code and data for the run. The program is sent to the secure processor (2), which proceeds to run it. The program enters TE mode by using the `enter_aegis` instruction (3), at that time, a hash of the program gets computed for later use. The program executes and produces a result (4). The result gets concatenated with the program's hash and signed (5). The processor returns the signed result to the job dispatcher along with a certificate from the manufacturer that certifies the processor's public key as belonging to a correct processor (6). The job dispatcher checks the signature (7) and the program hash (8) before accepting the program's output as correct.

5.2 Digital Rights Management

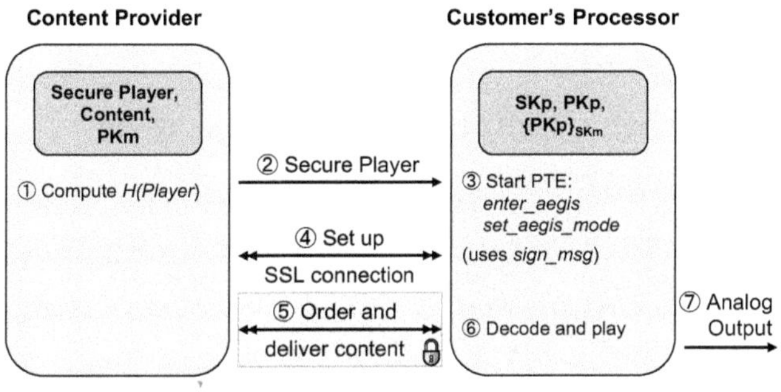

Figure 5: Digital rights management with PTR architecture.

Digital Rights Management (DRM) is a hot topic since the advent of large scale sharing of copyrighted media over the Internet. We are starting to see applications that attempt to enforce simple DRM policies [20]. A typical scenario is for an individual to buy a media file that can only be played once, or on a single computer. This type of policy is enforced by encrypting the the media file so that it can only be decoded by an authorized reader, which enforces the single use policy. Unfortunately, a determined attacker can use debugging tools to get the player to provide him with a decrypted version of the media file, thus breaking the DRM scheme.

In Figure 5, we show how a bidirectional private and authentic channel can be created between a content provider, and a trusted program, running in PTR mode on a customer's computer. This channel can be used to send digital content to the customer. Once it is on the customer's machine, the content is managed by the trusted program which is designed to enforce the content provider's policy concerning access to the content. Since the trusted program is running in PTR mode, the content cannot be accessed except in ways that are approved by the trusted program, even if an attacker tries to use debugging tools, or tries to modify the hardware of his machine. Only physical attacks on the AEGIS processor could break the privacy of the system.

The protocol is very simple. First the content provider produces a trusted player program to run on the customer's machine. Embedded in the program is the content provider's public key. The content provider calculates a hash of the program that he will use to identify it (1), before sending it to the customer (2). When the player runs on the customer's machine, it uses the `enter_aegis` and `set_aegis_mode` instruction to enter PTR mode (3). The player program now

Architectural parameters	Specifications
Clock frequency	1 GHz
L1 I-caches	64KB, 2-way, 32B line
L1 D-caches	64KB, 2-way, 32B line
L2 caches	Unified, 1MB, 4-way, 64B line
L1 latency	2 cycles
L2 latency	10 cycles
Memory latency (first chunk)	80 cycles
I/D TLBs	4-way, 128-entries
Memory bus	200 MHz, 8-B wide (1.6 GB/s)
Fetch/decode width	4 / 4 per cycle
issue/commit width	4 / 4 per cycle
Load/store queue size	64
Register update unit size	128
AES latency	40 cycles
AES throughput	3.2 GB/s
Hash latency	160 cycles
Hash throughput	3.2 GB/s
Hash buffer	32
Hash length	128 bits
Initial vectors	32 bits
Initial vector buffer	32 8-B entry

Table 2: Architectural parameters used in simulations.

has the public key of the server it wishes to access. It can use a standard protocol such as Secure Socket Layer (SSL) [16], with client authentication, to establish a bidirectional private and authenticated channel with the content provider (4), the `sign_msg` instruction being used to authenticate the client. In order to perform the SSL handshake, the player program requires a secure source of randomness. The AEGIS processor must therefore be equipped with a secure hardware random number generator that secure processes can use. Once the secure connection is established, it is used to transmit orders and content (5). Finally, the content is played (6) through a secure peripheral that gets encrypted content and outputs it in analog form (7).

6. EVALUATION

This section evaluates the performance overhead of the AEGIS processor architecture through detailed simulations.

Our experimental results are indicative of the performance of both the security kernel and the untrusted OS solutions. The two solutions have about the same performance because they both use the same hardware mechanisms for integrity verification and encryption, and those mechanisms are responsible for the only two major performance penalties in our architecture (see Section 3.5 for more detailed discussion).

6.1 Simulation Framework

Our simulation framework is based on the SimpleScalar tool set [3]. The simulator models speculative out-of-order processors. To model the memory bandwidth usage more accurately, separate address and data buses were implemented.

The architectural parameters used in the simulations are shown in Table 2. In the experiments, we use 4-B encryption random vector RV for each cache block while the memory bus is 8-B wide. To avoid wasting off-chip bandwidth, a processor always accesses two consecutive random vectors (8 Bytes) at a time, and uses small 32 entry buffer for them. SimpleScalar is configured to execute Alpha binaries, and all benchmarks are compiled for EV6 (21264) to maximize performance.

To capture the characteristics of benchmarks in the middle of computation, each benchmark is simulated for 100 million instructions after skipping the first 1.5 billion instructions. In the simulations, we ignore the initialization overhead of the integrity checking schemes. Given the fact that benchmarks run for a long time, the overhead should be negligible compared to the steady-state performance.

For all the experiments in this section, nine SPEC2000 CPU benchmarks [10] are used as representative applications: `gcc`, `gzip`, `mcf`, `twolf`, `vortex`, `vpr`, `applu`, `art`, and `swim`.

6.2 Tamper-Evident Processing

As discussed in Section 3.5, the performance overhead of the TE processing can be estimated by the performance overhead of the off-chip memory integrity verification.

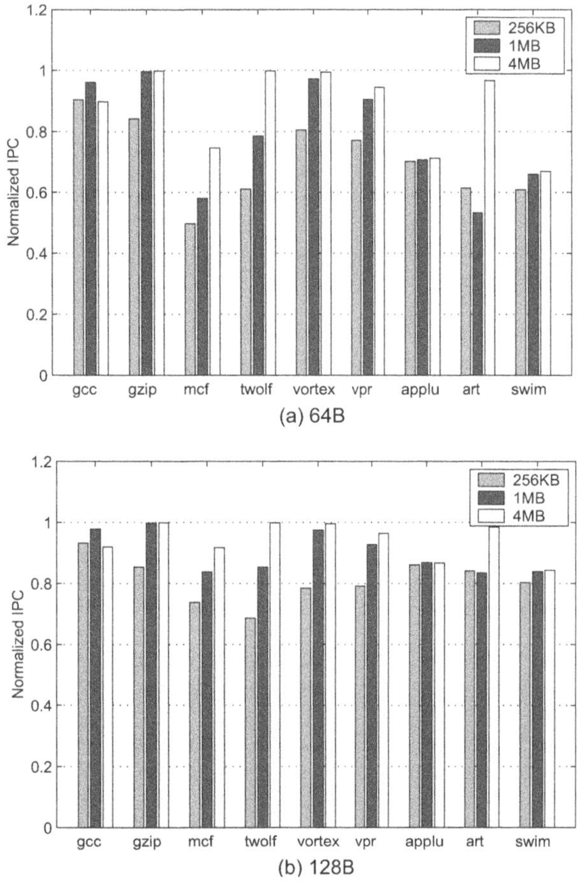

Figure 6: The performance overhead of TE processing. The results are shown for various L2 cache sizes with two block sizes (64B and 128B).

Figure 6 illustrates the impact of TE processing on application performance. For different L2 cache configurations, the IPCs are shown normalized by the corresponding IPC without TE processing. The figure first demonstrates that the performance overhead of the TE processing is relatively low. Even though the hash tree mechanism can cause over ten additional memory accesses per L2 cache miss, the performance degradation is less than 50% in the worst case.

Moreover, the performance degradation decreases rapidly as either the L2 cache size or the block size increases. Having a large L2 cache improves the performance by reducing the number of off-chip memory accesses. Integrity verification show less performance degradation with larger L2 blocks because the larger blocks reduce the levels in the hash tree. However, we note that a larger L2 block size can degrade the performance of applications that do not use integrity verification.

Obviously, the performance overhead of the TE processing also depends on the application characteristics. Because the major overhead occurs for off-chip memory accesses, applications with less off-chip accesses show less performance degradation. For example, `gzip` shows less than 15% performance degradation for all cases, while the performance of `mcf` can be degraded by as much as 50%.

In summary, with the hash tree mechanism, the TE processing can be done with less than 20% performance overhead for most cases, and 50% overhead in the worst case. For a more detailed discussion of memory integrity verification, see [8] and [22].

6.3 Private Tamper-Resistant Processing

PTR processing requires both memory encryption and memory integrity verification. As discussed in Section 3.5, the overhead of these two mechanisms are the only major concerns for our PTR architecture. We first study the performance overhead of the encryption mechanism. Then, we estimate the performance overhead of the PTR architecture by simulating memory encryption and memory integrity verification together.

6.3.1 Encryption Performance

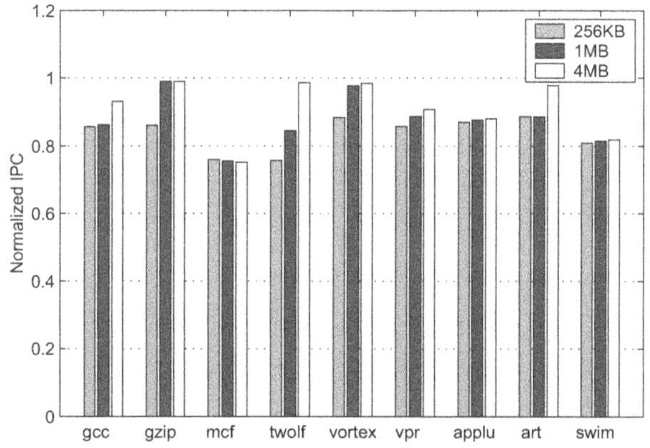

Figure 7: The performance overhead of the direct encryption scheme. Results for three different L2 caches with 64-B blocks are shown.

Figure 7 shows the performance overhead of the direct encryption mechanism compared to the standard case without encryption. In the experiments, we simulated the case where *all instructions and data are encrypted in memory.* The encryption degrades the processor performance by consuming additional memory bandwidth for random vectors, and by delaying the data delivery for decryption. Therefore, increasing the L2 cache size or L2 block size reduces the performance degradation for encryption as it does for integrity verification. In our experiments, the memory encryption results in up to 25% degradation.

Figure 8 shows the impact of changing the memory bandwidth on the encryption overhead. Our base configuration assumes the memory bandwidth of 1.6GB/s, which corre-

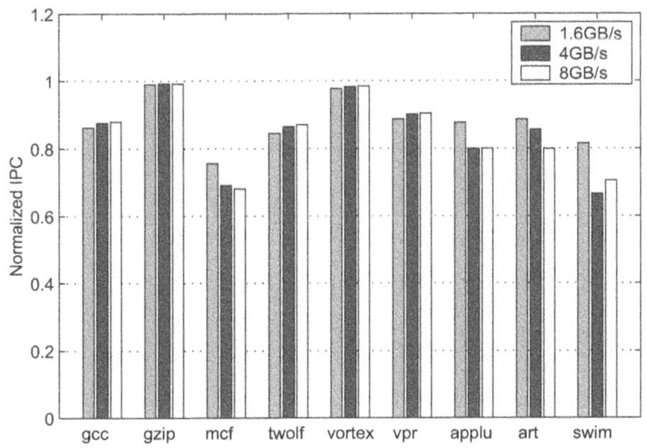

Figure 8: The impact of memory bandwidth on the memory encryption overhead.

sponds to 5 processor cycles per 8-B memory transfer in our case. Modern microprocessors are beginning to have higher bandwidth with the development of new memory and interconnect technologies. With higher bandwidth, the performance is more sensitive to the memory latency because it is not limited by the bandwidth anymore. At the same time, the memory latency without encryption decreases as we can transfer a cache block faster, which means that the decryption latency becomes more significant in comparison to the original memory latency. On the other hand, higher bandwidth mitigates the effect of the bandwidth overhead for accessing random vectors. Because there are effects on both positive and negative sides, the bandwidth change does not significantly change the relative performance degradation in one way although it always improves the absolute performance.

6.3.2 *Overall Performance*

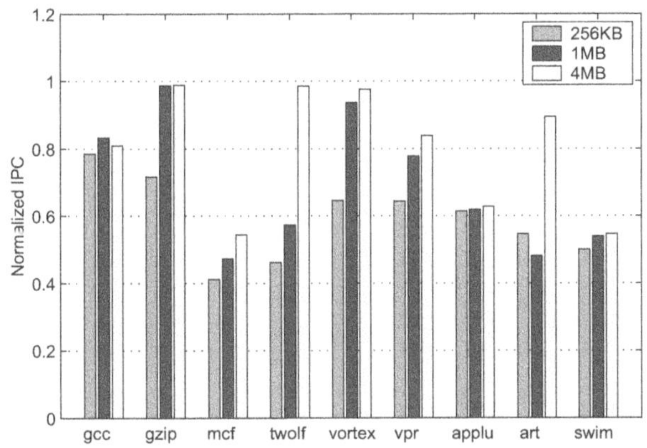

Figure 9: The performance overhead of PTR processing. Results for three different L2 caches with 64-B blocks are shown.

Finally, we study the performance of the PTR processing by simulating integrity verification and encryption together. Figure 9 demonstrates that PTR processing can be done with 60% overhead in the worst case (`mcf`), and less than 40% overhead in most cases. With the trend of larger on-chip caches and faster improvement of computation speed compared to the memory latency, the overhead should reduce with time. We also note that these numbers correspond to the case where all instructions and data are encrypted.

7. RELATED RESEARCH

7.1 Secure Processors

Secure co-processors have been proposed (e.g., [23], [21]) that encapsulate processing subsystems within a tamper-sensing and tamper-responding environment where one can run security-sensitive processes. A processing subsystem contains the private key of a public/private key pair [6] and uses classical public key cryptography algorithms such as RSA [17] to enable a wide variety of applications. To maintain performance, the processing subsystems have invariably been used as co-processors rather than primary processors. The processing subsystems of these processors typically assume that system software is trusted.

The eXecute Only Memory (XOM) architecture [12] is designed to run security requiring applications in secure compartments, where instructions are encrypted and from which data can escape only on explicit request from the application. Even the operating system cannot violate the security model. However, XOM's integrity mechanism is vulnerable to replay attacks, which was also pointed out in [20]. In particular, XOM will not notice if writes to memory are sometimes ignored. XOM can be fixed by using memory integrity verification to protect against replay attacks. In the AEGIS untrusted operating system solution, we have drawn insight from XOM, notably for the on-chip data tagging mechanism and the saving of contexts. Our implementation of the context manager is different because we use hash-trees to verify process state, which can be stored in off-chip memory. This allows us to support a much larger number of processes running in TE and PTR environments. Our architecture also provides flexibility for applications to use protection mechanisms only when they are necessary, avoiding unnecessary performance degradation.

7.2 Systems

The Trusted Computing Platform Alliance (TCPA) is an alliance led by Intel whose stated goal is 'a new computing platform for the next century that will provide for improved trust in the PC platform'. The proposed implementation in the first phase of TCPA is a *Fritz* chip - a smartcard chip or dongle soldered to the motherboard. When the PC boots up, the Fritz chip stores a hash of the boot ROM before executing it. The boot ROM stores a hash of the boot loader on the Fritz chip before executing it. This process is repeated throughout the boot process so that a trace of the system boot can be read from the Fritz chip. This is similar to the integrity-checking boot process described in [2]. Because the security mechanisms are implemented separately from the main processor, physical attacks on communication between off-chip components, such as memory and the Fritz chip, are possible.

Palladium [4], recently renamed to NGSCB, is software with minimal hardware support that Microsoft plans to incorporate in future versions of Windows. In Palladium, the *Nexus* is a trusted security kernel. Palladium protects software from software, but does not concern itself with physical attacks.

Because they are both vulnerable to hardware attacks, TCPA and Palladium can be enhanced, i.e., made secure against a larger set of attacks, using the components in the AEGIS processor, namely, integrity verification and memory encryption. With integrity verification, applications could get guarantees that their data has not been modified, even by a physical attacker. Encryption of data in main memory would prevent physical attacks that attempt to read private data from memory.

Moreover, in the AEGIS architecture, it is possible to perform secure computation while only trusting a processor and an application program. In TCPA and Palladium, the user has to trust the entire software stack or at least part of the operating system.

8. CONCLUSION

We have described the architecture of a processor that can be used to build secure computing systems where the processor is the only trusted component. This requires the integration of many architectural mechanisms into a conventional architecture, notably, memory integrity verification, memory encryption/decryption, and secure context management. Using simulation, we have shown that the performance overhead of integrating such mechanisms into a high-performance super-scalar processor is reasonable. We believe this overhead can likely be reduced with further architectural innovation.

Our current architecture focuses on a single processor system where a secure process always executes on the same processor. In multiprocessor systems, a process can run on multiple processors. Therefore, efficient ways for multiple processors to share off-chip memory while preserving the protection should be developed as future work.

9. ACKNOWLEDGEMENTS

This work was funded by Acer Inc., Delta Electronics Inc., HP Corp., NTT Inc., Nokia Research Center, and Philips Research under the MIT Project Oxygen partnership.

We would also like to thank Ron Rivest and Krste Asanovic for many constructive comments, as well as all the members of our group who helped proof-read this paper.

10. REFERENCES

[1] J. Agat. Transforming out timing leaks. In 27th *ACM Principles of Programming Languages*, January 2000.

[2] W. Arbaugh, D. Farber, and J. Smith. A Secure and Reliable Bootstrap Architecture. In *Proceedings of the 1997 IEEE Symposium on Security and Privacy*, pages 65–71, May 1997.

[3] D. Burger and T. M. Austin. The SimpleScalar Tool Set, Version 2.0. Technical report, University of Wisconsin-Madison Computer Science Department, 1997.

[4] A. Carroll, M. Juarez, J. Polk, and T. Leininger. Microsoft "Palladium": A Business Overview. In *Microsoft Content Security Business Unit*, August 2002.

[5] J. Claessens, B. Preneel, and J. Vandewalle. (how) can mobile agents do secure electronic transactions on untrusted hosts? a survey of the security issues and the current solutions. *ACM Transactions on Internet Technology*, 3, Feb. 2003.

[6] W. Diffie and M. E. Hellman. New Directions in Cryptography. *IEEE Transactions on Information Theory*, IT-22(6):644–654, 1976.

[7] B. Gassend, D. Clarke, M. van Dijk, and S. Devadas. Silicon Physical Random Functions . In *Proceedings of the Computer and Communication Security Conference*, May 2002.

[8] B. Gassend, G. E. Suh, D. Clarke, M. van Dijk, and S. Devadas. Caches and merkle trees for efficient memory integrity verification. In *Proceedings of Ninth International Symposium on High Performance Computer Architecture*, February 2003.

[9] O. Goldreich and R. Ostrovsky. Software protection and simulation on oblivious RAMs. *Journal of the ACM*, 43(3):431–473, 1996.

[10] J. L. Henning. SPEC CPU2000: Measuring CPU performance in the new millennium. *IEEE Computer*, July 2000.

[11] H. Kuo and I. M. Verbauwhede. Architectural optimization for a 1.82 gb/s vlsi implementation of the aes rijndael algorithm. In *Cryptographic Hardware and Embedded Systems 2001 (CHES 2001), LNCS 2162*, 2001.

[12] D. Lie, C. Thekkath, M. Mitchell, P. Lincoln, D. Boneh, J. Mitchell, and M. Horowitz. Architectural Support for Copy and Tamper Resistant Software. In *Proceedings of the* 9th *Int'l Conference on Architectural Support for Programming Languages and Operating Systems (ASPLOS-IX)*, pages 169–177, November 2000.

[13] R. C. Merkle. Protocols for public key cryptography. In *IEEE Symposium on Security and Privacy*, pages 122–134, 1980.

[14] A. C. Myers. JFlow: Practical Mostly-Static Information Flow Control. In 26th *ACM Principles of Programming Languages*, January 1999.

[15] National Institute of Science and Technology. FIPS PUB 197: Advanced Encryption Standard (AES), November 2001.

[16] E. Rescola. *SSL and TLS: Designing and Building Secure Systems*. Addison-Wesley, 2001.

[17] R. Rivest, A. Shamir, and L. Adleman. A Method for Obtaining Digital Signatures and Public-Key Cryptosystems. *Communications of the ACM*, 21:120–126, 1978.

[18] L. F. G. Sarmenta. *Volunteer Computing*. PhD thesis, Massachusetts Institute of Technology, June 2001.

[19] P. R. Schaumont, H. Kuo, and I. M. Verbauwhede. Unlocking the design secrets of a 2.29 gb/s rijndael processor. In *Design Automation Conference 2002*, June 2002.

[20] W. Shapiro and R. Vingralek. How to Manage Persistent State in DRM Systems. In *Digital Rights Management Workshop*, pages 176–191, 2001.

[21] S. W. Smith and S. H. Weingart. Building a High-Performance, Programmable Secure Coprocessor. In *Computer Networks (Special Issue on Computer Network Security)*, volume 31, pages 831–860, April 1999.

[22] G. E. Suh, D. Clarke, B. Gassend, M. van Dijk, and S. Devadas. Hardware mechanisms for memory integrity checking. In *Technical Report MIT-LCS-TR-872*, November 2002.

[23] B. S. Yee. *Using Secure Coprocessors*. PhD thesis, Carnegie Mellon University, 1994.

Energy Conservation Techniques for Disk Array-Based Servers *

Eduardo Pinheiro and Ricardo Bianchini
Department of Computer Science
Rutgers University
Piscataway, NJ 08554
{edpin,ricardob}@cs.rutgers.edu

ABSTRACT

In this paper, we study energy conservation techniques for disk array-based network servers. First, we introduce a new conservation technique, called Popular Data Concentration (PDC), that migrates frequently accessed data to a subset of the disks. The goal is to skew the load towards a few of the disks, so that others can be transitioned to low-power modes. Next, we introduce a user-level file server that takes advantage of PDC. In the context of this server, we compare PDC to the Massive Array of Idle Disks (MAID). Using a validated simulator, we evaluate these techniques for conventional and two-speed disks and a wide range of parameters. Our results for conventional disks show that PDC and MAID can only conserve energy when the load on the server is extremely low. When two-speed disks are used, both PDC and MAID can conserve significant energy with only a small fraction of delayed requests. Overall, we find that PDC achieves more consistent and robust energy savings than MAID.

Categories and Subject Descriptors

D.4 [**Operating systems**]: Storage management; B.4 [**Input/output and data communications**]: Input/output devices

General Terms

Experimentation, measurement

Keywords

Energy conservation, network servers, disk power

1. INTRODUCTION

Energy conservation has been extensively studied in the context of mobile devices. Recently, researchers have realized that energy conservation is also important for servers and server clusters. For these systems, energy conservation is obviously not intended to extend battery life, but nonetheless has serious economical and environmental implications. Economical because the energy consumption of these servers and their cooling systems is reflected in their electricity bills. Environmental because most power-generation technologies are harmful to the environment.

A few efforts [6, 12, 18] have been made to conserve energy in server clusters by tackling the high base power of traditional servers, i.e. the power consumption when the server is on but idle. Other efforts [2, 8, 9] have tackled the energy consumed by the servers' microprocessors. Finally, the energy consumption of disk array-based servers has received some attention as well [5, 7, 10, 11, 20, 21]. The energy consumed by the array can easily surpass that of the rest of the system, depending on the array size [5, 10].

In this paper, we propose a new energy conservation technique for disk array-based network servers, called Popular Data Concentration (PDC). The idea behind PDC is to dynamically migrate the popular disk data (i.e., the most frequently accessed data on disk) to a subset of the disks in the array, so that the load becomes skewed towards a few of the disks and others can be sent to low-power modes. PDC is based on the observation that network server workloads often exhibit files with widely different popularities. For instance, Web server workloads are known to exhibit highly skewed popularity towards a small set of files.

To demonstrate the benefits of PDC, we also propose a user-level file server, called Nomad FS, that takes advantage of our technique. We envision coupling Nomad FS with one or more front-end network servers. Nomad FS uses the MQ algorithm [19] for second-level cache replacement to guide the placement of files in the disk array dynamically. The current prototype of Nomad FS conserves energy by spinning disks down after a period of idleness. Unfortunately, spinning a disk back up to service a request increases the response time for the request significantly.

We also study Nomad FS in the context of disk arrays composed of two-speed disks [5]. These disks conserve energy by automatically reducing their rotational speeds under light load. Thus, Nomad FS does not have to explicitly effect power mode transitions when two-speed disks are used. Furthermore, requests are only delayed during rotational speed transitions, which means that only a small percentage of requests is delayed for stable workloads.

Because our work targets network servers, degrading the response time of a small fraction of requests is acceptable for Nomad FS. In fact, the overhead of multiple message exchanges per request in network servers means that higher server response times can be accommodated. Moreover, network servers typically interact with

*This research was supported in part by NSF grants CCR-0238182 (CAREER award) and EIA-0224428.

people (or background processes), so even substantial degradations may not be noticeable. For example, a degradation from 10 to 100 milliseconds is usually acceptable for network servers.

To put PDC in context, we compare Nomad FS against a very similar version of it that is based on the Massive Array of Idle Disks (MAID) [7]. Instead of relying on file popularity and migration, MAID relies on temporal locality to place copies of files on a subset of the disks. Each disk in this subset acts as a cache of the files and uses the LRU replacement policy. Non-cache disks then become more lightly loaded, allowing for energy conservation.

The behavior of the systems we consider is affected by several important parameters, such as the type of disks, the disk request rate, the size of the main memory cache, and the percentage of the stored files that is actually accessed. To understand the effect of these parameters and determine the "sweet spot" for each technique, we assess the parameter space extensively using a simulator and synthetic traces. We also simulate two real traces to confirm the observations from the parameter space exploration. To guarantee the accuracy of our results, we validate the simulator against real executions of our prototype implementation of Nomad FS.

Our results for arrays of conventional disks show that PDC and MAID can only conserve energy when the load on the server is extremely low. When arrays of two-speed disks are used, both PDC and MAID can conserve up to 30-40% of the disk energy with only a small fraction of delayed requests. Overall, PDC is more consistent and robust than MAID; the behavior of MAID is highly dependent on the number of cache disks. Furthermore, PDC achieves these properties without the overhead of extra disks. However, the PDC energy savings degrade substantially for long migration intervals. Based on these results, we conclude that the techniques we study will be very useful for disk array-based servers when multi-speed disks become available.

In summary, the contributions of this paper are:

- We propose a file popularity-based energy conservation technique for disk array-based network servers;
- We design and implement an energy-aware file server that takes advantage of the technique; and
- We assess the behavior of two energy conservation techniques for conventional and two-speed disk arrays and a wide range of parameters.

The remainder of this paper is organized as follows. The next section describes PDC, Nomad FS, and MAID. Section 3 describes our evaluation methodology, including our simulator and the parameter space we study. Sections 4 and 5 present our results for synthetic and real traces, respectively. Section 6 discusses the related work. Finally, section 7 concludes the paper.

2. ENERGY CONSERVATION IN ARRAYS

In this section we first describe two of our main contributions: the PDC energy conservation technique and Nomad FS. Next, we move on to describing MAID and the traditional fixed-threshold technique, and qualitatively comparing the approaches.

2.1 Popular Data Concentration

Several types of network servers exhibit workloads with highly skewed file access frequencies. For example, it has been shown that the frequency of file access by a Web server conforms to a Zipf distribution [3] with high coefficient. The same is true of other servers as well, e.g. [13]. More formally, Zipf's law predicts that the frequency of access or popularity τ of a file is proportional to the inverse of its rank r raised to some coefficient α, i.e. $\tau = 1/r^{\alpha}$. When α is high (close to 1), a relatively small number of files is accessed frequently, whereas a large number of files is accessed rarely. Workloads with high α often exhibit skewed popularity in terms of disk accesses as well (albeit with smaller α), even in the presence of large main memory caches [4].

PDC is inspired by such heavily clustered popularities. The idea behind PDC is to concentrate the most popular disk data (i.e., those that most frequently miss in the main memory cache) by migrating it to a subset of the disks. This concentration should skew the disk load towards this subset, while other disks become less loaded. These other disks can then be sent to low-power modes to conserve energy. More specifically, the goal of PDC is to lay data out across the disk array so that the first disk stores the most popular disk data, the second disk stores the next set of most popular disk data, and so on. The least popular disk data and the data that are never accessed will then be stored on the last few disks. In fact, the last few disks will also include the data that most frequently hit in the main memory cache.

To avoid performance degradation, it is important not to overload the disks that store popular data. Thus, the expected access rate for each disk needs to be considered explicitly. This is done by estimating the future load (in MBytes/second) on each disk to be the sum of the recent load directed to the data to be stored on it. PDC should then only migrate data onto a disk until the expected load on the disk is close to its maximum bandwidth for the workload.

Because data popularity can change over time, PDC may have to be applied periodically. In such cases, it might be necessary to free up space on a disk by migrating data out of it, before more popular data can be migrated in.

2.2 Nomad FS

PDC has been implemented in Nomad FS, a prototype energy-aware file server consisting of approximately 13k lines of C++ code. Nomad FS is a user-level, event-driven server that works on top of the local file system. The server associates a helper thread with each disk. This thread is the only part of the server that directly touches the disk, either for read/write operations or migrations. Although the server receives requests for 8-KByte file blocks, entire files are migrated according to PDC. This approach works fine for the workloads we are interested in, such as Web, proxy, ftp, and email server workloads, which access entire files at a time.

To conserve energy in disk arrays composed of conventional disks, PDC is used to idle disks, which are then spun down by the server after a fixed period of idleness (the idleness threshold). The server determines that it is time to spin down a disk by keeping the last access time per disk and periodically testing whether any disk has been idle for longer than the idleness threshold. A spun down disk is reactivated on the next access to it. When we consider disk arrays composed of two-speed disks, Nomad FS does not explicitly effect power mode transitions. Furthermore, Nomad FS does not migrate files out of disks that are already running in low speed to reduce the migration overhead.

The file server exports one single view of the file system, although multiple disks drives can be used. For simplicity of our prototype, each file is permanently stored on one disk only, i.e. no striping or mirroring is used at this time. The user has no control over where (on the disk array) files are stored, since that information can change dynamically. New files are created on any of the disks with enough free space. Metadata information is kept in a well-known location on the disk that stores the most popular files. The metadata for each file contains the file name (at most 128 bytes), the size of the file, the disk on which the file resides, the times of creation and last access, and bookkeeping information (pointers to next and previous files on the same disk, etc). Overall, each metadata entry consumes 168 bytes. The metadata for all files is kept in a large file that is memory mapped to the virtual address space of the server. Only when a file is actually opened is its metadata accessed and physical memory allocated for it.

Nomad FS caches data blocks in memory at the user level. Because the cache is not a first-level cache (it sits behind the clients' and/or network servers' caches), the standard LRU replacement policy would not work well for this cache. Instead, Nomad FS uses the Multi Queue (MQ) algorithm [19] to manage its block cache. MQ has been shown superior to other algorithms, including sophisticated variations of LRU.

The MQ cache works as follows. There are multiple LRU queues numbered Q_0, Q_1, ..., Q_{m-1}; in our prototype $m = 12$, but the system behavior is typically similar for other large numbers of queues. Blocks stay in the LRU queues for a given *lifetime*. This lifetime is defined dynamically by the MQ algorithm to be the maximum temporal distance between two accesses to the same file or the number of cache blocks, whichever is larger. If a block has not been referenced within its lifetime, it is demoted from Q_i to Q_{i-1} or evicted from the cache if it is in Q_0. Each queue also has a maximum access count. If a block in queue Q_i is accessed more than 2^i times, this block is then promoted to Q_{i+1} until it is accessed more than 2^{i+1} times or its lifetime expires. Within a given queue, blocks are ranked by recency of access, according to LRU.

During operation of the server, information about the files referenced in the past are summarized on a list in main memory. The summary for each file stores the file descriptor, the number of disk accesses for the file, a pointer to its metadata, and some other bookkeeping data (such as list pointers), totaling 60 bytes. The amount of memory dedicated to the list of summary information should be large enough to hold at least the number of files in the working set of a given workload.

The ranking of file popularity is done incrementally every time a file access requires a disk access. We do this by reusing the same MQ cache algorithm described above, but instead of using it on cache blocks, we use it on the summary information. More specifically, we keep the summary information on an MQ cache-like list. Every disk access causes the file's summary data to move on the list according to the MQ policy. More disk accesses cause the summary entry to move closer to the head of the list. After a while, popular files (in terms of disk accesses) will be close to the head of the list, while unpopular files will be towards the tail.

Periodically, files are migrated to disks based on this ranked list of disk accesses. The algorithm traverses the queues from Q_{m-1} to Q_0. Initially, files in queue Q_{m-1} are migrated to the first disk (numbered 0) until it is full or the expected load on the disk approaches its maximum bandwidth for the workload. The expected load associated with a file is estimated by dividing its size by its average inter-access time. The next set of files is migrated to the second disk (according to the same conditions) and so on. If the server needs to migrate a file F to disk drive i, there is no space available on i, and a file L on i is less popular than F, then file L is migrated to disk z. Disk z is selected as follows. First, the server tries the disks holding more popular files, starting from disk 0 and checking all disks until disk $i - 1$. If not enough space and bandwidth can be found there, the server checks the disks holding less popular data, starting from disk $i + 1$ and checking all higher numbered disks. This algorithm should always find space for the file, as long as the overall disk space is not excessively tight for the size of the file system. We have not developed an algorithm to deal with this last scenario, because it has not been a problem for us.

2.3 Comparison Against Other Approaches

MAID. The Massive Array of Idle Disks (MAID) [7] has been proposed as a replacement for old tape backup archives with hundreds or thousands of tapes. Because only a small part of the archive would be active at a time, the idea is to copy the required data to a set of "cache disks" and put all the other disks in low-power mode. Accesses to the archive may then find the data on the cache disk(s). Cache disk replacements are implemented using an LRU policy. Replaced data can simply be discarded if it is clean. If it is dirty, it has to be written back to the corresponding non-cache disk.

This same idea can be applied to file servers as well. In fact, we developed a version of Nomad FS that uses MAID to conserve energy. We used as much code from Nomad FS as possible for our MAID-based file server, so that the two servers can be directly compared. The main memory cache management, for instance, is exactly the same for both implementations. On an access to a cached file block, the access is performed on the corresponding cache disk. If the block accessed is not cached, the entire file is copied by the server from its location on one of the non-cache disks to one of the cache disks. If a replacement is required on a cache disk, an entire file that is large enough is replaced according to LRU.

The designers of MAID observed that cache disks can become overloaded [7]. To counter this problem, we optimize MAID by avoiding copying files to the cache disks when the recent load on these disks is approaching their maximum bandwidth. We find that the absence of this optimization always leads to a large percentage of delayed requests, as the cache disks become a bottleneck.

To conserve energy in configurations with conventional disks, the MAID version of our server explicitly spins disks down after a period of idleness. When considering two-speed disks, the server does not control power modes explicitly and does not copy data out of disks that are already at low speed.

In section 4, we quantitatively compare the MAID version of our file server against the PDC version. Here we focus on a qualitative comparison. PDC and MAID have the same objective, namely to increase idle times by moving data around the disk array and spinning disks down. As a result, both techniques sacrifice the access time of certain files in favor of energy conservation. However, instead of relying on file popularity and migration like PDC, MAID relies on temporal locality and copying to conserve energy. This has a few potential disadvantages in terms of energy savings: (1) the cache disk(s) represent energy overhead, since they are additional to the set of disks that are required to store the actual data; (2) the cache disk(s) might not have enough space to store the entire (dynamically changing) working set for a given workload, causing constant accesses to the non-cache disks; and (3) files are randomly spread on the non-cache disks, which may significantly reduce the opportunity for energy conservation if requests miss in the cache disk(s) frequently. Nevertheless, MAID does have a few potential advantages: (1) metadata management is significantly simpler, since it does not need to store and operate on file access information about all files, only those that are on cache disks; and (2) it adapts faster to changes in workload behavior, because file copying (and possibly replacement) take place on a per-file access basis.

FT. When considering disk arrays composed of conventional disks, we also study a fixed-threshold (FT) technique. FT is simple: a disk is spun down after it has been idle for a fixed period. The idleness threshold is the amount of time for which the energy consumed in idle state is the same as that of powering the disk down and later powering the disk back up. The rationale for this definition is similar to the competitive argument about renting or buying skis [15]. A spun down disk is reactivated on the next access to it.

FT does not involve any data movement or re-organization and, thus, is not very effective at conserving energy in busy servers. In contrast, it is very useful when combined with PDC or MAID, as described above. We use an FT-based version of our file server as a basis for comparison in section 4. Again, we re-used most of the Nomad FS code to implement our FT-based file server.

3. METHODOLOGY

Our main goals in this paper are to determine the conditions under which PDC is effective at conserving energy and how it compares to MAID and FT for two disk array types and a wide range of parameters. We explore this parameter space using the simulator that we describe in subsection 3.1.

The reason why we chose simulation rather than real experimentation is two-fold: (1) two-speed disks are not yet available on the market (although Sony already has a disk drive that allows for static speed setting [16]); and (2) using real experiments to perform such a comprehensive parameter space exploration would have taken extremely long. For example, each of our simulations involves 19 million requests at 750 requests/second. A real experiment with these parameters takes 7 hours, whereas a simulation takes less than 40 minutes. Note that accelerating a real execution and then scaling results back would not have worked, since it is not possible to accelerate real disk spin up/spin down operations, file copying, or file migration.

Nevertheless, we strongly believe in realistic simulations, so we carefully validated the simulator against executions of our prototype file server implementations on our own server hardware. We discuss the validation of the simulator in subsection 3.2.

Another advantage of using simulation is that we can easily vary parameters, which is a key component of this paper. In subsection 3.3 we discuss the set of parameters that we have found most relevant in evaluating and comparing the different file servers.

We drive the simulator with both synthetic and real traces. Subsection 3.4 describes our generator of synthetic traces, whereas subsection 3.5 describes our real traces.

3.1 Simulation

We have developed an execution-driven simulator of our prototype file servers. The simulator mimics the implementation of our servers as closely as possible. In fact, several parts of the real servers were reused in the simulator to avoid deviations from the real implementations. The MQ replacement algorithm implementation, for example, was copied straight out of the server code.

At the file system level, files are assumed to be laid out in consecutive blocks of the same disk, whereas i-nodes are assumed to be cached in memory. At a lower level, the simulator models an array of conventional Cheetah disks or an array of two-speed disks. The main characteristics of the conventional disk are shown in table 1. The table also lists the idleness threshold for this disk, which is the sum of the energies to spin the disk up and down divided by the idle power.

The main characteristics of the two-speed disks are shown in table 2. The high speed values are those of the Cheetah disk. These values were scaled down to produce the low speed values. In particular, the power and energy values were scaled down in quadratic fashion [10], assuming that $power = c \times speed^2 + 1.86$ where c is the constant $(5.26 - 1.86)/10K^2$. The disk controller slows the disk down when the offered load becomes lower than 80% of the disk throughput at low speed. Conversely, the controller transitions the disk to high speed when this same threshold is exceeded. The controller can trigger these transitions by observing the actual utilization of the disk. We assume that no accesses can proceed when a disk is transitioning speeds. The speed transition costs are set to half of the corresponding costs for the Cheetah disk. For example, going from low to high speed costs half of the energy and time to spin up the Cheetah disk. These transition cost settings are admittedly somewhat arbitrary. However, note that the transition costs make little difference in our simulations, since the frequency of speed transitions is low for the parameters we consider. This same effect has been observed in previous work [5].

Finally, the PDC and MAID-based servers involve four major sources of overhead that do not exist in the FT version of our server: migrations, copies, LRU processing, MQ processing. The CPU energy consumed by these operations has not been considered so far. To take this consumption into account, we determined these overheads by running three microbenchmarks. One of them isolates the CPU energy involved in each file block request to be about 37 μJ for both LRU and MQ processing. The other two microbenchmarks isolate the CPU energy consumed by each migration and copy operation, as a function of file size. We have approximated these costs to 1.5 μJ per byte moved. The simulator charges each request, migration, and copy with these CPU energy costs.

Description	Value
Disk model	Seagate Cheetah ST39205LC
Standard interface	SCSI
Storage capacity	9.17 GBytes
Number of platters	1
Rotational speed	10000 rpm
Avg. seek time	5.4 msecs
Avg. rotation time	3 msecs
Transfer rate	31 MBytes/sec
Idle power	5.26 Watts
Down power	1.86 Watts
Active energy (8-KB read)	61 mJoules
Spin up energy	65.91 Joules
Spin down energy	28.25 Joules
Spin up time	6.12 secs
Spin down time	11.24 secs
Idleness threshold	17.9 secs

Table 1: Main characteristics and measured power, energy, and time statistics of our SCSI disk.

Description	Value
Storage capacity	9.17 GBytes
Avg. seek time	5.4 msecs
High to low speed transition energy	14.13 Joules
High to low speed transition time	5.62 secs
Low to high speed transition energy	32.96 Joules
Low to high speed transition time	3.06 secs
High rotational speed	10000 rpm
Avg. rotation time at high speed	3 msecs
Transfer rate at high speed	31 MBytes/sec
Idle power at high speed	5.26 Watts
Active energy at high speed (8-KB read)	61 mJoules
Low rotational speed	3000 rpm
Avg. rotation time at low speed	10 msecs
Transfer rate at low speed	9.3 MBytes/sec
Idle power at low speed	2.17 Watts
Active energy at low speed (8-KB read)	43 mJoules

Table 2: Main characteristics and simulated power, energy, and time for our two-speed disk. The high speed values are those of our Cheetah disk (table 1). These values were scaled down to produce the low speed values. The speed transition costs are set to half of the corresponding costs in the Cheetah disk.

Description	Total energy consumed			Files moved		MBytes moved		Spin downs/ups		Delayed requests	
	Sim	Real	Error	Sim	Real	Sim	Real	Sim	Real	Sim	Real
PDC	152023	172843	12.0%	9715	10943	227	283	336	326	1.3%	1.2%
MAID	141349	156335	9.6%	8738	8716	204	204	300	304	1.1%	1.0%
FT	190374	200479	5.0%	n/a	n/a	n/a	n/a	10	13	0.2%	0.2%
EO	190346	200833	5.2%	n/a	n/a	n/a	n/a	n/a	n/a	0.0%	0.0%

Table 4: Summary of simulator validation. Energy values are in Joules.

Description	Value
Request rate	4 file requests/sec
Trace length	9033 secs (2.5 hours)
Number of files	43690 *
File size	20 KBytes *
Total file system size	853 MBytes *
Main memory cache size	64 MBytes *
Number of disks	4
Disk capacity	342 MBytes *
Idleness threshold	17.9 secs
Migration period	every 1.25 hours (PDC only)

Table 3: Values used in the simulator validation: workload characteristics (top), server settings and disk characteristics (bottom). Values marked with "*" are used for fast validation.

The simulator faithfully models the disk powers, energies, and times discussed above to determine disk energy consumption and response times. The CPU energy costs associated with PDC and MAID are added to their disk energy consumption.

3.2 Simulator Validation

It is important to build confidence in our simulator by validating it against real experiments. Unfortunately, we can only validate the simulations that assume conventional disks.

Our server hardware consists of an ASUS A7A133 motherboard with an Intel Pentium-4 1.9-GHz processor, 512 MBytes of memory, 4 Seagate Cheetah 9.1-GByte Ultra SCSI disks, one Adaptec 29160 Ultra 160 SCSI controller, and one Gigabit Ethernet network adaptor. The energy consumed by the disks is monitored by a TDS 3014 oscilloscope. The oscilloscope is connected to a remote computer that collects power consumption data at 1.25 Gsamples/second. These data are averaged every 10 milliseconds. A 1.2-GHz PC connected to the server via a Gigabit Ethernet connection generates load for the server.

We used a synthetic workload to validate the simulator against our prototype file servers running on this server hardware. Our workload generator (explained in detail below) keeps selecting a file to access randomly out of a set of files for a user-specified amount of time. All the blocks of each chosen file are requested in sequence. The timing of the file requests follows an exponential distribution. The main characteristics of the synthetic workload and the server settings are summarized in table 3. Note that some of the workload characteristics and server settings (those marked with "*") are not realistic; they are meant exclusively for fast validation.

We collected results for our file servers, as well as an energy-oblivious server (EO) under which disks are never powered down. The MAID version used one of the 4 disks as a cache disk, so it did not incur any energy overhead due to the cache disk. Table 4 compares the servers in terms of disk energy consumption, files and bytes moved between disks, number of disk spin downs/ups, and the percentage of delayed requests. We consider a file request to be delayed if it takes longer than 200 milliseconds.

The results show that the total energy consumed by each server matches closely (within 5 to 12%) that of the simulated system. The results also match the other metrics closely, especially the number of spin downs/ups, which is a key metric for energy conservation. These results give us confidence that our simulator can be used to illustrate the important trends across the parameter space.

3.3 Parameter Space

Three categories of parameters directly affect the energy conservation techniques and file servers we study: workload characteristics, server characteristics, and disk drive characteristics. Next, we discuss each of these categories in turn.

Workload characteristics. These are characteristics that are inherent to the workload imposed on the file server. Among the large set of parameters that describe a workload, we have identified five key characteristics: the request rate, the file popularity, the coverage of the file system, the percentage of writes, and the temporal correlation of accesses to files.

The *request rate* has to do with the rate at which file requests arrive at the server. We assume that inter-arrival times are exponentially distributed; the request rate is the average of the distribution.

File *popularity* corresponds to the frequency with which each file is accessed. We represent popularity by a value of the α coefficient in Zipf's power law. This coefficient determines how skewed the distribution of accesses to files is. A smaller α (close to 0) means that requests are more evenly distributed among files, whereas a larger α (close to 1) means that requests are more skewed towards a few files.

The file system *coverage* has to do with the percentage of the entire file repository that is actually accessed by the workload. A coverage of 100% means that all files in the file system are accessed at least once.

The *percentage of writes* corresponds to the frequency of file write operations in the workload.

Temporal locality describes how far apart in time consecutive accesses to the same files are. In particular, workloads with high temporal locality exhibit consecutive accesses to the same file that are "close" in time, whereas workloads with low temporal locality exhibit consecutive accesses to the same file that are "far apart" in time. Temporal locality has a direct relationship with popularity, i.e., popular files have a short inter-arrival time due to their popularity. However, temporal locality can also be an effect of *temporal correlation*, as discussed in [14]. Files with high temporal correlation are those for which accesses are close together in time regardless of the absolute popularity of the file. In this study, we are interested in the effect of both aspects of temporal locality on energy conservation.

File server characteristics. The configuration of the file server can impact the energy savings significantly. Important configuration parameters are the main memory cache size, the cache replacement policy, and the number of disks used. We consider the *cache size* and the *number of disks* in this study. We keep the cache replacement policy fixed on the MQ algorithm, which has been shown to be the best policy for second-level caches such as the ones used in our file servers [19].

Disk drive characteristics. Several characteristics of physical disk drives affect energy consumption directly, especially the power consumption in each mode and the spin up/down overheads. Rather than focusing on a detailed exploration of this space however, we concentrate on evaluating the systems we study for disk arrays composed of either *conventional* or *two-speed disks*.

3.4 Synthetic Trace Generator

To understand the impact of the parameters we just discussed, we built a workload generator that can produce request traces with user-specified request rate, popularity, coverage, temporal correlation, number of requests, file system size, and average file size. Currently the generator assumes that all files are of the same size for simplicity.

To generate a request trace, the generator must first compute the total number of files in the file system, by dividing the file system size by the file size. With the total number of files, the generator can determine the number of files that must be requested, according to the desired coverage. Each of the files to be requested then receives a probability weight, based on Zipf's formula $1/i^{\alpha}$, where i is the rank of the file from 1 to the number of files to be requested. Based on these probabilities, the generator randomly selects the actual file requests that will make up the trace. All blocks of a selected file are requested in sequence. Each new request is assigned a timestamp that is equal to the time of the last access plus an exponentially distributed random increment based on the request rate.

The generator continues to select files based on their weights until the number of requests reaches the desired number. If the desired coverage is still missing N files when the trace is missing N requests, a request for each of these N files is appended to the trace sequentially. However, to avoid having a long sequence of previously unreferenced files in the end of the trace, we randomize the trace once all the files have been selected. We have verified that this procedure produces the desired coverage without changing the desired popularity (α) by inspecting several generated workloads.

However, this generation procedure does not consider temporal correlation explicitly. As described, the temporal locality of the workload is the one inherent to the popularity of files. The workloads we consider have this form of temporal locality, except when we explicitly address the effect of temporal correlation. To generate a set of workloads with varying degrees of temporal correlation, the generator does the following. The probability weights described by the Zipf are split into a fixed number of groups with the same number of files per group. Instead of generating requests that span the whole range of files in the coverage, the generator selects files from the first group first, for as many requests as the first group of files should receive. After generating all the requests for the first group, the generator moves to the second group and so on. Grouping files in this way forces files to be selected more closely together in time. For a number of groups larger than 1, the result is a workload with higher temporal correlation. For large numbers of groups, even unpopular files will have much higher temporal correlation. The resulting workload might be unrealistic for more than 1 group, but it does exhibit a controlled temporal correlation behavior, which suffices for our purpose of observing trends.

3.5 Real Traces

We also simulate two real (proxy server) traces, which we call Hummingbird (HUM) and Point of Presence (POP). HUM was collected at AT&T from 01/16/99 to 01/31/99. The total footprint of HUM consists of 76.9 GBytes with an average requested file size of 294 KBytes. POP was collected between 10/15/01 and 10/26/01 at the Federal University of Minas Gerais, Brazil. POP was filtered to eliminate the proxy misses, leading to a total footprint of 39.4 GBytes and an average requested file size of 17 KBytes.

Description	Default Value
Request rate *	750 reqs/s (36 MBytes/sec)
File popularity *	0.85
Coverage *	40%
Percentage of writes *	0%
Temporal locality *	popularity-induced only
Trace length	19,000,000 requests
Main memory cache size *	1 GByte
Number of disks *	8 (PDC), 9 (MAID-1+), 10 (MAID-2+)
File size	48 KBytes
Total file system size	126 GBytes
Migration period *	every 1/2 hour (PDC only)
Cache disks	1 (MAID-1+), 2 (MAID-2+)
Disk characteristics	same as in tables 1 and 2

Table 5: Default parameters used in synthetic trace simulations: workload characteristics (top), server settings (middle), disk characteristics (bottom). We vary the parameters marked with "*".

4. PARAMETER SPACE RESULTS

In this section we present the results of our parameter space exploration. We break the evaluation into two parts: arrays of conventional disks and arrays of two-speed disks. In each part, we start by analyzing workload characteristics and later move on to file server characteristics. To study the effect of each parameter, we assess the energy savings of the PDC, MAID, and FT-based versions of our file server (in comparison to the energy-oblivious version, EO), as a function of different settings for the parameter. To isolate the effect of a single parameter at a time, all other parameters are fixed at their default values. Throughout this section, we refer to the name of each technique and the server that exploits it interchangeably.

The default values for our simulation parameters are listed in table 5. Note that MAID-1+ is the MAID version of our file server that uses one extra disk as cache; MAID-2+ assumes two cache disks. The "+" refers to the optimization we made to MAID to avoid overloading the cache disk(s). The values for our simulated hardware are based on our own real server hardware, except for the main memory cache size. The values for the workload characteristics were chosen because they are "reasonable" values that represent areas of the parameter space where PDC and MAID perform well. In particular, the default request rate was set to half of the peak load we would expect for our real server. Common provisioning practice suggests that a server should be provisioned such that its peak load reaches 80% of its maximum throughput; the 20% extra capacity can handle any unexpected increases in load. We followed these suggestions and determined the maximum throughput of our server, 125 MBytes/sec, when all file requests can be served from the main memory cache. Given that the load peaks and valleys of servers deployed in the field can vary by factors ranging from 3 to 10 [6], our default request rate corresponds to a period of light load, exactly when energy savings are possible. Previous works have made similar assumptions, e.g., [5]. Nevertheless, we do vary the parameters marked with "*" in the table in the next two subsections.

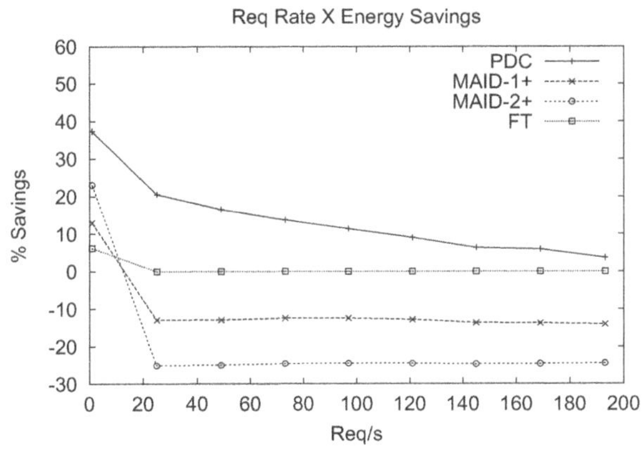

Figure 1: Energy savings per file request rate (conventional disks).

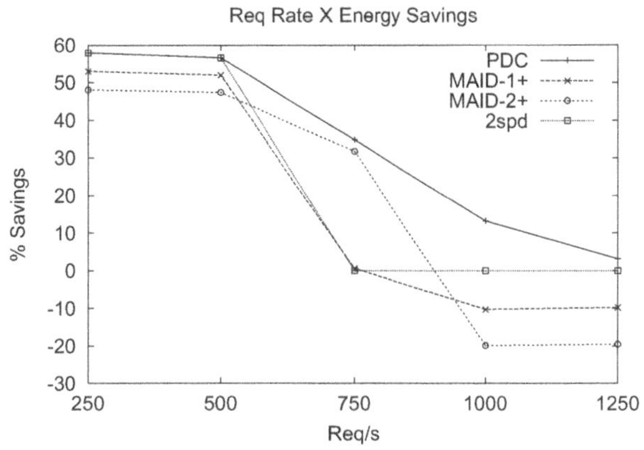

Figure 2: Energy savings per file request rate (two-speed disks).

4.1 Arrays of Conventional Disks

Figure 1 depicts the energy savings that can be accrued by the four versions of our file server, as different average file request rates are imposed on the servers. The energy savings are computed in comparison to EO.

As expected, low request rates show better energy savings. The maximum savings are substantial, reaching almost 40% in the case of PDC. However, note that non-trivial energy savings can only be achieved for very low request rates, less than 100 requests/second. These request rates are less than 10% of our default request rate. A file request rate of 25 request/second, for instance, is equivalent to a throughput of only 1.2 MBytes/second. Even worse, when request rates are very low, a significant percentage of requests is delayed by disk spin up operations. Note also that the MAID systems actually produce negative energy gains, i.e. they consume more energy than EO, across most of the space of request rates. The reason is that the cache disks do not reduce the load on the non-cache disks enough for them to be spun down; they are simply energy overhead.

These request rate and response time results clearly show that conventional disks are not useful when the goal is to conserve energy without noticeable performance degradation. When request rates are high, no energy savings can be accrued. When request rates are low, requests are frequently delayed by disk spin ups. These same negative effects are observed across the whole parameter space of workload and file server characteristics, so we do not present further results for arrays of conventional disks.

4.2 Arrays of Two-Speed Disks

4.2.1 Workload Characteristics

Request rate. Figure 2 depicts the energy savings that can be accrued by the four versions of our file server, as a function of the file request rate. The curve labeled "2spd" represents the version that uses two-speed disks, but no data movement. All energy savings are computed with respect to EO running on an array of conventional (Cheetah) disks.

Again, lower request rates show better energy savings. In fact, the maximum savings in comparison to EO are very substantial, reaching almost 60%, the energy differential between low and high speeds, for PDC and 2spd at 250 and 500 requests/second. In this part of the space, the MAID systems produce lower savings due to the cache disks, which are unnecessary. The energy savings decrease quickly as we increase the file request rate. At 750 requests/second, the 2spd and MAID-1+ systems stop producing energy gains, since all disks remain in high speed virtually all the time. At that request rate, PDC and MAID-2+ still produce gains of 30-40%, as data movement has the effect of reducing the load on several disks. At 1000 requests/second, the gains achievable by both MAID systems become negative, whereas PDC still produces gains of more than 10%. For higher request rates, the PDC gains are reduced and approach 3% at 1250 requests/second.

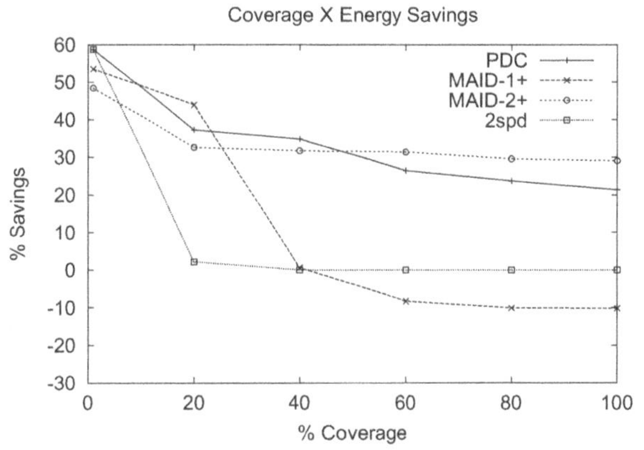

Figure 3: Energy savings per file system coverage.

These results demonstrate that PDC is more consistent and robust than other techniques for the range of request rates that can actually provide energy savings. PDC achieves the highest gains across the range, without ever consuming more energy than EO. The behavior of the MAID systems is heavily influenced by the number of cache disks used. Moreover, the overhead of cache disks is pronounced on both ends of the range. 2spd does not provide gains in most cases.

In terms of response time, we find that all versions of our server exhibit less than 2% delayed requests, regardless of the request rate. In fact, the percentage of delayed requests is consistently very low for all except the most extreme (and clearly unrealistic) of parameters for two-speed disks. For this reason and the fact that network servers can accommodate substantial response time degradations, hereafter we do not discuss response times.

File system coverage. Figure 3 presents the energy savings accrued by the four servers, as a function of file system coverage.

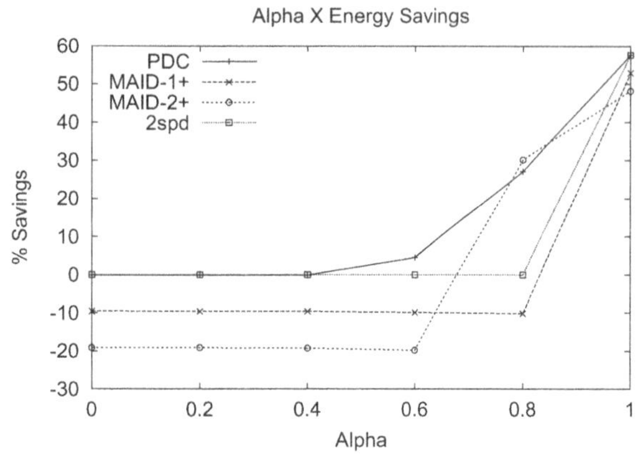

Figure 4: Energy savings per file popularity.

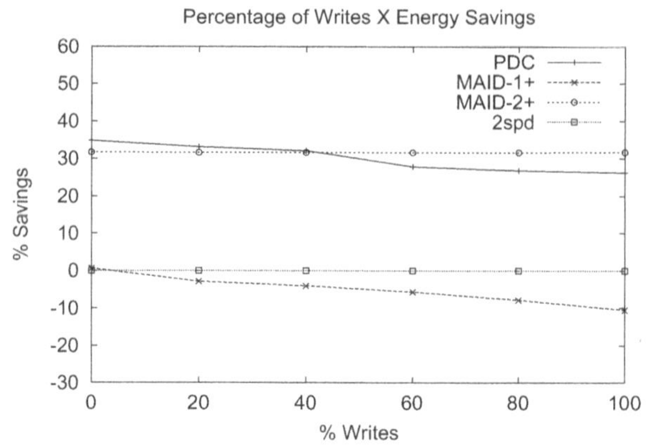

Figure 5: Energy savings per percentage of writes.

Recall that the default coverage we consider in our other analyses is 40%. As expected, higher coverages mean that disk loads increase and therefore the energy savings are reduced. On the other hand, higher coverage also allows the Nomad FS file placement algorithm (MQ) to place a larger number of files more intelligently in the array. As a result, the energy savings accrued by PDC degrade gracefully. MAID-2+ also degrades gracefully, since its two cache disks provide enough extra bandwidth at the default request rate to compensate for increases in coverage. In contrast, MAID-1+ suffers severely with increasing coverage, as a result of the extra pressure on the cache disk. When this disk becomes fully utilized, the non-cache disks also start operating at high speed.

File popularity. Figure 4 depicts the energy gains for different values of the Zipf coefficient (alpha). Alpha represents the file popularity as seen by the server, not the disk subsystem. Recall that the default popularity we assume in our other analyses is 0.85. The figure shows that all systems suffer as we decrease the popularity. The reason is that decreased popularity means lower main memory cache hit rates, which yield higher disk loads. Furthermore, the PDC file migration approach does not work as well when file popularity is decreased. Despite these problems, PDC degrades more gracefully than MAID or 2spd; it provides energy gains for popularities as low as 0.6. MAID does not behave as well as PDC because the files on its cache disks exhibit worse (popularity-induced) temporal locality with decreased popularity. This increases the load on the cache disks. When the cache disks become fully utilized, the traffic directed to the other disks increases further, forcing all disks to operate at high speed. As a result, the MAID systems consume more energy than EO for most of the parameter space.

Percentage of file write operations. Figure 5 shows the effect of the percentage of writes on the energy savings provided by the servers we consider. Recall that we have been considering read-only workloads by default. The figure shows that the energy savings provided by the different techniques decrease slightly (if at all) with increases in the percentage of writes. The reason for the slight decreases is that more writes increase the disk traffic when dirty blocks are evicted from the main memory cache. In fact, in the MAID-based servers, writes can cause even more traffic when dirty disk cache blocks have to be written back to their corresponding non-cache disks.

Temporal correlation. Figure 6 shows the effect of temporal correlation on the energy savings of the servers we consider. We compute the average number of file accesses between two consecutive accesses to each file and compute the overall average for all files. Recall that we assume no temporal locality besides that induced by file popularity in our other analyses. For each curve in the figure, this means the rightmost point.

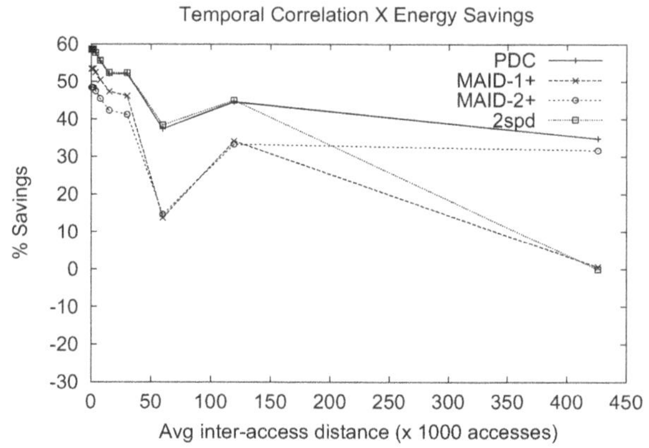

Figure 6: Energy savings per temporal correlation.

We can see that all systems benefit from higher temporal correlation (i.e., smaller average inter-access distance). The higher correlation increases the main memory cache hit rate and reduces the load on the disk subsystem. This effect is highly beneficial for 2spd. MAID has the added benefit that high temporal correlation causes the cache disks to work more effectively. However, the MAID systems have the energy overhead of the cache disks themselves. Again, PDC is the most consistent and robust system across the parameter space.

4.2.2 File Server Characteristics

Number of disks. Figure 7 shows the energy savings of the different versions of our server, as a function of the number of disks. The total storage size is not changed, therefore simulations with more disks have fewer files per disk and do not require additional cache disks for the MAID systems. Recall that the default number of disks we assume in our other analyses is 8 for PDC and 2spd, 9 for MAID-1+, and 10 for MAID-2+.

We can see that increasing the number of disks increases savings quite significantly, as one would expect. The smaller set of accesses directed to each disk allows all disks to operate at low speed. Note

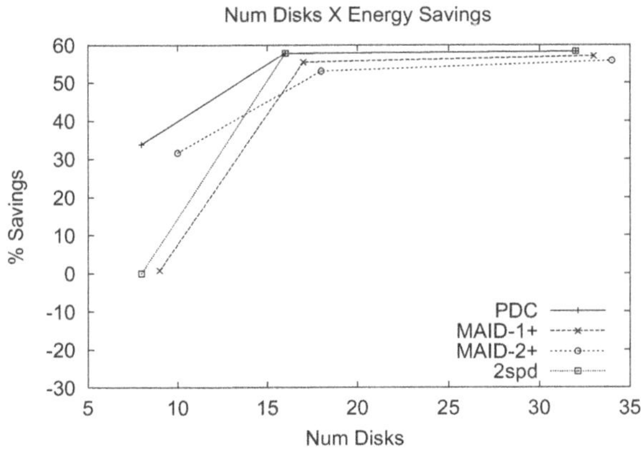

Figure 7: Energy savings per number of disks.

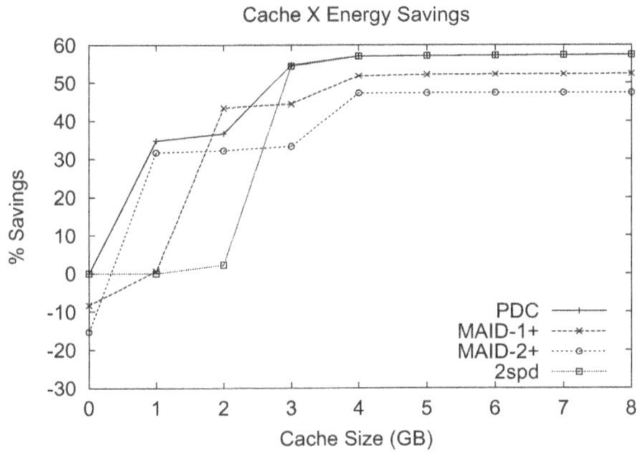

Figure 8: Energy savings per main memory cache size.

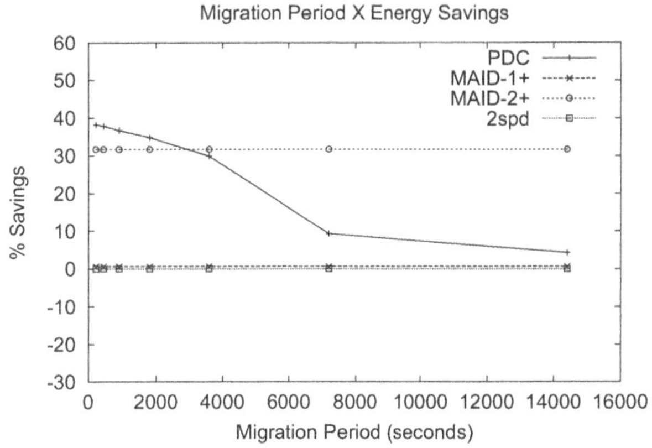

Figure 9: Energy savings per reconfiguration period.

Description	HUM	POP
Avg. request rate	241 reqs/sec	263 reqs/sec
Coverage	100%	100%
File popularity	0.70	0.93
Percentage of writes	35%	0%
Temporal correlation	467280 reqs	94568 reqs
Cache size	1 GByte	64 MBytes
Migration period	672 minutes	168 minutes

Table 6: Parameters of real traces and server settings. Request rate values correspond to the accelerated traces. Migration periods correspond to one week in the non-accelerated traces.

also that the energy overhead of cache disks is better amortized in larger array configurations. However, if we had assumed the number of cache disks to increase proportionally to the number of regular disks, we would have seen overheads of around 10% and 20% for the two MAID systems in these large configurations.

Main memory cache size. Figure 8 considers the effect of main memory cache size. Recall that the default size of the memory cache we assume in our other analyses is 1 GByte.

Cache size increases produce significant benefits for all servers. With caches of 5 GBytes or larger, both PDC and 2spd approach the maximum achievable energy savings of 60%, since the cache miss rate becomes so low that all disks start to operate at low speed. The MAID systems also benefit from larger main memory caches, but settle at lower energy savings with very large caches.

Migration frequency. Figure 9 shows the effect of changes in the migration period in Nomad FS. Recall that the default migration period we assume in our other analyses is every 1/2 hour. For very short migration periods, there may not be enough time to complete the migrations until the next round of migrations needs to start. In these cases, we simply stop the current migration process midway and start the next. Since MAID and 2spd do not involve migrations, we plot their energy gains as horizontal lines for comparison.

From the figure we can see that the frequency of migrations has a substantial impact on the gains achieved by PDC. With longer periods, PDC takes longer to adjust to access patterns. It is also interesting to note that short migration periods provide slightly higher energy savings than our default setting. The reason is that the energy cost of file placement changes is a small fraction of the energy consumed in between migrations. However, these shorter periods also come with substantial increases in the percentage of delayed requests, due to the intense file migration traffic.

5. REAL TRACE RESULTS

The results so far have assumed synthetic traces and exponential request arrivals with a fixed mean arrival rate. In this section, we study real traces that exhibit pronounced load intensity variations, with load peaks in the afternoon and valleys at night. Note however that we accelerated the traces by factors of 15 (HUM) and 60 (POP), because even the peak loads in the original traces are relatively low for our disk array.

We simulate a tight coupling between the file server and the network server; the file server forms the "bottom half" of the network server on a single machine. We assume a "warm up" period corresponding to one week of the original, non-accelerated traces. Table 6 lists the characteristics of the traces and server settings with respect to the parameters we just explored. All simulations assume two-speed disks and 8 (PDC), 9 (MAID-1+), or 10 (MAID-2+) disks in the array.

Table 7 lists the energy and percentage of requests delayed (by more than 200 milliseconds) for each technique and trace after their warm up periods. EO consumes 2022095 J (HUM) and 256745 J (POP) with virtually no delayed requests.

These results confirm the main observations of the previous section, i.e. under light load, PDC conserves a significant amount of

Technique	HUM	POP
PDC Energy	1472438 J	147332 J
MAID-1+ Energy	1605547 J	170232 J
MAID-2+ Energy	1700585 J	181815 J
2spd Energy	1538228 J	160114 J
PDC Delayed	5.3%	8.0%
MAID-1+ Delayed	14.3%	8.5%
MAID-2+ Delayed	11.2%	8.1%
2spd Delayed	6.0%	7.6%

Table 7: Real trace results: energy and percentage of requests delayed.

energy (27% for HUM and 43% for POP) while the cache disks in MAID reduce energy gains. The one exception is that 2spd conserves more energy than both MAID systems. 2spd performs well because, throughout most of the traces, the disk load is low enough that all disks can be at low speed. This characteristic makes these traces ideal for 2spd. Despite these good results, PDC still conserves more energy than 2spd (14% more for HUM and 13% more for POP) without an increase in the percentage of delayed requests.

Note also that the percentage of delayed requests is higher than in our parameter space exploration. The main reason for these results is that, going from each valley to the next peak, disk loads increase very quickly in the accelerated traces. Under this scenario, disk contention develops until the two-speed disks can transition to high speed. This should not be a problem in practice however, since load variations are substantially slower in real time.

6. RELATED WORK

We originally suggested PDC and our energy-aware file server at the work-in-progress session of SOSP'01 [17]. This paper is the first detailed and complete evaluation of our proposals. The inspiration for this work came from our work on Load Concentration (LC) and dynamic cluster reconfiguration for energy conservation [18]. PDC is an application of a similar concept to LC to storage systems. However, we found that it was much harder to successfully apply PDC than LC, given the information required to make intelligent migration decisions and the large number of important parameters involved.

As far as we know, there have been six other works on disk energy conservation for servers [5, 7, 10, 11, 20, 21]. Carrera *et al.* [5] and Gurumurthi *et al.* [10] considered multi-speed disks for standalone servers. These papers showed that significant energy savings can be accrued by adjusting speeds according to the load imposed on the disk. Carrera *et al.* also show that a combination of laptop and SCSI disks can be even more beneficial in terms of energy, but only for over-provisioned servers. Our work is orthogonal to these contributions in that we seek to conserve energy in the context of disk array-based servers. For these systems, exploiting data movement between disks can provide significant additional gains, as we demonstrate in section 4.2.

In terms of disk array-based servers, Gurumurthi *et al.* [11] considered the effect of different RAID parameters, such as RAID level, stripe size, and number of disks, on the performance and energy consumption of stand-alone database servers running transaction processing workloads. They also observed that it is not possible to exploit idleness in this context. However, they did not consider any other energy conservation techniques.

Colarelli and Grunwald [7] proposed MAID and evaluated it for a large scientific workload. Although they mentioned a migration-based version of MAID, they decided not to pursue it in favor of the copy-based version we studied here. For their workload, MAID conserves no more energy than FT. We extend their work by implementing a prototype file server based on MAID, validating our simulator against the prototype, considering a broader range of parameters, and comparing copying against migration.

Finally, Zhu *et al.* [20] recently considered storage cache replacement techniques that selectively keep blocks from certain disks in the main memory cache, so that the disks can stay in low-power mode for a longer period of time. In another paper, Zhu *et al.* [21] study a more elegant approach to the same problem. Their work is similar to ours in that it also attempts to affect the load directed to disks. As another similarity, their work evaluated replacement techniques for disk arrays composed of multi-speed disks. However, they did not consider data movement between disks, which can provide greater benefits.

Bianchini and Rajamony [1] surveyed these and other works on power and energy conservation for server systems.

7. CONCLUSIONS

We have introduced a new energy conservation technique called PDC for disk arrays. We have also designed and implemented an energy-aware file server called Nomad FS that exploits this technique. For comparison, we developed two versions of our server that use other energy conservation techniques, MAID and FT. Using a validated simulator, we performed a comprehensive study of the parameters that affect energy conservation the most, pinpointing the scenarios under which each technique is useful, for disk arrays composed of either conventional or two-speed disks. The study allowed us to map the areas of the parameter space for which no technique can conserve energy. We also studied the behavior of the different techniques for two real traces.

In summary, we found that it is possible to conserve a substantial amount of energy during periods of light load on the server, as long as two-speed disks are used. We have also found that Nomad FS can deal more gracefully with increases in request rate and decreases in file popularity than the other servers. In addition, PDC achieved consistent energy savings for most of the parameter space. However, the PDC gains degrade substantially for long migration intervals. In comparison, the behavior of MAID is heavily dependent on the number of cache disks used. Furthermore, the energy overhead of these disks is pronounced in several parts of the parameter space. For the real traces, PDC achieved the best results, confirming the observations from the synthetic traces. We also showed that using two-speed disks without data movement behaves well when real disk loads remain light most of the time.

Based on these results, we conclude that the techniques we study will be very useful for disk array-based network servers when multi-speed disks become available.

Further research is required on the reliability implications of PDC. In fact, it is clear that PDC negatively affects the reliability of conventional disks due the large number of power mode transitions it causes. However, we have shown that PDC is not useful for conventional disks anyway. For multi-speed disks, we expect PDC to have a negligible impact on reliability. The reason is that real network server workloads (which exhibit load peaks in the afternoon and valleys at night) should induce at most two speed transitions/disk/day in the presence of PDC.

Another interesting research issue is the interaction of PDC with storage system reliability approaches, such as mirroring and RAID. Extending Nomad FS to deal with mirroring should be easy, but combining PDC with data striping can be more challenging.

Finally, our parameter space exploration and experience with real traces suggest that PDC is highly sensitive to the length of the migration period and the estimation of the load to be imposed on disks after migrations. Another research topic is how to make Nomad FS automatically determine the best settings for these parameters.

Acknowledgements

We would like to thank Enrique V. Carrera and the other members of the Rutgers DARK Lab for comments that helped improve this paper. We would also like to thank Prof. Uli Kremer for lending us the power measurement infrastructure of the Energy Efficiency and Low-Power Lab at Rutgers. Finally, we would like to thank Prof. Arthur Goldberg from New York University for giving us the Hummingbird trace.

8. REFERENCES

[1] R. Bianchini and R. Rajamony. Power and Energy Management for Server Systems. Technical Report DCS-TR-528, Department of Computer Science, Rutgers University, June 2003.

[2] P. Bohrer, E. Elnozahy, T. Keller, M. Kistler, C. Lefurgy, C. McDowell, and R. Rajamony. The Case for Power Management in Web Servers. In Graybill and Melhem, editors, *Power-Aware Computing*. Kluwer Academic Publishers, January 2002.

[3] L. Breslau, P. Cao, L. Fan, G. Phillips, and S. Shenker. Web Caching and Zipf-like Distributions: Evidence and Implications. In *Proceedings of IEEE InfoCom'99*, March 1999.

[4] E. V. Carrera and R. Bianchini. Improving Disk Throughput in Data-Intensive Servers. In *Proceedings of the 10th International Symposium on High-Performance Computer Architecture*, February 2004.

[5] E. V. Carrera, E. Pinheiro, and R. Bianchini. Conserving Disk Energy in Network Servers. In *Proceedings of the 17th International Conference on Supercomputing*, June 2003.

[6] J. Chase, D. Anderson, P. Thackar, A. Vahdat, and R. Boyle. Managing Energy and Server Resources in Hosting Centers. In *Proceedings of the 18th Symposium on Operating Systems Principles*, October 2001.

[7] D. Colarelli and D. Grunwald. Massive Arrays of Idle Disks For Storage Archives. In *Proceedings of the 15th High Performance Networking and Computing Conference*, November 2002.

[8] E. N. Elnozahy, M. Kistler, and R. Rajamony. Energy-Efficient Server Clusters. In *Proceedings of the 2nd Workshop on Power-Aware Computing Systems*, February 2002.

[9] M. Elnozahy, M. Kistler, and R. Rajamony. Energy Conservation Policies for Web Servers. In *Proceedings of the 4th USENIX Symposium on Internet Technologies and Systems*, March 2003.

[10] S. Gurumurthi, A. Sivasubramaniam, M. Kandemir, and H. Franke. DRPM: Dynamic Speed Control for Power Management in Server Class Disks. In *Proceedings of the International Symposium on Computer Architecture*, June 2003.

[11] S. Gurumurthi, J. Zhang, A. Sivasubramaniam, M. Kandemir, H. Franke, N. Vijaykrishnan, and M. J. Irwin. Interplay of Energy and Performance for Disk Arrays Running Transaction Processing Workloads. In *Proceedings of the International Symposium on Performance Analysis of Systems and Software*, March 2003.

[12] T. Heath, B. Diniz, E. V. Carrera, W. Meira Jr., and R. Bianchini. Self-Configuring Heterogeneous Server Clusters. In *Proceedings of the Workshop on Compilers and Operating Systems for Low Power*, September 2003.

[13] S. Jin and A. Bestavros. GISMO: A Generator of Internet Streaming Media Objects and Workloads. *ACM SIGMETRICS Performance Evaluation Review*, 29(3), November 2001.

[14] S. Jin and A. Bestavros. Sources and Characteristics of Web Temporal Locality. In *Proceedings of IEEE/ACM International Symposium on Modeling, Analysis and Simulation of Computer and Telecommunication Systems*, August 2000.

[15] A. Karlin, M. S. Manasse, L. Rudolph, and D. D. Sleator. Competitive Snoopy Caching. *Algorithmica*, 3(1):79–119, 1988.

[16] K. Okada, N. Kojima, and K. Yamashita. A Novel Drive Architecture of HDD: "Multimode Hard Disk Drive". In *Proceedings of the International Conference on Consumer Electronics*, June 2000.

[17] E. Pinheiro and R. Bianchini. A Power-Aware Cluster-Based File System. Work-in-Progress Session, 18th Symposium on Operating Systems Principles. October, 2001.

[18] E. Pinheiro, R. Bianchini, E. Carrera, and T. Heath. Dynamic Cluster Reconfiguration for Power and Performance. In L. Benini, M. Kandemir, and J. Ramanujam, editors, *Compilers and Operating Systems for Low Power*. Kluwer Academic Publishers, September 2003. Earlier version published as "Load Balancing and Unbalancing for Power and Performance in Cluster-Based Systems" in the Proceedings of the Workshop on Compilers and Operating Systems for Low Power, September 2001.

[19] Y. Zhou, P.M. Chen, , and K. Li. The Multi-Queue Replacement Algorithm for Second-Level Buffer Caches. In *Proceedings of the 2001 USENIX Annual Technical Conference*, June 2001.

[20] Q. Zhu, F. M. David, Y. Zhou, C. F. Devaraj, P. Cao, and Z. Li. Reducing Energy Consumption of Disk Storage Using Power-Aware Cache Management. In *Proceedings of the 10th International Symposium on High-Performance Computer Architecture*, February 2004.

[21] Q. Zhu, A. Shankar, and Y. Zhou. PB-LRU: A Self-Tuning Power Aware Storage Cache Replacement Algorithm for Conserving Disk Energy. In *Proceedings of the 18th International Conference on Supercomputing*, June 2004.

A NUCA Substrate for Flexible CMP Cache Sharing

Jaehyuk Huh Changkyu Kim[†] Hazim Shafi Lixin Zhang [§]
Doug Burger Stephen W. Keckler[†]

[†]Dept. of Computer Sciences
The University of Texas at Austin

[§]Austin Research Laboratory
IBM Research

ABSTRACT

We propose an organization for the on-chip memory system of a chip multiprocessor, in which 16 processors share a 16MB pool of 256 L2 cache banks. The L2 cache is organized as a non-uniform cache architecture (NUCA) array with a switched network embedded in it for high performance. We show that this organization can support the spectrum of degrees of sharing: *unshared*, in which each processor has a private portion of the cache, thus reducing hit latency, *completely shared*, in which every processor shares the entire cache, thus minimizing misses, and every point in between. We find the optimal degree of sharing for a number of cache bank mapping policies, and also evaluate a per-application cache partitioning strategy. We conclude that a static NUCA organization with sharing degrees of two or four work best across a suite of commercial and scientific parallel workloads. We also demonstrate that migratory, dynamic NUCA approaches improve performance significantly for a subset of the workloads at the cost of increased power consumption and complexity, especially as per-application cache partitioning strategies are applied.

Categories and Subject Descriptors: C.1.2 [Processor Architectures]: Multiple Data Stream Architectures (Multiprocessors), B.3.2 [Memory Structures]: Design Styles – Shared memory, C.4 [Performance of Systems] – Design studies

General Terms: Performance, Design, Experimentation, Measurement

Keywords: chip-multiprocessor, cache sharing, non-uniform cache architecture

1. INTRODUCTION

Assuming that power ceilings do not limit continued CMP integration, future server-class processors are likely to contain large numbers of processors along with large caches. While level-one caches are likely to remain private to each processor, the degree of sharing for the integrated level-two caches will be a key design decision. The level-two caches may be shared by all processors, or may be separated into private per-processor partitions, or any point in between. In this paper, we explore this range of caching and sharing policies for a CMP targeted at 45 nanometer technologies, with 16MB of on-chip cache and 16 high-capability processors. The specific layout we propose, based on a non-uniform cache architecture (NUCA) designs, mitigates the effects of growing wire resistivity and thus intra-cache communication delays, and permits any degree of cache sharing in this single implementation. The underlying hardware is sufficiently flexible to have its degree of sharing chosen dynamically, adjusted by the operating system.

The tension between a greater versus lesser degree of sharing is driven by the reduced misses of greater cache sharing versus the reduced hit latencies of lesser cache sharing. More precisely, we call the *sharing degree* the number of processors that share a given pool of cache. In this terminology, a sharing degree of one means that each processor has its own private L2 partition, whereas a sharing degree of sixteen means that all processors are sharing a single large cache array.

Greater sharing degrees reduce misses in two ways. First, they reduce the number of shared copies of a single line existing on-chip, since each line maps to only one place in shared caches. Second, they provide a larger shared pool to tolerate imbalances across the sharers' working sets. However, larger sharing degrees result in longer cache latencies, as the shared cache is larger than the individual private partitions, assuming total cache area is held constant. An ideal design would somehow capture the benefits of both reduced misses *and* reduced hit latencies.

As shown in Figure 1, the floorplan we evaluate consists of a single large cache array, broken into numerous banks which are connected by a lightweight, switched 2-D mesh network. Processors span the top and bottom edges of the cache array, and each has a port into the L2 cache network. By adjusting the bits used to route memory addresses to a cache bank, the cache array is configurable by the system to use any degree of sharing. If each processor maps the same address bit string to a different bank, the sharing degree is one. If all processors map the same address bits to a single bank, the sharing degree is sixteen.

We first measured the optimal bank size and sharing degree for a cache in which the mapping of lines to banks does

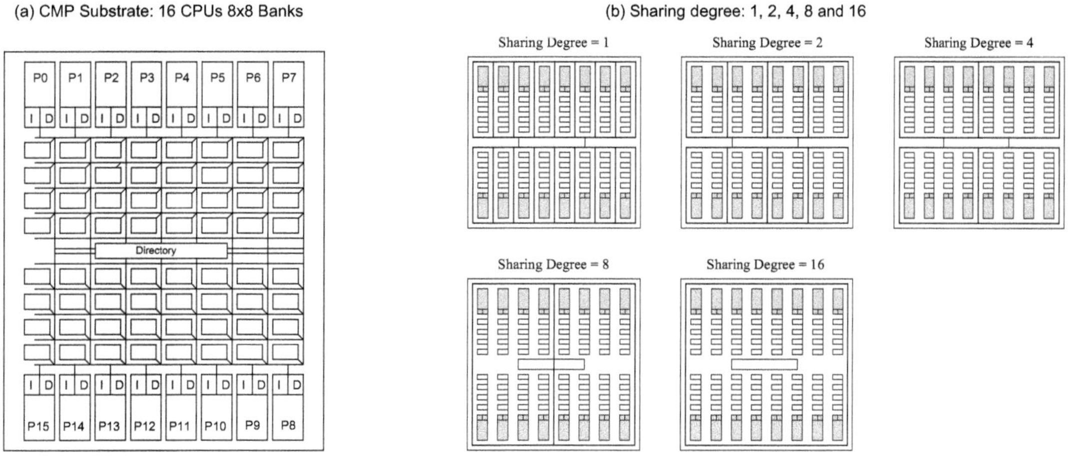

Figure 1: 16 Processor CMP Substrate

not change (this uniprocessor organization was called static NUCA, or S-NUCA, in prior work [13]). We then evaluated per-application sharing degrees, as well as different techniques, such as intra-cache line migration (called dynamic, or D-NUCA caches in prior work) and level-one prefetching, to reduce average L2 hit latencies and thus support larger sharing degrees. The results of this study are the following:

- The ideal bank size across all configurations is 64KB.
- We confirmed that significant latency reductions are possible for private L2 caches, and significant miss reductions are possible for shared L2 caches. The results showed 54% latency reduction with private L2 caches and 33% reduction of external memory accesses with fully shared caches.
- For shared S-NUCA organizations, low-to-medium sharing degrees, from one to four, provide the best performance for all applications except one. The best sharing degree across all benchmarks is four.
- Although dynamic mapping (D-NUCA) reduces hit latencies for high sharing degrees by 30%, performance improvement is relatively modest except two applications with 17% and 20% speedups. However, this improvement incurs considerable complexity and power overheads.
- Level-one prefetching improves performance proportionately to the L2 cache hit delay, but does not change the ideal sharing degree significantly.
- A priori, application-specific adaptation of the sharing degree provides an average 5% performance boost for the D-NUCA organization, but little gain for the S-NUCA organization.
- Per-line sharing degree, which provides two different sharing degrees for private and shared cache blocks, can mitigate the negative effect of large sharing degrees, thus reducing overall miss rates and avoiding slow hit latencies. The best private sharing degree is one or two, reducing hit latencies for private blocks, but the best shared sharing degree is 16, maximizing caching efficiency.

In Section 2, we describe the flexible NUCA substrate that supports reconfigurable sharing degrees. In Section 3, we describe the simulation environment that we use, evaluate per-application and per-class sharing degrees, and compare the performance of S-NUCA and D-NUCA. We also discuss the effect of L1 prefetching on the best sharing degree. In Section 4, we describe related work in CMP L2 cache designs. We conclude in Section 5.

2. CMP L2 CACHE DESIGN SPACE

Figure 1 (a) shows a multiprocessor chip projected for 45nm process technology in 2010. The chip has 16 processors and 16MB of L2 cache capacity on a die area of approximately $300mm^2$. The L2 cache resides in the middle of the chip and contains an array of banks connected by a lightweight routing network. Half of the 16 CPUs are at the top and the other half are at the bottom. Because of the large number of CPUs and cache banks, there are many possible design options for the L2 cache. In this paper, we search for the cache sharing organization that gives the best average performance across a range of commercial and scientific applications.

In the rest of this section, we first discuss the implications of varying the number of CPUs that can share a cache bank. We then describe both static and dynamic ways to map lines to cache banks. We then propose two approaches for reducing L2 latency and facilitating larger shared cache pools (thus reducing both latency *and* misses): an efficient migration policy that moves data to tiles closer to the requesting CPU, and partial tag arrays to speed up the lookup of remote cache banks.

2.1 Sharing Degree

Shared L2 caches have been adopted as an alternative to traditional private L2 caches for CMP L2 cache designs [3, 7, 11, 23]. One of the key factors in CMP shared caches is the number of CPUs that can share a L2 cache, called the *sharing degree* (SD for short). A sharing degree of N means that N CPUs share a L2 cache.

The basic trade-offs of varying the sharing degree are hit latency, hit rate, inter-processor communication, and coherence maintenance overhead. In general, for hit latency, a lower sharing degree is better as each L2 cache is smaller. For hit rates and inter-processor communication, higher sharing degrees are better because they make more efficient use of cache capacity. Since a higher sharing degree has more L1 caches sharing an L2 cache, it is more expensive to maintain L1 coherence. However, a lower sharing degree means more discrete L2 caches on a chip, making maintaining L2 coherence more expensive.

The main advantage of higher sharing degrees is higher L2 cache hit rates. If the working sets across CPUs are not well balanced, private L2 caches can make one CPU suffer from capacity misses while other CPUs have unused cache space. Shared caches, on the other hand, allow that otherwise unused cache space to be used by the space-hungry CPU. Furthermore, shared caches keep at most one copy of a block, not wasting space by storing multiple copies of the same block, unlike private L2 caches sharing copies of the same line. As a result, shared caches can effectively store more data, indirectly increasing hit rates. A shared cache also avoids the L2 coherence misses generated by private L2 caches [8].

Inter-processor communication through a shared L2 cache is normally faster than through private L2 caches connected by a coherent bus. With shared L2 caches, processors communicate through L2 cache blocks directly. With private L2 caches, processors have to communicate through private L2 caches and coherence fabric.

The main drawback of a higher sharing degree is the potential for higher average hit latency due to the larger size, longer wire delays, and increased bandwidth requirements. In future wire-dominated implementations, the effect of increased hit latency may outweigh the benefit of increased hit rate.

Another overhead of shared caches is that each L2 cache needs to maintain coherence for the L1 caches sharing the L2 cache. In this study, the system maintains L1 cache coherence by embedding sharing status vectors in the L2 tag arrays. The tag of an L2 cache line includes a bit mask to indicate which L1 caches have copies of the line. When a L2 cache receives an update request from an L1 cache, it sends invalidation messages to other L1 caches that have a copy of the requested block. Such directory-based L1 coherence was used in the Piranha CMP [3]. Although broadcast-based protocols can reduce the area overhead for sharing vectors [11, 23], we used the directory protocol because it is more scalable for these types of systems, demanding less L2-to-L1 bandwidth than broadcast protocols.

A lower sharing degree means that each chip will have more private L2 caches, thus it is more difficult to maintain L2 data coherence. As with the L1 caches, we use a centralized L2 tag directory to maintain on-chip L2 coherence. When a L2 miss is detected, the request is sent to the centralized L2 tag directory. The directory decides, without snooping other L2 caches in the chip, whether to get data from another L2 cache on the chip or whether to issue an off-chip memory request. The directory-based coherence protocol has a number of advantages over broadcast-based protocols. First, it relieves the coherence bus from becoming the bottleneck. Second, it detects on-chip cache misses faster because it does not need to snoop other L2 caches in the chip. Third, the directory functions as the single external coherence snoop point for requests from other chips, avoiding the need to have multiple L2 caches on the same chip snoop the global bus.

2.2 Organization

Shared caches require more bandwidth than private caches, since the data request rate is proportional to the number of processors. Two common ways of increasing bandwidth are i) adding more access ports and ii) splitting a monolithic cache into multiple independently operated banks. L2 caches typically use the latter because it is more cost-effective than having multiple ports. For instance, the dual-processor Power4 CMP [23] uses three banks, and the eight-processor Piranha CMP uses eight banks for each L2 cache.

As exemplified in Figure 1, a CMP chip can consist of many independently operated L2 cache banks. To enable high-speed clocking and reduce the space for wires, we use a switched network, instead of traditional dedicated wires, to connect cache banks and processors. A processor may access only one L2 cache directly and must use the coherence fabric to access other L2 caches. Figure 1 (b) shows five possible partitioning schemes in a 16 processor CMP that have sharing degrees of 1, 2, 4, 8, and 16, respectively. With a sharing degree of 1, there are sixteen 1 MB caches, each of which is private to one processor. With a sharing degree of 16, there is only one 16 MB cache, which is shared by all 16 processors.

To optimize bank organization, we evaluated 5 different bank sizes: 64KB, 128KB, 256KB, 512KB, and 1MB. We estimated bank access latencies using Cacti [18] and a wire delay model [1]. Network hop delays are derived from the dimension of banks, with switching overheads. Among the five bank configurations, our experiments show that the 64KB bank size has the best performance across all experimental configurations. For the remainder of this paper, we assume a 16x16 64KB bank array.

To change sharing degrees, the bank mapping tables in L1 cache controllers, bank controllers, and the central on-chip directory are updated by the operating system. For fully reconfigurable sharing degrees, the sharing status vectors both in L2 tags and the central directory should have enough bits to represent all processors in the CMP. In this substrate, the size of bit vectors in L2 tags and the central directory is the maximum 16.

2.3 Mapping Algorithms

With multiple banks per L2 cache, we have the choice of either always putting a block into a designated bank or allowing a block to reside in one of multiple banks (but not simultaneously). We call the former *static mapping* and the latter *dynamic mapping*.

In static mapping, a fixed hash function uses the lower bits of a block address to select the correct bank. L2 access latency is proportional to the distance from the issuing L1 cache to the L2 cache bank. By allowing non-uniform hit latencies, static mapping can reduce hit latencies of traditional monolithic cache designs, which fix the latency to the longest path [13]. Because a block can be placed into only one bank, its L2 access latency is essentially decided by its address. If frequently accessed blocks happen to map to banks with longer latencies, static mapping will not provide optimal performance.

Dynamic mapping (D-NUCA) addresses the problem faced by static mapping by allowing a block to go to multiple candidate banks, or a *bank set*. With proper placement and migration policies, D-NUCA enables the cache to place frequently accessed blocks in the banks closest to the CPU and less frequently accessed block in the banks that are farther away. Previous studies have shown that generational promotion that migrates blocks towards banks near the requesting processors yields good performance in uniprocessor systems [5, 13].

CMPs pose new challenges to dynamic mapping. First, migration in multiple directions can cause migration conflicts, with shared blocks ping-ponging between two processors. Second, searching blocks in bank sets becomes more complicated than single-processor D-NUCA organizations. Past studies have shown that centralized partial tags work well in uniprocessor D-NUCA [13]. In CMPs, however, besides increased bandwidth requirements on the central partial tag array, the central partial tags cannot be located close to all processors, thus requiring multi-hop latencies to access the tags.

We address the challenge with two mechanisms: distributed partial tags and a dynamic lookup mechanism.

2.3.1 *Migration Policies*

A simple migration policy permits a block to be mapped to only one column and restricts migration to the vertical dimension only (D-NUCA 1D, Figure 2 (a)). In this policy, the vertical migration does not reduce the network latency for the horizontal traversal of requests and data blocks. We assumed the following bank set policies for misses: new cache blocks are inserted at the tail of a column bank set. For 8 and 16 sharing degrees, the victim banks are selected from the banks in the middle.

The second migration policy allows blocks to be mapped to any bank without restriction. Migration can happen in both vertical and horizontal directions (D-NUCA 2D, Figure 2 (b)). This policy can further reduce hit latency by decreasing horizontal network latencies. However, it requires a more complicated search mechanism since an L1 miss might need to look up all banks in a shared cache. In D-NUCA 2D, new blocks are inserted at the column closest to the requesting processor.

Unlike single-processor D-NUCA caches, in which blocks are always promoted in one direction, multiple processors from different locations in CMPs can cause cache blocks to be promoted in conflicting directions. In a worst-case scenario, a block may ping-pong between two adjacent banks, with no reduction in hit latencies. To reduce unnecessary migration for conflicting promotion, we simulated two-bit saturated counters embedded in the cache tags, which allow a block to migrate only if the relevant counter for that moving direction is saturated.

2.3.2 *Lookup Mechanisms*

A partial tag structure replicates low-order bits of full cache tags as a way to reduce the number of requests to full tags [12]. In single-processor D-NUCA caches, centralized partial tags detect L2 misses early and reduce the number of requests to banks. However, the centralized partial tag approach has three drawbacks. First, since the global partial tag array is required to hold the information about all cache blocks in the cache, its access time and energy consumption will be relatively large. Second, since the centralized structure should be placed near the center of the cache, wire delays to and from it can be significant. Finally, the centralized tag array may require many ports since all primary cache misses must access it.

Parameter	Value
Processor frequency	10 GHz
Issue width	4
Window size	64-entry RUU
Number of CPUs	16
L1 I/D cache	32KB, 2-way, 64B block, 8 MSHRs
L2 cache	16x16 banks
L2 cache bank	64KB, 16-way, 5 cycle latency
Network	1 cycle latency between two adjacent banks
On-chip directory	10 cycle access latency
Main Memory	260 cycle latency, 360 GB/s bandwidth

Table 1: Simulated system configuration

Application	Dataset/Parameters
SPECWeb99	Apache web server, file set: 230MB
TPC-W	185MB databases using Apache & MySQL
SPECjbb	IBM JVM version 1.1.8, 16 warehouses
Ocean	258×258 grid
Barnes	16K particles
LU	512×512, 16×16 blocks
Radix	1M integers

Table 2: Workloads.

To overcome these drawbacks, we employ a distributed scheme: partial tags are distributed over the columns, and each column's partial tag array tracks the state of blocks cached in that column. Any changes in a bank column's contents must be reflected in its partial tags synchronously. Cache lookups for a bank column always start from the distributed partial tag array. In the SD=8 or 16 cases, we replicate the partial tags at both ends of a column. This doubles the space overheads of partial tags, but greatly decreases the distance from processors to column partial tags.

In D-NUCA 1D, the search mechanism is straightforward with column partial tags. L1 misses are sent to the head of statically mapped columns, and the first bank and partial tags are accessed simultaneously. For a miss in the first bank, the column partial tags can command further lookups of other banks in the same column or start an L2 refill request. In D-NUCA 2D, the partial tags of all columns that a block can map to may be searched. L1 misses are first sent to the column closest to the requesting processor. If the block is not found in that column, other columns' partial tags are searched.

3. EXPERIMENTAL RESULTS

3.1 Methodology

We evaluated our CMP cache designs using an execution-driven full-system simulator derived from IBM's SimOS-PPC, which uses AIX 4.3.1 as the simulated OS. The core timing model extends the SimpleScalar simulator with multiprocessor support. Table 1 shows a summary of the main architectural parameters. We used three commercial applications: SPECWeb99, TPC-W, and SPECjbb, and four scientific shared-memory benchmarks from the SPLASH-2 suite [24]: Ocean, Barnes, LU, and Radix. Table 2 shows the dataset size and other notable features of each application.

As previously discussed, we model an invalidation-based cache coherence protocol in the CMP. The L2 caches are the points of L1 coherence and maintain sharing vectors for L1 caches. The L2 cache bank array is embedded with a

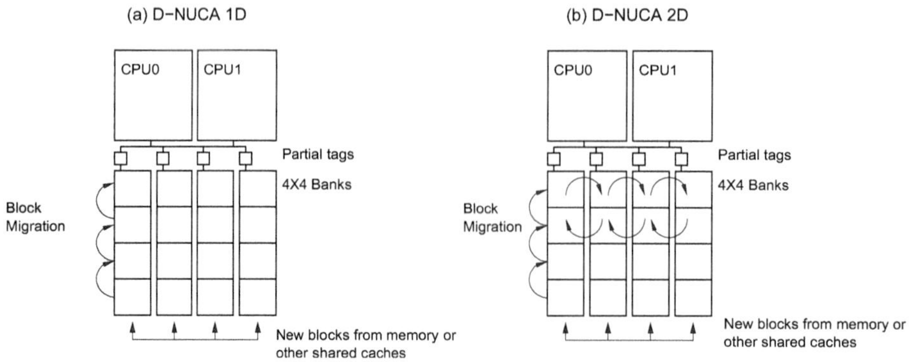

Figure 2: D-NUCA Block Migration Policies

Sharing Degree (SD)	SD=1	SD=2	SD=4	SD=8	SD=16
L2 hit time (cycles)	16.5	18.0	20.9	30.0	35.9
Norm. Remote L2 hits	1.00	0.75	0.60	0.36	n/a
Norm. Mem. accesses	1.00	0.88	0.78	0.78	0.66

Table 3: Average L2 hit times, and normalized remote L2 hits and memory accesses

2D-mesh point-to-point interconnection network comprised of links and switches. All messages for coherence and data migration are modeled to consume network bandwidth; however, we assume infinite buffering at each switching node. A centralized directory is used to track cache lines that are cached in the CMP and is consulted on a cache miss to enforce coherence and/or detect misses.

3.2 Degree of L2 Sharing

In this section, we study the performance effect of the varied L2 cache sharing degrees. In the baseline CMP with S-NUCA based shared caches, the sharing degree changes the effective L2 hit latency, communication frequency among shared caches (e.g., cache-to-cache transfers), and external memory accesses. Table 3 shows the trends in average L2 hit latencies, the number of remote L2 hits and memory accesses as the sharing degree (SD) is changed, with the latter two normalized to the SD=1 case. As the sharing degree increases, shared cache hit latencies increase monotonically from 17 cycles to 36 cycles.

Remote L2 accesses can occur in two cases: First, a read-only shared line is evicted from a local L2 cache, due to a conflict/capacity miss, and upon the next access that line is provided by another shared cache, which has an intact copy of that line. Second, a producer-consumer line is invalidated by another processor in a remote shared cache. In both cases, communication across shared cache boundaries is more expensive in terms of latency and energy consumption than intra-shared cache communication. After detecting a miss in the local shared cache, a miss request is sent to the centralized on-chip directory. The on-chip directory re-transmits the request to another shared cache to service the miss if the cache line is on-chip. Such remote L2 accesses (cache-to-cache transfers) decrease as the sharing degree increases since the likelihood that shared cache lines fall within the same L2 cache increases.

Memory accesses also decrease as the sharing degree increases. With a high sharing degree, processors can share the cache capacity dynamically, reducing the effect of a temporal working set imbalance, resulting in fewer capacity misses than smaller caches. Furthermore, by reducing the number of replicated copies of shared data, the limited on-chip cache capacity can be more efficiently utilized. As shown in Table 3, increasing the sharing degree to 16 can reduce the external memory accesses by 33% on average.

In several ways, the sharing degree affects L1 miss penalties. Figure 3 shows a breakdown of the average L1 miss penalty for each application as the L2 cache sharing degree is varied. L1 misses are served by either the local L2 cache, a remote L2 cache, or external memory. Each bar in the graph shows how much latency each component contributes to the average L1 miss penalty.

Across all benchmark applications, the L2 hit time component (black bar) increases monotonically as the sharing degree increases, due to the wire delay increase in the larger caches. The remote L2 and memory components decrease as the degree of L2 sharing is increased; however, those reductions in latency are often not enough to outweigh the increase in local L2 hit latency. For applications that have high local L2 hit rates and low sharing of cache lines like Barnes-Hut, an increased sharing degree beyond private L2 caches degrades performance.

Figure 4 shows the relative execution times for each application as the sharing degree is varied. As expected from Figure 3, SPECWeb99, Ocean, and LU have the best performance at sharing degree two or four. For Barnes and SPECjbb, increasing the sharing degree degrades performance, with the best performance at the sharing degree of one. The bar with the lowest average L1 miss penalty does not always correspond to the fastest execution time since each miss may affect the execution time with different weight (e.g., SPECWeb99 with SD=4). Critical misses that are not overlapped with other misses can increase execution times more than non-critical misses.

We draw three conclusions from these results. First, building high-degree shared caches for CMPs does not have any advantage in wire-delay dominated future technologies even when high degrees of application sharing exist. The increase in L2 hit latency in shared caches degrades performance more than the reduced misses improve it. Second, the sharing degree can change overall performance significantly. The difference between the best and worst sharing degree ranges from 9% to 22%. Third, no single sharing degree provides the best performance for all the benchmarks. The best performing sharing degree varies across applications. Nevertheless, the SD=4 design point has the best

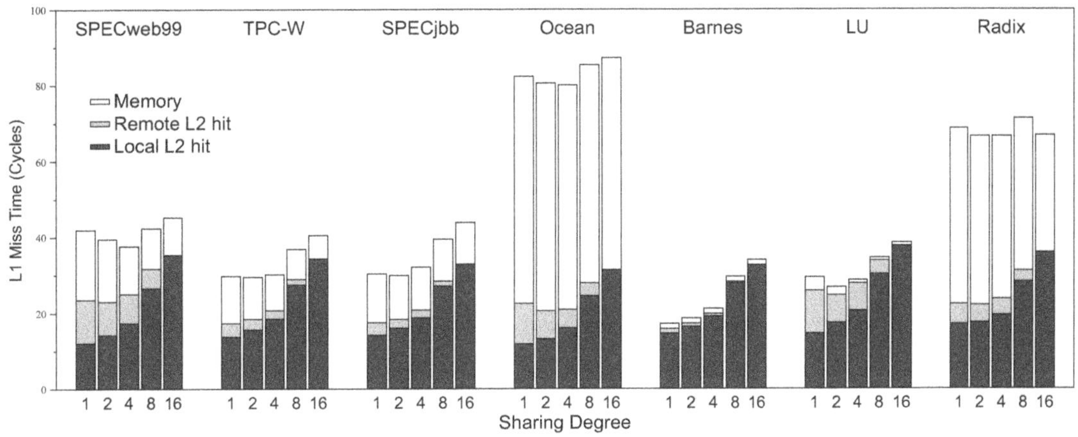

Figure 3: S-NUCA L1 miss latencies (16x16 banks)

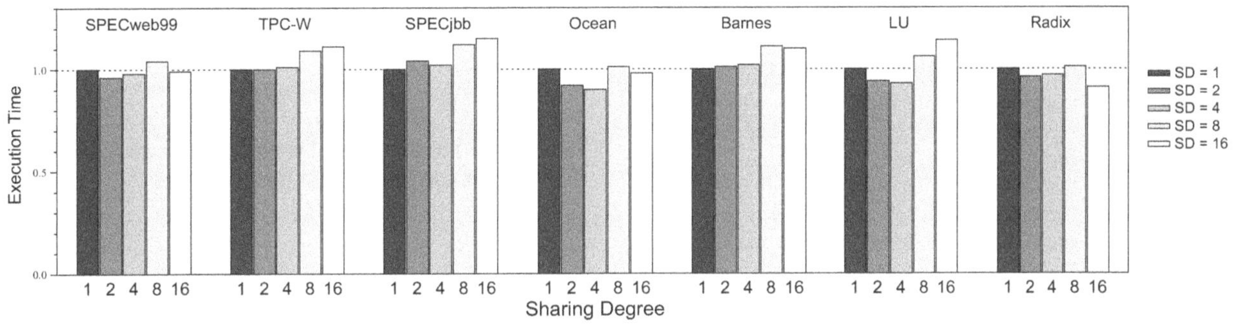

Figure 4: S-NUCA execution time (normalized to SD=1)

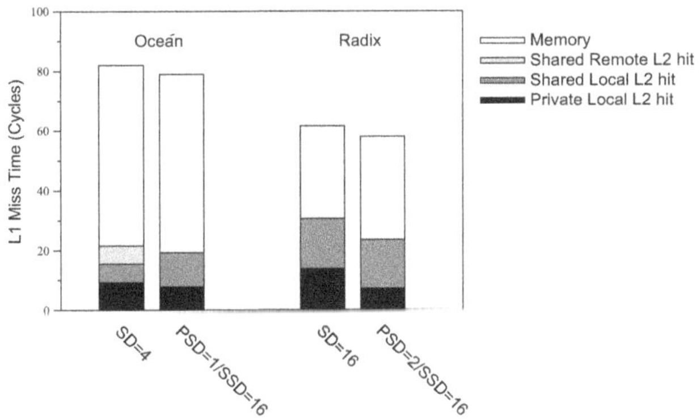

Figure 5: Per-line sharing degrees

average performance for the applications used in this evaluation, and would be the best compromise fixed design point for this mix of workloads for S-NUCA.

3.3 Per-line Sharing Degree

Sharing degree can affect individual cache blocks in different ways based on the sharing patterns of the block. For private blocks, which will never be replicated in other caches, a low sharing degree can reduce the access latencies without hurting caching efficiency. For shared blocks, a higher sharing degree may be more beneficial than lower sharing degree when the reduction of replicated blocks can decrease miss rates significantly. In this section, we investigate the potential benefit of multiple sharing degrees for different classes of blocks.

We divide the address space into private and shared block addresses, and assign different sharing degrees to the two address classes. To evaluate the per-line sharing degrees, we simulated S-NUCA with the two different sharing degrees, *private* and *shared* (PSD and SSD). Since our full-system simulator does not have support for distinguishing private and shared blocks, we used an approximate method of tracking access patterns for the entire address space during run time. Until more than one processor access a block address, the address is assumed to be a private block. Once an address is recognized as a shared block, the block is re-mapped to caches by shared sharing degree. We assumed that the shared sharing degree is always higher than or equal to the private sharing degree.

Figure 5 presents the breakdown of L1 miss penalties for the two applications in which per-line sharing degree is effective. We measured all combinations of private and shared sharing degrees. The two bars for each application represent the baseline ideal uniform sharing degree and the best per-line sharing degree configuration. We divided the local L2 hit latencies into private and shared accesses.

For the two applications, per-line sharing degree reduced execution time by 7% and 6%. With fixed sharing degree, the best sharing degree was 4 (Ocean) or 16 (Radix). When different sharing degrees are allowed for private and shared blocks, the best combination is 1 or 2 for private sharing degree and 16 for shared sharing degree. For these two

Sharing Degree	SD=1	SD=2	SD=4	SD=8	SD=16
S-NUCA	16.5	18.0	20.9	30.0	35.9
D-NUCA 1D Perfect	9.8	11.2	13.8	21.7	28.6
D-NUCA 1D Real	11.2	12.3	15.0	24.8	31.5
D-NUCA 2D Perfect	10.0	10.4	11.7	19.8	25.2
D-NUCA 2D Real	11.6	13.5	16.2	25.1	31.9

Table 4: Average D-NUCA L2 hit latencies

benchmarks, access latencies to private blocks are reduced by having lower sharing degrees (1 or 2), while replications are minimized with high shared a sharing degree (16). With a low private sharing degree, private blocks, which will never be accessed by other processors, are placed on a small range of banks close to processors. With a high shared sharing degree, block replication is reduced, although the shared blocks may be spread across a larger range of banks than private blocks, thus increasing access latencies. It is possible that a finer-grained distribution of lines to banks would improve performance.

3.4 Overcoming Wire Delay Dominance

In Section 3.2, we showed the performance trade-offs of changing the sharing degree in CMP S-NUCA L2 caches. In this section, we evaluate dynamic mapping policies which can potentially reduce long latencies with large sharing degrees. Performance improvements are achieved when the migration policy is successful and the reduction in latency dominates the increased latency of the more complex lookup mechanism. To isolate the effectiveness of dynamic migration from the overheads of the search mechanism, we evaluated two more configurations: perfect D-NUCA 1D and 2D caches. The two configurations assume an oracle searching mechanism that allows L1 misses to be sent directly to the L2 bank storing the requested block on a hit. L2 misses are detected without any overhead. The simulated system models other overheads such as network and bank bandwidth consumption for accesses and migration in detail.

Table 4 shows the average L2 hit times across all applications for five sharing degrees. With the perfect lookup mechanism, both 1D and 2D migration policies show significant reductions in L2 hit latencies. The latency reductions increase as the sharing degree increases. At SD=16, the perfect D-NUCA 1D and 2D policies reduce the average L2 hit latency by 22% and 33%, respectively compared to the S-NUCA design. However, with a realistic search mechanism with distributed partial tags, the latency reduction of D-NUCA is significantly reduced, confirming the search mechanism is a key design issue with D-NUCA.

Figure 6 shows the relative execution times of the best performing sharing degree for the S-NUCA and D-NUCA design points across all applications. Each bar shows the SD with the best performance noted at the top. This figure illustrates two issues: (1) the performance potential of the two perfect search and migration mechanisms (1D and 2D perfect) and how closely the realistic implementations can match them, and (2) performance of two realistic D-NUCA designs compared to S-NUCA with the best sharing degree.

The perfect search mechanisms with 1D and 2D dynamic migration can reduce execution time by 3-25%, except Ocean. For Ocean, although D-NUCA reduces average hit latencies, L2 miss rates are increased since blocks are not promoted quickly, and thus replaced by new blocks. For SPECjbb, the performance improvement is small, since SPECjbb does not take any advantage of the increased sharing degree, and the effect of dynamic migration is not high at low sharing degrees.

With realistic search mechanisms, performance improvement of D-NUCA can be lost (SPECWeb99 and TPC-W). For LU and Radix, both 1D and 2D migrations show large improvement by 17%-20%. LU has a relatively large L1 data miss rate of 12%, but the entire working set nearly fits in the L2 caches. The reduction in L2 hit latencies directly improves performance. In Radix however, external memory accesses dominate performance due to both capacity and conflict misses. The increased bank associativity with dynamic migration reduced conflict misses significantly. Since shared caches, especially with high sharing degrees, are prone to conflict misses, the increased associativity helps avoid certain pathological conflict miss cases.

Although dynamic migration improves the performance of shared caches, the improvement is still modest (less than 5%) for 5 tested applications. Considering the complexity of a D-NUCA implementation and the extra energy consumption due to lookups, it is unlikely that implementing dynamic migration is justified for CMPs.

3.5 Interaction Between L1 Prefetching and NUCA Design Alternatives

In this section, we investigate the effect of hardware-based strided prefetching [2, 10] on NUCA design alternatives. Since effective prefetching can tolerate L1 miss latencies, it can potentially diminish the effect of the increased L2 hit latency observed with larger sharing degrees. We evaluated the effect of strided prefetching on the CMP caches using an implementation similar to the one used by Beckmann et al [4], but restricted to L1 prefetching. The strided prefetching strategy uses three filters with 32 entries each to detect streams. The three filters, positive unit stride, negative unit stride, and non-unit stride use four consecutive misses before confirming a stream, and allocate an entry in an eight-entry stream table. As soon as a stream is detected, six consecutive prefetch requests are issued on behalf of the L1 caches. Prefetching can be stopped when all MSHR entries are used or prefetches cross physical page boundaries. Prefetched cache blocks are stored directly into the caches, which may cause cache pollution problems. If the processors access a prefetched block, another prefetch for the stream is issued from the stream table if the entry is still resident. Stream table entries are replaced using an LRU policy.

Table 5 shows the coverage and accuracy of L1 prefetching. *Coverage* is the ratio of prefetch hits to L1 misses, and *accuracy* is the ratio of prefetch hits to the total number of prefetches, ignoring any late prefetches that may partially hide latency. SPECjbb and LU have small coverage (0.5% for SPECjbb and 0.1% for LU) and relatively low accuracy. Prefetching is most effective for Ocean, with a coverage of 32% of the L1 data misses and 95% accuracy.

Figure 7 shows the relative execution times of S-NUCA and D-NUCA 2D with L1 prefetching compared to the baseline without prefetching using the best performing SD configuration for each run. For S-NUCA shared caches, L1 prefetching can reduce execution time for SPECweb99 (3%), Ocean (10%), and Radix (20%). For SPECjbb, L1 prefetching does not reduce execution time due to the low coverage. Although prefetching can improve performance for many applications for the different configurations, it does not change

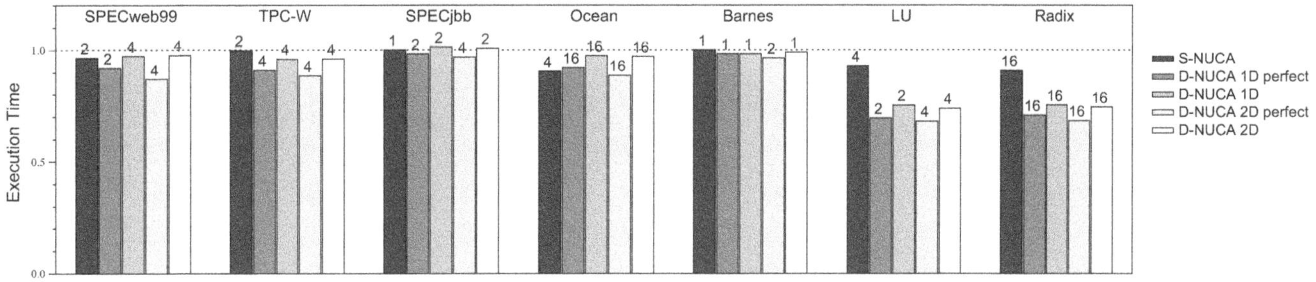

Figure 6: D-NUCA execution time (normalized to S-NUCA with SD=1)

	SPECweb99	TPC-W	SPECjbb	Ocean	Barnes	LU	Radix
L1 I Coverage	31.3%	14.1%	28.3%	20.3%	15.0%	14.8%	25.5%
L1 I Accuracy	46.4%	39.2%	34.0%	61.4%	50.4%	56.5%	49.4%
L1 D Coverage	14.0%	6.8%	0.5%	32.4%	12.2%	0.1%	10.3%
L1 D Accuracy	96.9%	90.0%	35.2%	95.3%	41.5%	0.1%	98.8%

Table 5: Prefetching coverage and accuracy for L1 instruction and data caches

the choice of the best average sharing degree for each design significantly. For six applications, the best sharing degrees with prefetching are either the same as or close to the best sharing degree without L1 prefetching.

We observe that prefetching can also improve dynamic migration. For applications where S-NUCA prefetching is effective, D-NUCA caches have similar performance improvements. This observation confirms that dynamic migration and prefetching are complementary memory latency reduction/tolerance techniques.

3.6 Energy Trade-Offs

One concern with dynamic migration designs is the increased energy consumption due to the complex search mechanism and cache line movement. Instead of estimating the actual energy consumption, we indirectly show the total number of bank accesses of S-NUCA and 2D D-NUCA. For each application, we compared the best sharing degree of the two configurations in Table 6. The numbers in parentheses in the 2D D-NUCA row show the percentage of extra bank accesses compared to the S-NUCA case.

As expected, block migration increases the total bank accesses significantly. The extra bank accesses for block migration constitute 28-48% for the tested applications. In shared caches, unnecessary block migration may occur more frequently than private D-NUCA caches. Although we reduced the unnecessary migration by 2-bit saturating counters, the number of bank accesses due to migration is still significant.

D-NUCA lookup mechanisms also consume energy. For each L2 access, at least a part of distributed partial tags should be accessed. With D-NUCA 2D, the number of partial tag lookups may increase, if blocks are not found in the closest column.

4. RELATED WORK

Shared Cache Designs: Shared caches have been studied in the context of chip multiprocessors and multithreaded processors. Sohi and Franklin's early study proposed the interleaved banks for extra ports in private L1 caches, which resembles multi-banking in shared caches [19]. Nayfeh et al. investigated shared caches for primary and secondary caches on a multi-chip module substrate with four CPUs [16]. They examined how the memory sharing patterns of different applications affect the best cache hierarchy. Subsequent work from the same authors showed the trade-offs of shared-cache clustering in multi-chip multiprocessors [17]. With eight CPUs, they observed for private L2 caches, a coherence bus becomes the performance bottleneck, suggesting shared caches to reduce the bus traffic.

Recent studies considered wire latency as a primary design factor in CMP caches. Beckmann et al. compared three latency reduction techniques including D-NUCA for CMPs with an 8-CPU shared cache [4]. Their study fixed the sharing degree to 8 and observed that combining the three latency reduction techniques can decrease the L2 hit latencies of CMPs. With NuRAPID-based CMP L2 designs, Chishti et al. studied optimizations to reduce unnecessary replication and communication overheads [6]. Speight et al. studied how CMP L2 caches interact with off-chip L3 caches and how on-chip L2 caches temporarily absorb modified replacement blocks from other caches [20].

Dynamic Partitioning: Several researches investigated dynamically re-allocating cache capacity for CMPs and multithreaded processors. Suh et al. studied a monitoring system for an optimal dynamic partitioning [21], and a hardware partitioning mechanism for set-associative caches [22]. Liu et al. proposed achieving dynamic bank allocation by re-mapping the banks [15]. Iyer proposed a priority-based cache management systems to allocate cache resources by OS-assigned priority [9]. To prevent thread starvation due to cache capacity sharing, Kim et al. investigated fairness issues in CMP cache sharing [14].

5. CONCLUSION

The CMP organization that we introduced in this paper is designed to support both low-latency, private logical caches as well as highly shared caches, simply by adjusting the mapping of the same address on different processors to the L2 cache.

The results showed that–compared to private, non-shared L2 partitions–the L2 latency more than doubled for a fully shared cache. The results also showed that the fully shared

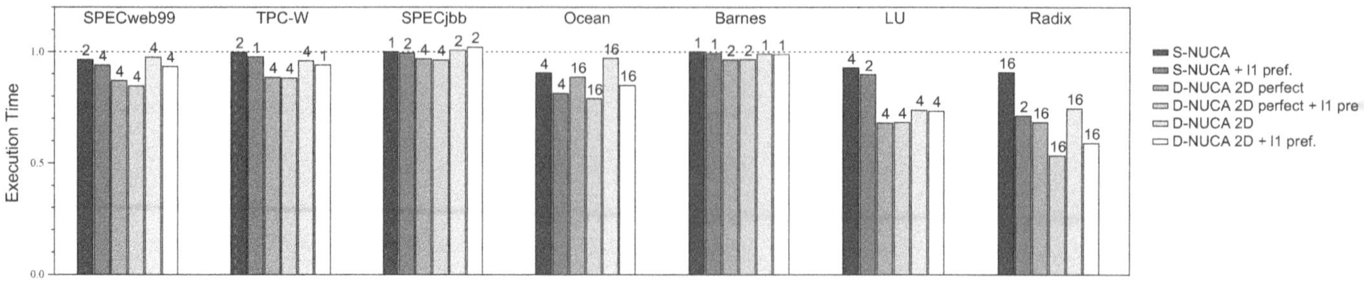

Figure 7: Prefetching execution time (normalized to S-NUCA with SD=1)

	SPECweb99	TPC-W	SPECjbb	Ocean	Barnes	LU	Radix
S-NUCA Best	44	25	4	10	12	31	20
D-NUCA 2D Best	72 (40%)	34 (28%)	6 (32%)	18 (49%)	15 (27%)	60 (43%)	49 (48%)

Table 6: Bank accesses per 1K instructions

cache could eliminate a third of off-chip misses. Clearly, a large opportunity exists if this gap can be bridged.

The S-NUCA organization worked best with a low-to-medium sharing degree for all applications; the extra hit latency was simply too detrimental with larger sharing degrees. Consequently, we evaluated L1 prefetching and dynamic migration of lines, attempting to reduce the average hit latencies and make the larger sharing degrees more effective. L1 prefetching worked uniformly well, but did not drive the ideal sharing degree significantly in one direction or the other, even though the L1 miss rates were reduced.

Dynamic migration (D-NUCA 1D and 2D) showed modest performance improvements, despite reductions in average hit latency. However, for a subset of applications, D-NUCA drove the ideal sharing degree to higher sharing degrees, showing that mechanisms to reduce latency can indeed make higher-degree shared caches the optimal point. It remains to be seen whether the added complexity and power consumption justify moving to a D-NUCA design since only a subset of the applications benefit appreciably; we think it unlikely to be justifiable.

Since the underlying cache framework permits different degrees of sharing on the same hardware, further opportunity exists: The cache can be configured differently to have the ideal sharing degree for each specific application or for individual cache lines. Figure 8 shows a comparison of the average execution time across all applications for the S-NUCA and D-NUCA designs normalized to the S-NUCA design with the best sharing degree of four. For each policy, we show the performance with the best fixed sharing degree across all applications, the worst fixed sharing degree, and a per-application "variable" degree. Choosing the best sharing degree at a finer granularity provides a small but measurable (5%) speedup for the more aggressive policies. In Table 7, we list the ideal per-application sharing degrees for each policy and show the percentage speedup over the best fixed sharing degree for that policy. For D-NUCA, SPECjbb, Ocean, and Radix showed a measurable boost of 5-25%.

Based on these results, we conclude that the simplest design is probably the best: an S-NUCA organization with a sharing degree of two or four. However, the D-NUCA results still hold promise, and we are continuing to explore ways to exploit the flexible mapping. Treating different classes of lines with different sharing degrees showed significant potential for two applications, and this approach is a subject of continuing effort.

6. ACKNOWLEDGMENTS

This research is supported by the Defense Advanced Research Projects Agency (DARPA) under contracts F33615-01-C-1892 and NBCH30390004, NSF infrastructure grant EIA-0303609, and two IBM University Partnership Awards. We thank the members of the IBM PERCS team for their technical feedback.

7. REFERENCES

[1] V. Agarwal, S. W. Keckler, and D. Burger. The effect of technology scaling on microarchitecture structures. Technical Report TR-00-02, Department of Computer Sciences, University of Texas at Austin, May 2001.

[2] J.-L. Baer and T.-F. Chen. Effective hardware-based data prefetching for high-performance processors. *IEEE Transactions on Computer*, 44(5):609–623, 1995.

[3] L. A. Barroso, K. Gharachorloo, R. McNamara, A. Nowatzyk, S. Qadeer, B. Sano, S. Smith, R. Stets, and B. Verghese. Piranha: A scalable architecture based on single-chip multiprocessing. In *The 27th Annual International Symposium on Computer Architecture*, pages 282–293, June 2000.

[4] B. M. Beckmann and D. A. Wood. Managing wire delay in large chip-multiprocessor caches. In *37th International Symposium on Microarchitecture (MICRO)*, December 2004.

[5] Z. Chishti, M. Powell, and T. N. Vijaykumar. Distance associativity for high-performance energy-efficient non-uniform cache architectures. In *The 36th Annual International Symposium on Microarchitecture (MICRO)*, pages 55–66, December 2003.

[6] Z. Chishti, M. D. Powell, and T. N. Vijaykumar. Optimizing replication, communication, and capacity allocation in cmps. In *Proceedings of the 32nd annual international symposium on Computer Architecture*, 2005.

[7] L. Hammond, B. A. Hubbert, M. Siu, M. K. Prabhu, M. Chen, and K. Olukotun. The Stanford Hydra

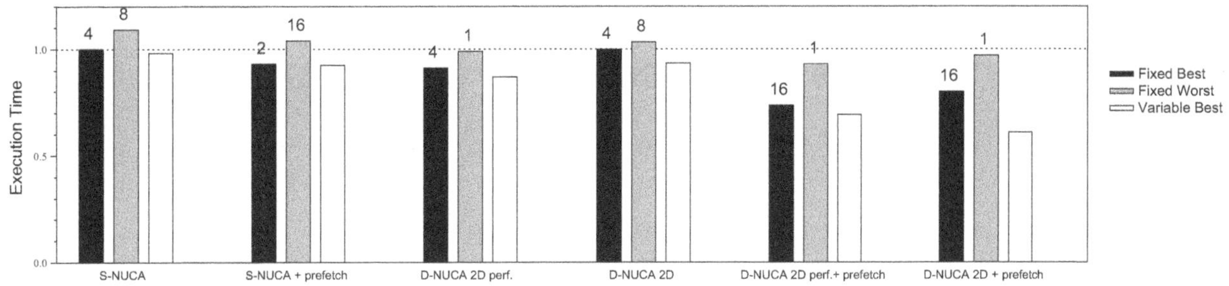

Figure 8: Execution time for fixed best, fixed worst and variable best sharing degree

	SPECweb99	TPC-W	SPECjbb	Ocean	Barnes	LU	Radix	Fixed Best
S-NUCA	2 (1.4%)	2 (1.4%)	1 (1.6%)	4 (0.0%)	1 (2.0%)	4 (0.0%)	16 (6.6%)	4
S-NUCA +pref.	4 (0.4%)	1 (0.4%)	2 (0.0%)	4 (2.4%)	1 (0.9%)	2 (0.0%)	2 (0.0%)	2
D-NUCA 2D	4 (0.0%)	4 (0.0%)	2 (9.4%)	16 (4.1%)	1 (3.6%)	4 (0.0%)	16 (25.4%)	4

Table 7: Per-application best sharing degrees

CMP. *IEEE Micro*, pages 71–84, December 2000.

[8] J. Huh, J. Chang, D. Burger, and G. S. Sohi. Coherence decoupling: Making use of incoherence. In *International Conference on Architectural Support for Programming Languages and Operating Systems (ASPLOS)*, Oct. 2004.

[9] R. Iyer. CQoS: a framework for enabling QoS in shared caches of cmp platforms. In *Proceedings of the 18th annual international conference on Supercomputing*, pages 257–266, 2004.

[10] N. P. Jouppi. Improving direct-mapped cache performance by the addition of a small fully-associative cache and prefetch buffers. In *Proceedings of the 17th annual international symposium on Computer Architecture*, pages 364–373, 1990.

[11] R. Kalla, B. Sinharoy, and J. M. Tendler. IBM Power5 Chip: A dual-core multithreaded processor. *IEEE Micro*, 24(2), Mar/Apr 2004.

[12] R. Kessler, R. Jooss, A. Lebeck, and M. Hill. Inexpensive implementations of set-associativity. In *Proceedings of the 16th Annual International Symposium on Computer Architecture*, pages 131–139, May 1989.

[13] C. Kim, D. Burger, and S. W. Keckler. An adaptive, non-uniform cache structure for wire-delay dominated on-chip caches. In *Proceedings of the 10th International Conference on Architectural Support for Programming Languages and Operating Systems (ASPLOS)*, pages 211–222, October 2002.

[14] S. Kim, D. Chandra, and Y. Solihin. Fair cache sharing and partitioning in a chip multiprocessor architecture. In *Proceedings of the 13th International Conference on Parallel Architecture and Compilation Techniques (PACT'04)*, pages 111–122, 2004.

[15] C. Liu, A. Sivasubramaniam, and M. Kandemir. Organizing the last line of defense before hitting the memory wall for cmps. In *Proceedings of the 10th International Symposium High Performance Computer Architecture*, Feb. 2004.

[16] B. A. Nayfeh, L. Hammond, and K. Olukotun. Evaluation of design alternatives for a multiprocessor microprocessor. In *Proceedings of the 23th Annual International Symposium on Computer Architecture*, pages 67–77, May 1996.

[17] B. A. Nayfeh, K. Olukotun, and J. P. Singh. The impact of shared-cache clustering in small-scale shared-memory multiprocessors. In *Proceedings of the 2nd IEEE Symposium on High-Performance Computer Architecture (HPCA)*, page 74, 1996.

[18] P. Shivakumar and N. P. Jouppi. Cacti 3.0: An integrated cache timing, power, and area model. Technical Report 2001-2, HP, Western Research Laboratory, 2001.

[19] G. Sohi and M. Franklin. High-performance data memory systems for superscalar processors. In *Proceedings of the Fourth Symposium on Architectural Support for Programming Languages and Operating Systems*, pages 53–62, Apr. 1991.

[20] E. Speight, H. Shafi, L. Zhang, and R. Rajamony. Adaptive mechanisms and policies for managing cache hierarchies in chip multiprocessors. In *Proceedings of the 32nd annual international symposium on Computer Architecture*, 2005.

[21] G. Suh, S. Devadas, and L. Rudolph. A new memory monitoring scheme for memory-aware scheduling and partitioning. In *Proceedings of the 8th International Symposium High Performance Computer Architecture*, Feb. 2002.

[22] G. E. Suh, L. Rudolph, and S. Devadas. Dynamic partitioning of shared cache memory. *Journal of Supercomputing*, 28(1):7–26, 2004.

[23] J. M. Tendler, S. Dodson, S. Fields, H. Le, and B. Sinharoy. Power4 system microarchitecture. *IBM Journal of Research and Development*, 46(1), 2002.

[24] S. C. Woo, M. Ohara, E. Torrie, J. P. Singh, and A. Gupta. The splash-2 programs: Characterization and methodological considerations. In *Proceedings of the 22nd International Symposium on Computer Architecture*, pages 24–36, 1995.

Design Tradeoffs for Tiled CMP On-Chip Networks

James Balfour* , William J. Dally
Computer Systems Laboratory
Stanford University
{jbalfour,billd}@cva.stanford.edu

ABSTRACT

We develop detailed area and energy models for on-chip interconnection networks and describe tradeoffs in the design of efficient networks for tiled chip multiprocessors. Using these detailed models we investigate how aspects of the network architecture including topology, channel width, routing strategy, and buffer size affect performance and impact area and energy efficiency. We simulate the performance of a variety of on-chip networks designed for tiled chip multiprocessors implemented in an advanced VLSI process and compare area and energy efficiencies estimated from our models. We demonstrate that the introduction of a second parallel network can increase performance while improving efficiency, and evaluate different strategies for distributing traffic over the subnetworks. Drawing on insights from our analysis, we present a concentrated mesh topology with replicated subnetworks and express channels which provides a 24% improvement in area efficiency and a 48% improvement in energy efficiency over other networks evaluated in this study.

1. INTRODUCTION

Chip multiprocessors (CMPs) use increasing transistor budgets to integrate multiple processors on a single die [17]. Tiled architectures provide a scalable solution for managing design complexity and effectively using the resources available in advanced VLSI technologies [20]. The complexity of designing efficient, scalable on-chip communication mechanisms will continue to increase as advances allow more processors to be integrated on a single die; furthermore, power dissipation and wire delay will continue to increase in significance as limiting design constraints [8, 9]. On-chip networks address many of the difficulties associated with managing the increasing complexity of on-chip communication: their modular construction facilitates design reuse and allows high-performance circuits to be used in the interconnect; the structured wiring allows the abundant wire resources to be efficiently used while maintaining well controlled electrical characteristics [4].

This work investigates the design of area-efficient and energy-efficient on-chip networks for tiled CMP architectures. Previous work has described efficient router architectures for on-chip networks [21, 15, 11]. We address the broader issue of the complete network's performance and efficiency. We develop comprehensive analytical area and energy models for on-chip networks. The energy models extend those presented in [21, 7] by incorporating the impacts of physical design and layout on energy dissipation. Our area and energy models incorporate design space attributes including topology, routing, channel design, switch architecture, and buffer sizing with sufficient detail to explore a broad design space. We demonstrate that using multiple on-chip networks to increase bandwidth and path diversity substantially improves performance without adversely affecting area or energy efficiency as measured by the area-delay product and energy-delay product, respectively. Drawing on insights from our analysis, we propose a *concentrated mesh* architecture which offers a 24% improvement in area efficiency and a 48% improvement in energy efficiency over other architectures evaluated in this work.

The remainder of this paper is organized as follows. In Section 2 we present network performance and technology models. In Section 3 we detail the motivating system architecture and constraints imposed by the VLSI technology. In Section 4 we present a canonical network architecture and develop our energy and area models. In Section 5 we describe the design space and present our architectures. In Sections 6 and 7 we describe evaluation methodologies and present results and analysis. We conclude in Section 8.

2. PRELIMINARIES

We begin by presenting a simple analytical model that provides insight into interconnection network performance and will motivate later design decisions. A complete treatment of the subject may be found in [5]. Because management of wire resources is critical to the design of efficient on-chip networks, we then proceed to describe wire models used in our analysis. We conclude this section by describing the technology models used in our evaluation.

2.1 Network Performance

Capacity and latency are two measures which are commonly used to compare networks. Capacity, defined as the injection bandwidth offered to each of the N terminal nodes for uniform random traffic, can be calculated from the bi-

*Supported by the Cadence Design Systems Stanford Graduate Fellowship

ICS06, June 28-30, Cairns, Queensland, Australia.

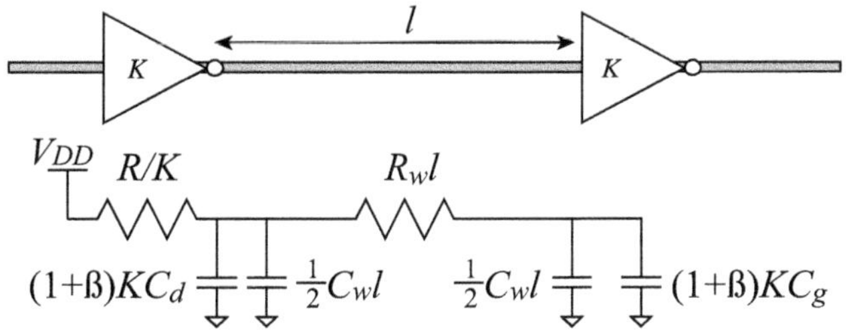

Figure 1: First-Order Repeated Wire Delay Model

section bandwidth (B_B) or the bisection channel count (B_C) and the channel bandwidth (b) as:

$$\text{Capacity} = \frac{2B_\mathrm{B}}{N} = \frac{2bB_\mathrm{C}}{N} \tag{1}$$

As the channel bisection provides an indicator of global wiring requirements, equation (1) can be interpreted as expressing a tradeoff between network performance and implementation complexity.

The average contention-free latency (T_0) from source s to destination d depends on a number of parameters, including: the average hop count (H) from s to d and router traversal latency (t_r), which determine the routing latency; the channel traversal latency (T_c); and the packet length (L) and channel bandwidth (b), which determine the serialization latency (T_s). We calculate T_0 as:

$$T_0(s,d) = H(s,d)\, t_\mathrm{r} + T_\mathrm{c}(s,d) + \frac{L}{b} \tag{2}$$

As the load on the network increases, greater resource contention contributes to longer router traversal latencies.

A well designed network exploits available resources to improve performance. Simple, regular topologies provide compact layouts and allow low-latency router architectures to be used. However, routing latency begins to dominate as more processors are added and hop counts increase. While topologies using high radix routers can reduce the the average hop count, wiring requirements complicate layout and may increase the area consumed by the network. Similarly, increasing the channel bandwidth improves throughput at the expense of additional demand for wiring resources, which may complicate layout or dilate the die area. For a fixed wire bandwidth, increasing the channel width to reduce serialization latency improves performance but occupies more area. As the die area expands and packets travel longer distances, both channel latency and energy consumption increase.

2.2 Wire Model

We use the first-order RC wire delay model described in [8] and depicted in Figure 1. The model incorporates the following intrinsic parameters: the input or gate capacitance (C_g); the output or diffusion capacitance (C_d); the equivalent resistance (R); the resistance per millimeter for a minimum pitch wire (R_w); and the capacitance per millimeter for a minimum pitch wire (C_w). Parameter values appear in Tables 1 and 2.

Inverters are identically sized and uniformly distributed along the path. The repeated wire delay (T_w) across the segment of length l with repeaters of size K and PMOS:NMOS ratio ß is calculated as:

$$\kappa_0 = R(1+ß)(C_d + C_g) \tag{3}$$

$$\kappa_1 = \frac{R}{K} C_w + K R_w (1+ß) C_g \tag{4}$$

$$\kappa_2 = \frac{1}{2} R_w C_w \tag{5}$$

$$T_w = \kappa_0 + \kappa_1 l + \kappa_2 l^2 \tag{6}$$

All wires are minimum pitch with an aspect ratio consistent with our representative technology, which maximizes the aggregate channel bandwidth [14].

We calculate the power (P_w) dissipated driving the wire segment with activity factor α as:

$$\kappa_a = \alpha\,(K(C_g + C_d) + C_w l)\, f V_\mathrm{DD}^2 \tag{7}$$

$$\kappa_l = \frac{1}{2} K (I_{\mathrm{off}_\mathrm{N}} + ß I_{\mathrm{off}_\mathrm{P}}) V_\mathrm{DD} \tag{8}$$

$$P_w = \kappa_a + \kappa_l \tag{9}$$

Here, $I_{\mathrm{off}_\mathrm{N}}$ is the NMOS leakage current, and $I_{\mathrm{off}_\mathrm{P}}$ is the PMOS leakage current.

Table 1: Interconnect Characteristics

Parameter	Local	Semi-global	Global
Metal Layers	4	2	2
Width (nm)	100	200	400
Pitch (nm)	200	400	800
Thickness (nm)	180	360	720
Aspect Ratio	1.8	1.8	1.8
Vertical Spacing (nm)	200	300	700
Resistivity (Ωmm)	2.8	2.5	2.3
Resistance (Ω/mm)	1550	350	80
Capacitance (fF/mm)	166	228	240

Table 2: Device Characteristics

Supply Voltage	V_{DD}	1.0	[V]
Gate Capacitance	C_g	1.34	[fF/um]
Diffusion Capacitance	C_d	0.85	[fF/um]
Equivalent Resistance	R	1.085	[kΩ/um]
NMOS Leakage Current	$I_{\mathrm{off}_\mathrm{N}}$	30	[nA/um]
PMOS Leakage Current	$I_{\mathrm{off}_\mathrm{P}}$	30	[nA/um]

2.3 Technology Model

Our technology model is intended to be representative of the 65nm processes disclosed in [2, 3, 13]. Device models are based on the predictive technology models described in [22]. Interconnect models were derived from [10, 2, 3, 13]. Tables 1 and 2 present relevant parameters.

3. SYSTEM ARCHITECTURE

In this section, we introduce the motivating tiled CMP architecture and identify the constraints imposed by the VLSI technology model used in the evaluation.

We consider a tiled CMP with 64 processors connected by a packet switched interconnection network implemented in a 65nm CMOS technology. Each tile includes an execution unit and 256KB of local memory. Because our focus is the interconnection network rather than on-chip coherence and consistency protocols, we model an abstract communication

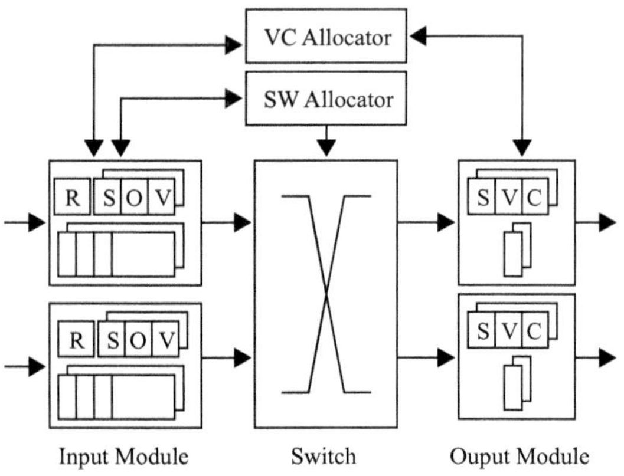

Figure 2: Router Architecture

protocol consisting of read and write transactions. Read transactions are initiated with a request sent to a remote tile and are completed when the requested memory block is received. Write transactions are initiated with a request that transfers a block to a remote tile and are completed when an acknowledgment from the remote tile is received. Transactions transfer 512-bit blocks of data. To model prefetching and similar latency hiding techniques, tiles may have up to four concurrent transactions pending. Read requests and write replies are mapped into short packets, which are nominally 64-bits in length. Read replies and write requests are mapped into longer packets that are constructed by appending the memory block to a header similar to the request packet, which yields a packet that is nominally 576-bits in length.

The processor tiles are nominally square, measuring 1.5mm along an edge. Local metal layers M1-M4 are reserved for the processor, leaving semi-global metal layers M5 and M6 available for routing network channels over the tiles. Global metal layers M7 and M8 are reserved for distributing power and ground, clocks, and critical control signals. The interconnection network is required to operate at the processor clock frequency of 2GHz, which corresponds to roughly 24 fan-out of 4 inverter delays. In-order packet delivery is not required.

4. NETWORK ARCHITECTURE

In this section we describe the network architecture and develop our area and energy models. We begin with a description of the router architecture in Section 4.1 and proceed to elaborate on the design of the datapath components in Sections 4.2 through 4.4. We describe the design of the channels in Section 4.5, and conclude with our area model for a complete router in Section 4.6.

4.1 Router Architecture

Figure 2 presents a block diagram of the pipelined input-queued virtual-channel router architecture used throughout this analysis. The architecture resembles that described in [18]. We use route lookahead to remove routing from the critical path. The virtual-channel allocator (VC Allocator) allows speculative assignment of output virtual-channels to packets arriving at the input modules. Similarly, the switch allocator (SW Allocator) permits speculative assignment of switch time slots to flow control digits (flits). The switch allocator prioritizes flits with non-speculative virtual-channel assignments ahead of speculative requests. With route lookahead and speculation, the nominal router traversal time is 2 cycles. Routing, virtual-channel allocation, and switch assignment are performed in the first cycle, with switch traversal occurring in the second.

The router architecture often differentiates between short packets (read requests, write acknowledgments) and long packets (read responses, write requests). We denote the width of flits used when routing short packets as w_s, and denote the width of flits used when routing long packets as w_l. Short packets are mapped into a single flit, while long packets are mapped into a sequence of L_l flits. Thus, for long packets we have: packet length $= w_l \times L_l$. The datapath width (w) corresponds to the maximum width of flits traversing the network: $w = \max(w_s, w_l)$.

4.2 Input Module

The input module manages the states of its virtual-channels and buffers flits until they can be forwarded. The following state, illustrated in Figure 2, is replicated per virtual-channel: the virtual-channel control state (S), which indicates whether the virtual-channel is in use; the destination output module (O); and the assigned output virtual-channel (V). We do not reuse a virtual-channel until the tail credit is received. Consequently, it is not necessary to track the number of credits available for the virtual-channel at the downstream router. Instead, the virtual-channel is held until the downstream router signals that the tail flit has been forwarded, freeing the virtual-channel for recycling. A routing unit (R) is implemented in each input module. With route lookahead, the routing unit simply decodes the routing information provided by the previous router to determine the output virtual-channel for a packet.

Flits arrive late in the clock cycle and are retimed by an input register before being buffered. The flit buffers are implemented in a dual-port memory. Each virtual-channel receives a disjoint allocation of contiguous memory words to allow rapid translation of virtual-channel identifiers to buffer locations. The flit buffers are bypassed when an arriving flit is immediately eligible for virtual-channel and switch allocation. Flits are written into the buffers regardless of whether the bypass path is enabled to allow recovery from a failed speculative allocation.

The memory width is matched to the datapath width to allow an entire flit to be accessed in one cycle. Because short flits can be accommodated by a narrower memory word, the memory includes two SRAM arrays of different widths. The arrangement of the arrays within the memory is illustrated in Figure 3 (which is described in more detail below). This construction improves the energy efficiency of the flit buffer and is possible because we statically assign virtual-channels locations in the memory. To avoid unnecessary transitions at the egress of the input module when forwarding short flits to the switch, the flit buffer includes a set of latches (QLatch) to preserve a quescient state on lines that are not used by short flits.

4.2.1 Input Module Area Model

The area of the input module is dominated by the flit buffer memory. Figure 3 illustrates the placement of blocks used to estimate the area of the input module. The datapath uses a bitslice construction, with the slice pitch selected to

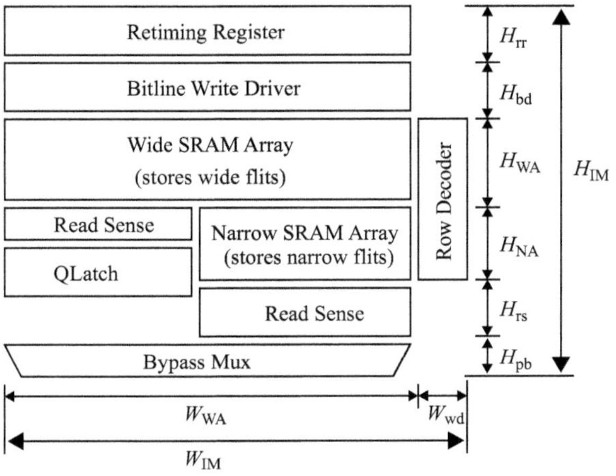

Figure 3: Router Input Buffer Area

accommodate both the memory cell pitch and and the switch input pitch. Arrays of elements whose pitch exceeds the slice pitch, such as the latches, are folded to preserve a constant pitch through the datapath pitch.

Because narrow memories result in more compact layouts for our floorplans, we assume no bitline multiplexing at the sense amps. For an SRAM cell with dimensions $H_{\text{cell}} \times W_{\text{cell}}$, the height of the wide array (H_{WA}) is determined by the number of virtual-channels provided for long packets (VC_l) and the buffer depth per virtual-channel (D_l):

$$H_{\text{WA}} = H_{\text{cell}} \times VC_l \times D_l \tag{10}$$

The height of the narrow array is similarly determined by the number of virtual-channels provided for short packets (VC_s) and the buffer depth per virtual-channel ($D_s = 1$) .

$$H_{\text{NA}} = H_{\text{cell}} \times VC_s \times D_s \tag{11}$$

The height of the bitline drivers (H_{bd}) and the read sense logic (H_{rs}) depends on the circuit topology. When detailed circuit designs are unavailable, we estimate the height of the bitline drivers based on the size of inverters needed to drive the bitlines and the area required for the bitline conditioning circuits. We estimate the height of the read sense logic assuming a cross-coupled inverter pair construction. The height of the flit buffer memory (H_{Mem}) is

$$H_{\text{Mem}} = H_{\text{WA}} + H_{\text{NA}} + H_{\text{bd}} + H_{\text{rs}} \tag{12}$$

When in the height of the retiming register (H_{rr}) and bypass multiplexer (H_{bp}) are included, the total height of the input module (H_{IM}) is:

$$H_{\text{IM}} = H_{\text{rr}} + H_{\text{Mem}} + H_{\text{bp}} \tag{13}$$

The width of the input module (W_{IM}) is determined by the width of the wide array (W_{WA}) and the row decoder driving the wordlines (W_{wd}):

$$W_{\text{IM}} = W_{\text{IM}} + W_{\text{wd}} = (w \times W_{\text{cell}}) + W_{\text{wd}} \tag{14}$$

The decoder width is estimated from the size of the final buffers required to drive the wordlines and the number of predecode wires routed along the length of the row decoder, parallel to the array bitlines. As will be illustrated in Figure 7, the placement of the row decoder allows its width to be partially hidden by the output modules described subsequently.

4.2.2 Input Module Energy Model

The wordline capacitance (C_{wl}) is calculated from the number of bits (N_{b}) per memory word, the gate capacitance of the passgate transistor (C_{pg}), and the wire capacitance associated with the length of the wordline spanning a cell (l_w). For the wide array $N_{\text{b}} = w_l$, while for the narrow array $N_{\text{b}} = w_s$. The wordline capacitance is calculated as:

$$C_{\text{wl}} = N_{\text{b}}(2C_{\text{pg}} + C_w l_w) \tag{15}$$

The bitline capacitance (C_{bl}) is calculated from the number of words in the array (N_{w}), the diffusion capacitance of the passgate transistor (C_{pd}), and the wire capacitance of the length of the bitline spanning the cell (l_b):

$$C_{\text{bl}} = 2N_{\text{w}}(C_{\text{pd}} + C_w l_b) \tag{16}$$

The energy expended in a write operation is calculated based on the discharging of the bitlines by the bitline driver with internal capacitance (C_{bd}) and the charging of the wordline by the wordline driver with internal capacitance (C_{wd}). The energy expended activating a wordline (E_{wl}) is:

$$E_{\text{wl}} = (C_{\text{wd}} + C_{\text{wl}})V_{\text{DD}}^2 \tag{17}$$

We include the internal capacitance of the input retiming register (C_{rr}) in the write energy because the register is always written in the cycle before the flit buffer. For modeling purposes, we assume that half of the enabled cells change state during a write. The state change requires charging the internal capacitance of the cross-coupled inverters (C_{cc}). Accordingly, the energy expended writing a flit of width w_f into the flit buffer (E_{wr}) is:

$$E_{\text{wr}} = E_{\text{wl}} + w_f(C_{\text{rr}} + C_{\text{bd}} + C_{\text{bl}} + 0.5\, C_{\text{cc}})V_{\text{DD}}^2 \tag{18}$$

The energy expended in a read operation is calculated similarly to that of a write operation except that we assume the bitlines have a signal swing of $0.25V_{\text{DD}}$ during a read operation. For modeling purposes, the capacitance associated with the read sense circuit (C_{rs}) absorbs that associated with the buffers required to drive the signals to the switch. The energy expended by a read of the flit buffer (E_{rd}) is:

$$E_{\text{rd}} = E_{\text{wl}} + C_{\text{rs}}V_{\text{DD}}^2 + 0.25 C_{\text{bl}}V_{\text{DD}}^2 \tag{19}$$

4.3 Switch

The switch is implemented as a segmented crossbar to allow a regular, compact layout and reduce power dissipation [21]. Figure 4 presents a simplified illustration of a 2-input, 2-output segmented crossbar. As suggested by Figure 4, the segmented crossbar is a refinement of the canonical matrix crossbar in which the input and output lines are broken into segments of approximately equal length with adjacent segments isolated by tri-state buffers. Control signals selectively enable the tri-state buffers to minimize the number of active line segments. All of our routers use segmented crossbars that divide the input and output lines into two segments of approximately equal length.

4.3.1 Switch Area Model

Each edge of the crossbar must be wide enough to accommodate $N_{\text{i}} \times w$ input signals or $N_{\text{o}} \times w$ output signals. The crossbars considered in this analysis are wire dominated,

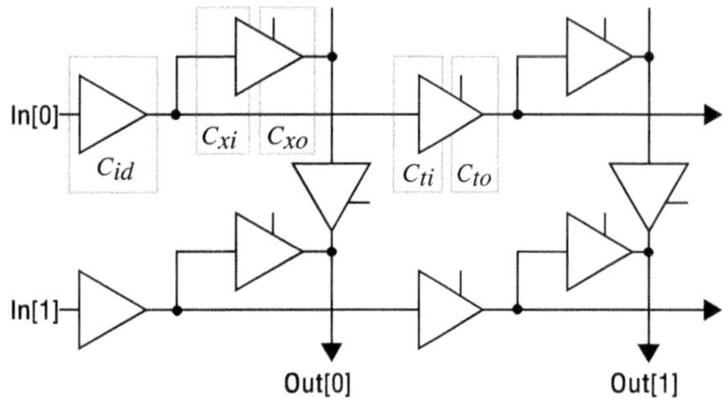

Figure 4: Crossbar annotated with Capacitances

with areas proportional to $(N_\text{i} \times w) \times (N_\text{o} \times w)$. When calculating the dimensions of a crossbar, we must account for metal tracks reserved for vias bringing signals from the upper wire matrix layers down to the crosspoints. We denote the spacing between wires as s_x. For a wire pitch of p_w, the crossbar width and height are calculated as:

$$W_x = N_\text{o} \times (w \times p_w \times s_x) \quad (20)$$
$$H_x = N_\text{i} \times (w \times p_w \times s_x) \quad (21)$$

4.3.2 *Switch Energy Model*

The model for the capacitive load contributed by the input lines incorporates the following parameters: the length of the input wire (l_{xb}); the capacitance contributed by the input driver (C_{id}); the capacitive contributed by the input of a cross-point (C_{xi}); the input capacitance of the tri-state buffer (C_{ti}); the output capacitance of the tri-state buffer (C_{to}); and, the wire capacitance per unit length (C_w). When only the first segment of an input line is driven, the load is calculated as:

$$C_{xbi} = C_{id} + 0.5(N_o C_{xo} + C_w l_{xb}) + C_{ti} \quad (22)$$

When both segments of an input line are driven, the load is calculated as:

$$C_{xbi} = C_{id} + N_o C_{xi} + C_w l_{xb} + C_{ti} + C_{to} \quad (23)$$

The model for the capacitive load contributed by the output lines incorporate the following additional parameters: the parasitic diffusion capacitance at the output of a cross-point switch (C_{xo}); and the capacitance associated with the output latch (C_l). When only the first segment of an output line is driven, the load is calculated as:

$$C_{xbo} = 0.5(N_i C_{xo} + C_w l_{xb}) + C_{to} + C_l \quad (24)$$

When both output segments are driven, the output load is calculated as:

$$C_{xbo} = N_i C_{xo} + C_w l_{xb} + C_{ti} + C_{to} + C_l \quad (25)$$

The energy associated with a flit of width w_f traversing the switch can be calculated as:

$$E_\text{sw} = w_f \times (C_{xbi} + C_{xbo}) V_\text{DD}^2 \quad (26)$$

4.4 Output Module

The output module forwards flits from the switch to the downstream router. Because traversing the switch consumes enough of the clock period to prohibit propagating the flit to the downstream router in what remains of the cycle, it is necessary to latch outgoing flits in the output module. To reduce energy consumption when sending flits that are narrower than the channel, the output latch preserves a quiescent state on those wires that are not used to transmit the flit. The state fields of interest are: the output virtual-channel control state (S), the input virtual-channel (V), and the number of flit buffer credits available at the downstream router (C). The control state indicates whether a virtual-channel is idle, active, or unavailable because the tail credit of the previous packet has yet to be returned.

4.4.1 *Output Module Area Model*

The output latch contributes most of the output module's area. Accordingly, we use the dimensions of the output latch to determine the height of the output module (H_OM) and the width of the output latch to determine the width of the output module (W_OM).

4.4.2 *Output Module Energy Model*

We limit the energy consumption attributed to the output module to that of the output latch not included in the crossbar and incorporate the energy expended switching the channel wires into the channel energy model. For a datapath of width w, the energy dissipated when forwarding a flit of width w_f through the output module (E_OM) is:

$$E_\text{OM} = w_f E_\text{L} + w C_{\text{L},in} V_\text{DD}^2 \quad (27)$$

Here, E_L is the energy associated with an active latch transition and $C_{\text{L},in}$ is the input latch capacitance loading a crossbar output. The later term correctly accounts for switched capacitance at crossbar outputs leading to disabled latches when forwarding short flits.

4.5 Channels

Figure 5 illustrate how the number (N) and size (K) of repeaters affects the distance a signal routed in semi-global metal layers will propagate in one cycle and the energy expended driving the repeated wire. At shorter wire lengths, the wire contributes 10 to 40 times the capacitance of the repeaters. At longer wire lengths where repeaters become larger and more frequent, the contribution of the wire capacitance declines to 6 to 10 times that of the repeaters. The similarity of the curves presented in Figure 5 results from the majority of the energy being expended in the wires.

Wires transporting signals traveling longer distances are broken into M segments separated by sequencing elements. With channel lengths determined by the placement of routers in the floorplan, we design channels by selecting K, N, and M to minimize the energy-delay measure KNM^2 subject to the constraint that the repeated segment wire delay (T_w) cannot exceed the cycle time less margin for setup time and clock skew.

4.5.1 *Channel Area Model*

The lateral capacitance between wires running parallel over long distances results in capacitive coupling which affects timing and leads to coupling noise injection. To mitigate these adverse effects, metal tracks are reserved at regular intervals within the channels for power and ground shields. We calculate the physical width of the region reserved for routing a channel (W_ch) from the width of the channel (w), the metal pitch (p_M) and the average signal

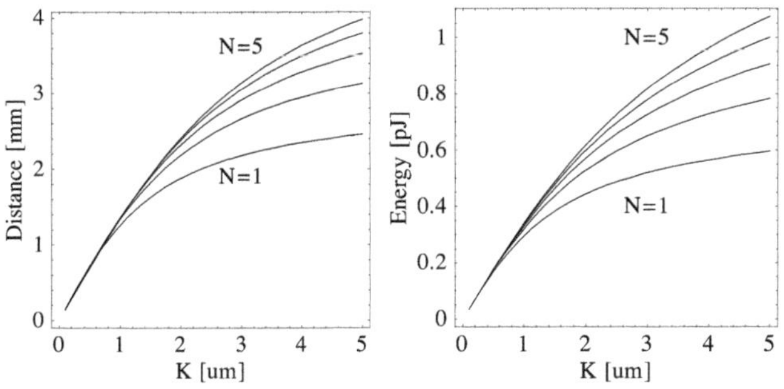

Figure 5: Channel Wire Performance

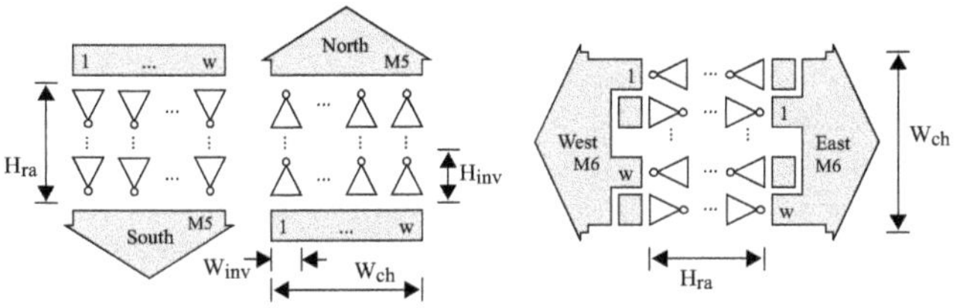

Figure 6: Channel Area Calculation

wire spacing within the channel (s_w):

$$W_{\rm ch} = w \times p_M \times s_w \tag{28}$$

We reserve area within the processor tiles for repeaters as necessary and increase the dimensions of the tiles appropriately. When allocating area for a collection of repeaters within a processor tile, we reserve a rectangular strip of uniform height across the tile. If necessary, we fold the repeater array maintain the signal wire pitch at the expense of an increase in the array's height. Folding causes the height of the reserved region to increase as signal densities increase in wider channels. Figure 6 illustrates the folding of repeaters. As illustrated in the right of Figure 6, wires from parallel channels may be interdigitated to allow a compact layout while maintaining the datapath pitch established in the routers. For an inverter cell of height $H_{\rm inv}$ and width $W_{\rm inv}$, we calculate the height of the repeater array ($H_{\rm ra}$) using the channel width from (28) as:

$$H_{\rm ra} = H_{\rm inv}\lceil wW_{\rm inv}/W_{\rm ch}\rceil \tag{29}$$

4.5.2 Channel Energy Model

The channel energy model is derived from the wire model of Section 2.2. The energy dissipated in a w-bit wide channel with M sequencing elements and N repeaters per segment is:

$$E_{\rm ch} = wM(E_{\rm sq} + NE_{\rm w}) \tag{30}$$

Here, the energy expended driving the wire ($E_{\rm w}$) is calculated from (7), and the energy dissipated in the sequencing element ($E_{\rm sq}$) is based on an analytic energy model of a hybrid-latch flip-flop we developed and verified with SPICE simulations.

4.6 Combined Router Area Model

The router area is determined by the placement of the datapath elements. For illustrative purposes, we present layouts for two router architectures used in our analysis. Figure

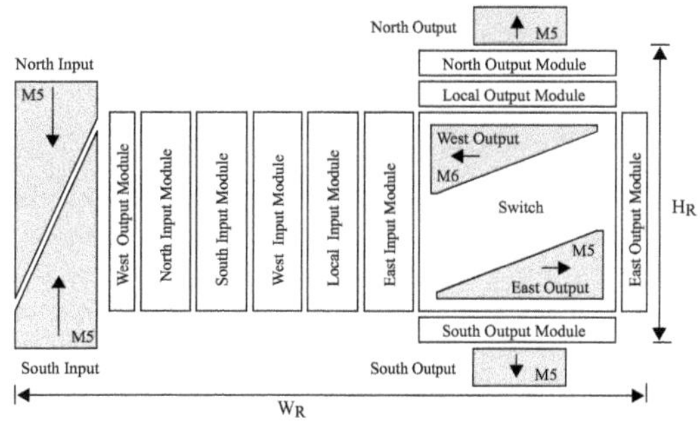

(a) 5 × 5 Router

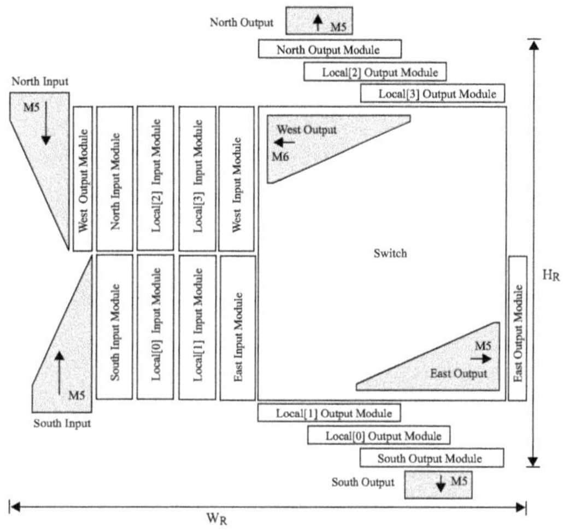

(b) 8 × 8 Router

Figure 7: Router Floorplan for Area Model

7(a) illustrates the arrangement of datapath elements in a 5-input, 5-output router suitable for a mesh or torus network. The input modules are collocated to one side of the switch to reduce the length of control signals traveling between the input modules and the arbiters. Vertical channels connecting to the North and South neighbors are implemented in M5, while horizontal channels connecting to the East and West neighbors are implemented in M6. Inputs from the North and South neighbors are brought down to the local metal layers at the left edge of the router before traveling horizontally to an input module. Inputs from the East and West neighbors are brought down from M6 over the destination input module. Outputs to the North and South neighbor leave from the top and bottom edges of the switch, respectively. Because output lines in the switch run vertically, the East and West neighbor outputs are brought up to the semi-global metal layers over the switch before traveling horizontally to the output modules. The connection from the switch to the West output module is implemented in M6; the required vias create a blockage in M5 that precludes routing vertical channels over the switch. The connection from the switch to the East output module is implemented in M5, which departs from our convention of routing only vertical signals in M5. However, there are too few tracks available in M6 to route both outputs and the East input channel over the switch in a single metal layer. The width ($W_{\rm R}$) and height ($H_{\rm R}$) of the 5 × 5 router depicted in Figure 7(a) are calculated as:

$$W_R = W_{ch} + 5H_{IM} + 2H_{OM} + W_x \quad (31)$$
$$H_R = 3H_{OM} + H_x \quad (32)$$

Figure 7(b) illustrates organization of an 8-input, 8-output router suitable for an indirect network. The increased switch height allows the input modules to be stacked vertically to reduce the width of the router while maintaining a consistent slice pitch across the router. The width (W_R) and height (H_R) of the 8×8 are calculated as:

$$W_R = W_{ch} + 4H_{IM} + 2H_{OM} + W_x \quad (33)$$
$$H_R = 6H_{OM} + H_x \quad (34)$$

5. NETWORKS

In this section we describe the networks evaluated in this analysis. The network topologies are illustrated in Figure 8. Figure 9 illustrates the placement of routers amongst the processor tiles in the lower left quadrant of the chips used to estimate chip areas. Channels connecting routers outside the quadrant are omitted for clarity.

5.1 Mesh/MeshX2

Topology: The mesh topology is depicted in Figure 8(a). The Mesh network leaves enough unused area between the tiles to implement a second network. The MeshX2 network increase wire and area utilization by introducing a second parallel network.

Routing: We use the O1TURN algorithm described in [19]. The algorithm is a randomized variant of dimension-order routing in which the order of dimension traversal, XY or YX, is chosen at random to evenly distribute the load over the XY and YX paths. Each subnetwork of the MeshX2 architecture transports a disjoint subset of the packet types. Assigning short packets to one subnetwork and long packets to the other reduces the complexity of the subnetworks because each transports packets of a single, fixed length. Alternately, assigning read request and response packets to one subnetwork and write request and response packets to the other, effectively creating a read subnetwork and a write subnetwork, allows a single network architecture to be used for both subnetworks. We shall show that partitioning the networks based on the packet lengths performs poorly when such a partitioning fails to maximize use of the available wiring resources.

Flow Control: Deadlock is avoided by introducing a deadlock free routing subfunction accessible through a distinguished subset of the virtual-channels [6]. We reserve one virtual-channel for XY dimension-order routing and one virtual-channel for YX dimension-order routing. The remaining virtual-channels are available for both XY and YX routing.

5.2 Torus

Topology: The Torus is constructed from the Mesh by adding end-around channels at the periphery. We use the folded topology depicted in Figure 8(b), which provides channels of uniform length at the expense of longer average channel lengths.

Routing: The Torus network uses dimension-order routing.

Flow Control: Intra-dimension deadlock is avoided by partitioning each ring and promoting packets into reserved sets of virtual channels when they cross the partition [5].

5.3 Concentrated Mesh (CMesh/CMeshX2)

Topology: The CMesh network reduces the Mesh described above to a radix-4 mesh in which each router services four processors. The decrease in the average hop count reduces the component of the zero-load latency due to router delay (T_r). We augment the mesh with express channels along the perimeter of the network to restore the bisection channel count lost to the reduction in the radix of the mesh. As with the Mesh networks, we can improve the wire and area utilization of the CMesh network by introducing a second parallel network. The CMeshX2 network provides two independent CMesh subnetworks.

Routing: The CMesh network uses dimension-order routing with the express links used when a packet travels more than one hop along the perimeter of the network. While we could conceivably reduce the average number of hops packets travels by preferentially routing over the express channels even when doing so violates the normal dimension order, such a routing strategy would introduce deadlock and is therefor disallowed.

Flow Control: The routing algorithm is deadlock free and therefor introduces no additional constraints on the flow control policy.

5.4 Fat-Tree (FTree)

Topology: The FTree topology is based on that described in [12]. As illustrated in Figure 8(d), we use a 4-ary fat-tree with a height of 3, which corresponds to an instance of the SPIN network described in [1]. Like the tapered fat-tree described below, the FTree is also an instance of a folded Clos network.

Routing: The FTree topology uses nearest-common ancestor routing. Packets are adaptively routed up to the common ancestor and deterministically down to the destination.

Flow Control: The fat-tree does not introduce addition restrictions on the allocation of virtual-channels beyond those required to prevent protocol deadlock.

5.5 Tapered Fat-Tree (TTree)

Topology: The TTree, illustrated in Figure 8(e), is an instance of a generalized fat-tree topology [16] in which the bandwidth decreases towards the root. The topology is equivalent to a tapered 5-stage folded Clos with reduced bandwidth in the interior of the network and interior nodes replicated to increase path diversity.

Routing: The routing algorithm is similar to that used for the FTree. Should a packet reach a root node while routing up the tree, the algorithm randomly forwards the packet to one of the two viable descendents.

Flow Control: The routing algorithm for the TTree network does not introduce any additional constraints on the allocation of virtual channels beyond those required to avoid protocol deadlock.

5.6 Network Comparison

Table 3 compares the network configurations that provided the best area and energy efficiencies. We identified these configurations by evaluating the impact of the following design parameters on the performance and efficiency: the number of virtual-channels assigned to each packet type and the allocation policy; the sharing of virtual-channels across

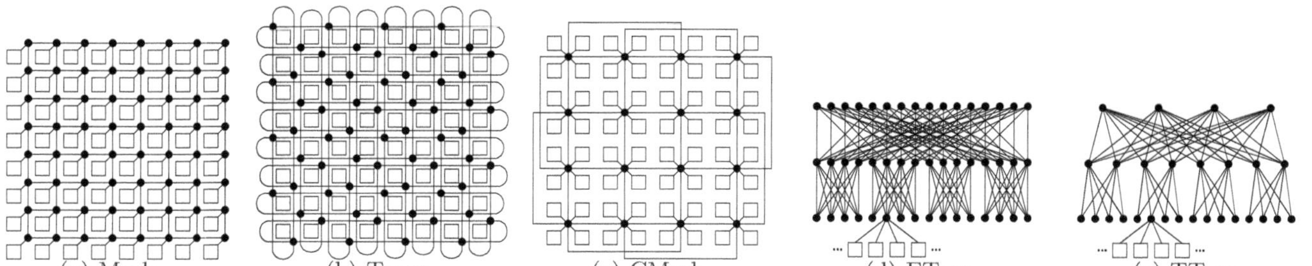

(a) Mesh (b) Torus (c) CMesh (d) FTree (e) TTree

Figure 8: Network Topologies

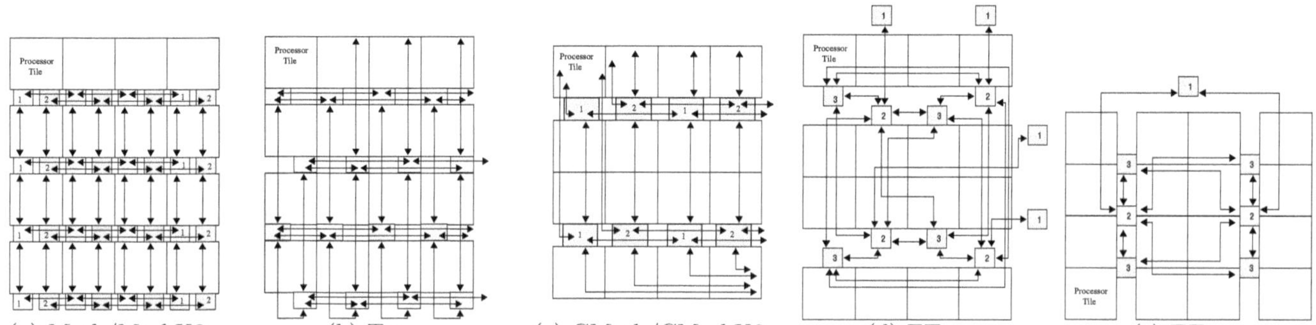

(a) Mesh/MeshX2 (b) Torus (c) CMesh/CMeshX2 (d) FTree (e) TTree

Figure 9: Floorplan for Estimating Area (Lower Left Quadrant of Die Shown)

packet types; the flit buffer depth provided for each packet type; the channel router datapath width; the assignment of packet types to subnetworks; the routing function; and the channel repeater sizing and spacing policy. The large switch used in the CMesh configurations introduces an additional router stage for switch preparation, which increases the router latency to 3 cycles. Table 4 lists the number of virtual-channels allocated for each packet type and the flit buffer depth per virtual-channel.

Table 3: Preferred Network Configurations

	H	t_r	B_C	w	B_B	T_c	T_s	T_0
Mesh	$6\frac{1}{4}$	2	16	192	3,072	5.3	3	17.8
MeshX2	$6\frac{1}{4}$	2	32	192	6,144	5.3	3	17.8
Torus	5	2	32	288	9,216	4.0	2	14.0
CMesh	$3\frac{1}{8}$	3	16	288	4,608	2.1	2	11.5
CMeshX2	$3\frac{1}{8}$	3	32	288	9,216	2.1	2	11.5
FTree	$4\frac{3}{8}$	2	64	144	9,216	4.4	4	13.1
TTree	$4\frac{3}{8}$	2	32	144	4,608	3.5	4	12.2

6. EVALUATION METHODOLOGY

We evaluate the networks based on their area and energy efficiency using a cycle-accurate interconnection network simulator that incorporates our area and energy models. Area efficiency is measured as the product of the workload completion time and the chip area; energy efficiency is measured as the product of the completion time and energy expended in the network. For each network, we evaluate the impact of varying the datapath width, number and partitioning of virtual-channels, flit-buffer depths, and placement of routers amongst the tiles to determine the configuration providing the most competitive area and energy efficiency. To accurately estimate energy dissipation in different configurations, our simulator automatically sizes repeaters based on the calculated channel lengths, accounts for the impact of the flit-buffer sizing on the memory circuitry, and adjusts driver sizes within the router datapath to match capacitive loads calculated using our energy models. The area model parameters used in the evaluation are presented in Table 5.

Table 4: Virtual-Channel Configurations

	Short Packet		Long Packet	
	Number	Depth	Number	Depth
Mesh(X2)	8	1	6	3
Torus	8	1	6	2
CMesh(X2)	8	1	8	2
FTree	8	1	4	4
TTree	8	1	4	4

We simulate a workload in which every processor performs a fixed number of transactions and measure the time required for all transactions to complete. We follow the convention of ensuring the number of messages exchanged during the simulation is large enough that those packets injected into the empty network at startup, which experience little queuing delay and therefore lower latency, do not unduly influence the reported results. Each processor issues at least 1,000 packets, which was determined to be sufficient to ensure that load-induced queuing delay develops.

Table 5: Area Model Parameter Values

Parameter	Value (M1 Tracks)
SRAM Cell Height (H_{cell})	8
SRAM Cell Width (W_{cell})	6
Latch Height	10
Latch Width	10
Read Sense Height (H_{rs})	40
Bitline Driver Height (H_{bd})	20
Inverter Height (H_{inv})	$10 + 3K/5$
Crossbar Wire Spacing (s_x)	2
Channel Wire Spacing (s_w)	2

The mixture of common synthetic traffic patterns included in the workload (bitreverse, nearest neighbor, tornado, and uniform random) was chosen to avoid biasing the workload in favor of one topology or routing algorithm. The taper pattern corresponds to an augmented uniform random pattern in which the probability of nodes communicating decreases with the distance between them. Rather than report throughput-latency curves, we simulate a closed-loop system in which each sender and receiver may have a limited number of messages in-flight, which is more reflective of a CMP. Aggregate workload completion times are reported because they better reflect the network's overall performance than the completion time of any single traffic pattern or trace.

7. RESULTS AND ANALYSIS

This section presents the results of our analysis. We contrast the performance of the networks described above to provide insight into the merits of the different architectures. Figure 10 compares the performance and efficiency of the preferred configuration of each network identified in Table 3. Figure 10(a) presents the relative workload completion times. Figure 10(b) separates chip area estimates into major components. Figure 10(c) contrasts the average power dissipation in the networks during the simulated workload. Normalized area-delay and energy-delay metrics are presented Figure 10(d). We discuss the preferred topology, network costs, benefits of a second network, and load balancing issues in the following subsections.

7.1 Preferred Topology

As Figure 10(a) illustrates, the CMeshX2 network provides the best aggregate completion time. Additionally, the CMeshX2 network provides the best completion time for uniform and tapered traffic patterns, which one might consider more representative of typical application behavior. Figure 11, which illustrates the distribution of packet latencies for the uniform pattern component of the workload, shows that the CMeshX2 network reduces the latency variability in addition to providing a lower average latency. While the distributions exhibit lengthy tails, indicating occasional long packet latencies, the networks are heavily loaded during the workload and operate near capacity.

Figure 10(d), which compares network efficiency, clearly shows that the CMeshX2 network is substantially more efficient. Concentration reduces the average hop count and improves load balance across the channels without increasing wiring complexity. While the tree networks also offer low hop counts, their wiring complexity limits the datapath

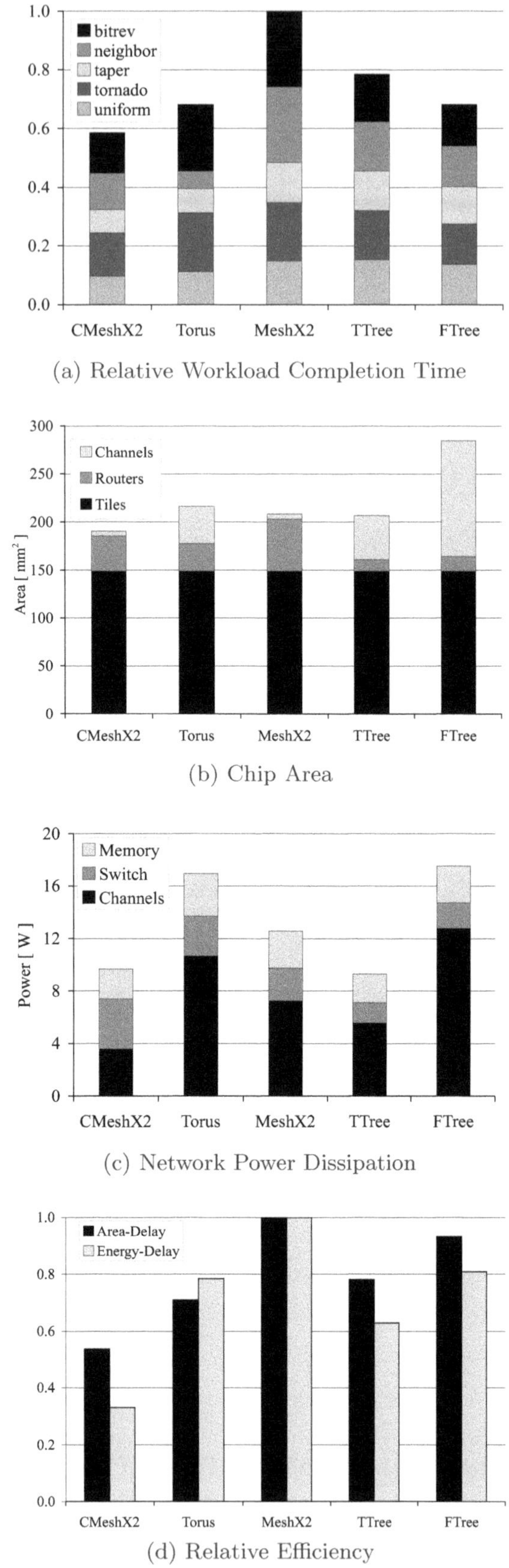

Figure 10: Performance Comparison

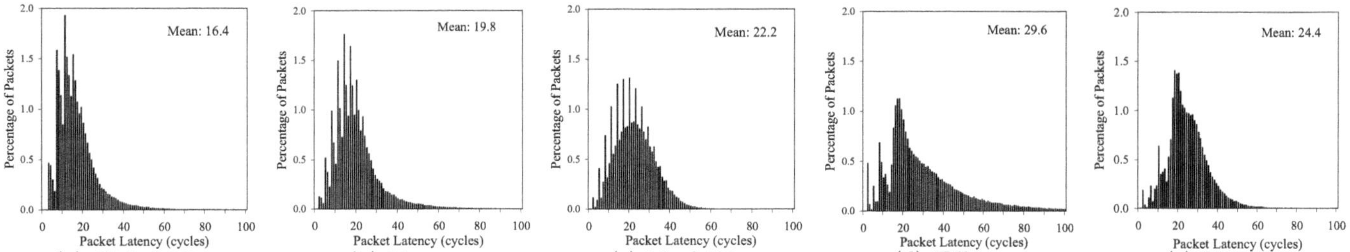

(a) CMeshX2 (b) Torus (c) MeshX2 (d) TTree (e) FTree

Figure 11: Workload Packet Latency Distribution for Uniform Random Traffic Pattern

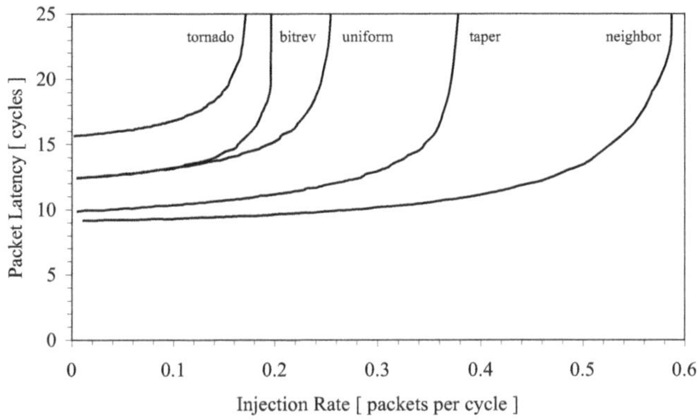

Figure 12: Offered Latency for CMeshX2 Network

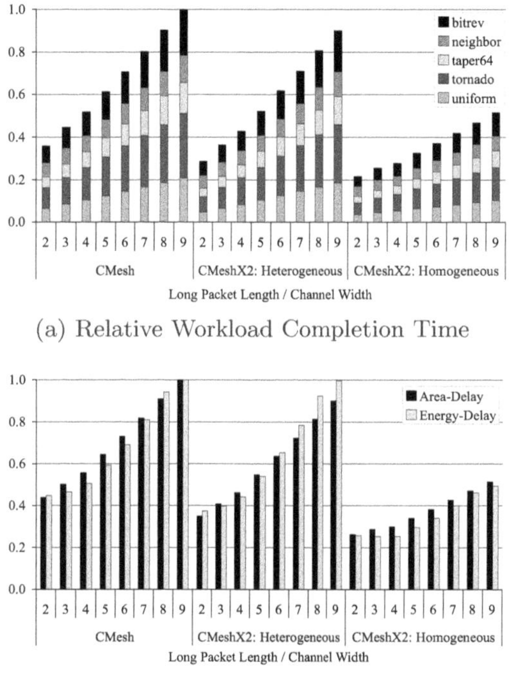

(a) Relative Workload Completion Time

(b) Relative Efficiency

Figure 13: CMesh Performance

width and results in long channels with significant traversal costs. The power dissipated in the channels relative to the bisection bandwidth is substantially greater in the tree networks as a consequence of the wiring complexity and ensuing area increase. The Torus network similarly suffers from excess energy dissipation in the channels. The Torus offers a compact layout but its average channel length is long, spanning two tiles and the bypassed router in between. The repeaters used to drive these long channels consume more energy per length of wire driven than those used in the CMeshX2 network, resulting in worse energy efficiency. The mesh networks, which are commonly proposed architectures for on-chip networks, perform poorly and offer the worst energy and area efficiency of all networks evaluated in this study.

Figure 12 plots measured latencies against packet injection rate for the CMeshX2 network for different traffic patterns. Measurements were taken using a uniform distribution of packet types. The curves effectively illustrate the network's ability to exploit locality in traffic flows to reduce latency.

7.2 Network Costs

Figure 10(b) illustrates the contributions of the processor tiles and network to the total die area. The channel component includes area allocated for routing channels over what might otherwise be unused die area. While the unused lower metal layers and diffusion area could be partially reclaimed for other purposes, the regions tend to be irregularly shaped with frequent interruption by repeater arrays and are consequently unsuitable for larger structures such as memories. Figure 10(b) shows that the direct topologies and sparse indirect topology incur similar area costs. However, the direct topologies afford wider datapaths by routing more channels above processor tiles rather, which avoids dedicating additional area to routing channels around the die. The regular planar structure of the direct networks renders them particularly amenable to compact layout and well suited to the inherent structure of a tiled CMP. The area consumed by the CMesh network is modest, contributing at most 23.6% of the total die area with two parallel 288-bit datapaths to as little as 8.4% with two parallel 64-bit datapath.

Figure 10(c) compares the power consumed by the networks, showing the contributions from the different datapath components. The power consumed in the networks is modest and would represent an acceptable component of the total power dissipated by the chip. While the TTree network dissipate slightly less power than the CMeshX2 network, the later is simply more active and Figure 10(d) clearly illustrates that the CMeshX2 network is more energy efficient.

This efficiency results from the lower hop count, which reduces the energy expended routing packets, and more compact layout, which reduces channel lengths and the energy dissipated driving wire capacitance in the channels.

7.3 Benefits of a Second Network

Introducing a second parallel network improves utilization of the abundant wire resources. While increasing the datapath width would also improve wire utilization, the larger crossbars required in wider datapaths consume more die area and dissipate more energy when forwarding packets. To quantify the benefits of a second network, we compare a single concentrated mesh network to duplicated configurations. We consider two strategies for distributing traffic over the subnetworks: the heterogeneous architecture, and the homogeneous architecture. The heterogeneous architecture uses one subnetwork to transport short packets (read requests, write replies) and the other to transport long packets (read replies, write requests). The homogeneous architecture uses one subnetwork to transport packets associated with read transactions (requests and replies) and one to transport packets associated with write transactions.

Figure 13 compares the performance of a single concentrated mesh network to the replicated architectures. We vary the datapath width to illustrate its effect on the network's performance. The widths in Figure 13 yield serialization latencies for long packets of 2 to 9 cycles. The datapath width of the short packet network in the heterogeneous architecture remains constant at 64-bits.

The addition of a second network significantly improves both performance and efficiency. The second network has negligible impact on the chip area because the additional routers reside in areas initially allocated for channels in the first network. While the presence of additional routers and channels increases power dissipation in the network, the greatly improved performance more than compensates, resulting in significant improvements in energy-efficiency.

While the performance of the two architectures is similar with wide datapaths, the homogeneous architecture consistently performs better. As Figure 13 illustrates, the performance advantage increases with narrower datapaths. For a wide datapath, the difference in performance results from the greater aggregate bandwidth provided by the homogeneous architecture. However, the homogeneous architecture performs significantly better even when both subnetworks provide identical 64-bit datapaths and equivalent aggregate bandwidth. The improvement arises from differences in how the two strategies distribute traffic over the subnetworks. The heterogeneous strategy routes all long packets through one subnetwork. Because the communication protocol generates short and long packets in equal numbers, the load on the long packet subnetwork is significantly greater and the short packet subnetwork is poorly utilized. Thus, the performance difference arises from the failure of the heterogeneous architecture to balance the load equitably across the subnetworks.

7.4 Contribution from Express Channels

To quantify the performance contributed by the express channels, we present the performance of the CMesh network when the express channels are removed. Table 6 compares the area and energy efficiency measured for the ensemble workload when the express channels are removed. With dimension-order routing (DOR), the workload completion time is reduced by 23.1%. Without express channels the area efficiency degrades by 23% and the energy efficiency degrades by 38%. Because the express channels are routed over processor tiles in otherwise unused metal tracks and use preexisting router ports, the area overhead is negligible. Energy efficiency improves both because the completion time decreases and because it is more efficient to route packets over express channels than through intermediate routers.

Table 6: Contribution of Express Channels

Express	Routing	Area-Delay	Energy-Delay
Present	O1TURN	0.800	0.713
	DOR	0.801	0.721
Absent	O1TURN	0.993	0.995
	DOR	1.000	1.000

Table 7: Permutation Completion Time

Network	Max	Min	Mean	Std.Dev
CMeshX2	0.649	0.600	0.689	0.007
Torus	0.903	0.876	0.890	0.004
MeshX2	1.000	0.928	0.991	0.002
FTree	0.662	0.641	0.649	0.003
TTree	0.949	0.890	0.924	0.009

7.5 Load Balancing

Non-deterministic routing can improve load balance. The CMeshX2 network performs equally well with deterministic and oblivious routing, illustrated by the similar performance of DOR and O1TURN (Table 6). The comparable performance is noteworthy because the workload heavily loads the networks and oblivious routing generally provides better throughput under heavy load. Because deterministic routing preserves message ordering between a source and destination, which reduces the complexity of cache coherence and similar protocols, we prefer DOR on the CMesh networks.

Table 7 presents the mean workload completion times for 5,000 random traffic permutations. While the FTree network provides a slight performance improvement over the CMeshX2 network, the advantage does not compensate for the increased overhead. The poor performance of the Torus network on the random permutations in comparison to its performance on synthetic patterns results from the Torus being better able to exploit locality in the neighbor and taper patterns (similar results were obtained using adaptive routing strategies on the Torus network).

8. CONCLUSION

In this work we present detailed analytical area and energy models for on-chip networks and explore tradeoffs in the design of high performance interconnects for CMPs. Our analysis shows that architectures commonly assumed in on-chip networks studies are unlikely to perform well in CMP systems as processor counts increase. Even with low-latency router architectures assumed, a two dimensional mesh scales poorly in an on-chip environment.

We address the issue of channel width selection and demonstrate that increasing the channel width in on-chip networks significantly improves both performance and area and energy efficiency. The serialization latency may contribute a significant component of the overall latency in an on-chip network, particularly when traffic is well localized or the network is lightly loaded. Wide channels exploit the availability of wires on-chip to provide significant improvements in the performance for packet sizes typical for CMP systems. The additional wiring complexity introduced by wide channels increases the importance of selecting a topology whose structure is well suited to the wiring constraints imposed on-chip. The indirect topologies evaluated in this work do not provide compact, area efficient layouts with wide channels, which adversely constrains the maximum channel width.

We demonstrate that replicating networks in an on-chip environment can improve performance while simultaneously improving area and energy efficiency. Topologies such as the Mesh and CMesh may accommodate a second network without increasing the die area, though the network will occupy more of the chip area. The placement of the routers and channels must be considered before estimating the area overhead of introducing a second network. Our results comparing different strategies for distributing traffic over the subnetworks illustrate the importance of equitably distributing load across the subnetworks.

Drawing on the above insights, we present the concentrated mesh architecture with replicated subnetworks and express channels. Concentration reduces hop counts and improves load balance without increasing wiring complexity. The regular structure efficiently exploits the abundant wiring resources available on chip by providing wide channels. Channel lengths are kept short to reduce energy dissipation. Express channels further improve energy efficiency by directing packets around routers while simultaneously improving performance by reducing hop counts between distant processors. Thoughtful planning allows us to introduce a second network without increasing die area. The result is a network that performs well while controlling area overhead and introducing a modest energy overhead.

Acknowledgments

We wish to acknowledge the contributions of Rebecca Schultz and thank the reviewers for insightful comments.

9. REFERENCES

[1] A. Adriahantenaina, H. Charlery, A. Greiner, L. Mortiez, and C. A. Zeferino. Spin: A scalable, packet switched, on-chip micro-network. In *DATE '03: Proceedings of the conference on Design, Automation and Test in Europe*, page 20070, Washington, DC, USA, 2003. IEEE Computer Society.

[2] P. Bai *et al.* A 65nm logic technology featuring 35nm gate lengths, enhanced channel strain, 8 cu interconnect layers, low-k ild and 0.57 μm^2 sram cell. In *Electronic Devices Meeting, 2004. IEDM Technical Digest*, pages 657–660. IEEE International, Dec 2004.

[3] A. Chatterjee *et al.* A 65 nm cmos technology for mobile and digital signal processing applications. In *Electronic Devices Meeting, 2004. IEDM Technical Digest*, pages 665–668. IEEE International, Dec 2004.

[4] W. J. Dally and B. Towles. Route packets, not wires: on-chip inteconnectoin networks. In *DAC '01: Proceedings of the 38th conference on Design automation*, pages 684–689, New York, NY, USA, 2001. ACM Press.

[5] W. J. Dally and B. Towles. *Principles and Practices of Interconnection Networks*. Morgan Kaufmann Publishers, 2004.

[6] J. Duato. A new theory of deadlock-free adaptive routing in wormhole networks. *IEEE Trans. Parallel Distrib. Syst.*, 4(12):1320–1331, 1993.

[7] N. Eisley and L.-S. Peh. High-level power analysis for on-chip networks. In *CASES '04: Proceedings of the 2004 international conference on Compilers, architecture, and synthesis for embedded systems*, pages 104–115, New York, NY, USA, 2004. ACM Press.

[8] R. Ho, K. Mai, and M. Horowitz. The future of wires. In *Proceedings of the IEEE*, volume 89, pages 490–504. IEEE, April 2001.

[9] R. Ho, K. Mai, and M. Horowitz. Managing wire scaling: a circuit perspective. In *Proceedings of the IEEE 2003 International Interconnect Technology Conference*, pages 177–179, June 2003.

[10] International technology roadmap for semiconductors. 2005 edition.

[11] J. Kim, D. Park, T. Theocharides, N. Vijaykrishnan, and C. R. Das. A low latency router supporting adaptivity for on-chip interconnects. In *DAC '05: Proceedings of the 42nd annual conference on Design automation*, pages 559–564, New York, NY, USA, 2005. ACM Press.

[12] C. E. Leiserson. Fat-trees: universal networks for hardware-efficient supercomputing. *IEEE Trans. Comput.*, 34(10):892–901, 1985.

[13] Z. Luo *et al.* High performance and low power transistors integrated in 65nm bulk cmos technology. In *Electronic Devices Meeting, 2004. IEDM Technical Digest*, pages 661–664. IEEE International, Dec 2004.

[14] M. L. Mui, K. Banerjee, and A. Mehrotra. A global interconnect optimization scheme for nanometer scale vlsi with implications for latency, bandwidth, and power dissipation. In *IEEE Transactions on Electron Devices*, volume 51, pages 195–202. IEEE, February 2004.

[15] R. Mullins, A. West, and S. Moore. Low-latency virtual-channel routers for on-chip networks. In *ISCA '04: Proceedings of the 31st annual international symposium on Computer architecture*, page 188, Washington, DC, USA, 2004. IEEE Computer Society.

[16] S. R. Öhring, M. Ibel, S. K. Das, and M. J. Kumar. On generalized fat trees. In *IPPS '95: Proceedings of the 9th International Symposium on Parallel Processing*, page 37, Washington, DC, USA, 1995. IEEE Computer Society.

[17] K. Olukotun, B. A. Nayfeh, L. Hammond, K. Wilson, and K. Chang. The case for a single-chip multiprocessor. *SIGOPS Oper. Syst. Rev.*, 30(5):2–11, 1996.

[18] L.-S. Peh and W. J. Dally. A delay model and speculative architecture for pipelined routers. In *HPCA '01: Proceedings of the 7th International Symposium on High-Performance Computer Architecture*, page 255, Washington, DC, USA, 2001. IEEE Computer Society.

[19] D. Seo, A. Ali, W.-T. Lim, N. Rafique, and M. Thottethodi. Near-optimal worst-case throughput routing for two-dimensional mesh networks. *SIGARCH Comput. Archit. News*, 33(2):432–443, 2005.

[20] M. B. Taylor, J. Kim, J. Miller, D. Wentzlaff, F. Ghodrat, B. Greenwald, H. Hoffman, P. Johnson, J.-W. Lee, W. Lee, A. Ma, A. Saraf, M. Seneski, N. Shnidman, V. Strumpen, M. Frank, S. Amarasinghe, and A. Agarwal. The raw microprocessor: A computational fabric for software circuits and general-purpose programs. *IEEE Micro*, 22(2):25–35, 2002.

[21] H. Wang, L.-S. Peh, and S. Malik. Power-driven design of router microarchitectures in on-chip networks. In *MICRO 36: Proceedings of the 36th annual IEEE/ACM International Symposium on Microarchitecture*, page 105, Washington, DC, USA, 2003. IEEE Computer Society.

[22] W. Zhao and Y. Cao. New generation of predictive technology model for sub-45nm design exploration. *ISQED*, 0:585–590, 2006.

Cooperative Cache Partitioning for Chip Multiprocessors

Jichuan Chang and Gurindar S. Sohi
Computer Sciences Department
University of Wisconsin-Madison

ABSTRACT

This paper presents **Cooperative Cache Partitioning** (CCP) to allocate cache resources among threads concurrently running on CMPs. Unlike cache partitioning schemes that use a single spatial partition repeatedly throughout a stable program phase, CCP resolves cache contention with multiple time-sharing partitions. Time-sharing cache resources among partitions allows each thrashing thread to speed up dramatically in at least one partition by unfairly shrinking other threads' capacity allocations, while improving fairness by giving different partitions equal chance to execute. Quality-of-Service (QoS) is guaranteed over the long term by orchestrating the shrink and expansion of each thread's capacity across partitions to bound the average slowdown. Time-sharing based cache partitioning is further integrated with CMP cooperative caching [6] to exploit the benefits of LRU-based latency optimizations, which leads to a simplified partitioning algorithm and better performance for workloads that do not benefit from cache partitioning.

We evaluate the effectiveness of CCP by simulating a 4-core CMP running all combinations of 7 representative SPEC2000 benchmarks. For workloads that can benefit from cache partitioning, CCP achieves up to 60%, and on average 12%, better performance than the exhaustive search of optimal static partitions. Overall, CCP provides the best results on almost all evaluation metrics for different cache sizes.

Categories and Subject Descriptors: B.3.2 [Memory Structures]: Design Styles – Cache memory, C.4 [Performance of Systems] – Design studies

General Terms: Algorithm, Design, Management, Performance

Keywords: Multiple time-sharing partitions, cooperative cache partitioning, CMP, fairness, QoS

1. INTRODUCTION

With an increasing number of processor cores being integrated onto a single chip, chip multiprocessors (CMPs) require efficient organization and management of the on-chip cache resources to provide fast data accesses for concurrently running threads. To efficiently use the aggregate cache capacity, most CMP proposals share cache resources between threads via either a logically shared cache [14, 1, 39, 43] or private caches augmented with capacity sharing policies [35, 8, 6, 2]. However, under high capacity pressure, conventional LRU-based sharing policies cause destructive interference between threads, leading to thrashing [9], unfairness [20] and lack of Quality-of-Service (QoS) [18] (e.g., no guarantee in providing certain baseline performance). Interference isolation for fairness and QoS is important for CMPs as they are used in consolidated servers, shared computing clusters, embedded systems, and other platforms, where meeting these requirements is as important as improving overall throughput. Without hardware solutions, their remedy can complicate the task of operating systems and server administration. In contrast to unconstrained sharing, a private cache design avoids inter-thread interference via design-time partition of the aggregate capacity between processor cores. This design is simple, fair and guarantees QoS, but often incurs many more expensive off-chip misses for thread mixes with non-uniform caching requirements.

To match the perceived requirements of different threads, CMP cache partitioning schemes orchestrate cache allocation with more flexible, usually heterogeneous partitions [38, 20, 42, 18, 21, 17, 27, 29, 11, 10]. Despite their differences in metrics, mechanisms, and policies, prior partitioning schemes have two common characteristics: (1) they use a single spatial partition repeatedly throughout a stable program phase; and (2) compared with LRU-based capacity sharing, they control the partitioning overhead via coarse-grained cache management: allocating large capacity units for long epochs (e.g., 64KB chunks for 5M-cycle epochs [29]). Consequently, prior proposals share two limitations. (1) **Limited functionality.** None of the previous proposals addresses all CMP caching requirements, including thrashing avoidance, fairness improvement, QoS guarantee and priority support, partially due to the difficulty of satisfying multiple, often conflicting, goals in a single cache partition. (2) **Limited scope of application.** Cache partitioning can only outperform LRU-based latency-reducing schemes for some multiprogrammed workloads. An attempt to solely use cache partitioning can cause sub-optimal performance for workloads that do not experience destructive inter-thread interference.

Our proposed solution, **Cooperative Cache Partitioning** (CCP), has two aspects to address the two limitations, respectively. First, CCP introduces Multiple Time-sharing Partitions (MTP) to improve throughput and fairness while maintaining QoS. Specifically, each MTP partition improves at least one thrashing thread's throughput by temporarily shrinking the capacity of other threads. By time-sharing cache resources among multiple unfair partitions that favor different threads, the problems of fairness improvement and priority support are translated into well-studied time-sharing resource management problems. Fairness can thus be improved by giving different threads equal opportunity to speed up, while priority can be supported by allocating different percentages of time slices to different partitions. The MTP partitioning algorithm further guarantees QoS over the long term by using partitions that, on average, can bound each thread's slowdown against the equal partitioning baseline. Comparing with the best single spatial partition based scheme without QoS constraints, MTP achieves up to 60%, and on average 12%, better performance for workloads that can benefit from cache partitioning.

Depending on whether destructive inter-thread interference ex-

ICS'07, June 18-20, 2007, Seattle, WA USA.

ists or not, a workload can either prefer cache partitioning or LRU-based sharing. In order to combine their strengths, the second aspect of CCP is to integrate MTP with CMP Cooperative Caching (CC) [6], an LRU-based caching optimization. The complementary advantages of MTP and CC are combined by dividing the total execution epochs into those controlled by either MTP or CC, according to the fraction of threads that can benefit from each of them. The integrated scheme is shown to achieve robust performance for both workloads with and without destructive inter-thread interference. Furthermore, having CC as the default policy can simplify the MTP partitioning algorithm by focusing only on threads with large speedup potentials, leading to a heuristic-based algorithm that can be practically implemented.

The rest of the paper is organized as follows. Section 2 defines the metrics for CMP cache partitioning, overviews cache partitioning proposals, and classifies benchmarks based on their speedup characteristics. We detail in Sections 3 and 4 the two aspects of our approach: MTP and its integration with CC. Our evaluation methodology and results are presented in Section 5. Related work is discussed in Section 6 and we conclude in Section 7.

2. BACKGROUND AND DEFINITIONS

To simplify later discussion, this section provides background information on CMP cache partitioning and workload characteristics, as well as defines metrics to evaluate different caching policies.

2.1 CMP Multiprogramming Metrics

To compare the effectiveness of CMP caching schemes for multiprogramming, we first need to find proper metrics to summarize the overall performance, fairness and QoS results for a thread schedule. A multiprogrammed workload's throughput can be simply measured as the sum of per-thread throughput (i.e., IPC for our workloads), but quantifying QoS and fairness can be hard, and requires an understanding of these notions in the context of CMP caching.

Our notions of performance, fairness and QoS are based on two principles: (1) proportional-share resource allocation and (2) Pareto efficiency. The first principle states that QoS and fairness is achieved when the shared resource is divided among sharers in proportion to their priorities or weights [41, 4, 40, 34][1]. Using proportional-share allocation to maintain the baseline fairness, the second principle further improve performance (efficiency) by allowing disproportional sharing if it helps some sharers without hurting the others. These principles have been used to define min-max fairness [3], which has wide applications in computer networks and scheduling policies (e.g., Generalized Processor Sharing [26]).

2.1.1 QoS Metric

QoS is the ability to provide a thread with guaranteed baseline performance (corresponding to a specific resource partition) regardless of the load placed on the shared resource from other co-scheduled threads [40]. We use **equal-share cache allocation** to define the performance bottom line for QoS, which corresponds to the special case of proportional-sharing when all threads have the same priority. Notice that equal-priority has been implicitly assumed by previous fair caching proposals [20, 42, 16], while our MTP scheme can also support threads with different priority levels (refer to Section 3.3). This baseline can be implemented either by uniform-sized private caches or an equal partitioning of shared cache capacity between on-chip cores, and it guarantees QoS because all threads get the same capacity and thus can achieve the same performance across different schedules. The equal-share allocation baseline also provides intuitive QoS results to multiprocessor users because it corresponds to traditional multiprocessors with private caches. For similar reasons, Yeh and Reinman [42] use this baseline implemented by private caches. Here we use the even partitioning of a shared cache as our baseline because most existing cache partitioning schemes assume a shared cache.

The QoS metric is thus defined as the sum of per-thread slowdowns (as negative percentages) over this baseline. Same as [42, 25], we claim a caching scheme can guarantee QoS if this measurement is bounded within a user-defined threshold (e.g., -5%). Other ways of measuring QoS exist (e.g., reporting the maximum slowdown or the number of threads that violate QoS), but we use the total slowdown because it captures the behavior of the entire workload and thus is a more stringent criteria.

$$QoS(scheme) = \sum_{i=1}^{\#app} min(0, \frac{IPC_i(scheme)}{IPC_i(base)} - 1)$$

2.1.2 Fair Speedup Metric

According to the principle of Pareto efficiency, CMP caching schemes should further improve performance while maintaining fairness, if uneven resource allocation can speed up some threads over the equal-share allocation baseline without hurting others. Now we consider how to measure the scale of performance improvement for co-scheduled threads.

Summarizing the overall performance of multiple benchmarks (co-scheduled threads in our context) has been an extensively discussed topic [32, 19]. We adopt prior wisdom and define the **Fair Speedup (FS)** metric to quantify the overall performance of co-scheduled threads. FS is calculated as the harmonic mean of per-thread speedups over the equal-share allocation baseline.

$$FS(scheme) = \#app / \sum_{i=1}^{\#app} \frac{IPC_i(base)}{IPC_i(scheme)}$$

Using harmonic mean of speedups, FS measures the execution time reduction against a baseline cache configuration that resembles traditional multiprocessors (so higher FS is better). FS is also a fair metric because using the harmonic mean (instead of the sum as used by [42]) rewards uniform speedups and penalizes slowdowns[2], which corresponds to the principle of Pareto efficiency.

The notion of fair speedup is similar to the fair slowdown metrics proposed by Kim et al. [20], which is measured against a single-thread execution baseline where one thread has exclusive use of all cache resources. Such a baseline is borrowed from SMT processors [33], where it corresponds to the single-thread execution mode that allocates all execution and cache resources to one thread. However, single-thread execution in a CMP will waste the majority of execution resources. Instead, we choose to use the equal-share allocation baseline because it has better resource utilization by supporting multiple concurrently running threads and performs similarly as in traditional multiprocessors. For the same reason, two other SMT performance metrics using a single-thread execution baseline—weighted speedup [33] (or WS, which is the sum of speedups) and harmonic mean of speedups [22]—are not used.

2.1.3 Metrics Comparison

The choice of evaluation metrics has a significant impact on CMP caching policies. Below we use two examples to demonstrate the differences between caching schemes that optimize for different metrics.

[1]Contention in other shared resources, especially the memory system, can also cause destructive interference. Here we focus on the impact of destructive interference occurring in the last-level CMP caches, assuming a fair memory system as proposed in [25].

[2]According to the power-mean inequality, the harmonic mean of a vector is maximized when all elements have the same value.

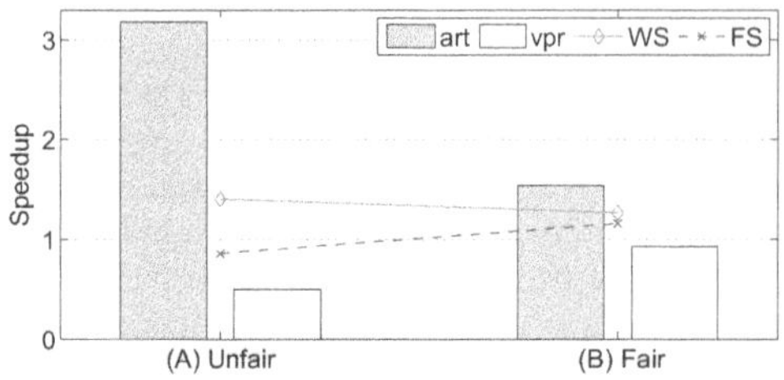

Figure 1: FS vs. WS for Two Example Schemes

Figure 1 shows the per-thread speedups of benchmarks `art` and `vpr` using two partitioning schemes (2 threads sharing a 2MB L2 cache). Scheme (A) maximizes weighted speedup (WS) by tripling the performance of `art`, however, its fair speedup (FS) measurement is worse than the baseline (FS = 1) due to unfair per-thread speedups. On the other hand, the fair scheme (B) optimizes FS at the cost of a lowered WS result because the low-speedup thread is given a more fair cache allocation. This example shows that (1) FS optimization has the side effect of avoiding unfair caching, (2) a scheme that optimizes FS may hurt the WS or IPC results, and vice versa, due to different optimization tradeoffs.

Metrics	Scheme A	<=>	Scheme B
Speedups	0.76/0.76/3.18/3.18		1.97/1.97/1.97/1.97
IPC	*0.52*	=	*0.52*
WS	*2.42*	=	*2.42*
QoS	**-52%**	<	**0%**
FS	**1.28**	<	**2.00**

Table 1: Performance Comparison Using Different Metrics

Table 1 compares the performance of two partitioning schemes for workload `art-art-art-art` (a co-schedule of 4 copies of `art`). Scheme A optimizes WS and throughput without considering its implications on fairness and QoS, while Scheme B aims to simultaneously optimize FS and maintain QoS. If only comparing throughput and WS results, the two schemes have the same performance (shown as *italic* in Table 1). However, our QoS and FS metrics (marked as **bold** in Table 1) reveal that Scheme A cannot guarantee QoS while Scheme B can, and Scheme B achieves better fairness and execution time than A. This example shows that our QoS and FS metrics are able to distinguish whether a scheme can maintain QoS and fairness, but the WS and IPC metrics cannot.

To summarize, using QoS and FS metrics together, we can measure a caching scheme's effectiveness in improving performance, fairness and QoS. We will report results using the FS and QoS metrics in this paper, but also provide WS and IPC results in the evaluation section for comparison.

2.2 Cache Partitioning Background

CMP cache partitioning schemes generally work in repetitive cycles, each consisting of three steps: (1) measurement, (2) partitioning, and (3) enforcement. The first step is to measure and estimate each thread's performance (in terms of miss rate or IPC) for candidate cache partitions. Then this information is used to determine the next cache partition to reach a given optimization goal. The new partition will be enforced in the next execution epoch, while new measurement will be gathered and used in the subsequent cycles. Measurement information can be gathered via profiling [20, 16], LRU stack hit position counting [42], monitoring [37], or dynamic set sampling [29]. This step can incur space or execution time overhead, while inaccurate information can lead to sub-optimal partitioning decisions.

Most prior proposals use coarse-grained **way partitioning** [7, 38] as the basic mechanism to enforce a cache partition (with the exceptions of STATSHARE [27] and cache-level-quota enforcement [31]). Assuming a set-associative cache, way partitioning allocates cache resources in units of cache ways (each way having the same number of cache sets). This mechanism can be implemented with a modified cache replacement policy to ensure that the number of blocks used by a thread at a cache set level does not exceed its way quota.

Cache partitioning proposals differ mainly in their optimization goals and partitioning policies, which are compared in Table 2. To avoid exhaustive search, cache partitioning algorithms use heuristics to prioritize capacity allocation according to the miss rate and speedup characteristics of co-scheduled threads. Unlike prior partitioning algorithms that select the best single spatial partition (SSP) for a given epoch, the proposed MTP scheme selects multiple partitions and allows them to be enforced in a time-sharing manner, possibly across multiple epochs within a stable program phase.

Because cache partitioning schemes are often coarse-grained, they are amenable to not only online simulation, but also offline analysis [21, 20, 16]. To do offline analysis, we first gather performance profiles for all possible (benchmark, capacity) combinations. Comparing against each benchmark's baseline IPC, we can calculate the per-thread speedups for all (benchmark, capacity) combinations and use them to calculate metrics such as FS, WS and QoS. For a given metric, we construct the candidate cache partition space for each workload and exhaustively search in the partition space for the optimal result. Compared with online simulation, offline analysis is idealized because (1) it uses accurate measurement information and (2) it searches for all possible partitions, which can be too slow to be practically implemented.

Due to its idealized nature, offline analysis can be used to estimate the performance upper bounds for given cache partitioning policies. We will use this approach to demonstrate the advantage of our proposed MTP policy over prior cache partitioning schemes, and avoid the need to compare against realistic implementations of prior proposals. We will also compare the offline analysis results of MTP with online simulation results of LRU-based caching schemes to identify the limitation of cache partitioning schemes. However, our final scheme CCP, which integrates MTP with CC, will be evaluated using a practical implementation, online measurement information, and execution-driven simulation results.

2.3 Benchmark Characteristics

Different cache partitioning schemes should be compared using a wide range of multiprogrammed workloads to evaluate their performance robustness. In this paper, we assume a CMP with 4 single-threaded cores and consider all 210 4-thread multiprogramming combinations (repetition allowed) from 7 SPEC benchmarks[3].

Figure 2 shows the performance of 7 SPEC benchmarks under different cache allocations. The IPC data are gathered using a 4-core CMP with 4MB 16-way total L2 cache. With way partitioning, cache resources are allocated in 256KB chunks. The equal-share allocation baseline (marked as the vertical line) is for each thread to use 1MB cache. At least 1 way is allocated to each thread. With three other cores on-chip, this leaves 13 ways ($13 = 16 - 3 * 1$), or 3.25MB, as the maximum capacity for one thread to have. This figure shows that our selected benchmarks have a wide variety of working set sizes and IPC curve shapes, therefore their combinations are able to generate a wide range of workload behaviors.

Figure 3 breaks the IPC curve of `art` into three distinctive regions as more capacity is allocated: (1) pre-working-set region

[3]With repetition, the number of K combinations selected from N objects is C_K^{N+K-1}. Therefore, selecting 4-thread combinations from 7 benchmarks can generate C_4^{7+4-1}=210 workloads.

	Optimization goals	Policies (threads with allocation priority)
Liu et al. [21]	Maximize throughput	Static partitioning
Suh et al. [38]	Minimize miss rate	Greedy (thread with best marginal miss reduction)
Fair Sharing [20]	Minimize slowdown difference	Greedy (thread with most extra misses)
Fast and Fair [42]	Maximize $\sum speedup$ under QoS	Greedy (thread with best speedup)
CQoS [18]	QoS	Generic framework, open policies
OS-managed [31], STATSHARE [27]	Open	Generic model/mechanism, open policies
Utility-based [29]	Maximize WS	Lookahead (thread with best marginal utility)
MTP	Maximize FS under QoS	Iterative (threads with high speedups)

Table 2: Comparing CMP Cache Partitioning Policies

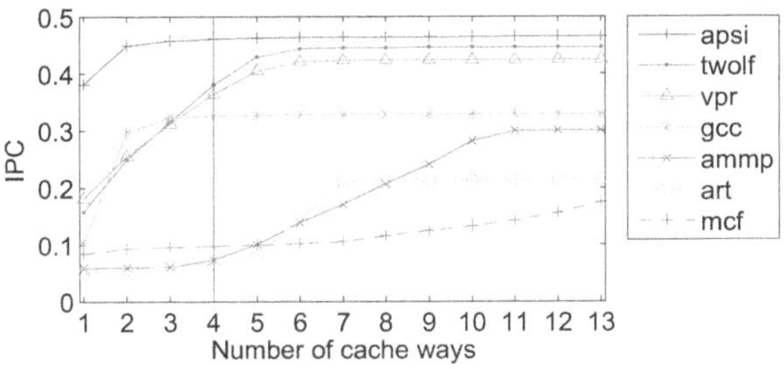

Figure 2: IPC Curves

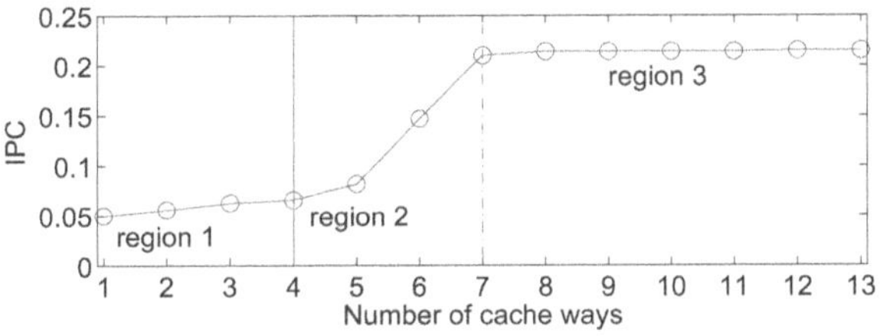

Figure 3: IPC of `art`

(from 1 way to 4 way) represents gradual speedups before the program's working set starts to fit into cache; (2) in-working-set region (from 5 way to 7 way) indicates dramatic throughput increases when the working set can be partly cached; (3) post-working-set region (starting from 7 way) shows saturated performance after the working set is fully cached. Except for benchmarks whose working sets are beyond the capacity of the on-chip cache (i.e., streaming threads), most threads demonstrate IPC curves that consist of regions with distinct slopes, albeit with different cache configurations. According to which region intersects with the equal-share allocation (which is dependent on both thread characteristic and cache configuration), we classify these threads into 3 categories.

- **Supplier threads**: These threads can supply some or all of their equal-share capacity for other threads while still achieving the same level of performance as using all cache resources. They include threads with very small working sets (e.g., `apsi` and `gcc` whose working set sizes are less than 1MB) and streaming threads (e.g., `swim` and `facerec` which are not included in Figure 2).
- **Sensitive threads**: `vpr` and `twolf` are benchmarks whose in-working-set regions are divided by the line of equal-share capacity. The performance of such programs changes significantly over the baseline as cache size varies, therefore judicious cache partitioning is needed when they are co-scheduled with other threads.
- **Thrashing threads**: `art`, `ammp` and `mcf` are benchmarks whose in-working-set regions are beyond their equal-share capacity. These threads usually slow down gradually with reduced capacity, but can speed up dramatically when a certain amount of extra capacity is allocated.

A similar classification can be found in [29], according to the benefit of increased capacity (or utility). Our classification is different by separating thrashing threads from sensitive threads, both called high-utility programs in [29] because they can speed up with more capacity.

3. MULTIPLE TIME-SHARING PARTITIONS

Prior CMP cache partitioning policies use the best single partition to achieve their optimization goals. However, it is an intrinsically hard problem to satisfy multiple goals (e.g., throughput, fairness and QoS) with a single partition when conflicts exist between competing threads. In this section we introduce the notion of Multiple Time-sharing Partitions (MTP) to resolve such conflicts over longer terms. Below we detail the development of MTP as we add support for different caching requirements.

3.1 Thrashing Avoidance

We first discuss when cache partitioning is needed by examining when destructive interference occurs. Starting with the equal-share allocation baseline, if this configuration can satisfy the caching requirements of every co-scheduled thread, then cache partitioning is not needed because little inter-thread interference exists. Cache partitioning is needed only if some threads experience thrashing with their current capacity allocations. These threads will attempt to acquire extra cache resources from each other and from other threads, which leads to performance, fairness and QoS problems.

Thrashing is a classic virtual memory management problem [9], and can be avoided by reducing the multiprogramming level: when the number of competing threads is reduced to a point that their working sets can be cached simultaneously, they can all run much faster. In the context of CMP caching, the number of co-scheduled threads is fixed by the operating system, but cache partitioning can intentionally manage capacity contention by unfairly starving some thrashing threads to make room for other thrashing threads.

Consider partitioning a 4MB 16-way L2 cache between 4 co-scheduled copies of `art`. With the equal-share allocation of a 1MB L2 cache, `art` has a low IPC of 0.066 due to thrashing (over 50 off-chip misses per thousand instructions) as previously shown in Figure 3. As more cache resources are allocated, its throughput increases quickly and reaches a saturating point of 0.215 IPC with 1.75MB capacity. At this point, thrashing can be avoided for 2 threads by unfairly allocating to each of them 1.75MB capacity, and starving the other threads each with a 256KB cache (0.05 IPC). This partition doubles the total throughput ($0.215*2+0.05*2=0.52$, which is two times of $0.066*4=0.264$), but is unfair to the threads being starved.

3.2 Fairness Improvement

Cache partitioning between 4 copies of `art` is an example of the throughput-fairness dilemma. When the available cache capacity cannot simultaneously satisfy the working set requirements of multiple large threads, a compromise has to be made within a single spatial partition. In this example, fair partitions cause thrashing for all threads, while thrashing avoidance requires unfair partitioning. Existing cache partitioning schemes all face this dilemma, but differ in the way they trade off between throughput and fairness.

We resolve this dilemma by learning from a similar example in game theory [12]. Consider two officemates who commute to their workplace: efficiency is doubled when they carpool, but it is unfair because the driver invests more effort and money. Not carpooling is a fair strategy, but is also inefficient. In real life, such games are played daily by the same players who often improve both performance and fairness by "taking turns" to drive when they carpool. We adopt the same cooperative policy to simultaneously improve throughput and fairness with multiple time-sharing partitions (MTP). Instead of using a single partition that is either low-throughput or unfair, multiple unfair but high-throughput partitions are selected and given equal opportunity to be used.

Specifically, individual threads are coordinated to shrink and expand their cache allocations in different cache partitions. Within a partition, the spare capacity collected from shrinking threads is used by expanding threads, and different threads are expanded in different partitions. As a thrashing thread goes through shrinking and expanding partitions, its average throughput can be much better than its baseline throughput. This is because a thrashing thread's baseline performance is already low by definition, and shrinking capacity usually causes insignificant slowdown. However, the thread can achieve dramatic speedup in expanding partitions (when the allocated cache can hold its working set) and, on average, the speedup in one expanding partition is often more than what is needed to compensate the slowdowns in multiple shrinking partitions. Overall, the workload's fair speedup (FS) is improved because all expandable threads get a fair chance to speedup.

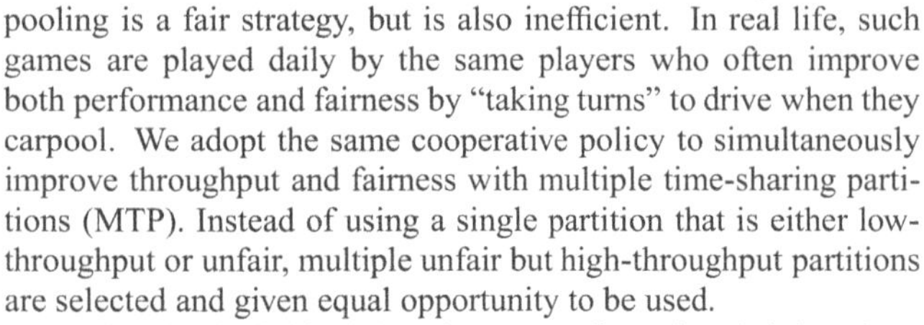

Figure 4: Cache Partitioning Options for `art-art-art-art`

Figure 4 compares three cache partitioning schemes for 4 copies of `art`. Single spatial partition (SSP) based schemes A and B provide the most fair and fast partitions, respectively. Based on MTP, scheme C can both maintain the same level of fairness as scheme A (by equalizing per-thread speedups) and achieve the same high throughput (IPC=0.52) and weighted speedup (WS=2.42) of scheme B. Such improvement is reflected by its high FS result (97% and 61% higher than scheme A and B, respectively), but can be overlooked if we only compare the IPC or WS results.

3.3 Priority Support

MTP extends the option of cache partitioning from the single dimension of space-sharing into two-dimensional time-sharing between spatial partitions. The time-sharing optimization can be applied to any proportional-sharing resource partition baseline, thus supporting priority if the priority levels of co-scheduled threads are reflected in the baseline.

Priority can also be supported through time-sharing. Instead of giving different threads equal opportunity to speedup, different time-sharing priorities can be assigned to different unfair partitions to deliver differentiated levels of performance. Because time-sharing based priority support has been well understood and implemented by operating systems [15, 41], MTP can serve as the cache management primitive to the high-level software by focusing on the determination and enforcement of multiple unfair partitions.

As priority specification and interpretation are usually conducted by end-users and operating systems, we leave the development and evaluation of priority algorithms for future work and assume the co-scheduled threads have the same priority for the rest of the paper.

3.4 QoS Guarantee

QoS can be guaranteed either in a real-time manner, or over the long term to meet different thread's timing requirements. Real-time QoS is needed only by certain programs (e.g., real-time video playback), and is not needed for many other programs. For example, users of SPEC-like programs are most concerned about total execution time, and thus long-term QoS, often measured over many millions of cycles.

To guarantee real-time QoS, fast and fair partitioning [42] reserves for each thread a **guaranteed partition**, which is the minimum amount of cache space required to achieve the same level of performance as using the equal-share cache allocation. Further speedup can be obtained by intelligently partitioning the remaining space. However, because only supplier threads (defined in Section 2.3) can have their guaranteed partitions smaller than the equal-share capacity, the cache partitioning algorithm is often left with a limited amount of space to optimize, resulting in lowered performance compared with schemes under no QoS constraints.

Single spatial partition (SSP) based cache partitioning schemes experience the same problem even for threads that require only long-term QoS. Because the same spatial partition is used repeatedly throughout a stable program phase, these schemes have to guarantee long-term QoS by guaranteeing QoS within every cache partition. In contrast, MTP's cooperative shrink/expand model can be used to guarantee long-term QoS with little loss of performance. To meet the QoS requirement, the MTP partitioning algorithm now uses multiple partitions to maximize FS, under the constraint that each thread's average throughput across multiple partitions is no worse than the equal-share baseline throughput.

To demonstrate MTP's advantage in guaranteeing long-term QoS, Figure 5 compares SSP and MTP based cache partitioning schemes that optimize FS under different QoS requirements: without QoS (SSP$_{noQoS}$ and MTP$_{noQoS}$), real-time QoS (SSP$_{QoS}$ and MTP$_{rtQoS}$) and long-term QoS (MTP$_{ltQoS}$). These results are obtained from an offline analysis to show the performance potential of an ideal MTP$_{ltQoS}$ implementation. In Sections 4 and 5, we will develop and evaluate its practical implementation.

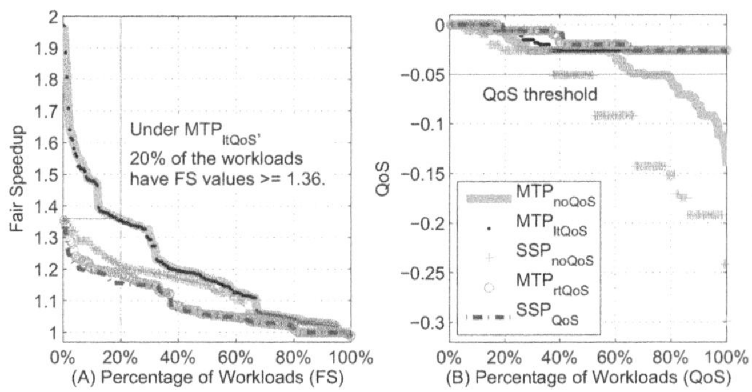

Figure 5: Comparing SSP and MTP Schemes

For each scheme, we plot the percentage of workloads that can achieve various metric values. These curves are essentially Cumulative Distribution Functions (CDF) being transposed, so that a higher curve indicates a better performing scheme. For example in Figure 5(A), each point (X%, Y) on the MTP$_{ltQoS}$ curve indicates that, X% of workloads have FS measurements equal to or large than (≥) value Y. Notice that for the same type of QoS guarantee, the ideal SSP scheme can never outperform the ideal MTP because single spatial partitioning is a special case in the MTP model, which is also empirically shown in the figure.

Figure 5(A) only shows 4 distinct curves for 5 schemes because MTP_{ltQoS} and MTP_{noQoS} have almost the same FS results. Similarly, the curves of the QoS guaranteeing schemes overlap in Figure 5(B). Figure 5 further shows that (1) SSP_{noQoS} and MTP_{noQoS} can not bound per-thread slowdown within the user-specified threshold (-5% in this paper); (2) SSP_{QoS} and MTP_{rtQoS} are the worst performing policies (their curves overlap for workloads with smaller FS values), indicating that real-time QoS guarantee can restrict performance optimization; and (3) MTP_{ltQoS} can maintain long-term QoS while achieving almost the same performance as the best performing scheme MTP_{noQoS}.

For its performance and QoS benefits, we now use MTP_{ltQoS} as the representative MTP policy in the rest of the paper, and denote it as MTP. MTP can support real-time QoS by simply reserving guaranteed partitions for real-time threads and optimizing the other threads with the remaining capacity.

3.5 Summary

MTP is a high-level cache partitioning policy that extends existing proposals with time-sharing multiple cache partitions. MTP addresses four cache partitioning requirements: (1) thrashing is avoided by unfair allocation within a partition; (2) fairness is improved with fair time-sharing between unfair partitions that each favors a different subset of co-scheduled threads; (3) priority can be supported with either prioritized proportional-share baselines or unfair time-sharing; and (4) different types of QoS can be guaranteed by bounding per-thread slowdown within each partition or across multiple partitions.

With multiple epochs in one iteration, MTP takes longer to adapt to phase/scheduling changes. MTP (and most partitioning schemes) cannot promptly adapt to frequent, irregular changes because their prediction of future execution relies on stable phases. In our infrastructure (Solaris-based full-system simulator), we observe stable thread-scheduling and repetitive phase changes. Our scheme works for such changes by using longer epochs (20M-cycles) to include multiple phases, whose aggregate behavior is stable enough for cache partitioning.

MTP can be implemented in different ways. A hardware-only solution is transparent but less flexible, especially considering priority support. Cooperation between hardware and software allows hardware to collect measurement and enforce partitioning decisions, and software to schedule partitions to meet high-level requirements. This section used offline analysis results to demonstrate the advantages of MTP without considering implementation details. Next we will present a practical, heuristic-based MTP partitioning algorithm by exploiting the benefits of CMP Cooperative Caching (CC) [6].

4. INTEGRATING MTP WITH CC

This section addresses another limitation of existing cache partitioning proposals—inadequacy for workloads that are well supported by LRU-based latency optimizations, where cache partitioning can hurt. We propose a new hybrid scheme, Cooperative Cache Partitioning (CCP), that combines the advantages of MTP and CMP Cooperative Caching (CC) [6]. Below, we motivate the need for the integration by showing the complementary advantages of MTP and CC on different workloads. We then develop a simple online heuristic to select MTP partitions based on the different characteristics of MTP and CC, and extend the CC design to implement the hybrid scheme.

4.1 Motivation

Figure 6 compares the FS and QoS results of MTP with two LRU-based caching schemes: CC and shared cache, using the same aggregate cache size and associativity. We use scatter plots to reveal the correlation between the best performing schemes and workload characteristics. To show the advantages of MTP and CC over shared cache, we normalize the FS values against the better results provided by MTP and CC (i.e., Max[FS(MTP), FS(CC)]). The 210 workloads are also clustered into two groups according to whether MTP outperforms CC (i.e., FS(MTP)>FS(CC)).

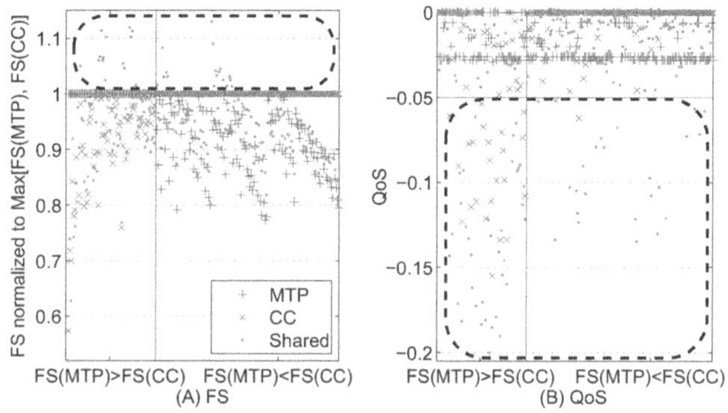

Figure 6: Comparing MTP with CC and Shared Cache. Each point on the X-axis represents a workload, and the corresponding Y-values are the measured results of the three schemes.

Focusing on the regions highlighted by the dotted rectangles, several observations can be made from Figure 6. First, Figure 6(A) shows that only a small number of dots (10%) are above 1 and fewer (3%) are above 1.1, indicating that a shared cache only outperforms both MTP and CC infrequently and insignificantly. Second, MTP only provides better performance than CC for 32% of the workloads, indicating the limited effectiveness of cache partitioning over CC for many workloads. Third, for workloads that benefit less from MTP, CC is almost always the best performing scheme (Figure 6(A)) and can guarantee QoS (Figure 6(B)), showing the complementary strengths of MTP and CC.

These observations imply that we can choose the best performing scheme (in both FS and QoS) for a given workload according to whether FS(MTP)>FS(CC): if MTP provides better FS result than CC, then MTP is very likely to perform the best; otherwise, CC is the best choice. Therefore, a hybrid scheme that integrates MTP and CC can potentially provide the best performance for all workloads by simply choosing the better scheme for any given workload. Below we analyze the reasons for CC and MTP's performance advantages, in order to achieve such an integration.

4.1.1 *Advantages of CC*

Two major reasons contribute to CC's performance advantage over MTP: (1) latency optimization over shared cache and (2) LRU-based fine-grained cache sharing. The first reason is unique to CC—it is the only private cache based CMP caching proposal that approximates global LRU replacement for multiprogrammed workloads; the second is supported by both CC and a shared cache.

CC reduces the average cache access latency by keeping a thread's data set locally in the processor's private L2 cache. Due to on-chip wire delay, local cache access latencies are much lower than remote access latencies. Comparing with a shared cache where data are distributed evenly across all banks, and a large fraction of L2 accesses are to remote banks, CC has the advantage of servicing most L2 accesses locally. For threads whose working sets can be mostly satisfied by a private cache, such reduced L2 cache latencies often translate into higher performance.

Similar to a shared cache, CC supports LRU-based capacity sharing by (1) allowing a local cache's victim block to be placed in a randomly picked peer cache (called spill in [6]), and (2) approximating global LRU replacement for multiprogrammed workloads via the combination of local LRU and global spill/reuse history. CC differs from a shared cache in that it allocates capacity according to the local thread's L2 reference stream and the remote threads' L2 miss streams, which are first filtered by their local L2 caches.

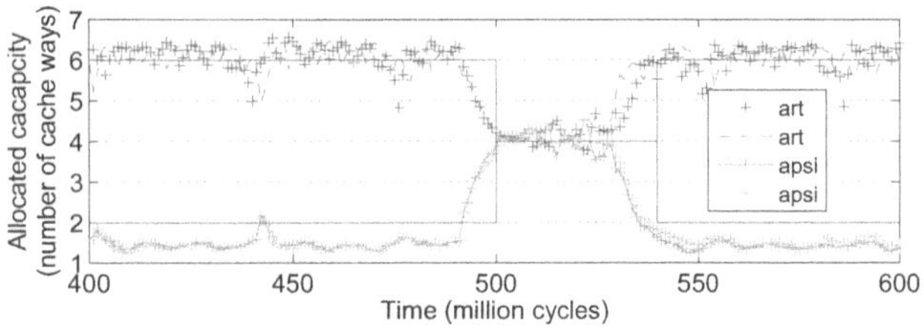

Figure 7: Cache Allocation for `art-art-apsi-apsi`

An LRU-based policy can provide near-optimal cache allocation for many workloads [36]. Figure 7 shows the amount of cache allocated by CC for individual threads in `art-art-apsi-apsi`. CC shows spatial fine-grained sharing by allocating on average 6.5 ways and 1.5 ways of capacity to `art` and `apsi` to better fit their capacity requirements, while way partitioning schemes can only allocate capacity in units of cache ways (the best partition allocates 6 ways to each `art` and 2 ways to each `apsi`). Temporal fine-grained sharing occurs during simulation time 500 to 530 million cycles, when `apsi` enters a phase that needs more capacity. CC adapts to this change swiftly without explicit phase tracking support or cache repartitioning. Due to spatial fine-grained sharing, `art` achieves 34% better speedup than way partitioning. The throughput of `apsi` is also slightly improved due to temporal fine-grained sharing (even though its average cache capacity is lower than way partitioning). This example also shows that CC is capable of managing workloads whose aggregate working set size modestly exceeds the total cache capacity, by dynamically balancing each individual thread's cache allocation.

Programs with highly non-uniform associativity demands across different cache sets [30] can also benefit from fine-grained sharing. For example, although ammp has a working set size of 1.5MB (or 6 cache ways), it can further speed up by 2X when the associativity requirements of certain hot sets are satisfied by a 16-way allocation.

4.1.2 Heuristics for MTP to Outperform CC

We now try to discover the characteristics of the workloads that can achieve better performance with MTP than with CC. Such characteristics will then be used to develop a simple heuristic to integrate MTP with CC.

To simplify discussion, we first assume that within one group of MTP partitions, a thread always uses the same capacity C_{expand} in all of its expanding partitions and the same capacity C_{shrink} in all shrinking partitions, thus achieving the same speedup Sp and slowdown Sd repeatedly. Offline analysis results show that this assumption has almost no performance impact on MTP. We further filter out supplier threads by allocating their guaranteed partitions to them, and allocate the remaining space among other threads.

To guarantee QoS and improve performance using MTP, each thread's total speedup has to exceed its total slowdown, and at least one thread should have a much larger total speedup. This can be achieved in two ways. The first way is to have a thrashing thread whose dramatic Sp can compensate the total slowdown in multiple shrinking partitions. The other way for a thread to achieve speedup using MTP, without a large Sp, is to have a modest Sp, but a steep speedup curve and a gradual slowdown curve, so that the speedups accumulated in multiple expanding partitions exceed the slowdown in one shrinking partition. However, achieving a modest Sp along with a steep speedup curve requires only a small amount of extra capacity, in which case CC is likely to achieve the same effect because the LRU policy is better at fine-turning cache allocation to achieve speedups (example shown in Figure 7).

The above analysis suggests that the common case for MTP to outperform CC is to have at least one thrashing thread, determined by whether its speedup Sp in one expanding partition is larger than the total slowdown accumulated in shrinking partitions. Here the Sp and Sd values are dependent on both the thread's IPC curve and the available capacity (which further depends on capacity allocated to co-scheduled threads). The test of a thrashing thread will be used as the partitioning heuristic for MTP.

The common case also explains why CC can guarantee QoS when its FS value is better than MTP (Figure 6(B)). A QoS violation occurs in CC only when a thread's private cache is overly used by blocks replaced from other threads (or spilled blocks [6]). Because CC's private cache has the same capacity as the equal-share baseline used to define thrashing, the aggressive spilling implies the existence of high miss rates and thus thrashing threads. Therefore, for workloads that prefer CC, the spilling should not be too invasive to affect QoS, otherwise thrashing will occur and cause MTP to be preferred.

4.2 Cooperative Cache Partitioning

We now develop Cooperative Cache Partitioning (CCP), a heuristic based hybrid cache allocation scheme that integrates MTP with CC. CCP consists of three components: (1) a heuristic-based partitioning algorithm to determine the MTP partitions, (2) a weight-based integration policy to decide when to use MTP and CC, and (3) modifications to the baseline CC design to enforce fine-grained cache partitioning decisions.

4.2.1 CCP Partitioning and Weighting Heuristics

Before MTP partitioning, CCP first gathers each thread's L2 cache miss rates under candidate cache allocations, and uses them to estimate the IPC curve. Miss rates are collected in our simulator in dedicated, online sampling epochs where each thread takes turns to use the maximum amount of cache. We use LRU stack hit counters to estimate miss rates under all possible cache associativities to reduce sampling overhead. Although such overhead can be avoided with the recently proposed UMON online sampling mechanism [29], we include it in our evaluation results.

Using IPC estimations, each thread's guaranteed partition (for real-time QoS guarantee) can be calculated. CCP also initializes each thread's C_{expand} to the minimum capacity needed to achieve the highest speedup, and C_{shrink} to the minimum capacity that can ensure long-term QoS when cooperating with C_{expand}. A thread is a supplier thread if its C_{shrink} and guaranteed partition are the same.

The CCP partitioning algorithm (shown in Table 3) then returns a set of MTP partitions that are likely to outperform CC, using the test of a thrashing thread as a simple heuristic. This algorithm has the following three steps: (1) filtering out supplier threads which cannot benefit from cache partitioning; (2) determine MTP partitions that each favors one thrashing thread by starving other thrashing threads with their C_{shrink} capacity; (3) for MTP partitions where one expanding thread can not use all the remaining space, expand other threads to further increase speedup. We will describe

```
Inputs: capacity C, thread set TS, sample results (IPC[i][c], guaranteed partitions g[i]);
Outputs: expanded[i], MTP partitions MTP[p][i];   /* Thread i's capacity in partition p */
--------------------------------------------------------------------------------
/* Step 1: Filter out supplier threads */
Identify supplier threads SupplierTS, subtract their g[i] from C;

/* Step 2: Determine the set of thrashing threads ThrashTS */
/* init stable = false; ThrashTS=TS-SupplierTS; */
while (ThrashTS is non-empty and !stable)
    stable=true;
    foreach thread i∈ThrashTS
        C_expand[i]=i's capacity usage when other threads use their C_shrink[j];
        stable &= thrashing_test(i, size(ThrashTS), C_expand[i], C_shrink[i]);

/* Step 3: Merge multiple expanding threads */
/* init p = 0; expanded[i] = false; MTP[p][j]=C_shrink[j]; */
foreach thread i∈ThrashTS, p++
    foreach thread j, start from i, in circular order
        MTP[p][j] += minimal remaining capacity for j to achieve its best speedup;
        if (MTP[p][j]≥C_expand[j]) expanded[j]=true;   /* Expanded in MTP */
--------------------------------------------------------------------------------
thrashing_test(i, nump, expand, shrink)        /* Key heuristic */
    if (IPC[i][expand]-IPC[i][base])≥(nump-1)*(IPC[i][base]-IPC[i][shrink]) return true; /* large speedup */
    C_shrink[i]=g[i]; C=C-g[i]; remove i from ThrashTS; return false;
```

Table 3: CCP Partitioning Algorithm

steps (2) and (3) in detail because step (1) is rather straightforward.

Step (2) determines the set of thrashing threads by removing threads whose speedups are not large enough to guarantee long-term QoS. Each candidate thread is tested by the function **thrashing_test**, to see whether its speedup in one expanding partition can compensate for the total slowdown accumulated in other (shrinking) partitions. The threads that fail the **thrashing_test** are assigned with their guaranteed partitions and removed from the candidate set, which will reduce the number of candidate partitions, the amount of remaining capacity and possibly remaining candidates' C_{expand} and speedups. Such tests are repeated until one of the two termination conditions is satisfied: (1) the candidate set is empty, or (2) all candidate threads pass the test. This step is guaranteed to terminate because each round of tests either reduces the candidate set size which leads to condition (1) in a finite number of steps, or satisfies condition (2).

After step (2), it is possible that in an MTP partition, the expanding thread does not need all the spare space provided by other shrinking threads. Step (3) merges multiple expandable threads in such a partition to further increase speedup. To be fair, the algorithm expands different sets of threads in different partitions.

This algorithm returns a set of MTP partitions and a vector $expanded$. A thread i benefits from MTP if it is allocated with C_{expand} capacity in at least one partition (*expanded*[i] is true), otherwise it is likely to benefit from CC. This observation leads to the CCP integration heuristic: the execution time is broken into epochs managed by either MTP or CC, weighted by how many threads can benefit from them respectively. For N co-scheduled threads, if M of them can be expanded by MTP partitions, then CCP will use MTP for every M out of N epochs and use CC for other epochs. A special case is when no thread is expanded because step (2) cannot find any MTP partitions, in which case CC should be used throughout the execution.

4.2.2 *Extending CC to Enforce Capacity Quota*

To enforce MTP partitions, CCP modifies the baseline CC design to monitor each thread's capacity usage and maintain capacity quota by throttling spill-based capacity sharing. For our evaluated 4-core CMP (assuming single-threaded cores), every cache block is augmented with 2 bits to indicate its owner thread ID. Each cache maintains 4 counters to reflect the numbers of blocks used by different threads. By periodically exchanging capacity usage information between caches, CCP can monitor the capacity usage of different threads. With such information, CCP maintains quota by disallowing over-quota threads to spill and disabling spills into under-quota threads.

5. EVALUATION AND RESULTS

We evaluate the effectiveness of different cache allocation schemes using Virtutech Simics-based [23] full-system simulation. The cache and memory simulator is derived from Ruby, which is part of the GEMS toolset [24]. A single-issue, in-order processor model is used, which allows us to simulate all 210 multiprogrammed workloads. We choose this methodology because, under the same simulation time, simulating a wide range of workload combinations allows us to recognize the limitations of different approaches on different workloads, which could have been missed by simulating a few combinations with a more detailed processor model.

Table 4 lists the relevant configuration parameters used in our simulations. The same total capacity and associativity are used for shared cache (both with and without way partitioning) and CC. We use the reference input sets for the selected SPEC benchmarks, except for `art` which uses the train input.[4] All benchmarks are fast forwarded by 800M instructions to bypass program initialization, and simulated for 700M cycles.

We compare the online simulation results of realistic CCP implementation with offline analysis results of ideal cache partitioning policies (e.g., MTP). Because the ideal MTP implementation results were shown to be the performance upper bound of existing cache partitioning schemes in Section 3, we do not compare CCP with realistic implementations of prior partitioning proposals.

We first compare CCP with its two baseline schemes CC and MTP in terms of FS, followed by comparison between CCP with

[4] `Art` with reference input is a streaming (thus supplier) thread. We do not include streaming threads because cache partitioning for them is very simple: their IPCs don't change with L2 cache allocations, so we can simply allocate the minimal capacity (e.g., 1 cache way) to them.

Component	Parameters
Processors	4-core, single-issue, in-order
Block size	128-byte
L1 I/D caches	32KB, 2-way, 2-cycle
L2 caches	sequential tag/data access, 15 cycles total
On-chip interconnect	Point-to-point, 5-cycle per-hop latency
Main Memory	300 cycles total
Coherence	MOSI-based directory protocols
CC	1MB per-core private cache, 4-way
shared cache	1MB per-bank capacity, 4 banks, 16-way

Table 4: Processor and Memory System Parameters

idealized offline analysis results on other metrics—QoS, throughput and weighted speedup. Lastly, we evaluate the performance robustness of CCP by halving the total cache size.

5.1 Effectiveness of CCP

In Section 4, MTP was shown to be better than CC for only a subset of workloads. Since the ideal MTP implementation represents the best cache partitioning results, we now refer to workloads that prefer CC over MTP as workloads where cache partitioning could hurt performance, and the other workloads as workloads that need the help of cache partitioning. Figure 8 compares the performance of CCP (realistic) with MTP (ideal) and CC (realistic) on both classes of workloads. Only FS results are reported because both CCP and MTP can guarantee QoS.

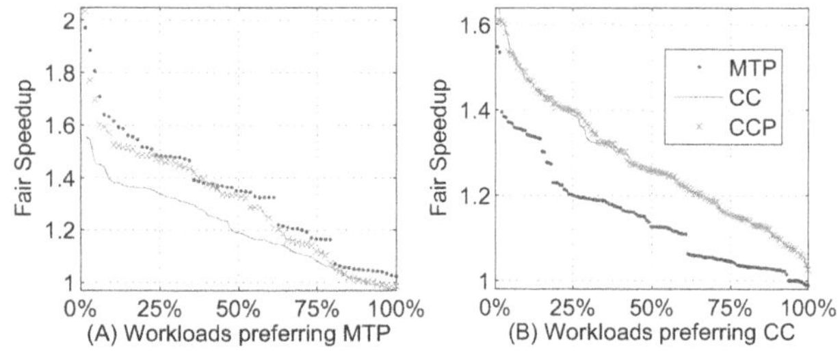

Figure 8: Comparing MTP, CC and CCP's FS Results

Same as in Figure 5, we use transposed CDF curves to show the percentage of workloads that can achieve various levels of performance. Here, a higher curve indicates a better scheme because it achieves better FS measurements across different fractions of the workloads, and the gaps between curves correspond to their performance differences.

Figure 8(A) shows that when cache partitioning is needed, CCP achieves comparable performance as MTP (the gap between CCP and MTP curves is small), and much better FS values than CC (the gap between CCP and CC is much larger). The performance difference between CCP and MTP reflects the difference between our practical partitioning heuristic and a less realistic, offline, exhaustive search of MTP partitions. For workloads where cache partitioning hurts, Figure 8(B) shows that CCP performs slightly better or the same as CC and significantly better than MTP. Together they demonstrate that CCP effectively combines the strengths of both MTP and CC.

5.2 Results of Different Metrics

Besides FS, CMP caching performance can also be evaluated using other metrics. We use transposed CDF plots to compare CCP (realistic) and MTP (ideal) against two single spatial partition (SSP) based schemes IPC_{opt} and WS_{opt}, which optimize offline for throughput and weighted speedup, respectively. Focusing on workloads that need cache partitioning, Figure 9 compares IPC_{opt}, WS_{opt}, MTP and CCP over 4 different metrics: (A) fair speedup, (B) QoS, (C) throughput, and (D) weighted speedup.

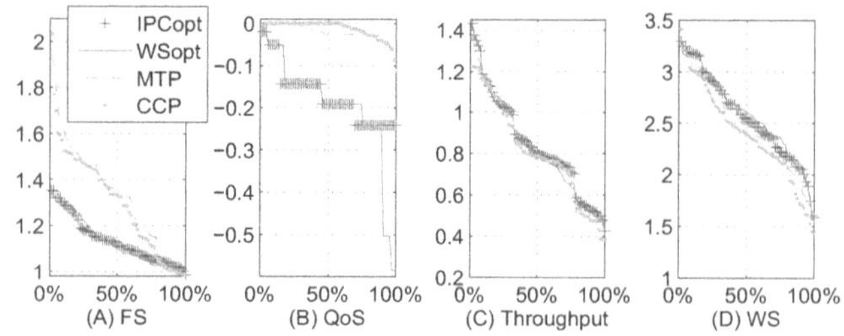

Figure 9: Results of Multiple Metrics for Workloads that Need Cache Partitioning (32% of All Workloads) for 4MB Cache

For the first two metrics (FS and QoS), MTP and CCP are both significantly better than IPC_{opt} and WS_{opt}. This is because the SSP-based schemes, when their goals conflict with fairness and QoS requirements, often optimize by favoring only a subset of threads while sacrificing the performance of other threads. For IPC and WS metrics, both IPC_{opt} and WS_{opt} are better, although the gap between different schemes are much smaller than in Figure 9(A) and Figure 9(B). As illustrated in Section 2.1.3's examples, this is because schemes optimizing for WS, IPC and FS have different tradeoffs between performance and fairness.

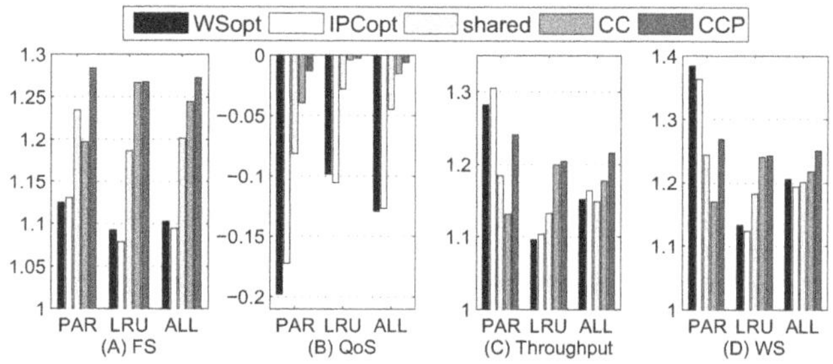

Figure 10: Average Improvement for 4MB L2 Cache

Figure 10 summarizes the average improvement of WS_{opt}, IPC_{opt}, shared cache, CC and CCP over the equal-share baseline for different metrics. The average improvements are calculated as geometric means of per-workload improvements[5]. The results are summarized over three groups of workloads: "PAR" represents workloads that prefer cache partitioning, "LRU" covers other workloads, while "ALL" includes all workload combinations. This figure shows that for workloads preferring cache partitioning (PAR), CCP performs much better than a shared cache and CC, while achieving similar or much better results than the two cache partitioning schemes. Considering workloads that prefer LRU-based sharing (LRU) and all workloads (ALL), CCP provides the best average results on all reported metrics.

5.3 Results for a 2MB L2 Cache

Now we evaluate the robustness of CCP when the total L2 cache capacity is reduced to 2MB. The reduction of cache size not only increases capacity contention between threads, but also causes some benchmarks to switch their categories (e.g., from supplier threads to sensitive threads, or from sensitive threads to thrashing threads) so the performance of CCP can be tested under new scenarios.

Figure 11 uses transposed CDF plots to compare 4 cache partitioning schemes (IPC_{opt}, WS_{opt}, MTP and CCP) on workloads that need cache partitioning. CCP again achieves comparable FS and QoS results as the ideal MTP implementation and outperforms the two SSP-based partitioning schemes. This shows the robustness

[5]QoS results are summarized using the arithmetic mean because the QoS measurements of many workloads are zero, which causes the average results to be the same (zero) with geometric means.

of CCP's heuristic-based partitioning algorithm. In terms of fairness and throughput tradeoff, the weighted speedup results of MTP and CCP are similar to IPC_{opt} and WS_{opt}, while their throughput results are 10% lower. Again, QoS constraint and fair speedup optimization are the two reasons that cause MTP and CCP's lower throughput, while IPC_{opt} and WS_{opt} can achieve better throughput without satisfying such constraints.

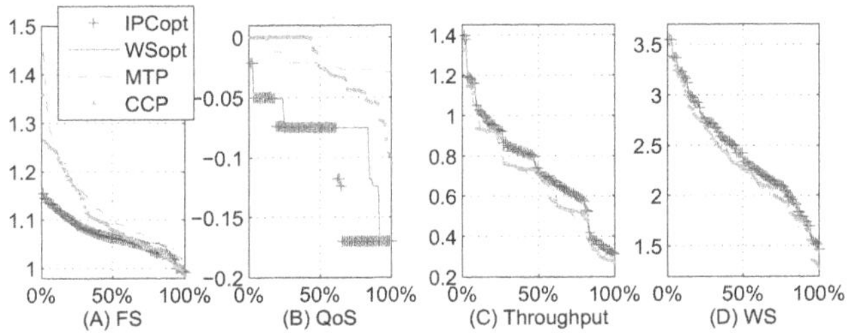

Figure 11: WS_{opt}, MTP and CCP on Workloads that Need Cache Partitioning (40% of All Workloads) with 2MB Cache

Figure 12 compares the average improvements of various schemes over the equal-share baseline. Due to higher cache contention, more workloads now prefer cache partitioning (increased from 32% to 40%). The performance of a shared cache also drops significantly and comes close to the equal-share baseline performance. In contrast, CCP still consistently outperforms other schemes for workloads where cache partitioning can hurt. However, the gap between cache partitioning schemes and CCP (as well as CC) is reduced because, due to capacity pressure, latency optimization contributes less to the overall speedup. Averaged over all 210 workloads, CCP achieves the best results on almost all metrics (except for throughput, where CCP is 1% lower than IPC_{opt}).

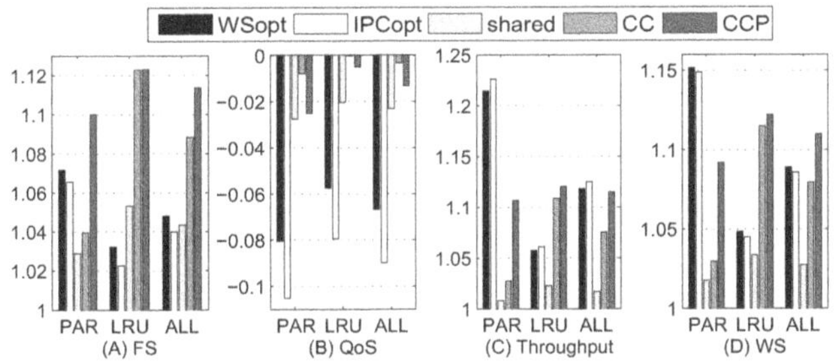

Figure 12: Average Improvement for 2MB L2 Cache

6. RELATED WORK

Cooperative cache partitioning is closely related to CMP cache partitioning research. Stone et al. [36] studied the problem of partitioning cache capacity between different reference streams, and identified LRU as the near-optimal policy for their workloads. Suh et al. [38, 37] first applied way partitioning to shared CMP caches, using in-cache monitoring mechanism and marginal gain based partitioning algorithm to reduce off-chip misses. Recently Qureshi and Patt [29] proposed UMON sampling mechanism to provide more precise measurement and lookahead partitioning to handle workloads with non-convex miss rate curves. The UMON mechanism can be combined with CCP to improve miss rate measurement and adapt to fine-grained program phase changes. Dybdahl et al. [11] extended way partitioning by overbooking cache capacity to account for non-uniform per-set requirements, and evaluated its effectiveness using private L1/L2 caches with a shared L3 cache. Dybdahl and Stenstrom [10] also proposed an adaptive shared/private partitioning scheme to both avoid inter-thread interference and exploit the locality benefits of private caches. Their partitioning algorithm is essentially the same as in [38], but instead of in-cache monitors, "shadow tags" are used to measure the benefit of having one extra cache way.

Kim et al. [20] emphasized the importance of fair CMP caching, and proposed a set of fairness metrics as their goal of optimization. Iyer [18] motivated the importance of QoS guarantee and prioritization with a general QoS framework. Yeh and Reinman [42] focused on throughput improvement with QoS guarantee and exploited the latency advantage of a NUCA design. Their notion of guaranteed partition is adopted in this paper. Rafique et al. [31] and Petoumenos et al. [27] proposed spatially fine-grained partitioning support, which is supported in CCP by throttling cooperative sharing activities. Hsu et al. [16] studied various partitioning metrics and policies, and recognized the difficulties of improving both throughput and fairness. CCP is the only partitioning proposal that simultaneously optimizes throughput, fairness, and QoS for a wide range of workload combinations.

Beside capacity optimization, CMP caching proposals also reduce on-chip access latency. CCP combines the strength of cache partitioning with such fine-grained latency reduction optimizations via the integration of MTP and CC [6]. MTP can also be integrated with other private cache based latency optimizations [35, 2] that do not support global LRU replacement. Planas et al. [28] provided a model to explain cache partitioning speedups over LRU-based fine-grained sharing.

CCP also borrows heavily from virtual memory management research. Verghese et al. [40] recognized the need for performance isolation for SMP-based systems, and proposed mechanisms to provide isolation under heavy load while allowing sharing under light load. CCP aims to support a broader sense of performance isolation that also balances between partitioning and sharing. The integration between MTP and CC resembles WSClock [5], a paging algorithm that integrates working-set based partitioning with global LRU replacement. CCP also uses other well-known operating system techniques such as thrashing avoidance and time-sharing based resource management, but differs from software-only schemes [13] that manage cache sharing solely in the operating system.

7. CONCLUSION

Current cache partitioning schemes have limited functionality and applicability because they can only support a subset of CMP caching requirements, and they can not compete with LRU-based latency-reducing caching schemes (e.g., CC) for many workloads. To answer these challenges, this paper introduces Multiple Time-sharing Partitions (MTP) to simultaneously improve throughput and fairness while guaranteeing QoS. MTP is further integrated with CMP Cooperative Caching (CC) to exploit its latency optimizations. The resulting Cooperative Cache Partitioning (CCP) scheme is evaluated and shown to provide the best overall performance over 210 combinations of 7 representative SPEC2000 benchmarks under different cache sizes. For a 4-core CMP with 4MB L2 cache, CCP on average improves performance (measured by fair speedup) by 12% and throughput by 4.5%, respectively, comparing against the best static partitioning schemes optimizing fair speedup and throughput, respectively, while maintaining long-term QoS.

CCP takes a first step in balancing partitioning-based capacity optimizations and LRU-based latency optimizations for multiprogrammed workloads. Future research is needed to extend CCP to better adapt to phase/scheduling changes, as well as to support large-scale CMPs and CMPs with SMT cores. For environments that prefer higher throughput over execution time reduction, fairness, and QoS guarantee, CCP can also be modified to use a single unfair partition that only optimizes throughput, which is also left as future work.

8. ACKNOWLEDGEMENTS

The authors thank Philip Wells, Koushik Chakraborty, Saisantosh Balakrishnan, Matthew Allen and Vikas Garg for helpful discussion and proofreading. We also thank Jim Smith and Kyle Nesbit for their valuable comments on the selection of baselines and metrics, and the anonymous reviewers for their comments. Special thanks to Philip Wells who first suggested time-sharing based cache partitioning.

This research is supported in part by NSF grants CCR-0311572 and CNS-0551401, funds from the John P. Morgridge Chair in Computer Science, and the University of Wisconsin Graduate School (a WARF Named Professorship). Sohi has a significant financial interest in Sun Microsystems. The views expressed herein are not necessarily those of the National Science Foundation.

9. REFERENCES

[1] L. A. Barroso, K. Gharachorloo, R. McNamara, A. Nowatzyk, S. Qadeer, B. Sano, S. Smith, R. Stets, and B. Verghese. Piranha: A Scalable Architecture Based on Single-Chip Multiprocessing. In *Proceedings of the 27th Annual International Symposium on Computer Architecture (ISCA-27)*, 2000.

[2] B. M. Beckmann, M. R. Marty, and D. A. Wood. ASR: Adaptive Selective Replication for CMP Caches. In *Proceedings of the 39th Annual International Symposium on Microarchitecture (MICRO-39)*, 2006.

[3] D. Bertsekas and R. Gallager. *Data Networks (2nd ed.)*. Prentice-Hall, 1992.

[4] J. Bruno, E. Gabber, B. Özden, and A. Silberschatz. The Eclipse Operating System: Providing Quality of Service via Reservation Domains. In *USENIX 1998 Annual Technical Conference*, 1998.

[5] R. W. Carr and J. L. Hennessy. WSClock - a Simple and Effective Algorithm for Virtual Memory Management. In *Proceedings of the 8th ACM Symposium on Operating Systems Principles (SOSP-8)*, 1981.

[6] J. Chang and G. S. Sohi. Cooperative Caching for Chip Multiprocessors. In *Proceedings of the 33th Annual International Symposium on Computer Architecture (ISCA-33)*, 2006.

[7] D. T. Chiou. *Extending the Reach of Microprocessors: Column and Curious Caching*. PhD thesis, MIT, 1999.

[8] Z. Chishti, M. D. Powell, and T. N. Vijaykumar. Optimizing Replication, Communication and Capacity Allocation in CMPs. In *Proceedings of the 32nd Annual International Symposium on Computer Architecture (ISCA-32)*, 2005.

[9] P. J. Denning. Thrashing: Its Causes and Prevention. In *AFIPS 1968 Fall Joint Computer Conference*, volume 33, pages 915–922, 1968.

[10] H. Dybdahl and P. Stenstrom. An Adaptive Shared/Private NUCA Cache Partitioning Scheme for Chip Multiprocessors. In *Proceedings of the 13th International Symposium on High-Performance Computer Architecture (HPCA-13)*, 2007.

[11] H. Dybdahl, P. Stenstrom, and L. Natvig. A Cache-Partition Aware Replacement Policy for Chip Multiprocessors. In *ACM 2006 Conference on High Performance Computing (HiPC-13)*, 2006.

[12] R. Fagin and J. H. Williams. A fair carpool scheduling algorithm. *IBM Journal of Research and Development*, 27(2):133–139, 1983.

[13] A. Fedorova, M. Seltzer, C. Small, and D. Nussbaum. Performance Of Multithreaded Chip Multiprocessors And Implications For Operating System Design. In *USENIX 2005 Annual Technical Conference*, 2005.

[14] L. Hammond, B. A. Hubbert, M. Siu, M. K. Prabhu, M. Chen, and K. Olukotun. The Stanford Hydra CMP. *IEEE Micro*, 20(2):71–84, 2000.

[15] J. L. Hellerstein. Achieving service rate objectives with decay usage scheduling. *IEEE Transaction of Software Engineering*, 19(8), 1993.

[16] L. R. Hsu, S. K. Reinhardt, R. Iyer, and S. Makineni. Communist, Utilitarian, and Capitalist Cache Policies on CMPs: Caches as a Shared Resource. In *Proceedings of the 15th International Conference on Parallel Architecture and Compilation Techniques (PACT-15)*, 2006.

[17] J. Huh, C. Kim, H. Shafi, L. Zhang, D. Burger, and S. W. Keckler. A NUCA Substrate for Flexible CMP Cache Sharing. In *Proceedings of the 19th ACM International Conference on Supercomputing (ICS-19)*, 2005.

[18] R. Iyer. CQoS: a Framework for Enabling QoS in Shared Caches of CMP Platforms. In *Proceedings of the 18th ACM International Conference on Supercomputing (ICS-18)*, 2004.

[19] L. K. John. More on Finding a Single number to Indicate Overall Performance of a Benchmark Suite. *SIGARCH Computer Architecture News*, 32(1), 2004.

[20] S. Kim, D. Chandra, and Y. Solihin. Fair Cache Sharing and Partitioning in a Chip Multiprocessor Architecture. In *Proceedings of the 13th International Conference on Parallel Architecture and Compilation Techniques (PACT-13)*, 2004.

[21] C. Liu, A. Sivasubramaniam, and M. Kandemir. Organizing the Last Line of Defense before Hitting the Memory Wall for CMPs. In *Proceedings of the 10th International Symposium on High-Performance Computer Architecture (HPCA-10)*, 2004.

[22] K. Luo, J. Gummaraju, and M. Franklin. Balancing Throughput and Fairness in SMT Processors. In *Proceedings of the 2001 IEEE International Symposium on Performance Analysis of Systems and Software (ISPASS-2001)*, 2001.

[23] P. Magnusson, M. Christensson, J. Eskilson, D. Forsgren, G. Hållberg, J. Högberg, F. Larsson, A. Moestedt, and B. Werner. Simics: A Full System Simulation Platform. *IEEE Computer*, 35(2):50–58, Feb 2002.

[24] M. M. Martin, D. J. Sorin, B. M. Beckmann, M. R. Marty, M. Xu, A. R. Alameldeen, K. E. Moore, M. D. Hill, and D. A. Wood. Multifacet's General Execution-driven Multiprocessor Simulator (GEMS) Toolset. *Computer Architecture News*, 2005.

[25] K. J. Nesbit, N. Aggarwal, J. Laudon, and J. E. Smith. Fair Queuing Memory Systems. In *Proceedings of the 39th Annual International Symposium on Microarchitecture (MICRO-39)*, 2006.

[26] A. K. Parekh and R. G. Gallager. A Generalized Processor Sharing Approach to Flow Control in Integrated Services Networks: the Single-node Case. *IEEE Transaction of Networks*, 1(3):344–357, 1993.

[27] P. Petoumenos, G. Keramidas, H. Zeffer, S. Kaxiras, and E. Hagersten. STATSHARE: A Statistical Model for Managing Cache Sharing via Decay. In *Second Annual Workshop on Modeling, Benchmarking and Simulation (MoBS 2006)*, 2006.

[28] M. M. Planas, F. Cazorla, A. Ramirez, and M. Valero. Explaining Dynamic Cache Partitioning Speed Ups. *IEEE Computer Architecture Letters*, 6(1), 2007.

[29] M. K. Qureshi and Y. N. Patt. Utility-Based Cache Partitioning: A Low-Overhead, High-Performance, Runtime Mechanism to Partition Shared Caches. In *Proceedings of the 39th Annual International Symposium on Microarchitecture (MICRO-39)*, 2006.

[30] M. K. Qureshi, D. Thompson, and Y. N. Patt. The V-way Cache: Demand Based Associativity via Global Replacement. In *Proceedings of the 32nd Annual International Symposium on Computer Architecture (ISCA-32)*, 2005.

[31] N. Rafique, W.-T. Lim, and M. Thottethodi. Architectural Support for Operating System-Driven CMP Cache Management. In *Proceedings of the 15th International Conference on Parallel Architecture and Compilation Techniques (PACT-15)*, 2006.

[32] J. E. Smith. Characterizing Computer Performance with a Single Number. *Communication of ACM*, 31(10), 1988.

[33] A. Snavely and D. M. Tullsen. Symbiotic Jobscheduling for a Simultaneous Multithreaded Processor. In *Proceedings of the 9th International Conference on Architectural Support for Programming Languages and Operating Systems (ASPLOS-IX)*, 2000.

[34] A. Snavely, D. M. Tullsen, and G. Voelker. Symbiotic jobscheduling with priorities for a simultaneous multithreading processor. In *Proceedings of 2002 ACM SIGMETRICS International Conference on Measurement and Modeling of Computer Systems*, 2002.

[35] E. Speight, H. Shafi, L. Zhang, and R. Rajamony. Adaptive Mechanisms and Policies for Managing Cache Hierarchies in Chip Multiprocessors. In *Proceedings of the 32nd Annual International Symposium on Computer Architecture (ISCA-32)*, 2005.

[36] H. S. Stone, J. Turek, and J. L. Wolf. Optimal partitioning of cache memory. *IEEE Transaction of Computers*, 41(9):1054–1068, 1992.

[37] G. E. Suh, S. Devadas, and L. Rudolph. A New Memory Monitoring Scheme for Memory-aware Scheduling and Partitioning. In *Proceedings of the 8th International Symposium on High-Performance Computer Architecture (HPCA-8)*, 2002.

[38] G. E. Suh, L. Rudolph, and S. Devadas. Dynamic Partitioning of Shared Cache Memory. *Journal of Supercomputing*, 28(1):7–26, 2004.

[39] J. M. Tendler, J. S. Dodson, J. S. F. Jr., H. Le, and B. Sinharoy. IBM Power4 system microarchitecture. *IBM Journal of Research and Development*, 46(1):5–26, 2002.

[40] B. Verghese, A. Gupta, and M. Rosenblum. Performance Isolation: Sharing and Isolation in Shared-memory Multiprocessors. In *Proceedings of the 8th International Conference on Architectural Support for Programming Languages and Operating Systems (ASPLOS-VIII)*, 1998.

[41] C. A. Waldspurger. Lottery and stride scheduling: Flexible proportional-share resource management. Technical Report MIT/LCS/TR-667, Cambridge, MA, USA, 1995.

[42] T. Y. Yeh and G. Reinman. Fast and Fair: Data-stream Quality of Service. In *Proceedings of the 2005 International Conference on Compilers, Architecture, and Synthesis for Embedded Systems (CASES'05)*, 2005.

[43] M. Zhang and K. Asanovic. Victim Replication: Maximizing Capacity while Hiding Wire Delay in Tiled CMPs. In *Proceedings of the 32nd Annual International Symposium on Computer Architecture (ISCA-32)*, 2005.

Biomedical Image Analysis on a Cooperative Cluster of GPUs and Multicores*

Timothy D. R. Hartley[1], Umit Catalyurek[1], Antonio Ruiz[2], Francisco Igual[3], Rafael Mayo[3], Manuel Ujaldon[2]
[1] Departments of Biomedical Informatics and Electrical and Computer Engineering, The Ohio State University, Columbus, OH, USA.
{hartleyt,umit}@bmi.osu.edu
[2] Computer Architecture Department, University of Malaga, Malaga, Spain.
{aruiz,ujaldon}@ac.uma.es
[3] Department of Computer Engineering and Computer Science, University Jaume I, Castellon, Spain.
{figual,mayo}@icc.uji.es

ABSTRACT

We are currently witnessing the emergence of two paradigms in parallel computing: streaming processing and multi-core CPUs. Represented by solid commercial products widely available in commodity PCs, GPUs and multi-core CPUs bring together an unprecedented combination of high performance at low cost. The scientific computing community needs to keep pace with application models and middleware which scale efficiently to hundreds of internal processing units. The purpose of the work we present here is twofold: first, a cooperative environment is designed so that both parallel models can coexist and complement one another. Second, beyond the parallelism of multiple internal cores, further parallelism is introduced when multiple CPU sockets, multiple GPUs, and multiple nodes are combined within a unique multi-processor platform which exceeds 10 TFLOPS when using 16 nodes. We illustrate our cooperative parallelization approach by implementing a large-scale, biomedical image analysis application which contains a number of assorted kernels including typical streaming operators, co-occurrence matrices, convolutions, and histograms. Experimental results are compared among different implementation strategies and almost linear speed-up is achieved when all coexisting methods in CPUs and GPUs are combined.

*This work was supported by the US National Science Foundation (CNS-0643969, CNS-0403342, CNS-0615155, CFF-0342615), NIH NIBIB BISTI (P20EB000591), US Department of Energy (ED-FC02-06ER25775), Ministry of Education of Spain (TIC2003-06623, PR-2007-0014), Junta de Andalucía of Spain (P06-TIC-02109), and Fundación Caixa-Castellón/Bancaixa and the Univ. Jaume I (P1-1B2007-32).

ICS'08, June 7–12, 2008, Island of Kos Aegean Sea, Greece.

Categories and Subject Descriptors

C.1 [**Processor Architectures**]: Multiple Data Stream Architectures (Multiprocessors)—*Parallel Processors* ; I.3 [**Computer Graphics**]: Hardware Architecture—*Graphics Processors* ; I.4 [**Image Processing and Computer Vision**]: Applications

General Terms

Algorithms, Languages, Performance

1. INTRODUCTION

Biomedical applications are becoming a major focus due to the large possible benefit to the public welfare as well as to the scientific community. In particular, imaging applications are emerging as a new opportunity for innovation at the meeting point between medicine and computer science. These applications are challenging for several reasons. From the practical concerns of fitting into a clinician's standard workflow to the performance-centric difficulties in using disruptive architectures for the maximum application throughput, biomedical image analysis applications provide many opportunities for novelty.

Computer technology has made a tremendous impact on medical imaging technology. The recent availability of whole slide digital scanners has made research on pathological image analysis more attractive, by enabling quantitative analysis tools to decrease the evaluation time pathologists spend for each slide. This also reduces the variation in decision-making processes among different pathologists or institutions and introduces reproducibility.

The analysis of pathology images is particularly challenging due to the large size of the data. Since uncompressed image sizes can be 30 gigabytes for one slice of tissue, typical datasets for case studies can easily stretch to terabyte scale. Further, the computation required to analyze these images can be extensive; analysis can often take hours on a single CPU. Several research studies on different cancer types have been conducted to develop computational methods within this field [7, 12, 14, 15, 19, 24, 26]. Most of these approaches only tested randomly selected image tiles, while some [18] have recently extended their methods to process-

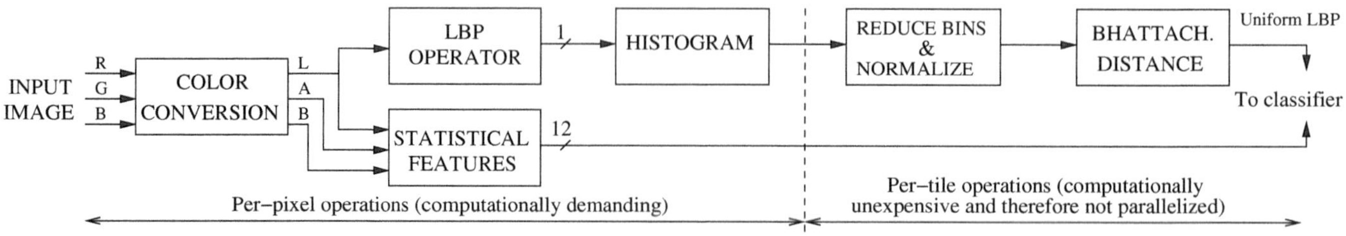

Figure 1: Flow chart for the stroma classification algorithm.

ing whole-slide images, but without discussing the computational burden. One of the most recent results [3] involves a parallelization technique, but the focus of the study was not strictly one of execution time performance, and processing a relatively small image took almost half an hour on a 16-node configuration, which is still impractical for clinical application.

With respect to improving the processing time of scientific applications, the newest versions of programmable Graphics Processing Units (GPU) provide an ideal platform, since they allow extremely high floating point arithmetic throughput for applications which fit their architectural idiosyncrasies [16]. This fact has attracted many researchers and encouraged the use of GPUs in many fields [10] including data mining [11], image segmentation and clustering [13], numerical methods for finite element computations used in 3D interactive simulations [30], and nuclear, gas dispersion and heat shimmering simulations [31]. In an earlier work [22, 23], we have also leveraged GPU processing power and introduced techniques based on shaders and Cg to accelerate the feature extraction by a factor of 321x versus a Matlab version and 45x versus an equivalent C++ version running on a single CPU.

GPU manufacturers have responded to the wide acceptance and use of GPUs in general-purpose computing with the introduction of CUDA (Compute Unified Device Architecture) [5], a more general programming interface, and Tesla [28], a new computational node with multiple GPUs, reaching near supercomputer performance levels starting at $1500. Recent announcements from Nvidia (GeForce 9 Series) and ATI (FireStream) [9] have also responded to the scientific computing community's widespread call for double-precision, floating-point arithmetic which does not incur a large performance penalty compared to single-precision.

In this work, our goal is the efficient execution of large-scale biomedical image analysis applications on a cooperative cluster of GPUs and multi-core CPUs. The advent of multi-core CPUs means that more computation can occur on a single computer than ever before. Traditional SMPs are now becoming hybridized, such that multiple multi-core CPUs are resident in a single compute node. Furthermore, new architectures can support more than one GPU card per node. Hence, our target hardware architecture is a cluster of compute nodes with multiple multi-core CPUs and multiple GPUs, and this work presents methods to make full use of all of the computational power such a hardware system offers.

On the software side, our cooperative approach is enabled by software libraries and middleware which ease both the GPU programming and the parallelization computation at many granularities. Nvidia's CUDA provides easier access to the high computational performance available in modern era GPUs. Additionally, it provides capabilities beyond that of other programming methods with respect to applications which do not entirely fit into the more traditional graphics processing paradigm. DataCutter [2] is a powerful middleware tool for data-parallel application decomposition, transparent task replication, and task graph execution. Its use here allows us to leverage all of the parallelism inherent in the hardware architecture. By analyzing the application bottlenecks appropriately, we are able to hide much of the latency incurred by the hardware when analyzing very large data sets. Additionally, DataCutter enables the overlap of computation and communication, which are still fundamental issues in the GPU and multi-core era.

The rest of the paper is organized as follows. Section 2 presents the neuroblastoma image analysis application which provides the testbed for this new paradigm of cooperation between multi-core CPUs and GPUs. The specifications and properties of an example state-of-the-art, multi-socket, multi-core, multi-GPU cluster are presented in Section 3. Section 4 focuses on the specifics of the GPU programming with CUDA and that of the parallelization strategies. The experimental results are presented in section 5, and section 6 concludes.

2. PATHOLOGICAL IMAGE ANALYSIS

Neuroblastoma is a cancer of the sympathetic nervous system which mostly affects children. The prognosis of the disease is currently based on visual examination under a microscope of tissue slides by expert pathologists. These tissue slides are classified into different prognostic groups depending on the differentiation grade of the neuroblasts among other issues [25]. Manual examination by pathologists is an error-prone and very time consuming process which also may lead to inter- and intra-reader variations. Therefore, together with our collaborators, we are developing a computerized pathological image analysis system [3, 12, 22, 23, 24] to assist in the determination of the prognosis of the neuroblastoma by automatically characterizing stroma regions.

2.1 The algorithm

Figure 1 shows the flowchart of the image analysis algorithm for the classification of stromal development in neuroblastoma images [22, 23]. The image analysis occurs in four stages:

Phase 1: Color conversion. The RGB input image is converted into the LA*B* color space, which provides color perceptual uniformity and enables the use of Euclidean distance in feature calculation [17].

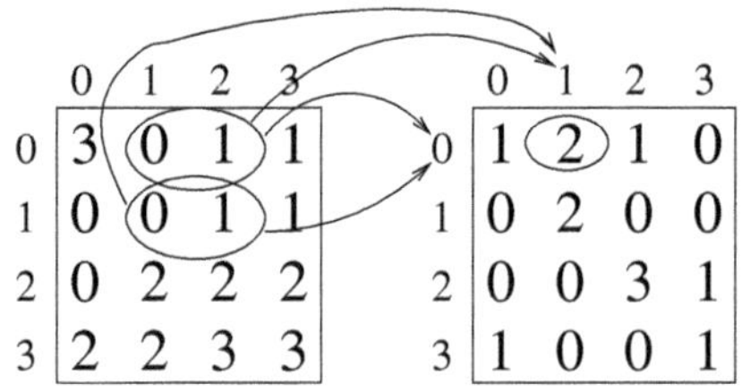

Figure 2: The computation of a co-occurrence matrix (right) from a 4x4 image (left) where pixel intensities are shown.

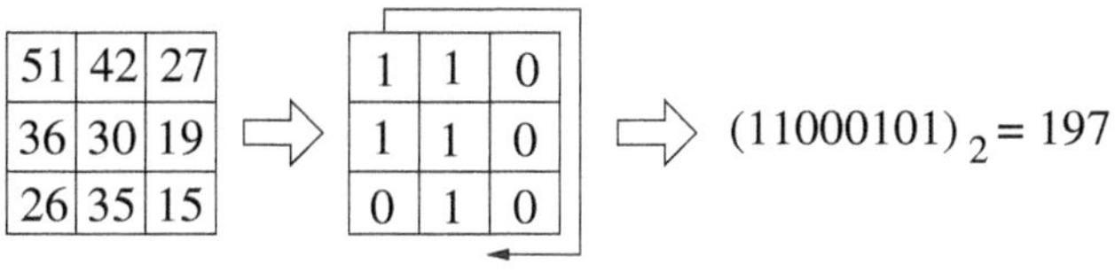

Figure 3: The LBP operator on a 3x3 grid.

Phase 2: Statistical features. Four second order statistical features are extracted from each color channel: contrast, correlation, homogeneity and energy [29]. An intermediate data structure used during the calculation of those twelve features is the co-occurrence matrix [6], which represents how often a pixel with the intensity value i occurs in a specific spatial relationship to a pixel with the intensity value j (see Figure 2). The size of the co-occurrence matrix has a major impact on the workload, but only a marginal influence on the algorithm's classification accuracy [23]. Therefore we have selected a 4×4 co-occurrence matrix for our experiments, which yields the fastest execution times.
Phase 3: LBP operator. The local binary pattern feature (LBP) is extracted from the L (luminance) channel to become the thirteenth feature for texture analysis. Widely used in many applications such as facial expression recognition and content based image retrieval [27], LBP is a rotationally invariant operator defined within a 3×3 neighborhood of each pixel, where the eight neighbors are examined to see if their intensity is greater than that of center pixel p. The results form a binary number $b_1b_2b_3b_4b_5b_6b_7b_8$ where $b_i = 0$ if the intensity of the ith neighbor is less than or equal to p and 1 otherwise (see Figure 3).
Phase 4: Histogram. Since LBP feature values are in the range $0 \rightarrow 255$, a histogram is constructed with 256 bins for the entire image, with each bin accumulating the number of pixels which have that LBP feature value. These bins are then reduced into ten canonical classes and normalized between 0 and 1 to become the components of a ten-dimensional vector. The Bhattacharyya distance [21] is then measured between the LBP feature vector and a $(1,1,1,1,1,1,1,1,1,1)$ vector to constitute the uniform LBP feature value used for the stroma classification. The subsequent classifier is a computationally inexpensive process, so we will not mention it further.

2.2 Major challenges

Input tissue samples are digitized at 40x magnification and stored in TIFF files using JPEG compression and the RGB color format. Each whole-slide image has a resolution of 110K×80K pixels in the worst case, which poses two major challenges:

- A single uncompressed image's size is well over the memory capacity of a single GPU. Additionally, providing balanced parallelization and effective use of cluster resources like disk I/O requires a smaller data granularity. In order to relieve memory usage and allow for an efficient parallelization of the computation across nodes, we decompose the image into 1K x 1K tiles.

- The algorithm takes several hours to run on a single CPU (see Table 5). This motivates us to study alternative platforms for its parallel execution. Our selection of multi-socket and multi-core CPUs combined with high-end GPUs will give us the opportunity for assessing scalability on both sides.

Tiling and parallelism are in fact tightly coupled, since the first strategy favors the latter. On a multi-processor system, each processor may independently perform the image analysis task on a subset of tiles and return a label indicating whether the particular image tile is stroma rich or stroma poor. Finally, labels are gathered on a central host and the classification map for the whole-slide image is constructed.

Apart from its implementation on a multi-processor system, our particular image analysis application is of great interest for evaluating the memory hierarchy and computational power of graphics architectures, because it meets a diverse number of features. For example, color conversion is a typical streaming operation with no data reuse. The LBP operator, on the other hand, exhibits a large degree of data reuse and locality, which typically favors more traditional, cache-based systems. Statistical features (through a co-occurrence matrix) and histogram construction both use extensive indirect array accesses such as those characterizing irregular computing and reduction operations often found in linear algebra. These two phases present undesirable features for both the CPU and the GPU. In our earlier work, we have investigated these in the context of Cg programming [23], while here we look at the trade-offs in the context of CUDA and a parallel implementation using cooperative cluster of multi-core, multi-socket CPUs and multiple GPUs.

3. GPU CLUSTER TESTBED

In this section we will present the specifications and properties of a typical, state-of-the-art, multi-socket, multi-core, multi-GPU cluster. For this purpose we picked the Ohio Supercomputer Center's BALE cluster [1]. The BALE cluster is comprised of a total of 71 Linux nodes, but our main focus is the newly added 16 visualization nodes, equipped with two dual-core AMD Opteron 2218 CPUs and two Nvidia Quadro FX 5600 GPUs each. The interconnection network for the BALE cluster is Infiniband. Figure 4 illustrates the architecture of the visualization nodes, and Table 1 shows the specifications of the CPU and GPU processors. Below we will go over some important specifications and features of the CPUs and GPUs used in our system.

On the CPU side, each node consists of two Opteron X2 2218 chips, which are dual-core processors running at 2.6 GHz. Each core in the system has a pair of 64 KB 2-way set associative L1 caches for holding data and instructions, and a 1 MB 4-way set associative L2 cache which is not shared among cores but are cache coherent. Each socket includes its own dual-channel DDR2-667 memory controller as well as a single HyperTransport link to access the other

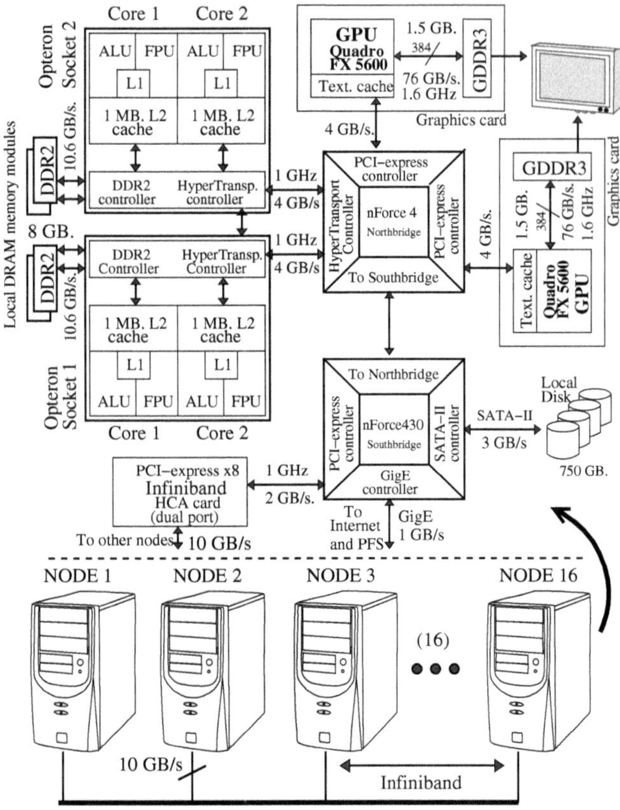

Figure 4: The BALE supercomputer at a glance.

socket's cache and memory. Each socket can thus deliver 10.6 GB/s for an aggregate memory bandwidth of 21.3 GB/s to each node's 8 GB of 667 MHz DDR2. The peak double-precision performance is 4.4 GFLOPS per core, 8.8 GFLOPS per socket, 17.6 GFLOPS per node. The peak single-precision performance per node is 35.2 GFLOPS, providing an aggregate single-precision performance of 563.2 GFLOPS for the 16 visualization nodes.

On the GPU side, each node has two Nvidia Quadro FX 5600 GPUs based on the G80 architecture. From a graphics viewpoint, the G80 can be seen as a 4-stage graphics pipeline for shading, texturing, rasterizing and coloring. As a parallel architecture, however, the G80 becomes a SIMD processor endowed with 128 cores, and CUDA is the programming interface to use it for general purpose computing. From the CUDA perspective, cores are organized into 16 multi-processors, each having a set of 32-bit registers, constants and texture caches, and a 16 KB memory shared by the eight cores inside each multi-processor. In any given cycle, each core executes the same instruction on different data, and communication between multi-processors is performed through global memory (see Figure 6).

4. TOOLS AND GPU IMPLEMENTATION

In order to give an example of the cooperative relationship between GPUs and multi-core CPUs, this section shows the details of the CUDA [5] implementation of the image analysis algorithm as well as the multi-node, multi-core and multi-GPU parallelization using DataCutter middleware [2]. We have used Matlab [3], C++ and Cg implementations [23] as

Table 1: Hardware features of the CPU and GPU used on each node of the testbed cluster. The GLFLOPS listed are for 32-bit, single-precision floating-point arithmetic.

Hardware feature	CPU from AMD	GPU from Nvidia
Board	ASUS KFN32-D SLI	Quadro FX 5600
Processor model	Opteron X2 2218	G80
Processor speed	2.6 GHz	600/1350 MHz
Number of sockets	2	2
Number of cores	2	128
Peak processing	2 x 8.8 GFLOPS	2 x 330 GFLOPS
Memory size	8 GB	2 x 1.5 GB
Memory bus width	2 x 64 bits	2 x 384 bits
Memory speed	667 MHz	1600 MHz
Memory bandwidth	2 x 10.8 GB/s.	2 x 76.8 GB/s

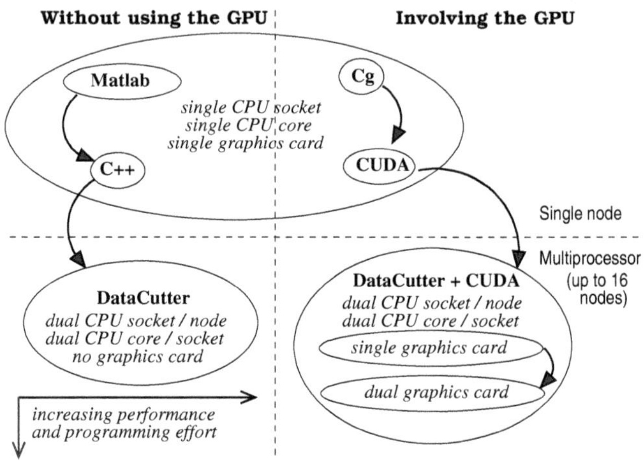

Figure 5: The programming approaches and their effect on performance, both single node and parallel.

a baseline for our performance comparisons. Programming tools and paradigms are summarized in Figure 5.

4.1 CUDA

The CUDA programming interface consists of a set of C language library functions, and the CUDA-specific compiler generates the executable code for the GPU. Since CUDA is designed for generic computing, it does not suffer from excessive constraints when accessing memory (as Cg [4] does), but memory access times do vary for different memory types.

4.1.1 Computation Paradigm

CUDA exposes a model to the developer consisting of a collection of threads running in parallel. There are several other elements involved in the execution which bear mentioning, since they are unique to graphics processor programming with CUDA:

- A program is decomposed into **blocks** that run *logically* in parallel (physically only if there are resources available). Assembled by the developer, a block is a group of threads that is mapped to a single multi-processor, where they can share 16 Kbytes of memory (see Figure 6). All threads of concurrent blocks on a single multi-processor divide the resources available

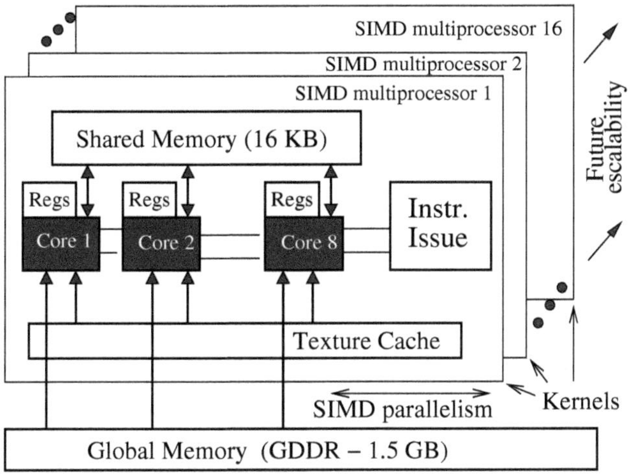

Figure 6: The CUDA hardware interface.

equally amongst themselves. The data is also divided amongst all of the threads in a SIMD fashion with a decomposition explicitly managed by the developer.

- A **warp** is a collection of threads that can actually run concurrently (with no time sharing) on all of the multi-processors. The size of the warp (32 threads on the G80) is less than the total number of available cores (128 on the G80) due to memory access limitations. The developer has the freedom to determine the number of threads to be executed (up to a limit intrinsic to CUDA), but if there are more threads than the warp size, they are time-shared on the actual hardware resources.

- A **kernel** is the actual code to be executed by each thread; the executable is shared among all of the threads in the system. Conditional execution of different operations on each multi-processor can be achieved based on a unique thread ID.

The CUDA documentation states that a single block should contain 128-256 threads to maximize execution efficiency, with a CUDA-imposed maximum of 512. Other hardware and software limitations are listed in Table 2, where we have ranked them according to their impact on the developer's implementation and overall performance based on our own experience.

4.1.2 Memory and registers

In the CUDA model, all of the threads can access all of the GPU memory, but, as expected, there is a performance boost when each thread reads data resident in the shared memory area, particularly when the data resides in several different memory banks (each bank can only support one memory access at a time, and therefore simultaneous accesses are serialized, hurting parallelism). The use of up to 16 KB of shared memory is explicit within a thread, which allows the developer to solve bank conflicts wisely. However, this type of optimization is often very difficult, but can also be very rewarding. Execution times may decrease by as much as 10x for vector operations and latency hiding may increase by up to 2.5x [8].

Table 2: Major hardware and software limitations with CUDA. Constraints are listed for the G80 GPU and categorized according to their difficulty of optimization and impact on the overall performance.

Parameter	Limitation	Impact
Multi-Processors per GPU	16	Low
Processors / Multi-Processor	8	Low
Threads / Warp	32	Low
Thread Blocks / Multi-Processor	8	Medium
Threads / Block	512	Medium
Threads / Multi-Processor	768	High
32-bit registers / Multi-Processor	8192	High
Shared Memory / Multi-Processor	16 Kbytes	High

When developing applications for GPUs with CUDA, the management of registers becomes important as a limiting factor for the amount of parallelism we can exploit. Each multi-processor contains 8,192 registers which will be split evenly among all the threads of the blocks assigned to that multi-processor. Hence, the number of registers needed in the computation will affect the number of threads able to be executed simultaneously, given the constraints outlined in Table 2. For example, if a kernel (and therefore a thread) consumes 16 registers, only 512 threads can be assigned to a single multi-processor, and this can be achieved by using 1 block with 512 threads, 2 blocks of 256 threads, and so on.

4.1.3 Implementation of Image Analysis Code

We have used a typical CUDA development cycle, which we will describe briefly. First, the code was compiled using the CUDA compiler and a special flag that outputs the hardware resources (memory and registers) consumed by the kernel. Using these values, we were able to analytically determine the number of threads and blocks that were needed to use a multi-processor with maximum efficiency. If a satisfactory efficiency could not be achieved, the code would need revision to reduce the memory footprint.

Due to the high floating point computation performance of the GPU, memory access becomes the bottleneck in many parts of our application. The input image tile (1K×1K×3 bytes) is much larger than the size of the multi-processor shared memory (16 KB), so we prioritize data structures like partial co-occurrence matrices (used in phase 2) and partial histograms (phase 4). However, in phase 1, even though the tile pixels are swept over without being reused, the execution time was lower when using shared memory (2.32 ms versus 2.77 ms - see Table 3). Also, in phase 3, the input pixels were moved to shared memory because the calculation of the LBP feature shows high data reuse.

In order to illustrate the progression of a typical CUDA implementation, we discuss the specific optimizations applied to each phase of the image analysis application below.

Phase 1: Color conversion.

As a departure point, we started using 24-bit `float3` data types for each color channel. However, extra performance can be obtained by padding the RGB input to match the expected data width of 32-bits, which simplifies all subsequent optimizations involving shared memory. This is called data *coalescing*, and for this phase it saved 35% of the computa-

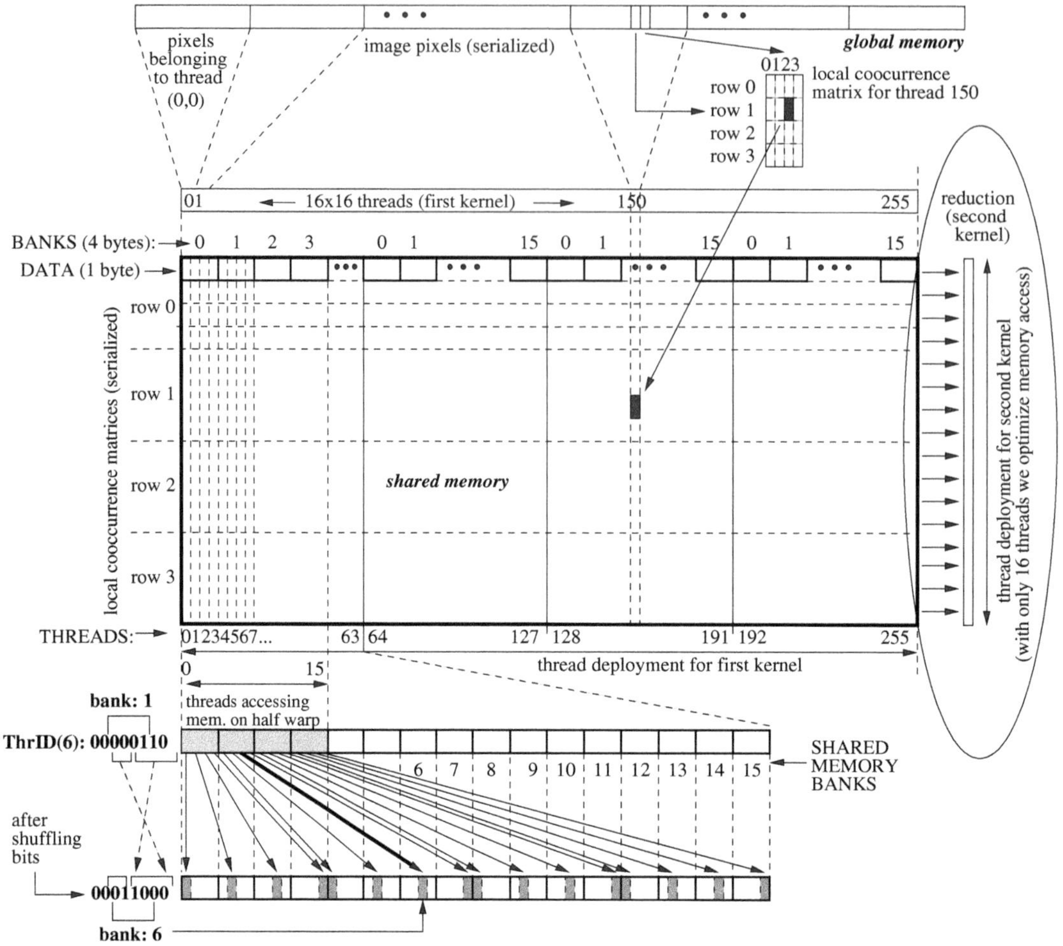

Figure 7: Phase 2: Local co-occurrence matrices in CUDA. Assigning banks in shared memory to each thread to avoid conflicts when computing co-occurrence matrices.

tion time at the expense of communication time (see code 1.11 in Table 3). Next, it was found that 8-bit `uchar` data types were sufficient for the precision of the application. As expected, this reduces the communication time by nearly a factor of 4.

We then used the special CUDA compilation flag to find that the color conversion kernel requires 13 registers and 1064 bytes of shared memory, leading to a maximum processor occupancy of 75% when allocating between 176 and 192 threads. However, we chose to allocate 256 threads instead, trading processor occupancy (from 75% down to 67%) for better load balance, since 256 is a multiple of 32 (maximum threads per warp) and a divisor of 768 (maximum threads per multi-processor) and 1024 (maximum pixels per image). The result was that the execution times improved slightly (see code 1.30 versus 1.40 in Table 3 - version 1.40 reports the minimum time obtained for all threads/block cases between 169 and 192, which turns out to be 169 threads). Unfortunately, maximum performance here is limited because each thread needs more than 10 registers (11 to be precise), which, as discussed earlier, prevents us from reaching the maximum occupancy of 768 threads within a multiprocessor. The optimal execution time for this phase was 2.98 ms for pixel transfer and 2.32 ms for computing the color conversion, as reflected in Table 3.

Phase 2: Statistical features.

This kernel requires 9 registers and 4132 bytes of shared memory, which allowed us to allocate 3 parallel blocks of 256 threads. This perfect usage of all 768 threads filled all of the G80 hardware resources for a 100% occupancy factor. Pixels are equally distributed among threads and local co-occurrence matrices are simultaneously computed within them. Finally, partial results are accumulated through a reduction operator.

It was found to be challenging to compute co-occurrence matrices in shared memory while avoiding conflicts accessing its 16 banks. With a grid of 256 threads arranged in a 16x16 grid, the naive thread deployment would force the 32 threads in a warp to access only 8 shared-memory banks, which would severely limit parallelism and performance. We found that by intelligently shuffling the active threads combined into a warp, the local matrix computation and the subsequent global matrix aggregation operation can proceed without forcing threads to wait for bank access (see Figure 7). This complex optimization solves all conflicts when accessing memory banks, reducing the execution time to 2.58 ms from 4.48 ms. Without using shared memory, a straightforward implementation consumes 15.40 ms instead (see Table 3).

Table 3: Major CUDA optimizations in the image analysis application. Execution times correspond to an isolated 1Kx1K tile on a single GPU. Phase 1 shows the times for CPU to GPU communication and actual GPU computation. Phases 2 and 3 show only GPU computation (no communication is required). Phase 4 shows the times for GPU to CPU communication and actual GPU computation. The fifth column in the table refers to conflicts arising when several threads simultaneously access the same bank of shared memory.

Analysis Phase	Code tag	Description / Optimizations	In shared memory	Conflicts solved	Execution time (millisecs.) Comm.	Comput.	Total
1:	1.10	Baseline version: Using float3 per color channel	All in global memory		8.49	3.71	12.20
RGB to	1.11	Coalescing (Alpha channel inserted) on float3	All in global memory		10.79	2.44	13.23
LA*B*	1.12	Replacing float3 by uchar (256 threads/block)	All in global memory		2.98	2.77	5.75
color	1.20, 1.30	**Using shared memory (256 threads/block)**	**Pixels**	**Unneeded**	**2.98**	**2.32**	**5.30**
conversion	1.40	Using between 169 and 192 threads/block	Pixels	Unneeded	2.98	2.43	5.41
2:	2.10	Baseline version: Using global memory	All in global memory		None	15.40	15.40
Statistical	2.20	Using shared memory for co-occurrence matrices	Co-oc. mat.	No	None	4.48	4.48
features	2.30	**Solving conflicts on shared memory banks**	**Co-oc. mat.**	**Yes**	**None**	**2.58**	**2.58**
3:	3.10	Baseline version: Special threads on grid borders	All in global memory		None	2.29	2.29
LBP	3.20, 3.30	**Blocks of 16x16 threads, 14x14 computing**	**Pixels**	**Unneeded**	**None**	**1.82**	**1.82**
operator	3.40	Blocks of 8x8 threads, 6x6 of them computing	Pixels	Unneeded	None	2.31	2.31
4:	4.10	Baseline version: Using global memory	All in global memory		4.02	2.08	6.10
Histogram	4.20	Using shared memory for local histograms	Local hist.	No	0.31	0.61	0.92
	4.30	**Solving inter-warp conflicts in mem. banks**	**Local hist.**	**Inter-warp**	**0.31**	**0.59**	**0.90**
Total	Σ(*.10)	Baseline version	All in global memory		12.51	23.48	35.99
GPU	Σ(*.20)	Involving shared memory	Enabled	No	3.29	9.23	12.52
time	Σ(*.30)	**Optimal version**	**Enabled**	**Most**	**3.29**	**7.31**	**10.60**
Total CPU time:		(1:) 880.31 ms. + (2:) 43.24 ms. + (3:) 156.28 ms. + (4:) 7.49 ms. = **1087.32**					

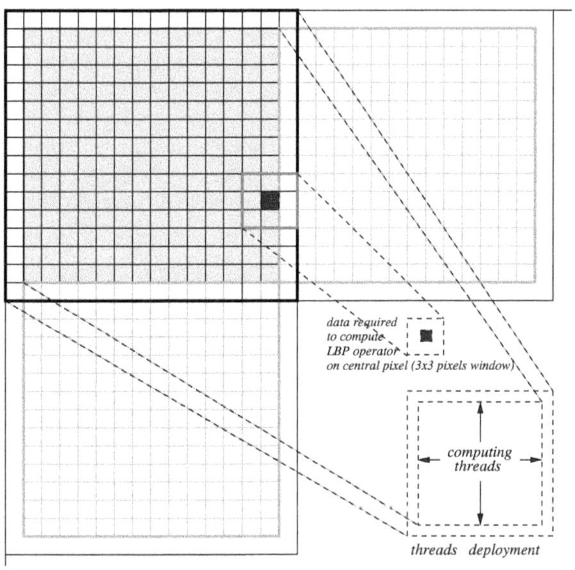

Figure 8: Phase 3: LBP operator in CUDA. We allocate more memory than computing threads and overlap two rows and columns of the external frame on neighbor blocks in order to cover the whole computational domain homogeneously.

Phase 3: LBP operator.

The computation of the LBP feature entails a convolution with a 3x3 mask, followed by a binary to decimal conversion (see Figure 3). Each thread requires 10 registers and each block of threads uses 296 bytes of shared memory. Due to the memory usage characteristics, we were able to allocate 256 threads in a 16 x 16 grid to reach 100% occupancy on the G80. Each thread reads a pixel from global memory and stores it in a shared memory data structure. Those threads located on the border of the grid are unable to compute, since they do not have access to their neighbor data (see Figure 8); they exit the kernel at this stage. The LBP for the border regions will be computed by the next block of threads, since we overlap the thread layout by two rows and two columns of pixels each time. By using this strategy, we incur 23% idle cycles and the associated redundant memory accesses, but the computation is more homogeneous and the threads are more lightweight. As compared to the heterogeneous version, where there are no idle cycles and no memory redundancy, the homogeneous version is faster by 1.25x, leading to the lowest execution time of 1.82 ms.

Since the LBP kernel is very regular, we can select different sizes of thread deployments, provided a square grid is used. Therefore, we investigated the effect of different thread/block ratios. We gathered values for grids of threads of sizes 20x20 (2.02 ms), 18x18 (1.90 ms), 16x16 (1.82 ms - optimal), 14x14 (1.89 ms), 12x12 (2.00 ms), 10x10 (2.16 ms), and 8x8 (2.31 ms - reported in Table 3 as version 3.40). A grid of 16x16 threads is a popular choice among expert programmers to maximize performance in CUDA; that said, our intention was more to quantify the penalty we may incur by making an inappropriate choice for thread allocation.

Phase 4: Histogram.

The implementation of this phase is based on a histogram kernel included with the CUDA library [20], where the global reduction is delegated to the CPU. We deemed this an appropriate solution, since the histogram is only computed once per tile, and does not incur a large execution time cost. The execution time for this last phase is 0.9 ms.

Table 3 summarizes all of the major optimizations performed within CUDA on each phase along with their execution times. Since the CUDA programming model does not allow the developer to assign different kernels to different multi-processors, the four phases are sequentially executed and the whole GPU is used during each phase independently.

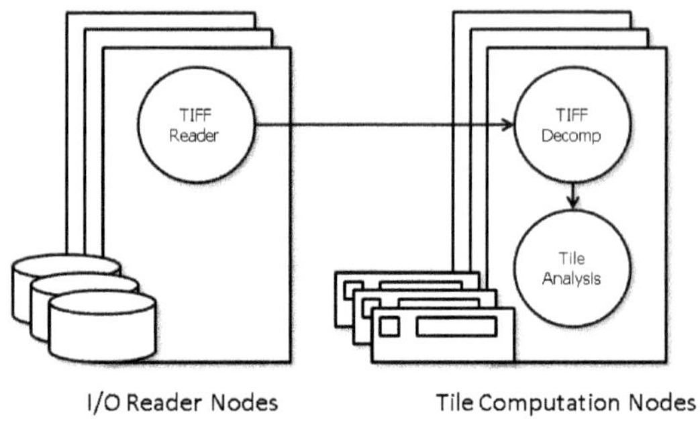

Figure 9: DataCutter layout of the image analysis application.

Overall, by using CUDA to implement the image analysis, we were able to reduce the execution time by a factor of 3-5 over the times obtained by Cg (see Table 5 for times on an entire image), by an additional factor of 3 when enabling shared memory, and by an extra 20% when solving memory conflicts as much as possible for an optimal execution.

4.2 DataCutter

We employed DataCutter middleware for the parallelization of the testbed image analysis computation. DataCutter [2] is a component-based middleware framework and provides a coarse-grained data flow system allowing combined use of task- and data-parallelism. Applications are decomposed into sequential tasks (*filters*) with data dependencies between them. Data flows from filter to filter through *logical streams* in a buffered, non-blocking manner. This buffering allows for the easy overlap of data communication and computation, which allows for the hiding of disk and inter-node communication latencies. The DataCutter runtime system supports efficient execution of filters on heterogeneous, multi-socket, and multi-core compute clusters. The runtime system performs all steps necessary to instantiate filters on the desired hosts, to connect all logical endpoints, and to call the filter's interface functions for processing work. Each filter executes within a separate POSIX thread, allowing for CPU, I/O and communication overlap. Data exchange between two filters on the same host is carried out by memory copy or pointer operations, while TCP sockets or MPI communications (in order to leverage low latency high bandwidth interconnects such as Infiniband) are employed for communication between filters on different hosts.

Our image analysis application is easily divided into three stages, each of which is implemented as a single filter type. These are: a *TIFF-Reader* filter that reads binary TIFF tiles, a *TIFF-Decompressor* filter that decompresses TIFF tiles and produces RGB images, and a *Tile-Analysis* filter where the real image analysis computation is carried out. A layout which includes one each of these three filter types constitutes a complete image analysis task graph, while multiple copies of each filter type allows for quick parallelization and efficient execution. Figure 9 shows the general layout of the system. One or more reader nodes (with one *TIFF-Reader* filter each) read the binary TIFF image tiles from the disk and write them to the stream leading to the *TIFF-Decompressor*. One or more *TIFF-Decompresser* filters are able to coexist on the same node and simply take the binary TIFF file and decompress it into the appropriate RGBA tuples. This decompressed image data is then written to the input stream to the *Image-Analysis* filter on the same node. When the *Tile-Analysis* filter makes use of the GPU, the ability for multiple *Tiff-Decompressor* filters to feed data to the GPU allows for full utilization of the GPU's throughput. Placing both the *TIFF-Decompressor* and the *Image-Analysis* filters on the same node has the benefit of saving memory bandwidth by leaving the largest representation of each TIFF tile in place and simply transferring the pointer.

Table 4: Properties of the three slides used in our experiments.

Name	Resolution in pixels	Number of 1Kx1K tiles
SMALL	32,980 x 66,426	33 x 65 = 2,145
MEDIUM	76,543 x 63,024	75 x 62 = 4,659
LARGE	109,110 x 80,828	107 x 79 = 8,453

Table 5: Execution times for the image analysis application for different programming methods and hardware platforms. These times do not include disk I/O or decompression overheads. The image tile size is 1Kx1K pixels. The co-occurrence matrix size is 4x4. The values in the CUDA column represent running on one and two GPUs.

	On the CPU		On the GPU	
Image size	Matlab	C++	Cg	CUDA
SMALL	2h 57' 29"	43' 40"	1' 02"	27", 14"
MEDIUM	6h 25' 45"	1h 34' 51"	2' 08"	58", 32"
LARGE	11h 39' 28"	2h 51' 23"	3' 54"	1' 47", 58"

The component-based programming model of DataCutter allows us to easily develop and deploy image analysis applications that utilize GPUs as co-processors. By simply replacing the C++ *Tile-Analysis* filters with filters using the GPU, we can quickly develop a parallel code that efficiently executes on a multi-socket, multi-core, multi-GPU cluster. The layout, the two *TIFF-Reader* and *TIFF-Decompressor* filters, and the entire parallelization system are reusable.

5. EXPERIMENTAL RESULTS

Our experiments were performed on the BALE cluster (see Section 3) using the 16 visualization nodes and an additional six compute nodes as reader nodes, in order to provide enough disk bandwidth to avoid the disk I/O bottleneck. Further, these reader nodes had their system file caches preloaded with several discarded experiments to ensure extremely high I/O from the upstream, *TIFF-READER* filters. We feel this is a suitable experimental setup to use; any production cluster designed to analyze this kind of image data with very high performance with multiple GPUs and a fast interconnect can reasonably be said to have parallel disks providing high I/O bandwidth.

In our experiments, we have used three different digitized pathology images. Table 4 summarizes their features.

The first set of experiments shows the single node CPU and GPU performance for the various implementations of the image analysis algorithm. Figure 10 shows the execution time and overhead time of each implementation when

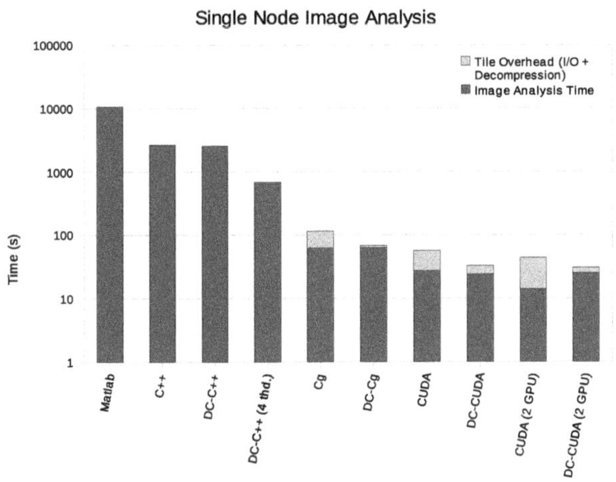

Figure 10: Execution time comparison of all implementations of the image analysis codes running on a single node using SMALL image.

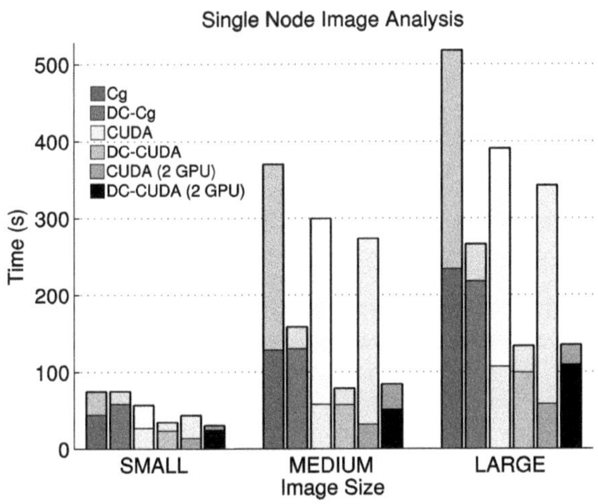

Figure 11: Execution time comparison of GPU and DataCutter implementations running on a single node using all three input images.

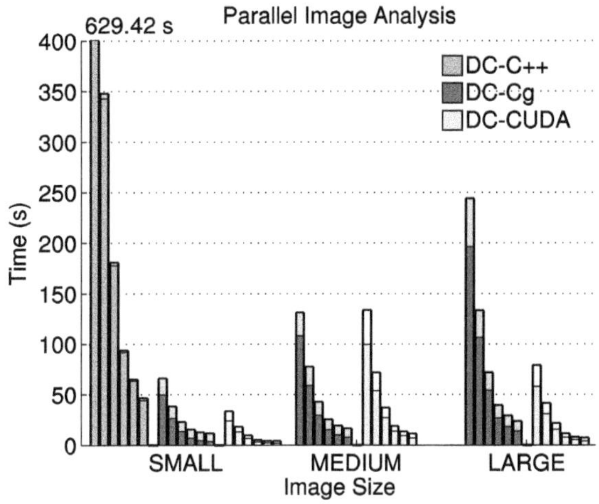

Figure 12: Parallel execution times of C++, Cg, and CUDA based DataCutter implementations using three input images while varying the number of nodes from 1 to 16.

analyzing the SMALL image. The first four stacked bars represent CPU-only implementations, while the last six stacked bars bring one or two GPUs into the fold. Those bars with labels beginning with 'DC' are results from those implementations using DataCutter and those without the 'DC' label are the basic, serial implementations.

The execution time in Figure 10 (shown by the lower, darker portion of each bar) is due solely to the actual image analysis, while the overhead (shown by the upper, lighter portion of each bar) is caused by disk I/O, TIFF decompression, remote process invocation, and network latencies, where applicable. In this experiment, the most important thing to note is the two to three orders of magnitude of performance speedup when moving from the CPU-based solutions to the GPU-based solutions. While a large amount of performance is gained by moving away from Matlab, the C++ implementations are still far slower than those which are GPU-based. Additionally, the DataCutter versions of the GPU-based image analysis algorithms are able to shorten the execution time for the entire image versus the non-DataCutter versions, since the decoupled, multi-threaded nature of DataCutter allows the image analysis to overlap with the TIFF tile decompression and the disk I/O. Unfortunately, the CUDA implementation of the image analysis algorithm is fast enough to cause the TIFF tile decompression stage to become a bottleneck when 2 GPUs are used. This stalling, incurred by the GPUs waiting for tiles to analyze, prevents both GPUs from being fully utilized. Since four C++ threads shows a clear advantage over running a single thread, all future C++ results will be comprised of the DataCutter version with four tile analysis threads per node.

Figure 11 shows the performance comparison of the GPU-based implementations of the analysis routine for our three images. The main point to take from this chart is that there is a linear relationship between the execution time and the overall size of the image under analysis in all of the implementations. Unfortunately, even when analyzing large images, making full use of 2 GPUs is hindered by the associated overheads; this being the case, we will not show 2 GPU results for the remainder of the experiments.

Figure 12 shows the scalability of our solution with respect to the number of nodes. The numbers of nodes involved in the image analysis are $1, 2, 4, 8, 12, 16$, and are represented by the bars in the figure from left to right, six in each color group. As in Figure 11, the lower, darker-colored portion of each bar represents the image analysis time, while the upper, lighter-colored portion of each bar shows the aggregated overhead. This type of image analysis computation scales extremely well, resulting in image analysis execution times which decrease nearly linearly with the number of nodes. Further, the total analysis times for the DataCutter/CUDA implementation are under four seconds for the SMALL image, under seven seconds for the MEDIUM image, and just over eleven seconds for the LARGE image, when running on sixteen nodes. Compared with the single node CPU Matlab

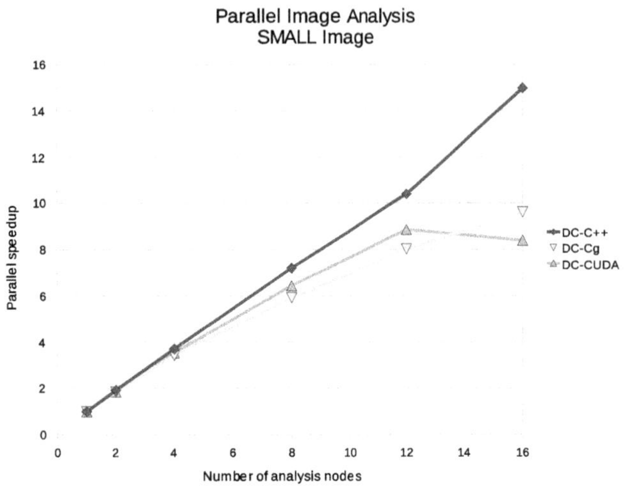

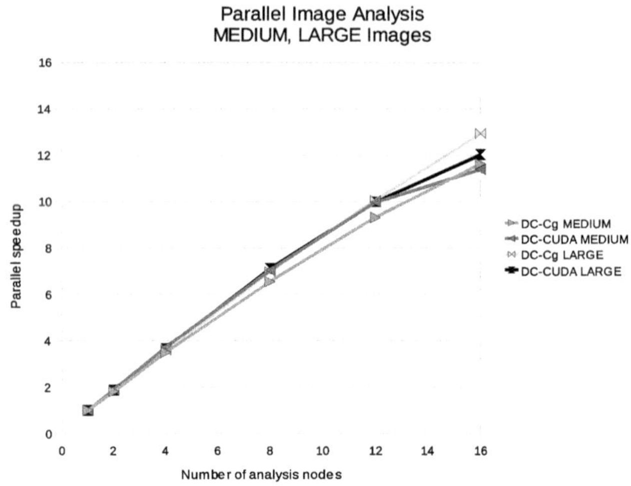

Figure 13: Parallel speedup results. Within DataCutter (DC) versions, we compare on the left a CPU-only case with two GPU-assisted ones for the `SMALL` image. On the right, we contrast the two GPU versions for the `MEDIUM` and `LARGE` images.

computation time of nearly three hours for the `SMALL` image and almost twelve hours for the `LARGE` image, this represents a tangible benefit of increased productivity. In the interest of increased chart legibility, we have cropped the single node C++ result. Its values are 629.42 seconds of image analysis time and 29.7 seconds of overhead. Additionally, since the main focus of this paper is the GPU results, and since the C++ result is shown to scale well in the worst-case (because it incurs the lowest proportional overhead), we have chosen to remove it from the figures showing results for the `MEDIUM` and `LARGE` images.

Figure 13 shows the parallel speedup of the execution time versus the number of nodes. As seen in the figures, there is nearly linear speedup since the tiles are able to be decompressed and processed entirely independently of each other. However, due to the small execution times in the GPU-based implementations, the various overheads (comprised of remote process startup, network, and TIFF decompression latencies) begin to become comparable in overall time to the total time spent per node processing the image tiles. For instance, on sixteen nodes, the CUDA implementation requires at most 1.80 seconds of computation to compute 2,145 tiles. However, despite concurrently running three *TIFF-Decompressor* filters, the decompression time alone for each node's allotment of 135 tiles could range from 0.3 seconds to 1.3 seconds.

Nearly linear speedup could be achieved in a production environment, however, since it is reasonable to assume that remote process invocation would only occur once for many images which are to be analyzed. Under these server-like circumstances, only the I/O system and network latencies would comprise the system overheads.

6. CONCLUSIONS

In this paper, we have presented design trade-offs and a performance evaluation of a sample biomedical image analysis application running on a cooperative cluster of CPUs and GPUs.

By implementing algorithms on GPUs using CUDA and using DataCutter to parallelize the computation within and across nodes, we establish a solid heterogeneous and cooperative multi-processor platform where all the granularities of parallelism inherent in the architecture and in the application are fully exploited: multi-node (using DataCutter for data partitioning across nodes), SMP and thread-level (using DataCutter to fully utilize the available on-node and on-chip hardware resources), SIMD (using CUDA to fully populate the 128 stream processors of the GPU with work), and finally, ILP (Instruction Level Parallelism, by setting up blocks of computational threads within the GPU execution).

Our experimental results show great success for our techniques, first by decreasing the execution time on a single CPU/GPU node by using different intra-node optimizations, and then extending those performance gains to inter-node parallelism for a scalable multi-processor execution. When analyzing the largest test image and including overheads, on the 16 node cluster configuration, the single GPU DataCutter-CUDA implementation is 31.3 times faster than the serial CUDA implementation. By using two GPUs per node, the single-node time to process the image is under one minute, if you ignore the overheads associated with disk I/O and tile decompression, proving that the CUDA method is extremely powerful. Additionally, the use of DataCutter to overlap the computation with disk I/O and tile decompression helps the GPU stay as busy as possible. This results in up to 12.94 speedup on 16 nodes using GPU-based DataCutter implementations.

GPUs are highly scalable and are evolving towards general-purpose architectures [10]; we envision biomedical image processing as one of the most exciting fields able to benefit from the use of GPUs. Additionally, new tools like CUDA [5] may assist non-computer scientists with a more friendly interface for adapting biomedical applications to GPUs. This computational power may then be combined with DataCutter to parallelize the computation across clusters of GPUs as outlined in this paper to provide real-time response to clinicians of all types.

7. ACKNOWLEDGEMENTS

We thank Metin Gurcan from the Department of Biomedical Informatics, Ohio State University, for providing us the input neuroblastoma images and Matlab code for the image analysis application. We also thank Dennis Sessanna and Don Stredney at the Ohio Supercomputer Center for support running our code on the BALE visualization cluster.

8. REFERENCES

[1] The BALE cluster at the Ohio Supercomputer Center. http://www.osc.edu/supercomputing/hardware.

[2] M. Beynon, K. T., U. Catalyurek, C. Chang, A. Sussman, and J. Saltz. Distributed processing of very large datasets with DataCutter. *Parallel Computing*, 27(11):1457–1478, October 2001.

[3] B. B. Cambazoglu, O. Sertel, J. Kong, J. Saltz, M. N. Gurcan, and U. V. Catalyurek. Efficient processing of pathological images using the grid: Computer-aided prognosis of neuroblastoma. In *Proceedings Intl. Workshop on Challenges of Large Applications in Distributed Environments*, 2007.

[4] The Cg language. Home page maintained by Nvidia. http://developer.nvidia.com/page/cg_main.html.

[5] CUDA. Home page maintained by Nvidia. http://developer.nvidia.com/object/cuda.html.

[6] L. Davis, S. Johns, and J. Aggarwal. Texture analysis using generalized co-occurrence matrices. *IEEE Transactions on Pattern Analysis and Machine Intelligence*, 3:251–259, 1979.

[7] A. N. Esgiar, R. N. G. Naguib, B. S. Sharif, M. K. Bennet, and A. Murray. Microscopic image analysis for quantitative measurement and feature identification of normal and cancerous colonic mucosa. *IEEE Transactions on Information Technology in Biomedicine*, 2:197–203, 1998.

[8] M. Fatica, D. Luebke, I. Buck, D. Owens, M. Harris, J. Stone, C. Phillips, and B. Deschizeaux. CUDA Tutorial at Supercomputing 2007.

[9] FireStream. GPU hardware solutions from AMD-ATI. http://ati.amd.com/products/streamprocessor/specs.html, 2008.

[10] GPGPU. General-purpose computation using graphics hardware. http://www.gpgpu.org.

[11] S. Guha, S. Krisnan, and S. Venkatasubramanian. Data visualization and mining using the GPU. *Tutorial at 11th ACM International Conference on Knowledge Discovery and Data Mining*, 2005.

[12] M. Gurcan, J. Kong, O. Sertel, B. Cambazoglu, J. Saltz, and U. Catalyurek. Computerized pathological image analysis for neuroblastoma prognosis. In *AMIA Annual Symposium*, 2007.

[13] M. Hadwiger, C. Langer, H. Scharsach, and K. Buhler. State of the art report on GPU-based segmentation. Technical Report TR-VRVIS-2004-17, VRVis Research Center, Vienna, Austria, 2004.

[14] K. J. Khouzani and H. S. Zadeh. Multiwavelet grading of pathological images of prostate. *IEEE Transactions on Biomedical Engineering*, 50(6):697–704, 2003.

[15] J. Kong, H. Shimada, K. Boyer, J. Saltz, and M. Gurcan. Image analysis for automated assessment of grade of neuroblastic differentiation. In *IEEE Intl. Symposium on Biomedical Imaging*, 2007.

[16] J. D. Owens, D. Luebke, N. Govindaraju, M. Harris, J. Kruger, A. E. Lefohn, and T. J. Purcell. A survey of general-purpose computation on graphics hardware. *Journal of Computer Graphics Forum*, 26:21–51, 2007.

[17] G. Paschos. Perceptually uniform color spaces for color texture analysis: An empirical evaluation. *IEEE Transactions on Image Processing*, 10:932–937, 2001.

[18] S. Petushi, F. U. Garcia, M. Habe, C. Katsinis, and A. Tozeren. Large-scale computations on histology images reveal grade-differentiating parameters for breast cancer. *BMC Medical Imaging*, 6(14), 2006.

[19] S. Petushi, C. Katsinis, C. Coward, F. Garcia, and A. Tozeren. Automated identification of microstructures on histology slides. In *IEEE Intl. Symposium on Biomedical Imaging*, 2004.

[20] V. Podlozhnyuk. Histogram calculation in CUDA, 2007.

[21] S. Ray. On a theoretical property of the bhattacharyya coefficient as a feature evaluation criterion. *Pattern Recognition Letters*, pages 315–319, 1989.

[22] A. Ruiz, O. Sertel, M. Ujaldón, U. Catalyurek, J. Saltz, and M. Gurcan. Stroma classification for neuroblastoma on graphics processors. *Intl. Journal of Data Mining and Bioinformatics*, 3(4), 2008.

[23] A. Ruiz, O. Sertel, M. Ujaldón, U. Catalyurek, J. Saltz, and M. Gurcan. Pathological image analysis using the GPU: Stroma classification for neuroblastoma. In *IEEE Intl. Conference on BioInformatics and BioMedicine (BIBM'07)*, November, 2007.

[24] O. Sertel, J. Kong, H. Shimada, U. Catalyurek, J. Saltz, and M. Gurcan. Computer-aided prognosis of neuroblastoma: classification of stromal development on whole-slide images. In *SPIE Medical Imaging*, San Diego, California, 2008.

[25] H. Shimada, I. M. Ambros, L. P. Dehner, J. Hata, V. V. Joshi, B. Roald, D. O. Stram, R. B. Gerbing, J. N. Lukens, K. K. Matthay, and R. P. Gastlebery. The Intl. neuroblastoma pathology classification (the Shimada system). *Cancer*, 86(2):364–372, 1999.

[26] M. A. Tahir and A. Bouridane. Novel round-robin tabu search algorithm for prostate cancer classification and diagnosis using multispectral imagery. *IEEE Transactions on Information Technology in Biomedicine*, 20:782–791, 2006.

[27] V. Takala, T. Ahanen, and M. Pietikainen. Block-based methods for image retrieval using local binary patterns. *Lecture Notes in Computer Science*, 3540:882–891, 2005.

[28] Nvidia Tesla GPU computing solutions for HPC. http://www.nvidia.com/object/tesla_computing_solutions.html

[29] M. Tuceryan and A. K. Jain. *Texture Analysis, in The Handbook of Pattern Recognition and Computer Vision (2nd Ed.)*. World Scientific Publishing Co, 1998.

[30] W. Wu and P. Heng. A hybrid condensed finite element model with GPU acceleration for interactive 3D soft tissue cutting: Research articles. *Computer Animation and Virtual Worlds*, 15(3-4):219–227, 2004.

[31] Zhao, Y., Y. Han, Z. Fan, F. Qiu, Y. Kuo, Kaufman, and K. A., Mueller. Visual simulation of heat shimmering and mirage. *IEEE Trans. on Visualization and Computer Graphics*, 13(1):179–189, 2007.

www.ingramcontent.com/pod-product-compliance
Ingram Content Group UK Ltd.
Pitfield, Milton Keynes, MK11 3LW, UK
UKHW051511290926
15471UKWH00008B/1552